An Introduction to Applied Econometrics:
A Time Series Approach

Other books by the same author:

Patterson, K.D. and Schott K.E. (eds) (1979), *The Measurement of Capital*, Macmillan, London.
Henry, S.G. and Patterson, K.D. (eds) (1990), *Economic Modelling at the Bank of England*, Chapman & Hall, London.

An Introduction to Applied Econometrics: A Time Series Approach

Kerry Patterson

First published 2000 by
MACMILLAN PRESS LTD
Houndmills, Basingstoke, Hampshire RG21 6XS
and London
Companies and representatives throughout the world

ISBN 0–333–80245–4 hardcover
ISBN 0–333–80246–2 paperback

A catalogue record for this book is available from the British Library.

This book is printed on paper suitable for recycling and made from fully managed and sustained forest sources.

10   9   8   7   6   5   4   3   2   1
09 08 07 06 05 04 03 02 01 00

Typeset in Great Britain by Aarontype Limited, Easton, Bristol

Printed in Great Britain by Antony Rowe Ltd, Chippenham, Wiltshire

To four Cs, D, E and F

Contents

List of figures

Preface

The last 15–20 years have seen something of a revolution in econometric techniques and how these are used in applications. As is often the case the seeds of the change were sown earlier and occasional 'buds' surfaced but were yet to reach 'full-flower'. Much but not all of the new direction came from the recognition that the econometric paradigm of stationary time series, which was the backbone of many texts and applications, was based on a very disputable assumption. In this paradigm positively trending time series were 'accounted' for as stationary deviations around a deterministic trend. This assumption had already been too much for time series analysts – see, for example, Box and Jenkins (1970) – who had moved away, generally much before the econometricians, to adopt the default that time series were nonstationary. The econometric 'buds' were there in, for example, the work of Sargan (1964) and Davidson et al. (1978) who developed the idea of an error correction model, ECM (which is also in an early paper by Phillips (1957) of Phillips curve fame). The ECM turned out to be intimately connected to related nonstationary series, so parts of a new paradigm were starting to look like a structure. An important paper by Granger and Weiss (1983), which was unfortunately not published in a widely available source, developed the ECM and nonstationarity connection further. Engle and Granger (1987) marked the turning point, with a high profile paper published in Econometrica. As with many influential techniques the formidable theory was balanced by some easily applied methods, with the result that there was an 'explosion' of applications of

the Engle–Granger procedure. Theory also followed suit with a particularly influential article by Johansen (1988), which, fortunately for applied econometricians, also came with methods that were readily applied. Thereafter the rest is, as they say, history. No serious application of economics that requires econometrics now fails to consider whether the time series on the candidate economic variables are stationary or nonstationary.

A second development of the 1980s, which although not as wide-reaching as the developments relating to error correction mechanisms and nonstationarity, was to have profound effects in financial econometrics, even though it was not introduced in that area. Engle (1982) introduced the idea that it would be possible to model the conditional variance of a regression model as a time varying process. The generic term for this concept is ARCH – for autoregressive conditional heteroscedasticty. This was important because the hitherto dominant assumption was that the conditional variance was constant. The dormancy period for this concept was fortunately not as long as for ECMs. Modelling the volatility of asset returns in a way that allowed volatility to vary over time was a concern for financial economists, but prior to Engle's article there was no readily available framework to do this. ARCH and its many subsequent extensions provided this. The result was a transformation and 'megaexplosion' of theoretical and empirical papers using the ARCH framework. For example, in a survey of ARCH modelling in finance Bollerslev, Chou and Kroner (1992) list over 200 published articles. Now no research involving financial variables would fail to consider the possibility of an ARCH effect.

Textbooks were somewhat slow to respond to these developments except at the more advanced level – see section **1.5** for some relevant books. This meant that students taking typical undergraduate and postgraduate degree programmes in economics were often only briefly introduced to the key concepts underlying much econometric practice of the last 10–15 years. Those majoring in econometrics would fare a little better, but the standard was by no means uniform. My interviewing for the UK Government Economic Service continues to reinforce this view. Rarely do I come across a potential government economist who is even moderately familiar with the importance of just knowing the difference between a stationary and a nonstationary time series. And ARCH is generally an alien word as well as an alien world! This has consequences for post-degree training for beginning professional economists in public and private service, as well as for postgraduates undertaking dissertations. Indeed, it was such a concern to the Bank of England that their intake of economists are not equipped with the right econometric techniques, that part of their in-service training includes a course on econometrics focusing, *inter alia*, on modelling with nonstationary time series. The textbook market is beginning to respond (again see section **1.5**) but leading texts in econometrics and applied econometrics, even though in second and third editions, still devote very little space to the topics covered here.

An overriding development of the last 20 years, not based on particular techniques (for example, Engle–Granger or ARCH) or distinctions among the properties of the variables (for example, stationary or nonstationary), relates to how economists do their empirical research. Hendry and his colleagues, in a number of papers – see, for example, Hendry and Richard (1983, 1989) and Hendry and Mizon (1990) – have argued for a progressive research strategy.

Not only should researcher A put forward a new explanation of an economic problem, supported by empirical work which is robust to tests of misspecification and specification, he should also be able to explain the previous results of researcher B. Otherwise we may find that contemporaneous views held simultaneously show that the world is both flat and spherical! Of course, it is not always easy to do this. In an economic context there is considerable debate over what determines the exchange rate; whether productivity shocks permanently affect the level of output; whether government spending crowds out private spending; whether expectations are best modelled as backward or forward looking and so on. Nevertheless, we can and should impose some systematisation on our research.

I hope in this book that I have dealt with the key developments in applicable econometric techniques, outlined above, in a way accessible to nonspecialists (by which I mean economists not taking time series econometrics as an elective). The potential audience is wide, including undergraduate and postgraduates as well as professional economists who need to occasionally do, but certainly must be able to interpret, empirical work. I have taken the view, as my students often tell me, that econometrics needs applications to understand what is going on. Illustrations, in the sense of skeletal applications, are not always enough, although they are often useful. Hence, several of the applications here are chapter length studies involving the interaction of economics and econometrics. Even so I am conscious that this book could have been much longer. Time series econometrics is a very vibrant area of research and, fortunately, much of this comes with interesting applications. With ease I could have introduced another ten techniques or variations on the existing ones; I have had to make a judgement or trade-off balancing the coverage of included areas with some other areas that I might have included if there had been no constraint on space. This judgement included omitting a detailed treatment of some areas I have worked on, for example fractional integration. I am confident, though, that such topics will be easily accessed following study of those I have included.

This book is *not* though just about nonstationary time series. It does, I hope, also provide a sound basis from which to undertake the empirical analysis of stationary time series analysis and covers the range of essential topics for this purpose found in similar level books on econometric techniques. The difference, I hope, is that the applications serve to show how economics and econometrics 'need each other'.

There is another development in econometric techniques that has had an important effect in the last ten years or so. The ready availability of personal computers, with the power of what were previously known as 'mainframe' computers, has meant that simulations are now easily carried out. For example, in studying the properties of a particular estimator the mechanism generating the data is specified and a large number of replications then follow; the estimator is calculated at each replication and the overall results are summarised. I have found simulations useful even where the available theory is good enough to tell us what the properties of a particular estimator are in finite samples. For example, even in the simplest case (see Chapter 4) where ordinary least squares (OLS) estimators are known to be unbiased in finite samples, students often have difficulty with what the expectation of the OLS estimator actually refers to, although they do not have difficulty with routinely restating, without really understanding, the proof of the Gauss–Markov theorem that OLS estimators are BLUE. Even in this situation a simulation serves to make it clear what is meant by the key concept of 'repeated sampling'. *A fortiori*, simulations are useful in more realistic situations, and have been used in this book in an illustrative way.

A full simulation analysis can, however, be quite demanding, requiring a detailed assessment of the sensitivity of the results to the design parameters and, if necessary, a full experimental design. I have taken the view that much of interest can be conveyed, keeping within the confines of the anticipated readership of this book. If there are doubts about the sensitivity of the simulation results to a particular design parameter they have been indicated and, indeed, it is a challenge on offer to follow up the results reported here.

I am grateful to a number of colleagues for reading and commenting on draft chapters. I would particularly like to thank Ólan Henry for reading several chapters and providing important references for, and some of the data used, in Chapters 11 and 16. I am also grateful to Bahram Pesaran for his help on a number of detailed points. I have been pleasantly surprised by the responses of several cohorts of my students on quantitative economics and econometrics courses who have offered, although they might not have been quite aware of it, constructive comments on draft chapters and the review questions. I am grateful to Brigitte Calderon of the Mathematics Department at the University of Reading, who rescued the word processing on some of the more difficult chapters after others had given up in despair. I would also like to thank Sue Salts for her help with the indices.

In a more general sense anyone carrying out empirical research is aware of the debt owed to some key econometricians who have managed to grasp a too often noted divide between econometric theory and applicable techniques. At the risk of offending by omission, with one exception I will limit my acknowledgements to those who have been publishing for 20 years or more. In this respect I think there can be no doubt that Robert Engle, Clive Granger and David Hendry have profoundly changed the way that time series empirical work is carried out. Their combination of a mastery of econometric theory and the ability to see how techniques can have an empirical impact in important areas of economics is enviable. The one exception is Søren Johansen, whose publications since 1988 had a profound effect on the way empirical work is carried out in the area of time series analysis.

I note from prefaces to a number of books, which I regard as 'classics' in their area, that the authors often thank colleagues for pointing out errors of commission and omission. At the time of reading these books, I was often puzzled by this frank admission of fallibility. Having completed this book I am now rather painfully aware of the importance of the pervasive feeling of fallibility, and especially that there is still much to know and learn even in relatively well-established areas of time series econometric methods.

All of the empirical results reported in this book are reproducible, and a website has been established for the purposes of offering an interactive response for queries, estimating the regressions reported in this book and drawing the graphics. If any errors or typos do slip through let me know on my email address! Reproducibility of existing results is essential if we are to discover how we can progressively improve the models upon which the results are based. Surprisingly reproducibility is often something of a novelty for economists! Colleagues have often expressed concern that they cannot 'match' the results published in a learned journal; conversely they express surprise when they can. There are legitimate reasons for nonreproducibility, especially where macroeconomic data, which is often heavily revised, is used. However, this would not be a problem if the original data was made available. Fortunately a number of journals now make it a requirement of publication that the data used in empirical articles is available to other researchers, often in an electronically readable form.

I am indebted to Stephen Rutt at Macmillan Business for sharing my enthusiasm for this project. I am also grateful to Ray Addicott at Chase Production Services and the team he organised, especially Alan Everett and Tracey Day, for the production of this book.

Website and email details

Author's website, http://www.rdg.ac.uk/~lespatsn
Author's email address, K.D.Patterson@reading.ac.uk
Macmillan Press Online, http://www.macmillan-press.co.uk
Macmillan email address, v.nash@macmillan.co.uk

Acknowledgements

Figure 1.1, p. 7, reprinted from E.W. Gilboy, 'The Propensity to Consume', *Quarterly Journal of Economics* 53: 1 (November 1938), pp. 120–140, by permission, and copyright © the President and Fellows of Harvard College.

Table A7.1, p. 315, extracted from W.A. Fuller, *Introduction to Statistical Time Series*, John Wiley, New York, 1976, by permission, and copyright © John Wiley.

Table A8.1, p. 372, reprinted from J. MacKinnon, 'Critical Values for Cointegration Tests' in R.F. Engle and C.W. Granger (eds) *Long Run Economic Relationships*, Oxford University Press, Oxford, 1991, by permission, and copyright © Oxford University Press.

Figure 12.1, p. 510, reprinted from A.W. Phillips, 'The Relation Between Unemployment and the Rate of Change of Money Wage Rates in the United Kingdom 1861–1957', *Economica* Vol 25, 1958, pp. 283–299, by permission of Blackwell Publishers, copyright © the London School of Economics.

Figures 12.2 and 12.3, pp. 512–513, reprinted from P.A. Samuelson and R.M. Solow, 'Analytical Aspects of Anti-inflation Policy', *American Economic Review*, Papers and Proceedings, Vol. 50, 1960, pp. 177–194, by permission, and copyright © the American Economic Association.

Tables 14.3–14.7, pp. 630–632, critical values extracted from M. Osterwald-Lenum, 'A Note on Quantiles of the Asymptotic Distribution of the Maximum Likelihood Cointegration Rank Test Statistic', *Oxford Bulletin of Economics and Statistics* Vol. 54, 1992, pp. 461–472, by permission of Blackwell Publishers, copyright © Blackwell Publishers/Institute of Economics and Statistics, University of Oxford.

Tables A1–A4, pp. 753–757, based on E.S. Pearson and H.O. Hartley (eds) *Biometrika Tables for Statisticians*, Cambridge University Press, Cambridge, 1970, by permission, and copyright © the Biometrika Trustees.

Table A5, pp. 758–759, based on J. Durbin and G.S. Watson, 'Testing for Serial Correlation in Least Squares Regression, II', *Biometrika* Vol. 38, 1951, pp. 159–178, by permission, and copyright © the Biometrika Trustees.

Part I
Foundations

CHAPTER 1
Economics and quantitative economics

1.1 Introduction

The aim in this chapter is twofold. The first is to provide some motivation for the need to study quantitative economics in general and the application of econometrics in particular. The second is to provide an introduction to the way this book is structured and how and by whom it could be used with benefit. Some directions are given to accessible articles and books and these are structured in two levels: those which are a useful complement and those which develop and extend the techniques in this book at a higher level of technical sophistication.

Section **1.2** considers a relative standard definition of economics and suggests how quantitative economics fits into the overall framework. Section **1.3** distinguishes between the descriptive and constructive roles of quantitative economics; the latter particularly emphasises the model building role of econometrics. This distinction is taken up further in section **1.4**, including a brief historical perspective which is then related to present-day concerns. Section **1.5** outlines the structure of the following chapters and, finally, section **1.6** contains some concluding remarks.

1.2 Defining economics

Most texts on the principles of economics start with a definition of economics similar to that offered by Paul Samuelson (1966):

Economics is the study of how men and society *choose*, with or without the use of money, to employ *scarce* resources, which could have alternative uses, to produce various commodities over time and distribute them for consumption, now and in the future, among various people and groups in society. (Emphasis in original)

As definitions go this is at a fairly high level of abstraction; by itself it gives little idea at a practical level of what economics is about. Most texts typically divide the scope of economics into two and sometimes three distinct areas of study. Of the obligatory two the first is microeconomics, that is the study of the behaviour of individuals or small groups of agents. An agent may be a single individual as in the study of consumer behaviour or a group of agents working together in a firm. The second is macroeconomics, which is the study of the aggregate relationships in the economy; for example, what determines total spending on consumer goods, the demand for imports of goods and services and the demand and supply of money.

In essence the distinction between microeconomics and macroeconomics is one of the degree of aggregation of individual units, but as this is a spectrum there is the real possibility of situations which do not fall neatly into one category or the other. While there have been some attempts to build up macro relationships by the aggregation of micro relationships this is the exception rather than the rule. As an example consider how we might determine the decisions of an individual consumer with a given amount of income to dispose of on a set of *n* different commodities. Economists typically approach this task by suggesting that the consumer has a utility function – that is a function which enables the consumer to rank the satisfaction he or she derives from consuming a particular selection of consumer goods. However, the consumer cannot choose any configuration of goods; what is chosen has to satisfy the budget constraint which states that expenditure cannot exceed income. The problem facing the consumer is usually then analysed as maximising utility subject to satisfying the budget constraint. Now given this micro framework one possibility for studying the consumption function, that is the relationship between total consumption and its determinants, is to add together all the underlying micro consumption functions. However, with millions of consumers this is unlikely to be practical and, instead, reference is usually made to a representative or average consumer whose behaviour can be mimicked at the aggregate level.

The third area of study is that of general equilibrium analysis which views the economy as comprising individual units, or relatively small groups of individual units, interacting together. The aim with general equilibrium analysis is to bring together the decisions which are made by individuals or individual entities (for example, firms) into a large model. It is a way of building up to a model of the macroeconomy which makes explicit reference to the micro 'units' comprising the economy. However, at a practical level, since there are typically millions of micro 'units' in an economy, some compromise is necessary if general equilibrium models are to be feasible.

In all three areas of economics the application of quantitative techniques has a great deal to offer. In microeconomics while we learn from demand theory that the demand for a particular good is likely to be a function of its price relative to other goods and real income, typically microeconomic theory is unable to specify the numerical values of the corresponding elasticities. In the theory of the firm we learn what conditions need to be satisfied if profits are to be maximised but not how to measure the cost and marginal revenue curves empirically. From macroeconomics we expect consumption to be a function of income, investment to be a function of the change in output, exports to be a function of relative prices and so on, and we rely on the techniques of quantitative economics to provide numerical values for these functions. Since general equilibrium analysis builds up from the behaviour of micro-units we encounter a similarly vital role for quantitative economics.

We must be careful, though, not to think of quantitative economics as just *numerically parameterising* consumption functions, import functions and the like. A good quantitative economist needs also to be a good economist; familiar with and able to develop the relevant economic theory; *and* competent to use and critically interpret quantitative techniques applied to the area being studied.

1.3 Description, construction and models in economics

A useful distinction in quantitative techniques is between its descriptive and constructive roles, although in practice these are often combined in a particular study. There are techniques, such as measures of the central tendency or the variability of a series of observations, which are an aid to a description of events. For example, we may be able to conclude that spending on consumption goods was more variable in one period compared to another, that the level of imports was higher on average in one decade compared to another. Description helps us to get a feel of the salient features of the subject under study, and is usually a prerequisite to the construction of an explanation, which we might regard as the higher level role for quantitative economics.

The constructive role for quantitative economics usually gives rise to the idea of a *model* of economic behaviour – a characterisation which extracts from the complexity of human behaviour those aspects which are of particular interest to an economist. For example, as economists we are interested in consumers' behaviour and are concerned to explain how much consumers spend and on what. But in so doing we must regard some of the details of such behaviour as inessential – for example, the time of day when purchases are made or the clothes a consumer is wearing are not generally matters of interest. A model extracts from this detail and is often given a mathematical form, especially if the purpose of the model is to provide some guidance on the empirical magnitudes of the parameters which are part of the characterisation – for example, price and income elasticities in a study of the demand for a consumer good. While the parameterisation of the model could be undertaken by intuition and guesswork, it seems likely that it will be possible to improve upon such methods by a more systematic method of *estimation*; this is one part of model building, but by no means the only part. A distinctive feature of best practice econometrics is the positive interaction between data and ideas about the way the economy works.

1.4 The scope of model building in quantitative economics

How much then can we achieve with our quantitative techniques towards an understanding of how the economy works? There is not a single answer to this question now or in the past. We first consider some early contributions to this general debate.

1.4.1 A historical debate

Economists formulate and use models almost as second nature. For example, in macroeconomics a subject of considerable attention has been the relationship between aggregate consumption and real personal disposable income. Keynes (1936) suggested that consumption was a function of income or to be more precise he introduced a relationship between aggregate consumption in terms of wage units, C_w, and aggregate income in terms of wage units, Y_w, and called this relationship the propensity to consume. This is a *model* of what has come to be called the consumption function. Of this he said (*op. cit.*, p. 95):

> in a given situation the propensity to consume may be considered a fairly stable function.

and he continued:

> The fundamental psychological law, upon which we are entitled to depend with great confidence both *a priori* from our knowledge of human nature and from detailed facts of experience, is that men are disposed, as a rule and on average, to increase their consumption as their income increases, but not by as much as the increase in their income. (*op. cit.*, p. 96)

How detailed a particular model is will depend upon its purpose. Keynes' specification of the consumption income relationship does not specify a precise form of the function which links C_w to Y_w, indeed there are many functions which will satisfy 'The fundamental psychological law', but Keynes was not concerned with those in making a general statement about the relative magnitude of changes in consumption and income. It is clear, though, that the truth or falsity of Keynes' two statements is an empirical rather than a theoretical matter; no amount of introspection will deliver a verdict on the stability of the propensity to consume or whether consumption actually increases as income increases but not by as much as the increase in income. These are matters for the techniques of quantitative economics. As Keynes recognised, in order to make statements about relative and absolute magnitudes, we need to make reference to the empirical evidence – the detailed facts of experience; and we would add that from these facts we would need to arrive at some numerical measures of stability and sensitivity of consumption to changes in income.

It was also clear that Keynes would have to undertake some calculations of a statistical nature to put a numerical magnitude to the multiplier – a concept closely related to that of the propensity to consume. (In the simplest macroeconomic model familiar to first year students, the multiplier is $1/(1 - b)$ where b is the marginal propensity to consume.) A method of estimation would have to be used together with some statistical data. Keynes (1936, pp. 127–128) used data provided by Kuznets for the United States to estimate the multiplier:

> If single years are taken in isolation, the results look rather wild. But if they are grouped in pairs, the multiplier seems to have been less than 3 and probably fairly stable in the neighbourhood of 2.5. This suggests a marginal propensity to consume not exceeding 60 to 70 per cent – a figure quite plausible for the boom, but surprisingly, and, in my judgement, improbably low for the slump.

This kind of calculation was quite rough and ready, but served to give an idea of the broad numerical magnitudes involved. In a similar way, a number of studies were published which sought to look at whether the empirical evidence supported Keynes' views on the propensity to consume and on the related concept of the elasticity of consumption with respect to income. In particular, Gilboy published a number of papers using US data. In her 1940 paper in the *Review of Economics and Statistics* she used income and expenditure data for the United States as a whole, and plotted average expenditure against average income using a logarithmic scale for both variables (this is known as a 'double logarithmic scale' so that the slope is an estimate of the elasticity of expenditure with respect to income). She then fitted a curve to the data by eye and with further approximate calculations concluded that:

> ...the collective propensity to consume for American families in 1935–36 appears to be approximately .74. (Gilboy 1940)

In another article entitled 'The Propensity To Consume' in the *Quarterly Journal of Economics*, Gilboy (1938/39a) made use of data on a number of regions of the United States to estimate the approximate expenditure–income elasticity for various expenditure items in those regions. The method used was to plot average income and average expenditure on a chart again with a double logarithmic scale, and fit by eye either a single straight line, or a small number of straight line segments, to the points; the slope of the line would then be an estimate of the expenditure–income elasticity for that item. One of Gilboy's charts, Chart II for farm operators in Michigan and Wisconsin, is reproduced here as Figure 1.1. Even though the method of fitting straight lines to the data is approximate the observations do suggest that the income elasticities vary for different expenditure items; for example, food is relatively income inelastic compared to expenditure on recreation. (Note that the symbol η is used on the chart to denote the income–expenditure elasticity.)

Although Gilboy's and Keynes' calculations are 'approximate', and not what we would expect, certainly as far as methodology, they are nonetheless laudable. It seems self-evident now, although it was not always so, that a considerable degree of quantification of economic relationships and testing of economic hypotheses is necessary if economics is to progress. Early attempts at quantification were thus an attempt to move in that direction.

There has not always been agreement on the role of the quantitative characterisation of economic relationships. Despite the quotations above Keynes himself was concerned about how much progress could be made in putting numerical magnitudes to economic relationships and he is sometimes viewed and quoted as being a

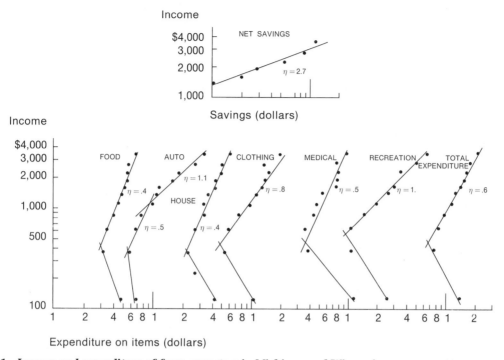

Figure 1.1 *Income and expenditure of farm operators in Michigan and Wisconsin*
Source: reprinted from Gilboy (1938a) by permission of MIT Press Journals; copyright © the President and Fellows of Harvard College

considerable sceptic of statistical methods applied to economic data. In a famous debate with Tinbergen, who had produced a 46 equation econometric model of the United States (Tinbergen 1939a, b), Keynes (1939) wrote:

> I hope that I have not done injustice to a brave pioneer effort. The labour it involved must have been enormous. The book is full of intelligence, ingenuity and candour; and I leave it with sentiments of respect for the author. But it has been a nightmare to live with, and I fancy that others will find the same. I have a feeling that Professor Tinbergen may agree with much of my comment, but that his reaction will be to engage another ten computers and drown his sorrows in arithmetic.

Students reading this book may take comfort from the fact that quantitative modelling, then – as now – is not to everyone's liking and maybe you have had your own nightmares! For Keynes it was a matter of balance: rough calcula-

tions were necessary to provide guidance but Tinbergen had gone too far. Keynes wrote very approvingly of the need for statistical analysis. Of Gilboy's (1938/39a) study Keynes wrote:

> Dear Mrs Gilboy:
> I have been much interested to read your article in the November Quarterly Journal of Economics on the Propensity to Consume. There is a great deal of useful and interesting work to be done on calculating the statistical value of the propensity to consume, both for different classes of the community and in different circumstances. This is a pioneer study for which we have hardly any material over here, but where I think there is a chance of making some sort of an approximation on the basis of American statistics. (Gilboy 1938/39b)

Perhaps then like now there was a barrier between 'informative' and usually simple calculations, and the use of techniques requiring a relatively considerable investment in statistics and mathematics as in Tinbergen's model and the developments in econometrics which were to bear fruit later in the 1940s – see Hendry and Morgan (1995) for an illuminating discussion. We develop this theme further in the next section which brings the debate into the present.

1.4.2 Present-day concerns: an 'indubitably complete analysis of the significant factors'?

While Keynes' views might be regarded as of historical interest only, they lead us into some very important present-day concerns. The quotations above raise an obvious point of interest since Keynes appears to be both supportive *and* critical of statistical analysis. Why? In order to understand the answer to this question and its present-day importance we will need a brief explanation of the statistical method of which Keynes was, on occasion, quite critical.

The primary method used by quantitative economists over the last 50 years to determine the empirical magnitude of such concepts as the propensity to consume is known as 'regression analysis', often referred to in Keynes' time as 'multiple correlation analysis', when its use was in its infancy. The basic idea behind this analysis is quite simple although the mathematics and computational aspects were off-putting to some economists.

Suppose we are interested, as Keynes suggests, in the relationship between consumption, income and the distribution of income, with the first of these depending on the remaining two, then we should observe some empirical regularities over time among these variables. For example, as income increases then, other things being equal (*ceteris paribus*), consumption should increase. However, in attempting to discern whether such a positive relationship holds over time it is likely that other factors will not conveniently remain constant. In order to assign a numerical parameter to the propensity to consume we will need to take into account the possible variation in other factors. In other words we will not assume that other things have been constant, and the relevant method used to do this is 'multiple correlation analysis'. Such a method must enable us to separate the influences of particular variables within a group of such variables. Of this regression analysis Keynes (1939) wrote:

> Am I right in thinking that the method of multiple correlation analysis depends on the economist having furnished not merely a list of the significant causes, which is correct as far as it goes, but a *complete* list? For example, suppose three factors are taken into account, it is not enough that these should be in fact *verae causae*; there must be no other significant factor. If there is a further factor, not taken account of, then the method is not able to discover the relative quantitative importance of the first three. If so, this means that the method is only applicable where the economist is able to provide beforehand a correct and indubitably complete analysis of the significant factors. (Emphasis in original)

Was Keynes right? Do we need 'a correct and indubitably complete analysis'? If so we must surely fail for such omniscience is rarely available in any scientific field of study. What Keynes sought was a counsel of perfection, rarely if ever met then or now. Despite its considerable relevance this issue was largely put aside but for many years, with books on econometric and quantitative methods written assuming that the task of the quantitative economist was that of estimating the parameters of the model as *efficiently* as possible, given that the specification of the model was correct – the 'axiom of correct specification' was assumed.

Although econometrics has long been regarded as that branch of economics dealing with the methods and techniques of mathematics and, particularly, statistics, which were developed for the study of economics, for a considerable time the textbook view of what econometrics had to offer was very limited. The role of econometrics was considered in a sense to be a lesser one than economics itself – a handmaiden to the princess! Given the theoretical model the role of econometrics was to put numerical values to the parameters of the model, with a related role being that of the corroboration or rejection of theoretical relationships; and while the techniques of econometrics might have seemed quite formidable to those without the right background, they might reasonably be viewed just as rather secondary tools to the main task of specifying theoretical relationships.

The central role of econometrics was often regarded as one of *estimating* the parameters of the model in as efficient a way as possible given a particular set of data with which to apply the statistical and mathematical techniques; given those estimated parameters the next stage would be to establish whether the values so obtained were different from some particular values of interest. A hypothesis would be set up and tested within a statistical framework about the role of the explanatory variables in determining a dependent variable; often the hypothesis would be formulated so that a particular parameter would be zero if the variable to which it corresponded had no influence on the dependent variable, and a conclusion pronounced on whether the empirical model was consistent with the theory – or, occasionally, that the theory was not corroborated by the data.

There are many studies that reflect this approach. For example, let us suppose a simple model with just two periods: now, designated as period t, and the future, designated as period $t + 1$. An individual has the choice of whether to spend all his or her income in period t or save some for future consumption, period $t + 1$. Any income not spent currently we assume is put into a financial asset which yields a real rate of return (that is after taking inflation into account) of $r\%$ p.a. It is likely that in planning how much to save the individual will be sensitive to the value of r expected at time t to

prevail from period t to period $t + 1$, designated r_t^e. An increase in r_t^e will indicate a greater return to unconsumed – or saved – income, and as a result we anticipate that this increase will lead to consumption being deferred into the future – that is to period $t + 1$. Therefore, c_{t+1} and r_t^e are positively related. The sensitivity of consumption over time to changes in the (expected) rate of interest is usually characterised as the intertemporal elasticity of the substitution of consumption.

The theory outlined here suggests that the change in consumption, comparing period $t + 1$ with period t, should be positively related to the (expected) rate of interest. Further, the larger is this elasticity the greater is the sensitivity of future consumption to changes in the expected rate of interest. With an appropriate set of data and statistical tools it appears that the empirical task is simple: a numerical parameterisation of the intertemporal elasticity of substitution and a hypothesis test on whether this quantity is zero. For many years this kind of definition of the task appeared to be the *methodological* role of the quantitatively minded economist. In essence it was a rather limited role, but many textbooks on econometrics portrayed the role in that way. In practice, though, things seemed to be rather different, and often a contrast with what one had been taught as an undergraduate or postgraduate. Usually many equations were estimated rather than one, there may have been experimentation with different empirical definitions of the variables, sometimes variables not initially in the analysis were subsequently included, there was experimentation as to the best functional form and so on. There often seemed to be many elements of choice that did not appear explicitly in these learned sources!

To see how the methodology of an empirical study might be different consider again attempting to numerically parameterise the intertemporal substitution of consumption. The first point to note is that there is a *theory model* which explains how consumption in the present and the future, and the expected real interest rate, are linked together, and also gives an anticipated sign to the intertemporal elasticity of consumption (positive) and a description of the meaning of the different magnitudes which might occur for this parameter. The theory model suggests a number of *theory variables*, namely, *present* and *future consumption*, and *the expected real rate of interest*. In estimating the theory model complications may arise; for example what if there are imperfect capital markets so it is not possible to transfer consumption into the future? And in a related context would data from liquidity constrained households be helpful in estimating the intertemporal elasticity of consumption?

Relating the theory model to empirical evidence requires the translation of *theory variables* into *observable variables* and often this translation is by no means straightforward. In this example there are three possible measures of consumption: expenditure on nondurable goods and services (those which are more or less actually consumed as they are paid for); total expenditure on consumption goods including expenditure on durable goods (such as computers and televisions which yield a stream of consumption services over a number of years); expenditure on nondurable goods and services, and the service flow from durable goods. While the last of these is the theoretically correct measure, in order to obtain such an empirical measure involves a large number of assumptions and approximations and, anyway, is not generally available, so one or both of the first two is usually used.

As to the expected rate of interest there are three problems: the first is that data is available on *actual* rather than *expected* series. The second is that there is a vast range of financial assets with associated interest rates – which one should we choose? The third is that the theory model specifies a *real* interest rate which will have to be constructed by subtracting the rate of inflation from a nominal interest rate, and that requires an empirical decision on the appropriate rate of inflation.

1.4.3 Stylisations of methodology

In practice undergraduates, postgraduates and professional researchers were aware that when they were 'doing' empirical work it was rarely in the manner suggested by the textbooks. The textbook approach could be characterised as:

1. Formulate theoretical model
2. Obtain data
3. Estimate model efficiently and test hypotheses
4. Report results

Generally, the tasks of formulating the theoretical model and estimating the model were regarded as being undertaken by separate individuals with the econometrician being given the somewhat lesser, if no doubt more technical, task of estimation – an application, perhaps, of the principle of comparative advantage! According to the textbooks the theoretical model must come first, to look at the data first was to 'cheat'; indeed, although this term was rarely levelled directly, many an empirical economist was accused in pejorative terms of 'data mining' – that is looking at the data first and trying more than one alternative characterisation of the model before reporting the results for the preferred model.

Yet, in contrast to the textbook model, 'data mining' seemed an informative way to proceed. Looking at the data gave one ideas and allowed the observation of potentially important *empirical regularities* which might be exploited in constructing a theoretical model of economic variables. Further, initial attempts at estimating models might be relatively unsuccessful, and allowing this information and the data to motivate a respecification of the theoretical model would often yield interesting and informative results. This approach suggests that economic theory and empirical specification interact rather than be kept in separate compartments. One example of this is where economic theory is informative about the equilibrium specification – for example, that consumption depends upon income – but relatively uninformative about how consumption *adjusts* to changes in income in the *short run*; this is something about which we expect the observed data to provide information.

Another confusing matter, for the undergraduate and professional economist alike, is that they would often read books or articles and find that two or more apparently incompatible theories were claimed to be consistent with an observed dataset. There often appeared no systematic approach to progressing economic knowledge by discarding particular theories (as being 'bettered' by another theory). It could appear that the earth was both spherical and flat, depending upon which author you read! Clearly there was a considerable need to construct a framework for economic research, which would describe a productive and progressive research strategy. Productive in the sense that it would incorporate the methods which successful researchers *actually* used, and progressive in that it would lead to an advancement by discarding models which could be shown to be inferior to others. This strategy would also serve to answer Keynes' criticism of 'multiple correlation analysis' that it seemed to require a complete specification of the significant factors. We would recognise that empirical specifications were only *tentatively adequate*, and that in time, with more data and the development of techniques, other specifications may well lead to improvements, which would enable an explanation of why previous results were inferior; progress would be made by *encompassing* previous empirical specifications.

At the centre of this research strategy is the concept of the *data generation process* – or *DGP*. This is the mechanism that generates the data we observe; in general it is a complex process that is almost certain to be unknown to us, involving a large number of variables and parameters. Were it to be known it would provide the 'indubitably complete list' of significant factors to which Keynes referred. Our task is to see how well we can approximate – or

reduce – the DGP; and in order to do this we can use any means that will advance that aim. Thus, while the first step in empirical analysis should always involve a theory model, we would not rule out the possibility that the theory model had been informed by 'looking at the data' first. This is part of the concept of *data instigated discovery*, which is the idea that being aware of what has been happening, as revealed by the data, is a catalyst to suggesting possible theoretical explanations. Indeed a familiarity with the main *empirical regularities* in the data is almost a prerequisite to successful modelling.

The first stage in modelling is not as simple as specifying a theory model, although that is part of it; rather it is the interaction of a theoretical framework, previous research, data instigated ideas and empirical regularities. The next stage is to relate the resulting theory and ideas, which might involve such broad concepts as consumption, prices, income and so on, to measurable variables which can be brought together in a particular sample of data. This is often a very difficult and much underrated stage in undertaking empirical work. If your 'ideal' variables are unobtainable, can you still go ahead? You may find that the available sample of data for some variables is longer than for others; that perhaps there has been a change in the definition of a variable on which you are collecting data; and, as often happens with data in index number forms there has been a change of base. The formulation of an empirical model is the next stage and will often involve a number of judgements. Quite often the theory model is relatively unspecific about the precise form of the relationship between the economic variables both in terms of functional form and dynamic specification. For example, in estimating a demand function the main explanatory variables are likely to be real disposable income and the relative prices of substitutes and complements, but the form which relates these variables together is not specified by theory nor how they adjust over time faced with a complex set of shocks and adjustments.

In practice, and in contrast to the idealised methodology of quantitative economics outlined above, carrying out an empirical study usually involves solving a large number of detailed problems of which the estimation one, regarded narrowly as using the most efficient method of estimation, while important is rarely likely to be the most central. An alternative stylisation of the methodological steps is as follows.

1. Theory model
   - Observation of empirical regularities
   - Assessment of past empirical and theoretical research
   - Data instigated ideas/discovery
2. Outline formulation of a model to be estimated
   - Problems of matching theory and observable variables
   - Empirical definitions of variables
   - Collection of data and choice of sample period
3. Estimation of the empirical model
   - Choice of estimation method
   - Estimation
4. Diagnostic evaluation of the empirical model
   - Is the model statistically adequate?
   - Does it pass diagnostic tests?
   - Is respecification necessary?
   - Is the model tentatively adequate?
5. Progressive evaluation of the empirical model
   - Does the model improve upon previous models?
   - Is the model able to encompass competing models?

In the first stage a combination of sources is brought together to suggest the way in which the model will be constructed; the key variables in the analysis and their likely interrelationships are identified through a combination of a study of the previous literature, covering both theoretical and empirical analyses, and original ideas perhaps prompted by plotting data series which suggest interesting empirical regularities. In the first stage the main aim is to reduce the range of possible explanations for the economic variables of interest, and to provide a theoretical background which will allow an interpretation of the subsequent empirical results.

In the second stage the form of the model should be specified. That is whereas the first stage might have been relatively vague on the precise functional relationship among the variables and the precise definitions of the variables to be used, in the second stage these essential details must be specified. For example, while the first stage might have led to the suggestion that consumption is determined by income and an interest rate, in the second stage the possible functional relationships must be specified by assessing questions such as whether these variables are linearly related – or is a form of nonlinear model to be considered? A much underrated step is matching the theoretical variables to the corresponding observable variables. This is often a source of considerable frustration for students and researchers alike. The consumption example referred to above is relevant in this context. Most theories of consumers' behaviour define consumption in terms of expenditure on nondurable goods and services and the service flow from durable consumer goods such as televisions and automobiles. Yet the student will look in vain for a corresponding empirical variable in official publications of statistics.

Thus, going into the third stage you should have a workable, but not yet parameterised, formulation of the model. It is very likely that there will be some matters to be determined by the data. You may be unsure, for example, whether a change in income affects consumption immediately or, perhaps, with a lag, and you may have had a choice of interest rate variables. Thus, although this stage has been described as estimating the model, in practice there are several related decisions to be made, of which estimation is just one.

Ideally, the outcome of the third stage should be a numerically parameterised model, which you have some confidence in as representing an accurate description of that part of the structure of the economy of interest. That confidence will be enhanced if your model passes some tests which indicate that no misspecification can be detected. Just as in the process of building physical models thorough checks are made, so such checks can be made on conceptual models. For example, you should not have omitted any systematic influence from your model. This is the fourth stage: a diagnostic checking that your model is not 'ill'! It is only if your model is healthy – that is not misspecified – that you can undertake testing hypotheses. Testing within a misspecified model is likely to be misleading.

However, resting easy at the fourth stage, even having established a 'healthy model', is not to be recommended. What students and professional economists alike find confusing is a multiplicity of different models all purporting to provide explanations for the same phenomena. In such a case there is unlikely to be any progression in our knowledge about the structure of the economy; much more likely is confusion given several competing explanations.

Hence, a fifth stage is necessary, that of an evaluation of competing models, and if your model is the best available it should be able to explain why other models get the results they do. This is the concept of one model encompassing another model, with the encompassing model to be preferred. This might seem a counsel of perfection, but it is an essential step if economics is to move forward – or progress – in discarding inadequate explanations. That is not to say that a particular encompassing model will always be dominant. It may subsequently prove inadequate, as did models of the UK consumption function built in the 1970s, which primarily depended upon income, when faced with developments which liberalised the financial markets in the 1980s. At a particular point what we can try and achieve is a *tentatively* adequate

model; and herein lies the resolution of Keynes' concerns about the role and scope of 'multiple correlation analysis'. While in principle we would like to be able to specify an indubitably complete list of significant factors, we know that we are rarely going to be able to know the full structure of the *data generation process.* Hence, we adopt a progressive strategy of building tentatively adequate – but, of course, 'healthy' – models which, in principle, improve upon previous models by encompassing them, so that multiple and competing explanations do not exist side by side. We undertake checks on a particular model to ensure that it is healthy but do not close our minds to the progressive strategy of assessing and improving that model as further data becomes available and econometric techniques are developed. Unlike the experimental scientist of the physical sciences we are rarely in the position of being able to replicate experiments to assess our explanation of a particular phenomenon. In most cases we simply have to wait for the real world to provide further observations which we can then use.

Tinbergen's approach to quantitative model building can be seen as a pioneer of the progressive and encompassing methodology. For example, in summarising his own approach he wrote:

> We do not claim to have proved, when constructing our models of the American, English and Dutch economies, all features laid down in these models to be inevitable. We have presented these models as possible structures, perhaps even as probable structures, which have the advantage that they are at least not contradictory to the statistics used in their construction. Hence, not all our conclusions on some business-cycle theories can actually be proved. Nevertheless we think that our attempts lead to useful suggestions and it is hoped that those who reject our conclusions will at least try to give alternative attempts to explain the real course of the crucial variables in a way similar to ours. (Tinbergen 1941)

1.5   The structure and aims of this book

This section describes the general aims of this book, relating it to recent developments in econometric technique, outlines the structure of the parts and chapters and suggests further reading.

1.5.1   General aims

The central aim of this book is to provide an accessible introduction to some key concepts and techniques which are now routinely found in modern empirical studies, but which are not adequately covered in entry level books of econometric methods or in books on applied econometrics. An important aspect of applications of econometrics to time series variables in the last ten years or so has been the emphasis on techniques which assess whether the data is what is known as stochastically trended. For example, even a casual look at macroeconomic data, such as GDP, consumption, investment and so on, for developed countries reveals an increase over time – but an increase which could not easily be explained as random deviations about an underlying deterministic trend. Rather the trend itself shows changes, perhaps a steeper increase at one time than at other times. The development might also be cyclical but the peak in one cycle is very likely to be above the peak in the previous cycle.

It has been known for a long time that typical time series data is trended, but with some notable exceptions – for example, Box and Jenkins (1970) – this has been dealt with by assuming that the trend is adequately captured by a deterministic specification. For example, suppose there were theoretical reasons to suppose that the variables Y_t and X_t were related; then if one was trended such a (bivariate) relationship would only make sense if the other was also trended. A typical reaction to the trending was either first to run a de-trending regression in which each variable was separately regressed on time, or to include a dummy variable to represent 'time' in the regression equation. (Regression is a method of using the data to obtain estimates of the coefficients of interest, and the dummy variable 'time' is one that increments by one unit each time period.)

Generally, there was little question of this practice until the early 1980s, when developments on two related fronts came to suggest serious criticisms of such an approach. First, a seminal empirical study by Nelson and Plosser (1982), using existing but somewhat overlooked technical developments in the study of time series variables, especially those due to Fuller (1976), concluded that the picture of time series being generated by deterministic trends was misleading. The alternative was that the trend was generated within the structure of the time series rather than 'added' on, and this seemed to fit the macroeconomic data better than the deterministic trend view for a large number of time series. Second, the view of trends as deterministic was uncomfortable at a theoretical level. For example, the implication of a stochastic shock to a deterministically trended series was that the effect of the shock would be relatively short-lived, the series in due course returning to its underlying deterministic trend – the series would 'mean revert'. In contrast in a stochastically trended world, stochastic shocks have permanent effects, they get built into the future levels of the series – they are 'integrated' into the series, hence such series are referred to as integrated series. The Nelson and Plosser article generated a debate which is still going on as different methods have been developed and brought to bear on their general theme. Whether or not the eventual verdict is the same as that suggested by Nelson and Plosser, their article has undoubtedly been a permanent shock to the development of econometric techniques.

Whereas Nelson and Plosser were concerned with individual series in a univariate analysis, in another important development at the beginning of the 1980s Granger and Weiss (1983) considered how to deal with two or more series each of which had a stochastic trend, that is each was integrated. They introduced the idea that two or more integrated series, which generally would have no tendency to move together, might well be tied together in the long run. A good example is consumption and income, each of which appears to be an integrated series and which could, therefore, in principle bear no relationship to each other in their stochastic trending. However, in practice consumption and income are tied together in the long run as economic theory suggests; thus, even though they are separately integrated their joint movement over time suggests they are *cointegrated*, the 'co' indicating the tying together. Although Granger's seminal article with Engle was not published until 1987, Engle and Granger (1987), it was clear that there was a seachange in the way that time series econometric theory was developing with an important effect on the techniques used in future empirical studies.

Almost chronologically parallel developments were taking place in the methodology of econometrics. Although these can be traced to Sargan's important article on wage inflation in 1964, Sargan (1964), a considerable impetus to the practice of econometrics was delivered by Davidson, Hendry, Srba and Yeo (1978), usually referred to as DHSY (and pronounced DAISY!), which anticipated the development of the analysis of cointegrated time series, and a series of articles by David Hendry and his co-authors, see, for example, Hendry and von Ungern-Sternberg (1981), Hendry and Richard (1982, 1983), Hendry and Mizon (1990). At the risk of simplifying their considerable contribution, they codified existing best practice in applied econometric research and provided a framework for a progressive research strategy in econometrics. Again these developments were a permanent shock to the way that subsequent empirical studies were structured.

By the end of the 1980s existing econometric textbooks and the few available books on applied econometrics were looking distinctly uncomfor-

table against a background of continual development in time series econometrics at both the theoretical and empirical level. While there was still a need for 'traditional' textbooks which covered the details of estimation theory and inference, there was also a need for books which were closer to what applied econometricians did. This gap was filled by a number of excellent books. Lütkepohl (1991) provided a thorough though theoretical treatment of multiple time series analysis in the context of integrated and cointegrated variables; Banerjee, Dolado, Galbraith and Hendry (1992) brought together the main theoretical contributions with an important emphasis on cointegrated variables and error correction models; Cuthbertson, Hall and Taylor (1993) emphasised applications in the context of cointegrated time series; Harris (1995) provided a very useful short guide to some key aspects of using cointegration techniques; and at the other end of the scale, Hamilton (1994) provided a comprehensive account of techniques applicable to integrated time series; and Enders (1995) provided an extremely useful mixture of techniques and applications linked to the commercially available time series econometric package, RATS (regression analysis of time series) – see Doan (1996). The applied econometrician often relies on others to provide the means to implement developing econometric techniques and there are a number of commercially available econometric packages. PCGIVE, Doornik and Hendry (1994, 1996), and MICROFIT, Pesaran and Pesaran (1997, Version 4.0) are available each with a book which serves as an excellent tutorial in econometric techniques. RATS and TSP – see Hall and Cummins (1996) – contain ready-made routines and a simple programming language which enables the user to build up their own purpose-made routines.

A second key development, which also had its origins in the 1980s, especially for the application of econometric methods to financial time series, is the set of techniques originating from Engle's (1982) seminal article on what are known as ARCH processes. Although not introduced in the context of financial time series, the ARCH concept was to have profound effects in that area. In a survey in 1992 Bollerslev, Chou and Kroner (1992) cited well over 200 articles developing and applying ARCH techniques to finance. To understand what an ARCH effect is, and its impact on modelling financial time series, consider a particular financial asset, the return on which is not certain – for example, the price of a particular stock or index of stocks on the New York Stock Exchange. Over time the price of the stock will vary with, perhaps, some periods of relative tranquillity of price movement interspersed with periods of quite substantial movement. These changes in price affect the return, defined as the rate of change in the price (sometimes the return is benchmarked in that it is defined relative to the return on a certain asset such as a 3-month Treasury Bill or a portfolio of assets available in the market). In broad terms the movement in returns is characterised as volatility, and an *ex ante* measure of volatility is vital to pricing the asset. The question then arises as how to form such a measure. As volatility is clearly not constant over time any scheme must take this aspect as fundamental. The ARCH scheme, with the acronym standing for autoregressive conditional heteroscedasticity, first extracts any predictable part to the return, what is left is then termed 'news'; the variance of the news at time *t* is then a function of past news. Usually volatility is positively related to past news (more precisely the square of past news) so that a process which has in the past been noisy will lead to an *ex ante* measure of volatility which is large. This simple idea has led to one of the biggest growth areas in the development of techniques and their practical application.

This book complements those mentioned in the last but one paragraph in the following ways. It is primarily an entry level book which is suitable for a wide audience of non-specialists. Very few prerequisites are required. For example, some knowledge of matrix algebra and calculus would help but is not generally essential. Some elementary aspects of matrix algebra are used in Chapters 2, 5, 14 and 15, but much progress can be made by the reader without the mathematical formalities. The book is structured so that basic techniques are introduced and then complemented in later chapters with applications. In contrast to a number of existing books on either econometric methods or applied econometrics, the applications chapters are generally full-length, self-contained studies of some areas of economics. They are deliberately not illustrations which just show how to use particular techniques, but omit the theoretical detail motivating the economic example. The detail of the economic argument is usually vital to understand the context of the application of econometric techniques. Many other areas of application could have been chosen and no doubt some would wish that a particular application topic should have been included. The techniques of time series econometrics are very widely applied and cover almost every area for which there is a theoretical interest. However, noting the constraint of space, the aim has been to show how economics and econometrics combine in an empirical study, sometimes leading to positive conclusions but sometimes leading to an agnostic conclusion and an almost insatiable desire for more research, more data and different techniques.

While this book does not sidestep the problem of integrated (or nonstationary) time series, and it recognises the impact of ARCH-type processes on modelling financial time series, it is meant also for the 'conventional' ground found in introductory and intermediate textbooks on econometrics. That is the basics of least squares estimation, inference and hypothesis testing are covered. Also, although the title of this book emphasises time series applications, there are very few techniques covered here that are not also applicable to cross-section data. However, there are some techniques particular to cross-section data and bringing these together with those from time series would have resulted in a much (and perhaps impracticably) longer book.

1.5.2 Parts and chapters

Part I is headed Foundations, and should not be treated as inessential. Much of the difficulty encountered by econometric nonspecialists in studying econometrics arises from a lack of familiarity with some of the commonly used language. Chapter 2 introduces some basic concepts in time series analysis. For example, the related concepts of lagging and leading time series together with the lag operator and its associated algebra are important building blocks in later analysis. Similarly, Chapter 3 introduces some basic concepts, first in probability and second in the distinction between stationary and nonstationary random variables.

Part II is concerned with regression analysis and its role in model building and comprises six chapters in all. Chapters 4 and 5 are a pair concerned with the common theme of estimation and inference but at different levels of complexity; at this stage no complications are introduced from nonstationarity. Chapter 4 starts with the analysis limited to two variables (the bivariate model). Even though this is a practical limitation most of the general principles of estimation and inference can be illustrated in this context. This chapter introduces estimation by ordinary least squares, OLS, and instrumental variables, IV, and the general principles of hypothesis testing. Toward the end of the Chapter 4 the bivariate model is extended as a precursor to Chapter 5, where the multiple linear regression model is covered. Estimation methods are also extended to cover generalised least squares, GLS. Econometric model building usually involves judgement about whether an initial specification is adequate, and Chapter 5 also details a number of standard tests, usually referred to as diagnostic tests, which are commonly applied.

Chapters 6 and 7 are also a pair with the common theme of distinguishing between stationary and nonstationary time series. The framework of these two chapters is the univariate model and the type of nonstationarity which can be removed by differencing the original series an appropriate number of times. For example, a nonstationary series which can be made stationary by differencing it once is said to be integrated of order 1. (Which is why a non-stationary series is sometimes referred to as being integrated.) The extension to the multivariate model is taken up later in Chapters 14 and 15. Chapter 6 deals with the basic model and test statistics due to Fuller (1976) and Dickey and Fuller (1979, 1981), usually referred to as DF (for Dickey–Fuller) or ADF (for augmented DF) tests. Chapter 7 extends the framework of Chapter 6 in a number of ways. The basic univariate time series model is extended and this naturally leads into other test statistics and their different properties. Chapter 7 also contains a discussion on the difficulty of distinguishing between a nonstationary series and a stationary series with a deterministic trend subject to one or more 'breaks'.

The last two chapters in Part II could also be considered a pair with a related theme. Chapter 8 brings together related aspects of regression analysis, which was the subject of Chapters 4 and 5, and the distinction between stationary and nonstationary series, which was the subject of Chapters 6 and 7. The key concepts of cointegration and error correction models are introduced in Chapter 8 together with a test procedure and choice of test statistics. While economists do not generally have access to experimental data in their empirical studies, they can generate their own data by means of simulation analysis and then evaluate the properties of different estimators and hypothesis testing techniques. This technique, sometimes referred to as Monte Carlo analysis, by analogy with the replicability of games of chance, involves specifying the mechanism generating the data (the data generation process) and usually involves a random or stochastic element which gives different outcomes their variability. Simulation analysis is used in Chapter 8 to illustrate some key points about estimation and inference in finite samples with variables that are nonstationary or very nearly nonstationary.

Until Chapter 9 the focus of analysis is very much the single regression equation with the variables in the analysis given an unequal status. One variable is designated as dependent on a number of other variables which are, therefore, regarded as explanatory for that choice of dependent variable; moreover the explanatory variable(s) are assumed to have particular properties which do not make them endogenous for the parameters of interest in the single equation. Chapter 9 makes a start on relaxing this assumption. One aim of this chapter is to introduce the modification of the OLS estimator applied to nonstationary time series due to Phillips and Hansen (1990), usually referred to as FMOLS (for fully modified OLS). However, setting up the framework to interpret the FMOLS estimator has much wider implications than just the derivation of an estimator; it serves to introduce a discussion of the conceptualisation of endogeneity, and the distinction among conditional, unconditional and long-run variance matrices, which is also useful in Chapter 16. Simulation analysis is also used in this chapter to illustrate some of the issues involved in practical choices about whether it is better to treat nearly integrated processes as stationary or nonstationary for purposes of estimation and inference.

Part III comprises four chapters with substantive applications involving economic theory and econometric methods. The overall aim of this part of the book is to go beyond illustrations to show how an empirical study necessarily involves quite detailed consideration of an underlying theoretical framework, combined with an interpretation of the relevant data and choice of econometric techniques. The results are not always positive for the economic theory involved; nevertheless, this serves to show what happens in practice and what may not, as well as what may, be reported in academic journals.

Chapter 10 opens Part III with a study of the demand for money in two disparate periods and countries. The first concerns a hyperinflationary period in post-First World War Germany which has attracted a lot of interest since Cagan's (1956) seminal study of hyperinflation in a number of countries. A drawback to the studies of this period is that they are based on a rather small sample size. Even so, the results are interesting and show how practical considerations do not always coincide with theoretical considerations. Ideally, the empirical study should be able to explain the transition in and out of particular hyperinflationary periods, rather than limit itself to one turbulent period. The second country and sample period are relatively standard in terms of the number of observations and stability of economic regime we have come to expect of contemporary empirical studies. The country is the United States with a sample period of over 200 observations from 1974 onwards.

Chapter 11 considers the expectations model of the term structure of interest rates when combined with the rational expectations hypothesis – a combination sometimes referred to as EM + REH. The 'term structure of interest rates' refers to the yield on financial securities which are alike in every respect except their term to maturity (that is the time when they can be redeemed). Whilst EM + REH is only one possible explanation of the term structure, it is the leading one which has led to a large number of different tests on different datasets. The results, in the existing literature and here, do not tend to give overwhelming support for the theory.

Chapter 12 switches focus to one of the most influential empirical studies in the period since 1945. In 1958 Phillips published an article which introduced a curve, representing the shape of a (possible) trade-off between unemployment and (nominal) wage inflation, which was to become synonymous with his name. Phillips' article generated a substantial body of empirical research into the existence, or nonexistence, of such a trade-off in different countries and over different periods. We take Phillips' first historical period, 1860–1913, to show what happens when the original and different methods of estimation and evaluation are used. Phillips' article was important not only because it was interesting at the time, but because it generated a lasting debate about the theory of a trade-off and the development of models of expectations and methods of estimation. Although the thrust of empirical research with post-1970s data has led to an assumption that there is no trade-off, it is my view that this still remains an open question. Although far from confirmatory it could be argued that the UK Government, at least, believes, in a broad sense, that there is a (reduced form) trade-off between activity and inflation; controlling activity (output and hence employment) through the instrument of nominal interest rates controls the intermediate target of inflation. Whatever the results of the theoretical and empirical reassessments of the Phillips curve, Phillips' 1958 article undoubtedly led to a permanent 'shock' to economics.

Chapter 13 is the last chapter in Part III and is concerned with the purchasing power parity (PPP) theory of the exchange rate. PPP is of interest in its own right and is central to most theories of the exchange rate even if part of a more general framework – for example, as part of the flexible price monetary model (FPMM). Although a heavily researched area, it is still not clear what determines the exchange rate. Chapter 13 is an introduction to this ongoing debate.

There is a general lesson from the four applications chapters. Throughout, based on the methodological precept of progressive empirical research outlined above, I hope that those with a particular interest in one chapter or another will be able to improve, or at least will be encouraged to try and improve, upon the results reported here; a progressive research framework applies here in particular as well as in general. The improvement may come in some cases through other studies which develop the theoretical or technical framework beyond the level of this book.

Part IV, headed Extensions, comprises three chapters. Chapters 14 and 15 are closely related being a pair, with the emphasis in the first on basic concepts and techniques and on developments and applications in the second. Apart from Chapter 9, the focus of previous chapters

has been single equation analysis, even though examples of the Phillips–Hansen FMOLS estimator were reported in some of the applications chapters, and GLS was applied to several real exchange rate equations in Chapter 13. Chapter 14 is based on the developments of multivariate integration and cointegration analysis due to Johansen – see, for example, Johansen (1995a) and Hansen and Johansen (1998). Much applied econometric work, in many different areas, now adopts the Johansen paradigm, and hence this should be included in a book intended to encourage empirical studies. Broadly the Johansen approach differs from the preceding analysis by its explicit recognition of the interaction of economic variables in a system context. If some variables can be treated asymmetrically and designated as (weakly) exogenous, as in a typical single equation analysis, then this must be part of a wider approach in which such assumptions are testable. In the Johansen framework we start with the assumption that, deterministic variables aside, all the variables in the analysis are endogenous, and are, therefore, to be explained from within. Chapter 14 lays out the basic theoretical framework which covers estimation and inference. Chapter 15 develops the basic framework of the preceding chapter in two ways: there are extensions to the framework which allow interesting and practically relevant special cases to arise, as in the case of weakly exogenous variables; there are a number of applications of the techniques which serve to illustrate how decisions are made in a practical context.

Finally, Chapter 16 is devoted to ARCH techniques, their specification, estimation and interpretation, especially in the context of financial econometrics. As in previous chapters the emphasis is on usable techniques and illustrations with genuine applicability.

1.5.3 General comments about the structure of this book

Finally, some comments on what this book is not. It is not primarily a textbook on econometric methods in the usual sense. There are many conventional books available at different levels of entry, and which are required reading on courses on econometric methods. Ideally, at least one of these books should be a compulsory item of purchase for the aspiring economist.

The point of this book is to enable the student and hopefully the nonspecialist professional to feel more comfortable about doing economic research and, at least, be able to read with greater confidence the empirical research in their own areas of interest. An example might make my point. My own area of research has not included development economics, yet recently I was called upon to read about and comment upon the connection between financial liberalisation, or more precisely the lack of it, and economic growth in some developing countries. A search of recent literature suggested that the articles by Demetriades and Hussein (1996) and Demetriades and Luintel (1997) would be of particular relevance to this topic. It transpired that the techniques used in those articles might well have equally been chosen to illustrate the theoretical and empirical concepts of Chapters 14 and 15.

The decision to make the applications substantive rather than illustrative has meant detailed coverage on a smaller number of topics rather than commentary on a larger number of illustrations. This was a conscious decision but, of course, may mean that a particular topic of interest to a reader is not explicitly covered here. The trade-off is a more detailed understanding of the scope of alternative techniques and their application and, like my own example on development economics, I hope the confidence to read and critically appraise areas not explicitly dealt with.

Each chapter is structured in a similar way. An introduction gives a brief idea of the areas to be covered in each section, or subsection where the detail is important. Sections define an overall topic with subsections breaking up the topic into smaller more 'digestible' parts. Finally, a section on concluding remarks either draws together the main conclusions or, if more appropriate

to the level of discussion, suggests qualifying remarks and extensions to the various arguments. A point-by-point review in summary form follows the final section. This is not meant to be a substitute for reading the chapter, but should be an aid to summarising the main points and for revision. Review questions are included and should be attempted as an integral part of each chapter.

While this book is intended to be at an entry level, it contains results which may well be of interest to the professional economist or specialist (either technically or in the areas of application considered here). At the least I hope it provides the means to move on to reading articles in the many journals that publish empirical work and to other books dealing with a similar subject matter at a different level.

1.5.4 Further reading

Good, but somewhat advanced, theoretical treatments of integration and cointegration are provided by Hamilton (1994), Hatanaka (1996) and Johansen (1995a). Charemza and Deadman (1992), Banerjee *et al.* (1993), Enders (1995), Harris (1995) and Hansen and Johansen (1998) provide an approach which should be easy to follow from this book; and Cuthbertson *et al.* (1992) is a useful reference for its emphasis on practical illustrations. Although not oriented toward applications of econometrics involving nonstationary data, Berndt (1991) is useful for the range of empirical studies covered. A highly recommended collection of survey articles in much the same spirit as in this book is provided by Oxley, George, Roberts and Sayer (1995). Engle (1995a) brings together a number of articles focusing on the development and application of ARCH techniques.

There are a large number of econometric textbooks at different levels of entry. At the introductory level Gujarati (1995) and Kennedy (1997) are to be recommended; also at this level, Thomas (1997) is useful because it recognises the importance of the distinction between stationary and nonstationary time series. At an intermediate level, Greene (1997) and Judge, Griffiths, Hill, Lütkepohl and Lee (1982) are market leaders; and at an advanced level, Hendry (1995) continues the theme of integrated variables and cointegration, while Judge, Griffiths, Hill, Lütkepohl and Lee (1985) is as compendious on standard techniques as their intermediate level book.

1.6 Concluding remarks

Writing a book suggests there is a gap that needs filling. The gap to be filled in this case is to enable nonspecialists access to a large and apparently quite complex set of techniques which are used in empirical studies. Even undergraduates and postgraduates specialising in econometrics may find the techniques and exposition here of interest. It is my experience that while econometric textbooks are lengthy there are few, as yet, which devote an amount of space on time series techniques for nonstationary series and ARCH which is necessary and commensurate with the demands made in the literature on econometric applications. Thus, even a final year undergraduate majoring in economics will most likely only have experienced the barest of introductions to the issues surrounding the use of standard techniques, for example OLS, when the time series in question are nonstationary or nearly nonstationary. Many will hang on to the interpretation of R^2 (the coefficient of determination) as a goodness of fit measure in regression analysis (see Chapter 4) even though its interpretation changes with nonstationary time series.

The role of econometric techniques and quantitative methods is vital if economics is going to take a view as to which theories are consistent with the data and which are not. However, progress is often not as clinical as this statement suggests. It is likely that the progression is first in terms of tentatively adequate conclusions which await further data, and then find confirmation in further results perhaps using different time periods. Also different techniques may be brought to bear which do not always lead to previous conclusions. A relevant example is the debate on whether the empirical evidence favours purchasing power parity (PPP) theory of the exchange rate, which in its simplest form states that the price of tradable goods should be the same in common currency units. In contrast to the 'intuition' (or 'warm, fuzzy feelings', Rogoff (1996)) of many economists, much of the empirical literature concludes that the data does not support PPP; in part this has generated a voluminous literature, using different time periods, different countries and different techniques, to see if there is any empirical support for PPP.

It is unlikely that we will ever have an indubitably complete list of significant factors in any area of empirical study – or in modern terminology that we will ever have complete knowledge of the DGP – but we do not 'sit on our hands'!

Review

1. Quantitative economics is an integral part of economics.
2. Quantitative economics has a descriptive and a constructive role to play in economics.
3. Models are abstract characterisations which focus on the essential detail of economic inquiry. How detailed a particular model is will depend upon its purpose.
4. While introducing many of the concepts we now regard as cornerstones of macroeconomics, Keynes expressed doubts as to the role of econometric model building. However, considerable progress was made in the 1930s in applying some of the techniques of quantitative economics.
5. One example of a model is Keynes' relationship between consumption and income. Whether the propensity to consume is stable or whether consumption actually

increases as income increases but not by as much as the increase in income are empirical matters: we need to make reference to 'the detailed facts of experience'.

6. By grouping years in pairs Keynes estimated the multiplier to be in the neighbourhood of 2.5.

7. Gilboy estimated the income elasticity of expenditure by plotting average expenditure against average income using a logarithmic scale for both variables and then fitting a curve to the data by eye. The resulting elasticity appeared to be approximately 0.74.

8. There has not always been agreement on the role of the quantitative characterisation of economic relationships. Keynes was critical of attempts by Tinbergen to construct macroeconomic models, suggesting he would 'engage another ten computers and drown his sorrows in arithmetic'.

9. Keynes' concerns arose because of what he saw as the apparent need for an 'indubitably complete analysis of the significant factors' in a 'multiple correlation analysis'.

10. Textbooks on econometrics often avoided confronting this issue by assuming the axiom of correct specification and focusing on estimating the parameters as efficiently as possible.

11. The practice of applied econometrics was, however, often very different from the simple methodology of: formulate model; obtain data; estimate the model; and test hypotheses.

12. Critical choices had to be made at almost every stage indicated in the simple methodology.

13. A concept which is central to the reconstruction of econometric methodology is the data generating process, the DGP. Like Keynes' indubitably complete list it is usually unknown; however, it forms the basis of empirical models which are reductions of the DGP. The important question is, then, whether a particular model is a valid reduction.

14. Accepting the central role of the underlying DGP, and the need to find a reduction consistent with the data, means a change in focus from estimating an axiomatically correct specification as efficiently as possible to finding a statistically and then tentatively adequate empirical model.

15. There is a valid role in this process for looking at the data and assessing several different empirical specifications. Indeed familiarity with the empirical regularities in the data is often essential to successful modelling.

16. A tentatively adequate model may be overcome – or encompassed – by a subsequent model which explains why the previous model was in error.

17. Tinbergen recognised this aspect of model building in stating: 'We have presented these models as possible structures, perhaps even as probable structures, which have the advantage that they are at least not contradictory to the statistics used in their construction ... it is hoped that those who reject our conclusions will at least try to give alternative attempts to explain the real course of the crucial variables in a way similar to ours.' (Tinbergen 1939)

18. The central aim of this book is to provide an accessible introduction to some key concepts and techniques which are now routinely found in modern empirical studies. It should be accessible to undergraduates and postgraduates not specialising in econometrics.

19. No book on econometric techniques or applications to economic time series would be complete without recognition of the distinction between stationary and nonstationary time series.

20. This distinction is important for economic time series because, and especially for macroeconomic data, many show a sustained increase over time.

21. There are two paradigms which account for such 'trend' increases. The first is that the

trend increases are deterministic subject only to a trendless random shock (the trend stationarity hypothesis); and the second is that the trend is itself stochastic and owes its trajectory to the (infinite) cumulation of shocks and hence long memory of the process.

22. An 'integrated' series cumulates – or integrates – previous and current shocks and is a nonstationary process.

23. The distinction is of interest for two reasons. First, the properties of a single series are of interest in their own right. There are several examples of economic models which generate a particular kind of nonstationary series.

24. Second, in an analysis of the relationship among economic variables, a necessary requirement for a tentatively adequate model is that it should be balanced in its time series properties.

25. For example, we would not seek to explain a nonstationary variable (solely) by a stationary variable.

Review questions

1. Read Keynes' article in the *Economic Journal* (1939) on 'Professor Tinbergen's method' and Tinbergen's reply in the *Economic Journal* (1940) 'On a method of statistical business-cycle research. A Reply', and write a brief imaginary dialogue between these two economists.

2. Think of examples from microeconomics and macroeconomics which illustrate: (a) the descriptive and (b) the constructive roles of quantitative economics.

3. Continuing your examples, are any problems likely to arise in matching the variables of your constructive models with data that is actually available?

4. The Quantity Theory of Money states that $MV = PT$ where M is the stock of money, V is the velocity of circulation, P is the price level and T is the level of transactions. Discuss the difficulties of translating these theoretical constructs into their empirical counterparts. For example, what is the appropriate measure of money? How should transactions be measured and so on?

5. (i) How does Gilboy's method of graphing the log of expenditure against the log of income by fitting a straight line by eye provide an estimate of the income elasticity of expenditure?
   (ii) As one person's 'eye' may result in a different line from another, suggest alternative methods of obtaining an estimate of the income elasticity using the data available to Gilboy.

6. (i) What is a data generation process (DGP)?
   (ii) Is the DGP a useful construct given that we rarely, if ever, know what it is?

7. Why would we be happy to accept an empirical model which was only tentatively adequate, would we not prefer a model which was definitive?

8. Suppose Smith proposes an empirical model of the demand for money which he claims is better than Jones's previous model, what criteria would enable you to decide whether Smith was correct?

9. (i) Suppose the data on a variable Y_t is generated according to the model $Y_t = Y_{t-1} + \varepsilon_t$ where ε_t is a random shock with a zero mean, by repeatedly substituting for past values of Y_t show that this generates a path for Y_t which depends upon all past shocks.
   (ii) What difference does it make if a constant is added to the specification, which is now:

$$Y_t = \kappa + Y_{t-1} + \varepsilon_t?$$

CHAPTER 2
Some preliminaries

2.1 Introduction

This chapter introduces some important preliminaries to the subsequent analysis. In later chapters reference will often be made to some underlying concepts such as: time series data; units of measurement and frequency of the data; static and dynamic models; the lag operator and lag polynomial function and so on. The idea of this chapter is to bring these basic concepts together to establish a language and common framework that is used in the remaining chapters.

The plan of this chapter is as follows. In section **2.2** consideration is first given to what kinds of data are available to economists; this section highlights some distinguishing characteristics of the data as they relate to aggregation, time series, cross-section, frequency, dimension and simulation (Monte Carlo experiments). Of particular importance in this book, which emphasises time series applications, are the related concepts of lagging and leading a time series of observations, y_t. These ideas are introduced in section **2.3**. An economical notation for lagging and leading is explained in section **2.4** together with some illustrations of its use, especially in the context of a univariate dynamic model which specifies y_t as a function of its past values. This leads on to models and representations of bivariate relationships in section **2.5**, especially the class of autoregressive distributed lag – or ADL – models which are widely used in practical, modelling applications. These preliminaries are sufficient in a single equation context; however, there are many examples in

this book of multi-equation modelling – see, especially, Chapters 14 and 15; thus, it is also necessary, for example, to extend the notation and lag operator to the more complex modelling framework and this is done in section **2.6**. The final section contains some concluding remarks.

2.2 Distinguishing characteristics of the data

There are several dimensions on which data can be distinguished. It might, for example, relate to individuals or to organisations, to annual or even hourly observations and to variables measured as rates or in current prices. This section considers some basic distinctions with examples, including graphical illustrations.

2.2.1 Time series and cross-section data

The data economists use can be distinguished in a number of ways. It may, for example, relate to an individual (or entity) or a group of individuals (or entities), and to a particular commodity or group of commodities. In going from the individual to a group, whether for an economic agent or a particular commodity, some degree of entity aggregation is involved. For example, an observation on consumers' expenditure on nondurables involves (a) aggregation over different consumers and (b) aggregation over different kinds of consumers' goods.

A further distinction arises with the identifying index attached to particular observations. For example, the data may relate to a sequence of observations over time on an individual, or group of individuals; or to a sequence of observations on different individuals, or groups of individuals, at a particular time. The distinction is between observations which form a *time series* – so that time, t, is the identifying index – and those which relate to a particular point in time – so that the individual entity, i, is the identifying index. The latter type of observations are often referred to as *cross-section* data, that is a cross-section of individuals – or entities – all with the same time index. In the first case, that of time series of observations, a convenient notation for a single (random) variable of interest is y_t, for observations $t = 1, \ldots, T$; for example, the sequence of observations on aggregate expenditure on consumer goods for the years 1955 ($t = 1$) through to 1997 ($t = T$). In the second case, time is de-emphasised and a usual notation is y_i, for $i = 1, \ldots, N$. It is possible to have a time series of observations on cross-sectional data; for example, sales on N retail outlets for T consecutive months, which is represented by the notation y_{it} for $i = 1, \ldots, N$ and $t = 1, \ldots, T$. This notational convention is not, however, adhered to in multi-equation models applied to time series data (see Chapters 14 and 15); when it is necessary to distinguish conceptually among time series on different variables the notation y_{it} is often convenient, and in this case, for example, y_{1t} and y_{2t} are time series observations on the variables y_1 and y_2, respectively.

Besides being entity aggregated, the data economists' work may also be temporally aggregated. For example, original data might relate to expenditure over a month on a particular commodity, which would give rise to a time series sequence of monthly observations. If the monthly expenditure is summed over three months to relate to a quarter, the original data has been temporally aggregated. The data could be temporally aggregated further with, for example, temporal aggregation of the monthly data into yearly data. While temporal aggregation is more likely to take place with time series data it may also occur with cross-section data. For example, data on monthly sales of N retail outlets could be temporally aggregated into the annual sales of those outlets.

It is important to be aware of how the data economists use is constructed, which is why concepts such as entity aggregation and temporal aggregation are relevant. One reason for this is that economic theory often relates to a particular level of aggregation – frequently referring to individual economic agents or individual commodities – yet the data we have available rarely matches this level. It is important to be aware, therefore, even if it is a counsel of perfection, that matching the theory and the available data may not be straightforward.

2.2.2 Time series graphs

A sequence of time series observations for a single variable can be conveniently recorded on a two-dimensional graph with time on the horizontal axis and values of the observations on the vertical axis. One of the characteristics of time series data is that the index of time serves to naturally order the observations; for example, the observation for 1989 precedes that for 1990, while that for 1990 precedes 1991 and so on. In contrast in cross-sectional data there may be no ordering – or index – which is generally of interest to economists, although in particular cases an ordering may exist. For example, in analysing the sales of retail outlets, distance from the town centre to the retail outlet may serve to order the observations.

Then graphing y_t for different values of t gives a visual impression of the time series and may be helpful in revealing characteristics of the series which were not apparent just from the sequence of observations; for example, the series may tend to increase or decrease according to a regular pattern or may tend to fluctuate more widely at different periods in the overall plot. Initially, in this chapter, only one variable is considered, a situation referred to as univariate analysis; at a later stage further variables are introduced.

Before illustrating some times series graphs – or plots – some distinctions in the kinds of data that could be plotted may be helpful. First, economists tend to work with observations which are of a quantitative nature; for example, the amount of expenditure on a commodity, the level of wages, the rate of inflation and so on are all variables which can be measured quantitatively. Variations on this theme are possible as with a variable that takes a limited range of values; for example, in considering whether an individual purchases a particular commodity in a sequence of weeks we could assign the value 0 to no purchase and the value 1 to a purchase. This particular kind of quantitative variable is usually referred to as a categorical variable. A quantitative variable can be created from a binary decision, for example assigning the value 1 if you went to your last economics lecture and 0 if you did not.

2.2.3   Frequency

An important distinguishing feature of data ordered by time is the frequency of the data, which refers to how often the observations are recorded. For example, data on many macroeconomic variables, such as aggregate consumption and investment, is published four times a year corresponding to four (approximately) equally spaced quarters and so a frequency of four times a year; this data is also built up – or temporally aggregated – into an annual observation which corresponds to a frequency of one a year and is usually regarded as data of a low frequency. Data of a high frequency is often available for financial variables such as exchange rates or share prices which have been recorded as frequently as every hour during the trading day, and may even be available on a minute-by-minute basis.

2.2.4   Dimension of a variable

Another distinction is the dimension of a variable. The essence of this distinction is between variables that are measured as a flow, those which are measured as a stock and those which are measured as a rate. An analogy may be useful. Turning the bath tap on gives rise to a flow of water into the bath. For example, suppose that in a minute the tap discharges 10 litres of water, then the flow is 10 litres per minute – a flow necessarily involves the dimension of time. If this flow is constant for 3 minutes then the bath will contain 30 litres of water, so that the stock position after 3 minutes is 30 litres. In contrast to the dimension of a flow, a stock refers to a particular point in time. As a variation, suppose the bath leaks 1 litre per minute through the overflow; after 3 minutes the leakage rate relative to the stock is 1/30.

Many economic examples of flow and stock variables should come to mind. Expenditure on consumer goods is usually recorded for a period of time – for example, so much expenditure a quarter. For durable goods, which are not completely consumed within the quarter, we could also record their stock position – that is the current level of accumulation of the past flows less any depreciation – at the end of the quarter. This distinction can give rise to some minor difficulties in plotting time series of flows and stocks. In principle we should plot the flow observation for period t at a representative point between t and $t + 1$ and the midpoint is usually taken, whereas an observation on a stock usually relates to the end of a period.

A variable that has the dimension of a rate can be created in one of two ways. First, consider a durable good which depreciates by an amount d_t in period t and has a corresponding (opening period) stock of K_{t-1}, then the rate of depreciation is defined as d_t/K_{t-1}. Thus, the flow of depreciation has been expressed relative to the stock and has the interpretation as the rate of depreciation, that is the proportion of the stock which depreciates during period t.

Another way of creating a rate, and one that has some importance in economics, is to express the proportionate change in a variable over time. The symbol Δ_i is used to define the difference between y_t and y_{t-i}; that is,

$$\Delta_i y_t \equiv y_t - y_{t-i} \qquad (2.1)$$

If the frequency of the data is annual then taking $i = 1$ gives the annual change in y_t; if the frequency of the data is quarterly then taking $i = 1$ gives the quarterly change in y_t and $i = 4$ gives the annual change in y_t. A convention, followed here, is that if there is no subscript to the symbol Δ it is referring to the case of $i = 1$, that is, the first difference. It is often useful in economics to express the difference relative to the level of the variable, which gives the rate of change, and for convenience this is often expressed in percentage terms. The rate of change of y_t using the first difference, denoted g_t is

$$g_t \equiv \Delta y_t / y_{t-1} \qquad (2.2)$$

Occasionally there is ambiguity as to the appropriate divisor in defining a rate of change. For example, the rate of change could be defined relative to y_t or $0.5(y_t + y_{t-1})$, each of which defines a rate of change; however, the convention adopted here is that the rate of change should satisfy

$$y_t = (1 + g_t)y_{t-1} \qquad (2.3)$$

so that applying the rate of growth, g_t, to last period's flow results in y_t. If, for example, the frequency of the data is quarterly and interest is in annual rates of change then use

$$g_t = \Delta_4 y_t / y_{t-4} \qquad (2.4)$$

which is the rate of growth in y_t over the year comprising the four quarters $t - 4$ to t.

Finally, note the units of measurement of the three different types of variables that have been distinguished. A flow is measured in the units of y, for example millions of $, expressed per unit of time. A stock is also measured in the units of

the variable but refers to a particular point in time. A rate is a dimensionless – or pure – number that is expressed per unit of time, for example a depreciation rate of 0.05 per quarter.

One way of looking at how to obtain the units of measurement of the rate is to note that the two components of the rate, that is the numerator and the denominator, are both expressed in units of y_t and these cancel leaving the rate as a pure number. The importance of matching the units of measurement of economic variables in explaining one variable by another is often overlooked.

2.2.5 Some examples of time series data

Figure 2.1 graphs consumers' expenditure in the United States over the period 1960 quarter 1 to 1991 quarter 4 (seasonally adjusted, billions, 1987 dollars, annualised). The frequency of this data, which is the interval between successive observations, is quarterly; that is one observation every quarter. Higher frequency data, such as monthly or weekly data, has a shorter interval between successive observations and lower frequency data, such as annual data, has a longer interval between successive observations. The data on consumers' expenditure is a flow variable – so much expenditure per time period – and the source for the US data plotted in Figure 2.1 is Business Statistics 1963–1991 (Bureau of Economic Analysis 1992). Note that as the data is presented in Figure 2.1, and published in its source, it is 'annualised'; that is while the data refers to observations at a quarterly frequency, the quarterly figure is multiplied by 4, the idea being that if a year was comprised of 4 like quarters that is the annual total that would result. This is a convention that is not universally adopted and can cause confusion when comparing international sources of statistics. For example, in contrast to the US practice, quarterly flow data published by the United Kingdom's National Statistics Office is not 'annualised'

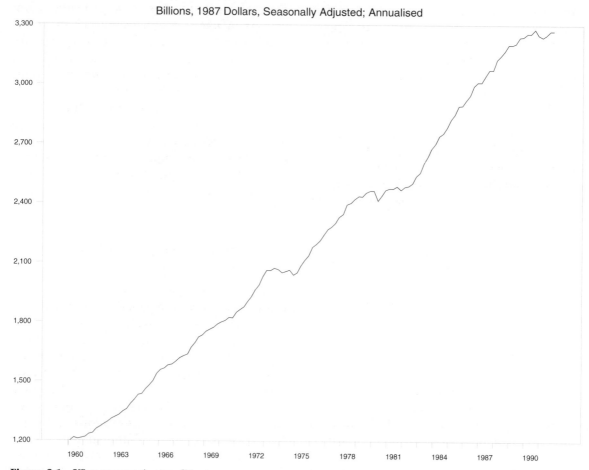

Figure 2.1   *US consumers' expenditure*

The pattern displayed by the data in Figure 2.1 contains features that are common to a large number of industrialised and industrialising countries over the same period. There is a distinct tendency for the series to increase over the period. For example, in only 11 of the 128 quarterly observations in Figure 2.1 is there a decline for consecutive quarters, and considering the annual figures there are declines in just two years (1974 and 1980).

Figure 2.2 illustrates stock data with an annual frequency, here the stock of consumer durables for the United States over the period 1925 to 1989. This stock includes, for example, autos and other motor vehicles, furniture, durable household furnishings, video and audio products, computers, musical instruments and so on. For a detailed definition consult the source for this data, which is Fixed Reproducible Tangible Wealth in the United States 1925–1989 (Bureau of Economic Analysis 1993a). An observation for stock data refers to a particular point in time, here the measurement of the stock is at the end of the year. For example, the stock of consumer durables is measured at 140,205 million (1987 US$) for the end of 1925 and 1,830,323 million (1987 US$) for the end of 1989. It is evident from Figure 2.2 that the stock of consumer durables was fairly flat until the end of the Second World

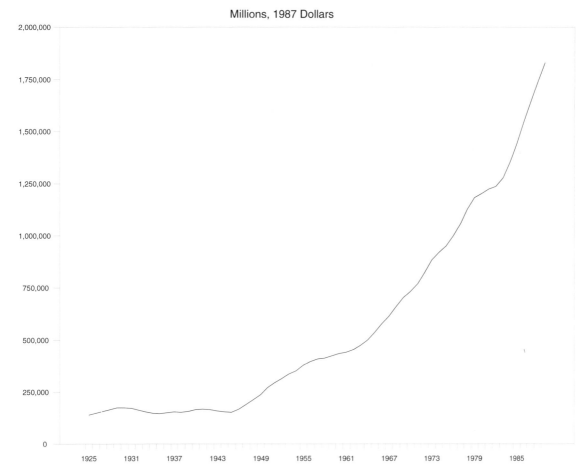

Millions, 1987 Dollars

Figure 2.2 *US stock of consumers' durables*

War, after which there was sustained growth through to the end of the period.

Figure 2.3 illustrates data expressed in rate form. In this case the rate of depreciation on consumers' durables measured as the ratio of depreciation to the opening period stock of consumers' durables. Unlike the two preceding series the rate of depreciation is dimensionless; for example, the figure for 1989 is 0.193 (or 19.3%) per year. Also in contrast the rate of depreciation does not show the sustained increase evident in the two preceding series.

Finally, Figure 2.4 illustrates a series without a sustained increase, in this case the change in US

business inventories (seasonally adjusted, billions, 1987 US$ annualised; source: Business Statistics 1963–1991 (Bureau of Economic Analysis 1992)). The change is defined as the first difference, and it is quite often the case that transforming the data in this way removes the dominant tendency of a series to increase. This is a matter that is of importance in later chapters. For the moment note from Figure 2.4 that there is a tendency for the amplitude of the series to increase over time, which is a salient characteristic of this data.

Many of the key features of data can often be informed by visual representations. This in turn

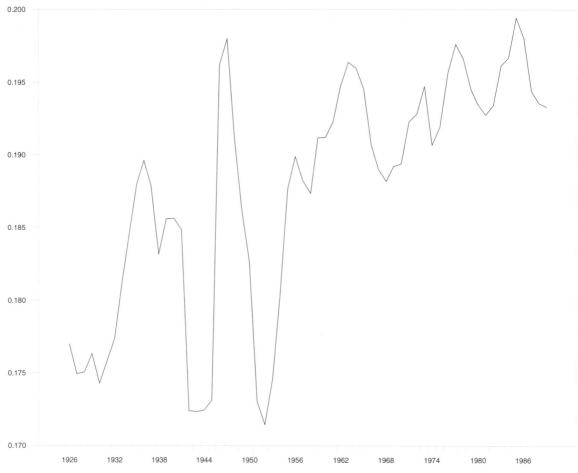

Figure 2.3   *US rate of depreciation on consumers' durables*

can lead to, what was termed in Chapter 1, data instigated discovery as an explanation of the characteristics of the data.

2.2.6   Nonexperimental data

The data economists use is mostly of a non-experimental kind. Although economics has been likened to the natural sciences such as physics and chemistry in its use of mathematically formulated theories and hypotheses, it is generally unlike such sciences in the kind of data it uses. Although economists are able to formulate hypotheses of this type they are not generally able to set up an experiment and

compare the results of the experiment with the predictions of their theory. Economists do not usually have the facility to undertake experiments in laboratory conditions; an experiment that might be repeated again and again in order to establish whether a particular scientific hypothesis is able to predict a particular outcome. Although there are exceptions to this situation economists usually have to make do with the 'experiments' which are captured in history and which are not capable of replication by an economist. Thus, the data available to economists usually relates to historical and non-replicable events usually in the form of a record over time (a time series) for particular economic

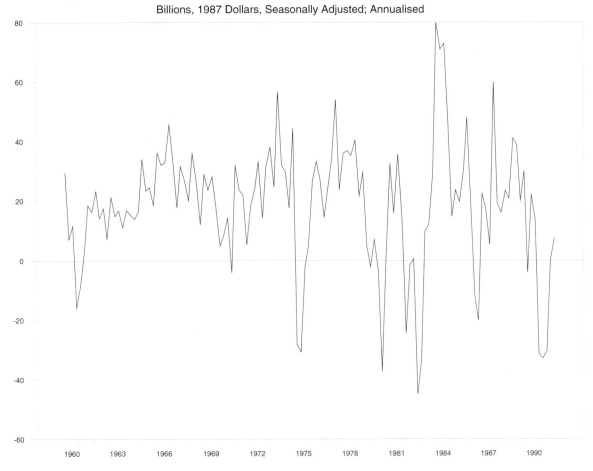

Figure 2.4 *US change in real business inventory*

agents or a record for a particular point in time of many different agents (a cross-section); sometimes the combination – or pooling – of both sources of data is possible in a particular study. As we shall see later, though, the idea of replication, particularly through Monte Carlo experiments, is an important concept which economists borrow from science and mathematics, and it motivates the framework underlying much of the way that economists seek to explain how the data they work with – whether of a time series or cross-section nature – is generated. The paradigm for the generation of data from apparently nonreplicable events is important: the observations forming a sample

are *realisations* or outcomes from inherently random variables such as prices, consumption, investment and so on.

2.2.7 Experimental data

A number of later chapters make reference to data simulated by Monte Carlo experiments, and a brief description of this process is given here. As noted above economic data usually relates to historical and nonreplicable events generated by an unknown DGP, and the purpose of empirical analysis is to use this data to approximate the relevant features of the DGP to derive a quantitative understanding of the links among variables. But how good are the techniques used in the empirical analysis? By assuming that the characteristics of the DGP are known it is possible to generate different sample realisations, and then to evaluate the quantitative techniques.

The econometric techniques chosen for analysis of the data will usually be thought to have desirable properties; for example, that an estimator $\hat{\theta}$ of a DGP parameter θ is unbiased in the sense that were it possible to obtain a number, say M, of further samples of data drawn from the same DGP then the average of the numerical values of $\hat{\theta}$ over the M samples, as M tends to infinity (written $M \to \infty$), would be equal to θ. The numerical values of $\hat{\theta}$ for different samples differ in this conceptual framework because the DGP variables are random rather than deterministic; so one sample differs from another because the sample observations are different realisations (or outcomes) from the same set of random variables. If the variables were deterministic, the outcomes would always be the same.

To check the unbiasedness property of the estimator, $\hat{\theta}$, the unknown DGP could be replaced by a DGP specified by the researcher. All the parameters of the DGP are numerically specified including the precise nature of randomness of each variable and the connections between variables. For the purposes of these experiments the researcher *knows* the DGP, a very simple example is that data on y_t is generated by $y_t = 1.0 + 0.5x_t + u_t$ for $t = 1, \ldots,$ $T = 100$, with x_t a set of $(T = 100)$ fixed numbers which are the same for each experiment and u_t is a random variable which follows the normal distribution with the same parameters for each value of $t = 1, \ldots, 100$. In this set-up differences between samples arise only because the sample values of u_t differ. Now suppose the objective is to evaluate the performance of an estimator, $\hat{\theta}$, of $\theta = 0.5$, then M different samples can be generated from the DGP and the numerical estimates of θ, calculated according to the rule given by $\hat{\theta}$, and then recorded and averaged. If the estimator is

unbiased the average value of $\hat{\theta}$ will converge to θ as M increases. This 'experiment' could be repeated for different values of T and θ to see if the results of the experiment are sensitive to these parameters.

2.3 Lagging and leading time series data

The application of economic models often involves the specification of lags and leads. For example, consumption may depend not only upon current income but also income in previous periods; the current yield on a Treasury Bond of a particular maturity may well depend upon the future yield on a bond that is identical except that it has a shorter time to maturity. It turns out that introducing what seems initially just a shorthand for lagging and leading variables is a very powerful device, often allowing considerable simplification of complex calculations. Section **2.3.1** introduces the idea of lagging variables and data, while section **2.3.2** does the same for leading; section **2.4** then builds upon these ideas to introduce the lag/lead operator with subsections showing how this offers an economy of notation as well as analytical advantages.

2.3.1 Lagging time series data

Economists working with time series data often use lagged data. There were several examples of this above; for example, in defining an annual growth rate the value of y in period t is compared with the value of y one year before that. If the data is of a quarterly frequency that means a lag of 4 quarters, so the comparison is of y_t with y_{t-4}; if the data is of an annual frequency the comparison is of y_t with y_{t-1}. The subscript on y indicates the number of lags to be taken. To see how this works in practice consider the hypothetical values of the y series in Table 2.1.

The observations in this case run from y_1 through to y_{10} for the unlagged series – that is

Table 2.1 *Lagging a variable*

Current value y_t	Lagged once y_{t-1}	Lagged twice y_{t-2}	Lagged three times y_{t-3}	Lagged four times y_{t-4}	$\Delta y_t/y_{t-1}$	$\Delta_4 y_t/y_{t-4}$
$y_1 = 100$	n.a.	n.a.	n.a.	n.a.	n.a.	n.a.
$y_2 = 110$	100	n.a.	n.a.	n.a.	10/100	n.a.
$y_3 = 125$	110	100	n.a.	n.a.	15/110	n.a.
$y_4 = 130$	125	110	100	n.a.	5/125	n.a.
$y_5 = 140$	130	125	110	100	10/130	40/100
$y_6 = 120$	140	130	125	110	$-20/140$	10/110
$y_7 = 160$	120	140	130	125	40/120	35/125
$y_8 = 165$	160	120	140	130	5/160	35/130
$y_9 = 150$	165	160	120	140	$-15/165$	10/140
$y_{10} = 145$	150	165	160	120	$-5/150$	25/120

the series y_t has 10 observations distinguished by the subscript $t = 1, \ldots, 10$. Now if this series is lagged once the values of y_t are displaced by one row; in effect this creates a new variable but to avoid problems in thinking of new symbols or letters for each new variable, the convention is to indicate the lag on the subscript of the variable. For example, for observation 2, that is $t = 2$, $y_t = 110$ and $y_{t-1} = 100$; however, it is not possible to obtain y_{t-2} because there are not any values for y_t before $t = 1$. For observation 3, that is $t = 3$, $y_t = 125$, $y_{t-1} = 110$, $y_{t-2} = 100$ but no further lagged values are available. By now you should be able to see the (diagonal) pattern being created by successively lagging variables.

If reference is needed to a general lag, as yet unspecified, then the notation is y_{t-i}, indicating the ith lag on variable y_t. To indicate the creation of a set of time series with different lags – as in Table 2.1 – the notation is y_{t-i} for $i = p_1, \ldots, p_n$, where p_1 is the starting lag and p_n is the highest lag. In Table 2.1 above, the set of time series is y_{t-i} for $i = 0, \ldots, 4$ (so $p_1 = 0$ and $p_n = 4$).

One point to note which becomes obvious from inspection of Table 2.1 is that in lagging the series y_t once, one observation is 'lost'; so y_{t-1} runs from observations 2 through to 10. Similarly when y_t is lagged twice two observations are 'lost' and y_{t-2} runs from observations 3 through to 10. In general, creating a series y_{t-i} by

lagging y_t will result in a sample with i fewer observations than the original series.

The creation of lagged variables allows the calculation of differences and growth rates of the variable y_t. The penultimate and final columns of Table 2.1 give the quarterly and annual growth rates, respectively, of y_t. For a series with a quarterly frequency the quarterly growth rate is $(y_t - y_{t-1})/y_{t-1}$ and the annual growth rate is $(y_t - y_{t-4})/y_{t-4}$; these are expressed on a percentage basis by multiplying by 100. For example, the quarterly growth rate for y_t at $t = 5$ is 10/130 $= \frac{1}{13}$, which is 7.692% per quarter; the annual growth rate for y_t at $t = 5$ is $0.4 = (140 - 100)/100$, which is 40% per year.

2.3.2   Leading time series data

As well as 'lagging' a variable economists do sometimes consider the 'leading' of a time series, particularly in the context of theoretical developments which emphasise forward looking behaviour. From a practical viewpoint leading is the opposite of lagging. For example, the first lead of y_t is denoted y_{t+1}, the second lead is y_{t+2} and so on. This process is illustrated in Table 2.2. Now the displacement of the observations is in the opposite direction to that for lagging: y_t for $t = 3$ is 125, whereas y_{t+1} is 130. The one period lead looks forward whereas the one period lag looks back. Continuing the same principle at

Table 2.2 *Leading a variable*

Current value y_t	Lead once y_{t+1}	Lead twice y_{t+2}	Lead three times y_{t+3}	Lead four times y_{t+4}
$y_1 = 100$	110	125	130	140
$y_2 = 110$	125	130	140	120
$y_3 = 125$	130	140	120	160
$y_4 = 130$	140	120	160	165
$y_5 = 140$	120	160	165	150
$y_6 = 120$	160	165	150	145
$y_7 = 160$	165	150	145	n.a.
$y_8 = 165$	150	145	n.a.	n.a.
$y_9 = 150$	145	n.a.	n.a.	n.a.
$y_{10} = 145$	n.a.	n.a.	n.a.	n.a.

$t = 3$ then $y_{t+2} = 140$, which looks forward two periods, $y_{t+3} = 120$, which looks forward three periods and so on. Notice that now observations are 'lost' at the end of the sample as the one period lead of y_{10} is y_{11}, which is not available.

2.4 The lag operator

This section introduces and then uses the lag operator. Although in principle the lag operator seems like shorthand notation it can be put to very powerful uses. For an extensive analysis of the lag operator and its use in dynamic models see Dhrymes (1981).

2.4.1 Definition of the lag operator

Notice that lags and leads of a variable involve a similar kind of operation on the variable y_t. In the former case the subscript is moved 'back' to y_{t-i} for the ith lag and in the latter case the subscript is moved 'forward' to y_{t+i} for the ith lead. It is convenient to introduce what is known as an *operator* for the lagging and leading of variables, which turns out to offer much more than just the efficiency of a shorthand notation. In particular define the lag operator L^j such that:

$$L^j y_t \equiv y_{t-j} \qquad (2.5)$$

for example, $L^1 y_t \equiv y_{t-1}$ and $L^4 y_t \equiv y_{t-4}$.

So a positive power, j, of L applied to the variable y_t is the same as lagging y_t by j periods. If j is negative then the operation implies taking the jth lead of y_t. For example

$$L^{-2} y_t \equiv y_{t+2}$$

For completeness note that $L^0 y_t \equiv y_t$, that is L^0 is the identity operator as it leaves y_t unchanged. Also L^1 is usually just written as L. Finally, note that the lag operator satisfies what is known as the law of exponents, that is

$$L^i L^j y_t \equiv L^{i+j} y_t \equiv y_{t-(i+j)}$$

2.4.2 The lag polynomial

A lag polynomial is a function of L, usually a linear function, with the 'order' of the polynomial given by the highest power of L in the polynomial. For example, the linear combination of lags of y_t given by

$$y_t - \phi_1 y_{t-1} - \phi_2 y_{t-2} - \cdots - \phi_p y_{t-p}$$

can be rewritten as

$$y_t - \phi_1 L y_t - \phi_2 L^2 y_t - \cdots - \phi_p L^p y_t$$

Now factoring out the common element y_t this can be written as:

$$(1 - \phi_1 L - \phi_2 L^2 - \cdots - \phi_p L^p) y_t \equiv \phi(L) y_t \qquad (2.6)$$

which defines the pth order lag polynomial $\phi(L)$, and the original linear combination is, therefore, rewritten in an equivalent way as $\phi(L) y_t$.

2.4.3 Obtaining the sum of the lag coefficients

There are many uses of the lag operator which justify its introduction. For example, if $L = 1$ in the pth order lag polynomial, $\phi(L)$, a notation for which is $\phi(L = 1)$ or sometimes even more concisely written as simply $\phi(1)$, the result is the sum of the lag coefficients. This is easy enough to see in the simple model (2.6) since

$$\phi(L = 1) = 1 - \phi_1 1^1 - \phi_2 1^2 - \cdots$$

$$- \phi_p 1^p = 1 - \sum_{i=1}^{p} \phi_i \qquad (2.7)$$

While this might seem like a trivial application consider obtaining the sum of the lag coefficients in the following example in which $\phi(L)$ is an infinite order lag polynomial with geometrically declining lag coefficients. In this case

$$\phi_1 = k^1, \phi_2 = k^2, \ldots, \phi_p = k^p, \ldots$$
$$\text{where } 0 < k < 1$$

and $\phi(L)$ is given by

$$\phi(L) = (1 - kL - k^2 L^2 - \cdots - k^p L^p \cdots)$$

In order to simplify the expression in brackets on the right-hand side some results on infinite sums are needed, which are proved in more advanced texts – see Dhrymes (1981). First note that $\sum_{i=0}^{\infty} z^i = 1/(1 - z)$ for $0 < |z| < 1$, then

$$1 - \sum_{i=1}^{\infty} z^i = 1 - \left(\sum_{i=0}^{\infty} z^i - 1 \right)$$

$$= 1 - \left(\frac{1}{1 - z} - 1 \right)$$

$$= 1 - z/(1 - z)$$

$$= (1 - 2z)/(1 - z)$$

For z use kL to obtain,

$$\phi(L) = (1 - 2kL)/(1 - kL)$$

Now set $L = 1$ to obtain the sum:

$$\phi(L = 1) = (1 - 2k)/(1 - k)$$

For example, if $k = 0.5$ then $\phi(L = 1)$ is $(1 - 1)/0.5 = 0$; if $k = 0.25$ then $\phi(L = 1)$ is $(1 - 0.5)/(1 - 0.75) = 0.666$.

2.4.4 A univariate dynamic model

The simplest point at which to start modelling y_t is to relate it to its past values in a linear, univariate, dynamic model:

$$y_t = \phi_1 y_{t-1} + \phi_2 y_{t-2} + \cdots + \phi_p y_{t-p} \qquad (2.8)$$

The process (2.8) is *linear in the parameters* because it involves no powers (other than the first) of the ϕ_i coefficients; it is *linear in the variables* because it involves no powers of the lagged variables, y_{t-i}. The process (2.8) is *autoregressive and so dynamic* because the current value y_t is related to past values of itself. As written it is also *deterministic* because there is no element of doubt in the outcome y_t given the coefficients ϕ_1 to ϕ_p and lags y_{t-1} to y_{t-p}. Using the newly introduced lag operator notation this equation can be written as:

$$(1 - kL - k^2 L^2 - \cdots - k^p L^p)y_t = 0$$

or, for simplicity,

$$\phi(L)y_t = 0 \qquad (2.9)$$

A deterministic function such as (2.8) will often seem unrealistic as a description or representation of an economic time series. The distinction between deterministic and stochastic processes is taken up again in section **2.5.2** and in Chapter 3. For the moment the additive, stochastic term ε_t is introduced to give

$$\phi(L)y_t = \varepsilon_t \qquad (2.10)$$

ε_t is assumed to be a zero mean process with a constant variance. The importance of introducing ε_t is that the outcome for y_t given lagged values of itself and values of ϕ_i is no longer one particular value but a range of values: the process is no longer deterministic.

2.5 Bivariate relationships

The usual aim in economics is to understand the interrelationships among variables. Empirically this means that while something can be learnt from studying the history of individual variables this is only part of an approach which has, as its central aim, to model how variables interact. To illustrate this development consider a *bivariate* model, that is one which involves two variables y_t and x_t.

2.5.1 A deterministic bivariate model

The simplest bivariate model to start with is a linear deterministic function, say

$$y_t = \beta_1 + \beta_2 x_t \qquad (2.11)$$

This implies that given a value of x_t, y_t is completely determined from that value and the parameters β_1 and β_2. Imagine an experimental situation in which different values of x_t are chosen and the resulting values of y_t are recorded, then if x_t is the same in two or more experiments the value of y_t will also be identical for those experiments. A plot of y_t will show no deviations from the straight line with intercept $= \beta_1$ and slope $= \beta_2$.

Some reflection on the deterministic model, though, suggests that it may well be inappropriate for modelling economic interrelationships. Suppose y_t is consumption and x_t is income, a relationship suggested in general terms by economic theory and, to fix ideas, assume that these variables refer to your consumption and income. Now if your income was observed for a large number of successive months and in two of those months income was the same, would consumption be the same? Even assuming that there are no other variables which determine your consumption it seems unlikely that it will be identical in those months. There is the suggestion here that human behaviour is not well described by deterministic functions, and that the variables of economic analysis would be

better analysed as realisations from random rather than deterministic processes. This was the idea behind making the univariate process in the previous section stochastic. The concept of a random process is an important one in economics and it is taken up more formally in Chapter 3. For the moment the purpose is motivational and it will suffice to appeal to the intuitive idea that modelling with nondeterministic functions better represents human behaviour.

In contrast to a deterministic process, in a random process if x_t is the same in two or more experiments it is unlikely that the resulting values of y_t will be the same; they will only be the same by *chance*. Instead of a single possible outcome, as in a deterministic process, there is a range of possible outcomes each of which is consistent with $y_t = \beta_1 + \beta_2 x_t$ *provided* allowance is made for a random component. The deterministic function is not an adequate description of the process which generates the realisations which are recorded as y_t. Neither, in general, is the view that x_t is a deterministic (nonrandom) variable. An appropriate framework is to view y_t and x_t as being jointly generated as the outcomes of a (bivariate) random process.

2.5.2 A stochastic bivariate model

What, therefore, is meant by an equation with y_t as the dependent variable and x_t as the explanatory variable? The answer is that y_t is the outcome *conditional* on a value for x_t. In a sense the value of x_t is fixed, and the equation gives the result for y_t given that value of x_t. This is an example of what is known as conditioning, for which there is a particular notation; the notation $y_t \mid x_t$ is a shorthand for the value of y_t conditional on the value of x_t. Sometimes, where it is clear from the context, this explicit notation is not used. Now the deterministic part of the function, $\beta_1 + \beta_2 x_t$, is the average of the conditional values for a given x_t; that is the average of $y_t \mid x_t$ is $\beta_1 + \beta_2 x_t$. The outcome for

$y_t \mid x_t$ can then be viewed as the average plus the deviation from the average conditional on x_t. (For example, your height can always be represented as the average height plus your deviation from the average.) The conditional deviation is written $\varepsilon_t \mid x_t$ and sometimes referred to as the *innovation* relative to x_t. The outcome for $y_t \mid x_t$ can, therefore, be represented as:

$$y_t \mid x_t = \beta_1 + \beta_2 x_t + \varepsilon_t \mid x_t \qquad (2.12)$$

The deviation, $\varepsilon_t \mid x_t$, will, in general, have a distribution of values, some large, some small, some positive and some negative, but its average must be zero.

The explicit notation to indicate conditioning is sometimes omitted and (2.12) is written

$$y_t = \beta_1 + \beta_2 x_t + \varepsilon_t \qquad (2.13)$$

While this is an often convenient shorthand, the underlying rationale should not be forgotten. Models like this are considered in greater detail in Chapter 4.

2.5.3 Visual representation of 2 variables

A useful visual device in a bivariate relationship is the scatter diagram which is a plot of the

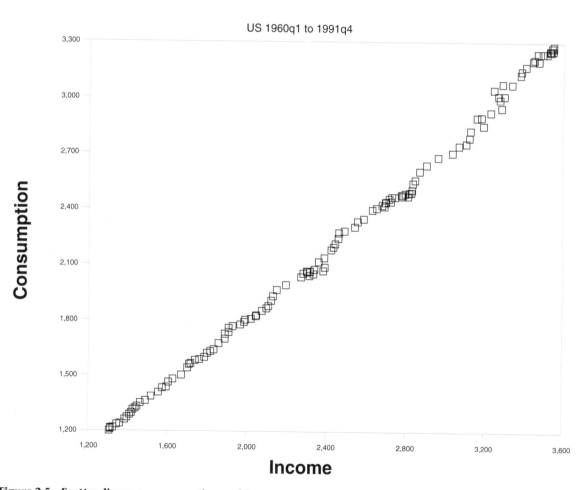

Figure 2.5 *Scatter diagram: consumption and income*

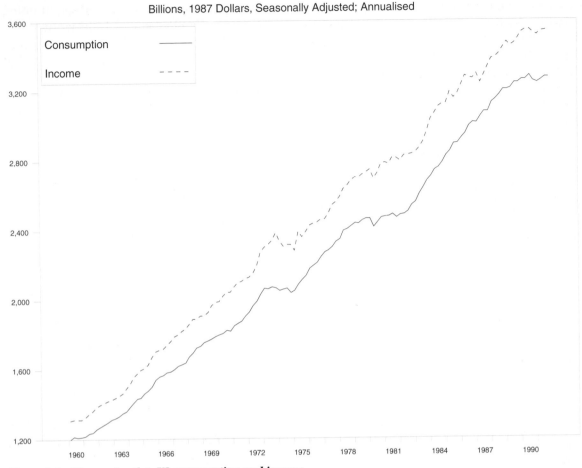

Billions, 1987 Dollars, Seasonally Adjusted; Annualised

Figure 2.6   *Time series plot: US consumption and income*

ordered pairs of values (y_1, x_1), (y_2, x_2), ..., (y_T, x_T). It is the convention that y_t takes the vertical axis and x_t the horizontal axis. An illustration of a scatter diagram is provided by Figure 2.5, which plots real, consumption and real personal disposable income for the United States for the sample period 1960q1 to 1991q4. The visual impression is of two series which are very closely associated with the relationship looking very close to being linear but, bearing out the argument above, deviations from linearity being apparent throughout the range.

Another complementary visual device, which is not limited to just two series, is to plot y_t and x_t on the same time series graph. Continuing the consumption–income example refer to Figure 2.6. From this graph note that both series share a common tendency to increase over time; moreover the visual impression is of two series which not only increase over time, which is a pattern shared by a multitude of economic series, but also are linked together. In later chapters procedures are developed to determine whether this visual impression is apparent, and hence spurious, or real.

2.5.4   Dynamic bivariate models

A common feature of models of economic behaviour is that they involve a dynamic relationship, that is one in which time, or more precisely the difference in time, has a role to play.

Consider the illustration provided by the partial adjustment model, PAM, applied to the stock of consumers' durables which is denoted y_t. Suppose that consumers have a 'target' for their stock of consumer durables, denoted y_t^*. In equilibrium $y_t = y_t^*$, that is the actual and target stocks are equal; however, because of adjustment costs, either or both actual or psychological, consumers are not able to adjust immediately to any changes in the target value. This suggests the model

$$y_t - y_{t-1} = \delta(y_t^* - y_{t-1}) + \varepsilon_t \quad |\delta| \leq 1 \quad (2.14)$$

The interpretation of this model is that the change in the stock of consumer durables is proportional to the difference between any gap which has opened up between the target value, y_t^*, and the opening period stock, y_{t-1}. The closer δ is to 1, the quicker is this adjustment. By a simple rearrangement the PAM can be rewritten with y_t as the dependent variable,

$$y_t = \delta y_t^* + (1 - \delta)y_{t-1} + \varepsilon_t$$

Notice that if $\delta = 1$ this reduces to $y_t = y_t^* + \varepsilon_t$. The model can be further developed by letting $y_t^* = \lambda_0 x_t$, so that the target relationship is modelled as a simple function of an explanatory variable x_t. Substituting for y_t^*

$$y_t = \delta \lambda_0 x_t + (1 - \delta)y_{t-1} + \varepsilon_t \quad (2.15)$$

This model is an illustration of a dynamic process since y_t depends in a fundamental way not just upon the contemporaneous value of x_t but also the one period lag of itself. Letting $\beta_0 = \delta \lambda_0$ and $\gamma_1 = (1 - \delta)$, (2.14) can be rewritten as

$$(1 - \gamma_1 L)y_t = \beta_0 x_t + \varepsilon_t \quad (2.16)$$

This is the standard way of writing a distributed lag model which has one lag on the dependent variable and no lags on the explanatory variable.

The basic PAM can be generalised to show how more complex distributed lag models can be generated. Suppose that adjustment depends not just on the current difference $y_t^* - y_{t-1}$, but also the lagged difference, $y_{t-1}^* - y_{t-2}$, then the PAM becomes

$$y_t - y_{t-1} = \delta_1(y_t^* - y_{t-1})$$
$$+ \delta_2(y_{t-1}^* - y_{t-2}) + \varepsilon_t \quad (2.17)$$

which on substituting for $y_t^* = \lambda_0 x_t$, and rewriting in the standard form, gives

$$(1 - \gamma_1 L - \gamma_2 L^2)y_t = (\beta_0 + \beta_1 L)x_t + \varepsilon_t \quad (2.18)$$

with $\gamma_1 = (1 - \delta_1)$, $\gamma_2 = -\delta_2$, $\beta_0 = \delta_1 \lambda_0$ and $\beta_1 = \delta_2 \lambda_0$. Thus, this generates a distributed lag model with two lags on the dependent variable and one lag on the explanatory variable.

2.5.5 Autoregressive distributed lag (ADL) models

Models such as the PAM written in standard form are known as autoregressive distributed lag models. A model with p lags on the dependent variable and q lags on the explanatory variable is referred to as an ADL(p, q) model. That is,

$$\left(1 - \sum_{i=1}^{p} \gamma_i L^i\right)y_t = \alpha_0 + \sum_{j=0}^{q} \beta_j L^j x_t + \varepsilon_t$$
$$(2.19)$$

A constant, α_0, has also been included. Let

$$\gamma(L) = \left(1 - \sum_{i=1}^{p} \gamma_i L^i\right) \quad \text{and}$$

$$\beta(L) = \sum_{j=0}^{q} \beta_j L^j \quad (2.20)$$

then the ADL(p, q) model can equivalently be written as

$$\gamma(L)y_t = \alpha_0 + \beta(L)x_t + \varepsilon_t \quad (2.21)$$

Now if $\gamma(L)$ was a scalar (that is a single number) it would be straightforward to divide both sides of this equation by $\gamma(L)$ to obtain an expression for y_t. The fact that $\gamma(L)$ is a lag polynomial is not, however, a problem because a meaning can be attached to $1/\gamma(L) \equiv \gamma(L)^{-1}$. Dividing (2.21) through by $\gamma(L)$ gives

$$y_t = \alpha_0^* + [\beta(L)/\gamma(L)]x_t + v_t \qquad (2.22)$$

where $\alpha_0^* = \alpha_0/\gamma(L)$ and $v_t = \varepsilon_t/\gamma(L)$. To simplify this further define $w(L) = \beta(L)/\gamma(L)$ then

$$y_t = \alpha_0^* + w(L)x_t + v_t \qquad (2.23)$$

where $w(L)$ is known as a distributed lag function; $w(L)$ is a function of L, say

$$w(L) = \sum_{s=0}^{\infty} w_s L^s \qquad (2.24)$$

with lag weights w_s in a potentially infinite sequence.

2.5.6   The distributed lag function

The lag weights in (2.24) depend upon the coefficients in $\gamma(L)$ and $\beta(L)$ and, in general, are quite complicated functions of these. However, introducing the function $w(L)$ is useful for two reasons. First, it shows the explicit dependence of y_t on current and past values of x_t, that is

$$y_t = \alpha_0^* + w_0 x_t + w_1 x_{t-1} + \cdots + v_t \qquad (2.25)$$

Second, it is particularly useful in obtaining the long-run relationship between y_t and x_t. For example, if x_t settles to a constant level, what will be the resulting value of y_t? Let x_c be the common value of x then

$$\sum_{s=0}^{\infty} w_s L^s x_t = \sum_{s=0}^{\infty} w_s x_c \quad \text{because} \quad L^s x_t = x_c$$

$$= x_c \sum_{s=0}^{\infty} w_s \quad \text{because } x_c \text{ is a constant}$$

$$(2.26)$$

The coefficient on x_c is simply the sum of the lag weights $\sum_{s=0}^{\infty} w_s$, for convenience let $\lambda_0 \equiv \sum_{s=0}^{\infty} w_s$. Notice that evaluating $\sum_{s=0}^{\infty} w_s L^s$ by setting $L = 1$ gives the sum of the lag weights, $\sum_{s=0}^{\infty} w_s$.

In practice the values of the coefficients in $\gamma(L)$ and $\beta(L)$ will be available rather than the lag weights, so how is the long-run coefficient λ_0 obtained? As noted, the answer is to use the 'trick' introduced earlier, that is set $L = 1$ in the lag function $w(L)$, the notation for which is $w(1)$ or if emphasis is needed $w(L = 1)$. Then

$$\lambda_0 = w(1)$$
$$= \gamma(1)/\beta(1)$$

To see how this works consider the modified PAM with

$$(1 - \gamma_1 L - \gamma_2 L^2)y_t = (\beta_0 + \beta_1 L)x_t + u_t$$
$$(2.27)$$

Then

$$y_t = w(L)x_t + v_t$$

where $w(L) = (\beta_0 + \beta_1 L)/(1 - \gamma_1 L - \gamma_2 L^2)$ and $v_t = \varepsilon_t/(1 - \gamma_1 L - \gamma_2 L^2)$.

Now set $L = 1$ to obtain:

$$\lambda_0 \equiv w(1)$$
$$= (\beta_0 + \beta_1)/(1 - \gamma_1 - \gamma_2)$$

Substituting for values of β_0, β_1, γ_1 and γ_2 gives the sum of the lag weights but without actually evaluating the sum directly.

If the distributed lag model has a constant α_0^* then the same trick can be applied to obtain the long-run value of the constant, denoted k. That is

$$k = \alpha_0 / \left(1 - \sum_{i=1}^{p} \gamma_i \right)$$

Specifically in the case of the extended PAM the long run is

$$y_t = k + \lambda_0 x_t \qquad (2.28)$$

where $k = \alpha_0/(1 - \gamma_1 - \gamma_2)$
and $\lambda_0 = (\beta_0 + \beta_1)/(1 - \gamma_1 - \gamma_2)$

($v_t = 0$ on the assumption that the random disturbance has a zero value in the long run.)

It might be helpful to follow through these developments with a numerical example. The motivation for the example is the extended PAM given by

$$\Delta y_t = 0.5(y_t^* - y_{t-1}) + 0.3(y_{t-1}^* - y_{t-2}) + \varepsilon_t$$

with $y_t^* = 0.75 + 2x_t$. Then $\alpha_0 = 0.6$, $\beta_0 = 1.0$, $\beta_1 = 0.6$, $\gamma_1 = 0.5$ and $\gamma_2 = -0.3$. The distributed lag function is:

$$w(L) = (1.0 + 0.6L)/(1 - 0.5L + 0.3L^2)$$

evaluating $w(L)$ at $L = 1$, to obtain the sum of the lag weights, then

$$\lambda_0 = w(1)$$
$$= 1.6/0.8 = 2.0$$

and $k = 0.6/(1 - 0.5 + 0.3)$
$$= 0.6/0.8 = 0.75$$

The long-run solution is, therefore,

$$y_t = 0.75 + 2x_t$$

Of course, the long-run solution just reproduces the target value of y_t. If x_t is constant at 100 then

$$y_t = 0.75 + 2(100)$$
$$= 200.75$$

Now suppose x_t increases to 110 and stays at this increased level then, in the long run, what is the revised value of y_t? In order to answer this

question just substitute the revised value of x_t into the long-run equation to obtain

$$y_t = 0.75 + 2(110)$$
$$= 220.75$$

The difference between the two long-run solutions is 20, that is $\lambda_0 \Delta x_t$, where $\lambda_0 = 2$ and $\Delta x_t = 10$.

2.5.7 More than one conditioning variable

The models introduced so far are generally too simple to form the basis of a realistic empirical analysis. One direction of generality is to extend the number of conditioning variables; for example, consumption is likely to depend upon wealth and interest rates as well as income, and it may well depend upon lags of these variables. The set of $k + 1$ variables in the analysis is $(y_t, x_{t1}, x_{t2}, \ldots, x_{tk})$, note the distinguishing notation between the endogenous variable y_t and the conditioning variables $x_t = (x_{t1}, x_{t2}, \ldots, x_{tk})$ and the use of two subscripts, the first to indicate time, and the second to indicate the variable. The extension of the simple bivariate model of (2.12) is:

$$y_t \,|\, x_t = \beta_1 x_{t1} + \beta_2 x_{t2} + \beta_3 x_{t3} + \cdots$$
$$+ \beta_k x_{tk} + \varepsilon_t \,|\, x_t \qquad (2.29a)$$

If a constant is included in the model then the convention is to set $x_{t1} = 1$ for all $t = 1, \ldots, T$, so that $\beta_1 x_{t1} = \beta_1$, and this is the constant. The extended model is now:

$$y_t \,|\, x_t = \beta_1 + \beta_2 x_{t2} + \beta_3 x_{t3} + \cdots$$
$$+ \beta_k x_{tk} + \varepsilon_t \,|\, x_t \qquad (2.29b)$$

Apart from the inclusion of more variables the interpretation of (2.29b) is the same as (2.12): conditional on x_t the outcome for y_t is given by the average response, which is a linear function of the x_{ti} variables, that is

$\beta_1 + \beta_2 x_{t2} + \beta_3 x_{t3} + \cdots + \beta_k x_{tk}$, and a deviation or innovation relative to the information in the set x_t, $\varepsilon_t | x_t$. As before, but with the occasional risk of confusion, the notation indicating the conditioning is dropped and the model is simply represented as

$$y_t = \beta_1 + \beta_2 x_{t2} + \beta_3 x_{t3} + \cdots + \beta_k x_{tk} + \varepsilon_t$$

(2.30)

which is the multiple regression model of Chapter 5.

A dynamic model involves lags on some or all of the variables in (2.29). For example, denote as ADL($p, q_2, q_3, \ldots, q_k$), the autoregressive distributed lag model with p lags on y_t and q_i lags on the conditioning variable x_{ti}. Say

$$\gamma(L)y_t = \beta_1 + \beta_2(L)x_{t2}$$
$$+ \beta_3(L)x_{t3} + \cdots + \beta_k(L)x_{tk} + \varepsilon_t$$

(2.31)

with $\gamma(L)$ as before and $\beta_i(L) = \sum_{j=0}^{q_i} \beta_{ij}L^j$ for $i = 2, \ldots, k$.

2.5.8 Notation in more complex models

Notation in econometrics can be quite a difficult obstacle for students to overcome. A student just becomes comfortable with one notational convention when it is changed in a later variation! The purpose of this short digression is to alert the student to an important example of this situation. When several variables are involved in time series analysis there are two dimensions that need to be identified: the index indicating the variable and the index indicating which observation is being referred to. The notation introduced in the previous section is to put the time index first, followed by the variable index. This is useful because it enables the T observations on all the k variables to be collected into a matrix with T rows and k columns. Thus the matrix X of dimension $T \times k$ is defined by:

k columns (the variables)

$$X \equiv \begin{bmatrix} x_{11} & x_{12} & \cdots & \cdots & x_{1k} \\ x_{21} & x_{22} & \cdots & \cdots & x_{2k} \\ x_{31} & x_{32} & \cdots & \cdots & x_{3k} \\ \vdots & \vdots & \cdots & \cdots & \vdots \\ x_{T1} & x_{T2} & \cdots & \cdots & x_{Tk} \end{bmatrix}$$

There are T observations ordered by rows and k variables ordered by columns. This notation is the convention when a single variable, usually denoted y_t, is explained by the k variables, x_{t1}, $x_{t2}, \ldots, x_{tk}$.

A different convention is usually adopted if there are equations for several variables. This is the situation in what are known as vector autoregressions, to be described briefly in the next section and used extensively in Chapters 14 and 15. In this case the convention reverses the roles of the two indices: now the first index indicates the variable, and the second is the index indicating time. Further, the variables are partitioned into two sets, the first – the y variables – are explained by the second – the x variables. Thus, if there are two y variables and two x variables the notation is: y_{1t} and y_{2t} and x_{1t} and x_{2t} for $t = 1, \ldots, T$.

The reversal of the previous single equation notational convention offers the following economy when dealing with dynamic multi-equation models. A one-period lag of y_{1t} is written y_{1t-1}, which is simple to write and interpret. If the convention had been to put the time index first so y_{1t} becomes y_{t1}, the one-period lag is y_{t-11}, which is confusing and would have to be written $y_{t-1,1}$ to distinguish the one-period lag from the 11-period lag. This different notational convention is illustrated in the next section.

2.6 Several equations together

Chapters 14 and 15 deal extensively with models which involve the joint determination of several variables that are treated symmetrically. For example, suppose economic theory suggests a relationship between consumption and income, which are designated y_{1t} and y_{2t}. A single equation approach would either condition consumption on income or income on consumption; however, as subsequent chapters show (see especially Chapters 9 and 15) this will not be a generally valid approach unless certain conditions are met. These conditions can be viewed as restrictions on a more general approach in which the variables are initially treated symmetrically. It is not the purpose of this section to detail these conditions but rather to extend some of the basic concepts of previous sections to include the multi-equation case.

The first aim is to extend the univariate, autoregressive model starting with the two variables y_{1t} and y_{2t}. A simple extension is to the vector autoregressive model, usually referred to as a VAR. In a VAR y_{1t} is related not just to its own lagged values but also to lagged values of y_{2t}, and similarly y_{2t} is related to its own lagged values and the lagged values of y_{1t}. A VAR has two dimensions: the length, or order, p of the longest lag in the autoregression; and the number, k, of variables being jointly modelled. For example, a second order, $p = 2$, bivariate, $k = 2$, VAR is:

$$y_{1t} = \mu_{10} + \pi_{11.1}y_{1t-1} + \pi_{12.1}y_{2t-1}$$
$$+ \pi_{11.2}y_{1t-2} + \pi_{12.2}y_{2t-2} + \varepsilon_{1t} \quad (2.32a)$$

$$y_{2t} = \mu_{20} + \pi_{21.1}y_{1t-1} + \pi_{22.1}y_{2t-1}$$
$$+ \pi_{21.2}y_{1t-2} + \pi_{22.2}y_{2t-2} + \varepsilon_{2t} \quad (2.32b)$$

Each of these equations is like a univariate, autoregressive model but, in addition, includes lagged values of the other variable(s). The 'innovations', or unpredictable stochastic elements of y_{1t} and y_{2t} are ε_{1t} and ε_{2t}, respectively. The subscripts on the π coefficients, which at first sight seem somewhat complex, need a word of explanation. In this case the first subscript refers to the equation number, the second subscript refers to the variable and the third subscript to

the lag; for example, $\pi_{12.1}$ is the coefficient in the first equation on the first variable lagged once, $\pi_{21.2}$ is the coefficient in the second equation on the first variable lagged twice.

Using the lag operator these equations can be written

$$y_{1t} = \mu_{10} + \pi_{11.1}Ly_{1t} + \pi_{12.1}Ly_{2t}$$
$$+ \pi_{11.2}L^2 y_{1t} + \pi_{12.2}L^2 y_{2t} + \varepsilon_{1t} \quad (2.33a)$$

$$y_{2t} = \mu_{20} + \pi_{21.1}Ly_{1t} + \pi_{22.1}Ly_{2t}$$
$$+ \pi_{21.2}L^2 y_{1t} + \pi_{22.2}L^2 y_{2t} + \varepsilon_{2t} \quad (2.33b)$$

The next step is to write the equations together using a vector/matrix notation:

$$y_t = \mu + \Pi_1 Ly_t + \Pi_2 L^2 y_t + \varepsilon_t \quad (2.34)$$

The advantage of this form is seen immediately from its simplicity relative to (2.32). The variables in (2.34) are defined as follows: $y_t = (y_{1t}, y_{2t})'$; $\mu = (\mu_1, \mu_2)'$ is the vector of constants; $\varepsilon_t = (\varepsilon_{1t}, \varepsilon_{2t})'$, the vector of innovations; and

$$\Pi_1 L = \begin{bmatrix} \pi_{11.1}L & \pi_{12.1}L \\ \pi_{21.1}L & \pi_{22.1}L \end{bmatrix} \quad \text{and}$$

$$\Pi_2 L^2 = \begin{bmatrix} \pi_{11.2}L^2 & \pi_{12.2}L^2 \\ \pi_{21.2}L^2 & \pi_{22.2}L^2 \end{bmatrix}$$

The multivariate equivalent of (2.10) for the univariate model is

$$(I - \Pi_1 L - \Pi_2 L^2)y_t = \mu + \varepsilon_t \quad (2.35)$$

say $A(L)y_t = \mu + \varepsilon_t$ where

$$A(L) = (I - \Pi_1 L - \Pi_2 L^2)$$

$A(L)$ is sometimes referred to as a *matrix lag polynomial*. Just as in the univariate case the sum of the lag weights is obtained by setting $L = 1$ in the lag polynomial $A(L)$, the shorthand for which is $A(1)$ or equivalently if emphasis is needed $A(L = 1)$.

The VAR given by (2.32) is said to be *closed* in the sense that there are the same number of equations as variables; an *open* VAR has more variables than equations, which implies that the variables are now not treated symmetrically, there is a distinction between those variables which are modelled and those which are not. This is the multi-equation extension of the multiple regression model (2.29). To illustrate, let $k = 4$, with the variables divided into the 'endogenous', $y_t = (y_{1t}, y_{2t})'$, for which there are equations, and the 'exogenous', $x_t = (x_{1t}, x_{2t})'$ which are the conditioning variables; $p = 2$ as in the previous example. In this example there are just two equations:

$$y_t = \mu + \Pi_1 L y_t + \Pi_2 L^2 y_t + \Theta_2 L x_t + \varepsilon_t \quad (2.36)$$

where $x_t = (x_{1t}, x_{2t})'$ and

$$\Theta_1 = \begin{bmatrix} \theta_{11.1}, & \theta_{12.1} \\ \theta_{21.1}, & \theta_{22.1} \end{bmatrix} \quad \text{and}$$

$$\Theta_2 L = \begin{bmatrix} \theta_{11.2}L, & \theta_{12.2}L \\ \theta_{21.1}L, & \theta_{22.2}L \end{bmatrix}$$

Just as in the single-equation case the long-run value of y_t can be obtained conditional on constant values for the 'exogenous' variables. First write (2.36) collecting terms:

$$(I - \Pi_1 L y_t - \Pi_2 L^2) y_t = \mu + (\Theta_1 + \Theta_2 L) x_t + \varepsilon_t \quad (2.37)$$

and $\qquad A(L) y_t = \mu + B(L) x_t + \varepsilon_t$

where $A(L)$ is as defined before and $B(L) = (\Theta_1 + \Theta_2 L)$; multiplying through by $A(L)^{-1}$ gives

$$y_t = A(L)^{-1} \mu + A(L)^{-1} B(L) x_t + A(L)^{-1} \varepsilon_t$$

say

$$y_t = \mu^* + C(L) x_t + v_t \quad (2.38)$$

where $\mu^* = A(L)^{-1} \mu$, $C(L) = A(L)^{-1} B(L)$ and $v_t = A(L)^{-1} \varepsilon_t$. The inverse of $A(L)$ will exist if the determinant of $A(z)$, written $\det[A(z)]$ or $|A(z)|$, for the artificial variable z, is not equal to zero. The equation (2.38) is sometimes referred to as the final form of the open VAR, and the matrix $C(L)$ is referred to as the transfer function that summarises the effect of a unit change in the exogenous variables on the endogenous variables. $C(L)$ is the analogue of the rational lag function $w(L)$ in the single-equation case and, like that function, is of infinite order; that is $C(L) = \sum_{i=0}^{\infty} C_i L^i$, where each C_i is a matrix, in this case of dimension 2×2. The long-run relationship between y_t and x_t is obtained on setting $L = 1$ in (2.38), that is (assuming ε_t is set to its mean of zero)

$$y_t = A(1)^{-1} \mu + C(1) x_t \quad (2.39)$$

$C(1)$ is the matrix of long-run multipliers, the element $C_{ij}(1)$ is the long-run effect on y_{it} of a one unit change in x_{jt}.

As an example of the preceding models consider the two-equation system in the four variables y_{1t}, y_{2t}, x_{1t} and x_{2t}

$$\begin{aligned} y_{1t} = {}& 0.50 + 0.625 y_{1t-1} + 0.3125 y_{2t-1} \\ & - 0.125 y_{1t-2} + 0.250 y_{2t-2} \\ & + 0.250 x_{1t} + 0.125 x_{2t} \\ & + 0.750 x_{1t-1} + 0.375 x_{2t-1} + \varepsilon_{1t} \end{aligned}$$

$$(2.40a)$$

$$\begin{aligned} y_{2t} = {}& 0.75 + 0.750 y_{1t-1} + 0.1875 y_{2t-1} \\ & - 0.250 y_{1t-2} + 0.750 y_{2t-2} \\ & - 1.500 x_{1t} + 0.200 x_{2t} \\ & - 0.50 x_{1t-1} + 0.050 x_{2t-1} + \varepsilon_{2t} \quad (2.40b) \end{aligned}$$

which can be written as

$$\begin{aligned} \begin{pmatrix} y_{1t} \\ y_{2t} \end{pmatrix} = {}& \begin{pmatrix} 0.5 \\ 0.75 \end{pmatrix} \\ & + \begin{bmatrix} 0.625 & 0.3125 \\ 0.750 & 0.1875 \end{bmatrix} \begin{pmatrix} y_{1t-1} \\ y_{2t-1} \end{pmatrix} \\ & + \begin{bmatrix} -0.125 & 0.250 \\ -0.250 & 0.750 \end{bmatrix} \begin{pmatrix} y_{1t-2} \\ y_{2t-2} \end{pmatrix} \\ & + \begin{bmatrix} 0.250 & 0.125 \\ -1.500 & 0.200 \end{bmatrix} \begin{pmatrix} x_{1t} \\ x_{2t} \end{pmatrix} \\ & + \begin{bmatrix} 0.750 & 0.375 \\ -0.500 & 0.050 \end{bmatrix} \begin{pmatrix} x_{1t-1} \\ x_{2t-1} \end{pmatrix} \end{aligned}$$

The following vectors and matrices are needed:

$$\mu = (0.50 \quad 0.75)'$$

$$A(L) = \begin{bmatrix} 1 & 0 \\ 0 & 1 \end{bmatrix} - \begin{bmatrix} 0.625L & 0.3125L \\ 0.750L & 0.1875L \end{bmatrix}$$

$$- \begin{bmatrix} -0.125L^2 & 0.250L^2 \\ -0.250L^2 & 0.750L^2 \end{bmatrix}$$

$$B(L) = \begin{bmatrix} 0.250 & 0.125 \\ -1.500 & 0.200 \end{bmatrix}$$

$$+ \begin{bmatrix} 0.750L & 0.375L \\ -0.500L & 0.050L \end{bmatrix}$$

So

$$A(1) = \begin{bmatrix} 0.50 & -0.5625 \\ -0.50 & 0.0625 \end{bmatrix}$$

$$A(1)^{-1} = \begin{bmatrix} -0.25 & -2.25 \\ -2.00 & -2.00 \end{bmatrix}$$

$$\det[A(1)] = -0.25 \neq 0$$

$$B(1) = \begin{bmatrix} 1.00 & 0.50 \\ -2.00 & 0.25 \end{bmatrix}$$

$$A(1)^{-1}\mu = \begin{bmatrix} -0.25 & -2.25 \\ -2.00 & -2.00 \end{bmatrix} \begin{pmatrix} 0.50 \\ 0.75 \end{pmatrix}$$

$$= \begin{bmatrix} -1.8125 \\ -2.50 \end{bmatrix}$$

$$A(1)^{-1}B(1) = \begin{bmatrix} -0.25 & -2.25 \\ -2.00 & -2.00 \end{bmatrix} \begin{bmatrix} 1 & 0.50 \\ -2 & 0.25 \end{bmatrix}$$

$$= \begin{bmatrix} 4.25 & -0.6875 \\ 2.00 & -1.50 \end{bmatrix}$$

The determinant of $A(1)$ is -0.25, hence $A(1)$ is nonsingular and its inverse exists and, therefore, the operation $A(1)^{-1}B(1)$ is possible in this example.

The long run of this model is:

$$y_{1t} = -1.8125 + 4.25x_{1t} - 0.6875x_{2t}$$

$$y_{2t} = -2.50 + 2.00x_{1t} - 1.50x_{2t}$$

So in the long run a unit increase in x_{1t} increases y_{1t} by 4.25 and increases y_{2t} by 2; and in the long run, a unit increase in x_{2t} leads to a decrease of -0.6875 in y_{1t} whereas y_{2t} decreases by -1.5. The coefficients in $C(1) = A(1)^{-1}B(1)$ are the long-run multipliers. Referring back to (2.40) we see that they differ from the impact effects; for example, from (2.40a) the effect of a one unit change in x_{1t} on y_{1t} in the same period is 0.25, and the effect of a one unit change in x_{2t} on y_{1t} in the same period is 0.125. The difference between the impact and long-run effects is due to the presence of a dynamic structure captured by non-zero values of the coefficients on lagged values of y_{1t} and y_{2t}.

The statements as to long-run effects presuppose one qualification, which should now be made explicit. They assume that the model is stable; that is, following changes to x_{1t} or x_{2t} the values of y_{1t} and y_{2t} will change from one equilibrium value to another. Whether this is or is not the case depends upon the dynamic structure. For linear models like this one, stability can be checked analytically or computationally. The analytical conditions refer to what are known as the eigenvalues (sometimes called characteristic values) of $A(L)$ and are dealt with in detail in Chapter 14, especially section **14.2.4**; for now we note that the model is stable (this requires the eigenvalues of $A(L)$ to have modulus less than 1 and in this case the eigenvalues are 0.8549 and -0.2924). Computationally we can calculate the impulse response function, which follows from shocking, say, x_{1t} by one unit and tracing out the response path for y_{1t} and y_{2t} using equations (2.40a) and (2.40b).

2.7 Concluding remarks

Although this chapter has dealt with several topics, there has been throughout the unifying theme of the importance of time and dynamic relationships in economics. While obviously present in time series analysis, the importance of dynamic connections should not be overlooked in cross-section data; for example, a cross-section study to examine the competitive behaviour of retail stores in a shopping catchment is likely to need a dynamic aspect.

Some important concepts have been introduced in this chapter; concepts which will appear again and again in the following chapters. An essential element in constructing models to explain time series data, whether such models are univariate, bivariate or multivariate, is the connection between series at different points of time. With this in mind, the idea of lagging and leading a time series and constructing dynamic models is of central importance. A convenient 'shorthand' in dynamic models, which turns out also to offer a tool of analysis, is the lag operator defined by $L^j y_t \equiv y_{t-j}$ and the associated lag polynomial function.

At a less erudite level knowledge of the types of data available for empirical analysis is important as is a clear understanding of the units of measurement of data series. A common mistake, in undergraduate projects involving the collection and analysis of data, is to mismatch variables in their units of measurement; for example, relating a variable measured in current prices to one measured in constant prices or, in specifying a demand function, relating a variable measured in constant prices to its own absolute price rather than, as economic theory suggests, its own *relative* price. A lot of these mistakes can be removed by taking a preliminary look at the data using graphical means such as the scatter diagram or time series plot. This is also useful in the related context of obtaining a balanced equation. To illustrate, consider the simple bivariate equation given by $y_t = \beta_1 + \beta_2 x_{2t} + \varepsilon_t$ then, for example, if the data y_t contains a trend then there must be an equivalent matching property in x_{2t}, otherwise the equation does not achieve an empirical balance. Alternatively, suppose y_t shows a distinct seasonal pattern as in the case of personal consumption expenditures, which show a marked increase in the fourth quarter of each year, then this must be matched on the right-hand side of the equation otherwise the latter cannot be an explanation of the former.

Sections **2.4–2.6** above introduced the idea of a random variable, this is taken up further in Chapter 3 which also considers the distribution of two or more random variables. Chapters 4 and 5 consider the problem of estimating the coefficients in the regression model and testing hypotheses.

Review

1. The aim of this chapter was to introduce some basic but important concepts and models which underlie the analysis of economic data.

2. A number of distinctions were made on the kind of data economists use. An important distinction was in the degree of aggregation. Data could relate to an individual entity, for example a consumer or firm, or to a group of entities. In addition to entity aggregation it could relate to temporal aggregation. As the adjective suggests this is aggregation over time. The sum of expenditures over the 13 weeks of a quarter is an example of temporal aggregation.

3. Much of the data economists use is of a nonexperimental kind and usually relates to historical and nonreplicable events. However, in recent years economists have started to explore experimental situations and have for some time used simulation techniques that can be likened to replicable experiments.

4. The data analysed in this book is of a time series nature where the index of time serves to naturally order the observations. For example, the observation for 1989 precedes that for 1990, while that for 1990 precedes 1991 and so on.

5. We emphasised the importance of time series graphs of economic data. The convention is to put the index of time on the horizontal axis and values of the variable, y_t, on the vertical axis.

6. A distinguishing feature of time series data is its frequency, which refers to how often the observations are recorded. An economic activity might be taking place continuously but only a sample of observations is possible, frequency then refers to how often, in a given period, for example a year, the data is actually recorded.

7. High frequency data is often available for financial variables such as exchange rates or share prices, which have been recorded as frequently as every hour (or even minute) during the trading day.

8. Another distinction among economic data is the dimension of a variable. We distinguished among flows, stocks and rates with examples of each.

9. An important aspect in the analysis of time series data is that there is often a link between a variable at time t, say y_t, and its lagged value y_{t-1}. Table 2.1 gave an example of what happens to a time series when it is lagged a number of times.

10. The creation of lagged variables allows the calculations of differences and growth rates. For example, the annual percentage growth rate for quarterly data is

$$100(\Delta_4 y_t / y_{t-4})$$

where $\Delta_4 y_t = y_t - y_{t-4}$.

11. As well as lagging variables, economists sometimes consider the leading of a time series. For example, the first lead of y_t is y_{t+1}. Table 2.2 gave an example of what happens to a time series when it is subject to a lead. Leads are useful in modelling expectations.

12. Figure 2.1 illustrated time series data of a quarterly frequency with a flow dimension. Figure 2.2 illustrated time series data of an annual frequency with a stock dimension. Figure 2.3 illustrated time series data of a quarterly frequency expressed in rate form. Finally, Figure 2.4 illustrated quarterly time series (flow) data without the dominant tendency, so apparent in Figures 2.1 and 2.2, of the series to increase.

13. Visual representation of data is to be encouraged in an initial stage of investigation. This should not, though, be done without reference to available economic theory. Measurement and theory are symbiotic, rather than exclusive, partners.

14. The next section introduced the lag (and lead) operator, L^j. This was necessary as a stepping stone to considering dynamic bivariate models. The operator L^j applied to a series y_t is defined by $L^j y_t \equiv y_{t-j}$, with $L^0 y_t \equiv y_t$. With j negative L^j is the lead operator.

15. A simple example of a lag polynomial is $\phi_0 L^0 + \phi_1 L^1 + \phi_2 L^2$. This is a second order polynomial as the highest power of L is L^2. In general a pth order polynomial will have terms up to and including $\phi_p L^p$, and is sometimes written as $\phi(L)$. The ϕ_i are the lag coefficients.

16. The sum of the lag coefficients is obtained by setting $L = 1$ in the lag polynomial. For example, if $\phi(L) = (1 - 2kL)/(1 - kL)$, then the sum of lag coefficients is $\phi(L = 1) = (1 - 2k)/(1 - k)$.

17. A stochastic, autoregressive process for the variable y_t is given by

$$y_t = \phi_1 y_{t-1} + \phi_2 y_{t-2} + \cdots + \phi_p y_{t-p} + \varepsilon_t$$

where ε_t is a random component.

18. In economics we seek to understand the interrelationships between variables. Thus while the history of individual variables can be useful it is usual to move on to consider how several variables interact. The simplest extension of univariate analysis is to bivariate analysis.

19. We started with a deterministic bivariate model but argued that the variables of economic analysis are better viewed as outcomes of stochastic – or random – rather than deterministic processes.

20. We introduced the idea that we could represent the relationship between y_t and x_t as $y_t = \alpha + \beta x_t + \varepsilon_t$, provided that we viewed the outcome, y_t, as being conditional on the

value of the input, x_t. ε_t is a random term which has properties determined from the joint distribution of y_t and x_t.

21. A useful visual device for a bivariate relationship is to plot y_t on the vertical axis and x_t on the horizontal axis. This was illustrated in Figure 2.5 with US data on per capita consumption and per capita income.

22. A complementary visual device is to plot both series on the same time series graph. (In some cases different left- and right-hand scales might be needed.)

23. Having introduced a bivariate model and lag polynomials we are then able to bring both aspects together in some illustrative dynamic models. For example, the partial adjustment model (PAM) is

$$\Delta y_t = \delta(y_t^* - y_{t-1}) + \varepsilon_t \quad 0 < \delta \le 1.$$

24. A dynamic model with p lags on the dependent variable, y_t, and q lags on the explanatory variable, x_t, is referred to as an autoregressive distributed lag, ADL(p, q), model and written as

$$\gamma(L)y_t = \alpha_0 + \beta(L)x_t + \varepsilon_t$$

or

$$y_t = \alpha_0^* + w(L)x_t + v_t$$

with $w(L) = \beta(L)/\gamma(L)$ and $v_t = \varepsilon_t/\gamma(L)$

25. The coefficients in $w(L) = \sum_{s=0}^{\infty} w_s L^s$ are known as lag weights. We can obtain the sum of the lag weights, which is the long-run coefficient between y_t and x_t, by setting $L = 1$. That is

$$\lambda_0 = w(L = 1)$$
$$= \beta(L = 1)/\gamma(L = 1)$$
$$= \sum_{j=0}^{q} \beta_j \Big/ \left(1 - \sum_{i=1}^{p} \gamma_i\right)$$

26. The long-run constant is

$$\alpha_0^* = \alpha_0 \Big/ \left(1 - \sum_{i=1}^{p} \gamma_i\right).$$

27. An extension of the simple bivariate model is:

$$y_t \,|\, x_t = \beta_1 + \beta_2 x_{t2} + \beta_3 x_{t3} + \cdots$$
$$+ \beta_k x_{tk} + \varepsilon_t \,|\, x_t$$

Conditional on x_t the outcome for y_t is given by the average response, which is a linear function of the x_{ti} variables, that is $\beta_1 + \beta_2 x_{t2} + \beta_3 x_{t3} + \cdots + \beta_k x_{tk}$ and a deviation or innovation relative to the information in the set x_t, $\varepsilon_t \,|\, x_t$. This is the multiple regression model.

28. The autoregressive distributed lag model with p lags on y_t and q_i lags on the conditioning variable x_{ti}, referred to as ADL$(p, q_2, \ldots, q_k)$, is

$$\gamma(L)y_t = \beta_1 + \beta_2(L)x_{t2} + \beta_3(L)x_{t3} + \cdots$$
$$+ \beta_k(L)x_{tk} + \varepsilon_t$$

29. Later chapters also involve models that specify the joint determination of variables. A simple extension of the univariate autoregressive model is the vector autoregressive model, usually referred to as a VAR.

30. In a two variable VAR y_{1t} is related not just to its own lagged values but also to lagged values of y_{2t}, and similarly y_{2t} is related to its own lagged values and the lagged values of y_{1t}.

31. A VAR has two dimensions: the length, or order, p of the longest lag in the autoregression; and the number, k, of variables being jointly modelled.

32. A second order, $p = 2$, VAR can be written very compactly using vector/matrix notation as: $(I - \Pi_1 L - \Pi_2 L^2)y_t = \mu + \varepsilon_t$, say $A(L)y_t = \mu + \varepsilon_t$ where

$$A(L) = (I - \Pi_1 L - \Pi_2 L^2);$$

and $y_t = (y_{1t}, \ldots, y_{kt})'$ a vector of k variables.

33. A VAR is said to be closed if there are the same number of equations as variables; an open VAR has more variables than equations.

34. Just as in the single equation case the long-run value of y_t can be obtained conditional on constant values for the 'exogenous' variables. In the open VAR,

$$A(L)y_t = \mu + B(L)x_t + \varepsilon_t,$$

the long-run solution is obtained by evaluating the final form $y_t = \mu^* + C(L)x_t$, where $C(L) = A(L)^{-1}B(L)$, for $L = 1$.

Review questions

1. Distinguish between entity aggregation and temporal aggregation of data with examples of each.
2. What distinguishes time series data from cross-section data?
3. Give examples of low-frequency and high-frequency time series data.
4. Categorise the following variables as either flow variables or stock variables and state their units of measurement:
   (i)   US imports of merchandise.
   (ii) US direct investment abroad.
   (iii) Net US official reserve assets.
   (iv) Employees in manufacturing industry.
   (v)   Gross domestic product.
5. The following data is US imports of goods and services (billions, 1987 US$) from 1989q1 to 1991q4: 532.4, 541.3, 550.3, 555.7, 552.2, 554.5, 567.4, 553.7, 531.1, 548.0, 576.3, 579.3. Lay this data out as in Table 2.1, obtaining lags 1 through to 4 and the quarterly and annual rates of change.
6. Continuing question 5, now layout the data as in Table 2.2 with leads 1 through to 4 and the forward looking quarterly and annual rates of change.
7. Express the quarterly and annual rates of change using the lag operator.
8. (i) Show that

$$\Delta_1\Delta_4 y_t = (y_t - y_{t-1}) - (y_{t-4} - y_{t-5});$$

   and, hence, interpret this variable.
   (ii) Interpret $\Delta_1^2 y_t$.

9. Explain what is meant by a polynomial in the lag operator L. What is the order of such a polynomial?
10. Suppose the lag coefficients, ϕ_i, $i = 0, \ldots, \infty$ are obtained from the following sequence

$$\phi_0 = 1, \ \phi_1 = r, \ \phi_2 = r^2, \ldots, \phi_p = r^p, \ldots$$

   What is the sum of the lag coefficients?
11. Explain what is meant by a linear, deterministic, autoregressive process. Give some examples of such processes.
12. (i) How does a bivariate model differ from a univariate model?
    (ii) Give two economic examples of bivariate models.
13. Do you think that deterministic or stochastic models are more likely to be suitable for economic modelling?
14. Plot the following data on a scatter diagram and describe the visual impression given by the data.

	Money stock measure, M1 (billions, US$)	Disposable personal income (billions, US$)
1980	396.0	1,952.9
1981	425.1	2,174.5
1982	453.2	2,319.6
1983	503.4	2,493.7
1984	538.9	2,759.5
1985	587.3	2,943.0
1986	666.8	3,131.5
1987	744.1	3,289.5
1988	775.8	3,548.2
1989	783.3	3,788.6
1990	812.0	4,058.8

Source: Business Statistics, 1963–1991 (Bureau of Economic Analysis 1992).

15. What is the interpretation of δ in the partial adjustment model? Illustrate your answer by choosing different values for δ.
16. Suppose that in the PAM given by (2.14) initially $y_{t-1} = y_{t-1}^*$, $y_{t-2} = y_{t-2}^*$ and so on, but then $y_t^* = y_{t-1}^* + 1$. Trace out the path of

y over the subsequent periods. What do you conclude about the adjustment path?

17. Obtain the long-run coefficients in the following ADL(3, 2) model,

$$(1 - 0.5L - 0.1L^2 - 0.05L^3)y_t$$
$$= 0.7 + (0.2 + 0.1L + 0.05L^2)x_t + \varepsilon_t$$

18. (i) Put the following VAR into vector/matrix form:

$$y_{1t} = 0.4 + 0.35y_{1t-1} - 0.1y_{1t-2}$$
$$+ 0.1y_{1t-3} + 0.3y_{2t-1}$$
$$+ 0.2y_{2t-2} + 0.05y_{2t-3} + \varepsilon_{1t}$$

$$y_{2t} = 0.6 + 0.2y_{1t-1} - 0.05y_{1t-2}$$
$$+ 0.05y_{1t-3} + 0.15y_{2t-1}$$
$$+ 0.3y_{2t-2} + 0.15y_{2t-3} + \varepsilon_{2t}$$

(ii) Obtain and interpret the long run of this VAR.

(iii) Modify the VAR to add $0.3x_{1t} + 0.5x_{2t-1}$ to the first equation and $1.5x_{1t-1} + 0.25x_{2t}$ to the second equation, and answer parts (i) and (ii) of this question.

19. What is the difference between an open VAR and a closed VAR?

20. What are the advantages/disadvantages of VAR over a single-equation model?

CHAPTER 3

An introduction to stationary and nonstationary random variables

3.1   Introduction

It is apparent from the time series graphs of many economic series that they share certain characteristics. In particular there is a tendency, especially noticeable for macroeconomic aggregates, to increase (or more unusually decrease) over time. For example, while we would not predict that GDP will increase next quarter, over a longer period it will almost certainly increase. Informally we characterise a typical series as having a positive trend. Of course there are other patterns, but they often fit the description as being trended. For example, nominal exchange rates tend to have sustained 'walks' in one direction before 'walking' in the other direction – see Chapter 13 for further details and graphs of four leading nominal exchange rates against the US dollar which illustrate this typical pattern. A framework for the explanation of economic time series must be able to account for this kind of pattern.

There are two aspects of a stylisation of how economic time series are generated which are important for this chapter. First, the realisations of economic data are viewed as being generated by stochastic processes; a particular realisation of one variable at a specific point in time is just one possible outcome from an inherently random variable. While the variables would be the same if history could be rerun, the realisations would not be the same. The second aspect draws on the pattern illustrated in Figure 3.1 of section **3.2**. Typically the realisations from the stochastic

processes generating economic data show a distinct tendency to sustain movements in one direction. Given this observation we need a framework, which at the least allows the random variable – for example, GDP, consumption or income – to have a mean that is not constant. In an intuitive sense the stochastic process generating the observed data does not 'stay still' over time. This chapter introduces some basic concepts in the analysis of stochastic processes that do not 'stay still'.

Section **3.2** suggests some difficulties with viewing economic time series as being generated by stationary processes. Section **3.3** is an overview of some basic concepts of probability, which are the building blocks for later work. Some simple and familiar examples are used in that section to motivate the ideas of sample space, probability and joint probability distributions. Section **3.4** introduces the related concepts of: covariance, autocovariance and autocorrelation. Particularly important in this section is the idea that where two variables are involved it is possible to fix – or 'condition' on – one variable and obtain a conditional probability distribution for the other variable. The concept of a nonstationary process is also introduced in section **3.4**, and taken up with a simple example – the random walk – in section **3.5**. A brief comparison of the estimation of familiar concepts such as the mean and variance, when the underlying process is stationary or nonstationary, is contained in section **3.6**, and section **3.7** contains some concluding remarks.

3.2 Time series with a varying mean

Consider Figure 3.1 that graphs US imports of goods (constant prices, quarterly, seasonally adjusted at annual rates) and Figure 3.2 that graphs the US price index for food (index number, 1987 = 100, quarterly, seasonally adjusted). For comparison both are plotted over the period 1967q1 to 1988q4. It is evident from a visual inspection of these series that there is a general tendency for each to trend upwards over time, although the regularity of the upward movements differs between the series. At certain times, in both cases, the series may increase or decrease

rather more rapidly than we would expect from a simple projection of the recent pattern, but over the sample a substantial increase characterises both series. It appears, though, and this is a topic we return to at length in Chapter 6, that the trend is not a simple deterministic one, there appears to be a random element in the movement from one observation to the next. One possible explanation of the trend is that the realisations are outcomes from a stochastic process where the mean is increasing over time.

3.2.1 Some examples

Denote by X_t a random variable which at time t has a range of possible outcomes – or

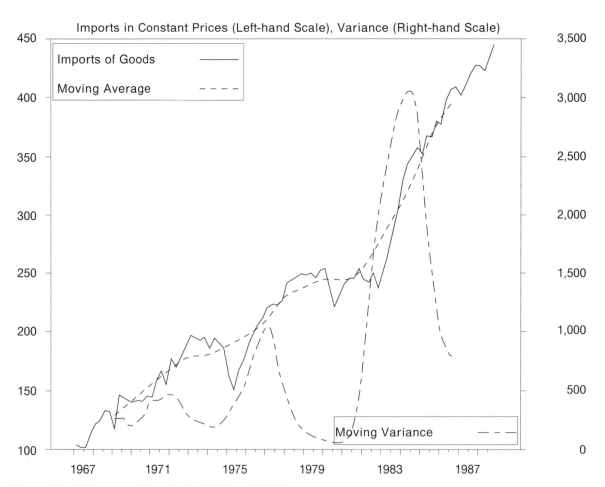

Figure 3.1 *US imports of goods: level, CMA and CMV*

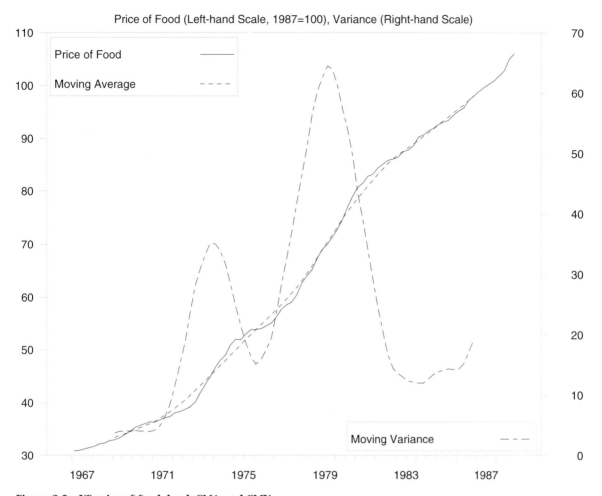

Price of Food (Left-hand Scale, 1987=100), Variance (Right-hand Scale)

Figure 3.2   US price of food: level, CMA and CMV

realisations – and denote by $\mu(t)$ the mean of the series X_t, or, if emphasis is needed that this is the mean of variable X, rather than variable Y, then $\mu_X(t)$ is used. We will return to these definitions more formally below. For the moment we comment on the notational conventions used in this chapter.

Typically a time series variable has time indexed by a subscript, for example X_t and Y_t for the random variables X and Y at time t. However, at times, when there are multiple dimensions to a variable, other conventions that do not overburden the subscript notations are adopted. A mixture of subscripts and super-scripts may be used, alternatively the dependence on one or more classifiers may be shown in parentheses, which is the solution we adopt here. Later in this chapter we need to distinguish on more than one dimension; for example, between the mean of variable X at time t and the mean of variable Y at time s. Given that we wish to emphasise the importance of time these means are written as $\mu_X(t)$ and $\mu_Y(s)$, respectively. Also on occasion there is a need to distinguish among three dimensions while emphasising the importance of the time index. With this in mind, for example, the variance of variable 1 at time t is denoted $\sigma_1^2(t)$ and the covariance between variables 1 and 2 at time t is denoted $\sigma_{12}(t)$ or between the same variable at different points of time as $\sigma(t, s)$.

It is evident from considering Figures 3.1 and 3.2 that the realisations we see there do not support the idea that $\mu_X(t)$ is constant for $t = 1967q1$ to 1988q4. So what sort of process do we imagine is generating the observations, that are realisations of X_t, for each t in the sample? Is it plausible that they are generated by a process in which $\mu_X(t)$ is a constant for each t? The answer to this last question is that this seems most unlikely – a rationale for X_t increasing in a systematic way is that they are realisations from a process in which $\mu_X(t)$ is increasing.

By analogy with how an average is obtained it might be tempting to think we can obtain an estimator of $\mu_X(t)$ by averaging the values of X_t over the sample period; say

$$\bar{X} = \sum_{t=1}^{T} X_t/T \qquad (3.1)$$

where $\bar{X}$ is the estimator of $\mu_X(t)$. However, although such an estimator is commonly employed it rests upon the assumption that $\mu_X(t)$ is a constant for $t = 1, \ldots, T$. Where this assumption is not tenable $\bar{X}$ is *not* a sensible estimator of $\mu_X(t)$. It might still be a useful descriptive device to say that the average of the sample observations is $\bar{X}$. For example, the average of US imports of goods over the sample period is 239.5 (US$ billion, 1987 prices), but this figure is *not* an estimate of $\mu_X(t)$ for any particular period. $\bar{X}$ would only be an estimator of $\mu_X(t)$, and a particular value (such as 239.5) would only be an estimate, if $\mu_X(t)$ was constant for $t = 1, \ldots, T$.

A better indicator, although still not formally a good estimator, of $\mu_X(t)$ would be to take a moving average of the realisations of X_t. For example, we define the centred moving average, CMA, as:

$$\bar{X}_J(t) = \sum_{i=-J}^{+J} X_{t-i}(J)/(2J + 1) \qquad (3.2)$$

for $t = J + 1, \ldots, T - (J + 1)$. What this formula does is to take the value of X_t at time t and add to it the J observations either side, so in all there are $2J + 1$ observations. Then dividing by $2J + 1$ gives an average which is centred about t, but changes as t increments by 1 and one new realisation is added and one old one removed. Instead of calculating the mean for the whole sample size we initially calculate the average for a window of $2J + 1$ observations, we then drop the first observation and add the $(2J + 2)$th, we then drop the second observation and add the $(2J + 3)$rd and so on. Each time we keep our selected sample size constant but calculate the average by moving the sub-sample through the complete sample. If the series displays an upward or downward tendency this should be revealed in differences between the sub-sample average and the overall average. At an informal level we could regard these means as providing a rough and ready estimate of the central tendency – or trend – of the series. Referring again to Figures 3.1 and 3.2 we also graph the centred moving average, with $J = 8$, for each series. In both cases the centred moving average confirms the tendency for each series to increase over time.

A series X_t which shows a regular increase over time may follow the pattern which we stylise as

$$X_t = \kappa + X_{t-1} + \varepsilon_t \qquad (3.3)$$

that is X_t increments each period by a constant, κ, sometimes called the *drift* in the series, although clear recognition of this process is obscured by a random disturbance term ε_t with a zero mean. (A convention in the literature on random walks, of which (3.3) is an example, is to denote the drift as μ; however, in this chapter this notation risks a confusion with the mean of a series, hence here we denote the drift κ, reverting to the more common notation in later chapters.)

It turns out that these processes are of particular interest to economists. Subtracting X_{t-1} from both sides we have

$$\Delta X_t = \kappa + \varepsilon_t \qquad (3.4)$$

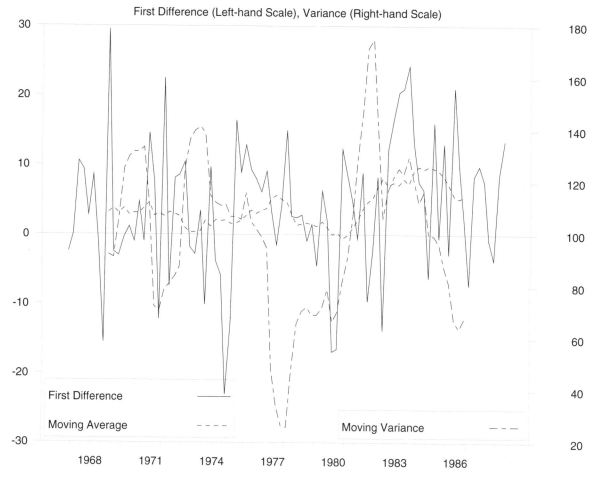

Figure 3.3   *US imports of goods: first difference, CMA and CMV*

So that apart from ε_t the first difference of X_t is a constant. Thus, although X_t does not have a constant mean ($\mu_X(t) \neq \mu_X(t-s)$ for $s \neq 0$), the first difference of X_t does have a constant mean $= \kappa$.

Figures 3.3 and 3.4 show the first difference of the US imports of food and price index of food, respectively, and the centred moving average (with $J = 8$). Considering Figure 3.3, first we see that there is not now a tendency for the series to increase over time. The CMA confirms this; although we note that in the latter part of the sample (post 1983) there is an increase in the CMA. Turning to Figure 3.4 for the price of food,

the CMA suggests a pattern of increase peaking in the early 1980s.

This is enough by way of motivation for the theme of this chapter. Economic time series often share the characteristic that they could not be viewed as being generated by a process with a constant mean. In particular, expenditure, income and price series typically display a tendency to increase over time. In an intuitive sense, with a more formal definition offered below, we say that such a series is not stationary. To study this concept further we need some basic building blocks.

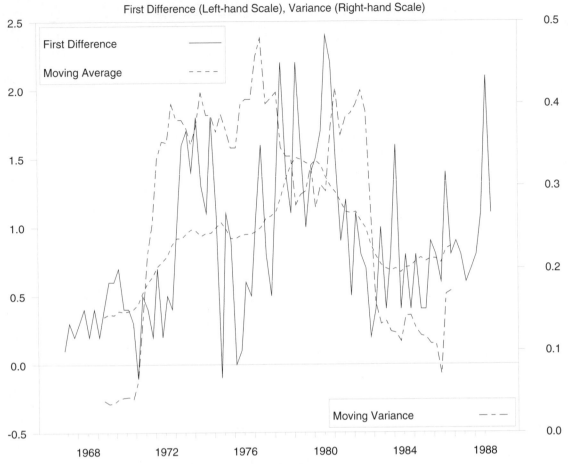

First Difference (Left-hand Scale), Variance (Right-hand Scale)

Figure 3.4   *US price of food: first difference, CMA and CMV*

3.3   Random variables

This section formalises the concept of a random variable. As a motivational device it primarily deals with discrete random variables. Examples of these are readily to hand and the ones used, at least in their simplest form, are likely to be familiar. However, the idea of continuous random variables is needed for Chapter 4 and a brief outline of the key concepts is also included here.

3.3.1   The expected value of a random variable

Let X_t denote a random variable that can take a range of N possible values at each time t. This

variable may either be a stock variable, for which t is then interpreted as a point in time, or a flow variable, in which case t is a period of time. Whichever is the case the N outcomes for X_t are viewed as being generated from a probability distribution. For simplicity we will assume in this section that the possible values, known as the *sample space*, of X_t are discrete; continuous random variables are introduced in section **3.3.3**. A notation for the probability of each of the discrete outcomes is $P_t(X_t = x_{ti})$, which is read as the probability at time t of the random variable X_t having the ith outcome. There is an important distinction captured here in this notational convention; while X_t is a random variable x_{ti} is not, it is a particular realisation from the $i = 1, \ldots, N$

distinct possible outcomes. It does not mean that $X_t = i$ although there will be some examples where the two concepts coincide. A simple example where the two are the same is if each day ($=t$) a dice was rolled and the outcome, X_t, was recorded. In this case the probability distribution for each day is that a probability of $\frac{1}{6}$ is assigned to each of the 6 possible outcomes $x_{t1} = 1, x_{t2} = 2, \ldots, x_{t6} = 6$.

Sometimes it is necessary to transform the original sample space so that the new sample space is a region on the real line, referred to as R^1, that is the sample space consists of all or part of the set $[-\infty, +\infty]$. For example, if the random variable is the result of a football match for a particular team, the original sample space is [lose, draw, win]; this could be transformed into [0, 1, 2]; however, such a mapping may not be unique as when the scoring system for football was changed into the set [0, 1, 3]. Another example, and one used extensively in this chapter, is tossing a coin and noting whether it lands heads or tails, which is the original sample space; a possible mapping into the real line is to assign 0 if the coin lands tails and 1 if the coin lands heads.

The notation $P_t(X_t = x_{ti})$ is sometimes cumbersome, and where no confusion can be caused this is simplified to P_{ti}. If the probability distribution remains the same for all t, this can be simplified further to P_i. Also as a shorthand, we will on occasion use $(X_t = x_{ti})$ to indicate that X_t takes the ith outcome.

Let us proceed further by considering a simple coin-tossing experiment. Suppose on the day that you are reading this chapter you toss a coin and note whether it lands heads or tails. If it lands tails you set the realisation of the variable $X_t = 0$, this is outcome 1 (that is $x_{t1} = 0$), and if it lands heads you set $X_t = 1$ (that is $x_{t2} = 1$); t is the index which indicates which day you are tossing the coin. X_t is a random variable, we cannot say in advance of the coin being tossed whether X_t will certainly equal 1 – it *might* equal 1 but it also *might* equal zero; the outcome is not certain. The probability that the coin lands

Table 3.1 *Tossing a fair coin*

Sample space		Probability, $P_t(X_t = i)$
outcome 1: $x_{t1} = 0$	the coin lands on tails	0.5
outcome 2: $x_{t2} = 1$	the coin lands on heads	0.5
	$\sum_{i=1}^{2} P_{ti} = 1.0$	

on heads is a parameter of the experiment; we will assume that the coin is fair so that a probability of 0.5 is assigned to each outcome. The range of values X_t can take is the sample space, in this case it is summarised in Table 3.1.

Multiplying each element in the sample space by its corresponding probability and summing these elements together gives the expected value, or mean, of X_t and is written $E\{X_t\}$.

That is, in general,

$$E\{X_t\} = \sum_{i}^{N} (X_{ti} = x_{ti})P_t(X_{ti} = x_{ti}) \qquad (3.5)$$

or, more simply,

$$\mu_X(t) \equiv E\{X_t\} = \sum_{i}^{N} X_t P_{ti} \qquad (3.6)$$

The summation ranges over the discrete outcomes $i = 1, \ldots, N$. $E\{X_t\}$ is also sometimes referred to as the mean or average value of X_t. In the coin-tossing experiment $E\{X_t\}$ is:

$$E\{X_t\} = 0 * 0.5 + 1 * 0.5 = 0.5 \qquad (3.7)$$

The expected, or average, value of x on day t is 0.5. The index t may or may not be important; if, for example, the conditions of the coin-tossing experiment are replicated exactly on days $t + 1$, $t + 2, \ldots$, and so on then we can dispense with the t subscript on the probability, and the expected value is:

$$E\{X_t\} = \sum_{i=1}^{N} (X_t = x_{ti})P(X_t = i)$$

$$= \sum_{i=1}^{N} (X_s = x_{si})P(X_s = i) \quad \text{for } s \neq t$$

$$= \sum_{i=1}^{N} (X_t = x_{ti})P_i \tag{3.8}$$

In an intuitive way we can see that, in this case, an important characteristic of the probability distribution is constant, with the result that the mean of X_t does not change as the index t changes. Otherwise if $P(X_t = x_{ti})$ does vary with the index t we must be sure to refer to the expected value of x on day t.

Suppose, to continue the coin-tossing example, we toss a fair coin twice each day, and again let X_t be the variable that 'counts' the number of heads. We need to adjust the sample space and probabilities to reflect the change in the experiment. The three outcomes for X_t are shown in Table 3.2.

The probabilities are obtained as follows. Outcome 1 is no heads on either toss of the coin. The probability of no heads on the first toss is 0.5, as is the probability of no heads on the second toss. What happens on the first toss does not affect the outcome on the second toss, the events are independent and to obtain the probability of this joint event we simply multiply the two probabilities together to get $0.5^2 = 0.25$. If the probability of heads on the second toss was affected by what happened on the first toss the events would not be independent, and we could not just multiply the individual probabilities together to get the probability of the joint event.

Outcome 2 is the combination of two events. The first event is heads on the first toss, with probability equal to 0.5, and tails on the second toss, also with probability of 0.5. Multiplying these probabilities together we get the probability of this event equal to $0.5^2 = 0.25$. The second event is when we obtain tails on the first toss and heads on the second toss. By the same argument we obtain a probability of $0.5^2 = 0.25$. Since outcome 2 does not distinguish between whether the head was on the first toss or the second toss, to obtain its probability we add together the probabilities of the two mutually exclusive events which make up the outcome, that is $0.25 + 0.25 = 0.5$.

Finally, outcome 3, that is heads on the first toss and tails on the second toss, has, by an argument which should now be straightforward to follow, a probability of 0.25. To make sure that we have done our probability arithmetic correctly we should undertake two checks. First, is the sample space comprised of events that are mutually exclusive and together exhaust all the possibilities; and second, do the probabilities of the outcomes sum to unity? In this case both checks are satisfied so we have defined the sample space (of outcomes) and probabilities correctly.

Table 3.2 Tossing 2 fair coins

Sample space		Probability $P_t(X_t = x_{ti})$
outcome 1: $x_{t1} = 0$	no heads on either toss	0.25
outcome 2: $x_{t2} = 1$	either heads on the first toss and tails on the second toss; or tails on the first toss and heads on the second toss	0.5
outcome 3: $x_{t3} = 2$	heads on the first toss *and* heads on the second toss	0.25
		$\sum_{i=1}^{3} P_{ti} = 1.0$

The expected value of X_t is:

$$E\{X_t\} = 0*0.25 + 1*0.5 + 2*0.25$$
$$= 1 \tag{3.9}$$

On average, if the circumstances of this experiment are unchanged, X_t on day 1 (that is $t = 1$) will take the value 1. Suppose that the experiment is also carried out on days 2, 3, 4 and so on until T, so that we obtain a sequence of random variables $[X_t] = [X_1, X_2, X_3, \ldots, X_T]$. Each random variable is indexed by the appropriate value of $t = 1, \ldots, T$, that is $X_1, X_2, X_3, \ldots, X_T$. Note that in each case the expected value of X_t is the same. In such a case we say that X_t is stationary in the mean; in a sense the series X_t is static as far as its mean is concerned. This is an important property of a time series as we shall show below. We highlight the importance of this property by the following definition:

A random variable X_t that has a constant mean is said to be stationary to the first order.

Now suppose that the conditions of the experiment are changed for $t + 1$, $t + 2, \ldots, T$. For illustrative purposes imagine that the coin becomes biased at $t + 1$ with a probability of 0.4 for a head; then while the sample space is unchanged, the probabilities are changed as shown in Table 3.3. To ease the notation we let $s = t + 1$.

The probability of 0 in the sample space is now $0.6 * 0.6 = 0.36$; the probability of 1 in the sample space corresponds to either a head on the first toss and a tail on the second toss with a probability of $0.6 * 0.4 = 0.24$, or a tail on the first toss and a head on the second toss with probability of $0.4 * 0.6 = 0.24$; adding these probabilities together we get $0.24 + 0.24 = 0.48$; finally we could get a head on the first toss and a head on the second toss with probability $0.4 * 0.4 = 0.16$. The expected, or mean, value of X_s is:

$$E\{X_s\} = 0 * 0.36 + 1 * 0.48 + 2 * 0.16$$
$$= 0.80 \tag{3.10}$$

Notice that the expected value of X_s is $0.8 < 1.0$, and the sequence $[X_t, X_s]$ is not now a series which is stationary to the first order as $\mu_X(t) \neq \mu_X(s)$.

Before moving on there is an important point to note about how we obtained the expected value of X_t. At each point t, X_t can conceptually take a range of values each with an associated probability and, in order to calculate the expected value of X_t, we multiply each possible value of X_t by its probability and then sum them; that is the meaning of $E\{X_t\}$. When we are recording a particular set of realisations of X_t, $t = 1, \ldots, T$, that will give rise to a set of numbers; for example, for $t = 1, \ldots, 5$. Sample realisations are put in lower case, thus x_t is the sample realisation of the random variable X_t. Thus, we might observe the set $[x_t] = [0, 0, 1, 2, 0]$; we do not calculate the expected value of X_t by multiplying these realised values of X_t by their probabilities and summing them because this mixes values of X_t for different values of t.

Table 3.3   *Tossing a biased coin*

Sample space	Probability, $P_s(X_s = x_{si})$
outcome 1: $x_{s1} = 0$	0.36
outcome 2: $x_{s2} = 1$	0.48
outcome 3: $x_{s3} = 2$	0.16
	$\sum_{i=1}^{3} P_{ti} = 1.0$

3.3.2   The variance of a random variable

Another characteristic of X_t, which will interest us, is the variability of the realisations. There are several possible measures of variability and we will concentrate here on the variance, which is defined as follows

$$\sigma^2(t) \equiv E\{X_t - \mu_X(t)\}^2$$

$$\equiv \sum_{i=1}^{N} ((X_t = x_{ti}) - \mu_X(t))^2$$

$$\times P_t(X_t = x_{ti}) \qquad (3.11)$$

For a variable stationary to the first order $\mu_X(t) = \mu_X$, and simplifying the notation, this reduces to

$$\sigma^2(t) = \sum_{i=1}^{N} ((X_t = x_{ti}) - \mu_X)^2 P_{ti} \qquad (3.12)$$

The rationale of $\sigma^2(t)$ as a measure of variability is as follows. First, imagine a random variable X_t which can only take one value, say $X_t = c$, then this variable shows no variability and any measure thereof should be zero. Trivially $\mu_X(t) = c * 1 = c$, the mean of the series is equal to the constant c. Now suppose X_t can take the values 0 and 1 with equal probability, then a measure of variability for this case should be positive to reflect some (if not much) variation. We could try measuring variability by adding together the differences from the mean and weighting them by their respective probabilities, but, as this example shows, these deviations always sum to zero. In the example we get $(0 - 0.5) * 0.5 + (1 - 0.5) * 0.5 = 0$. If, however, we square the differences from the mean, these must be nonzero, and then weight these by the probability of that outcome we obtain a nonnegative measure; continuing the example we obtain $(-0.5)^2 * 0.5 +$ $(0.5)^2 * 0.5 = 0.25$ which is a positive number and reflects some variability in the series. Suppose we change the outcomes slightly so that X_t is more variable and takes the values 0 and 2 with equal probability, then squaring the deviations from the mean and weighting by the respective probabilities we obtain $(-1)^2 * 0.5 + (1)^2 * 0.5 = 1.0$. Our measure records this increase in variability. Other measures would be possible, for example ignoring the sign of the deviation from the mean, but $\sigma^2(t)$ is the most widely used measure of variability. Where it is necessary to distinguish the variances of different variables we will introduce a subscript, for example $\sigma_X^2(t)$; if there is no risk of confusion this subscript is omitted.

These examples show that the rationale of $\sigma^2(t)$ is that a variable, which has large deviations about its mean, will have a large variance measure: each deviation is squared and weighted by the probability that that particular value of X_t will occur. Let us see how this works by revisiting the example in Table 3.2 with the calculations necessary to obtain the variance shown in Table 3.4.

The variance for the coin-tossing example of Table 3.3, in which there was a probability of 0.4 for a head, is calculated in Table 3.5.

The variance is 0.48 which has decreased compared to the original case where $\sigma^2(t) = 0.5$. Thus, if the coin became biased at $t + 1 = s$, the series $X_1, \ldots, X_t, X_s, \ldots, X_T$, would not be stationary, although in a particular sample of observations from such a coin-tossing experiment the change in the mean and variance, which are here quite small, might be quite difficult to detect.

Table 3.4   Calculating the variance for a fair coin

	Sample space	μ_X	$X_t - \mu_X$	$(X_t - \mu_X)^2$	$(X_t - \mu_X)^2 P_t$
outcome 1	$x_{t1} = 0$	1	-1	1	0.25
outcome 2	$x_{t2} = 1$	1	0	0	0
outcome 3	$x_{t3} = 2$	1	1	1	0.25
					$\sigma^2(t) = 0.5$

Table 3.5 *Calculating the variance for a biased coin*

	Sample space	μ_X	$X_t - \mu_X$	$(X_t - \mu_X)^2$	$(X_t - \mu_X)^2 P_t$
outcome 1	$x_{t1} = 0$	0.8	−0.8	0.64	0.2304
outcome 2	$x_{t2} = 1$	0.8	0.2	0.04	0.0192
outcome 3	$x_{t3} = 2$	0.8	1.2	1.44	0.2304
					$\sigma^2(t) = 0.48$

Table 3.6 *Calculating the variance for a biased coin*

	Sample space	μ_X	$X_t - \mu_X$	$(X_t - \mu_X)^2$	$(X_t - \mu_X)^2 P_t$
outcome 1	$x_{t1} = 0$	0.4	−0.4	0.16	0.1024
outcome 2	$x_{t2} = 1$	0.4	0.6	0.36	0.1152
outcome 3	$x_{t3} = 2$	0.4	1.6	2.56	0.1024
					$\sigma^2(t) = 0.32$

Table 3.7 *Summary table*

	Probability		$\mu_X(t)$	$\sigma^2(t)$
	Heads	Tails		
Experiment 1	0.5	0.5	1.0	0.50
Experiment 2	0.4	0.6	0.8	0.48
Experiment 3	0.2	0.8	0.4	0.32

We will now consider one final variation in the coin-tossing example. Suppose at $t + 1 = s$ the biased coin has a probability of 0.2 for heads and, hence, 0.8 for tails. You should confirm the following calculations in Table 3.6 for $\mu_X(s)$ and $\sigma^2(s)$.

In this case the difference in variance between the unbiased coin and the biased coin is quite noticeable. The variance of the former is 0.5 whereas the variance of the latter is 0.32, which is, perhaps, the kind of difference we should be able to detect quite quickly if faced with several replications tossing the biased coin.

The results of the experiments with different values of obtaining a head on the coin are summarised in Table 3.7.

3.3.3 Continuous random variables

So far we have considered a particular kind of random variable. Specifically, we have assumed that the sample space for X_t contains a finite number of possible outcomes, as in the dice-rolling or coin-tossing examples. The sample space for throwing a six-sided dice is [1, 2, 3, 4, 5, 6]; for the coin-tossing experiment we mapped the original sample space $[T, H]$ into the sample space [0, 1]. In general we assume that if necessary a mapping has been made from the original sample space to points on the real line $[-\infty$ to $+\infty]$. Associated with each sample space was a probability distribution which defined $P(X_t = x_{ti})$ for each of the $i = 1, \ldots, N$ possible outcomes. The probabilities in this distribution sum to 1, that is $\Sigma P(X_t = x_{ti}) = 1$, where the summation is over the range of all possible outcomes. We can also define the cumulative distribution function for this random variable as $F(X_t \leq x_{tj}) \equiv \Sigma P(X_t = x_{ti})$ where the summation is for all $i \leq j$; this is the probability that X_t takes any of the outcomes i, for $i = 1, \ldots, j$. Sometimes $F(.)$ is just referred to as the distribution function, with no reference to cumulative. Note that $P(X_t = x_{tj}) = F(X_t \leq x_{tj}) - F(X_t \leq x_{tj-1})$, so that we can alternatively work with the probabilities or the distribution function.

Some processes can generate a sample space that is a continuum on the real line, and may in some cases be the real line. We typically think of economic variables, particularly macroeconomic aggregates, as falling into this category –

for example, in principle, GDP could take any value on the positive side of the real line. Although in practice the lowest unit of measurement will limit the continuum, it is likely to be a more useful paradigm to think of the range of possible outcomes as infinite rather than finite. Consider the random walk model given by $X_t = \kappa + X_{t-1} + \varepsilon_t$, where ε_t is a random variable, sometimes referred to as the innovation or disturbance to the X_t process. A usual specification of ε_t is that its range of possible outcomes is any number in the (infinite) interval $-\infty$ to $+\infty$, although some range of outcomes may be more likely than others and the mass of observations is in a fairly narrow range.

Probability in a continuum involves a slightly different notation and concepts compared to finite probability distributions. The first difficulty arises because the probability of a particular number in the continuum is zero. What is defined is the probability that the outcome lies between two values in the sample space. To simplify the notation denote the random variable as X with realisation x; more precisely the realisations are elements from a set $[x] \in R^1$. Then the probability density function, or pdf, is usually written $f(x)$ and regarded as a function of x as x varies across the continuum of outcomes in R^1. By analogy with the probabilities in a finite probability distribution summing to 1, integrating $f(x)$ across its range will give the value 1. In practical examples the pdf will be given a parametric form. Also, as in the discrete case, we can define the distribution function $F(x)$, which is the partial integral (partial sum in the finite case) from the lowest part of the range, for convenience assumed to be $-\infty$, to the point x. The relation between the pdf and the distribution function is $F(x) = \int_{-\infty}^{x} f(x)\,dx$. Perhaps the best known of the probability density functions is that for the normal distribution; the range is $-\infty$ to $+\infty$ and $f(x)$ is symmetric and bell shaped. Specifically:

pdf for the normal distribution:
$$f(x) = (2\pi\sigma^2)^{-\frac{1}{2}}\exp\{-(x - \mu_X)/2\sigma^2\}$$

Continuous distributions can also be defined across some part of the real line. For example, the exponential distribution with parameter $\lambda > 0$ has the pdf: $f(x) = \lambda \exp(-\lambda x)$ for $x \geq 0$ and $f(x) = 0$ for $x < 0$, so only nonnegative values of x are defined in this process.

The concepts associated with finite probability distributions are easily extended to the continuous case. For example, the expectation of X_t is $E\{X_t\} \equiv \int_{-\infty}^{+\infty} f(x_t)\,dx_t$ and the variance is $\sigma^2 \equiv \int_{-\infty}^{+\infty} (x_t - \mu_X)^2 f(x_t)\,dx_t$ where $E\{X_t\} = \mu_X$. Other extensions of these concepts are considered in Chapter 4.

3.4 Joint events, covariance, autocovariance and autocorrelation

In addition to measuring the variability of a single random variable, X_t, economists are interested in measuring the degree of association between different variables, for example X_t and Y_t. They are also interested in the degree of association between the same variable but at different points of time, for example X_t and X_s for $t \neq s$; and different variables at different points of time, for example X_s and Y_s for $t \neq s$. This section starts by considering the concept of joint events, which is the basic building block of these measures of association. This concept is then developed in order to define covariance, autocovariance, correlation and autocorrelation and their associated functions.

3.4.1 Joint events

The covariance is a measure that captures the idea that there may be dependence between random variables, although the two concepts (covariance and dependence) are not quite the same. Consider X_t and X_s where $t \neq s$, then we have two random variables separated by the difference in the index, $k = t - s$; if, for example, $s = t - 1$ then we are considering random variables at adjacent points in time. We are now going to consider these random variables together in which case we are interested not just in the individual probabilities for the realisations in X_t and X_s separately, but also in the probability of joint events which involve an outcome in X_t and an outcome in X_s.

For example, let us return to the coin-tossing experiment with one toss of the same unbiased coin on days t and s. Now there are four possible outcomes, called joint events, and we associate with each of these a probability, which we summarise in Table 3.8.

For example, the outcome $x_{t1} = 0$ and $x_{s1} = 0$ is tails on the first day ($=t$) and tails on the second day ($=s$). We assume that the outcome on day s is unaffected by the outcome on day t, that is X_t and X_s are (stochastically) independent. In this case the probability of the joint events in the table is the product of the probabilities of the individual events which comprise the joint event. For example, the probability of the outcomes $x_{t1} = 0$ and $x_{s1} = 0$ is 0.5 times $0.5 = 0.25$, and the other probabilities are obtained in the same way.

Independence of stochastic events is a useful starting point for constructing probability tables for joint events. Each entry is the product of the corresponding entries for the (marginal) probability distributions. The marginal distribution is what we referred to earlier in the chapter simply as the distribution, for example the probability distribution of X_t. The adjective marginal is now useful because it refers us to the margin of the joint event table. If the probabilities in the joint

event table are not the product of the probabilities from the marginal distributions then the events are dependent.

We need to establish a notation for joint events and their probabilities. Our notation here will be a little more complex than that in introductory texts as we will, in due course, need to emphasise the possibility of nonstationary series. As joint events are the intersection of two (or more) separate events the intersection symbol ∩ is often used instead of 'and'. The probability of the joint event X_t takes the ith outcome and X_s takes the jth outcome is written as

$$P_{ts}(X_t = x_{ti} \cap X_s = x_{sj}) \quad \text{for } i, j = 0, 1 \quad (3.13)$$

A shorthand for this is $P_{ti,sj}$; the subscripts indicate that the probability is specific to the time indices t and s. In the coin-tossing example the probabilities are unchanged whichever time indices we consider; however, in some cases these probabilities may depend on the values taken by the indices t and s. In the special case of independence of events, the probability of the joint event is the product of the probabilities of the separate events, indeed this is a definition of stochastic independence:

$$P_{ti,sj} = P_{ti}P_{sj} \quad (3.14)$$

For (stochastic) independence (3.14) must hold for *all* events in the joint sample space. P_{ti} and P_{sj} are sometimes referred to as the marginal probabilities, since in a joint event table they are the (unconditional) probabilities shown in the

Table 3.8 *Joint events and their probabilities, first example*

	tails on day s $x_{s1} = 0$	heads on day s $x_{s2} = 1$	$P(X_t)$
tails on day t $x_{t1} = 0$	$x_{t1} = 0$ and $x_{s1} = 0$ 0.5 times $0.5 = 0.25$	$x_{t1} = 0$ and $x_{s1} = 1$ 0.5 times $0.5 = 0.25$	0.5
heads on day t $x_{t2} = 1$	$x_{t2} = 1$ and $x_{s1} = 0$ 0.5 times $0.5 = 0.25$	$x_{t2} = 1$ and $x_{s2} = 1$ 0.5 times $0.5 = 0.25$	0.5
$P(X_s)$	0.5	0.5	1.0

margins (the last column and the last row) of the table. Similarly the last column and the last row of the joint event table give the marginal probability distributions for each of the two random variables. A joint event table with independent random variables has cell entries that are just the product of the corresponding (marginal) probabilities.

3.4.2 Covariance and autocovariance

Covariance is a measure of the association between two variables. These variables can either be the same variable but at different points in time, for example consumption at times t and $t - k$, or distinct variables, for example consumption and income. In the former case the covariance is referred to as the kth order autocovariance, where k is the lag or lead between the variables.

The covariance between the random variables X_t and Y_t is given by:

$$\sigma(X_t, Y_t)$$
$$\equiv E\{(X_t - \mu_X(t))(Y_t - \mu_Y(t))\} \quad (3.15)$$
$$= \sum_i^{N_I} \sum_j^{N_J} [(X_t = x_{ti}) - \mu_X(t)]$$
$$\times [(Y_t = y_{tj}) - \mu_Y(t)]$$
$$\times P(X_t = x_{ti} \cap Y_t = y_{tj}) \quad (3.16)$$

where $P(X_t = x_{ti} \cap Y_t = y_{tj})$ is the probability of the joint event comprising the ith outcome for X_t and the jth outcome for Y_t. The notation assumes that there are N_I distinct outcomes in the sample space for X_t and N_J distinct outcomes in the sample space for Y_t. In all there are, therefore, N_I times N_J joint outcomes (or events), with associated probabilities. For example, if X_t is the random variable corresponding to tossing a coin on day t, and Y_t is the random variable corresponding to rolling a six-sided dice, also on day t, then a joint events table of dimensions 2 by 6 could be drawn up with 12 entries. These correspond to all possible joint outcomes, here tails on the coin toss and one from 1 to 6 on the roll of the dice, and heads on the coin throw

and one from 1 to 6 on the roll of the dice. If the coin and dice are fair the joint probabilities are the same in each cell of the table, and the covariance will be zero. A simple extension of the basic definition would consider the covariance between the two variables at different times, say X_t and Y_s where $t \neq s$.

The autocovariance is a special case of the covariance. For convenience define $s = t - k$ then the kth order autocovariance is $\text{Cov}(X_t, X_s)$

$$\text{Cov}(X_t, X_s)$$
$$= E\{(X_t - \mu_X(t))(X_s - \mu_X(s))\} \quad (3.17a)$$
$$= \sum_i^{N_I} \sum_j^{N_J} [(X_t = x_{ti}) - \mu_X(t)]$$
$$\times [(X_s = x_{si}) - \mu_X(t)]P_{ti,sj} \quad (3.18a)$$

If $\mu_X(t) = \mu_X(s) = \mu_x$ then (3.17a) simplifies to

$$\text{Cov}(X_t, X_s)$$
$$= E\{(X_t - \mu_X)(X_s - \mu_X)\} \quad (3.17b)$$

and (3.18a) simplifies to

$$= \sum_i^{N} \sum_j^{N} [(X_t = x_{ti}) - \mu_X]$$
$$\times [(X_s = x_{si}) - \mu_X]P_{ti,sj} \quad (3.18b)$$

Note that as the sample space is the same for X_t and X_s the upper limit on the double summations is also the same. For example, in the simple coin-tossing game on days t and s, the summations are just over the two outcomes corresponding to tails (outcome 1) or heads (outcome 2).

A commonly used and convenient notation for the autocovariance of order k for a (stationary) series is $\gamma(k)$. A special case of the autocovariance is the variance since this corresponds to a zero lag; hence $\gamma(0)$ is the variance of X_t. One drawback with this notation is that it only indicates the difference between the time subscripts and not the original points in time. For example, $\gamma(k)$ could be the covariance between X_t and X_{t-k} or X_{t+j} and X_{t-k+j} for any choice of $j \neq 0$; hence only if these are the same is the $\gamma(k)$

shorthand useful. Alternatively, if we want to emphasise the possibility that autocovariance may depend upon the points in time t and s, then the full notation can be shortened to $\sigma(t, s)$.

Although the covariance is a measure of association between two variables we cannot, in general, infer the strength of the relationship from a particular numerical value. This difficulty arises for two possible reasons. First, because there is an element of arbitrariness if the mapping from the original sample is not the identity mapping; for example, the original sample space for the coin-tossing game is $[T, H]$ which is usually mapped into $[0, 1]$ but could equally be mapped into $[1,000, 2,000]$, and the latter would not, in general, lead to the same measure of covariance with other random variables. The exception is where there is no (linear) association between random variables which always results in a zero covariance. The second problem arises because even if there is no ambiguity over the mapping into the R^1 sample space, each random variable will usually have units of measurement, and the covariance will have units of measurement equal to the product of the units of measurement of the component random variables. For example, suppose two random variables of interest are turnover in $\$1,000 = X_t$ and distance from the city centre for retail outlets in miles (kilometres) $= Y_s$, then the covariance between X_t and Y_s has units of measurement of $\$1,000$ times miles (kilometres). For these reasons the covariance, or autocovariance, is not generally taken to indicate the strength of

the association between two random variables, although a nonzero value indicates that such a relationship exists and the sign indicates the direction of the relationship. The correlation – or autocorrelation – coefficient, which is a unit-free measure achieved by dividing the covariance by the product of the standard deviations of the component random variables, is usually used as a measure of the strength of a bivariate relationship; this concept is considered in detail in section **3.4.7**.

From the definition note that to obtain the covariance directly:

(i) subtract the mean from each possible event for X_t and X_s;

(ii) multiply these deviations from means together;

(iii) weight each by the probability of the joint event; and

(iv) finally sum all these components.

(A practical alternative to the direct calculation is to multiply out the various components in the definition of the covariance, but that would not aid the interpretation here.)

To see how this works consider the covariance for the 4 joint events of the previous example in Table 3.8. The calculations are organised in Table 3.9. The 4 joint events are the combinations resulting from columns (1) and (3), for example $X_t = 0$ and $X_s = 0$ is the first joint event. Columns (2) and (4) then subtract the expected values of X_t and X_s, respectively, which are in this case both equal to 0.5. Finally, these

Table 3.9 *Calculation of the covariance for the first example*

(1)	(2)	(3)	(4)	(5)
$X_t = x_{ti}$	$x_{ti} - \mu_X(t)$	$X_s = x_{sj}$	$x_{sj} - \mu_X(s)$	$[(X_t = x_{ti}) - \mu_X(t)][(X_s = x_{sj}) - \mu_X(s)]P_{ti,sj}$
0	-0.5	0	-0.5	$(-0.5)(-0.5)(0.25) = \frac{1}{16}$
1	$+0.5$	0	-0.5	$(+0.5)(-0.5)(0.25) = -\frac{1}{16}$
0	-0.5	1	$+0.5$	$(-0.5)(+0.5)(0.25) = -\frac{1}{16}$
1	$+0.5$	1	$+0.5$	$(+0.5)(+0.5)(0.25) = \frac{1}{16}$
				$\sigma(t, s) = 0$

Table 3.10 Joint events and their probabilities, second example

	tails on day s $x_{s1} = 0$	heads on day s $x_{s2} = 1$	$P(X_t)$
tails on day t $x_{t1} = 0$	$x_{t1} = 0$ and $x_{s1} = 0$ 0.2	$x_{t1} = 0$ and $x_{s1} = 1$ 0.3	0.5
heads on day t $x_{t2} = 1$	$x_{t2} = 1$ and $x_{s1} = 0$ 0.3	$x_{t2} = 1$ and $x_{s2} = 1$ 0.2	0.5
$P(X_s)$	0.5	0.5	1.0

deviations from the means are multiplied by the respective probabilities of the joint events to obtain column (5). The sum of the entries in this last column is the covariance of X_t and X_s. In this case $\sigma(t, s)$ is zero which follows from the independence of X_t and X_s. (Independence implies a zero covariance but a zero covariance does not imply independence.)

For a further illustration of the calculation of the covariance consider the joint probabilities in Table 3.10.

Your calculations should confirm that $\mu_X(t) = \mu_X(s) = 0.5$, and the covariance is

$$\sigma(t, s) = (-0.5)(-0.5)(0.2)$$
$$+ (0.5)(-0.5)(0.3)$$
$$+ (-0.5)(0.5)(0.3)$$
$$+ (+0.5)(+0.5)(0.2)$$
$$= 0.05 - 0.075 - 0.075 + 0.05$$
$$= -0.05$$

Another nonzero covariance is obtained from the joint probabilities in Table 3.11.

With further calculations as follows:

$$\mu_X(t) = 0 * 0.3 + 1 * 0.7 = 0.7$$
$$\mu_X(s) = 0 * 0.6 + 1 * 0.4 = 0.4$$

$$\sigma(t, s) = (-0.7)(-0.4)(0.2)$$
$$+ (0.3)(-0.4)(0.4)$$
$$+ (-0.7)(0.6)(0.1) + (0.3)(0.6)(0.3)$$
$$= 0.02$$

3.4.3 Conditional expectation

The joint event and probabilities table, as in Tables 3.9 to 3.11, also serve to define what are known as the conditional expectations as well as the familiar (marginal) expectations. For example, consider Table 3.11 where we have seen that $E\{X_t\} = 0.7$ and $E\{X_s\} = 0.4$, these are the unconditional or marginal expectations of X_t and X_s, respectively; now suppose we fix $X_s = 0$, what is the expectation of X_t conditional on this now-given value of X_s? In order to calculate

Table 3.11 Joint events and their probabilities, third example

	tails on day s $x_{s1} = 0$	heads on day s $x_{s2} = 1$	$P(X_t)$
tails on day t $x_{t1} = 0$	$x_{t1} = 0$ and $x_{s1} = 0$ 0.2	$x_{t1} = 0$ and $x_{s1} = 1$ 0.1	0.3
heads on day t $x_{t2} = 1$	$x_{t2} = 1$ and $x_{s1} = 0$ 0.4	$x_{t2} = 1$ and $x_{s2} = 1$ 0.3	0.7
$P(X_s)$	0.6	0.4	1.0

this expectation we need the appropriate probabilities, which are known as conditional probabilities. We need the following:

$$P(X_t = 0 \mid X_s = 0)$$

and

$$P(X_t = 1 \mid X_s = 0)$$

where the vertical line indicates that the probability of the event to the left of the line is conditional on the event to the right of the line. We cannot take the probabilities in the column headed $X_s = 0$ because while they cover the exhaustive events $X_t = 0$ and $X_t = 1$ they do not sum to unity and, hence, cannot be the appropriate probabilities. However, they are easily normalised to sum to unity by dividing by the column sum. That is

$$P(X_t = 0 \mid X_s = 0) = 0.2/0.6 = \tfrac{1}{3}$$
$$P(X_t = 1 \mid X_s = 0) = 0.4/0.6 = \tfrac{2}{3}$$

The conditional expectation $E\{X_t \mid X_s\}$ is now obtained in the usual way as

$$E\{X_t \mid X_s = 0\} = 0(\tfrac{1}{3}) + 1(\tfrac{2}{3}) = \tfrac{2}{3}$$

In words the expectation of X_t given $X_s = 0$ is equal to $\tfrac{2}{3}$; note that this is not equal to the unconditional expectation of 0.7.

In a similar way we can obtain

$$E\{X_t \mid X_s = 1\} = 0(0.1/0.4) + 1(0.3/0.4)$$
$$= 0.75$$

which is the expectation of X_t given $X_s = 1$. Again this differs from the unconditional expectation.

We can obtain the unconditional expectation from the conditional expectations if we sum the latter each weighted by the probability of the conditioning event. For example

$$E\{X_t\} = E\{X_t \mid X_s = 0\}P(X_s = 0)$$
$$\quad + E\{X_t \mid X_s = 1\}P(X_s = 1)$$
$$= \tfrac{2}{3}(0.6) + 0.75(0.4)$$
$$= 0.7$$

We can also condition the outcomes in X_s on a given outcome in X_t. As in the previous case there are two possibilities

$$P(X_s \mid X_t = 0) \quad \text{and} \quad P(X_s \mid X_t = 1)$$

with corresponding conditional expectations

$$E\{X_s \mid X_t = 0\} \quad \text{and} \quad E\{X_s \mid X_t = 1\}$$

Calculations analogous to the first case give

$$P(X_s = 0 \mid X_t = 0) = 0.2/0.3 = \tfrac{2}{3}$$
$$P(X_s = 0 \mid X_t = 1) = 0.4/0.7 = \tfrac{4}{7}$$
$$P(X_s = 1 \mid X_t = 0) = 0.1/0.3 = \tfrac{1}{3}$$
$$P(X_s = 1 \mid X_t = 1) = 0.3/0.7 = \tfrac{3}{7}$$
$$E\{X_s \mid X_t = 0\} = 0(\tfrac{2}{3}) + 1(\tfrac{1}{3}) = \tfrac{1}{3}$$
$$E\{X_s \mid X_t = 1\} = 0(\tfrac{4}{7}) + 1(\tfrac{3}{7}) = \tfrac{3}{7}$$

and

$$E\{X_s\} = \tfrac{1}{3}(0.3) + \tfrac{3}{7}(0.7) = 0.4$$

3.4.4 Autocovariances and second order stationarity

In these simple examples the explicit notation used in the definition of $\sigma(t,s)$ may seem superfluous; however, we now introduce a possibility which makes this notation worthwhile and develops the original definition of the autocovariance given in section **3.4.2**. It also leads on to the definition of a random variable that is second order stationary.

Suppose X_t is in essence a time series, that is the index t refers to time so X_t is a generic notation for a time series random variable. As noted, the covariance is then referred to as the autocovariance, that is the covariance between the random variable at time t and the random variable at time s, a time difference $k = t - s$ (when $t = s$ the covariance becomes the variance). If, for example, $s = t - 1$ then there is a one period difference in the time index. $\sigma(t, t - 1)$ is the first order autocovariance at time t; and similarly $\sigma(t - 1, t - 2)$ is the first order autocovariance at

$t - 1$. Higher order autocovariances are defined by analogy; for example, $\sigma(t, t - 2)$ is the second order autocovariance at t; $\sigma(t - 1, t - 3)$ is the second order autocovariance at $t - 1$. It may be the case that these autocovariances just depend on the difference in the time index. In the first order case, $\sigma(t, t - 1) = \sigma(t - 1, t - 2)$ and so on; in the second order case $\sigma(t, t - 2) = \sigma(t - 1, t - 3)$ and so on. In a sense these co-variances are stationary, depending not upon the point in time, t, but just on their order or difference in time index, k. There is then no ambiguity in the notation $\gamma(k)$, as the kth order autocovariance, which makes no reference to the particular location in time of the autocovariance.

If, in addition to the constancy of the auto-covariances for each $k \neq 0$, the expected value of X_t is constant, and the variance, $\sigma^2(t)$, is a constant independent of t, then the time series X_t is said to be stationary to the second order (also known as weak stationarity or covariance stationarity). Sometimes the qualification is omitted and the series is just said to be stationary. In summary the conditions are:

1. $\mu_X(t) = \mu_X$, a constant independent of t.
2. $\sigma^2(t) = \sigma^2$, a constant independent of t.
3. $\sigma(t, s) = \sigma(t + j, t + j - s)$.

The last condition states that shifting the time index by j periods leaves the kth order auto-correlations unchanged (recall that $k = t - s$ is the time difference). Then $\gamma(k)$ unambiguously indicates the kth order autocorrelation.

Second order stationarity is not the only concept of stationarity used in econometric analysis, although it is the most widely used and the 'default' usage of the term. While it may seem obscure now it is important for Chapter 16 to distinguish between second order stationarity and 'strict' stationarity. To see that an alternative definition is possible note that second order stationarity refers to the constancy of the first and second moments, that is the mean (first moment) and variance and covariance (second

moments), of the process generating X_t. Now, for some distributions some or all the moments do not exist, does that mean that such a distribution could not be stationary? The answer to this question is no, provided the definition of stationarity is clear. An appropriate starting point is what is known as complete or strict stationarity. That is, a process $[X_t] = [X_1, X_2, \ldots, X_T]$ is said to be completely stationary if the joint probability distribution of $[X_t]$ is identical to that for $[X_{t+k}]$. Intuitively, if the probability process governing the generation of the sequence of random variables stays the same whatever displacement in time takes place, the process is completely stationary. This definition does not require that the moments (means, variance, covariances and so on) exist. An example is given by a continuous distribution known as the Cauchy distribution, which does not have a well-defined mean (that is the integral defining the mean does not converge). If all moments exist a completely stationary process is stationary up to all orders (Priestley 1981). So to answer the question posed earlier, a series without well-defined moments could be completely stationary. Thus, in assessing stationarity care has to be taken in the special circumstance that, for example, a mean is not defined.

3.4.5 Linear combinations of random variables

It will occasionally be necessary to consider linear combinations of random variables. For example, if X_{1t} and X_{2t} are random variables with means, variances and covariance given by: $\mu_1(t), \mu_2(t), \sigma_1^2(t), \sigma_2^2(t)$ and $\sigma_{12}(t)$, respectively, what is the mean and variance of $X_t = X_{1t} + X_{2t}$? These and some other relevant results are summarised below.

1. $E(c) = c$
2. $E(cX_{1t}) = cE(X_{1t})$ where c is a constant
3. $\text{Var}(cX_{1t}) = c^2\sigma_1^2(t)$
4. $\text{Var}(X_{1t} + c) = \sigma_1^2(t)$

The following results are for linear combinations of the random variables X_{1t} and X_{2t}:

5. $E\{X_{1t} + X_{2t}\} = E\{X_{1t}\} + E\{X_{2t}\}$
6. $E\{X_{1t} - X_{2t}\} = E\{X_{1t}\} - E\{X_{2t}\}$
7. $\mathrm{Var}(X_{1t} + X_{2t}) = \sigma_1^2(t) + \sigma_2^2(t) + 2\sigma_{12}(t)$
8. $\mathrm{Var}(X_{1t} - X_{2t}) = \sigma_1^2(t) + \sigma_2^2(t) - 2\sigma_{12}(t)$

Result 1 is trivial and states that the expected value of a constant, c, is that constant. Results 2 and 3 say that if each possible outcome is scaled by the factor c then the expected value is also scaled by that factor, whereas the variance is scaled by c^2. Notice the ratio of the mean to the standard deviation is unchanged and this ratio is said to be scale-invariant. Result 4 states that adding a constant, c, to each possible outcome leaves the variance unchanged. Results 5 and 6 state that the expectations operator is a linear function: the expectation of a sum is the sum of the expectations, and the expectation of a difference is the difference in the expectations.

Results 7 and 8 relate to the variance of the sum and difference, respectively. The variance of a sum of random variables is the sum of the variances plus twice the covariance, $\sigma_{12}(t)$. The variance of the difference of random variables is the sum of the variances minus twice the covariance, $\sigma_{12}(t)$. Only if the covariance is zero is the variance of a linear combination equal to the linear combination of the variances.

There are two further results of interest to later chapters. These concern the implications for the linear combination of random variables. Suppose there are two random variables X_{1t} and X_{2t} then a linear combination of these is defined as: $Z_t = X_{1t} + \lambda_2 X_{2t}$ (we have assumed, without loss, that the coefficient on X_{1t} is 1). Then:

9. a linear combination of stationary random variables is stationary
10. a linear combination of nonstationary variables is, in general, nonstationary.

The first result is straightforward; the second less so because there is an important exception to the general rule. That is while the general result is that nonstationary random variables combine to become a nonstationary variable, in some special cases nonstationary variables combine to become stationary; in an intuitive sense the nonstationarity of one component series has a balancing counterpart in the other series. In a time series context this situation takes on particular importance and is known as cointegration, a theoretical and practical concept that appears at length in later chapters.

3.4.6 An example of a nonstationary time series

Earlier in (3.3) we considered the generation of X_t as a random walk, that is

$$X_t = \kappa + X_{t-1} + \varepsilon_t \qquad (3.19)$$

where ε_t is a zero mean, random variable with constant variance, σ_ε^2, independent increments ε_t and hence zero autocovariances. Suppose the initial value X_0 is fixed then the sequence of X_t follows the pattern:

$$X_1 = \kappa + X_0 + \varepsilon_1$$
$$X_2 = \kappa + X_1 + \varepsilon_1 + \varepsilon_2$$
$$= \kappa + \kappa + X_0 + \varepsilon_1 + \varepsilon_2$$

and in general,

$$X_t = t\kappa + X_0 + \sum_{s=1}^{t} \varepsilon_s \qquad (3.20)$$

As κ and X_0 are fixed, the stochastic (or random) properties of X_t are determined entirely by ε_t.
Using the above results we have:

Expectation	**Variance**
$\mu_X(1) = \kappa + X_0$	$\sigma^2(1) = \sigma_\varepsilon^2$
$\mu_X(2) = 2\kappa + X_0$	$\sigma^2(2) = 2\sigma_\varepsilon^2$
$\mu_X(t) = t\kappa + X_0$	$\sigma^2(t) = t\sigma_\varepsilon^2$

For example, consider

$$E\{X_2\} = E\{\kappa + \kappa + X_0 + \varepsilon_1 + \varepsilon_2\}$$
$$= 2\kappa + X_0 + 0 + 0$$

and

$$\sigma^2(2) = \text{Var}(\varepsilon_1 + \varepsilon_2) \text{ because } 2\kappa + X_0$$
$$\text{is a constant,}$$
$$= \sigma_\varepsilon^2 + \sigma_\varepsilon^2$$
$$= 2\sigma_\varepsilon^2$$

The second last line uses the fact that ε_t has a constant variance and zero autocovariances – hence $\text{Cov}(\varepsilon_1, \varepsilon_2) = 0$.

The process generating X_t is not stationary since neither its mean nor its variance is constant. Indeed if κ is positive the mean increases linearly with t, as does the variance; X_t is, therefore, an example of a nonstationary process.

3.4.7 Correlation and the autocorrelation function

Having defined the covariance and autocovariance in section **3.4.2**, it is a simple extension to consider the correlation between two random variables and the autocorrelation function. After a brief review of the concept of covariance we define correlation and autocorrelation.

Correlation has a specific meaning in statistics, it is a measure of the degree of linear association between *two* random variables (although the extension to more than two variables is possible through the concept of canonical correlation). The covariance between X_t and Y_s, where these are two distinct, not necessarily stationary, random variables, is

$$\text{Cov}(X_t, Y_s) \equiv E\{(X_t - \mu_X(t))(Y_s - \mu_Y(s))\}$$

Where $\mu_X(t) = E\{X_t\}$ and $\mu_Y(s) = E\{Y_s\}$. If X_t forms a sequence of random variables indexed by $t = 1, \ldots, s, \ldots, T$, so that $Y_t \equiv X_t$ this definition is of the *autocovariance* of the X_t process.

Notice that the definition allows for the possibility that X_t and X_s, or X_t and Y_s, are nonstationary processes. If X_t and Y_s are stationary to the first order then $\mu_X(t) = \mu_X$ and $\mu_Y(s) = \mu_Y$ and the definition simplifies to

$$\text{Cov}(X_t, Y_s) \equiv E\{(X_t - \mu_X)(Y_s - \mu_Y)\}$$

A positive covariance for X_t and Y_s indicates a tendency for positive association between the realisations of X_t and Y_s, but the magnitude of the numerical value cannot, generally, be interpreted as a measure of the strength of the association. As noted in section **3.4.2** the reason for this is that the covariance is not a scale-invariant measure. For example, suppose that X_t and Y_s are random variables – say male and female earnings, respectively – measured in US$. Now if we change the scale of X_t and Y_s by measuring earnings in cents, what will happen to the covariance? In this case the scaling factor is $c = 100$ so we define $W_t = cX_t$ and $V_s = cY_s$, then:

$$\text{Cov}(W_t, V_s) = c^2 \text{Cov}(X_t, Y_s)$$
$$= (100^2) \text{Cov}(X_t, Y_s) \quad (3.21)$$

We could use the covariance as a relative measure of association provided the comparison is between the same variables (and there is no change of scale, or change in the units of measurement, over time). But generally we seek a measure of association that will not change with the units of measurement.

Such problems of interpretation can be removed by defining a scale-invariant measure of association. One such is the correlation coefficient given by,

$$\rho(X_t, Y_s)$$
$$\equiv \text{Cov}(X_t, Y_s)/[\text{Var}(X_t) \text{Var}(Y_s)]^{\frac{1}{2}} \quad (3.22)$$

That is the correlation coefficient is the covariance between X_t and Y_s divided by the product of the standard deviations of X_t and Y_s. When

Y_s is a random variable from the sequence X_t, $t = 1, \ldots, s, \ldots, T$, that is $Y_s \equiv X_s$, then the correlation coefficient is known as the autocorrelation coefficient. It is easy to check that correlation is a scale-invariant measure. Scaling X_t by c_1 and Y_s by c_2, scales the covariance by c_2c_2, $\mathrm{Var}(X_t)$ by c_1^2, $\mathrm{Var}(Y_s)$ by c_2^2 and hence their standard deviations by c_1 and c_2, respectively. Thus, the scaling cancels out in the numerator and denominator. The correlation coefficient has the limits $-1 \le \rho(X_t, Y_s) \le +1$; the lower limit indicating perfect negative linear association and the upper limit perfect positive linear association.

A special notation is reserved for the autocorrelation function when X_t and X_s are stationary to the first order. Recall from the definition of stationarity that $\mu_X(t) = \mu_X(t + |k|) = \mu_X$. The autocorrelation coefficient between X_t and X_s where $s = t - k$, with $k \ne 0$, is denoted

$$\rho(k) = \mathrm{Cov}(X_t, X_{t-k})/[\mathrm{Var}(X_t)\,\mathrm{Var}(X_{t-k})]^{\frac{1}{2}}$$
$$\text{for} \quad k \ne 0 \tag{3.23}$$

$\rho(k)$ as a function of k is the autocorrelation function, and indicates the correlation between pairs of X_t, $t = 1, \ldots, T$, separated by k units of time. Clearly $\rho(0) = 1$. In the special but important case where X_t is stationary the variance is constant, and we can take advantage of the shorthand $\gamma(0)$ for the variance and $\gamma(k)$ for the autocovariance – see section **3.4.2** – to rewrite (3.23) as:

$$\rho(k) = \gamma(k)/\gamma(0) \tag{3.24}$$

where we have used

$$[\mathrm{Var}(X_t)\,\mathrm{Var}(X_{t-k})]^{\frac{1}{2}} = [\gamma(0)\gamma(0)]^{\frac{1}{2}} = \gamma(0)$$

Note also that in the stationary case $\rho(k) = \rho(-k)$ since all that matters is the difference in time not its position on the time axis.

With the concepts developed so far we can establish two shorthand descriptions of random variables which occur frequently in econometrics. A sequence of random variables, that is $[X_t] = [X_1, X_2, \ldots, X_T]$, is said to be 'white noise' if it has the following three properties:

(a) $E\{X_t\} = 0$ for all t;
(b) the variance of X_t is constant and hence independent of time, that is $\sigma^2(t) = \sigma^2$ for all t – in a terminology to be used extensively in later chapters the variance is said to be *homoscedastic*;
(c) all autocorrelations, $|k| \ge 1$, are equal to 0.

A white noise process is stationary since it has a constant mean, constant variances and autocorrelations that do not depend on time (but a stationary process is not necessarily white noise).

A closely related concept is that of independent and identically distributed random variables, a description often shortened to iid. A sequence of random variables, that is $[X_t] = [X_1, X_2, \ldots, X_T]$, is said to be iid if it has the following three properties:

(a) $E\{X_t\} = \mu_X$, a constant not necessarily equal to 0, for all t;
(b) the variance of X_t is constant and hence independent of time, that is $\sigma^2(t) = \sigma^2$;
(c) X_t is independent of X_s for all t and s, $t \ne s$, in the set $1, \ldots, T$.

The first property allows the constant mean to be nonzero; the second condition is the same as for white noise; the third is a strengthening of the third white noise condition since a sequence of independent random variables has zero autocorrelations but zero autocorrelations do not imply independence except in some special cases. A special case of interest is where the X_t are normally distributed, in which case zero autocorrelations do imply independence. An iid sequence is stationary. Where the distribution of the random variables is normal the sequence of random variables is referred to as niid; similarly if the white noise sequence comprises normally distributed variables it is described as normal white noise; normal white noise is niid because normality and zero auto-correlations imply independence.

3.4.8 The variance decomposition

A result used on several occasions in later chapters is known as the variance decomposition. Given two random variables Y_t and X_t the variance of Y_t can be written as:

$$\text{Var}(Y_t) = E_X\{\text{Var}(Y_t \mid X_t)\} + \text{Var}_X(E\{Y_t \mid X_t\})$$

In words, this says the variance of Y_t is the sum of the expected value of the conditional variance of Y_t given X_t as X_t varies, plus the variance of the conditional expectation of Y_t given X_t as X_t varies. Another way of interpreting the variance decomposition is to note that the left-hand side is the unconditional variance of Y_t (that is the variance of the marginal distribution), while the right-hand side involves the conditional variance $\text{Var}(Y_t \mid X_t)$ and another term; it emphasises that the unconditional variance and the conditional variance are not generally equal.

An example is likely to be helpful here, and we base one on the probabilities used in Table 3.11, here summarised in Table 3.12.

Direct calculation of the variance of Y_t gives:

$$\text{Var}(Y_t) = (0 - 0.7)^2(0.3) + (1 - 0.7)^2(0.7)$$
$$= 0.49(0.3) + 0.09(0.7) = 0.21$$

Table 3.12 *Joint events and their probabilities, third example*

	$x_{t1} = 0$	$x_{t2} = 1$	$P(Y_t)$
$y_{t1} = 0$	0.2	0.1	0.3
$y_{t2} = 1$	0.4	0.3	0.7
$P(X_t)$	0.6	0.4	1.0

Using the variance decomposition we require:

$$E\{Y_t \mid X_t = x_{t1}\} = 0(\tfrac{1}{3}) + 1(\tfrac{2}{3}) = \tfrac{2}{3}$$
$$E\{Y_t \mid X_t = x_{t2}\} = 0(\tfrac{1}{4}) + 1(\tfrac{3}{4}) = \tfrac{3}{4}$$
$$\text{Var}(Y_t \mid X_t = x_{t1}) = (0 - \tfrac{2}{3})^2(\tfrac{1}{3})$$
$$+ (1 - \tfrac{2}{3})^2(\tfrac{2}{3}) = \tfrac{2}{9}$$
$$\text{Var}(Y_t \mid X_t = x_{t2}) = (0 - \tfrac{3}{4})^2(\tfrac{1}{4})$$
$$+ (1 - \tfrac{3}{4})^2(\tfrac{3}{4}) = \tfrac{3}{16}$$

The first term in the variance decomposition is $E_X\{\text{Var}(Y_t \mid X_t)\}$. Now the conditional variance is the random variable with the two outcomes $\tfrac{2}{9}$ and $\tfrac{3}{16}$; these outcomes have probabilities 0.6 (the probability that $X_t = x_{t1}$) and 0.4 (the probability that $X_t = x_{t2}$), respectively. Hence,

$$E_X\{\text{Var}(Y_t \mid X_t)\} = (\tfrac{2}{9})0.6 + (\tfrac{3}{16})0.4$$
$$= 0.2083$$

The second term in the variance decomposition is $\text{Var}_X(E\{Y_t \mid X_t\})$. Now the conditional expectation is the random variable with the two outcomes $\tfrac{2}{3}$ and $\tfrac{3}{4}$, with probabilities 0.6 and 0.4, respectively; and the overall mean is, therefore, $\tfrac{2}{3}(0.6) + \tfrac{3}{4}(0.4) = 0.7$. Hence,

$$\text{Var}_X(E\{Y_t \mid X_t\}) = (\tfrac{2}{3} - 0.7)^2 0.6$$
$$+ (\tfrac{3}{4} - 0.7)^2 0.4$$
$$= 0.00167$$

Bringing these two terms together then, as required:

$$\text{Var}(Y_t) = E_X\{\text{Var}(Y_t \mid X_t)\} + \text{Var}_X(E\{Y_t \mid X_t\})$$
$$= 0.00167 + 0.2083 = 0.210$$

Of course, in general, it is not intended that the variance decomposition is actually how the unconditional variance should be calculated: the result is of theoretical rather than practical importance. For example, if the expectation of Y_t given X_t is constant across the range of outcomes for X_t, then $\text{Var}_X(E\{Y_t \mid X_t\}) = 0$ and $\text{Var}(Y_t) = E_X\{\text{Var}(Y_t \mid X_t)\}$. (This result is relevant to Chapter 4.)

3.4.9   Iterating expectations

The concept of conditional expectation was introduced in section **3.4.3**. Incidentally we also gave an example of iterating expectations, which deserves a special mention as this concept occurs in several areas of economics. Conditional expectations can be defined in the following circumstances, which we illustrate initially with two variables. Let Y_t and X_t be two random variables with joint pdf defined by $f(y_t, x_t)$, then we can either obtain the expectation by conditioning on X_t or Y_t, using the conditional pdf $f(y_t \mid x_t)$ or $f(x_t \mid y_t)$, respectively. Three examples of this were given for the discrete case in Tables 3.8, 3.10 and 3.11. Suppose we initially obtain $E\{Y_t \mid X_t\}$, then we can 'undo' the conditioning by evaluating the conditional expectation $E\{Y_t \mid X_t\}$ with respect to X_t. We write this as $E\{Y_t\} = E_X\{E\{Y_t \mid X_t\}\}$, where the X subscript on E indicates that we are now evaluating the conditional expectation with respect to X_t. In this context $E\{Y_t \mid X_t\}$ is a random variable viewed as a function of X_t.

Suppose X_t has two outcomes x_{t1} and x_{t2} with (marginal) probabilities $P(x_{t1})$ and $P(x_{t2})$ and Y_t has two outcomes y_{t1} and y_{t2} with (marginal) probabilities $P(y_{t1})$ and $P(y_{t2})$. The conditional probabilities are: $P(y_{t1} \mid x_{t1})$, $P(y_{t2} \mid x_{t1})$, $P(y_{t1} \mid x_{t2})$ and $P(y_{t2} \mid x_{t2})$ where $P(y_{t1} \mid x_{t1}) + P(y_{t2} \mid x_{t1}) = 1$ and $P(y_{t1} \mid x_{t2}) + P(y_{t2} \mid x_{t2}) = 1$. Then:

$$E\{Y_t \mid X_t = x_{t1}\} = y_{t1}P(y_{t1} \mid x_{t1})$$
$$+ y_{t2}P(y_{t2} \mid x_{t1})$$
$$E\{Y_t \mid X_t = x_{t2}\} = y_{t1}P(y_{t1} \mid x_{t2})$$
$$+ y_{t2}P(y_{t2} \mid x_{t2})$$

and

$$E\{Y_t\} = E_X\{E\{Y_t \mid X_t\}\}$$
$$= E\{Y_t \mid X_t = x_{t1}\}P(x_{t1})$$
$$+ E\{Y_t \mid X_t = x_{t2}\}P(x_{t2})$$

An example was given earlier where

$$E\{Y_t \mid X_t = x_{t1}\} = \tfrac{2}{3}$$

$P(x_{t1}) = 0.6$, $E\{Y_t \mid X_t = x_{t2}\} = 0.75$ and $P(x_{t2}) = 0.4$; hence,

$$E_x\{E\{Y_t \mid X_t\}\} = \tfrac{2}{3}(0.6) + 0.75(0.4) = 0.7$$

We can extend the iterative process if there are more than two variables. For example, consider three variables Y_t, X_t and Z_t. Then we could first condition the expectation of Y_t on X_t and Z_t, that is $E\{Y_t \mid X_t, Z_t\}$; we could then iterate on X_t, that is $E_X\{E\{Y_t \mid X_t, Z_t\}\}$ keeping Z_t constant but varying X_t; and, finally, iterate on Z_t, that is $E_Z\{E_X\{E\{Y_t \mid X_t, Z_t\}\}\}$, which is now $E\{Y_t\}$. The notation looks complex, but work out from the central set of brackets to understand what is happening.

Economic models often require the specification of an expected variable given a particular set of information, and rational expectations, RE, figures prominently as the adopted solution to this problem. Consider the example given by the probabilities in Table 3.12 where

$$E\{Y_t \mid X_t = x_{t1}\} = 0(\tfrac{1}{3}) + 1(\tfrac{2}{3}) = \tfrac{2}{3}$$

From this conditional expectation we can also define the difference

$$(\varepsilon_t \mid X_t = x_{t1}) \equiv (Y_t \mid X_t = x_{t1})$$
$$- E(Y_t \mid X_t = x_{t1})$$

which has the two outcomes $\varepsilon_{t1} = 0 - \tfrac{2}{3} = -\tfrac{2}{3}$ with probability $\tfrac{1}{3}$, and $\varepsilon_{t2} = 1 - \tfrac{2}{3} = \tfrac{1}{3}$ with probability $\tfrac{2}{3}$. We refer to ε_t as an innovation and to $\varepsilon_t \mid X_t = x_{t1}$ as a conditional innovation. Notice that the expected value of the conditional innovation is zero, that is $E\{\varepsilon_t \mid X_t = x_{t1}\} = -\tfrac{2}{3}(\tfrac{1}{3}) + \tfrac{1}{3}(\tfrac{2}{3}) = 0$. This is a mathematical feature of conditional expectations, which holds generally. A simple rearrangement of the conditional innovation gives

$$(Y_t \mid X_t = x_{t1}) \equiv E(Y_t \mid X_t = x_{t1})$$
$$+ (\varepsilon_t \mid X_t = x_{t1}) \quad \text{with}$$
$$E\{(\varepsilon_t \mid X_t = x_{t1})\} \equiv 0$$

The rational expectation, RE, of Y_t given $X_t = x_{t1}$ is simply the mathematical conditional expectation $E(Y_t \mid X_t = x_{t1})$, with the consequence that the difference between the outturn $(Y_t \mid X_t = x_{t1})$ and the rational expectation is necessarily zero on average. Rational expectations are often used where values of a variable in the future are involved. For example, conditional on an information set Ω_t, what is the rational expectation of Y_{t+1}? The RE answer is $E_t\{Y_{t+1} \mid \Omega_t\}$, where the subscript on E indicates when the expectation is formed. Now consider the rational expectation of Y_{t+2} formed at $t + 1$ given Ω_{t+1} (and Ω_t and so on). This is $E_{t+1}\{Y_{t+2} \mid \Omega_{t+1}, \Omega_t\}$, with iterated expectation

$$E_t\{E_{t+1}\{Y_{t+2} \mid \Omega_{t+1}, \Omega_t\}\} = E_t\{Y_{t+1} \mid \Omega_t\}$$

From the last equality note that

$$E_t\{(E_{t+1}\{Y_{t+2} \mid \Omega_{t+1}, \Omega_1\} - Y_{t+1} \mid \Omega_t)\} = 0$$

with the RE interpretation that the revision to Y_{t+1} to obtain the expectation of Y_{t+2} is not predictable at time t.

3.5 A random walk

In this section we bring together concepts from previous sections to illustrate the generation of a nonstationary process. The example we use is an extension of the coin-tossing game due to Feller (1968). In using this example we are building upon the simple illustrations of coin tossing games given in section **3.2**, to generate a process, that of a random walk, which has considerable importance in the construction and application of time series models.

3.5.1 The coin-tossing game

The extension of the coin-tossing game is very simple. We suppose that an unbiased coin is tossed at regular intervals and $1 is paid if the coin lands heads while $1 is deducted if the coin lands tails. Thus for each individual toss of the coin the outcomes are $+1, -1$ with equal proba-

bility. The game consists of T tosses of the coin, and the random variable we are interested in is the net gain to the player. What does your intuition suggest should be the outcome of the game if the coin is tossed a large number of times, for example suppose $T = 10,000$? Note your answer down now and see if it agrees with the Feller's argument.

First, it will be helpful to introduce some notation. Let ε_t denote the random variable with outcomes $+1, -1$ at time t; then the net gain at time T is $X_T = \sum_{t=1}^{T} \varepsilon_t$ and note that

$$X_t = X_{t-1} + \varepsilon_t \tag{3.25}$$

The variance of ε_t is denoted $\sigma_\varepsilon^2(t)$ and the variance of X_t is denoted $\sigma_X^2(t)$. ε_t is a random variable with zero mean and variance $= (1-0)^2 * 0.5 + (-1-0)^2 * 0.5 = 1.0$. In this process the differences $X_t - X_{t-1} = \varepsilon_t$ are uncorrelated (indeed they are independent). Equation (3.25) says that the gain in period t equals the gain last period plus a zero mean random term with constant variance. The idea of a random *walk* comes across strongly when the realisations are plotted on a graph. Initially, because the random walk idea is conveyed more easily, we set T to be a fairly small number, here $T = 50$. The resulting random walk is illustrated in Figure 3.5. The walk starts in the positive half but then 'sets' off in the negative half in a direction which is sustained and the lead (that is the positive half) is never regained. Even with $T = 50$ this pattern seems counter-intuitive. Intuition seems to suggest that if the game is even, that is a $1 gain is as likely as a $1 loss, then the zero axis should be crossed frequently by the path of the gain. However, we do not see this pattern; rather once the lead is lost, as it is in this case, it is lost for long periods. Indeed for the example in Figure 3.5, the lead is only held for the first twelve tosses. The expected gain is zero since:

$$E\{X_t\} = E\left\{\sum_{t=1}^{T} \varepsilon_t\right\} = \sum_{t=1}^{T} E\{\varepsilon_t\} = 0 \tag{3.26}$$

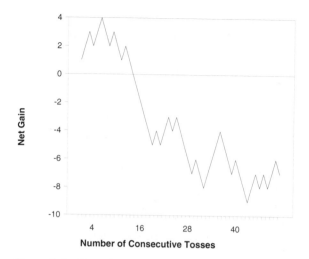

Figure 3.5 *Net gain in coin-tossing game, T = 50*

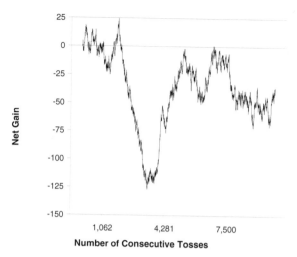

Figure 3.6 *Net gain in coin-tossing game, T = 10,000*

but this does not seem to be reflected in what happens.

The problem for our intuition is that while ε_t is a stationary stochastic process, X_t is not. For example, suppose the process starts at $t = 1$ then:

$$X_1 = \varepsilon_1 \quad \text{and} \quad \sigma_X^2(1) = \sigma_\varepsilon^2(1)$$

and

$$X_2 = \varepsilon_2 + \varepsilon_1 \quad \text{with} \quad \sigma_X^2(2) = 2\sigma_\varepsilon^2(1)$$

$$X_3 = \varepsilon_3 + \varepsilon_2 + \varepsilon_1 \quad \text{with} \quad \sigma_X^2(3) = 3\sigma_\varepsilon^2(1)$$

$$\vdots$$

$$X_T = \sum_{t=1}^{T} \varepsilon_t \quad \text{with} \quad \sigma_X^2(T) = T\sigma_\varepsilon^2(1) \quad (3.27)$$

In deriving the variance we have used the result that, for example,

$$\sigma_X^2(2) = \text{Var}(\varepsilon_2 + \varepsilon_1) = \sigma_\varepsilon^2(2) + \sigma_\varepsilon^2(1)$$
$$+ 2\,\text{Cov}(\varepsilon_1, \varepsilon_2)$$
$$= \sigma_\varepsilon^2(2) + \text{because the covariance}$$
$$\text{is zero}$$
$$= 2\sigma_\varepsilon^2(1) \text{ because } \sigma_\varepsilon^2(2) = \sigma_\varepsilon^2(1)$$

The covariance is zero because successive tosses are independent.

We now increase the number of tosses to $T = 10,000$. The net gain is illustrated in Figure 3.6. Note that once the gain is lost, at about $t = 2,000$, it is regained (just) once only! This is a result quite contrary to our unguided intuition that the 'law of averages' should result in the lead being regained and then lost, and so on, with considerable frequency.

As we shall later see the autocorrelations of a random walk do not die out and in Figure 3.7 we see that even at a lag of 100 the autocorrelations are above 0.94. However, taking the first

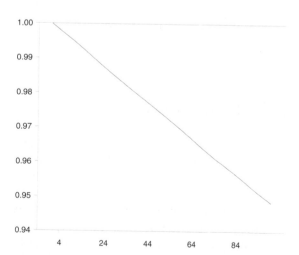

Figure 3.7 *Autocorrelations of coin-tossing game, T = 10,000*

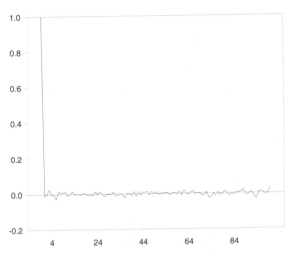

Figure 3.8 *Autocorrelations, difference of coin-tossing game, T = 10,000*

difference of X_t results in a stationary process for which the autocorrelations do die out quickly – see Figure 3.8.

A stochastic process is a martingale if it satisfies $E\{X_{t+1} \mid \Omega_t\} = X_t$. In the case of (3.25), $E\{X_{t+1} \mid \Omega_t\} = X_t + E\{\varepsilon_{t+1}\} = X_t$, so the process $[X_t]$ is also a martingale. The current total gain, X_t, is obviously in the information set Ω_t, and cannot be improved upon as a forecast of X_{t+1}. The difference $\varepsilon_{t+1} = X_{t+1} - X_t$ is known as a martingale difference sequence, mds. In general an mds only requires uncorrelated rather than the independent increments required for a random walk; that is ε_t and ε_t are uncorrelated but not necessarily independent for $t \neq s$.

3.6 Estimation

While estimation is the central topic in Chapters 4 and 5 it is useful to introduce some basic concepts to familiarise the idea in this chapter. In part the idea here is to use a simple illustration to show how nonstationarity complicates the process of estimation. Introductory courses in quantitative methods typically show how to calculate the mean and variance for some typical economic time series. To be specific in order to

calculate the sample mean a number of realisations, $t = 1, \ldots, T$ (that is outcomes), from a particular series are given, then summed and divided by the number of observations, T, to give a numerical value. The point here is what interpretation should be given to the resulting numerical figure? In the terms of this chapter, if the sample mean is intended as an estimate of the corresponding mean of the sequence of random variables, then an implicit assumption is that the sequence is of first order stationary random variables. However, it is not difficult to find examples where the mean is calculated for series that are clearly not stationary.

3.6.1 Nonstationary processes

A little thought about the nature of nonstationary processes will suggest how difficult, and perhaps impossible, it is in general to estimate parameters such as the mean, variance and autocovariances. Consider the mean, $\mu_X(t)$, associated with the sequence $[X_t]$. First recall that X_t is a random process, that is a sequence of random variables $[X_1, \ldots, X_T]$ with a corresponding sequence of means $[\mu_X(1), \ldots, \mu_X(T)]$. While each X_t has a range of possible outcomes with associated probabilities, in practice we are only likely to observe one actual outcome – that is the sample observation at t for X_t. We may have no alternative but to take this outcome as the estimator of $\mu_X(t)$. If there was some structure to the evolution of $\mu_X(t)$ we might be able to exploit that to obtain a better estimator for each $\mu_X(t)$. If the process X_t is nonstationary with a nonconstant variance then the difficulties of estimation will be apparent in trying to estimate $\sigma^2(t)$. Taking the sample outcome of X_t as an estimate of $\mu_X(t)$, runs into immediate difficulty when trying to form an estimate of $\sigma^2(t)$ by squaring the difference between the outcomes and the mean – this must be identically zero for each t!

However, estimation of the parameters is relatively straightforward for stationary processes. Although there is one subtlety which we first consider. Note that $E\{X_t\}$ refers to the weighted sum of the range of outcomes of X_t, at time t, weighted by their probabilities. It is what Priestley (1981) calls an ensemble average. The ensemble is the range of possible outcomes at t; however, and in this there is no difference between nonstationary and stationary processes, in general we will only have one sample outcome for each t. The difference for stationary processes is that since the X_t process has certain constant characteristics, we can collect a time series sample of outcomes, that is realisations of X_t at different points in time and treat them as if they came from the ensemble. We can use the fact that the process is stationary to use the time average, for example, as an estimator of the ensemble average. Having obtained an estimator of the mean we can then obtain estimators of the variance and covariances.

3.6.2 Stationary processes

In the following we are considering a sequence of discrete random variables $[X_t]$ which constitute a stationary process, that is:

$$E\{X_t\} = \mu, \text{Var}\{X_t\} = \sigma^2,$$
$$\text{Cov}(X_t, X_{t+k}) = \gamma(k) \quad \text{for all } k \qquad (3.28)$$

For simplicity and where there is no ambiguity in this section, the mean of X_t is referred to simply as μ. We now emphasise the notational distinction between a random variable and particular realisations of that variable. To recap, the notation X_t refers to the random variable X at time t; X_t takes a range of outcomes which are finite in number and indexed from $i = 1, \ldots, N$. When we take a sample of T observations one from each period 1 through to T we are recording a particular set of realisations of X_t, $t = 1, \ldots, T$. To emphasise we distinguish the actual realisations from the random variable by denoting the former as x_t and the latter as X_t.

This notational distinction is cumbersome but necessary if we are to distinguish between an estimator and an estimate – an important distinction taken up in the next chapter. Given a parameter of interest, for example the constant mean, μ_X, a possible estimator of this parameter is the sample mean

$$\bar{X} = \frac{1}{T} \sum_{t=1}^{T} X_t \qquad (3.29)$$

This 'rule' or estimator is framed in terms of the random variables $X_1, \ldots, X_T$, not the realisations $x_1, \ldots, x_T$ of these random variables. Given a particular set of realisations we have an estimate, sometimes referred to as a point estimate, from a particular sample – a numerical value given a particular set of realisations. The estimate of the sample mean is

$$\bar{x} = \frac{1}{T} \sum_{t=1}^{T} x_t \qquad (3.30)$$

An important property of an estimator is whether it is biased. In general an estimator $\hat{\theta}$ of a parameter of interest θ, which is a characteristic of the sequence of (stationary) random variables $[X_t]$, will be a function of that sequence, which we summarise as $\hat{\theta}(X_1, \ldots, X_T)$. The estimator $\hat{\theta}$ is an unbiased estimator of θ if and only if

$$E\{\hat{\theta}\} = \theta \qquad (3.31)$$

otherwise $\hat{\theta}$ is biased and the bias is given by

$$\text{bias}(\hat{\theta}) = E\{\hat{\theta}\} - \theta \qquad (3.32)$$

Notice that bias is a concept applied to the estimator not the estimate. It is easy to show that $\bar{X}$ is an unbiased estimator of μ:

$$E\{\bar{X}\} = \frac{1}{T} \sum_{t=1}^{T} E\{X_t\} = \frac{1}{T} T\mu = \mu \qquad (3.33)$$

Notice that we are applying the expectations operator to the random variable $\bar{X}$, not to a numerical estimate from a particular sample. We have used the properties that the expectation of a sum of random variables is the sum of the expectations and X_t is a stationary random variable with constant mean, that is $E\{X_t\} = \mu$ for all t.

Just as the sample mean is a candidate estimator for μ, the sample variance is also a candidate estimator for σ^2. The sample variance is

$$S^2 = \frac{1}{T} \sum_{t=1}^{T} (X_t - \bar{X})^2 \tag{3.34}$$

However, S^2 is a biased estimator of σ^2. To show this we use the following identity

$$\sum (X_t - \bar{X})^2 = \sum [(X_t - \mu) - (\bar{X} - \mu)]^2$$
$$= \sum (X_t - \mu)^2 + T(\bar{X} - \mu)^2$$
$$- 2(\bar{X} - \mu) \sum (X_t - \mu)$$
$$= \sum (X_t - \mu)^2 + T(\bar{X} - \mu)^2$$
$$- 2T(\bar{X} - \mu)^2$$
$$= \sum (X_t - \mu)^2$$
$$- T(\bar{X} - \mu)^2 \tag{3.35}$$

Using this result we can now evaluate the expected value of S^2:

$$E(S^2) = \frac{1}{T} E\left\{ \sum_{t=1}^{T} (X_t - \bar{X})^2 \right\}$$

$$= \frac{1}{T} E\left\{ \sum_{t=1}^{T} (X_t - \mu)^2 \right\}$$

$$- \frac{T}{T} E\{(\bar{X} - \mu)^2\} \tag{3.36}$$

$$= \frac{1}{T} T\sigma^2 - E\{(\bar{X} - \mu)^2\}$$

$$= \sigma^2 - \frac{1}{T} \sigma^2 \tag{3.37}$$

The penultimate line uses the following:

$$E\{(\bar{X} - \mu)^2\} = E\left[\frac{1}{T} \left(\sum_{t=1}^{T} X_t - T\mu \right) \right]^2$$

$$= \frac{1}{T^2} E\{(X_1 - \mu + X_2$$
$$- \mu + \cdots + X_T - \mu)^2\}$$

$$= \frac{1}{T^2} E\{(X_1 - \mu)^2$$
$$+ (X_2 - \mu)^2 + \cdots + (X_T - \mu)^2\}$$

$$= \frac{1}{T^2} T\sigma^2$$

$$= \frac{1}{T} \sigma^2$$

A feature of a random sample with independent random variables is that $E\{X_t X_s\} = 0$ for $t \neq s$, and this is used in going from the second to third line.

Notice that S^2 on average underestimates σ^2, the difference in expectation being σ^2/T which tends to zero as $T \to \infty$. We can find an unbiased estimator quite easily since

$$E(S^2) = \sigma^2 - \frac{1}{T} \sigma^2 = \sigma^2 \left(1 - \frac{1}{T} \right) \tag{3.38}$$

$$= \sigma^2 \left(\frac{T-1}{T} \right) \tag{3.39}$$

So correcting S^2 by the factor $(T/(T-1))$ will give an unbiased estimator. That is define $\hat{\sigma}^2$

$$\hat{\sigma}^2 = \frac{T}{(T-1)} S^2$$

$$= \frac{1}{(T-1)} \sum_{t=1}^{T} (X_t - \bar{X})^2 \tag{3.40}$$

An estimator of the autocovariance function for a stationary process is provided by

$$\hat{\gamma}(k) = \frac{1}{T - |k|} \sum_{t=1}^{T-|k|} (X_t - \bar{X})$$
$$\times (X_{t-|k|} - \bar{X}) \tag{3.41}$$

where $|k|$ is the absolute value of k, for example $|-4| = 4$, $|4| = 4$. $\hat{\gamma}(k)$ can be viewed as the time (or sample over time) average of the product of and $X_t - \bar{X}$ and $X_{t-|k|} - \bar{X}$. If μ rather than $\bar{X}$ is used in (3.41), $\hat{\gamma}(k)$ is an unbiased estimator of $\gamma(k)$. However, if μ is replaced by $\bar{X}$ then $\hat{\gamma}(k)$ is only unbiased as the sample size T tends to infinity (a property known as asymptotic unbiasedness); the proof of this is beyond the scope of this book, interested readers may consult Priestley (1981, p. 322).

3.6.3 Centred moving variance

Where X_t is a stationary process we note that the centred moving average defined earlier is also an unbiased estimator but, in general, it will not be such a good estimator of the ensemble average as the average over the whole sample. By analogy to the centred moving average we can also define a centred moving variance, CMV,

$$\hat{\sigma}_J^2(t) = \sum_{t=-J}^{+J} (X_t - \bar{X}_J(t))^2/(2J+1) \qquad (3.42)$$

As with the CMA, the CMV will not be a good estimator if the process is nonstationary. However, $\bar{X}_J(t)$ and $\hat{\sigma}_J^2(t)$ have a use as indicators of nonstationarity in the mean and variance, respectively. That is moving a 'window' of observations through the complete sample can help in suggesting whether the assumption of a constant mean and constant variance (and by a simple extension constant covariance) is consistent with the data.

Returning to Figures 3.1 and 3.2 for US import of goods and the US price of food, respectively, we can now draw attention to the right-hand scale on each of these figures. This refers to the CMV of the series using, as with the CMA, a window of 17 observations. The CMV for US imports indicates a nonstationary series with estimates ranging from close to zero to just over 3,000 with a sustained increase in the mid-1980s. Taking the first difference of US imports

of goods does not settle the CMV estimates down enough to suggest constancy, but there is a diminution in the strength of pattern observed in the levels of the series.

Turning to the US price of food in Figure 3.2, the CMV estimates suggest an increase in the variance until the early 1980s with a steady decline thereafter. The CMV estimates of the first difference series are graphed in Figure 3.4. Again there is a flattening-out of the steady increase observed in the levels. Without coming to any firm conclusions, it does appear that the first difference of each series seems closer to a stationary process than is the case for the levels series. This is a view which suggests that developments of models based on the simple random walk model of equation (3.3) could provide a useful description of trended economic time series – this issue considered at length in Chapter 6.

3.7 Concluding remarks

The motivation for this chapter is that we can often make little sense of how economic data is generated if we maintain the assumption that the mean, and possibly the variance and covariances, of a series are constant over time. The levels of many economic time series share the characteristic that they have trended upwards since the 1940s, and we need a stochastic framework to explain this characteristic. One framework is that this data is generated by nonstationary processes in contrast to the stationary processes that are often the focus of many introductory texts in economics and statistics. However, to understand the nature of nonstationary processes we have first to understand what is meant by a stationary process. For students who have taken an introductory course in statistics it is likely that the probability examples given in sections **3.3** and **3.4** are familiar and seem relatively simple. That is intentional: they serve to show how elementary variations in the underlying assumptions can lead to nonstationary processes.

In general terms a nonstationary time series process is one in which any aspect of its probability structure is not constant. Quite often, though, the nonstationarity typical of economic time series has an easily characterisable form and for that purpose we introduced definitions of processes stationary to the first order and stationary to the second order. In the former case the mean is not constant, and in the second case either or both the variance and the covariances are not stationary.

In section **3.5** the simple coin-tossing experiment was extended to show how to generate a random walk, and in one of the review questions this is extended to a random walk with drift. The net gain, in a game in which there was a sequence of tosses of a coin with $1 paid if the coin lands heads and $1 deducted if the coin lands tails, was shown to be a nonstationary time series which took the form of a random walk. This was an interesting introduction to an important class of nonstationary processes that have been widely used in economics.

We return to the concept of a nonstationary time series in Chapters 6 and 7. Chapters 4 and 5 consider the basic tools of econometric model building; the former introduces regression analysis, estimation and hypothesis testing in the context of a bivariate model, and the latter extends this to a multivariate model.

Review

1. This chapter introduces some concepts that are central to the developments in other chapters. It is motivated by the need to establish a conceptual framework for interpreting random variables and random processes.
2. Formally a random variable is a function defined on a sample space. Random variables are easy to illustrate, for example the number of heads in T tosses of a coin, the number of sixes in T throws of a dice. Each of these examples illustrates that a random variable for time t has a range of outcomes

and we can associate a probability with each element – or outcome – in the range.

3. A random process is a sequence of random variables X_t, indexed by the symbol t. The particular processes of interest in this book are time series processes where the symbol t is an index of time.
4. At the beginning of the chapter we graphed two series, US imports of goods and the US price index of food. It is series such as these that we regard as outcomes of a (time series) random process. Such outcomes often share similar characteristics, for example note the tendency for the outcomes to increase over time in a trend like fashion.
5. An important question to consider when describing or analysing time series processes is whether they appear to be generated by a process which is static. At an informal level it seemed unlikely that this was the case for the two time series considered here. Regarding each outcome as a realisation from a random process it did not seem plausible that they were being generated by a process with a constant mean.
6. A useful first assessment of a time series can be provided by calculating the centred moving average and comparing it with the mean calculated over the whole sample of outcomes.
7. The expectation or mean of a random variable X_t is the sum of all possible outcomes weighted by the probability of the outcomes, that is

$$E\{X_t\} \equiv \sum_{i=1}^{N} (X_t = x_{ti})P_t(X_{ti} = x_{ti})$$

the shorthand for this is $\mu_X(t)$.

8. On several occasions in this chapter we used the example provided by variations of a coin-tossing experiment. This gives rise to a random variable which in the first experiment had just two outcomes, $X_t = 0$ and $X_t = 1$, with equal probability. In this case $\mu_X(t) = 0.5$.

9. If the first experiment was repeated on consecutive days, indexed by the symbol t, then $\mu_X(t)$ would be constant at 0.5. This is an example of a process that is said to be stationary to the first order.

10. In a variation to the first experiment we consider tossing two coins each day, this changed the set of outcomes to $X_t = 0$, $X_t = 1$, $X_t = 2$, and the expectation to $\mu_X(t) = 1$. Then, in experiment 2, we supposed that on day $s = t + 1$ the coin was biased, with a probability of 0.4 for a head. Now $\mu_X(s) = 0.8$ and so the random process $\{X_t, X_s\}$ was no longer stationary to the first order.

11. A measure of variability of the random variable X_t is provided by the variance defined as:

$$\mathrm{Var}(X_t) \equiv E\{X_t - \mu_X(t)\}^2$$

$$\equiv \sum_{i=1}^{N} ((X_t = x_{ti}) - \mu_X(t))^2$$

$$\times P_t(X_t = x_{ti})$$

the shorthand for this is $\sigma^2(t)$.

12. Substituting the biased coin with probability of heads $= 0.4$, for the unbiased coin reduced the variance from 0.5 to 0.48. This suggested a second aspect of nonconstancy for a random process X_t, that is when the variance is not constant.

13. When we consider either two, or more, distinct random variables or a random process with a sequence of random variables a further aspect of description and analysis concerns the connections between, or among, the random variables.

14. One such measure is the covariance defined as

$$\mathrm{Cov}(X_t, Y_s)$$
$$\equiv E\{(X_t - \mu_X(t))(Y_s - \mu_Y(s))\}$$
$$= \sum_{i}^{N_t} \sum_{i}^{N_j} [(X_t = x_{ti}) - \mu_X(t)]$$
$$\times [(Y_s = y_{sj}) - \mu_Y(s)]P_{ti,sj}$$

the shorthand for this, which emphasises potential nonstationarity, is $\sigma(t,s)$.

15. The covariance is constructed by subtracting the mean from each possible outcome, for each variable, and weighting the joint outcomes by the probability of those joint outcomes.

16. The autocovariance is the special case of the covariance when X_t and Y_s are pairs of random variables from the same random process or sequence. For example, the covariance between X_t and X_{t-1} is known as the first order autocovariance. For a process with a constant mean the autocovariance function is given by:

$$\mathrm{Cov}(X_t, X_{t-k}) = E\{(X_t - \mu_X)(X_{t-k} - \mu_X)\}$$

17. The covariance between X_t and Y_s has units of measurement equal to the units of measurement of X_t times the units of measurement of Y_s. It is not, therefore, invariant to a change in the units of measurement of either variable. For example, changing from measuring in US dollars to US cents.

18. A unit-free measure of association is provided by the correlation coefficient, that is $\rho(X_t, Y_s) = \mathrm{Cov}(X_t, X_s)/[\mathrm{Var}(X_t)\,\mathrm{Var}(X_s)]^{\frac{1}{2}}$.

19. When X_t and Y_s are pairs of variables from the same sequence or process, with $s = t - k$, then we have the autocorrelation coefficient

$$\rho(X_t, X_{t-k})$$
$$= \mathrm{Cov}(X_t, X_{t-k})/[\mathrm{Var}(X_t)\,\mathrm{Var}(X_{t-k})]^{\frac{1}{2}}$$

Denoted more simply as $\rho(k)$ for a stationary process.

20. The (auto)correlation coefficient lies between -1, indicating perfect negative linear association and $+1$, indicating perfect positive linear association.

21. A process which has a constant mean, constant variance and for which the autocovariances are constant for each difference, k, in the index t, is said to be stationary to the second order. Sometimes this is referred

to as (weak) stationarity. A process which is not stationary is said to be nonstationary.

22. An example of a nonstationary process is given by the random process,

$$X_t = \kappa + X_{t-1} + \varepsilon_t$$

which has mean $\mu_X(t) = t\kappa + X_0$, where X_0 is the initial value, assumed fixed, and variance $\sigma^2(t) = t\sigma_\varepsilon^2$, where σ_ε^2 is the variance of ε_t, assumed constant. This process is a random walk with drift which we study further in Chapter 6.

23. Estimation of the means, variances and covariances for nonstationary processes depends in a critical way on the nature and structure of the nonstationarity. If nothing more is known than that these parameters vary over time then little can usually be done. A transformation of a nonstationary process may be stationary and this is a possibility we explore in Chapter 6.

24. Estimation of the parameters of a stationary process is much more straightforward. For example, if the process has a constant mean, $E\{X_t\} = \mu$ for all t, then estimation of the ensemble average by the time average yields an unbiased estimator.

25. Similarly if the process is stationary to the second order an unbiased estimator of the (common) variance is

$$\hat{\sigma}^2 = \frac{T}{(T-1)} S^2$$

$$= \frac{1}{(T-1)} \sum_{t=1}^{T} (X_t - \bar{X})^2$$

where

$$S^2 = \frac{1}{T} \sum_{t=1}^{T} (X_t - \bar{X})^2$$

26. An asymptotically unbiased estimator of the kth order autocovariance is

$$\hat{\gamma}(k) = \frac{1}{T - |k|} \sum_{t=1}^{T-|k|} (X_t - \bar{X})(X_{t-|k|} - \bar{X})$$

27. Dividing $\hat{\gamma}(k)$ by $\hat{\sigma}^2$ (or S^2) gives an asymptotically unbiased estimator of the autocorrelation coefficient, $\hat{\rho}(k)$.

28. Analogous to the centred moving average, CMA, a centred moving variance, CMV, can be defined:

$$\hat{\sigma}_J^2(t) = \sum_{t=-J}^{+J} (X_t - \bar{X}_J(t))^2/(2J + 1)$$

where

$$\bar{X}_J(t) = \sum_{i=-J}^{+J} X_{t-i}(J)/(2J + 1)$$

is the CMA. $(2J + 1)$ is sometimes referred to as the 'window' of observations on which the moving average is based. The CMV can be useful in assessing nonstationarity of the variances as illustrated with imports of goods and the price of food for the US.

Review questions

1. Explain, with examples, what is meant by a discrete random variable.

2. What is the meaning of the following notation:

$$P_t(X_t = x_{ti}) \quad i = 1, \ldots, N;$$
$$P_{ti} \quad\quad\quad i = 1, \ldots, N;$$
$$P_i \quad\quad\quad\; i = 1, \ldots, N.$$

3. (i) Let X_t denote the random variable which is the sum of the number of points on two dice which are rolled at the same time. What is the set of possible values of X_t and their associated probabilities? What are the mean and variance of X_t? Is X_t a stationary random variable?

   (ii) Let Y_t be the random variable which is the number on a fair roulette wheel (an evenly divided circle of 36 numbers).

What is the set of possible values of X_t and their associated probabilities? What are the mean and variance of X_t? Is X_t a stationary random variable?

(iii) What is the joint sample space of X_t and Y_t?

4. Let X_t be the random variable with $X_t = 0$ if a tossed coin lands tails and $X_t = 1$ if the coin lands heads; and let $Y_t = i$, $i = 1, \ldots, 6$, be the number of points on the single roll of a dice. Draw up a table of these joint events and their probabilities.

5. Continuing the example calculate the following:
   (i) $E\{X_t\}$ and $E\{Y_t\}$
   (ii) $E\{X_t \mid Y_t = i\}$ for $i = 1, \ldots, 6$;
   (iii) $E\{Y_t \mid X_t = j\}$ for $j = 1, 2$;
   (iv) $\sigma_X^2(t)$ and $\sigma_Y^2(t)$;
   (v) $\sigma_{XY}(t)$.
   Are X_t and Y_t independent random variables?

6. Consider the following table of joint events and associated probabilities.

	$Y_t = 0$	$Y_t = 1$	$P(X_t)$
$X_t = 0$	0.1	0.4	0.1
$X_t = 1$	0.4	0.1	0.9
$P(Y_t)$	0.7	0.3	1.0

   (i) Calculate the covariance between X_t and Y_t.
   (ii) Are the variables X_t and Y_t independent?
   (iii) Given the marginal probabilities what would the table entries have to be if the random variables were independent?

7. Prove the following:

$$E\{X_{1t} + X_{2t}\} = E\{X_{1t}\} + E\{X_{2t}\}$$
$$\text{Var}\{X_{1t} + X_{2t}\} = \sigma_1^2(t) + \sigma_2^2(t) + 2\sigma_{12}(t)$$

Where X_{1t} and X_{2t} are random variables, $\sigma_i^2(t)$ is the variance of X_{it} and $\sigma_{12}(t)$ is the covariance between X_{1t} and X_{2t}.

8. Return to the examples in questions 4 and 6 and calculate and interpret the correlation coefficient in each case.

9. It is usual to map the sample space of the random variable, X_t, which is toss of the coin with outcomes tails, T, and heads, H, into the real line as $(0, 1)$; suppose instead you assign the value 1,000 to a tail and 2,000 to a head, what is the mean and variance of X_t in the new sample space?

10. (i) What is the difference between the correlation coefficient and the autocorrelation coefficient?
    (ii) Under what circumstances does it make sense to use the shorthand notation $\gamma(0)$ and $\gamma(k)$?
    (iii) Is it always the case that the autocovariance is the same for $s = t - k$ and $s = t + k$? Explain your answer.

11. (i) What is the difference between an 'ensemble' average and a time average?
    (ii) If X_t is a stationary random variable, is the (sample) time average a good estimator of the 'ensemble' average?
    (iii) Suppose that X_t is a random variable, which is not stationary to the first order, reconsider your answer to the first part of this question.

12. Explain what is meant by
    (i) a centred moving average (CMA);
    (ii) a centred moving variance (CMV).
    Why might the CMA and CMV be useful informal indicators of the stationarity or otherwise of a random process?

13. Give examples of random variables that are:
    (i) not stationary to the first order but which have a constant variance and constant covariances; and
    (ii) not stationary to the second order.

14. Reconsider the coin-tossing game in section **3.5** with the variation that it now costs 10¢ to play each game in the sequence with $1 paid if the coin lands heads and $1 lost if the coin lands tails. Show that the net gain is now a random walk with drift. What difference does this make to:

(i) the mean net gain;

(ii) the variance of the net gain; and

(iii) the kind of graphical picture generated by $T \to \infty$ tosses of the coin.

15. Suppose now that the coin used in question 14 is biased with a probability of heads of 0.6. Reconsider your answers to the previous question.

16. Consider the sequence of random variables given by the autoregressive process $X_t = \kappa + \rho X_{t-1} + \varepsilon_t$ where ε_t is white noise.

(i) Derive the first order autocovariance and the first order autocorrelation coefficients.

(ii) Derive the kth order autocovariance and the kth order autocorrelation coefficient where $k > 1$.

(iii) Examine the stationarity of this process for the following range of values of ρ: $-1 < \rho < 1$; $\rho = 1$; $\rho > 1$; $\rho < -1$.

17. (i) The following result was used in the derivation of equation (3.35) in the text:

$$\sum (X_t - \mu)^2 + T(\bar{X} - \mu)^2 - 2T(\bar{X} - \mu)^2$$
$$= \sum (X_t - \mu)^2 - T(\bar{X} - \mu)^2$$

Confirm this result.

(ii) Also confirm the following result

$$E\{(\bar{X} - \mu)^2\} = \frac{1}{T} \sigma^2$$

and hence show that S^2 is a biased estimator of σ^2.

(iii) Let X_t, $t = 1, \ldots, T$, denote a sequence of stationary random variables with constant mean μ. Which of the following is true and why?

$$\sum_{t=1}^{T} (X_t - \bar{X}) = 0; \quad \sum_{t=1}^{T} (X_t - \mu) = 0.$$

18. Consider the joint distribution defined by the following joint events table:

Probability of joint events

	$x_{t1} = 0$	$x_{t2} = 1$	$P(Y_t)$
$y_{t1} = 0$	0.4	0.15	0.55
$y_{t2} = 1$	0.1	0.35	0.45
$P(X_t)$	0.5	0.50	1.00

(i) Confirm that the variance decomposition for this example is:

$$\mathrm{Var}(Y_t) = E_X\{\mathrm{Var}(Y_t \mid X_t)\}$$
$$+ \mathrm{Var}_X(E\{Y_t \mid X_t\})$$
$$0.2475 = 0.185 + 0.0625$$

Probability of joint events

	$x_{t1} = 0$	$x_{12} = 1$	$P(Y_t)$
$y_{t1} = 0$	0.4	0.4	0.8
$y_{t2} = 1$	0.1	0.1	0.2
$P(X_t)$	0.5	0.5	1.0

(ii) Confirm that the variance decomposition for this example is:

$$\mathrm{Var}(Y_t) = E_X\{\mathrm{Var}(Y_t \mid X_t)\}$$
$$+ \mathrm{Var}_X(E\{Y_t \mid X_t\})$$
$$0.16 = 0.16 + 0$$

(iii) What is special about this last example?

Part II
Estimation and Simulation

CHAPTER 4

Estimation and hypothesis testing in simple regression models

4.1 Introduction

This and the next chapter are concerned with several related issues. The first is the estimation of unknown parameters in linear regression equations. For example, suppose the problem, in its simplest form, is that the numerical values of β_1 and β_2 are unknown in the (regression) equation

$$E\{Y_t \mid X_t\} = \beta_1 + \beta_2 X_t \qquad (4.1)$$

where the left-hand side of this equation is the expected value of Y_t conditional on X_t. The process of estimation implies specifying a rule, or function, which transforms random variables, or, exceptionally, fixed quantities, into an *estimator* of an unknown coefficient. Then substitution of the values from a particular sample of the realisations of the random variables into the estimator rule or function results in a numerical *estimate* of the unknown coefficient. In the context of (4.1) we anticipate that the estimators for β_1 and β_2 will depend upon the random variables Y_t and X_t and the corresponding numerical estimates will depend upon a sample of the realisations of Y_t and X_t.

In section **4.2** we set the background – or statistical paradigm – for model specification and estimation. The emphasis in these sections is different from the usual emphasis in introductory texts. We take the view that it is important to introduce the idea of jointly distributed random variables as soon as pos-

sible, rather than emphasise the classical linear regression model, CLRM, which, in its simplest form, considers X_t as fixed in repeated samples. In section **4.3** we consider the difference between estimators and estimates, and outline the least squares and instrumental variable principles of obtaining estimators. There will often exist several different estimators for a particular parameter of interest and in section **4.4** we consider criteria that distinguish among the properties of an estimator. In section **4.5** the ordinary least squares, OLS, estimator is evaluated according to the criteria introduced in the previous section. While the previous sections have considered linear models, non-linear models are introduced in section **4.6**. The goodness of fit of a regression model is considered in section **4.7**, where a distinction is made between the population and sample coefficient of determination – the R^2 – of a regression equation. Some of the complications arising from dynamic models, that is those which involve lags of the variables, are introduced in section **4.8**; in part this is a precursor to later chapters, especially Chapters 6 and 8, which consider the problems arising from lagged dependent variables in greater detail. The difference between structure and regression is introduced in section **4.9**, which also serves to provide an application of the instrumental variables, rather than the OLS, estimator. Tests of hypotheses are routinely applied in econometrics and the basic principles are considered in section **4.10**. In section **4.11** an empirical example illustrates some of the techniques, and concluding remarks are contained in section **4.12**. For later reference appendix **A4.1** gives a brief introduction to the method of maximum likelihood. Finally, as practically regressions and test statistics are calculated from widely available econometric programs, in appendix **A4.2** typical computer output from four widely available econometric programs illustrates what to expect.

The next chapter builds upon several of the principles introduced in this chapter. In particular while the emphasis in this chapter is on the bivariate model, this is extended to the multivariate model in the next chapter. Also a distinction is made between hypothesis tests which are tests of specification, and hypothesis tests which are tests of misspecification. This distinction is central to the idea of assessing the adequacy of an empirical model as a base for statistical inference. The next chapter also contains several illustrations of estimated models.

4.2 Statistical background

This section gives an introduction to some key statistical concepts that provide a background to regression analysis. It builds upon the ideas in Chapter 3 to develop the concepts of conditional expectation and conditional expectation function. A more advanced reference to the statistical background for econometric model building is provided by Spanos (1986).

The notation used in this chapter is that a capital letter denotes a random variable, which is assumed to have a continuous range of possible values, the realisations of which are distinguished by using a lower case letter. For example, X_t is a random variable with the realisation x_t. The range of possible realisations (at time t) is called the ensemble of X_t (see Priestley (1981, p. 101)). The other dimension of X_t is the index t; a sequence, for example, $X_1, \ldots, X_T$, is indicated by square brackets; thus $[X_t]_1^T$ is a family of random variables over the range of the index $t = 1, \ldots, T$. For simplicity the range will usually

be omitted. The *family* of random variables indicated by the sequence $[X_t]$ is sometimes called a random or stochastic *process*.

4.2.1 Factorisation of the joint density

X_t is assumed to be a stationary, continuous random variable with values on the real line $[-\infty, +\infty]$ with probability density function, pdf, denoted $f(x_t)$. The probability that X_t lies between a and b with $b > a$ is given by

$$\Pr(a \leq X_t \leq b) = \int_a^b f(x_t)\,dx_t \qquad (4.2)$$

The expectation (or mean value) of X_t is

$$E\{X_t\} \equiv \int_{-\infty}^{+\infty} x_t f(x_t)\,dx_t \qquad (4.3)$$

Sometimes it is convenient to denote the expectation of X_t as μ_x. For a continuous variable:

$$\Pr(-\infty \leq X_t \leq +\infty) = \int_{-\infty}^{+\infty} f(x_t)\,dx_t \qquad (4.4)$$
$$= 1$$

That is the probability must sum to 1 over the range of the random variable. The variance of X_t is

$$\mathrm{Var}(X_t) \equiv \int_{-\infty}^{+\infty} (x_t - \mu_x)^2 f(x_t)\,dx_t \qquad (4.5)$$

Sometimes it is convenient to denote this variance as σ_x^2. In some cases the expectation and/or the variance may not exist as when the integrals do not converge.

The cumulative distribution function of X_t is $F(x_t)$, and is the probability that X_t is less than or equal to x_t. For a continuous random variable

$$F(x_t) = \int_{-\infty}^{x_t} f(s)\,ds \qquad (4.6)$$

where s is the (artificial) variable of integration varying over the range $-\infty$ to x_t. On occasion we will need to use the percentiles of the distribution of a random variable. For example, the 95%

percentile is the value, say $x_t(0.95)$, which cuts off 95% of the distribution to the left of this point and hence 5% to the right. That is

$$F(x_t(0.95)) = \int_{-\infty}^{x_t(0.95)} f(s)\, ds = 0.95$$

and hence

$$1 - F(x_t(0.95)) = 0.05 \tag{4.7}$$

A leading example of a univariate distribution is the normal distribution with pdf given by

$$f(x_t) = \frac{1}{(2\pi\sigma_X^2)^{\frac{1}{2}}} \exp\left\{ -\frac{(x_t - \mu_x)^2}{2\sigma_X^2} \right\} \tag{4.8}$$

The normal distribution is symmetric and bell shaped. A linear function of a normally distributed random variable is also normally distributed, and a particularly useful transformation is to what is known as the standard (univariate) normal. That is define

$$Z_t = (X_t - \mu_x)/\sigma_x \tag{4.9}$$

where $E\{X_t\} = \mu_x$ and $\mathrm{Var}(X_t) = \sigma_x^2$, then $\mu_z = 0$ and $\sigma_z^2 = 1$. The pdf for Z_t is

$$f(z_t) = \frac{1}{(2\pi)^{\frac{1}{2}}} \exp(-z_t^2/2) \tag{4.10}$$

Using this transformation only one table of the percentiles of the normal distribution is needed. Any normally distributed random variable can be transformed to this standard form and then, if necessary, transformed back to its original units as $X_t = \mu_x + \sigma_x Z_t$. To illustrate the use of Table A1, The Normal Distribution (see Appendix), consider the entry for $Z = \pm 0.5$. The table gives the area of the normal distribution between $Z = -0.5$ and $Z = 0.5$ as 0.3829, or 38.29% of the total area. Alternatively transforming back to X this is the area between $\mu_x - 0.5\sigma_x$ and $\mu_x + 0.5\sigma_x$; for example, if $\mu_x = 10.0$ and $\sigma_x = 2$ then 38.29% of the total area lies between $10 - 0.5(2) = 9$ and $10 + 0.5(2) = 11$. The normal distribution is symmetric so if a

one-sided area is required, it would be one-half the table entry. For example, the area between $Z = 0$ and $Z = 0.5$ is $0.5(0.3829) = 0.19145$, or returning to X the area between 10 and 11 is 0.19145. An alternative use of the standard normal table is to ask what value of Z corresponds to a particular quantile. For example, the 95% percentile is that value of Z that cuts off 5% of the distribution to the right and, from Table A1, is 1.645. Alternatively, to find the central 95% of the distribution requires the 2.5% and 97.5% quantiles; these are -1.96 and $+1.96$, respectively.

Next consider two random variables, Y_t and X_t, each of which is continuous. The joint pdf of Y_t and X_t is written $f(y_t, x_t)$, and the probability that Y_t lies between the interval a and b and X_t lies between the interval c and d is given by

$$\Pr(a \leq Y_t \leq b \text{ and } c \leq X_t \leq d)$$

$$= \int_a^b \int_c^d f(y_t, x_t)\, dy_t\, dx_t \tag{4.11}$$

A special case of interest is the bivariate normal (bvn) distribution, with joint pdf given by

$$f(y_t, x_t) = \frac{1}{2\pi\sigma_Y\sigma_X(1 - \rho^2)^{0.5}}$$

$$\times \exp\left(\frac{-(z_{Y_t}^2 + z_{X_t}^2 - 2\rho z_{Y_t} z_{X_t})}{2(1 - \rho^2)} \right) \tag{4.12}$$

where

$$Y_t \sim N(\mu_Y, \sigma_Y^2), \qquad X_t \sim N(\mu_X, \sigma_X^2)$$

$$z_{Y_t} = (Y_t - \mu_Y)/\sigma_y, \qquad z_{X_t} = (X_t - \mu_X)/\sigma_X$$

and ρ is the correlation coefficient between Y_t and X_t. A graph of $f(y_t, x_t)$ against y_t and x_t reveals a symmetric bell shape in three dimensions.

Now consider the joint distribution but with the random variable X_t fixed at a given value, say

$X_t = x_t$; this gives rise to the distribution of Y_t conditional on $X_t = x_t$. The probability that X_t lies between a and b with $X_t = x_t$ is given by

$$\Pr(a \leq Y_t \leq b \mid X_t = x_t) = \int_a^b f(y_t \mid x_t)\, dy_t$$

$$\text{(4.13)}$$

where $f(y_t \mid x_t)$ denotes the conditional pdf for Y_t. Reversing the roles of Y_t and X_t gives the conditional pdf for X_t. The probability that X_t lies between c and d with $Y_t = y_t$ is given by

$$\Pr(c \leq X_t \leq d \mid Y_t = y_t) = \int_c^d f(x_t \mid y_t)\, dx_t$$

$$\text{(4.14)}$$

where $f(x_t \mid y_t)$ is the conditional pdf for X_t. Analogous to the expectation and variance in a univariate distribution the conditional expectation and the conditional variance are defined as follows:

conditional expectation of Y_t:

$$\mu_{Y|x} \equiv E\{Y_t \mid X_t = x_t\}$$

$$\equiv \int_{-\infty}^{\infty} y_t f(y_t \mid x_t)\, dy_t \qquad \text{(4.15a)}$$

conditional expectation of X_t:

$$\mu_{X|y} \equiv E\{X_t \mid Y_t = y_t\}$$

$$\equiv \int_{-\infty}^{\infty} x_t f(x_t \mid y_t)\, dx_t \qquad \text{(4.15b)}$$

conditional variance of Y_t:

$$\sigma_{Y|x}^2 \equiv \mathrm{Var}\{Y_t \mid X_t = x_t\}$$

$$\equiv \int_{-\infty}^{\infty} (y_t - \mu_{Y|x})^2 f(y_t \mid x_t)\, dy_t$$

$$\text{(4.16a)}$$

conditional variance of X_t:

$$\sigma_{X|y}^2 \equiv \mathrm{Var}\{X_t \mid Y_t = y_t\}$$

$$\equiv \int_{-\infty}^{\infty} (x_t - \mu_{X|y})^2 f(x_t \mid y_t)\, dx_t$$

$$\text{(4.16b)}$$

The conditional pdfs are usually most easily obtained as

$$f(y_t \mid x_t) = f(y_t, x_t)/f(x_t) \qquad \text{(4.17a)}$$

and

$$f(x_t \mid y_t) = f(y_t, x_t)/f(y_t) \qquad \text{(4.17b)}$$

That is the conditional pdf is the ratio of the joint pdf to the (marginal) pdf of the conditioning variable. The reader should recognise these expressions as being the analogues of the equivalent expressions for discrete random variables – see Chapter 3.

A simple rearrangement of the conditional pdfs is useful, that is

$$f(y_t, x_t) = f(y_t \mid x_t) f(x_t) \qquad \text{(4.18a)}$$

and

$$f(y_t, x_t) = f(x_t \mid y_t) f(y_t) \qquad \text{(4.18b)}$$

In this representation the joint pdf is 'factorised' into a conditional pdf and a marginal pdf. The reason this factorisation is useful is that while the DGP can be viewed as generating the joint pdf, the focus of empirical enquiry is often just on the conditional distribution; this raises the question of when such a limited focus is valid – which we consider further in section **4.9**.

4.2.2   The conditional expectation function, CEF, as the regression function

As noted above the conditional expectation of Y_t given $X_t = x_t$ is

$$E\{Y_t \mid x_t\} = \int_{-\infty}^{\infty} y_t f(y_t \mid x_t)\, dy_t$$

With X_t fixed at x_t, $f(y_t \mid x_t)$ is a univariate pdf which is then used to evaluate the (conditional) expectation of Y_t. There are as many of these expectations as there are distinct values of X_t; for example, if X_t is a continuous random variable there is an infinite number of conditional expectations. When the conditional expectation is written as $E\{Y_t \mid X_t\}$, it is known as the conditional expectation *function* of Y_t. Note the important difference in notation between $E\{Y_t \mid x_t\}$ and $E\{Y_t \mid X_t\}$. In the former only one value of $X_t = x_t$ is considered, whereas in the latter this condition is relaxed to consider the complete range of X_t giving rise to the concept of a function. By a simple substitution of variables we can also define the conditional expectation of X_t given Y_t, written as $E\{X_t \mid Y_t\}$.

There are some bivariate distributions, the best known being the bivariate normal, for which the CEF is linear. That is

$$E\{Y_t \mid X_t\} = \beta_1 + \beta_2 X_t \qquad (4.19a)$$

which is known as the *regression* of Y_t on X_t; and

$$E\{X_t \mid Y_t\} = \alpha_1 + \alpha_2 Y_t \qquad (4.19b)$$

which is known as the *regression* of X_t on Y_t. The parameters of the CEF are functions of the moments of Y_t and X_t, specifically:

$$\beta_1 = \mu_Y - \beta_2 \mu_X; \quad \beta_2 = \sigma_{XY}/\sigma_X^2;$$
$$\sigma_{Y|X}^2 = \sigma_Y^2 - \beta_2^2 \sigma_X^2$$

and

$$\alpha_1 = \mu_X - \alpha_2 \mu_Y; \quad \alpha_2 = \sigma_{XY}/\sigma_Y^2;$$
$$\sigma_{X|Y}^2 = \sigma_X^2 - \alpha_2^2 \sigma_Y^2$$

For future reference we also define the correlation coefficient between X_t and Y_t:

$$\rho_{XY} \equiv \frac{\sigma_{XY}}{\sigma_X \sigma_Y}$$

β_1, β_2, α_1 and α_2 and α_2 are often referred to as the (population) regression coefficients. σ_{XY} is the covariance between X and Y; $\sigma_{Y|X}^2$ is the variance of Y conditional on X as a function of X (that is the extension to a function of $\sigma_{Y|x}^2$); and $\sigma_{X|Y}^2$ is the variance of X conditional on Y as a

function of Y (that is the extension to a function of $\sigma_{X|y}^2$). We will concentrate on the CEF for Y_t since with just a change of notation analogous results for the CEF for X_t can be obtained. Also where there is no risk of confusion the conditional variance (function) $\sigma_{Y|X}^2$ will be referred to in subsequent sections as σ^2.

In more advanced texts, see, for example, Goldberger (1991, Chapter 7), the relationship between the regression parameters in (4.19a) and (4.19b) and the moments of Y_t and X_t, that is the means, variances and covariance, are derived explicitly. Here we state rather than derive the relationship. However, there is one result that will be needed in Chapter 9, which we consider here. Specifically, given two variables Y_t and X_t that have a bivariate normal distribution then

$$\begin{aligned} E\{Y_t \mid X_t\} &= \beta_1 + \beta_2 X_t \\ &= (\mu_Y - \beta_2 \mu_X) + \beta_2 X_t \\ &\quad \text{on substituting for } \beta_1 \\ &= \mu_Y + \frac{\sigma_{XY}}{\sigma_X^2}(X_t - \mu_X) \\ &\quad \text{on substituting for } \beta_2 \\ &= \mu_Y + \rho_{XY}\left(\frac{\sigma_Y}{\sigma_X}\right)(X_t - \mu_X) \quad (4.20) \end{aligned}$$

This way of writing the conditional expectation shows how the conditional expectation differs from the unconditional expectation by a term that depends upon the correlation between Y_t and X_t. If $\rho_{XY} = 0$, that is Y_t and X_t are uncorrelated, then the conditional and unconditional expectations are equal. (Y_t is then said to be 'mean independent' of X_t and, by symmetry in a bvn, X_t is mean independent of Y_t.)

When the joint pdf is bivariate normal there are some important characteristics of the corresponding conditional pdfs and conditional expectations, which are stated here without proof.

(i) If $f(y_t, x_t)$ is bvn then $f(y_t \mid x_t)$ and $f(x_t \mid y_t)$ are normally distributed, that is the conditional pdfs are normal.

(ii) If $f(y_t, x_t)$ is bvn then the conditional expectations, $E(Y_t \mid x_t)$ and $E(X_t \mid y_t)$, are linear in x_t and y_t, respectively.

(iii) The conditional variances, of Y_t given $X_t = x_t$ and X_t given $Y_t = y_t$, are constant.

We can summarise these three characteristics as follows:

$$(Y_t \mid x_t) \sim N(\beta_1 + \beta_2 x_t, \sigma^2_{Y|x})$$

$$(X_t \mid y_t) \sim N(\alpha_1 + \alpha_2 y_t, \sigma^2_{X|y})$$

Recall that the factorisation of the joint density in (4.18) is into a conditional density and a marginal density – in a sense there are two parts to the information in the joint density, but the regression function just concerns one of these. When the information in the marginal density, say for X_t, can be ignored without loss, while obtaining the parameters of interest from the conditional density, X_t is said to be weakly exogenous. This and the question of which conditional density or regression function is of interest – the conditional expectation of Y_t given X_t or the conditional expectation of X_t given Y_t – are issues to which we return in section **4.9.1**.

It will not always be the case that the regression function is linear. While there are some joint pdfs, the leading example being that of the bivariate normal distribution, which imply linear regression functions, there are many others which imply nonlinear regression functions. We return to this aspect in section **4.6**.

To anticipate the later sections, if interest centres on the regression coefficients, substitution of the sample moments for the unknown population movements offers an easy method of obtaining estimates of the unknown coefficients. For example, let s_{xy} and s^2_x denote the covariance and variance in a particular sample of observations then a numerical estimate of $\beta_2 = \sigma_{XY}/\sigma^2_X$ is obtained as the ratio of s_{xy} to s^2_x.

Define $\varepsilon_t \mid x_t$ as the random variable which is the difference between Y_t and its expectation

conditional on $X_t = x_t$, call this the conditional innovation; that is

$$(\varepsilon_t \mid x_t) \equiv Y_t - E\{Y_t \mid x_t\} \qquad (4.21)$$

For consistency we could use the notation $Y_t \mid x_t$ rather than Y_t in (4.21), but the conditioning would be superfluous as the range of Y_t is not affected by the conditioning. A simple illustration may help in fixing the concepts in (4.21). For simplicity consider a discrete bivariate distribution with just two outcomes for each of Y_1 and X_1, the four possible outcomes are indicated by y_{11}, y_{12}, x_{11} and x_{12}, respectively, with the following joint probability table

		X_1	
		$x_{11} = 10$	$x_{12} = 20$
Y_1	$y_{11} = 1$	0.4	0.2
	$y_{12} = 2$	0.1	0.3

Then

$$E\{Y_1 \mid X_1 = 10\} = 1(0.4/0.5)$$
$$+ 2(0.1/0.5) = 1.2$$

and

$$(\varepsilon_{11} \mid X_1 = 10) \equiv y_{11} - E\{Y_1 \mid X_1 = 10\}$$
$$= 1 - 1.2 = -0.2$$
$$(\varepsilon_{12} \mid X_1 = 10) \equiv y_{12} - E\{Y_2 \mid X_1 = 10\}$$
$$= 2 - 1.2 = 0.8$$

and

$$E\{\varepsilon_t \mid X_1 = 10\} \equiv -0.2(0.4/0.5)$$
$$+ 0.8(0.1/0.5) = 0$$

Note from the last result that the conditional innovation has an expected value of zero. More generally

$$E\{\varepsilon_t \mid x_t\} = E\{Y_t - E\{Y_t \mid x_t\} \mid x_t\} \qquad (4.22)$$
$$= E\{Y_t \mid x_t\} - E\{Y_t \mid x_t\}$$
$$= 0$$

By allowing x_t to vary across the range of values taken by the random variable X_t we can define the conditional innovation function, CIF, that is $\varepsilon_t \mid X_t$. As (4.22) holds for each x_t it also holds for the random variable X_t, so $E\{\varepsilon_t \mid X_t\} = 0$ and the expected value of the conditional innovation is always zero.

A simple rearrangement of (4.21) allows the equation to be viewed as 'determining' Y_t, that is:

$$Y_t \equiv E\{Y_t \mid x_t\} + \varepsilon_t \mid x_t \qquad (4.23)$$

This says that Y_t is (identically) equal to its conditional expectation plus the conditional innovation. For simplicity assume that the conditional expectation of Y_t is linear, specifically

$$E\{Y_t \mid x_t\} = \beta_1 + \beta_2 x_t \qquad (4.24)$$

Then (4.23) becomes

$$Y_t = \beta_1 + \beta_2 x_t + \varepsilon_t \mid x_t \qquad (4.25)$$

In this representation the random variables are Y_t and $\varepsilon_t \mid x_t$, with X_t fixed equal to x_t. It is important to note here that even though X_t is fixed, Y_t is a random variable with properties and realisations 'determined' by the conditional innovation, $\varepsilon_t \mid x_t$. We enclose 'determined' by apostrophes because although in many introductory texts $\varepsilon_t \mid x_t$ is viewed as a separate entity – an 'error' or 'disturbance' term to be added to $\beta_1 + \beta_2 x_t$ – it is, as is apparent from (4.21), a derived, rather than an independent, construct. Nevertheless, with this caveat in mind it is often useful to focus on (4.23) as the mechanism determining Y_t. For example, by repeatedly sampling from the ensemble of $\varepsilon_t \mid x_t$, an ensemble of values of Y_t is generated; so even with X_t fixed the outcome for Y_t is not fixed.

A typical time series of observations can be viewed as being generated from (4.23) by allowing the time index t to vary, say from $t = 1, \ldots, T$ giving a sample of T observations. Within this framework X_t is a sequence of random variables, $[X_t]$, with a sequence of fixed values corresponding to particular realisations: $X_1 = x_1, X_2 = x_2, \ldots, X_T = x_T$.

As noted above the conditional innovation function is defined by:

$$\varepsilon_t \mid X_t \equiv Y_t - E\{Y_t \mid X_t\} \qquad (4.26)$$

The difference between this expression and (4.21) for the conditional innovation is that the conditional expectation function $E\{Y_t \mid X_t\}$ replaces the conditional expectation $E\{Y_t \mid X_t = x_t\}$, so X_t is no longer fixed; $E\{Y_t \mid X_t\}$ and hence ε_t are functions of X_t. Another way of looking at the difference is that (4.26) is the general representation from which the special case of fixing X_t, as in (4.21), results. As before we can give $\varepsilon_t \mid X_t$ the look of a separate entity by rewriting (4.26) as,

$$Y_t \equiv E\{Y_t \mid X_t\} + \varepsilon_t \mid X_t \qquad (4.27)$$

which, with linearity of the CEF, gives,

$$Y_t = \beta_1 + \beta_2 X_t + \varepsilon_t \mid X_t \qquad (4.28)$$

For simplicity of representation ε_t is often used rather than $\varepsilon_t \mid X_t$ so that (4.28) is written as

$$Y_t = \beta_1 + \beta_2 X_t + \varepsilon_t \qquad (4.29)$$

Other properties of the innovation, which are of interest, are as follows:

(i) $E\{\varepsilon_t\} \quad = E_X\{E\{\varepsilon_t \mid x_t\}\}$
$\quad\quad\quad\quad = E_X\{0\} = 0$

(ii) $\mathrm{Cov}\{X_t, \varepsilon_t\} = 0$

The first of these properties states that the unconditional expectation of the innovation is zero; this is trivial given that the conditional expectation is zero for every choice of x_t. The second property states that the covariance of X_t and the (unconditional) innovation is zero. We need to show that $\mathrm{Cov}\{X_t, \varepsilon_t\} = 0$, for which the following result is used, see Goldberger (1991, p. 49):

$$\mathrm{Cov}\{X_t, \varepsilon_t\} = \mathrm{Cov}\{X_t, E\{\varepsilon_t \mid X_t\}\} \qquad (4.30)$$

That is the covariance of X_t and ε_t is equal to the covariance of X_t and the conditional expectation of ε_t given X_t. Substituting for $E\{\varepsilon_t \mid X_t\}$ then

$$\text{Cov}\{X_t, \varepsilon_t\} = \text{Cov}\{X_t, 0\} \qquad (4.31)$$
$$= 0$$

The last result follows since the covariance of a random variable with a constant, in this case, a set of zeros, is zero. A review question considers an extended example to distinguish among the concepts introduced in this section.

Equation (4.29) is the representation of the 'linear regression model', which may be familiar to those who have previously studied an introductory text on regression models. However, the emphasis here is likely to be different since Y_t and X_t are inherently random variables with the consequence that ε_t is a derived construct that owes its origin to the generating process of the random variables Y_t and X_t. In the classical linear regression model, CLRM, X_t is assumed to be 'fixed in repeated samples', and the disturbance ε_t, as it is usually called in this context, is accorded a separate existence due to omitted influences on Y_t, measurement errors, the inherent randomness in human behaviour and so on. The CLRM is useful at an introductory level as its conceptual basis is much simpler than the CEF approach and students may initially find it easier to think of *the* regression model as (4.29) with ε_t having the following properties:

(i) $E\{\varepsilon_t\} = 0$ for all t: the disturbance has a zero mean for all t;

(ii) $E\{\varepsilon_t - E\{\varepsilon_t\}\}^2 = E\{\varepsilon_t\}^2 = \sigma_\varepsilon^2$, a constant for all t: the disturbance has a constant variance – it is said to be homoscedastic (the opposite is heteroscedastic);

(iii) $E\{(\varepsilon_t - E\{\varepsilon_t\})(\varepsilon_{t-s} - E\{\varepsilon_{t-s}\})\} = E\{\varepsilon_t \varepsilon_{t-s}\}$ $= 0$ for $t \neq s$: the disturbances at different points in time are uncorrelated; they are said to be serially uncorrelated;

(iv) if X_t is fixed in repeated samples then (trivially since X_t is a constant) the covariance of X_t and ε_t is zero.

These four assumptions are the standard assumptions of the CLRM. A traditional approach to estimation is then to derive the 'best' estimator given these assumptions, and then consider the implications for estimation of the breakdown of each of the assumptions in turn. While this is a useful introductory device it is also important for further work to be aware of the conceptual basis which treats the variables Y_t and X_t as random variables and hence starts with the idea of approximating the data generation process for Y_t and X_t.

4.2.3 Some important distributions

Two important univariate distributions used extensively in applied econometrics, both related to the normal distribution, are the χ^2 (chi-squared) and 't' distributions; and an important bivariate distribution related to the χ^2 distribution is the F distribution. The χ^2 distribution has a degrees of freedom parameter denoted g and is written $\chi^2(g)$. Relevant details are as follows.

(i) If Z is standard normal, that is $Z \sim N(0, 1)$, then $Z^2 \sim \chi^2(1)$. In words, the square of a standard normal variable has the χ^2 distribution with 1 degree of freedom. The $\chi^2(1)$ distribution is skewed with a mean $= 1$ and variance $= 2$.

(ii) If Z_1 and Z_2 are each standard normal and independent, for which it is sufficient that the covariance between them is 0, then $Z_1^2 + Z_2^2 \sim \chi^2(2)$. In words the sum of two independent standard normal variables has the $\chi^2(2)$ distribution with 2 degrees of freedom. The $\chi^2(2)$ distribution is skewed with a mean $= 2$ and variance $= 4$. The $\chi^2(2)$ generalisation to the $\chi^2(g)$ distribution should now be obvious.

(iii) If Z_i, $i = 1, \ldots, g$ are independent, standard normal variables then $\sum_{i=1}^{g} Z_i^2$ is distributed as $\chi^2(g)$. The mean and variance of a variable distributed as $\chi^2(g)$ are g and $2g$, respectively.

(iv) The '*t*' distribution is a combination of a standard normal variable, Z_t, and an independent $\chi^2(g)$ variable, W_t. Specifically if $Z_t \sim N(0, 1)$ and $W_t \sim \chi^2(g)$, and Z_t and W_t are independent, then 't'$(g) = Z_t/(W_t/g)^{0.5}$. In words, the ratio of a standard normal variable to the square root of an independent $\chi^2(g)$ variable divided by its degrees of freedom, has the '*t*' distribution with *g* degrees of freedom. As *g* gets larger the '*t*' distribution looks more and more like the normal distribution; otherwise it has fatter tails. For example, with $g = 20$ the 2.5% and 97.5% quantiles are -2.086 and $+2.086$, respectively, compared to ± 1.96 for the normal distribution. (This distribution is due to W.S. Gosset writing as 'Student' (1908) rather than under his own name; his distribution was sometimes referred to as 'Student's *t*' – we shorten that reference here keeping the superfluous apostrophes.)

(v) The *F* distribution is a combination of two independent χ^2 variables. Specifically if Z_1 and Z_2 are independent χ^2 variables with g_1 and g_2 degrees of freedom, respectively, then $F(g_1, g_2) = (Z_1/g_1)/(Z_2/g_2)$ has the *F* distribution with g_1 numerator degrees of freedom and g_2 denominator degrees of freedom. From the definition of the '*t*' and *F* distributions observe that $F(1, g_2) = {'t'}(g_2)^2$, that is the square of the '*t*' distribution with g_2 degrees of freedom is equal to the *F* distribution with 1 and g_2 degrees of freedom.

4.3 Estimation, estimators and estimates

In practice, as discussed in the introduction, the application of econometrics is much more than the estimation of unknown parameters in otherwise completely known specifications. A closer description of what econometrics is concerned with is that of model building and evaluation.

Nevertheless estimation is an important part of this process and it is natural to proceed first by assuming that the present situation just concerns a known specification apart from parameters, such as the coefficients of the CEF and the variance of Y_t. The task of estimation is to determine a rule or function that specifies the unknown parameters in terms of random variables or, exceptionally, fixed quantities, realisations of which are, in principle, observable. The bivariate case is considered in this section with Y_t and X_t random variables; the multivariate case is considered in Chapter 5.

This section introduces two important estimation rules: instrumental variables and ordinary least squares, often referred to as IV and OLS, respectively. In the bivariate model of this section – see (4.29) – the IV and OLS estimators coincide and we concentrate on the latter in this section. It will not always be the case that the IV and OLS estimators are the same and section **4.9** details an example. (An appendix describes the method of maximum likelihood estimation.)

4.3.1 The least squares principle

The problem considered here is to predict Y_t from a given X_t: what is the best predictor? The answer to this question depends in part upon how deviations from the true value are penalised. The deviation or prediction error as a random variable is denoted

$$\hat{\varepsilon}_t \mid X_t = Y_t - \hat{Y}_t \mid X_t \qquad (4.32)$$

where $\hat{Y}_t$ is the predicted value of Y_t. In general $\hat{Y}_t$ is a function of X_t, say $\hat{Y}_t = f(X_t)$; in the linear case $\hat{Y}_t = \hat{\beta}_1 + \hat{\beta}_2 X_t$, where $\hat{\beta}_1$ and $\hat{\beta}_2$ are estimators of β_1 and β_2, respectively. Note that the 'hat' notation, which places ˆ above a coefficient or variable, is reserved for the OLS principle.

One possible penalty function is the least squares penalty function; that is choose $\hat{Y}_t$ to minimise $E\{\hat{\varepsilon}_t^2 \mid X_t\}$. It turns out that whether or not $f(X_t)$ is linear, $E\{\hat{\varepsilon}_t^2 \mid X_t\}$ is minimised by choosing $\hat{Y}_t = E\{Y_t \mid X_t\}$; the least squares predictor of Y_t given X_t is the CEF (Goldberger 1991, p. 51). A simple extension of this result is that the least squares criterion applicable to the sequence of random variables $\hat{\varepsilon}_t^2$, $t = 1, \ldots, T$, that is $\sum_{t=1}^{T} E\{\hat{\varepsilon}_t^2\} = E\{\sum_{t=1}^{T} \hat{\varepsilon}_t^2\}$, is minimised by choosing $\hat{Y}_t = E\{Y_t \mid X_t\}$ for $t = 1, \ldots, T$. The CEF is assumed to be linear unless otherwise stated.

First, consider the generic problem of obtaining estimators of β_1 and β_2, say $\hat{\beta}_1$ and $\hat{\beta}_2$ with given x_t and Y_t a random variable. The following function is minimised to obtain the estimators:

$$\sum_{t=1}^{T} (\hat{\varepsilon}_t \mid x_t)^2 = \sum_{t=1}^{T} (Y_t - (\hat{\beta}_1 + \hat{\beta}_2 x_t))^2$$

$$\text{(4.33)}$$

The OLS residual is defined as $\hat{\varepsilon}_t \mid x_t = Y_t - (\hat{\beta}_1 + \hat{\beta}_2 x_t)$, and (4.33) is usually referred to as the residual sum of squares, RSS. For economy of notation, where no confusion is likely to arise, the explicit conditioning on x_t is omitted with the residual referred to as $\hat{\varepsilon}_t$.

The $\hat{}$ notation indicates that the function has been minimised and the resulting parameters, $\hat{\beta}_1$ and $\hat{\beta}_2$, are the least squares estimators. A necessary condition for minimisation is that the derivatives with respect to $\hat{\beta}_1$ and $\hat{\beta}_2$ are set to zero; that is

$$\frac{\partial \sum \hat{\varepsilon}_t^2}{\partial \hat{\beta}_1} = -2 \sum (\hat{\varepsilon}_t \mid x_t) = 0$$

$$= \sum (Y_t - \hat{\beta}_1 - \hat{\beta}_2 x_t) = 0 \quad \text{(4.34a)}$$

$$\frac{\partial \sum \hat{\varepsilon}_t^2}{\partial \hat{\beta}_2} = -2 \sum x_t(\hat{\varepsilon}_t \mid x_t) = 0$$

$$= \sum x_t(Y_t - \hat{\beta}_1 - \hat{\beta}_2 x_t) = 0 \quad \text{(4.34b)}$$

The second condition uses the function of a function rule. The derivative of $\hat{\varepsilon}_t^2$ is $2\hat{\varepsilon}_t$ and the

derivative of $\hat{\varepsilon}_t$ with respect to $\hat{\beta}_2$ is $-x_t$, hence, overall, the derivative is $-2x_t \sum \hat{\varepsilon}_t$.

To check that a minimum, rather than a maximum, has been achieved (4.34a) and (4.34b) are differentiated again to obtain

$$\frac{\partial \left(-2 \sum \hat{\varepsilon}_t \right)}{\partial \hat{\beta}_1}$$

$$= \frac{\partial}{\partial \hat{\beta}_1} \left(-2 \left(\sum Y_t - \hat{\beta}_1 - \hat{\beta}_2 x_t \right) \right)$$

$$= \frac{\partial}{\partial \hat{\beta}_1} \left(-2 \sum Y_t + 2T\hat{\beta}_1 + \hat{\beta}_2 \sum x_t \right)$$

$$= +2T > 0 \quad \text{(4.35a)}$$

$$\frac{\partial}{\partial \hat{\beta}_2} \left(-2 \sum x_t \hat{\varepsilon}_t \right)$$

$$= \frac{\partial}{\partial \hat{\beta}_2} \left(-2 \sum x_t(Y_t - \hat{\beta}_1 - \hat{\beta}_2 x_t) \right)$$

$$= \frac{\partial}{\partial \hat{\beta}_2} \left(-2 \sum x_t Y_t + 2\hat{\beta}_1 \sum x_t \right.$$

$$\left. + 2\hat{\beta}_2 \sum x_t^2 \right)$$

$$= +2 \sum x_t^2 > 0 \quad \text{(4.35b)}$$

Both derivatives are both positive as required for a minimum of the objective function.

Note that (4.34a) and (4.34b) imply the following.

(i) From (4.34a), $\sum (\hat{\varepsilon}_t \mid x_t) = 0$, the sum of the residuals, $\sum (Y_t - \hat{\beta}_1 - \hat{\beta}_2 x_t) = 0$.
(ii) From (4.34b), $\sum x_t(\hat{\varepsilon}_t \mid x_t) = 0$, the residuals are orthogonal to the regressor, that is $\sum x_t(Y_t - \hat{\beta}_1 - \hat{\beta}_2 x_t) = 0$.

Equations (4.34a) and (4.34b) are sometimes referred to as the normal equations. Notice that they are a pair of simultaneous equations, which can be solved for $\hat{\beta}_1$ and $\hat{\beta}_2$ as a function of Y_t

and x_t. To obtain the solutions, first solve for $\hat{\beta}_1$ conditional on $\hat{\beta}_2$ from (4.34a); that is

$$\sum (Y_t - \hat{\beta}_1 - \hat{\beta}_2 x_t) = 0 \Rightarrow$$

$$\sum Y_t - T\hat{\beta}_1 - \hat{\beta}_2 \sum x_t = 0 \Rightarrow$$

$$\hat{\beta}_1 = \bar{Y}_t - \hat{\beta}_2 \bar{x} \qquad (4.36)$$

Now from (4.34b), and substituting for $\hat{\beta}_1$, the solution for $\hat{\beta}_2$ is obtained:

$$\sum x_t (Y_t - \hat{\beta}_1 - \hat{\beta}_2 x_t) = 0 \Rightarrow$$

$$\sum x_t Y_t - \hat{\beta}_1 \sum x_t - \hat{\beta}_2 \sum x_t^2 = 0 \Rightarrow$$

$$\sum x_t Y_t - (\bar{Y}_t - \hat{\beta}_2 \bar{x}) \sum x_t$$

$$- \hat{\beta}_2 \sum x_t^2 = 0 \Rightarrow$$

$$\hat{\beta}_2 = \frac{\sum x_t Y_t - \bar{Y} \sum x_t}{\sum x_t^2 - \bar{x} \sum x_t} \qquad (4.37a)$$

$$= \frac{\sum (x_t - \bar{x})(Y_t - \bar{Y}_t)}{\sum (x_t - \bar{x})} \qquad (4.37b)$$

All summations are over $t = 1, \ldots, T$. (4.36) and (4.37a), or (4.37b), give the OLS estimators of β_1 and β_2.

(To show the equivalence of (4.37a) and (4.37b) first expand the numerator in (4.37b), that is:

$$\sum (x_t - \bar{x})(Y_t - \bar{Y})$$

$$= \sum x_t Y_t - \bar{x} \sum Y_t - \bar{Y} \sum x_t + T\bar{x}\bar{Y}$$

$$= \sum x_t Y_t - \bar{x} \sum Y_t$$

$$- \bar{Y} \sum x_t + T\bar{x} \sum Y_t/T$$

$$= \sum x_t Y_t - \bar{Y} \sum x_t$$

as required. Second, the denominator of (4.37b) is

$$\sum (x_t - \bar{x})(x_t - \bar{x}) = \sum x_t^2 - 2\bar{x}$$

$$\times \sum x_t + T\bar{x}^2$$

$$= \sum x_t^2 - \bar{x} \sum x_t$$

as required.)

Equations (4.36) and (4.37b) define estimators rather than estimates because even though x_t is fixed, Y_t is a random variable. Estimates of $\hat{\beta}_1$ and $\hat{\beta}_2$, denoted in **bold** for emphasis $\boldsymbol{\hat{\beta}_1}$ and $\boldsymbol{\hat{\beta}_2}$, respectively, for the purposes of this section only, result from a particular sample of realisations of the sequence of random variables $[Y_t]$, say $y_1, \ldots, y_T$. These numerical estimates are calculated from:

$$\boldsymbol{\hat{\beta}_1} = \bar{y} - \boldsymbol{\hat{\beta}_2}\bar{x} \quad \text{and} \quad \boldsymbol{\hat{\beta}_2} = \frac{\sum (x_t - \bar{x})(y_t - \bar{y})}{\sum (x_t - \bar{x})^2}$$

and the estimated (or fitted) value of y_t is given by

$$\hat{y}_t = \boldsymbol{\hat{\beta}_1} + \boldsymbol{\hat{\beta}_2} x_t \qquad (4.38)$$

The sample residuals are defined by $\hat{\varepsilon}_t = y_t - \hat{y}_t$ for $t = 1, \ldots, T$, and $\sum \hat{\varepsilon}_t^2$ is the sample residual sum of squares (SRSS).

The mean of the fitted values equals the sample mean of the realisations of Y_t, implying that the mean of the residuals is zero. Second, from (4.34b), observe that the product of x_t and the OLS residuals, $\hat{\varepsilon}_t$, from a particular sample is zero. This implies that

$$\sum (x_t - \bar{x})(\hat{\varepsilon}_t - \bar{\hat{\varepsilon}})$$

$$= \sum (x_t - \bar{x})\hat{\varepsilon}_t \quad \text{because } \bar{\hat{\varepsilon}}_t = 0 \quad (4.39a)$$

$$= \sum x_t \hat{\varepsilon}_t \quad \text{because } \bar{x} \sum \hat{\varepsilon}_t = 0 \quad (4.39b)$$

but this is zero by (4.34b) applied to a particular sample. This is an important property of OLS estimation mimicking the population property that the covariance of X_t and ε_t is zero. Thus minimisation of the RSS in a particular sample implies $\sum \hat{\varepsilon}_t = 0$ and $\sum x_t \hat{\varepsilon}_t = 0$. Indeed in this case we could have started from the principle that we want to match the moment properties in the population that $E\{\varepsilon_t\} = 0$ and $Cov\{X_t, \varepsilon_t\} = 0$, and then derived estimators that matched these properties in the sample.

A useful way of rewriting (4.37b) is to define the following set of (fixed) weights:

$$w_t = \frac{(x_t - \bar{x})}{\sum (x_t - \bar{x})^2} \quad \text{for} \quad t = 1, \ldots, T \quad (4.40)$$

There are two properties of w_t that are useful for later.

(i) $\sum w_t = 0$ and (ii) $\sum w_t x_t = 1$

The first,

$$\sum w_t = \frac{\sum (x_t - \bar{x})}{\sum (x_t - \bar{x})^2} = 0,$$

follows because

$$\sum (x_t - \bar{x}) = \sum x_t - T \sum x_t / T = 0$$

The second,

$$\sum w_t x_t = \frac{\sum (x_t - \bar{x}) x_t}{\sum (x_t - \bar{x})^2} = 1,$$

follows because the denominator $\sum (x_t - \bar{x})^2 = \sum (x_t - \bar{x}) x_t$ using $\bar{x} \sum (x_t - \bar{x}) = 0$.

In terms of the weights the OLS estimator of β_2 is:

$$\hat{\beta}_2 = \sum w_t (Y_t - \bar{Y})$$
$$= \sum w_t Y_t - \bar{Y} \sum w_t$$
$$= \sum w_t Y_t \quad (4.41)$$

For the estimate of $\hat{\beta}_2$:

$$\hat{\beta}_2 = \sum w_t y_t \quad (4.42)$$

It is apparent that $\hat{\beta}_2$ and $\hat{\beta}_2$ are linear functions of Y_t and y_t, respectively, since the weights w_t are fixed. For this reason $\hat{\beta}_2$ ($\hat{\beta}_2$) is said to be a linear estimator (estimate) of β_2. From (4.36) it is evident that if $\hat{\beta}_2$ is a linear estimator then so is $\hat{\beta}_1$. This use of 'linear' is separate and should be distinguished from the concept of a linear CEF.

To make it apparent that the realisations of Y_t (and y_t) are conditional on the realisations of the sequence of values of X_t it is sometimes useful to emphasise this by writing $\hat{\beta}_2 = \sum w_t(Y_t \mid x)$ or $\hat{\beta}_2 = \sum w_t(y_t \mid x)$, as the case may be, where $X = X_1, \ldots, X_T$ and $x = x_1, \ldots, x_T$.

4.3.2 Instrumental variables estimation

Consider the bivariate regression model:

$$Y_t = \beta_1 + \beta_2 X_t + \varepsilon_t$$

We assume this is a CEF, and if X_t was observed would cause no problems in estimation. However, suppose X_t is not directly observed but has a measurement counterpart, X_t^*, which is observed and has the property that is the true value plus a measurement error v_t. A leading economic example is where X_t is 'permanent income' and X_t^* is measured income. Then

$$X_t^* = X_t + v_t \quad (4.43)$$

Substituting this relationship into the CEF we obtain:

$$Y_t = \beta_1 + \beta_2(X_t^* - v_t) + \varepsilon_t$$
$$Y_t = \beta_1 + \beta_2 X_t^* + (\varepsilon_t - \beta_2 v_t) \quad (4.44)$$
$$Y_t = \beta_1 + \beta_2 X_t^* + \eta_t$$

Where $\eta_t = (\varepsilon_t - \beta_2 v_t)$; this disturbance is now a composite comprising the original innovation minus a function of the measurement error.

The disturbance is no longer orthogonal to the regressor X_t^*. Assume, for simplicity, that the measurement error, v_t, has a zero mean and is uncorrelated with ε_t and X_t, and ε_t and X_t are uncorrelated, then

$$\begin{aligned}
\text{Cov}(X_t^*, \eta_t) &= E\{(X_t^* - \bar{X}^*)\eta_t\} \\
&= E\{(X_t^* - \bar{X}^*)(\varepsilon_t - \beta_2 v_t)\} \\
&= E\{(X_t - \bar{X}_t + v_t)(\varepsilon_t - \beta_2 v_t)\} \\
&= E\{-\beta_2 v_t^2\} = -\beta_2 \sigma_v^2 \neq 0
\end{aligned}$$

That is X_t^* and η_t are correlated because of the common measurement error component. The regression model (4.44) is not a CEF and estimation of it by OLS will not deliver estimates of the parameters of interest β_1 and β_2. (A review question is concerned with the bias in the OLS estimators.)

How do we make progress in this case? Presently we cannot satisfy the orthogonality condition because $\text{Cov}(X_t^*, \eta_t) \neq 0$ and we cannot observe X_t, although if we could it would satisfy the orthogonality condition $\text{Cov}(X_t, \varepsilon_t) = 0$. What is needed is some more information. One possibility is that there exists a variable Z_t, which is correlated with the unobservable X_t but uncorrelated with ν_t, so that $\text{Cov}(Z_t, X_t) \neq 0$ and $\text{Cov}(Z_t, \nu_t) = 0$. This variable will be termed an instrumental variable. Conditional on $Z_t = z_t$, and focusing on the observable equation (4.44), the analogue of $\text{Cov}(z_t, \nu_t) = 0$ in the sample is:

$$\sum z_t(Y_t - \tilde{\beta}_1 - \tilde{\beta}_2 x_t^*) = 0 \qquad (4.45a)$$

We also require the sample to mimic the condition in the population that $E\{\varepsilon_t\} = 0$:

$$\sum \tilde{\varepsilon}_t = \sum (Y_t - \tilde{\beta}_1 - \tilde{\beta}_2 x_t^*) = 0 \qquad (4.45b)$$

Where, for example, the estimator has been denoted $\tilde{\beta}_2$ rather than $\hat{\beta}_2$ to distinguish the resulting IV estimator from the OLS estimator. Solving these two conditions (just as for (4.36) and (4.37)) for the unknowns $\tilde{\beta}_1$ and $\tilde{\beta}_2$ we obtain:

$$\tilde{\beta}_1 = \bar{Y} - \tilde{\beta}_2 \bar{x}^* \qquad (4.46a)$$

$$\tilde{\beta}_2 = \frac{\sum (z_t - \bar{z}_t)(Y_t - \bar{Y})}{\sum (z_t - \bar{z}_t)(x_t^* - \bar{x}^*)} \qquad (4.46b)$$

These are the instrumental variable(s), IV, estimators. IV estimation is a general principle of estimation, which is relevant in many areas of application (for example, especially in 'simultaneous equation' models – see, for example, section **4.9**).

The key point clearly relates to whether instrumental variables exist. In the present context there are, at least, two possibilities. The first is that a lagged value of X_t^*, say X_{t-1}^*, could be used. This is a valid choice if X_t^* is serially correlated, so X_{t-1}^* has predictive power for X_t^*, and provided the measurement errors are not serially correlated. For example, if $\nu_t = \rho\nu_{t-1} + \omega_t$ then X_{t-1}^* is not a valid instrument because it is correlated with ν_{t-1}. In practical cases, in the absence of further information, the default choice is often a lag of the 'problem' variable. In this case consideration could also be given to whether a measure of wealth could be the instrumental variable. A further example of IV estimation is given in section **4.9**.

4.4 Properties of estimators

An important part of econometric theory concerns the properties of estimators, in turn these properties assist in discriminating among alternative estimators which are alike in some characteristics but not in others. The properties considered here are bias, consistency, asymptotic bias and efficiency. For a more rigorous discussion of these and related topics see Davidson (1994) and Amemiya (1985).

4.4.1 Bias

Let $\hat{\theta}(T)$ be an estimator of the parameter θ based on a sample of T observations. $\hat{\theta}(T)$ is said to be unbiased if its expectation, $E\{\hat{\theta}(T)\}$, is equal to θ. If there is no qualification to the word unbiased then $\hat{\theta}(T)$ is unbiased whatever the sample size T. The bias of an estimator is defined as

$$\text{bias}(\hat{\theta}(T)) = E\{\hat{\theta}(T)\} - \theta \qquad (4.47)$$

That is, the bias of an estimator is the expected value of the estimator minus the population (true) value of the parameter.

4.4.2 Consistency

Consistency and asymptotic bias are large sample properties of an estimator; by allowing $T \to \infty$ the *asymptotic* properties of the estimator can be studied. A consistent estimator is defined as follows:

an estimator $\hat{\theta}(T)$ of θ is consistent if

$$\text{plim } \hat{\theta}(T) = \theta \text{ as } T \to \infty \qquad (4.48)$$

The expression plim $\hat{\theta}(T)$ as $T \to \infty$ refers to the probability limit of the random variable $\hat{\theta}(T)$. For simplicity, the reference $T \to \infty$ is often omitted when writing 'plim'.

4.4.2a Examples

While much estimation theory is concerned with continuous random variables it is often helpful initially to consider some simple examples, first with discrete nonstochastic variables and then with discrete random variables. For example, consider the infinite sequence

$$c^0, c^1, c^2, c^3, \ldots, c^T, \ldots, \quad \text{for } c \geq 0$$

The limiting value in this sequence as $T \to \infty$ depends upon the value of c; for example,

$$\lim(c^T) = \infty \quad \text{for } c > 1$$
$$\lim(c^T) = 0 \quad \text{for } 0 < c < 1$$

The notation lim is short for 'in the limit as T tends to infinity'. In this case c is a fixed constant; if c is greater than 1 then c^T tends to infinity as $T \to \infty$; if c is between zero and 1 then c^T tends to zero as $T \to \infty$. If $c = 1$, $c^T = 1$, whatever the value of T.

Suppose now that $\hat{\theta}(T)$ is a random variable with the following (two) discrete outcomes and probabilities:

$$\hat{\theta}(T) = \theta \quad \text{with probability } (T-1)/T$$
$$\hat{\theta}(T) = T \quad \text{with probability } 1/T$$

What is the probability limit – or plim – of $\theta(T)$? As T increases the probability of outcome $\hat{\theta}(T) = \theta$ becomes ever more likely while that of $\hat{\theta}(T) = T$ becomes even less likely: in the limit $\hat{\theta}(T)$ converges on θ which is said to be the probability limit – or plim – of $\hat{\theta}(T)$. That is:

$$\text{plim } \hat{\theta}(T) = \theta$$

When this condition is satisfied the estimator is said to be consistent.

Notice that while $\hat{\theta}(T)$ in the last example is consistent it is not unbiased. For example, for $T = 10$,

$$E\{\hat{\theta}(10)\} = \theta(\tfrac{9}{10}) + 10(\tfrac{1}{10}) = 0.9\theta + 1 \neq \theta$$

$$(4.49)$$

and the bias is

$$\text{bias}(\hat{\theta}(10)) = (0.9\theta + 1) - \theta$$
$$= -0.1\theta + 1 \qquad (4.50)$$

The bias, however, gets smaller in absolute value as the sample size increases. For $T = 100$

$$E\{\hat{\theta}(100)\} = 0.99\theta + 1 \qquad (4.51)$$

and, therefore,

$$\text{bias}(\hat{\theta}(100)) = -0.01\theta + 1 \qquad (4.52)$$

In this example even though the first term on the right-hand side of (4.52) becomes negligible in the limit, the second term does not and so the bias remains asymptotically. An estimator that is consistent but asymptotically biased is said to have second order bias.

4.4.2b Speed of convergence

Consider the sequence $\hat{\theta}(T) = \theta + bT^\alpha$, then α determines both whether θ is the limit of the sequence as $T \to \infty$ and the speed of divergence or convergence to the limit. For example, if $\alpha = 1$

then $\hat{\theta}(T) \to \infty$ as $T \to \infty$; similarly if $\alpha = 2$ then $\hat{\theta}(T) \to \infty$ as $T \to \infty$. In neither of these cases does $\hat{\theta}(T) \to \theta$, but the divergence is clearly faster for $\alpha = 2$. Next consider $\alpha = -1$, now $\hat{\theta}(T) \to \theta$ as $T \to \infty$, because $bT^{-1} \to 0$ as $T \to \infty$. Finally consider $\alpha = -2$, now it is also the case that $\hat{\theta}(T) \to \theta$ as $T \to \infty$ but, because $bT^{-2} \to 0$ more quickly than $bT^{-1} \to 0$, convergence is faster. While this discussion concerns a particular deterministic sequence it readily conveys the idea that another aspect of interest in describing deterministic or stochastic sequences is the speed of convergence (or divergence) of the sequence. To do this we introduce the O and o notation. The sequence $\hat{\theta}(T)$ is said to be at most of order T^{α} if $T^{-\alpha}\hat{\theta}(t)$ is bounded; this is written as $\hat{\theta}(T)$ is $O(T^{\alpha})$. If $\hat{\theta}(T) = \theta + bT^{\alpha}$ with $\alpha > 0$ then $T^{-\alpha}\hat{\theta}(T) = T^{-\alpha}\theta + b$, and as $T \to \infty$ then $T^{-\alpha}\theta(T) = b$, which is finite and so $T^{-\alpha}\hat{\theta}(T)$ is bounded. Notice that $\hat{\theta}(T)$ is not $O(T^{\alpha-1})$ because $T^{-(\alpha-1)}\hat{\theta}(t) = T^{-(\alpha-1)}\theta + bT$, which is not bounded as $T \to \infty$. If the sequence $T^{-\alpha}\hat{\theta}(T) \to 0$ as $T \to \infty$ then it is said to be of smaller order than T^{α}, written $o(T^{\alpha})$.

In more advanced texts a distinction is made between the notation for deterministic and random sequences and a subscript p is used for the latter. A formal definition is as follows: a stochastic sequence $\hat{\theta}(T)$ is $O_p(T^{\alpha})$ if $T^{-\alpha}\hat{\theta}(T)$ is bounded in probability as $T \to \infty$; that is there is a δ such that $\Pr[|T^{-\alpha}\hat{\theta}(T)| \le A_{\delta}] \ge 1 - \delta$. To interpret this definition suppose δ is small, say 0.01, then normalising (that is multiplying) the sequence $\hat{\theta}(T)$ by $T^{-\alpha}$ means that its limit is bounded ($\le A_{\delta}$) with probability 0.99 ($= 1 - \delta$) as $T \to \infty$; and however small we choose δ a finite bound always exists with probability $1 - \delta$.

To see the importance of this definition note that many random variables that feature in econometric estimators are unbounded, for example the residual sum of squares $\sum_{t=1}^{T} \hat{\varepsilon}_t^2$, which is a random variable, is generally unbounded as $T \to \infty$. That is adding observations adds residuals, which are then squared and added to the sum. However, dividing by T, generally, results in the normalised (by T^{-1})

residual sum of squares being bounded. (Indeed this is closely related to the OLS estimator of the conditional variance of the regression.) In this case we say that $\sum_{t=1}^{T} \hat{\varepsilon}_t^2$ is $O_p(T)$.

Note that the order of a sequence can be negative, that is $\alpha < 0$. Consider two estimators of θ one biased, $\hat{\theta}_1(T)$, and the other unbiased, $\hat{\theta}_2(T)$, where $\hat{\theta}_1(T) = bT^{-1}$, $\hat{\theta}_2(T) = b(T-k)^{-1}$ and k is fixed. Then in the limit the ratio of these two is 1 because the fixed k becomes negligible as $T \to \infty$. Define the random variable $r(T)$ as the ratio of the two estimators minus 1, that is:

$$r(T) \equiv \frac{\hat{\theta}_1(T)}{\hat{\theta}_2(T)} - 1 = -\frac{k}{T}$$

The sequence is of order T^{-1}, that is $O_p(T^{-1})$, since $T^1 r(T) = -T(k/T) = -k$, which is finite and clearly bounded. (Note, obviously $T^1 = T$, but the superfluous power is written explicitly to link back to the general definition.) In intuitive terms this is telling us that the limit is being approached at the 'speed' $1/T$. Consider a variation on this example, suppose

$$\hat{\theta}_1(T) = b \frac{1}{T^{0.5}} \quad \text{and} \quad \hat{\theta}_2(T) = b \frac{1}{(T^{0.5} - k)}$$

then

$$r(T) \equiv \frac{\hat{\theta}_1(T)}{\hat{\theta}_2(T)} - 1 = -\frac{k}{T^{0.5}}$$

So as before the limit of the ratio of $\hat{\theta}_1(T)$ and $\hat{\theta}_2(T)$ is 1; however, the speed of convergence is slower, because the series is $O_p(T^{-0.5})$. To check note that $T^{0.5} r(T) = -k$, whereas T times $r(T) = -T(k/T^{0.5}) = -T^{0.5}k$ which is not bounded. The limit, although the same in both examples, is now approached more slowly in the second example.

Given two estimators of an unknown parameter θ, apart from the speed of convergence to θ, the one with the faster speed – or rate – of convergence would be preferred. The notion of a rate of convergence shows that consistency can be quite a weak property of an estimator. For example, if $\hat{\theta}(T)$ has the probability limit θ and is, say, $O(T^{-0.1})$ then it is consistent but increases in the sample size have relatively little impact. Alternatively if $\hat{\theta}(T)$ is $O_p(T^{-1.5})$ then convergence is fast. Typically, in econometrics with stationary variables, consistent estimators are $O_p(T^{-0.5})$. However, in some circumstances (with nonstationary variables) higher rates of convergence are obtained, and an estimator that approaches θ with a rate of convergence $O_p(T^{-1})$ is termed superconsistent, and hyperconsistent if the rate of convergence is $O_p(T^{-1.5})$.

The rate of convergence has another use. For a consistent estimator $\hat{\theta}(T)$ of θ the mass of probability converges on θ as $T \to \infty$, so that the difference $\hat{\theta}(T) - \theta$ converges to 0. However, from the definition of $O_p(T^{\alpha})$ we know that $T^{-\alpha}(\hat{\theta}(T) - \theta)$ is bounded so that even though $\hat{\theta}(T) - \theta$ tends to 0 with the mass of probability centred on this point, the normalised difference $T^{-\alpha}(\hat{\theta}(t) - \theta)$ has a distribution not a single point. The term $T^{-\alpha}$ is sometimes called the normaliser – see, for example, Hatanaka (1996, Chapter 4). Typically the normaliser is $T^{0.5}$ for many econometric estimators involving stationary variables and T for (some) nonstationary variables. Suppose we wanted to know if $\hat{\theta}(T) - \theta$ was normally distributed, then it would be useless to plot $\hat{\theta}(T) - \theta$ for increasing T because the mass of probability converges on 0 for a consistent estimator; what we need to consider is $T^{-\alpha}(\hat{\theta}(T) - \theta)$. For example, for a series of order $O_p(T^{-0.5})$ we consider $T^{0.5}(\hat{\theta}(T) - \theta)$, for a series of order $O_p(T^{-1})$ we consider $T(\hat{\theta}(T) - \theta)$ and for a series of order $O_p(T)$ we consider $T^{-1}(\hat{\theta}(T) - \theta)$.

4.4.3 Asymptotic bias

More formally the definitions of asymptotic expectation and asymptotic bias are as follows,

asymptotic expectation,

$$AE[\hat{\theta}(T)] = \lim E\{\hat{\theta}(T)\} \quad \text{as } T \to \infty \quad (4.53)$$

In words, the asymptotic expectation is the limit as $T \to \infty$ of the expectation of $\hat{\theta}(T)$. The definition of asymptotic bias then follows naturally as,

asymptotic bias,

$$AB[\hat{\theta}(T)] = \lim E\{\hat{\theta}(T)\} - \theta \quad \text{as } T \to \infty$$
$$(4.54)$$

An unbiased estimator is also asymptotically unbiased but this reverse is not necessarily true. For example, suppose the previous example is modified so that

$$\hat{\theta}(T) = \theta \quad \text{with probability } (T - 1)/T$$
$$\hat{\theta}(T) = T^{\frac{1}{2}} \quad \text{with probability } 1/T$$

then
$$\begin{aligned} E\{\hat{\theta}(T)\} &= \theta(T - 1)/T + T^{\frac{1}{2}}/T \\ &= \theta - \theta/T + (1/T^{\frac{1}{2}}) \quad (4.55a) \end{aligned}$$

and the small sample bias is

$$\begin{aligned} E\{\hat{\theta}(T)\} - \theta &= \theta - \theta/T + (1/T^{\frac{1}{2}}) - \theta \\ &= -\theta/T + (1/T^{\frac{1}{2}}) \quad (4.55b) \end{aligned}$$

However, in the limit:

$$\lim E\{\hat{\theta}(T)\} = \theta$$

So as $T \to \infty$, $E\{\hat{\theta}(T)\} \to \theta$ and $\hat{\theta}(T)$ is asymptotically unbiased; however, its small sample bias is $-(\theta/T) + (1/T^{\frac{1}{2}})$. Notice that the 'speed' at which the bias is removed depends upon the square root of the sample size T.

There is an alternative definition of asymptotic expectation to be found in the literature. For example, Amemiya (1985, pp. 93–95) defines the asymptotic expectation of the random variable $\hat{\theta}(T)$ as $\int_{-\infty}^{\infty} \hat{\theta} \, dF(\hat{\theta})$, where $F(\hat{\theta})$ is the limiting distribution function. In some cases, the example in the text being one of them, the definitions will differ in their implications. In Amemiya's definition $\hat{\theta}(T)$ is unbiased. The definition in the text seems widely accepted – see Dhrymes (1970, pp. 86–90) and, more recently, Hendry (1995, pp. 714–715).

4.4.4 Efficiency

Efficiency refers to the variance of an estimator. An estimator with a smaller variance is said to be more efficient than one with a larger variance. Usually the comparison between variances is made within a particular class of estimator. For example, two estimators that are alike in some properties, say in a lack of bias or consistency, can then be compared in terms of their respective variances. Usually, within a class, the estimator with the smaller variance is preferred as its distribution is more tightly concentrated about the true value of the parameter.

4.4.5 Linearity

Linearity has already been briefly discussed in connection with the specification of a CEF. Linearity as a property of an estimator, which should be distinguished from linearity of the CEF, refers to the structure of an estimator in terms of the random variables $Y_1, \ldots, Y_t$. Consider $\hat{\beta}_2$ from equation (4.41), that is:

$$\hat{\beta}_2 = \sum w_t Y_t$$

where $w_t = \dfrac{(x_t - \bar{x})}{\sum (x_t - \bar{x})^2}$

Note that $\hat{\beta}_2$ is a weighted function of Y_t with weights, w_t, which are not a function of Y_t. Hence $\hat{\beta}_2$ is said to be linear in Y_t, $t = 1, \ldots, T$.

4.5 Properties of the OLS estimators $\hat{\beta}_1$ and $\hat{\beta}_2$

The properties of the OLS estimators $\hat{\beta}_1$ and $\hat{\beta}_2$ are considered in this section. It should be clear now that $\hat{\beta}_1$ and $\hat{\beta}_2$ are random variables, which

depend in principle upon the joint distribution of the sequences of random variables $[Y_t] = [Y_1, Y_2, \ldots, Y_T]$ and $[X_t] = [X_1, X_2, \ldots, X_T]$. To focus ideas consider $\hat{\beta}_2$. We first obtain the expectation and bias of $\hat{\beta}_2$ conditional on $X = x$, where $x = [x_1, x_2, \ldots, x_T]$, and then obtain the unconditional expectation and bias of $\hat{\beta}_2$.

4.5.1 Conditionally and unconditionally unbiased

Conditional on $X = x$, $\hat{\beta}_2$ is a linear function of Y_t with fixed weights given by w_t in (4.40). Notice that the conditioning also affects Y_t since $Y_t \mid x = \beta_1 + \beta_2 x_t + \varepsilon_t \mid x$ and $E\{Y_t \mid x\} = \beta_1 + \beta_2 x_t$. The expectation of $\hat{\beta}_2$ conditional on x is

$$E\{\hat{\beta}_2 \mid x\} = E\left\{ \sum w_t(Y_t \mid x) \right\}$$
$$= \sum w_t E\{(Y_t \mid x)\} \tag{4.56}$$

The last line uses the property that the expectation operator is linear, together with the fact that the weights, w_t, are fixed for given $X = x$. To continue substitute $E\{Y_t \mid x\} = \beta_1 + \beta_2 x_t$ into (4.56) to obtain:

$$E\{\hat{\beta}_2 \mid x\} = \sum w_t(\beta_1 + \beta_2 x_t)$$
$$= \beta_1 \sum w_t + \beta_2 \sum w_t x_t \tag{4.57}$$

Note that $\sum w_t = 0$ and $\sum w_t x_t = 1$, therefore

$$E\{\hat{\beta}_2 \mid x\} = \beta_2 \tag{4.58}$$

Conditional on $X = x$, $\hat{\beta}_2$ is unbiased for all sample sizes; it is, therefore, also consistent and asymptotically unbiased. (Goldberger (1991, p. 141) points out a subtlety often overlooked in these proofs, namely that the conditioning is initially on the complete set of realisations. That is, in evaluating $E\{\hat{\beta}_2 \mid X = x\}$ we implicitly use $E\{Y_t \mid x\} = E\{Y_t \mid x_t\}$; this follows from the assumptions that each sequence of Y_t and X_t is iid.)

Now consider $\hat{\beta}_1$. Recall that, conditional on $X = x$,

$$\hat{\beta}_1 \mid x = (\bar{Y} \mid x) - \hat{\beta}_2 \bar{x} \qquad (4.59)$$

Therefore,

$$E\{\hat{\beta}_1 \mid x\} = E\{\bar{Y} \mid x\} - \bar{x} E\{\hat{\beta}_2 \mid x\} \qquad (4.60)$$

To evaluate $E\{\bar{Y} \mid x\}$ note that

$$\bar{Y} \mid x = \sum Y_t/T = \beta_1 + \beta_2 \bar{x} + \sum (\varepsilon_t \mid x)/T \qquad (4.61)$$

hence,

$$E\{\bar{Y} \mid x\} = \beta_1 + \beta_2 \bar{x} + E\left\{\sum (\varepsilon_t \mid x)/T\right\}$$
$$= \beta_1 + \beta_2 \bar{x} + T^{-1} \sum E\{(\varepsilon_t \mid x)\}$$
$$= \beta_1 + \beta_2 \bar{x} \quad \text{using } E\{(\varepsilon_t \mid x)\} = 0 \qquad (4.62)$$

Substituting (4.62) into (4.60) gives:

$$E\{\hat{\beta}_1 \mid x\} = \beta_1 + \beta_2 \bar{x} - \beta_2 \bar{x}$$
$$= \beta_1 \qquad (4.63)$$

Therefore, $\hat{\beta}_1$ is also conditionally unbiased, consistent and asymptotically unbiased.

So far the expectations of $\hat{\beta}_1$ and $\hat{\beta}_2$ have been evaluated conditional on $X = x$, for example $E\{\hat{\beta}_2 \mid x\}$ is the conditional expectation of $\hat{\beta}_2$ given $X = x$. This conditioning is relaxed if $E\{\hat{\beta}_2 \mid x\}$ is evaluated across all possible realisations of X, the notation for which is $E_x\{E\{\hat{\beta}_2 \mid X\}\}$. As the conditional expectation of $\hat{\beta}_2$ is just β_2, which is not a function of X, then trivially:

$$E_x\{E\{\hat{\beta}_2 \mid X\}\} = E_x\{\beta_2\}$$
$$= \beta_2 \qquad (4.64)$$

$\hat{\beta}_2$ is unconditionally unbiased. By similar reasoning $\hat{\beta}_1$ is also unconditionally unbiased.

4.5.2 Minimum variance in the class of linear unbiased estimators

If the DGP and the regression model are the same, the OLS estimators $\hat{\beta}_1$ and $\hat{\beta}_2$ are conditionally and unconditionally unbiased. They are also linear estimators in the sense defined earlier. However, there are many other linear unbiased estimators and a natural question then arises as to whether within this class of estimators the OLS are to be preferred. The answer to this question is usually formulated in what is known as the Gauss–Markov theorem, which states that within the class of linear unbiased estimators the OLS estimators are efficient in the sense that no other estimator has a smaller variance than the OLS estimator. These properties give rise to the acronym BLUE, which stands for Best (minimum variance), Linear, Unbiased, Estimator. This section contains a derivation of the variances of $\hat{\beta}_1$ and $\hat{\beta}_2$, and a proof that the OLS estimator $\hat{\beta}_2$ has minimum variance in the class of linear unbiased estimators.

(Coincidence of the DGP and the regression model is actually a sufficient rather than a necessary condition for $\hat{\beta}_1$ and $\hat{\beta}_2$ to be unbiased. For example, omission of a variable, which is in the DGP but which is orthogonal to the included regressors, will not affect the bias property. Also it is assumed here that X_t is not a lagged value of Y_t.)

It should be clear now that $\hat{\beta}_1$ and $\hat{\beta}_2$ are random variables. Even with X_t fixed, Y_t is a random variable with pdf, $f(y_t \mid x_t)$, defined by the univariate conditional distribution. As $\hat{\beta}_1$ and $\hat{\beta}_2$ are linear functions of Y_t, the properties of the latter are transmitted to the former. Different sample realisations from the sequence of random variables $[Y_t]$, with $[X_t]$ fixed, will give rise to different numerical values of $\hat{\beta}_1$ and $\hat{\beta}_2$. It is instructive to think of how this theoretical framework is mimicked in a simulation experiment where the DGP is known, the distributions of the random variables are specified and there is repeated sampling according to the specified distribution(s). Suppose M samples are drawn and in each case $\hat{\beta}_2$ is calculated according to the estimator rule, then, provided M is sufficiently large, the properties of $\hat{\beta}_2$ should become apparent. For example, if the regression model and the DGP are the same, the mean of $\hat{\beta}_2$ over the M samples should be close to $\hat{\beta}_2$. The simulation set-up could also be used to compare different estimators. For example, if $\tilde{\beta}_2$ is another linear unbiased estimator, $\hat{\beta}_2$ and $\tilde{\beta}_2$ could be compared in terms of the variances of $\hat{\beta}_2$ and $\tilde{\beta}_2$. In the case of OLS estimators in a linear regression model the relevant results can be obtained analytically, but the simulation approach is still intuitively useful and is considered further in Chapter 8.

4.5.2a The variance of $\hat{\beta}_2$

We start with the variance of $\hat{\beta}_2$ conditional on $X = x$:

$$\text{Var}(\hat{\beta}_2 \mid x) = \text{Var}\left(\sum w_t (Y_t \mid x) \right)$$

using

$$\hat{\beta}_2 \mid x = \sum w_t (Y_t \mid x)$$

It will be helpful in obtaining this variance first to take some simple examples. If $T = 2$ then:

$$
\begin{aligned}
\text{Var}(\hat{\beta}_2 \mid x) &= \text{Var}(w_1(Y_1 \mid x) + w_2(Y_2 \mid x)) \\
&= w_1^2 \text{Var}(Y_1 \mid x) + w_2^2 \text{Var}(Y_2 \mid x) \\
&\quad + 2w_1 w_2 \text{Cov}(Y_1, Y_2 \mid x)
\end{aligned}
$$

We have made use of rules 3 and 7 of section **3.4.5** on combining random variables. If $T = 3$ then:

$$
\begin{aligned}
\text{Var}(\hat{\beta}_2 \mid x) &= \text{Var}(w_1 Y_1 + w_2 Y_2 + w_3 Y_3) \\
&= \sum_{t=1}^{3} w_t^2 \text{Var}(Y_t \mid x) \\
&\quad + 2w_1 w_2 \text{Cov}(Y_1, Y_2 \mid x) \\
&\quad + 2w_1 w_3 \text{Cov}(Y_1, Y_3 \mid x) \\
&\quad + 2w_2 w_3 \text{Cov}(Y_2, Y_3 \mid x)
\end{aligned}
$$

Now we can move to the general result:

$$
\begin{aligned}
\text{Var}(\hat{\beta}_2 \mid x) &= \sum_{t=1}^{T} w_t^2 \text{Var}(Y_t \mid x) \\
&\quad + \sum_{t=1}^{T} \sum_{s \neq t}^{T} w_t w_s \text{Cov}(Y_t, Y_s \mid x) \\
&= \sum_{t} w_t^2 \text{Var}(Y_t \mid x)
\end{aligned}
\tag{4.65}
$$

The last line follows the previous one as we are assuming that Y_t and Y_s for $t \neq s$ have a zero covariance. Independence, which occurs if Y_t and Y_s are jointly normally distributed with zero covariance, is sufficient but not necessary for this assumption to hold.

$\text{Var}(Y_t \mid x)$ is the variance of Y_t conditional on $X = x$; as X varies this defines the conditional variance function, $\text{CVF} \equiv \text{Var}(Y_t \mid X)$. An important special case is when the CVF is constant whatever the value of X; this is the homoscedastic case with $\text{Var}(Y_t \mid X) = \sigma^2$, a constant. On the assumption of homoscedasticity, the conditional variance of $\hat{\beta}_2$ is:

$$
\begin{aligned}
\text{Var}(\hat{\beta}_2 \mid x) &= \sum_{t=1}^{T} w_t^2 \sigma^2 \\
&= \sigma^2 \sum_{t=1}^{T} w_t^2
\end{aligned}
\tag{4.66}
$$

From the definition of w_t

$$
\begin{aligned}
\sum w_t^2 &= \sum \left(\frac{(x_t - \bar{x})}{\sum (x_t - \bar{x})^2} \right)^2 \\
&= \left(\frac{\sum (x_t - \bar{x})^2}{\left(\sum (x_t - \bar{x})^2 \right)^2} \right) \\
&= \left(\frac{1}{\sum (x_t - \bar{x})^2} \right)
\end{aligned}
\tag{4.67}
$$

Therefore the variance of $\hat{\beta}_2$ conditional on $X = x$ is:

$$\text{Var}(\hat{\beta}_2 \mid x) = \sigma^2 \left(\frac{1}{\sum (x_1 - \bar{x})^2} \right) \qquad (4.68)$$

The conditional variance of $\hat{\beta}_2$ is σ^2 divided by the sum of squared deviations of x_t in the sample.

4.5.2b   The variance of $\hat{\beta}_1$

For the conditional variance of $\hat{\beta}_1$ start with

$$\hat{\beta}_1 = \bar{Y} - (\hat{\beta}_1 \mid x)\bar{x}$$

and

$$\text{Var}(\hat{\beta}_1 \mid x) = \text{Var}(\bar{Y}) - \bar{x}^2 \, \text{Var}(\hat{\beta}_2 \mid x) \qquad (4.69)$$

because $\bar{x}$ is a constant

$$= \frac{\sigma^2}{T} + \sigma^2 \bar{x}^2 \left(\frac{1}{\sum (x_t - \bar{x})^2} \right)$$

$$= \sigma^2 \left[\frac{1}{T} + \bar{x}^2 \left(\frac{1}{\sum (x_t - \bar{x})^2} \right) \right]$$

$$(4.70)$$

The derivation in the line following (4.69) uses the following result:

$$\text{Var}(\bar{Y}) = \text{Var}\left[\frac{\sum Y_t}{T} \right]$$

$$= \frac{1}{T^2} \text{Var}\left(\sum Y_t \right)$$

$$= \frac{1}{T^2} T\sigma^2$$

$$= \frac{1}{T} \sigma^2$$

The third line makes use of the assumptions of homoscedasticity and zero covariance between Y_t and Y_s for $t \neq s$.

The constant σ^2 is generally unknown, so operational expressions for $\text{Var}(\hat{\beta}_1 \mid x)$ and $\text{Var}(\hat{\beta}_2 \mid x)$ require an estimator of σ^2. An (unbiased) estimator of σ^2 is given by

$$\hat{\sigma}^2 = \frac{\sum \hat{\varepsilon}_t^2}{(T - k)} \qquad (4.71)$$

where k is the number of regressors including the constant; in the bivariate regression $k = 2$. $\hat{\sigma}$, the square root of $\hat{\sigma}^2$, also known as the estimated standard error of the equation, is routinely reported in econometric software programs.

With $\hat{\sigma}^2$ replacing σ^2, given a particular set of sample realisations, (4.70) and (4.68) are operational expressions for the conditional variances of $\hat{\beta}_1$ and $\hat{\beta}_2$. The square roots of these expressions are the respective estimated standard errors, the numerical counterparts of which are routinely reported with the estimates of $\hat{\beta}_1$ and $\hat{\beta}_2$ in econometric software packages. These are referred to below as $\hat{\sigma}(\hat{\beta}_1)$ and $\hat{\sigma}(\hat{\beta}_2)$, respectively. In the (unlikely) event that σ^2 is known, the standard errors are referred to as $\sigma(\hat{\beta}_1)$ and $\sigma(\hat{\beta}_2)$, respectively.

4.5.2c   The unconditional variances of $\hat{\beta}_1$ and $\hat{\beta}_2$

The variances in (4.68) and (4.70) are, as the notation makes clear, the variances conditional on $X = x$. These are the variances, the square roots of which (that is the standard errors) are reported in econometric software programs, and form the basis of inference for Z and 't' statistics.

If the conditioning is relaxed the unconditional variances are obtained. In the classical linear regression model, used in many introductory econometric texts, the regressor X_t (or set of regressors in the multiple regression model) is fixed in repeated samples, and is, therefore, a nonstochastic variable. In that special case the conditional and unconditional variances are the same. However, an essential part of the framework used here is to regard Y_t and X_t as being jointly distributed random variables and, hence, the unconditional variance is not the same as the conditional variance. The unconditional variance of $\hat{\beta}_2$ is

$$\text{Var}(\hat{\beta}_2) = E_x\{\text{Var}(\hat{\beta}_2 \mid X)\}$$

where the subscript indicates that expectations are taken across X. Continuing

$$\text{Var}(\hat{\beta}_2) = E_x\left\{\sigma^2\left(\frac{1}{\sum (X_t - \bar{X})^2}\right)\right\}$$

$$\text{Var}(\hat{\beta}_2) = E_x\left\{\frac{\sigma^2/T}{S_x^2}\right\}$$

$$= \frac{\sigma^2}{T} E_x\left\{\frac{1}{S_x^2}\right\} \qquad (4.72)$$

where $S_x^2 = \sum (X_t - \bar{X})^2/T$

For $\text{Var}(\hat{\beta}_1)$ we obtain

$$\text{Var}(\hat{\beta}_1) = E_x\{\text{Var}(\hat{\beta}_1 \mid X)\}$$

$$= E_x\left\{\frac{\sigma^2}{T} + \sigma^2\bar{X}^2\left(\frac{1}{\sum (X_t - \bar{X})^2}\right)\right\}$$

$$= \frac{\sigma^2}{T}\left(1 + E_x\left\{\frac{\bar{X}^2}{S_x^2}\right\}\right) \qquad (4.73)$$

An assumption implicit in this derivation which will turn out to have wider consequences in later chapters is that $[X_t]$, and $[Y_t]$, are sequences of stationary random variables. This assumption is necessary to give a meaning to S_x^2 as an estimator of the variance of X_t, and to $\bar{X} = \sum X_t/T$ as an estimator of the mean of X_t, for $t = 1, \ldots, T$. Second order stationarity requires that both the mean and variance are constant. The unconditional variances are generally *not* reported in econometric software programs. They could be calculated in Monte Carlo simulations, where the $[X_t]$ process could be specified as part of the data generation process.

4.5.2d The Gauss–Markov theorem

The Gauss–Markov theorem states that the OLS estimators, $\hat{\beta}_1$ and $\hat{\beta}_2$, are best linear unbiased, which gives rise to the acronym BLUE (best linear unbiased estimator). That is in the class of linear unbiased estimators the OLS estimators have minimum variance, and hence are best. Linearity and unbiasedness have already been noted. The property of minimum variance, which is considered here, completes the proof. We will concentrate on the proof for $\hat{\beta}_2$. The proof is not difficult, but without the use of matrix algebra it is quite lengthy; nevertheless, the steps involved are simple and follow through logically.

First define an arbitrary linear unbiased estimator $\check{\beta}_2$:

$$\check{\beta}_2 \mid x = \sum a_t Y_t \qquad (4.74)$$

The idea being that the OLS estimator $\hat{\beta}_2$ will arise as a special case of the general linear unbiased estimator. To establish the conditions which ensure $\check{\beta}_2$ is unbiased, substitute for $Y_t = \beta_1 + \beta_2 x_t + \varepsilon_t \mid x$ to obtain:

$$\check{\beta}_2 \mid x = \sum a_t(\beta_1 + \beta_2 x_t + \varepsilon_t \mid x)$$

$$= \beta_1 \sum a_t + \beta_2 \sum a_t x_t$$

$$+ \sum a_t(\varepsilon_t \mid x) \qquad (4.75)$$

and taking expectations

$$E\{\check{\beta}_2 \mid x\} =$$

$$E\left\{\beta_1 \sum a_t + \beta_2 \sum a_t x_t + \sum a_t(\varepsilon_t \mid x)\right\}$$

$$= \beta_1 \sum a_t + \beta_2 \sum a_t x_t$$

$$+ \sum a_t E\{(\varepsilon_t \mid x)\}$$

$$= \beta_1 \sum a_t + \beta_2 \sum a_t x_t$$

$$\text{because } E\{(\varepsilon_t \mid x)\} = 0 \quad (4.76)$$

Unbiasedness requires $E\{\breve{\beta}_2 \mid x\} = \beta_2$, which will be satisfied if and only if $\sum a_t = 0$ and $\sum a_t x_t = 1$. Imposing these conditions on (4.75) then

$$\breve{\beta}_2 \mid x - \beta_2 = \sum a_t(\varepsilon_t \mid x) \qquad (4.77)$$

Hence,

$$\text{Var}(\breve{\beta}_2 \mid x) = E\left\{\left[\sum a_t(\varepsilon_t \mid x)\right]^2\right\} \qquad (4.78)$$

For a comparison with $\hat{\beta}_2$ it is useful to define the weights as $a_t = w_t + v_t$, that is the OLS weights, w_t, plus any difference, v_t. The conditions for unbiasedness in $\breve{\beta}_2$ are then

$$\sum a_t = \sum (w_t + v_t) = 0$$
$$\Rightarrow \sum v_t = 0 \quad \text{as} \quad \sum w_t = 0, \text{ and}$$
$$\sum a_t x_t = \sum (w_t + v_t)x_t = 1$$
$$\Rightarrow \sum v_t x_t = 0 \quad \text{as} \quad \sum w_t x_t = 1$$

Another preliminary step is to express $\hat{\beta}_2$ in a convenient way, that is:

$$\hat{\beta}_2 \mid x = \sum w_t Y_t$$
$$= \sum w_t(\beta_1 + \beta_2 x_t + \varepsilon_t \mid x)$$
$$= \beta_2 + \sum w_t(\varepsilon_t \mid x_t)$$
$$\text{using} \sum w_t = 0$$
$$\text{and} \sum w_t x_t = 1 \qquad (4.79)$$

Hence,

$$\hat{\beta}_2 \mid x - \beta_2 = \sum w_t(\varepsilon_t \mid x) \qquad (4.80)$$

and

$$\text{Var}(\hat{\beta}_2 \mid x) = E\{[(\hat{\beta}_2 \mid x) - \beta_2]^2\}$$
$$= E\left\{\left[\sum w_t(\varepsilon_t \mid x)\right]^2\right\}$$
$$\text{using (4.80)} \qquad (4.81)$$

Returning to $\breve{\beta}_2$ the aim is to express $\text{Var}(\breve{\beta}_2 \mid x)$ in terms of $\text{Var}(\hat{\beta}_2 \mid x)$ and a difference, which can be signed. To this end note that

$$\text{Var}(\breve{\beta}_2 \mid x) = E\left\{\left[\sum a_t(\varepsilon_t \mid x)\right]^2\right\}$$
$$= E\left\{\left[\sum (w_t + v_t)(\varepsilon_t \mid x)\right]^2\right\}$$
$$= E\left\{\left[\sum w_t(\varepsilon_t \mid x)\right.\right.$$
$$\left.\left. + \sum v_t(\varepsilon_t \mid x)\right]^2\right\}$$
$$= E\left\{\left[\sum w_t(\varepsilon_t \mid x)\right]^2\right.$$
$$+ \left[\sum v_t(\varepsilon_t \mid x)\right]^2$$
$$+ 2\sum w_t(\varepsilon_t \mid x)$$
$$\left. \times \sum v_t(\varepsilon_t \mid x)\right\} \qquad (4.82a)$$

On multiplying out the terms inside $\{.\}$ in (4.82a), there will be some with equal subscripts, for example $w_1^2(\varepsilon_1 \mid x)^2$ in the first summation, $v_1^2(\varepsilon_1 \mid x)^2$ in the second summation and $w_1 v_1(\varepsilon_1 \mid x)^2$ in the third summation. There will also be terms with unequal subscripts, for example $w_2 w_1(\varepsilon_2 \mid x)(\varepsilon_1 \mid x)$ in the first summation, $v_2 v_1(\varepsilon_2 \mid x)(\varepsilon_1 \mid x)$ in the second summation and $w_2 v_1(\varepsilon_2 \mid x)(\varepsilon_1 \mid x)$ in the third summation. Taking the expectation of such terms, only those with equal subscripts will remain as the covariances, that is $E\{(\varepsilon_t \mid x)(\varepsilon_s \mid x)\} = E\{(\varepsilon_t \varepsilon_s \mid x)\}$ for $t \neq s$, are equal to zero. The last line, that is (4.82a), therefore, simplifies to:

$$\text{Var}(\breve{\beta}_2 \mid x) = E\left\{\sum w_t^2(\varepsilon_t \mid x)^2\right.$$
$$+ \sum v_t^2(\varepsilon_t \mid x)^2$$
$$\left. + 2\sum w_t v_t(\varepsilon_t \mid x)^2\right\}$$

$$= \text{Var}(\hat{\beta}_2 \mid x) + \sigma^2 \sum v_t^2$$

$$+ 2E\left\{\sum w_t v_t (\varepsilon_t \mid x)^2\right\}$$

$$= \text{Var}(\hat{\beta}_2 \mid x) + \sigma^2 \sum v_t^2$$

$$+ 2\sigma^2 \sum w_t v_t$$

$$= \text{Var}(\hat{\beta}_2 \mid x) + \sigma^2 \sum v_t^2 \quad (4.82b)$$

The second line uses

$$E\left\{\sum w_t^2 (\varepsilon_t \mid x)^2\right\} = \sigma^2 \sum w_t^2 = \text{Var}(\hat{\beta}_2 \mid x)$$

and

$$E\left\{\sum v_t^2 (\varepsilon_t \mid x)^2\right\} = \sigma^2 \sum v_t^2.$$

The last line uses:

$$\sum w_t v_t = \sum v_t (x_t - \bar{x}) \bigg/ \sum (x_t - \bar{x})^2$$

$$= \sum v_t x_t \bigg/ \sum (x_t - \bar{x})^2$$

$$- \bar{x} \sum v_t \bigg/ \sum (x_t - \bar{x})^2$$

$$= 0 \quad \text{using} \ \sum v_t x_t = 0$$

$$\text{and} \ \sum v_t = 0$$

The interpretation of (4.82b) is straightforward. It states that the (conditional) variance of $\breve{\beta}_2$ is equal to the variance of the OLS estimator $\hat{\beta}_2$ plus a quadratic term $\sigma^2 \sum v_t^2$. This latter term will only be zero if and only if $v_t = 0$ for all t (assuming $\sigma^2 > 0$); but if that is the case then $\breve{\beta}_2$ and $\hat{\beta}_2$ are the same. Thus, in the class of linear unbiased estimators of β_2, the OLS estimator $\hat{\beta}_2$ achieves the minimum variance – in that sense it is best. (The proof that the OLS estimator of the constant, $\hat{\beta}_1$, is best is left to a review question.)

4.6 A nonlinear CEF

So far the CEF for Y_t has been assumed to be linear in the regression coefficients β_1 and β_2, and linear in variable X_t. The second assumption is easy to relax and is not fundamental to the derivation of the OLS estimators. For example, consider the following CEF that is nonlinear in X_t:

$$E\{Y_t \mid X_t\} = \beta_1 + \frac{\beta_2}{X_t} \quad (4.83a)$$

and conditioning on $X_t = x_t$

$$E\{Y_t \mid x_t\} + \frac{\beta_2}{x_t} \quad (4.83b)$$

This is nonlinear in x_t because the first derivative of $E\{Y_t \mid x_t\}$ with respect to x_t is a function of x_t, specifically:

$$\frac{\partial E\{Y_t \mid x_t\}}{\partial x_t} = -\frac{\beta_2}{x_t^2}$$

However, define $Z_t \equiv 1/X_t$, then the CEF is a linear function of $Z_t = z_t$. That is, conditioning on $Z_t = z_{1t}$

$$E\{Y_t \mid z_t\} = \beta_1 + \beta_2 z_t$$

$$\frac{\partial E\{Y_t \mid z_t\}}{\partial z_t} = \beta_2$$

which is not a function of z_t

Nonlinearity in β_1 and β_2 requires the development of other methods of estimation. First, note that a CEF which is nonlinear in the variables is not necessarily nonlinear in the coefficients. For example, $E\{Y_t \mid X_t\} = \beta_1 + \beta_2/X_t$ is linear in β_1 and β_2; the partial derivatives with respect to β_2 and β_2, respectively are 1 and $1/x_t$ and neither is a function of β_1 or β_2. However, consider the nonlinear CEF given by

$$E\{Y_t \mid X_t\} = \beta_1 + X_t^{\beta_2}$$

With β_2 unknown the CEF is nonlinear in X_t *and* nonlinear in β_2. It is still possible, though, to use the method of least squares to derive an estimator but in this case it will be a nonlinear least squares, NLLS, estimator. Define the residual sum of squares:

$$\sum \hat{\varepsilon}_t^2 = \sum (Y_t - \hat{\beta}_1 - X_t^{\hat{\beta}_2})^2$$

then

$$\frac{\partial \left(\sum \hat{\varepsilon}_t^2 \right)}{\partial \hat{\beta}_1} = -2 \sum \hat{\varepsilon}_t$$

and

$$\frac{\partial \left(\sum \hat{\varepsilon}_t^2 \right)}{\partial \hat{\beta}_2} =$$
$$- 2 \sum (X_t^{\beta_2} \ln X_t (Y_t - \hat{\beta}_1 - X_t^{\beta_2}))$$

The last line uses the result that the derivative of $X_t^{\beta_2}$ with respect to β_2 is $X_t^{\beta_2} \ln X_t$.

The first order conditions set these derivatives to zero giving a pair of nonlinear, rather than linear, equations to solve for $\hat{\beta}_1$ and $\hat{\beta}_2$ (a review question considers the second order conditions). The technical details, although not the principle, of the solution are beyond our scope here; interested readers should consult Hendry (1995, Chapter A5). In a later chapter we have occasion to estimate a nonlinear model and the estimation method is an application of NLLS. (Goldberger (1991, p. 143), shows that the NLLS and IV estimators will not always coincide when the CEF is nonlinear.)

4.7   Goodness of fit

The question of how well a regression fits often arises in empirical work, with much emphasis placed on obtaining a high sample R^2 (the coefficient of determination). This section reviews and evaluates some concepts of goodness of fit, and suggests that the importance of a high R^2 is often wrongly emphasised. An important distinction is between a measure of goodness of fit in the population, η^2, that is between the random variables Y_t and X_t, and in a particular sample, that is between realisations of the random variables denoted y_t and x_t, R^2.

4.7.1   Goodness of fit in the population, η^2

The starting point is the bivariate distribution of the random variables Y_t and X_t. For simplicity we assume that the CEF is linear and consider the analysis with X_t as the conditioning variable. First consider the linear CEF

$$E\{Y_t \mid X_t\} = \beta_1 + \beta_2 X_t$$

and

$$Y_t \equiv E\{Y_t \mid X_t\} + \varepsilon_t$$
$$= \beta_1 + \beta_2 X_t + \varepsilon_t$$

We are adopting the conventional shorthand of ε_t for $(\varepsilon_t \mid X_t)$. For later use in this section note that $Var(E\{Y_t \mid X_t\}) = \beta_2^2 Var(X_t)$. Now consider the variance of $Y_t = Var(E\{Y_t \mid X_t\} + \varepsilon_t)$:

$$Var(Y_t) = Var(E\{Y_t \mid X_t\})$$
$$+ Var(\varepsilon_t) + 2 Cov(E\{Y_t \mid X_t\}, \varepsilon_t)$$
$$(4.84)$$

Given that $Cov(X_t, \varepsilon_t) = 0$ the last term is zero – see (4.31) – and, therefore, (4.84) simplifies to

$$Var(Y_t) = Var(E\{Y_t \mid X_t\}) + Var(\varepsilon_t) \quad (4.85)$$

In words this says that the variance of Y_t can be 'decomposed' into the variance of the conditional expectation considered as a function of X_t and the variance of the innovation. In an appealing description $Var(E\{Y_t \mid X_t\})$ is the *regression variance* and $Var(\varepsilon_t)$ is the *innovation variance*. (In the classical linear regression model $Var(\varepsilon_t)$ is usually referred to as the 'disturbance' variance.)

Dividing (4.85) through by $\text{Var}(Y_t)$ gives:

$$1 = \frac{\text{Var}(E\{Y_t \mid X_t\})}{\text{Var}(Y_t)} + \frac{\text{Var}(\varepsilon_t)}{\text{Var}(Y_t)} \tag{4.86}$$

This shows how the *proportion* of the variance of Y_t is allocated or decomposed between the regression variance and the innovation variance. Now define

$$\eta^2 = \frac{\text{Var}(E\{Y_t \mid X_t\})}{\text{Var}(Y_t)} \tag{4.87}$$

and by a rearrangement of (4.86)

$$\eta^2 = 1 - \frac{\text{Var}(\varepsilon_t)}{\text{Var}(Y_t)} \tag{4.88}$$

η^2 is usually called the (population) coefficient of determination.

To see how a goodness of fit measure could be obtained consider the case when Y_t is mean independent of X_t. That is $E\{Y_t \mid X_t\} = E\{Y_t\}$, so the conditioning on X_t does not affect the mean of Y_t. Since $E\{Y_t\} = \mu_Y$, for all t, on the assumption that Y_t is, at least, first order stationary then $\text{Var}(E\{Y_t \mid X_t\}) = \text{Var}(E\{Y_t\}) = \text{Var}(\mu_Y) = 0$, because the variance of a constant is zero. Thus, when Y_t is mean independent of X_t, $\text{Var}(Y_t) = \text{Var}(\varepsilon_t)$, and the regression variance contributes nothing to accounting for the unconditional variance of Y_t and $\eta^2 = 0$.

Now consider how Y_t depending on X_t alters this decomposition and η^2. First, note that $E\{Y_t \mid X_t\} = E\{Y_t\}$ must imply $\beta_2 = 0$, hence now assume $\beta_2 \neq 0$. From the CEF for Y_t then $\text{Var}(E\{Y_t \mid X_t\}) = \beta_2^2 \text{Var}(X_t)$ and, therefore, (4.85) becomes

$$\text{Var}(Y_t) = \beta_2^2 \text{Var}(X_t) + \text{Var}(\varepsilon_t) \tag{4.89}$$

Now part of the variance of Y_t is accounted for by the variance of the CEF. In the limiting case all of the variance of Y_t is accounted for by the variance of the CEF and $\text{Var}(\varepsilon_t) = 0$ which, given that $E\{\varepsilon_t\} = 0$, implies that $\varepsilon_t = 0$. In this case $\eta^2 = 1$. However, note that all that is

required for the variance of $E\{Y_t \mid X_t\}$ to contribute to the variance of Y_t is that $\beta_2 \neq 0$ which will result in $0 < \eta^2 \leq 1$. (For more on the decomposition of the variance see Goldberger (1991), Greene (1997) and Rao (1973).) We could have also used the variance decomposition in the form $\text{Var}(Y_t) = \text{Var}(E\{Y_t \mid X_t\}) + E\{\text{Var}(Y_t \mid X_t)\}$; Goldberger (1991) shows that $\text{Var}(\varepsilon_t) = E\{\text{Var}(Y_t \mid X_t)\}$.)

Recall that ε_t can also be interpreted as the prediction error, that is $\varepsilon_t = Y_t - E\{Y_t \mid X_t\}$, with $\text{Var}(\varepsilon_t)$ the variance of the prediction error. In an appealing way the better the (conditional) predictions, $E\{Y_t \mid X_t\}$, in terms of squared error, ε_t^2, the better the goodness of fit. This motivates the interpretation of η^2 as a measure of the goodness of fit of the regression function. However, it can be quite misleading as to whether there is a relationship between Y_t and X_t: provided $\beta_2 \neq 0$ then $\eta^2 > 0$. A low value of η^2 is not by itself an indication there is no relation between Y_t and X_t in the population, this is a tempting but incorrect conclusion. What we can say is that η^2 is a useful indicator of the signal-to-noise ratio. Looking again at (4.86) we can interpret the first term as the relative 'signal' and the second term as the relative 'noise', that is

$$1 = \text{relative signal} + \text{relative noise}$$

where

$$\text{relative signal} = \frac{\text{Var}(E\{Y_t \mid X_t\})}{\text{Var}(Y_t)}$$

and

$$\text{relative noise} = \frac{\text{Var}(\varepsilon_t)}{\text{Var}(V_t)}.$$

A noisier, that is large, variance for $\text{Var}(\varepsilon_t)$, masks the signal from $E\{Y_t \mid X_t\}$.

4.7.2 Goodness of fit in the sample, R^2

A standard statistic reported with other regression details is R^2, defined precisely below. This is the sample coefficient of determination, which is often used as a measure of the goodness of fit of the *sample* regression. As such it is subject to the same caveat as the population coefficient of determination.

The derivation and interpretation of the sample (centred) R^2 is as follows where reference is to a sample or realised values of the random variables. First note that identically

$$\hat{\varepsilon}_t \equiv y_t - \hat{y}_t \qquad (4.90a)$$

or

$$y_t \equiv \hat{y}_t + \hat{\varepsilon}_t \qquad (4.90b)$$

The residual is defined as the actual minus the fitted value of y_t, where $\hat{y}_t = \hat{\beta}_1 + \hat{\beta}_2 x_t$. Subtracting $\bar{y}$, the sample mean of y_t for $t = 1, \ldots, T$, from both sides of (4.90b) and then squaring, gives:

$$(y_t - \bar{y})^2 = (\hat{y}_t - \bar{y})^2 \\ + \hat{\varepsilon}_t^2 + 2(\hat{y}_t - \bar{y})\hat{\varepsilon}_t \qquad (4.91)$$

This is the variation in a particular observation measured about the mean. Sum both sides, where the summation is over 1 to T,

$$\sum (y_t - \bar{y})^2 \equiv \sum (\hat{y}_t - \bar{y})^2 + \sum \hat{\varepsilon}_t^2 \\ + 2 \sum (\hat{y}_t - \bar{y})\hat{\varepsilon}_t \qquad (4.92)$$

The left-hand side is the total (sample) variation in y_t; and on the right-hand side this is decomposed into the variation of the fitted values plus the residual variation – that is the residual sum of squares – and a cross-product.

Provided that there is a constant in the regression the cross-product equals zero. Note that $\sum (\hat{y}_t - \bar{y})\hat{\varepsilon}_t = \sum \hat{y}_t \hat{\varepsilon}_t - \bar{y} \sum \hat{\varepsilon}_t = \sum \hat{y}_t \hat{\varepsilon}_t$, because $\sum \hat{\varepsilon}_t = 0$ from (4.34a). Further, $\sum \hat{y}_t \hat{\varepsilon}_t = \sum (\hat{\beta}_1 + \hat{\beta}_2 x_t)\hat{\varepsilon}_t = \hat{\beta}_1 \sum \hat{\varepsilon}_t + \hat{\beta}_2 \sum x_t \hat{\varepsilon}_t = 0$, this time using both first order conditions for a minimum, that is $\sum \hat{\varepsilon}_t = 0$ and $\sum x_t \hat{\varepsilon}_t = 0$, (4.34b).

Thus, if there is a constant in the regression, (4.92) becomes:

$$\sum (y_t - \bar{y})^2 \equiv \sum (\hat{y}_t - \bar{y})^2 + \sum \hat{\varepsilon}_t^2 \qquad (4.93)$$

and so the total variation is decomposed into the regression variation and the residual variation. Dividing through by $\sum (y_t - \bar{y})^2$ gives a relative decomposition

$$1 = \frac{\sum (\hat{y}_t - \bar{y})^2}{\sum (y_t - \bar{y})^2} + \frac{\sum \hat{\varepsilon}_t^2}{\sum (y_t - \bar{y})^2} \qquad (4.94)$$

Now define the sample coefficient of determination

$$R^2 = \frac{\sum (\hat{y}_t - \bar{y})^2}{\sum (y_t - \bar{y})^2} \qquad (4.95)$$

which is the ratio of the regression variation to the total variation, then

$$R^2 = 1 - \frac{\sum \hat{\varepsilon}_t^2}{\sum (y_t - \bar{y})^2} \qquad (4.96)$$

That is R^2 is one minus the ratio of the (sample) residual sum of squares to the total (sample) variation in y_t, with limits 0 and 1. The lower limit occurs when $\sum (\hat{y}_t - \bar{y})^2 = 0$, which is only satisfied for $\hat{y}_t - \bar{y}$ for all t, hence $\hat{\beta}_2 = 0$ and the fitted line is horizontal in the (y, x) plane. At the other extreme each residual must be zero, since then and only then will the sample residual sum of squares equal zero implying $R^2 = 1$. The goodness of fit interpretation of R^2 is motivated by noting that the smaller the residual sum of squares relative to the total variation, the less variation is left in the particular sample unaccounted for by the regression.

We highlight four areas of caution in interpreting R^2.

(i)   For the decomposition in (4.93) to be valid the regression has to include a constant. If this is not the case $\sum (\hat{y}_t - \bar{y})\varepsilon_t \neq 0$, and is only equal to zero by chance. Consider the bivariate regression without a constant, $y_t = \beta_2 x_t + \varepsilon_t$. Then minimising the residual sum of squares in a particular sample, $\sum \hat{\varepsilon}_t^2 = \sum (y_t - \hat{\beta}_2 x_t)^2$, gives the first order condition $-2\hat{\beta}_2 \sum x_t \hat{\varepsilon}_t = 0$, which implies, as when there is a constant, $\sum x_t \hat{\varepsilon}_t = 0$; however, it does not imply $\sum \hat{\varepsilon}_t = 0$. In this case the cross-product term in (4.92) becomes:

$$\sum (\hat{y}_t - \bar{y})\hat{\varepsilon}_t = \sum \hat{y}_t \hat{\varepsilon}_t - \bar{y} \sum \hat{\varepsilon}_t$$

$$= \hat{\beta}_2 \sum x_t \hat{\varepsilon}_t - \bar{y} \sum \hat{\varepsilon}_t$$

$$= -\bar{y} \sum \hat{\varepsilon}_t$$

Where the last line uses $\sum x_t \hat{\varepsilon}_t = 0$. So now R^2 is

$$R^2 = 1 - \frac{\sum \hat{\varepsilon}_t^2}{\sum (y_t - \bar{y})^2} - \frac{\bar{y} \sum \hat{\varepsilon}_t}{\sum (y_t - \bar{y})^2}$$

Comparing this with (4.96) observe that there is an extra term, which will only be zero by coincidence; thus, the exhaustive allocation of the total variation between the regression and the residual no longer holds. Without a constant in the regression, R^2 should not be interpreted as a measure of goodness of fit.

The usual alternative when a constant is not included is what is known as the *uncentred R^2*. By way of contrast, the previous definition referred to the *centred R^2* in the sense of subtracting the mean of the sample observations in defining the variation, $\sum (\hat{y}_t - \bar{y})^2$, to be accounted for by the regression. The derivation of the uncentred R^2 starts from

$$y_t \equiv \hat{y}_t + \hat{\varepsilon}_t \tag{4.97}$$

with

$$\sum y_t^2 \equiv \sum \hat{y}_t^2$$
$$+ \sum \hat{\varepsilon}_t^2 + 2 \sum \hat{y}_t \hat{\varepsilon}_t \tag{4.98}$$

But $\sum \hat{y}_t \hat{\varepsilon}_t = \hat{\beta}_2 \sum x_t \hat{\varepsilon}_t = 0$, from the first order condition for a minimum (4.34b), which holds whether or not there is a constant in the regression; therefore,

$$\sum y_t^2 = \sum \hat{y}_t^2 + \sum \hat{\varepsilon}_t^2 \tag{4.99}$$

and

$$1 = \frac{\sum \hat{y}_t^2}{\sum y_t^2} + \frac{\sum \hat{\varepsilon}_t^2}{\sum y_t^2} \tag{4.100}$$

Define the uncentred R^2 denoted R_{uc}^2:

$$R_{uc}^2 = \frac{\sum \hat{y}_t^2}{\sum y_t^2} = 1 - \frac{\sum \hat{\varepsilon}_t^2}{\sum y_t^2} \tag{4.101}$$

The uncentred R^2 is the sum of the squared fitted values divided by the sum of the squared y_t values. (A review question considers the limits of the uncentred R^2.)

(ii) Both versions of R^2 are not invariant to the definition of the dependent variable in the regression function. For example, suppose in the regression

$$Y_t = \beta_1 + \beta_2 x_{2t} + \beta_3 x_{3t} + \varepsilon_t \tag{4.102}$$

the sample data supports the hypothesis $\beta_2 = 1$ so that (4.102) is:

$$Y_t = \beta_1 + x_{2t} + \beta_3 x_{3t} + \varepsilon_t \tag{4.103a}$$

Then an equivalent formulation of the regression equation is

$$Y_t - x_{2t} = \beta_1 + \beta_3 x_{3t} + \varepsilon_t \tag{4.103b}$$

However, even though the regression models and coefficients are the same in equations (4.103a) and (4.103b), the R^2 will differ because in the former the dependent variable is y_t whereas in the latter it is $y_2 - x_{2t}$.

(iii) At best the interpretation of R^2 as a goodness of fit measure can be maintained in regression models with *stationary* random variables. When the random variables are nonstationary the regression R^2 is misleading. This is an issue that is considered in greater depth in Chapter 8.

(iv) R^2 is not a direct analogue of η^2. To see this compare

$$\eta^2 = 1 - \frac{\text{Var}(\varepsilon_t)}{\text{Var}(Y_t)}$$

and

$$R^2 = 1 - \frac{\sum \hat{\varepsilon}_t^2}{\sum (y_t - \bar{y})^2}$$

For a measure of the goodness of fit to be more directly motivated as the sample counterpart of η^2 we would need to replace $\text{Var}(\varepsilon_t)$ and $\text{Var}(Y_t)$ with their respective sample estimates. In the former case $\hat{\sigma}^2 = \sum \hat{\varepsilon}_t^2/(T - k)$ provides an unbiased estimator of $\text{Var}(\varepsilon_t)$; and in the latter case $\sum (Y_t - \bar{Y})^2/(T - 1)$ is an unbiased estimator of the (unconditional) variance of Y_t. Their sample counterparts are $\hat{\sigma}^2 = \sum \hat{\varepsilon}_t^2/(T - k)$, where $\hat{\varepsilon}_t$ is now interpreted as the sample residual, and $\sum (y_t - \bar{y})^2/(T - 1)$. Using these gives the following measure of goodness of fit.

$$\bar{R}^2 = 1 - \frac{\sum \hat{\varepsilon}_t^2 / (T - k)}{\sum (y_t - \bar{y})^2 / (T - 1)} \quad (4.104a)$$

$$\bar{R}^2 = 1 - \frac{\sum \hat{\varepsilon}_t^2}{\sum (y_t - \bar{y})^2} \frac{(T - 1)}{(T - k)} \quad (4.104b)$$

This measure is usually called the adjusted R^2, but is often motivated rather differently in introductory texts. Specifically, notice that R^2 cannot decrease if a variable is added to the regression and will usually increase. The logic of this is simple: OLS minimises the residual sum of squares. Adding another variable to a regression does not rule out achieving the previous value of the RSS, which can be obtained by setting the estimated coefficient on the new variable to zero,

and so getting exactly the same R^2. However, adding the variable allows the minimisation routine to add an extra dimension to its search for a minimum, if the estimated coefficient on the new variable is nonzero the RSS for the new regression must be smaller than for the original regression and so R^2 has increased.

So adding variables generally increases R^2 making the goodness of fit look better; effectively there is no 'penalty' cost to the new variables. $\bar{R}^2$ is one of a number of goodness of fit criterion that impose a penalty on adding variables. (See Goldberger (1991, p. 179) for an elaboration of these concepts.) Consider adding one variable to an already estimated regression with $k = 2$ variables then, in general, the sample residual sum of squares, $\sum \hat{\varepsilon}_t^2$, will decrease and so, *ceteris paribus*, $\bar{R}^2$ increases. However, to counter this increase, $1/(T - k)$ in the numerator of (4.104a) increases to $1/(T - k - 1)$ as a result of the additional variable in the regression. For example, suppose initially $\sum \hat{\varepsilon}_t^2 = 16$, with $T = 10$ and $k = 2$, then, in the numerator of (4.104a), $\sum \hat{\varepsilon}_t^2/(T - k) = 16/(10 - 2) = 2$. Suppose another variable is added to the regression and $\sum \hat{\varepsilon}_t^2$ declines to 15, then $\sum \hat{\varepsilon}_t^2/(T - k - 1) = 15/(10 - 3) = 2\frac{1}{7}$, so the smaller residual sum of squares is multiplied by a larger adjustment or penalty factor, the product increases and $\bar{R}^2$ declines. In general $\bar{R}^2$ may increase, stay the same or decline depending upon the balance of the two competing factors.

4.7.3 %$\hat{\sigma}$ as a measure of goodness of fit

In multiplicative models which are linear in the logarithms, an interesting interpretation can be attributed to $\hat{\sigma}$, the estimated standard error of the regression. Suppose the regression function in logarithms of the variables is

$$Y_t^* = \beta_1 + \beta_2 x_t^* + \varepsilon_t \quad (4.105)$$

where $Y_t^* = \ln(Y_t)$, $x_t^* = \ln(x_t)$ and logarithms are to the base e. In levels of the variables this model corresponds to

$$Y_t = e^{\beta_1} x_t^{\beta_2} e^{\varepsilon_t} \qquad (4.106)$$

and

$$Y_t = \hat{Y}_t e^{\hat{\varepsilon}_t} \qquad (4.107)$$

Where $\hat{Y}_t = e^{\hat{\beta}_1} x_t^{\hat{\beta}_2}$, which is the antilogarithm of the fitted value of Y_t from the regression (4.105). In passing, and because it is a frequently used feature of loglinear models, note that β_2 is the elasticity, E_{Yx} of Y_t with respect to x_t. This is simple to show:

$$E_{Yx} \equiv \frac{\partial Y_t}{\partial x_t} \frac{x_t}{Y_t} = \beta_2 e^{\beta_1} x_t^{\beta_2 - 1} e^{\varepsilon_t} \frac{x_t}{Y_t}$$

$$= \beta_2 \frac{Y_t}{x_t} \frac{x_t}{Y_t}$$

$$= \beta_2$$

To continue note from (4.107) that multiplying through by $e^{-\hat{\varepsilon}_t} Y_t^{-1}$ gives

$$e^{-\hat{\varepsilon}_t} = \frac{\hat{Y}_t}{Y_t} \qquad (4.108)$$

If $\hat{\varepsilon}_t$ is small then $e^{-\hat{\varepsilon}_t} \approx 1 - \hat{\varepsilon}_t$, therefore

$$1 - \hat{\varepsilon}_t \approx \frac{\hat{Y}_t}{Y_t} \qquad (4.109)$$

and

$$\hat{\varepsilon}_t \approx 1 - \frac{\hat{Y}_t}{Y_t}$$

$$= \frac{(Y_t - \hat{Y}_t)}{Y_t} \qquad (4.110)$$

Therefore $\hat{\varepsilon}_t$ can be interpreted as the *proportionate* residual, which is free of units and, hence, $100\hat{\varepsilon}_t$ is the percentage residual; for example, $\hat{\varepsilon}_t = 0.04$ indicates that the tth residual is (approximately) 4% of Y_t. The standard error of $\hat{\varepsilon}_t$ is also unit free and multiplied by 100 gives the % standard error of the regression, denoted %$\hat{\sigma}$. In loglinear models it is, therefore, sensible

to interpret %$\hat{\sigma}$ as a measure of the goodness of fit of the regression; given a particular sample, estimates replace estimators and the sample residuals are used to estimate $\hat{\sigma}$. Also as $\hat{\sigma}$ is invariant to linear reparameterisations, which change the dependent variable, it does not suffer from the drawback of R^2 which changes with linear reparameterisations.

4.8 Estimation of dynamic models

Dynamic models in the form of autoregressive distributed lag models were introduced in Chapter 2, and the importance of these models in empirical research was emphasised. The partial adjustment model, PAM, of (2.14), provides a simple illustration of a dynamic model that is

$$Y_t - Y_{t-1} = \delta(Y_t^* - Y_{t-1}) + \varepsilon_t \qquad (4.111)$$

(Upper case letters are used in this chapter to indicate reference to random variables rather than sample realisations.) A partial adjustment model is sometimes specified for stock variables, for example the stock of consumers' durables. Y_{t-1} is then the end-period stock for $t-1$ or, equivalently, the opening period stock for period t; in a PAM, Y_t adjusts from its opening period stock as a proportion δ of the difference between the target end-period stock, Y_t^*, and the opening period stock. If $\delta = 1$ there is full adjustment to the target otherwise, for $0 < \delta < 1$, adjustment is partial. To operationalise the model the target end-period stock, Y_t^*, has to be specified. For example, suppose $Y_t^* = \lambda_0 X_t$, where X_t is known, on substitution into (4.111) we obtain

$$Y_t = \beta_1 Y_{t-1} + \beta_2 X_t + \varepsilon_t \qquad (4.112)$$

with $\beta_1 = (1 - \delta)$ and $\beta_2 = \delta\lambda_0$. This is an example of an autoregressive distributed lag model, referred to as ADL(p, q), for the bivariate model, with $p = 1$ and $q = 0$.

Another type of dynamic model that occurs frequently in empirical work can be illustrated with a simple error correction model, usually referred to as an ECM. This has the form:

$$Y_t - Y_{t-1} = \theta_1 \Delta X_t$$
$$+ \theta_2(Y_{t-1} - Y_{t-1}^\star) + \varepsilon_t \quad (4.113)$$

The target value of Y_t is $Y_t^* = \lambda_0 X_t$ with X_t described as the 'forcing' variable, hence $Y_{t-1} - Y_{t-1}^*$ can be interpreted as lagged disequilibrium. For this reason the model is sometimes referred to as an equilibrium (rather than error) correction model, or EqCM; another description is that it is a model capturing differences plus differences from equilibrium giving rise to the acronym DDE. The acronym ECM is in widespread use, and we will use this in later chapters; however, the reader should be aware that the use of EqCM is gaining ground.

In an ECM the change in Y_t is related to last period's disequilibrium, with adjustment coefficient θ_2, and any changes induced by a change in the forcing variable between t and $t - 1$, with coefficient θ_1. Since the equation involves Y_{t-1}, X_t and X_{t-1} it is a reparameterisation of an ADL(1, 1) model.

Some of the differences between dynamic and static models can be illustrated with an AR(1) model given by

$$Y_t = \beta_2 + \beta_2 Y_{t-1} + \varepsilon_t \quad (4.114)$$

In terms of section **4.2** the genesis of (4.114) is the joint distribution of the random variables Y_t and Y_{t-1}, with pdf given by $f(y_t, y_{t-1})$. Given that Y_{t-1} precedes Y_t it seems natural to adopt Y_{t-1} as the conditioning variable, so that the joint pdf is factored as:

$$f(y_t, y_{t-1}) = f(y_t \mid y_{t-1}) f(y_{t-1})$$

That is the joint pdf is factored into the conditional pdf of Y_t given Y_{t-1} and the (marginal) pdf for Y_{t-1}. Assuming that Y_t and Y_{t-1} are

jointly normally distributed a linear CEF for Y_t conditional on Y_{t-1} follows. That is

$$E\{Y_t \mid Y_{t-1}\} = \beta_1 + \beta_2 Y_{t-1} \quad (4.115)$$

with innovation defined by

$$\varepsilon_t \mid Y_{t-1} = Y_t - E\{Y_t \mid Y_{t-1}\}$$
$$= Y_t - (\beta_1 + \beta_2 Y_{t-1}) \quad (4.116)$$

The regression coefficients are, as in section **4.2.2**, functions of the population variances and covariances. Recall that, generally, $\beta_1 = \mu_Y - \beta_2 \mu_X$ and $\beta_2 = \sigma_{XY}/\sigma_X^2$; in this case $X_t = Y_{t-1}$ so $\mu_Y = \mu_X$, σ_{XY} is the first order autocovariance $\gamma(1)$ and σ_X^2 is the zero order autocovariance denoted $\gamma(0)$. In these terms

$$\beta_1 = (1 - \beta_2)\mu_Y \quad \text{and} \quad \beta_1 = \gamma(1)/\gamma(0)$$

So far the statistical framework is, if anything, simpler than the previous case because it seems natural to condition the present, Y_t, on the past, Y_{t-1}.

One important difference of note between static and dynamic regression models concerns the properties of the OLS estimator, $\hat{\beta}_2$, of β_2. In the case of an autoregressive model, with or without additional variables, $\hat{\beta}_2$ is biased in small samples but consistent and asymptotically unbiased – see Goldberger (1991, sections 25.5 and 26.3). The small sample bias can be substantial – see Stine and Shaman (1989) – and this is an issue to which we return in Chapter 8.

4.9 Structure and regression

There is a rather obvious point about conditional expectation functions which has some important consequences for how to approach estimating the parameters of interest. This point is most simply illustrated in the bivariate case with random variables Y_t and X_t. From the joint distribution of Y_t and X_t it is possible to obtain two CEFs, namely $E\{Y_t \mid X_t\}$ and $E\{X_t \mid Y_t\}$. For example, if Y_t, consumption, and X_t, income, are bivariate-normally distributed then there is a linear CEF for consumption given income and a linear CEF for income given consumption. The choice, usually taken in applied work, to estimate the first of these rests upon economic theory which suggests that consumption is a function of income, otherwise *both* are valid CEFs.

This section introduces some important concepts and distinctions. The structure of an economic relationship may involve the joint determination of several variables; thus to analyse one separately (for example, Y_t) may be invalid in the sense of not locating the parameters of interest. In such a situation the OLS estimators may not have the properties attributed to them in the single equation case, and an alternative estimation method is required.

4.9.1 Weak exogeneity and the parameters of interest

Sometimes the dynamics of a particular example suggest a natural choice of the conditioning variable. For example, if, as in the previous section, Y_t and Y_{t-1} are bivariate-normally distributed then although it is possible to specify both $E\{Y_t \mid Y_{t-1}\}$ and $E\{Y_{t-1} \mid Y_t\}$, the natural order of time suggests that the former of these is likely to be of interest. As noted the expectation of Y_t being conditioned on the past event leads to

$$E\{Y_t \mid Y_{t-1}\} = \beta_1 + \beta_2 Y_{t-1}$$

The choice of CEF will also be guided by whether its parameters are the parameters of interest.

Consider the demand function which specifies the quantity demanded, Q_t^d, as a linear function of its own (relative) price, P_t, and a demand shock ε_{1t}.

$$Q_t^d = \beta_1 + \beta_2 P_t + \varepsilon_{1t} \tag{4.117}$$

In addition the market for this good clears so that the quantity supplied, Q_t^s, equals the quantity demanded, the transaction (or common) quantity is referred to without superscripts, that is Q_t. The demand function in the observable variables Q_t and P_t is:

$$Q_t = \beta_1 + \beta_2 P_t + \varepsilon_{1t} \tag{4.118}$$

Whether it is appropriate to condition Q_t on P_t in order to determine the parameters of interest β_1 and β_2 amounts to asking whether P_t is *weakly exogenous* for β_1 and β_2. Suppose the quantity supplied is, as in the simplest microeconomic model, also a function of price P_t and, say, an additional variable, R_t, which represents the climatic conditions. For convenience we write this relationship with P_t as the left-hand side variable in what is known as the inverse supply function:

$$P_t = \alpha_1 + \alpha_2 Q_t + \alpha_3 R_t + \varepsilon_{2t} \tag{4.119}$$

The stochastic specification is $\varepsilon_{1t} \sim (0, \sigma_1^2)$, $\varepsilon_{2t} \sim (0, \sigma_2^2)$ and $R_t \sim (\mu_R, \sigma_R^2)$ and, for simplicity, all pairwise correlations are assumed to be zero.

The CEF of (4.118) is

$$E(Q_t \mid P_t) = \beta_1^* + \beta_2^* P_t + \varepsilon_{1t} \tag{4.120}$$

with $\quad \beta_1^* = \mu_Q - \beta_2^* \mu_P \quad$ and $\quad \beta_2^* = \dfrac{\sigma_{PQ}}{\sigma_P^2}$

In order to obtain σ_{PQ} and σ_P^2 we first solve for what is known as the *reduced form* of Q_t and P_t. To obtain the solution of the simultaneous equations for Q_t and P_t, first substitute the expression for P_t into that for Q_t and simplify so that Q_t is on the left-hand side. Similarly substitute the equation for Q_t into that for P_t and simplify. The solutions are known as the *reduced form* equations. In this case they are:

$$Q_t = (\beta_1 + \beta_2 \alpha_1 + \beta_2 \alpha_3 R_t + \varepsilon_{1t} + \beta_2 \varepsilon_{2t})$$
$$/(1 - \alpha_2 \beta_2) \tag{4.121}$$

$$P_t = (\alpha_1 + \alpha_2 \beta_1 + \alpha_3 R_t + \alpha_2 \varepsilon_{1t} + \varepsilon_{2t})$$
$$/(1 - \alpha_2 \beta_2) \tag{4.122}$$

We are now in a position to obtain σ_{PQ} and σ_P^2:

$$\sigma_{PQ} = (\beta_2\alpha_3^2\sigma_R^2 + \alpha_2\sigma_1^2 + \beta_2\sigma_2^2)/(1 - \alpha_2\beta_2)^2 \tag{4.123}$$

$$\sigma_P^2 = (\alpha_3^2\sigma_R^2 + \alpha_2^2\sigma_1^2 + \sigma_1^2)/(1 - \alpha_2\beta_2)^2 \tag{4.124}$$

The covariance σ_{PQ} is obtained by multiplying Q_t in (4.121) by P_t in (4.122), and then taking the expectation of the product. Using (4.123) and (4.124) we obtain

$$\begin{aligned}
\beta_2^* &= \sigma_{PQ}/\sigma_P^2 \\
&= \frac{\beta_2\alpha_3^2\sigma_R^2 + \alpha_2\sigma_1^2 + \beta_2\sigma_2^2}{\alpha_3^2\sigma_R^2 + \alpha_2^2\sigma_2^2 + \sigma_2^2} \\
&= \beta_2 \frac{(\alpha_3^2\sigma_R^2 + \sigma_2^2)}{(\alpha_3^2\sigma_R^2 + \alpha_2^2\sigma_1^2 + \sigma_2^2)} \\
&\quad + \frac{\alpha_2\sigma_1^2}{(\alpha_3^2\sigma_R^2 + \alpha_2^2\sigma_1^2 + \sigma_2^2)} \\
&\neq \beta_2 \tag{4.125}
\end{aligned}$$

In general $\beta_2^* \neq \beta_2$; so if β_2 is a parameter of interest, which seems likely given that it is the price coefficient in the demand equation, we cannot learn about it from the regression of Q_t on P_t. (This problem also affects the constant in the regression $\beta_1^* = \mu_Q - \beta_2^*\mu_P \neq \beta_1$, where $\mu_Q = (\beta_1 + \beta_2\alpha_1 + \beta_2\alpha_3\mu_R)/(1 - \dot{\alpha}_2\beta_2)$ and $\mu_P = (\alpha_1 + \alpha_2\beta_1 + \alpha_3\mu_R)/(1 - \alpha_2\beta_2)$.)

It is instructive to consider what happens if $\alpha_2 = 0$. Then, in the inverse supply function, price is a function of climate, R_t, and not quantity, Q_t, and $\beta_2^* = \beta_2$; in this case P_t is determined by R_t and not simultaneously with Q_t. When it is possible to learn about the parameter of interest just from the CEF, here of Q_t conditioned on P_t, P_t is said to be weakly exogenous and, in effect, it can be ignored as far as estimation and inference on the parameters of interest are concerned. (For an extensive discussion of various concepts of exogeneity see Hendry (1995).)

4.9.2 Instrumental variables estimation

If β_1 and β_2 are the parameters of interest, then can progress be made in obtaining estimators which have some desirable properties? One possibility is the method of instrumental variables, IV, estimation – see section **4.3.2**.

In the system comprising the random variables Q_t, P_t and R_t we assume that it is valid to condition on R_t, although it is not valid to condition on P_t or Q_t. That is while the following conditioning is not valid

$$f(q_t, p_t, r_r) = f_1(q_t \mid p_t, r_t)f_2(p_t \mid r_t)f_3(r_t)$$

it is valid to consider

$$f(q_t, p_t, r_t) = f_0(q_t, p_t \mid r_t)f_3(r_t) \tag{4.126}$$

The last factorisation embodies the assumption that R_t is weakly exogenous for the parameters of interest. Alternatively R_t can be regarded as determined outside of the demand and supply equations. Given this status for R_t its covariance with ε_{1t} and ε_{2t} is zero, that is $\text{Cov}(R_t, \varepsilon_{1t})$ and $\text{Cov}(R_t, \varepsilon_{2t}) = 0$; in addition $E\{\varepsilon_{1t}\} = 0$ and $E\{\varepsilon_{2t}\} = 0$. The IV method exploits the analogy of making the corresponding sample quantities zero. For the first equation use is made of the sample analogues of $E\{\varepsilon_{1t}\} = 0$ and $\text{Cov}(R_t, \varepsilon_{1t}) = 0$, that is:

$$\sum_{t=1}^{T} \tilde{\varepsilon}_t = 0 \quad \text{and} \quad \sum_{t=1}^{T} r_t\tilde{\varepsilon}_t = 0$$

Using the first condition we obtain:

$$\begin{aligned}
\sum_{t=1}^{T} \tilde{\varepsilon}_t &= \sum_{t=1}^{T} (Q_t - \tilde{\beta}_1 - \tilde{\beta}_2 P_t) = 0 \\
&= \sum_{t=1}^{T} Q_t - T\tilde{\beta}_1 - \beta_2 \sum_{t=1}^{T} P_t = 0
\end{aligned}$$

This last condition solves for an estimator of β_1, that is

$$\tilde{\beta}_1 = \bar{Q} - \tilde{\beta}_2 \bar{P} \qquad (4.127a)$$

A particular estimate results from using sample values, distinguished by lower case letters for variables and **bold** for coefficients, that is:

$$\hat{\boldsymbol{\beta}}_1 = \bar{q} - \tilde{\boldsymbol{\beta}}_2 \bar{p} \qquad (4.127b)$$

The second condition, $\sum_{t=1}^{T} r_t \tilde{\varepsilon}_t = 0$, can be solved for an estimator, $\tilde{\beta}_2$, of β_2 and, given a sample of realisations, an estimate $\tilde{\boldsymbol{\beta}}_2$.

$$\sum_{t=1}^{T} r_t \tilde{\varepsilon}_t = \sum_{t=1}^{T} r_t (Q_t - \tilde{\beta}_1 - \tilde{\beta}_2 P_t) = 0$$

Expanding brackets and substituting for $\tilde{\beta}_1$ we obtain:

$$\sum_{t=1}^{T} r_t Q_t - (\bar{Q} - \tilde{\beta}_2 \bar{P}) \sum_{t=1}^{T} r_t - \tilde{\beta}_2 \sum_{t=1}^{T} r_t P_t$$

$$= \sum_{t=1}^{T} r_t Q_t - \bar{Q} \sum_{t=1}^{T} r_t$$

$$- \tilde{\beta}_2 \left(\sum_{t=1}^{T} r_t P_t - \bar{P} \sum_{t=1}^{T} r_t \right)$$

Setting the right-hand side to 0 and solving for $\tilde{\beta}_2$ gives:

$$\tilde{\beta}_2 = \frac{\displaystyle\sum_{t=1}^{T} r_t Q_t - \bar{Q} \sum_{t=1}^{T} r_t}{\displaystyle\sum_{t=1}^{T} r_t P_t - \bar{P} \sum_{t=1}^{T} r_t}$$

the estimator (conditional on $R_t = r_r$)

$$= \frac{\displaystyle\sum_{t=1}^{T} (r_t - \bar{r})(Q_t - \bar{Q})}{\displaystyle\sum_{t=1}^{T} (r_t - \bar{r})(P_t - \bar{P})} \qquad (4.128a)$$

$$\tilde{\beta}_2 = \frac{\displaystyle\sum_{t=1}^{T} r_t q_t - \bar{q} \sum_{t=1}^{T} r_t}{\displaystyle\sum_{t=1}^{T} r_t p_t - \bar{p} \sum_{t=1}^{T} r_t}$$

an estimate (with sample values of the variables)

$$= \frac{\displaystyle\sum_{t=1}^{T} (r_t - \bar{r})(q_t - \bar{q})}{\displaystyle\sum_{t=1}^{T} (r_t - \bar{r})(p_t - \bar{p})} \qquad (4.128b)$$

The last line follows from:

$$\sum (r_t - \bar{r})(q_t - \bar{q}) = \sum r_t q_t - \bar{r} \sum q_t$$

$$- \bar{q} \sum r_t + T \, \bar{r}\bar{q}$$

$$= \sum r_t q_t - \bar{r} \sum q_t - \bar{q}$$

$$\times \sum r_t + T\bar{r} \sum q_t / T$$

$$= \sum r_t q_t - \bar{q} \sum r_t$$

and use the same procedure for the denominator.

These expressions give IV estimators for β_1 and β_2 which are consistent but biased – see, for example, Goldberger (1991, p. 343), Judge et al. (1985, pp. 168–169).

The IV estimation principle does not in general provide unique estimators. Any choice of Z_t such that $\text{Cov}(Z_t, \varepsilon_t) = 0$ provides the basis of an IV estimator. Sometimes the structure of the problem suggests a 'natural' IV estimator. In the case of the two equations determining Q_t and P_t, the reduced form equation for P_t shows that P_t is a linear function of R_t, hence R_t seems an obvious choice as an instrumental variable for P_t. See Godfrey (1999) and Shea (1997) for further suggestions on choosing instruments.

Where the structure of an equation system is incomplete there may be no single obvious choice. For example, suppose that in the single equation model

$$Y_t = \beta_1 + \beta_2 X_t + \varepsilon_t$$

it is known that $\text{Cov}(X_t, \varepsilon_t) \neq 0$ but otherwise no further specification is known. As noted in section **4.3.2**, what is sought is an instrumental variable Z_t for X_t such that $\text{Cov}(Z_t, \varepsilon_t) = 0$ and $\text{Cov}(Z_t, X_t) \neq 0$. A common choice for Z_t is X_{t-p} for $p \geq 1$, that is lagged values of X_t, the argument being that as economic time series are generally highly autocorrelated, X_{t-p} has predictive power for X_t and, provided ε_t is not autocorrelated, is a valid instrument for X_t. If, for example, X_t and X_{t-1} are not autocorrelated, X_{t-1} is not a good instrument for X_t as $\text{Cov}(X_t, X_{t-1}) = 0$. Also X_{t-1} is, generally, not a good instrument for X_t if ε_t is autocorrelated. Suppose $\rho(1) \neq 0$ for the $[\varepsilon_t]$ sequence, then ε_t is correlated with ε_{t-1}, and as ε_{t-1} is a function of X_{t-1} (which is apparent on lagging the equation for Y_t), ε_t is correlated with X_{t-1}. A review question considers further the choice of instruments.

When there is just one violation of the orthogonality condition only one instrumental variable is required; however, there are situations where more than one may be available. Suppose that in the quantity–price example the inverse supply function also included a further variable, say F_t, for fertiliser, which was a valid conditioning variable. Then F_t is also a candidate instrumental variable, but the estimates of β_1 and β_2 alternatively using r_t and f_t will, save for a coincidence, differ. An alternative is to use a single instrumental variable formed by regressing P_t on R_t and F_t and using the estimated values of P_t. (A constant would also, generally, be included so that the regression is not forced through the origin.) This is the 'natural' choice given that the suggested regression is just the reduced form regression. In this situation the instrumental variable formed from the reduced form is the optimal choice in the sense of

minimising the variance of the estimators – see, for example, Greene (1997, Chapter 16).

Finally, it will not always be the case that empirical estimates of the parameters of interest can be retrieved from simultaneous systems such as the quantity–price example. In econometric textbooks this is referred to as the problem of identification (of the parameters of interest) a detailed treatment of which is beyond the scope of this book. However, we can gain some insight into the problem by considering the inverse supply function, in our example, with parameters α_1, α_2 and α_3. In contrast to the quantity equation we see that no instrumental variables are available within the system to remedy the problem caused by the correlation between Q_t and ε_{2t}. R_t is not a valid instrument because it already appears in the price equation. What is needed, but not specified in the original system, is a (valid conditioning) variable in the quantity equation which is not in the price equation. For example, if the quantity equation was originally misspecified and should have included, say, an income variable then that provides an instrumental variable for the price equation. In the terminology of the identification literature the price equation becomes *identified* by the inclusion of income in the quantity equation; previously it was *not identified*. This informal discussion suggests that in order for the parameters of interest to be identified, the quantity and price equations have to be distinct from each other. The quantity equation includes price and income and the price equation includes quantity and climate, the income and climate variables serve to distinguish the two equations. Indeed they are just distinguished from each other leading to the terminology that the respective parameters of interest are *just identified*. When the price equation is modified to include fertiliser, F_t, there is, in a sense, a choice of identifying variables (corresponding to the choice of instrumental variables) for the quantity equation which is now said to be *over-identified*.

4.10 Tests and associated concepts

Estimation is usually just part of an overall model-building process. Typically an initial specification is subject to alteration following tests of hypotheses which relate to (i) whether there is any indication that the empirical model is not adequate and (ii) whether (specification) hypotheses are consistent with the data. In the latter category there may be interest about a single parameter, linear combination of parameters or several linear combinations of parameters. The concern of this section is to establish a general framework for testing hypotheses. First, we establish some general principles and notation. In the discussion of this section we assume the existence of a statistical model which is congruent with the data (Hendry 1995).

4.10.1 Significance tests

The null hypothesis, usually denoted H_0, implies that some aspect of the distribution of Y_t is being specified. For example, the null hypothesis that, in the bivariate regression model, the coefficient $\beta_2 = 0$, implies that the expectation of the conditional distribution of Y_t given X equals the expectation of the marginal distribution of Y_t; that is conditioning on X_t does not affect the expectation of Y_t. A null hypothesis might also relate directly to the conditional distribution of Y_t; for example, it might be hypothesised that the distribution is normal.

In order to assess the consistency of the null hypothesis with the data we require a test statistic, in general denoted $TS(Y \mid X)$. The notation is explicit and perhaps initially cumbersome but this is necessary to establish the paradigm of hypothesis testing. As indicated here, TS is a function of the random variable Y conditional on X and hence is itself a random variable. The distribution of TS will, therefore, depend upon the distribution of Y conditional

on X. Further, according to the null hypothesis some aspect of the conditional distribution is restricted. If we are considering the distribution of $TS(Y \mid X)$ with the restriction(s) of the null hypothesis imposed, we refer to the distribution of the test statistic as being 'under the null hypothesis'. For the moment this is the only distribution which is specified. Given a sample of observations – or realisations – of Y and X the sample value of the test statistic can be calculated, this is denoted $ts(y, x)$ or, for simplicity, just ts; similarly TS will be used where there is no ambiguity.

Following Cox and Hinkley (1974), TS is a test statistic for H_0 if two conditions are satisfied:

(a) the distribution of TS under H_0 is known;
(b) the larger the value of ts or abs(ts) the greater the evidence of departure from H_0.

Where abs(w) is the absolute value of w (that is ignore the sign) which is used in this section rather than $|w|$ to avoid confusion with the conditioning statement.

The conditions do not, in general, lead to a unique test statistic for H_0. Under condition (b) we allow for the possibility that large positive or large negative values of ts indicate a departure from H_0. It might be that the particular circumstances of H_0 suggest that departures in one direction only are to be taken as evidence against H_0.

Given a particular sample value $ts(y, x)$ – or realisation – of the test statistic the one-sided and two-sided *marginal levels of significance* or p-values are defined as follows:

one-sided positive msl: $msl^+ = pr(TS \geq ts \mid H_0)$
one-sided negative msl: $msl^- = pr(TS \leq ts \mid H_0)$
two-sided msl: $msl = pr(abs(TS) \geq abs(ts) \mid H_0)$

These marginal significance levels are read and interpreted as follows: the one-sided positive marginal significance level is the probability under H_0 that the random variable TS is greater than or equal to the realisation of the test statistic. To illustrate this calculation suppose that under the null hypothesis TS is normally distributed with zero mean and unit variance and that the value of ts from a particular sample is $+1.96$. Then

$$\text{msl}^+ = \text{pr}(\text{TS} \geq +1.96 \mid \text{TS} \sim N(0, 1))$$
$$= 0.025 \quad \text{or } 2.5\%$$

and

$$\text{msl}^- = \text{pr}(\text{TS} \leq +1.96 \mid \text{TS} \sim N(0, 1))$$
$$= 0.975 \quad \text{or } 97.5\%$$

There is a 2.5% probability of TS being greater than or equal to $+1.96$ under the null hypothesis and a 97.5% probability of TS being less than or equal to 1.96 under the null hypothesis. Suppose now that $ts = -1.96$, which is the realised value of TS, then the one-sided negative msl, that is msl^-, is

$$\text{msl}^- = \text{pr}(\text{TS} \leq -1.96 \mid \text{TS} \sim N(0, 1))$$
$$= 0.025$$

and

$$\text{msl}^+ = \text{pr}(\text{TS} \geq -1.96 \mid \text{TS} \sim N(0, 1))$$
$$= 0.975$$

These values follow from the symmetry of the (standard) normal distribution about zero. The two-sided msl for $ts = \text{abs}(1.96)$ is

$$\text{msl} = \text{pr}\{\text{abs}(\text{TS}) \geq \text{abs}(1.96) \mid \text{TS} \sim N(0, 1)\}$$
$$= 0.025 + 0.025 = 0.05$$

There is a 5% chance that TS will be greater than or equal to $+1.96$ or less than or equal to -1.96.

Sometimes, as in the case of the standard F test statistic, described in detail in Chapter 5, which compares the residual sum of squares in a restricted and an unrestricted model, a test statistic is inherently two sided. Suppose, for example, a test statistic, TS, was defined which could take either negative or positive values with large abs(ts) indicating departures from the null hypothesis. Then defining a new test statistic $\tau = \text{TS}^2$ with corresponding realisations $(ts)^2$, τ would be inherently two sided, being unable to distinguish the direction of departure.

When the only distribution specified is that under H_0, the test for departures from H_0 using TS is known as a pure significance test. In this framework a large value of ts or abs(ts) is evidence of a departure from H_0 without itself indicating the nature of an alternative hypothesis which could satisfactorily account for the realised value of the test statistic. For example, a test of the normality of the distribution of Y_t could be based on measures of symmetry and kurtosis which are combined in the test statistic TS, large values of which indicate a departure from the null. However, the realised value of TS does not by itself have anything to say about the nature of the departure from the null, there being a plethora of distributions that are either or both asymmetric and skew. Pure tests of significance are rare in applied econometrics. Usually the direction of departure from the null is informed by economic theory, which then aids in the choice of an alternative hypothesis and test statistic. The next section illustrates this development.

Now consider the compatibility of H_0 with the sample evidence. A *critical value or values* are chosen which divide the distribution of H_0 under the null hypothesis into two kinds of region: *the nonrejection region and the rejection region*. Suppose that both large negative and large positive values of ts are evidence of departure from H_0 and that these 'large' values are treated equally irrespective of their sign. Then 'large' values of abs(ts) suggest rejection of H_0 while small values of abs(ts) suggest nonrejection. The chosen critical values are those associated with a reference value of the two-sided msl of the test. This reference value is usually denoted α and is called the significance level of the test; typical reference values are $\alpha = 0.01$, $\alpha = 0.05$ and $\alpha = 0.10$ (that is 1%, 5% and 10%). For example, if the test statistic is normally distributed with zero mean and unit variance under H_0, and $\alpha = 0.10$, then the two-sided critical values are ± 1.645. The rejection regions are $-\infty$ to -1.645 and $+1.645$ to ∞; a value of ts falling into these regions suggests the conclusion that H_0 is not compatible with the sample evidence – in a frequently used terminology the hypothesis is not consistent with the data. The nonrejection region is -1.645 to $+1.645$, and a value of ts in this region suggests that H_0 is not rejected; it does not, though, carry the implication that H_0 is accepted which is a much stronger conclusion. For example, suppose the test statistic is for the null hypothesis that a particular coefficient takes the value 1, and the test statistic falls in the nonrejection region. Then it is also likely that the hypothesis that the coefficient is $1 - \delta$, where δ is 'small', will also lead to nonrejection: accepting both null hypotheses is a contradiction, not rejecting both is, however, consistent.

If departures in one direction only are to be taken as evidence against H_0, there is just one critical value with a corresponding one-sided rejection region. For example, if as before $TS \sim N(0, 1)$ but only large positive values of ts are evidence against H_0 then keeping $\alpha = 0.10$ the critical value is $+1.28$, so the nonrejection region is $-\infty$ to $+1.28$ and the rejection region is $+1.28$ to $+\infty$. One of the problems with this approach is that the assessment of H_0 by the choice of the a reference value tells us very little about the *strength* of the rejection or nonrejection of H_0. A more attractive procedure is to assess the msl of sample test statistics. If large or small values of TS indicate departure from H_0 then it is much more informative to report the two-sided msl. For example, suppose $TS \sim N(0, 1)$ and $ts = 1.8$ then the two-sided msl is

$$pr(abs(TS) \geq 1.8 \mid H_0) = 2(0.0359)$$
$$= 0.0718 (=7.18\%)$$

This calculation tells us that the significance level at which we would just be indifferent between rejecting and not rejecting H_0 is 7.18%.

Had $\alpha = 0.05$ been adopted, H_0 would not have been rejected and we would not have known how close to rejection we were. This procedure is easily modified for departures in one direction. For example, if only large values of ts are taken as evidence against H_0, then report msl^+. In this case

$$msl^+ = pr(TS \geq 1.8 \mid H_0)$$
$$= 0.0359 (=3.59\%)$$

So the one-sided (positive) msl is just 3.59%: if the null hypothesis is true, the chance of observing a value of $ts = 1.8$ or greater is 3.59%.

4.10.2 The alternative hypothesis

As noted above it is not often the case that the model builder is just interested in a pure test of significance without the specification of an hypothesis that is an alternative to the null hypothesis. For example, in the bivariate regression model $Y_t = \beta_1 + \beta_2 X_t + \varepsilon_t$, where Y_t and X_t are consumption and income, respectively, interest is likely to centre on whether $\beta_2 > 0$ which will form an explicit alternative hypothesis to the null of $\beta_2 = 0$. Another possibility is the two-sided alternative that $\beta_2 \neq 0$. In each case the null hypothesis is a statement to the effect that Y_t and X_t are unrelated or more precisely that $E\{Y_t \mid X_t\} = E\{Y_t\}$, that Y_t is 'mean independent of X_t'; whereas the alternative hypothesis contradicts the null hypothesis. The alternative hypothesis is usually denoted H_a; for example, for the two-sided alternative $H_a: \beta_2 \neq 0$. According to the null hypothesis $E\{\hat{\beta}_2 \mid X\} = \beta_2 = 0$, that is the OLS estimator $\hat{\beta}_2$ is distributed about $\beta_2 = 0$. To proceed further we will need an assumption about the nature of this distribution, the most usual assumption being that $\hat{\beta}_2$ and $\hat{\beta}_1$ are normally distributed. Since $\hat{\beta}_2$ is a linear function of Y_t, that is $\hat{\beta}_2 = \sum w_t Y_t$, this assumption can be justified by the normality of Y_t.

To obtain a test statistic, TS, for the null hypothesis recall that a standardised random variable is obtained by subtracting the true value according to H_0, and dividing by the standard error of the random variable. Standardising $\hat{\beta}_2$ under the null hypothesis we obtain what is usually known as the Z statistic

$$Z = \frac{\hat{\beta}_2 - \beta_2 \mid H_0}{\sigma(\hat{\beta}_2)} = \frac{\hat{\beta}_2}{\sigma(\hat{\beta}_2)}$$

$$\text{given } H_0: \beta_2 = 0 \quad (4.129)$$

where $\sigma(\hat{\beta}_2)$ is the standard error of $\hat{\beta}_2$. The notation $\beta_2 \mid H_0$ indicates the value of β_2 under H_0. According to the null hypothesis $Z \sim N(0, 1)$ so we can tabulate the probability of abs$(Z) > c$ where c is an arbitrary constant. For example, from standard normal tables

$$\text{pr}(\text{abs}(Z)) > 1 = 0.1587(2) = 0.3174,$$

$$\text{pr}(\text{abs}(Z)) > 2 = 0.0228(2) = 0.0456$$

and

$$\text{pr}(\text{abs}(Z)) > 3 = 0.0013(2) = 0.0026.$$

It is clear from these probabilities that large values of abs(z), the sample value of abs(Z), are improbable if the null hypothesis is correct. The critical values associated with $\alpha = 0.05$ and $\alpha = 0.10$, for the two-sided alternative, are ± 1.96 and $+1.645$ respectively. If the sample value, abs(z), exceeds 1.96 the conclusion is that at the 5% significance level, the null hypothesis is rejected as not consistent with the data, against H_a: $\beta_2 \neq 0$. If $1.645 < \text{abs}(z) < 1.96$, the null hypothesis is rejected at $\alpha = 10\%$ but not at $\alpha = 5\%$. Generally it is more informative to report the msl of z or abs(z) rather than just assess it against a particular reference value of α.

When the standard error of $\hat{\beta}_2$ is unknown, $\sigma(\hat{\beta}_2)$ is replaced by its estimated standard error $\hat{\sigma}(\hat{\beta}_2)$. This change leads to the t statistic, 't'; that is

$$'t' = \frac{\hat{\beta}_2 - \beta_2 \mid H_0}{\hat{\sigma}(\hat{\beta}_2)} = \frac{\hat{\beta}_2}{\hat{\sigma}(\hat{\beta}_2)}$$

$$\text{if } \beta_2 = 0 \text{ under } H_0 \quad (4.130)$$

The 't' distribution has an extra parameter compared to the normal distribution, that parameter being the degrees of freedom, $T - k$, in the regression where k is the number of regressors including the constant. As $T - k$ increases the 't' distribution looks increasingly like the normal distribution but, otherwise, is 'flatter' than the normal with a greater mass in the tails of the distribution. This implies that, for a given level of significance, the critical values are larger, in absolute value, for the 't' distribution compared to the normal distribution. Intuitively, estimation of the standard error of β_2 implies that a greater range of values of the test statistic is consistent with the distribution of the test statistic under the null hypothesis. For example, suppose $T - k = 20$ then the 5% and 10% two-sided critical values are ± 2.086 and ± 1.725, respectively, compared to ± 1.96 and $+1.645$ from the normal distribution. Apart from the different distribution of the test statistic the testing procedure is as before with a preference to report the marginal significance level of a test statistic wherever possible.

The specification of the alternative as a one-sided rather than a two-sided hypothesis requires some care in deciding what is evidence against H_0. For example, when Y_t is consumption and X_t is income, economic theory suggests $\beta_2 > 0$ rather than $\beta_2 < 0$. Hence, rejection of the null hypothesis, $\beta_2 = 0$, comes from the alternative hypothesis that $\beta_2 > 0$, so 'large' positive values of Z, or 't', will lead to rejection of the null in the direction of the alternative hypothesis. For example, the 5% critical value arising from the right-hand, or positive, side of the normal distribution is $+1.645$. If $z > 1.645$ this is evidence, at the 5% significance level, against the null hypothesis; that is the data is more consistent with the view that $\beta_2 > 0$ than $\beta_2 = 0$. Again reporting the msl of a test statistic is to be preferred to simply reporting whether a null hypothesis has, or has not, been rejected at a particular significance level. Most econometric software routinely calculates the msl for an implicit two-sided rather than one-sided alternative. This does not present a problem, provided the realised value of the test statistic is on the side favouring the alternative, because symmetry of the distribution of the test statistic implies that the msl for the one-sided alternative is half the reported msl for the two-sided alternative. To illustrate, suppose, as before, that the realised value of Z is $z = 1.8$; then the two-sided marginal significance level of this test statistic is $0.0359(2) = 0.0718$, whereas the one-sided msl[+] is 0.0359. Notice that this implies that rejection of the null hypothesis is more likely for positive values of z (or 't' as the case may be).

If the null hypothesis suggests that a particular coefficient takes a value other than zero, the testing procedure is easily modified to take this into account. Suppose the null hypothesis is H_0: $\beta_2 = c$, where c is nonzero, then the modified Z and 't' statistics are:

$$Z = \frac{\hat{\beta}_2 - c}{\sigma(\hat{\beta}_2)} \quad \text{and} \quad 't' = \frac{\hat{\beta}_2 - c}{\hat{\sigma}(\hat{\beta}_2)}$$

With this change the testing procedure is as before. The same principle applies to a null hypothesis involving several coefficients. For example, suppose in the linear regression model given by

$$Y_t = \beta_1 + \beta_2 X_{t2} + \beta_3 X_{t3} + \varepsilon_t \quad (4.131)$$

Where Y_t is the log of output, X_{t2} and X_{t3} are the logs of capital and labour services, respectively, an hypothesis of interest is that there are constant returns to scale. This translates into the null hypothesis:

$$H_0: \beta_2 + \beta_3 = 1$$

The two-sided alternative is

$$H_a: \beta_2 + \beta_3 \neq 1$$

The 't' statistic is

$$'t' = \frac{(\hat{\beta}_2 + \hat{\beta}_3) - 1}{\hat{\sigma}(\hat{\beta}_2 + \hat{\beta}_3)} \quad (4.132)$$

where

$$\hat{\sigma}(\hat{\beta}_2 + \hat{\beta}_3)$$
$$= (\hat{\sigma}^2(\hat{\beta}_2) + \hat{\sigma}^2(\hat{\beta}_3) + 2\,\text{Côv}(\hat{\beta}_2, \hat{\beta}_3))^{\frac{1}{2}} \quad (4.133)$$

and $\text{Côv}(\hat{\beta}_2, \hat{\beta}_3)$ is the estimated covariance between $\hat{\beta}_2$ and $\hat{\beta}_3$.

4.10.3 Power

The sample realisation of a test statistic is an aid to taking a view about the consistency of an hypothesis and the data. In the usual approach, the framework for decision making involves setting up a null hypothesis about a coefficient or coefficients and assessing the data consistency of that hypothesis against an alternative that is less restrictive in at least one direction. For example, in the bivariate regression a null hypothesis was proposed which was 'simple' in the sense of concerning the single coefficient β_2, and the alternative hypothesis could be $\beta_2 \neq 0$ or either $\beta_2 < 0$ or $\beta_2 > 0$. The realised value of the test statistic would provide evidence from *one* sample as to the data consistency of the null hypothesis, with small values of the msl indicating a lack of consistency of the null hypothesis and data. In the event that a decision is made based on this procedure there are two errors that could be made, which are summarised below.

	Decision	
	Do not reject H_0	Reject H_0
H_0 correct	Confidence level $= 1 - \alpha$	Type 1 error $=$ significance level $=$ size $= \alpha$
H_0 incorrect	Type 2 error $= \phi$	Power $= 1 - \phi$

If H_0 is correct and H_0 is not rejected, a correct decision has been made: this is the confidence level of the test. If H_0 is correct but H_0 is rejected an error, known as a type 1 error, has been made;

this is also the significance level, or size, of the test usually referred to as α. The confidence level of the test is, therefore, $1 - \alpha$ since if H_0 is true we can either make a correct decision or an incorrect decision. The ability of a test procedure to reject H_0 when H_0 is incorrect is the power of the test. Finally, if H_0 is incorrect but it is not rejected an error, known as a type 2 error, has been made; the type 2 error is referred to as ϕ and, therefore, the power of the test is $1 - \phi$. In practice, a balance has to be made between controlling the type 1 error (with implications for the confidence level) and power (with implications for the type 2 error) of a test procedure. By never rejecting H_0 we would ensure a type 1 error of zero but such a procedure will have no power. Generally, as the type 1 error is increased the power of the test is improved. While statistical decisions are often made with reference to the 5% and 10% significance levels these are chosen for convenience or perhaps to fill a vacuum in the sense of there being no obvious criteria with which to replace them.

Within a particular test procedure there is a trade-off between setting the type 1 and type 2 errors. It is not possible to minimise one kind of error without implications for the other. The element of choice open to the researcher is in choosing a test procedure which, for a given significance level, achieves the lowest possible type 2 error and hence the highest possible power. The test statistics presented in this chapter are generally in this class of most powerful tests but, in exploiting this property, care does have to be taken in specifying the alternative and using the appropriate testing procedure. As a matter of course many econometric programs routinely report the 't' statistic and the two-sided (marginal) significance level, msl, for an estimated coefficient. If the alternative hypothesis is two sided this is the appropriate msl and, generally, the most powerful test procedure. However, often economic theory suggests an alternative hypothesis which is one sided; for example, that quantity demanded depends negatively upon price, that consumption depends

positively on income. In these cases a more powerful test procedure uses the appropriate one-sided critical value. Suppose the realised value of the test statistic Z, for $\beta_2 = 0$ against $\beta_2 > 0$, is $z = 1.80$. The two-sided alternative for a 5% significance level gives critical values of ± 1.96; against this criteria 1.80 would be judged insignificant. However, concentrating the significance level on the positive side of the distribution of Z as suggested by economic theory, the 5% critical value is 1.645, against which $z = 1.80$ is significant.

Generally, the power of a test will increase with the extent of the departure from the null hypothesis. For example, *ceteris paribus*, it is more likely that we will conclude against the null hypothesis of $\beta_2 = 0$ if $\beta_2 = 0.9$ compared to $\beta_2 = 0.1$. The power function is the function that relates the power of the test to the departure of β_2 (or other coefficient of interest) from the value hypothesised under the null. When there is no departure of β_2 from the null value the power of the test equals the size of the test, otherwise as the difference between β_2 and $\beta_2 \mid H_0$ increases, the power also increases.

The significance level and power are the *characteristics* of a test statistic. Notice that these characteristics are not, generally, constant as the sample size increases since, for a given significance level, the power increases with the sample size. Keeping the characteristics of a test constant suggests allowing the significance level to vary with the sample size rather than permitting all the benefit from the increased sample size to be in the increased power of the test.

4.11 Summary of OLS estimators and an empirical example

Section **4.11.1** draws together the results on the OLS estimators of the constant and slope coefficients in a bivariate model and their variances; and section **4.11.2** provides an example, using Phillips' original data, which gave rise to the Phillips curve.

4.11.1   Tabular summary

This subsection gathers together some of the results so far in a tabular form.

4.11.2   Typical computer output

Practically, regressions are usually estimated using commercially available econometric software. In this section the same regression is estimated using the following four widely available programs: MICROFIT, TSP, RATS and PCGIVE with the output shown in the appendix.

The regression is based on a simple version of the Phillips curve using the data period 1861–1913 suggested by Phillips (1958). This

Table 4.1   *Summary of results*

OLS estimators and variances		
OLS estimator	Conditional variance	Unconditional variance
$\hat{\beta}_1$	$\mathrm{Var}(\hat{\beta}_1 \mid x) \equiv \sigma^2(\hat{\beta}_1)$	$\mathrm{Var}(\hat{\beta}_1)$
$= \bar{Y} - \hat{\beta}_2 \bar{x}$	$= \sigma^2 \left[\dfrac{1}{T} + \bar{x}^2 \left(\dfrac{1}{\sum (x_t - \bar{x})^2} \right) \right]$	$= \dfrac{\sigma^2}{T} (1 + E_x\{\bar{X}^2/S_x^2\})$
$\hat{\beta}_2$	$\mathrm{Var}(\hat{\beta}_2 \mid x) \equiv \sigma^2(\hat{\beta}_2)$	$\mathrm{Var}(\hat{\beta}_2)$
$= \dfrac{\sum (x_t - \bar{x})(Y_t - \bar{Y})}{\sum (x_t - \bar{x})}$	$= \sigma^2 \left(\dfrac{1}{\sum (x_t - \bar{x})^2} \right)$	$= \dfrac{\sigma^2}{T} E_x\left\{ \dfrac{1}{S_x^2} \right\}$

Note: $S_x^2 = \sum (X_t - \bar{X})^2/T$

Test statistic for the null hypothesis H_0: $\beta_i = 0$ against the alternative H_a: $\beta_i \neq 0$

If σ^2 known:

$Z = \dfrac{\hat{\beta}_1}{\sigma(\hat{\beta}_1)}$

If σ^2 unknown:

$'t' = \dfrac{\hat{\beta}_1}{\hat{\sigma}(\hat{\beta}_1)}$

If σ^2 is known

$Z = \dfrac{\hat{\beta}_2}{\sigma(\hat{\beta}_2)}$

If σ^2 unknown

$'t' = \dfrac{\hat{\beta}_2}{\hat{\sigma}(\hat{\beta}_2)}$

Test statistic normally distributed

Test statistic t distributed

Estimated variances of the coefficients: replace the unknown σ^2 by $\hat{\sigma}^2 = \sum \hat{\varepsilon}_t^2/(T - k)$. Estimated standard errors of the coefficients: replace σ^2 by $\hat{\sigma}^2$ in the variance and take the square root of the estimated variance.

Goodness of fit

Population η^2	Sample (centred) R^2	Sample (uncentred) R_{uc}^2
$1 - \dfrac{\mathrm{Var}(\varepsilon_t)}{\mathrm{Var}(Y_t)}$	$1 - \dfrac{\sum \hat{\varepsilon}_t^2}{\sum (y_t - \bar{y})^2}$	$\dfrac{\sum \hat{y}_t^2}{\sum y_t^2} = 1 - \dfrac{\sum \hat{\varepsilon}_t^2}{\sum y_t^2}$

topic is covered in detail in Chapter 12. The regression captures, in a simple form, a nonlinear relationship between the rate of change of money wage rates, denoted π_{wt}, referred to as wage inflation, and the unemployment rate, u_t. The nonlinear relationship is captured by using the inverse of the unemployment rate as the regressor, denoted $uinv_t = 1/u_t$. Estimation details are as follows:

$$\hat{\pi}_{wt} = -2.322 + 10.925 uinv_t \qquad (4.134)$$

$\hat{\sigma}(\hat{\beta}_i)$	(0.332)	(0.930)
't'	(−6.976)	(11.749)
msl	[0.000]	[0.000]

$$R^2 = 0.730; \quad \bar{R}^2 = 0.725; \quad \hat{\sigma} = 1.287.$$

Sample period: 1861–1913; number of observations: $T = 53$; degrees of freedom: $T - k = 53 - 2 = 51$.

This is the general format followed in reporting estimated equations. The estimated standard errors and standard 't' statistics are given beneath the estimated coefficients, although generally only one of these, usually the 't' statistic, is given. Square brackets [.] are reserved throughout for the two-sided msl of the test statistic, in this case the 't' statistic.

The OLS estimate of β_1 is −2.322 and the OLS estimate of β_2 is 10.925. The estimated standard errors are 0.332 and 0.930 for $\hat{\sigma}(\hat{\beta}_1)$ and $\hat{\sigma}(\hat{\beta}_2)$, respectively. The standard 't' test statistic is simply the ratio of the estimated coefficient to its estimated standard error. For illustrative purposes we assume at this stage that the regression forms a valid basis for inference, although we explore below how it can be improved.

The 't' statistic for the null hypothesis H_0: $\beta_2 = 0$ against the two-sided alternative H_a: $\beta_2 \neq 0$ is $11.749 = 10.925/0.930$; at the 5% significance level, the two-sided critical values for $T - k = 53 - 2 = 51$ degrees of freedom are ±2.01. As the sample value of 11.749 exceeds 2.01, the null hypothesis is rejected. Additionally note that the msl for this value of the test statistic is 0.000, hence the null hypothesis is rejected for all choices of significance level.

The regression is linear in $uinv_t$ and, hence, is linear in the variables and is estimated by OLS. It is, however, nonlinear in u_t as $uinv_t = 1/u_t$. The estimated derivative $\partial \pi_{wt}/\partial u_t = -10.925/u_t^2$, which is a negative slope that varies with u_t. In particular, the slope decreases (in absolute value) as u_t increases. This is what we anticipate if Phillips was correct about the negative nonlinear relationship between wage inflation and unemployment. Thus, a natural alternative hypothesis is not $\beta_2 \neq 0$ but $\beta_2 > 0$, as then the derivative is negative. Given that the estimated 't' statistic at 11.749 is so large this change of alternative hypothesis will make no difference to the msl. However, suppose that the test statistic was 1.90, then it becomes important to the power of the test which side the alternative is specified. The two-sided msl is 0.063, or 6.3%, and hence is not significant against the two-sided alternative at the 5% level; whereas, the one-sided msl^+ is 0.0315, or 3.15% which is significant against the one-sided positive alternative hypothesis.

The sample goodness of fit measure (the centred) R^2 can be given its standard interpretation given that the variables in the regression are stationary (see Chapter 7); with $R^2 = 0.730$, 73% of the variation in the dependent variable, π_{wt}, is accounted for by the regressor $uinv_t$. The estimated standard error of the regression $\hat{\sigma} = 1.287$. To interpret this value note that the standard deviation of the dependent variable is 2.453, hence conditioning on $uinv_t$ reduces this by $100(2.453 - 1.287)/2.435 = 47.534\%$.

Journal articles usually report the final estimates rather than estimates of the intermediate steps, which may have involved some searching for an acceptable specification. Some likely steps are illustrated in greater detail in Chapter 5. For now note that the reported equation does not validly exclude further lags of $uinv_t$. For example, consider the regression model:

$$\pi_{wt} = \beta_1 + \sum_{j=0}^{4} \beta_{2j} uinv_{t-j} + \varepsilon_t \qquad (4.135)$$

Table 4.2 *General to specific search using marginal 't' statistics*

Reduction	4 to 3	3 to 2	2 to 1	1 to 0
't' value	(−0.180)	(−1.908)	(−3.003)	(−0.684)
msl	[0.857]	[0.063]	[0.004]	[0.497]

Common sample period: 1866–1913.

which allows for up to 4 lags of $uinv_t$. Such a model might be specified if it was thought that wage inflation responded to unemployment but with a lag. The model with four lags is more general than the specific model without lags. One way of testing down from the general model is to exclude one lag at a time in the sequence from 4 lags through to 0 lags, using the 't' statistic on the marginal coefficient. To illustrate, the relevant marginal 't' statistics are given in Table 4.2.

To interpret Table 4.2, note that the first model to be estimated included 4 lags of $uinv_t$. In that model the 't' statistic on the fourth lag was −0.180 with msl = 0.857; hence, the fourth lag can be removed. The model was then estimated with 3 lags of $uinv_t$ and the 't' statistic on the third lag was −1.908 with msl⁻ = 0.063. Whether this lag is excluded depends upon the alternative hypothesis and the significance level. In contrast to the simple model with just $uinv_t$ as the regressor we cannot sign the lag coefficients a priori. All we anticipate is that the sum of the lag coefficients is positive, in order to give the result that the long-run relationship between wage inflation and the inverse of unemployment is positive and, hence, equivalently the long-run relationship between wage inflation and unemployment is negative. We cannot sign individual coefficients in the sum and a two-sided alternative is, therefore, appropriate.

The significance level is also important because carrying out more than one test at a particular significance level means that the overall significance level is (generally) larger than the individual test significance level. For example, in testing whether lags 4 and 3 can be

excluded because they are zero, a wrong decision, that is a type one error, occurs if either or both lags 4 and 3 are excluded when they should not be. A general result is that the upper limit on the overall (or cumulative) significance level is $\alpha_c = 1 - (1 - \alpha)^n$, where n is the number of tests in the sequence and α is the common significance level of each test in the sequence. In the sequence being considered here $n = 4$. To control the upper limit on the overall significance level to, say, 5% we need to solve for $0.05 = 1 - (1 - \alpha)^n$; this implies $\alpha_c = 1 - (1 - 0.05)^{1/n} = 1 - (0.95)^{1/n}$, and for $n = 4$, $\alpha_c = 0.0127$. Alternatively if we keep to a 5% significance level for each test in the sequence then with $\alpha = 0.05$, $\alpha_c = 0.185$ or 18.5%.

Returning to the decision as to whether lag 3 should be excluded if we choose $\alpha_c = 0.05$ then 't' $= -1.908$ is not significant. Reducing the model by removing the fourth and third lags, the marginal 't' statistic for the second lag is −3.003, with msl = 0.004. Now this is significant and the model should not be reduced further. (Note that in order to ensure the comparison is made across the same sample period, 4 observations are 'lost' at the beginning of the sample period due to lagging.) The resulting 'reduced' model is:

$$\hat{\pi}_{wt} = -1.749 + 8.800uinv_t + 5.047uinv_{t-1} - 4.955uinv_{t-2}$$

$\hat{\sigma}(\hat{\beta}_i)$	(0.387)	(1.652)	(2.379)	(1.650)
't'	(−4.525)	(5.327)	(2.121)	(−3.003)
msl	[0.000]	[0.000]	[0.040]	[0.004]

$$(4.136)$$

$$R^2 = 0.781; \quad \bar{R}^2 = 0.795; \quad \hat{\sigma} = 1.169.$$

Sample period: 1866–1913; number of observations: $T = 48$; degrees of freedom: $48 - 4 = 42$.

Compared to the simpler model R^2 has increased, but note that it cannot decrease by including more variables, more relevant is $\bar{R}^2$ which has increased and also $\hat{\sigma}$ which has decreased, the latter by nearly 10%. The sum of the lag coefficients is 8.892 so the implied long-run relationship between wage inflation and inverse unemployment is:

$$\pi_{wt} = -1.749 + 8.892 uinv_t$$

and

$$\frac{\partial \pi_{wt}}{\partial u_t} = \frac{-8.892}{u_t^2} < 0$$

There is a negative long-run relationship between wage inflation and unemployment.

To examine this regression further requires greater consideration as to whether there are any indications of misspecification, and whether other specifications might result in further improvements. These topics are beyond the scope of this chapter and they are dealt with in Chapter 5 (in general terms) and Chapter 12 (specific to the Phillips curve).

4.12 Concluding remarks

It could be argued that economic theories are vacuous without the means to assess whether they are consistent with the data; discarding those which seem not to be consistent with the data and favouring those which are offers a way forward. The framework for such decisions usually involves a number of stages. In summary these are as follows:

1. The conversion of the central ideas of an economic theory into a potentially estimable model.
2. The specification of the relationship between the theoretical variables and their observable counterparts.
3. The formulation of an empirical model which is an adequate base from which to conduct inference about the parameters of interest.
4. An assessment of the robustness of any conclusions to realistic changes in specification or data period.
5. Assessment of competing empirical models.

Each of these stages usually involves several components and there may be interaction among them. For example, stage 3 may first involve estimating a general model that is statistically adequate (see the next chapter for an elaboration of this concept), which is then simplified provided the restrictions leading to the simplified model are theoretically justified and consistent with the data. Thus, the overall process of model building and evaluation is much more than just estimation of a given relationship.

The technical means behind this framework can seem off-putting to many students of economics, a view that is likely to be confirmed on reference to the econometrics section of the library or bookshop! However, a lot of progress *can* be made with limited technical ability since, despite its seeming complexity, there are several important, and moreover, constructive, principles in econometrics. The purpose of this chapter and the next is to provide some usable tools and simple principles which enable progress in both assessing published empirical work and in undertaking empirical investigations of your own. The next chapter contains a number of illustrations of estimated models and hypothesis testing.

This chapter has introduced the principles of OLS and IV estimation in a simple model usually involving just two variables. The next chapter builds upon this with an extension to more than two variables. Although the detail is naturally more complex there is no change in principle. The bivariate model is also a good place to introduce the concepts of hypothesis testing and the size and power of a test. The next chapter extends hypothesis testing to multiple hypotheses and different principles for the construction of test statistics but, again, the foundation has been laid in this chapter.

Review

1. Estimation is that part of an overall process of model building and evaluation concerned

with the numerical parameterisation of functional relationships.

2. For an empirical model to become tentatively adequate it must satisfy some evaluation criteria which are a combination of economic and econometric criteria.

3. A bivariate model with two random variables Y_t and X_t was introduced in this chapter; Y_t and X_t were assumed to be continuous random variables with probability density function, pdf, $f(y_t, x_t)$.

4. If the random variable X_t is fixed at $X_t = x_t$, the conditional pdf is written as $f(y_t \mid x_t)$ and the conditional expectation is $E\{Y_t \mid x_t\} = \int_{-\infty}^{\infty} y_t f(y_t \mid x_t)\, dy_t$.

5. Considering the conditional expectation $E\{Y_t \mid x_t\}$ as a function of X_t, we obtain the conditional expectation function, CEF, written as $E\{Y_t \mid X_t\}$.

6. In general the CEF will be nonlinear in X_t, but there are some bivariate distributions, the best known being the bivariate normal, for which the CEF is linear: $E\{Y_t \mid X_t\} = \beta_1 + \beta_2 X_t$.

7. (i) By reversing the roles of Y_t and X_t we can obtain the conditional expectation of X_t given $Y_t = y_t$ and the corresponding CEF; that is

$$E\{X_t \mid Y_t\} = \int_{-\infty}^{\infty} x_t f(x_t \mid y_t)\, dy_t.$$

(ii) The linear CEF in this case is

$$E\{X_t \mid Y_t\} = \alpha_1 + \alpha_2 Y_t.$$

8. CEFs are also known as regression functions and β_1, β_2, α_1 and α_2 are the regression coefficients, which are functions of the population moments. Specifically:

$$\beta_1 = \mu_Y - \beta_2 \mu_X; \quad \beta_2 = \sigma_{XY}/\sigma_X^2;$$
$$\alpha_1 = \mu_X - \alpha_2 \mu_Y; \quad \alpha_2 = \sigma_{XY}/\sigma_Y^2.$$

9. An economic model will serve to define some *parameters of interest*.

10. The joint pdf for Y_t and X_t can be factored in the following two ways:

$$f(y_t, x_t) = f(y_t \mid x_t) f(x_t)$$

or

$$f(y_t, x_t) = f(x_t \mid y_t) f(y_t)$$

11. Although there are two parts to the joint pdf, the CEF or regression function ignores the information from the marginal pdf (for X_t in $E\{Y_t \mid X_t\}$ and for Y_t in $E\{X_t \mid Y_t\}$).

12. The direction of conditioning will depend upon which CEF captures the parameters of interest. If, for example, the parameters of interest are β_1 and β_2 the appropriate statistical model is $E\{Y_t \mid X_t\}$.

13. The deviation of Y_t from its CEF is called the innovation error or sometimes just the innovation; that is: $\varepsilon_t = Y_t - E\{Y_t \mid X_t\}$.

14. Some important properties of ε_t are $E\{\varepsilon_t\} = 0$ and $E\{X_t, \varepsilon_t\} = 0$. The latter property is known as the orthogonality of the regressor and the innovation. In a multiple regression model the innovation is orthogonal to all the regressors.

15. An estimator is a function or rule that relates an unknown parameter to random variables and/or fixed quantities. An estimate is obtained by substituting the sample realisations for the random variables in the estimator function.

16. Suppose Y_t is a stationary random variable with mean μ_Y then an estimator of μ_Y is the time average $\bar{Y} = \sum_{t=1}^{T} Y_t/T$. An estimate of the mean is obtained by substituting the realisations from a particular sample into the estimator rule, which is $\bar{y} = \sum_{t=1}^{T} y_t/T$. An estimate is not a random variable.

17. The criteria for deciding how to form estimators of (population) parameters are not unique although different criteria may result in the same estimator in particular circumstances.

18. Replacing the unknown population moments by their counterparts from random

sampling, that is $\bar{Y}$, $\bar{X}$, s_{XY} and s_X^2, results in estimators for the regression coefficients β_1 and β_2 – see review point 8.

19. The instrumental variables, IV, analogy derives estimators by mimicking the population properties in the sample. For example, in the population the following properties are satisfied $E\{\varepsilon_t\} = 0$ and $E\{X_t, \varepsilon_t\} = 0$; whereas in the sample the IV analogy requires: $\sum_{t=1}^{T} \tilde{\varepsilon}_t/T = 0$ and $\sum_{t=1}^{T} x_t \tilde{\varepsilon}_t/T = 0$ or equivalently

$$\sum_{i=1}^{T} \tilde{\varepsilon}_t = 0 \quad \text{and} \quad \sum_{t=1}^{T} x_t \tilde{\varepsilon}_t = 0$$

20. The least squares principle derives estimators by noting that the CEF is the best predictor of Y_t in the sense of minimising the expected squared prediction errors. The analogy in random sampling is to minimise $\sum_{t=1}^{T} \hat{\varepsilon}_t^2/T$ or equivalently $\sum_{t=1}^{T} \hat{\varepsilon}_t^2$, the latter being known as the residual sum of squares – or more simply the RSS.

21. If the CEF is linear, ordinary least squares, OLS, estimators of β_1 and β_2 can be derived analytically as

$$\hat{\beta}_1 = \bar{Y} - \hat{\beta}_2 \bar{x}$$

$$\hat{\beta}_2 = \frac{\sum (x_t - \bar{x})}{\sum (x_t - \bar{x})^2} Y_t$$

These are conditional on the observed values of $X_t = x_t$.

22. If the CEF is linear, and the regression coefficients are the parameters of interest, the IV and least squares analogies give the same estimators.

23. Let $\hat{\theta}(T)$ be an estimator of the parameter θ based on a sample of T observations. $\hat{\theta}(T)$ is said to be unbiased if $E\{\hat{\theta}(T)\} = \theta$ for all T for which $\hat{\theta}(T)$ exists.

24. An estimator $\hat{\theta}(T)$ is said to be consistent if plim $\hat{\theta}(T) = \theta$.

25. A consistent estimator is not necessarily unbiased.

26. The asymptotic expectation of $\hat{\theta}(T)$ is the limit of $E\{\hat{\theta}(T)\}$ as $T \to \infty$. The asymptotic bias of $\hat{\theta}(T)$ is $\lim E\{\hat{\theta}(T)\} - \theta$. An unbiased estimator is asymptotically unbiased, but an asymptotically unbiased estimator is not necessarily unbiased.

27. A consistent estimator is not necessarily asymptotically unbiased.

28. An efficient estimator in a class of estimators is one with minimum variance.

29. The OLS estimators are conditionally and unconditionally unbiased. Conditionally unbiased refers to conditioning on $X = (X_1, \ldots, X_T) = x = (x_1, \ldots, x_T)$.

30. An estimator is unconditionally unbiased (with respect to X) if it is unbiased whatever the value of X; that is, for example, for $\hat{\beta}_2$, $E_X\{E\{\hat{\beta}_2 \mid X\}\} = E_X\{\beta_2\} = \beta_2$.

31. The conditional variances of the OLS estimators are

$$\text{Var}(\hat{\beta}_1 \mid x) = \sigma^2 \left[\frac{1}{T} + \bar{x}^2 \left(\frac{1}{\sum (x_t - \bar{x})^2} \right) \right]$$

$$\text{Var}(\hat{\beta}_2 \mid x) = \sigma^2 \left(\frac{1}{\sum (x_t - \bar{x})^2} \right)$$

32. An unbiased estimator of σ^2 is provided by $\hat{\sigma}^2 = \sum \hat{\varepsilon}_t^2/(T - k)$.

33. Nonlinear CEFs pose different problems depending whether they are nonlinear in the variables, for example $1/X_t$ or X_t^2, or nonlinear in the parameters, for example X_t^β. A CEF which is nonlinear in the parameters is more fundamentally nonlinear, with the first order conditions from minimising the residual sum of squares resulting in nonlinear equations.

34. There is a distinction between the population coefficient of determination, η^2, and the sample coefficient of determination, R^2, both of which can easily be subject to misinterpretation.

35. All that is required for the variance of $E\{Y_t \mid X_t\}$ to contribute to the variance of

Y_t is that $\beta_2 \neq 0$. Nevertheless $\eta^2 = 1 - \text{Var}(\varepsilon_t)/\text{Var}(Y_t)$ is often interpreted as measuring the strength of the relationship between Y_t and X_t with $0 \leq \eta^2 \leq 1$.

36. The sample coefficient of determination is defined as $R^2 \equiv 1 - \sum \hat{\varepsilon}_t^2 / \sum (y_t - \bar{y})^2$, with $0 \leq R^2 \leq 1$ provided there is a constant in the regression. If Y_t and X_t are (stochastically) trended R^2 is a misleading indicator of the goodness of fit (see Chapter 8). R^2 is not invariant to the definition of the dependent variable.

37. When the parameters of interest are not those in the regression function (the CEF), a potentially viable method of estimation is instrumental variables, IV, estimation.

38. IV estimation requires at least as many instrumental variables as there are violations of the condition that the disturbance and the regressors are uncorrelated. The instrumental variables should be uncorrelated with the disturbance but correlated with the regressor(s).

39. Where a simultaneous system of equations is specified a 'natural' choice of instrumental variables is provided by the reduced form equations.

40. It will not always be possible to estimate the parameters of interest. An example was provided in the text of an (inverse) supply function which had 'unidentified' parameters of interest.

41. The situation when the parameters of interest do not coincide with the regression coefficients is sometimes characterised as a conflict between *structure*, which determines the parameters of interest, and *regression*.

42. The null hypothesis restricts some aspect of the parameter space of a model. A particularly important null hypothesis in a bivariate model is H_0: $\beta_2 = 0$, with the interpretation that the conditioning of Y_t on X_t is irrelevant.

43. A test statistic, TS, is a random variable whose distribution under H_0 is known. A realisa-

tion of TS from a sample of observations is denoted ts, and the larger the value of ts or $\text{abs}(ts)$ the greater the evidence of departure from H_0.

44. The (one-sided) positive marginal significance level, msl^+, is defined by $msl^+ = \text{pr}\{\text{TS} \geq ts \mid H_0\}$. The positive msl is the probability that the test statistic exceeds a realised value given that the null hypothesis is true.

45. The (one-sided) negative marginal significance level, msl^-, is defined by $msl^- = \text{pr}\{\text{TS} \leq ts \mid H_0\}$.

46. If departures either on the positive side or the negative side represent equivalent departures from the null hypothesis; that is $\text{TS} \geq ts$ and $\text{TS} \leq -ts$ are treated equally the two-sided or simply the msl is $msl = \text{pr}\{\text{abs}(\text{TS}) \geq \text{abs}(ts) \mid H_0\}$.

47. Usually the direction of departure from the null is informed by economic theory and is captured by the alternative hypothesis, usually written H_a.

48. A two-sided alternative considers a large negative or a large positive value of the TS as evidence against the null hypothesis.

49. If H_a is a one-sided alternative, only one of a large negative or a large positive value of ts is evidence against the null hypothesis.

50. In a bivariate regression we are often interested in whether X_t is irrelevant to the mean of Y_t so that $E\{Y_t \mid X_t\} = E\{Y_t\}$. This is the null hypothesis $\beta_2 = 0$; possible alternatives are $\beta_2 \neq 0$, $\beta_2 < 0$ or $\beta_2 > 0$.

51. Generally we seek a test statistic, with known distribution under the null hypothesis, which is put into a standard form. Leading examples are the test statistics Z and 't' which have standard normal and t distributions, respectively.

52. The usual test statistic for the null hypothesis $H_0 \mid \beta_2 = 0$ is the 't' statistic

$$'t' = \frac{\hat{\beta}_2 - (\beta_2 \mid H_0)}{\hat{\sigma}(\hat{\beta}_2)}$$

53. Large negative values of 't' will lead to rejection of H_0 in favour of H_a: $\beta_2 < 0$; large positive values of 't' will lead to rejection of H_0 in favour of H_a: $\beta_2 > 0$; and either will lead to rejection of H_0: $\beta_2 = 0$ in favour of H_a: $\beta_2 \neq 0$.

54. Nonrejection of the null hypothesis does not necessarily imply its acceptance. The data will often be consistent with a range of different null hypotheses.

55. Provided interest centres on one coefficient, or one linear combination of coefficients, the same principles of testing apply in models with more than one regressor.

56. In the regression model $Y_t = \beta_1 + \beta_2 X_{t2} + \beta_3 X_{t3} + \varepsilon_t$, a test of the null hypothesis H_0: $\beta_2 + \beta_3 = 1$ against any of the alternatives $\beta_2 + \beta_3 < 1$, $\beta_2 + \beta_3 > 1$, $\beta_2 + \beta_3 \neq 1$ is provided by the 't' statistic

$$'t' = \frac{\hat{\beta}^* - (\beta^* \mid H_0)}{\hat{\sigma}(\hat{\beta}^*)}$$

where $\beta^* = \beta_2 + \beta_3$ and $\hat{\beta}^* = \hat{\beta}_2 + \hat{\beta}_3$.

57. A type 1 error is the probability of rejecting H_0 when H_0 is true, this is also the (marginal) significance level and size of the test. One minus the significance level is the confidence level of the test.

58. A type 2 error is the probability of not rejecting H_0 when it is incorrect; and one minus the type 2 error, which is the probability of rejecting H_0 when it is false, is the power of the test.

59. Ideally we would like to minimise both the type 1 and type 2 errors; however, with a particular test statistic, reducing the type 1 error (for example, by reducing the significance level of the test from 10% to 5%) increases the type 2 error.

60. For a particular significance level, choose the test procedure that minimises the type 2 error or equivalently gives the greatest power. The test procedures considered here are in this class of most powerful tests (provided a one-sided test procedure is used for a one-sided alternative).

Review questions

1. Explain the difference between $E\{Y_t \mid X_t = x_t\}$ and $E\{Y_t \mid X_t\}$; which one of these is the conditional expectation function?

2. Consider the following table of joint probabilities:

		X_t					
		0	1	2	3	4	
Y_t	4	$\frac{1}{10}$	$\frac{1}{5}$	$\frac{1}{20}$	$\frac{3}{20}$	$\frac{1}{20}$	$\frac{11}{20}$
	5	$\frac{1}{10}$	$\frac{1}{10}$	$\frac{3}{20}$	$\frac{1}{20}$	$\frac{1}{20}$	$\frac{9}{20}$
		$\frac{2}{10}$	$\frac{3}{10}$	$\frac{2}{10}$	$\frac{2}{10}$	$\frac{1}{10}$	1

Calculate
(i) $E\{Y_t \mid X_t = x_t\}$ for the ensemble of X_t;
(ii) $\varepsilon_t = Y_t - E\{Y_t \mid X_t\}$;
(iii) $E\{\varepsilon_t \mid X_t = x_t\}$ for the ensemble of X_t;
(iv) $Cov\{X_t, \varepsilon_t\}$;
(v) $E\{\varepsilon_t\}$.

3. Consider the linear bivariate CEF. Given the following population moments calculate the regression parameters:

$$\mu_X = 10.8; \quad \mu_Y = 11.0; \quad \sigma_{XY} = 0.075;$$
$$\sigma_X^2 = 0.085; \quad \sigma_Y^2 = 0.067$$

4. Explain why it is necessarily the case in the bivariate CEF that
(i) $E\{\varepsilon_t\} = 0$ and
(ii) $Cov\{X_t, \varepsilon_t\} = 0$.

5. What is the difference between an estimator and an estimate?

6. (i) Consider the linear, bivariate CEF with $Y_t =$ consumption and $X_t =$ income. In a particular sample the following are obtained:

$$\bar{y} = 52.38; \quad \bar{x} = 62.52; \quad s_{xy} = 247.0;$$
$$s_x^2 = 328.7; \quad s_y^2 = 189.0$$

calculate and interpret the sample regression coefficients.

(ii) Given the following sample information calculate and interpret the estimated standard errors of the sample regression coefficients:

$$\sum \hat{\varepsilon}_t^2 = 184.6, \quad T = 154$$

(iii) Carry out the 't' test of the null hypothesis $\beta_2 = 0$ against the following alternative hypotheses: $H_{a1} : \beta_2 \neq 0$; $H_{a2} : \beta_2 > 0$ for illustrative purposes choose the reference value $\alpha = 5\%$ for the size of the test).

7. Continuing question 6, calculate and interpret the sample regression coefficients and estimated standard errors from the regression that reverses the order of conditioning.

8. Evaluate the plim, expectation, bias, asymptotic expectation and asymptotic bias of the following estimator, $\hat{\theta}(T)$:

$\hat{\theta}(T) = \theta$ with probability $(T - 1)/T$
$\hat{\theta}(T) = T^2$ with probability $1/T$

9. Explain the difference between the conditional expectation and the unconditional expectation of the OLS estimator $\hat{\beta}_2$.

10. In the bivariate linear regression model, prove that the OLS estimator $\hat{\beta}_1$ of β_1 is unbiased.

11. Explain how you would construct a Monte Carlo simulation to assess whether the OLS estimators, for different sample sizes, in a bivariate regression model were unbiased.

12. Explain what is meant by the acronym BLUE applied to OLS estimators.

13. (i) Are the following models (a) nonlinear in the parameters, (b) nonlinear in the variables or (c) both?
A. $Y_t = \beta_1 X_t^{\beta_2} + \varepsilon_t$
B. $Y_t = \beta_1 + \beta_2/X_t^2 + \varepsilon_t$
C. $Y_t = \beta_1 + \beta_2 \ln X_t + \varepsilon_t$
D. $Y_t = \beta_1(\exp X_t^{\beta_2}) + \varepsilon_t$
(ii) In each case form the residual sum of squares and differentiate with respect to the regression parameters. Comment on whether the resulting equations are linear or nonlinear.

(iii) If $E\{Y_t \mid X_t\} = \beta_1 + X_t^{\beta_2}$, derive the first and second order conditions for a minimum.

14. Consider the population coefficient of determination η^2. Show that if Y_t is mean independent of X_t then $\eta^2 = 0$. Calculate and interpret the sample R^2 for question 6 where Y_t is consumption and X_t is income.

15. What is the difference between the centred R^2 and uncentred R^2? What are the limits of the uncentred R^2?

16. Explain why in a loglinear model $100\hat{\sigma}$ can be interpreted as the percentage standard error of the regression. Is this measure invariant to a linear transformation of the dependent variable?

17. (i) Consider the demand and supply functions of section **4.9** with the relationship between the regression coefficient β_2^* and the parameter of interest β_2 given by (4.125). Students who regress quantity on price, thinking that they are estimating a demand function, are often puzzled when they obtain a positive coefficient on the price variable: show that the sign and magnitude of α_2 offers an explanation of this puzzle.

(ii) Suppose $\sigma_1^2 = 0$, how does this change the relationship between β_2^* and β_2? Interpret the revised model.

18. Suppose a test statistic TS is distributed $\sim N(0, 1)$, obtain: msl^+ and msl^- for $ts = 1.80$; and obtain the two-sided msl for $ts = 1.80$.

19. Suppose only large positive values of ts are evidence against H_0 then with $\alpha = 0.05$ and TS $\sim N(0, 1)$ what are the nonrejection and rejection regions? Suppose only large negative values of ts are evidence against H_0, obtain the nonrejection and rejection regions for $\alpha = 0.05$.

20. Tabulate the following probabilities assuming that $Z \sim N(0, 1)$ and 't' follows the

t distribution with $T - k = 20$ degrees of freedom:

$$pr(Z) \geq 1.0 \quad pr(abs(Z)) \geq 1.0$$
$$pr(Z) \geq 1.5 \quad pr(abs(Z)) \geq 1.5$$
$$pr(Z) \geq 2.0 \quad pr(abs(Z)) \geq 2.0$$
$$pr(t) \geq 1.0 \quad pr(abs(t)) \geq 1.0$$
$$pr(t) \geq 1.5 \quad pr(abs(t)) \geq 1.5$$
$$pr(t) \geq 2.0 \quad pr(abs(t)) \geq 2.0$$

21. Consider the measurement error model of section **4.3.2**, that is

$$Y_t = \beta_1 + \beta_2 X_t + \varepsilon_t$$
$$X_t^* = X_t + \nu_t$$

   (i)   Show that OLS applied to the regression model results in 'biased' estimators of β_1 and β_2.
   (ii) Relate the bias in the OLS estimator of β_2 to the variance of the measurement error relative to the variance of X_t (see, for example, Goldberger (1991, section 31.2) or Greene (1997, section 9.5.1)).
   (iii) Interpret these results for likely magnitudes of the variance ratio. In particular which is more damaging to OLS: large errors of measurement with small variance or small errors of measurement with large variance?

22. Consider the following specification of the DGP:

$$Y_t = \beta_1 + \beta_2 X_t + \varepsilon_t$$
$$X_t = \phi X_{t-1} + u_t + \kappa \varepsilon_t$$

where $\varepsilon_t \sim N(0, 1)$, $0 < \phi < 1$ and $u_t \sim N(0, 1)$.
   (i)   Derive and interpret $E\{X_t, \varepsilon_t \mid X_{t-1}\}$.
   (ii) What problems are likely to arise with OLS estimation of the bivariate regression?
   (iii) A simulation study was based on the following values for the parameters: $\beta_1 = 5.0$, $\beta_2 = 0.5$, $\kappa = 0.5$. Two values of ϕ were chosen: $\phi = 0.0$ and $\phi = 0.9$.

Estimation was alternately by OLS and by IV using X_{t-1} as an instrument (as well as the constant).

Interpret the following simulation results:

Median value of estimated regression coefficients

	$\phi = 0.0$	
OLS	5.000	0.899
IV	5.001	0.908

	$\phi = 0.9$	
OLS	5.000	0.577
IV	5.000	0.498

Simulation details: based on 5,000 replications with $T = 500$.

23. Consider the following specification of the DGP:

$$Y_t = \beta_1 + \beta_2 X_t + \varepsilon_t$$
$$X_t = \phi X_{t-1} + u_t + \kappa \varepsilon_t$$

where $\varepsilon_t \sim N(0, 1)$, $0 < \phi < 1$ and $u_t \sim N(0, 1)$. In addition ε_t is autocorrelated according to one of the following schemes:
   (i) $\varepsilon_t = \rho \varepsilon_{t-1} + \omega_t$ with $\omega_t \sim N(0, 1)$ or
   (ii) $\varepsilon_t = \omega_t + \theta \omega_{t-1}$
Would X_{t-1} or X_{t-2} be a valid instrument in either case?

Appendices

A4.1   Maximum likelihood estimation

Maximum likelihood estimation – or MLE – is an alternative, and quite general, principle for the estimation of unknown parameters. MLE is widely used in econometrics and statistics, and in contrast to OLS (and other least squares methods), requires the specification of the probability density function, which contains the parameters of interest. This appendix outlines the general principle of MLE and applies it first to a nonregression example and then to the regression problem. The intention here is to motivate the idea of maximum likelihood estimation with some simple examples applied first to a nonregression example, and then to two regression examples. The first is the bivariate regression model used in the first part of this chapter and the second is the structural model, and its generalisation, used in section **4.9**.

Maximum likelihood methods are widely used in two important empirical contexts (multivariate cointegration and ARCH estimation) that feature in three of the later chapters, that is Chapters 14, 15 and 16. Often what the user needs in order to interpret regression output sensibly is a broad understanding of the principle of MLE rather than detailed knowledge of the technical details. If that is required the reader could usefully consult Spanos (1986) and Amemiya (1985). *The reader is advised to delay A4.1.4 of this appendix until after a more detailed consideration of the multiple regression model in the next chapter.*

A4.1.1   The likelihood function

Data on the random variables Z_t is generated by the pdf $f(z_t; \theta)$, where θ is the set of DGP parameters; for example, Z_t could be the regression variables Y_t and X_t, θ the regression coefficients and $f(.)$ is the density which states that Y_t and X_t are jointly normally distributed; alternatively Z_t could be the random variable which is tossing a coin, and θ the probability of heads which is sufficient to define the function $f(.)$ – for example, the binomial, see below.

Suppose $f(z_t; \theta)$ is stationary and we take a random sample of size T, then the joint pdf for all T random variables is

$$h(z_1, \ldots, z_T; \theta) = \Pi_{t=1}^{T} f(z_t; \theta) \qquad (A4.1)$$

where $\Pi_{t=1}^{T}$ indicates the product from $t = 1$ to T, and note that random sampling implies independence so that the individual pdfs can be multiplied together.

The usual problem is that the DGP is unknown and we want to infer key characteristics of it from a given sample of observations. From

this perspective, the outcomes of Z_t are known, $t = 1, \ldots, T$, but θ is unknown. To emphasise this distinction we write $L(.)$ reversing the order of z_t and θ, and in this form it is known as the *likelihood function*:

$$L(\theta; z_1, \ldots, z_T) = \Pi_{t=1}^{T} f(z_t; \theta) \qquad (A4.2)$$

The maximum likelihood principle maximises $L(.)$, or some simple monotonic transformation of it, by choosing the value of θ, say $\hat{\theta}$, regarding the sample information as given. A usual transformation is to take the (natural) log of the likelihood function since the log of a product is the sum of the logs. That is

$$LL(\theta; z_1, \ldots, z_T) \equiv \ln[L(\theta; z_1, \ldots, z_T)]$$

$$= \sum_{t=1}^{T} \ln[f(z_t; \theta)] \qquad (A4.3)$$

If θ is a single parameter then maximisation requires $\partial LL/\partial \theta = 0$ which is solved for $\hat{\theta}$, the maximum likelihood estimator; and, as a check, $\partial^2 LL/\partial(\theta)^2 < 0$ is also required. If θ is a vector of k elements then each of the derivatives $\partial LL/\partial \theta_i = 0$, $i = 1, \ldots, k$, which provides k conditions to solve for the unknowns; and, as a check, $\partial^2 LL/\partial \theta \, \partial \theta'$ should be a negative definite matrix. To emphasise that this is the ML solution it is often useful to write $\partial LL/\partial \hat{\theta}$, that is the derivative is taken with respect to the estimator $\hat{\theta}$, since it is anyway the estimator and *not* the parameter θ, which is variable in this maximisation problem. (Quite often in a practical problem there are constants in the log-likelihood function and these can be neglected without loss as they do not involve θ.)

A4.1.2   The binomial distribution of probabilities

We illustrate the ML principle using a development of the simple coin-tossing example used in Chapter 3. That example was an illustration of a random variable with a binomial distribution, with the reference to binomial emphasising that there are only two outcomes to the random variable. The model could be applied to many situations with dichotomous outcomes, for example whether a coin lands head, whether an individual drawn at random from a particular population has blue eyes, whether a throw of a dice lands on a number divisible by 3 without remainder. A common terminology is that if the characteristic is present the event is called a 'success', whereas otherwise it is a 'failure'; the probabilities are denoted p and q respectively, where $p + q = 1$. The binomial set-up often considers n independent 'trials', each of which could take one of the dichotomous outcomes. In effect there are n independent random variables, but we assume that each random variable is simply a clone of the others with the probability structure unchanged.

The sample space and the associated probabilities depend upon the number of trials. In the simplest case $n = 1$ with outcomes (S, F) with probabilities p and q, respectively. If $n = 2$ the sample space comprises (S, S), (S, F), (F, S), (F, F) with probabilities p^2, pq, qp and q^2. If the sample space has been completely enumerated these probabilities should sum to 1. Do they? The easiest way to show this is to note that $p^2 + pq + qp + q^2 = (p + q)^2 = (1)^2 = 1$. Continuing this line of argument, note that if there are n trials the probabilities are given by the expansion of $(p + q)^n$. In the binomial expansion the order of the S and F entries in the sample space is not important, in the last example (S, F) is the same as (F, S) and hence the associated probability is $2pq$. Bearing this in mind the binomial expansion is given by

$$(p + q)^n = \sum_{r=0}^{n} {}_nC_r p^r q^{n-r} \quad \text{where}$$

$$_nC_r = \frac{n(n-1)(n-2)\ldots(n-s+1)}{s!}$$

$$\text{and} \quad s! = s(s-1), \ldots, 1$$

$_nC_r$ is the binomial coefficient which gives the number of ways of obtaining r from n without regard to order. Note that $_nC_1 = n$, $_nC_n = 1$ and

$_nC_0 \equiv 1$; and $s!$ is pronounced s factorial. To see how this expansion works consider some simple examples:

$$(p + q)^2 = q^2 + {}_2C_1 pq + p^2 = q^2 + 2pq + p^2$$
$$(p + q)^3 = q^3 + {}_3C_1 pq^2 + {}_3C_2 p^2 q + p^3$$
$$= q^3 + 3pq^2 + 3p^2 q + p^3$$
$$(p + q)^4 = q^4 + {}_4C_1 pq^3 + {}_4C_2 p^2 q^2$$
$$+ {}_4C_3 p^3 q + p^4$$
$$= q^4 + 4pq^3 + 6p^2 q^2 + 4p^3 q + p^4$$

This completes the set-up from the viewpoint of the probability structure.

Suppose now we know that a random variable has the binomial distribution but we do not know the probability p. The problem is one of inferring p, that is estimating it, from n (independent) trials. To fix ideas suppose $n = 10$ of which 6 resulted in S, and hence 4 in F. Given this sample we ask what value of the estimator of p, say $\hat{p}$, would make this outcome the most likely among all possible outcomes? To obtain this we maximise the likelihood of the sample as a function of the estimator $\hat{p}$ – see, for example, Kendall and Stuart (1977). If p was known the probability of 6 successes in 10 is given by $_{10}C_6 p^6 q^4$. When p is not known we replace this by $_{10}C_6 \hat{p}^6 (1 - \hat{p})^4$. This becomes linear in the logs, making it easier to maximise, that is $\ln(_{10}C_6) + 6\ln(\hat{p}) + 4\ln(1 - \hat{p})$. Differentiating with respect to $\hat{p}$, setting the derivative to 0 and solving for $\hat{p}$ we obtain:

$$\frac{\partial LL}{\partial \hat{p}} = \frac{6}{\hat{p}} - \frac{4}{(1 - \hat{p})} = 0 \Rightarrow \hat{p} = \frac{6}{10} \quad \text{(A4.4)}$$

This is, perhaps, the solution you anticipated, but ML estimation will not always lead to the 'obvious' outcome. Note that

$$\frac{\partial^2 LL}{\partial(\hat{p})^2} = -\frac{6}{\hat{p}^2} - \frac{4}{(1 - \hat{p})^2} \quad \text{(A4.5)}$$

$$= -41\tfrac{2}{3} < 0$$

as required for a maximum

A4.1.3 Maximum likelihood estimation: the regression model

In this section we show how the maximum likelihood approach is applied to the bivariate regression model. The framework in this section is that of section **4.2**: there are two random variables, Y_t and X_t, which are jointly normally distributed; in shorthand, $f(y_t, x_t) \sim$ bvn(ρ). Now we restate for convenience the result on the conditional distributions from section **4.2.2**:

(i) If $f(y_t, x_t)$ is bvn then $f(y_t \mid x_t)$ and $f(x_t \mid y_t)$ are normally distributed, that is the conditional pdfs are (univariate) normal.

(ii) If $f(y_t, x_t)$ is bvn then the conditional expectations, $E(Y_t \mid x_t)$ and $E(X_t \mid y_t)$, are linear in x_t and y_t, respectively.

As in the OLS case we assume that the parameters of interest are in the conditional density of y_t given x_t. Treating X_t as fixed, $X_t = x_t$ for $t = 1, \ldots, T$, the conditional pdf $f(y_t \mid x_t)$ is univariate normal with mean $\beta_1 + \beta_2 x_t$ and variance $\sigma^2_{Y|x}$. Thus, the pdf for an individual observation is – see (4.8):

$$f(y_t \mid x_t) = \frac{1}{(2\pi\sigma^2_{Y|x})^{\frac{1}{2}}} \exp\left\{ -\frac{(y_t - \mu_{Y|x})^2}{2\sigma^2_{Y|x}} \right\}$$

(A4.6a)

$$= \frac{1}{(2\pi\sigma^2_{Y|x})^{\frac{1}{2}}}$$

$$\times \exp\left\{ -\frac{(y_t - \beta_1 - \beta_2 x_t)^2}{2\sigma^2_{Y|x}} \right\}$$

(A4.6b)

If we randomly sample T such observations, then the density function of the sample is simply the product of the T individual densities. (Randomness implies independence, and the pdf for a joint event, where the component events are independent, is simply the product of

the individual pdfs.) That is:

$$\Pi^T_{t=1} f(y_t \mid x_t; \beta_1, \beta_2, \sigma^2_{Y|x})$$

$$= \Pi^T_{t=1} \frac{1}{(2\pi\sigma^2_{Y|x})^{\frac{1}{2}}} \exp\left\{ -\frac{(y_t - \beta_1 - \beta_2 x_t)^2}{2\sigma^2_{Y|x}} \right\}$$

(A4.7)

To emphasise that this is a function of the regression parameters β_1, β_2 and $\sigma^2_{Y|x}$, these have been explicitly introduced into the conditional pdf.

To interpret this as the likelihood function, we regard y_t and x_t as given; then treat the parameters, β_1 and β_2, as unknown; and ask what values $\hat{\beta}_1$ and $\hat{\beta}_2$ would make this sample of y_t, given $X_t = x_t$, most likely? The likelihood function for the sample is:

$$L(\beta_1, \beta_2, \sigma^2_{Y|x}; y_t \mid x_t)$$

$$= \Pi^T_{t=1} f(y_t \mid x_t, \beta_1, \beta_2, \sigma^2_{Y|x})$$

$$= \Pi^T_{t=1} \frac{1}{(2\pi\sigma^2_{Y|x})^{\frac{1}{2}}} \exp\left\{ -\frac{(y_t - \beta_1 - \beta_2 x_t)^2}{2\sigma^2_{Y|x}} \right\}$$

(A4.8a)

$$= \frac{1}{(2\pi\sigma^2_{Y|x})^{\frac{T}{2}}} \exp\left\{ -\frac{\sum\limits_{t=1}^{T}(y_t - \beta_1 - \beta_2 x_t)^2}{2\sigma^2_{Y|x}} \right\}$$

(A4.8b)

To illustrate how the third line follows from the second, first note that $(2\pi\sigma^2_{Y|x})^{\frac{1}{2}}$ is a constant which is multiplied T times; then note, for example, $\exp(\varepsilon_t)\exp(\varepsilon_s) = \exp(\varepsilon_t + \varepsilon_s)$, where $\varepsilon_t = y_t - \beta_1 - \beta_2 x_t$.

Differentiating $L(.)$ with respect to β_1 and β_2, which are regarded as variable in the likelihood function, and solving for the values which yield a maximum, denoted $\hat{\beta}_1$ and $\hat{\beta}_2$, gives the maximum likelihood estimators. In practice it is easier to maximise the log of the likelihood function, which is

$$LL(\beta_1, \beta_2, \sigma^2_{Y|x}; y_t \mid x_t)$$

$$= \sum_{t=1}^{T} f(y_t \mid x_t; \beta_1, \beta_2, \sigma^2_{Y|x})$$

$$= -\frac{T}{2} \ln 2\pi - \frac{T}{2} \ln \sigma^2$$

$$-\frac{1}{2\sigma^2} \sum_{t=1}^{T} (y_t - \beta_1 - \beta_2 x_t)^2 \qquad \text{(A4.9)}$$

Where for simplicity we have defined $\sigma^2 \equiv \sigma^2_{Y|x}$. LL is then maximised with respect to β_1, β_2 and σ^2. The first order conditions are:

$$\frac{\partial LL}{\partial \beta_1} = -\frac{(-2)}{2\sigma^2}$$

$$\times \sum_{t=1}^{T} (y_t - \beta_1 - \beta_2 x_t) = 0 \qquad \text{(A4.10a)}$$

$$\frac{\partial LL}{\partial \beta_2} = -\frac{(-2)}{2\sigma^2}$$

$$\times \sum_{t=1}^{T} x_t(y_t - \beta_1 - \beta_2 x_t) = 0 \qquad \text{(A4.10b)}$$

$$\frac{\partial LL}{\partial \sigma^2} = -\frac{T}{2\sigma^2} + \frac{1}{2\sigma^4}$$

$$\times \sum_{t=1}^{T} (y_t - \beta_1 - \beta_2 x_t)^2 = 0 \qquad \text{(A4.10c)}$$

The first two conditions are, apart from the constant $-1/(2\sigma^2)$, the same as the normal equations that result from minimisation of the residual sum of squares, hence the solutions $\hat{\beta}_1$ and $\hat{\beta}_2$ are the same as the OLS estimators $\hat{\beta}_1$ and $\hat{\beta}_2$. There is, however, a difference when the last condition is solved for $\hat{\sigma}$, the ML estimator of σ^2. Specifically defining $\hat{\varepsilon}_t \equiv y_t - \hat{\beta}_1 - \hat{\beta}_2 x_t$, the solution is:

$$\hat{\sigma}^2 = \frac{\sum_{t=1}^{T} \hat{\varepsilon}_t^2}{T}$$

compared to the OLS estimator

$$\hat{\sigma}^2 = \frac{\sum_{t=1}^{T} \hat{\varepsilon}_t^2}{(T-k)}$$

When, as is usually the case, σ^2 is unknown, the maximum likelihood estimators of the variances of $\hat{\beta}_1$ and $\hat{\beta}_2$ are the same as those for the OLS estimators of the variances of $\hat{\beta}_1$ and $\hat{\beta}_2$ with one exception. The exception is that $\hat{\sigma}^2$ is used in place of $\hat{\sigma}^2$, a difference that is negligible as $T \to \infty$.

A4.1.4 Estimation in simultaneous models

At this stage it does not appear that MLE has much to offer over OLS estimation. However, it offers a way into the more complex case, of much practical importance, where it is invalid to condition on $X_t = x_t$. In a least squares context an example was given in section **4.9**. We recall the essence of the problem with a modification of that example. There are two jointly determined endogenous variables, with equations interpreted as the demand function and the inverse supply function:

$$Q_t = \beta_1 + \beta_2 P_t + \beta_3 I_t + \varepsilon_{1t} \qquad \text{(A4.11)}$$

$$P_t = \alpha_1 + \alpha_2 Q_t + \alpha_3 R_t + \varepsilon_{2t} \qquad \text{(A4.12)}$$

Compared to the earlier example real income, I_t, with coefficient β_3, has been added to the demand function to ensure that the inverse supply function is identified. In order to obtain the parameters of interest, β_1, β_2 and β_3, it is not valid to condition Q_t on P_t (and I_t and R_t), nor is it valid in order to obtain the parameters of interest α_1, α_2 and α_3, to condition P_t on Q_t (and I_t and R_t).

We start from the joint density $f(q_t, p_t, i_t, r_t)$. Then this can be factored as:

$$f(q_t, p_t, i_t, r_t)$$

$$= f_1(q_t \mid p_t, i_t, r_t) f_2(p_t \mid i_t, r_t) f_3(i_t \mid r_t) f_4(r_t)$$

$$\text{(A4.13)}$$

It is tempting, by analogy with treating all 'right-hand side' variables in the regression as legitimate regressors, to take $f(q_t \mid p_t, i_t, r_t)$ as the (univariate) density on which to base MLE, so excluding $f_2(p_t \mid i_t, r_t)$, $f_3(i_t \mid r_t)$ and $f_4(r_t)$. However, this, as we saw in the slightly simpler example of section **4.9.1**, is invalid. The correct factorisation is:

$$f(q_t, p_t, i_t, r_t) = f_0(q_t, p_t \mid i_t, r_t) f_3(i_t \mid r_t) f_4(r_t) \tag{A4.14}$$

It is legitimate to consider the joint density defined by $f_0(q_t, p_t \mid i_t, r_t)$ to the exclusion of $f_3(i_t \mid r_t) f_4(r_t)$, or equivalently the exclusion of $f_5(r_t \mid i_t) f_6(i_t)$. (Note that both $f_3(i_t \mid r_t) f_4(r_t)$ and $f_5(r_t \mid i_t) f_6(i_t)$ are equal to the joint density $f_7(r_t, i_t)$.) This then offers a way to maximum likelihood estimation with the relevant density being $f_0(q_t, p_t \mid i_t, r_t)$, with Q_t and P_t jointly normally distributed. The valid conditioning variables are I_t and R_t in the joint distribution of Q_t and P_t. To go further requires some mathematics, which may lose the overriding simplicity of the argument. Here we just sketch out the detail. For those who would like to take this further, Spanos (1986, Chapters 24 and 25) provides an excellent technical exposition.

We have four variables, two of which are 'endogenous' and two of which are conditioning variables. To simplify the notation we define $Y_t = (Y_{1t}, Y_{2t})'$ and $X_t = (X_{1t}, X_{2t})'$, so both are 2×1 (column) vectors, respectively. We assume that the four variables have a multivariate normal distribution with contemporaneous variance matrix of dimension 4×4:

$$\mathrm{Var}\begin{pmatrix} Y_t \\ X_t \end{pmatrix} = \begin{bmatrix} \Sigma_{11} & \Sigma_{12} \\ \Sigma_{21} & \Sigma_{22} \end{bmatrix} \equiv \Sigma \tag{A4.15}$$

and conditional expectation function, which is linear in $X_t = x_t$:

$$E\{Y_t \mid X_t = x_t\} = B'x_t \tag{A4.16}$$

where $\quad B' = \begin{bmatrix} \beta_{11} & \beta_{12} \\ \beta_{21} & \beta_{22} \end{bmatrix} \tag{A4.17}$

B' is the matrix of regression coefficients, the first row being relevant for the conditional expectation of Y_{1t} and the second row relevant for the conditional expectation of Y_{2t}.

MLE proceeds by defining the joint pdf as bivariate normal in Y_t conditional on X_t. In more advanced texts, see, for example, Spanos (1986, especially Chapter 24), it is shown that

$$B = \Sigma_{22}^{-1} \Sigma_{21} \tag{A4.18a}$$

$$E\{\zeta_t \zeta_t'\} \equiv \Omega = \Sigma_{11} - \Sigma_{12} \Sigma_{22}^{-1} \Sigma_{21} \tag{A4.18b}$$

$$E\{\zeta_t \zeta_s'\} = 0 \quad \text{for } t \neq s \tag{A4.18c}$$

where $\zeta_t = Y_t - B'x_t$. Although all this looks more complex, it is really not much more so than the univariate case. All the principles are just the same. The dimensions of these matrices and vectors help to indicate to what they are referring. B is the 2×2 matrix of regression coefficients, given as a function of the moments, that is the variances and covariances, of the data. ζ_t is the 2×1 vector of 'disturbances', hence, $\zeta_t \zeta_t'$ is a 2×2 matrix and $E\{\zeta_t \zeta_t'\}$ is the contemporaneous, as the time subscripts are the same on each element, variance–covariance matrix; the diagonal elements refer to variances and off-diagonal elements to covariances between the two equations. $E\{\zeta_t \zeta_s'\}$ is the noncontemporaneous (or temporal) covariance matrix, for example the first element is the covariance between ζ_{1t} and ζ_{1s} for $t \neq s$, and these are zero.

Where the problem becomes more complex is that the parameters in the statistical model, that is B and Ω, may not be the parameters of interest. A hint that this is likely to be the case can be gained by noting that the conditional expectation $E\{Y_t \mid X_t = x_t\} = B'x_t$, does not contain the coefficients on the endogenous variables. For example, the coefficient on Y_{2t} in the Y_{1t} equation is not in this formulation, yet it is a parameter of interest. The way forward is to reparameterise $Y_t = B'x_t + \zeta_t$, so that it contains the parameters of interest. First, separate out Y_{1t} from the other endogenous variables, here just Y_{2t}.

$$(Y_{1t} \mid X_t = x_t) = b_1' x_t + \zeta_{1t} \qquad \text{(A4.19a)}$$

$$(Y_{2t} \mid X_t = x_t) = b_2' x_t + \zeta_{2t} \qquad \text{(A4.19b)}$$

Where $b_1' = (\beta_{11}, \beta_{12})$ is the first row of B', and $b_2' = (\beta_{21}, \beta_{22})$ is the second row of B'. The variance–covariance matrix is:

$$\Omega = \begin{bmatrix} \Omega_{11} & \Omega_{12} \\ \Omega_{21} & \Omega_{22} \end{bmatrix} \qquad \text{(A4.20)}$$

Where Ω was defined by (A4.18b). In general with m 'endogenous' variables, Y_t, and g 'exogenous' variables, X_t, Ω_{22} is a $(m-1) \times (m-1)$ matrix rather than a scalar and b_2' is a $(m-1) \times g$ matrix rather than a vector.

Now condition on Y_{2t} and $X_t = x_t$:

$$Y_{1t} = \gamma_{12} Y_{2t} + \delta_{11} x_{1t} + \delta_{12} x_{2t} + \varepsilon_{1t} \qquad \text{(A4.21)}$$

Define $\delta_1' \equiv (\delta_{11}, \delta_{12})$. Then $\gamma_{12} = \Omega_{22}^{-1}\Omega_{21}$ and $\delta_1 = b_1 - b_2\Omega_{22}^{-1}\Omega_{21}$ – see Spanos (1986). Equation (A4.21) is in the form we recognise as a 'structural' equation, with structural coefficients $(\gamma_{12}, \delta_{11}, \delta_{12})$, which are related back to the parameters and moments of the underlying joint distribution of the four variables Y_1, Y_2, X_1 and X_2 given by (A4.15) and (A4.16).

We have deliberately turned full circle since, apart from a constant, (A4.21) with $\delta_{12} = 0$ has a direct correspondence with (A4.11). Neither is the zero restriction $\delta_{12} = 0$ incidental, since that relates back to the discussion at the end of section **4.9.2** concerning identification. In general, there are $m \times g$ parameters in B and $\frac{1}{2}m(m+1)$ parameters in the covariance matrix

Ω, a total of $mg + \frac{1}{2}m(m+1)$; in the example this is $4 + 3 = 7$. Now if each endogenous variable is reparameterised into the form (A4.21) that will define $m \times ((m-1)+g)$ structural coefficients and $\frac{1}{2}m(m+1)$ parameters in the corresponding covariance matrix, Θ. The difference is $m(m-1)$, which is the number of restrictions necessary if the structural parameters are to be identified. In our example, $m(m-1) = 2(2-1) = 2$, and this was achieved because R_t was excluded from (A4.11) and I_t was excluded from (A4.12).

In general, the complete set of parameters in the m structural equations is denoted $\varphi \equiv (\Gamma, D, \Theta)$, where Θ is the variance–covariance matrix of ε_{it}, $i = 1, \ldots, m$. In the example of this section, the system in structural form is:

$$Y_{1t} - \gamma_{12} Y_{2t} = \delta_{11} x_{1t} + \delta_{12} x_{2t} + \varepsilon_{1t} \qquad \text{(A4.22a)}$$

$$-\gamma_{21} Y_{1t} + Y_{2t} = \delta_{21} x_{1t} + \delta_{22} x_{2t} + \varepsilon_{2t} \qquad \text{(A4.22b)}$$

This can be rewritten in a more convenient matrix form in two equivalent ways:

$$\begin{bmatrix} 1 & -\gamma_{12} \\ -\gamma_{21} & 1 \end{bmatrix} \begin{pmatrix} Y_{1t} \\ Y_{2t} \end{pmatrix}$$
$$= \begin{bmatrix} \delta_{11} & \delta_{12} \\ \delta_{21} & \delta_{22} \end{bmatrix} \begin{pmatrix} x_{1t} \\ x_{2t} \end{pmatrix} + \begin{pmatrix} \varepsilon_{1t} \\ \varepsilon_{1t} \end{pmatrix} \qquad \text{(A4.23a)}$$

$$(Y_{1t} \quad Y_{2t}) \begin{bmatrix} 1 & -\gamma_{21} \\ -\gamma_{12} & 1 \end{bmatrix}$$
$$= (x_{1t} \quad x_{2t}) \begin{bmatrix} \delta_{11} & \delta_{21} \\ \delta_{12} & \delta_{22} \end{bmatrix} + (\varepsilon_{1t} \quad \varepsilon_{2t}) \qquad \text{(A4.23b)}$$

Note that (A4.23b) is the transpose of (A4.23a). Which representation we use depends upon convenience. (A4.23a) can be written even more compactly as:

$$\Gamma Y_t = D x_t + \varepsilon_t \qquad \text{(A4.24)}$$

Incidentally the reduced form of (A4.24) is now easily obtained by premultiplying (A4.24) by Γ^{-1} to give:

$$Y_t = \Gamma^{-1}Dx_t + \Gamma^{-1}\varepsilon_t \qquad (A4.25)$$

The reduced form differs from the structural form by expressing the endogenous variables entirely in terms of the variables in X_t.

There are several maximum likelihood-based methods of estimation which differ depending upon how much information is used in estimation, varying from information on one equation to information on the complete system of equations. These methods are usually referred to as limited information and full information maximum likelihood, respectively, denoted LIML and FIML. Although the technical details of estimation are not needed for the remaining chapters, reference to FIML estimation is made later, especially in Chapters 15 and 16, so an outline of the method is included here.

First, define the parameters in the conditional multivariate normal model given by (A4.19) and (A4.20) as $\theta \equiv (B, \Omega)$. The conditional pdf for the system comprising Y_t conditional on X_t and θ is:

$$f(Y_t \mid X_t; \theta) = \frac{1}{(2\pi)^{\frac{m}{2}}[\det(\Omega)]^{\frac{1}{2}}}$$
$$\times \exp\{-\tfrac{1}{2}(Y_t - B'x_t)'$$
$$\times \Omega^{-1}(Y_t - B'x_t)\} \qquad (A4.26)$$

Where $\det(\Omega)$ is the determinant of Ω. If the parameters in θ are to be related to a structural (simultaneous equations) model with identified parameters then restrictions must be imposed upon ML estimation based on (A4.26). The resulting ML estimator can be viewed as determining the structural coefficients in $\varphi \equiv (\Gamma, D, \Theta)$ as functions of the parameters in the restricted multivariate model. The technical details are beyond the scope of this book – see Hendry (1976) or Spanos (1986).

Alternatively, working directly in terms of the structural representation (A4.23b) it is first convenient to define the complete set of T observations:

$$Y\Gamma' = xD' + \varepsilon'$$

where Y is the T by m matrix of observations on the Y_t variables, x is the T by g matrix of observations on the x_t variables and ε' is the T by m matrix of 'disturbances'. The coefficient matrices Γ and D are assumed to have sufficient restrictions imposed to identify them. The log-likelihood function is:

$$
\begin{aligned}
LL(Y_t \mid X_t; \varphi) = &-\frac{mT}{2}\log(2\pi) \\
&+ T\log[|\det(\Gamma)|] \\
&- \frac{T}{2}\log[\det(\Theta)] \\
&- \frac{1}{2}\operatorname{tr}(\Theta^{-1})(\Gamma Y - Dx) \\
&\times (Y'\Gamma' - x'D') \qquad (A4.27)
\end{aligned}
$$

Where $|\det(\Gamma)|$ is the absolute value of the determinant of Γ, and $\operatorname{tr}(A)$ stands for the trace, that is the sum of the diagonal elements, of A. Obtaining the FIML estimator proceeds by maximising the log-likelihood function with respect to Θ, Γ and D. Again the details are technical and a good reference is Amemiya (1985).

A4.1.5 Hypothesis testing

Given the set-up of maximum likelihood estimation, it is fairly simple to derive a test statistic, that has wide applicability. Let H_0 denote a set of j linear restrictions on the regression model, these might be restrictions on individual coefficients or combinations of the coefficients. The log-likelihood of the regression model without the restrictions imposed is denoted LL_{ur}, whereas with the restrictions imposed it is LL_r, and note that $LL_{ur} \geq LL_r$, so that $(LL_r / LL_{ur}) \leq 1$ and is only 1 if the restrictions are satisfied in the particular sample. Then

$$LLR \equiv -2(LL_r - LL_{ur}) = 2(LL_{ur} - LL_r)$$

is asymptotically distributed as $\chi^2(j)$ if the null hypothesis is correct where *LLR* is the logarithm of the likelihood ratio. Hence large values of *LLR* relative to the $(1 - \alpha)\%$ quantile of the $\chi^2(j)$ distribution lead to rejection of the null hypothesis. For example, if H_0 comprises two restrictions and $\alpha = 0.05$, then the 95% quantile of the $\chi^2(2)$ distribution is 5.99; a sample value exceeding 5.99 is, therefore, not consistent with the null hypothesis at the 5% significance level.

A4.2 Computer output

Typical computer output from four leading econometric programs is shown in normal type; comments are in **bold** and show relation to Chapters 4 and 5. Reference back to this section after reading Chapter 5 will be useful.

A4.2.1 MICROFIT

Ordinary Least Squares Estimation

Dependent variable is WDOT
53 observations used for estimation from 1861 to 1913

Regressor	Coefficient	Standard Error	T-Ratio[Prob]
constant	$\hat{\beta}_1$	$\hat{\sigma}(\hat{\beta}_1)$	$\text{`}t\text{'} = \hat{\beta}_1/\hat{\sigma}(\hat{\beta}_1)$ [msl of 't']
INPT	-2.3225	.33286	$-6.9775[.000]$
$1/u_t$	$\hat{\beta}_2$	$\hat{\sigma}(\hat{\beta}_2)$	$\text{`}t\text{'} = \hat{\beta}_2/\hat{\sigma}(\hat{\beta}_2)$ [msl of 't']
UINV	10.9252	.92986	11.7493[.000]

Centred R^2		**See Chapter 5.**	
R-Squared	.73022	F-statistic $F(1, 51)$	138.0463[.000]
$\bar{R}^2$		$\hat{\sigma}$	
R-Bar-Squared	.72494	S.E of Regression	1.2868
$\sum \hat{\varepsilon}_t^2$		$\bar{y} = \sum y_t/T$	
Residual Sum of Squares	84.4486	Mean of Dependent Variable	.99137
$\left[\sum (y_t - \bar{y})^2/(T - 1)\right]^{0.5}$		**Chapter 4 appendix.**	
S.D. of Dependent Variable	2.4535	Maximum of Log-likelihood	-87.4388
See Chapter 5.			
DW-statistic	1.8847		

A4.2.2   TSP

TSP Version 4.2A
Copyright (C) 1993 TSP International
ALL RIGHTS RESERVED
TSP International
P.O. Box 61015, Station A
Palo Alto, CA 94306
USA

1 freq a;	**Sets frequency to annual.**
2 smpl 1861:1 1913:1;	**Defines sample period.**
3 read(file = '\data\ch4wdot.dat') wdot uinv;	**Reads data from data directory.**
4 print wdot uinv;	**Prints data as a check.**
5 smpl 1861:1 1913:1;	**Defines estimation period.**
6 olsq wdot c uinv;	**OLS instructions.**
EXECUTION	

Current sample: 1861 to 1913

Equation 1
Method of estimation = Ordinary Least Squares

Dependent variable: WDOT
Current sample: 1861 to 1913
Number of observations: 53

$$T$$

Mean of dependent variable = .991367

$$\bar{y} = \sum y_t/T$$

Std. dev. of dependent var. = 2.45354

$$\left[\sum (y_t - \bar{y})^2/(T - 1)\right]^{0.5}$$

Sum of squared residuals = 84.4486

$$\sum \hat{\varepsilon}_t^2$$

Variance of residuals = 1.65586

$$\hat{\sigma}^2 = \sum \hat{\varepsilon}_t^2/(T - k)$$

Std. error of regression = 1.28680 $\qquad\hat{\sigma}$
R-squared = .730225 $\qquad$**Centred R^2**
Adjusted R-squared = .724935 $\qquad$**$\bar{R}^2$**
Durbin-Watson statistic = 1.88468 $\qquad$**See Chapter 5.**
F-statistic (zero slopes) = 138.046 $\qquad$**See Chapter 5.**
Schwarz Bayes. Info. Crit. = .615674 $\qquad$**See Chapter 6.**
Log of likelihood function = −87.5488 $\qquad$**Chapter 4 appendix.**

Variable	Estimated Coefficient	Standard Error	t-statistic
	$\hat{\beta}_1$	$\hat{\sigma}(\hat{\beta}_1)$	$'t' = \hat{\beta}_1/\hat{\sigma}(\hat{\beta}_1)$
C	−2.32250	.332856	−6.97747
	$\hat{\beta}_2$	$\hat{\sigma}(\hat{\beta}_2)$	$'t' = \hat{\beta}_2/\hat{\sigma}(\hat{\beta}_2)$
UINV	10.9252	.929863	11.7493

END OF OUTPUT.

A4.2.3 RATS

RATS386 4.10c.
(c) 1992–4 Thomas A. Doan. All rights reserved
cal 1861 1 1   **Set calendar for data.**
allocate 1913:1   **Allocate enough space for the sample.**
* SIMPLE PHILLIPS CURVE
OPEN \DATA\ch4wdot.dat   **Location of data.**
DATA(FORMAT = FREE,ORG = OBS) / wdot uinv   **Names of data series.**
linreg wdot   **Instructions for OLS regression.**
#constant uinv   **Names of regressors.**

Dependent Variable WDOT – Estimation by
Least Squares

Annual Data From 1861:01 To 1913:01			**Sample period.**		
Usable Observations	53	**T**	Degrees of Freedom	51	**$T - k$.**
Centered R**2	0.730225	**R^2**	R Bar **2	0.724935	**$\bar{R}^2$**
Uncentered R**2	0.768711	**R^2_{uc}**	$T \times R$**2	40.742	**T times R^2**

Mean of Dependent Variable	0.9913668302	$\bar{y} = \sum y_t/T$
Std Error of Dependent Variable	2.4535427104	$\left[\sum (y_t - \bar{y})^2/(T - 1) \right]^{0.5}$
Standard Error of Estimate	1.2868005246	$\hat{\sigma}$
Sum of Squared Residuals	84.448635092	$\sum \hat{\varepsilon}_t^2$
Regression $F(1, 51)$	138.0463	**See Chapter 5.**
Significance Level of F	0.00000000	**msl of above F test.**
Durbin-Watson Statistic	1.884681	**See Chapter 5.**
Q(13–0)	25.038305	**Ljung-Box Serial correlation test – see Chapter 5**
Significance Level of Q	0.02281766	**msl of Q test.**

Variable	Coeff	Std Error	T-Stat	Signif
	$\hat{\beta}_1$	$\hat{\sigma}(\hat{\beta}_1)$	$'t' = \hat{\beta}_1/\hat{\sigma}(\hat{\beta}_1)$	**msl of 't' (2-sided)**
1. Constant	−2.32249716	0.33285639	−6.97748	0.00000001
	$\hat{\beta}_2$	$\sigma(\hat{\beta}_2)$	$'t' = \hat{\beta}_2/\hat{\sigma}(\hat{\beta}_2)$	**msl of 't' (2-sided)**
2. UINV	10.92524793	0.92986297	11.74931	0.00000000

A4.2.4 PCGIVE

PcGive 9.00 session

EQ(1) Modelling WDOT by OLS (using Ch4wdot.dat) **data read in as .dat file**
The present sample is: 1861 to 1913 **sample period**

Variable	Coefficient	Std.Error	t-value	t-prob	PartR^2
	$\hat{\beta}_1$	$\hat{\sigma}(\hat{\beta}_1)$	$\hat{\beta}_1/\hat{\sigma}(\hat{\beta}_1)$	**msl**	
Constant	−2.3225	0.33286	−6.977	0.0000	0.4884
	$\hat{\beta}_2$	$\hat{\sigma}(\hat{\beta}_2)$	$\hat{\beta}_2/\hat{\sigma}(\hat{\beta}_2)$	**msl**	
UINV	10.925	0.92986	11.749	0.0000	0.7302

R^2	F test	$\hat{\sigma}$	DW test
↓	see Chapter 5	↓	see Chapter 5
$\hat{R}2 = 0.730225$	$F(1,51) = 138.05$ [0.0000]	sigma = 1.2868	DW = 1.88

$\sum \hat{\varepsilon}_t^2$ ↓

RSS = 84.44863515 for 2 variables and 53 observations

AR 1–2 F(2, 49)	= 0.098229 [0.9066]	**LM test serial correlation test**
ARCH 1 F(1, 49)	= 5.6414e-005 [0.9940]	**ARCH test – see Chapter 16**
Normality Chî2(2)	= 0.94107 [0.6247]	**Jarque-Bera (JB) test for normality**
Xî2 F(2, 48)	= 0.57853 [0.5646]	**White's test for heteroscedasticity[a]**
Xi*Xj F(2, 48)	= 0.57853 [0.5646]	**White's test for heteroscedasticity[b]**
RESET F(1, 50)	= 1.8534 [0.1795]	**Ramsey's RESET test**

The tests in MICROFIT and PCGIVE are described in Chapter 5 as follows: LM test for serial correlation, 5.6.1b; the normality test, 5.7; the RESET test for functional form, 5.8.2; MICROFIT test for heteroscedasticity, 5.5.2c; PCGIVE, White's tests for heteroscedasticity, 5.5.2a. PCGIVE note: a, b, for White's tests for heteroscedasticity in PCGIVE: a uses the squared regressor(s), b uses the regressor cross-product(s); because there is only 1 regressor in this case, they are the same. MICROFIT gives LM and F versions of all but the normality test. These diagnostic tests are easily programmed in TSP and RATS.

Notes for all programs: the DW test is described in section 5.6.1a; the F test (the regression F test) is described in 5.4.2.

CHAPTER 5

Extending estimation and model building to several regressors

5.1 Introduction

The CEF of Chapter 4 has been kept deliberately simple, restricted to the bivariate case involving just the variables Y_t and X_t. While there are very few applications in which only two variables are involved most of the important principles in estimation can be illustrated with this simple case. The extension to the multivariate case is straightforward given the framework outlined in the bivariate case. For example, the method of ordinary least squares still proceeds by defining the residual sum of squares and seeking the estimators that result in a minimum. Similarly the principles of hypothesis testing are the same, with the classical testing procedure involving the specification of a null and an alternative hypothesis. Where there is a difference is in testing hypotheses which involve more than one of the regression coefficients; in that case the distribution of a suitable test statistic under the null hypothesis is likely to lead to the χ^2 or F distribution. The central point is that while the technical details may seem more complex in the multivariate case, if the reader is confident with the bivariate model, there are no 'surprises' awaiting in the extension to more variables.

Section **5.2** extends the linear regression model to more than two variables. This extension is made very much easier if matrix–vector notation is used. Complications that arise from serial correlation and heteroscedasticity in ε_t are considered in section **5.3**; and the generalised least squares, GLS, estimator is introduced and compared to the OLS estimator. Testing multiple hypotheses and principles for the construction of test statistics are considered in section **5.4**. A number of frequently used misspecification tests are introduced in sections **5.5** to **5.9**; these tests serve to assist in establishing whether an empirical model is adequate for the purposes of drawing inference through specification tests. Section **5.10** views the process of model building and evaluation as an iterative one rather than one of simply assigning numerical values to the unknown coefficients. Section **5.11** uses a model of consumption expenditure to provide an extended illustration of the process of model building and assessment. Section **5.12** contains some concluding remarks.

5.2 Extending the bivariate model: more than two regressors

There are several ways to approach an extension of the bivariate model. One possibility is to extend the CEF paradigm with the assumption that there are now $k \geq 2$ random variables for which there is a joint pdf. If the k variables are jointly normally distributed, that is they are *multivariate normal*, then conditioning on $k - 1$ of the variables results in a conditional pdf which is univariate normal. It also results in a

CEF which is linear in the conditioning variables. Since, in principle, it is possible to condition on any one of the k variables there are k CEFs differing in the conditioning variables. In this paradigm, just as in the bivariate case, a choice has to be made as to which CEF is the one containing the parameters of interest; and we have to recognise that it may be necessary to analyse a joint distribution of say $k_1 < k$ variables conditional on the remaining $k - k_1$ variables in order to obtain the parameters of interest. This is one point of principle that does differ between bivariate and multivariate models. The CEF framework accommodates deterministic variables quite easily, as they can be regarded as always taking the role of conditioning variables. The CEF approach fits in more naturally to the view that the aim of estimation and model building is to find an empirical reduction of the DGP, which jointly determines a set of inherently stochastic variables.

An alternative paradigm is to extend the classical linear regression model so that the regressors are $X_{t2}, \ldots, X_{tk}$ (X_{t1} is reserved notation for the constant in the model, so $X_{t1} = 1$ for all t) and these are regarded, in the simplest case, as being fixed in repeated samples and, hence, nonstochastic. As in the bivariate CLRM ε_t, which is usually referred to as the 'disturbance' in this context, is an entity in its own right with an assumed set of properties, for example zero mean, constant variance and no serial correlation, which can be subjected in a particular sample to a number of diagnostic tests. The CLRM can be extended in the direction of nonstochastic regressors and it is relatively easy to do so – see, for example, Greene (1997), especially Chapter 6). In practice, whichever paradigm is adopted the resulting estimation methods are common, for example OLS, instrumental variables and generalised least squares; a preference for one paradigm over another is more to do with the process of model building, for example responding to a significant test statistic for misspecification, rather than estimation.

5.2.1 Multiple regressors: the basic set-up

In a multivariate context the vector of random variables is $Z_t = (Y_t, X_{t2}, \ldots, X_{tk})$ and, as in the bivariate case, each of these random variables is assumed to be stationary. One of the random variables has been designated Y_t to distinguish its status from the remaining variables. In particular we are interested in the conditional expectation of Y_t given $X_{t2}, \ldots X_{tk}$, on the grounds that the resulting CEF contains the parameters of interest. Assuming multivariate normality for the vector Z_t means that the CEF for Y_t is linear in the conditioning variables. Alternatively in the CLRM paradigm we can simply assume that there is a linear regression function with Y_t as the dependent variable and $(X_{t2}, \ldots, X_{tk})$ is the set of regressors. Whichever paradigm is adopted the CEF (regression function) is

$$E\{Y_t \mid X_{t2}, \ldots, X_{tk}\} = \beta_1 + \beta_2 X_{t2} + \cdots$$
$$+ \beta_k X_{tk} \tag{5.1}$$

and the conditional innovation (disturbance) is

$$(\varepsilon_t \mid X_{t2}, \ldots, X_{tk})$$
$$= Y_t - E\{Y_t \mid X_{t2}, \ldots, X_{tk}\} \tag{5.2}$$

therefore

$$Y_t = \beta_1 + \beta_2 X_{t2} + \cdots + \beta_k X_{tk}$$
$$+ (\varepsilon_t \mid X_{t2}, \ldots, X_{tk}) \tag{5.3}$$

Sometimes the notational convenience of using ε_t rather than $(\varepsilon_t \mid X_{t2}, \ldots, X_{tk})$ is adopted here, although this will not be the case where it is necessary to emphasise the conditioning. When this convention is adopted the linear regression model is conveniently written as:

$$Y_t = \beta_1 + \beta_2 X_{t2} + \cdots + \beta_k X_{tk} + \varepsilon_t$$
$$= \beta_1 + \sum_{j=2}^{k} \beta_j X_{tj} + \varepsilon_t \tag{5.4}$$

For further analysis it is convenient to define matrices and vectors of the variables as follows:

$$Y = (Y_1, Y_2, \ldots, Y_T)'$$
$$\beta = (\beta_1, \beta_2, \ldots, \beta_k)'$$
$$\varepsilon = (\varepsilon_1, \varepsilon_2, \ldots, \varepsilon_T)'$$

$$X = \begin{bmatrix} 1 & X_{12} & \cdots & X_{1k} \\ 1 & X_{22} & \cdots & X_{2k} \\ \vdots & \vdots & & \vdots \\ 1 & X_{T2} & \cdots & X_{Tk} \end{bmatrix}$$

Notice that the first column of X has a 1 in every row; this is a dummy variable in the sense that it allows a constant β_1 in the regression model. In matrix notation the regression model of T observations is:

$$Y = X\beta + \varepsilon \tag{5.5}$$

That is:

$$\begin{pmatrix} Y_1 \\ Y_2 \\ \vdots \\ Y_T \end{pmatrix} = \begin{bmatrix} 1 & X_{22} & \cdots & X_{1k} \\ 1 & X_{22} & \cdots & X_{2k} \\ \vdots & \vdots & & \vdots \\ 1 & X_{T2} & \cdots & X_{Tk} \end{bmatrix} \begin{pmatrix} \beta_1 \\ \beta_2 \\ \vdots \\ \beta_k \end{pmatrix}$$

$$+ \begin{pmatrix} \varepsilon \\ \varepsilon_2 \\ \vdots \\ \varepsilon_T \end{pmatrix} \tag{5.6}$$

Y is $T \times 1$; X is $T \times k$ and conformal with β which is $k \times 1$, so $X\beta$ is also $T \times 1$; finally, ε_t is $T \times 1$ and, therefore, conformal with Y and $X\beta$. Particular observations are read off across the rows of $Y = X\beta + \varepsilon$. Where a particular row (=observation) is needed the following notation is used:

$$Y_t = X_t\beta + \varepsilon_t$$

where X_t is the $1 \times k$ vector of observations on the tth row of the matrix X.

The specification of the stochastic properties of ε_t is as follows:

(i) $E\{\varepsilon \mid X\} = 0$;
(ii) $E\{\varepsilon\varepsilon' \mid X\} = \sigma^2 I$, where I is the identity matrix of order T.

The meaning of $E\{\varepsilon \mid X\}$ is that the expectations operator is understood to be applied to every element of $\varepsilon \mid X$; thus $E\{\varepsilon \mid X\}$ is a shorthand for $(E\{\varepsilon_1 \mid X\}, E\{\varepsilon_2 \mid X\}, \ldots, E\{\varepsilon_T \mid X\})'$ and $E\{\varepsilon \mid X\} = 0$ means that every element in the vector is equal to 0. The typical element of $E\{\varepsilon \mid X\}$ is $E\{\varepsilon_t \mid X\}$, which is interpreted as the expectation of ε_t conditional on the whole set of T observations in X. If $E\{\varepsilon \mid X\} = \mu_\varepsilon \neq 0$ then the constant in the regression can be redefined as $\beta_1 + \mu_\varepsilon$ and the 'disturbances' as $\varepsilon_t^* = \varepsilon_t - \mu_\varepsilon$, hence $E\{\varepsilon^* \mid X\} = 0$.

$E\{\varepsilon\varepsilon' \mid X\} = \sigma^2 I$ comprise two sets of assumptions. First, note that $\varepsilon\varepsilon'$ is a $T \times T$ matrix

$$\varepsilon\varepsilon' = \begin{bmatrix} \varepsilon_1^2 & \varepsilon_1\varepsilon_2 & \varepsilon_1\varepsilon_3 & \cdots & \varepsilon_1\varepsilon_T \\ \varepsilon_2\varepsilon_1 & \varepsilon_2^2 & \varepsilon_2\varepsilon_3 & \cdots & \varepsilon_2\varepsilon_T \\ \vdots & \vdots & \cdots & & \vdots \\ \varepsilon_T\varepsilon_1 & \varepsilon_T\varepsilon_2 & \varepsilon_T\varepsilon_3 & \cdots & \varepsilon_T^2 \end{bmatrix}$$

The typical diagonal element of $\varepsilon\varepsilon'$ is ε_t^2 with conditional expectation $E\{\varepsilon_t^2 \mid X\}$. The conditional variance of ε_t^2 is $E\{(\varepsilon_t - E\{\varepsilon_t \mid X\})^2 \mid X\}$; however, as $E\{\varepsilon_t \mid X\} = 0$ this reduces to $E\{\varepsilon_t^2 \mid X\}$; hence, $E\{\varepsilon_t^2 \mid X\} = \sigma^2$ for all t is interpreted as the conditional variance of ε_t is constant, usually referred to as *homoscedasticity*.

The off-diagonal elements of $\varepsilon\varepsilon'$ relate to terms where the time index differs; in general we can represent this as $\varepsilon_t\varepsilon_s$ for $t \neq s$. The conditional covariance of ε_t and ε_s is

$$E\{[(\varepsilon_t - E\{\varepsilon_t \mid X\}) \mid X][(\varepsilon_s - E\{\varepsilon_s \mid X\}) \mid X]\}$$

however, because $E\{\varepsilon_t \mid X\} = E\{\varepsilon_s \mid X\} = 0$ this reduces to $E\{\varepsilon_t\varepsilon_s \mid X\}$, hence the off-diagonal elements of $E\{\varepsilon\varepsilon' \mid X\}$ are the covariances between ε_t and ε_s (conditional on X) which are assumed to be 0. Because the covariance between ε_t and

ε_s is the numerator of the serial correlation coefficient between ε_t and ε_s, zero covariance implies (and is implied by) zero serial correlation. In summary $E\{\varepsilon\varepsilon' \mid X\} = \sigma^2 I$ embodies homoscedasticity and zero serial correlation.

5.2.2 Deriving the OLS estimator

As in the bivariate case it is necessary to define the estimated values, $\hat{Y}$, and the residuals, $\hat{\varepsilon}$; specifically

$$\hat{Y} = X\hat{\beta} \quad \text{and} \quad \hat{\varepsilon} = Y - \hat{Y}$$

Then the residual sum of squares to be minimised is:

$$\begin{aligned}
\text{RSS} &= \hat{\varepsilon}'\hat{\varepsilon} \\
&= (Y - X\hat{\beta})'(Y - X\hat{\beta}) \\
&= (Y'Y - 2\hat{\beta}'X'Y + \hat{\beta}'X'X\hat{\beta} \\
&\quad \text{using } \hat{\beta}'X'Y = Y'X\hat{\beta} \quad (5.7)
\end{aligned}$$

The $\hat{\ }$ notation is reserved for the OLS estimator that leads to a minimum in the RSS. The necessary conditions for a minimum are that the partial derivatives with respect to the elements of $\hat{\beta}$ are set equal to zero; that is

$$\frac{\partial \text{RSS}}{\partial \hat{\beta}} = -2(X'Y + X'X\beta) = 0 \quad (5.8)$$

which implies $X'X\hat{\beta} = X'Y$; this is a set of k simultaneous equations, sometimes referred to as the normal equations, to be solved for $\hat{\beta}$. If $X'X$ is of full rank ($=k$) then the solution is:

$$\hat{\beta} = (X'X)^{-1}X'Y \quad (5.9)$$

which is the ordinary least squares, OLS, estimator. To check that this is a minimum, differentiate again

$$\frac{\partial^2(\text{RSS})}{\partial(\hat{\beta})^2} = -2X'X \quad (5.10)$$

A matrix of the form $X'X$ is positive definite, hence $-X'X$ is negative definite and, therefore, the OLS estimator locates a minimum rather

than a maximum in the RSS. (A useful reference for the mathematical analysis used here is Sydsaeter and Hammond (1995).)

The normal equations imply some interesting properties:

$$\begin{aligned}
\text{from} \quad & X'X\hat{\beta} = X'Y \\
& X'\hat{Y} = X'Y \quad \text{using } \hat{Y} = X\hat{\beta} \\
\Rightarrow \quad & X'(Y - \hat{Y}) = 0 \\
\text{that is} \quad & X'\hat{\varepsilon} = 0 \quad \text{using } \hat{\varepsilon} = Y - \hat{Y} \quad (5.11)
\end{aligned}$$

The last of these states that the OLS residuals are orthogonal to the regressors, which mimics the property in the population that the regressors and innovations (disturbances) are uncorrelated. If the first column of X has a 1 in each row, so that the regression includes a constant, then $\sum \hat{\varepsilon}_t = 0$, so that the sum of the OLS residuals is zero.

The OLS estimator, $\hat{\beta} = (X'X)^{-1}X'Y$, is conditionally and unconditionally unbiased. Consider

$$\begin{aligned}
E\{\hat{\beta} \mid X\} &= E\{(X'X)^{-1}X'Y \mid X\} \\
&= (X'X)^{-1}X'E\{Y \mid X\} \quad \text{because} \\
&\qquad \text{expectations are taken} \\
&\qquad \text{conditional on } X \\
&= (X'X)^{-1}X'X\beta \\
&\qquad \text{using } E\{Y \mid X\} = X\beta \\
&= \beta \quad (5.12)
\end{aligned}$$

hence $\hat{\beta}$ is conditionally unbiased; also since $E\{\hat{\beta} \mid X\} = \beta$, which does not depend on X, $\hat{\beta}$ is unconditionally unbiased.

5.2.3 The variance–covariance matrix of $\hat{\beta}$

It is convenient at this stage to derive the conditional and unconditional variance matrix for $\hat{\beta}$. Consider

$$\begin{aligned}
\hat{\beta} &= (X'X)^{-1}X'Y \\
&= (X'X)^{-1}X'(X\beta + \varepsilon) \\
&= (X'X)^{-1}X'X\beta + (X'X)^{-1}X'\varepsilon \\
&= \beta + (X'X)^{-1}X'\varepsilon
\end{aligned}$$

hence

$$\hat{\beta} - \beta = (X'X)^{-1}X'\varepsilon \qquad (5.13)$$

The conditional variance matrix of $\hat{\beta}$ (which we refer to henceforth more simply as the variance matrix) is

$$
\begin{aligned}
E\{(\hat{\beta} &- \beta)(\hat{\beta} - \beta)' \mid X\} \\
&= E\{((X'X)^{-1}X'\varepsilon)((X'X)^{-1}X'\varepsilon)' \mid X\} \\
&= ((X'X)^{-1}X')E\{\varepsilon\varepsilon' \mid X\}X(X'X)^{-1} \\
&\quad \text{because of the conditioning on } X \\
&= (X'X)^{-1}X'(\sigma^2 I)X(X'X)^{-1} \\
&\quad \text{using } E\{\varepsilon\varepsilon' \mid X\} = \sigma^2 I \\
&= \sigma^2(X'X)^{-1} \quad \text{using } \sigma^2 \text{ is a scalar} \\
&\quad \text{and constant} \qquad\qquad (5.14)
\end{aligned}
$$

Thus, the variance matrix of $\hat{\beta}$ conditional on X is $\sigma^2(X'X)^{-1}$; if in a particular sample the realisations of X are $X = x$ then $\text{Var}(\hat{\beta} \mid x) = \sigma^2(x'x)^{-1}$. The diagonal elements of this matrix are particularly important because they provide the variances of the individual elements of $\hat{\beta}$; for example, the ith diagonal element of $\sigma^2(X'X)^{-1}$ is the variance of $\hat{\beta}_i$. The square root of this is the standard error of $\hat{\beta}_i$. In general an estimator of σ^2 is required in order to obtain an operational expression for the variances and standard errors. We return to this problem shortly.

The unconditional variance of $\hat{\beta}$ is obtained by using the variance decomposition. That is

$$
\begin{aligned}
\text{Var}(\hat{\beta}) = E_X\{\text{Var}(\hat{\beta} \mid X)\} \\
+ \text{Var}_X(E\{\hat{\beta} \mid X\}) \qquad (5.15)
\end{aligned}
$$

This simplifies because $E\{\hat{\beta} \mid X\} = \beta$, and hence does not vary with X, so $\text{Var}_X(E\{\hat{\beta} \mid X\})$; therefore,

$$
\begin{aligned}
\text{Var}(\hat{\beta}) &= E_X\{\text{Var}(\hat{\beta} \mid X)\} \\
&= E_X\{\sigma^2(X'X)^{-1}\} \\
&= \sigma^2 E_X\{(X'X)^{-1}\} \qquad (5.16)
\end{aligned}
$$

and the unconditional variance of $\hat{\beta}$ depends upon the 'average' value of $(X'X)^{-1}$. In order to go further we would need to specify in greater detail the stochastic properties of X. From a practical point of view, that is in a particular set of realisations from the random variables in X, operational expressions are provided from the conditional variance–covariance matrix of $\hat{\beta}$.

An estimator of σ^2 with desirable properties is provided by

$$\hat{\sigma}^2 = \frac{\hat{\varepsilon}'\hat{\varepsilon}}{(T - k)} \qquad (5.17)$$

That is the residual sum of squares divided by the degrees of freedom. This estimator is the best quadratic unbiased estimator of σ^2. That is in the class of estimators which are quadratic functions of $\hat{\varepsilon}$ and unbiased, $\hat{\sigma}^2$ has minimum variance. Other estimators of σ^2 are possible; for example, $\hat{\varepsilon}'\hat{\varepsilon}/T$, the maximum likelihood estimator, is consistent but not unbiased.

5.3 Generalised least squares, GLS

In the linear regression model $Y = X\beta + \varepsilon$, if $E\{\varepsilon \mid X\} = 0$ and $E\{\varepsilon\varepsilon' \mid X\} = \sigma^2 I$ the OLS estimator $\hat{\beta}$ is unbiased and has minimum variance in the class of linear unbiased estimators. Serial correlation and/or heteroscedasticity in ε imply $E\{\varepsilon\varepsilon' \mid X\} = \Omega \neq \sigma^2 I$ and then, generally, it will be the case that the OLS estimator $\hat{\beta}$ no longer has minimum variance and the usual expression for $\text{Var}(\hat{\beta})$ is incorrect. The qualification 'generally' reflects the technical detail that $E\{\varepsilon\varepsilon' \mid X\} = \sigma^2 I$ is a sufficient rather than a necessary condition for the Gauss–Markov theorem to hold, and there are some cases (which are not likely to be frequently encountered in practice) where $E\{\varepsilon\varepsilon' \mid X\} = \Omega$ but OLS is still efficient provided the correct expression is used for $\text{Var}(\hat{\beta})$.

5.3.1 The GLS estimator

The purpose of this section is to consider estimation when $E\{\varepsilon\varepsilon' \mid X\} = \Omega$. This provides a common background against which to assess the impact of serial correlation, heteroscedasticity and incorrect functional form in later sections. It will be helpful to consider the structure of Ω first in terms of its off-diagonal elements and second in terms of its diagonal elements. The off-diagonal elements of Ω are $E\{\varepsilon_t\varepsilon_s \mid X\}$ for $t \neq s$; in a time series context these are the autocovariances. (We continue to maintain the assumption that $E\{\varepsilon\} = 0$.) Non-zero values of $E\{\varepsilon_t\varepsilon_s \mid X\}$ indicate that the disturbances are related over time (hence they are not innovations). This is the problem of serial correlation of ε_t, considered below in section **5.6.1**. The diagonal elements of Ω are $E\{\varepsilon_t^2 \mid X\}$ which are the conditional variances for $t = 1, \ldots, T$. If these are not equal for all values of t then the variances are heteroscedastic. Typically, the problems of serial correlation and heteroscedasticity are analysed separately from each other, although they might both be present in a particular application. To make progress in a practical situation we need to have some structure for Ω, but at this stage we consider the problem in general terms with $\Omega \neq \sigma^2 I$.

In some texts we find Ω written as $\sigma^2\Phi$ and, as we will use this convention several times in this chapter, it is worth explaining the difference. σ^2 is a scalar which has been factored out of Ω and can sometimes be given an interpretation, for example in the special case when $\Phi = I$ then $\Omega = \sigma^2 I$ and σ^2 is the constant (conditional) variance of ε_t; similarly, when ε_t is serially correlated according to either an AR or MA process – see section **5.6.1** below – σ^2 can be interpreted as the variance of the white noise part of the process; at its simplest σ^2 could be taken as the largest common factor of the diagonal elements of Ω, for example suppose Ω is a 3×3 matrix with diagonal elements $3, 6, 9$, then we can factor out $\sigma^2 = 3$ with the diagonal elements of Φ equal to $1, 2, 3$.

Returning to the general case, progress could be made when $E\{\varepsilon\varepsilon' \mid X\} = \Omega$ if the regression model $Y = X\beta + \varepsilon$ could be transformed to $Y^* = X^*\beta + \varepsilon^*$ so that $E\{\varepsilon^*\varepsilon^{*\prime} \mid X\} = \sigma^2 I$, where $Y^* = PY$, $X^* = PX$ and $\varepsilon^* = P\varepsilon$. P is a $T \times T$ non-singular matrix that transforms, that is weights and combines in linear combinations if necessary, the observations in the underlying model. For simplicity we assume that P comprises non-stochastic elements. Suppose such a transformation exists, then what is required of it? Consider the variance–covariance matrix of ε^* in the transformed model,

$$
\begin{aligned}
E\{\varepsilon^*\varepsilon^{*\prime} &\mid X\} \\
&= E\{P\varepsilon(P\varepsilon)' \mid X\} \\
&= E\{P\varepsilon\varepsilon'P' \mid X\} \\
&= PE\{\varepsilon\varepsilon' \mid X\}P' \quad \text{using } P \text{ is nonstochastic} \\
&= P\Omega P' \quad \text{using } E\{\varepsilon\varepsilon' \mid X\} = \Omega \\
&= \sigma^2 P\Phi P' \quad \text{using } \Omega = \sigma^2\Phi \qquad (5.18)
\end{aligned}
$$

From the last line, we see that for the transformation to work then $P\Phi P' = I$. As P is nonsingular it has an inverse, then premultiplying $P\Phi P$ by P^{-1} and postmultiplying by P'^{-1} results in $P^{-1}P\Phi P'P'^{-1} = \Phi$; carrying out the same operations to the right-hand side gives $P^{-1}P'^{-1}$, hence $\Phi = P^{-1}P'^{-1}$ and, therefore, $\Phi^{-1} = P'P$. (This last expression uses the result that if $A = BC$ then $A^{-1} = C^{-1}B^{-1}$ provided both B and C are nonsingular.) Given a complex structure for Φ, P can be quite difficult to obtain; however, there are some simple and commonly occurring cases. If Φ is diagonal, but the diagonal elements are not equal, there is (just) heteroscedasticity and in this case P is diagonal and, hence, $P = P'$; in this case $\Phi^{-1} = P^2$ and P is a diagonal matrix with the ith diagonal element equal to the reciprocal of the square root of the ith diagonal element of Φ. Other cases that have been worked out include serial correlation in ε_t, where the generating process is either a low order autoregressive scheme, for example $\varepsilon_t = \rho\varepsilon_{t-1} + u_t$, or a low order moving average scheme, for example $\varepsilon_t = u_t + \theta u_{t-1}$.

Deriving an efficient estimator is straightforward if P is known, since the effect of the transformation is to ensure that Var$(\varepsilon^* \mid X) = \sigma^2 I$, and OLS can be applied to the transformed model. The resulting estimator is

$$\beta^0 = (X^{*\prime}X^*)^{-1}X^{*\prime}Y^* \quad \text{by analogy}$$
$$\text{with the standard case}$$
$$\text{where } \hat{\beta} = (X'X)^{-1}X'Y$$
$$\beta^0 = [(PX)'PX]^{-1}(PX)'PY$$
$$= [X'P'PX]^{-1}X'P'PY \qquad (5.19)$$

The original model does not literally have to be transformed, since we can now substitute $P'P = \Phi^{-1}$ to obtain

$$\beta^0 = [X'\Phi^{-1}X]^{-1}X'\Phi^{-1}Y \qquad (5.20)$$

To distinguish β^0 from $\hat{\beta}$, the OLS estimator, the former is referred to as the generalised least squares, GLS, estimator.

5.3.2 The variance–covariance matrix of the GLS estimator, Var(β^0)

The variance–covariance matrix of β^0 is

$$\text{Var}(\beta^0) = \sigma^2(X^{*\prime}X^*)^{-1} \quad \text{by analogy with}$$
$$\text{the standard case where}$$
$$\text{Var}(\hat{\beta}) = \sigma^2(X'X)^{-1}$$
$$= \sigma^2[X'P'PX]^{-1}$$
$$= \sigma^2[X'\Phi^{-1}X]^{-1} \qquad (5.21)$$

An unbiased estimator of σ^2 is again obtained by analogy with the standard OLS set-up; specifically, the GLS estimator of σ^2 is

$$\tilde{\sigma}^2 = \hat{\varepsilon}^{*\prime}\hat{\varepsilon}^*/(T-k)$$

where $\hat{\varepsilon}^*$ is the vector of residuals from GLS estimation.

The GLS estimator β^0 is unbiased and, provided Φ is known, is more efficient than the OLS estimator $\hat{\beta}$. This is not, however, a typical situation. Usually Φ is an unknown and estima-

tion proceeds in two steps. First, a consistent estimator Φ, say $\tilde{\Phi}$, is obtained; then this is used in place of the unknown Φ in β^0 and Var(β^0) so that the GLS procedure is feasible. The resulting estimator $\beta^0 = [X'\tilde{\Phi}^{-1}X]^{-1}\tilde{\Phi}^{-1}Y$ is usually referred to as the FLGS estimator. (Note that β^0 can also be written as $\beta^0 = [X'\tilde{\Omega}^{-1}X]^{-1}X'\tilde{\Omega}^{-1}Y$ because σ^2 will cancel out.) There is not usually a need to make a notational distinction between the GLS and FGLS estimator, since it is apparent from the context whether the feasible procedure is being described. Unfortunately the GLS estimator loses its clear-cut advantage over the OLS estimator when Φ has to be estimated; the FGLS estimator is now only asymptotically more efficient than the OLS estimator. This raises the interesting question of whether it would be worth reconsidering the OLS estimator.

5.3.3 OLS or GLS?

A standard proof that $\hat{\beta}$ remains unbiased when $E\{\varepsilon\varepsilon' \mid X\} = \Omega \neq \sigma^2 I$ is as follows. The OLS estimator is $\hat{\beta} = (X'X)^{-1}X'Y$, hence substituting $Y = X\beta + \varepsilon$ then

$$\hat{\beta} = \beta + (X'X)^{-1}X'\varepsilon$$

This is unbiased since

$$E\{\hat{\beta} \mid X\} = \beta + (X'X)^{-1}X'E\{\varepsilon \mid X\}$$
$$= \beta \quad \text{using } E\{\varepsilon \mid X\} = 0$$

This proof, while correct for the conditions stated, can be somewhat misleading when the reason for $E\{\varepsilon\varepsilon' \mid X\} = \Omega \neq \sigma^2 I$ arises from a misspecification which also affects $E\{\varepsilon \mid X\}$ – we consider this situation below.

An important point to note is that when $E\{\varepsilon\varepsilon' \mid X\} = \Omega \neq \sigma^2 I$, the usual expression for Var$(\hat{\beta}) = \sigma^2(X'X)^{-1}$ is incorrect. The variance matrix of $\hat{\beta}$ is

$$E\{(\hat{\beta}) - \beta)(\hat{\beta} - \beta)'\}$$
$$= E\{(X'X)^{-1}X'\varepsilon\varepsilon'X(X'X)^{-1}\} \qquad (5.22)$$

evaluating this conditionally on X

$$E\{(\hat{\beta} - \beta)(\hat{\beta} - \beta)' \mid X\}$$
$$= E\{(X'X)^{-1}X'\varepsilon\varepsilon'X(X'X)^{-1} \mid X\}$$
$$= (X'X)^{-1}X'E\{\varepsilon\varepsilon' \mid X\}X(X'X)^{-1}$$
$$= (X'X)^{-1}X'\Omega X(X'X)^{-1}$$
$$\text{using } E\{\varepsilon\varepsilon' \mid X\} = \Omega$$
$$= \sigma^2(X'X)^{-1}X'\Phi X(X'X)^{-1}$$
$$\text{using } \Omega = \sigma^2\Phi \qquad (5.23)$$

and, in general,

$$\sigma^2(X'X)^{-1} \neq (X'X)^{-1}X'\Omega X(X'X)^{-1}$$

hence using $\sigma^2(X'X)^{-1}$ as the expression for $\text{Var}(\hat{\beta})$ is incorrect.

The correct combinations when $E\{\varepsilon\varepsilon' \mid X\}$ are:

OLS	**GLS**
estimator:	
$\hat{\beta} = (X'X)^{-1}X'Y$	$\beta^0 = [X'\Omega^{-1}X]^{-1}X'\Omega^{-1}Y$
variance matrix:	
$\text{Var}(\hat{\beta}) = (X'X)^{-1}$ $\times X'\Omega X(X'X)^{-1}$	$\text{Var}(\beta^0) = [X'\Omega^{-1}X]^{-1}$

A feasible GLS estimator results from replacing the generally unknown Ω with a consistent estimator, $\tilde{\Omega}$.

5.4 Testing hypotheses

Estimation is only one part of model building. An second important component is hypothesis testing, whether for misspecification analysis or for specification testing. This section first outlines three general principles for hypothesis testing, which apply in a bivariate or multivariate context. The hypothesis tests introduced in Chapter 4 are then extended to testing multiple hypotheses.

5.4.1 Testing principles: Lagrange-Multiplier, likelihood ratio, Wald

The general concern outlined so far is to test a null hypothesis H_0 against an alternative hypothesis H_a. The model specified by H_0 is a restriction of that specified by H_a; that is $H_0 \subset H_a$. For example, in the case of the simplest 't' statistic H_0 restricts a particular regression coefficient, say β_i, to zero, whereas it is allowed to be nonzero under H_a. Testing H_0 only involves estimation under the alternative hypothesis. That is we estimate the regression model including the ith regressor, X_{ti}, and then assess whether the estimated coefficient provides evidence against the null hypothesis. This is an example of the Wald principle of hypothesis testing, which only requires estimation under H_a.

There are two other principles, which are used in the construction of test statistics. In the Lagrange-Multiplier, LM, principle it is only the model according to H_0 which is estimated. This is convenient where the model according to H_a is complex and/or difficult to estimate. Suppose $\varepsilon_t = u_t + \theta_1 u_{t-1}$ where u_t is white noise, which is known as a moving average error, then H_0 is $\theta_1 = 0$ and H_a is $\theta_1 \neq 0$; estimation under the null is considerably easier than estimation under the alternative since $\theta_1 = 0$ just leads to the standard regression model. Although estimation under H_a will have to be considered if H_0 is rejected, using the LM procedure will be particularly economical when H_0 is not rejected. Finally, the likelihood ratio principle involves estimation of both the null model and the alternative model and hence a direct comparison of how well each fits the data. The origin of this principle is estimation of both models according to the principle of maximum likelihood; the maximised likelihood under the restricted model of H_0 cannot exceed the maximised likelihood under the (more) general model of H_a. A comparison of the restricted and unrestricted maximised likelihoods is the basis of a likelihood ratio test statistic – see also **A4.1.5**.

H_0 is assumed to be a linear hypothesis on H_a. For example, $\beta_i = 0$ is a straightforward linear hypothesis involving one coefficient; another example, this time involving two coefficients, is $\beta_2 + \beta_3 = c$, where c is a constant. An H_0 which simultaneously restricts several coefficients with linear hypotheses is $\beta_i = 0$ for $i = 2, \ldots, k$. An example of a nonlinear hypothesis is $\beta_i\beta_j = c \neq 0$. Given a specification of H_0 as a set of linear restrictions on H_a and test statistics W, LR and LM calculated according to the Wald, Likelihood Ratio and Lagrange-Multiplier principles, respectively, then in finite samples $W \geq LR \geq LM$ with the equality holding asymptotically. If an asymptotic critical value is used in a finite sample, then W is more likely to lead to rejection of H_0 compared to LR, and LR is more likely to lead to rejection of H_0 compared to LM. The obverse of this result is that if the asymptotic critical value is used the actual size (percentage rejections of the null when the null is true) of the W test will be larger than for LR, and larger for LR compared to LM; and in finite samples none could actually equal the nominal size! There are two practical responses to this problem apart from no action. Either the test statistic or the critical value can be adjusted. In the first case an adjustment factor, usually depending on the sample size and the number of parameters being estimated, is applied to the test statistic.

The second practical response is to obtain finite sample critical values. There are some special cases where the finite sample distribution of the test statistic is known, for example the standard 't' and F statistics when the regression model is linear with nonstochastic variables and ε_t is normal white noise. However, as soon as we move away from this set-up, for example if one of the regressors is a lagged dependent variable, the finite sample distribution is either intractable or simply unknown, and reliance is again placed on the asymptotic distribution to provide critical values. An alternative is simulation with finite samples of varying size to obtain the empirical distribution of the test statistic and hence relevant critical values. If the Monte Carlo simulation is detailed enough it may be possible to identify the dependence of the empirical distributions on the sample size; this dependence could be used to estimate a relationship between the critical values, the sample size and other

factors, for example the lag length in a dynamic regression, which affect the empirical distribution. This relationship is usually known as a response function, an example of which will be used in Chapter 6.

5.4.2 Extension to multiple hypotheses

Both the normal and t distributions apply to situations where there is just one linear combination of coefficients in the null and alternative hypotheses; however, situations often arise in applications of econometrics which involve simultaneous consideration of several linear combinations of coefficients. In this context perhaps the simplest example arises in a multiple regression when the null hypothesis is that simultaneously all of the β coefficients, apart from the constant, are zero. In this case the null hypothesis is

$$H_0: \beta_2 = 0; \ \beta_3 = 0; \ldots; \beta_k = 0$$

and the alternative hypothesis is

$$H_a: \quad \text{at least one of } \beta_j \neq 0, j = 2, \ldots, k$$

Notice that H_0 restricts the parameter space of H_a by constraining all the β_j, $j = 2, \ldots, k$, to equal zero; H_a 'nests' H_0 as a special case, written $H_0 \subset H_a$. The regression implied by the null hypothesis is simply that of Y_t on a constant, whereas that of the alternative is the regression of Y_t on a constant and the regressors $X_{t2}, \ldots, X_{tk}$. The residual sums of squares from these regressions are:

$$H_0: \text{RRSS} \equiv \sum_{t=1}^{T} \hat{\varepsilon}_t^2 = \sum_{t=1}^{T} (Y_t - \hat{\beta}_1)^2 \quad (5.24)$$

$$H_a: \text{URSS} \equiv \sum_{t=1}^{T} \hat{\varepsilon}_t^2$$

$$= \sum_{t=1}^{T} \left(Y_t - \sum_{j=1}^{k} \hat{\beta}_j X_{tj} \right)^2 \quad (5.25)$$

If X_{tj}, $j = 2, \ldots, k$, have something to add by way of accounting for the variation in Y_t then URSS < RRSS, but we know anyway that URSS cannot exceed RRSS because the unconstrained optimum will never be worse than the constrained optimum. The residual sum of squares in the restricted model is always available in the unrestricted model if the coefficient restrictions are exactly satisfied in the data. Hence

$$RRSS - URSS \geq 0$$

It might be thought that a test statistic could be based on the difference between the residual sum of squares because a 'large' difference implies that the restrictions of the null hypothesis are being forced on the data. However, this difference is not scale invariant and this is important for two reasons: change in the units of measurement throughout the regression will change the size of the difference; and the judgement of whether a particular difference is large or small should be normalised by a factor which gives the relative cost of imposing the restrictions.

A relative measure of the cost of imposing the restrictions of the null hypothesis is given by what is known as the F statistic:

$$F = \frac{(RRSS - URSS)/g}{URSS/(T - k)}$$

$$= \frac{RRSS - URSS}{URSS} \frac{(T - k)}{g} \qquad (5.26)$$

which is distributed as $F(g, T - k)$ under the null hypothesis. (An implicit assumption here is that ε_t is normal white noise.) This result holds if the regressors are nonstochastic or stochastic – see Greene (1997). The parameters g and $T - k$ are known, respectively, as the numerator and denominator degrees of freedom; g is the number of (independent) restrictions comparing the null and alternative hypotheses and $T - k$ is the degrees of freedom in the regression under the alternative hypothesis, that is the unrest-

ricted regression. The sample value of the F statistic is compared to the critical value for the $\alpha\%$ significance level from the right-hand tail of the F distribution with g and $T - k$ degrees of freedom, with sample values exceeding the critical value leading to rejection of the null hypothesis. As the critical value is taken from the right-hand tail an equivalent terminology for the $\alpha\%$ critical value is the $(1 - \alpha)\%$ quantile.

To illustrate suppose in a regression of y_t on a constant and three regressors x_{t2}, x_{t3} and x_{t4}, where lower case letters indicate a particular sample, URSS = 100, whereas in the regression of y_t on the constant the residual sum of squares is RRSS = 150; assume $T = 24$. The test statistic for testing the null hypothesis $\beta_2 = \beta_3 = \beta_4 = 0$ against the alternative that at least one of β_2, β_3, β_4 is not equal to zero is calculated as follows,

$$F = \frac{(150 - 100)/3}{100/20}$$

$$= \frac{50}{100} \frac{20}{3}$$

$$= 3.333$$

From standard F tables, given in the statistical appendix, with 3 and 20 degrees of freedom the 5% critical value of $F(3, 20)$ is 3.10; therefore at the 5% significance level, as $3.333 > 3.10$, the null hypothesis is not consistent with the data. Where possible it is useful to report the msl of the test statistic and a standard practice is to indicate the msl of the sample value of the test statistic in parentheses. For example, 3.333[0.040] indicates that this value of the test statistic has an msl of 4%. We will use [.] brackets after a test statistic to give the msl.

Any linear hypothesis can be put in the framework that leads to an F test. For example, suppose in the regression

$$Y_t = \beta_1 + \beta_2 X_{t2} + \beta_3 X_{t3} + \beta_4 X_{t4} + \varepsilon_t \quad (5.27)$$

The null hypothesis is

$$H_0: \beta_2 = 1 \quad \text{and} \quad \beta_4 = 0$$

and the alternative is

$$H_a: \beta_2 \neq 1 \quad \text{and/or} \quad \beta_4 \neq 0$$

Then, as before, H_a leads to a (relatively) unrestricted model compared to H_0. The restricted model is

$$Y_t = \beta_1 + X_{t2} + \beta_3 X_{t3} + \varepsilon_t \qquad (5.28)$$

which is easily estimated by subtracting X_{t2} from both sides, that is

$$Y_t - X_{t2} = \beta_1 + \beta_3 X_{t3} + \varepsilon_t \qquad (5.29)$$

The unrestricted model is given by (5.27). Estimation of both models gives the RRSS and URSS required for the F test. Suppose in a particular sample RRSS $= 60$ and URSS $= 55$ with $T = 30$, then the sample value of the F statistic is

$$F = \frac{(60 - 55)/2}{55/(30 - 4)}$$

$$= \frac{5}{55} \frac{26}{2}$$

$$= 1.182[0.323]$$

From standard F tables, the 5% critical value for F with 2 and 26 degrees of freedom is 3.37, hence as $1.182 < 3.37$ the null hypothesis is not rejected. Alternatively note that the msl of 1.182 is 32.3% which gives us much more information than a simple comparison with the 5% critical value. The null hypothesis would not be rejected using significance levels up to 32.3%.

There are two points to note about the framework for testing joint hypotheses of the kind illustrated here. First, the reason for rejection of the null hypothesis could be due to any one or any combination of the component hypotheses in the alternative. A value of the test statistic falling in the critical region does not identify the source of the rejection. For example, in the second illustration above had the null hypoth-

esis been rejected, that rejection could have occurred for the following reasons:

$$H_{a1}: \beta_2 \neq 1, \ \beta_4 = 0; \quad H_{a2}: \beta_2 = 1, \ \beta_4 \neq 0;$$
$$H_{a3}: \beta_2 \neq 1, \ \beta_4 \neq 0$$

From the F statistic alone we cannot say which of the component alternative hypotheses led to a significant test statistic. Both H_{a1} and H_{a2} are effectively one-dimensional hypotheses and the implied regression models are:

$$H_{a1}: Y_t = \beta_1 + \beta_2 X_{t2} + \beta_3 X_{t3} + \varepsilon_t \qquad (5.30)$$

and

$$H_{a2}: Y_t = \beta_1 + X_{t2} + \beta_3 X_{t3}$$
$$+ \beta_4 X_{t4} + \varepsilon_t \qquad (5.31)$$

While, given a rejection of the null hypothesis, it is likely to be useful to test each of these individually against the alternative model (5.27) there is no guarantee that a decision reached on this basis will be consistent with the decision reached on the basis of the original F test. Resolving this problem is an issue beyond the scope of this book, interested readers may consult Hendry (1995, section 13.10.5), Judge et al. (1985, section 6.5.2) and Seber (1977, Chapter 5); in general, though, this subject is rather poorly treated in textbooks on econometrics.

Second, note that this testing framework is not appropriate for components of the alternative hypothesis which are one sided. This is because departures from the null hypothesis in either direction are treated symmetrically in calculating the F test statistic. Again testing a joint hypothesis where some of the components involve one-sided alternatives is beyond the scope of this book – see, for example, Greene (1997).

It is useful for later chapters to put linear hypotheses in a notation which exploits their linearity. To start consider the single hypothesis $\beta_j = 0$, and to simplify the exposition suppose that k, the number of regressors, is 4 and $j = 2$, then this can be expressed as

$$(0 \quad 1 \quad 0 \quad 0) \begin{pmatrix} \beta_1 \\ \beta_2 \\ \beta_3 \\ \beta_4 \end{pmatrix} = 0$$

Now suppose the restriction $\beta_3 + \beta_4 = 1$ is added to the restriction $\beta_2 = 0$, then this combination can be expressed as

$$\begin{bmatrix} 0 & 1 & 0 & 0 \\ 0 & 0 & 1 & 1 \end{bmatrix} \begin{pmatrix} \beta_1 \\ \beta_2 \\ \beta_3 \\ \beta_4 \end{pmatrix} = \begin{pmatrix} 0 \\ 1 \end{pmatrix}$$

In general linear restrictions can be expressed as

$$R\beta = r \qquad (5.32)$$

where R is $g \times k$ so that there are g restrictions, $g < k$, and r is a $g \times 1$ vector of constants. If $r = 0$ the restrictions are said to be homogeneous, if $r \neq 0$ they are inhomogeneous. The restrictions are assumed to be independent and, therefore, the rank of R is g. The null hypothesis is H_0: $R\beta = r$; the alternative hypothesis is usually specified as $R\beta \neq r$ but the one-sided alternatives $R\beta > r$ and $R\beta < r$ are also possible and, indeed, may be desirable to increase power on the likely side of the alternative; they may also, though, be difficult to test against in some specifications.

Writing $R\beta = r$ stresses that restrictions are put on certain coefficients of the regression model and is known as an indirect parameterisation of the restrictions. An alternative way of representing the restrictions arises from noting that if there are g restrictions on the k regression coefficients there are really only $k - g$ free coefficients. To illustrate we assume the restrictions are homogeneous, that is $R\beta = 0$. What is needed is a transformation which takes us from the k coefficients in β to $k - g$ coefficients in, say, φ; the transformation is captured by a matrix of dimensions $k \times (k - g)$, denoted H, of rank $k - g$.

That is $\beta = H\varphi$, which says that β 'maps' down into a smaller number of coefficients φ. This is the direct parameterisation of the restrictions. Of course H cannot be arbitrary, it must satisfy some connection with the original way of writing the restrictions; to see what this implies note that $R\beta = RH\varphi$ which must equal 0; since φ is not equal to 0 this must imply that $RH = 0$. H is not unique, since postmultiplying H by S and defining $H^* = HS$ also gives $RH^* = 0$.

To illustrate, first consider the example used above with $\beta_2 = 0$ and $k = 4$ so $k - g = 3$, then H must be 4×3 and φ is 3×1; an H matrix which satisfies $RH = 0$ is

$$R\beta = 0$$

$$(0 \quad 1 \quad 0 \quad 0) \begin{pmatrix} \beta_1 \\ \beta_2 \\ \beta_3 \\ \beta_4 \end{pmatrix} = 0$$

$$\beta = H\varphi$$

$$\begin{pmatrix} \beta_1 \\ \beta_2 \\ \beta_3 \\ \beta_4 \end{pmatrix} = \begin{bmatrix} 1 & 0 & 0 \\ 0 & 0 & 0 \\ 0 & 1 & 0 \\ 0 & 0 & 1 \end{bmatrix} \begin{pmatrix} \varphi_1 \\ \varphi_2 \\ \varphi_3 \end{pmatrix} \qquad (5.33)$$

In this simple case the elements of H have been chosen not only to satisfy $RH = 0$ but to give the simple relationships $\beta_1 = \varphi_1$, $\beta_3 = \varphi_3$ and $\beta_4 = \varphi_4$; another choice which satisfies $RH = 0$ is

$$R\beta = 0$$

$$(0 \quad 1 \quad 0 \quad 0) \begin{pmatrix} \beta_1 \\ \beta_2 \\ \beta_3 \\ \beta_4 \end{pmatrix} = 0$$

$$\beta = H\varphi$$

$$\begin{pmatrix} \beta_1 \\ \beta_2 \\ \beta_3 \\ \beta_4 \end{pmatrix} = \begin{bmatrix} 1 & 1 & 0 \\ 0 & 0 & 0 \\ 1 & 0 & 1 \\ 0 & 1 & 1 \end{bmatrix} \begin{pmatrix} \varphi_1 \\ \varphi_2 \\ \varphi_3 \end{pmatrix} \qquad (5.34)$$

The direct parameterisation is $\beta_1 = \varphi_1 + \varphi_2$, $\beta_2 = 0$, $\beta_3 = \varphi_1 + \varphi_3$ and $\beta_4 = \varphi_2 + \varphi_3$.

More interesting cases arise with linear combinations of coefficients or multiple restrictions. For example, consider the restrictions $\beta_2 = 0$ and $\beta_3 + \beta_4 = 0$, now R is 2×4 and H is 4×2, so there are two free coefficients:

$$R\beta = 0$$

$$\begin{bmatrix} 0 & 1 & 0 & 0 \\ 0 & 0 & 1 & 1 \end{bmatrix} \begin{pmatrix} \beta_1 \\ \beta_2 \\ \beta_3 \\ \beta_4 \end{pmatrix} = 0$$

$$\beta = H\varphi$$

$$\begin{pmatrix} \beta_1 \\ \beta_2 \\ \beta_3 \\ \beta_4 \end{pmatrix} = \begin{bmatrix} 1 & 0 \\ 0 & 0 \\ 0 & 1 \\ 0 & -1 \end{bmatrix} \begin{pmatrix} \varphi_1 \\ \varphi_2 \end{pmatrix} \qquad (5.35)$$

The direct parameterisation says $\beta_1 = \varphi_1$, $\beta_3 = \varphi_2$ and $\beta_4 = -\varphi_2$.

Imposing the restrictions is particularly easy using the direct parameterisation. The regression model is $Y = X\beta + \varepsilon$ and the restrictions are $\beta = H\varphi$, so substituting for β in the regression model results in $Y = XH\varphi + \varepsilon$, say $Y = Z\varphi + \varepsilon$ with $Z = XH$, which can then be estimated by OLS. The resulting OLS estimators $\hat{\varphi}$ and $\hat{\beta} = H\hat{\varphi}$ will be unbiased and minimum variance provided the restrictions are correctly imposed.

All the test statistics considered in this and the previous chapter can be derived by first putting them in the form $R\beta = r$. Then if $g > 1$ an obvious candidate to test the null hypothesis H_0: $R\beta = r$ against the alternative hypothesis H_a: $R\beta \neq r$ is the F statistic given earlier – see (5.26) – with g and $T - k$ degrees of freedom. We conclude this section by briefly revisiting the F test using the notation that the restrictions are specified as $R\beta = r$.

A random variable is distributed as F with g and $T - k$ degrees of freedom if it is the ratio of independent χ^2 each divided by their degrees of freedom, with g degrees of freedom for the numerator and $T - k$ degrees of freedom for the denominator. The numerator χ^2 random variable of the F test is

$$\Theta_1 = \delta'[\text{Var}(R\hat{\beta})]^{-1}\delta$$
$$= \delta'[R(X'X)^{-1}R']^{-1}\delta/\sigma^2 \qquad (5.36)$$

where $\delta = R\hat{\beta} - r$ and $\text{Var}(R\hat{\beta}) = \sigma^2[R(X'X)^{-1}R']$. Θ_1 is distributed as $\chi^2(g)$ under the null hypothesis. The left-hand side of (5.36) is easy to interpret. δ measures the extent to which the restrictions are not satisfied using the unrestricted estimator $\hat{\beta}$; the test statistic is the weighted sum of these squared differences where the weights are the appropriate elements in the variance matrix of the estimator of the restrictions, $R\hat{\beta}$. (The simple 't' statistic works in the same way by weighting, or scaling, the difference between the estimated coefficient and the coefficient under the null by the reciprocal of its estimated standard error.)

If σ^2 is known then Θ_1 is an operational statistic with sample values of $\Theta_1 > \chi^2(g)_\alpha$ leading to rejection of the null, where $\chi^2(g)_\alpha$ is the critical value, for the $\alpha\%$ significance level, from the right-hand tail of the $\chi^2(g)$ distribution. Again, as with the F distribution, since the critical value is taken from the right-hand tail an equivalent terminology is the $(1 - \alpha)\%$ quantile. In general σ^2 is unknown; however, $\hat{\sigma}^2$, or any consistent estimator, could replace σ^2 and Θ_1 would then be asymptotically distributed as $\chi^2(g)$. In finite samples the actual size of the test, with estimated σ^2, is likely to be larger than the nominal size of the test ($=\alpha$). If σ^2 is unknown there is an alternative to Θ_1, namely the F statistic which is valid in finite samples.

A random variable distributed as $\chi^2(T - k)$, which is independent of Θ_1, is

$$\Theta_2 = (T - k)\hat{\sigma}^2/\sigma^2$$

This is a good choice of denominator because in forming the ratio of χ^2 variables for the F statistic the unknown σ^2 will cancel. The F

statistic is the ratio of Θ_1 and Θ_2 each divided by their degrees of freedom; that is

$$\frac{\Theta_1/g}{\Theta_2/(T-k)} = \frac{(\delta'[R(X'X)^{-1}R']^{-1}\delta)/g}{\hat{\sigma}^2}$$

$$= \frac{(\delta'[R(X'X)^{-1}R']^{-1}\delta)}{g\hat{\sigma}^2} \qquad (5.37)$$

It can be shown that this expression is identical to the one given earlier for the F statistic – see (5.26).

5.5 Heteroscedasticity: implications for OLS estimation and tests

Another assumption critical to hypothesis testing is that the conditional variance σ^2 is constant. On this assumption an estimator with desirable properties is given by dividing the residual sum of squares by the degrees of freedom, that is $\hat{\sigma}^2$. There are a number of test statistics available to test this assumption, the differences among them are generally due to the specification of the alternative assumption. The discussion in this section is divided into three parts. We first consider the implications of heteroscedasticity for OLS estimation; and then consider some leading tests for heteroscedasticity; finally, we consider what to do if heteroscedasticity is thought to be a feature of the regression model.

5.5.1 Implications of heteroscedasticity

In a heteroscedastic specification the variances of ε_t are not constant so a time subscript is needed to distinguish them: $E\{\varepsilon_t^2\} = \sigma_t^2$, so that $Var(\varepsilon_t) = \Omega \neq \sigma^2 I$, where Ω is a diagonal matrix with diagonal elements equal to σ_t^2; the shorthand for this is $\Omega = \text{diag}(\sigma_t^2)$. What are the consequences of heteroscedasticity for the OLS estimators? At an intuitive level since heteroscedasticity is a property of the second moment

of ε_t, and since $E\{\varepsilon_t\} = 0$ is maintained, there will be no consequences for first moments such as $E\{\beta\}$. More formally returning to the proof of the Gauss–Markov theorem, then $\hat{\beta}$ remains conditionally and unconditionally unbiased. Recall that

$$\hat{\beta} = \beta + (X'X)^{-1}X'\varepsilon$$

which remains unbiased since

$$E\{\hat{\beta} \mid X\} = \beta + (X'X)^{-1}X'E\{\varepsilon \mid X\}$$
$$= \beta \quad \text{using} \quad E\{\varepsilon \mid X\} = 0$$

This last expression does not involve any assumption about the variance of ε_t. The (conditional) variance matrix of $\hat{\beta}$ is

$$(X'X)^{-1}X'\Omega X(X'X)^{-1}$$

but this will simplify because in the case of heteroscedasticity Ω is diagonal although the diagonal elements are not equal.

If Ω was known, or could be replaced by a consistent estimator, it would be possible to compute $Var(\hat{\beta})$, or a consistent estimator for $Var(\hat{\beta})$, which would then provide a basis for inference on the elements of $\hat{\beta}$. We return to this consideration after describing a number of tests for heteroscedasticity.

5.5.2 Tests for heteroscedasticity

This section describes a number of leading tests for heteroscedasticity and the following section suggests what to do in the event of a significant test statistic. Heteroscedasticity is considered again, in a slightly different context, in Chapter 16, where the ARCH process is introduced.

5.5.2a White's (1980) test

The first test procedure we consider is due to White (1980), which also has important implications for the calculation of standard errors of the estimated coefficients which are consistent in the presence of heteroscedastic variances. White's paper is remarkable because it shows that our intuition can let us down quite badly – there is no substitute for good analysis.

Our starting point is that there is, *a priori*, no known formal structure for the heteroscedasticity which may be present in the regression model. The most we are willing to entertain is that there might well be some candidates, for example the variances can be partitioned by groups or subsets of the observations, or the variances depend upon some other variables; but equally we are not certain that the hypothesised structure is correct, so testing the null of constant variances against the structured alternative may be misleading since all of the candidate alternatives are incorrect. It might be thought that this is not a very fruitful way to proceed, since if all we hypothesise is that $E\{\varepsilon_t^2 \mid X\} = \sigma_t^2$, while maintaining $E\{\varepsilon_t \mid X\} = 0$ and $E\{\varepsilon_t\varepsilon_s \mid X\} = 0$ for $t \neq s$, implying that Ω is diagonal, but not scalar diagonal, then there are simply too many unknown parameters – the σ_t^2, of which there are T, and the k regression coefficients, $T + k$ in all – to proceed: we should give up! However, White showed that this line of reasoning is misleading. To understand the derivation note that for the correct variance matrix of the OLS estimator (and the GLS estimator) what we need is a consistent estimator of $X'\Omega X$; this could be obtained by first obtaining a consistent estimator of Ω, but this is not necessary and may be impossible. In contrast to Ω, $X'\Omega X$ is a $k \times k$ matrix so perhaps looking at this will be useful. Let us return briefly to the derivation of the OLS estimator when $E\{\varepsilon\varepsilon' \mid X\} = \Omega$. The relevant steps are:

(i) $E\{(\hat{\beta} - \beta)(\hat{\beta} - \beta)' \mid X\}$
     $= E\{(X'X)^{-1}X'\varepsilon\varepsilon'X(X'X)^{-1} \mid X\}$
(ii) $= (X'X)^{-1}E\{X'\varepsilon\varepsilon'X \mid X\}(X'X)^{-1}$
(iii) $= (X'X)^{-1}X'\Omega X(X'X)^{-1}$

Rather than go to step (iii) if we pause at step (ii) it is evident that we need $E\{X'\varepsilon\varepsilon X \mid X\}$. Consider the situation with $k = 3$ and $T = 4$, these values

are kept small to illustrate the algebra not to be indicative of practical situation, then

$$X'$$

$$\begin{bmatrix} 1 & 1 & 1 & 1 \\ X_{12} & X_{22} & X_{32} & X_{42} \\ X_{13} & X_{23} & X_{33} & X_{43} \end{bmatrix}$$

$$\varepsilon\varepsilon' \qquad\qquad X$$

$$\times \begin{bmatrix} \varepsilon_1^2 & 0 & 0 & 0 \\ 0 & \varepsilon_2^2 & 0 & 0 \\ 0 & 0 & \varepsilon_3^2 & 0 \\ 0 & 0 & 0 & \varepsilon_4^2 \end{bmatrix}\begin{bmatrix} 1 & X_{12} & X_{13} \\ 1 & X_{22} & X_{23} \\ 1 & X_{32} & X_{33} \\ 1 & X_{42} & X_{43} \end{bmatrix}$$

$$= \begin{bmatrix} \sum_{t=1}^{4} \varepsilon_t^2 & \sum_{t=1}^{4} \varepsilon_t^2 X_{t2} & \sum_{t=1}^{4} \varepsilon_t^2 X_{t3} \\ \sum_{t=1}^{4} \varepsilon_t^2 X_{t2} & \sum_{t=1}^{4} \varepsilon_t^2 X_{t2}^2 & \sum_{t=1}^{4} \varepsilon_t^2 X_{t2} X_{t3} \\ \sum_{t=1}^{4} \varepsilon_t^2 X_{t3} & \sum_{t=1}^{4} \varepsilon_t^2 X_{t2} X_{t3} & \sum_{t=1}^{4} \varepsilon_t^2 X_{t3}^2 \end{bmatrix}$$

$$= \sum_{t=1}^{4} \varepsilon_t^2 \begin{pmatrix} 1 \\ X_{t2} \\ X_{t3} \end{pmatrix}(1 \quad X_{t2} \quad X_{t3})$$

$$= \sum_{t=1}^{4} \varepsilon_t^2 X_t' X_t$$

where $X_t = (1 \quad X_{t2} \quad X_{t3})$ (5.38)

In general the time subscript runs from $t = 1$ to T and X_t will have k columns. Taking the expectation is what is required, see step (ii) above:

$$E\{X'\varepsilon\varepsilon'X\} = E\left\{\sum_{t=1}^{T} \varepsilon_t^2 X_t' X_t\right\}$$

Normalising by the sample size T gives

$$E\{X'\varepsilon\varepsilon'X\}/T = E\left\{\sum_{t=1}^{T} \varepsilon_t^2 X_t' X_t\right\}\Big/ T \qquad (5.39)$$

and is useful because this can now be interpreted as the average expectation. It is not necessary to estimate each of the T expectations separately; all that is required is an estimator of the symmetric $k \times k$ matrix, $E\{X'\varepsilon\varepsilon'X\}/T$.

White (*op. cit.*) shows that $\{\sum_{t=1}^{T} \varepsilon_t^2 X_t'X_t\}/T$ is a consistent estimator of $E\{X'\varepsilon\varepsilon'X\}/T$. Also the OLS estimator $\hat{\beta}$ is consistent, even with heteroscedastic variances, provided the model specification is correct and the regressors are fixed in repeated samples or if stochastic are independent of ε_t. The OLS residuals $\hat{\varepsilon}_t$ are then consistent for ε_t. So the feasible and consistent estimator of $E\{X'\varepsilon\varepsilon'X\}/T$ is:

$$\sum_{t=1}^{T} \hat{\varepsilon}_t^2 X_t'X_t/T$$

This is simple to compute given the OLS residuals.

Step (iii) in deriving the variance–covariance matrix of $\hat{\beta}$ is replaced with

(iii) $E\{(\hat{\beta} - \beta)(\hat{\beta} - \beta)' \mid X\}$
$\qquad = T^{-1}(X'X/T)^{-1}[E\{X'\varepsilon\varepsilon'X \mid X\}/T]$
$\qquad \times (X'X/T)^{-1}$

The operational or feasible version of this is (which is now the asymptotic variance matrix because a consistent estimator has replaced the unknown matrix):

$$T^{-1}(X'X/T)^{-1}\left[\sum_{t=1}^{T} \hat{\varepsilon}_t^2 X_t'X_t/T\right](X'X/T)^{-1}$$

$$= (X'X)^{-1}\left[\sum_{t=1}^{T} \hat{\varepsilon}_t^2 X_t'X_t\right](X'X)^{-1} \quad (5.40)$$

When the variance–covariance matrix is computed in this way rather than as $\sigma^2(X'X)^{-1}$ it is known as the heteroscedasticity consistent variance matrix; equivalently it may be referred to as the *robust* (to heteroscedasticity) variance matrix, and the square roots of the diagonal elements, which are the estimated standard errors

of the regression coefficients are described as *robust standard errors*. These standard errors allow inference, and the construction of confidence intervals, in the presence of heteroscedasticity of unknown structure.

No test statistic has yet been offered for the null of homoscedasticity but it should now be clear how one could be motivated. Under heteroscedasticity $\hat{\sigma}^2(X'X/T)^{-1}$ is not a consistent estimator of $T(\text{Var}(\hat{\beta}))$, whereas

$$(X'X/T)^{-1}[E\{X'\varepsilon\varepsilon'X \mid X\}/T](X'X/T)^{-1}$$

is consistent, so a test statistic could be based on the extent to which these two differ; if the variances are homoscedastic they will not differ by much. As described the test statistic would be based on the likelihood principle requiring estimation of both variance matrices. A more attractive alternative is to use the Lagrange-Multiplier principle, which only initially requires estimation under the null hypothesis of homoscedasticity. To illustrate we assume the same regression model as before with $k = 3$ including a constant in the regression. The first step is to obtain the OLS residuals $\hat{\varepsilon}_t$ and the second step is to run the following auxiliary regression

$$\hat{\varepsilon}_t^2 = \alpha_1 + \alpha_2 X_{t2} + \alpha_3 X_{t3} + \alpha_4 X_{t2}^2 + \alpha_5 X_{t3}^2$$
$$+ \alpha_6 X_{t2}X_{t3} + \zeta_t \quad (5.41)$$

The regressors in this auxiliary regression are the product of the regressors 1, X_{t2} and X_{t3} with each regressor in turn excluding double-counted variables which will be redundant. Thus if a constant was included in the original regression the regressors in the auxiliary regression are: all the regressors in the original equation; plus the products and cross-products of the regressors; in this case in all there are six regressors and, in general, there will be $k(k+1)/2$ regressors less any redundant regressors. If any of the products or cross-products were included in the original regression they are redundant and only included once in the auxiliary regression. The null hypothesis is that apart from the constant all the regression coefficients are zero, that is $\alpha_i = 0$ for $i = 2, \ldots, 6$, and the alternative is that at least one of these is nonzero. According to the null the variances are constant, for all t, equal to α_1.

White's test statistic can be calculated in its χ^2 form as $\mathrm{WT}(5) = T$ times R^2, where R^2 is the (centred) R^2 from the auxiliary regression, which will be distributed as $\chi^2(5)$ under the null with 'large' values leading to rejection of the null. In general, with a constant in the original regression, $\mathrm{WT}(g) = T$ times R^2 will be distributed as $\chi^2(g)$ under the null where $g = k(k+1)/2 - 1 - rd$ and rd is the number of redundant (double-counted) regressors. Alternatively the test statistic can be calculated in its F form as the F test of $\alpha_i = 0$, $i \neq 1$, with g and $T - (g+1)$ degrees of freedom. (The test statistic presented here assumes that $E\{\varepsilon_t^4\}$ is constant; White's test has been modified by Hseih (1983) to relax this assumption.)

If a constant was not included in the original regression, a constant is still included in the auxiliary regression, because it provides the constant variance under the null, but the levels of the original regressors are not included as they do not result from any of the cross-products. If there are no redundant regressors, T times R^2 is then distributed as $\chi^2(k(k+1)/2)$.

The implicit null hypothesis of White's test is more general than homoscedasticity, which has a bearing on the interpretation of a significant test statistic and the power of the test. The original regression model is assumed to be correctly specified, otherwise the disturbance in the incorrectly specified model contains the specification error, for example an omitted variable, which could be heteroscedastic, serially correlated and correlated with the included regressors! Also anything that leads to a correlation between the disturbance and the included regressors, for example a measurement error or endogenous regressor, will lead to an inconsistency in $\hat{\sigma}^2(X'X/T)^{-1}$. Hence, White's test could also be considered a general misspecification test. *If* the model is correctly specified and the ε_t are independent of the regressors *then* a significant test

statistic can be interpreted as evidence against the null in the direction of heteroscedasticity.

White notes that there are some specifications of heteroscedasticity which do not result in inconsistency of $\hat{\sigma}^2(X'X/T)^{-1}$ and so for these cases his test will have low power. This also means that nonrejection of the null of homoscedasticity could occur because there is homoscedasticity or because one of the 'special' cases is present (this is an example where nonrejection of a null hypothesis does not imply its acceptance). This is not such a problem as it might at first seem since it says that heteroscedasticity will most likely be detected where it makes a difference to inference. However, we should distinguish between inference and estimation. The efficiency of the OLS estimator could be improved by taking into account the heteroscedasticity and forming the feasible GLS estimator, which will be a weighted least squares estimator. In the example (5.38) given above define the weights,

$$\hat{\omega}_t = \hat{\alpha}_1 + \hat{\alpha}_2 X_{t2} + \hat{\alpha}_3 X_{t3} + \hat{\alpha}_4 X_{t2}^2$$
$$+ \hat{\alpha}_5 X_{t3}^2 + \hat{\alpha}_6 X_{t2} X_{t3} \qquad (5.42)$$

where $\hat{\alpha}_i$ is the OLS estimator of $\hat{\alpha}_i$ from (5.41); and, hence, define $\tilde{\Omega}$ as the diagonal matrix with $\hat{\omega}_t$ on the diagonal and then use the feasible GLS estimator $\beta^0 = [X'\tilde{\Omega}^{-1}X]^{-1}X'\tilde{\Omega}^{-1}Y$ and variance matrix $\mathrm{Var}(\beta^0) = [X'\tilde{\Omega}^{-1}X]^{-1}$. (The estimated weights are here assumed to be positive, if they are not they are replaced with an arbitrary $\delta > 0$ – see White (*op. cit.*, p. 827).)

White's procedure for obtaining robust standard errors is attractive because it means that even in the presence of heteroscedasticity of an unknown structure it is still possible to carry out standard inference, for example on the significance of coefficients. Similarly White's test is useful when there is no prior information concerning the structure of the heteroscedasticity, although its interpretation as a test for heteroscedasticity rests upon that being the only source of misspecification in the model. In practice where heteroscedasticity is suspected the dominant theme in applied work is to find the OLS, rather than the FGLS, estimates reported along with their robust standard errors.

There may also be cases when a view can be taken on how the heteroscedasticity arises, and this information can be exploited to provide a test statistic which can improve upon the power of White's test in finite samples (White *op. cit.*, p. 826). The Goldfeld–Quandt, GQ, and Breusch–Pagan, BP tests, which are described next, are of this kind. As we shall see there is a similarity between White's test and certain specifications of the BP test.

5.5.2b The Goldfeld–Quandt (1965) test

In the Goldfeld–Quandt test the sample is divided into two groups of T_1 and T_2 observations, each of which is large enough to estimate the regression model. Subscripts now indicate which sample the disturbances or residuals have been generated from. The null hypothesis is H_0: $\sigma_1^2 = \sigma_2^2$ and the alternative is H_a: $\sigma_1^2 > \sigma_2^2$. The specification of the alternative reflects the view that the variance is larger in the first sample. The GQ test statistic is

$$GQ = \hat{\sigma}_1^2 / \hat{\sigma}_2^2 \tag{5.43}$$

where $\hat{\sigma}_1^2 = \hat{\varepsilon}_1' \hat{\varepsilon}_1 / (T_1 - k)$ and $\hat{\sigma}_2^2 = \hat{\varepsilon}_2' \hat{\varepsilon}_2 / (T_2 - k)$. Thus GQ is very simple to compute being the ratio of the estimated variances for the two subsamples. GQ is distributed as F with $T_1 - k$ numerator degrees of freedom and $T_2 - k$ denominator degrees of freedom, if the disturbances are normally distributed and none of the regressors are lagged dependent variables. A large value of GQ leads to rejection of the null hypothesis in the direction of the alternative hypothesis. If the alternative hypothesis is that H_a: $\sigma_2^2 > \sigma_1^2$, then the subscripts are reversed in the test statistic. If no view is expressed *a priori* as to which subsample has the larger variance, a two-sided α level test can be carried out by putting the *ex post* larger estimated variance into

the numerator and carrying out the test using the critical F value for a significance level of $\frac{1}{2}\alpha$.

The structure of the GQ test statistic suggests that it will be useful when the sample naturally separates into two groups or subsamples; it is also not conditional on equality of the regression coefficients between groups. Omitting some observations in the middle of the sample is likely to make the sample separation more marked and increase the power of the test.

5.5.2c The Breusch–Pagan/Godfrey test

Another form of heteroscedasticity arises when the disturbance variances are systematically related to a variable or variables. For example, suppose

$$\sigma_t^2 = \alpha_1 + \alpha_2 Z_{t2} + \alpha_3 Z_{t3} \tag{5.44}$$

so that the variance varies systematically with Z_{t2} and Z_{t3}, which may be variables included in the regression but there is no constraint that this should be so. If either of the coefficients on these variables is nonzero ε_t is heteroscedastic, otherwise $\sigma_t^2 = \alpha_1$ and ε_t is homoscedastic. In the simplest case Z_{t2} and Z_{t3} are assumed nonstochastic. The null hypothesis is H_0: $\alpha_2 = \alpha_3 = 0$ against the two-sided alternative H_a: $\alpha_2 \neq 0$ and/ or $\alpha_3 \neq 0$. The extension to more variables is straightforward. Define $\alpha' = (\alpha_1, \alpha_2, \ldots, \alpha_g)$ and $Z_t' = (1, Z_{2t}, \ldots, Z_{gt})$ then the variance function is

$$\sigma_t^2 = \alpha' Z_t \tag{5.45}$$

The null hypothesis is H_0: $\alpha^* = 0$ and the alternative hypothesis is H_a: $\alpha^* \neq 0$, where $\alpha^* = (\alpha_2, \ldots, \alpha_g)'$.

A χ^2 test statistic for this form of heteroscedasticity due to Breusch and Pagan (1979) and Godfrey (1978a), usually referred to as the Breusch–Pagan, or BP, test for heteroscedasticity, is obtained as follows:

(i)   run the regression $Y = X\beta + \varepsilon$ to obtain the residuals $\hat{\varepsilon}$, compute $\hat{\sigma}^2 = \hat{\varepsilon}'\hat{\varepsilon}/T$ and $r_t = (\hat{\varepsilon}_t^2/\hat{\sigma}^2) - 1$;

(ii) regress r_t on a constant and the explanatory variables in the variance function, here Z_{t2} and Z_{t3};

(iii) calculate the LM test for heteroscedasticity as $\frac{1}{2}$ESS, where ESS is the explained sum of squares from the regression in (ii), which is asymptotically distributed as $\chi^2(g-1)$ where g is the number of regressors in the variance function including the constant;

(iv) reject H_0 for 'large' values relative to the chosen critical value from the right-hand tail of $\chi^2(g-1)$.

In the BP version of the test the ε_t are assumed to be normally distributed. A variation, due to Koenker (1981), results in a test statistic that is robust to departures from the normality assumption. The test statistic is T times R^2 from the regression in (ii) above which is asymptotically distributed as $\chi^2(g-1)$ under the null hypothesis. Equivalently we can exploit the structure of White's test for heteroscedasticity to note that this is the same as T times R^2 from the regression of the squared OLS residuals $\hat{\varepsilon}_t^2$ on $1, Z_{2t}, \ldots, Z_{gt}$; this is the variation reported as BP$(g-1)$ in this and subsequent chapters.

Based on this last statement an F version of this test is easily constructed – see Godfrey (1988). The test statistic is simply the F test that the coefficients $\alpha_i, i = 2, \ldots, g$ are jointly zero, this is H_0, against the standard two-sided alternative that at least one of the coefficients is not zero. Large values of the sample test statistic relative to the $\alpha\%$ critical value from the right-hand tail of the $F(g-1, T-g)$ distribution lead to rejection of H_0.

Godfrey (1988) shows that an asymptotically equivalent version of the GQ test can be obtained as a special case of the procedure described above. Define Z_{2t} as the dummy variable which splits the sample into two groups with $Z_{2t} = 0$ for observations in the first group and $Z_{2t} = 1$ for observations in the second group, then run the regression $\hat{\varepsilon}_t^2 = \alpha_1 + \alpha_2 Z_{t2} + \psi_t$ and test the significance of α_2.

The application of the BP test and its variants requires some thought about the likely nature of the heteroscedasticity present in the regression model. If cross-section data is being used there may well be a single scale variable to which the disturbance variances can be related. For example, in a cross-section study of the determinants of employment, with data from companies of considerably different size, the assumption of homoscedasticity is likely to be untenable; output – or sales – may well provide an appropriate scale variable. Typically time series data using expenditure or income series shows a sustained upward trend; in this context the assumption of homoscedasticity in a linear functional form implies that the ratio of the variance of the disturbances to the mean, $E\{Y \mid x\} = x\beta$, declines as $E\{Y \mid x\}$ increases. This implication is likely to be uncomfortable in a sample that spans a large period of time. A test procedure based on this idea is to specify σ_t^2 as a monotonic function of the estimated mean, say $\sigma_t^2 = f(\hat{Y}_t) = f(X_t\hat{\beta})$; this function acts as a scale variable in the same way as choosing a single regressor or nonincluded variable, and could be justified in a cross-section as well as a time series context. This idea forms the basis of the routine test for heteroscedasticity in MICRO-FIT, Pesaran and Pesaran (1997), and see also Bickel (1978), where the auxiliary regression for the F test is

$$\hat{\varepsilon}_t^2 = \alpha_1 + \alpha_2 \hat{Y}_t^2 + \psi_t \tag{5.46}$$

Where ψ_t is a regression disturbance, which arises because $\hat{\varepsilon}_t^2 \neq \sigma^2$. The null is $\alpha_2 = 0$, in which case $E\{\hat{\varepsilon}_t^2\} = \alpha_1$ and the variance of ε_t is constant. The simplest form of test statistic is HS$(1) = T$ times R^2 from this regression, distributed as $\chi^2(1)$ under the null hypothesis that $\alpha_2 = 0$. The F version of the test is also simple in this case since it is just the square of the 't' statistic for the null that $\alpha_2 = 0$, distributed as $F(1, T-2)$. These versions of the test for heteroscedasticity are referred to as the 'standard' tests.

In both these cases the test statistic is a quadratic form so there is an implicit assumption that the alternative is two sided; however, since $\hat{\varepsilon}_t^2 \geq 0$ and, therefore, setting ψ_t to its expected value of 0, $\alpha_1 + \alpha_2 \hat{y}_t^2 \geq 0$. For arbitrary y_t we require $\alpha_2 > 0$ (that is if $\alpha_1 > 0$ and $\alpha_2 < 0$, we can always find $\hat{y}_t$ such that the contradiction $\hat{\varepsilon}_t^2 < 0$ is obtained), which suggests a one-sided test, such as the 't' test, would be more powerful.

5.5.3 Interpretation of significant test statistics for heteroscedasticity

The finding that a test for homoscedasticity indicates rejection of the null hypothesis naturally raises the question of what to do. There are two possible reactions to a finding of heteroscedasticity. The first is to use the structure of heteroscedasticity as described in the alternative hypothesis of the test to provide a consistent estimator, $\tilde{\Phi}$, of Φ which is then used to obtain a feasible GLS estimator of β; and the second is to use OLS, which is still unbiased, to provide an estimator of β but replace the estimator of the variance–covariance matrix with a consistent estimator of the correct expression $(=(X'X)^{-1}X'\Omega X(X'X)^{-1})$.

Before discussing these solutions in detail it is helpful to recall what the GLS estimator looks like when the only problem is one of heteroscedasticity; and to illustrate a very simple example is used. Consider the bivariate regression

$$Y_t = \beta_1 + \beta_2 X_t + \varepsilon_t$$

with $t = 1, 2, 3$. The (only) problem is that ε_t is heteroscedastic with $E\{\varepsilon_t\} = \sigma_t^2$; otherwise there is no serial correlation and ε_t is normally distributed with zero mean. The variance–covariance matrix of ε_t is

$$\mathrm{Var}(\varepsilon_t) = \begin{bmatrix} \sigma_1^2 & 0 & 0 \\ 0 & \sigma_2^2 & 0 \\ 0 & 0 & \sigma_3^2 \end{bmatrix}$$

For convenience, and to make a point, it is useful to factor out σ_1^2 so that

$$\Omega = \begin{bmatrix} \sigma_1^2 & 0 & 0 \\ 0 & \sigma_2^2 & 0 \\ 0 & 0 & \sigma_3^2 \end{bmatrix}$$

$$= \sigma_1^2 \begin{bmatrix} 1 & 0 & 0 \\ 0 & \kappa_2 & 0 \\ 0 & 0 & \kappa_3 \end{bmatrix} \quad \text{say } \Omega = \sigma_1^2 \Phi \quad (5.47)$$

The following variance ratios have been defined: $\kappa_2 \equiv \sigma_2^2/\sigma_1^2$ and $\kappa_3 \equiv \sigma_3^2/\sigma_1^2$. If $\kappa_2 = \kappa_3 = 1$ the set-up is standard and OLS is efficient. At an intuitive level it is easy to see what we need to do to exploit the structure of Φ. Suppose κ_3 is 'large', to fix ideas say $\kappa_3 = 4$, and $\sigma_1^2 = 100$ so $\sigma_1 = 10$, and $\sigma_3 = \sqrt{400} = 20$, then Y_t is generated by a 'noisy' process at $t = 3$ compared to $t = 1$; the probability of $\varepsilon_1 > 20 (=2\sigma_1)$ is 0.0228 (from normal tables), but the probability of $\varepsilon_3 > 20 \ (=1\sigma_3)$ is 0.242, thus an observation from Y_1 is much more informative than an observation from Y_3. What we need to do is give a greater weight to period 1 observations relative to period 3 observations; the weights should be inversely related to the variance ratio.

Following this idea further note that the standard set-up has all the variance ratios equal to 1, so in minimising the residual sum of squares each observation is given an *equal* weight. Hence an interesting question is what is the transformation of the regression model which will result in a variance–covariance matrix for the transformed disturbances, say $\mathrm{Var}(\varepsilon_t^*)$, which is scalar diagonal? Since Φ is diagonal (but not scalar diagonal) a simple transformation to the identity matrix is $\Phi^{-1}\Phi = I$, then in the transformed model $\Omega = \sigma_1^2 I$, and since there is now no ambiguity we can write this as $\sigma^2 I$, which is just what is specified in the standard set-up. Also since Φ is diagonal then so is Φ^{-1}; indeed this matrix has diagonal elements which are just the reciprocals of the diagonal elements of Φ. If the software is not available to calculate the GLS estimator directly then OLS can be applied to the transformed model where the transformation results in $\text{Var}(\varepsilon_t^*) = \sigma^2 I$. In general terms – see section **5.3.1** – a transformation results from multiplying through $Y = X\beta + \varepsilon$ by a $T \times T$ non-singular matrix P; in this case we anticipate that because Φ is diagonal then P will also be diagonal. For the simple case considered here this is

$$
\begin{bmatrix} P_1 & 0 & 0 \\ 0 & P_2 & 0 \\ 0 & 0 & P_3 \end{bmatrix} \begin{pmatrix} Y_1 \\ Y_2 \\ Y_3 \end{pmatrix}
$$

$$
= \begin{bmatrix} P_1 & 0 & 0 \\ 0 & P_2 & 0 \\ 0 & 0 & P_3 \end{bmatrix} \begin{pmatrix} \beta_1 \\ \beta_1 \\ \beta_1 \end{pmatrix}
$$

$$
+ \begin{bmatrix} P_1 & 0 & 0 \\ 0 & P_2 & 0 \\ 0 & 0 & P_3 \end{bmatrix} \begin{pmatrix} X_{12}\beta_2 \\ X_{22}\beta_2 \\ X_{32}\beta_2 \end{pmatrix}
$$

$$
+ \begin{bmatrix} P_1 & 0 & 0 \\ 0 & P_2 & 0 \\ 0 & 0 & P_3 \end{bmatrix} \begin{pmatrix} \varepsilon_1 \\ \varepsilon_2 \\ \varepsilon_3 \end{pmatrix} \quad (5.48)
$$

Because P is diagonal this simplifies to:

$$
P_1 Y_1 = P_1\beta_1 + P_1 X_{12}\beta_2 + P_1\varepsilon_1
$$
$$
\text{say } Y_1^* = P_1\beta_1 + X_{12}^*\beta_2 + \varepsilon_1^*
$$
$$
P_2 Y_2 = P_2\beta_1 + P_2 X_{22}\beta_2 + P_2\varepsilon_2 \quad (5.49)
$$
$$
\text{say } Y_2^* = P_2\beta_1 + X_{22}^*\beta_2 + \varepsilon_2^*
$$
$$
P_3 Y_3 = P_3\beta_1 + P_3 X_{32}\beta_2 + P_3\varepsilon_3
$$
$$
\text{say } Y_3^* = P_3\beta_1 + X_{32}^*\beta_2 + \varepsilon_3^*
$$

and the disturbance variances, conditional on X and P, are:

$$
E\{(\varepsilon_1^* \mid X, P)^2\} = E\{(P_1\varepsilon_1)^2 \mid X, P)\}
$$
$$
= P_1^2 E\{\varepsilon_1^2 \mid X, P)) = P_1^2\sigma_1^2
$$
$$
= \sigma_1^2 \Rightarrow P_1^2 = 1 \Rightarrow P_1 = 1
$$
$$
E\{(\varepsilon_2^* \mid X, P)^2\} = E\{(P_2\varepsilon_2)^2 \mid X, P)\}
$$
$$
= P_2^2 E\{\varepsilon_2^2 \mid X, P)) = P_2^2\sigma_2^2
$$
$$
= \sigma_1^2 \Rightarrow P_2^2 = \sigma_1^2/\sigma_2^2
$$
$$
\Rightarrow P_2 = \sigma_1/\sigma_2
$$

$$
E\{(\varepsilon_3^* \mid X, P)^2\} = E\{(P_3\varepsilon_3)^2 \mid X, P)\}
$$
$$
= P_3^2 E\{\varepsilon_3^2 \mid X, P)) = P_3^2\sigma_3^2
$$
$$
= \sigma_1^2 \Rightarrow P_3^2 = \sigma_1^2/\sigma_3^2
$$
$$
\Rightarrow P_3 = \sigma_1/\sigma_3
$$

The implications, if these variances are to satisfy the homoscedasticity assumption, are drawn out at the end of each line following the $\Rightarrow$ symbol. Specifically the transformation weights are:

$$
P_1 = 1, \quad P_2 = \sigma_1/\sigma_2 = \sqrt{(1/\kappa_2)}
$$
$$
P_3 = \sigma_1/\sigma_3 = \sqrt{(1/\kappa_3)} \quad (5.50)
$$

Extending to more than $T = 3$ observations is straightforward, with $P_t = \sigma_1/\sigma_t = \sqrt{(1/\kappa_t)}$.

Notice that in the transformed model the first column in the data matrix is now $(1, P_2, P_3, \ldots, P_T)$. The transformation weights are normalised on the first observation so $P_1 = 1$, then the weight for the second observation is the square root of the reciprocal of the variance ratio; the larger is the variance σ_2^2 relative to σ_1^2 the smaller is the weight given to the second observation and, in general, the weights vary inversely with the square root of the variance ratio – the larger the variance the smaller the weight. With the weights defined in this way, OLS can be applied to the transformed equation and is efficient if the weights are known. This procedure is, for reasons that should now be clear, known as weighted least squares, WLS, which is a special case of GLS. In practice whether this procedure is feasible depends upon the availability of a consistent estimator of Φ. If a consistent estimator is available the procedure becomes *feasible*.

An example of a feasible procedure is the Goldfeld–Quandt case where the observations are split into two mutually exclusive groups. The variance specification is:

$$
\Omega = \begin{bmatrix} \sigma_1^2 I_1 & 0 \\ 0 & \sigma_2^2 I_2 \end{bmatrix} = \sigma_1^2 \begin{bmatrix} I_1 & 0 \\ 0 & \kappa_2 I_2 \end{bmatrix} \quad (5.51)
$$

where I_i is the identity matrix of order T_i and $\kappa^2 = \sigma_2^2/\sigma_1^2$. The variance ratio κ_2 can be consistently estimated by $\hat{\sigma}_2^2/\hat{\sigma}_1^2$, where $\hat{\sigma}_i^2$ is the OLS estimator of σ_i^2 from the ith sample. The transformation matrix P is particularly simple since its effect must be to leave the first T_1 observations unchanged and the remaining T_2 observations divided by $\sqrt{\kappa_2}$, specifically:

$$P = \begin{bmatrix} I_1 & 0_1 \\ 0_2 & \Lambda \end{bmatrix} \tag{5.52}$$

where Λ is a diagonal matrix with $\sqrt{(1/\kappa_2)} = \sigma_1/\sigma_2$ on the diagonal, 0_1 is a $T_1 \times T_2$ matrix with 0 in every element and $0_2 = 0_1'$.

Even in this simple case there are some potential problems. It requires $T_i > k$, so changes in variance closer to k periods from the beginning or end of the sample are not allowed. If some of the middle observations from the sample have been omitted to improve the power of the test, a view has to be taken as to which regime generated these observations.

If the variance function is specified as $\sigma_t^2 = \alpha'Z_t$, then a consistent estimator, $\tilde{\alpha}$, of α can be obtained from OLS estimation of the regression

$$\hat{\varepsilon}_t^2 = \alpha'Z_t + \psi_t \tag{5.53}$$

where $\hat{\varepsilon}_t$ are the OLS residuals from the primary regression, $Y = X\beta + \varepsilon$. With α estimated from the auxiliary regression then a consistent estimator of σ_t^2 is obtained as

$$\tilde{\sigma}_t^2 = \tilde{\alpha}'Z_t \tag{5.54}$$

and $\tilde{\Omega} = \text{diag}(\tilde{\sigma}_t^2)$. The feasible GLS estimator, β^0, can then be obtained

$$\beta^0 = (X'\tilde{\Phi}^{-1}X)^{-1}X'\tilde{\Phi}^{-1}Y \tag{5.55}$$

and

$$\text{Var}(\beta^0) = \hat{\sigma}^2(X'\tilde{\Phi}^{-1}X)^{-1} \tag{5.56}$$

An alternative strategy to feasible GLS is to continue to use the OLS estimator $\hat{\beta}$ but in conjunction with the correct variance matrix $(X'X)^{-1}X'\Omega X(X'X)^{-1}$. The latter requires a consistent estimator of $\Omega = \sigma^2\Phi$, as in the feasible GLS procedure, which uses the specification of heteroscedasticity under the alternative hypothesis. However, White's (1980) procedure provides a different approach. First note that $\Omega = \text{diag}(\sigma_t^2)$ if the disturbance variances are heteroscedastic; then a consistent estimator of Ω is obtained on replacing σ_t^2 by the squared OLS residuals $\hat{\varepsilon}_t^2$. A heteroscedasticity consistent estimator of $\text{Var}\,\hat{\beta}$ is then

$$\text{Var}(\hat{\beta}) = (X'X)^{-1}X'\tilde{\Omega}X(X'X)^{-1} \tag{5.57}$$

where $\tilde{\Omega} = \text{diag}(\hat{\varepsilon}_t^2)$. The standard errors for the individual elements of $\hat{\beta}$ resulting from this procedure are sometimes referred to as (heteroscedasticity) robust standard errors. This procedure is particularly useful if the form of the heteroscedasticity is unknown; and robust standard errors are an option in several commercially available econometric software packages.

5.6 Misspecification: diagnosis and effects

Specification tests assume that the model as specified is an adequate basis for inference and are then concerned with particular aspects of the model. For example, a test of the null hypothesis that a regression coefficient is zero, against the alternative that it is not, is a specification test.

Misspecification tests are concerned with the adequacy of a model as a basis for inference – for example, can the assumption of normality be maintained, are the residuals consistent with innovation errors, are the parameters constant over time? Misspecification tests are in practice prior to tests of specification of the type described in the previous section. The null hypothesis in this context is usually that some aspect of the model is adequate, the alternative being that it is not. A rejection of the null hypothesis does not usually lead to the conclusion that there is a unique alternative, even if the set-up of the test gives that impression. For example, the DW test – see section **5.6.1a** below – for a first order autoregressive disturbance, is also able to detect other types of autocorrelation, incorrect functional form and omitted (autocorrelated) variables. Hence, rejection of the null hypothesis using the DW test statistic does not automatically imply acceptance of the alternative for which it was originally designed.

5.6.1   Serial correlation of ε_t

A familiar concern in the econometrics literature is the time series properties of the sequence ε_t, $t = 1, \ldots, T$. Recall that ε_t is a derived construct given by

$$\varepsilon_t \equiv Y_t - E\{Y_t \mid X\}$$

An empirical model is *data coherent* if its error process $[\varepsilon_t]$ is white noise, which requires homoscedasticity, $E\{\varepsilon_t^2\} = \sigma^2$, and no serial correlation, $E\{\varepsilon_t \varepsilon_s\} = 0$ for $t \neq s$. Tests for heteroscedasticity were considered in section **5.5.2**, whereas this section considers tests for serial correlation of ε_t.

If ε_t follows the first order autoregressive scheme, AR(1), then

$$\varepsilon_t = \rho \varepsilon_{t-1} + u_t \quad |\rho| < 1 \tag{5.58}$$

with $E\{\varepsilon_{t-1} u_t\} = 0$, and u_t is white noise with $\mathrm{Var}(u_t) = E\{u_t^2\} = \sigma_u^2$. Note that $E\{\varepsilon_t\} = 0$ and $\mathrm{Var}(\varepsilon_t) = E\{\varepsilon_t^2\}$, and denote this variance σ^2, then

$$\begin{aligned}
\sigma^2 &= E\{(\rho \varepsilon_{t-1} + u_t)^2\} \\
&= E\{\rho^2 \varepsilon_{t-1}^2 + u_t^2 + 2\rho \varepsilon_{t-1} u_t\} \\
&= \rho^2 E\{\varepsilon_{t-1}^2\} + E\{u_t^2\} + 2\rho E\{\varepsilon_{t-1} u_t\} \\
&= \rho^2 \sigma^2 + \sigma_u^2 \quad \text{using } E\{\varepsilon_{t-1}^2\} = E\{\varepsilon_t^2\} = \sigma^2 \\
&\quad \text{and} \quad E\{\varepsilon_{t-1} u_t\} = 0
\end{aligned}$$

hence

$$\sigma^2 = \sigma_u^2/(1 - \rho^2) \tag{5.59}$$

The first order autocovariance is

$$\begin{aligned}
E\{\varepsilon_t \varepsilon_{t-1}\} &= E\{(\rho \varepsilon_{t-1} + u_t)\varepsilon_{t-1}\} \\
&= \rho E\{\varepsilon_{t-1}^2\} + E\{u_t \varepsilon_{t-1}\} \\
&= \rho \sigma^2 \neq 0
\end{aligned} \tag{5.60}$$

and the first order autocorrelation coefficient is

$$\begin{aligned}
\rho(1) &= \rho \sigma^2 / \sigma^2 \\
&= \rho
\end{aligned} \tag{5.61}$$

Hence $[\varepsilon_t]$ is not a white noise sequence, and in particular it is serially correlated. Because the serial correlation is in the nature of an autoregression of ε_t on lagged values of itself, ε_t is said to be autocorrelated. It will also be useful later to derive some of higher order autocovariances and autocorrelations.

$$\begin{aligned}
E\{\varepsilon_t \varepsilon_{t-2}\} &= E\{(\rho \varepsilon_{t-1} + u_t)\varepsilon_{t-2}\} \\
&= \rho E\{\varepsilon_{t-1} \varepsilon_{t-2}\} + E\{u_t \varepsilon_{t-2}\} \\
&= \rho^2 \sigma^2 \quad \text{using } E\{\varepsilon_{t-1} \varepsilon_{t-2}\} = \rho \sigma^2 \\
&\quad \text{and} \quad E\{u_t \varepsilon_{t-2}\} = 0
\end{aligned} \tag{5.62}$$

hence

$$\begin{aligned}
\rho(2) &= \rho^2 \sigma^2 / \sigma^2 \\
&= \rho^2
\end{aligned} \tag{5.63}$$

These expressions generalise in a straightforward manner to $E\{\varepsilon_t \varepsilon_{t-s}\} = \rho^s \sigma^2$ and $\rho(s) = \rho^s$.

The AR(1) scheme could be generalised to higher order processes, that is AR(p) with $p > 1$,

$$\varepsilon_t = \sum_{i=1}^{p} \rho_i \varepsilon_{t-i} + u_t \tag{5.64}$$

Another possibility is that ε_t follows a moving average, MA, scheme. An MA(1) process is given by

$$\varepsilon_t = u_t + \theta_1 u_{t-1} \tag{5.65}$$

where u_t is white noise with variance σ_u^2. The variance of ε_t is

$$\begin{aligned}
\text{Var}(\varepsilon_t) &= \text{Var}(u_t) + \theta_1^2 \, \text{Var}(u_{t-1}) \\
&\quad + 2\theta_1 \, \text{Cov}(u_t, u_{t-1}) \\
&= \sigma_u^2(1 + \theta_1^2) \quad \text{as} \quad \text{Cov}(u_t, u_{t-1}) = 0 \\
&\quad \text{and} \quad \text{Var}(u_t) = \text{Var}(u_{t-1}) = \sigma_u^2 \tag{5.66}
\end{aligned}$$

The first order autocovariance, $E\{\varepsilon_t \varepsilon_{t-1}\}$, is

$$\begin{aligned}
E\{(u_t &+ \theta_1 u_{t-1})(u_{t-1} + \theta_1 u_{t-2})\} \\
&= E\{u_t u_{t-1} + \theta_1 u_{t-1}^2 + \theta_1 u_t u_{t-2} \\
&\quad + \theta_1^2 u_{t-1} u_{t-2}\} \\
&= \theta_1 \sigma_u^2 \neq 0 \tag{5.67}
\end{aligned}$$

the last line uses

$$E\{u_t u_{t-1}\} = E\{u_t u_{t-2}\} = E\{u_{t-1} u_{t-2}\} = 0$$

because u_t is white noise. So again $[\varepsilon_t]$ is serially correlated and is, therefore, not a white noise sequence. Note that the first order autocorrelation coefficient is:

$$\begin{aligned}
\rho(1) &= E\{\varepsilon_t \varepsilon_{t-1}\}/\sqrt{E\{\varepsilon_t^2\}}\sqrt{E\{\varepsilon_{t-1}^2\}} \\
&= \theta_1 \sigma_u^2 / \sigma_u^2(1 + \theta_1^2) \\
&= \theta_1/(1 + \theta_1^2) \tag{5.68}
\end{aligned}$$

As in the AR case, the MA scheme can be generalised to an MA(p) process,

$$\varepsilon_t = u_t + \theta_1 u_{t-1} + \cdots + \theta_p u_{t-p} \tag{5.69}$$

which generates nonzero autocorrelations.

In the next sections we describe two test statistics which are designed to detect particular kinds of departures from the hypothesis that there is no serial correlation structure in the $[\varepsilon_t]$

sequence. The first of these is the Durbin–Watson statistic, which was originally designed for the AR(1) alternative; and the second is the LM statistic, which is applicable for both AR(p) and MA(p) alternatives.

5.6.1a The Durbin–Watson, DW, statistic

Durbin and Watson (1950, 1951) derived what is usually referred to as the DW statistic. Originally it was intended for the following regression model

$$Y_t = \beta_1 + \sum_{j=2}^{k} \beta_j X_{tj} + \varepsilon_t \tag{5.70}$$

with

$$\varepsilon_t = \rho \varepsilon_{t-1} + u_t \tag{5.71}$$

That is the standard linear regression model with the additional specification that ε_t follows an AR(1) process with $|\rho| < 1$; a constant is included in the regression, none of the X_{tj} is a lagged value of Y_t and u_t is white noise. The DW statistic is appropriate for the null hypothesis

$$H_0 \colon \rho = 0$$

with specification of H_a given by one of the following:

$$H_{a1} \colon \rho > 0; \quad H_{a2} \colon \rho < 0; \quad H_{a3} \colon \rho \neq 0$$

That is the null hypothesis is no autocorrelation in the ε_t, whereas the alternative can be positive or negative autocorrelation or both.

The DW statistic, which provides a test statistic for H_0, is

$$\text{DW} = \frac{\displaystyle\sum_{t=2}^{T}(\hat{\varepsilon}_t - \hat{\varepsilon}_{t-1})^2}{\displaystyle\sum_{t=1}^{T}\hat{\varepsilon}_t^2} \tag{5.72}$$

where $\hat{\varepsilon}_t$ is the OLS residual from estimation of (5.50). Some motivation for the DW statistic can be provided by considering the sample correlation coefficient $\tilde{\rho}$ between $\hat{\varepsilon}_t$ and $\hat{\varepsilon}_{t-1}$.

$$\tilde{\rho} = \frac{\sum\limits_{t=2}^{T} \hat{\varepsilon}_t \hat{\varepsilon}_{t-1}}{\sum\limits_{t=1}^{T} \hat{\varepsilon}_t^2} \tag{5.73}$$

Expanding the numerator in the DW statistic we obtain

$$\text{DW} = \frac{\sum\limits_{t=2}^{T} \hat{\varepsilon}_t^2}{\sum\limits_{t=1}^{T} \hat{\varepsilon}_t^2} + \frac{\sum\limits_{t=2}^{T} \hat{\varepsilon}_{t-1}^2}{\sum\limits_{t=1}^{T} \hat{\varepsilon}_t^2}$$

$$- 2 \frac{\sum\limits_{t=2}^{T} \hat{\varepsilon}_t \hat{\varepsilon}_{t-1}}{\sum\limits_{t=1}^{T} \hat{\varepsilon}_t^2} \tag{5.74}$$

Note that the first term is approximately equal to 1, the denominator including the extra term $\hat{\varepsilon}_1^2$; also the second term is close to 1, the difference between numerator and denominator being the exclusion of $\hat{\varepsilon}_T^2$ in the former. Finally, the last term is $-2\tilde{\rho}$. The implication is that

$$\text{DW} \cong 2(1 - \tilde{\rho}) \tag{5.75}$$

Thus, approximately, the values of DW corresponding to $\tilde{\rho} = +1, 0, -1$ are $\text{DW} = 0, 2, 4$, respectively. This implies that a sample value of DW between 0 and (less than) 2 suggests positive first order autocorrelation, a value of DW close to 2 suggests no first order autocorrelation, and a value of DW above 2 but less than 4 suggests negative first order autocorrelation. The slight complication in using the DW statistic is that its distribution depends upon the matrix of regressors; for a given significance level Durbin and Watson provided bounds d_L and d_U to the critical value rather than a single critical value.

(Critical values are provided in a statistical appendix at the end of the book.) Consider a particular sample value of DW denoted dw, then with H_0: $\rho = 0$ and H_{a2}: $\rho > 0$, H_0 is rejected at the 5% significance level if $dw < d_L$; if $dw > d_U$, H_0 is not rejected. This leaves an inconclusive region between d_L and d_U which can be quite large for small T and/or large values of $k - 1$. For example, for $T = 20$ and $k - 1 = 2$, $d_L = 1.100$ and $d_U = 1.537$.

With H_0: $\rho = 0$ and H_{a3}: $\rho < 0$ the bounds are $4 - d_L$ and $4 - d_U$. If $dw < 4 - d_U$, H_0 is not rejected; if $dw > 4 - d_L$, H_0 is rejected. Again this leaves the inconclusive region from $4 - d_U$ to $4 - d_L$. For example, for $T = 20$ and $k - 1 = 2$ this is 2.900 and 2.463.

With H_0: $\rho = 0$ and the two-sided alternative H_{a1}: $\rho \neq 0$, the bounds are

$$d_L \text{ and } d_U \quad and \quad 4 - d_U \text{ and } 4 - d_L$$

For $T = 20$, $k - 1 = 2$:

$$d_L = 1.100 \text{ and } d_U = 1.537 \quad and$$
$$4 - d_U = 2.463 \text{ and } 4 - d_L = 2.900$$

Thus, for the two-sided test the test procedures for each one-sided test are combined, with H_0 rejected if $dw < d_L$ or $dw > 4 - d_L$; H_0 is not rejected if $d_U < dw < 4 - d_U$. This leaves the two inconclusive regions, d_L to d_U and $4 - d_U$ to $4 - d_L$. Note also that combining the two one-sided tests each at a 5% significance level yields a test with an overall significance level of 10%.

←Reject→ H_0	Incon-clusive region	←Nonrejection→ region	Incon-clusive region	←Reject→ H_0
0 $\quad$ d_L	d_U	2	$4 - d_U$ $\quad$ $4 - d_L$	4

The problem with the inconclusive regions has been addressed by a number of authors including Durbin and Watson (1971). The proposed solutions, however, tend to be rather complex, especially so when there are alternative tests which are simple to compute – see, for example, the LM test for pth order serial correlation described below. For a summary of ways to avoid an inconclusive region see Judge *et al.* (1985). Nevertheless the DW statistic is often reported in empirical work. A conservative but simple rule of thumb is to treat d_U, and hence $4 - d_U$, as the critical value.

The DW test has proved resilient and is routinely included in econometric software packages. Apart from its original design purpose there are at least two reasons why this is the case. First, the DW test, although derived in the context of detecting a particular (first order autoregressive) structure, turns out also to be quite powerful in detecting first order serial correlation when it is generated by a first order moving average process, $\varepsilon_t = \varepsilon_t + \theta_1 \varepsilon_{t-1}$ or higher order autoregressive or moving average processes – see, for example, Greene (1997). Second, the DW test has proved rather ubiquitous as a general misspecification test; a significant value could be generated because, for example, linearity of the regression model is not consistent with the data, or variables, which are themselves autocorrelated, have been omitted – see, for example, Harvey (1981, Chapter 1). The limitations of the DW test should not, however, be forgotten. For example, if a lagged dependent variable is included in the regression the DW statistic is biased towards nonrejection of the null hypothesis; hence, in such a case *dw* close to 2 should not be taken as evidence of nonrejection of the null hypothesis, though $dw < d_L$ can be taken as evidence of rejection of the null hypothesis.

5.6.1b The Lagrange-Multiplier (LM) test for serial correlation

A test of the null hypothesis

$$H_0: E\{\varepsilon_t, \varepsilon_{t-s}\} = 0 \quad \text{for } t \neq s, s = 1, \ldots, p$$

against the alternative

$$H_a: E\{\varepsilon_t, \varepsilon_{t-s}\} \neq 0$$

due to Breusch (1978) and Godfrey (1978b, c), known as the LM test for pth order serial correlation, is simple to compute. The test statistic is based on the LM principle, hence its common description as the LM test for serial correlation, which only requires estimation under the null hypothesis. This is particularly attractive because imposing the null means that the test is based upon the OLS residuals assuming no serial correlation.

The first step is to estimate the (primary) regression model of Y_t on a constant and the regressors, $X_{2t}, \ldots, X_{kt}$ and obtain the OLS residuals, $\hat{\varepsilon}_t$ for $t = 1, \ldots, T$. In the second step an auxiliary regression is estimated with the tth residual, $\hat{\varepsilon}_t$, regressed on the original set of regressors (although if the sample size is reasonable large the constant may be omitted because $\hat{\varepsilon}_t$ will have a zero mean by construction) *and* $\hat{\varepsilon}_{t-1}, \ldots, \hat{\varepsilon}_{t-p}$. The test is of the joint significance of $\hat{\varepsilon}_{t-1}, \ldots, \hat{\varepsilon}_{t-p}$ in the auxiliary regression. The test statistic can be calculated in either its original LM form or as an F test. In its LM form the test statistic is

$$SC(p) = T^+(R_{uc}^2) \tag{5.76}$$

where R_{uc}^2 is the uncentred R^2 from the auxiliary regression. Note that in forming the lagged OLS residuals p observations are lost from the original sample so the auxiliary regression is based on $T^+ = (T - p)$ observations. In some applications of this test statistic the p 'lost' starting observations are set equal to 0, so the auxiliary regression is then based on T observations; however, as Godfrey (1988, p. 117) notes: '... the asymptotic irrelevance of such starting values does not guarantee that their impact in small samples can always be neglected'. Whichever strategy is adopted, $SC(p)$ is asymptotically distributed as $\chi^2(p)$ under the null hypothesis, so a 'large' value relative to the $(1-\alpha)\%$ quantile from the $\chi^2(p)$ distribution leads to rejection of the null hypothesis.

In its F form the test statistic is simply the F test that simultaneously the coefficients on $\hat{\varepsilon}_{t-1}, \ldots, \hat{\varepsilon}_{t-p}$ are 0, whereas the alternative hypothesis is that they are not. If the 'lost' starting values $\hat{\varepsilon}_1, \ldots, \hat{\varepsilon}_p$ are not artificially replaced the F test will have p and $T^+ - (p+k)$ degrees of freedom; otherwise the F test will have p and $T - (p+k)$ degrees of freedom. Large values of the test statistic again lead to rejection. The test statistic is valid (asymptotically) if lagged dependent variables are included in the set of regressors.

If p is large relative to T it is usually wise to retain the constant in the auxiliary regression because the mean of the residuals over the smaller sample will only be approximately zero. Similarly as the χ^2 version of the test statistic makes reference to asymptotic critical values it is usually wise to check the results in small samples, as a working guide say $T^+ < 30$, against the F version of the test. In later chapters the $\chi^2(p)$ version of the test is reported but there is always a check with the F version of the test.

5.6.1c   Box–Pearce and Ljung–Box tests

Box and Pearce (1970) suggested a test statistic based on the autocorrelations of the residuals. As in the LM and DW tests, first, estimate the regression model by OLS and obtain the residuals $\hat{\varepsilon}_t$, $t = 1, \ldots, T$; define the rth order autocorrelation coefficients by:

$$\hat{\rho}_r = \frac{\sum_{t=r+1}^{T} \hat{\varepsilon}_t \hat{\varepsilon}_{t-r}}{\sum_{t=1}^{T} \hat{\varepsilon}_t^2} \qquad r = 1, \ldots, m \qquad (5.77)$$

Then the Box–Pearce test statistic, usually referred to as $Q(m)$, is T times the sum of the squared autocorrelation coefficients from 1 to m, that is: $Q(m) \equiv T \sum_{r=1}^{m} \hat{\rho}_r^2$. Sample values of Q are to be compared with the $(1 - \alpha)\%$ quantile from the χ^2 distribution with m degrees of freedom. For example, with $m = 4$ degrees of freedom, the 95% quantile of $\chi^2(4)$ is 9.488, so sample values

in excess of this lead to rejection of the null hypothesis at the 5% significance level. Ljung and Box (1979) suggested a modified Q statistic, say $MQ(m)$. Specifically:

$$MQ(m) \equiv T(T+2) \sum_{r=1}^{m} \frac{\hat{\rho}_r^2}{(T-r)} \qquad (5.78)$$

Which, as in the Box–Pearce case, is asymptotically distributed as $\chi^2(m)$ under the null hypothesis of no serial correlation. The modified Q statistic is part of the routine output in a number of econometric packages.

5.6.2   An illustration of the DW and LM tests

Consider the following regression of the percentage rate of change of money wages, π_{wt}, on a constant and the inverse of the unemployment rate, $z_t = 1/u_t$, for the United Kingdom using the sample period 1862 to 1913. The following results were obtained:

$$\pi_{wt} = -2.307 + 10.914 z_t + \hat{\varepsilon}_t$$
$$(-6.849) \ (11.646)$$

Sample period 1862–1913, $T = 52$, $R^2 = 0.731$, dw $= 1.877$, RSS $= 84.043$; and 't' statistics in parentheses.

The sample value of the DW statistic is dw $= 1.877$; with $T = 52$ and $k = 2$ the 10% two-sided critical values are $d_L = 1.51$, $d_U = 1.59$ and $4 - d_U = 2.41$, $4 - d_L = 2.49$. Hence we conclude, as $1.877 > d_U$ and $1.877 < 4 - d_U$, against an AR(1) error process.

To illustrate the LM test procedure consider the following null and alternative hypotheses:

$$H_0: E\{\varepsilon_t, \varepsilon_{t-s}\} = 0 \quad \text{for } t \neq s, \, s = 1, \ldots, 4$$
$$H_a: \varepsilon_t = \rho_1 \varepsilon_{t-1} + \rho_2 \varepsilon_{t-2} + \rho_3 \varepsilon_{t-3}$$
$$+ \rho_4 \varepsilon_{t-4} + u_t \quad \text{or}$$
$$\varepsilon_t = u_t + \theta_1 u_{t-1} + \theta_2 u_{t-2}$$
$$+ \theta_3 u_{t-3} + \theta_4 u_{t-4}$$

The auxiliary regressions are:

$$\hat{\varepsilon}_t = -0.133 + 0.221 z_t$$
$$\quad\quad (0.397)\ (0.233)$$

$$R^2 = 0.001;\ \text{RSS} = 73.238$$

$$\hat{\varepsilon}_t = 0.080 - 0.403 z_t - 0.031 \hat{\varepsilon}_{t-1}$$
$$\quad\quad (0.220)(-0.392)\ (-0.206)$$

$$\quad + 0.092 \hat{\varepsilon}_{t-2} + 0.251 \hat{\varepsilon}_{t-3} + 0.168 \hat{\varepsilon}_{t-4}$$
$$\quad\ (0.596)\quad\quad (1.736)\quad\quad (1.166)$$

$$R^2 = 0.001;\ R_{uc}^2 = 0.108;\ \text{RSS} = 65.545$$

Sample period: 1866–1913, $T^+ = 52 - 4 = 48$; 't' statistics in parentheses.

Note that the constant is included in the auxiliary regressions. The LM test statistic is:

$$\text{SC}(4) = T^+(R_{uc}^2) = 48(0.1088)$$
$$= 5.220[0.265]$$

Compared to the $\chi^2(4)$ distribution, 5.22 has a marginal significance level of 26.5%, hence the null hypothesis of no serial correlation is not rejected at all conventional significance levels. The F version of this test compares residual sums of squares for the two auxiliary regressions, that is without and with the lagged residuals as regressors, estimated over the same sample period. The sample value of F is

$$F = \frac{(73.238 - 65.545)}{65.545}\frac{(48 - 6)}{4}$$
$$= 1.232[0.311]$$

The marginal significance level of this last statistic is 31.1%, the slight difference between the χ^2 and F tests being attributable to the small sample adjustments in the F test statistic.

5.6.3 Interpretation of significant test statistics for serial correlation

The LM test for serial correlation is in widespread use for a number of reasons. As noted it is simple to compute; it is (asymptotically) valid in the presence of lagged dependent variables; and it is valid against autoregressive and moving average schemes of serial correlation. Because of

the last point a significant value of the test statistic does not usually lead to a constructive outcome which indicates the alternative model to be fitted to the data; in this sense the test is a misspecification test. Although this is generally the case there are some circumstances where there is a constructive outcome. For example, the temporal aggregation of a relationship with white noise disturbances induces a moving average disturbance – see, for example, Ermini (1989) and Patterson and Pesaran (1992); forecasting a process with a white noise disturbance n periods ahead also induces a moving average disturbance – see Hansen and Hodrick (1980). The point is that the response to a significant test statistic should depend upon the theoretical background. If there is *a priori* justification for the serial correlation, the next problem to be addressed is how to take this into account for estimation and inference. If the serial correlation test is being used as a misspecification test then a significant test is interpreted as model inadequacy and the next problem is how to respecify the model. We deal with these different responses separately starting with a brief but somewhat misleading proof of the implications for estimation of serial correlation in ε_t. Although some of the ground covered here is common to the section on heteroscedasticity it is provided here for completeness of the argument.

The standard proof that $\hat{\beta}$ remains unbiased in the presence of $E\{\varepsilon\varepsilon' \mid X\} = \Omega \neq \sigma^2 I$ was presented in section **5.2**. If serial correlation is present in ε_t then $E\{\varepsilon_t, \varepsilon_{t-s}\} \neq 0$, for some s not equal to t, and hence $\Omega \neq \sigma^2 I$; in particular, and in contrast to the case for heteroscedasticity, the off-diagonal elements of Ω are nonzero. $E\{\varepsilon_t\} = 0$ is maintained *if* the serial correlation does not arise from a misspecification such as an omitted variable and the proof is correct in this case. Remember, though, that the correct OLS variance matrix for is

$$\text{Var}(\hat{\beta}) = (X'X)^{-1}X'\Omega X(X'X)^{-1}$$

and not $\sigma^2(X'X)^{-1}$.

Assuming no misspecification, an emphasis can then be appropriately placed on efficient methods of estimation. Perhaps the most obvious route is to see whether a feasible GLS estimator exists. We consider this approach first and then a popular alternative that uses the OLS estimator.

If a consistent estimator $\tilde{\Omega}$ of Ω can be found then the FGLS estimator,

$$\beta^0 = (X'\tilde{\Omega}^{-1}X)^{-1}X'\tilde{\Omega}^{-1}Y$$

can be used together with $\text{Var}(\beta^0) = (X'\tilde{\Omega}^{-1}X)^{-1}$. Two examples of a two-step procedure follow in which the first step is to obtain a consistent estimator of $\tilde{\Phi}$ and the second step is to use that in the FGLS estimator.

The first example is the AR(1) process $\varepsilon_t = \rho\varepsilon_{t-1} + u_t$. In this case Ω is given by:

$$\Omega = \frac{\sigma_u^2}{(1 - \rho^2)}$$

$$\times \begin{bmatrix} 1 & \rho & \rho^2 & \rho^3 & \cdots & \rho^{T-1} \\ \rho & 1 & \rho & \rho^2 & \cdots & \rho^{T-2} \\ \rho^2 & \rho & 1 & \rho & \cdots & \rho^{T-3} \\ \vdots & \vdots & \vdots & \vdots & & \vdots \\ \rho^{T-1} & \rho^{T-2} & \rho^{T-3} & \rho^{T-4} & \cdots & 1 \end{bmatrix}$$

$$(5.79)$$

A consistent estimator of ρ can be obtained from the OLS residuals. One possibility is to use $\tilde{\rho}$ given above; a slight variation is the OLS estimator $\hat{\rho} = \sum_{t=2}^T \hat{\varepsilon}_t\hat{\varepsilon}_{t-1}/\sum_{t=2}^T \hat{\varepsilon}_{t-1}^2$ which differs from $\tilde{\rho}$ in not including $\hat{\varepsilon}_T^2$ in the denominator. Both estimators are consistent and several others have been proposed – for a summary see Judge *et al.* (1985, p. 286).

Another example is provided when ε_t is generated by a first order MA process, $\varepsilon_t = u_t + \theta_1 u_{t-1}$, then $\text{Var}(\varepsilon_t) = \sigma_u^2(1 + \theta_1^2)$, $E\{\varepsilon_t, \varepsilon_{t-1}\} = \theta_1\sigma_u^2 \neq 0$ and $E\{\varepsilon_t, \varepsilon_{t-s}\} = 0$ for $s > 1$. In this case Ω is a band diagonal matrix:

$$\Omega = \sigma_u^2 \begin{bmatrix} (1+\theta_1^2) & \theta_1 & 0 & & & & \\ \theta_1 & (1+\theta_1^2) & \theta_1 & & & & \\ 0 & \theta_1 & (1+\theta_1^2) & & & & \\ \vdots & \vdots & \vdots & & & & \\ & & & & & & \\ 0 & 0 & 0 & & & & \end{bmatrix}$$

$$\begin{matrix} \cdots & 0 & 0 & 0 \\ \cdots & 0 & 0 & 0 \\ \cdots & 0 & 0 & 0 \\ \vdots & \vdots & \vdots & \vdots \\ & \theta_1 & (1+\theta_1^2) & \theta_1 \\ \cdots & 0 & \theta_1 & (1+\theta_1^2) \end{matrix}$$

$$(5.80)$$

$$= \sigma_u^2(1 + \theta_1^2)$$

$$\times \begin{bmatrix} 1 & \rho(1) & 0 & \cdots & 0 & 0 & 0 \\ \rho(1) & 1 & \rho(1) & \cdots & 0 & 0 & 0 \\ 0 & \rho(1) & 1 & \cdots & 0 & 0 & 0 \\ \vdots & \vdots & \vdots & \vdots & \vdots & \vdots & \vdots \\ & & & & \rho(1) & 1 & \rho(1) \\ 0 & 0 & 0 & \cdots & 0 & \rho(1) & 1 \end{bmatrix}$$

$$(5.81)$$

where $\rho(1) = \theta_1/(1 + \theta_1^2)$ is the first order autocorrelation coefficient. The elements of Ω can be consistently estimated from the OLS residuals since $\sum_{t=2}^T \hat{\varepsilon}_t\hat{\varepsilon}_t/T$ is a consistent estimator of $\text{Var}(\varepsilon_t) = \sigma_u^2(1 + \theta_1^2)$ and $\sum_{t=2}^T \hat{\varepsilon}_t\hat{\varepsilon}_{t-1}/T$ is a consistent estimator of $E\{\varepsilon_t, \varepsilon_{t-1}\} = \theta_1\sigma_u^2$.

A second option is to continue to use the OLS estimator $\hat{\beta} = (X'X)^{-1}X'Y$ but in combination with the correct variance–covariance matrix $\text{Var}(\hat{\beta}) = (X'X)^{-1}X'\tilde{\Omega}X(X'X)^{-1}$. The latter method is quite popular in applied work because, although β^0 and $\hat{\beta}$ remain unbiased in this setup, GLS only dominates OLS in efficiency, in finite samples, when Ω is known. However, the extent to which the GLS gain is carried over in finite samples when Ω is consistently estimated is not known in general (although it has been worked out in some special cases – for a summary see Judge *et al.* (1985, pp. 278 *et seq.*)). The OLS procedure seems to hedge one's bets in the sense of using an unbiased estimator with a variance matrix which is 'robust' to serial correlation. Generalisations of either procedure to higher order AR and MA processes are relatively straightforward. Direct one-step estimation based on maximum likelihood or nonlinear least squares is also possible.

It is important at this stage to remember two assumptions underlying the previous discussion. The first is that the serial correlation is 'pure' in the sense of not arising from a misspecification of the regression model such as omitting a variable, which should have been included. The second is that none of the regressors is a lagged dependent variable. To illustrate the importance of the first assumption consider the following model

$$Y_t = \beta_1 + \beta_2 X_t + \beta_3 Z_t + \varepsilon_t \qquad (5.82)$$

where ε_t satisfies the usual assumptions. Suppose Z_t is omitted from the regression so that the model becomes

$$Y_t = \beta_1 + \beta_2 X_t + \xi_t \quad \text{where } \xi_t = \beta_3 Z_t + \varepsilon_t$$
$$(5.83)$$

Then

$$E\{\xi_t \mid X_t\}$$
$$= E\{(\beta_3 Z_t + \varepsilon_t) \mid X_t\}$$
$$= \beta_3 E\{Z_t \mid X_t\} + E\{\varepsilon_t \mid X_t\}$$
$$= \beta_3 E\{Z_t \mid X_t\} \quad \text{using } E\{\varepsilon_t \mid X_t\} = 0$$

Hence, the first problem to arise is that

$$E\{\xi_t \mid X_t\} = \beta_3 E\{Z_t \mid X_t\} \neq 0$$

if $E\{Z_t \mid X_t\} \neq 0$. In this case the OLS estimator of β_1 will be biased because it is actually an estimator of $\beta_1 + \beta_3 E\{Z_t \mid X_t\}$.

Now consider

$$E\{\xi_t \xi_{t-1} \mid X_t\}$$
$$= E\{(\beta_3 Z_t + \varepsilon_t)(\beta_3 Z_{t-1} + \varepsilon_{t-1}) \mid X_t\}$$
$$= \beta_3^2 E\{Z_t Z_{t-1} \mid X_t\}$$
$$\text{using } E\{\varepsilon_t \varepsilon_{t-1} \mid X_t) = 0$$
$$\text{and} \quad E\{\varepsilon_t Z_{t-1} \mid X_t\} = E\{Z_t \varepsilon_{t-1} \mid X_t\} = 0$$

If Z_t is serially correlated, which is likely with time series data, then $E\{Z_t Z_{t-1} \mid X_t\} \neq 0$ and $E\{\xi_t \xi_{t-1} \mid X_t\} \neq 0$. Given a test statistic, which indicates serial correlation, then the appropriate response is to respecify the model rather than seek an efficient method of estimation for the existing model.

A case, which often arises in empirical work, is that the response to a significant test for serial correlation is to include lags of the dependent variable. This can sometimes be justified by reference to the theoretical derivation of the model; for example, we know that partial adjustment and error correction models are essentially dynamic involving lagged dependent variables and lagged regressors. In the above example suppose $Z_t = Y_{t-1}$, then $E\{Y_t Y_{t-1} \mid X_t\} \neq 0$ is highly probable for time series data. A typical practice in applied work is to allow the data to determine the lag length for dynamic models; this will be done partly by reference to the usual 't' and F tests for the exclusion of variables, but also by reference to whether there is any indication of residual serial correlation. Care has to be taken with this approach to model building for while, as in the case above with $Z_t = Y_{t-1}$, misspecification can arise from an omitted lag of the dependent variable it may also arise because another variable has been omitted.

The impact of the second assumption of the absence of lagged dependent variables can be illustrated with the following model

$$Y_t = \beta_1 + \beta_2 X_t + \beta_3 Y_{t-1} + \varepsilon_t \qquad (5.84)$$

If ε_t is white noise, then OLS estimation in (5.84) is biased in finite samples but consistent. If, however,

$$\varepsilon_t = \rho\varepsilon_{t-1} + u_t \qquad (5.85)$$

then ε_t is no longer an innovation relative to Y_{t-1}: Y_{t-1} and ε_t are correlated. The implication of this correlation is that the OLS estimators are biased and inconsistent. To see how the correlation arises note that ε_t depends upon ε_{t-1} and from (5.84), $\varepsilon_{t-1} = Y_{t-1} - (\beta_1 + \beta_2 X_{t-1} + \beta_3 Y_{t-2})$: so ε_{t-1}, and hence ε_t, is in part determined by Y_{t-1}; therefore Y_{t-1} and ε_t are correlated.

Note that it is valid to use the LM test for serial correlation in a model with lagged dependent variables, that is a virtue of a test which is based upon estimation under the null hypothesis of no serial correlation. The importance of the observation that if serial correlation is detected, then OLS estimation will no longer remain consistent rests upon what is the appropriate response to this finding. As before, the serial correlation may arise from omitted variables, and the omission of further lags of the dependent variable could be the prime candidate in time series analysis; as noted above a typically model-building strategy is to select the lag length to ensure no residual serial correlation, although care must be taken in the mechanical application of this procedure. If the serial correlation is 'pure', then the FGLS or OLS procedures described above are inappropriate because, when the null hypothesis of no serial correlation is incorrect, neither recognise the correlation between one or more of the regressors and the disturbance term. An appropriate method of estimation is instrumental variables. Instrumental variables should be correlated with the regressors they replace but uncorrelated with the disturbance term. To illustrate the choice in (5.84) note that the constant and X_t can act as their own instruments, the real problem is Y_{t-1}. Lagging (5.84) shows that Y_{t-1} is by hypothesis correlated with X_{t-1} and Y_{t-2}, either or both of which can serve as instruments. X_{t-1} is a valid instrument

because it is not correlated with ε_t (or ε_{t-1}); lags of the problem regressor can also serve as valid instruments provided they are lagged one more than the degree of serial correlation. Recall the problem is that Y_{t-1} is correlated with ε_t through the latter's serial correlation with ε_{t-1}, choosing Y_{t-2}, or Y_{t-s} with $s \geq 2$, is a valid because a second lag or higher order lag is predetermined at $t - 1$.

The estimation procedure could end here since the IV estimator is consistent and the variance matrix of the IV estimator, $\tilde{\beta}$, of β is valid for inference. Alternatively, IV estimation could be regarded as the first step in an FGLS procedure, just as OLS usually provides the first step when the regressors and the disturbances are not correlated. Starting with

$$\begin{aligned} Y_t &= \beta_1 + \beta_2 X_t + \beta_3 Z_t + \varepsilon_t \\ Z_t &= Y_{t-1} \end{aligned} \qquad (5.86)$$

the IV procedure replaces Z_t with the instrumental variable $\tilde{Z}_t$ where $Z_t = \tilde{Z}_t + \tilde{v}_t$; substituting into (5.86) then

$$\begin{aligned} Y_t &= \beta_1 + \beta_2 X_t + \beta_3 \tilde{Z}_t + \omega_t \\ \omega_t &= \varepsilon_t + \beta_3 \tilde{v}_t \end{aligned} \qquad (5.87)$$

OLS applied to (5.87) produces consistent estimators, $\hat{\beta}_1$, $\hat{\beta}_2$ and $\hat{\beta}_3$ with OLS residuals $\hat{\omega}_t$; further, ε_t can then be consistently estimated by $\hat{\varepsilon}_t = \hat{\omega}_t - \hat{\beta}_3 \tilde{v}_t$. The residuals $\hat{\varepsilon}_t$ can then be used to obtain a consistent estimator $\tilde{\Omega}$ for use in the FGLS estimator $\beta^0 = (X'\tilde{\Omega}^{-1}X)^{-1}X'\tilde{\Omega}^{-1}Y$.

5.6.4 The Newey–West estimator of the variance(–covariance) matrix of $\hat{\beta}$

This subsection introduces an approach to serial correlation which is part of a more inclusive view of what can be done if $\Omega \neq \sigma^2 I$. Chronologically, the development started with White's (1980) estimator of the variance matrix for the OLS estimator when the sole problem was heteroscedasticity of a generally unknown form. Newey and West (1987) extended White's approach to serial correlation of a generally unknown form and Andrews (1991) provides further extensions.

Recall that the variance matrix of $\hat{\beta}$ is:

$$E\{(\hat{\beta} - \beta)(\hat{\beta} - \beta)' \mid X\}$$
$$= T^{-1}(X'X/T)^{-1}[E\{X'\varepsilon\varepsilon'X \mid X\}/T]$$
$$\times (X'X/T)^{-1}$$
$$= (X'X)^{-1}X'\Omega X(X'X)^{-1}$$

and the point at which we are 'stuck' is in determining an estimator for

$$E\{X'\varepsilon\varepsilon'X \mid X\} = X'\Omega X$$

when Ω is, generally, of unknown form.

To see how to progress, as in the case of heteroscedasticity, it will be useful to choose a simple example with manageably low values for T and k and then generalise; as before we choose $T = 4$ and $k = 3$. Then

$$X'$$
$$\begin{bmatrix} 1 & 1 & 1 & 1 \\ X_{12} & X_{22} & X_{32} & X_{42} \\ X_{13} & X_{23} & X_{33} & X_{43} \end{bmatrix}$$

$$\varepsilon\varepsilon'$$
$$\times \begin{bmatrix} \varepsilon_1^2 & \varepsilon_1\varepsilon_2 & \varepsilon_1\varepsilon_3 & \varepsilon_1\varepsilon_4 \\ \varepsilon_1\varepsilon_2 & \varepsilon_2^2 & \varepsilon_2\varepsilon_3 & \varepsilon_2\varepsilon_4 \\ \varepsilon_1\varepsilon_3 & \varepsilon_2\varepsilon_3 & \varepsilon_3^2 & \varepsilon_3\varepsilon_4 \\ \varepsilon_1\varepsilon_4 & \varepsilon_2\varepsilon_4 & \varepsilon_3\varepsilon_4 & \varepsilon_4^2 \end{bmatrix}$$

$$X$$
$$\times \begin{bmatrix} 1 & X_{12} & X_{13} \\ 1 & X_{22} & X_{23} \\ 1 & X_{32} & X_{33} \\ 1 & X_{42} & X_{43} \end{bmatrix}$$

Also

$$X'$$
$$\begin{bmatrix} 1 & 1 & 1 & 1 \\ X_{12} & X_{22} & X_{32} & X_{42} \\ X_{13} & X_{23} & X_{33} & X_{43} \end{bmatrix}$$

$$\Omega \qquad\qquad X$$
$$\times \begin{bmatrix} \sigma_{11} & \sigma_{12} & \sigma_{13} & \sigma_{14} \\ \sigma_{21} & \sigma_{22} & \sigma_{23} & \sigma_{24} \\ \sigma_{31} & \sigma_{32} & \sigma_{33} & \sigma_{34} \\ \sigma_{41} & \sigma_{42} & \sigma_{43} & \sigma_{44} \end{bmatrix} \begin{bmatrix} 1 & X_{12} & X_{13} \\ 1 & X_{22} & X_{23} \\ 1 & X_{32} & X_{33} \\ 1 & X_{42} & X_{43} \end{bmatrix}$$

$$= \begin{bmatrix} \displaystyle\sum_{t=1}^{T}\sum_{s=1}^{T} \sigma_{ts} & \displaystyle\sum_{t=1}^{T}\sum_{s=1}^{T} \sigma_{ts}X_{s2} \\[2em] \displaystyle\sum_{t=1}^{T}\sum_{s=1}^{T} \sigma_{ts}X_{t2} & \displaystyle\sum_{t=1}^{T}\sum_{s=1}^{T} \sigma_{ts}X_{t2}X_{s2} \\[2em] \displaystyle\sum_{t=1}^{T}\sum_{s=1}^{T} \sigma_{ts}X_{t3} & \displaystyle\sum_{t=1}^{T}\sum_{s=1}^{T} \sigma_{ts}X_{t2}X_{s3} \end{bmatrix}$$
$$\begin{matrix} \displaystyle\sum_{t=1}^{T}\sum_{s=1}^{T} \sigma_{ts}X_{s3} \\[2em] \displaystyle\sum_{t=1}^{T}\sum_{s=1}^{T} \sigma_{ts}X_{t2}X_{s3} \\[2em] \displaystyle\sum_{t=1}^{T}\sum_{s=1}^{T} \sigma_{ts}X_{t3}X_{s3} \end{matrix}$$

$$= \sum_{t=1}^{T}\sum_{s=1}^{T} \sigma_{ts} \begin{pmatrix} 1 \\ X_{t2} \\ X_{t3} \end{pmatrix} \begin{pmatrix} 1 & X_{s2} & X_{s3} \end{pmatrix}$$

$$= \sum_{t=1}^{T}\sum_{s=1}^{T} \sigma_{ts} X_t'X_s$$

where $X_S = (1\ X_{s2}\ X_{s3})$.

Notice the structure of this expression. σ_{ts} provides the weights on observations which differ in time by $t - s$ periods; if $\sigma_{ts} = 0$ for $t \neq s$, so there is no serial correlation, then all terms not at the same point in time disappear and the only weights left are those which allow for heteroscedasticity. Define ℓ as the difference in time between t and s, that is $\ell \equiv t - s$ so that $s \equiv t - \ell$, then $\sigma_{ts} \equiv \sigma_{t,t-\ell}$ is the autocovariance of order ℓ. We have introduced a superfluous comma in the subscripts to clarify this point, but also to note that $\sigma_{t,t-\ell} = \sigma_{t-\ell,t}$. Now, for example, if only the first order autocovariances are nonzero, as would be the case if ε_t is generated by an MA(1) process, then all terms for which $|\ell| > 1$ are zero.

The Newey–West consistent estimator of the variance(–covariance) matrix of $\hat{\beta}$ involves three points. First, σ_{ts} is replaced by $\hat{\varepsilon}_t \hat{\varepsilon}_s$ where $s = t - \ell$, and $\hat{\varepsilon}_t$ are the OLS residuals; this is just like White's estimator but also applied to the off-diagonal elements. The second point concerns how many autocovariances to include. Sometimes there is theoretical guidance that a particular order MA process, say MA($\mathcal{L}$) should be present – see, for example, Hansen and Hodrick (1980) – so that lags on the autocovariances should not exceed $\mathcal{L}$; otherwise for autoregressive processes some experimentation is necessary to establish the point at which further lags can be neglected. A third point is that Newey and West (*op. cit.*) introduce weights, w_ℓ, on the products $\hat{\varepsilon}_t \hat{\varepsilon}_s$, where $s = t - \ell$, to ensure that the estimator of the variance matrix is positive definite. These weights, which follow the Bartlett window, are $w_\ell = 1 - [\ell/(\mathcal{L} + 1)]$ for $\ell = 1, \ldots, \mathcal{L}$, thus the weights decline from $\mathcal{L}/(\mathcal{L} + 1)$ to $1/(\mathcal{L} + 1)$. Thus, with these three points, the Newey–West estimator of $E\{X'\varepsilon\varepsilon'X \mid X\}$ is:

$$\hat{\Xi} = \left[\sum_{t=1}^{T} \hat{\varepsilon}_t^2 X_t' X_t \right.$$

$$\downarrow$$

heteroscedasticity
adjustment

$$\left. + \sum_{\ell=1}^{\mathcal{L}} \sum_{t=\ell+1}^{T} w_\ell \hat{\varepsilon}_t \hat{\varepsilon}_{t-\ell} (X_t' X_{t-\ell}' + X_{t-\ell}' X_t) \right]$$

$$\downarrow$$

serial correlation
adjustment

Hence, the Newey–West estimator of the variance matrix, $(X'X)^{-1}X'\Omega X(X'X)^{-1}$, of $\hat{\beta}$ is:

$$\text{Var}(\hat{\beta})_{\text{NW}} = (X'X)^{-1}\hat{\Xi}(X'X)^{-1}$$

Just as in the simplest OLS case with $E\{\varepsilon\varepsilon'\} = \sigma^2 I$, the square roots of the diagonal elements of $\text{Var}(\hat{\beta})_{\text{NW}}$ are the estimated standard errors. Standard errors computed according to this method are said to be heteroscedastic and autocorrelation consistent.

Other choices of weights are possible; for example, MICROFIT, Pesaran and Pesaran (1997, pp. 403–404), allows the user to choose equal weights with $w_\ell = 1$, which is recommended for MA processes of known order, although this could, especially where $\mathcal{L}$ is large relative to T, result in a negative definite estimate. MICROFIT also makes the small sample adjustment to White's heteroscedastic consistent estimator and to the Newey–West estimator recommended by MacKinnon and White (1985). Specifically, multiply the Newey–West estimator by $T/(T - k) > 1$; the estimated standard errors will be smaller without this adjustment.

If the diagonal elements of Ω are equal the problem is just that of serial correlation. If the problem is just that of heteroscedasticity all the terms with $t \neq s$ are set to zero so setting $\mathcal{L} = 0$ in standard econometric packages with the Newey–West option will give just the heteroscedasticity correction.

5.7 Normality and the Jarque–Bera test

Normality is important for hypothesis testing, as the test statistic under consideration requires specification of its distribution under the null hypothesis. The usual specification is that of the normal distribution so an important part of the econometric toolkit is a test for normality. The leading test, due to Jarque and Bera (1980,

1987), is described in this section. If nonnormality is indicated then a typical response is not that another distribution should be specified, although there are circumstance when that route might be justified – see Chapter 16 on ARCH – but rather that there are 'outlying' residuals suggesting that the regression model is misspecified. In this sense tests for normality fall into the category of diagnostic or misspecification tests.

5.7.1 Normality of ε_t

A test for normality of the disturbances is a standard part of most econometric packages and is routinely applied in empirical work. Such a test serves two purposes. First, hypothesis testing requires specification of the distribution of a test statistic under the null hypothesis. In regression analysis the test statistic often depends upon the disturbances, which are usually assumed to be normally distributed. Alternatively, even if the disturbances are not normally distributed some weaker assumptions, for example that they are independent and identically distributed, are sufficient for normality of the OLS estimators to hold asymptotically. Second, a test for normality can be useful in identifying periods that indicate possible deficiencies in the empirical model. For example, a test for normality of the disturbances is based on the residuals from a fitted model; if normality holds then (in large) samples the probability of a residual exceeding $3\hat{\sigma}$ is 0.0013 and, hence, almost zero. Thus residuals of this size not only indicate that the residuals are not normal they also suggest that the model is not fitting well – there are 'outliers' not accounted for by the explanatory variables. Tests of normality are misspecification rather than specification tests: rejection of the null hypothesis does not, in general, identify the cause of the rejection.

5.7.2 The Jarque–Bera test

Several tests for normality are available, and a useful summary is given in Jarque and Bera (1987). The most commonly used and programmed test for normality of the regression disturbances is due to Jarque and Bera (1980). Before stating the test statistic it is helpful to review some characteristics of the normal distribution. Perhaps the most obvious characteristic is that the normal distribution is symmetric, so that mean = mode = median; a distribution which is not symmetric is *skew*; hence, one direction of departure to test for is the skewness of the distribution. One possible measure, due to Pearson, is

$$Psk = (\text{mean} - \text{mode})/\sigma \qquad (5.88)$$

where σ is the standard deviation of the distribution; Psk = 0 indicates a symmetric distribution. This measure is particular useful for a class of distributions known as Pearson's distributions, which include the normal, 't' and F distributions, for which the mode can be expressed exactly in terms of what are known as the central moments of the distribution.

The jth central moment of Y_t is $\mu_j = \sum (Y_t - \bar{Y})^j / T$; if $\bar{Y} = 0$ then this simplifies to $\sum Y_t^j / T$. Note that $\mu_1 = 0$ as $\sum Y_t = T\bar{Y}$. A symmetrical distribution also has odd order moments, for $j \geq 3$, which are 0 (but it is also the case that some asymmetrical distributions have odd order moments which are 0). Define

$$b_1 = \mu_3^2/\mu_2^3 \quad \text{and} \quad b_2 = \mu_4/\mu_2^2 \qquad (5.89)$$

then Pearson's measure of skewness is (Kendall and Stuart 1977)

$$Psk = \frac{b_1^{\frac{1}{2}}(b_2 + 3)}{2(b_2 - 6b_1 - 9)} \qquad (5.90)$$

It is also possible to base a measure of skewness just on the square root of b_1 since as $\mu_3 = 0$ for a symmetric distribution then this implies $b_1 = b_1^{\frac{1}{2}} = 0$. The square root of b_1 is

$$b_1^{\frac{1}{2}} = \frac{\mu_3}{\mu_2^{\frac{3}{2}}} \qquad (5.91)$$

and this is sometimes called the skewness coefficient (its use in this context rests on the implicit assumption that those asymmetric distributions with $\mu_3 = 0$ are unlikely to occur).

The second important characteristic of the normal distribution is its 'peakedness' or kurtosis. Thus even if a distribution is symmetric it could be more or less peaked than the normal distribution. A measure of kurtosis is provided by b_2, with $b_2 = 3$ for the normal distribution; hence define $\kappa = b_2 - 3$ with the departure of κ from 0 indicating excess kurtosis. In particular distributions for which $\kappa = 0$ are known as mesokurtic; when $\kappa > 0$ the distribution is more peaked, and hence with more probability in the 'tails' than the normal, and is known as leptokurtic; and when $\kappa < 0$ the distribution is flatter than the normal and is known as platykurtic. Leptokurtic distributions occur frequently in the study of financial variables, such as the return calculated from stock prices; there is a higher probability of excess returns, either large profits or large losses, than would be consistent with a normal distribution.

It should be clear from this discussion that tests for normality could be based on either or both $b_1^{\frac{1}{2}}$, for skewness, and b_2, for kurtosis. The particular test statistic due to Jarque and Bera (1980), sometimes referred to as the JB test for normality, combines both these measures. Applying the definition of the jth moment to the regression residuals, note first that if a constant is included in the regression then $\sum \hat{\varepsilon}_t = 0$, so the mean of $\hat{\varepsilon}_t$ is 0. In this case the jth moment of $\hat{\varepsilon}_t$ is $\hat{\mu}_j = \sum \hat{\varepsilon}_t^j / T$, thus $\hat{\mu}_1 = \sum \hat{\varepsilon}_t / T = 0$, $\hat{\mu}_2 = \sum \hat{\varepsilon}_t^2 / T$ and so on; also, for example, $\hat{\mu}_3^2$ is the square of the third moment and $\hat{\mu}_2^3$ is the cube of the second moment. The notation $\hat{\mu}_j$, rather than μ_j, is used to indicate that the residuals are estimators of the corresponding, but unobserved, disturbances. H_0 is that the disturbances are normally distributed; the JB test statistic is

$$JB = T\left[\frac{b_1}{6} + \frac{\hat{\kappa}^2}{24}\right] \tag{5.92}$$

This test statistic is asymptotically distributed as $\chi^2(2)$ under the null hypothesis; thus large values of JB, relative to quantiles from the $\chi^2(2)$ distribution, lead to rejection of the null hypothesis.

If the regression does not include a constant then $\sum \hat{\varepsilon}_t \neq 0$, and hence $\hat{\mu}_1 \neq 0$, and the modified JB test statistic is

$$JB = T\left[\frac{\hat{b}_1}{6} + \frac{\hat{\kappa}^2}{24}\right] + T\left[\frac{3\hat{\mu}_1^2}{2\hat{\mu}_2} + \frac{\hat{\mu}_1\hat{\mu}_3}{\hat{\mu}_2^2}\right] \tag{5.93}$$

which is asymptotically distributed as $\chi^2(2)$ under H_0.

Jarque and Bera (1987) report simulations to assess the power of the JB and some other tests of normality of regression disturbances. Of particular interest are the results where the alternative is the 't' distribution that is symmetric but fatter tailed than the normal distribution. Jarque and Bera (*op. cit.*) generate observations using the 't' distribution with 5 degrees of freedom (which gives considerably fatter tails than the normal) and use a significance level of 10%; the reported results for $T = 20$ and $T = 50$ show that the JB test is the most powerful of the seven tests considered with, for example, power of 46.4% for $T = 50$.

One point to note in the use of the JB test for normality is that the test statistic is asymptotically distributed as $\chi^2(2)$, but there is some evidence from Deb and Sefton (1996) that the asymptotic distribution is not a particularly good approximation for small samples. Deb and Sefton first consider the case where the JB test is applied directly to a set of observations (that is not a set of regression residuals) and generate critical values for the 5% and 10% significance levels some of which are extracted in Table 5.1.

The asymptotic critical values are shown in the last column and, on comparison, it is evident that there is considerable variation according to sample size. Using the asymptotic critical value will distort the actual size of the test in small samples. As the finite sample critical values are

Table 5.1   *Critical values of the JB test for normality of observations*

$T =$	20	40	50	75	100	150	200	500	$\infty = \chi^2(2)$
10%	2.332	2.994	3.188	3.491	3.670	3.903	4.046	4.352	4.605
5%	3.773	4.740	5.002	5.303	5.437	5.598	5.711	5.887	5.991

smaller, using the asymptotic critical value will result in an undersized test; that is there will be fewer rejections than there should be using the small sample critical value. For example, with $T = 100$, the actual size of the test at a nominal 10% significance level using the asymptotic critical value is 6.68%. This result will not carry over without qualification to a normality test using regression residuals. This is because the residuals will depend upon the matrix of regressors X, and the finite sample critical values will thus also depend upon X. To assess the sensitivity of the comparison between actual and nominal size to the regressor set, Deb and Sefton (*op. cit.*) used four datasets varying in the generating process assumed for the regressors. Their results strongly suggested that using the small sample critical values given in Table 5.1 led to a negligible difference between the actual and nominal size of the test, whereas using the critical values from $\chi^2(2)$ again resulted in an undersizing of the tests.

5.8   Functional form and the RESET test

The CEF is usually assumed to be linear in the conditioning variables, which follows if the distribution of the stochastic variables in the analysis is multivariate normal. In the alternative paradigm of the CLRM the direct assumption is usually made that the regression model is linear in the regressors. In contrast economic theory usually has little to say about the precise functional specification of the relationship among the variables of interest; linearity often seems to be the simplest practical choice. Of course,

linearity is not as restrictive as might at first seem the case, since all it really requires is that there is a linear relationship among some transformation of the variables. A leading case is the model which is multiplicative in the levels but linear in the logarithms. For example, suppose the consumption function is specified as $C_t = KY_t^\beta \exp(\varepsilon_t)$, then taking logs of both sides results in $\ln C_t = \ln K + \beta \ln Y_t + \varepsilon_t$, which is linear in the transformed variables.

5.8.1   Developing a test for nonlinearity

Nevertheless linearity is still restrictive and an assumption which it would seem desirable to test. To provide some motivation for a test statistic consider the following specification of a regression model:

$$Y_t = \beta_1 + \beta_2 X_t + \beta_3 X_t^2 + \varepsilon_t \qquad (5.94)$$

such a specification might arise, for example, as a quadratic cost function. Suppose the quadratic term is omitted and the regression is specified as

$$Y_t = \beta_1 + \beta_2 X_t + \xi_t \qquad (5.95)$$

Then $\xi_t = \beta_3 X_t^2 + \varepsilon_t$; now even if $E\{\varepsilon_t | X_t\} = 0$ it is not the case that $E\{\xi_t \mid X_t\} = 0$ because $E\{\beta_3 X_t^2 \mid X_t\} \neq 0$. In this case a test is straightforward, since adding X_t^2 to the regression (5.95) and testing its significance by a standard 't' test should reveal its incorrect omission. Similarly higher order powers of X_t could be added and tested either individually with 't' tests or simultaneously with an F test. These tests could be viewed as tests for: incorrect functional form, for example a quadratic should have been used; or omitted variables, for example X_t^2 was incorrectly excluded; or the disturbance has a non-zero mean.

Another way of viewing the assumption of linearity is as a first order approximation to an arbitrary function. Taylor's theorem provides the basis for this statement. Under certain conditions it states that an arbitrary function $f(X_t)$ can be approximated about the point $X_t = X_0$, by a polynomial function and a remainder. If the arbitrary function is a polynomial the approximation is a lower order polynomial and the remainder is also a polynomial.

More formally $f(X_t)$ can be expanded as follows:

$$f(X_t) = [f(X_0) + f'(X_0)(X_t - X_0)/1! \\ + f''(X_0)(X_t - X_0)^2/2! \\ + f'''(X_0)(X_t - X_0)^3/3! + \cdots \\ + f^n(X_0)(X_t - X_0)^n/n!] + R_n \quad (5.96)$$

where $f'(X_0)$ is the first derivative of $f(X_t)$ with respect to X_t evaluated at $X_t = X_0$; $f''(X_0)$ is the second derivative evaluated at $X_t = X_0$; and f^n is the nth derivative evaluated at $X_t = X_0$. The expression in square brackets is the polynomial approximation, say P_n where n indicates the order of the polynomial, to the unknown function and R_n is the remainder. Choosing $n = 1$ for P_n results in a linear approximation, specifically

$$f(X_t) = [f(X_0) + f'(X_0)(X_t - X_0)/1!] + R_1 \quad (5.97)$$

To see how this expansion works suppose the arbitrary function is known and specifically is the quadratic function $Y_t = \beta_1 + \beta_2 X_t + \beta_3 X_t^2$, which is expanded about $X_0 = 0$. In this case if $n = 2$ the expansion is exact. The required functions and derivatives evaluated at $X_t = 0$ are:

$$f(0) = \beta_1$$
$$f'(0) = \beta_2 + 2\beta_3(X_t = 0) = \beta_2$$
$$f''(0) = 2\beta_3$$

Hence, the second order expansion is

$$Y_t = \frac{f(0)}{0!} + \frac{f'(0)}{1!} X_t + \frac{f''(0)}{2!} X_t^2 \\ = \beta_1 + \beta_2 X_t + \beta_3 X_t^2 \quad (5.98)$$

Since $n = 2$ this exactly reproduces the original function; however, if $n = 1$ the remainder is $f''(0)X_t^2/2$. The point of this example is that the higher the order of the approximation, the better the approximation to the original function. Adding terms in the powers of X_t to a linear regression can, therefore, be regarded as assessing how good the linear approximation is to an arbitrary function in X_t.

5.8.2 Ramsey's RESET test

A procedure due to Ramsey (1969, 1970) called RESET, which is usually interpreted as a test of functional form, adds the squared fitted values of Y_t to the linear regression and tests for the significance of this additional variable. That is first estimate

$$Y_t = \beta_1 + \beta_2 X_t + \varepsilon_t \\ \text{to get the fitted values } \tilde{Y}_t = \tilde{\beta}_1 + \tilde{\beta}_2 X_t$$

then form $\tilde{Y}_t^2$ and carry out the regression

$$Y_t = \alpha_1 + \alpha_2 X_t + \alpha_3 \tilde{Y}_t^2 + \omega_t \quad (5.99)$$

to obtain

$$\hat{Y}_t = \hat{\alpha}_1 + \hat{\alpha}_2 X_t + \hat{\alpha}_3 \tilde{Y}_t^2 \quad (5.100)$$

and test the significance of $\hat{\alpha}_3$. To see why this works expand $\tilde{Y}_t^2$ and substitute in (5.100):

$$\hat{Y}_t = \hat{\alpha}_1 + \hat{\alpha}_2 X_t \\ + \hat{\alpha}_3(\tilde{\beta}_1^2 + 2\tilde{\beta}_1\tilde{\beta}_2 X_t + \tilde{\beta}_2^2 X_t^2) \quad (5.101)$$

then rearranging

$$\hat{Y}_t = (\hat{\alpha}_1 + \hat{\alpha}_3\tilde{\beta}_1^2) + (\hat{\alpha}_2 + 2\hat{\alpha}_3\tilde{\beta}_1\tilde{\beta}_2)X_t \\ + \hat{\alpha}_3\tilde{\beta}_2^2 X_t^2 \quad (5.102)$$

The direct approach is to estimate (5.102) and obtain

$$\hat{Y}_t = \hat{\beta}_1 + \hat{\beta}_2 X_t + \hat{\beta}_3 X_t^2 + \varepsilon_t \qquad (5.103)$$

and on equating coefficients in (5.102) and (5.103)

$$\hat{\alpha}_1 + \hat{\alpha}_3 \tilde{\beta}_1^2 = \hat{\beta}_1$$
$$\hat{\alpha}_2 + 2\hat{\alpha}_3 \tilde{\beta}_1 \tilde{\beta}_2 = \hat{\beta}_2$$
$$\hat{\alpha}_3 \tilde{\beta}_2^2 = \hat{\beta}_3$$

Hence the RESET procedure is an indirect way of testing whether the square of the regressor is significant.

So far the discussion has been limited to just two variables, Y_t and X_t; however, most empirical applications involve more than two variables. The RESET procedure is again applicable and consists of including the squared fitted values in a second regression with the original variables. As in the bivariate case the RESET test is a one-dimensional test on the significance of the regression coefficient on the squared fitted values. This can be computed in its F form, which is the square of the 't' statistic on the regression coefficient, or a χ^2 form, which we refer to as FF(1). The RESET test can be generalised to include higher order powers of the fitted values. For example, if the powers from 2 to p are included, the F test has $p - 1$ and $T - k - (p - 1)$ degrees of freedom, and the χ^2 version has $p - 1$ degrees of freedom which we refer to as FF($p - 1$). An alternative in the case of more than one regressor is to separately include powers of the individual regressors. This will not be equivalent to the RESET procedure. For example, if the regressor set is $(1, X_{t2}, \ldots, X_{tk})$, adding the squares of the regressors will add $k - 1$ variables resulting in a test with $k - 1$ numerator degrees of freedom, whereas the RESET test will have 1 numerator degree of freedom. The RESET test can be interpreted as a test for incorrect functional form, which is the motivation here, or a test for omitted variables which are proxied by powers of the mean function as estimated by the fitted values of Y_t. RESET is included as a routine test of functional form in MICROFIT – see Pesaran and Pesaran (1997).

5.9 Stability of the regression coefficients

An important assumption of the regression model is that the regression coefficients are constant so that it is valid to consider the sample of $t = 1, \ldots, T$ observations as being realisations from a process which is stationary. The simplest example of a process which violates this assumption is where, as in the set-up of the GQ test for heteroscedasticity, there is a single breakpoint at $T_1 + 1$, with the first T_1 observations generated from one regime and the remaining $T - T_1 = T_2$ observations generated from another regime; the difference between the regimes is assumed to be confined to the regression coefficients. Because of the change in the regression coefficients there is a change in the mean function, $E\{Y_t \mid X\}$, for $t = 1, \ldots, T_1$, $\neq E\{Y_t \mid X\}$ for $t = T_1 + 1, \ldots, T$ so the process is not first order stationary.

5.9.1 Chow's (first) test

There are two tests for the constancy of the regression coefficients due to Chow (1960) which are frequently programmed into commercially available econometric software packages. In the first test, sometimes called Chow's analysis of covariance (AOC) test or Chow's first test, there are sufficient observations in each regime to estimate the regression model; that is $T_1 > k$ and $T_2 > k$. We start from the following specification

$$Y_1 = X_1 \beta_1 + \varepsilon_1 \quad \text{with } E\{\varepsilon_1 \varepsilon_1' \mid X_1\} = \sigma^2 I_1 \qquad (5.104)$$

$$Y_2 = X_2 \beta_2 + \varepsilon_2 \quad \text{with } E\{\varepsilon_2 \varepsilon_2' \mid X_2\} = \sigma^2 I_2 \qquad (5.105)$$

where the subscript indicates the first or second regime; Y_i is $T_i \times 1$, X_i is $T_i \times k$, β_i is $k \times 1$, and ε_i is $T_i \times 1$ for $i = 1, 2$. The breakpoint $T_1 + 1$ is assumed to be known. According to the null hypothesis, $H_0: \beta_1 = \beta_2 = \beta$, so the observations can be pooled into one sample with constant regression coefficients (and homoscedastic disturbances). That is the regression model is

$$\begin{pmatrix} Y_1 \\ Y_2 \end{pmatrix} = \begin{pmatrix} X_1 \\ X_2 \end{pmatrix} \beta + \begin{pmatrix} \varepsilon_1 \\ \varepsilon_2 \end{pmatrix} \qquad (5.106)$$

The alternative hypothesis is $H_a: \beta_1 \neq \beta_2$, or equivalently say $\beta_2 = \beta_1 + \delta$ and $H_0: \delta = 0$ with $H_a: \delta \neq 0$. Under H_a we can write regime 2 as

$$\begin{aligned} Y_2 &= X_2 \beta_2 + \varepsilon_2 \\ &= X_2 \beta_1 + X_2 \delta + \varepsilon_2 \end{aligned} \qquad (5.107)$$

and the complete model

$$\begin{aligned} Y_1 &= X_1 \beta_1 + \varepsilon_1 \\ Y_2 &= X_2 \beta_1 + X_2 \delta + \varepsilon_2 \end{aligned}$$

$$\begin{pmatrix} Y_1 \\ Y_2 \end{pmatrix} = \begin{bmatrix} X_1 & 0 \\ X_2 & X_2 \end{bmatrix} \begin{pmatrix} \beta_1 \\ \delta \end{pmatrix} + \begin{pmatrix} \varepsilon_1 \\ \varepsilon_2 \end{pmatrix} \qquad (5.108)$$

Where 0 is a $T_1 \times k$ matrix with 0 in every element. This regression modifies the standard set-up by adding a $T \times k$ data matrix with the first T_1 rows 0, and the remaining T_2 rows as in the X_2 matrix. The test statistic is simply the F test of $\delta = 0$ with k numerator degrees of freedom and $T - 2k$ denominator degrees of freedom; a large value of the test statistic compared to the $\alpha\%$ critical value from the right-hand tail of the $F(k, T - 2k)$ distribution leads to rejection of the null hypothesis.

Chow (1960) presented his test statistic slightly differently. First, note that in general an F statistic can be calculated as

$$\begin{aligned} F &= \frac{(\text{RRSS} - \text{URSS})/g}{\text{URSS}/(T - k)} \\ &= \frac{(\text{RRSS} - \text{URSS})}{\text{URSS}} \frac{(T - k)}{g} \end{aligned}$$

where RRSS is the residual sum of squares from a restricted version of a more general model from which the unrestricted residual sum of squares, URSS, is calculated. Equivalently RRSS comes from the regression model with the null hypothesis imposed and URSS comes from the regression model according to the alternative hypothesis. In this case the restricted model imposes just one set of regression coefficients for T observations with residual sum of squares $\sum_{t=1}^{T} \hat{\varepsilon}_t^2 = \hat{\varepsilon}' \hat{\varepsilon}$ and $T - k$ degrees of freedom. According to the alternative hypothesis the regression should be estimated separately for the first and second regimes resulting in residual sums of squares

$$\sum_{t=1}^{T_1} \hat{\varepsilon}_{1t}^2 = \hat{\varepsilon}_1' \hat{\varepsilon}_1 \quad \text{and} \quad \sum_{t=T_1+1}^{T} \hat{\varepsilon}_{2t}^2 = \hat{\varepsilon}_2' \hat{\varepsilon}_2$$

with $T_1 - k + T_2 - k = T - 2k$ degrees of freedom. The test statistic is

$$\begin{aligned} &CT(k, T - 2k) \\ &= \frac{(\hat{\varepsilon}' \hat{\varepsilon} - (\hat{\varepsilon}_1' \hat{\varepsilon}_1 + \hat{\varepsilon}_2' \hat{\varepsilon}_2))}{(\hat{\varepsilon}_1' \hat{\varepsilon}_1 + \hat{\varepsilon}_2' \hat{\varepsilon}_2)} \frac{(T - 2k)}{k} \end{aligned} \qquad (5.109)$$

This is exactly the test statistic which results from the F test of $\delta = 0$. The test statistic is sometimes presented in the χ^2 – or LM – form:

$$LM(k) = k \frac{(\hat{\varepsilon}' \hat{\varepsilon} - (\hat{\varepsilon}_1' \hat{\varepsilon}_1 + \hat{\varepsilon}_2' \hat{\varepsilon}_2))}{\tilde{\sigma}} \qquad (5.110)$$

where $\tilde{\sigma} = (\hat{\varepsilon}_1' \hat{\varepsilon}_1 + \hat{\varepsilon}_2' \hat{\varepsilon}_2)/(T - 2k)$. $LM(k)$ is asymptotically distributed as $\chi^2(k)$ under the null hypothesis. (Note also that $LM(k) = k$ times $CT(k, T - 2k)$.)

5.9.2 Predictive/forecast failure tests

5.9.2a Chow's (second) test: a test for predictive failure

When $T_2 < k$ (or $T_1 < k$) there are insufficient observations in one of the regimes to run the regression and the Chow AOC test statistic cannot be calculated. To motivate a test statistic in this case consider the following. As before, observations in the first regime are generated by

$$Y_1 = X_1\beta_1 + \varepsilon_1 \tag{5.111}$$

If there is no change in regime using β_1 to predict Y_2, the observations in the second regime should result in

$$E\{Y_2 \mid X_2\} = X_2\beta_1 \tag{5.112}$$

and the regression model

$$Y_2 = X_2\beta_1 + \varepsilon_2 \tag{5.113}$$

If there is a change in regime then

$$E\{Y_2 \mid X_2\} = X_2\beta_1 + I_2\gamma_2 \tag{5.114}$$

where $I_2\gamma \neq 0$, and the regression model is

$$Y_2 = X_2\beta_1 + I_2\gamma + \varepsilon_2 \tag{5.115}$$

where I_2 is the $T_2 \times T_2$ identity matrix and γ is $T_2 \times 1$; that is there is one γ_i coefficient for each of the T_2 observations in the second regime. These can be interpreted as the prediction errors that result from using the regression coefficients from regime 1 to predict the mean of the dependent variable for regime 2. If these are all zero there has been no change of regime. The null hypothesis is H_0: $\gamma = 0$ and the alternative is H_a: $\gamma \neq 0$. If the null hypothesis is rejected the regression coefficients from the first regime fail to predict the (mean of the) observations on the dependent variable in the second regime; hence this test is usually referred to as Chow's test of *predictive failure* – or *Chow's second test*. According to the alternative hypothesis the observations have been generated by

$$Y_1 = X_1\beta_1 + \varepsilon_1 \tag{5.116a}$$

$$Y_2 = X_2\beta_1 + I_2\gamma + \varepsilon_2 \tag{5.116b}$$

which can be written as

$$\begin{pmatrix} Y_1 \\ Y_2 \end{pmatrix} = \begin{pmatrix} X_1 \\ X_2 \end{pmatrix}\beta_1 + \begin{pmatrix} \bar{0} \\ I_2 \end{pmatrix}\gamma + \begin{pmatrix} \varepsilon_1 \\ \varepsilon_2 \end{pmatrix}$$

where $\bar{0}$ is the $T_1 \times T_2$ matrix with 0 in every element. The test statistic is the F test of $\gamma = 0$ with T_2 numerator degrees of freedom and $T - (T_2 + k) = T_1 - k$ denominator degrees of freedom. The test statistic is calculated in the usual way as:

$$
\begin{aligned}
& PF(T_2, T_1 - k) \\
&= \frac{(RRSS - URSS)/T_2}{URSS/(T_1 - k)} \\
&= \frac{(RRSS - URSS)}{URSS} \frac{(T_1 - k)}{T_2}
\end{aligned}
\tag{5.117}
$$

The RRSS comes from estimating the regression over the complete sample imposing $\gamma = 0$; as before this is $\hat{\varepsilon}'\hat{\varepsilon}$. The URSS results from estimating the unrestricted model, which allows $\gamma \neq 0$; conceptually this is as in Chow's first test, that is $\hat{\varepsilon}_1'\hat{\varepsilon}_1 + \hat{\varepsilon}_2'\hat{\varepsilon}_2$ but the fit in the second period is exact because there is one γ_i for each of the T_2 observations so $\hat{\varepsilon}_2'\hat{\varepsilon}_2 = 0$ and $URSS = \hat{\varepsilon}_1'\hat{\varepsilon}_1$. The predictive failure test statistic is:

$$PF(T_2, T_1 - k) = \frac{(\hat{\varepsilon}'\hat{\varepsilon} - \hat{\varepsilon}_1'\hat{\varepsilon}_1)}{\hat{\varepsilon}_1'\hat{\varepsilon}_1} \frac{(T_1 - k)}{T_2} \tag{5.118}$$

An LM version of the test statistic is also available

$$LM(T_2) = \frac{(\hat{\varepsilon}'\hat{\varepsilon} - \hat{\varepsilon}_1'\hat{\varepsilon}_1)}{\hat{\sigma}_1^2} \tag{5.119}$$

where $\hat{\sigma}_1^2 = \hat{\varepsilon}_1'\hat{\varepsilon}_1/(T_2 - k)$. $LM(T_2)$ is distributed as $\chi^2(T_2)$ under the null hypothesis. (Note also that $LM(T_2) = T_2$ times $PF(T_2, T_1 - k)$.)

Although the predictive failure test statistic was designed for the situation where there are insufficient observations in one of the regimes (which we assume to be the second) to estimate the regression, it can also be used when $T_2 > k$ as a supplement to Chow's first test. Notice that if there is a change in regime then

$$E\{Y_2 \mid X_2\} = X_2\beta_1 + I_2\gamma \qquad (5.120)$$

If $I_2\gamma \neq 0$ this could arise because there is a change in the regression coefficients or some variables, other than those in X_2, which are relevant to the second regime have been omitted. Hence, the predictive failure test can be interpreted as a misspecification test with power against changes in regime arising from nonconstant regression coefficients or omitted variables.

5.9.2b A forecast (deterioration) test

An alternative test of predictive – or forecast – failure works directly on the idea of forecasting the observations in the second (first) period using the estimated coefficients from the first (second) period. The model for the second period is:

$$Y_2 = X_2\beta_2 + \varepsilon_2 \qquad (5.121)$$

but if there is no change in regime, interpreted here as no change in the β coefficients, then this is the same as

$$Y_2 = X_2\beta_1 + \varepsilon_2 \qquad (5.122)$$

or for a particular observation, say the tth,

$$Y_{2t} = X_{2t}\beta_1 + \varepsilon_{2t} \qquad (5.123)$$

where X_{2t} is the $1 \times k$ vector of observations on the tth row of X_2. If β_1 is estimated from the first T_1 observations then the conditional forecast errors are defined as $(\hat{\varepsilon}_{2t} \mid \hat{\beta}_1) = Y_{2t} - \tilde{Y}_{2t}$ for $t = T_1 + 1, \ldots, T$, where $\tilde{Y}_{2t} = X_{2t}\hat{\beta}_1$. Under the null hypothesis of no regime change then the following test statistic is distributed as $\chi^2(T_2)$:

$$\mathrm{HF}(T_2) = \sum_{t=T_1+1}^{T} (\hat{\varepsilon}_{2t} \mid \hat{\beta}_1)^2 / \hat{\sigma}_1^2 \qquad (5.124)$$

Large values of $\mathrm{HF}(T_2)$ indicate deterioration in the fit of the equation, relative to the first period, and lead to rejection of the null hypothesis. 'Large' is used in the usual sense of exceeding the $(1 - \alpha)\%$ quantile of the null distribution, here $\chi^2(T_2)$. The test statistic can be written as:

$$\mathrm{HF}(T_2) = T_2\tilde{\sigma}_2^2 / \hat{\sigma}_1^2 \qquad (5.125)$$

where $\tilde{\sigma}_2^2 = \sum_{t=T_1+1}^{T} (\hat{\varepsilon}_{2t} \mid \hat{\beta}_1)^2 / T_2)$ is a consistent estimator of σ_2^2 under the null that $\beta_2 = \beta_1$. On the assumption that $\sigma_1^2 = \sigma_2^2$, $\mathrm{HF}(T_2)$ should not be far from T_2 and so 'large' values of the test statistic suggest that the fit in the second period does not match the fit in the first period. If $\sigma_1^2 = \sigma_2^2$, this is due to either $\beta_2 \neq \beta_1$ or some change in the determinants of Y_2 compared to Y_1; another possibility is $\sigma_1^2 \neq \sigma_2^2$, which is why it is useful to undertake a prior test of this assumption before calculating the test.

5.9.3 Unknown breakpoint(s)

The Chow and Predictive Failure tests assume that the breakpoint is known; however, this knowledge is rarely available with the required certainty. An alternative is to compute sequential Chow/Predictive Failure tests and allow the breakpoint to move through the sample from observations $k_1 + 1$ to $T - (k + 1)$ for Chow's first test, or $k_1 + 1$ to $T - 1$ for Chow's second test. Notice also that in Chow's first test the two regimes are treated symmetrically, but in Chow's second test they are treated asymmetrically; hence it would be possible to have a forward and a backward predictive failure test. The forward sequential predictive failure test first uses observations 1 to $k_1 + 1$ to predict the remaining observations, and then adds observations one at a time so that the final test uses observations 1 to $T - 1$ to predict the Tth observation. The backward sequential predictive failure test first uses observations T to $T - (k + 1)$, then adds observations one at a time until the sample for the last regression consists of observations T to 2 to predict the first observation.

There are three complications arising from an uncertain breakpoint. First, there is a cumulation of type one error in carrying out a sequence of tests, so that the chances of falsely rejecting the null hypothesis generally increase with the number of tests; if n tests are carried out at the $\alpha\%$ significance level the upper limit on the overall significance level is $n\alpha$; it will be less than this where the tests are dependent but, typically, the degree of dependence is not known. The upper limit of the cumulated type one error could be controlled by reducing the significance level for each test; for example, by carrying out each individual test at the $(1/n)\alpha\%$ significance level. Second, when the breakpoint is unknown the critical values from the F distribution are not appropriate, although they are still often used by researchers; the true critical values will be larger to take account of the uncertainty as to where the breakpoint is located. Finally, as the sequential procedure may well indicate, there may be more than one possible change in regime; for example, if there are two changes in regime Chow's first test statistic becomes (in an obvious extension of the previous notation):

$$CT(2k, T - 3k) = \frac{(\hat{\varepsilon}'\hat{\varepsilon} - (\hat{\varepsilon}_1'\hat{\varepsilon}_1 + \hat{\varepsilon}_2'\hat{\varepsilon}_2 + \hat{\varepsilon}_3'\hat{\varepsilon}_3))}{(\hat{\varepsilon}_1'\hat{\varepsilon}_1 + \hat{\varepsilon}_2'\hat{\varepsilon}_2 + \hat{\varepsilon}_3'\hat{\varepsilon}_3)}$$

$$\times \frac{(T - 3k)}{2k} \qquad (5.126)$$

which is distributed as $F(2k, T - 3k)$ under the null hypothesis of no change.

Maintaining the assumption of homoscedasticity between regimes may be difficult when the regression coefficients are not constant. Indeed it might be thought that the combination $\beta_1 \neq \beta_2$ and $\sigma_1^2 \neq \sigma_1^2$ is quite probable, with the change of regime affecting the disturbance variance as well as the regression coefficients. The GQ test for heteroscedasticity does not assume $\beta_1 \neq \beta_2$, hence it could be used first to test the homoscedasticity assumption. If there is a rejection of this assumption then use $\hat{\sigma}_1^2$ and $\hat{\sigma}_2^2$ to form the transformation matrix P defined above in (5.52), the effect of which is to leave the first T_1 observations unchanged while the remaining T_2 observations are divided by $\sqrt{\kappa_2} = \hat{\sigma}_2/\hat{\sigma}_1$. The disturbances are homoscedastic in the transformed model, which can then be used for Chow's first test.

5.10 Model building and evaluation

The wider role of econometrics is in building and evaluating models. Estimation is an important part of this process but it is only one part. The idea of model building suggests that the structure, for example the form and number of equations and whether particular variables are treated as determined within or outside the system, is not known with certainty. In Chapter 1 we outlined an approach in which the aim was to construct models that were tentatively adequate, and informed in their construction by theory and data.

The concept of a tentatively adequate model captures the idea that the data generation process is unknown and we hope to approximate some part of it in an empirical enquiry. Part of this enquiry will involve the numerical parameterisation of the equation(s), for example the value of the elasticity of consumption with respect to income or the value of the elasticity of the nominal exchange rate with respect to relative prices, a problem which is usually solved by estimation. With numerical estimates replacing the unknown parameters it will be possible to evaluate the adequacy of the empirical model. Should this stage reveal that this model is not adequate, it will be necessary to reconsider the structure of the model, requiring respecification and further estimation. This suggests a 'loop' between initial and subsequent model specification, estimation and evaluation rather than a simple 'one-off' process which just requires estimation of some regression coefficients.

Assessing whether a particular empirical model is (tentatively) adequate requires an economic as well as an econometric evaluation.

As an example of the former suppose the (aggregate) long-run elasticity of consumption with respect to income was estimated at 0.2; then an uncomfortable implication of this estimate is that in the long run the asset to income ratio is increasing. An econometric evaluation comprises, at least, tests of specification and misspecification, diagnostic testing and post-sample model performance. Tests of specification usually concern sharply defined null and alternative hypotheses, for example in the context of a simple bivariate model with Y_t consumption and X_t income, a null hypothesis of interest is that the income elasticity is unity, that is $\beta_2 = 1$, against the alternative hypothesis of $\beta_2 \neq 1$. To be valid specification tests the estimated model, which provides the empirical framework for testing, should be data and theory consistent (more extensively it should be what Hendry (1995, p. 365) describes as congruent). For example, an empirical model in which the residuals can be explained, in part, by a variable, say Z_t, not included in the equation, is not data consistent; it can be improved by respecification to include Z_t.

As noted in section **5.6** tests designed to assess the adequacy of the tentative empirical model are usually referred to as tests of misspecification or diagnostic tests. A test for serial correlation in the residuals, which revealed a positive correlation between successive residuals, could have alerted the researcher to the possibility of an omitted variable but, equally, might have indicated a number of other possible failings in the specification – for example, misspecification of the dynamic structure of the model or incorrect imposition of a linear form to the equation.

The application of tests of specification, misspecification and diagnostic checking involves an extensive use of sample data to design a data and theory consistent (congruent) model. A further check on the adequacy of the model uses out of sample data (usually post-sample but it could be pre-sample) to check the forecasting accuracy of the empirical model. The analysis of such tests suggests the need for some interpretative and detective abilities on the part of the model builder.

5.11 An estimated regression model

In this section an empirical model is used to illustrate the techniques of this and the previous chapter. The example, which considers US personal consumption expenditure, is based on the work of Davidson, Hendry, Srba and Yeo (1978) and Deaton (1977).

5.11.1 The basic model

In equilibrium consumers are assumed to maintain a constant ratio between their consumption expenditure, C_t, and disposable income Y_t. That is

$$C_t = KY_t \tag{5.127}$$

or with lower case letters denoting natural logarithms

$$c_t = k + y_t \tag{5.128}$$

A measure of disequilibrium is, therefore, given by

$$\xi_t = c_t - (k + y_t) \tag{5.129}$$

Faced with a changing environment, for example suppose at least $\Delta y_t \neq 0$, consumers adopt a decision rule to keep on track with equilibrium and take into account short-run changes. One possible decision rule is that of an error correction mechanism, ECM – see also Chapter 8 – given by

$$\begin{aligned}
\Delta c_t &= \theta_1 \Delta y_t + \theta_2 \xi_{t-1} + \varepsilon_t \\
&= \theta_1 \Delta y_t + \theta_2 (c_t - k - y_t) + \varepsilon_t \\
&= \theta_0 + \theta_1 \Delta y_t + \theta_2 (c_t - y_t)_{-1} + \varepsilon_t
\end{aligned} \tag{5.130}$$

where $\theta_0 = -k\theta_2$.

The interpretation of this ECM is as follows: consumption is changed, $\Delta c_t \neq 0$, if either there was disequilibrium last period, $\xi_{t-1} \neq 0$, in which case some change in consumption is necessary to restore equilibrium, and/or there was a change in income in the current period which, because of the equilibrium condition (5.128), implies that consumption should also change. The anticipated signs and magnitudes of the coefficients are as follows: θ_2 is the error correction – or disequilibrium correction – coefficient. If $\xi_{t-1} > 0$ there is a 'surplus' of consumption, hence $\Delta c_t < 0$ is required to restore equilibrium; if $\xi_{t-1} < 0$ there is a 'deficiency' of consumption and $\Delta c_t > 0$ is required to restore equilibrium. We anticipate $-1 \leq \theta_2 < 0$, with $\theta_2 = -1$ implying that all of last period's disequilibrium is removed, otherwise $-1 < \theta_2 < 0$ implies that only a proportion is removed. We also anticipate $\theta_1 > 0$ as the equilibrium relationship (5.128) tells us that consumption is positively related to income; further, $\theta_1 \leq 1$ as the coefficient on y_t in the equilibrium relationship is 1. In summary $0 \leq \theta_1 \leq 1$.

It is also useful to write the model given by (5.130) in its autoregressive distributed lag form in which the level of consumption, c_t, is related to the level and lags of y_t and lagged c_t. To do this write Δc_t as $c_t - c_{t-1}$, Δy_t as $y_t - y_{t-1}$ and collect all like terms; that is

$$
\begin{aligned}
c_t - c_{t-1} &= \theta_0 + \theta_1(y_t - y_{t-1}) \\
&\quad + \theta_2(c_t - y_t)_{-1} + \varepsilon_t \\
\Rightarrow c_t &= c_{t-1} + \theta_0 + \theta_1 y_t - \theta_1 y_{t-1} \\
&\quad + \theta_2 c_{t-1} - \theta_2 y_{t-1} + \varepsilon_t \\
&= \theta_0 + (1 + \theta_2)c_{t-1} + \theta_1 y_t \\
&\quad - (\theta_1 + \theta_2)y_{t-1} + \varepsilon_t \\
&= \beta_1 + \beta_2 y_t + \beta_3 y_{t-1} \\
&\quad + \gamma_1 c_{t-1} + \varepsilon_t
\end{aligned}
\tag{5.131}
$$

where $\beta_1 = \theta_0$, $\beta_2 = \theta_1$, $\beta_3 = -(\theta_1 + \theta_2)$ and $\gamma_1 = (1 + \theta_2)$.

It is easier to interpret (5.131) in the terms introduced in Chapter 4. (5.131) is a dynamic

extension of a bivariate model with the variables c_t and y_t; c_t is conditioned on y_t and the lagged variables c_{t-1} and y_{t-1}. It assumes that the joint distribution of c_t and y_t is normal, and hence the joint distribution of c_t, c_{t-1}, y_t and y_{t-1} is (multivariate) normal. This assumption implies that the conditional expectation functions are linear. The conditioning on the lagged values, c_{t-1} and y_{t-1}, is uncontentious. Conditioning on the current value of y_t assumes that the univariate conditional pdf, $f(c_t \mid c_{t-1}, y_t, y_{t-1})$, contains the parameters of interest, β_1, β_2, β_3 and γ_1. We are in effect assuming two things in this approach. First, that the parameters of interest can be obtained from $f(c_1 \mid c_t, y_t, y_{t-1})$ rather than from, for example, the joint pdf $f(c_t, y_t \mid c_{t-1}, y_{t-1})$; the former is a marginalisation of y_t relative to the latter. Second, that given this marginalisation the univariate conditional pdf does not contain more lagged values, for example $f(c_t \mid c_{t-1}, c_{t-1}, y_t, y_{t-1}, y_{t-2})$; $f(c_t \mid c_{t-1}, y_t, y_{t-1})$ is a reduction relative to this pdf.

In the context of the CLRM paradigm, y_t is a stochastic variable (it is not sensible to think of y_t as being fixed in repeated samples), and ε_t is a random disturbance which is assumed to be normally distributed with constant variance, no serial correlation and uncorrelated with y_t. The specification in (5.131) is assumed to be correct.

Note that there are three coefficients, θ_0, θ_1 and θ_2, in (5.130) but four, β_1, β_2, β_3 and γ_1, in (5.131). However, as the connections between the coefficients given beneath (5.131) show the following restriction holds: $\beta_1 + \beta_2 = 1 - \gamma_1$. The interpretation of this restriction is straightforward since it implies that the long-run coefficient (which here is interpreted as elasticity since c_t and y_t are in logs) is 1. To see this assume that c_t has settled to an equilibrium in the sense that there is no change in c_t; further as c_t is determined (just) by y_t there must have been no change in y_t for as long as necessary to work out any previous changes in y_t; hence, at least, $c_t = c_{t-1}$ and $y_t = y_{t-1}$. So for the purposes of deriving the implied long run of (5.131) the lag subscripts can be ignored. Assuming that ε_t has taken its mean value of 0, this results in

$$c_t = \beta_1 + \beta_2 y_t + \beta_3 y_t + \gamma_1 c_t$$
$$\Rightarrow$$
$$c_t = \beta_1/(1 - \gamma_1) + [(\beta_2 + \beta_3)/(1 - \gamma_1)]y_t$$
$$(5.132)$$

The coefficient on y_t is $(\beta_2 + \beta_3)/(1 - \gamma_1)$ which equals 1 if $\beta_1 + \beta_2 = 1 - \gamma_1$. This is as expected because in the ECM interpretation equilibrium consumption is specified as $c_t = k + y_t$; hence on comparison of (5.129) and (5.132), $\beta_1/(1 - \gamma) = k$ and $(\beta_2 + \beta_3)/(1 - \gamma_1) = 1$.

5.11.2   Estimation of the basic model

The data for this example is from the National Income and Product Accounts of the United States (Bureau of Economic Analysis 1993b, Vol. 2). C_t and Y_t are quarterly observations on personal consumption expenditure and personal disposable income in 1987 billions of US dollars, seasonally adjusted at annual rates. Lower case letters indicate logarithms of the corresponding upper case variable. As a first step Figure 5.1 graphs the data on the logarithms of consumption and income. The general impres-

sion is of two series that share a similar positive trend, although short-run movements in c_t are not always related to short-run movements in y_t.

Initial estimation of the simple ECM given by (5.130) produced the following estimates for 1960q2 to 1989q4

$$\Delta c_t = 0.00003 + 0.338\Delta y_t$$
$$(0.007) \quad (5.322)$$
$$- 0.055(c_t - y_t)_{-1} + \hat{\varepsilon}_t$$
$$(-1.356) \qquad\qquad (5.133)$$

't' statistics in parentheses.
Sample period: 1960q2 to 1989q4; $R^2 = 0.196$; dw $= 1.997$.

The estimated coefficients are of the anticipated sign but otherwise the regression is not entirely satisfactory. This conclusion is informed by the diagnostic or misspecification tests which were outlined in sections **5.5** to **5.9**; these are reported below.

5.11.3   Diagnostic and misspecification tests

5.11.3a   Serial correlation

The residuals are plotted in Figure 5.2; the pattern suggested in this figure is of some positive serial correlation, note that once the residuals

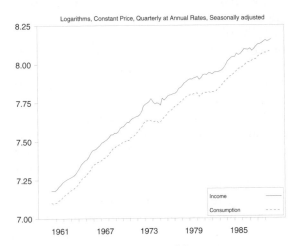

Figure 5.1   US consumption and income

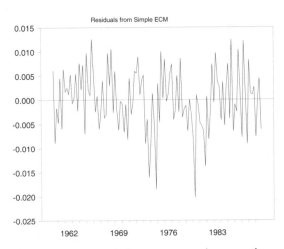

Figure 5.2   Residuals from consumption equation

are positive they tend to stay positive for a number of observations, and similarly when they are negative they tend to stay negative. Whether or not there is a pattern can be assessed more formally by the serial correlation test statistic. To allow for the possibility of serial correlation related to the seasonal frequency the LM test is calculated for fourth order serial correlation, SC(4). In its χ^2 form this is T times the R^2 from the auxiliary regression of the OLS residuals $\hat{\varepsilon}_t$ on the original regressors plus $\hat{\varepsilon}_{t-1}$ to $\hat{\varepsilon}_{t-4}$; in its F form it is the F statistic for the hypothesis that the coefficients on the lagged residuals are 0. The auxiliary regression is:

$$\hat{\varepsilon}_t = -0.004 - 0.021\Delta y_t - 0.045(c_t - y_t)_{-1}$$
$$\quad\quad (-0.838)(-0.321)\quad (-0.913)$$

$$+ 0.007\hat{\varepsilon}_{t-1} + 0.239\hat{\varepsilon}_{t-2} + 0.214\hat{\varepsilon}_{t-3}$$
$$\quad (0.065)\quad\quad (2.432)\quad\quad (2.201)$$

$$+ 0.019\hat{\varepsilon}_{t-4} + \hat{\psi}_t$$
$$\quad (0.195) \quad\quad\quad\quad\quad\quad (5.134)$$

't' statistics in parentheses.
Sample period: 1961q2 to 1989q4; $T = 115$;
$R^2 = 0.0883$.

The LM statistic for fourth order serial correlation is $SC(4) = T$ times $R^2 = 115 \times 0.0883 = 10.159$ with an msl of 3.78%; hence there is an indication of serial correlation in the residuals. In particular the auxiliary regression suggests significant serial correlation at lags 2 and 3. The F version of this test is 2.593 with 4 and 108 degrees of freedom, which has an msl of 4.050%. A constant is included in the auxiliary regression since although the mean of $\hat{\varepsilon}_t$ is 0 across the whole sample, 1960q2 to 1989q4, there are 4 fewer observations in the auxiliary regression due to the lagging of $\hat{\varepsilon}_t$. Excluding the constant gives $SC(4) = 9.477$ with msl = 5.02% and $F(4, 109) = 2.449$ with msl = 5.04%. An alternative to omitting the first 4 observations is to replace each missing $\hat{\varepsilon}_t$ with a 0. The SC(4) test statistic is then 11.360 with msl = 2.28% and $F(4, 112) = 2.944$ with msl = 2.30%. Since the justification for excluding the constant rests

upon a zero mean for $\hat{\varepsilon}_t$, which will not generally be satisfied exactly, and the justification for 'padding' out the missing observations with 0 is asymptotic, in finite samples the suggested procedure is to use actual observations with a constant in the regression.

The Durbin–Watson test statistic is $dw = 1.997$; however, although this value is not significant with $d_L = 1.532$ and $d_U = 1.607$ hence $d_U < dw < 4 - d_U$, DW is biased toward 2 when a lagged dependent variable is included in the regression. It may not be obvious that there is a lagged dependent variable in the regression since the dependent variable is Δc_t which does not appear in lagged form on the right-hand side. However, a regression with the same residuals is $c_t = \beta_1 + \beta_2 y_t + \beta_3 y_{t-1} + \gamma_1 c_{t-1}$, see (5.131), subject to the restriction $\beta_2 + \beta_3 = 1 - \gamma_1$, hence there is an implicit lagged dependent variable and the Durbin–Watson statistic cannot be interpreted literally.

5.11.3b   Heteroscedasticity

The 'standard' test
The squared residuals are plotted in Figure 5.3. There is some evidence of heteroscedasticity from two periods, broadly around 1974 and

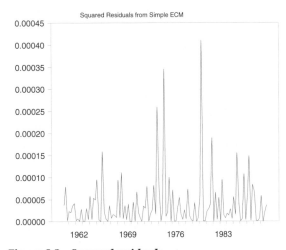

Figure 5.3   *Squared residuals*

1981, but overall the visual evidence for heteroscedasticity across the whole period is not pronounced. It will be interesting to see what the more formal tests show. A routine test statistic for heteroscedasticity, which we refer to later as the 'standard' test, involves an auxiliary regression of the squared OLS residuals on the squared fitted values from the original regression. The auxiliary regression is

$$\hat{\varepsilon}_t^2 = \alpha_1 + \alpha_2 \hat{Y}_t^2 + \psi_t \qquad (5.135)$$

The test statistic can be calculated in χ^2 form as T times R^2 from the auxiliary regression, which is distributed as $\chi^2(1)$ under the null hypothesis; as an F test with 1 and $T - k$ degrees of freedom; or a one-sided 't' test against the alternative that $\alpha_2 > 0$. These three forms give:

$$HS(1) = 119 \times 0.0211 = 2.514[0.113]$$
$$F(1, 117) = 2.524[0.115]$$
$$'t' = -1.589[0.943]$$

The $\chi^2(1)$ and F forms of the test statistic give essentially the same information because the sample size, $T = 119$, is large enough for the finite sample correction of the F test to make a negligible difference; both suggest nonrejection of the null with an msl of just over 11%. The 't' test is of the wrong sign to provide evidence in favour of the alternative hypothesis that $\alpha_2 > 0$ with $\hat{\alpha}_2 = -0.153$; inspection of the fitted values reveals one negative value.

White's test

White's test, which is a test for heteroscedasticity if the model is correctly specified but is otherwise a test for misspecification, involves estimating an auxiliary regression with the products and cross-products of the regressors in the original regression. In this case the auxiliary regression is of the form:

$$\hat{\varepsilon}_t^2 = \alpha_1 + \alpha_2 X_{t2} + \alpha_3 X_{t3} + \alpha_4 X_{t2}^2 + \alpha_5 X_{t3}^2$$
$$+ \alpha_6 X_{t2}X_{t3} + \zeta_t \qquad (5.136)$$

where $X_{t2} \equiv \Delta y_t$, $X_{t3} \equiv (c_t - y_t)_{-1}$ and there are no redundant regressors. White's test can be calculated in χ^2 form as $WT(5) = T$ times R^2, which is distributed as $\chi^2(5)$ in this case, or as the F test that $\alpha_2 = \cdots = \alpha_6 = 0$. The estimated auxiliary regression is as follows:

$$\hat{\varepsilon}_t^2 = 0.000 - 0.009 X_{t2} - 0.001 X_{t3}$$
$$(0.037)(-1.963) \quad (-0.228)$$
$$+ 0.090 X_{t2}^2 - 0.006 X_{t3}^2$$
$$(3.090) \quad (-0.243)$$
$$- 0.057 X_{t2}X_{t3} + \hat{\zeta}_t$$
$$(-1.264) \qquad (5.137)$$

't' statistics in parentheses.

The test statistics are:

$$WT(5) = T \text{ times } R^2 = 119 \times 0.181$$
$$= 21.594[0.000]$$
$$F(5, 113) = 5.018[0.000]$$

Because there is evidence of serial correlation, White's test is not interpreted in this case as purely a test for heteroscedasticity but rather a test for misspecification. The test statistics are significant, both have marginal significance levels which are effectively 0.

Breusch–Pagan test

As an example of the BP testing procedure we consider the possibility that there is heteroscedasticity with the variance related to the regressor $X_{t2} \equiv \Delta y_t$ and its square X_{t2}^2. The auxiliary regressions are specialisations of those for White's test, that is:

$$\hat{\varepsilon}_t^2 = \alpha_1 + \alpha_2 X_{t2} + \zeta_t \qquad (5.138a)$$

$$\hat{\varepsilon}_t^2 = \alpha_1 + \alpha_2 X_{t2} + \alpha_3 X_{t2}^2 + \zeta_t \qquad (5.138b)$$

Estimation of these regressions gave:

$$\hat{\varepsilon}_t^2 = 0.000 - 0.002 X_{t2} + \hat{\zeta}_t$$
$$(7.775)(-3.446)$$

The test statistics are:

$$\chi^2 \text{ version, BP}(1) = 10.965[0.000]$$
$$F \text{ version, } F(1, 117) = 11.876[0.000]$$

$$\hat{\varepsilon}_t^2 = 0.000 - 0.003X_{t2} + 0.079X_{t2}^2 + \hat{\zeta}_t$$
$$(7.669)(-4.163) \quad (2.939)$$

The test statistics are:

$$\chi^2 \text{ version, BP}(2) = 18.454[0.000]$$
$$F \text{ version, } F(2, 116) = 110.645[0.000]$$

There is evidence from both auxiliary regressions, with marginal significance levels of the test statistics effectively 0, that there is heteroscedasticity although, as in the White test, this may be indicating misspecification in a more general sense.

The Goldfeld–Quandt, GQ, test

The null hypothesis for the GQ test is H_0: $\sigma_1^2 = \sigma_2^2$ and the alternative, if *a priori*, the variance in the first subsample is thought to be larger than the variance in the second subsample, is H_a: $\sigma_1^2 > \sigma_2^2$. Where there is no prior information H_a is $\sigma_1^2 \neq \sigma_2^2$ which can be thought of as comprising H_{a1}: $\sigma_1^2 > \sigma_2^2$ and H_{a2}: $\sigma_2^2 > \sigma_1^2$.
The GQ test statistics are then:

$$GQ_{a1} = \hat{\sigma}_1^2/\hat{\sigma}_2^2 \quad \text{and} \quad GQ_{a2} = \hat{\sigma}_2^2/\hat{\sigma}_1^2$$

where $\hat{\sigma}_1^2 = \hat{\varepsilon}_1'\hat{\varepsilon}_1/(T_1 - k)$ and $\hat{\sigma}_2^2 = \hat{\varepsilon}_2'\hat{\varepsilon}_2/(T_2 - k)$. A large value of GQ_{ai}, $i = 1, 2$, leads to rejection of the null hypothesis in the direction of the alternative hypothesis. Periods 1 and 2 are taken with approximately equal numbers of observations and 20 observations are omitted from the middle of the sample to increase the power of the test; period 1 is 1960q2 to 1972q4 and period 2 is 1978q1 to 1989q4. The estimated variances are: $\hat{\sigma}_1^2 = 0.0000269$ and $\hat{\sigma}_2^2 = 0.0000456$, hence the test statistics are:

$$GQ_{a1} = \hat{\sigma}_1^2/\hat{\sigma}_2^2 = 269/456$$
$$= 0.590[0.963] \sim F(48, 45)$$

$$GQ_{a2} = \hat{\sigma}_2^2/\hat{\sigma}_1^2 = 456/269$$
$$= 1.695[0.037] \sim F(45, 48)$$

While neither test statistic is significant at the 5% significance level, with 2.5% in each tail, there is some evidence from GQ_{a2} with an msl of 3.7% = 7.4% on a two-sided test, that the second period variance may well be larger than the first period variance. Inspection of the residuals and their squared values suggests that much of this significance is contributed by the observation for 1980q2, which is an 'outlier' in the sense that the residual at −0.020 is over three times the estimated standard error of the regression, $\hat{\sigma} = 0.006$. While this was not sufficient by itself to trigger a significant value of the JB test for normality of ε_t, which is often where 'outliers' are highlighted, the GQ test can be sensitive to such observations. Introducing a dummy variable, which is 1 in 1980q2 and 0 elsewhere, leads to the following revised GQ test statistics:

$$GQ_{a1} = 0.763[0.820] \sim F(48, 44)$$
$$GQ_{a2} = 1.310[0.179] \sim F(44, 48)$$

In this case neither of the test statistics is significant at conventional levels.

However, the introduction of a dummy variable is not a satisfactory resolution to the problem indicated by the first set of GQ test statistics; they correctly indicated a potential problem in the second period. The problem could arise because of a 'special event' not captured by the existing regressors or some other kind of structural change. This procedure demonstrated that GQ tests will have power not only in cases of 'pure' heteroscedasticity but also in situations where the estimated variance in the second period increases because of a structural change in the regression; for example, factors which were quiescent in the first period may become relevant in the second period. These possibilities should be considered before heteroscedastic adjustments are made to the variance–covariance matrix of the OLS estimators. We consider this aspect further below.

5.11.4 Normality

A standard test for normality of the residuals is the Jarque–Bera test, which is distributed as $\chi^2(2)$ under the null hypothesis. The JB test statistic, where the regression includes a constant, is

$$JB = T\left[\frac{\hat{b}_1}{6} + \frac{\hat{\kappa}^2}{24}\right]$$

where $\hat{b}_1 = \hat{\mu}_3^2/\hat{\mu}_2^3$, $\hat{\kappa} = \hat{b}_2 - 3$ and $\hat{b}_2 = \hat{\mu}_4/\hat{\mu}_2^2$; $\hat{b}_1$ is a measure of skewness and $\hat{b}_2$ is a measure of kurtosis. In this case the sample value of the JB statistic is 3.906 with an msl of 14.20%, hence the null hypothesis that the $\hat{\varepsilon}_t$ are normally distributed is not rejected.

5.11.5 Functional form: the RESET test

A standard test of functional form is Ramsey's RESET test. The original regression is first estimated and the fitted values of the dependent variable are obtained; the regression is estimated again with the powers, $2, \ldots, p$, of the fitted values as additional regressors. The RESET test is a test of the significance of the coefficients on the powers of the fitted values. The test statistic can be calculated in χ^2 form with $p - 1$ degrees of freedom or in F form with $p - 1$ and $T - k - (p - 1)$ degrees of freedom. MICROFIT routinely calculates the RESET test with the squared fitted values, resulting in a test statistic which in its χ^2 form has 1 degree of freedom and in its F form has 1 and $T - k - 1$ degrees of freedom.

The RESET regressions for $p = 2$ and $p = 3$ gave:

$$\Delta c_t = -0.001 + 0.440\Delta y_t - 0.075(c_t - y_t)_{-1}$$
$$\quad (-0.270) \quad (1.164) \quad (-0.961)$$
$$\quad - 15.950(\Delta\hat{c}_t)^2 - 67.520(\Delta\hat{c}_t)^3 + \hat{\varepsilon}_t$$
$$\quad (-0.961) \quad (-0.060)$$

't' statistics in parentheses. $\qquad\qquad$ (5.139)

RESET test statistics:
$$\chi^2 \text{ version, FF(2)} = 0.405[0.817]$$
$$F \text{ version, } F(2, 114) = 0.199[0.819]$$

$$\Delta c_t = -0.001 + 0.445\Delta y_t - 0.075(c_t - y_t)_{-1}$$
$$\quad (-0.305) \quad (2.471) \quad (-1.453)$$
$$\quad - 17.969(\Delta\hat{c}_t)^2 + \hat{\varepsilon}_t$$
$$\quad (-0.635)$$

't' statistics in parentheses.

RESET test statistics:
$$\chi^2 \text{ version, FF(1)} = 0.403[0.525]$$
$$F \text{ version, } F(1, 115) = 0.403[0.526]$$

From these statistics there is no evidence that the functional form is misspecified in the direction for which the RESET tests have power. For example, when the squared fitted values are added to the original regression the additional coefficient has a 't' statistic of -0.635, and the RESET statistics in their χ^2 or F versions have an msl of about 52.5%.

5.11.6 Chow tests

5.11.6a Chow's first test

Chow's first test is a test that the regression coefficients are constant across two mutually exclusive regimes of T_1 and T_2 observations, conditional on equality of the variances, that is $\sigma_1^2 = \sigma_2^2$. The test statistic was given earlier as equation (5.109).

There was some evidence earlier – see the GQ test statistics – against $\sigma_1^2 = \sigma_2^2$; however, to illustrate the procedure we assume that this assumption can be maintained. Also, for illustrative purposes, we assume no serial correlation in the residuals and the normality of ε_t so that the only problem is that the regression coefficients may not be constant.

Ideally the breakpoint, T_1, for the Chow test should be informed by some potential source of structural change. Using critical values from an appropriate F distribution will only be valid if the selection of the breakpoint is not data

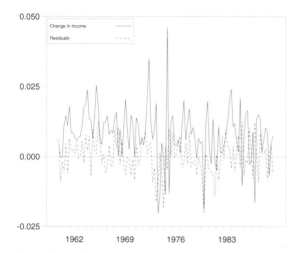

Figure 5.4 *Change in real income and residuals*

assessed visually by graphing the equation residuals on the same figure. Despite the prior view that the budget may have led to a structural break the evidence from the residuals is not particularly strong and this is confirmed by the Chow test – see Table 5.2; taking the breakpoint as 1975q2, the F statistic is $CT(3, 113) = 1.310$, with an msl of 17.9% there is no strong suggestion of structural change at this breakpoint.

The picture is different if the breakpoint is taken to be sometime in the early 1980s; moving the Chow test forward sequentially by 4 quarters at a time, from an initial breakpoint of 1980q1 suggests that the null hypothesis of constant regression coefficients should be rejected up to 1984q4. Significant test statistics are usually taken to indicate misspecification rather than the literal interpretation of the alternative hypothesis that the regression coefficients, in this case in the second period, should be allowed to differ from those in the first; nevertheless, it can sometimes be informative to see if the change is concentrated on certain coefficients. This can be done by defining three dummy variables, one for each coefficient, first define $dv_t = 0$ for $t = 1, \ldots, T_1$ and $dv_t = 1$ for $t \geq T_1 + 1$, and take the breakpoint as 1980q4; then define $dv\Delta y_t = dv$ times Δy_t and $dv(c_t - y_t)_{-1} = dv$ times $(c_t - y_t)_{-1}$. The three dummy variables are, therefore, dv_t, $dv\Delta y_t$ and $dv(c_t - y_t)_{-1}$. These will capture changes to the constant, the coefficient on Δy_t and the coefficient on $(c_t - y_t)_{-1}$,

dependent; if the breakpoint is unknown and is searched for, the critical values will be larger than those of the F distribution. Notwithstanding this point it is common practice to calculate the Chow test for several periods, for example a sequence of breakpoints advancing in time for the forward version of the test, and compare these with the critical value from the F distribution. We illustrate both possibilities here. One possible source of structural change was the Reagan budget of 1975, which led to an exceptional increase in income through tax rebates. The change in real personal disposable income is clearly apparent in Figure 5.4. Whether the consumption equation coped with this can be

Table 5.2 *(Forward) Chow and predictive failure test statistics*

	Breakpoint:									
	1975q2	1979q4	1980q4	1981q4	1982q4	1983q4	1984q4	1985q4	1986q4	1987q4
	Forward Chow test statistics									
CT	1.310	0.413	2.306	4.277	4.933	5.072	4.781	2.292	1.368	0.743
[msl]	[0.179]	[0.744]	[0.080]	[0.007]	[0.008]	[0.002]	[0.004]	[0.082]	[0.256]	[0.528]
	Forward predictive failure test statistics									
PF	0.858	1.344	1.076	1.007	1.028	1.090	1.227	0.974	1.032	0.386
[msl]	[0.465]	[0.133]	[0.384]	[0.472]	[0.443]	[0.370]	[0.250]	[0.490]	[0.415]	[0.926]

Notes: degrees of freedom for the CT tests are 3 and 113; degrees of freedom for the PF tests are 59 and 57 for breakpoint of 1975q2, 40 and 76 for breakpoint of 1979q4, then the numerator degrees of freedom decrease by 4 and the denominator degrees of freedom increase by 4 moving from left to right in the table.

respectively. The F test that the coefficients on these three dummy variables are zero will give precisely the same result as the Chow test. The regression with dummy variables resulted in:

$$\Delta c_t = 0.000 + 0.443\Delta y_t - 0.038(c_t - y_t)_{-1}$$
$$(0.092) \quad (6.101) \quad (-0.678)$$
$$- 0.001 dv_t - 0.434 dv\Delta y_t$$
$$(-0.201) \quad (-3.023)$$
$$- 0.063 dv(c_t - y_t)_{-1} + \hat{\varepsilon}_t$$
$$(0.078) \quad\quad\quad\quad\quad (5.140)$$

't' statistics in parentheses.

On an individual basis the dummy variable for Δy_t is significant and the coefficient on Δy_t after the break is virtually 0 at $0.443 - 0.434 = 0.009$; the coefficient on $(c_t - y_t)_{-1}$ becomes larger negative at $-0.038 - 0.063 = -0.101$. These are quite substantial changes and it is not surprising that the Chow test failed.

5.11.6b   Chow's second test: predictive failure

A final illustration concerns Chow's second test, known as the predictive failure test. Although originally intended for the case where there are insufficient observations in one of the regimes to calculate the Chow test, it can be applied where there are sufficient observations with the interpretation of a general misspecification test. The test statistic was given earlier as either equation (5.117) or equation (5.118).

This is a *forward predictive failure* test in that T_2 is the sample of observations after (or forward of) T_1. The roles of T_1 and T_2 could be reversed if $T_1 > k$ and $T_2 > k$, resulting in the *backward predictive failure* test. We illustrate with the *forward predictive failure* test using the same set of dates as for the forward version of the Chow test. The breakpoint was first taken to be 1975q2 which resulted in PF(59, 57) = 0.858[0.465]; the msl of this test statistic is 46.5%, hence the null of no predictive failure is not rejected. In contrast to the Chow tests this is also the case when the breakpoint is moved through the

1980s with none of the test statistics significant. Evidently although the hypothesis of constant regression coefficients can be rejected for some sub-periods, the changes are offsetting and do not result in predictive failure.

Returning to the estimated model it might be tempting to drop the variable $(c_t - y_t)_{-1}$ as its coefficient, while correctly signed, is 'insignificant' in conventional terms with a 't' statistic of -1.356. However, deleting 'insignificant' variables is not a safe strategy if the estimated regression is not a satisfactory empirical model from which to draw conclusions about insignificant variables, and there are indications from the various tests, especially in the serial correlation statistics, that the empirical model is misspecified.

5.11.7   An extended model

To assess whether the regression can be improved we consider a suggestion by Deaton (1977) to include the inflation rate, π_t, in the dynamic model but not in the definition of equilibrium. In this way inflation has a short-term but not a long-term effect. The model is also amended to extend the dynamics, including a lag of Δy_t as well as π_t and π_{t-1}. The extended model is:

$$\Delta c_t = \theta_0 + \theta_1 \Delta y_t + \theta_2 \Delta y_{t-1} + \theta_3(c_t - y_t)_{-1}$$
$$+ \theta_4 \pi_t + \theta_5 \pi_{t-1} + \varepsilon_t \quad\quad (5.141)$$

This specification gives the same equilibrium relationship between consumption and income as before when the variables are constant, that is $\Delta c_t = \Delta y_t = \pi_t = 0$, but allows short-run adjustments through changes in inflation as well as changes in income. If θ_4 and/or $\theta_5 \neq 0$, positive or negative inflation will affect the change in consumption with the rationalisation that in an inflationary (or deflationary) environment prices of the many goods that comprise consumption do not change smoothly and uniformly together. Consumers might, therefore, mistake price changes which are a result of

Table 5.3 *An extended version of the consumption model*

$$\Delta c_t = -0.0009 + 0.250\Delta y_t + 0.099\Delta y_{t-1} - 0.101(c_t - y_t)_{-1} + 0.002\pi_t - 0.005\pi_{t-1} + \hat{\varepsilon}_t$$
$$(-0.257) \quad (4.286) \quad (1.786) \quad (-2.631) \quad (2.027) \;\; (-4.455)$$
$$\{-0.236\} \;\; \{3.883\} \quad \{2.169\} \quad \{-2.535\} \quad \{2.017\} \;\; \{-3.872\}$$

inflationary movements for relative price changes to which they should respond; however, this is a short-term effect because in the long run consumers are not subject to this kind of 'money illusion'. On this basis we anticipate $\theta_4 + \theta_5 < 0$. The variable π_t is measured as the % change per quarter in the seasonally adjusted, implicit deflator for consumers' expenditure.

Re-estimation gave the results reported in Table 5.3. Standard 't' statistics in (.); robust 't' statistics in {.}.

$$R^2 = 0.398; \; \hat{\sigma} = 0.056; \; dw = 2.108$$

The diagnostic test statistics for this equation are reported in Tables 5.4 and 5.5.

The revised empirical model is a considerable improvement on the previous model. There is now no evidence of serial correlation. The LM test for fourth order serial correlation is SC(4)=5.194 with an msl of 26.70%. Although there is still an inequality in the estimated variances, the GQ test for heteroscedasticity is not now significant at the 5% level. White's test, which can be interpreted as a test for heteroscedasticity if other aspects of the model are correctly specified, is satisfactory at the 5% significance level with the F version of the test $F(20, 97) = 1.602$ with an msl of 6.3%. In contrast to the earlier results the Chow tests no longer suggest a problem in the 1980s. The only test statistic to remain significant is

Table 5.4 *Diagnostic statistics for revised consumption equation*

Serial correlation

Tests for fourth order serial correlation:
  χ^2 version, SC(4) = 5.194[0.267]; F version, $F(4, 104) = 1.055[0.382]$

Heteroscedasticity

'Standard' test:
  χ^2 version, HS(1) = 0.709[0.400]; F version, $F(1, 116) = 0.700[0.404]$

Breusch–Pagan, BP, test with Δy_t:
  χ^2 version, BP(1) = 6.136[0.013]; F version, $F(1, 113) = 6.369[0.013]$

BP with Δy_t and $(\Delta y_t)^2$:
  χ^2 version, BP(2) = 9.081[0.010]; F version, $F(2, 112) = 4.801[0.010]$

White's test:
  χ^2 version, WT(20) = 29.548[0.077]; F version, $F(20, 97) = 1.620[0.063]$

Goldfeld–Quandt, subsamples, 1960q2 to 1972q4 and 1978q1 to 1989q4; null hypothesis, $\sigma_1^2 = \sigma_2^2$
Alternative hypothesis, $\sigma_1^2 > \sigma_2^2$: $F(44, 42) = 0.651[0.920]$
Alternative hypothesis, $\sigma_1^2 < \sigma_2^2$: $F(42, 44) = 1.536[0.081]$

Functional form

RESET test with $(\Delta \hat{c}_t)^2$:
  χ^2 version, FF(1) = 1.844[0.174]; F version, $F(1, 111) = 1.858[0.176]$

RESET test with $(\Delta \hat{c}_t)^2$ and $(\Delta \hat{c}_t)^3$:
  χ^2 version, FF(2) = 4.880[0.087]; F version, $F(2, 110) = 2.440[0.092]$

Table 5.5 *(Forward) Chow and predictive failure test statistics for the amended consumption model*

	1975q2	1979q4	1980q4	1981q4	1982q4	1983q4	1984q4	1985q4	1986q4	1987q4
	Breakpoint:									
				Forward Chow test statistics						
CT	1.183	0.209	1.142	1.813	1.778	1.784	1.701	1.530	1.608	0.977
[msl]	[0.321]	[0.973]	[0.343]	[0.103]	[0.110]	[0.109]	[0.128]	[0.176]	[0.154]	[0.444]
				Forward predictive failure test statistics						
PF	1.226	1.141	1.125	1.032	1.073	1.018	1.150	1.270	1.270	0.529
[msl]	[0.225]	[0.308]	[0.327]	[0.440]	[0.389]	[0.453]	[0.316]	[0.232]	[0.247]	[0.832]

Notes: degrees of freedom for the CT tests are 6 and 106; degrees of freedom for the PF tests are 59 and 53 for breakpoint of 1975q2, 40 and 72 for breakpoint of 1979q4, then the numerator degrees of freedom decrease by 4 and the denominator degrees of freedom increase by 4 moving from left to right in the table.

the BP test for heteroscedasticity using the regressors Δy_t and $(\Delta y_t)^2$ in the auxiliary regression. As there is no evidence of misspecification apart from the BP test it seems sensible to follow White's procedure of calculating heteroscedastic consistent – or robust – standard errors using $\mathrm{Var}(\hat{\beta}) = (X'X)^{-1} X' \Omega X (X'X)^{-1}$. The robust '$t$' statistics are given beneath the ordinary 't' statistics; comparing the two, the changes are fairly slight.

All of the regression coefficients, except the constant, are significant with the anticipated sign. The coefficient on Δy_t is positive indicating a short-run elasticity of consumption with respect to income of 0.250 with a further adjustment after a one period lag of 0.099. The coefficient on the error correction term is negative with a robust 't' statistic of -2.535; the implication of this coefficient is that 10.1% of last period's disequilibrium is removed in the current period. The sum of the coefficients on inflation is negative which provides some support for the view that an increase in inflation temporarily depresses consumption, but note that the initial effect is to increase consumption. An estimate of the constant, K, is obtained from $\theta_0 = -k\theta_3$, so with $\hat{\theta}_0 = -0.00098$ and $\hat{\theta}_3 = -0.101$ then $\hat{k} = -0.00098/-0.101 = 0.0097$ and $\hat{K} = e^{0.0097} \approx 1.0097$. However, notice that the constant is not significant and the regression without a constant (not reported) shows only very minor differences from the equation

reported above, implying that $\hat{K}$ is not statistically distinguishable from 1.

The implied static equilibrium, assuming that inflation is zero in equilibrium, is obtained by setting $\Delta c_t = \Delta y_t = 0$ and $\pi_t = 0$ in the estimated model; this gives

$$c_t = (-0.00098/-0.101)y_t \qquad (5.142)$$

or in levels

$$C_t = e^{0.0097} Y_t \approx 1.0097 Y_t \qquad (5.143)$$

The F statistic for the null hypothesis that the regression coefficients apart from the constant are 0, sometimes referred to as the regression F statistic, is:

$$F = \frac{(\mathrm{RRSS} - \mathrm{URSS})}{\mathrm{URSS}} \frac{(T - k)}{(k - 1)} \qquad (5.144)$$

where RRSS is the residual sum of squares imposing the null hypothesis and URSS is the residual sum of squares from the unrestricted model. In this case we obtain a sample value of:

$$F = \frac{(0.00585 - 0.00352)}{0.00352} \frac{(118 - 6)}{(6 - 1)}$$

$$= 14.831[0.000]$$

which is distributed as $F(5, 118)$ under the null hypothesis. The msl of $F = 14.831$ is zero, so the null hypothesis is firmly rejected: the regression coefficients considered as a group are significantly different from zero. Also of interest is the null hypothesis that the model could be reduced to the previous one, which involves setting the coefficients on Δy_{t-1}, π_t and π_{t-1} to zero. The F statistic for this null is

$$F = \frac{(0.00468 - 0.00352)}{0.00352} \frac{(118 - 6)}{3}$$

$$= 12.303[0.000]$$

which is distributed as $F(3, 112)$ under the null hypothesis. An F statistic of 12.303 has an msl of 0, so we conclude against the null hypothesis, hence the previous model was an invalid reduction of this more general model. (Note that these standard F tests assume homoscedasticity but we have some evidence against this assumption from the BP test; however, the adjustment due to heteroscedasticity is slight – see the robust 't' statistics – and does not materially affect the F test statistics.)

The last question to ask is whether the extended model is itself a valid reduction of a more general model. In this context what we are referring to by 'general' is a model with the same set of variables but longer lags; obviously we could extend this definition to include more explanatory variables but the assumption here is that if there were such candidate variables they would have been included in the initial analysis. The 'general' model also includes Δc_{t-1}, Δc_{t-2}, Δy_{t-2} and π_{t-2}. The F test that the coefficients on these variables are jointly zero is:

$$F = \frac{(0.00334 - 0.00320)}{0.00320} \frac{(117 - 10)}{4}$$

$$= 1.179[0.324]$$

which is distributed as $F(4, 107)$ under the null hypothesis; $F = 1.179$ has an msl of 32.4%, so we conclude that the reported model is a valid reduction of the more general dynamic model.

R^2 is 0.398, which is not large by 'conventional' standards; however, this refers to the

R^2 for *changes* in consumption. Rerunning the regression with c_t as the dependent variable and c_{t-1} as a regressor but with a coefficient of $+1$ imposed gives an R^2 of 0.999, which is high by conventional standards and illustrates the dependence of R^2 on the choice of dependent variable and the care that has to be taken in not misinterpreting R^2. An alternative measure of the goodness of fit is $\hat{\sigma}$ which at 0.056 is just over a half of 1% of the level of consumption, indicating that the margin for improvement is quite slight.

5.12 Concluding remarks

The process of empirical model building necessarily involves several stages of estimation and evaluation. Even if published articles give the impression of presenting an empirical model as if it were the one first thought of, it is most unlikely that the actual process was as simple as that. A typical strategy is to initially seek guidance from previously published work and relevant economic theory. If a new explanation of a particular economic variable, or set of variables, is being proposed, a minimum aim should be to explain the results of previous researchers. For example, suppose that previous research suggested that consumption could be modelled according to the error correction mechanism $\Delta c_t = \theta_0 + \theta_1 \Delta y_t + \theta_2(c_t - y_t)_{-1} + \varepsilon_t$: however, as we saw, fitting such a model to the data revealed a number of inadequacies, notably residuals which were serially correlated and some evidence of nonconstant regression coefficients. Developing the basic framework of this model to incorporate short-run effects from inflation and further dynamics on income remedied these deficiencies (we refer to this as the extended model). The serial correlation and nonconstant regression coefficients in the initial model are explained by the omission of relevant variables.

The extended model encompasses the initial model in two respects. First, theoretically, it provides an explanation of why the short-run adjustment of consumption was not adequately modelled. Second, statistically, the initial model was not a valid reduction of the extended model, while the extended model was itself a valid reduction of a model with further dynamics. The argument for a *progressive research* strategy whereby newly proposed and estimated models can explain previous results as well as offering something new should not be controversial. It does not rule out 'maverick' explanations; for example, that consumption is determined by the number of hours of sunlight or millimetres of rainfall. It offers a strategy that aids the evaluation of competing explanations. Despite claims, which may be made to the contrary, even the 'best' explanation is likely to be superseded and the 'best' equation is open to improvement. New methods and new theory lead to new research on established topics.

This chapter and the last have outlined some basic methods of estimation, hypothesis testing and model evaluation. There is, of course, much more to econometric technique, for example the leading econometric textbooks run to 1000 pages or so; however, it is possible to undertake some interesting empirical research based on the techniques covered here and in the next two chapters, in conjunction with one of the commercially available econometric software packages. In applied econometrics there is no substitute for 'doing'.

Review

1. This chapter considers estimation, hypothesis testing and model building when $k > 2$ variables are included in the analysis.

2. If k variables are jointly normally distributed then conditioning on $k - 1$ of the variables results in a conditional pdf which is univariate normal and a linear CEF.

3. An alternative framework is to extend the classical linear regression model so that the regressors are fixed in repeated samples and hence nonstochastic.

4. (i) The CEF (regression function) is

$$E\{Y_t \mid X_{t2}, \dots, X_{t2}\}$$
$$= \beta_1 + \beta_2 X_{t2} + \cdots + \beta_k X_{tk}$$

   (ii) The conditional innovation (disturbance) is

$$(\varepsilon_t \mid X_{t2}, \dots, X_{tk}) = Y_t$$
$$- E\{Y_t \mid X_{t2}, \dots, X_{tk}\}$$

5. In matrix notation the linear regression model is: $Y = X\beta + \varepsilon$ where ε has the following properties:
   (i) $E\{\varepsilon \mid X\} = 0$; (ii) $E\{\varepsilon\varepsilon' \mid x\} = \sigma^2 I$.

6. (i) The OLS estimator is $\hat{\beta} = (X'X)^{-1}X'Y$ which is conditionally and unconditionally unbiased.

   (ii) The conditional variance–covariance matrix of $\hat{\beta}$ is $\sigma^2(X'X)^{-1}$.

   (iii) The unconditional variance of $\hat{\beta}$ is $\sigma^2 E_X\{(X'X)^{-1}\}$.

   (iv) An unbiased estimator of σ^2 is $\hat{\sigma}^2 = \hat{\varepsilon}'\hat{\varepsilon}/(T - k)$.

7. Serial correlation and/or heteroscedasticity in ε imply $E\{\varepsilon\varepsilon' \mid X\} = \Omega = \sigma^2\Phi \neq \sigma^2 I$ and then, generally, the OLS estimator $\hat{\beta}$ no longer has minimum variance.

8. (i) The GLS estimator is

$$\beta^0 = [X'\Phi^{-1}X]^{-1}X'\Phi^{-1}Y$$

   (ii) The variance–covariance matrix of β^0 is $\text{Var}(\beta^0) = \sigma^2[X'\Phi^{-1}X]^{-1}$.

   (iv) An unbiased estimator of σ^2 is $\tilde{\sigma} = \hat{\varepsilon}^{*\prime}\hat{\varepsilon}^*/(T - k)$ where $\hat{\varepsilon}^*$ is the vector of residuals from GLS estimation.

9. The GLS estimator β^0 is unbiased and provided Φ is known is more efficient than the OLS estimator $\hat{\beta}$, but loses its clear-cut advantage over the OLS estimator when Φ has to be estimated. Feasible estimators result from replacing the generally unknown Ω with a consistent estimator, $\tilde{\Omega}$.

10. The correct expression for $\text{Var}(\hat{\beta})$ is

$$(X'X)^{-1}X'\Omega X(X'X)^{-1}$$

11. Tests which take the estimated model as adequate and then test some detailed aspect of the specification, for example that a particular regression coefficient equals a specified value, are known as specification tests.

12. Tests to assess the adequacy of an estimated model, for example whether the residuals are consistent with white noise, are known as misspecification tests. By their nature these are usually prior to specification tests.

13. (i) The Wald principle of hypothesis testing only requires estimation under H_a.
    (ii) The Lagrange-Multiplier, LM, principle only requires estimation under H_0.
    (iii) The likelihood ratio principle requires estimation under H_0 and H_a.

14. A test statistic which finds general application is the F test given by $F = [(\text{RRSS} - \text{URSS})/\text{URSS}](T - k)/g$ where g is the number of restrictions; F is distributed as $F(g, T - k)$ under the null hypothesis.

15. The sample value of the F statistic is compared to the critical value for the $\alpha\%$ significance level from the right-hand tail of the F distribution with g and $T - k$ degrees of freedom, with sample values exceeding the critical value leading to rejection of the null hypothesis. As the critical value is taken from the right-hand tail an equivalent terminology for the $\alpha\%$ critical value is the $(1 - \alpha)\%$ quantile.

16. In general linear restrictions can be expressed in an indirect parameterisation as $R\beta = r$ or a direct parameterisation as $\beta = H\varphi$.

17. Misspecification tests are concerned with the adequacy of a model as a basis for inference.

18. The Durbin–Watson statistic was intended for the specification of serial correlation as $\varepsilon_t = \rho\varepsilon_{t-1} + u_t$ in a linear regression model with a constant and no lagged dependent variables. The critical values involve an inconclusive region.

19. The LM test for pth order serial correlation is simple to compute: estimate an auxiliary regression where the OLS residuals are regressed on the variables in the original model plus p lagged residuals. The test statistic is either T times R^2 from the auxiliary regression or an F test that the coefficients on the lagged residuals are 0.

20. In a heteroscedastic specification the variances of ε_t are not constant; $\hat{\beta}$ remains conditionally and unconditionally unbiased.

21. White has suggested a test for heteroscedasticity which involves an auxiliary regression of the squared OLS residuals on the products and cross-products of the regressors excluding redundant regressors. The test statistic can be calculated in its T times R^2 form or as an F test.

22. In the Goldfeld–Quandt test for heteroscedasticity the sample is divided into two groups of T_1 and T_2 observations, each of which is large enough to estimate the regression model. The null hypothesis is H_0: $\sigma_1^2 = \sigma_2^2$ and if the alternative is H_a: $\sigma_1^2 > \sigma_2^2$ then the test statistic is $\text{GQ} = \hat{\sigma}_1^2/\hat{\sigma}_2^2 \sim F(T_1 - k, T_2 - k)$. If the alternative hypothesis is that H_a: $\sigma_1^2 < \sigma_2^2$, then the subscripts are reversed in the test statistic.

23. The Breusch–Pagan/Godfrey test for heteroscedasticity is similar to the White test, with an auxiliary regression of the squared OLS residuals on variables thought to determine the heteroscedasticity.

24. White has shown that it is possible to consistently estimate the variance matrix of $\hat{\beta}$ without imposing any structure on the heteroscedasticity. This results in robust standard errors so an alternative strategy to feasible GLS is to continue to use the OLS estimator $\hat{\beta}$ but in conjunction with an estimator of the correct variance matrix $(X'X)^{-1}X'\Omega X(X'X)^{-1}$.

25. The most commonly used and programmed test for normality of the regression disturbances is due to Jarque and Bera (1980, 1987). H_0 is that the disturbances are normally distributed; the JB test statistic for the regression without a constant is

$JB = T[\hat{b}_1/6 + \hat{\kappa}^2/24]$ which is asymptotically distributed as $\chi^2(2)$ under the null hypothesis.

26. Ramsey's RESET test adds powers (for example, the square) of the fitted values of Y_t to the original linear regression and tests for the significance of the additional variables.

27. An important assumption of the regression model is that the regression coefficients are constant. Chow's first test is often used to test this assumption. The sample is split into two mutually exclusive groups, and conditional on $\sigma_1^2 = \sigma_2^2$, the following test statistic is used:

$$CT(k, T - 2k) = \frac{(\hat{\varepsilon}'\hat{\varepsilon} - (\hat{\varepsilon}_1'\hat{\varepsilon}_1 + \hat{\varepsilon}_2'\hat{\varepsilon}_2))}{(\hat{\varepsilon}_1'\hat{\varepsilon}_1 + \hat{\varepsilon}_2'\hat{\varepsilon}_2)}$$

$$\times \frac{(T - 2k)}{k}$$

which is distributed as $F(k, T - 2k)$ under the null.

28. When $T_2 < k$ (or $T_1 < k$) there are insufficient observations to compute the regression in the second (first) regime and an alternative to the CT test is Chow's (second) test of predictive failure:

$$PF(T_2, T_1 - k) = \frac{(\hat{\varepsilon}'\hat{\varepsilon} - \hat{\varepsilon}_1'\hat{\varepsilon}_1)}{\hat{\varepsilon}_1'\hat{\varepsilon}_1} \frac{(T_1 - k)}{T_2}$$

which is distributed as $F(T_2, T_1 - k)$ under the null of no predictive failure.

29. The predictive failure test statistic can also be used when $T_2 > k$ as a general misspecification test.

30. An empirical model of consumption was used to illustrate the use of a number of techniques. The simplest model was an example of an error correction mechanism:

$$\Delta c_t = \theta_0 + \theta_1 \Delta y_t + \theta_2 (c_t - y_t)_{-1} + \varepsilon_t$$

31. There was evidence that this model was misspecified with a significant test statistic for serial correlation, heteroscedasticity and structural change.

32. The revised model included inflation and more dynamics:

$$\Delta c_t = \theta_0 + \theta_1 \Delta y_t + \theta_2 \Delta y_{t-1}$$
$$+ \theta_3 (c_t - y_t)_{-1} + \theta_4 \pi_t$$
$$+ \theta_5 \pi_{t-1} + \varepsilon_t$$

and the only test statistics to remain significant were those for heteroscedasticity.

33. Robust 't' statistics were calculated for the revised model; these showed some minor changes from the conventional 't' statistics. The extended model was empirically more satisfactory than the initial model.

34. The extended model encompasses the simpler model theoretically and statistically without being encompassed by a more general model.

Review questions

1. Consider the MA(2) process for ε_t given by

$$\varepsilon_t = u_t + \theta_1 u_{t-1} + \theta_2 u_{t-2}$$

 (i) Derive the variance of ε_t.
 (ii) Derive the following autocovariances and autocorrelations of ε_t: $E\{\varepsilon_t\varepsilon_{t-1}\}$, $E\{\varepsilon_t\varepsilon_{t-2}\}$, $E\{\varepsilon_t\varepsilon_{t-3}\}$ and $\rho(1)$, $\rho(2)$ and $\rho(3)$.
 (iii) Hence, show that the variance matrix of ε_t, Ω, is band diagonal.
 (iv) Explain how to obtain a consistent estimator of Ω and hence obtain a consistent estimator of the variance matrix of the OLS estimator $\hat{\beta}$.
 (v) Explain how to test for second order serial correlation using the LM test.

2. Consider the regression model given by

$$Y_t = \beta_1 + \beta_2 X_{t2} + \beta_2 X_{t2}^2 + \varepsilon_t$$

 (i) What auxiliary regression would you estimate to implement White's test for heteroscedasticity?

(ii) Explain how to calculate and interpret White's test statistic in its χ^2 and F forms.

(iii) Explain why White's test could, under some conditions, be interpreted as a general misspecification test.

3. (i) Explain how to use the Goldfeld–Quandt test for heteroscedasticity when it is not known *a priori* which variance in each of two sub-periods is the larger.

(ii) Using the data set provided through the website for the example in section **5.11**, and the extended model, calculate and interpret the GQ test for a number of different sub-periods.

(iii) Suppose that it is suspected the sample splits into three sub-groups each with a different variance for ε_t, explain how to test for heteroscedasticity using a modified GQ procedure.

4. (i) Explain why, when the only problem is that of heteroscedasticity, the GLS estimator is usually described a weighted least squares estimator.

(ii) Suppose, as in question 3(iii), there are three sub-groups each with a different variance, explain how you can obtain an FGLS estimator of the β coefficients.

5. (i) Explain with examples the difference between a specification test and a misspecification test.

(ii) Illustrate with an example how a test intended as a specification test is often interpreted in practice as a misspecification test.

6. What are the differences among the three principles of constructing test statistics; give examples of each procedure?

7. (i) Explain why the Jarque–Bera test for normality is described as a Lagrange-Multiplier test for normality.

(ii) Suppose the distribution of ε_t is 't' rather than normal; what structure in the JB test picks up this departure from normality?

(iii) Suppose the distribution of ε_t is known to be symmetric but not normal: explain how a more powerful test than the JB test could be constructed.

8. (i) Explain how to obtain the static long run of the following equation:

$$\Delta c_t = \theta_0 + \theta_1 \Delta y_t + \theta_2 \Delta y_{t-1}$$
$$+ \theta_3 (c_t - y_t)_{-1} + \theta_4 \pi_t$$
$$+ \theta_5 \pi_{t-1} + \varepsilon_t$$

(ii) Why is this model described as an error correction mechanism?

(iii) Suppose instead of the static long run it is assumed that consumption, income and inflation are on a steady growth path, for example $\Delta c_t = g \neq 0$, what difference does this make to the implied equilibrium?

9. Consider the following simple version of the Phillips curve, where the percentage rate of change of money wages, π_{wt}, is regressed on a constant and the inverse of the unemployment rate, z_t. The annual data is from Phillips' (1958) original study for the United Kingdom, 1860–1914. The regression model is

$$\pi_{wt} = \beta_1 + \beta_2 z_t + \varepsilon_t$$

with the following empirical results:

$$\pi_{wt} = -2.437 + 10.991 z_t + \hat{\varepsilon}_t$$
$$(-7.346) \ (11.922)$$

Sample period 1865 to 1914; $T = 50$; RSS $= 75.176$; dw $= 1.959$; $R^2 = 0.747$; SC(4) $= 5.349[0.253]$; 't' statistics in parentheses.

(i) Evaluate the regression model from an economic and an econometric perspective.

(ii) A second regression is estimated based on augmenting the initial model with lagged values of price inflation, π_t. Specifically the revised model is:

$$\pi_{wt} = \beta_1 + \beta_2 z_t + \sum_{j=1}^{4} \beta_j \pi_{t-j} + \varepsilon_t$$

with the empirical model given by

$$\pi_{wt} = -2.437 + 10.786z_t + 0.048\pi_{t-1}$$
$$\qquad (5.927) \quad (9.413) \quad (0.0592)$$

$$\qquad - 0.019\pi_{t-2} - 0.002\pi_{t-3}$$
$$\qquad (-0.245) \quad (-0.028)$$

$$\qquad + 0.040\pi_{t-4} + \hat{\varepsilon}_t$$
$$\qquad (0.054)$$

Sample period: 1865 to 1914; $T = 50$; RSS $= 74.497$; $R^2 = 0.750$; dw $= 2.2$; SC(4) $= 6.389[0.172]$; 't' statistics in parentheses.

(ii) Test the hypotheses that none of the lagged inflation terms have an influence on π_{wt}.

10. Consider the following regression model to explain the change in consumers' expenditure on nondurable goods and services, CND_t, in terms of the change in real personal disposable income, $RPDI_t$, and lagged disequilibrium. Equilibrium is defined as

$$CND_t = k + \lambda_0 RPDI_t$$

hence disequilibrium is given by

$$\xi_t = CND_t - (k + \lambda_0 RPDI_t)$$

Estimates of k and λ_0 obtained from a prior regression are $\hat{k} = 7029.75$ and $\hat{\lambda}_0 = 0.718$, and $\hat{\xi}_t = CND_t - (7029.5 + 0.718RPDI_t)$. All data is for the United Kingdom in constant prices, quarterly and seasonally adjusted. The regression model is formulated as a simple error correction mechanism.

$$\Delta CND_t = \beta_1 + \beta_2 \Delta RPDI_t + \beta_3 \hat{\xi}_{t-1} + \varepsilon_t$$

with coefficient estimates:

$$\hat{\beta}_1 = 160.444(3.876);$$
$$\hat{\beta}_2 = 0.205(3.392);$$
$$\hat{\beta}_3 = -0.219(-2.592)$$

't' statistics are in parentheses. Sample 1955q2 to 1970q2; $T = 61$; RSS $= 4714571$; dw $= 2.685$; $R^2 = 0.385$.

(i) Interpret the estimated regression model. The following auxiliary regressions were also estimated:

$$\hat{\varepsilon}_t = 5.882 - 0.012\Delta RPDI_t + 0.008\hat{\xi}_{t-1}$$

Sample: 1956q2 to 1970q2; $T^+ = 57$; $T^+ - k = 57 - 3 = 54$; RSS $= 4629372$; $R^2 = 0.001$.

$$\hat{\varepsilon}_t = 3.188 - 0.014\Delta RPDI_t + 0.193\hat{\xi}_{t-1}$$
$$\qquad - 0.554\hat{\varepsilon}_{t-1} - 0.014\hat{\varepsilon}_{t-2}$$
$$\qquad (-2.980) \quad (-0.095)$$
$$\qquad + 0.058\hat{\varepsilon}_{t-3} + 0.044\hat{\varepsilon}_{t-4}$$
$$\qquad (0.390) \quad (0.310)$$

Sample: 1956q2 to 1970q2; $T^+ = 57$;

$$T^+ - p - k = 57 - 4 - 3 = 50$$
$$RSS = 3767116$$

$R^2 = 0.186$; $R^2_{uc} = 0.186$; 't' statistics are in parentheses.

(ii) Use the information in these two auxiliary regressions to calculate and evaluate the LM test for fourth order serial correlation in its χ^2 and F forms. Comment on the differences between the test outcomes.

(iii) Following your test for fourth order serial correlation consider the auxiliary regressions and assess whether it would be sensible to undertake a further test for first order serial correlation. From the following information undertake such a test and comment on your results.

$$\hat{\varepsilon}_t = -0.962 - 0.000\Delta RPDI_t + 0.000\hat{\xi}_{t-1}$$

Sample: 1955q3 to 1970q2; $T^+ = 60$; $T^+ - k = 60 - 3 = 57$; RSS $= 4710391$; $R^2 = 0.001$.

$$\hat{\varepsilon}_t = -2.099 - 0.000\Delta RPDI_t$$
$$\qquad + 0.179\hat{\xi}_{t-1} - 0.518\hat{\varepsilon}_{t-1}$$
$$\qquad (-3.438)$$

Sample: 1955q3 to 1970q2; $T^+ = 60$;
$T^+ - p - k = 60 - 1 - 3 = 56$;

RSS $= 3889311$; $R^2 = 0.174$

$R_{uc}^2 = 0.174$

(iv) Given that the total sum of squares of CND_t about its mean is 1,108,528,300 calculate and interpret the R^2 for the level of CND_t rather than ΔCND_t. What do you conclude from the difference in R^2?

CHAPTER 6

An introduction to nonstationary univariate time series models

6.1 Introduction

This chapter and the next consider some of the properties of univariate time series. In particular a class of nonstationary processes is examined which is of particular relevance for economic data. This class concerns those nonstationary series that can be 'differenced to stationarity'. The initial approach is to consider some simple time series models and simulated time series realisations from these models in order to get an understanding of the properties they generate. An important distinction, introduced previously in Chapter 3, is whether a process is stationary or not; and in this context the related ideas of the order of integration and the number of unit roots in a time series process are introduced.

The overall purpose of this chapter is twofold. First, the univariate analysis of economic time series is of interest in its own right, and the approach described here offers a way of assessing the salient characteristics of a particular series. For example, an article by Nelson and Plosser (1982), on the nonstationarity of some US macroeconomic time series, led to a large number of methodological and empirical studies on the univariate properties of macroeconomic and microeconomic time series data.

Second, suppose interest centres on explaining what accounts for the variable Y_t, and a candidate variable for this explanation is X_t; and it is apparent from an assessment of the salient characteristics of Y_t that it has a pronounced positive trend, then X_t must also contain such a trend if an equation explaining Y_t by X_t is to be 'balanced' in its time series properties. The need for balance is essential whether a bivariate relationship is considered, as in this illustration, or a multivariate relationship. If the latter is the case the requirement of balance suggests the need for at least a pair of variables with the dominant characteristic; otherwise no matching or balancing can take place. This chapter is a precursor to further analysis, since an essential aspect of economic enquiry is to explain the interrelationships among variables.

The basic models and concepts are introduced in section **6.2**. A number of test statistics are then described in section **6.3** to determine whether a time series is nonstationary, or more precisely whether the hypothesis of nonstationarity is consistent with the data. As a large number of tests have been proposed for this purpose an element of selectivity has been exercised in choosing the ones described in this chapter. Frequency of use in applied work and availability are two of the criteria that have been used here. In practice the tests due to Dickey and Fuller (Fuller 1976, Dickey and Fuller 1979, 1981), widely referred to as DF tests, are dominant in empirical work and programmed into commercially available econometric software such as RATS, TSP, MICROFIT and PCGIVE.

Even within the confines of a particular class of tests there is often a number of decisions to be made which can confuse the uninitiated user.

A frequently used DF test is a simple variant of a standard 't' test statistic usually referred to as a $\hat{\tau}$ test statistic because, although it is constructed as the ratio of an estimated coefficient to its estimated standard error, it does not have the standard 't' distribution. However, the $\hat{\tau}$ test statistic comes in three versions depending upon whether the maintained regression has a deterministic trend and an intercept, just an intercept or neither a trend nor an intercept. Sometimes the conclusions from applying these $\hat{\tau}$ tests to a particular time series can hinge critically on which variant is used. A framework, which aids such decisions, is an essential part of the practical application of such tests and is considered in section **6.4**. Section **6.5** contains some concluding remarks.

6.2 Nondeterministic time series

As noted in Chapter 2 economic time series usually have a nondeterministic, or random, element that generates a more 'ragged' pattern than that associated with purely deterministic functions. To get an understanding of the kinds of patterns associated with univariate models of economic time series some of the simple examples of the univariate autoregressive processes introduced in Chapter 2 are considered again.

6.2.1 A pure random walk

An autoregressive process for the time series variable Y_t is one in which the current value of Y_t depends upon past – that is lagged – values of Y_t and a stochastic 'disturbance' term; for example, in a first order autoregressive process Y_t depends only upon Y_{t-1} and a disturbance term, ε_t. A convenient shorthand for an autoregressive process is AR(p), where AR indicates the process is autoregressive and p indicates the maximum lag of Y_t, upon which Y_t depends, that is Y_{t-p}; in this notation lags are assumed

to be present from 1 through to p. AR(1) is thus shorthand for the first order autoregressive process given by

$$Y_t = \phi_1 Y_{t-1} + \varepsilon_t \tag{6.1}$$

where ε_t is an innovation relative to Y_{t-1} with variance σ_ε^2; if there is no ambiguity the subscript on the variance will be omitted.

A special but very interesting case arises when $\phi = 1$, then

$$Y_t = Y_{t-1} + \varepsilon_t \tag{6.2}$$

This is the equation of a *pure random walk*, which is studied in detail below. The likely range of ϕ_1, given typical economic time series, is $0 < \phi_1 \leq 1$. If $\phi_1 < 0$ then successive values of Y_t will tend to oscillate in sign; if $\phi_1 > 1$ the process is explosive in that Y_t will tend to grow without limit. If $\phi_1 = 0$ then $Y_t = \varepsilon_t$ and Y_t has the properties of the stochastic term ε_t. ε_t is assumed to have a constant mean, which for convenience we will take to equal zero, a constant variance and zero autocorrelations, and hence is said to be 'white noise'. Thus if $Y_t = \varepsilon_t$ and if ε_t is white noise then so is Y_t.

The idea of a random walk is an important one in several areas of economics, especially where the concept of fully efficient markets rules out the possibility of profitable speculation on the course of, for example, the prices of financial assets. The random walk model implies that the best guess of Y_{t+1}, given information at time t, is Y_t; this is because there is no predictive structure in the AR process or the ε_t process as the latter has, by assumption, zero mean, constant variance and zero autocorrelations at all lags. The random walk model is often taken, therefore, as a baseline model for financial and foreign exchange markets. For example, if Y_t is the bilateral exchange rate between the $US and £UK and follows a pure random walk, it is not possible to exploit the past history of Y_t or ε_t to systematically make profits by speculating on the future course of the exchange rate.

Another important property of a random walk relates to the persistence of random shocks. This can be seen in the following way. If in (6.2) the random walk process starts in $t = 0$, then in $t = 1$ the process is $Y_1 = Y_0 + \varepsilon_1$ and in $t = 2$, $Y_2 = Y_1 + \varepsilon_2 = Y_0 + \varepsilon_1 + \varepsilon_2$. In general:

$$Y_t = Y_0 + \sum_{i=1}^{t} \varepsilon_i \qquad (6.3)$$

So that Y_t can be viewed as the initial value, Y_0, plus the cumulative sum of all the random disturbances or 'shocks' since the process began. This means that the impact of a particular shock does not die away. If, for example, $\varepsilon_2 = 1$ rather than, say, $\varepsilon_2 = 0$ then all values of Y from Y_2 onwards will be 1 unit higher as a result of this positive shock – the shock is persistent, its effect never dies out. The random walk is said to have an infinite memory: it 'remembers' the shock forever.

To illustrate the kinds of patterns associated with a random walk 4 sets of 500 realisations from the random walk given by (6.2) were generated. The distribution of ε_t is assumed to be normal with a zero mean and unit variance, and the initial value, Y_0, is zero. These realisations are graphed in Figure 6.1. Notice how the values

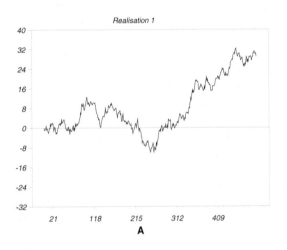

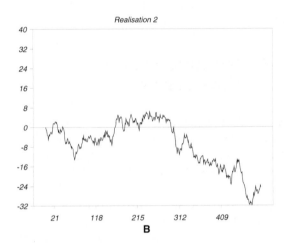

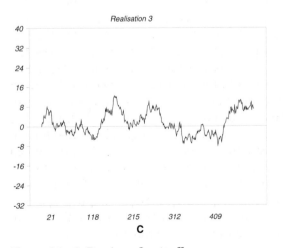

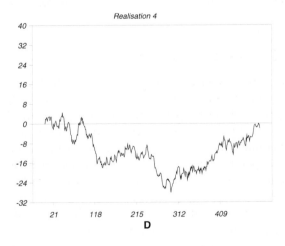

Figure 6.1   A–D – A random walk

of Y_t wander with no settled mean to which they return. As each of the different sets of realisations shows, the wandering may give rise to a sustained move away from zero in either a positive or negative direction. It cannot be predicted, *a priori*, which way the wandering will go. What is clear is that once the wandering starts it is sustained – this is an aspect of the persistence of shocks.

There is another characteristic of a random walk that helps to identify whether a particular process is reasonably described as a random walk. To understand this characteristic it is useful to use the autocorrelations of the (uni-variate) time series – see section **3.4.7**. Recall that an autocorrelation of order k is the correlation coefficient of a series Y_t with itself lagged τ times, that is Y_{t-k}. The notation for this is $\rho(k)$, with limits $-1 \le \rho(k) \le +1$; thus, the autocorrelation coefficient is just a rather simple extension of the ordinary correlation coefficient, applied to a single time series and its lags and, as such, it has an identical interpretation. A $\rho(k) = +1$ indicates perfect positive correlation, whereas $\rho(k) = 0$ indicates no correlation, and $\rho(k) = -1$ indicates perfect negative correlation, where correlation refers to the linear association between two series.

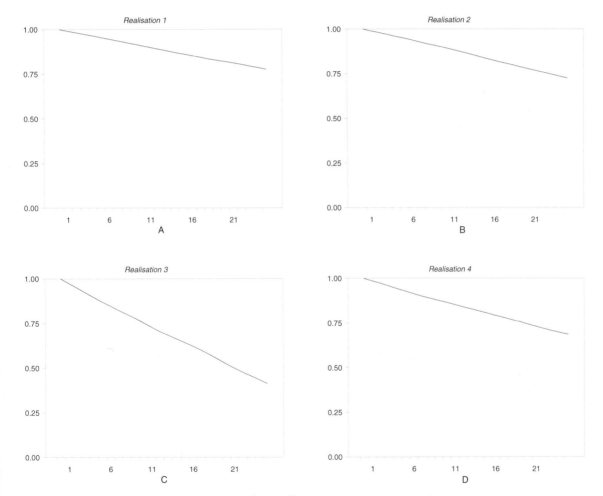

Figure 6.2   A–D – *Autocorrelations for a random walk*

In Figure 6.2 the values of $\rho(k)$ are plotted with $k = 0, \ldots, 25$ for the realisations of Y_t given in Figure 6.1. Notice that the $\rho(k)$ are large even for long lags. This is another aspect of a process with an infinite memory, which could equally be defined as one in which the autocorrelations, for all $|k| \neq 0$, die out 'very slowly'. It is possible to go further for a random walk and be more precise about what is meant by a 'slow' decay of the autocorrelations. In this case the theoretical value of the autocorrelation coefficient $\rho(Y_t, Y_{t-k})$ for all $k > 0$ is $[1 - (k/t)]^{0.5}$ where $t = 0$ is the starting date of the process. Therefore, for a fixed sample size, the anticipated

pattern of autocorrelations for a random walk with $k = 0, 1, \ldots, n$ is a slow decline from 1 for $k = 0$ to $[1 - n/t]^{0.5}$ for $k = n$; for example, with $t = 100$ and $n = 40$ the autocorrelations will decline slowly from 1 to 0.774. For fixed k this autocorrelation tends to 1 as $t \rightarrow \infty$ since $k/t \rightarrow 0$. This persistence or 'memory' of the process is apparent intuitively if you consider the effect of a shock at, say, period 1 on all the subsequent periods. *Ceteris paribus*, all values of Y from Y_1 onward will be changed by the magnitude of the shock: the process always remembers the shock. In practice, as with the realisations in Figure 6.1, there will be sampling

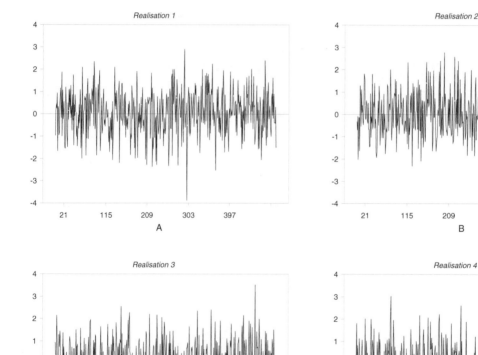

Figure 6.3   A–D – *White noise*

variations and the sample autocorrelations will not exactly equal their theoretical values. A plot of the autocorrelations of a series is, nevertheless, a useful descriptive device in assessing whether a particular time series is consistent with a random walk.

A third aspect of a random walk, which is of interest, is illustrated by taking the first difference of Y_t in (6.3); that is

$$Y_t - Y_{t-1} = \varepsilon_t \qquad (6.4)$$

Taking the first difference of a pure random walk results in a white noise process, ε_t, with a well-defined mean, in this case equal to zero and, as illustrated in Figure 6.3, frequent crossing of the axis at the value of the mean. The pattern displays no tendency to wander and stay on one side of the mean rather than theother. If a particular value of $\Delta y_t = \varepsilon_t$ is positive it cannot be said that the next value is more likely to be positive than negative or vice versa. In contrast to the random walk itself, the variance is constant: there is no tendency for the amplitude of the random disturbances to change over the sample. This is the pattern associated with 'white noise'. As reference to Figure 6.4 shows apart from some variations due to chance the

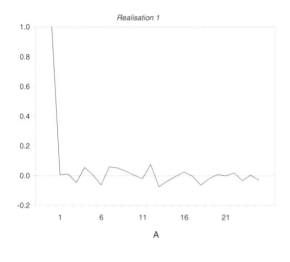

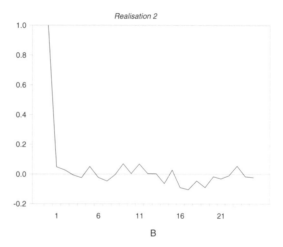

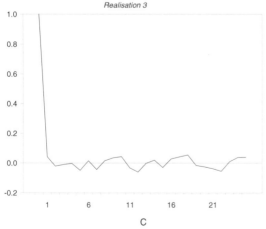

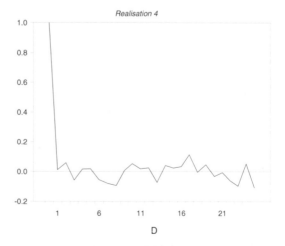

Figure 6.4   A–D – *Autocorrelations for white noise*

autocorrelations, $\rho(k)$, for $k = 1, \ldots, \infty$, are zero. A process with $\rho(k) \neq 0$, for at least one value of $k > 0$, is referred to as 'coloured noise'.

6.2.2   A near random walk

We have already seen what happens if $\phi_1 = 1$ in equation (6.1). Does it make much difference to the characteristics of the process if ϕ_1 is close to but actually below 1? To see whether it does consider $\phi_1 = 0.95$ so that Y_t is an autocorrelated time series, in this case a 'near random walk'. Before turning to Figure 6.5, which graphs 4 sets of 500 realisations for this process, ask yourself:

will this minor change make much difference? Now refer to Figure 6.5 and notice that Y_t does not wander and crosses the zero axis quite frequently. Even if Y_t temporarily diverges, perhaps suggesting that it might wander, it again crosses the zero axis. This small change of reducing ϕ_1 from 1 to 0.95 has had a marked effect on the pattern of realisations for Y_t. There is now a different structure in the patterns shown in Figure 6.5 compared to Figure 6.1. Positive values tend to be followed by more positive values, but then this sequence will be broken by Y_t crossing the zero axis to a negative value which then tends to be followed by

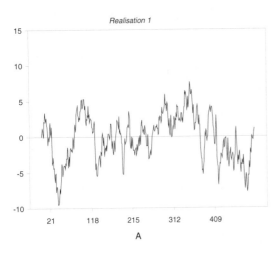

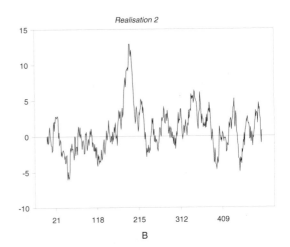

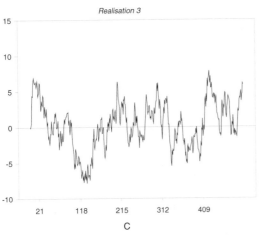

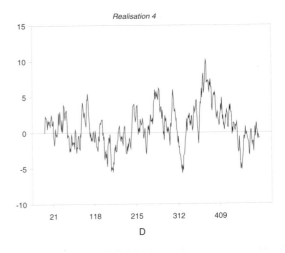

Figure 6.5   A–D – Autocorrelated time series, $\phi_1 = 0.95$

more negative values. When there are sequences of observations with the *same* sign the series is *positively* autocorrelated; whereas when there are sequences of observations with the *opposite* sign the series is *negatively* correlated. The positive autocorrelation in these realisations follows from the positive value of ϕ_1. The $\rho(k)$ for the realisations in Figure 6.5 are plotted in Figure 6.6. There are two points to note from this figure: the autocorrelations are initially positive and tend to remain positive; however, they decline to zero as the lag length τ increases, and this contrasts with the $\rho(k)$ shown for the random walk. With $\phi_1 = 0.95$ the process, Y_t, still has a relatively long memory – the autocorrelations are dying out quite slowly – but it is no longer a process with an infinite memory.

The difference between the model for Y_t with $\phi_1 = 1$ and $\phi_1 = 0.95$ is also apparent with the first difference of Y_t and the autocorrelations of the first differences. Taking the first difference of $Y_t = 0.95Y_{t-1} + \varepsilon_t$:

$$\Delta Y_t = (0.95 - 1)Y_{t-1} + \varepsilon_t$$

say

$$\Delta Y_t = v_t$$

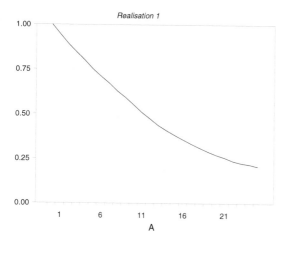

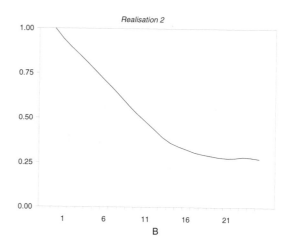

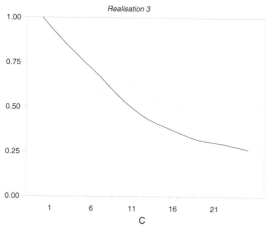

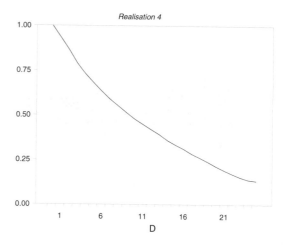

Figure 6.6 A–D – *Autocorrelations for $\phi_1 = 0.95$*

where

$$v_t = -0.05Y_{t-1} + \varepsilon_t$$

The first difference of Y_t is very close to, but not actually, white noise because of the dependence on time captured by the term $-0.05Y_{t-1}$. The noise is said to be 'coloured' rather than white noise. The first differences of the 4 sets of realisations in Figure 6.5 are shown in Figure 6.7 and while the pattern looks at first sight to be like white noise there is a very slight tendency of deviations from zero of opposite sign to follow each other. The autocorrelations of the

first differences are shown in Figure 6.8; again, because the deviation from white noise is so slight in this case, these look very close to those in Figure 6.6 illustrating that it may be difficult in practice to distinguish between a random walk and a near random walk.

6.2.3 A random walk with drift

A characteristic of a random walk, which is apparent from the 4 particular realisations shown in Figure 6.1, is that the 'walk' may, once it is underway, result in either a sustained

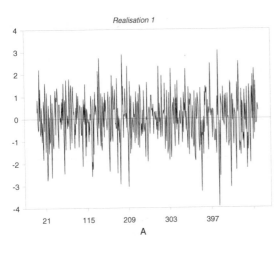

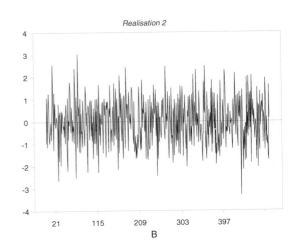

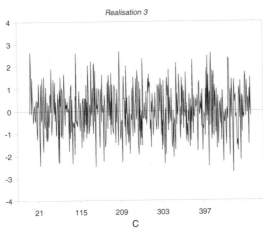

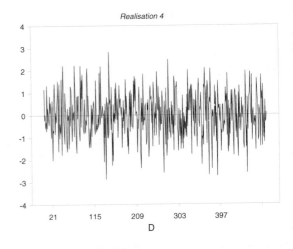

Figure 6.7   A–D – *Coloured noise (mild case)*

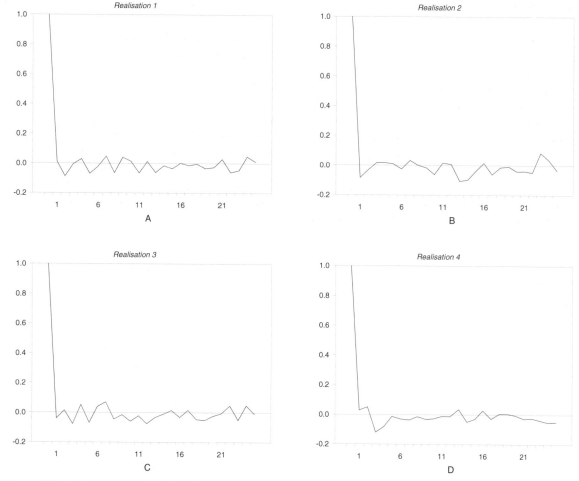

Figure 6.8 A–D – *Autocorrelations for coloured noise (mild case)*

positive wandering or a sustained negative wandering. We cannot predict, *a priori*, which way the wandering will go. While this kind of pattern characterises some economic time series, a more prevalent characteristic is of a series with a continuing upward trend so that taking a span of observations the central tendency in the series is for a sustained increase.

To capture this possibility a constant, μ, is added to the pure random walk model which becomes

$$Y_t = \mu + Y_{t-1} + \varepsilon_t \tag{6.5}$$

The coefficient μ is the 'drift' term; Y_t will increase by μ compared to Y_{t-1} whatever the particular realisation of ε_t. Further insight into this process can be gained by imagining it starting at $t = 1$, with Y_0 a fixed value. Then

$$Y_1 = \mu + Y_0 + \varepsilon_1$$
$$Y_2 = \mu + (\mu + Y_0 + \varepsilon_1) + \varepsilon_2$$
$$\vdots$$

$$Y_t = Y_0 + \mu t + \sum_{i=1}^{t} \varepsilon_i \tag{6.6}$$

Unlike the pure random walk this process has a trend represented by the term μt, so that there is a (deterministic) increment of μ each time period.

To assess the effect of introducing drift into the random walk model the same set of realisations as for the random walks shown in Figure 6.1 are used with the difference that the drift term, with $\mu = 0.1$, is added. These random walks with drift are shown in Figure 6.9. Now the wandering associated with the random walk is dominated by the drift term, which gives the positive trend in the series. The autocorrelations for these series are graphed in Figure 6.10

and, as before, they show a pattern of sustained persistence.

Taking the first difference of a random walk with drift we obtain

$$Y_t - Y_{t-1} = \mu + \varepsilon_t \tag{6.7}$$

so that if ε_t has a zero mean, the mean of the first differenced series is μ. Apart from this change the white noise properties of the first difference series, and the pattern of the autocorrelations, is as shown previously for the pure random walk model – see Figure 6.4 – and so are not replicated here.

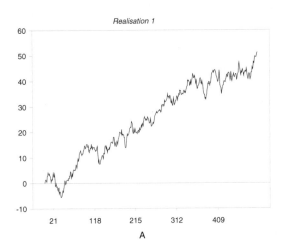

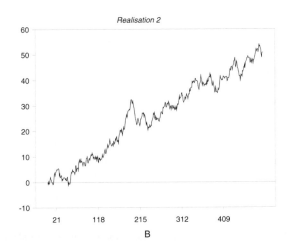

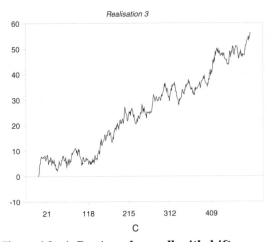

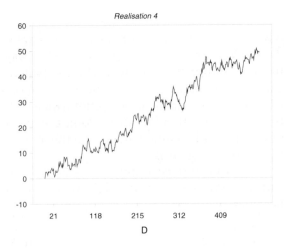

Figure 6.9   A–D – A random walk with drift

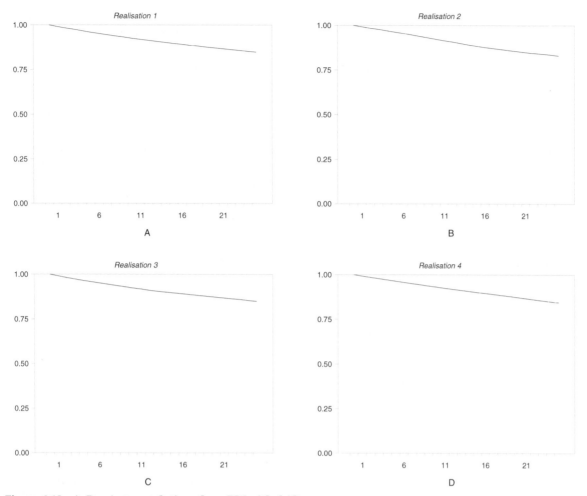

Figure 6.10   A–D – *Autocorrelations for a RW with drift*

The presence of μ tends to impart a trend to (6.7), for example a positive trend if $\mu > 0$; however, a positive value for Y_t is not guaranteed in such a case without further conditions. What we have in mind – see Granger, Inoue and Morin (1997) – is that a symmetric $(1 - \alpha)\%$ confidence interval centred on the mean could be negative because of increasing spread of the distribution. The mean of the random walk with drift, Y_t, is μt, and, from Chapter 3, the variance is $t\sigma^2$ (recall that the variance of ε_t is σ^2, assumed constant). Then the limit of the $100(1 - \alpha)\%$ confidence interval is $\mu t - b(t\sigma^2)^{0.5}$ where b is a constant determined by the size of α, which

increases as α decreases. Hence, for positivity $\mu t - b(t\sigma^2)^{0.5} > 0$, which implies the condition $\sigma^2 < ct$ where $c = (\mu/b)^2$; as intuition suggests this is more easily satisfied as μ increases thus increasing the strength of the drift, and b decreases thus increasing the significance level α and so decreasing the $(1 - \alpha)\%$ confidence interval.

It will now be useful to recall the definition of a stationary series introduced in section **3.4.4**. A second order – or weakly stationary – time series has a constant mean, a constant variance, and autocovariances (and autocorrelations) which depend only upon the difference in the time index and not upon their location in time. A nonstationary time series is one in which one or all of these conditions do not hold. Broadly speaking a stationary time series is generated by a process that stays the same over time – the index of time is not essential to characterising the properties of the series. However, in a nonstationary time series the index of time is an important characteristic of the series: the mean, variance or autocovariances may all depend upon the particular point in time at which they are measured.

In section **3.4.6** the process which we know as a random walk with drift was shown to be an example of a nonstationary time series. In the context of (6.6) with Y_0 fixed, the expected value of Y_t is $E\{Y_t\} = Y_0 + \mu t$ and the variance is $\mathrm{Var}(Y_t) = t\sigma_\varepsilon^2$ where σ_ε^2 is the (constant) variance of ε_t, hence both the mean and the variance increase with t. The covariance is $E\{Y_t Y_{t+\tau}\} = t\sigma_\varepsilon^2$ and so also depends upon t. Even if the drift term is zero, so the process is a pure random walk, the series is still nonstationary because the variance increases with t. However, taking the first differences of a random walk with drift gives a stationary series since $E\{\Delta Y_t\} = \mu$ and $\mathrm{Var}\{\Delta Y_t\} = \sigma_\varepsilon^2$, and the autocorrelations are constant and equal to zero in this case as ε_t is white noise.

This development leads to the following definition of an integrated series:

> a series which is stationary after being differenced once is said to be integrated of order 1, and is denoted I(1). In general a series which is stationary after being differenced d times is said to be integrated of order d, denoted I(d). A series, which is stationary without differencing, is said to be I(0).

This definition assumes that d is an integer; it is, though, possible to extend this definition to the case of fractional value of d but that is beyond the scope of this book – the interested reader will find a useful introduction to fractional integration/differencing in Mills (1993, 1999). A random walk, with or without drift, is I(1), and its first difference is I(0).

Note that the definition above does not imply that all nonstationary series are I(1), or more generally I(d) with $d \geq 1$. It may not be possible to difference a nonstationary series to stationarity, see Leybourne, McCabe and Tremayne (1996); and a series with fractional d with $0.5 \leq d < 1$ is nonstationary, see Hosking (1981) and Sowell (1992a). The definition, although widely used, also implies no distinction between stationary series and I(0) series; while not made here, it could be argued that such a distinction is necessary – see Granger (1997) for a further discussion.

6.2.4 Unit roots

A series, which is I(1), is also said to have a unit root and a series, which is I(d), has d unit roots. To understand this further consider the simple AR(1) model,

$$Y_t = \mu + \phi_1 Y_{t-1} + \varepsilon_t$$

or

$$Y_t - \phi_1 Y_{t-1} = \mu + \varepsilon_t \tag{6.8}$$

When $\phi_1 = 1$ this is the random walk with drift, which is an I(1) series; if $|\phi_1| < 1$, then as we show below, the series is I(0). Rewriting the last equation using the lag operator introduced in **2.4** gives

$$(1 - \phi_1 L)Y_t = \mu + \varepsilon_t \tag{6.9}$$

Consider the term $(1 - \phi_1 L)$ which on dividing through by ϕ_1 gives $([1/\phi_1] - L)$. The root of this equation is the value of L, say L^*, which satisfies $([1/\phi_1] - L^*) = 0$; the solution of this equation is $L^* = (1/\phi_1)$, and this value, L^*, is called the root of the equation. If $\phi_1 = 1$ then $L^* = 1$ and the equation has a unit root. In this case the first difference of Y_t is stationary since substituting in for $\phi_1 = 1$ gives $Y_t - Y_{t-1} = \mu + \varepsilon_t$, which is stationary. The I(1) series therefore has 1 unit root, whereas the I(0) series has no unit roots.

If the AR model is second order or higher it is possible that there are two unit roots. To see this consider the AR(2) model

$$Y_t = \mu + \phi_1 Y_{t-1} + \phi_2 Y_{t-2} + \varepsilon_t \qquad (6.10)$$

which can be rearranged as

$$(1 - \phi_1 L - \phi_2 L^2)Y_t = \mu + \varepsilon_t \qquad (6.11)$$

The term in brackets is a second order polynomial with two roots and to obtain these it is necessary to solve the quadratic equation

$$(1 - \phi_1 L - \phi_2 L^2) = 0 \qquad (6.12)$$

A solution is obtained upon factoring the quadratic equation into

$$(1 - a_1 L)(1 - a_2 L) = 0 \qquad (6.13)$$

where $a_1 + a_2 = \phi_1$ and $a_1 a_2 = -\phi_2$. Let $L_1^* = 1/a_1$ and $L_2^* = 1/a_2$ denote the solutions, or roots, of the quadratic equation in that substitution of either of these values into (6.13) will result in the equation being satisfied. A special case obtains when $\phi_1 = 2$ and $\phi_2 = -1$, so that $a_1 = 1$ and $a_2 = 1$, then $L_1^* = 1$ and $L_2^* = 1$ so that there are two unit roots. The existence of two unit roots in an AR(p) model implies that it needs to be differenced twice to become stationary and the series is said to be integrated of order 2, or I(2) for convenience.

Taking the case of $\phi_1 = 2$ and $\phi_2 = -1$, the AR(2) model is

$$Y_t = \mu + 2Y_{t-1} - Y_{t-2} + \varepsilon_t \qquad (6.14)$$

Which can be rewritten as:

$$Y_t - 2Y_{t-1} + Y_{t-2} = \mu + \varepsilon_t$$

that is $(1 - L)(1 - L)Y_t = \mu + \varepsilon_t$

This model will generate an I(2) series as it has 2 unit roots. Differencing Y_t once will not be sufficient to generate a stationary series: the

difference of an I(2) series is I(1) and hence still nonstationary. An I(2) series has to be differenced twice to become stationary. To see this subtract Y_{t-1} from both sides of (6.14) to obtain

$$\Delta Y_t = \mu + \Delta Y_{t-1} + \varepsilon_t \qquad (6.15)$$

For convenience define $Z_t \equiv \Delta Y_t$, then (6.15) can be rewritten as

$$Z_t = \mu + Z_{t-1} + \varepsilon_t \qquad (6.16)$$

But note that this is random walk with drift in the first difference of Y_t which is I(1) and hence nonstationary. Taking the first difference again – so that two differences have been taken overall – gives

$$\Delta Z_t = \mu + \varepsilon_t \qquad (6.17)$$

and now the series is stationary. Thus, if $\phi_1 = 2$ and $\phi_2 = -1$ there are two unit roots and two differences have to be taken before the original series Y_t becomes stationary.

An AR(2) model could also generate an I(1) series. In this case only one of the roots is 1 while the other has a modulus greater than one if the process is stable. We will return to the concept of stability below; for the moment consider the following example of an AR(2) model,

$$Y_t = \mu + 1.25 Y_{t-1} - 0.25 Y_{t-2} + \varepsilon_t \qquad (6.18)$$

that is

$$(1 - 1.25L + 0.25L^2)Y_t = \mu + \varepsilon_t$$

The polynomial in L factors into $(1 - L)$ $(1 - 0.25L)$, setting this equal to zero and solving gives the roots of the polynomial as $L_1^* = 1$ and $L_2^* = 4$; thus there is one unit root. Using this factorisation the model can be written as

$$(1 - L)(1 - 0.25L)Y_t = \mu + \varepsilon_t$$

that is $(1 - 0.25L)Z_t = \mu + \varepsilon_t$ or equivalently $Z_t = \mu + 0.25Z_{t-1} + \varepsilon_t$, where $Z_t \equiv \Delta Y_t$.

In general the AR(p) model is written as

$$\phi(L)Y_t = \mu + \varepsilon_t \tag{6.19}$$

where $\phi(L) = 1 - \sum_{i=1}^{p} \phi_i L^i$. Then if a unit root exists $\phi(L)$ can be factored into the product of $(1 - L)$ and $\phi^*(L) = 1 - \sum_{i=1}^{p-1} \phi_i^* L^i$ that is $\phi(L) = \phi^*(L)(1 - L)$, so that (6.19) can be written as

$$\phi^*(L)(1 - L)Y_t = \mu + \varepsilon_t \tag{6.20}$$

and

$$\Delta Y_t = \mu + \sum_{i=1}^{p-1} \phi_i^* L^i \Delta Y_t + \varepsilon_t$$

which is an AR($p - 1$) model in the first difference $\Delta Y_t \equiv (1 - L)Y_t$. Similarly if there are two unit roots $\phi(L)$ can be factored into the product of $(1 - L)^2$ and $\phi^{**}(L) = 1 - \sum_{i=1}^{p-2} \phi_i^{**} L^i$, so that (6.19) can be written as

$$\phi^{**}(L)(1 - L)^2 Y_t = \mu + \varepsilon_t \tag{6.21}$$

and

$$\Delta^2 Y_t = \mu + \sum_{i=1}^{p-2} \phi_i^{**} L^i \Delta Y_t + \varepsilon_t$$

which is an AR($p - 2$) model in the second difference $\Delta^2 Y_t \equiv (1 - L)^2 Y_t$.

Stability concerns the response of Y_{t+h} to a (one-off) perturbation in, or shock to, ε_t. If the response dies out, that is tends to zero, as $h \to \infty$, the model is stable. A necessary and sufficient condition for stability is that the roots of the polynomial $\phi(L) = 1 - \phi_1 L - \cdots - \phi_p L^p$, should have modulus greater than unity. Thus a model with a unit root is not stable, it is persistent to shocks, but we are alert to this already from the discussion of the random walk case. In an AR(2) model with one unit root, factoring out the unit root may result in a stable model in ΔY_t depending upon the other root;

for example, $Z_t = \mu + 0.25Z_{t-1} + \varepsilon_t$ is stable because the second root is $(1/0.25) = 4$ which is greater than 1.

There is an intimate connection between stability and stationarity which is explored further in the following sections; for now note that a stable process is stationary: *stability implies stationarity* (however, the converse is not true – see Lütkepohl (1991)).

6.2.5 A near random walk with drift

A random walk with drift can – see (6.6) – be expressed in the form:

$$Y_t = Y_0 + \mu t + \sum_{i=1}^{t} \varepsilon_i \tag{6.22}$$

or assuming, for simplicity, that $Y_0 = 0$, then

$$Y_t = \mu t + \sum_{i=1}^{t} \varepsilon_i \tag{6.23}$$

where $E\{Y_t\} = \mu t$ and $\text{Var}\{Y_t\} = t\sigma_\varepsilon^2$, and so a random walk, with or without drift, is an I(1) process, with its first difference an I(0) process. The random walk model is a particular example of an AR(1) process with $\phi_1 = 1$. The situation we have yet to consider is whether such a process, without the restriction $\phi_1 = 1$, is stationary. First, consider the AR(1) process given by

$$Y_t = \mu + \phi_1 Y_{t-1} + \varepsilon_t \tag{6.24}$$

Then with an initial value of Y_0 the sequence $Y_1, \ldots, Y_t$ is

$$Y_1 = \mu + \phi_1 Y_0 + \varepsilon_1$$
$$Y_2 = \mu + \phi_1(\mu + \phi_1 Y_0 + \varepsilon_1) + \varepsilon_2$$
$$= \mu + \phi_1 \mu + \phi_1^2 Y_0 + \phi_1 \varepsilon_1 + \varepsilon_2$$
$$\vdots$$

$$Y_t = \mu \sum_{i=0}^{t-1} \phi_1^i + \phi_1^t Y_0 + \sum_{i=0}^{t-1} \phi_1^i \varepsilon_{t-i} \tag{6.25}$$

Setting $\phi_1 = 1$ gives a random walk with drift, that is

$$Y_t = \mu t + Y_0 + \sum_{i=0}^{t-1} \varepsilon_{t-i} \tag{6.26}$$

where use has been made of $\sum_{i=0}^{t-1} \phi_1^i = t$ and $\phi_1^t = 1$ for $\phi_1 = 1$. On comparison with (6.6), note that $\sum_{i=1}^{t} \varepsilon_i = \sum_{i=0}^{t-1} \varepsilon_{t-i}$.

Now compare (6.25) when $0 < \phi_1 < 1$ with the random walk, (6.26). Note that in the former case the past is not as influential as in the random walk. This is evident from the nature of an autoregressive process – see (6.24) – but it is also useful to compare (6.25) and (6.26) term by term. Comparing first terms note that $t > \sum_{i=0}^{t-1} \phi_1^i$; then, comparing the second terms, $\phi_1^t \to 0$ as t increases so $\phi_1^t Y_0$ also tends to zero with t; finally taking the difference between the last terms we have

$$\sum_{i=0}^{t-1} \varepsilon_{t-i} - \sum_{i=0}^{t-1} \phi_1^i \varepsilon_{t-i}$$

$$= \sum_{i=0}^{t-1} (1 - \phi_1^i) \varepsilon_{t-i} \tag{6.27}$$

(6.27) is positive, indicating that the past matters more for (6.26), because $(1 - \phi_1^i) > 0$ given $0 < \phi_1^i < 1$. Overall, note that whereas the random walk, (6.26), has an infinite memory (that is the effect of a shock is persistent) when $0 < \phi_1 < 1$ the memory of the process is finite, being longer the closer ϕ_1 is to 1. This condition can be related to the stability of the AR(1) model. From the previous section the condition for stability is that the roots of $\phi(L) = 1 - \phi_1 L - \cdots - \phi_p L^p$, should have modulus greater than unity. In this case $\phi(L) = 1 - \phi_1 L$, hence the root is $L_1^* = 1/\phi_1$ which has a modulus greater than unity for $|\phi_1| < 1$, so if $0 < \phi_1 < 1$ the AR(1) is stable and stationary. The stationarity of the AR(1) process is considered in section **6.2.7**. The related notion of persistence is considered next.

6.2.6 The persistence of shocks

At various points in previous sections we have alluded to the persistence of shocks in AR processes and to emphasise that this is a key difference between nonstationary and stationary series some important results are summarised here. The random walk model with drift is given by (6.26), now consider the effect in that model of a one unit shock in period 1 so that the total disturbance in that period is $\varepsilon_1 + 1$; then the shocked value of Y_t is

$$Y_t = \mu t + Y_0 + \sum_{i=0}^{t-1} \varepsilon_{t-i} + 1 \tag{6.28}$$

and Y_t is one unit larger for all values of t after the shock. The shock is persistent: its effect never dies out.

In contrast in a stationary AR(1) model the shock is not infinitely lived. To see this refer to (6.25) with $0 < \phi_1 < 1$, then after the shock Y_t is

$$Y_t = \mu \sum_{i=0}^{t-1} \phi_1^i + \phi_1^t Y_0$$

$$+ \sum_{i=0}^{t-1} \phi_1^i \varepsilon_{t-i} + \phi_1^{t-1} \tag{6.29}$$

and Y_t is larger by ϕ_1^{t-1}; for example, Y_2 is larger by ϕ_1, Y_3 is larger by ϕ_1^2 and so on. As $0 < \phi_1 < 1$ then $\phi_1^{t-1} \to 0$ as $t \to \infty$ and so the shock is not persistent. As noted earlier the closer ϕ_1 is to 1 the greater is the persistence or, in an alternative terminology, the longer is the 'memory' of the process.

6.2.7 The mean, variance and autocorrelations of an AR(1) process

Is the AR(1) process with $0 < \phi_1 < 1$ a stationary process? That is does it have a constant mean, constant variance and autocovariances which depend only upon the time difference k? Taking the expectation of Y_t defined by (6.25)

$$E\{Y_t\} = \mu \sum_{i=0}^{t-1} \phi_1^i + \phi_1^t E\{Y_0\}$$

$$+ \sum_{i=0}^{t-1} \phi_1^i E\{\varepsilon_{t-i}\} \tag{6.30}$$

The expectation operator can be passed through the first term because both μ and ϕ_1 are constants. Assuming Y_0 is a constant, say $Y_0 = 0$ for simplicity (and this can always be ensured by subtracting the initial value from every observation), then the second term disappears. The random disturbance – or process innovation – has a zero mean so that the last term is zero. $E\{Y_t\}$ therefore reduces to

$$E\{Y_t\} = \mu \sum_{i=0}^{t-1} \phi_1^i \tag{6.31}$$

The summation in (6.31) runs from $i = 0$ to $t - 1$, this can be rewritten as

$$\sum_{i=0}^{t-1} \phi_1^i = \sum_{i=0}^{\infty} \phi_1^i - \sum_{i=t}^{\infty} \phi_1^i$$

$$= [1/(1 - \phi_1)] - \phi_1^t/(1 - \phi_1)$$

$$= (1 - \phi_1^t)/(1 - \phi_1)$$

where twice use has been made of the result that the infinite sum $\sum_{i=0}^{\infty} \phi_1^i$ has the limit $1/(1 - \phi_1)$ if $|\phi_1| < 1$; if $\phi_1 = 1$, then $\sum_{i=0}^{t-1} \phi_1^i = t$. With this derivation (6.31) is now written as

$$E\{Y_t\} = \mu(1 - \phi_1^t)/(1 - \phi_1) \tag{6.32}$$

This is equal to zero and independent of time if $\mu = 0$. Otherwise $E\{Y_t\}$ is a function of time and is not, therefore, strictly stationary. Notice though that as $t \to \infty$ then

$$E\{Y_t\} = \mu/(1 - \phi_1) \quad \text{because } \phi_1^t \to 0$$
$$\text{as } t \to \infty \quad \text{for } |\phi_1| < 1$$

Taking the limit of an expression is known as finding the 'asymptotic' value. The process Y_t has a constant mean in the limit and is said to be 'asymptotically stationary'.

The variance of Y_t is obtained in a similar fashion, although the derivation is slightly more complex and the result is just stated here (Priestley (1981, p. 118) proves the result and see Chapter 9 for a more detailed treatment of the variance of a time series process which includes this result.)

$$\text{Var}(Y_t) = \sigma_\varepsilon^2(1 - \phi_1^{2t})/(1 - \phi_1^2) \tag{6.33}$$

and note that as t gets increasingly large

$$\text{Var}(Y_t) \to \sigma_\varepsilon^2/(1 - \phi_1^2) \quad \text{because } \phi_1^{2t} \to 0$$
$$\text{as } t \to \infty \quad \text{for } |\phi_1| < 1 \tag{6.34}$$

So that the variance of Y_t is asymptotically constant for $|\phi_1| < 1$. From Chapter 3 we know that if $\phi_1 = 1$ then $\text{Var}(Y_t) = t\sigma_\varepsilon^2$.

Also in a similar way the autocovariance, $\gamma(k) \equiv \text{Cov}(Y_t Y_{t+k})$, can be derived (see Priestley (*op. cit.*) and Chapter 3). For $|\phi_1| < 1$, this is:

the autocovariance function:

$$\gamma(k) = \sigma_\varepsilon^2 \phi_1^k (1 - \phi_1^{2t})/(1 - \phi_1^2)$$

As with the variance, $\phi_1^{2t} \to 0$ as $t \to \infty$ and, therefore, we obtain:

the (asymptotic) autocovariance function:

$$\gamma(k) = \sigma_\varepsilon^2 \phi_1^k/(1 - \phi_1^2) \quad \text{as } t \to \infty$$

which depends on k but not on t. The autocorrelation function is $\rho(k) \equiv \gamma(k)/\gamma(0)$. As $t \to \infty$, we obtain:

the (asymptotic) autocorrelation function:

$$\rho(k) \equiv [\gamma(k)/\gamma(0)] \to \phi_1^{|k|}$$
$$\text{for } k = 0, \pm 1, \pm 2 \tag{6.35}$$

The correlation coefficient, $\rho(k)$, between pairs of Y_t separated by k points in time, tends to ϕ_1^k for $k > 0$, and ϕ_1^k for $k < 0$.

The mean, variance, autocovariances and autocorrelations of a stable AR(1) process *do*, in general, depend on time and are not, therefore, strictly stationary; however, the dependence on time disappears in the limit (as the sample size tends to infinity). In such a case the series is said to be asymptotically stationary. Quite often, and although the usage is admittedly wrong, the series is just said to be stationary if $|\phi_1| < 1$ and the limiting (or asymptotic) autocovariance and autocorrelation functions are taken to be *the* autocovariance and autocorrelation functions.

6.2.8 Difference stationary and trend stationary series

A common feature of many economic time series is that they have a positive trend, of the kind displayed by the stylised random walk with drift model. A characterisation of these time series is that they are stationary – or integrated – series in which shocks have persistent effects. An alternative and contrasting view is that these series contain a deterministic trend, which accounts for the sustained increase in the series over time, and a random disturbance term which is stationary. Such a series is described as being trend stationary. In this alternative view shocks have transitory rather than permanent effects. A trend stationary series is contrasted here with an I(1) series which is stationary after being differenced once and is, therefore, described as being difference stationary. In practice it can be difficult to distinguish between these two kinds of series and it is possible that a particular series contains both a deterministic trend and an I(1) component. However, the distinction between difference stationarity and trend stationarity is an important one and it is considered further now.

The simplest trend stationary model is

$$Y_t = \mu + \beta t + \varepsilon_t \qquad (6.36)$$

where ε_t is I(0) and, for simplicity, ε_t is assumed to be white noise. Y_t is clearly stationary without any differencing since its stochastic properties are entirely determined by ε_t. *Ceteris paribus* Y_t will increase by β each period. Adding an AR(1) component (6.36) becomes:

$$Y_t = \mu + \phi_1 Y_{t-1} + \beta t + \varepsilon_t \qquad (6.37)$$

The model represented by (6.37) includes several interesting special cases. For example, when $\beta = 0$, $\mu \neq 0$ and $\phi_1 = 1$, the model is that of a random walk with drift and so is nonstationary, generating a series with a sustained positive trend if $\mu > 0$ and sufficiently large to dominate the stochastic shocks. If $\beta = 0$, $\mu = 0$, and $\phi_1 = 1$ then the model is a pure random walk. If $\phi_1 = 0$ the model is that of a deterministic trend plus stationary noise, that is (6.36). At its most general the model allows for $\mu \neq 0$, $\phi_1 \neq 0$ and $\beta \neq 0$. If $\phi_1 = 1$ in this combination then the model is that of a random walk, with drift if $\mu \neq 0$, about a deterministic trend, although this may be thought an unlikely mixture of deterministic and stochastic trends.

A summary of the types of model which can be generated from (6.37) is shown in Table 6.1. The difference between Models 1 and 2 is simply the unit root hypothesis that $\phi_1 = 1$; both models also contain a deterministic trend. Alternatively, Model 3 is a random walk with drift but no deterministic trend, and Model 4 is a pure deterministic trend. The similarity in these models is that they are all capable of producing a series with the sustained (usually positive) trend associated with many economic time series. The pure random walk, Model 5, can produce a trend but, *a priori*, we cannot be sure that it will, for example, be positive, and it can change direction. It will not, therefore, be appropriate for typical macroeconomic time series like GDP and expenditure on consumer goods.

Some examples of the realisations from these models are plotted in Figures 6.11A and 6.11B. The nature of these realisations is broadly as before; for convenience we set $Y_0 = 0$, and make

Table 6.1 *Types of model from the maintained regression $Y_t = \mu + \phi_1 Y_{t-1} + \beta t + \varepsilon_t$*

Model No.	Parameter set	Description	Properties
1	$\mu \neq 0$, $\lvert\phi_1\rvert < 1$, $\beta \neq 0$	Deterministic trend with stationary AR(1) component	I(0)
2	$\mu \neq 0$, $\phi_1 = 1$, $\beta \neq 0$	Random walk with drift *and* deterministic trend	I(1)
3	$\mu \neq 0$, $\phi_1 = 1$, $\beta = 0$	Random walk with drift	I(1)
4	$\mu \neq 0$, $\phi_1 = 0$, $\beta \neq 0$	Deterministic trend	I(0)
5	$\mu = 0$, $\phi_1 = 1$, $\beta = 0$	Pure random walk	I(1)

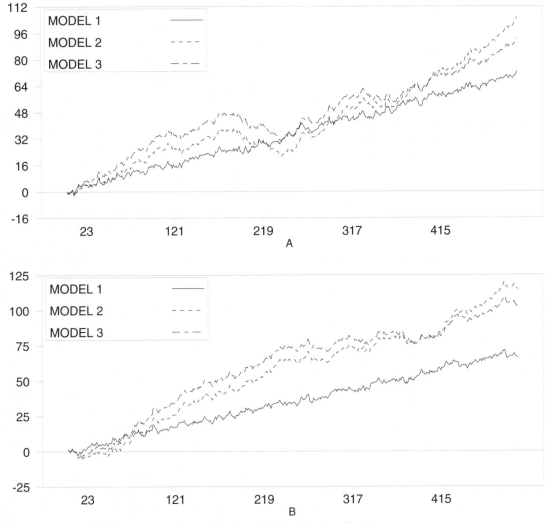

Figure 6.11 A – *Different time series models.* B – *Another set of realisations*

Table 6.2 *Parameter values for Models 1 to 3 maintained regression $Y_t = \mu + \phi_1 Y_{t-1} + \beta t + \varepsilon_t$*

	μ	ϕ_1	β	Properties
Model 1	0.1	0.80	0.028	I(0)
Model 2	0.1	1.00	0.0005	I(1)
Model 3	0.2	1.00	0.00	I(1)

replications of the model drawing each time from a normal distribution for ε_t with mean zero and unit variance and zero autocorrelations. For ease of comparison the realisations of these random numbers are kept the same across the different models for each figure. The parameter values for each of the sets of realisations are given in Table 6.2.

To emphasise the point that Models 1 to 3 can all generate a similar upward trend, depending on the particular realisations of ε_t, note the clustering of observations from the different models shown in Figure 6.11A. Taking another set of realisations but keeping the same parameter values generates another set of data, and this is shown in Figure 6.11B. The same upward trend is apparent although the series are not so closely tied together.

There are two reasons for establishing the nature of the process generating, or least describing, the data. First, the persistence of shocks is very different with an I(1) series, that is one which is difference stationary, compared to an I(0) series such as one which is trend stationary. Second, when analysing two or more series together, as is usually the case in economics, it makes a considerable difference whether the series are I(1) or I(0). This suggests testing to determine whether a time series contains a unit root (more precisely, is consistent with the data). It is possible, also, that a particular series contains more than one unit root, that is it is I(d) with $d > 1$ and this situation is dealt with in the next chapter.

The realisations in Figures 6.11A and 6.11B also imply a cautionary tale, especially those in Figure 6.11A. If it is possible for an I(0) model,

that is Model 1, to generate realisations which are 'close' to those of an I(1) model, for example Models 2 and 3, will it be possible, given this (finite) sample of realisations to infer the model that generated them? A test designed to assess whether realisations have been generated from an I(1) model rather than an I(0) model carries the risk of wrongly inferring the former rather than the latter. This relates to the 'power' of the test to reject the null, I(1), when the alternative, I(0), is true. We return to this problem in section **6.3.4** and again in the next chapter. Sections **6.3.1** to **6.3.3** first describe the range of Dickey–Fuller test statistics which are routinely included in econometric software packages, and might be regarded as the standard tests in this area.

6.3 Testing for a unit root

The tests described here are due to Fuller (1976) and Dickey and Fuller (1979, 1981). A review of an appropriate testing strategy is to be found in Dickey and Rossana (1994) and see also Dolado, Jenkinson and Sarvilla-Rivero (1990). The tests due to Dickey and Fuller are referred to as DF tests. There are many other tests for a unit root, especially those due to Phillips and his co-workers – see, for example, Phillips (1987) and Phillips and Perron (1988); some of these are considered in the next chapter.

6.3.1 $\hat{\tau}$ test

To understand the motivation for the DF test procedure we start with Model 5 from Table 6.1, the pure random walk, as the simplest example and then consider more complex models. Model 5 is the AR(1) model with $\phi_1 = 1$ and without an intercept, that is

$$Y_t = \phi_1 Y_{t-1} + \varepsilon_t \qquad (6.38)$$

The ε_t, $t = 1, \ldots, T$, are assumed to have a zero mean and be independent and identically distributed, in shorthand this is $\varepsilon_t \sim \text{iid}(0, \sigma^2)$;

normality is not required for validity of the DF tests. Subtract Y_{t-1} from both sides and define $\gamma \equiv \phi_1 - 1$, then

$$\Delta Y_t = \gamma Y_{t-1} + \varepsilon_t \qquad (6.39)$$

and if $\phi_1 = 1$, so that there is a unit root, then $\gamma = 0$. Now even if $\gamma = 0$ the presence of ε_t, a random disturbance term, will prevent us from reaching this conclusion with certainty from a particular dataset. To illustrate this point 100 realisations were generated from Model 5 with $\phi_1 = 1$ and ε_t drawn from a normal distribution with zero mean and unit variance; γ was then estimated by ordinary least squares on this dataset. The estimator of γ is denoted $\hat{\gamma}$. This procedure was carried out 10 times and the results obtained reported in Table 6.3.

Of course no firm conclusions can be drawn from just 10 replications, but Table 6.3 does illustrate that because of the 'noise' term, ε_t, the actual estimate of γ will not be identically zero. The 't' statistic for the hypothesis that $\gamma = 0$ is given in the second row of the table, and following Fuller (1976) this 't' statistic is denoted $\hat{\tau}$. The $\hat{\tau}$ test statistic does not have a normal distribution so that it would be inappropriate to use conventional normal or 't' tables to look up critical values. Appropriate critical values, which depend on the sample size, have been tabulated by Fuller (1976, p. 373) based on Dickey (1975). These critical values were obtained by simulation, which is a process we have used several times. In the simulation, step 1 is to generate data of a given sample size, T, according to a specified DGP. Data is generated by first specifying a DGP, here the pure random walk, $Y_t = Y_{t-1} + \varepsilon_t$, that is $\Delta Y_t = \varepsilon_t$, with ε_t a random variable with zero mean, unit

variance and zero autocorrelations, and specifying an initial value for the process, which is usually taken to be zero. The values of ε_t, for $t = 1, \ldots, T$, are obtained from a random number generator with distribution as specified, here standard normal. This process is repeated M times and so generates M samples of size T.

Step 2 is to estimate a regression model using the data for each sample generated in step 1. With M samples there will be M estimated models. The choice of regression model in this step is important and can have a substantial influence on the way the subsequent critical values are used. In the case of the DF $\hat{\tau}$ test, the regression model is the simplest extension of the DGP which includes the pure random walk model as a special case. That is the estimated model is $\Delta Y_t = \gamma Y_{t-1} + \varepsilon_t$, so $\gamma = 0$ corresponds to the pure random walk. Notice that a constant is not included in the regression, so the regression model matches the DGP in that respect. The values of $\hat{\gamma}$ and its estimated 't' statistic, $\hat{\tau}$, from each of the M samples are recorded. Even though $\gamma = 0$ in the DGP there will be a distribution of the $\hat{\gamma}$, with nonzero values occurring. If the estimation method is unbiased then this should be picked up if M is 'large' enough (for example, 10,000) by an average of $\hat{\gamma}$ over the M samples equal to the value in the DGP (here in the DGP $\gamma = 0$); similarly a bias will show up in the difference between the average $\hat{\gamma}$ and the corresponding DGP value. For each realisation (sample) of $\hat{\gamma}$ its 't' statistic $\hat{\tau}$ is recorded, and so the distribution of these values is obtained over the M samples. Now the distribution of $\hat{\tau}$ is known when the DGP is $\Delta Y_t = \varepsilon_t$ and the (maintained) regression model is $\Delta Y_t = \gamma Y_{t-1} + \varepsilon_t$. Given this distribution, critical values for particular significance levels can be extracted just

Table 6.3 *Estimating γ from samples of 100 realisations of a pure random walk*

Sample No.	1	2	3	4	5	6	7	8	9	10
$\hat{\gamma}$	−0.0016	−0.0010	−0.264	−0.0088	−0.006	−0.0778	−0.0203	−0.0004	0.0044	−0.0095
$\hat{\tau}$	−0.234	−0.150	−1.014	−1.221	−0.947	−2.124	−1.018	−0.043	−0.383	−0.694

as in the case of the ordinary 't' statistic, the usual choice of significance levels being 1%, 5% and 10%.

The critical values will also depend upon the specification of the null and alternative hypotheses. The null hypothesis is straightforward since it corresponds to the existence of a single unit root, that is H_0: $\gamma = 0$ implying $Y_t = Y_{t-1} + \varepsilon_t$ and the series is I(1). The alternative hypothesis should be chosen to maximise the power of the test in the likely direction of departure from the null. A two-sided alternative $\gamma \neq 0$, comprising $\gamma > 0$ and $\gamma < 0$, is *not* chosen in general because $\gamma > 0$ corresponds to $\phi_1 > 1$ and in that case the process generating Y_t is not stable; instead the one-sided alternative H_a: $\gamma < 0$, that is $\phi_1 < 1$, is chosen because departures from the null are expected to be in this direction corresponding to an I(0) process. Thus the critical values are *negative*, with sample values more negative than the critical values leading to rejection of the null hypothesis in the direction of the one-sided alternative. A sample value less negative than the critical value implies nonrejection of the null that the series is I(1); *a fortiori* a positive sample value would imply nonrejection of the null hypothesis. The test statistic is referred to as $\hat{\tau}$ without any subscripts to distinguish it from cases where a constant and/or time trend is included.

These steps are repeated for different values of the sample size, T, to see whether they are sensitive to that parameter. The critical values of the $\hat{\tau}$ test for the 1%, 5% and 10% significance levels for the one-sided alternative H_a: $\gamma < 0$ and a range of sample sizes are given in Table 6.4. The critical values vary only slightly with the different sample sizes. An alternative to using this table (and related tables in this chapter) to obtain the critical values is to use the 'response surfaces' calculated by MacKinnon (1991) and Cheung and Lai (1995). A response surface relates the critical values to a (usually) simple function of the sample size and other parameters of relevance. This approach is described in greater detail in section **6.3.6** and Cheung and

Table 6.4 *Critical values of the DF test statistic $\hat{\tau}$ for the null hypothesis $\gamma = 0(\phi_1 = 1)$ in the maintained regression $\Delta Y_t = \gamma Y_{t-1} + \varepsilon_t$*

Sample size T	Critical values		
	1%	5%	10%
25	−2.677	−1.981	−1.605
40	−2.645	−1.984	−1.637
50	−2.600	−1.961	−1.603
75	−2.604	−1.948	−1.619
100	−2.589	−1.945	−1.600
200	−2.581	−1.938	−1.619
500	−2.536	−1.943	−1.610
1,000	−2.593	−1.961	−1.624
5,000	−2.558	−1.952	−1.624

Notes: DGP is $\Delta Y_t = \varepsilon_t$, i.e. a pure random walk. Tabulated values are obtained from 25,000 replications.

Lai's response function is given in equation (6.53) and tabulated in Table 6.11.

To illustrate how to use Table 6.4 consider the entries for a sample size, T, of 100; these are −2.589, −1.945 and −1.600 for the 1%, 5% and 10% significance levels. Thus, for example, there is a 5% probability of a value of $\hat{\tau}$ smaller (more negative) than −1.945 if the null hypothesis $\gamma = 0$ is true. Suppose that in a single empirical example the sample value of $\hat{\tau}$ of −2.10 was obtained, then since this is more negative than −1.945, the 5% critical value, the conclusion is that −2.10 is significant at the 5% level. That is, at the 5% significance level the null hypothesis of a unit root, $\gamma = 0$, is not consistent with the sample data. Choosing a 1% significance level results in a different decision since the critical value is −2.589 and the sample value, in the example, is greater than that value. In this case the conclusion is that at the 1% significance level the null hypothesis is consistent with the data.

6.3.2 Φ_1 and $\hat{\tau}_\mu$ test statistics

The general principle in constructing tests to distinguish between null and alternative hypotheses is that the maintained regression must include both as special cases, so that either rather than just one can be 'discovered' with the sample data. The maintained regression for the τ test is $Y_t = \gamma Y_{t-1} + \varepsilon_t$ which 'nests' the null $\gamma = 0$ and the alternative $\gamma < 0$; however, this regression is restrictive because under the null and the alternative, Y_t has a zero mean (or the mean has been subtracted from each observation). This is particularly restrictive under the alternative because a stationary process frequently crosses its mean; if, therefore, the mean of Y_t is nonzero the maintained regression for the $\hat{\tau}$ test is not an appropriate starting point. The maintained regression should be extended to include an intercept so that a nonzero mean is allowed in the alternative hypothesis.

The extended maintained regression is:

$$Y_t = \mu + \phi_1 Y_{t-1} + \varepsilon_t \qquad (6.40)$$

which can be written as

$$\Delta Y_t = \mu + \gamma Y_{t-1} + \varepsilon_t \qquad (6.41)$$

where $\gamma \equiv \phi_1 - 1$. Now the maintained regression (6.41) allows a nonzero mean under the alternative since if $|\phi_1| < 1$ then, setting ε_t to its expected value of 0, in the long run $Y_t = \mu/(1 - \phi_1)$ which will be nonzero if $\mu \neq 0$.

An appropriate null hypothesis in this set-up is the joint hypothesis $H_0: \mu = 0$ and $\gamma = 0$; adopting this as the null hypothesis focuses on the role of μ since $\gamma = 0$ obviously corresponds to the existence of a unit root. Under the null the series Y_t is generated by a pure random walk without drift and it is, therefore, equally likely to exhibit a sustained positive walk (trend) as a sustained negative walk; *a priori* we do not know which way the walk will go. If $\Delta Y_t = \mu + \varepsilon_t$ and $\mu \neq 0$, Y_t is a random walk with drift which will trend in the direction of the sign of μ unless the 'noise', $\sum_{i=1}^{t} \varepsilon_t$, is particularly strong relative to the 'signal', $Y_0 + \mu t$ – see (6.6). The alternative hypothesis to put against the random walk with drift model, ($\mu \neq 0, \gamma = 0$), must also be able to account for a sustained movement in one

direction, so (6.41), with $\gamma < 0$, is clearly not appropriate as there is no mechanism to generate a trend. Under the alternative (6.41) generates a series stationary about a constant mean. Hence, if $\mu \neq 0$ the maintained regression (6.41) is not the place to start; an appropriate set-up is described in the next section.

The first test statistic to be considered is due to Dickey and Fuller (1981) and is an F type statistic known as Φ_1. The null hypothesis is $H_0: \mu = 0$ and $\gamma = 0$ whereas the alternative is H_a: either or both $\mu \neq 0$ and $\gamma \neq 0$. Under the alternative there are three possibilities corresponding to $\mu \neq 0$ and $\gamma \neq 0$, $\mu \neq 0$ and $\gamma = 0$ or $\mu = 0$ and $\gamma \neq 0$. In the first and third of these Y_t is a stationary series, with nonzero mean in the first case and a zero mean in the third case. In the second case, a drift, μ, is present in the random walk. We expect to find that either $\mu = 0$ and $\gamma = 0$, or $\mu \neq 0/\mu = 0$ and $\gamma < 0$. Although $\mu \neq 0$ and $\gamma = 0$ is not formally ruled out we anticipate $\mu \approx 0$, otherwise there will be a noticeable drift and hence, as noted above, a trend in the data, in which case this maintained regression is not the appropriate starting point. (Note that this does not rule out a significant but numerically small (≈ 0) value of μ.)

One possible strategy is to start with a test of the joint null using the DF Φ_1 test statistic. Nonrejection stops the sequence of tests in favour of the null; although, since $\mu = 0$ has not been rejected, it would also be possible to move down to the most restricted maintained regression without a constant. If the series does not display a sustained trend and the joint null is rejected there is a presumption in favour of the alternative of stationarity, even though rejection could formally come from either or both $\mu \neq 0$ and $\gamma \neq 0$.

The critical values for Φ_1 are obtained by simulation with the DGP set up, as before, as $\Delta Y_t = \varepsilon_t$ while the maintained regression is (6.41); denoting the residual sum of squares from the latter as URSS, and RRSS $= \sum_{t=2}^{T} (\Delta Y_t)^2$ respectively, the test statistic is calculated as $\Phi_1 = [(\text{RRSS} - \text{URSS})/\text{URSS}](T^+ - 2)/2$, where

Table 6.5 *Critical values of the DF test statistic* Φ_1 *test for the null hypothesis* $\gamma = 0(\phi_1 = 1)$ *and* $\mu = 0$ *in the maintained regression* $\Delta Y_t = \mu + \gamma Y_{t-1} + \varepsilon_t$

Sample size T	Critical values		
	1%	5%	10%
25	7.770	5.140	4.064
40	7.430	5.020	4.019
50	6.964	4.809	3.917
75	6.837	4.790	3.908
100	6.732	4.740	3.855
200	6.730	4.696	3.835
500	6.387	4.646	3.803
1,000	6.370	4.620	3.787
5,000	6.365	4.596	3.797

Notes: DGP is $\Delta Y_t = \varepsilon_t$, i.e. a pure random walk. Tabulated values are obtained from 25,000 replications.

$T^+ = T - 1$ and T^+ is the effective sample size after one observation is lost through lagging. 1%, 5% and 10% critical values for a number of sample sizes are given in Table 6.5. Sample values of Φ_1 less than the tabulated values are evidence for nonrejection of the null hypothesis; for example, suppose the sample value of the test statistic Φ_1 is 3.0 with $T = 100$, then the 5% critical value from Table 6.5 is 4.740 and the null hypothesis is not rejected. A sample value of Φ_1 greater than 4.740 would lead to rejection of the null hypothesis at the 5% significance level.

A potential drawback of using Φ_1 is that the alternative hypothesis is two sided, which does not maximise power in the likely direction of departure from the null hypothesis. The latter is $\gamma < 0$, corresponding to the stationary alternative. An alternative test statistic, which has found widespread use, is the 't' type statistic on γ in the maintained regression (6.41); here the null hypothesis is H_0: $\gamma = 0$ against the alternative H_a: $\gamma < 0$, and the test statistic is referred to as $\hat{\tau}_\mu$, where the subscript μ distinguishes the maintained regression (6.41) from (6.39). While $\hat{\tau}_\mu$ focuses on γ it turns out that μ is also important in the sense that the distribution of $\hat{\tau}_\mu$, and so the appropriate critical values,

depends upon the value of μ. We deal with the simplest case first, where $\mu = 0$ in the DGP.

The $\hat{\tau}_\mu$ test statistic is due to Dickey (1975) and Fuller (*op. cit.*). Critical values, generated by simulation using the DGP $\Delta Y_t = \varepsilon_t$ (that is, $\mu = 0$), are tabulated in Fuller (*op. cit.*, Table 8.5.2, p. 373). Critical values were also generated for this book using the same set-up but a wider range of sample sizes and these are reported in Table 6.6 for the row $\mu = 0$. Notice two important points about the entries for $\mu = 0.0$. First, as expected, they are very close to the corresponding entries in Table 8.5.2 of Fuller (*op. cit.*); a comparison for $T = 50$ is given below:

% significance level:	1%	5%	10%
$\mu = 0.0$			
Table 6.6	-3.572	-2.921	-2.592
Fuller Table 8.5.2	-3.580	-2.930	-2.600

Second, they are not the same as those in Table 6.4 because the maintained regression now includes an intercept, which leads to $\hat{\tau}_\mu < \hat{\tau}$ for a given significance level. Otherwise the testing procedure is as before with sample values of $\hat{\tau}_\mu$ more negative than the critical value leading to rejection of the null hypothesis of a unit root in favour of the alternative. For example, with $T = 50$ a sample value of $\hat{\tau}_\mu = -3.0$ would lead to rejection of the null at the 5% significance level, critical value $= -2.921$, but nonrejection at the 1% significance level, critical value -3.572. Critical values for *any* sample size can be obtained from Cheung and Lai's (*op. cit.*) response function for $\hat{\tau}_\mu$ with $\mu = 0$ – see equation (6.53) and Table 6.11 below.

Complications arise when $\mu \neq 0$ in the DGP. West (1988) has shown that the distribution of $\hat{\tau}_\mu$ is asymptotically normal for $\mu \neq 0$. However, in small samples the distribution is not normal – see Hylleberg and Mizon (1989a) – and is dependent on the size of μ; as μ increases in magnitude the finite sample distribution looks more and more like the normal distribution. To illustrate the small sample dependence, the critical values were also obtained by simulation for $\mu \neq 0$, and these are reported in Table 6.6 for 6 nonzero values of μ. The procedure for obtaining critical values is as before except that an intercept (drift) is now included in the DGP (step 1) and in the maintained model (step 2). This procedure, therefore, includes the Dickey–Fuller test statistic as a special case since it corresponds to setting $\mu = 0$ in the DGP while keeping the constant in the maintained regres-

sion. There is a different distribution of the test statistic $\hat{\tau}_\mu$ for each value of μ. More precisely the row entries in Table 6.6 refer to the standardised drift, μ/σ_ε, but because $\sigma_\varepsilon = 1$, which is a standard procedure in simulations, $\mu/\sigma_\varepsilon = \mu$. More generally, therefore, what matters is μ/σ_ε – see Banerjee et al. (1993, p. 170).

If $\mu = 0$ and $T = 100$ the 5% critical value is -2.897, whereas if $\mu = 10$ the 5% critical value

Table 6.6 *Critical values of the DF test statistic $\hat{\tau}_\mu$ for the null hypothesis $\gamma = 0(\phi_1 = 1)$ in the maintained regression $\Delta Y_t = \mu + \gamma Y_{t-1} + \varepsilon_t$*

	Critical values					
Sample size	1%	5%	10%	1%	5%	10%
		$T = 25$			$T = 40$	
$\mu = 0.00$	−3.716	−2.992	−2.641	−3.629	−2.933	−2.616
0.05	−3.697	−2.964	−2.624	−3.573	−2.907	−2.579
0.10	−3.697	−2.954	−2.600	−3.575	−2.900	−2.558
0.25	−3.611	−2.830	−2.457	−3.375	−2.696	−2.340
0.50	−3.273	−2.459	−2.059	−3.055	−2.262	−1.885
1.00	−2.860	−2.047	−1.668	−2.702	−1.948	−1.569
10.00	−2.517	−1.721	−1.346	−2.479	−1.734	−1.334
		$T = 50$			$T = 75$	
$\mu = 0.00$	−3.572	−2.921	−2.592	−3.501	−2.897	−2.583
0.05	−3.533	−2.890	−2.575	−3.508	−2.885	−2.565
0.10	−3.491	−2.868	−2.544	−3.421	−2.816	−2.510
0.25	−3.319	−2.629	−2.271	−3.189	−2.511	−2.161
0.50	−2.903	−2.171	−1.800	−2.837	−2.102	−1.722
1.00	−2.623	−1.897	−1.541	−2.543	−1.852	−1.495
10.00	−2.474	−1.714	−1.331	−2.406	−1.677	−1.316
		$T = 100$			$T = 200$	
$\mu = 0.00$	−3.520	−2.897	−2.591	−3.446	−2.878	−2.569
0.05	−3.462	−2.868	−2.553	−3.418	−2.837	−2.529
0.10	−3.447	−2.807	−2.471	−3.361	−2.717	−2.387
0.25	−3.067	−2.393	−2.041	−2.854	−2.156	−1.790
0.50	−2.743	−2.018	−1.641	−2.586	−1.888	−1.513
1.00	−2.515	−1.823	−1.463	−2.452	−1.763	−1.407
10.00	−2.367	−1.685	−1.310	−2.318	−1.647	−1.288
		$T = 500$			$T = 1,000$	
$\mu = 0.00$	−3.444	−2.851	−2.569	−3.431	−2.864	−2.563
0.05	−3.362	−2.763	−2.440	−3.255	−2.669	−2.336
0.10	−3.126	−2.461	−2.116	−2.947	−2.247	−1.875
0.25	−2.602	−1.933	−1.572	−2.518	−1.848	−1.477
0.50	−2.475	−1.811	−1.456	−2.423	−1.737	−1.367
1.00	−2.389	−1.719	−1.340	−2.390	−1.699	−1.340
10.00	−2.326	−1.659	−1.293	−2.336	−1.635	−1.272

Notes: DGP is $\Delta Y_t = \mu + \varepsilon_t$, i.e. a random walk with drift. Tabulated values are obtained from 25,000 replications. Standard Dickey–Fuller critical values correspond to row entries for $\mu = 0.00$.

is -1.685, which is getting close to the 5% critical value of -1.645 from the normal distribution. However, for moderate, but realistic, values of μ, for example $\mu = 0.05$, $\mu = 0.10$, there is relatively little variation in the critical values. This is relevant because for many economic time series Y_t will be the log of the series and the appropriate range of values for μ will be where there is relatively little variation in the critical values.

Care has to be taken in using Table 6.6 for the rows with $\mu \neq 0$ in the following sense. As noted above if $\mu \neq 0$ then it is unlikely that the maintained regression (6.41) is the appropriate starting point for inference about a unit root compared to a stationary alternative, since the latter is penalised because no mechanism is present to allow the generation of a trend. Table 6.6, for the rows with $\mu \neq 0$, could find use where the stationary, nontrended alternative is a viable competing explanation to the random walk with drift, but in the latter the noise-to-signal ratio does not allow the trend generated by the drift, μt, to dominate. A consistent estimator of μ *under the null* is obtained from OLS estimation of $\Delta Y_t = \mu + \varepsilon_t$.

μ could be regarded as a nuisance parameter for inference on γ, since the critical values for $\hat{\tau}_\mu$ depend upon the, generally unknown, value of μ. Two test statistics which avoid this dependence and which are based upon a more realistic alternative hypothesis to compete with the null of a random walk with drift are described in the next section.

6.3.3 Φ_3 and $\hat{\tau}_\beta$ test statistics

Recall that the purpose of unit root tests is to determine whether, given the sample data, a series is consistent with an I(1) process, that is difference stationary and has a stochastic trend, or is, alternatively, consistent with an I(0) process, that is it is stationary and may have a deterministic trend. The models under the alternative hypothesis for the $\hat{\tau}$ and $\hat{\tau}_\mu$ test statistics are unlikely practical alternatives in

this situation, because they cannot generate the trended behaviour typical of economic time series. For $\hat{\tau}$ and $\hat{\tau}_\mu$ the alternative to a unit root is $|\phi_1| < 1$ in $Y_t = \phi_1 Y_{t-1} + \varepsilon_t$ or $Y_t = \mu + \phi_1 Y_{t-1} + \varepsilon_t$, respectively but, as noted above, such a model has no mechanism for generating a trend; in the long run Y_t tends to a constant given by $\mu/(1 - \phi_1)$. If there is trend in the data neither $\hat{\tau}$ nor $\hat{\tau}_\mu$ is a relevant starting point; the maintained regression is more appropriately $Y_t = \mu + \phi_1 Y_{t-1} + \beta t + \varepsilon_t$, which 'nests' the null and alternative hypotheses as special cases.

As before it is usually simpler to rewrite the maintained regression as

$$\Delta Y_t = \mu + \gamma Y_{t-1} + \beta t + \varepsilon_t \tag{6.42}$$

where $\gamma = \phi_1 - 1$. The choice of null hypothesis is quite important in this context, as is the set of alternative explanations of how the data could have been generated. The most likely null hypothesis is of a random walk with drift, that is $H_0: \gamma = 0$ (unit root) and $\beta = 0$ (no deterministic trend), which can be conveniently written as

$$H_0: (\mu, \gamma, \beta) = (\mu, 0, 0) \tag{6.43}$$

This is read as μ is unrestricted, $\gamma = 0$ so there is a unit root, and $\beta = 0$ so there is no deterministic trend. The null hypothesis H_0 could be rejected for one of the following three reasons:

H_{a1}: $(\mu, \gamma, \beta) = (\mu, \gamma, \beta)$ no unit root, deterministic trend present, that is Model 1;

H_{a2}: $(\mu, \gamma, \beta) = (\mu, 0, \beta)$ unit root, deterministic trend present, that is Model 2;

H_{a3}: $(\mu, \gamma, \beta) = (\mu, \gamma, 0)$ no unit root, no deterministic trend, that is a restricted version of Model 1.

Thus H_0 could be rejected because any of H_{a1}, H_{a2} or H_{a3} is true, and that is a problem to which we will turn in a moment. First, consider how to test H_0 against the most general of the alternatives, that is H_{a1}.

The null hypothesis restricts the parameter space in two, rather than one, dimensions and, an appropriate test statistic is a version of the standard F test – see Dickey and Fuller (1981) – known as Φ_3. Although the F statistic is calculated in the usual way, as in the case of Φ_1, it does not have a standard distribution. The critical values for Φ_3, obtained by simulation, are given in Table 6.7. The set-up of the simulations is as follows: the DGP has $\mu \neq 0$, $\gamma = 0$ and $\beta = 0$; this is the DGP according to the null hypothesis. The maintained model is $\Delta Y_t = \mu + \gamma Y_{t-1} + \beta t + \varepsilon_t$. The F statistic for the null hypothesis, $H_0: \gamma = 0$ and $\beta = 0$, is calculated for each of the M samples in the simulation against the alternative hypothesis H_{a1}. The test statistic is invariant to the choice of μ, so we do not have to worry about this aspect of the design of the simulation. For each sample two regressions are estimated: the restricted model with $\gamma = 0$ and $\beta = 0$, and the unrestricted model with $\gamma \neq 0$ and $\beta \neq 0$; the former provides a restricted residual sum of squares, RRSS, and the latter the unrestricted residual sum of squares, URSS. The F statistic is then formed in the standard way as $\Phi_3 = [((\text{RRSS} - \text{URSS})/\text{URSS})(T^+ - 3)/2]$, where $T^+ = T - 1$.

To illustrate the use of Table 6.7 consider a sample size of 50 for which the 5% critical value

Table 6.7 *Critical values of the DF test statistic Φ_3 test for the null hypothesis $(\mu, \gamma, \beta) = (\mu, 0, 0)$ in the maintained regression $\Delta Y_t = \mu + \gamma Y_{t-1} + \beta t + \varepsilon_t$*

| Sample size T | Critical values | | |
	1%	5%	10%
25	10.492	7.223	5.906
40	9.459	6.771	5.657
50	9.839	6.776	5.667
75	9.013	6.578	5.556
100	9.042	6.606	5.555
200	8.542	6.397	5.433
500	8.326	6.238	5.321
1,000	8.328	6.209	5.309
5,000	8.209	6.218	5.349

Notes: DGP is $\Delta Y_t = \mu + \varepsilon_t$, i.e. a random walk with drift. Tabulated values are obtained from 25,000 replications.

is 6.776. If the particular sample value is less than this, then the null hypothesis $(\mu, \gamma, \beta) = (\mu, 0, 0)$ is not rejected and we conclude that a random walk with drift is consistent with the data. If, however, the sample value is greater than 6.776 the null hypothesis is rejected. The likely cause of the rejection is considered next.

The only one of the three alternatives with a unit root is $H_{a2}: \gamma = 0$ and $\beta \neq 0$, for which a relevant question is whether this case is likely to arise in practice. According to this hypothesis $\Delta Y_t = \mu + \beta t + \varepsilon_t$ which implies (on integration of the difference) that the level of Y_t must contain a term in μt *and* a term in βt^2. Such situations with a *quadratic* trend in the level seem unlikely to occur in practice, except perhaps on a very localised basis, and should be relatively easy to detect graphically. That leaves H_{a1} and H_{a3} which are alike in rejecting the unit root, but differ in that a deterministic trend is present in the former but not in the latter. However, H_{a3} is not likely if the data is evidently trended since it contains no inherent mechanism for generating the trend; if $\beta = 0$, given that $\gamma \neq 0$, then a trend cannot be generated by this model. That leaves H_{a1} as the prime candidate leading to rejection of the null hypothesis, that is Y_t is stationary about a deterministic trend. Hence, if the data is trended, rejection of the null hypothesis carries a presumption in favour of the stationary trend model.

As in the case of Φ_1, the alternative hypothesis for Φ_3 is two sided and, therefore, loses power against the stationary alternative, $\gamma < 0$. A test statistic with the one-sided alternative is the 't' type statistic on γ in the maintained regression (6.42) which includes a deterministic trend. This test statistic is denoted $\hat{\tau}_\beta$ with critical values for $\hat{\tau}_\beta$ given in Fuller (*op. cit.*, Table 8.5.2) and in Table 6.8 for a larger number of sample sizes (there is a notational difference compared to Fuller (*op. cit.*) who uses $\hat{\tau}_\tau$ rather than $\hat{\tau}_\beta$ for the case of $\beta = 0$ in the DGP; the β subscript is consistent with our use of β as the trend coefficient). The test procedure is as before with sample

Table 6.8 *Critical values of the DF test statistic $\hat{\tau}_\beta$ for the null hypothesis $\gamma = 0(\phi_1=1)$ in the maintained regression $\Delta Y_t = \mu + \gamma Y_{t-1} + \beta t + \varepsilon_t$*

	Critical values					
Sample size	1%	5%	10%	1%	5%	10%
		$T = 25$			$T = 40$	
$\beta = 0.00$	−4.402	−3.617	−3.247	−4.191	−3.531	−3.198
0.05	−4.106	−3.304	−2.925	−3.429	−2.642	−2.251
0.10	−3.621	−2.716	−2.303	−2.930	−2.204	−1.808
0.25	−2.886	−2.103	−1.718	−2.651	−1.880	−1.497
0.50	−2.745	−1.937	−1.516	−2.533	−1.792	−1.406
1.00	−2.614	−1.797	−1.414	−2.456	−1.727	−1.363
10.00	−2.544	−1.746	−1.334	−2.402	−1.672	−1.299
		$T = 50$			$T = 75$	
$\beta = 0.00$	−4.143	−3.485	−3.157	−4.066	−3.482	−3.167
0.05	−3.172	−2.376	−2.006	−2.759	−2.056	−1.674
0.10	−2.730	−2.036	−1.646	−2.588	−1.884	−1.500
0.25	−2.558	−1.821	−1.451	−2.499	−1.768	−1.385
0.50	−2.454	−1.746	−1.360	−2.417	−1.699	−1.325
1.00	−2.432	−1.721	−1.358	−2.381	−1.683	−1.309
10.00	−2.447	−1.686	−1.307	−2.420	−1.692	−1.310
		$T = 100$			$T = 200$	
$\beta = 0.00$	−4.073	−3.464	−3.162	−3.989	−3.433	−3.141
0.05	−2.670	−1.918	−1.538	−2.409	−1.729	−1.377
0.10	−2.505	−1.805	−1.425	−2.393	−1.715	−1.341
0.25	−2.376	−1.704	−1.325	−2.354	−1.655	−1.284
0.50	−2.413	−1.678	−1.316	−2.326	−1.653	−1.296
1.00	−2.407	−1.696	−1.320	−2.386	−1.667	−1.304
10.00	−2.356	−1.652	−1.284	−2.345	−1.636	−1.269
		$T = 500$			$T = 1,000$	
$\beta = 0.00$	−3.977	−3.424	−3.128	−3.970	−3.408	−3.123
0.05	−2.395	−1.683	−1.316	−2.320	−1.642	−1.298
0.10	−2.335	−1.646	−1.290	−2.326	−1.663	−1.304
0.25	−2.322	−1.625	−1.279	−2.315	−1.631	−1.269
0.50	−2.344	−1.643	−1.284	−2.306	−1.662	−1.291
1.00	−2.336	−1.615	−1.264	−2.340	−1.633	−1.275
10.00	−2.375	−1.671	−1.299	−2.373	−1.656	−1.298

Notes: DGP is $\Delta Y_t = \mu + \beta t + \varepsilon_t$, i.e. a random walk with drift about a deterministic time trend. Tabulated values are obtained from 25,000 replications with $\mu = 0.1$. Standard Dickey–Fuller critical values correspond to row entries for $\beta = 0.00$.

values more negative than the, say, 5% critical value leading to rejection of the null $\gamma = 0$ in favour of the alternative $\gamma < 0$. Note that for a given significance level $\hat{\tau}_\beta < \hat{\tau}_\mu < \hat{\tau}$.

The critical values of $\hat{\tau}_\beta$ are invariant to the value of μ but are affected by the value of β, which is analogous to the situation with $\hat{\tau}_\mu$. If this was thought critical, invariance could be obtained by further extending the maintained

regression to include a squared trend, say δt^2. The dependence is illustrated in Table 6.8 where the critical values are given for 6 nonzero values of $\beta/\sigma_\varepsilon = \beta$, given $\sigma_\varepsilon = 1$ in the simulations, from 0.05 to 10. There are three points to note about the critical values in Table 6.8 for the nonzero values of β. First, a relatively small value of β does affect the critical values even with moderate sample sizes; for example, with

$T = 100$ and $\beta = 0$ the 5% critical value is -3.464, but with $\beta = 0.05$ the 5% critical value is -1.918. Second, as T increases the convergence to the normal distribution is quick and noticeably faster than for $\hat{\tau}_\mu$. Third, for fixed T the larger is β the faster is this convergence; the 5% one-sided critical value from the normal distribution is -1.645 while with $T = 100$ and $\beta = 0.05$ and $\beta = 10.0$ the critical values are -1.918 and -1.652, respectively. Increasing the sample size to $T = 500$ the analogous critical values are -1.683 and -1.671.

Table 6.9 *Empirical power of some Dickey–Fuller tests for a unit root; 0.05 size of tests*

	$\phi_1 = 0.80$	$\phi_1 = 0.90$	$\phi_1 = 0.95$
Φ_1	0.80	0.24	0.09
Φ_3	0.59	0.16	0.07
$\hat{\tau}_\mu$ (t-s)	0.74	0.19	0.06
$\hat{\tau}_\mu$ (o-s)	0.86	0.30	0.12
$\hat{\tau}_\beta$ (t-s)	0.48	0.11	0.05
$\hat{\tau}_\beta$ (o-s)	0.64	0.18	0.08

Source: Extracted from Dickey and Fuller (1981, Tables VIII and IX); and Dickey *et al.* (1986, Table 2) for a sample size of 100.

6.3.4 The empirical power of some Dickey–Fuller test statistics

Dickey and Fuller (1981) and Dickey *et al.* (1986) report the results of simulations to assess the power of a number of the Dickey–Fuller test statistics. In these simulations the alternative model is $Y_t = \phi_1 Y_{t-1} + \varepsilon_t$ with $\phi_1 \neq 1$, and we report in Table 6.9 the power for $\phi_1 = 0.80, 0.90$ and 0.95 with $T = 100$ for the following test statistics: Φ_1, Φ_3, $\hat{\tau}_\mu$ and $\hat{\tau}_\beta$. The simulation set-up is most useful for Φ_1 and $\hat{\tau}_\mu$, since the alternative is the one for which they were designed, rather than Φ_3 and $\hat{\tau}_\beta$ which are designed to detect the trend stationary alternative. Where there is no trend in the alternative we expect $\hat{\tau}_\beta$ to be less powerful than $\hat{\tau}_\mu$. Φ_1 and Φ_3 are inherently two-sided tests, whereas $\hat{\tau}_\mu$ and $\hat{\tau}_\beta$ can be used in one-sided (o-s) or two-sided (t-s) tests and in practical applications are usually used as one-sided (negative) tests.

To see how Table 6.9 is interpreted, note that in 80% of the simulations with $\phi_1 = 0.80$, using Φ_1 and a 5% critical value, the null hypothesis of $\phi_1 = 1$ was rejected; this fell to 24% when $\phi_1 = 0.90$ and 9% when $\phi_1 = 0.95$. As expected Φ_3 is less powerful in each case because it contains a superfluous regressor (the time trend). Φ_1 is also more powerful than the two-sided version of $\hat{\tau}_\mu$ but not when the negative one-sided critical value is used. As expected in each case $\hat{\tau}_\beta$ is less powerful than $\hat{\tau}_\mu$. In every case as ϕ_1 gets

closer to 1 the power of the tests approaches the size (= significance level) of the test.

These empirical power calculations illustrate the general problem with unit root tests that where the alternative is close to 1 power is low, with false nonrejection of the null, that is a type 2 error, a frequent outcome. Also in a study of the theoretical power of a number of test statistics for a unit root Abidir (1993) notes '…it is hard to distinguish stable from unit roots'; and some very sceptical views have been expressed about whether it is possible to determine whether a process contains a unit root and whether it matters anyway – see, for example, Christiano and Eichenbaum (1990). This issue is taken up further in Chapter 7.

Part of the problem of low power lies in the set-up in classical hypothesis testing, where typically quite small significance levels are used in an asymmetric framework which places the null hypothesis in a primary position. One possibility is to reverse the roles of the hypotheses of nonstationarity and stationarity, and this is considered in Chapter 7 (but note that this does not avoid the 'near observational equivalence' problem – see Faust (1996) and Campbell and Perron (1991, rules 7 and 9)). Another is to increase the significance level of the test from the typically used 5%, and so trade off type 1 and type 2 errors. In addition other test statistics may be more powerful, even though there is no one test statistic which is uniformly more powerful;

some examples of other test statistics are considered in Chapter 7. Evaluating the empirical power to mimic the practice of applied econometricians is also more complex than presented here. Typically there are a number of decisions which have to be made (for example, is the maintained regression an adequate statistical base for inference?) and a number of 'pre-tests' are undertaken before the hypothesis of primary interest is assessed. We, therefore, return to an assessment of power in the next chapter.

The results of the empirical power simulations suggest caution against too rigid an application of the various unit root tests. In practice there is considerable uncertainty in knowing the exact nature of the DGP, and so where a decision is marginal, one way or another, there is sense in remaining agnostic and seeking further evidence rather than coming down firmly for the null hypothesis or the alternative hypothesis. One course of action is to use the unit root statistics as indicative of the properties of a time series rather than 'proving' that they do have certain properties. Other evidence, for example a plot of the autocorrelations, should be sought to provide further information.

6.3.5 Distribution of the test statistics on the intercept and trend

Whether or not an intercept or deterministic trend should be included in the maintained regression is an issue that also has to be considered. A complication in assessing the significance of the intercept or trend is that while under the alternative hypothesis, when there is no unit root, the distribution of the OLS estimators of μ and β are standard ('t' or normal), under the null this is not the case. The asymptotic, and some small sample, percentiles of the 't' statistics for $\mu = 0$ and $\beta = 0$ under the null of a unit root have been tabulated by Dickey and Fuller (1981, Tables I–III). The critical values of the 't' (type) statistic for $\mu = 0$ depend upon whether a time trend is included

in the maintained regression. The 't' (type) test statistics for $\mu = 0$, without and with a time trend in the maintained regression, are denoted $t(\mu)$ and $t(\mu)_\beta$, respectively; and the 't' (type) test statistic for $\beta = 0$ is denoted $t(\beta)$. Haldrup (1991) has shown that the critical values for $t(\beta)$ depend upon the value of μ in the DGP and that Dickey and Fuller's critical values assume $\mu = 0$; he has provided a set of tables for $t(\beta)$ for different values of μ. (More precisely Haldrup's results refer to the standardised drift, μ/σ_ε, but it is standard procedure in simulations to set $\sigma_\varepsilon = 1$.) Haldrup's results show that for $\mu \neq 0$, as the sample size, T, tends to infinity the distribution of $t(\beta)$ tends to the mirror image of the distribution of $\hat{\tau}_\beta$ (for $\beta = 0$ in the DGP), and that this result is more pronounced the larger is μ. A summary of relevant critical values is provided in Table 6.10.

The distributions $t(\mu)$, $t(\beta)_\beta$ and $t(\beta)$, with $\mu = 0$ in the DGP, are symmetric; for example, the two-sided 10% critical values for $T = 100$, for a test of $\mu = 0$ in a maintained regression model with time trend, are $t(\mu)_\beta = \pm 3.11$; and the two-sided 10% critical values for $\beta = 0$, with $\mu = 0$ in the DGP, are $t(\beta) = \pm 2.79$. The 5% one-sided critical values are obtained by halving the significance level and taking the appropriate sign; for example, the 5% one-sided critical value for the null $\beta = 0$ against the alternative $\beta > 0$, with $T = 100$, is $t(\beta) = 2.79$. Under the null of a unit root the critical values are substantially larger (in absolute value) compared to the stationary case.

As noted in the previous paragraph when $\mu \neq 0$ in the DGP then the distribution of $t(\beta)$ is not symmetric but the mirror image of the distribution of $\hat{\tau}_\beta$; for example, with $\mu = 0.10$ and $T = 100$, the 5% two-sided critical values are -2.41 and 3.46, and when $\mu = 1.0$ the 5% two-sided critical values are 0.58 and 3.67. These critical values arise because although when $\mu = 0$ the OLS estimator of the trend coefficient, β, is unbiased, it is biased for $\mu \neq 0$. The median value of $t(\beta)$ for $\mu = 1.0$ and $T = 100$ is 2.14, not 0 and the first percentile is 0.23; thus, effectively,

Table 6.10 *Two-sided critical values of* t *statistics for* $\mu = 0$ *and* $\beta = 0$ *when there is a unit root*

	Maintained regression model:					
DGP(null):	$\Delta Y_t = \mu + \gamma Y_{t-1} + \varepsilon_t$ $\mu = 0$ and $\gamma = 0$		$\Delta Y_t = \mu + \gamma Y_{t-1} + \beta t + \varepsilon_t$ $\mu = 0,\ \gamma = 0,\ \beta = 0$			
	$t(\mu)$		$t(\mu)_\beta$		$t(\beta)$	
	10%	5%	10%	5%	10%	5%
$T = 25$	±2.61	±2.97	±3.20	±3.59	±2.85	±3.25
$T = 50$	±2.56	±2.89	±3.14	±3.47	±2.81	±3.18
$T = 100$	±2.54	±2.86	±3.11	±3.42	±2.79	±3.14
$T = 250$	±2.53	±2.84	±3.09	±3.39	±2.79	±3.12
$T = 500$	±2.52	±2.83	±3.08	±3.38	±2.78	±3.11

	$t(\beta)$ for selected values of $\mu \neq 0$					
DGP(null):	$\mu \neq 0,\ \gamma = 0,\ \beta = 0$					
	$\mu = 0.1$		$\mu = 0.5$		$\mu = 1.0$	
	10%	5%	10%	5%	10%	5%
$T = 25$	−2.49/3.10	−2.94/3.48	0.17/3.53	−0.36/3.89	0.75/3.59	0.39/3.95
$T = 50$	−2.27/3.12	−2.71/3.44	0.65/3.46	0.25/3.75	0.84/3.49	0.51/3.78
$T = 100$	−1.91/3.16	−2.41/3.46	0.82/3.41	0.49/3.68	0.87/3.40	0.58/3.67
$T = 250$	−1.01/3.28	−1.74/3.55	0.91/3.44	0.60/3.70	0.92/3.43	0.63/3.69
$T = 500$	0.00/3.33	−0.69/3.60	0.94/3.41	0.64/3.67	0.92/3.41	0.63/3.66

Notes: Source, $t(\mu)$, $t(\mu)_\beta$ and $t(\beta)$, with $\mu = 0$, extracted from Dickey and Fuller (1981, p. 1062); critical values for $T = \infty$ are the same as for $T = 500$; two-sided critical values are shown; if a one-sided critical value is required halve the significance level and take the appropriate sign. Critical values for $t(\beta)$, with $\mu \neq 0$, from Haldrup (1991, Table 1).

none of the critical values are negative. The important question following these results is whether Haldrup's case, that is where $\mu \neq 0$ in the DGP, is likely to be important. To recap the framework, the maintained regression includes a deterministic time trend and an intercept, the latter having the interpretation of drift when the joint null hypothesis $\gamma = 0$ and $\beta = 0$ is not rejected. The trend is included in the maintained regression since the data is trended and the competing explanations according to the null and alternative hypotheses are: a random walk with drift and stationarity about a time trend, respectively. Thus, *a priori*, under the null a nonzero drift *is* anticipated; further μ and σ_ε, and hence the standardised drift μ/σ_ε, can be con-

sistently estimated under the null by imposing $\gamma = 0$ and $\beta = 0$ in the regression (6.42). However, as noted in section **6.3.3** the occurrence of $\mu \neq 0$, $\gamma = 0$ and $\beta \neq 0$, which corresponds to a random walk with drift *and* a deterministic trend, is unlikely since it implies a *quadratic* not a linear trend in the DGP.

6.3.6 The augmented Dickey–Fuller, ADF, test

The time series models in this chapter have, so far, been variations of an AR(1) process. However, this is a particularly simple model which may not adequately describe the more complex patterns exhibited in actual economic time series. A simple generalisation is the AR(p) process given by

$$Y_t = \mu + \phi_1 Y_{t-1} + \phi_2 Y_{t-2} + \cdots$$
$$+ \phi_p Y_{t-p} + \varepsilon_t \qquad (6.44)$$

If this is the process generating the data but an AR(1) model is fitted, say

$$Y_t = \mu + \phi_1 Y_{t-1} + v_t,$$

then

$$v_t = \phi_2 Y_{t-2} + \cdots + \phi_p Y_{t-p} + \varepsilon_t$$

and the autocorrelations of v_t and v_{t-k}, for $k > 1$, will be nonzero because of the presence of the lagged Y_t terms. Thus, an indication of whether it is appropriate to fit an AR(1) model can be aided by considering the autocorrelations of the residuals from the fitted model. If there is evidence of nonzero autocorrelations then one strategy is to increase the order of the AR process. Alternatively, in what is known as a 'general to specific' search strategy, select a maximum lag length, say p^*, that seems likely to ensure white noise residuals in the fitted equation and certainly is no less than the minimum order one would expect the true order to be. For example, if the data is of a monthly frequency then choose $p^* \geq 12$, and fit successively lower order models $p^* - 1$, $p^* - 2$, and so on until the point at which there are no nonzero autocorrelations in the residuals. The Lagrange-Multiplier (LM) test for serial correlation is used extensively for this purpose in the examples that follow in this and other chapters. Another aspect of the general to specific search strategy is to fit successively lower order models, $p^* - j$ for $j \geq 1$, by using a sequence of test statistics, for example an F statistic, say $F(j)$, that the last j lag coefficients are simultaneously zero, $1 \leq j \leq p^*$. The sequence stops at the first significant test statistic; that is the hypothesis that the last j lag coefficients are zero is rejected.

In addition there are a number of examples in the literature of choosing the lag length by an information criteria. In general terms the idea is to choose the lag order, p, to minimise a function of the form

$$\text{IC}(p) = T \ln \hat{\sigma}^2(p) + p[f(T)]$$
$$\text{for } p = 1, \ldots, p^*$$

where $\hat{\sigma}^2(p)$ is the estimated regression variance, which depends upon the sample size and order p of the ADF model. $p[f(T)]$ can be interpreted as the *penalty* function for increasing the order of the model, and comprises p times the function $f(T)$. Different choices of $f(T)$ give different information criteria. The Akaike (1974) Information Criterion, AIC, results from $f(T) = 2$; the Schwarz (1978) Information Criterion, SIC, results from $f(T) = \ln T$ and the Hannan–Quinn (1979) Information Criterion, HQIC, results from $f(T) = \ln(\ln T)$. AIC and SIC are often programmed into commercially available econometric software. Thus, for example, using the AIC, the information criterion is calculated for $p = 1, \ldots, p^*$ and p is chosen, say $\hat{p}(\text{AIC})$, where the criterion is at a minimum. In practice the information criterion is usually joined by the requirement that the resulting model has residuals which are consistent with a lack of serial correlation. The AIC penalty function is not as severe as that for SIC, with the result that the former may often result in a larger value of p compared to the SIC. Indeed we know that $\hat{p}(\text{AIC}) \leq \hat{p}(\text{SIC})$ for $T \geq 8$, Lütkepohl (1991). It is also known, Lütkepohl (*op. cit.*), that asymptotically (as $T \to \infty$) AIC overestimates the true order of the autoregression with positive probability, whereas SIC and HQIC do not; the former is said to be inconsistent whereas the latter are consistent. Nevertheless, the AIC is still frequently used because its *finite* sample performance in choosing the right model is not necessarily inferior to SIC (or HQIC). For an interesting study comparing model selection by different information criteria see Koreisha and Pukkila (1995).

If $p > 1$ an interesting way of rewriting the AR(p) was suggested by Fuller (1976, p. 374).

To illustrate first consider the AR(2) model

$$Y_t = \mu + \phi_1 Y_{t-1} + \phi_2 Y_{t-2} + \varepsilon_t \qquad (6.45)$$

then notice that this is the same as

$$Y_t = \mu + (\phi_1 + \phi_2) Y_{t-1} - \phi_2 (Y_{t-1} - Y_{t-2}) + \varepsilon_t \qquad (6.46)$$

and subtracting Y_{t-1} from both sides gives

$$\Delta Y_t = \mu + \gamma Y_{t-1} + \alpha_1 \Delta Y_{t-1} + \varepsilon_t \qquad (6.47)$$

where the following have been defined

$$\gamma = \phi_1 + \phi_2 - 1 \quad \text{and} \quad \alpha_1 = -\phi_2$$

This means that if the appropriate order of the AR process is 2 rather than 1, the term ΔY_{t-1} should be added to the regression model. A test on whether there is a unit root can be carried out in the same way as before, with the test statistic provided by the 't' statistic on the γ coefficient. If $\gamma = 0$ then there is a unit root in the AR(2) process – see section **6.2.4** above. In a useful terminology the standard Dickey–Fuller model has been 'augmented' by ΔY_{t-1} with coefficient α_1. In this case the regression model and 't' test are referred to as the ADF(1) model and ADF(1) test statistic, $\hat{\tau}_\mu$, respectively, where the number in brackets indicates the order of augmentation and the subscript on $\hat{\tau}$ indicates whether a constant or time trend is included in the regression model.

Now consider the AR(3) model, which is

$$Y_t = \mu + \phi_1 Y_{t-1} + \phi_2 Y_{t-2} + \phi_3 Y_{t-3} + \varepsilon_t \qquad (6.48)$$

With a little more algebraic dexterity this can be arranged as

$$Y_t = \mu + (\phi_1 + \phi_2 + \phi_3) Y_{t-1} - (\phi_2 + \phi_3) \Delta Y_{t-1} - \phi_3 \Delta Y_{t-2} + \varepsilon_t \qquad (6.49)$$

and subtracting Y_{t-1} from both sides gives

$$\Delta Y_{t-1} = \mu + \gamma Y_{t-1} + \alpha_1 \Delta Y_{t-1} + \alpha_2 \Delta Y_{t-2} + \varepsilon_t \qquad (6.50)$$

where the following have been defined

$$\gamma = \phi_1 + \phi_2 + \phi_3 - 1,$$
$$\alpha_1 = -(\phi_2 + \phi_3) \quad \text{and} \quad \alpha_2 = -\phi_3$$

(6.50) is an ADF(2) model as there are 2 augmentation terms given by ΔY_{t-1} and ΔY_{t-2}. The test procedure is as before with a 't' test on the γ coefficient denoted $\hat{\tau}_\mu$.

In general an ADF(p) model is given by

$$\Delta Y_t = \mu + \gamma Y_{t-1} + \sum_{j=1}^{p} \alpha_j \Delta Y_{t-j} + \varepsilon_t \qquad (6.51)$$

but note that this corresponds to an AR model of one higher order, that is an AR($p + 1$) model. The test statistic is as before being the 't' statistic, $\hat{\tau}_\mu$, on γ. If the intercept is omitted – see section **6.3.1** – the appropriate test statistic is $\hat{\tau}$ but otherwise the principle of augmenting the estimated model is the same.

Similarly (6.41) can be extended by adding a deterministic trend and augmenting by p terms to give the following model:

$$\Delta Y_t = \mu + \gamma Y_{t-1} + \sum_{j=1}^{p} \alpha_j \Delta Y_{t-j} + \beta t + \varepsilon_t \qquad (6.52)$$

Otherwise the testing procedure, whether for Φ_3 or the τ statistic $\hat{\tau}_\beta$, is as before.

The ADF(p), $p \geq 1$, model involves additional terms relative to the ADF(0) $\equiv$ DF model, which in slightly different forms is the regression model underlying the simulations giving the critical values of Tables 6.4 to 6.8; hence, there is the prospect that additional tables are needed for different values of p. Some evidence on this issue is provided by Cheung and Lai (1995). In that article the authors set up the DGP as a pure random walk, as in Fuller (1976), and estimate three regression models: the no constant, no trend case; the constant, no trend case; and the constant and trend case. These correspond to the test statistics $\hat{\tau}$, $\hat{\tau}_\mu$ and $\hat{\tau}_\beta$ and to the critical values in Table 6.4, Table 6.6 (first row) and Table 6.8 (first row), respectively. They find that there are some adjustments to the resulting finite sample critical values if the fitted regression model includes p augmented terms. To see how this works we introduce the idea of a response surface which relates the critical values, cv, of the test statistics to the sample size, T, and the order of the fitted ADF. The response surface is the calibration of this relationship. Cheung and Lai (op. cit.) fit the following

$$cv(T, p) = \kappa_0 + \kappa_1/T$$
$$+ \kappa_2/T^2 + \omega_1[(p/T)]$$
$$+ \omega_2[(p/T)]^2 + \eta_{T,p} \qquad (6.53)$$

The estimated coefficients are reported in Table 6.11.

The coefficients κ_1 and κ_2 capture the dependence of the critical values on the sample size and ω_1 and ω_2 capture the dependence on the lag order of the fitted ADF regression model (for comparison with Cheung and Lai (op. cit.) note

that their $k - 1$ is here p, since in their article k refers to the order of the AR model not the ADF model). $\eta_{T,p}$ is the regression disturbance. The adjustment due to fitting an ADF(p) model involves ω_1 and ω_2; however, note that the estimates of these coefficients are of opposite sign and, therefore, tend to offset each other. For example, with $T = 100$ and $p = 4$ the adjustment due to the lags for $\hat{\tau}_\mu$ at the 5% critical value is $0.748(4)/100 - 1.077(16)/10000 = 0.028$ and for $p = 6$ it is $0.748(6)/100 - 1.077(36)/10,000 = 0.041$. The adjustments are relatively slight and suggest that unless p is particularly large and T is small their consequence is secondary. More generally, Cheung and Lai's results suggest that the dependence of the finite sample critical values on the lag order is relatively slight where the DGP is a pure random walk and the fitted regressions are variants of equation (6.52). It seems likely that these results carry over to the case where the DGP includes a drift or deterministic trend although this has not been shown formally.

6.4 A framework for testing

The large number of test statistics and procedures for a unit root can sometimes lead to

Table 6.11 *Determining critical values by response surface coefficients, Cheung and Lai (1995)*

	$cv(T, p) = \kappa_0 + \kappa_1/T + \kappa_2/T^2 + \omega_1[(p/T)] + \omega_2[(p/T)]^2$				
Estimated coefficients:		Sample size adjustment		ADF(p) adjustment	
	κ_0	κ_1	κ_2	ω_1	ω_2
$\hat{\tau}$					
5%	−1.931	−1.289	−5.719	0.380	−0.722
10%	−1.609	−0.285	−4.090	0.321	−0.525
$\hat{\tau}_\mu(\mu = 0)$					
5%	−2.857	−2.675	−23.558	0.748	−1.077
10%	−2.566	−1.319	−15.086	0.667	−0.650
$\hat{\tau}_\beta(\beta = 0)$					
5%	−3.406	−4.060	−40.552	1.021	−1.501
10%	−3.122	−2.850	−15.813	0.907	−0.804

the cynical view that test statistics can be chosen to validate whatever prior view is held by a researcher. There are many examples reported in the empirical literature where a DF test statistic is given without reference to whether the underlying framework is appropriate. An important first step is to choose the right maintained regression for the characteristics of the data at hand and, therefore, to be sure that the competing explanations according to the null and alternative hypotheses are encompassed by the maintained regression.

Even if limited to the null of nonstationarity, in the form of a single unit root, and the alternative of stationarity together with the three DF $\hat{\tau}$ statistics, and Φ_1 and Φ_3, the order of tests needs to be determined and some thought needs to be given to an appropriate testing strategy to determine whether the evidence is consistent with the view that a series is nonstationary. This section outlines a possible approach and discusses alternatives. The strategy could be more inclusive, for example in extending the range of test statistics and reversing the roles of the null hypothesis of nonstationarity and the alternative hypothesis of stationarity; however, where there are alternative test statistics it should be clear at which point in the strategy they could be used as alternatives or complements to the DF test statistics. The maintained regression within which inference takes place is assumed to be statistically adequate; for example, it may have been necessary to augment the DF regression to 'whiten' the residuals.

6.4.1   Is the data series trended?

In choosing a test statistic, and an appropriate alternative hypothesis, consideration should be given to the nature of the time series, for example is there a trend? If the answer is yes, the appropriate starting point is the maintained regression with an intercept and deterministic time trend and the test statistics Φ_3 and/or $\hat{\tau}_\beta$. Given a sustained positive or negative trend in a time series, the nonunit root alternative hypothesis is that the series is stationary but trended, otherwise it cannot reproduce the central characteristics of the series.

A first step is to graph the data to become familiar with its central characteristics; and, as a matter of course, it is also good practice to graph the autocorrelations of the levels and first differences. For simplicity the data is assumed not to be seasonal or it has been seasonally adjusted, where this is not the case the strategy also has to take into account the possibility of seasonal unit roots, this is considered in the next chapter.

A more formal testing procedure starts with a maintained model which allows either the null hypothesis of a stochastic trend, $\gamma = 0$, or the alternative hypothesis of a deterministic trend, $\beta \neq 0$, to be discovered using the Φ_3 test of section **6.3.3**, with critical values given in Table 6.7. Starting here with a maintained regression, which includes a deterministic trend, is part of a general principle which states that the maintained regression *must* nest the models under the null and alternative hypotheses as special cases. The initial choice of null hypothesis is of a random walk with drift, which generates a stochastic trend but not a deterministic trend. Nonrejection of the null hypothesis implies that within a model in which the drift μ is unrestricted, a random walk *without* a deterministic trend is consistent with the data.

While it would be possible to stop at this point, the finding that $\beta = 0$ is consistent with the data suggests moving to the maintained model that excludes the deterministic trend. The valid exclusion of the deterministic time trend from the maintained regression generally results in a more powerful test of the unit root hypothesis. Given this observation the following alternate strategy might be tempting: start with the maintained regression with a deterministic time trend and test $\beta = 0$; if $\beta = 0$, proceed to test for a unit root. The problem with this strategy is that the distribution of the 't' statistic $t(\beta)$ depends upon whether there is a unit root, which is the primary hypothesis of interest (and whether there is a nonzero drift – see Table 6.10). The critical values of $t(\beta)$, for $\mu = 0$, are much larger in absolute value if there is a unit root than if there is not, so, if the alternative hypothesis is true, using the unit root critical values will not lead to a very powerful procedure.

If the null hypothesis $\gamma = 0$ and $\beta = 0$ is rejected, in order to determine which component hypothesis has led to rejection retain the maintained regression model with a trend but revise the null hypothesis so that both μ and β are unrestricted and $\gamma = 0$; this is a random walk with drift and deterministic trend unrestricted. The test statistic for the alternative hypothesis now concerns just the coefficient γ, with $\gamma < 0$ for a stationary, autoregressive model with β unrestricted. The appropriate test statistic is $\hat{\tau}_\beta$ of section **6.3.3** with critical values given in Table 6.8. An apparent difficulty here is that locating the appropriate entry in this table presupposes knowledge of β, a problem we consider in the next paragraph.

The problem is that if $\beta \neq 0$ then *asymptotically* the distribution of $\hat{\tau}_\beta$ is standard normal, whereas if $\beta = 0$ the distribution of $\hat{\tau}_\beta$ is given by simulation – see West (1988) and Choi (1993). There are three possible strategies to solve this dilemma which turns out to be more apparent than real. In the Perron (1988) strategy, the first test in the sequence is not the Φ_3 test but the $\hat{\tau}_\beta$ test assuming $\beta = 0$ in the DGP and hence using critical values from Table 6.8 for the row $\beta = 0$, or from Fuller's Table 8.5.2 which assumes $\beta = 0$ or from the response surfaces calibrated by MacKinnon (1991) or Cheung and Lai (1995). If the first test is not rejected then the joint hypothesis $\gamma = \beta = 0$ is tested using Φ_3; if that leads to rejection then given that the first test did not reject $\gamma = 0$ the implication is that $\beta \neq 0$, hence standard normal tables could be used, according to West's asymptotic results, for a revisit to $\hat{\tau}_\beta$ but now assuming $\beta \neq 0$ but otherwise unknown.

There are some difficulties with this approach. The distribution of $\hat{\tau}_\beta$, for given $\beta \neq 0$,

approaches the standard normal *asymptotically* as the sample size increases; however, as Table 6.8 indicates even with $T = 200$, which is usually regarded as a large sample, the empirical distribution is not standard normal unless β is 'substantial', although it provides a better guide than the Dickey–Fuller distribution (that is assuming $\beta = 0$). How substantial β has to be for the standard normal to be a good approximation is suggested by considering the rows of Table 6.8 for given T. For $T = 200$ the empirical distribution needs $\beta > 0.25$ to get close to the standard normal and $\beta > 1.00$ to be almost indistinguishable. These values of β, which are in units of the standard error of the regression, seem unlikely to occur in practice especially in log regressions. For smaller sample sizes, when $\beta \neq 0$, use of either the standard normal or Dickey–Fuller distribution is likely to be misleading. Thus, one potential problem with this strategy is that the wrong critical values are used in the third stage. Another possible problem is that, ideally, the fewer tests involved in a strategy the better since, unless the significance level of each test is adjusted to control the overall significance level, more tests generally mean a larger chance of falsely rejecting a true null hypothesis (type 1 error). Also, in the first stage, critical values from the Dickey–Fuller distribution are used so β is assumed to be 0; however, if $\beta \neq 0$ then given that $\hat{\tau}_\beta$ (for $\beta = 0$) $< \hat{\tau}_\beta$ (for $\beta \neq 0$) this procedure will have poor power which adds to a problem already endemic to unit root testing.

A second possible strategy recognises that β is a nuisance parameter for testing the hypothesis $\gamma = 0$. If there is no reasonable way of determining β then an alternative is to use the maintained regression which includes δt^2 as well as βt, and the DGP has $\gamma = 0$ with μ and β unrestricted, with, by analogy, the test statistic denoted $\hat{\tau}_\delta$. The distribution of the test statistic $\hat{\tau}_\delta$ is then invariant to the value of β. This strategy would require another table of critical values but these are relatively easy to compute. The problem, however, is again one of power since

$\hat{\tau}_\delta < \hat{\tau}_\beta$ (for $\beta = 0$) $< \hat{\tau}_\beta$ (for $\beta \neq 0$), and so the cost of making the test statistic invariant is a lower probability of correctly detecting that the series is stationary.

The third strategy is the one suggested here. Start with the Φ_3 since there is no ambivalence over which critical values to use. If the data suggests nonrejection of the null, then that is a straightforward conclusion except for the problem common to any strategy using this test that some power is sacrificed because the alternative not only has $\beta \neq 0$ but also $\gamma \neq 0$. Ideally a joint test designed with the alternative $\beta \neq 0$ and $\gamma < 0$ would be preferred since it is likely to give higher power in the probable direction of rejection of the null, but this is not available. If there is rejection using the Φ_3 test then either or both $\beta \neq 0$ and $\gamma \neq 0$, and in a second step, to determine whether $\gamma < 0$, use $\hat{\tau}_\beta$ with a consistent estimate of β under the null guiding the appropriate row entry. A variant on this procedure is to use critical values – see Table 6.10 – for the 't' statistic, $t(\beta)$, on β in the maintained regression to determine whether the auxiliary step of obtaining a consistent estimate of β under the null is necessary (in this step an estimate of μ is also needed). If only one test is used, in order to control the cumulation of type one error and preserve power, most researchers have opted for $\hat{\tau}_\beta$. Bear in mind that if the data is trended and the joint null $\gamma = 0$ and $\beta = 0$ is rejected using Φ_3, the presumption is in favour of the alternative of stationarity around a deterministic trend because, otherwise, there is no mechanism to generate the trend.

As a final comment on the problems arising within this set-up, *a priori*, the finding of $\beta \neq 0$ and $\gamma = 0$ is likely to be a rare occurrence. This combination implies a *quadratic* trend, that is a t^2 term, in the process generating Y_t (just as in the simpler model $Y_t = \mu + Y_{t-1}$ the presence of drift implies a linear trend) as well an infinite memory to shocks. A quadratic trend only seems likely on a localised basis rather than being a long-run property of the data.

6.4.2 The data is not obviously trended and the mean under the alternative is nonzero

When $\beta = 0$ the alternative to the unit root null hypothesis is a stationary, autoregressive model *without* a time trend; hence, the appropriate maintained regression is $\Delta Y_t = \mu + \gamma Y_{t-1} + \varepsilon_t$ (which may be augmented by lags of ΔY_t as in section **6.3.6**). The null hypothesis $\mu = 0$ and $\gamma = 0$ with test statistic Φ_1 is a sensible starting point; at this level we anticipate $\mu \approx 0$ otherwise there is likely to be a trend in the direction given by the sign of μ, for which the competing model is a stationary autoregressive model *with* a time trend. This does not, though, rule out a significant but numerically small estimated drift, as we shall see in the following chapter.

Nonrejection of the joint null ends the sequence. Starting with Φ_1 is also sensible because if the researcher has not noticed that the data is trended, the likely outcome is rejection of the null: there is no mechanism to generate the trend under the alternative, that leaves the data to be 'explained' by the model under the null, the necessary combination being $\mu \neq 0$ and $\gamma = 0$. The slight drawback in using Φ_1 is the lack of power against this alternative.

If the series does not display a sustained trend and the joint null is rejected there is a presumption in favour of the alternative of stationarity, even though rejection could formally come from either of $\mu \neq 0$ and $\gamma \neq 0$, or both. If Φ_1 leads to rejection, in a second step use $\hat{\tau}_\mu$ to test the null hypothesis $\gamma = 0$ against the alternative $\gamma < 0$, with critical values from Table 6.6, Fuller's Table 8.5.2 or from the response surfaces calibrated by MacKinnon (1991) or Cheung and Lai (1995). What we expect the tests, with the maintained regression $\Delta Y_t = \mu + \gamma Y_{t-1} + \varepsilon_t$, to find is that either $\mu = 0$ and $\gamma = 0$, or $\mu \neq 0$ and $\gamma < 0$. Although $\mu \neq 0$ and $\gamma = 0$ is not formally ruled out we anticipate $\mu \approx 0$ otherwise there will be a noticeable drift and hence a trend in the data, in which case this maintained regression is not the appropriate starting point. The use of $\hat{\tau}_\mu$ in a single step rather than Φ_1 is widespread. While there is some evidence – see Table 6.9 – that $\hat{\tau}_\mu$ is more powerful than Φ_1, when the direction of departure from the null is $\gamma < 0$, the null hypothesis for Φ_1 provides a useful focus on the role of μ to suggest whether the maintained regression is the appropriate starting point.

Using $\hat{\tau}_\mu$ runs into an analogous problem to $\hat{\tau}_\beta$ in that its distribution depends upon an unknown parameter, here μ. The Perron strategy applied in this case comprises: first, a test with $\hat{\tau}_\mu$ using critical values from the DF distribution, that is from, for example, Table 6.6 with $\mu = 0$; then if this test does not lead to rejection it is followed by a test with Φ_1 of the joint null $\mu = 0$ and $\gamma = 0$; if this test leads to rejection then given that in the first step $\hat{\tau}_\mu$ did not reject the implication is that $\mu \neq 0$, hence revisit $\hat{\tau}_\mu$ but with critical values from the standard normal distribution. The problems outlined earlier, for application of this strategy with a deterministic trend in the maintained regression, apply equally here. Reference to Table 6.6 indicates that either T or μ have to be large, with μ having to be larger the smaller is T, for the standard normal distribution to provide a good approximation to the small sample distribution of $\hat{\tau}_\mu$. Hence, it seems preferable to obtain a consistent estimate of μ under the null and use that to inform choice of the appropriate row entry in Table 6.6. Notice that the estimate of the constant in the maintained regression is not used since the small sample distributions are generated on the assumption that the null is correct; if the alternative is correct the constant in the maintained regression is not an estimate of the drift. However, in order to assess whether this auxiliary step is necessary, the 't' statistic, $t(\mu)$, on the constant in the maintained regression can be used with critical values from Table 6.10. A significant value of $t(\mu)$ is prima facie evidence against a unit root if the data is not trended.

The strategy suggested here is to use Φ_1, because there is no ambiguity over the critical values, and $\hat{\tau}_\mu$ in a second step (with μ estimated imposing the null) if the joint hypothesis of the first stage is rejected. Note though that, as with the difficulties which arise if $\beta \neq 0$ in using the $\hat{\tau}_\beta$ test, problems which arise from not knowing whether $\mu \neq 0$ are more apparent than real. If $\mu \neq 0$ then the maintained regression $\Delta Y_t = \mu + \gamma Y_{t-1} + \varepsilon_t$ does not nest the different explanations of the data corresponding to the null and alternative hypotheses; a time trend should be included and $\hat{\tau}_\beta$ is then invariant to the value of μ.

Care has to be taken in using $\Delta Y_t = \mu + \gamma Y_{t-1} + \varepsilon_t$. An almost certain way of finding in favour of a unit root, when there may not be one, is to use this maintained regression when the data is trended: nonrejection of the null is then the *likely* outcome as the alternative contains no mechanism to generate the trend.

6.4.3 The data is not obviously trended and the mean under the alternative is zero

If the null hypothesis $\mu = 0$ and $\gamma = 0$ is not rejected, it would be possible to move to an even more restricted maintained model. In this last case the null hypothesis is of a pure random walk against the alternative hypothesis of a stationary, autoregressive model without an intercept and a time trend. The test statistic is $\hat{\tau}$ of section **6.3.1** with critical values given in Table 6.4 or the sources cited for $\hat{\tau}_\mu$. However, the test statistic $\hat{\tau}$ is likely to be rarely used. The maintained regression $\Delta Y_t = \gamma Y_{t-1} + \varepsilon_t$ must nest the models under the null and alternative hypotheses. Under the null $\gamma = 0$, hence the process is a random walk without drift, and with a zero mean for Y_t, although nonstationarity will imply that there will be few crossings of the zero axis. The alternative is $\gamma < 0$, also with a zero mean for Y_t but, because of the stationarity, there will be frequent crossings of the zero axis. There are relatively few economic time series for which this will be a reasonable assumption.

Thus, if under the alternative the mean of the series is nonzero, this is not an appropriate starting point; fitting the maintained regression will distort inference since the regression is inappropriately forced through the origin.

It may, of course, be necessary to augment the appropriate maintained model to ensure that it has white noise residuals but the testing strategy is unaffected by this change. The ADF model, which forms the basis of inference, should at least have residuals free from serial correlation and model selection criteria are applicable here as well as in multivariate regression models. It is also important to detect outliers or step changes, which may suggest structural breaks and affect the conclusions of the testing strategy. These issues are considered at greater length in Chapter 7.

6.4.4 Cumulation of type 1 error

As with any strategy, which entertains the possibility of carrying out more than one test, there are problems with pre-testing and cumulation of type 1 error. In general the overall type 1 error is greater than the type 1 error of any constituent test, although how much more will be affected by the dependencies among the tests. Recall that type 1 error is the probability of falsely rejecting the null hypothesis, which in this strategy is generally that the time series contains a (single) unit root. So, for example, carrying out two tests, say sequentially $\hat{\tau}_\beta$ then $\hat{\tau}_\mu$, each at the 5% significance level, leads to a cumulated type 1 error, here the total probability of falsely rejecting the unit root, greater than 5%. In this case the cumulated type 1 error will lie between 5% and 10%, and in general the upper limit of the cumulated type 1 error is the sum of the significance levels at each stage, but will be less where the tests are dependent; however, how much less is not generally known. To guard against a cumulated type 1 error that is too large the significance level at each stage can be reduced. However, the power of unit root tests is low when the root is close to,

but not actually, 1 – an alternative that is quite reasonable with many economic time series. Hence, to guard against the testing procedure having inherently low power one possibility is to increase the significance level above conventionally used levels. This consideration offsets the first.

Sections **6.4.1–3** summarised a basic strategy, which can be developed in a number of ways. The *robustness* of the decisions can be assessed with reference to other unit root test statistics. Various simulation studies have indicated that the ADF tests, and their variants, have particular problems where the time series contains a moving average error and that ARIMA($p, 1, 1$) models, with a negative MA coefficient, often provide a good fit to the data – see section **7.2** for a definition of these terms and an elaboration of the problem. In such cases reversing the roles of the null and alternative hypotheses as in the KPSS and LMc tests described in section **7.5**, which have power against ARIMA($p, 1, 1$) alternatives, offers a more sensible approach.

The assumption in this strategy is that the possible nonstationarity in the series occurs through the presence of 1 unit root. However, other forms of nonstationarity may be relevant. The simplest extension is that there are 2 unit roots, that is the series is I(2) and where this is a possibility a testing strategy would need to take this into account. Section **7.6** considers how to test for 2 or more unit roots. Alternatively a series may be I(d) where d is not an integer, the series being nonstationary if $|d| \geq 0.5$; in this case the series is said to be fractionally integrated – see Hosking (1981). This extension is very promising since it offers an alternative to the standard unit root paradigm. Given an estimate and an estimated standard error for d it is possible to set up a confidence interval for d and see whether particular values, for example $d = 1$ or $d = 0$, fall within that interval. On a related approach where d is not fractional see Stock (1991). There are a number of methods to estimate d – see, for example, Geweke and Porter-Hudak (1982), Sowell (1992a, b), Beveridge and

Oickle (1993) and for an application see Patterson and Sowell (1995) – which differ in their degree of parameterisation of the model. The methods are beyond the scope of this book, the interested reader could usefully consult Mills (1993, 1999).

6.5 Concluding remarks

This chapter has introduced some frequently used concepts and techniques in assessing whether a time series is nonstationary. More precisely, in keeping with the statistical nature of the decision-making framework adopted here, we ask whether, given a sample of observations on a time series variable, the hypothesis of (a particular kind of) nonstationarity is consistent with the data. If the series is nonstationary then it can be differenced to stationarity; it is said to be integrated of order d, I(d), with d unit roots, where d is an integer indicating how many differences need to be taken before the series becomes stationary. Other forms of nonstationary time series, which cannot be differenced to stationarity, also arise in economics – see Leybourne, McCabe and Tremayne (1996).

The importance of assessing the dominant characteristics, such as the nonstationarity, of economic time series has been stressed in this chapter, because it is a subject of interest in its own right and it is a precursor to analysing the interrelationships among variables. As to the former much of the recent interest in assessing whether a time series is nonstationary is due to Nelson and Plosser's (1982) seminal study of US macroeconomic time series, which concluded that most of the series studied had a unit root. However, earlier work due to Box and Jenkins (1970) has also been influential; their approach to modelling univariate time series emphasised the importance of taking d differences of a variable integrated of order d, and so using stationary variables in a regression analysis designed, primarily, to provide forecasts. Although a number

of authors after Nelson and Plosser queried their conclusions, there was no doubt that a dominant view was emerging that it was important to assess whether an economic time series was nonstationary.

This view gained impetus with an important study of multiple integrated variables due to Engle and Granger (1987). They extended the univariate framework to consider how time series, which were individually integrated, might move together over time in a way which suggested that they were tied together; such series were said to be cointegrated. This extension was to have a radical influence on the techniques of empirical analysis and the theory of econometrics. It is standard now in applied econometric analysis to consider the time series properties of the data, and very few studies of time series variables are now published which do not consider whether the series are nonstationary. As to the latter whether or not series are nonstationary has significant implications for the properties of OLS estimators in univariate and multivariate regressions. To anticipate one result, which may help to motivate the concepts in this chapter, the R^2, that is coefficient of determination from a regression, which is often used by students (and professionals!) to gauge the goodness of fit, is inherently misleading when the variables in the regression include nonstationary series – see Chapter 8 for more details.

The integration/cointegration methodological approach to the analysis of economic time series is not, though, without its problems and critics. For example, in an AR(1) model the power of unit root tests is low when ϕ_1 is close to, but not actually, 1, for example 0.95, yet the long-run properties will be very different for these parameter values. This problem highlights an inherent difficulty in trying to infer the long-run properties of a series from a finite sample. A difficulty we return to in the next chapter. For the moment note the results from a simulation undertaken by Campbell and Perron (1991): (i) they simulated data from a stationary process which was close to being nonstationary with a near unit root; (ii) then fitted an autoregressive forecasting model alternately in levels and first differences, which would be appropriate for a stationary series and nonstationary series, respectively; (iii) they calculated one and 20 period ahead forecasts from these models; (iv) and evaluated the alternate models in terms of mean squared error of the forecasts. Their findings strongly suggested that the stationary, although nearly integrated, series were better forecast assuming they were integrated.

Treating a series which is nearly integrated as integrated may have other uses. For example, the limiting (as $T \to \infty$) distribution of the OLS estimator of ϕ_1 in the AR(1) model $Y_t = \phi_1 Y_{t-1} + \varepsilon_t$ is normal if $|\phi_1| < 1$ but it is not normal if $\phi_1 = 1$. However, if ϕ_1 is close to 1, the unit root distribution provides a better approximation in finite samples than the normal distribution – see Campbell and Perron (1991) and Evans and Savin (1981, 1984). Also, as we have seen in this chapter, for example in Tables 6.6 and 6.8 where the distributions of $\hat{\tau}_\mu$ and $\hat{\tau}_\beta$ depend upon μ and β, respectively, although the limiting distributions of $\hat{\tau}_\mu$ and $\hat{\tau}_\beta$ are normal the small sample distributions are much better approximated by the unit root distributions.

This chapter has described a widely used class of tests, those due to Dickey and Fuller, to implement a strategy to determine whether a series is nonstationary. In the next chapter we consider complications arising from developments of this basic framework and also illustrate application of the various tests to a number of economic time series.

Review

1. This chapter considers univariate models of economic time series which incorporate a stochastic – or random – component.
2. One of the simplest models of an economic time series is that of an autoregressive (AR) process. The order of an AR process is the length of the longest lag; for example, an AR(p) process is given by

$$Y_t = \mu + \sum_{i=1}^{p} \phi_i Y_{t-i} + \varepsilon_t$$

where ε_t is an innovation relative to the information set comprising lagged values of Y_t.

3. An interesting AR(1) process is the *pure random walk* model given by

$$Y_t = Y_{t-1} + \varepsilon_t$$

where ε_t is a random variable with zero mean, constant variance and zero autocorrelations.

4. A random walk can wander in either a positive or negative direction: once the wandering starts it tends to be sustained. *A priori* we do not know which direction the walk will take.

5. A random walk with drift is a special case of the following AR(1) model

$$Y_t = \mu + \phi_1 Y_{t-1} + \varepsilon_t$$

with $\mu = 0$ and $\phi_1 = 1$. The drift term is μ and the random walk will tend to 'walk' in the direction indicated by the sign of μ.

6. By substitution we can obtain an alternative representation of the random walk with drift. That is

$$Y_t = Y_0 + \mu t + \sum_{i=1}^{t} \varepsilon_i$$

7. An 'innovation', that is a shock to the random component ε_t has an infinite effect as it is incorporated into the cumulative sum, $\sum_{i=1}^{t} \varepsilon_i$.

8. The kth autocorrelation of a time series is denoted $\rho(k)$ and is just the correlation coefficient between Y_t and Y_{t-k}. The autocorrelations of a random walk do not die out as the lag length, k, increases. This is another

aspect of the infinite memory characteristic of a random walk.

9. A stationary time series has: (a) a constant mean; (b) a constant variance; (c) constant autocorrelations, $\rho(k)$, which depend only upon the difference k and not upon their location in time.

10. A random walk, with or without drift, is not a stationary series; it is an example of a *nonstationary* series.

11. A series which is stationary after being differenced once is said to be *integrated of order one*; this is denoted as I(1).

12. A series which is stationary after being differenced d times is said to be integrated of order d, denoted I(d). The order of integration of a series is the minimum number of times the series has to be differenced to become stationary.

13. An autoregressive series which is I(1) has 1 unit root.

14. An autoregressive series which is I(d) has d unit roots.

15. The characteristics of an AR(1) process, $Y_t = \mu + \phi_1 Y_{t-1} + \varepsilon_t$, with $|\phi_1| < 1$, even if ϕ_1 is close to 1, are quite different in the limit from those of a random walk. If $|\phi_1| < 1$ the series is stationary. The effect on Y_t of shocks to ε_t is far less persistent than in the random walk. Even if ϕ_1 is very close to 1 the Y_t process will not wander without limit as can happen in the random walk case.

16. Many economic time series exhibit a distinct trend. Alternative explanations of this pattern are the: trend stationary, TS, model and the difference stationary, DS, model which has a unit root and drift. A trend stationary series is I(0).

17. In order to distinguish between a difference stationary, DS, and a trend stationary, TS, model the maintained regression (in its simplest form) is set up as:

$$\Delta Y_t = \mu + \gamma Y_{t-1} + \beta t + \varepsilon_t$$

where $\gamma = \phi_1 - 1$. The DS model corresponds to $\phi_1 = 1$ ($\Rightarrow \gamma = 0$), with $\mu \neq 0$ for

drift and $\beta = 0$, and the TS model to $-1 < \phi_1 < 1$ ($\Rightarrow -2 < \gamma < 0$) and $\beta \neq 0$.

18. It may be necessary to add p lagged values of ΔY_t in the maintained regression to ensure that the regression residuals are consistent with the assumption that ε_t is not serially correlated These lagged values are said to 'augment' the Dickey–Fuller regression, giving rise to the notation ADF(p).

19. The maintained regressions, test statistics, null and alternative hypotheses introduced in this chapter are:

$$\Delta Y_t = \mu + \gamma Y_{t-1} + \beta t + \varepsilon_t$$
$$\hat{\tau}_\beta, \quad H_0: \gamma = 0, \ H_a: \gamma < 0;$$
$$\Phi_3, \quad H_0: \gamma = 0, \ \beta = 0,$$
$$H_a: \gamma \neq 0 \quad \text{and/or} \quad \beta \neq 0$$

$$\Delta Y_t = \mu + \gamma Y_{t-1} + \varepsilon_t$$
$$\hat{\tau}_\mu, \quad H_0: \gamma = 0, \ H_a: \gamma < 0;$$
$$\Phi_1, \quad H_0: \mu = 0, \ \gamma = 0,$$
$$H_a: \mu \neq 0 \quad \text{and/or} \quad \gamma \neq 0$$

$$\Delta Y_t = \gamma Y_{t-1} + \varepsilon_t$$
$$\hat{\tau}, \quad H_0: \gamma = 0, \ H_a: \gamma < 0$$

20. Where an economic time series has a discernible trend first test the joint null hypothesis $\gamma = 0$ and $\beta = 0$ using Φ_3, with critical values from Table 6.7. Non-rejection of this hypothesis implies that the series is consistent with a difference stationary process without a deterministic trend; it has a unit root.

21. The null hypothesis $\gamma = 0$ and $\beta = 0$ could be rejected because (i) $\gamma \neq 0$ and $\beta = 0$; (ii) $\gamma = 0$ and $\beta \neq 0$; (iii) or $\gamma \neq 0$ and $\beta \neq 0$ if the data is trended the first case is implausible because there is no mechanism to generate the trend; the second case is unlikely because it corresponds to a unit root and deterministic trend which implies a quadratic trend in the DGP; the third, and most likely, case is trend stationarity (assuming $\gamma < 0$).

22. A frequently used test statistic for the null hypothesis $\gamma = 0$ against the alternative $\gamma < 0$ in the maintained regression with a deterministic trend is $\hat{\tau}_\beta$, with critical values obtained from Cheung and Lai's response surface – see Table 6.11.

23. If $\beta \neq 0$ and there is a unit root ($\gamma = 0$) then *asymptotically* the distribution of $\hat{\tau}_\beta$ is standard normal, whereas if $\beta = 0$ the distribution of $\hat{\tau}_\beta$ is given by simulation. This creates uncertainty as to which critical values to use; however, the finding of $\beta \neq 0$ and $\gamma = 0$ is likely to be a rare occurrence. This combination implies a *quadratic* trend, that is a t^2 term, in the process generating Y_t which only seems likely on a localised basis rather than being a long-run property of the data.

24. The next level of tests is appropriate when the data is not obviously trended and the mean under the alternative is nonzero. The maintained regression is $\Delta Y_t = \mu + \gamma Y_{t-1} + \varepsilon_t$, augmented by lags of ΔY_t if necessary, with the null hypothesis $\mu = 0$ and $\gamma = 0$ and test statistic Φ_1. Nonrejection of the joint null ends the sequence.

25. If the joint null is rejected there is a presumption in favour of the alternative of stationarity, even though rejection could formally come from either of $\mu \neq 0$ and $\gamma \neq 0$, or both. More formally use $\hat{\tau}_\mu$ to test the null hypothesis $\gamma = 0$ against the alternative $\gamma < 0$, with critical values from Cheung and Lai's (1995) response surface.

26. What we expect the tests with the maintained regression $\Delta Y_t = \mu + \gamma Y_{t-1} + \varepsilon_t$ to find is that either $\mu = 0$ and $\gamma = 0$ which is the null hypothesis for Φ_1, or $\mu \neq 0$ and $\gamma < 0$. Although $\mu \neq 0$ and $\gamma = 0$ is not formally ruled out we anticipate $\mu \approx 0$ otherwise there will be a noticeable drift and hence a trend in the data, in which case this maintained regression is not the appropriate starting point.

27. If $\mu \neq 0$ and there is a unit root ($\gamma = 0$) then *asymptotically* the distribution of $\hat{\tau}_\mu$ is standard normal, whereas if $\mu = 0$ the distribution of $\hat{\tau}_\mu$ is given by simulation.

28. If $\mu \neq 0$ be careful in the use of $\hat{\tau}_\mu$ because it is likely that the maintained regression $\Delta Y_t = \mu + \gamma Y_{t-1} + \varepsilon_t$ does not nest the different explanations of the data corresponding to the null and alternative hypotheses; a time trend should be included and $\hat{\tau}_\mu$ is then invariant to the value of μ.

29. Using the maintained regression $\Delta Y_t = \mu + \gamma Y_{t-1} + \varepsilon_t$ when the data is trended is likely to (mis)lead to nonrejection of the null as the alternative contains no mechanism to generate the trend.

30. When the data is not obviously trended and the mean under the alternative is zero the maintained regression $\Delta Y_t = \gamma Y_{t-1} + \varepsilon_t$ nests the competing explanations of how the data is generated.

31. There are critics of 'unit root methodology' – see Christiano and Eichenbaum (1990), Cochrane (1991) and Miron (1991). The most frequent criticism is that a process which is difference stationary can be closely approximated in finite samples by another process which is trend stationary, and vice versa.

Review questions

1. Describe some economic models which suggest that time series should have a unit root.

2. What is the connection between a stochastic process with a unit root and the persistence of shocks to the stochastic component?

3. For a pure random walk show that $\text{Var}(Y_t) = t\sigma_\varepsilon^2$ and $E\{Y_t Y_{t+k}\} = t\sigma_\varepsilon^2$; hence, show that the autocorrelation coefficient

$$\rho(k) = E\{Y_t Y_{t+k}\} / [\text{Var}(Y_t)\,\text{Var}(Y_{t+k})]^{0.5}$$
$$= [t/(t+k)]^{0.5}$$

Also show that

$$\rho(-k) = E\{Y_t Y_{t-k}\}/[\text{Var}(Y_t)\,\text{Var}(Y_{t-k})]^{0.5}$$
$$= (1 - k/t)^{0.5}$$

Interpret these autocorrelations.

4. Consider the AR(1) model and explain what is meant by the root of the equation.

5. What is the root of the following AR(1) model?

$$Y_t = 0.1 + 0.9Y_{t-1} + \varepsilon_t$$

6. Is this AR(1) model (with $\phi_1 = 0.9$) stationary or nonstationary?

7. What is the root of the following AR(1) model?

$$Y_t = 0.1 + 1.0Y_{t-1} + \varepsilon_t$$

8. Is this AR(1) model (with $\phi_1 = 1$) stationary or nonstationary?

9. Consider the AR(2) model and explain what is meant by the roots of the equation.

10. What are the roots of the following AR(2) model?

$$Y_t = 0.1 + 1.5Y_{t-1} - 0.5Y_{t-2} + \varepsilon_t$$

11. Is the AR(2) model of question 10 stationary or nonstationary?

12. What are the roots of the following AR(2) model?

$$Y_t = 0.1 + 2Y_{t-1} - Y_{t-2} + \varepsilon_t$$

13. Explain what is meant by random walk models without drift and with drift. What is the effect of drift in a random walk?

14. Show that a random walk model, with or without drift, is a special case of an AR model.

15. Explain how the autocorrelations of a time series are useful in informally assessing whether there is a unit root.

16. Draw a stylised graph of the following nonstationary series: a time series with a nonconstant mean but a constant variance; a time series with a constant mean but a nonconstant variance; a time series with a nonconstant mean and a nonconstant variance.

17. Distinguish between a series which is difference stationary and a series which is trend stationary, and draw a stylised graph to illustrate possible distinguishing features.

18. Are shocks persistent in a trend stationary series?

19. In the context of the maintained model given by

$$\Delta Y_t = \mu + \gamma Y_{t-1} + \beta t + \varepsilon_t$$

explain what is meant by the null hypothesis

$$H_0 : (\mu, \gamma,, \beta) = (\mu, 0, 0)$$

and further explain how you would test this null against the alternative given by

$$H_a : (\mu, \gamma, \beta) = (\mu, \gamma, \beta)$$

20. What are the differences among the test statistics $\hat{\tau}_\beta$, $\hat{\tau}_\mu$ and $\hat{\tau}$ why do we require different sets of critical values for each test statistic?

21. A researcher reports the following test statistics for one unit root in the series Y_t: $\hat{\tau}_\beta = -2.115$, $\hat{\tau}_\mu = 0.043$ and $\hat{\tau} = 4.469$.
   (i) What do you conlcude about the process generating Y_t?
   (ii) What other information would you like to inform your judgement about the process generating Y_t?

22. Consider the AR(4) model

$$Y_t = \mu + \phi_1 Y_{t-1} + \phi_2 Y_{t-2} + \phi_3 Y_{t-3}$$
$$+ \phi_4 Y_{t-4} + \varepsilon_t$$

rearranged as an ADF(3) model,

$$\Delta Y_t = \mu + \gamma Y_{t-1} + \alpha_1 \Delta Y_{t-1} + \alpha_2 \Delta Y_{t-2}$$
$$+ \alpha_3 \Delta Y_{t-3} + \varepsilon_t$$

Show that $\gamma = \phi_1 + \phi_2 + \phi_3 + \phi_4 - 1$, $\alpha_1 = -(\phi_2 + \phi_3 + \phi_4)$, $\alpha_2 = -(\phi_3 + \phi_4)$ and $\alpha_3 = -\phi_4$.

23. Discuss the following statement by Miron (1991, p. 211): 'The starting point for my perspective on unit roots is the observation that we will never know whether the data are difference stationary or trend stationary.'

CHAPTER 7

Developments of nonstationary univariate time series models

7.1 Introduction

In this chapter we consider a number of extensions and developments of the concepts and techniques introduced in the previous chapter. The first extension, in section **7.2**, is to autoregressive integrated moving average, ARIMA, time series models. In the previous chapter the dynamics just came through an autoregression on Y_t, now we recognise that dynamics may also come through the stochastic component ε_t.

In practical applications of unit root tests often a number of prior decisions have to be made before the test of substantive interest is applied; for example, using a unit root test statistic from an ADF(p) regression requires prior specification of the order of the ADF model for which several strategies, such as choosing the lag length by an information criterion or a general-to-specific search strategy, are available. The power of various unit root testing procedures when there is a pre-test for the lag length is considered in section **7.3**.

While the previous chapter concentrated on introducing some of the most frequently used test statistics for a unit root, there are a number of other important tests available, and several of these are considered in section **7.4**. In particular mention should be made of the class of tests due to Phillips and his co-workers – see, for example, Phillips (1987) and Phillips and Perron (1988). The Phillips–Perron (PP) tests differ from the Dickey–Fuller tests in the way that

they account for residual serial correlation in the basic DF regression (that is, the unaugmented regression); the DF procedure is to augment the basic maintained regression model with additional lags of the dependent variable. In the PP tests a correction, which depends upon the auto-covariances of the residuals, is made to the DF test statistics from the unaugmented regression. Another test statistic described in section **7.4**, which may have greater power in situations of practical interest, is based on the weighted symmetric estimator – see Pantula, Gonzalez-Farias and Fuller (1994).

Section **7.5** considers the distinction between structural and reduced form univariate time series models. This distinction is of interest in its own right but also has the advantage of allowing the formulation of the null hypothesis, rather than the alternative, that the series is stationary; hence, the alternative hypothesis is that the series is nonstationary. This reverses the roles of the null and alternative hypotheses compared to the DF and PP tests. In this context the tests, due to Kwiatkowski, Phillips, Schmidt and Shin (1992), usually referred to as KPSS, and Leybourne and McCabe (1994), look for evidence to reject stationary in the direction of nonstationarity.

The tests described in the previous chapter and section **7.4** are framed in the context of assessing whether the nonstationarity of a series, say Y_t, is of the form that can be removed by differencing once. If so the series is said to be integrated of order one, or I(1) in a common notation, and it has one unit root – see sections **6.2.3** and **6.2.4** for definitions of these terms. However, a practical complication for some series is that they may be integrated of a higher order than one; for example, if Y_t is I(2) then the first difference, ΔY_t, is still nonstationary but the second difference, $\Delta \Delta Y_t$, is stationary, and Y_t therefore has two unit roots. Section **7.6** considers an extension of the DF tests to processes that may have two or more unit roots; the extension to other test statistics follows in a straightforward way from this development.

Quite often economists work with seasonally adjusted data implying that the original data had a distinct seasonal pattern which has been removed in a transformation of the original series. Dickey, Hasza and Fuller (1984) suggested how some of the DF test statistics could be applied directly to the (untransformed) seasonal time series. Hylleberg, Engle, Granger and Yoo (1990), usually referred to as HEGY, extended this work, and their approach is described in section **7.7**.

A potentially critical issue in testing for unit roots relates to whether a finding of nonstationarity is spurious because the testing framework has failed to take account of possible structural breaks in the underlying process. Such an argument forms the basis of the Perron (1989, 1997) critique of Nelson and Plosser's (1982) assessment that most of the macroeconomic time series they consider have a unit root. The Perron framework is considered in section **7.8** together with the related idea of outliers.

Application of some of the tests to a number of economic time series is reported in section **7.9**, where the opportunity is taken to bring together some of the problems which have been highlighted in the previous chapter and the earlier sections of this chapter.

The sharp distinction between an integrated process and a stationary process is relaxed in section **7.10**. For some purposes a stationary but 'nearly' integrated process may be better treated as integrated, and an integrated but 'nearly' stationary process may be better treated as

stationary. This aspect is particularly important because finite sample distributions of, for example, the 't' statistic on $\hat{\phi}_1$ in the maintained regression $Y_t = \mu + \phi_1 Y_{t-1} + \varepsilon_t$, do not have the sharp discontinuity at $\phi_1 = 1$ which is present in the asymptotic distribution. Finally, section **7.11** contains some concluding remarks.

7.2 ARIMA models

The models of the DGP have so far assumed that the dynamics arise purely from an autoregressive structure on Y_t. An alternative and popular class of models also includes a moving average component, specifically

$$\phi(L)Y_t = \mu + \theta(L)\varepsilon_t \tag{7.1}$$

where $\phi(L) = 1 - \sum_{i=1}^{p} \phi_i L^i$, $\theta(L) = 1 + \sum_{j=1}^{q} \theta_j L^j$ and ε_t is white noise. This is known as an autoregressive moving average model of orders p and q, or more simply an ARMA(p, q) model. For example, a simple MA(1) model is

$$Y_t = \mu + (1 + \theta_1 L)\varepsilon_t \tag{7.2}$$

This has an alternative representation as an AR(∞) model provided $|\theta_1| < 1$, in which case the MA model is said to be invertible. Multiplying through by the inverse of $(1 + \theta_1 L)^{-1} = 1 - \theta_1 L - \theta_1^2 L^2 - \theta_1^3 L^3 - \cdots - \theta_1^s L^s - , \ldots$, gives

$$(1 - \theta_1 L - \theta_1^2 L^2 - \cdots - \theta_1^s L^s - \cdots)Y_t$$
$$= \mu^* + \varepsilon_t \tag{7.3}$$

so that

$$Y_t = \mu^* + (\theta_1 L + \theta_1^2 L^2 + \cdots$$
$$+ \theta_1^s L^s + \cdots)Y_t + \varepsilon_t$$
$$= \mu^* + \sum_{j=1}^{\infty} \theta_j L^j Y_t + \varepsilon_t \tag{7.4}$$

where $\mu^* = (1 + \theta_1 L)^{-1}\mu$. The coefficients in the infinite autoregression, θ_1^s, decline monotonically in absolute value given $|\theta_1| < 1$ and, therefore, an AR(p) model, with p finite so the infinite lag in the autoregression is truncated, may be a reasonable approximation to the original MA model. More generally, the inversion of an ARMA(p, q)) model to an ARMA($\infty, 0$) requires that the roots of $\theta(L)$ must have modulus greater than 1. In the simple case considered here there is just one root, equal to $1/\theta_1$.

If $\phi(L)$ contains a unit root then it can be factored into $\phi(L) = \phi^*(L)(1 - L)$, and the ARMA($p, q$) model $\phi(L)Y_t = \mu + \theta(L)\varepsilon_t$ can be rewritten as $\phi^*(L)(1 - L)Y_t = \mu + \theta(L)\varepsilon_t$. In this case Y_t is integrated of order 1, and the model is referred to as an ARIMA(p, d, q) model, with $d = 1$ in this case. The inversion into a pure AR($\infty, 1, 0$) model is still possible provided the roots of $\theta(L)$ have modulus greater than 1.

On this basis an ADF(p) model with $p > 0$, which only has autoregressive dynamics, may arise as an approximation to moving average dynamics in ε_t, although care has to be taken in the use of ADF(p) models in such cases. Said and Dickey (1985) show that an unknown ARIMA($p, 0, q$) process can be adequately approximated by an ARIMA($l, 0, 0$) process provided l increases with the sample size, such that $l/T^{\frac{1}{3}} \to 0$ and there exists a $C > 0$ and $r > 0$ such that $l > C(T^{\frac{1}{r}})$. The first part of this 'rule' provides the rate of increase of l with the sample size and the second part the lower bound to l. This rule does not provide a value of l for a given T, which is the typical situation with a single sample, what it says is that l should not remain fixed as the sample size increases but should increase at a rate such that $(l/T^{\frac{1}{3}}) \to 0$. The rule is, therefore, relevant in Monte Carlo simulations that investigate the effect of changing the sample size on the AR approximation or establishing the asymptotic properties of estimators or test statistics. Of particular relevance, Said and Dickey (1984) show that provided l increases at an appropriate rate then the limiting distributions, and so critical values, of $\hat{\tau}$, $\hat{\tau}_\mu$, and (by extension) $\hat{\tau}_\beta$, are the same as in the standard case. They also show that normality of ε_t is not necessary for this result, which holds if the ε_t are independently and identically distributed (iid).

Although the results of Said and Dickey (*op. cit.*) are useful, two problems arise in finite samples. First, in a given finite sample, judgement, aided by diagnostic tests, still has to be used to determine an appropriate lag length for the test statistic. One possibility is to select l by an information criterion subject to no serial correlation in the residuals; another is to select l by a general-to-specific search strategy – see sections **6.3.6** and **7.3**. Schwert (1987) used two alternative fixed rules, l_4 and l_{12}, to select l in his simulation study (reported below), which suggested that a longer lag was preferable. Application of these rules, subject to no serial correlation in the residuals, could also provide guidance on choosing l. Second, as Schwert (*op. cit.*) shows, in finite samples the limiting distribution (that is, Dickey–Fuller) critical values may not be a good guide to the true critical values.

Schwert (*op. cit.*) argues that many economic time series are not pure AR processes and it is important not only to model them as ARIMA processes but also to consider what happens if an AR approximation is used. Schwert (*op. cit.*) reports some simulations in which the DGP is a parameterisation of an ARIMA(0, 1, 1), which thus has a unit root and a single MA coefficient. He computes 5% critical values for $\hat{\tau}_\mu$ and $\hat{\tau}_\beta$ where a pure AR approximation is used with the number of lags determined according to either:

$$l_4 = \mathrm{Int}[(4/100^{\frac{1}{4}})T^{\frac{1}{4}}] \quad \text{or}$$
$$l_{12} = \mathrm{Int}[(12/100^{\frac{1}{4}})T^{\frac{1}{4}}]$$

where Int[.] refers to the integer part of the expression in square brackets. When $T = 140$, $l_4 = 4$ and $l_{12} = 13$ and when $T = 444$, $l_4 = 5$ and $l_{12} = 17$, so on either rule the truncation lag increases with the sample size, and l_{12} gives a longer lag. To check whether these choices converge to 0 at the rate required by the Said and Dickey rule, divide each by $T^{\frac{1}{3}}$, so that apart from a constant the relevant term in both cases is $T^{\frac{1}{4}}/T^{\frac{1}{3}}$ which tends to 0 as $T \to \infty$. The rule for choosing l must have a lower bound, since making l increase at any rate less than $T^{\frac{1}{3}}$ will give the required convergence. As noted above the lower bound is provided by the condition that $l > C(T^{\frac{1}{r}})$, Said and Dickey (*op. cit.*, p. 600), where C and r are positive constants, which says that l is bounded from below by a positive multiple of $T^{\frac{1}{r}}$ for some $r > 0$; that is obviously satisfied here for $0 \le r < 4$ and $C = 4/100^{\frac{1}{4}}$ for l_4, and $C = 12/100^{\frac{1}{4}}$ for l_{12}. Some simulation results for $T = 140$ are reported in Table 7.1.

Note from the first part of Table 7.1 that the critical values calculated from Cheung and Lai's (C–L) response surface coefficients, which correspond to $\theta_1 = 0$ and take into account the number of lags in an ADF model, are very close to Schwert's simulated values. However, the real merit in the first part of Table 7.1 is in illustrating how the critical values vary for different values of θ_1, with the situation of interest being when $\theta_1 \neq 0$ but the critical values for $\theta_1 = 0$ are used

in an autoregressive approximation. The distortion is greatest when θ_1 is -0.8 and the lag is truncated using the l_4 rule. When $\theta_1 > -0.5$ and l_{12} is used there is relatively little variation in the critical values, and hence using the critical values for $\theta_1 = 0$ remains reasonably accurate. That the l_{12} rule gives a better approximation than using l_4 is perhaps not surprising, especially for large values of θ_1; for example, if $\theta_1 = 0.8$ the theoretical value of the last coefficient in the approximating autoregression is $0.8^4 = 0.4096 \neq 0$ for l_4 and $0.8^{12} = 0.069$ for l_{12}. The simulation results are least comforting where there seems the greatest chance that typical values of θ_1 are found. Schwert (*op. cit.*) finds that a typical ARIMA(0, 1, 1) model for 17 macroeconomic time series has a large negative MA coefficient, so use of a long lag is imperative to minimise distortion problems if critical values for $\theta_1 = 0$ are used.

Table 7.1 *5% critical values when the DGP is ARIMA(0, 1, 1) and empirical power*

| | 5% critical values for $\hat{\tau}_\mu \hat{\tau}_\beta$ | | | | | |
| | $\hat{\tau}_\mu$ $T = 140$ | | | $\hat{\tau}_\beta$ $T = 140$ | | |
θ_1	ARIMA(1, 0, 1)	AR(l_4)	AR(l_{12})	ARIMA(1, 0, 1)	AR(l_4)	AR(l_{12})
-0.8	-2.98	-4.38	-2.92	-3.19	-5.09	-3.49
-0.5	-2.78	-3.02	-2.82	-2.66	-3.61	-3.36
0	-2.83	-2.87	-2.82	-3.12	-3.41	-3.36
0 C–L[a]		-2.88	-2.82		-3.42	-3.36
0.5	-2.87	-2.93	-2.85	-3.30	-3.30	-3.36
0.8	-3.03	-3.02	-2.87	-3.43	-3.61	-3.38

Empirical power when the true model is ARIMA(1, 0, 1) for different values of ϕ_1 and θ_1

| | $\phi_1 = 0.80$ | | $\phi_1 = 0.90$ | | $\phi_1 = 0.95$ | | $\phi_1 = 1.00$ | |
| $T = 99$ | | | | | | | | |
θ_1	$\hat{\tau}$	$\hat{\tau}_\mu$	$\hat{\tau}$	$\hat{\tau}_\mu$	$\hat{\tau}$	$\hat{\tau}_\mu$	$\hat{\tau}$	$\hat{\tau}_\mu$
-0.8	0.88	0.71	0.75	0.46	0.46	0.27	0.10	0.11
-0.5	0.92	0.63	0.63	0.28	0.31	0.12	0.05	0.05
0.5	1.00	0.83	0.73	0.30	0.30	0.11	0.05	0.05

Notes: (a) C–L refers to the 5% critical value calculated from Cheung and Lai's response surface – see Table 6.11. Source of critical values in the first part of the table: from Schwert (1987, Table 7); note that Schwert (*op. cit.*, p. 75) defines the MA polynomial as $\theta(L) = 1 - \sum_{j=1}^{q} \theta_j L^j$ so, for example, 0.5 in his table is -0.5 here. Empirical power calculations are from Said and Dickey (1985, Table 3).

The second part of Table 7.1 reports some illustrative empirical power calculations for $\hat{\tau}$ and $\hat{\tau}_\mu$ extracted from Said and Dickey (1985). The DGP is ARIMA(1, 0, 1), that is $Y_t = \phi_1 Y_{t-1} + \varepsilon_t + \theta_1 \varepsilon_{t-1}$ with $\phi_1 = 0.80, 0.90, 0.95, 1.00$ and $\theta_1 = 0.5, -0.5, -0.8$. (Said and Dickey (op. cit.) also calculated the power for $\theta_1 = 0.8$ but, as this was virtually the same as for $\theta_1 = 0.5$, it is not reported in their study.) The critical values used by Said and Dickey (op. cit.), from the distributions of $\hat{\tau}$ and $\hat{\tau}_\mu$, are -1.95 and -2.89, respectively – see, for example, Fuller (1976, Table 8.5.2). Given that these critical values are from an ARIMA(0, 1, 0) model, one issue is how well the actual size of the tests relates to the nominal size, here 5%. To assess this consider the column for $\phi_1 = 1.0$ so that the DGP is ARIMA(0, 1, 1), then the empirical size equals the nominal size for $\theta_1 = 0.5$ and -0.5, but is virtually double the nominal size for $\theta_1 = -0.8$. This finding can be explained from Schwert's results in the first part of Table 7.1. Consider using $\hat{\tau}_\mu$ then the finite sample 5% critical value for an ARIMA(1, 0, 1) model is greater negative, at about -2.98, than the corresponding critical value of $\hat{\tau}_\mu$ of -2.89; using the latter will lead to more rejections of the null and hence the actual size will exceed the nominal size. However, for $\theta_1 = 0.5$, and to a lesser extent for $\theta_1 = -0.5$, the finite sample critical values for the ARIMA(0, 1, 1) and ARIMA(1, 1, 0) models are closer and so the actual and nominal sizes are similar. The oversizing of the tests for $\theta_1 = -0.8$ means that, in this case, the power is not as great as suggested in the table.

Using $\hat{\tau}$ for $\theta_1 = -0.5$ there are 92% rejections of the null when $\phi_1 = 0.8$, 63% rejections when $\phi_1 = 0.90$, and 31% rejections when $\phi_1 = 0.95$. Using $\hat{\tau}_\mu$ for $\theta_1 = -0.5$, there are 63% rejections when $\phi_1 = 0.8$, 28% rejections when $\phi_1 = 0.90$, and 12% rejections when $\phi_1 = 0.95$. Note that the power, generally, improves further when $\theta_1 = 0.5$. The starting value, Y_0, in the simulations is 0 so $\hat{\tau}$, which is specifically designed for this set-up, is more powerful than $\hat{\tau}_\mu$. The power for $1.0 > \theta_1 \geq -0.5$ is comparable with the

standard Dickey–Fuller case – see Table 6.9. Problems that arise, for example in the case of $\theta_1 = -0.8$, are associated with 'near cancellation' of the AR and MA coefficients. The ARIMA model is $(1 - \phi_1 L)Y_t = (1 + \theta_1 L)\varepsilon_t$, so if θ_1 is close to $-\phi_1$ there will be near cancellation of $\phi(L) = (1 - \phi_1 L)$ and $\theta(L) = (1 + \theta_1 L)$; in the example here $(1 - L)$ and $(1 - 0.8L)$, respectively, and then the model will look like $Y_t \approx \varepsilon_t$, which is stationary, and the tests find it difficult to distinguish stationarity from nonstationarity.

An alternative response to the possibility of moving average errors is due to Phillips (1987) and Phillips and Perron (1988), who have suggested a class of Dickey–Fuller type tests which allow the dynamics to arise from either or both autoregressive or moving average components. These tests are described in greater detail in section **7.4**. In this alternative approach the standard Dickey–Fuller test statistics from unaugmented regressions are adjusted by a factor which depends upon l sample autocorrelations of the regression residuals, where l is again a choice parameter. Schwert's (op. cit.) simulations show that, especially for large negative values of θ_1, the standard Dickey–Fuller critical values, which assume $\theta_1 = 0$, are not a good guide to the correct critical values. They are generally not as good as in the Said and Dickey approach, which truncates the infinite autoregressive approximation to the moving average model. This is a problem that is present even if the lag length is chosen by l_{12} rather than by l_4.

7.3 Pre-testing, power and model selection strategies using ADF test statistics

Hall (1994) points out that a typical strategy implementing the ADF procedure involves what is known as a pre-test estimator. For example, as suggested in section **6.3.6** suppose the lag order is chosen by an information criterion or a general-to-specific model choice criterion (for example, by a 't' or F test sequentially from p^* to the chosen order), then this is a pre-test before implementing the test of direct interest, that is the ADF test in one of its 't' statistic variants, $\hat{\tau}$, $\hat{\tau}_\mu$, $\hat{\tau}_\beta$. It is known that the use of a pre-test can bias an otherwise unbiased estimator or procedure – see Judge and Bock (1978). What we are interested in is whether the distribution of the test statistic when the true order, say p_0, of the $ADF(p) \equiv AR(p+1)$ regression is known is the same as when this order is estimated by some criterion. Hall (*op. cit.*) shows that the following two conditions are sufficient for this result to hold. First, the probability that the chosen order is less than the true order should be zero. Second, that the outcome of the model selection procedure and the unit root test should be unrelated (under the null hypothesis). Fortunately Hall's results show that the limiting distribution of the ADF $\hat{\tau}$ statistics is the same if a pre-test based on AIC, SIC or HQIC is used to choose p as when p_0 is used; this is also the case if a pre-test based on a general-to-specific search strategy is used. Interestingly, if a specific-to-general strategy is used, that is working outwards from a low to high lag order, then the resulting ADF $\hat{\tau}$ statistic variants do not, in general, have the same limiting distribution as the ADF model with the true order, p_0. Intuitively this occurs because there is a nonzero probability of underfitting, that is choosing a lag order less than the true lag order.

Another consideration in choosing a test procedure is how powerful it is in correctly inferring in favour of the alternative *when the alternative is true*. Given two test statistics, or strategies distinguished by differences in pretesting procedure, to choose between, which are used at the same significance level, we would prefer to use the more powerful one. A number of authors have pointed out that unit root tests are generally not very powerful when the true alternative is close to the unit root – see section **6.3.4** and Table 6.9. In a sense this is not a problem unique to unit root tests. The power of a standard 't' test of say β_i, a regression coefficient, equal to zero will not be high when the alternative is that the true β_i is close to zero. However, the 'sharpness' of the unit root null in terms of the implied persistence of shocks (infinite if there is a unit root, finite for a stable model) and the implications for the properties of the OLS estimators of the regression coefficients and their 't' statistics (see Chapter 8) highlight the importance of rejecting the null if it is incorrect. Further, the difficulty of making the right decision is compounded by the possibility that a stationary series with a deterministic trend but no unit root can look very like a unit root with drift model – this is something we saw in Figure 6.11.

Hall (*op. cit.*) provides a useful set of simulations that gives an idea of the power of the ADF test. In particular Hall combines the use of several pre-testing procedures with an evaluation of the actual size of the test, compared to its nominal size, and power for some near unit root alternatives. Hall used 10 model variants to generate the data and two sample sizes in his results. We choose two of these variants to illustrate the general results. These are:

(i) an $ADF(1) \equiv AR(2)$ model,

$$y_t = (\rho + 0.65)y_{t-1} - 0.65\rho y_{t-2} + \varepsilon_t$$

with $\rho = 1.00$ (unit root), 0.95, 0.90; the lag polynomial factors into $(1 - 0.65L)(1 - \rho L)$. This model can alternatively be written as an ADF(1) model:

$$\Delta y_t = 0.35(\rho - 1)y_{t-1} + 0.65\rho\Delta y_{t-1} + \varepsilon_t$$

so that if there is a unit root, the first term on the right-hand side disappears.

(ii) an $ADF(4) \equiv AR(5)$ model,

$$y_t = \rho y_{t-1} + 0.4y_{t-4} - 0.4\rho y_{t-5} + \varepsilon_t$$

with $\rho = 1.00$ (unit root), 0.95, 0.90; the lag polynomial factors into $(1 - 0.4L^4)(1 - \rho L)$.

This model can alternatively be written as an ADF(4) model:

$$\Delta y_t = 0.6(\rho - 1)y_{t-1} + 0.4(\rho - 1)\Delta y_{t-1}$$
$$+ 0.4(\rho - 1)\Delta y_{t-2}$$
$$+ 0.4(\rho - 1)\Delta y_{t-3}$$
$$+ 0.4\rho\Delta y_{t-4} + \varepsilon_t$$

The size and power are reported for five order selection strategies in Table 7.2. First, p is fixed at 4 whatever the model order. Alternatively, to mimic what happens in practice, AIC and SIC are used to select the model order, indicated by $\hat{p}$(AIC) and $\hat{p}$(SIC), respectively; as further alternatives the model order is selected by a general-to-specific strategy, $\hat{p}$(GS), or a specific-to-general strategy, $\hat{p}$(SG), using a χ^2 test on the marginal coefficients. The critical values used by Hall are for $\hat{\tau}$ from Fuller (op. cit., Table 8.5.2); the 5% critical value is -1.95 irrespective of the sample size.

We first consider the size of the various testing strategies. Fixing $p = 4$ is only right when the model is ADF(4). In this case for $T = 100$ the empirical size, that is the proportion of false rejections of the null in the simulations, at 6.2%

is greater than the nominal size of 5% and the test is said to be 'oversized'. This is improved for $T = 250$ where the empirical size at 4.8% is close to the nominal size of 5%. When $p = 4$ is the wrong model, the right model being ADF(1), the empirical size is 6.6% for $T = 100$ and 7.4% for $T = 250$.

Generally, when the order is estimated by AIC, SIC or GS, the empirical size is greater than the nominal size and this is more pronounced for the smaller sample size; for example, with an ADF(1) model $\hat{p}$(AIC) has an empirical size of 9.3% for $T = 100$ and 7.1% for $T = 250$. Using SG the test is undersized when the true model is ADF(4). As to size, fixing $p = 4$ does not generally do markedly worse than a strategy which estimates the lag order.

We now consider the power of the various strategies. In this case $\rho = 0.95$ or 0.90 and interest centres on the proportion of rejections of the null hypothesis since now the null is false. With the ADF(1) model fixing p at 4 with $\rho = 0.95$ gives 14.9% rejections for $T = 100$ and 36.7% for $T = 250$; choosing the lag order by AIC these figures are 19% and 40.5%. Moving further away from the unit root with $\rho = 0.90$, fixing p at 4

Table 7.2 Size and power of the ADF test, $\hat{\tau}$, with a pre-test: simulation results, Hall (1994)

	ρ	$p = 4$	$\hat{p}$(AIC)	$\hat{p}$(SIC)	$\hat{p}$(GS)	$\hat{p}$(SG)
$T = 100$						
ADF(1)	1.00	0.066	0.093	0.081	0.116	0.065
	0.95	0.149	0.190	0.138	0.198	0.136
	0.90	0.221	0.290	0.246	0.306	0.243
ADF(4)	1.00	0.062	0.080	0.056	0.087	0.038
	0.95	0.123	0.164	0.104	0.172	0.050
	0.90	0.210	0.238	0.181	0.235	0.125
$T = 250$						
ADF(1)	1.00	0.074	0.071	0.062	0.074	0.061
	0.95	0.367	0.405	0.382	0.389	0.388
	0.90	0.744	0.825	0.844	0.765	0.840
ADF(4)	1.00	0.048	0.054	0.050	0.059	0.023
	0.95	0.327	0.334	0.327	0.334	0.091
	0.90	0.727	0.704	0.719	0.674	0.447

Notes: Source, extracted from Hall (1994, Tables 1 and 2); GS is the general-to-specific strategy and SG the specific-to-general strategy.

gives 22.1% rejections for $T = 100$ and 74.4% for $T = 250$; choosing the lag length by AIC these figures are 29% and 82.5%. For $T = 100$ the best strategy in this case is general to specific, but this is not an advantage carried across to the larger sample size where the rejection proportions are similar for all strategies involving a choice. Generally, and here reference is being made to the full set of model variants reported by Hall (*op. cit.*), choosing the lag order by a pre-test improves the power of the test relative to a preset choice unless by chance the preset value is right. So while size is similar whether p is preset or strategically chosen, there are some improvements in power in making a strategic choice.

None of the pre-test criteria is uniformly superior. Even the specific-to-general strategy, which is not usually advocated as a good principle, stands relatively well with the other criteria. Obviously the further ρ is away from 1 the more likely is rejection of the null, and all criteria find it difficult to distinguish between $\rho = 1$ and $\rho = 0.95$. This is improved greatly with an increase in the sample size from 100 to 250; for $\rho = 0.90$ and an ADF(1) model, the rejection frequency is 82.5% for $\hat{p}(\text{AIC})$.

However, to an extent the tests are not as powerful as the proportions in Table 7.2 suggest because of their oversizing. One way to improve the power of a test is to increase the significance level which, *ceteris paribus*, leads to more rejections of the null hypothesis (but at the cost of more false rejections of the null hypothesis); hence, if the empirical size is larger than the nominal size the test will lead to more rejections than the same test with the empirical size equal to the nominal size. Again this suggests caution in applying unit root tests without reference to other criteria, even if these latter are just visual aids including a graph of the autocorrelations.

7.4 Other tests

There are a large number of tests designed to detect one or more unit roots. The choice of $\hat{\tau}$, $\hat{\tau}_\mu$ and $\hat{\tau}_\beta$ in sections **6.3.1–6.3.3** was influenced by the fact these are usually programmed in commercially available econometric software, and Φ_1 and Φ_3 are easily calculated. Some other test statistics are described in this section.

7.4.1 Dickey and Fuller's $\hat{\rho}$, $\hat{\rho}_\mu$ and $\hat{\rho}_\beta$

Another statistic due to Dickey and Fuller arises from consideration first of the simplest AR(1) model

$$Y_t = \phi_1 Y_{t-1} + \varepsilon_t \quad t = 1, \ldots, T \quad (7.5)$$

that is

$$(1 - \phi_1 L)Y_t = \varepsilon_t$$

with root equal to $1/\phi_1$, and the unit root case is $\phi_1 = 1$. Fuller (1976, pp. 366 *et seq.*) notes that $(\hat{\phi}_1 - 1)$ is of order $1/T$ in probability when $\phi_1 = 1$ and $\hat{\phi}_1$ is the OLS estimator of ϕ_1 based on $T - 1$ observations; hence, $T(\hat{\phi}_1 - 1)$ should have a distribution, when $\phi_1 = 1$, which shows little variation with the overall sample size, T, and can be used to test the null hypothesis that $\phi_1 = 1$ against the stationary one-sided alternative $0 \leq \phi_1 < 1$. Fuller (*op. cit.*, Table 8.5.1) provides a table of critical values which is used in the same way as the tables for the three $\hat{\tau}$ statistics. The critical values depend upon whether the regression model (but not the DGP which is a pure random walk in the Dickey–Fuller set-up) has: no intercept; an intercept; an intercept and a time trend. These give rise to the three test statistics denoted $\hat{\rho}$, $\hat{\rho}_\mu$ and $\hat{\rho}_\beta$ (in Fuller's (1976) notation the latter is $\hat{\rho}_\tau$). Table A7.1 in the appendix to this chapter reproduces Fuller's Table 8.5.1 of small sample critical values for these statistics.

To illustrate, suppose in an overall sample of 100 observations the OLS estimator of ϕ_1, in a regression model with an intercept, is 0.95, then $\hat{\rho}_\mu = 100(0.95 - 1) = -5.0$ whereas the 5% critical value is -13.7 and the 10% critical value is -11.0; hence, the null of a unit root is not rejected. The variation in the critical values due to sample size is slight; for example, the 5% critical values of $\hat{\rho}_\mu$ are -12.5 for $T = 25$ and -14.1 for $T = 500$. Also if the null is $\phi_1 = -1$, for which the alternative is more reasonably $0 \leq \phi_1 < -1$, Fuller's Table 8.5.1 can also be used, as the distribution for $\phi_1 = -1$ is the mirror image of the distribution for $\phi_1 = 1$.

More generally we consider the procedure if the starting point is an AR$(p+1)$ model with $p > 0$, that is

$$Y_t = \mu + \phi_1 Y_{t-1} + \cdots + \phi_p Y_{t-(p+1)} + \varepsilon_t$$
$$t = 1, \ldots, T \qquad (7.6)$$

say $\phi(L)Y_t = \varepsilon_t$ where $\phi(L) = 1 - \sum_{j=1}^{p+1} \phi_j L^j$.

Suppose we factor $\phi(L) = \theta(L)(1 - \rho L)$, where ρ is the largest root and $\theta(L) = 1 - \sum_{i=1}^{p} \theta_i L^i$ is a polynomial of order p; and note that

$$\phi(1) = \theta(1)(1 - \rho) \qquad (7.7)$$

The AR$(p+1)$ model can be rearranged, as in the development of (6.48), to the form

$$\Delta Y_t = \mu + \gamma Y_{t-1}$$
$$+ \sum_{j=1}^{p} \alpha_j (Y_{t-j} - Y_{t-(j+1)}) + \varepsilon_t$$
$$t = 1, \ldots, T \qquad (7.8)$$

where $\gamma = \sum_{j=1}^{p+1} \phi_j - 1$ and $\alpha_j = -\sum_{k=j+1}^{p+1} \phi_k$ for $j = 1, \ldots, p$. Note that

$$\gamma = -\phi(1) = -\theta(1)(1 - \rho)$$
$$= \theta(1)(\rho - 1) \qquad (7.9)$$

The coefficient on Y_{t-1} is now the product of $\theta(1)$ and $(\rho - 1)$, and will be zero under the null hypothesis. If consistent estimators of γ and $\theta(1)$, say $\tilde{\gamma}$ and $\tilde{\theta}(1)$, are available then $\tilde{\gamma}/\tilde{\theta}(1) = (\tilde{\rho} - 1)$; $T(\tilde{\rho} - 1)$ is approximately distributed as $\hat{\rho}_\mu$ – see Dickey, Bell and Miller (1986) – and so approximate critical values can be obtained from Table 8.5.1 of Fuller (*op. cit.*). A similar procedure

can be followed if there is no constant in the regression or a constant and a deterministic time trend.

The OLS estimator of γ in (7.8) is consistent. To illustrate how to obtain a consistent estimator of $\theta(1)$ consider the AR(3) model of (6.48)

$$Y_t = \mu + \phi_1 Y_{t-1} + \phi_2 Y_{t-2}$$
$$+ \phi_3 Y_{t-3} + \varepsilon_t \qquad (6.48) \text{ again}$$

rearranged as

$$\Delta Y_{t-1} = \mu + \gamma Y_{t-1} + \alpha_1 \Delta Y_{t-1}$$
$$+ \alpha_2 \Delta Y_{t-2} + \varepsilon_t \qquad (6.50) \text{ again}$$

with $\gamma = \phi_1 + \phi_2 + \phi_3 - 1$, $\alpha_1 = -(\phi_2 + \phi_3)$ and $\alpha_2 = -\phi_3$.

Note from expanding both sides of $\phi(L) = \theta(L)(1 - \rho L)$ and equating coefficients on like powers of L that the following relationships hold:

$$\phi_1 = \theta_1 + \rho, \quad \phi_2 = \theta_2 - \theta_1\rho, \quad \phi_3 = -\theta_2\rho$$

so $\alpha_1 = -[\theta_2(1 - \rho) - \theta_1\rho]$, $\alpha_2 = \theta_2\rho$ and hence $\gamma = (1 - \theta_1 - \theta_2)(\rho - 1)$. With estimates of α_1, α_2 and γ from (6.50) there are three (nonlinear) equations which could be solved for the three unknowns θ_1, θ_2 and ρ; or (6.50) could be estimated by least squares with the nonlinear constraints imposed. Dickey, Bell and Miller (*op. cit.*) note that all that is required is a consistent estimator of $\theta(1) = (1 - \theta_1 - \theta_2)$ under the null $\rho = 1$; but notice that when this is the case $\alpha_1 = \theta_1$ and $\alpha_2 = \theta_2$, so summing the coefficients on the lags ΔY_{t-j} for $j = 1, \ldots, p$, which are consistently estimated in the ADF regression (6.50), provides $\tilde{\theta}(1)$, which can then be divided into $\tilde{\gamma}$ to obtain $(\tilde{\rho} - 1)$, and $T(\tilde{\rho} - 1)$ is asymptotically distributed as $\hat{\rho}_\mu$. While the Dickey, Bell and Miller (*op. cit.*) procedure provides an operational test statistic it seems likely that a more powerful procedure would follow from not assuming $\rho = 1$ in obtaining $\theta(1)$.

The following is an example from Dickey, Bell and Miller (*op. cit.*). Fitting an ADF(1) model to the time series of US iron and steel exports, 1937 to 1980, resulted in

$$\Delta \hat{Y}_t = 0.867 - 0.603 Y_{t-1} + 0.224 \Delta Y_{t-1}$$
$$(0.218)\ (0.151) \qquad (0.153)$$

$$(7.10)$$

estimated standard errors in parentheses.

Recall that the coefficient on Y_{t-1}, -0.603, is an estimate of $\gamma = (1 - \theta_1)(\rho - 1)$ and that under the null of a unit root $\hat{\theta}_1 = 0.224$, so $1 - \hat{\theta} = 0.776$ and, therefore,

$$T(\tilde{\rho} - 1) = T(-0.603/0.776) = 44(-0.777)$$
$$= -34.190$$

which is asymptotically distributed as $\hat{\rho}_\mu$, with 5% critical value from Fuller's Table 8.5.1 of -13.7 for $T = 100$ or -14.1 for $T = \infty$; hence, the null of a unit root is rejected. The 't' statistic on ΔY_{t-1} is $0.224/0.153 = 1.464$; using standard tables this is not significant at conventional levels and could be omitted from the regression. If this is done the estimated model is

$$\Delta \hat{Y}_t = 0.695 - 0.490 Y_{t-1} \qquad (7.11)$$
$$(0.196)\ (0.135)$$

estimated standard errors in parentheses, and $T(\tilde{\rho} - 1) = 44(-0.490) = -21.56$ compared to a 5% critical value for $\hat{\rho}_\mu$ of -13.7; note also that $\hat{\tau}_\mu = -0.490/0.135 = -3.630$ compared to a 5% critical value from Table 6.6, assuming $\mu = 0$ in the DGP as in Fuller's set-up, of -2.897.

Dickey, Bell and Miller (*op. cit.*) report some power calculations for the pure random walk DGP with sample sizes of $T = 50$, 100 and test statistics, $\hat{\rho}$ and $\hat{\tau}$, $\hat{\rho}_\mu$ and $\hat{\tau}_\mu$, and $\hat{\rho}_\beta$ and $\hat{\tau}_\beta$. Where the regression model matches the DGP, there is little to choose between $\hat{\rho}$ and $\hat{\tau}$ in terms of power or size. If, however, the regression model overfits the DGP by including a constant or a time trend, $\hat{\rho}$ is more powerful than $\hat{\tau}$ and $\hat{\rho}_\beta$ is more powerful than $\hat{\tau}_\beta$. In turn the cost of the overfitting is that, within each class of test statistic, the test statistic in the model closest to the DGP is most powerful; so, for example, in

this case $\hat{\tau}$ is more powerful than $\hat{\tau}_\mu$ which is more powerful than $\hat{\tau}_\beta$. This emphasises the need to match the regression model to the DGP, as the reduction in power can be substantial.

7.4.2 The weighted symmetric (WS) estimator, Pantula et al. (1994)

Many other test statistics have been developed primarily in response to two motivations.

1. To find test statistics more powerful than the Dickey–Fuller statistics.
2. To accommodate situations where the regression disturbance is not independently and identically distributed (iid), which is the standard assumption in the Dickey–Fuller regression model.

Improving power for a given size is clearly an important motivation. Pantula *et al.* (1994) consider 10 test statistics which are alternatives to and generally more powerful than the standard Dickey–Fuller statistics. As their alternatives are very similar in power we will describe just one of these here, based on the weighted symmetric estimator.

To illustrate consider the simplest AR(1) model

$$Y_t = \mu + \phi_1 Y_{t-1} + \varepsilon_t, \quad t = 1, \ldots, T \quad (7.12)$$

For present purposes this is referred to as the backward looking model. Then OLS estimation is based on minimising the (backward) residual sum of squares, BRSS, over the $T - 1$ observations $2, \ldots, T$; that is minimise:

$$\mathrm{BRSS}(\phi_1) = \sum_{t=2}^{T} (y_t - \phi_1 y_{t-1})^2 \qquad (7.13)$$

where $y_t = Y_t - \bar{Y}$ and $\bar{Y} = T^{-1} \sum_{t=1}^{T} Y_t$. Minimisation results in the OLS estimator $\hat{\phi}_1 = \sum_{t=2}^{T} (y_t y_{t-1}) / \sum_{t=2}^{T} y_{t-1}^2$. If the AR(1) model is stationary it can also be written in a forward rather than backward form as

$$Y_t = \mu + \phi_1 Y_{t+1} + \eta_t, \quad t = 1, \ldots, T - 1$$

$$(7.14)$$

with the OLS estimator derived from minimising the forward residual sum of squares, FRSS,

$$\text{FRSS}(\phi_1) = \sum_{t=1}^{T-1} (y_t - \phi_1 y_{t+1})^2 \quad (7.15)$$

A natural development of these two approaches is to minimise the sum of the weighted backward and forward squared residuals, that is minimise

$$\text{WRSS}(\phi_1, w_t) = \sum_{t=2}^{T} w_t(y_t - \phi_1 y_{t-1})^2$$

$$+ \sum_{t=1}^{T-1} (1 - w_{t+1})(y_t - \phi_1 y_{t+1})^2 \quad (7.16)$$

where WRSS denotes the weighted residual sum of squares from the backward and forward AR(1) models with weight w_t on observation t. Setting $w_t = 1$ gives the standard OLS estimator. Alternatively other weights can be chosen, for example $w_t = 0.5$ which results in the simple symmetric estimator – see Dickey, Hasza and Fuller (1984). A more popular choice is Park and Fuller's (1993) specification of $w_t = (t-1)/T$ so $w_2 = 1/T$, $w_3 = 2/T$, $w_T = (T-1)/T$, with the resulting estimator designated the weighted symmetric (WS) estimator by Pantula et al. (op. cit.); here this is referred to as $\hat{\phi}_1^{ws}$. Analogous to the Dickey–Fuller case two easily formed test statistics in the first order case are $T(\hat{\phi}_1^{ws} - 1)$ and the 't' statistic on $\phi_1^{ws} - 1$. These are:

$$\hat{\phi}_1^{ws} = \sum_{t=2}^{T} y_t y_{t-1} / Z(T) \quad (7.17)$$

where $Z(T) = \sum_{t=2}^{T-1} y_t^2 + T^{-1} \sum_{t=1}^{T} y_t^2$

and $\hat{\tau}_\mu^{ws} = (\hat{\phi}_1^{ws} - 1)Z(T)^{0.5}/\hat{\sigma}^{ws}$

where $\hat{\sigma}^{ws} = \text{WRSS}(\hat{\phi}_1^{ws}, w_t)/(T-2)$. Empirical 5% critical values for different sample sizes are

Table 7.3 *5% critical values for test statistics based on the weighted symmetric estimator, Pantula et al. (1994)*

	$T = 25$	50	100	250	∞
$T(\hat{\phi}_1^{ws} - 1)$	−12.03	−12.48	−12.69	−12.88	−13.07
$\hat{\tau}_\mu^{ws}$		−2.66	−2.61	−2.56	−2.54	−2.50

Note: Source, Table 2 of Pantula *et al.* (1994).

obtained by simulation; these are extracted in Table 7.3 from Table 2 of Pantula *et al.* (*op. cit.*).

The power (and critical value) calculations in Pantula *et al.* (*op. cit.*) are obtained with the DGP a pure random walk and the regression an AR(1) model including a constant. We consider the case where the starting value Y_1 and ε_t are independent standard normal variables. Although the increase in power over the standard Dickey–Fuller equivalents is not marked for a sample of 25, for larger sample sizes (50, 100, 250) it is broadly doubled for interesting alternatives. For example, with $T = 100$ and $\phi_1 = 0.95$ the probability of rejection of the null increases from 11.7% for $\hat{\tau}_\mu$ to 26.08% for $\hat{\tau}_\mu^{ws}$, and for $\phi_1 = 0.90$ from 31.06% to 60.22%, respectively. Pantula *et al.* (*op. cit.*) also report power calculations where the regression model is alternately AR(2) or an ARMA(1, 1) model, with and without a trend and where the model order is selected by the AIC. There was generally an improvement in power using the weighted symmetric estimator compared to OLS, although the spurious inclusion of the time trend in the regression model effectively held back the improvement in power compared to when the time trend was excluded. For example, in an AR(2) model in the with-trend case where $T = 100$ and $\phi_1 = 0.95$, the power of the ADF and WS tests was virtually identical at 6%; whereas if the trend was excluded power was more than doubled from around 8% to 19%. An incidental feature of the Pantula results confirms Hall's (1994) observation that the various tests tend to be oversized, although not greatly so, when the lag order is estimated.

7.4.3 Phillips and Perron versions of the DF tests, Phillips (1987) and Phillips and Perron (1988)

The second motivation for alternative unit root test statistics is to allow for disturbance processes, ε_t, which are not iid $\sim (0, \sigma^2)$. Phillips (1987), Phillips and Perron, PP, (1988) generalised the DF tests to situations where, for example, the ε_t are serially correlated, other than by augmenting the initial regression with lagged dependent variables as in the ADF procedure. The PP approach is to add a correction factor to the DF test statistic; for example, consider the AR(1) model

$$Y_t = \mu + \phi_1 Y_{t-1} + \varepsilon_t, \quad t = 1, \ldots, T$$

with $\mathrm{Var}(\varepsilon_t) \equiv \sigma_\varepsilon^2$. If ε_t is serially correlated the ADF approach is to add lagged ΔY_t to 'whiten' the residuals. To illustrate the alternative approach consider the test statistic $T(\hat{\phi}_1 - 1)$ which is distributed as $\hat{\rho}_\mu$ – see section **7.4.1** – from the maintained regression with an intercept but no time trend. The PP modified version of this is

$$Z\hat{\rho}_\mu = T(\hat{\phi}_1 - 1) - \mathrm{CF} \tag{7.18}$$

where the correction factor CF is

$$\mathrm{CF} = 0.5(s_{Tl}^2 - s_\varepsilon^2) \bigg/ \left(\sum_{t=2}^{T} (Y_{t-1} - \bar{Y}_{-1})^2 / T^2 \right) \tag{7.19}$$

and

$$s_\varepsilon^2 = T^{-1} \sum_{t=1}^{T} \hat{\varepsilon}_t^2,$$

$$s_{Tl}^2 = s_\varepsilon^2 + 2 \sum_{s=1}^{l} w_{sl} \sum_{t=s+1}^{T} \hat{\varepsilon}_t \hat{\varepsilon}_{t-s} / T \tag{7.20}$$

$$w_{sl} = 1 - s/(l+1) \quad \text{and}$$

$$\hat{\varepsilon}_t = Y_t - \hat{\mu} - \hat{\phi}_1 Y_{t-1}$$

$$\bar{Y}_{-1} = \sum_{t=2}^{T} Y_t / (T - 1)$$

Although the correction factor looks complex it breaks down quite simply. Note that s_ε^2 is an estimator of σ_ε^2; s_{Tl}^2 is an estimator of the long-run variance,

$$\sigma^2 \equiv \lim(T \to \infty) \left[T^{-1} E \left\{ \sum_{t=1}^{T} \varepsilon_t \right\}^2 \right]$$

s_ε^2 and s_{Tl}^2 differ to the extent that the latter takes into account possible nonzero autocovariances, through the inclusion of $\hat{\varepsilon}_t \hat{\varepsilon}_{t-s}$; if these are zero the correction is also zero.

The PP version of the $\hat{\tau}_\mu$ test statistic, denoted $Z\hat{\tau}_\mu$, makes use of the same factors though the correction is slightly more complex:

$$Z\hat{\tau}_\mu = (s_\varepsilon/s_{Tl})\hat{\tau}_\mu - 0.5(s_{Tl}^2 - s_\varepsilon^2)$$

$$\bigg/ \left(s_{Tl} \left[T^{-2} \sum_{t=2}^{T} (Y_{t-1} - \bar{Y}_{-1})^2 \right]^{0.5} \right) \tag{7.21}$$

The correction factor for the maintained regression without an intercept is obtained as a special case by setting $\bar{Y}$ to zero and defining the residuals from the regression without an intercept. The correction factor for the maintained regression with an intercept and time trend is rather more complex – see Phillips and Perron (1988), and for a convenient reference consult Banerjee *et al.* (1993, p. 112). In general a Z in front of the Dickey–Fuller test statistic indicates that it is the Phillips–Perron version; for example, $Z\hat{\tau}_\beta$ is the PP version of $\hat{\tau}_\beta$.

The weights applied to the autocovariances, sometimes known as the Newey–West (1987) weights, ensure a positive estimate of the long-run variance. The 'truncation' lag of the autocovariances, l, is a choice parameter. In practice guidance on the choice of l can be obtained by calculating the autocorrelation function and applying a standard test to determine the last significant nonzero autocorrelation; as a check calculating the correction factor for a range of values of l should reveal when the numerical value of the correction stabilises. Andrews (1991) shows that consistency of $s_T^2 l$ requires that $l \to \infty$ as $T \to \infty$ at the rate $O(T^{\frac{1}{3}})$; for example, if $T = 100$, $l = 5$ (to the nearest integer), whereas if $T = 200$, $l = 6$. In terms of frequency of inclusion of unit root tests in commercially available econometric software packages, the range of ADF τ statistics is usually included as a matter of course, with some packages also providing the PP versions.

The PP versions of the DF tests are flexible in that the serial correlation between disturbances can be of an autoregressive or moving average form. However, as Campbell and Perron (1991) note, where the autocorrelations of ε_t are predominantly negative the PP tests suffer severe size distortions, with the actual size much greater than the nominal size – see Schwert (1989), Phillips and Perron (1988) and Campbell and Perron (*op. cit.*, Table 1). On correcting for this distortion in size, it appears that the PP tests can deliver more power than the ADF tests. Plotting the autocorrelation function can be an aid to detecting situations where it would be unwise to rely on the PP tests. However, the problem remains that situations do arise with economic time series where the autocorrelations, especially at lag one, are negative. One possibility is to use a Monte Carlo analysis to simulate the appropriate critical values, but this is often not an attractive proposition.

In the next section an alternative approach to the specification of time series modelling is described which offers three benefits: first, a structural interpretation of univariate time series models offers an insight into how nonstationary models may arise; second, the relationship between the structural and reduced forms of a time series model leads to a test of the null hypothesis of stationarity against the alternative of nonstationarity; and third, MA processes which generate negative first order autocorrelations arise quite naturally in the context of structural time series models.

7.5 Structural and reduced form univariate time series models

In the tests so far described the null hypothesis is of *nonstationarity* rather than *stationarity*; the alternative hypothesis represents the latter. Because of the different roles of the null and alternative hypotheses in the classical testing set-up these hypotheses are not treated symmetrically; with conventional significance levels of 5% or 10% the evidence is not weighed to determine which of the hypotheses is *more* likely. The asymmetry accords the null hypothesis the dominant role, and where the power of a test is low this can be uncomfortable. While staying within the classical testing framework an alternate is to set up the null hypothesis as that of stationarity with the alternative of nonstationarity. Tests within this approach include Kwiatkowski, Phillips, Schmidt and Shin (1992), usually referred to as KPSS, and Leybourne and McCabe (1994), referred to here as LMc. This section describes the LMc test. However, in order to accomplish this it is necessary to introduce an alternative way of looking at univariate time series models which distinguishes structural models from reduced form models. It transpires that this is worthy of study in itself as it offers insights into how nonstationary models arise quite naturally in time series modelling. This section considers some basic models and motivation; for an excellent treatment of this area of modelling the interested reader should consult Harvey (1989).

7.5.1 Structural univariate time series models

Note that the evidence on conventional unit root tests is that they lose power dramatically against stationary alternatives with a low order MA process; and such processes fit well to a number of macroeconomic time series. To see how these issues can be dealt with in a different framework we start with a simple *structural* time series model, which is then developed. Suppose a time series is observed with irregular movements but without a tendency for sustained movements in one direction or another. Such a series could be viewed as composed of a level component and an irregular component with the representation:

$$Y_t = \alpha_t + \xi_t \qquad (7.22)$$

where the level is α_t and the irregular component is ξ_t. Specification of the level is important if it is to match the characteristics of the observed series. The simplest specification is that the level is constant, say $\alpha_t = \alpha$, with recorded observations contaminated by noise or other irregular, random movements, ξ_t.

It seems unlikely that such a simple specification will have any general applicability; more likely is the case where the level changes over time. One possibility is

$$\alpha_t = \alpha_{t-1} + \eta_t \qquad (7.23)$$

so that the underlying level is a random walk which cumulates previous disturbances. This is known as a local-level model – see Harvey (1989). The random terms ξ_t and η_t are assumed to be zero mean, uncorrelated, normally distributed variables with variances σ_ξ^2 and σ_η^2. The effect of nonzero values of η_t is to shift the level up or down, to which is added the irregular component, ξ_t. A sequence of positive values of η_t will, *ceteris paribus*, build into an increase in the level. The magnitude of the variances is an important part of the specification. Suppose $\sigma_\xi^2 = 0$, then there is no irregular component and the Y_t follow an uncontaminated random walk as $Y_t = \alpha_t$ and $\alpha_t = \alpha_{t-1} + \eta_t$. If $\sigma_\eta^2 = 0$ then the level is constant, contaminated by the irregular component, ξ_t, if $\sigma_\xi^2 \neq 0$.

The model is easily generalised. For example, suppose in addition to a changing level we allow for a changing slope. First, start with a completely deterministic specification of the trend:

$$\alpha_t = \mu + \beta t \qquad (7.24)$$

from which it is easy to see that

$$\alpha_t = \alpha_{t-1} + \beta \qquad (7.25)$$

so β is the slope of the trend: the trend changes by β each period. To allow the level to change add the stochastic term η_t:

$$\alpha_t = \alpha_{t-1} + \beta + \eta_t \qquad (7.26)$$

so the level changes but the slope is constant. To allow the slope and level to change, let β_t designate the changing slope that also evolves according to a random walk:

$$\alpha_t = \alpha_{t-1} + \beta_t + \eta_t \qquad (7.27a)$$

$$\beta_t = \beta_{t-1} + \varsigma_t \qquad (7.27b)$$

The model is completed by

$$Y_t = \alpha_t + \xi_t \qquad (7.28)$$

where ξ_t is again the measurement error/irregular component. This is now quite a flexible model that can accommodate a trend, which changes both in the level, for example shifting up, and the slope, for example becoming steeper. However, note that these changes can be reversed by a different sequence of η_t and ς_t, so the changes are *local* rather than *global*; for this reason the model is much more flexible than its deterministic but stationary counterpart where η_t and ς_t are identically zero.

The LMc test is based on a variant of the changing level/fixed slope structural time series model. The simplest version is

$$Y_t = \alpha_t + \xi_t$$

and

$$\alpha_t = \alpha_{t-1} + \beta + \eta_t \qquad (7.29)$$

substitution of the latter into the former gives

$$Y_t = \alpha_{t-1} + \beta + \eta_t + \xi_t \qquad (7.30)$$

Note that

$$Y_t - Y_{t-1} = \alpha_t + \xi_t - \alpha_{t-1} + \xi_{t-1} \quad (7.31a)$$
$$= \beta + \eta_t + \xi_t - \xi_{t-1} \quad (7.31b)$$

Assuming that η_t and ξ_t are uncorrelated (at all lags) it is easy to show (see the review questions) that the variance, autocovariances and autocorrelations of ΔY_t are:

$$\text{Var}(\Delta Y_t) = \sigma_\eta^2 + 2\sigma_\xi^2 \quad (7.32a)$$
$$\gamma(1) = -\sigma_\xi^2$$
$$\rho(1) = -\sigma_\xi^2/(\sigma_\eta^2 + 2\sigma_\xi^2) \quad (7.32b)$$
$$\gamma(k) = 0 \quad \rho(k) = 0 \quad \text{for } k > 1 \quad (7.32c)$$

so there is a cut-off at $k = 1$. This is also the pattern characteristic of an MA(1) process in ΔY_t, that is:

$$\Delta Y_t = \beta + \varepsilon_t + \theta\varepsilon_{t-1} \quad (7.33)$$

where ε_t is white noise with variance σ_ε^2. This is an ARIMA(0, 1, 1) process with variance, auto-covariances and autocorrelations of ΔY_t given by

$$\text{Var}(\Delta Y_t) = \sigma_\varepsilon^2(1 + \theta^2) \quad (7.34a)$$
$$\gamma(1) = \theta\sigma_\varepsilon^2 \quad \rho(1) = \theta/(1 + \theta^2) \quad (7.34b)$$
$$\gamma(k) = 0$$
$$\rho(k) = 0 \quad \text{for } k > 1 \quad (7.34c)$$

The ARIMA(0, 1, 1) model is the reduced form of the structural, local level/constant slope, model: it does not directly interpret the disturbances η_t and ξ_t in structural terms, these are composited in ε_t. The connection between the structural and reduced forms can be seen by equating the nonzero autocovariances and autocorrelations, here these are just the first order. That is

$$\gamma(1) = \theta\sigma_\varepsilon^2 = -\sigma_\xi^2 \Rightarrow \sigma_\varepsilon^2 = -\sigma_\xi^2/\theta \quad (7.35)$$

and note that since σ_ε^2 and σ_ξ^2 are nonnegative, and generally positive, θ must be negative. Equating the first order autocorrelations gives

$$-\sigma_\xi^2/(\sigma_\eta^2 + 2\sigma_\xi^2) = \theta/(1 + \theta^2) \quad (7.36)$$

which can be solved for θ (the detail of the solution is covered in a review question)

$$\theta = [(q^2 + 4q)^{0.5} - q - 2]/2 \quad (7.37)$$

Where $q = \sigma_\eta^2/\sigma_\xi^2$ is the signal-to-noise ratio with limits $0 \leq q \leq \infty$. Note that when $q = 0$, $\theta = -1$ and when $q = \infty$, $\theta = 0$.

To illustrate suppose $\sigma_\xi^2 = 1$ and $\sigma_\eta^2 = 2$ so $q = 2$, then $\theta = [(4 + 8)^{0.5} - 2 - 2)]/2 = -0.268$, and the reduced form model is

$$\Delta Y_t = \beta + \varepsilon_t - 0.268\varepsilon_{t-1} \quad (7.38)$$

with first order autocorrelation coefficient of $\rho(1) = \theta/(1 + \theta^2) = -0.268/1.072 = -0.25$.

Alternately suppose $\sigma_\xi^2 = 1$ and $\sigma_\eta^2 = 0.5$ so $q = 0.5$, then $\theta = [(0.25 + 2)^{0.5} - 0.5 - 2)]/2 = -0.5$ and, therefore,

$$\Delta Y_t = \beta + \varepsilon_t - 0.5\varepsilon_{t-1} \quad \text{with}$$
$$\rho(1) = \theta/(1 + \theta^2) = -0.5/1.25$$
$$= -0.4 \quad (7.39)$$

The limits, $\theta = -1$ and $\theta = 0$, are also interesting. Suppose $q = \sigma_\eta^2/\sigma_\xi^2 = 0$, and thus $\theta = -1$, corresponding to $\sigma_\eta^2 = 0$, that is all $\eta_t = 0$, and σ_ξ^2 is positive, then the structural model is

$$Y_t = \alpha_t + \xi_t \quad \text{and} \quad \alpha_t = \alpha_{t-1} + \beta \quad (7.40)$$

The latter is a deterministic trend as it corresponds to $\alpha_t = \alpha_0 + \beta t$ where α_0 is α_t at $t = 0$. To check note that $\alpha_{t-1} = \alpha_0 + \beta(t-1)$, subtracting this from α_t confirms the result. In terms of the reduced form model

$$\Delta Y_t = \beta + \varepsilon_t + \theta\varepsilon_{t-1} \quad (7.41)$$

with $\theta = -1$ this becomes:

$$(1 - L)Y_t = \beta + (1 - L)\varepsilon_t \quad (7.42)$$

so $(1 - L)$ is a common factor. Multiplying both sides through by the summation operator

$S(L) = (1-L)^{-1} = (1 + L + L^2 + \cdots)$, and note that $S(L)\beta = \beta t + \sum_{i=t+1}^{\infty} L^i \beta$, then

$$Y_t = S(L)\beta + \varepsilon_t$$
$$= \alpha_0 + \beta t + \varepsilon_t \qquad (7.43)$$

where $\alpha_0 = \sum_{i=t+1}^{\infty} L^i \beta = \alpha_{-1} + \beta$. Also note that $\sigma_\varepsilon^2 = \sigma_\xi^2$. Whether the result is obtained through the structural or the reduced form of the time series model $\sigma_\eta^2 = 0$; that is all $\eta_t = 0$, and σ_ξ^2 positive results in the trend stationary model. At the other extreme $q = \infty$ implies $\theta = 0$. The reduced form model with $\theta = 0$ is a random walk (with drift)

$$\Delta Y_t = \beta + \varepsilon_t \qquad (7.44)$$

These examples illustrate that much hinges on whether $\sigma_\eta^2 = 0$, for when that is the case the model is trend stationary but otherwise it is an integrated process with a unit root.

7.5.2   Stationarity as the null hypothesis

In the LMc test the structural time series model is generalised to allow for lags on Y_t, so the basic model becomes

$$\phi(L)Y_t = \alpha_{t-1} + \beta + \eta_t + \xi_t \qquad (7.45)$$

where $\phi(L) = \phi(L) = 1 - \phi_1 L - \cdots - \phi_p L^p$. The reduced form of this model is ARIMA$(p, 1, 1)$, that is

$$\phi(L)\Delta Y_t = \beta + \varepsilon_t + \theta \varepsilon_{t-1} \quad \text{with } \theta \text{ negative} \qquad (7.46)$$

A testing strategy, which takes the null of stationarity against the alternative of nonstationarity, can be approached from the relation between structural and reduced form representations of time series models. The null is that the model is ARIMA$(p, 0, 0)$, more simply put as AR(p) with deterministic trend, whereas the

alternative is ARIMA$(p, 1, 1)$. Assuming a usable sample of T observations the test statistic is calculated as follows.

Step 1: Estimate the ARIMA$(p, 1, 1)$ model, $\Delta Y_t = \tilde{\beta} + \sum_{j=1}^{p} \tilde{\phi}_j \Delta Y_{t-j} + \varepsilon_t + \tilde{\theta} \varepsilon_{t-1}$.

Step 2: Calculate $Y_t^* = Y_t - \sum_{j=1}^{p} \tilde{\phi}_j \Delta Y_{t-j}$, where $\tilde{\phi}_j$ are obtained from step 1.

Step 3: Estimate $Y_t^* = \hat{\alpha} + \hat{\beta} t$.

Step 4: Calculate $\hat{\zeta}_t = Y_t^* - \hat{\alpha} - \hat{\beta} t$ and form the vector $\hat{\zeta}' = (\hat{\zeta}_1, \ldots, \hat{\zeta}_T)$.

Step 5: Calculate $\hat{\sigma}_\zeta^2 = \sum_{t=1}^{T} \hat{\zeta}_t^2 / T$.

Step 6: Calculate the test statistic, LMc $= \hat{\zeta}' V \hat{\zeta} / (T^2 \hat{\sigma}_\zeta^2)$, where V is a $T \times T$ matrix with ijth element equal to the minimum of i and j.

Step 7: The test statistic is a quadratic form with 'large' values indicating rejection of the null hypothesis of stationarity against the ARIMA$(p, 1, 1)$ nonstationary alternative.

Step 8: Critical values are from KPSS and are reproduced below. There are two versions of the test statistic depending on whether $(\beta = 0, \alpha \neq 0)$ or $(\beta \neq 0, \alpha \neq 0)$, referred to as LMc$_\alpha$ and LMc$_\beta$; for LMc$_\alpha$ steps 1, 3 and 4 omit the time trend, that is any term involving a β coefficient.

As with estimation of the ADF regression it is necessary to choose p, the order of the autoregression; and it is clearly sensible, by means of the usual diagnostic tests and information criteria, to establish that an ARIMA$(p, 1, 1)$ model is an adequate one to fit to the time series under consideration. In particular actual series for which this approach is relevant are likely to exhibit significant first order autocorrelations. An alternative test statistic is due to KPSS, this starts from the basic local level model

$$Y_t = \alpha_{t-1} + \beta + \eta_t + \xi_t \qquad (7.47)$$

While the autoregressive component of the LMc approach is captured by including lags on Y_t, in the KPSS test it is captured in the process generating ξ_t which may be serially correlated (and heteroscedastic). The KPSS test statistic has the same form as the LMc test, that is

$$KPSS = \hat{\zeta}'V\hat{\zeta}/(T^2\hat{\sigma}^2_{\zeta\zeta}) \qquad (7.48)$$

with two differences: first, steps 1 and 2 of the LMc procedure are not necessary, so that the residuals $\hat{\zeta}$ are calculated from either a regression of Y_t on just an intercept or an intercept and a trend for $KPSS_\alpha$ and $KPSS_\beta$, respectively; second, that $\hat{\sigma}^2_{\zeta\zeta}$ replaces $\hat{\sigma}^2_{\zeta}$, where

$$\hat{\sigma}^2_{\zeta\zeta} = T^{-1}\sum_{t=1}^{T}\hat{\zeta}^2_t$$

$$+ 2T^{-1}\sum_{s=1}^{1}w_{sl}\sum_{t=s+1}^{T}\hat{\zeta}_t\hat{\zeta}_{t-s} \qquad (7.49)$$

which we have seen before in the Phillips–Perron versions of the Dickey–Fuller tests. l is the lag truncation parameter, which has to be chosen in a practical application of the test. As in the LMc case there are two versions of the test statistic depending on whether $(\beta = 0, \alpha \neq 0)$ or $(\beta \neq 0, \alpha \neq 0)$, referred to as $KPSS_\alpha$ and $KPSS_\beta$.

Critical values from the asymptotic distribution under the null, for conventional significance levels, are given in KPSS (op. cit.) and reproduced below in Table 7.4. These are the same for the KPSS and LMc versions of the test statistic. Leybourne and McCabe (op. cit.) provide some simulations to determine whether the critical values are sensitive to the order, p, of

the autoregression and the comparative performance of the KPSS test. In summary, when the DGP is simple white noise, that is $Y_t = \varepsilon_t$, (so $p = 0$), and $T = 100$, the asymptotic critical values are a reasonable good guide to the actual size even when $p = 1, 2, 3$ for the LMc test. This result is maintained, although there is some very slight oversizing, when the (stationary) DGP is $Y_t = 0.7Y_{t-1} + \varepsilon_t$. When the DGP is more realistically set at $Y_t = 0.9Y_{t-1} + \varepsilon_t$ the 5% tests have an actual size of about 6.5%, but this may just result from a difference between the small sample and asymptotic critical values. In contrast the KPSS tests while accurate in size for the white noise DGP are severely oversized for the other DGPs with nonzero AR coefficients.

Turning to the power of the LMc and KPSS tests, the simulations reported in Leybourne and McCabe (op. cit., Table 4), where the critical values are adjusted to correct for the oversizing – that is the power is size adjusted – indicate that: overfitting p does not markedly affect the power of the LMc test; the LMc is more powerful than the KPSS test; the power of the KPSS test declines noticeably as the truncation lag parameter, l, increases. Hence, on the basis of this evidence the LMc test is preferred, especially as it appears robust both on size and power to not knowing the true value of p.

Leybourne and McCabe (op. cit.) apply their test and the KPSS test to 11 US macroeconomic time series originally studied by Schwert (1987). To illustrate some of the practical issues we

Table 7.4 *LMc and KPSS test statistics for the US CPI, Leybourne and McCabe (1994)*

LMc$_\beta$(0)	LMc$_\beta$(1)	LMc$_\beta$(2)	LMc$_\beta$(3)	LMc$_\beta$(4)
1.112	0.850	0.717	0.279	0.423
KPSS$_\beta$(0)	KPSS$_\beta$(3)	KPSS$_\beta$(9)	KPSS$_\beta$(15)	KPSS$_\beta$(21)
1.112	0.474	0.251	0.183	0.157

Asymptotic critical values for the LMc/KPSS test			
	10%	5%	1%
LMc$_\alpha$; KPSS$_\alpha$	0.347	0.463	0.739
LMc$_\beta$; KPSS$_\beta$	0.119	0.146	0.216

Source: Table 1, KPSS (op. cit.).

consider the US consumer price index, CPI. The data used was January 1949 to December 1985, giving 444 monthly observations, large enough not to expect problems using the asymptotic critical values. Since it is evident that the series is trended the relevant test statistics are $LMc_\beta(p)$ and $KPSS_\beta(l)$, with the number in brackets indicating the order of the autoregressive process or lag truncation parameter, respectively. The sample values of the test statistics and appropriate (large sample) critical values are given in Table 7.4.

Note that the sample values are sensitive to the particular choice of the autoregressive or truncation lag parameters, so this is an important practical issue. As to the former $p = 3$ was chosen by deleting marginal coefficients with insignificant t ratios; and for the latter $444^{\frac{1}{3}} = 8$ (to the nearest integer). In this case, at the 5% significance level, the asymptotic critical value of 0.146 – see Table 7.4 – is below all tabulated values of LMc_β and $KPSS_\beta$, so the choice is not critical and the null hypothesis of stationarity is rejected.

7.6   Testing for 2 unit roots

It is evident from the graphs of some economic time series that stationarity is not always induced by first differencing. This is particularly so for nominal (as opposed to relative) price series where the first difference in logs is an approximation to the rate of inflation, which in turn is a candidate for an I(1) series. An I(2) series appears smoother and more slowly changing than an I(1) series. A log-transformed series, which is I(2), will have an I(1) growth rate; thus shocks to the series will result in persistence in the growth rate and level of the series.

Some series may, therefore, contain 2 unit roots and have to be differenced twice to become stationary. Where this possibility is likely, it is important to start with a test for the largest number of unit roots rather than start with a test

for 1 unit root in an I(1) series. If the latter strategy is followed it is possible to wrongly conclude either that the series does not contain a unit root or it contains just one unit root. In the sense that the existence of 2 unit roots imposes 1 more restriction than 1 unit root, the suggested procedure tests from the specific to the general and is the reverse of the advice usually given to test from the general to the specific.

Broadly there are two strategies available if, for example, it is suspected that a series is I(2). One possibility is to test directly for the existence of 2 unit roots – see, for example, Hasza and Fuller (1979). Referring back to the AR(2) model of equations (6.10) and (6.14) of section **6.2.4**, note that the hypothesis of 2 unit roots corresponds to the joint hypothesis $\phi_1 = 2$, $\phi_2 = -1$, and a test procedure could be based on simultaneous testing of this hypothesis against the alternative that the restrictions are not valid. While this procedure has merits a simpler alternative exists which just uses the test statistics for 1 unit root. This alternative is a sequential procedure due to Dickey and Pantula (1987) beginning 'with the highest (practical) degree of differencing and work downward toward a test on the series level ...' (*op. cit.*, p. 456).

To illustrate the sequential procedure suppose that we want to allow for the possibility that a series might have 2 unit roots, then the first step is to define $Z_t \equiv \Delta Y_t$; then carry out the testing sequence described in section **6.3** using Z_t rather than Y_t. As 1 unit root has been imposed by taking the first difference of Y_t, the tests are, in effect, assessing whether a second unit root exists conditional on the existence of 1 unit root. If the null hypothesis, which now corresponds to 2 unit roots, is not rejected we are able to conclude that the hypothesis is data consistent. If, on the other hand, the null hypothesis is rejected the next move in the sequence is to see if the null hypothesis of 1 unit root is consistent with the data. In testing this latter hypothesis we revert to Y_t rather than Z_t as the variable we are analysing.

It is possible to extend this procedure to test for 3 or more unit roots – although such cases are likely to be rare in practice; however, Harvey (1989, p. 295) notes that a local quadratic trend structural time series model results in a reduced form with 3 unit roots which may be plausible for the log of the price level. For example, a test for 3 unit roots is a simple extension of the test for 2 unit roots. First define $W_t \equiv \Delta Z_t (\equiv \Delta\Delta Y_t)$, that is the second difference of Y_t, and use W_t as the variable to analyse. Move down to Z_t if the null hypothesis of 3 unit roots is rejected; then move down to Y_t if the null hypothesis of 2 unit roots is rejected.

When testing whether there are d unit roots, with $d > 1$ and assuming d is an integer, there is a choice to be made at which level to enter the testing strategy. For example, in testing for 2 unit roots Dickey and Pantula (1987) suggest the maintained models given by either

$$\Delta Z_t = \mu + \gamma Z_{t-1} + \sum_{j=1}^{p} \alpha_j \Delta Z_{t-j} + \varepsilon_t \quad (7.50)$$

or

$$\Delta Z = \gamma Z_{t-1} + \sum_{j=1}^{p} \alpha_j \Delta Z_{t-j} + \varepsilon_t \quad (7.51)$$

with corresponding test statistics $\hat{\tau}_\mu$ and $\hat{\tau}$. An alternative is to enter the testing strategy where the maintained model includes a deterministic time trend, that is:

$$\Delta Z_t = \mu + \gamma Z_{t-1}$$
$$+ \sum_{j=1}^{p} \alpha_j \Delta Z_{t-j} + \beta t + \varepsilon_t \quad (7.52)$$

The argument for using (7.52) as the first level is that we would not want to rule out the possibility of a unit root *and* a deterministic time trend at least in the I(1) case. The argument against using (7.52) is that when $d > 1$ it is unlikely that there are multiple roots, that is $d \geq 2$, *and* a deterministic time trend. The

procedure adopted in the next section and in succeeding chapters is to start with (7.52) but move onto (7.51) if there is evidence that the time trend is not needed. Indeed, to anticipate some of the results in later chapters, the usual case, when initially testing for 3 or 2 unit roots, is to find that β is numerically very close to zero –often zero to 3 or 4 decimal places even when normalised by the estimated equation standard error. Although the emphasis here is on using the DF $\hat{\tau}$ and Φ statistics the sequence is equally applicable with the Phillips–Perron versions of these test statistics which are likely to be relevant where the underlying process is not a finite order AR.

An alternative to the Dickey–Pantula procedure due to Hasza and Fuller (1979) results from a slight modification of (7.50) to include Y_{t-1} as a regressor,

$$\Delta Z_t = \mu + \gamma_1 Y_{t-1} + \gamma_2 Z_{t-1}$$
$$+ \sum_{j=1}^{p} \alpha_j \Delta Z_{t-j} + \varepsilon_t \quad (7.53)$$

The first unit root corresponds to $\gamma_1 = 0$ and the second to $\gamma_2 = 0$; therefore, the joint null hypothesis of 2 unit roots corresponds to $\gamma_1 = \gamma_2 = 0$ which can be tested by an F test with a nonstandard distribution, critical values are given in Hasza and Fuller (1979). If the first unit root is imposed $\gamma_1 = 0$, then the regression model reduces to that suggested by Dickey and Pantula (*op. cit.*). If there is one unit root the Dickey–Pantula procedure will be more powerful than the Hasza–Fuller procedure, as the unit root is imposed under both the null and alternative hypotheses.

Nevertheless Haldrup (1994) makes the point that Hasza–Fuller procedure is likely to be useful where the alternative to a double unit root is an explosive root. In the latter case differencing d times with $d \geq 2$ will not result in a stationary series, but we might misleadingly conclude so if a unit root has already been imposed. An alternative is to carry out the joint F test in the Hasza–Fuller procedure; following rejection carry out the next step in the Dickey–Pantula procedure, which is the ADF test for a single unit root; an explosive root will be indicated by a large *positive* value of the relevant $\hat{\tau}$ statistic.

Haldrup (*op. cit.*) also shows how to construct a Phillips and Perron type test for double unit roots which makes a 'semi-parametric' correction for serial correlation, rather than augmenting the original regression with lagged dependent variables as in the Dickey–Fuller/ Dickey–Pantula procedure. Monte Carlo simulations reported by Haldrup (*op. cit.*) show that the semi-parametric Hasza–Fuller test is generally more powerful than the Dickey–Pantula test where the alternative is a (mildly) explosive root. (Incidentally in a theme common to a number of parametric and semi-parametric test statistics for a single unit root, the simulations indicate that there are severe problems with the size of the test when the DGP includes a negative MA parameter.)

7.7 Seasonality and seasonal integration

Reference to official statistical sources shows that many series are available on a seasonally adjusted as well as unadjusted basis. There is a general recognition of seasonality in economic activity giving rise to distinct patterns in the associated economic time series. For example, 4th quarter consumers' expenditure tends to be high and 1st quarter expenditure low compared to the yearly average. The data to which the techniques so far described are applied is assumed to be without a seasonal pattern. Where this is not the case there are two possibilities. The most prevalent is to use data that has been seasonally adjusted, so that no seasonal pattern remains. Seasonal adjustment procedures take several forms. The simplest involves a prior regression of Y_t on seasonal dummy variables. For example, for quarterly data with the quarters indicated by $i = 1, 2, 3, 4$,

define $d_i = 1$ for quarter i but 0 for the other 3 quarters; then regress Y_t on d_1, d_2, d_3 and d_4 or, equivalently omit one of the dummy variables and include an intercept. In this case the seasonality is assumed to be deterministic; whichever year is considered the seasonal effect is the same. Official sources tend to use a more detailed seasonal adjustment process based on a complex filtering of the unadjusted data; for example, the US Census Bureau seasonal adjustment programme, X-11, which is used throughout the world, uses a sequence of moving average filters. In this procedure the seasonal adjustment pattern can evolve over time, so it is not fixed as in the simple dummy variable regression, but it does so in a deterministic fashion. An alternative is to develop a structural time series model that allows the seasonality to evolve stochastically over time – see, for example, Harvey (1989).

7.7.1 Integration in seasonal processes

The implicit assumption in applying unit root tests to data which has been deseasonalised is that the adjustment method does not affect inference regarding the stationarity or otherwise of the time series. This assumption implies that applying appropriate tests to the seasonally adjusted data and also to the unadjusted data, taking into account the effect that seasonality can have on the nature of the time series process, should not lead to different conclusions. Unfortunately several authors have shown that this assumption turns out to be at risk in finite samples where the unadjusted data is filtered by a moving average process – see Ghysels (1990), Jaeger and Kunst (1990) and Ghysels and Perron (1993). Monte Carlo simulations suggest that the power of standard unit root tests, applied to seasonally adjusted data, is reduced in finite samples, so that the null of nonstationarity is not rejected often enough. The Monte Carlo simulations in Olekalns (1994) indicate that the power loss in deseasonalising by using preliminary regression with seasonal dummy variables is not as great in finite samples as an X-11 procedure, which uses a moving average process.

Some have gone as far as suggesting that unit root testing should only take place with seasonally unadjusted data – see Olekalns (*op. cit.*); however, often this is not practical since unadjusted data is not always available, or the purpose of modelling is to provide predictions of the adjusted data which tend to be the focus of policy analysis. While in principle unadjusted data could be used in the modelling stage and then adjusted to be comparable with published adjusted data, access would be needed to the same adjustment filters used by the publishing source to ensure comparability.

The possibility of seasonality in economic time series has led to a modification of the definition of integration. The simplest extension is that seasonal differencing may be necessary to reduce a series to stationarity. For example, suppose a series is generated by

$$Y_t = \phi_{1s} Y_{t-s} + \varepsilon_t \tag{7.54}$$

where $s \geq 1$ and ε_t is white noise; that is

$$(1 - \phi_{1s} L^s) Y_t = \varepsilon_t \tag{7.55}$$

In this model $s = 4$ for quarterly data, $s = 12$ for monthly data, and the idea is that the autoregression relates observations in the same season one year apart; for example, consumers' expenditure in quarter 4 in year t to expenditure in quarter 4 in year $t - 1$ and so on. Stability requires $|\phi_{1s}| < 1$ and this implies stationarity. If $\phi_{1s} = 1$ there is a unit root at the sth *seasonal* frequency and the sth difference of Y_t removes the unit root, that is if:

$$Y_t = Y_{t-s} + \varepsilon_t \tag{7.56}$$

then

$$Z_t \equiv (1 - L^s) Y_t = \varepsilon_t$$

and $Z_t \equiv Y_t - Y_{t-s}$ is white noise, and hence stationary. This model is a random walk at the seasonal frequency, implying that the seasonal pattern is not constant over time with implications that are not entirely comfortable. For example, Hylleberg (1992) notes: 'As the existence of a seasonal unit root in the data-generating process implies that summer may become winter in the sense that the seasonal pattern may change dramatically, the finding of a seasonal unit root is best interpreted as an indication of a varying and changing seasonal pattern and against a constant seasonal pattern.'

7.7.2 Testing for a unit root in a seasonal process

Testing for a unit root in this framework is a straightforward extension of the Dickey–Fuller procedure – see Dickey *et al.* (1984) – with seasonal differences rather than first differences being taken in the Dickey–Fuller regressions. Dickey *et al.* (*op. cit.*) provide critical values for the seasonal model for $T(\hat{\phi}_{1s} - 1)$ and seasonal versions of $\hat{\tau}$ and $\hat{\tau}_\mu$ for $s = 2$, 4 and 12. Augmented Dickey–Fuller tests are easily constructed based on 'whitening' the residuals with the inclusion of lagged seasonal differences.

The pure seasonal model in (7.54) is, however, likely to be too simple in constraining Y_t to depend only upon seasonal differences. For example, quarterly consumers' expenditure may be related to last quarter's expenditure as well as last year's expenditure in the same quarter. A natural extension of the pure seasonal model is:

$$\phi(L)\phi_s(L^s) Y_t = \varepsilon_t \tag{7.57}$$

$$\text{say} \quad \phi^+(L) Y_t = \varepsilon_t \tag{7.58}$$

$$\text{where} \quad \phi^+(L) = \phi(L)\phi_s(L^s)$$

and $\phi_s(L^s) = (1 - \phi_{1s}L^s - \cdots - \phi_{rs}L^{rs})$, so the seasonal averaging is over r years and is referred to as the seasonal polynomial; and, as before,

$\phi(L) = 1 - \phi_1 L - \cdots - \phi_p L^p$, which to distinguish it is referred to as the regular polynomial. For example, if $p = r = 1$, then

$$(1 - \phi_1 L)(1 - \phi_{1s} L^s) Y_t = \varepsilon_t \qquad (7.59)$$

multiplying out the lag polynomials

$$
\begin{aligned}
Y_t &= \phi_1 Y_{t-1} + \phi_{1s} Y_{t-s} \\
&\quad - \phi_1 \phi_{1s} Y_{t-(s+1)} + \varepsilon_t
\end{aligned} \qquad (7.60)
$$

The coefficient on $Y_{t-(s+1)}$ is the negative of the product of the coefficients on Y_{t-1} and Y_{t-s}. This extension of the pure seasonal model suggests that unit roots could exist in both the $\phi(L)$ and $\phi_s(L^s)$ polynomials; continuing with the $p = r = 1$ example this would be

$$(1 - L)(1 - L^s) Y_t = \varepsilon_t \qquad (7.61)$$

So that a first and a seasonal difference must be taken to ensure stationarity; taking one or the other only would not result in stationarity.

The interesting question then arises as to how to test for unit roots in the regular and in the seasonal polynomials. The test often applied is due to Hylleberg, Engle, Granger and Yoo (1990), usually referred to as HEGY. Some simple definitions are required first:

(i) first difference operator: $\Delta \equiv 1 - L$;
(ii) seasonal difference operator: $\Delta_s \equiv 1 - L^s$;
(iii) the summation operator of order s: $S_s(L) \equiv 1 + L + L^2 + \cdots + L^{s-1}$.

The following relationship holds between these operators:

$$
\begin{aligned}
1 - L^s &= (1 - L)(1 + L + L^2 + \cdots + L^{s-1}) \\
&= (1 - L) S_s(L)
\end{aligned} \qquad (7.62)
$$

For example, it is straightforward to verify the following: for $s = 2$

$$1 - L^2 = (1 - L)(1 + L) \qquad (7.63)$$

and for $s = 4$

$$1 - L^4 = (1 - L)(1 + L + L^2 + L^3) \qquad (7.64)$$

We will concentrate on $s = 4$ as it corresponds to the frequently occurring case of quarterly data. Note that, as far as seasonal effects are concerned, with quarterly data within a year there could be a quarterly pattern *and* a (semi-annual) six monthly pattern, giving one cycle (of the 4 seasons) per year for the quarterly pattern and two cycles (of the half-years) for the semi-annual pattern. Therefore, at least theoretically, seasonal integration could be present at either or both of these frequencies as well as at the conventional long run of no cycles per year. With this in mind the following factorisations are used in the decomposition of $1 - L^4$, that is

$$(1 + L + L^2 + L^3) = (1 + L)(1 + L^2) \qquad (7.65)$$

and

$$(1 + L^2) = (1 - iL)(1 + iL) \qquad (7.66)$$

where i is the imaginary unit $(-1)^{0.5}$, so $i^2 = -1$ and $-i^2 = 1$; hence, using these results

$$
\begin{aligned}
1 - L^4 &= (1 - L)(1 + L + L^2 + L^3) \\
&= (1 - L)(1 + L)(1 - iL)(1 + iL)
\end{aligned}
$$
$$(7.67)$$

From the decomposition into the four bracketed terms on the right-hand side, the roots are: $+1, -1, +i, -i$. These roots correspond to the following interpretation: $+1$ to the long run of no cycles (the standard unit root), -1 to the semi-annual frequency of two cycles per year (the semi-annual frequency with a half cycle per quarter) and $+i$ and $-i$ to one cycle per year (the quarterly frequency with a quarter cycle per quarter). The possibility of unit roots at frequencies other than zero suggests that an amendment is required to the usual notation to indicate an integrated series. HEGY suggest $I_\theta(d)$ to indicate that the series is integrated of order d at the θ frequency; for example, with quarterly data and $d = 1$, the possibilities are:

zero frequency, $I_0(1)$; semi-annual frequency, $I_{\frac{1}{2}}(1)$; quarterly frequency, $I_{\frac{1}{4}}(1)$. Osborn, Chui, Smith and Birchenall (1988) suggest the notation $I(d, D)$, with d indicating the number of one-period differences and D the number of seasonal differences necessary to induce stationarity, for example with quarterly data $I(1, 4)$ indicates that a first difference and a fourth difference are necessary to induce stationarity. The HEGY definition conveys information about all the seasonal roots so that is used here.

To use the decomposition (7.67), HEGY show that a polynomial, $\phi^+(L)$, can be expanded about its roots with a remainder $\phi^*(L)(1 - L^4)$ as:

$$\phi^+(L) = -\gamma_1 L(1 + L + L^2 + L^3)$$
$$- \gamma_2(-L)(1 - L + L^2 - L^3)$$
$$- (\gamma_3 L + \gamma_4)(-L)(1 - L^2)$$
$$+ \phi^*(L)(1 - L^4) \qquad (7.68)$$

Substituting for $\phi^+(L)$ in the model $\phi(L)^+Y_t = \varepsilon_t$ – see (7.58) – we obtain

$$\phi^*(L)\Delta_4 Y_t = \gamma_1 L(1 + L + L^2 + L^3)Y_t$$
$$+ \gamma_2(-L)(1 - L + L^2 - L^3)Y_t$$
$$+ (\gamma_3 L + \gamma_4)(-L)$$
$$\times (1 - L^2)Y_t + \varepsilon_t$$
$$= \gamma_1 Y_{1t-1} + \gamma_2 Y_{2t-1} + \gamma_3 Y_{3t-2}$$
$$+ \gamma_4 Y_{3t-1} + \varepsilon_t \qquad (7.69)$$

where the following variables have been defined:

$$Y_{1t} \equiv (1 + L + L^2 + L^3)Y_t$$
$$Y_{2t} \equiv -(1 - L + L^2 - L^3)Y_t$$
$$Y_{3t} \equiv -(1 - L^2)Y_t$$

Y_{1t} is effectively seasonally adjusting Y_t since the seasonal components average out over a year

Table 7.5 *Seasonal unit roots: implications and availability of critical values*

Null	Implication	Alternative	Implication	Test statistic
		Implications		
$\gamma_1 = 0$:	$I_0(1)$	$\gamma_1 < 0$	$I_0(0)$	$\hat{\tau}$ type
$\gamma_2 = 0$:	$I_{\frac{1}{2}}(1)$	$\gamma_2 < 0$	$I_{\frac{1}{2}}(0)$	$\hat{\tau}$ type
$\gamma_3 = \gamma_4 = 0$:	$I_{\frac{1}{4}}(1)$	$\gamma_3 \neq 0$ and/or $\gamma_4 \neq 0$	$I_{\frac{1}{4}}(0)$	F type

Alternative strategy to test the null $I_{\frac{1}{4}}(1)$
(i) $\gamma_4 = 0$ against $\gamma_4 \neq 0$ use $\hat{\tau}$ type test statistic
If null not rejected continue with:
(ii) $\gamma_3 = 0$ against $\gamma_3 < 0$ use $\hat{\tau}$ type test statistic
and if $\gamma_4 = 0$ and $\gamma_3 = 0$ do not reject $I_{\frac{1}{4}}(1)$

No seasonal unit roots are present if: $\gamma_2 \neq 0$ and either γ_3 or $\gamma_4 \neq 0$: $I_{\frac{1}{2}}(0)$ and $I_{\frac{1}{4}}(0)$; no standard unit root is present if $\gamma_1 < 0$: $I_0(0)$.

Critical values available for specification of deterministic components in maintained regressions

Intercept (I)	Seasonal dummies (SD)	Trend (Tr)
✗	✗	✗
✓	✗	✗
✓	✓	✗
✓	✗	✓
✓	✓	✓

whether there are two cycles as in the semi-annual pattern or one cycle as in the quarterly pattern.

A test of $\gamma_1 = 0$ corresponds to a test of the standard unit root hypothesis against the one-sided alternative $\gamma_1 < 0$. Y_{2t} leaves in the semi-annual root, if present, of -1 and corresponds to a test of $\gamma_2 = 0$ against the one-sided alternative $\gamma_2 < 0$. The test statistics for these hypotheses are extensions of the $\hat{\tau}$ statistics of Dickey and Fuller which do not, in general, have the 't' distribution. Seasonal roots at the quarterly frequency, that is $\pm i$, correspond to $\gamma_3 = \gamma_4 = 0$. There will be no seasonal unit roots at the quarterly or semi-annual frequency if $\gamma_2 \neq 0$ *and* either γ_3 or $\gamma_4 \neq 0$; hence, this corresponds to rejection of $\gamma_2 = 0$ *and* rejection of the joint test $\gamma_3 = \gamma_4 = 0$.

Critical values are provided in HEGY for the $\hat{\tau}$ statistics on γ_1, γ_2, γ_3, against one-sided negative alternatives; for the $\hat{\tau}$ statistic on γ_4 against the two-sided alternative; and the F test on the joint hypothesis $\gamma_3 = \gamma_4 = 0$. The critical values depend upon the specification of the deterministic components in the maintained regressions, the DGP being $\Delta Y_t = \varepsilon_t$, with $\varepsilon_t \sim \text{nid}(0, 1)$. A summary of the tests, their implications and the deterministic components, is provided in Table 7.5. Small sample 5% critical values for the different specifications of the deterministic terms are provided in Table 7.6.

The basic model $\phi(L)^+ Y_t = \varepsilon_t$ may need to be amended in two ways. First, as in the standard ADF case, if the residuals need to be whitened, then lagged dependent variables, here in the

Table 7.6 5% critical values for HEGY test

Deterministic terms	T	Null: $\gamma_1 = 0$ Alternative: $\gamma_1 < 0$	$\gamma_2 = 0$ $\gamma_2 < 0$	$\gamma_3 = 0$ $\gamma_3 < 0$	$\gamma_4 = 0$ $\gamma_4 \neq 0$ $\gamma_4 < 0$	$\gamma_4 > 0$	$\gamma_3 \cap \gamma_4 = 0$ $\gamma_3 \neq 0$ and/or $\gamma_4 \neq 0$
No intercept	48	-1.95	-1.95	-1.93	-2.11	2.05	3.26
No seasonal dummies	100	-1.97	-1.92	-1.90	-2.01	2.00	3.12
No trend	136	-1.93	-1.94	-1.92	-1.99	1.99	3.14
	200	-1.94	-1.95	-1.92	-1.98	1.97	3.16
Intercept	48	-2.96	-1.95	-1.90	-2.06	2.04	3.04
No seasonal dummies	100	-2.88	-1.95	-1.90	-1.99	1.97	3.08
No trend	136	-2.89	-1.91	-1.88	-1.98	1.97	3.00
	200	-2.87	-1.92	-1.90	-1.98	1.96	3.12
Intercept	48	-3.08	-3.04	-3.61	-2.37	2.35	7.68
Seasonal dummies	100	-2.95	-2.94	-3.44	-2.32	2.29	7.72
No trend	136	-2.94	-2.90	-3.44	-2.31	2.28	7.66
	200	-2.91	-2.89	-3.38	-2.33	2.32	7.53
Intercept	48	-3.56	-1.91	-1.92	-2.05	1.96	2.95
No seasonal dummies	100	-3.47	-1.94	-1.89	-1.97	1.98	2.98
Trend	136	-3.46	-1.96	-1.90	-1.97	1.92	3.04
	200	-3.44	-1.95	-1.92	-1.97	1.96	3.07
Intercept	48	-3.71	-3.08	-3.66	-2.26	2.34	6.55
Seasonal dummies	100	-3.53	-2.94	-3.48	-2.32	2.28	6.60
Trend	136	-3.52	-2.93	-3.44	-2.78	2.31	6.62
	200	-3.49	-2.91	-3.41	-2.27	2.31	6.57

Source: HEGY (*op. cit.*) Tables 1A and 1B.

Table 7.7   Testing for seasonal unit roots in the log of UK consumption

(Augmented) Regression model: $\Delta_4 Y_t = \mu_t + \gamma_1 Y_{1t-1} + \gamma_2 Y_{2t-1} + \gamma_3 Y_{3t-2} + \gamma_4 Y_{3t-1} + \phi_1^* \Delta_4 Y_{t-1} + \phi_4^* \Delta_4 Y_{t-4} + \phi_5^* \Delta_4 Y_{t-5} + \varepsilon_t$					
Null hypothesis Frequency	$\gamma_1 = 0$ zero	$\gamma_2 = 0$ semi-annual	$\gamma_3 = 0$ quarterly	$\gamma_4 = 0$ quarterly	$\gamma_3 = \gamma_4 = 0$ quarterly
Deterministic components, μ_t					
None	2.45(−1.93)	−0.31(−1.94)	0.22(−1.92)	−0.84(−1.99)	0.38(3.14)
I	−1.62(−2.89)	−0.32(−1.91)	0.22(−1.88)	−0.87(−1.98)	0.40(3.00)
I, SD	−1.64(−2.94)	−2.22(−2.90)	−1.47(−3.44)	−1.77(−2.31)	2.52(7.66)
I, Tr	−2.43(−3.46)	−0.35(−1.96)	0.18(−1.90)	−0.85(−1.97)	0.38(3.04)
I, SD, Tr	−2.33(−3.52)	−2.16(−2.93)	−1.53(−3.44)	−1.65(−2.78)	2.43(6.62)

5% critical values in parentheses.
Source: HEGY (*op. cit.*, Table 2; 5% critical values, for $T = 136$, from Table 1);
overall sample period 1955q1 to 1984q4.

form $\Delta_4 Y_{t-j}$, $j = 1, \ldots, p$, could be added. Second, deterministic terms could be added, not only an intercept and trend but also seasonal dummy variables. The possibilities are: no deterministic terms; an intercept; an intercept and seasonal dummies – see the second part of Table 7.5 for a summary of the available critical values and Table 7.6 for the critical values.

HEGY consider the seasonal integration properties of the log of UK consumption expenditures on nondurables, c_t, for the period 1955q1 to 1984q4. An extract from their Table 2 is shown in Table 7.7.

The first column in Table 7.7 gives the sample value of the test statistic for the null hypothesis $\gamma_1 = 0$ against $\gamma_1 < 0$, for different specifications of the deterministic terms; in no case is the sample value more negative than the 5% critical value, so the null hypothesis of a unit root at the zero frequency is not rejected. The picture is the same for the null $\gamma_2 = 0$ against $\gamma_2 < 0$, hence the null of a seasonal unit root at the semi-annual frequency is not rejected. Considering the quarterly frequency (and hence annual cycle) the F (type) test of $\gamma_3 = \gamma_4 = 0$ is not rejected, the sample values being well below the 5% critical values whichever specification of the deterministic terms is used. The null of a seasonal unit root at the annual cycle is, therefore, not rejected. This conclusion is confirmed

by first testing the null of $\gamma_4 = 0$ against the alternative $\gamma_4 \neq 0$ from the penultimate column, and then testing $\gamma_3 = 0$ against $\gamma_3 < 0$ from the middle column. The conclusion from these test statistics is that the log of UK consumption is consistent with the hypotheses of a unit root at the zero, quarterly and semi-annual frequencies, that is $I_0(1)$, $I_{\frac{1}{4}}(1)$ and $I_{\frac{1}{2}}(1)$. HEGY also calculate these test statistics for the log of personal disposable income, y_t, and the log difference of consumption and income, $c_t - y_t$. They conclude that there is a unit root at the zero frequency in y and $c_t - y_t$, and that there is a unit root at the semi-annual frequency in y_t and $c_t - y_t$, as well as in c_t, as we saw in Table 7.7. In contrast to the results for c_t, HEGY did not find evidence of a seasonal unit root in y_t at the quarterly frequency.

7.8   Structural breaks

One criticism of unit root testing is that a stationary series subject to a structural break, for example a change in the intercept or trend, can look like a nonstationary series, with the result that if the structural break(s) is not taken into account the unit root test leads to false nonrejection of the null of nonstationarity. Thus, too often series are concluded to be nonstationary. In an approach suggested by Perron (1989) a single breakpoint is assumed, which is incorporated into the regression model and tests similar to the standard Dickey–Fuller unit root tests are applied. Zivot and Andrews (1992) and Perron (1997) have extended the original methodology to allow the breakpoint to be unknown, which affects the distribution of the unit root test statistics. Franses and Haldrup (1994) have undertaken related work in the context of multiple additive outliers. The next section outlines the Perron/Zivot–Andrews approach.

7.8.1   The Perron (1989) approach to a single structural break

Suppose given a sample $1, \ldots, T$ of observations on Y_t, it is known that there is a structural break in the series at T_b, where $1 < T_b < T$. Consider the following three extensions of the random walk with drift model, $Y_t = \mu + Y_{t-1} + \varepsilon_t$, where Y_t is assumed to be in logarithms and, for simplicity, no further dynamics are assumed present.

Model A: change in the level effective in $T_b + 1$:

$$Y_t = \mu + \delta_1 \text{DVTB}_t + Y_{t-1} + \varepsilon_t;$$
$$\text{DVTB}_t = 1 \quad \text{if } t = T_b + 1, \ \text{DVTB}_t = 0$$
$$\text{if } t \neq T_b + 1 \tag{7.70}$$

Model B: change in the growth rate effective at $T_b + 1$:

$$Y_t = \mu + \delta_2 \text{DVU}_t + Y_{t-1} + \varepsilon_t;$$
$$\text{DVU}_t = 0 \quad \text{if } t \leq T_b$$
$$\text{and} \quad \text{DVU}_t = 1 \quad \text{if } t > T_b \tag{7.71}$$

Model C: change in the level and in the growth rate effective at $T_b + 1$:

$$Y_t = \mu + \delta_1 \text{DVTB}_t + \delta_2 \text{DVU}_t + Y_{t-1} + \varepsilon_t \tag{7.72}$$

The dummy variable coefficients are δ_1 for the effect on the level and δ_2 for the effect on the growth rate μ. The difference between the two dummy variables is that DVTB_t is a one-off, or 'impulse', dummy, zero everywhere except $T_b + 1$ when it is 1; the effect in $T_b + 1$ is to increase Y_t by δ_1 which, because of the unit root, also changes the level thereafter by δ_1; *ceteris paribus*, Y_t is shifted by δ_1 from $T_b + 1$ onwards. The effect of the change is not distinguishable from a change of δ_1 in the innovation ε_t. The growth dummy variable, DVU_t, is 0 before T_b and 1 thereafter and so maintains the change; the growth rate becomes $\mu + \delta_2$ at $T_b + 1$ and so changes the underlying slope of the (stochastic) trend.

The alternative hypotheses are:

Model A: trend stationary, one-time change in the level:

$$Y_t = \mu + \beta t + \delta_2 \text{DVU}_t + \varepsilon_t \tag{7.73}$$

Model B: trend stationary, change in the trend slope (growth):

$$Y_t = \mu + \beta t + \delta_3 \text{DVT}_t^* + \varepsilon_t;$$
$$\text{DVT}_t^* = 0 \quad \text{if } t \leq T_b,$$
$$\text{DVT}_t^* = t - T_b \quad \text{if } t > T_b \tag{7.74}$$

Model C: change in the level and change in the trend slope (growth):

$$Y_t = \mu + \beta t + \delta_2 \text{DVU}_t + \delta_3 \text{DVT}_t + \varepsilon_t;$$
$$\text{DVT}_t = 0 \quad \text{if } t \leq T_b, \ \text{DVT}_t = t \quad \text{if } t > T_b \tag{7.75}$$

As drift is included in Models A to C of the null hypothesis, the alternative includes a deterministic trend, otherwise the null and alternative models are mismatched in being able to explain economic time series. In Model A the null hypothesis is a unit root with level change and the alternative is trend stationary with a change in the intercept to $\mu + \delta_2$. In Model B the null hypothesis is a unit root with change in the drift and the alternative is trend stationary with a change in the slope to $\beta + \delta_3$. In Model C the null hypothesis is a unit root with change in the level and drift, and the alternative is trend stationary with changes in the intercept and slope. In practice further dynamics may need to be added to whiten the residuals.

By means of some simple Monte Carlo simulations Perron (*op. cit.*) demonstrates that if the data is generated according to the alternative hypothesis, and so is trend stationary but with a structural break, the mean of the OLS estimator of ϕ_1^* in $Y_t = \mu^* + \phi_1^* Y_{t-1} + \beta^* t + \varepsilon_t^*$ gets closer to 1 as the size of the structural break increases, as indicated by either of the dummy variable coefficients δ_2 or δ_3, thus falsely suggesting a unit root.

Perron (*op. cit.*) suggests two procedures depending on whether adjustment following the break is assumed to be instantaneous or gradual. The former is referred to as the additive outlier, AO, case, which is a one-off effect at the time of the break; whereas the latter is referred to as the innovation outlier, IO, case, the effect is the same as a shock to the innovation at the time of the break, which in a dynamic equation is spread over several, and possibly an infinite number of, periods.

In the AO framework the first step is to construct residuals by regressing Y_t on the set of deterministic terms specified by the alternative hypothesis. These differ depending which model is relevant:

Model A, regress Y_t on a constant, a time trend and DVU_t;
Model B, regress Y_t on a constant, a time trend and DVT_t^*;
Model C, regress Y_t on a constant, a time trend, DVU_t and DVT_t.

Denote the residuals as $\tilde{Y}_t^{(i)}$ for $i = $ A, B, C and, as in an augmented DF regression, regress $\tilde{Y}_t^{(i)}$ on its first lag and, if necessary, p lagged first differences. That is

$$\tilde{Y}_t^{(i)} = \tilde{\phi}_1 \tilde{Y}_{t-1}^{(i)} + \sum_{j=1}^{p} \alpha_j \Delta \tilde{Y}_{t-j}^{(i)} + \tilde{\varepsilon}_t \qquad (7.76)$$

and subtracting $\tilde{Y}_{t-1}^i$ from both sides results in the familiar ADF regression which is then estimated by OLS,

$$\Delta \tilde{Y}_t^{(i)} = \tilde{\gamma} \tilde{Y}_{t-1}^{(i)} + \sum_{j=1}^{p} \alpha_j \Delta \tilde{Y}_{t-j}^{(i)} + \tilde{\varepsilon}_t \qquad (7.77)$$

where $\tilde{\gamma} = \tilde{\phi}_1 - 1$. To distinguish the set-up we refer to this ADF as an Additive Outlier ADF, AOADF$_i$, with $i = $ A in this case. Perron obtains the asymptotic critical values for $T(\tilde{\phi}_1 - 1)$ and the 't' statistic on $\tilde{\gamma}$, which depend upon the model, (A, B or C) and relative breakpoint $\lambda = T_b/T$. The 't' statistics do not have the 't' distribution and are referred to here as $\tilde{\tau}$ statistics: $\tilde{\tau}_A$, $\tilde{\tau}_B$ and $\tilde{\tau}_C$. The variations with respect to λ are quite slight, peaking at $\lambda = 0.5$; what is noticeable is that the critical values are larger in absolute value than the standard DF critical values. For example, the 5% critical value of $\tilde{\tau}_A$ for $\lambda = 0.5$ is -3.76, whereas the 5% critical value of $\hat{\tau}_B$, (for $\beta = 0$ in the DGP) is -3.41 (Fuller *op. cit.*, Table 8.5.2). Perron's asymptotic critical values for 5% and 10% significance levels are reproduced in Table 7.8 on page 283. It is relevant to note that, for a given significance level and λ, $\tilde{\tau}_A < \tilde{\tau}_B < \tilde{\tau}_C$. Illustrative examples of the use of these test statistics follow a description of the alternative IO approach.

In the IO approach the deterministic terms (constant, trend and dummy variables) are incorporated directly into the ADF regression in the untransformed variables, Y_t and ΔY_{t-i}. In this way the 'impulses' captured by the dummy variables, for example DVU_t is a sustained impulse of 1 for $t > T_b$, are treated as if they were changes to the innovations, ε_t. Because of this their effect is distributed over current and future Y_t, just as a one-unit change in ε_t would be – see (6.3) and (6.6).

Consider the following extension of the ADF regression model with time trend, which is relevant to distinguishing between the null and alternative hypotheses of Model A:

$$\Delta Y_t = \mu + \gamma Y_{t-1} + \beta t + \delta_1 \mathrm{DVTB}_t$$

$$+ \delta_2 \mathrm{DVU}_t + \sum_{j=1}^{p} \alpha_j \Delta Y_{t-j} + \varepsilon_t \qquad (7.78)$$

with $\gamma = \phi_1 - 1$. This type of model is referred to as a Innovation Outlier ADF, IOADF$_i$; $i = $ A in this case; it is a standard ADF regression with the addition of the dummy variable effects $\delta_1 DVTB_t$ and $\delta_2 DVU_t$, which are specified under the null and alternative hypotheses of Model A, respectively; thus the null and alternative hypotheses are nested as special cases of this model. A unit root corresponds to $\phi_1 = 1$, that is $\gamma = 0$, which can be tested with the τ type statistic for $\gamma = 0$ against the usual one-sided alternative $\gamma < 0$; the hat notation $\hat{\tau}$ is used for 't' (type) statistics from this (IO) model. The asymptotic critical values for $\hat{\tau}_A$ are the same as for $\tilde{\tau}_A$ in the AO model, Perron (*op. cit.*, Table IV.B), reproduced in Table 7.8 for the 10% and 5% significance levels and depend upon $\lambda = T_b/T$. Model A is appropriate where the structural break is a change in the level.

Model B is relevant where the structural break is a change in the slope. The relevant IOADF regression model for Model B is

$$\Delta Y_t = \mu + \gamma Y_{t-1} + \beta t + \delta_2 DVU_t$$
$$+ \delta_3 DVT_t^* + \sum_{j=1}^{p} \alpha_j \Delta Y_{t-j} + \varepsilon_t \quad (7.79)$$

with the 't' test statistic for $\gamma = 0$ against $\gamma < 0$ denoted $\hat{\tau}_B$. The asymptotic distribution of $\hat{\tau}_B$ is *not* the same as the asymptotic distribution of $\tilde{\tau}_B$; this is considered further below after the test procedure for Model C.

In Model C the structural break is simultaneously a change in the level and a change in the slope. The relevant IOADF regression model is:

$$\Delta Y_t = \mu + \gamma Y_{t-1} + \beta t + \delta_1 DVTB_t$$
$$+ \delta_2 DVU_t + \delta_3 DVT_t$$
$$+ \sum_{j=1}^{p} \alpha_j \Delta Y_{t-j} + \varepsilon_t \quad (7.80)$$

with the 't' test statistic for $\gamma = 0$ against $\gamma < 0$ denoted $\hat{\tau}_C$. The asymptotic critical values for $\hat{\tau}_C$ are the same as for $\tilde{\tau}_C$ in the AO model.

Now compare the specification of the deterministic components in calculating $\tilde{Y}_t^{(i)}$ and in the IOADF$_i$ models. On the pairwise comparison between AOADF and IOADF, in each case Models A and C differ only by $DVTB_t$; and since $DVTB_t$ is a pure impulse dummy, which takes the value 1 in only *one* period and is zero elsewhere, the asymptotic distribution of the test statistics will be the same. Hence, the asymptotic distributions of $\hat{\tau}_A$ and $\tilde{\tau}_A$ are the same, and the asymptotic distributions of $\hat{\tau}_C$ and $\tilde{\tau}_C$ are the same. However, this is not the case for τ_B and τ_B because the underlying regressions differ by DVU_t (needed under the null) which is *not* a pure impulse dummy and, therefore, affects the distribution of the test statistic. Note that the deterministic terms in the IOADF for Models B and C differ only by $DVTB_t$, but by the previous argument this does not change the asymptotic distribution of the test statistic; hence, the asymptotic distribution of $\hat{\tau}_B$ is the same as that of $\tilde{\tau}_C$. However, since $\tilde{\tau}_C > \tilde{\tau}_B$ there will be a loss of power in using the IOADF for Model B rather than the AOADF.

Perron (*op. cit.*) suggests the following variation which just includes the deterministic components of the alternative hypothesis of Model B, a constant, time trend and DVT_t^*, and thus matches the derivation of $\tilde{Y}_t^{(B)}$, and to distinguish the model it is denoted Model B*; That is

Model B*: $\Delta Y_t = \mu + \gamma Y_{t-1} + \beta t + \delta_3 DVT_t^*$
$$+ \sum_{j=1}^{p} \alpha_j \Delta Y_{t-j} + \varepsilon_t \quad (7.81)$$

In this model the asymptotic distribution of $\hat{\tau}_B$ is the same as $\tilde{\tau}_B$.

Perron (*op. cit.*) gives several examples of his testing procedure. A preliminary analysis of the 62 annual observations, 1909 to 1970, for US real GNP, suggested that there was potentially a structural break following the 'Great Crash' of 1929 which could be characterised as a gradual change in the level but no change in the slope.

The candidate model based on a gradual adjustment to the break was, therefore, Model A specified as an IOADF regression. Estimation gave, with 't' statistics in parentheses:

$$\Delta Y_t = 3.441 - 0.718Y_{t-1} + 0.0267t$$
$$\quad\;\; (5.07)\;(-5.03)\qquad\quad (5.05)$$

$$\quad -0.018\text{DVTB}_t - 0.189\text{DVU}_t$$
$$\quad\;\; (-0.30)\qquad\quad (-4.28)$$

$$\quad + \sum_{j=1}^{p} \alpha_j \Delta Y_{t-j} + \varepsilon_t \qquad (7.82)$$

't' statistics in parentheses.

Perron chose $p = 8$ with a general-to-specific strategy where the stopping rule is when the first significant coefficient is found. The procedure is to work down from a maximum of p^* (also equal to 8 in this case) deleting insignificant, marginal coefficients judged as the 't' statistic being less than 1.60 in absolute value. The 5% asymptotic critical value for for $\hat{\tau}_A$ for $\lambda = 0.33$ is -3.75, whereas the sample value is -5.03; hence the null within this maintained regression is rejected. Note also that the coefficient on Y_{t-1} is a long way from 0; the time trend is significant with a 't' statistic of 5.05, as is the dummy variable, DVU_t, for the change in the intercept, with a 't' statistic of -4.28 confirming the view that a trend stationary model with a level change in 1929 is consistent with the data (although Perron (*op. cit.*) notes rejection of the null of a unit root in favour of the alternative of stationary fluctuations around a breaking trend function does not imply acceptance of the alternative).

A different picture seems to characterise post-war quarterly GNP following the 1973 oil price shock. Perron (*op. cit.*, p. 1382) suggests that while there was not a step change in the level there was a slow down in the growth rate. The appropriate model is, therefore, Model B; however, because of the difficulty of testing for a unit root allowing for lagged effects (IOADF$_B$) the alternative test procedure using Model B* was adopted. With a sample of $T = 159$ observations, 1947q1 to 1986q3, with $T_b = 1973$q1 and thus $\lambda \approx 0.66$, the model was estimated in two stages and is an example of an additive rather than innovation outlier model. A preliminary regression was run of Y_t on a constant, a trend and DVT$_t^*$, which defined the residuals $\tilde{Y}_t$:

$$\tilde{Y}_t = Y_t - (6.977 + 0.0087t - 0.0031\text{DVT}_t^*)$$
$$\qquad\quad (1160.51)\;(97.73)\;(-12.06)\quad (7.83)$$

't' statistics in parentheses.

Then an ADF regression is run using the residuals:

$$\Delta \tilde{Y}_t = -0.14Y_{t-1} + \sum_{j=1}^{10} \alpha_j \Delta \tilde{Y}_{t-j} + \hat{\varepsilon}_t \quad (7.84)$$
$$\qquad\quad (-3.98)$$

't' statistics in parentheses.

A standard ADF regression model without any structural breaks gave

$$\Delta Y_t = 0.386 - 0.054Y_{t-1} + 0.0004t$$
$$\qquad (2.90)\;(-2.85)\qquad\quad (2.71)$$

$$\quad + \sum_{j=1}^{2} \alpha_j \Delta Y_{t-j} + \hat{\varepsilon}_t \qquad (7.85)$$

't' statistics in parentheses.

The 5% asymptotic critical value for $\tilde{\tau}_B$ with $\lambda = 0.66$ is -3.89, while the sample value for $p = 10$ is -3.98 indicating rejection of the null hypothesis of a unit root. To the extent that the small sample critical value (not given in Perron (*op. cit.*)) will be larger than the asymptotic critical value for a given size, use of the latter will bias the test to rejection of the null; this point is addressed again below. Note that in (7.83) the time trend and the dummy variable capturing a change in the slope are both significant.

In the standard ADF regression $\hat{\tau}_B$ is -2.85 compared to a 5% asymptotic critical value of -3.41 or small sample critical value of -3.46 from Table 6.8 for $T = 100$ (-3.43 for $T = 200$, both assume $\beta = 0$); the conclusion here is that the null hypothesis of a unit root is not rejected. With $p = 2$, rather than 10 in Perron's model, to match the standard ADF model, the test statistic is -3.97 so there is virtually no change. However, this is not so for $p = 1$, or $p = 3, \ldots, 9$, where the test statistics are less negative than the 5% critical value implying nonrejection of the null hypothesis of a unit root. Thus, as usual, much hinges on an appropriate choice of the lag length, whichever version of the ADF model is used; in this respect Perron (*op. cit.*, fn 10) notes that the 10th lagged first difference was significant with a 't' statistic of 2.29 whereas the 11th and 12th lagged first differences were not.

Extensions of the Perron approach involving multiple structural breaks are easy to deal with by a suitable definition of dummy variables, although the appropriate critical values would have to be obtained by simulation. Also Zivot and Andrews (1992) argue that under the alternative hypothesis the breakpoint should be treated as unknown and by not doing so Perron biases his results in favour of rejection of the unit root hypothesis. In the Zivot and Andrews framework the null, for series like GNP, would be a unit root process with drift, in which case the Great Crash would be viewed as a realisation from the left tail of the distribution of the underlying DGP; this explanation does not need a special event dummy variable. Zivot and Andrews' testing procedure leads to a reversal of Perron's conclusion of rejection of the unit root hypothesis in four out of 10 cases for the Nelson–Plosser series, and also reverses Perron's conclusion for rejection of the unit root for post-war quarterly GNP.

In the Zivot–Andrews' framework the null hypothesis is $Y_t = \mu + Y_{t-1} + \varepsilon_t$, so the series is integrated of order 1 without any form of structural break. The alternative hypotheses for Models A, B and C are as in Perron with two differences. First, because under the null there is no structural break the dummy variable $DVTB_t$ is absent from Models A and C; second, Model B* is used rather than Model B. Within this context the breakpoint is assumed to be one time at an

unknown point: 'The goal is to estimate the breakpoint that gives the most weight to the trend-stationary alternative', Zivot and Andrews (*op. cit.*, p. 254). λ is chosen to minimise the one-sided 't' (type) statistic for testing $\gamma^i = 0$, $i = $ A, B, C, where small (that is, in this context, large negative) values of the test statistic lead to rejection of the null hypothesis; denote the value of λ which yields the minimum as $\hat{\lambda}^i$ for model i. In all $T - 2$ regressions are estimated by allowing λ to vary over the range $2/T$ to $(T - 1)/T$. Because λ is estimated the critical values are now no longer the same as those used by Perron and are smaller, that is more negative, for a given size. For example, with Model A the 5% asymptotic critical value is -4.80 whereas the average over λ of Perron's critical values is -3.74. A summary of the 5% and 10% critical values, extracted from those in Zivot and Andrews (*op. cit.*), is provided in Table 7.8.

Zivot and Andrews (*op. cit.*) estimated the breakpoint for the 13 annual series and one quarterly series considered by Perron (*op. cit.*). Perron (*op. cit.*) selected Model A for 11 series; for the same series the Zivot–Andrews estimated breakpoint agreed with Perron's choice of 1929 in eight cases. For the other two annual series, common-stock prices and real wages, Perron selected Model C; in these cases the estimated breakpoints were 1936 and 1940, respectively. For the quarterly series of real GNP the minimising breakpoint with Model B* was 1972q2 compared to Perron's choice of 1973q1.

Perron (1997) has contributed further to the methodology and empirical analysis of unit root testing within the framework of breaking trend functions. He introduces the selection criterion of choosing λ where the 't' statistic on the parameter associated with the change shows greatest evidence of change. Prior information may be included in this selection criterion by looking for large negative values of the 't' statistic, which are associated with the negative one-sided alternative of a 'crash'; small sample and asymptotic critical values are provided in Perron (*op. cit.*). The last column of Table 7.8

Table 7.8 *Asymptotic critical values of $\tilde{\tau}_A$, $\tilde{\tau}_B$, $\tilde{\tau}_C$, for: λ known; λ unknown; and selection of breakpoint by minimising the 't' statistic on change variable*

λ	0.1	0.2	0.3	0.4	0.5	0.6	0.7	0.8	0.9	λ unknown	Min. 't' statistic
				λ known							
5%										Zivot–Andrews	Perron (1997)
$\tilde{\tau}_A$	−3.68	−3.77	−3.76	−3.72	−3.76	−3.76	−3.80	−3.75	−3.69	−4.80	−4.64
$\tilde{\tau}_B^*$	−3.65	−3.80	−3.87	−3.94	−3.96	−3.95	−3.85	−3.82	−3.68	−4.42	−4.08
$\tilde{\tau}_C$	−3.75	−3.99	−4.17	−4.22	−4.24	−4.24	−4.18	−4.04	−3.80	−5.08	−4.62
10%											
$\tilde{\tau}_A$	−3.40	−3.47	−3.46	−3.44	−3.46	−3.47	−3.51	−3.46	−3.38	−4.58	−4.37
$\tilde{\tau}_B^*$	−3.36	−3.49	−3.58	−3.66	−3.68	−3.66	−3.57	−3.50	−3.35	−4.11	−3.77
$\tilde{\tau}_C$	−3.45	−3.66	−3.87	−3.95	−3.96	−3.95	−3.86	−3.69	−3.46	−4.82	−4.28

Source: Extracted from Zivot and Andrews (*op. cit.*, Tables 2, 3 and 4) and Perron (1997, Table 1); $\lambda = T_b/T$. In the Zivot–Andrews methodology λ is unknown *a priori*, and the test statistic is chosen to maximise the evidence against the null. $\tilde{\tau}_A$, $\tilde{\tau}_B^*$ and $\tilde{\tau}_C$ are the test statistics from Models A, B* and C, respectively.

gives the asymptotic critical values for the case where the breakpoint is assumed be one-time and the criterion for choice is: minimising the 't' statistic on δ_2, the coefficient on DVU_t in the IOADF, for Model A; minimising the 't' statistic on δ_3, the coefficient on DVT_t in the IOADF, for Model C. The variant of Model B is the additive outlier model with a prior regression of Y_t on a constant, t and DVT_t^*, saving the residuals for the subsequent ADF regression, with the selection criterion minimising the 't' statistic on DVT_t^* in the prior regression. These critical values are smaller in absolute value than when the breakpoint is chosen by the Zivot and Andrews method and larger in absolute value than when the breakpoint is assumed known.

In Perron (1989), Model A was the basis of an evaluation of 11 of the Nelson–Plosser time series for a unit root in the context of the possibility of a structural break with 1929 as the fixed breakpoint. Perron's (1997) re-evaluation included data dependent selection of the breakpoint and a general-to-specific strategy for selecting the lag order in the ADF. As to the former the Zivot–Andrews method of choosing the breakpoint and minimising the 't' statistic on the change coefficient were used; these suggested that 1929 remained the breakpoint

for two of the series, with 1928 for six series and breakpoints 9 years or more away from 1929 for the remaining three series. In the original study Perron (1989) concluded that the unit root hypothesis can be rejected for eight and not rejected for three of the 11 series relevant here. In his re-evaluation 'The only series offering a markedly different picture from the fixed T_b case is the GNP deflator', Perron (*op. cit.*, p. 370). With T_b fixed *a priori* at 1929, $\hat{\tau}_A = -4.04$ compared to the 5% asymptotic critical value of −3.76 ($\lambda = 0.5$) suggesting rejection of the null of a unit root, whereas in the re-evaluation T_b is chosen to be 1928 according to the Zivot–Andrews criterion, with $\hat{\tau}_A = -4.14$ compared to the 5% asymptotic critical value of −4.80, suggesting nonrejection; according to the Perron criterion $T_b = 1919$ with $\hat{\tau}_A = -3.24$ compared to the 5% asymptotic critical value of −4.64, which again suggests nonrejection.

7.8.2 Additive outliers, Franses and Haldrup (1994)

Franses and Haldrup (1994) consider the effect of additive outliers on unit root (and cointegration) tests. An additive outlier has a one-off impact. For example, in the AR(1) model $Y_t = \phi_1 Y_{t-1} + \varepsilon_t$, an additive outlier of magnitude θ means that the observed time series is $Z_t = Y_t + \theta$; if the presence of the outlier is not certain, say it occurs with probability π, the observed time series is $Z_t = Y_t + \theta\delta_t$ where δ_t takes the value 1 with probability π and 0 with probability $1 - \pi$. For an outlier to be additive it must affect observations in isolation. For example, an anticipated change in expenditure tax may induce hoarding behaviour; a dock strike may temporarily affect imports and exports. In contrast to the implications of structural breaks suggested by Perron's work, additive outliers, which by definition only have a temporary effect, may give the impression that a series is stationary when it is not; this is especially so when there are multiple additive outliers. Franses and Haldrup (*op. cit.*) call this spurious stationarity. They find that if the probability of an additive outlier is positive, the Dickey–Fuller $\hat{\tau}$ test has an actual size greater than its nominal size, with the implication that the unit root hypothesis is rejected too often. Additive outliers usually show up in the residuals of regression models, with the likely consequence being rejection of the null of normally distributed residuals. If additive outliers can be detected then they can be removed with impulse dummy variables, which do not affect the limiting distribution of the test statistics, included in an otherwise standard DF regression. If the regression is ADF(p), $p > 0$, $p + 1$ lags of the dummy variable should also be included (recall ADF(p) = AR($p + 1$)). For example, suppose a prior analysis suggests the presence of 2 events leading to additive outliers with impulse dummy variables AODV$_i$, $i = 1, 2$, then the ADF(p) is

$$\Delta Y_t = \mu + \gamma Y_{t-1} + \beta t + \sum_{j=1}^{p} \alpha_j \Delta Y_{t-j}$$

$$+ \sum_{j=0}^{p+1} \delta_{1j} \text{AODV}_{1t-j}$$

$$+ \sum_{j=0}^{p+1} \delta_{2j} \text{AODV}_{2t-j} + \varepsilon_t \qquad (7.86)$$

Inference on γ then proceeds as usual. Franses and Haldrup's result that the presence of the dummy variables does not alter the distribution of the $\hat{\tau}$ test statistic presumes that the location of the additive outliers is known through a method that is not data dependent. Otherwise, as shown in Zivot and Andrews (*op. cit.*) and Perron (1997), a data dependent selection procedure does have implications for the asymptotic distribution.

7.8.3   Summary

This section has outlined two possible approaches to outliers in the regression model that forms the basis of inference on the unit root hypothesis. In the Perron approach a single structural break is assumed, where the break may affect the level or growth rate or both. The breakpoint may be assumed known as with the 'Great Crash' of 1929 or 'the oil price crisis' of 1973. If the breakpoint is known this results in a more powerful test compared to an unknown breakpoint, which has to be estimated. For a given significance level the absolute value of the critical value is smaller if the breakpoint is known.

Perron's argument is that the great crash and oil price shocks had persistent effects; however, because the standard unit root framework does not allow for the structural break it mistakenly leads to the conclusion that the observed persistence in the macroeconomic time series is due to a unit root rather than these special 'exogenous' events. Standard tests without allowance for the structural break are biased toward nonrejection of the null of a unit root; hence the finding of nonstationarity is spurious. Franses and Haldrup's (1994) additive outliers framework leads to the opposite conclusion in the presence of 'one-shot' effects. Multiple additive outliers with one-off impulse effects could be confused with stationary deviations, hence leading to a spurious finding of stationarity (and spurious cointegration in a multivariate context).

The Perron framework assumes one breakpoint so, for example, none of the Nelson–Plosser annual series considered by Perron (1989) cover both the great crash and the oil price shock, although there would be no problem in extending the data, otherwise at least two breakpoints would need to be considered. It might seem somewhat restrictive to set the framework so that only a single breakpoint is allowed. A generalisation of both Perron's single structural break and Franses and Haldrup's multiple additive outlier analysis would allow switching between regimes so that at t there are several possible states each with positive probability. Thus over the course of T observations there could be several changes in level or slope and multiple outliers. For a useful framework in the context of a structural univariate model see Harrison and Stevens (1976).

7.9 Applications to some economic time series

7.9.1 UK consumers' expenditure on nondurables

In this section some of the procedures described in this and the previous chapter are applied to some economic time series. The first series is the log of the UK per capita consumers' expenditure on nondurable goods, seasonally adjusted, quarterly from 1955q1 to 1990q2 giving a sample, before lagging, of 142 observations. Taking the logarithm of the series is sensible in order to allow for the possibility that the rate of growth of consumers' expenditure, which is the first difference of the log of the level, is stationary. As a shorthand the variable, in logarithms, is referred to as cnd_t. In this section a standard set of test statistics for unit roots is applied, which is often the kind of empirical analysis found in published empirical work. However, in addition the sensitivity and robustness of the results are assessed, particularly with respect to aspects of

model selection and choice of test statistic. In the case of cnd_t this sensitivity analysis illustrates the care which should be taken in forming conclusions about whether a series is nonstationary.

cnd_t is graphed in Figure 7.1A from which it is evident that there is a clear positive trend, so that the series is an I(d) candidate with $d \geq 1$. The first and second differences of the series are graphed in Figures 7.1C and 7.1E; the autocorrelations are graphed in Figures 7.1B, 7.1D and 7.1F. The autocorrelations of the levels die away but rather slowly indicating a series with a long memory – see Figure 7.1B – raising the problem that if the series is stationary it may be difficult to distinguish from a nonstationary series. If cnd_t is I(1) its first difference should be stationary. The first difference, graphed in Figure 7.1C, has a nonzero mean and some positive, but not excessively persistent, autocorrelation. This is confirmed in Figure 7.1D where, in contrast to the autocorrelations for the levels, the autocorrelations die out quite quickly; overall, the visual evidence is for a series with 1 unit root at most. To confirm this consider the second difference of the series in Figure 7.1E; now the series looks stationary, a picture also suggested by the autocorrelations in Figure 7.1F which are close to zero very quickly.

Given the distinct trend present in cnd_t the maintained regression should initially include the term βt. In order to ensure that the residuals are not serially correlated it is necessary to augment the regression with ΔZ_{t-j} for $j = 1, \ldots, 4$ when testing for 2 unit roots, that is an ADF(4) model with trend, and ΔY_{t-j} for $j = 1, \ldots, 5$ when testing for 1 unit root, that is an ADF(5) model with trend. Rationalisation of this choice is given in detail below. Explicitly the maintained regressions in testing for 2 unit roots are

$$\Delta Z_t = \mu + \gamma Z_{t-1}$$
$$+ \sum_{j=1}^{4} \alpha_j \Delta Z_{t-j} + \beta t + \varepsilon_t \qquad (7.87)$$

Constant Prices, sa

A

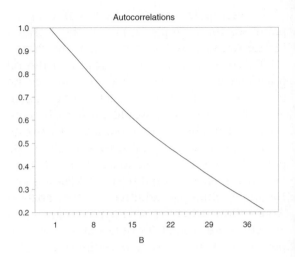

Autocorrelations

B

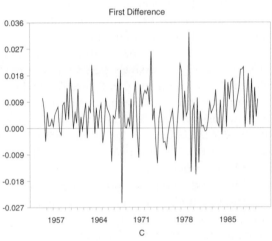

First Difference

C

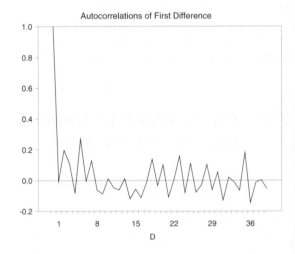

Autocorrelations of First Difference

D

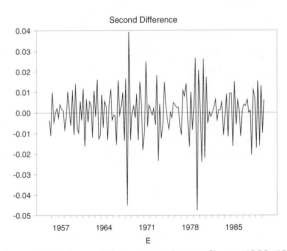

Second Difference

E

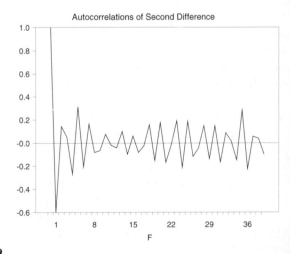

Autocorrelations of Second Difference

F

Figure 7.1   A–F – *UK consumers' expenditure, 1955–1990*

with

$$Z_t \equiv \Delta Y_t$$

and testing for 1 unit root the maintained regression is

$$\Delta Y_t = \mu + \gamma Y_{t-1}$$

$$+ \sum_{j=1}^{5} \alpha_j \Delta Y_{t-j} + \beta t + \varepsilon_t \qquad (7.88)$$

Table 7.9 provides a summary of the unit root test statistics, with more detailed results from the regressions underlying the various test statistics provided in Table 7.10. In later chapters the general format is to report a summary table, which is usually sufficient to inform decisions about the number of unit roots; however, information from the ADF regressions, especially the numerical magnitude of the coeffi-

cient on Y_{t-1}, should not be overlooked in any practical application. Table 7.10 is provided here so that the connection between the estimated models and test statistics is readily apparent.

As noted above an ADF(4) regression was necessary in testing for 2 unit roots; the Lagrange-Multiplier test statistic for up to fourth order serial correlation in this model was SC(4) = 4.544, with a marginal significance level of 33.7%. The last lagged difference ΔZ_{t-4} was significant with a 't' statistic of -2.733. In Table 7.9 the Φ_3 statistic for the joint hypothesis of a second (marginal) unit root, conditional on 1 unit root, and no time trend is 7.875. From Table 6.7 the 5% critical value of the Φ_3 test for $T = 100$ is 6.606 (and 6.397 for $T = 200$); as $7.875 > 6.606$ the null hypothesis is rejected. Notice from Table 7.10 that the estimated coefficient on Z_{t-1} is -0.666 which seems numerically quite a long way from the null

Table 7.9 *Unit root tests for cnd_t, $UKUR_t$ and $USUR_t$*

Variable	Model	$\hat{\tau}$	Φ_1	$\hat{\tau}_\mu$	$\hat{\mu}$	$\hat{\tau}_\beta$	$\hat{\beta}$	Φ_3
			Test statistics for 2 unit roots					
cnd_t	ADF(4)	-2.108	6.841	-3.804	0.003	-3.963	0.000	7.875
$USUR_t$	ADF(3)	-4.814	11.553	-4.805	-0.002	-4.907	-0.000	12.125
			Test statistics for 1 unit root					
cnd_t	ADF(5)	3.039	5.017	1.032	-0.021	-1.466	0.000	1.855
$UKUR_t$	ADF(1)	-2.144	14.481	-5.381	2.499	-5.456	0.014	14.889
$USUR_t$	ADF(4)	-0.410	4.629	-3.039	0.186	-3.145	-0.000	5.539

Critical values

		$\hat{\tau}$	Φ_1	$\hat{\tau}_\mu$	$\hat{\tau}_\beta$	Φ_3
			$T = 50$, $p = 1$			
	5%	-1.952	4.809	-2.905	-3.484	6.776
	10%	-1.610	3.917	-2.585	-3.168	5.667
			$T = 140$, $p = 4$			
	5%	-1.923	4.740	-2.857	-3.402	6.606
	10%	-1.600	3.855	-2.553	-3.112	5.555
			$T = 270$, $p = 4$			
	5%	-1.930	4.696	-2.856	-3.407	6.397
	10%	-1.605	3.835	-2.561	-3.120	5.433

Critical values of $\hat{\tau}$, $\hat{\tau}_\mu$ and $\hat{\tau}_\beta$ obtained using Cheung–Lai response surface coefficients; critical values of Φ_1 and Φ_3 obtained by simulation for $T = 50$, $T = 100$ and $T = 200$, respectively – see Chapter 6.

Table 7.10 *Regression results corresponding to unit root tests*

Variable: cnd_t
Sample: 1955q1 to 1990q2 (before lagging)

2 unit roots

$\Delta Z_t = 0.002 - 0.666Z_{t-1} - 0.332\Delta Z_{t-1} - 0.150\Delta Z_{t-2} - 0.101\Delta Z_{t-3} - 0.233\Delta Z_{t-4} + 0.000t$
$\quad\quad (1.406)(-3.963) \quad (-2.186) \quad\;\; (-1.076) \quad\;\; (-0.839) \quad\;\; (-2.133) \quad\quad\;\; (1.118)$
$\hfill$ SC(4)
$\hfill$ 4.544[0.337]

$\Delta Z_t = 0.003 - 0.604Z_{t-1} - 0.382\Delta Z_{t-1} - 0.189\Delta Z_{t-2} - 0.130\Delta Z_{t-3} - 0.249\Delta Z_{t-4}$
$\quad\quad (3.137)(-3.804) \quad (-2.635) \quad\;\; (-1.400) \quad\;\; (-1.097) \quad\;\; (-2.941)$
$\hfill$ 3.862[0.424]

$\Delta Z_t = \quad\quad\quad - 0.221Z_{t-1} - 0.675\Delta Z_{t-1} - 0.402\Delta Z_{t-2} - 0.277\Delta Z_{t-3} - 0.326\Delta Z_{t-4}$
$\quad\quad\quad\quad\quad\;\; (-2.108) \quad\;\; (-5.891) \quad\quad (-3.337) \quad\quad (-2.475) \quad\quad (-3.898)$
$\hfill$ 3.789[0.435]

1 unit root

$\Delta Y_t = 0.262 - 0.042Y_{t-1} + 0.036\Delta Y_{t-1} + 0.211\Delta Y_{t-2} + 0.085\Delta Y_{t-3} - 0.087\Delta Y_{t-4} + 0.271\Delta Y_{t-5} + 0.000t$
$\quad\quad (1.476) \;\; (1.466) \quad\;\; (0.416) \quad\quad\;\; (2.435) \quad\quad\;\; (0.968) \quad\quad\;\; (0.971) \quad\quad\;\; (3.022) \quad\quad\;\; (1.623)$
$\hfill$ 3.751[0.441]

$\Delta Y_t = -0.021 + 0.004Y_{t-1} + 0.001\Delta Y_{t-1} + 0.181\Delta Y_{t-2} + 0.051\Delta Y_{t-3} + 0.134\Delta Y_{t-4} + 0.229\Delta Y_{t-5}$
$\quad\quad (-0.898) \; (1.032) \quad\;\; (0.016) \quad\quad\;\; (2.119) \quad\quad\;\; (0.587) \quad\quad (-1.564) \quad\quad\;\; (2.654)$
$\hfill$ 4.285[0.369]

$\Delta Y_t = \quad\quad\quad 0.000Y_{t-1} + 0.013\Delta Y_{t-1} + 0.192\Delta Y_{t-2} + 0.062\Delta Y_{t-3} - 0.121\Delta Y_{t-4} + 0.241\Delta Y_{t-5}$
$\quad\quad\quad\quad\quad\;\; (3.039) \quad\quad\;\; (0.154) \quad\quad\;\; (2.269) \quad\quad\;\; (0.717) \quad\quad (-1.437) \quad\quad\;\; (2.816)$
$\hfill$ 4.231[0.375]

Variable: $UKUR_t$
Sample: 1861 to 1913 (before lagging)
1 unit root

$\Delta Y_t = 2.176 - 0.583Y_{t-1} + 0.551\Delta Y_{t-1} + 0.014t$
$\quad\quad (3.460)(-5.456) \quad (4.512) \quad\quad\;\; (0.941)$
$\hfill$ 3.311[0.507]

$\Delta Y_t = 2.499 - 0.565Y_{t-1} + 0.538\Delta Y_{t-1}$
$\quad\quad (4.739)(-5.381) \quad (4.440)$
$\hfill$ 2.775[0.596]

$\Delta Y_t = \quad\quad - 0.114Y_{t-1} + 0.309\Delta Y_{t-1}$
$\quad\quad\quad\quad\;\; (-2.144) \quad\;\; (2.322)$
$\hfill$ 10.994[0.027]

Sample 1972m1 to 1995m2 (before lagging)
Variable: $USUR_t$
2 unit roots

$\Delta Z_t = 0.025 - 0.439Z_{t-1} - 0.525\Delta Z_{t-2} - 0.332\Delta Z_{t-2} - 0.161\Delta Z_{t-3} - 0.000t$
$\quad\quad (1.104)(-4.907) \quad (-5.905) \quad\quad (-4.028) \quad\quad (-2.622) \quad\quad (-1.069)$
$\hfill$ 14.570[0.265]

$\Delta Z_t = -0.002 - 0.426Z_{t-1} - 0.534\Delta Z_{t-1} - 0.338\Delta Z_{t-2} - 0.163\Delta Z_{t-3}$
$\quad\quad (-1.140)(-4.805) \quad (-6.042) \quad\quad (-4.098) \quad\quad (-2.662)$
$\hfill$ 7.177[0.845]

$\Delta Z_t = \quad\quad\quad - 0.425Z_{t-1} - 0.534\Delta Z_{t-2} - 0.338\Delta Z_{t-2} - 0.163\Delta Z_{t-3}$
$\quad\quad\quad\quad\quad\;\; (-4.814) \quad\;\; (-6.053) \quad\quad (-4.106) \quad\quad (-2.668)$
$\hfill$ 14.340[0.279]

1 unit root

$\Delta Y_t = 0.222 - 0.028Y_{t-1} + 0.033\Delta Y_{t-1} + 0.198\Delta Y_{t-2} + 0.193\Delta Y_{t-3} + 0.188\Delta Y_{t-4} - 0.000t$
$\quad\quad (3.305)(-3.145) \quad (0.553) \quad\quad\;\; (3.307) \quad\quad\;\; (3.208) \quad\quad\;\; (3.086) \quad\quad (-1.346)$
$\hfill$ 15.341[0.223]

$\Delta Y_t = 0.186 - 0.027Y_{t-1} + 0.037\Delta Y_{t-1} + 0.203\Delta Y_{t-2} + 0.195\Delta Y_{t-3} + 0.190\Delta Y_{t-4}$
$\quad\quad (3.014)(-3.039) \quad (0.626) \quad\quad\;\; (3.392) \quad\quad\;\; (3.251) \quad\quad\;\; (3.117)$
$\hfill$ 5.783[0.976]

$\Delta Y_t = \quad\quad\quad - 0.006Y_{t-1} + 0.040\Delta Y_{t-1} + 0.196\Delta Y_{t-2} + 0.175\Delta Y_{t-3} + 0.164\Delta Y_{t-4}$
$\quad\quad\quad\quad\quad\;\; (-0.410) \quad\;\; (0.652) \quad\quad\;\; (3.236) \quad\quad\;\; (2.889) \quad\quad\;\; (2.675)$
$\hfill$ 14.263[0.283]

value of 0. The ADF test statistic for testing the unit root hypothesis directly in a maintained model with a time trend is $\hat{\tau}_\beta = -3.963$, in this case to be compared with a 5% critical value of -3.402 using the response surface coefficients in Table 6.11; hence, the null hypothesis of a second root is also rejected on this criterion. The sequence of tests could stop here – see section **6.4** – although it may be of interest to see what further tests in the sequence indicate.

Note that the estimate of β is zero to 4 decimal places with a 't' statistic, $t(\beta)$, of 1.118, so whether the null or alternative hypothesis is true, and whether μ is nonzero, these values suggest the time trend could be excluded without loss – see Table 6.10 for critical values of $t(\beta)$. Hence, in the next stage the regression model has an intercept but no time trend. The joint hypothesis $\mu = 0$ and $\gamma = 0$ is rejected with $\Phi_1 = 6.841$ compared to a 5% critical value of approximately 4.74 (from the nearest entry in Table 6.5 of $T = 100$). Considering the likely cause of rejection note that $\hat{\tau}_\mu = -3.804$, with $\hat{\mu} = 0.003$ and $t(\mu) = 3.137$ which is significant under the null hypothesis – see Table 6.10 where the 5% two-sided critical value is ± 2.86 for $T = 100$ – and also under the alternative hypothesis. We should stop at this point with a significant if numerically small intercept. Imposing the null, $\gamma = 0$, then $\hat{\mu} = 0.00017$ and $\hat{\sigma}_\varepsilon = 0.00863$; the ratio of these two, equal to 0.019, is an estimate of the standardised drift, which is close enough to zero not to affect the critical values. Using the response surface coefficients in Table 6.11 the 5% critical value for $\hat{\tau}_\mu$, with $\mu = 0$, is -2.857; hence, as $-3.803 < -2.857$, the earlier decision to reject the null hypothesis of a (marginal) second unit root is confirmed.

Having rejected the null hypothesis of a (marginal) second unit root the next stage is to consider whether the hypothesis of 1 unit root is consistent with the data. In this case the initial maintained regression model is ADF(5) with time trend. ΔY_{t-5} is necessary to ensure that the residuals are free from serial correlation; in ADF(5), SC(4) $= 3.751$ with a marginal significance level of 44.1%. The coefficient on Y_{t-1}, which is an estimate of $\gamma = \sum_{i=1}^{p+1} \phi_i - 1$, at -0.042 is now numerically quite close to the null value of 0. The Φ_3 statistic for a unit root and no time trend is 1.855 compared with the 5% critical value for $T = 100$ of 6.606, so the joint null hypothesis of 1 unit root and no time

trend is not rejected. Confirmation of nonrejection of the null of a unit root comes from $\hat{\tau}_\beta = -1.466$ compared to the 5% critical value of -3.407. Although the sequence of tests could stop here it will be of interest to see what happens if the sequence is continued.

The absence of a time trend is suggested by the estimate of β which is 0.00022 with $t(\beta) = 1.623$. Omitting the time trend we obtain $\hat{\tau}_\mu = 1.032$, with $\hat{\mu} = -0.021$ and $t(\mu) = -0.898$ which is not significant (under the null or alternative hypothesis). One might be tempted into the conclusion, from these individual tests, that the null hypothesis of a unit root and the null hypothesis of a zero intercept cannot be rejected. However, this is incorrect and counterintuitive. If there is a unit root *and* no drift it is only by chance that cnd_t has trended up for over 30 years, and it could equally start a (stochastic) trend down for a long period. The resolution of this counterintuitive statement is that the hypothesis $\gamma = 0$ and $\mu = 0$ should be tested using a joint test, for example using Φ_1, and not by way of the two separate tests; we then anticipate finding $\gamma = 0$ and $\mu \neq 0$. Carrying out the joint test then $\Phi_1 = 5.017$, which exceeds the 5% critical value of 4.74 from Table 6.5 (for $T = 100$) and hence the joint null, $\gamma = 0$ and $\mu = 0$, should be quite firmly rejected. Imposing the unit root, since Φ_3 and $\hat{\tau}_\beta$ did not lead to rejection and $\hat{\tau}_\mu = 1.032$ is wrong signed to find in favour of the alternative, the estimate of μ is 0.003, with a t statistic of 2.994. An estimate of the long-run drift (with the null imposed) is obtained from:

$$\Delta cnd_t = 0.00338 + 0.016 \Delta cnd_{t-1}$$
$$+ 0.195 \Delta cnd_{t-2} + 0.064 \Delta cnd_{t-3}$$
$$+ 0.1186 \Delta cnd_{t-4} + 0.244 \Delta cnd_{t-5}$$
$$(7.89)$$

setting $\Delta cnd_t = \Delta cnd_{t-1} = \Delta cnd_{t-2} = \cdots$, then

$$\Delta cnd_t = 0.00338/(1 - 0.4)$$
$$= 0.0056 \qquad (7.90)$$

where 0.4 is the sum of the coefficients on the lagged Δcnd_t terms, which converts to a plausible long-run annual rate of growth of $(1 + 0.0056)^4 - 1 = 2.25\%$ p.a.

In any study of the characteristics of a time series there are decisions which have to be taken which may affect the outcome, and often in published work these are details which are not reported. Some of these aspects are illustrated here, particularly concerning the sensitivity and robustness of the results reported so far using the model and test statistics for a single unit root.

In the context of the Dickey–Fuller test statistics an important issue is the number of lagged differences, p, in the ADF. The suggested progression is from an ADF(p) model that initially includes a deterministic time trend, so p has first to be determined. The model selection criteria used here was a joint one combining the absence of evidence of serial correlation in the residuals of the ADF with lack of significance of additional coefficients in the ADF. A general-to-specific selection strategy was part of the design. The general model was $p* = 6$. Estimation is first based on a common sample period being the largest sample available for the longest lag length, in this way the regressions with different lag lengths are compared over a uniform period. If the chosen model has fewer lags than $p*$, the preferred model can then be re-estimated over the longer period. Simplification of the general model can proceed either on the basis of individual coefficients through insignificant marginal 't' statistics, or jointly through insignificant F values of the joint hypothesis that the coefficients on the last j lags are zero. Using

the general-to-specific *individual strategy*, the 't' statistic on ΔY_{t-6} was 0.728 with an msl of 46.8%; excluding ΔY_{t-6} the 't' statistic on ΔY_{t-5} was 1.622 with an msl of 10.7%. Although just not significant at a conventional 10% level, ΔY_{t-5} was included because it also ensured that the LM(4) test statistic for serial correlation was satisfactory. The first step is the same in a general-to-specific *joint* strategy since only one coefficient is involved; however, at the next step the comparison is between ADF(6) and ADF(4) with $F(2, 126) = 4.863$; compared to a 5% critical value of 3.05 this leads to rejection of the null that the two marginal coefficients are zero, hence this is a step too far and we conclude in favour of ADF(5).

Serial correlation was assessed through the SC(4) test statistic with the following sample values (msl in parentheses) ADF(1): 16.442 [0.003]; ADF(2): 12.793[0.012]; ADF(4): 12.656 [0.013]; ADF(4): 12.219[0.015]; ADF(5), 3.751 [0.441]; ADF(6), 3.340[0.501]. On this basis only ADF(5) and ADF(6) are 'clean'. The three information criteria: AIC, HQIC and SIC, were also calculated, and these are reported in Table 7.11; the minimum in each case corresponds to the choice of $p = 5$. Rather unusually (in the author's experience), there is no conflict in the model selection criteria.

The need to whiten the residuals, by including lagged differences in the maintained regression, suggests that it may also be of interest to calculate the Phillips–Perron versions of the test statistics which make a semi-parametric correction for serially correlated residuals. In Table 7.12, $Z\hat{\rho}_\beta$ and $Z\hat{\tau}_\beta$ are given for a range of 1 to 8 for the truncation lag parameter l in a

Table 7.11 *Information criteria for ADF(p) models of cnd$_t$*

$p =$	1	2	3	4	5	6
AIC	−1289.11	−1291.93	−1292.01	−1291.79	**−1299.17**	−1287.25
HQIC	−1290.75	−1293.97	−1294.47	−1294.65	**−1302.44**	−1290.94
SIC	−1277.46	−1277.37	−1274.54	−1271.41	**−1275.87**	−1261.10

Note: Bold indicates minimum.

Table 7.12 *Phillips–Perron $Z\hat{\rho}_\beta$ and $Z\hat{\tau}_\beta$ unit root statistics for cnd$_t$*

l	1	2	3	4	5	6	7	8
$Z\hat{\rho}_\beta$	−0.294	−0.986	−1.433	−1.537	−2.077	−2.426	−2.848	−3.079
$Z\hat{\tau}_\beta$	−0.089	−0.257	−0.397	−0.423	−0.549	−0.627	−0.716	−0.763

Notes: For comparison the standard ADF statistics are as follows. $\hat{\rho}_\beta$ for ADF(5) is −11.896; $\hat{\tau}_\beta$ for ADF(5) is −1.466. $\hat{\rho}_\beta$ for ADF(0) is −0.459; $\hat{\tau}_\beta$ for ADF(0) is −0.136. Asymptotic 5% critical values are −21.8 and −3.41, respectively.

maintained regression that included a time trend. Note that with $T^{\frac{1}{3}} = 142^{\frac{1}{3}} = 6$ rounding up to the nearest integer.

The asymptotic critical values for the PP statistics are the same as for the DF versions, which are −21.8 and −3.41, respectively. With $l = 6$, $Z\hat{\rho}_\beta = -2.426$ and $Z\hat{\tau}_\beta = -0.627$ suggesting nonrejection of the null hypothesis of a unit root and confirming the results of the standard augmented Dickey–Fuller tests. Also of interest is the comparison of the PP and ADF versions of the same test statistic, both make corrections for 'non-white' residuals but in different ways. The ADF(5) version of $\hat{\rho}_\beta$ is −11.896, and $\hat{\tau}_\beta$ is −1.466, both larger negative values than the PP versions with $l = 6$. Although the PP corrections do not make a difference here to the outcome of the unit root tests, it is still of interest to note that the correction factors are numerically quite important. The comparison now is with the test statistics from the *unaugmented*, that is simple, Dickey–Fuller regression, where $\hat{\rho}_\beta = -0.459$ and $\hat{\tau}_\beta = -0.136$ compared to the PP versions ($l = 6$), $Z\hat{\rho}_\beta = -2.426$ and $Z\hat{\tau}_\beta = -0.627$.

To assess the robustness of the results so far to the Perron critique, we consider the possibility that the finding of nonstationarity is spurious, an alternative account being that cnd$_t$ is stationary around a split trend. The suggestion that this may be the case is data dependent in the sense that the graph of cnd$_t$ – see Figure 7.1A – displays what appears to be a change in the slope, which is the growth rate of consumers' expenditure, in the early 1980s. *Ex post* this possible structural break may be associated with the change of government in the United King-

dom in 1979, and the subsequent effect of its policies following the deregulation of the financial markets and the liberalisation of credit availability. Given this scenario the appropriate null and alternative hypotheses in Perron's framework are those associated with Model B* which, because the change seems to be gradual rather than abrupt, is used in its innovation, rather than additive, outlier form (this is also Model (2') of Zivot and Andrews (1992, p. 254)). For reference the alternative hypothesis is

Model B*:

$$\Delta Y_t = \mu + \gamma Y_{t-1} + \beta t + \delta_3 \text{DVT}_t^*$$
$$+ \sum_{j=1}^{p} \alpha_j \Delta Y_{t-j} + \varepsilon_t \qquad (7.91)$$

whereas the null is

$$\Delta Y_t = \mu + \gamma Y_{t-1}$$
$$+ \sum_{j=1}^{p} \alpha_j \Delta Y_{t-j} + \varepsilon_t \qquad (7.92)$$

with $\gamma = 0$.

Using the Zivot–Andrews (1992) criterion, of choosing the breakpoint where the evidence against the null is greatest, leads to $T_b = 1984q4$ with the regression:

$$\Delta Y_t = 1.176 - 0.189 Y_{t-1} + 0.0008t$$
$$(4.357)(-4.345) \qquad (4.363)$$

$$+ 0.0013 \text{DVT}_t^* + \sum_{j=1}^{5} \alpha_j \Delta Y_{t-j} + \hat{\varepsilon}_t$$

$$(4.303) \qquad (7.93)$$

't' statistics in parentheses.

An ADF(5) model is again preferred with the standard test for serial correlation SC(4) = 5.736 and an msl of 22%. The relevant test statistic is the 't' statistic on Y_{t-1}, denoted $\hat{\tau}_\beta$ earlier; here the sample value is −4.345. The 5% asymptotic critical value is −4.42 – see Table 7.9 – or Zivot and Andrews (1992, Table 3). Perron (1997) provides some small sample critical values, although in this context for the additive outlier version of Model B*, Perron (*op. cit.*, Table 1); making a similar adjustment for $T = 150$, the nearest relevant entry from Perron, suggests a small sample 5% critical value of −4.65 and a 10% critical value of −4.35. With $\hat{\tau}_\beta = −4.345$ the evidence is now far from as conclusive as it seemed earlier, especially as both the trend and the change in the trend have 't' statistics exceeding 4. The trend coefficients suggest a shift, dating from 1984q4, in 'autonomous' growth from 0.32 of 1% p.a. to 0.84 of 1% p.a. following the break associated with financial deregulation.

This example illustrates some of the difficulties associated with what seems a straightforward problem of inference: does a series have a unit root? Initially the evidence seemed clear cut that this was the case, whether conventional Dickey–Fuller or Phillips–Perron tests were used, and careful model selection procedures were followed. Considering the possibility of a (single) structural break in a nonstationary series led to some doubts about the earlier, apparently robust, conclusions. The crucial coefficient on Y_{t-1} in the ADF regression moved from −0.042 to −0.189 on the inclusion of a dummy variable to capture a possible change in the growth rate. Further aspects of this example are explored in a review question.

7.9.2 UK unemployment rate

The second illustration is the unemployment series used by Phillips (1958) in his famous study of the relation between wage inflation and unemployment. The data is annual for the United Kingdom between 1861 and 1913 measured as % p.a., the series is referred to as UKUR$_t$. The level of the series is graphed in Figure 7.2A; there is no sustained tendency to trend or wander, and there are frequent crossings of the mean. The autocorrelations, graphed in Figure 7.2B, confirm this picture; they die out quickly and do not lend support to the view that UKUR$_t$ has a long memory. The first difference of UKUR$_t$ is shown in Figure 7.2C and the second difference in Figures 7.2E, with the autocorrelation functions in Figures 7.2D and 7.2F, respectively. Overall, the visual impression is of a series that is stationary without any differencing. This conclusion is also suggested from the theoretical bounds on the unemployment rate of 0 and 1, which could in principle be breached by an unrestricted random walk.

The summary test results are reported in Table 7.9 with the more detailed regression results in Table 7.10. In this case there is no need to test for 2 unit roots so the test statistics start with those for 1 unit root. An ADF(1) model is required to ensure that the residuals are free from serial correlation. The visual impression from Figure 7.2 is of a series without a trend, hence economy of estimation would suggest that it is appropriate to use the maintained regression without a deterministic trend; however, for illustrative purposes we will see what the test statistics indicate if a trend is included. The Φ_3 statistic for the joint null of a unit root and no deterministic trend is 14.889, which is well above the 5% critical value of 6.776 for $T = 50$ from Table 6.7. On this basis the null hypothesis is rejected. Note from the regression details in Table 7.10 that the estimate of γ at −0.583 is numerically a long way from the value under the null of 0. The estimate of μ is 2.176, which is large relative to the estimated standard error of the equation of 1.587, and not consistent with the view that this an estimate of the drift in a random walk process; if this was the case the series would exhibit a pronounced positive trend, which it does not. The estimated trend coefficient is 0.014 with a 't' statistic, $t(\beta)$, of 0.941 which is not significant under

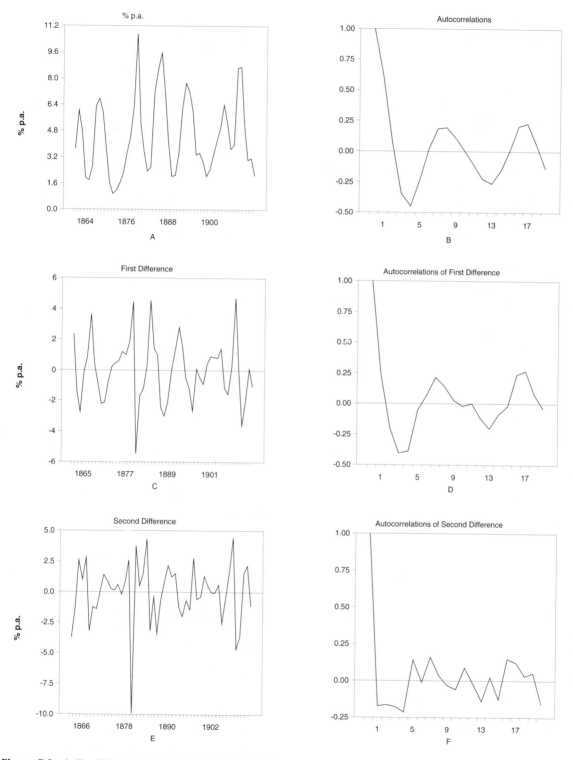

Figure 7.2   A–F – *UK unemployment rate, 1861–1913*

the null or alternative hypotheses. Further, $\hat{\tau}_\beta = -5.456$ compared to the 5% critical value of -3.484 (from Table 6.11 for $\beta = 0$) which suggests rejection of the null $\gamma = 0$.

The next step is to reduce the maintained regression so that it does not include a time trend. Starting with the joint null hypothesis $\mu = 0$ and $\gamma = 0$, the sample value of the test statistic Φ_1 is 14.481 which unambiguously indicates rejection of the null hypothesis. The estimate of μ is 2.499 with a 't' statistic of 4.739, and the estimate of γ is -0.565 with $\hat{\tau}_\mu = -5.381$ (the 5% critical value for $\hat{\tau}_\mu$ is -2.905, with $\mu = 0$, using the coefficients in Table 6.11). The estimate of μ is too large to suggest it is an estimate of the drift in a random walk process. If the null $\gamma = 0$ is imposed (to obtain a consistent estimate of μ under the null) the estimate of μ is -0.075 with a 't' statistic of -0.267; standardised by the estimated standard error of 2.007 this is -0.037, which is not large enough to affect the critical values for $\hat{\tau}_\mu$. Overall, the evidence is that rejection of the joint null $\mu = 0$ and $\gamma = 0$ occurs because both $\mu \neq 0$ and $\gamma \neq 0$; and UKUR$_t$ is stationary around a nonzero mean.

To obtain an estimate of the mean, consider the ADF(1) model with ε_t set equal to its expected value of 0:

$$\Delta Y_t = \mu + \gamma Y_{t-1} + \alpha_1 \Delta Y_{t-1} \tag{7.94}$$

or in terms of the AR coefficients

$$\begin{aligned} Y_t = {}& \mu + (\phi_1 + \phi_2)Y_{t-1} \\ & - \phi_2(Y_{t-1}Y_{t-2}) \end{aligned} \tag{7.95}$$

where $\gamma = \phi_1 + \phi_2 - 1$ and $\alpha_1 = -\phi_2$. Now in a static long run $Y_t = Y_{t-1} = Y_{t-2} = Y_{t-3} = \cdots$, therefore

$$\begin{aligned} Y_t ={}& [\mu/(1 - (\phi_1 + \phi_2)] \\ ={}& -(\mu/\gamma) \end{aligned} \tag{7.96}$$

For UKUR$_t$ the estimated long-run mean is:

$$-(\hat{\mu}/\hat{\gamma}) = -(2.499/-0.565) = 4.421\% \text{ p.a.}$$

which is near to the sample mean of 4.470% p.a. We conclude that UKUR$_t$ is stationary about a mean of close to 4.4% p.a. Note that this conclusion is based on a consideration of all of the regression details, hence the importance of the interpretation of, for example, the estimates of μ and γ, rather than just a comparison of $\hat{\tau}_\mu$ with a particular critical value.

The conclusion of stationarity seems relatively secure, nevertheless a sensitivity analysis is still important. As there is no suggestion that the series trends the relevant results here are for the model without a deterministic time trend. Setting the maximum lag for the ADF at 4 and estimating over the longest common sample period (1866–1913) gave the following sequence of SC(4) test statistics for serial correlation, with msl in parentheses: ADF(0): 13.738[0.008]; ADF(1): 2.220[0.695]; ADF(2): 0.696[0.951]; ADF(3): 1.156[0.885]; ADF(4): 0.776[0.942]. On this basis ADF(0) is ruled out and a minimum of ADF(1) is required. The longer sample period used in Table 7.10 gives SC(4) = 2.775 for ADF(1).

On a general-to-specific strategy none of the 't' statistics on the marginal lag working down from ADF(4) to ADF(3), from ADF(3) to ADF(2) and then from ADF(2) to ADF(1) are significant; the first significant 't' statistic on the lag coefficient is in the ADF(1) model. The sequence of F statistics on the lag coefficients is, with msl in parentheses: from ADF(4) to ADF(3), 0.507[0.480]; from ADF(4) to ADF(2), 0.283[0.755]; from ADF(4) to ADF(2), 0.777[0.513]; from ADF(4) to ADF(0), 5.190[0.002]. Hence, as the last of these is significant, ADF(0) is rejected in favour of at least ADF(1); further, since ADF(1) is not rejected against ADF(4) stop at ADF(1). Two of the information criteria, AIC and SIC, also lead to the selection of ADF(1); HQIC has a minimum at lag 2.

The sequence of $\hat{\tau}_\mu$ statistics is: ADF(0), -3.308; ADF(1), -5.381; ADF(2), -4.851; ADF(3), -4.166; ADF(4), -3.127. There is no material change in the test statistics between ADF(1) and ADF(2); however, choosing ADF(4) would make the decision more marginal (5% cv $= -2.868$ with $\mu = 0$) but not enough to change the decision. There is an important point here: since the evidence is that 4 lags are not needed, ADF(4) is profligate relative to ADF(1), leading to poor power to pick up the stationary alternative, the message is *do not overparameterise*.

In the preferred ADF(1) model the residuals are free from serial correlation, and there is no evidence of heteroscedasticity with the standard test HS(1) $= 0.513$ and msl $= 47.4\%$. However, the residuals are not consistent with normality, the standard test gives JB(2) $= 11.270$ with msl virtually zero. Although not necessary for the validity of the ADF tests Franses and Haldrup (*op. cit.*) suggest it may be useful to look at tests of normality to the extent that they are indicative of possible additive outliers. In this case there are four 'large' residuals judged by their scale relative to estimated equation standard error of 1.585, namely 4.48 in 1879, -4.29 in 1880, 3.39 in 1884 and 4.30 in 1908. None of these seem to be associated with structural breaks in the series (which would suggest a Perron type analysis); rather, even under the alternative there is just a one-off impulse effect so that the intercept is not permanently changed. The 1879/1880 effects seem to be approximately equal and offsetting, so the dummy variable DV7980$_t$ is set to $+1$ in 1879 and -1 in 1880 and zero elsewhere; the other dummy variables are 0 except for a 1 in 1884 for DV1884$_t$ and 1 in 1908 for DV1908$_t$. Re-estimation with 't' statistics in parentheses gave:

$$\Delta Y_t = 1.829 - 0.452Y_{t-1} + 0.527\Delta Y_{t-1}$$
$$\quad (5.155)(-6.486) \quad\quad (6.676)$$
$$+ 4.630DV7980_t + 3.772DV1884_t$$
$$\quad (6.238) \quad\quad\quad (3.590)$$
$$+ 4.533DV1908_t + \hat{\varepsilon}_t$$
$$\quad (4.353) \quad\quad\quad\quad\quad\quad (7.97)$$

Lags of the dummy variables, as suggested by Franses and Haldrup (*op. cit.*), were not significant; as expected the unlagged dummy variables

are significant and the normality statistic is now not significant with JB(2) $= 2.745$ [0.253]. The ADF(1) test statistic is now more negative at -6.486, so the conclusion of rejecting the null of nonstationarity for UKUR$_t$ remains quite secure.

7.9.3 US unemployment rate

The next series considered is the US unemployment rate, USUR$_t$, measured as % p.a., with monthly data from 1975m1 to 1995m2, a total of 278 observations. The data is graphed in Figure 7.3 with the levels in Figure 7.3A, the first difference in Figure 7.3C and the second difference in Figure 7.3E; the corresponding autocorrelations are in Figures 7.3B, D and F.

An important point to note first, and one that applies equally to the previous illustration with UKUR$_t$, is whether an unemployment rate could conceptually be I(1). The presence of a unit root implies that shocks are persistent, this is seen most simply in the case of a pure random walk but is also a characteristic of more complex I(1) processes. It is evident from Figure 7.3B that there is persistence in the level of USUR$_t$, more so than for UKUR$_t$. However, the persistence of shocks in turn implies that the series is potentially unbounded, which is not a characteristic of some economic time series including the unemployment rate and variables defined as shares, for example the share of liquid assets in total assets. The unemployment rate is bounded by 0 and 1; if the series was to undertake a persistent 'random walk', the limit is one of these boundaries; that these boundaries are not reached, nor approached, in the data series is evidence that the persistence, which is undoubtedly present, is a 'local' property. Unit root tests applied to such bounded series may find at best that, over the sample range of the series, the integration properties are not distinguishable from the series as if it was not bounded; if the unit root tests indicate that the null hypothesis that the series is I(d), $d \geq 1$ cannot be rejected on the sample evidence, the series can only be

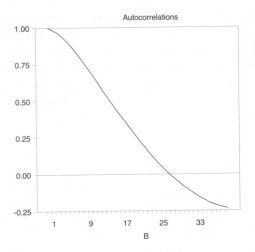

A

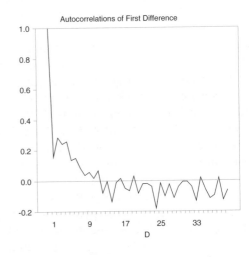

C

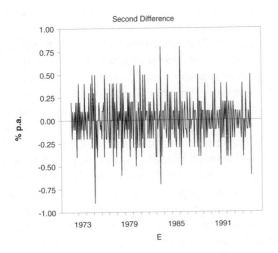

E

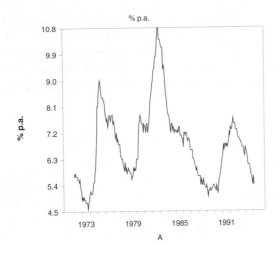

B

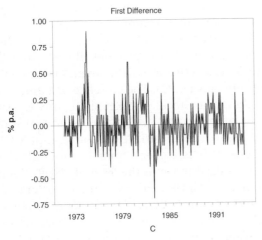

D

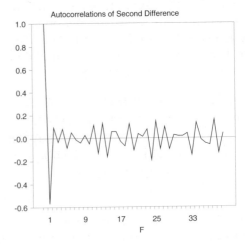

F

Figure 7.3   A–F – *US unemployment rate, 1975–1995*

locally not globally I(*d*). The unit root tests in this section are undertaken with this caveat in mind. The choice of USUR$_t$ here is because the series illustrates a number of important points of interpretation of unit root tests and associated techniques. Also, among others, Nelson and Plosser (*op. cit.*) included the unemployment rate in their influential study.

The characteristics of USUR$_t$ are less clearly discernible than for the two previous series. Figure 7.3A hints at a series that wanders but not in the sustained way that was apparent for cnd$_t$. The autocorrelations in Figure 7.3B suggest a series with a long memory but not necessarily a unit root as the autocorrelations approach zero as the lag length increases. Taking the first difference gives a series that looks stationary, although with some positive autocorrelation. Similarly taking the second difference also suggests a stationary series but the negative first order autocorrelation shown in Figure 7.3F suggests overdifferencing has taken place. In summary, the visual impression is of a series that is probably I(0) although perhaps one for which the formal tests may have low power.

The test statistics for USUR$_t$ are reported in summary form in Table 7.9 and in greater detail in Table 7.10. As we cannot rule out the possibility of finding 1 unit root (subject to the caveat at the beginning of this section) then, following the suggestion in Dickey and Pantula (1987) to begin with the highest (practical) degree of differencing, we start with tests for 2 unit roots. An ADF(3) model was selected with Φ_3 equal to 12.125, indicating rejection of the joint null hypothesis of a (marginal) unit root and no time trend. (The 5% critical value from Table 6.7 for $T = 200$ is 6.397.) The estimate of β is zero to 3 decimal places, with a '*t*' statistic, $t(\beta)$, of -1.069. The critical values of $t(\beta)$ depend upon μ in the DGP, which has a (marginal) unit root; with the null $\gamma = 0$ imposed, the estimate of μ is 0.010 and $\hat{\sigma}_\varepsilon = 0.195$, so the standardised estimate, 0.010/0.195, is 0.052 which is not sufficiently large to affect the critical values for $t(\beta)$ or $\hat{\tau}_\beta$. Thus $t(\beta) = -1.069$ is insignificant;

further $\hat{\tau}_\beta = -4.907$ which is larger negative than the 5% critical value of -3.407, so rejection of the joint null is most likely due to the rejection of the (marginal) unit root.

When the time trend is omitted, $\Phi_1 = 11.553$ compared to the 5% critical value from Table 6.5 for $T = 200$ of 4.696, so the joint null hypothesis $\mu = 0$ and $\gamma = 0$ is rejected. The estimate of μ is -0.002 and insignificant with $t(\mu) = -0.140$. The estimate of γ is -0.426, which is some way from the null of 0; also $\hat{\tau}_\mu = -4.805$ which is larger negative than any relevant critical value, so we conclude firmly for rejection of $\gamma = 0$. These results suggest that the maintained regression could omit both the time trend and the intercept. Omitting both, $\hat{\tau} = -4.814$ compared to the 5% critical value of -1.938, calculated from Chueng and Lai's response surface coefficients, again leading to firm rejection of 2 unit roots in USUR$_t$. We now consider the tests for 1 unit root.

An ADF(4) model was selected to test for 1 unit root (model selection details and sensitivity analysis are given below). On testing for 1 unit root with a deterministic time trend in the regression, $\Phi_3 = 5.539$ which is below the 5% critical value of 6.397 (for $T = 200$ from Table 5.7), suggesting that the null hypothesis, of a unit root and no time trend, is consistent with the data. However, this conclusion might be misleading if the time trend is superfluous to the model, and hence Φ_3 loses power against the I(0) alternative. That this is so is suggested by the estimate of β which is zero to 3 decimal places with a '*t*' statistic, $t(\beta)$, of -1.346. The critical values of $t(\beta)$ depend upon μ in the DGP, which has a unit root; with $\gamma = 0$ imposed the estimate of μ is 0.025 and the estimate standardised drift is $\hat{\mu}/\hat{\sigma}_\varepsilon = 0.025/0.187 = 0.133$. This is not large enough to affect the conclusion that the time trend is superfluous – see Table 6.10. Thus, although $\hat{\tau}_\beta = -3.145$ is a smaller negative than the 5% critical value of -3.407, and therefore by itself suggests nonrejection of the null of a unit root, this conclusion is not yet firmly enough based.

The visual impression from Figure 7.3A is of a series without a deterministic trend which suggests estimating a model with an intercept but no time trend. In this case $\Phi_1 = 4.629$ compared to the 5% critical value of 4.696 (for $T = 200$), so the decision is marginal at the 5% level but not at the 10% level, where the critical value is 3.835 and the joint null $\mu = 0$ and $\gamma = 0$ would be rejected. The estimate of μ is 0.186 with $t(\mu) = 3.014$, which is significant (under the null as well as the alternative); the estimate of μ seems too large to be interpreted as the drift in a random walk. If the unit root is imposed the estimate of μ falls to 0.0016, and the estimated standardised drift is $0.0016/0.187 = 0.008$, which is near enough to zero not to make any difference to the critical values of $\hat{\tau}_\mu$.

The estimate of γ is -0.027, which looks as though it might sustain the view that USUR_t has a unit root; however, the estimated standard error of γ is also small and $\hat{\tau}_\mu = -3.039$, which is larger negative than the 5% critical value of -2.857 (with $\mu = 0$) and hence the null is rejected. This rejection of the null is not so marked as in the case of UKUR_t, which reflects, in part, the long memory in USUR_t compared to UKUR_t. We conclude that the joint null $\mu = 0$ and $\gamma = 0$ is rejected because both $\mu \neq 0$ and $\gamma \neq 0$. This is consistent with the view that USUR_t is stationary about a long-run mean, which is estimated as follows: from the unrestricted model

$$\text{USUR}_t = 0.186 + (1 - 0.027)\text{USUR}_{t-1}$$
$$+ \sum_{j=1}^{4} \alpha_j \Delta \text{USUR}_{t-j} + \hat{\varepsilon}_t \qquad (7.98)$$

which in steady state with constant unemployment, that is $\Delta \text{USUR}_{t-j} = 0$ for $j = 0, 1, \ldots$, will revert to a mean of

$$\text{USUR}_t = -0.186/(-0.027)$$
$$= 6.89\% \text{ p.a} \qquad (7.99)$$

which is consistent with what we observe, the sample mean being 6.86% p.a. This combines with the picture from Figure 7.3A: in the early part of the sample there was an increase in unemployment, with the 1974 average of 5.6% increasing to a 1975 average of 8.5%, which then reverted; in a more gradual progression the 1979 average of 5.8% increased to 9.6% in 1983, but again reverted. In both cases the shocks were mean reverting suggesting a stationary process with a long memory rather than a process with a unit root.

Since the rejection of 2 unit roots seems unambiguous details of model selection and robustness of the results are confined to the tests for 1 unit root. Following previous guidelines the maximum lag in the ADF model was set at $p^* = 12$ (for monthly data). A general-to-specific individual ('t') strategy led to selection of ADF(4); all 't' statistics at the margin working down from ADF(12) to ADF(5) were insignificant, the lowest msl being 11.6% for ADF(11), generally the 't' statistics were well below $|1|$. Following a general-to-specific joint (F) strategy did not lead to the same choice, but this is not surprising since the significant lag tends to get 'swamped' by the large number of insignificant lags in a joint test. This was the case with the F test leading to selection of ADF(3), the first

Table 7.13 Model selection criteria for USUR$_t$ and unit root test statistics, $\hat{\tau}_\mu$

ADF(p)	1	2	3	4	5	6	7	8	9	10	11	12
SC(12)	40.688	24.060	15.910	5.783	14.646	13.407	14.132	16.780	16.787	16.817	16.917	14.984
msl	[0.000]	[0.020]	[0.195]	[0.926]	[0.261]	[0.340]	[0.292]	[0.158]	[0.158]	[0.162]	[0.242]	[0.110]
AIC	−854.56	−873.13	−882.74	**−890.50**	−888.80	−887.27	−885.31	−883.70	−881.87	−879.94	880.54	879.88
HQIC	−855.56	−874.25	−884.15	**−892.19**	−890.76	−889.52	−887.84	−886.51	−884.96	−883.31	−884.19	−883.81
SIC	−843.98	−858.81	−864.84	**−869.02**	−863.74	−858.64	−853.09	−847.90	−842.49	−836.99	−834.00	−829.76
$\hat{\tau}_\mu$	−1.651	−2.122	−2.573	−3.039	−3.082	−3.150	−3.062	−2.908	−2.930	−2.929	−3.149	−2.906

Note: Bold indicates minimum. Marginal significance level of serial correlation test statistic, χ^2 version, in [.].

rejection being from ADF(12) to ADF(2) with $F = 2.772$, msl $= 0.3\%$. The SC(12) tests for serial correlation showed that at least ADF(3) is necessary with SC(12) $= 15.910$ and msl of 19.5%, but note that for ADF(4), SC(12) $= 5.783$ and msl of 92.6% – see Table 7.13. Also note that the information criteria all have a minimum at $p = 4$. On balance the various criteria favour $p = 4$. The values of $\hat{\tau}_\mu$ stabilise at about -3 for $p \geq 4$, so the conclusion against a unit root is robust against choosing a longer lag.

7.9.4 Testing for seasonal nonstationarity: UK employees

The last series to be considered provides an example of testing for unit roots with seasonally unadjusted data. The data is the number of employees in employment in the UK, referred to as E_t, with an overall sample, before lags are taken, of 1959q2 to 1993q2; natural logarithms, indicated by lower case letters, are taken with the implication that if the series is I(1) the rate of growth will be I(0). The seasonally unadjusted data and seasonally adjusted data, both in logs, are graphed in Figures 7.4A and 7.4B, respectively. The difference between the seasonally unadjusted and seasonally adjusted data, $e(\text{nsa})_t - e(\text{sa})_t$, which shows the seasonal pattern, is graphed in Figure 7.4C for the whole sample period and in Figure 7.4D for sub-period 1978q1 to 1981q4. Figure 7.4A suggests that, the seasonal pattern apart, the series shows signs of nonstationarity. There are sustained movements away from the sample mean and there is little visual evidence of a deterministic trend. It is evident from Figure 7.4C that there is a seasonal pattern in employment. To illustrate this further in Figure 7.4D we take a four-year 'window' of 1978q1 to 1981q4, which shows that employment builds up from an annual trough in the first quarter, increasing in the second and peaking in the third quarter before falling slightly in the fourth quarter, and then falling markedly in the following first quarter.

Testing for nonstationarity follows the HEGY methodology described in section **7.7.2**. The augmented Dickey–Fuller regression modified to allow for the possibility of unit roots at the zero, biannual and quarterly frequencies is:

$$\Delta_4 Y_t = \mu_t + \gamma_1 Y_{1t-1} + \gamma_2 Y_{2t-1}$$
$$+ \gamma_3 Y_{3t-2} + \gamma_4 Y_{3t-1}$$
$$+ \sum_{j=1}^{p} \phi_j^* \Delta_4 Y_{t-j} + \varepsilon_t \qquad (7.100)$$

where

$$Y_{1t} = (1 + L + L^2 + L^3)Y_t$$
$$Y_{2t} = -(1 - L + L^2 - L^3)Y_t$$
$$Y_{3t} = -(1 - L^2)Y_t$$

and μ_t contains the deterministic components, for example a constant and time trend ($\mu_t = \mu + \beta t$). As a reminder the relevant null hypotheses for the seasonally unadjusted data are:

$\gamma_1 = 0$: unit root at the zero frequency

$\gamma_2 = 0$: unit root at the biannual frequency

$\gamma_3 = \gamma_4 = 0$: unit root at the quarterly frequency

As the emphasis here is on testing for unit roots at various frequencies we will condense the discussion on model selection, although that is just as important a decision as in the case of seasonally adjusted data. The maximum lag was set at $p = 8$ which meant that the longest lag was $\Delta_4 Y_{t-8}$ and the estimation sample period was 1962q2 to 1993q2 $= 125$ observations. The estimated model initially include a deterministic trend, but as its estimated coefficient was 0 to four decimal places and insignificant ($t(\beta) = -2.307$) it was subsequently excluded. In the model without a trend the SC(4) test for serial correlation showed a break at $p = 6$, smaller values having an msl below 5% whereas at $p = 6$, SC(4) $= 7.683$ with an msl of 10.4%. The information criteria, AIC, HQIC and SIC, all

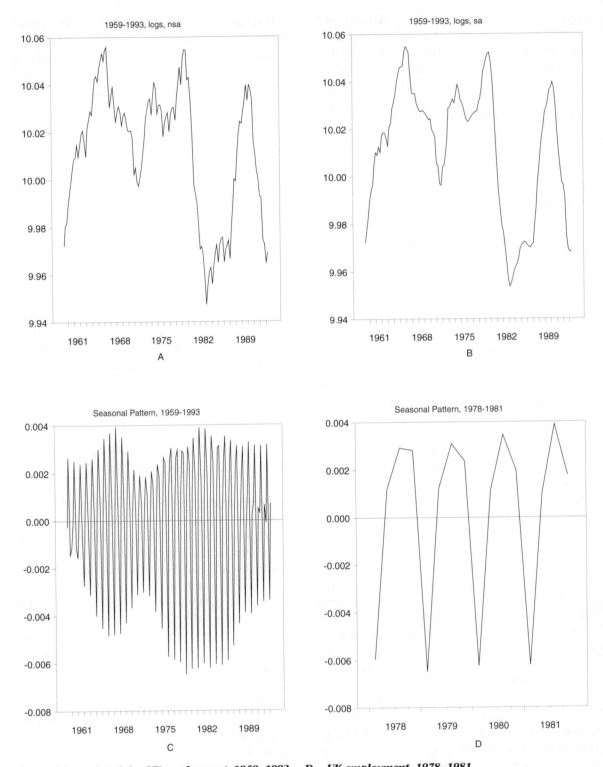

Figure 7.4   A, B and C – *UK employment, 1959–1993*.   D – *UK employment, 1978–1981*

suggested $p = 6$ so the reported results are based on that choice.

The estimated model, with 't' or $\hat{\tau}$ statistics in parentheses, is:

$$\Delta_4 Y_t = 0.416 - 0.010 Y_{1t-1} - 0.080 Y_{2t-1}$$
$$(2.113)(-2.114) \quad (-1.007)$$
$$5\% \text{ cv} \quad -2.89 \quad -1.91$$

$$- 0.059 Y_{3t-2} - 0.121 Y_{3t-1}$$
$$(-0.829) \quad (-1.687)$$
$$-1.88 \quad -1.98/+1.97$$

$$+ \sum_{j=1}^{p} \phi_j^* \Delta_4 Y_{t-j} + \hat{\varepsilon}_t \qquad (7.101)$$

5% critical values from Table 7.6 are given beneath the 't'/$\hat{\tau}$ statistics. The null hypothesis $\gamma_1 = 0$ is not rejected with a test statistic of -2.114 which is less, in absolute value, than the 5% cv of -2.89. Similarly the null hypothesis $\gamma_2 = 0$ is not rejected with a test statistic of -1.007 which is less, in absolute value, than -1.91. On this basis the hypotheses of one unit root at the zero frequency and one at the biannual frequency are not rejected. The simplest way to test for a unit root at the quarterly frequency is to test the joint null hypothesis $\gamma_3 \cap \gamma_4 = 0$; in this case the sample value of the test statistic is 1.775, which is less than the 5% critical value of 3.00 from Table 7.6, with the implication that the data is also consistent with a unit root at the quarterly frequency. Alternatively, test the null hypothesis $\gamma_4 = 0$ against the two-sided alternative with a test statistic of -1.687 with 5% two-sided critical values of $-1.98/+1.97$, hence do not reject the null hypothesis; and then test $\gamma_3 = 0$ against $\gamma_3 < 0$. In the latter case the test statistic is -0.829 against the 5% critical value of -1.88, hence the null of a unit root at the quarterly frequency is not rejected. Overall, the conclusion is that the data is consistent with unit roots at the long-run frequency, zero frequency and the two seasonal frequencies; in the notation of section **7.7**, $e(\text{nsa})_t$ is integrated at the zero frequency, $I_0(1)$, the quarterly frequency, $I_{\frac{1}{4}}(1)$, and the semiannual frequency, $I_{\frac{1}{2}}(1)$.

7.10 'Nearly' integrated and 'nearly' stationary time series

There are two primary uses of unit root tests. There is a considerable body of research, especially since the seminal article by Nelson and Plosser (1982) and the re-evaluation by Perron (1989), which considers the unit root hypothesis to be of interest for its own sake; and it is possible to find many examples of published articles which pose the question of whether particular series have been generated by a process with a unit root. There is also a widespread use of unit root tests as a diagnostic tool, effectively as a pre-test for the specification of empirical models. For example, in a bivariate regression a pre-test would be a unit root test on each of the variables to see if they are integrated of the same order to ensure that the regression model is 'balanced', and hence to offer guidance on whether it is appropriate to use the normal or a non-standard distribution for inference. These two uses of unit root tests are, or should be, related. For example, while Nelson and Plosser (*op. cit.*) were interested in the unit root hypothesis, their article should be taken against a background of a common empirical practice at that time of assuming that the nonstationarity which was clearly apparent in many macroeconomic time series could be accounted for by including a deterministic time trend in a regression or, equivalently, first estimating a (secondary) detrending regression of each variable on a time trend and using the residuals in the primary regression.

The use of unit root tests as diagnostic tools raises different points of emphasis compared to their use as 'own sake' tests. From a practical point of view we often encounter difficulties in distinguishing between unit root and nonunit root processes. Haldrup and Hylleberg (1991) argue that 'For practical purposes the question of whether a time series is integrated is not a question of whether the root is exactly one or strictly less than one, but rather whether the time series contains a strongly autocorrelated component that can justify the series to be *approximated* as an integrated process... Does it really have any meaning, for instance, that interest rates or the rate of unemployment, provided such series contain unit roots, can tend to plus or minus infinity if we permit the time horizon to tend to infinity?' (italics in original). Thus, it may be that for some purposes a 'nearly' integrated process should be treated as an integrated process. Similarly a unit root process may be 'nearly' stationary and it may be better for some purposes to treat it as a stationary process. This is a line of argument also considered by Blough (1992) who suggests that: 'A unit root test which falsely rejects the null of a unit root for a given process may properly be indicating that that process should be treated as stationary for purposes of finite sample inference.' In this section we therefore consider some aspects of unit root testing once we relax the constraint that the only distinction of interest is whether a series has been generated by a process which does – or does not – contain a unit root. Rather, we recognise that for some purposes it may be better to treat a stationary series as if it was integrated and a nonstationary series as if it was stationary.

We first consider processes that are 'nearly' integrated. The basis of discussion being a simple AR(1) DGP, $Y_t = \phi_1 Y_{t-1} + \varepsilon_t$, where ϕ_1 is estimated by OLS in the maintained regression $Y_t = \mu_t + \phi_1 Y_{t-1} + \varepsilon_t$ with μ_t specified as either null (level 1), including a constant (level 2) or a constant and a trend (level 3), and the 't' statistic for $\phi_1 = 0$ is formed. There is a discontinuity in the asymptotic distribution of the 't' statistic for ϕ_1 when $\phi_1 = 1$ in the DGP (which is, therefore, $\Delta Y_t = \varepsilon_t$). Asymptotically, even if the true value of ϕ_1 is, say, $1 - 10^{-6}$, the distribution of the OLS estimator $\hat{\phi}_1$ of ϕ_1 is normal, and the distribution of the 't' statistic is standard normal (because the 't' distribution converges to the normal as $T \rightarrow \infty$), but if $\phi_1 = 1$ the 't' statistic has a Dickey–Fuller distribution which is

skew to the left. However, there is a continuum of finite sample distributions and the discontinuity in the asymptotic distributions is not present in finite samples. An interesting question is then: which distribution, the normal (or 't') or Dickey–Fuller better approximates the finite sample distribution? For example, in moderate sized samples with $\phi_1 < 1$ but ≈ 1, so the DGP is stationary but 'nearly' has a unit root – that is it is 'nearly integrated' – will the Dickey–Fuller distribution provide a better approximation than the normal or 't'? This question is related to the evidence from simulations, with the DGP an AR(1) process, which showed that standard unit root tests have low power when ϕ_1 is close to 1 in the DGP; for example, typically with $\phi_1 = 0.95$ the power is only just above the size (see Table 6.9) and approaches the size as ϕ_1 gets closer to 1. These results suggest that in finite samples a nearly integrated process may well have a distribution close to the DF distribution.

To illustrate what happens in finite samples we simulated the DGP $Y_t = \phi_1 Y_{t-1} + \varepsilon_t$, where ε_t is (normal) white noise, with $\phi_1 = 0.99$, 0.95, 0.5, 0.1 and 0; the first two values are 'near' unit roots, the third is a stationary but autocorrelated process, the fourth is nearly white noise and the fifth is white noise. The maintained regression was Y_t on a constant and Y_{t-1}; the quantiles of the distribution of the 't' statistic, $t(\phi_1) = (\hat{\phi}_1 - \phi_1)/\hat{\sigma}(\hat{\phi}_1)$ where $\hat{\sigma}(\hat{\phi}_1)$ is the estimated standard error of $\hat{\phi}_1$, were recorded, some of which are reported in Table 7.14. Two 'moderate' sample sizes, of the kind encountered in practice, $T = 52$ and $T = 102$, were used. The quantiles from the Dickey–Fuller distribution, which assumes $\phi_1 = 1$, the 't' distribution with $T - 2$ degrees of freedom, and the normal distribution are also reported for comparison.

There are several points to note from Table 7.14. We start with $\phi_1 = 0$, which then allows an interpretation of the quantiles for nonzero values of ϕ_1. The quantiles for $\phi_1 = 0$ are not the same as for the normal (or 't') distribution because $\hat{\phi}_1$ is only *asymptotically*

Table 7.14 *Some quantiles of the distribution of* t(ϕ_1) *for* $\phi_1 = 0.99, 0.95, 0.5, 0.1, 0.0$

	1%	5%	10%	50%	90%	95%	99%
				$T = 52$			
$\phi_1 = 0.99$							
$t(\phi_1)$	−3.526	−2.839	−2.510	−1.440	−0.315	0.057	0.719
$\phi_1 = 0.95$							
$t(\phi_1)$	−3.230	−2.555	−2.221	−1.051	0.081	0.445	1.122
$\phi_1 = 0.5$							
$t(\phi_1)$	−2.673	−1.947	−1.561	−0.306	0.946	1.306	1.996
$\phi_1 = 0.1$							
$t(\phi_1)$	−2.491	−1.794	−1.413	−0.156	1.104	1.462	2.159
$\phi_1 = 0.0$							
$t(\phi_1)$	−2.470	−1.754	−1.400	−0.137	1.107	1.474	2.168
DF	−3.547	−2.914	−2.597	−1.552	−0.407	−0.033	0.662
't'	−2.403	−1.676	−1.299	0.000	1.299	1.676	2.403
Normal	−2.325	−1.645	−1.282	0.000	1.282	1.645	2.325
				$T = 102$			
$\phi_1 = 0.99$							
$t(\phi_1)$	−3.371	−2.727	−2.406	−1.335	−0.241	0.126	0.815
$\phi_1 = 0.95$							
$t(\phi_1)$	−3.065	−2.384	−2.035	−0.834	0.365	0.710	1.368
$\phi_1 = 0.5$							
$t(\phi_1)$	−2.563	−1.849	−1.476	−0.222	1.038	1.413	2.093
$\phi_1 = 0.1$							
$t(\phi_1)$	−2.466	−1.764	−1.390	−0.114	1.140	1.514	2.207
$\phi_1 = 0.0$							
$t(\phi_1)$	−2.470	−1.743	−1.374	−0.092	1.167	1.540	2.258
DF	−3.502	−2.893	−2.584	−1.553	−0.421	−0.061	0.649
't'	−2.364	−1.660	−1.290	0	1.290	1.660	2.364
Normal	−2.325	−1.645	−1.282	0	1.282	1.645	2.325

Note: Table entries are $t(\phi_1) = (\hat{\phi}_1 - \phi_1)/\hat{\sigma}(\hat{\phi}_1)$ for $\phi_1 = 0.99, 0.95, 0.5. 0.1, 0.0$.

unbiased, it is negatively biased in *finite* samples with the implication that the mean and median are less than the true ϕ_1. In finite samples, use of the critical values from the '*t*' distribution will lead to an overrejection of the null hypothesis (of no relation); for example, the 5% one-sided (negative) quantile from the '*t*' distribution with $T - k = 50$ degrees of freedom is −1.676, whereas the simulated 5% quantile is −1.754; the over-rejection will be even more marked if the quantiles from the normal distribution are used.

With $T = 52$ and $\phi_1 = 0.99$, the empirical quantiles of $t(\phi_1)$ are very close to those of the DF distribution; for example, the 5% quantiles are, respectively, −2.839 and −2.914. Although there is some movement away for $\phi_1 = 0.95$, the quantiles of $t(\phi_1)$ are still quite close to those from the DF distribution, and a lot closer than for the distribution with Y_t white noise, and either the '*t*' or normal distributions; and the distribution of $t(\phi_1)$ is substantially skewed. Inference assuming the '*t*' or normal distributions would still be very misleading. With $\phi_1 = 0.5$, the quantiles have moved away from those of the DF distribution, and while they are getting closer to those for Y_t white noise there is still some way to go. Even at this stage the distribution is not symmetric; the 5% one-sided (negative/positive) quantile is −1.947/+1.306

for $t(\phi_1)$ and $-1.676/+1.676$ for the 't' distribution. The quantiles for different values of ϕ_1 illustrate that the finite sample distributions do not reflect the discontinuity in the asymptotic distributions; there is a continuum of finite sample distributions, which depend upon the value of ϕ_1.

Although there is slightly greater movement away from the DF distribution when the sample size is increased to 102, the previous conclusions are not materially altered. The results for $\phi_1 = 0.99$ and 0.95 are as anticipated; those for $\phi_1 = 0.5$ and 0.1 emphasise that the finite sample distributions are a continuum in ϕ_1; for example, while $\phi_1 = 0.5$ obviously generates a stationary process, the quantiles have not converged on those for Y_t white noise, and the negative finite sample bias in the OLS estimator means that the quantiles are still some way from those of the 't' distribution.

In summary the three central points to note from Table 7.14 are:

(i) $\hat{\phi}_1$ has a negative bias in finite samples;
(ii) the finite sample distribution of $t(\phi_1)$ for $\phi_1 = 0$ is not the 't' or normal distribution;
(iii) for a 'nearly' integrated process the distribution assuming a unit root is a better guide than any of the three alternatives (assuming Y_t white noise, the 't' or normal).

An example of a process which has a unit root but which is 'nearly' stationary is $\Delta Y_t = (1 + \theta_1 L)\varepsilon_t$ with $\theta_1 > -1$ but ≈ -1; and recall that if $\theta_1 = -1$ the unit roots on the left- and right-hand sides cancel to leave $Y_t = \varepsilon_t$. What do we know so far about this situation? One problem is the size distortion of standard unit root tests when the DGP is a first order MA process in ΔY_t – see, for example, Schwert (1987, 1989). (See also Pantula (1991) for the derivation of the asymptotic distributions of some unit root tests in this case.) In particular, the null of nonstationarity is rejected too often when the unaugmented DF regression and DF critical values are used; the correct critical values for this

set-up, with $0 > \theta_1 > -1$, are more negative than the DF critical values so that the actual size of the test (false rejections of the null of nonstationarity) is much greater than the nominal size of the test: the unit root test too often falsely indicates that the series is stationary. However, this could be useful in the sense that it may be better to treat a 'nearly' stationary variable as stationary, although we need to be clear for what purposes it is 'better'. If the purpose is to decide, in an absolute sense, whether a series has a unit root then it is not better. However, if the purpose is whether in, for example, a bivariate regression a 'nearly' stationary variable is like a stationary variable and a 'nearly' integrated variable is like an integrated variable, in terms of the distribution of estimators and test statistics, it may well be better. We have already seen in Table 7.14 that the distribution of the conventional 't' statistic in 'nearly' integrated AR(1) processes is close to the distribution assuming a unit root.

This line of argument is followed up in Blough (1992) who considers a bivariate regression when the variables are 'nearly' stationary and when they are 'nearly' integrated. It is well known that using two variables which are unrelated random walks and judging the significance of the relationship by the conventional 't' test, the actual size of the test greatly exceeds the nominal size; a test at a nominal 5% size will have over 70% (false) rejections. In this case the regression is *spurious*; it falsely indicates that unrelated variables are related. If the two variables are unrelated (normal) white noise (and hence stationary) the actual and nominal sizes of the conventional 't' test are equal. The percentage of false rejections in finite samples can be seen as a continuum in a measure of how close a process is to being integrated on the one hand, and (normal) white noise on the other. A unit root test is then useful as a diagnostic tool if the pattern of its rejection probabilities matches the rejection pattern of the regression 't' statistic. In this context what we want from a unit root test is that for unit root processes which are nearly white noise there should be a high probability of false rejection of the null of nonstationarity; the process should be treated as stationary since that matches what we find in the bivariate regression. In the context of stationary processes which are 'nearly' integrated we want the unit root test to indicate that they are integrated if it matches the pattern of rejection of the 't' statistic and, with some qualifications, this is what Blough (*op. cit.*) finds.

7.11   Concluding remarks

This chapter and the last have covered a number of topics with the common theme that they are related to the distinction between nonstationary and stationary time series. Knowing about this distinction, even if there are problems in discerning it in practice, is important in understanding much of the recent literature in applied econometrics and econometric theory. It is also important as a building block in more complex models involving the interrelationships among variables. For example, the idea of 'balance' in a multiple regression model is crucial in understanding how spurious regressions arise, a central feature of which is a high R^2, which is usually interpreted as a model which fits well, but a residual which is I(1). At the least the literature on unit roots has led to a radical evaluation of the practice of including a time trend, or other filtering device, among the regressors in a regression model as a means of capturing the trending properties of the 'dependent' variable.

The difference between processes that are trend stationary and difference stationary is important from economic and econometric perspectives. It is evident that many macroeconomic time series can be characterised as including a secular growth component which dominates over the long run and produces a series which clearly cannot have a constant mean and may not have a constant variance. One view of the generation of a series with a nonconstant mean is that the series is stationary around a deterministic trend; hence, detrending is a simple matter (regress the series on a trend), and what is left can be explained by, for example, traditional theories of the business cycle. A shock, for example a policy variation, does not have a permanent effect on the trend; although it might have quite a persistent effect its impact will eventually die out. In contrast if the series is difference stationary, the shock has a permanent effect, changing the trend pattern, which is consistent with real business cycle theories – see Campbell and Mankiw (1987). In the trend stationary case the increase in the mean of a series is accounted for by a deterministic trend function, whereas if the series is difference stationary the increase in the mean is accounted for by a stochastic trend (unit root) process with drift. One of the impacts of Nelson and Plosser's (1982) study was to call into question the routine practice of detrending variables prior to regression analysis; and the work of Nelson and Kang (1981) and Durlauf and Phillips (1988) has shown that detrending (by regressing on a time trend) a random walk variable can have important statistical and econometric implications. As a result of the impact of the distinction between unit root and non-unit root processes Ouliaris, Park and Phillips (1988) suggest that 'In practical applications it is important to determine whether each series (once purged of its deterministic part) possesses a unit root.'

Whether this advice can be followed is a point on which some authors disagree. In finite samples, stationary and nonstationary processes are 'nearly observational equivalent' in the sense that a stationary process has unit root processes arbitrarily nearby and vice versa – see section **7.10** above, Blough (1992) and for other views critical of unit root testing see Christiano and Eichenbaum (1990), Cochrane (1988) and Faust (1996). In the extreme view it has been argued since we cannot know (in finite samples) whether a series has been generated by a nonstationary or stationary process we should not care about the distinction, Miron (1991, p. 206).

However, there are two points which mitigate against this critical view. First, as indicated in section **7.10**, the closeness of stationary but 'nearly' integrated and integrated processes, on the one hand, and integrated but 'nearly' stationary and stationary processes on the other, can be useful for the wider purpose of finite sample estimation and inference. Second, taking a view about the integration properties of particular series is a useful discipline that relates theoretical prior considerations to sample information. *Bounded* variables, such as portfolio shares (for example, personal sector wealth components as shares of total wealth) or some rates (for example, unemployment rates), should be I(0); and real interest rates, although not technically bounded in the same way, are bounded practically and likely to be I(0). If unit root tests indicate that such series are I(1) this must be a 'local' or approximation property.

As in other areas of translating econometric tools into useful practice, the 'unit root kit' of test statistics has to be used sensibly with an awareness of the requirements and limitations of the test statistics, especially when the outcome of a particular testing process suggests a decision is marginal. It is important to frame the maintained regression so that it nests both an explanation of the data under the nonstationary and stationary alternatives, and to use all the information from the regression, not just one of the DF $\hat{\tau}$ statistics (which is still, regrettably, common practice), to inform a decision; and even then that decision should be tentative, subject to further data and techniques. The maintained regression should be a statistically adequate basis for inference, and the results should be assessed for sensitivity and robustness to reasonable departures from standard assumptions; this is just good econometric practice applied to this particular area. The scope for a sensitivity analysis is considerable in any practical application. There are decisions on the test statistic which usually also involves a decision on a lag length and whether there are structural breaks or outliers in the series.

Perhaps even more so than in other areas of hypothesis testing, nonrejection of the null hypothesis (of a unit root) is just that: *nonrejection is not necessarily acceptance*, hence the terminology that the hypothesis is consistent with the data; if the null that $\gamma = 0$ is not rejected, implying nonstationarity, it is likely that, in the finite samples available to economists, the null $\gamma = -0.01$, implying stationarity, will also be 'not rejected'. (On constructing confidence intervals for the largest root see Stock (1991).) Accepting $\gamma = 0$ can only be tentative; it must give some advantages, such as a better approximation to the small sample distribution of estimators involving the series, over accepting $\gamma = -0.01$. It would also, ideally, find some support from economic theory.

Despite the critical view expressed by some on the value of unit root tests, this area is one of much active research both on the general framework and particular tests. We mention two particularly interesting developments by way of conclusion. An extension of the unit root testing paradigm associated with Dickey and Fuller is to allow the operator d in the transformation $(1 - L)^d Y_t$ to be a fraction. In the DF paradigm the simplest DGP is $(1 - L)^d Y_t = \varepsilon_t$ where d is an integer, usually $d = 0$, the stationary case, or $d = 1$, the unit root/nonstationary case. For fractional d if $0 < d < 0.5$ then Y_t is stationary, whereas for $1 > d \geq 0.5$, Y_t is nonstationary. It turns out that there may be some advantages associated with allowing d to be fractional. First, it nests the standard unit root case allowing a test of the null hypothesis $d = 1$. Second, while Y_t is nonstationary for $d \geq 0.5$ it is nonexplosive; the transition from stationarity to nonstationarity is gradual relative to the standard framework where there is a sharp discontinuity at $\phi_1 = 1$ (with stationarity for $|\phi_1| < 1$, nonstationarity for $\phi_1 = 1$ and explosiveness for $\phi_1 > 1$). Third, and more technically, the econometric properties of test statistics associated with the fractional d paradigm do not (generally) give rise to nonstandard distributions. For example, Gil-Alana and Robinson

(1997) derive a test statistic for the null hypothesis H_0: $d = d_0$ against one-sided or two-sided alternatives, which is asymptotically normally distributed and does not vary for different specifications of the intercept and polynomial trend terms. The emphasis in standard unit root tests on the ARIMA class of models reflects a historical interest.

The second development concerns a related set of problems. First, although normality of the regression errors is not required for validity of the asymptotic critical values of the Dickey–Fuller test statistics, a distributional assumption for the errors is required in order to simulate the finite sample critical values (for example, those reported in the various tables in the previous chapter and in Fuller (1976)). That assumption is that the errors are normally distributed. There is considerable evidence, however, particularly with financial data, that the distribution of errors has fatter tails than the normal distribution; and that some moments may not exist. This suggests the need for a test that is robust to differing assumptions about the distribution of the errors. Second, although sometimes there is guidance from economic theory about which units of measurement, for example a variable should be measured as a rate, or transformation, for example transform to logs so that the growth rate is stationary, should be used for the variable of interest, in many practical situations there is sometimes no presumption other than that the variable of interest or some as yet unspecified transformation of it is stationary/nonstationary. It would be useful to have a test that was invariant to the choice of transformation.

A procedure, which addresses both of these problems, is a rank test for a unit root. For example, in a ranked Dickey–Fuller, RDF, test the data on the variable Y_t is first ranked by magnitude to give a revised dataset Z_t of the ranks. For example, if $Y_t = \{100, 200, 50, 10, 400\}$ then $Z_t = \{3, 2, 4, 5, 1\}$. The mean is then subtracted from Z_t, say $r_t = Z_t - \bar{Z}$ to obtain to a zero mean variable. In general $\bar{Z} = (T + 1)/2$; in the exam-

ple $r_t = \{0, -1, 1, 2, -2\}$. The RDF test is based on the Dickey–Fuller regression using the ranks, r_t, that is

$$r_t = \alpha r_{t-1} + \zeta_t$$

with the test statistic being the Dickey–Fuller test on α. An alternative to subtracting the mean from the ranks is to include a constant in the regression. This test is due to Granger and Hallman (1991); extensions to random walks with drift and correlated innovations are considered in Breitung and Gouriéroux (1997).

In summary, based on the volume of published articles on unit root testing, and the continued interest among theoreticians and applied researchers alike, it is necessary for anyone interested in the time series analysis of economic data to be aware of the main techniques and developments in this area; otherwise much research is not accessible. A sceptical view leads to caution in a too literal interpretation on whether it is possible to distinguish between stationary and nonstationary series given a finite sample of data; the least that can be offered is that the spectrum of processes ranging from stationary and near-stationary to nearly integrated and integrated is useful in understanding the relationship between (or among) economic variables. Part of the problem, which prevents a definite resolution of whether the paradigm of stochastic versus nonstochastic trends is useful, rests upon the simplification that it is framed in a univariate context. In this context the idea of a deterministic trend which suggests an invariant movement in one direction, apart from short memory stochastic shocks, seems inherently unsatisfactory and is a description rather than an explanation of movements in the series; this discomfort is only partially resolved by allowing a split trend. The deterministic trend is an artificial device which captures the effects of capital accumulation, technical progress, population growth and so on which would be better, in principle, modelled in a multivariate context – see Chapters 14 and 15.

Review

1. An alternative to the AR model is the ARMA(p, q) model which includes a moving average component, specifically $\phi(L)Y_t = \mu + \theta(L)\varepsilon_t$ where

$$\phi(L) = 1 - \sum_{i=1}^{p} \phi_i L^i$$

$$\theta(L) = 1 + \sum_{j=1}^{q} \theta_j L^j$$

If the ARMA model has a unit root it is known as an autoregressive integrated moving average, ARIMA ($p, 1, q$), model.

2. An ADF(p) model with $p > 0$, which only has autoregressive dynamics, may arise as an approximation to a moving average model; provided p increases at an appropriate rate, then the limiting distributions of $\hat{\tau}$, $\hat{\tau}_\mu$, and $\hat{\tau}_\beta$, are the same as in the standard case.

3. Schwert (1987) argues that many economic time series should be modelled as ARIMA rather than AR processes, and using the DF critical values when the DGP is an ARIMA can lead to distortions in the size of the test, especially for large negative values of θ_1.

4. Hall (1994) points out that a typical strategy implementing the ADF procedure involves a pre-test to choose the lag order, and he shows that, provided certain conditions are met, the limiting distributions of the ADF $\hat{\tau}$ statistics are the same if a pre-test based on AIC, SIC or HQIC or general-to-specific search, GS, strategy is used, but not if a specific-to-general, SG, strategy is used.

5. Hall's simulation results suggest that when the lag order is estimated by AIC, SIC or GS, the empirical size is greater than the nominal size (oversized) but using SG the test is undersized.

6. Generally choosing the lag order by a pre-test improves the power of the test relative to a preset choice unless by chance the preset value is right.

7. There is a large number of other test statistics for a unit root. Among these is the normalised bias test statistic due to Fuller (1976). For example, in the AR(1) model,

$$Y_t = \phi_1 Y_{t-1} + \varepsilon_t, \quad t = 1, \ldots, T$$

$T(\hat{\phi}_1 - 1)$ can be used to test the null hypothesis that $\phi_1 = 1$ against the stationary one-sided alternative $0 \leq \phi_1 < 1$. This test statistic is called $\hat{\rho}$ in Fuller (*op. cit.*).

8. Critical values depend upon whether the regression model has: no intercept; an intercept; an intercept and a time trend. These give rise to the three test statistics: $\hat{\rho}$, $\hat{\rho}_\mu$ and $\hat{\rho}_\beta$.

9. In an AR($p + 1$) model with $p > 0$:

$$\gamma = -\phi(1) = -\theta(1)(1 - \rho)$$
$$= \theta(1)(\rho - 1)$$

10. The coefficient on Y_{t-1} is now the product of $\theta(1)$ and $(\rho - 1)$, and will be zero under the null hypothesis. Given consistent estimates of γ and $\theta(1)$, then dividing the former by the latter gives a consistent estimate of $(\rho - 1)$; multiplied by T this is approximately distributed as $\hat{\rho}_\mu$ with critical values from Table 8.5.1 of Fuller (*op. cit.*).

11. Another class of test statistics, analogous to the DF $\hat{\tau}$ statistics, is based on the weighted symmetric estimator which combines, with weights w_t and $1 - w_t$, respectively, the usual OLS (backward) residual sum of squares and the forward residual sum of squares, FRSS.

12. Choosing $w_t = (t - 1)/T$, so $w_2 = 1/T$, $w_3 = 2/T$, $w_T = (T - 1)/T$, gives the weighted symmetric (WS) estimator, $\hat{\phi}_1^{ws}$. Test statistics analogues to the Dickey–Fuller case are then easily formed.

13. There is generally an improvement in power in using the weighted symmetric estimators rather than in the (simple) OLS estimator.

14. Apart from seeking an increase in power, a second motivation for alternative unit root test statistics is to allow for disturbance

processes, ε_t, which are not iid $\sim (0, \sigma^2)$. Another class of tests which has found widespread use is due to Phillips (1987), Phillips and Perron (1987, 1988), known as PP tests.

15. There are PP modified versions of Φ_1, Φ_3, $\hat{\tau}$, $\hat{\tau}_\mu$, $\hat{\tau}_\beta$ and $\hat{\rho}$, $\hat{\rho}_\mu$ and $\hat{\rho}_\beta$. For example, the PP version of $\hat{\tau}_\mu$ test statistic, denoted $Z\hat{\tau}_\mu$:

$$Z\hat{\tau}_\mu = (s_\varepsilon^2/s_{Tl}^2)\hat{\tau}_\mu - 0.5(s_{Tl}^2 - s_\varepsilon^2)$$

$$\bigg/ \left(s_{Tl} \left[T^{-2} \sum_{t=2}^{T} (Y_{t-1} - \bar{Y}_{-1})^2 \right]^{0.5} \right)$$

16. The 'truncation' lag of the autocovariances, l, is a choice parameter. Calculating $\hat{\tau}_\mu$ for a range of values of l should reveal when the numerical value of the correction factor stabilises. Andrews (1991) shows that consistency of s_{Tl}^2 requires that $l \to \infty$ as $T \to \infty$ at the rate $O(T^{\frac{1}{3}})$; for example, if $T = 100$, $l = 5$ (to the nearest integer).

17. Campbell and Perron (1991) note that when the autocorrelations of ε_t are predominantly negative the PP tests are sometimes considerably oversized, but on correcting for this distortion the PP tests can deliver more power than the ADF tests.

18. A complementary view on how univariate time series should be modelled arises from a distinction between the structural and reduced forms and owes much to the work of Harvey, for example Harvey (1989).

19. A series could be viewed as composed of a level component and an irregular component with the representation: $Y_t = \alpha_t + \xi_t$. The local level model specifies $\alpha_t = \alpha_{t-1} + \eta_t$.

20. The local level model is easily generalised to allow for a trend, then $\alpha_t = \alpha_{t-1} + \beta + \eta_t$ so the level changes but the slope is constant. To allow the slope and level to change, let β_t designate the changing slope, which also evolves according to a random walk $\beta_t = \beta_{t-1} + \varsigma_t$.

21. The simplest changing level/fixed slope structural time series model, $Y_t = \alpha_{t-1} + \beta + \eta_t + \xi_t$, has autocovariances which are the same as an MA(1) process in ΔY_t, so the ARIMA(0, 1, 1) model is the reduced form of the structural, local level/constant slope, model.

22. Specifying the univariate time series model in its structural form enables a test of the unit root hypothesis in which the null hypothesis is that the series is stationary, whereas the alternative is that it is nonstationary. Two leading test statistics are due to Leybourne and McCabe, LMc, (1994) and KPSS (1992).

23. In the LMc test the local level/fixed slope structural time series model is generalised to allow for lags on Y_t, so the basic model becomes $\phi(L)Y_t = \alpha_{t-1} + \beta + \eta_t + \xi_t$. The reduced form of this model is ARIMA(p, 1, 1), that is $\phi(L)\Delta Y_t = \beta + \varepsilon_t + \theta\varepsilon_{t-1}$ with θ negative. The null is ARIMA(p, 1, 1) whereas the alternative is ARIMA (p, 1, 1).

24. An alternative test statistic is due to KPSS which also starts from the basic local level model $Y_t = \alpha_{t-1} + \beta + \eta_t + \xi_t$ but captures dynamics in the process generating ξ_t.

25. Leybourne and McCabe (*op. cit.*) provide some simulations, which suggest that the LMc test is more powerful than the KPSS test.

26. Some processes may generate series with 2 unit roots and have to be differenced twice to become stationary. An I(2) series appears smoother and more slowly changing than an I(1) series.

27. Hasza and Fuller (1979) suggest a procedure to test directly for the existence of 2 unit roots. Alternatively, Dickey and Pantula (1987) suggest a sequential procedure beginning 'with the highest (practical) degree of differencing and work downward toward a test on the series level . . .' (*op. cit.*, p. 456).

28. The Dickey–Pantula procedure is just a repeated application of the ADF procedure, which is now interpreted as testing for a marginal unit root. For example, if testing for two unit roots define $Z_t \equiv Y_t - Y_{t-1}$ and use Z_t where Y_t was previously specified in tests for one unit root.

29. Hasza and Fuller (1979) suggest using

$$\Delta Z_t = \mu + \gamma_1 Y_{t-1} + \gamma_2 Z_{t-1}$$

$$+ \sum_{j=1}^{p} \alpha_j \Delta Z_{t-j} + \varepsilon_t$$

The first unit root corresponds to $\gamma_1 = 0$ and the second to $\gamma_2 = 0$ so the joint null hypothesis of 2 unit roots corresponds to $\gamma_1 = \gamma_2 = 0$ which can be tested by an F test with a nonstandard distribution, critical values are given in Hasza and Fuller (1979).

30. Seasonal differencing may be necessary to reduce a series to stationarity. For example, suppose a quarterly series is generated by $Y_t = \phi_{14} Y_{t-4} + \varepsilon_t$, then if $\phi_{14} = 1$ there is a unit root at the quarterly seasonal frequency and the seasonal difference $Y_t - Y_{t-4}$ is stationary.

31. Testing for a unit root in this framework is a straightforward extension of the Dickey–Fuller procedure – see Dickey *et al.* (1984) – with seasonal differences rather than first differences being taken in the Dickey–Fuller regressions.

32. In practice a pure seasonal model is unlikely. For example, the following is an AR(1) model in the sth seasonal difference: $(1 - \phi_1 L)(1 - L^s)Y_t = \varepsilon_t$ which results in lags of order 1, s and $s + 1$. If $\phi_1 = 1$ there are unit roots at the long-run (zero) and quarterly seasonal frequencies.

33. A test often applied to seasonal data is due to Hylleberg, Engle, Granger and Yoo (1990), usually referred to as HEGY. It tests for the possibility of unit roots at the long-run, semi-annual and quarterly frequencies.

34. The HEGY test is based on the regression:

$$\phi^*(L)\Delta_4 Y_t = \gamma_1 Y_{1t-1} + \gamma_2 Y_{2t-1}$$

$$+ \gamma_3 Y_{3t-2} + \gamma_4 Y_{3t-1} + \varepsilon_t$$

where:

$$Y_{1t} = (1 + L + L^2 + L^3)Y_t,$$
$$Y_{2t} = -(1 - L + L^2 - L^3)Y_t,$$
$$Y_{3t} = -(1 - L^2)Y_t$$

The tests are linked to the following unit root null hypotheses: $\gamma_1 = 0$ for the long-run frequency; $\gamma_2 = 0$ for the semi-annual frequency; $\gamma_3 = \gamma_4 = 0$ for the quarterly frequency. The critical values, obtained by simulation, depend upon the deterministic terms included in the maintained regression.

35. Perron (1989) has suggested that one-time structural breaks can make a stationary series seem nonstationary when assessed by the usual unit root procedures. Events such as the 'Great Crash' of 1929 or the 'oil price rise' in 1973 may lead to structural changes.

36. Perron's framework assumes a known structural break at time T_b. Under the null of a unit root this break, effective at $T_b + 1$, can take the form of A, a change in the level; B, a change in the growth rate; C, a change in the level and growth rate.

37. Appropriate alternative hypotheses are: A, trend stationary with a one-time change in the level; B, trend stationary with a change in the trend slope; C, a change in the level and the slope.

38. If adjustment following the break is immediate an additive outlier, AO, model is used; if adjustment is gradual an innovation outlier, IO, model is used.

39. In the AO framework the first step is to construct residuals by regressing Y_t on the set of deterministic terms specified by the alternative hypothesis, then the residuals from this prior regression are used in a standard augmented DF regression.

40. In the IO approach the deterministic terms (constant, trend and dummy variables) are incorporated directly into the ADF regression in the untransformed variables, Y_t and ΔY_{t-j}.

41. The critical values are obtained by simulation and depend upon the model and the relative breakpoint $\lambda = T_b/T$.

42. Perron (*op. cit.*) gives several examples of his testing procedure. For example, a

preliminary analysis of the 62 annual observations 1909 to 1970, for US real GNP, suggested that there was potentially a structural
break following the 'Great Crash' of 1929,
which could be characterised as a gradual
change in the level but no change in the
slope so the appropriate model is Model A
specified as an IOADF regression.

43. Extensions of the Perron approach involving
multiple structural breaks are easy to deal
with by a suitable definition of dummy
variables, although the appropriate critical
values would have to be obtained by
simulation.

44. Zivot and Andrews (1992) suggested the
breakpoint T_b should be treated as unknown
and by not doing so Perron biases his results
in favour of rejection of the unit root
hypothesis.

45. In the Zivot and Andrews' framework T_b is
chosen where the evidence against the null
is greatest, and the critical values, obtained
by simulation, are more negative for a given
significance level than in Perron's case.

46. Zivot and Andrews' testing procedure leads to
a reversal of Perron's conclusion of rejection
of the unit root hypothesis in 4 out of 10
cases for the Nelson–Plosser series, and also
reverses Perron's conclusion for rejection of
the unit root for post-war quarterly GNP.

47. Perron (1997) introduces the selection criterion of choosing λ where the 't' statistic on
the parameter associated with the change
shows greatest evidence of change. The
critical values are smaller in absolute value
than when the breakpoint is chosen by the
Zivot and Andrews method and larger in
absolute value than when the breakpoint is
assumed known.

48. Franses and Haldrup (1994) consider the
effect of additive outliers, which have a
one-off impact, on unit root (and cointe-
gration) tests. In the AR(1) model $Y_t = \phi_1 Y_{t-1} + \varepsilon_t$, an additive outlier of magnitude
h means that the observed time series is
$Z_t = Y_t + \theta$.

49. Additive outliers, which by definition only
have a temporary effect, may give the
impression that a series is stationary when
it is not; the series is 'spuriously stationary'.

50. If the probability of an additive outlier is
positive the Dickey–Fuller $\hat{\tau}$ test has an
actual size greater than its nominal size,
with the implication that the unit root
hypothesis is rejected too often.

51. Some of the techniques of this and the
previous chapter were applied to economic
time series in section **7.9**. The first series was
quarterly, post-war data on the log of UK per
capita consumers' expenditure on nondurable goods, denoted cnd_t.

52. The graph of cnd_t suggested a distinct trend
hence the maintained regression included
βt. The hypothesis of 2 unit roots was firmly
rejected whereas the hypothesis of 1 unit
root was consistent with the data, with
$\Phi_3 = 1.855$ compared to a 5% cv of approximately 6.606. Also $\hat{\tau}_\beta = -1.466$ compared to
the 5% cv of -3.402.

53. If a change in the slope is allowed, associated
with the change of government in the
United Kingdom in 1979 and following
Perron's structural break framework, the
conclusion of a unit root is less firmly based.

54. The next series considered was UK unemployment used by Phillips (1958) in his
famous article. This series 'looked stationary', which was confirmed with the formal
tests. Of interest in this context was the
interpretation of the intercept in the maintained regression which was important in
estimating the stationary mean to which the
series reverted.

55. Applying unit root tests to an unemployment rate, which is bounded by 0 and 1,
raised the theoretical issue of whether such a
series can be a random walk, with the
conclusion that this is likely to be a 'local'
rather than global property.

56. There was some ambiguity when the formal tests were applied to the post-war US
unemployment rate. Although $\hat{\tau}_\beta = 3.145$ is

smaller negative than the 5% critical value of -3.407, suggesting nonrejection of the null of a unit root, the time trend was superfluous and reduced the power of the test.

57. Without a time trend in the maintained regression $\Phi_1 = 4.629$ compared to the 5% cv of about 4.696 and $\hat{\tau}_\mu = -3.039$ compared to the 5% cv of -2.856; on balance the unit root null was rejected, with $USUR_t$ stationary about a mean of approximately 6.89%.

58. The last series considered, the log of employees in employment in the UK, was an example of using seasonally unadjusted data. Within the HEGY framework tests were applied for unit roots at the zero, semi-annual and quarterly frequencies.

59. None of the HEGY tests led to rejection of the null hypothesis, with the conclusion that the data is consistent with unit roots at the long-run frequency and the two seasonal frequencies.

60. There is a widespread use of unit root tests as a diagnostic tool, effectively as a pre-test for the specification of empirical models to ensure that the regression model is 'balanced'. This use of unit root tests raises different points of emphasis compared to their use as 'own sake' tests.

61. From a practical point of view it is often difficult to distinguish between unit root and nonunit root processes; and it may be that for some purposes a 'nearly' integrated process should be treated as an integrated process. Similarly a unit root process may be 'nearly' stationary and it may be better for some purposes to treat it as a stationary process.

62. The closeness of stationary but 'nearly' integrated and integrated processes, on the one hand, and integrated but 'nearly' stationary and stationary processes on the other, can be useful for the wider purpose of finite sample estimation and inference.

63. As in other areas of translating econometric tools into useful practice, the 'unit root kit'

of test statistics has to be used sensibly with an awareness of the requirements and limitations of the test statistics.

64. Nonrejection of the null hypothesis (of a unit root) is just that: *nonrejection is not necessarily acceptance.*

65. An extension of the unit root testing paradigm associated with Dickey and Fuller is to allow the operator d in the transformation $(1 - L)^d Y_t$ to be a fraction. With d fractional the transition from stationarity to nonstationarity is gradual relative to the unit root case.

66. A test which is robust to differing assumptions about the distribution of the errors and which transformation of the data should be used is the ranked Dickey–Fuller, RDF, test.

67. The deterministic trend is an artificial device, which captures the effects of capital accumulation, technical progress, and population growth, and so on that would be better, in principle, modelled in a multivariate context.

Review questions

1. Consider the AR(4) model

$$Y_t = \mu + \phi_1 Y_{t-1} + \phi_2 Y_{t-2} + \phi_3 Y_{t-3} + \phi_4 Y_{t-4} + \varepsilon_t$$

rearranged as an ADF(3) model,

$$\Delta Y_t = \mu + \gamma Y_{t-1} + \alpha_1 \Delta Y_{t-1} + \alpha_2 \Delta Y_{t-2} + \alpha_3 \Delta Y_{t-3} + \varepsilon_t$$

For this model consider the factorisation $\phi(L) = \theta(L)(1 - \rho L)$:
   (i)   Show that $\phi(1) = \theta(1)(1 - \rho)$.
   (ii) Show that $\phi_1 = \theta_1 + \rho$, $\phi_2 = \theta_2 - \theta_1 \rho$, $\phi_3 = \theta_3 - \theta_2 \rho$ and $\phi_4 = -\theta_3 \rho$.
   (iii) Show that $\gamma = \theta(1)(\rho - 1)$.

(iv) Explain how to obtain an estimator of $T(\rho - 1)$ which has the same asymptotic distribution as Fuller's (1976) $\hat{\rho}_\mu$ statistic.

2. Consider the AR(2) model

$$Y_t = \mu + \phi_1 Y_{t-1} + \phi_2 Y_{t-2} + \varepsilon_t$$

which can be rearranged as an ADF(1) model

$$\Delta Y_t = \mu + \gamma Y_{t-1} + \alpha_1 \Delta Y_{t-1} + \varepsilon_t$$

Suppose estimation of the latter with an overall sample of $T = 100$ gives

$$\Delta Y_t = 0.1 - 0.02 Y_{t-1} + 0.72 \Delta Y_{t-1} + \varepsilon_t$$

Using the factorisation $\phi(L) = \theta(L)(1 - \rho L)$ and not assuming $\rho = 1$ obtain an estimate of $\theta(1)$, and hence obtain an estimate of the test statistic ρ_μ.

3. Reconsider the example from Dickey, Bell and Miller (*op. cit.*) used in section **7.4.1** of the text:

$$\Delta \hat{Y}_t = 0.867 - 0.603 Y_{t-1} + 0.224 \Delta Y_{t-1}$$

Not assuming $\rho = 1$, obtain an estimate of $\theta(1)$, and hence obtain an estimate of ρ_μ. Compare this to the value cited in the text.

4. (i) Interpret the following structural time series model and describe the kind of economic time series for which it would be appropriate:

$$Y_t = \alpha_t + \xi_t$$
$$\alpha_t = \alpha_{t-1} + \beta_t + \eta_t$$
$$\beta_t = \beta_{t-1} + \zeta_t$$

(ii) Simplify the model so it is appropriate for (a) a constant level and (b) a changing level but not a changing slope.

5. Show that the steps in obtaining the connection between the structural parameters and the reduced form parameters in the local level/changing trend model are:

(i) $(1 + \theta^2)(-\sigma_\xi^2/(\sigma_\eta^2 + 2\sigma_\xi^2)) = \theta$

(ii) $-\sigma_\xi^2/(\sigma_\eta^2 + 2\sigma_\xi^2) - \theta$
$-[\sigma_\xi^2/(\sigma_\eta^2 + 2\sigma_\xi^2)]\theta^2 = 0$

(iii) $1 + [(\sigma_\eta^2 + 2\sigma_\xi^2)/\sigma_\xi^2]\theta + \theta^2 = 0$

(iv) $1 + (q + 2)\theta + \theta^2 = 0$

(v) Hence, use the standard formula,

$$[\pm (b^2 - 4ac)^{0.5} - b]/2a$$

for the roots of the quadratic $c + bx + ax^2$ to obtain:

$$\theta = [(q^2 + 4q)^{0.5} - q - 2]/2$$

(vi) Explain why the solution with the negative of the square root is dropped (Harvey 1989, p. 68).

(vii) Show that when $q = 0$ this reduces to $\theta = -1$ and when $q = \infty$, $\theta = 0$; and interpret these special cases.

6. What advantages are there to specifying the null hypothesis as stationarity rather than nonstationarity?

7. What is the difference between the LMc and KPSS tests for a unit root?

8. Further diagnostic tests on the ADF(5) model, reported in section **7.9.1** above, with trend and split trend suggest that the residuals are homoscedastic with the standard test $HS(1) = 0.367$ and msl $= 54.5\%$, but not normal with $JB(2) = 17.537$ and msl $= 0\%$. The ADF and PP tests do not require the residuals to be normally distributed to be valid; lack of serial correlation and homoscedasticity is sufficient. While normality is not necessary, nonnormality may signal some important one-off impacts, leading to exceptional or outlying residuals. Consider the empirical case for impulse dummy variables in 1968q2, 1971q1, 1973q1 and 1979q2; the first could be associated with the sterling crisis in 1968, the third with the oil price crisis and the last with the anticipated increase in VAT from 8% to 15%. (What explanation could account for the second dummy variable?)

9. (i) From Figure 7.3 it is evident that there are two significant periods of change in the sample period for $USUR_t$. First, in the early part of the sample there was a marked increase in unemployment, with the 1974 average of 5.6% increasing to a 1975 average of 8.5%; second, in a more gradual progression the 1979 average of 5.8% increased to 9.6% in 1983. In both cases $USUR_t$ decreases following its peak. Do you think that these could be regarded as: (a) structural breaks; (b) innovation outliers; (c) responses to shocks from a stationary process with long, but not infinite, memory?

(ii) Define the dummy variables $DVU746_t = 0$ if $t < 1974m6$ and 1 for $t \geq 1974m6$; analogously define $DVU756_t$, $DVU805_t$ and $DVU831_t$. Interpret the following regression:

$$\Delta Y_t = 0.213 - 0.039 Y_{t-1}$$
$$(3.271)(-4.025)$$

$$+ 0.305 DVU746_t$$
$$(4.063)$$

$$- 0.274 DVU756_t$$
$$(-0.274)$$

$$+ 0.167 DVU805_t$$
$$(0.168)$$

$$- 0.175 DVU831_t$$
$$(-4.354)$$

$$+ \sum_{j=1}^{4} \alpha_j \Delta Y_{t-j} + \varepsilon_t$$

where $Y_t \equiv USUR_t$ and 't' statistics are in parentheses.

10. How would you test for a seasonal unit root in the following model (Dickey, Hasza and Fuller 1984)?

$$Y_t = \phi_{1s} Y_{t-s} + \varepsilon_t \quad \text{for } s > 1$$

11 (i) Show that

$$1 - L^4 = (1 - L)(1 + L + L^2 + L^3)$$
$$= (1 - L)(1 + L)(1 - iL)(1 + iL)$$

(ii) Interpret $(1 - L)(1 + L + L^2 + L^3)Y_t$.

(iii) Consider $(1 + L)Y_t = \varepsilon_t$ and show that, apart from ε_t, this is a process that repeats itself every two periods.

(iv) Consider $(1 - iL)Y_t = \varepsilon_t$ and show that, apart from ε_t, this is a process that repeats itself every four periods (Banerjee et al. 1993).

12. Explain how to test for unit roots at the seasonal frequencies in the following model (HEGY 1990):

$$\phi^*(L)\Delta_4 Y_t = \gamma_1 Y_{1t-1} + \gamma_2 Y_{2t-1}$$
$$+ \gamma_3 Y_{3t-2} + \gamma_4 Y_{3t-1} + \varepsilon_t$$

where

$$Y_{1t} = (1 + L + L^2 + L^3)Y_t$$
$$Y_{2t} = -(1 - L + L^2 - L^3)Y_t$$
$$Y_{3t} = -(1 - L^2)Y_t$$

Appendix

Table A7.1 *Empirical cumulative distribution of $T(\hat{\phi}_1 - 1)$ for $\phi_1 = 1$*

Sample Size T	Probability of a smaller value							
	0.01	0.025	0.05	0.10	0.90	0.95	0.975	0.99
	$\hat{\rho}$ (no constant in the maintained regression)							
25	−11.9	−9.3	−7.3	−5.3	1.01	1.40	1.79	2.28
50	−12.9	−9.9	−7.7	−5.5	0.97	1.35	1.70	2.16
100	−13.3	−10.2	−7.9	−5.6	0.95	1.31	1.65	2.09
250	−13.6	−10.3	−8.0	−5.7	0.93	1.28	1.62	2.04
500	−13.7	−10.4	−8.0	−5.7	0.93	1.28	1.61	2.04
∞	−13.8	−10.5	−8.1	−5.7	0.93	1.28	1.60	2.03
	$\hat{\rho}_\mu$ (constant in the maintained regression)							
25	−17.2	−14.6	−12.5	−10.2	−0.76	0.01	0.65	1.40
50	−18.9	−15.7	−13.3	−10.7	−0.81	−0.07	0.53	1.22
100	−19.8	−16.3	−13.7	−11.0	−0.83	−0.10	0.47	1.14
250	−20.3	−16.6	−14.0	−11.2	−0.84	−0.12	0.43	1.09
500	−20.5	−16.8	−14.0	−11.2	−0.84	−0.13	0.42	1.06
∞	−20.7	−16.9	−14.1	−11.3	−0.85	−0.13	0.41	1.04
	$\hat{\rho}_\beta$ (constant and trend in the maintained regression)							
25	−22.5	−19.9	−17.9	−15.6	−3.66	−2.51	−1.53	−0.43
50	−25.7	−22.4	−19.8	−16.8	−3.71	−2.60	−1.66	−0.65
100	−27.4	−23.6	−20.7	−17.5	−3.74	−2.62	−1.73	−0.75
250	−28.4	−24.4	−21.3	−18.0	−3.75	−2.64	−1.78	−0.82
500	−28.9	−24.8	−21.5	−18.1	−3.76	−2.65	−1.78	−0.84
∞	−29.5	−25.1	−21.8	−18.3	−3.77	−2.66	−1.79	−0.87

Note: Source, reproduced from *Introduction to Statistical Time Series* by W.A. Fuller (1976), Table 8.5.1, p. 371, by permission, and copyright © John Wiley.

CHAPTER 8

Stationarity and nonstationarity in single-equation regression analysis

8.1 Introduction

Chapters 4 and 5 dealt with basic issues of estimation and inference in a bivariate and then multivariate model; throughout the variables in the regression model were assumed to be stationary. Chapters 6 and 7 introduced the concept of nonstationary variables with the emphasis on how to test for the existence of unit roots in a single series. In this chapter, to draw a link between the theoretical results in the earlier chapters and the properties of OLS estimators in finite samples, we first consider the most basic of regression models using stationary variables. When dealing with stationary variables it is often possible to derive theoretical results that are applicable to finite samples. For example, if the regressors are fixed in repeated samples then the OLS estimator will be unbiased, and this is so whatever the sample size. In contrast if the regressors are nonstationary we generally only know the theoretical properties of estimators as the sample size tends to infinity. In order to study the properties of estimators in finite samples we, therefore, use simulation analysis. Starting with stationary variables in a simple regression model serves to introduce a technique that has found considerable application in more complex models.

After consideration of the simplest case the complications arising from allowing nonstationary variables in bivariate or multivariate regression models are considered. This is stage 1 of the analysis and development, the limitation in this chapter being that the emphasis is on estimating a single equation. Stage 2 of the analysis comes first in Chapter 9, where some of the issues related to endogeneity – or connections between equations – are raised and then, more substantively, in Chapters 14 and 15, where multiple equations are considered.

Specific sections deal with the issues as follows. Sections **8.2.1**–**8.2.3** consider some simple 'starting' cases, which involve the distributions of the OLS estimators and 't' statistics; first, in section **8.2.1**, the DGP is a bivariate regression with X_t fixed in repeated samples; and in sections **8.2.2** and **8.2.3**, is alternately a stationary and then nonstationary variable. Section **8.2.4** considers a spurious regression and section **8.2.5** looks at the distribution of R^2. A clear message from section **8.2** is the need to distinguish between spurious and cointegrating regressions, and this is the subject of section **8.3**.

Section **8.3** outlines the basic concept of cointegration applied to the bivariate case. The multivariate case is taken up in section **8.4.4**. Section **8.4.1** outlines the Dickey–Fuller-based test for noncointegration; critical values can be obtained by simulation as described in section **8.4.2** or, more economically, by using MacKinnon's response surface approach described in section **8.4.3**. The testing procedure is generalised to the case of more than two variables in section **8.4.4**, and illustrated with a cointegrating regression in section **8.4.5** and a spurious regression in section **8.4.6**. The link between cointegration and error correction models, due

316

to Gra⌐   ⌐em, is outlined
in ⌐   ⌐ion **8.5.1**,
                              ⌐ovide
                          ⌐nd
                        ⌐

stationary, distinguishing whether X_t is white noise or serially correlated. Finally, X_t is generated from a nonstationary, stochastic process and two cases are distinguished according to whether Y_t and X_t are, or are not, cointegrated. The latter case is an example of a spurious regression and distinguishing between this and a ⌐ointegrating regression is of vital importance. ⌐e DF and ADF tests for noncointegration are ⌐ribed in a following section.

⌐⌐l X_t is fixed in repeated samples

$(\text{⌐⌐}/\text{⌐⌐}(⌐⌐))$ ⌐⌐xed in repeated samples' is the central case by most introductory textbooks on econo- ics and is a useful starting point even gh interpreted literally it is unlikely to r in practice. The usual idea is that X_t is ause of Y_t, and the only source of stochastic ⌐⌐⌐tion in Y_t is due to the disturbance term ε_t. In this paradigm the disturbance looks like a separate entity and is often described in introductory texts as representing omitted but minor influences on Y_t, measurement error (in Y_t) and the 'inherent randomness' in human behaviour. We can, however, interpret this set-up differently – and more realistically – given the alternative paradigm outlined in Chapter 4, in which Y_t and X_t are jointly generated random variables, but regression analysis proceeds by conditioning on one of the variables. In that case X_t is regarded as the conditioning variable as in writing $E\{Y_t \mid X_t\}$, but with X_t fixed at a particular sample value, $X_t = x_t$. On this basis we can regard 'X_t fixed in repeated sampling' as a means of obtaining the conditional distribution of Y_t given $X_t = x_t$.

The idea that X_t can literally be fixed in repeated samples could also be justified in an experimental setting, in which it is possible to design and then repeat an experiment. We can illustrate this set-up with two artificial examples, one from agriculture and one from economics. In this example X_t is the amount of seed, and Y_t is the resulting crop. Imagine a large number of identical 10 metre squares of cultivated land

⌐⌐⌐⌐⌐⌐ ⌐⌐ ⌐⌐⌐⌐⌐⌐⌐⌐ ⌐
by simulation

An important distinguishing feature of regression analysis concerns the time series properties of the dependent variable and the regressors. As we shall see the properties of the OLS estimator of the coefficients and the distribution of this estimator depend crucially upon these properties. We will distinguish three cases of interest all of which can be illustrated with a single regressor, X_t:

(i) X_t is fixed in repeated samples,
(ii) X_t is a stationary, stochastic variable,
(iii) X_t is a nonstationary, stochastic variable.

In this section we consider each of these cases in turn with an emphasis on the empirical distributions of the OLS estimators of the constant and slope coefficient and their 't' statistics. The first case of X_t fixed in repeated samples is rather unrealistic but does serve to provide a useful base point from which to evaluate different, and more realistic, situations. Then we consider the case where X_t, and hence Y_t, are stochastic but each split into 100 square metre sections. Each of these sections is given a location index t which, therefore, runs from 1 to 100. To each of the 100 square metres we apply a different amount of seed, with the amount for each square fixed according to a design. For example, we might set the design so that the amount of seed X_t is proportional to the index t, but there are obviously many other possibilities. The important point is that X_t is fixed by a design and that design can be repeated over and over again on the 10 square metre sections of land. In experiment 1 we carry out the design so that X_t is fixed for $t = 1, \ldots, 100$, for each one of the 10 metre squares. The corresponding values of Y_t are recorded; thus we have one sample of 100 pairs of ordered observations (Y_t, X_t), $t = 1, \ldots,$ 100. With these observations, which constitute one sample, we can carry out the regression of Y_t on $X_t = x_t$ and record the OLS estimates of the coefficients β_1 and β_2. Notice that X_t fixed, that is $X_t = x_t$, does not mean $x_t = x_s$ for $t \neq s$; there can (and indeed must) be variation across the index; what stays constant is that in the next and subsequent repeated samples, x_t (and x_s and so on) are kept the same as in the first sample. The experiment can be repeated again and again on the 10 metre squares; however, to emphasise, each time the *design*, as fixed in experiment 1, of $X_t = x_t$, $t = 1, \ldots, 100$, is repeated. This makes X_t nonstochastic for the purposes of the experiments. The variation in Y_t, $t = 1, \ldots, 100$ between samples is accounted for by the different values of the stochastic element ε_t that are drawn on each sample.

It is rather more difficult to think of a plausible economic example of the fixed regressor case but the idea of an experiment again provides some motivation. Consider the aggregate consumption of a group of T homogeneous households and associate the index $t = 1, \ldots, T$ with these households; let Y_t and X_t denote their consumption and income, respectively. In order to observe the consumption behaviour of these households each is given a different amount of monthly income, denoted $X_t = x_t$ and varying

for the different households, $t = 1, \ldots, 100$. The resulting values of Y_t are recorded to obtain T pairs of ordered observations $(Y_t, X_t = x_t)$, $t = 1, \ldots, T$; this is sample 1, which can be used in the regression of Y_t on $X_t = x_t$ with resulting estimates $\hat{\beta}_{1,1}$ and $\hat{\beta}_{2,1}$; the second subscript, separated by a comma, which was not necessary in Chapter 4 has been introduced to indicate that these estimates are obtained from the first sample. The experiment is repeated the following month, with income for each household fixed as in the first month; thus, if consumption for household t for experiment 2 differs from that for experiment 1 the variation is entirely due to the different value of the disturbance term ε_t between the two experiments. Hypothetically we imagine this experiment being repeated again and again over successive months generating M samples, all of which can be used to regress consumption on income, with corresponding estimates of the regression coefficients, $\hat{\beta}_{1,j}$ and $\hat{\beta}_{2,j}, j = 1, \ldots, M$. The M sample estimates can then be used to obtain empirical – or more precisely experimental – counterparts of relevant theoretical concepts.

Rather than conduct experiments with human subjects it is easier to design an experiment that can be run on a computer; usually called Monte Carlo experiments or simulations – these were used extensively to provide critical values for the test statistics for a unit root in Chapter 6. In this case we are interested in a simulation to examine the properties of the OLS estimators when X_t is fixed in repeated sampling (and in other cases which are reported later in this section). In this simulation we first generated just one set of T random numbers which were then saved and used as the 'fixed' values of $X_t = x_t$ for $t = 1, \ldots, T$. The next step was to generate Y_t from the bivariate regression model

$$Y_t = \beta_1 + \beta_2(X_t = x_t) + \varepsilon_t$$
$$\text{for } t = 1, \ldots, T \tag{8.1}$$

with $\beta_1 = 10$ and $\beta_2 = 0.5$; ε_t is normal white noise, drawn from a standard normal distribu-

Table 8.1   OLS estimators with X_t fixed in repeated samples and $Y_t = 10 + 0.5X_t + u_t$; u_t is white noise

	Mean	$\hat{\sigma}$	1%	5%	10%	25%	50%	75%	90%	95%	99%	% rejection at 10% level
Sample size $T = 50$												
$\hat{\beta}_1$	10.000	0.142	9.673	9.768	9.819	9.904	10.000	10.097	10.182	10.232	10.332	
't'($\hat{\beta}_1$)	0.004	1.020	−2.370	−1.664	−1.291	−0.677	0.000	0.688	1.309	1.684	2.421	
$\hat{\beta}_2$	0.500	0.130	0.200	0.287	0.333	0.411	0.499	0.587	0.667	0.713	0.803	10.224
't'($\hat{\beta}_2$)	0.000	1.026	−2.410	−1.691	−1.310	−0.687	−0.006	0.686	1.309	1.685	2.432	
't' value	0.000		−2.406	−1.677	−1.299	−0.680	0.000	0.680	1.299	1.677	2.406	
Sample size $T = 100$												
$\hat{\beta}_1$	10.000	0.101	9.764	9.834	9.870	9.932	10.000	10.067	10.129	10.166	10.236	
't'($\hat{\beta}_1$)	0.002	1.011	−2.361	−1.672	−1.291	−0.676	0.005	0.675	1.293	1.669	2.354	
$\hat{\beta}_2$	0.500	0.085	0.300	0.360	0.391	0.422	0.499	0.557	0.609	0.641	0.700	9.876
't'($\hat{\beta}_2$)	0.002	1.012	−2.377	−1.658	−1.287	−0.677	−0.003	0.676	1.277	1.677	2.412	
't' value	0.000		−2.365	−1.660	−1.290	−0.677	0.000	0.677	1.290	1.660	2.365	
Sample size $T = 500$												
$\hat{\beta}_1$	10.000	0.044	9.896	9.926	9.943	9.700	10.000	10.030	10.057	10.073	10.104	
't'($\hat{\beta}_1$)	0.002	0.998	−2.329	−1.642	−1.267	−0.670	0.003	0.674	1.278	1.638	2.330	
$\hat{\beta}_2$	0.500	0.046	0.394	0.426	0.441	0.469	0.500	0.531	0.558	0.575	0.607	10.340
't'($\hat{\beta}_2$)	0.003	1.007	−2.349	−1.643	−1.297	−0.678	0.009	0.685	1.294	1.647	2.376	
't' value	0.000		−2.333	−1.645	−1.282	−0.675	0.000	0.675	1.282	1.645	2.333	

tion with zero mean and unit variance. *This is the DGP.* Next for each sample of size T run the regression of Y_t on a constant and $X_t = x_t$ and record the estimated values of β_1 and β_2 denoted $\hat{\beta}_{1,j}$ and $\hat{\beta}_{2,j}$, $j = 1, \ldots, M$, so that M is the number of samples being taken. In Monte Carlo terminology M is the number of 'draws' or replications in the experiment, taken here to be 25,000. To assess the effect of changing the sample size on the results we take $T = 50$, 100 and 500. Another design feature is the values of the regression coefficients in the DGP; here, to illustrate, we only take one pair of values but if the results were thought to be sensitive to this aspect of the design these could be varied. For each value of T a number of statistics are recorded which will help in interpreting the results of the Monte Carlo experiments. In particular: the mean over the M replications, the distribution of $\hat{\beta}_{1,j}$ and $\hat{\beta}_{2,j}$, and the distribution of the following 't' statistics,

$$t(\hat{\beta}_1) = (\hat{\beta}_{1,j} - \beta_1)/\hat{\sigma}(\hat{\beta}_{1,j})$$

$$t(\hat{\beta}_2) = (\hat{\beta}_{2,j} - \beta_2)/\hat{\sigma}(\hat{\beta}_{2,j})$$

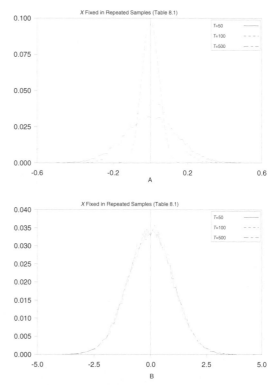

Figure 8.1   A – Distribution of bias of OLS estimator of slope. B – Distribution of 't' statistic for slope

where $\hat{\sigma}(\hat{\beta}_{i,j})$ is the estimated standard error for regression coefficient i in sample j.

A summary of the results with $T = 50$, 100, 500 is given in Table 8.1. Even with the relatively small sample size of $T = 50$ OLS does well, with the mean of the estimates of β_1 and β_2 equal to their corresponding population values of 10.00 and 0.5, respectively. The empirical distribution of the bias, $\hat{\beta}_{2,j} - \beta_2$, is shown in Figure 8.1A. That is the horizontal axis is the bias in estimating the slope coefficient β_2 and the vertical axis is the relative frequency. As the sample size increases the distribution concentrates about the population value of $\beta_2 = 0.5$, indicating that β_2 is more precisely estimated as T increases.

The empirical distribution of the 't' statistics for each of the three sample sizes is shown in Figure 8.1B. These distributions are close to their theoretical distributions; for example, the final

column of Table 8.1 records the percentage of rejections of the null hypothesis $\beta_2 = 0$ which would have occurred using the critical values from the 't' distribution at a 10% significance level (on a two-sided test). For $T = 50$, 100 and 500 we obtained 10.224%, 9.876% and 10.340% rejections, respectively; all of these are very close to the nominal 10% level of the test. For $T = 50$ the central 98% of the values of $\hat{\beta}_2$ lie between 0.200 and 0.803, a range of $0.803 - 0.200 = 0.603$; whereas for $T = 500$ the corresponding range is $0.607 - 0.394 = 0.213$, indicating a substantial increase in the concentration of the distribution around the population value $\beta_2 = 0.5$. The purpose of this simulation was largely illustrative in two respects. First, in indicating how a simple Monte Carlo experiment is set up; and, second, in showing whether the theoretical results concerning the properties of estimators, which were summarised in Chapters 4 and 5, provide a good indication as to what will happen in finite samples. In this case, they do.

8.2.2 X_t is a stationary, stochastic variable

8.2.2a X_t stationary: white noise

The next situation to be considered is where X_t is a stationary, stochastic variable, otherwise the simulation – or Monte Carlo – set-up is exactly as before. Here the intention is to mimic the more realistic case where we do not have control over the values of X_t; now not only are the values of X_t drawn again in each experiment – or sample – so are the values of X_t upon which they depend. Thus, if there are M replications, giving rise to M samples, the values of X_t are not the same in each sample. This corresponds to the situation covered in section **4.5**.

The first case we consider is where X_t is white noise, with a number of summary statistics reported in Table 8.2. The performance of the OLS estimator, compared to the fixed regressor case, is relatively unaffected by this change. For example, consider $T = 50$ and the distribution

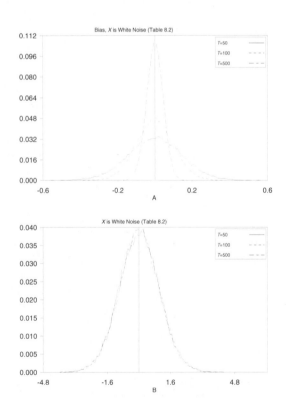

Figure 8.2 A – *Distribution of bias of OLS estimator of slope*. B – *Distribution of 't' statistic for slope*

Table 8.2 *OLS estimators with X_t white noise and $Y_t = 10 + 0.5X_t + u_t$; u_t is white noise*

	Mean	$\hat{\sigma}$	1%	5%	10%	25%	50%	75%	90%	95%	99%	% rejection at 10% level
Sample size $T = 50$												
$\hat{\beta}_1$	9.999	0.143	9.668	9.766	9.817	9.902	9.998	10.094	10.180	10.235	10.335	
't'($\hat{\beta}_1$)	0.008	1.020	−2.392	−1.686	−1.299	0.686	0.012	0.662	1.278	1.689	2.429	
$\hat{\beta}_2$	0.499	0.146	0.158	0.260	0.313	0.403	0.499	0.597	0.686	0.740	0.840	10.324
't'($\hat{\beta}_2$)	0.000	1.025	−2.391	−1.681	−1.308	−0.679	−0.002	0.685	1.308	1.681	2.403	
't' value	0.000		−2.406	−1.677	−1.299	−0.680	0.000	0.680	1.299	1.677	2.406	
Sample size $T = 100$												
$\hat{\beta}_1$	9.999	0.101	9.765	9.833	9.870	9.931	9.999	10.067	10.129	10.167	10.236	
't'($\hat{\beta}_1$)	0.004	1.017	−2.350	−1.679	−1.300	−0.686	0.005	0.669	1.292	1.672	2.393	
$\hat{\beta}_2$	0.499	0.102	0.263	0.331	0.369	0.431	0.498	0.567	0.628	0.666	0.739	10.236
't'($\hat{\beta}_2$)	0.009	1.014	−2.337	−1.679	−1.298	−0.689	−0.016	0.672	1.283	1.654	2.381	
't' value	0.000		−2.365	−1.660	−1.290	−0.677	0.000	0.677	1.290	1.660	2.365	
Sample size $T = 500$												
$\hat{\beta}_1$	10.000	0.044	9.895	9.267	9.943	9.970	10.000	10.031	10.058	10.074	10.103	
't'($\hat{\beta}_1$)	0.009	1.001	−2.352	−1.645	−1.263	−0.665	0.013	0.692	1.289	1.649	2.319	
$\hat{\beta}_2$	0.499	0.045	0.394	0.425	0.441	0.469	0.500	0.529	0.557	0.574	0.604	9.990
't'($\hat{\beta}_2$)	0.010	1.005	−2.350	−1.669	−1.308	−0.686	0.007	0.665	1.281	1.651	2.329	
't' value	0.000		−2.333	−1.645	−1.282	−0.675	0.000	0.675	1.282	1.645	2.333	

of $\hat{\beta}_2$ and its 't' statistic. There is a negligible small sample bias – the mean of $\hat{\beta}_2$ is 0.4999 compared to the population value of 0.5, with a slight increase in the range of the estimates compared to the fixed regressor case. The distributions of $\hat{\beta}_2$ and the 't' statistics are very close to those in the fixed regressor case – see Figures 8.2A and 8.2B. The distribution of $\hat{\beta}_2$ is again symmetric and the % rejections at the 10% significance level, 10.324% for $T = 50$, 10.236% for $T = 100$ and 9.990% for $T = 500$, are all close to the nominal 10% level of the test.

8.2.2b X_t stationary: an AR(1) process

The next situation we consider is where X_t is stationary but serially correlated and, in particular, it will be of interest to construct X_t as close to, but not actually, a random walk. We specify $X_t = 0.99X_{t-1} + \omega_t$, where ω_t, is normal white noise with zero mean and unit variance, so that

X_t is 'nearly' integrated. The Monte Carlo results are reported in Table 8.3 and Figures 8.3A and 8.3B. In summary we find that the OLS estimator continues to exhibit a negligible bias. The distributions of the 't' statistics for each sample size change but only marginally from those in Table 8.2 where X_t was white noise, and these in turn are close to their theoretical 't' distributions. There is, however, one important point of difference compared to the results reported in Tables 8.1 and 8.2. Comparing corresponding like sample sizes we see that there is a marked increase in the concentration of the distribution of $\hat{\beta}_2$. For example, for $T = 100$ and X_t white noise, the estimated standard deviation of the distribution is 0.102, whereas for X_t serially correlated the estimated standard deviation is around one-third of that at 0.035. For $T = 500$ the estimated standard deviation for $\hat{\beta}_2$ in Table 8.2 is 5 times that in Table 8.3. The increase in the concentration of the distribution is shown very clearly in Figure 8.3A, note

Table 8.3 OLS estimators with X_t stationary but serially correlated, $Y_t = 10 + 0.5X_t + u_t$; u_t is white noise

	Mean	$\hat{\sigma}$	1%	5%	10%	25%	50%	75%	90%	95%	99%	% rejection at 10% level
Sample size $T = 50$												
$\hat{\beta}_1$	10.004	0.454	8.675	9.316	9.557	9.817	10.004	10.194	10.447	10.689	11.344	
$'t'(\hat{\beta}_1)$	0.013	1.016	−2.371	−1.652	−1.282	−0.669	0.016	0.701	1.301	1.667	2.392	
$\hat{\beta}_2$	0.500	0.068	0.328	0.390	0.419	0.461	0.500	0.539	0.581	0.610	0.674	10.304
$'t'(\hat{\beta}_2)$	−0.005	1.023	−2.399	−1.678	−1.307	−0.690	−0.008	0.674	1.317	1.665	2.387	
$'t'$ value	0.000		−2.406	−1.677	−1.299	−0.680	0.000	0.680	1.299	1.677	2.406	
Sample size $T = 100$												
$\hat{\beta}_1$	10.000	0.232	9.321	9.653	9.766	9.890	9.999	10.111	10.238	10.344	10.654	
$'t'(\hat{\beta}_1)$	0.000	1.012	−2.359	−1.659	−1.290	−0.677	−0.004	0.673	1.299	1.674	2.388	
$\hat{\beta}_2$	0.500	0.035	0.406	0.443	0.458	0.479	0.500	0.520	0.542	0.558	0.591	10.180
$'t'(\hat{\beta}_2)$	−0.006	1.016	−2.400	−1.666	−1.294	−0.681	−0.111	0.672	1.295	1.678	2.382	
$'t'$ value	0.000		−2.365	−1.660	−1.290	−0.677	0.000	0.677	1.290	1.660	2.365	
Sample size $T = 500$												
$\hat{\beta}_1$	10.000	0.057	9.862	9.910	9.931	9.965	10.000	10.035	10.069	10.093	10.139	
$'t'(\hat{\beta}_1)$	0.001	1.000	−2.340	−1.639	−1.284	−0.671	−0.006	0.671	1.295	1.665	2.347	
$\hat{\beta}_2$	0.500	0.009	0.478	0.486	0.489	0.495	0.500	0.505	0.510	0.514	0.522	10.068
$'t'(\hat{\beta}_2)$	0.003	1.000	−2.361	−1.645	−1.272	−0.661	−0.010	0.678	1.288	1.656	2.340	
$'t'$ value	0.000		−2.333	−1.645	−1.282	−0.675	0.000	0.675	1.282	1.645	2.333	

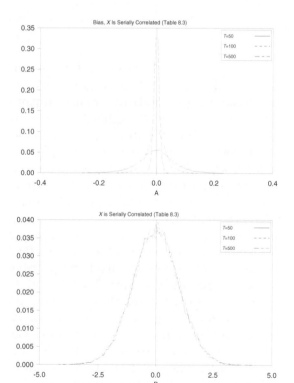

Figure 8.3 A – Distribution of bias of OLS estimator of slope. B – Distribution of 't' statistic for slope

especially the case when $T = 500$ compared to Figures 8.1A and 8.2A. The message we draw from this comparison is that for a 'nearly' integrated variable the estimator $\hat{\beta}_2$ converges faster, and the distribution of $\hat{\beta}_2$ is 'tighter' than when X_t is white noise.

8.2.3 X_t is a nonstationary, stochastic variable

The next simulation is a precursor to the more detailed simulations involving cointegrated and nonstationary variables reported in section **8.4**. In this case the generating process for X_t is a random walk, that is $X_t = X_{t-1} + \omega_t$ and, as before, $Y_t = 10 + 0.5X_t + \varepsilon_t$, a situation we recognise as cointegration between Y_t and X_t; ε_t and ω_t are uncorrelated, $N(0, 1)$ variables. A design parameter of this experiment is the variance ratio $\sigma_\omega^2/\sigma_\varepsilon^2$, which is here set to 1, but in a more comprehensive study would be varied to assess the sensitivity of the results. We should be careful to note here the simple nature of the DGP and the assumption that ω_t and ε_t are uncorrelated; in

Table 8.4 OLS estimators with X_t a random walk and $Y_t = 10 + 0.5X_t + u_t$; u_t is white noise

	Mean	$\hat{\sigma}$	1%	5%	10%	25%	50%	75%	90%	95%	99%	% rejection at 10% level
Sample size $T = 50$												
$\hat{\beta}_1$	9.990	0.844	7.439	8.701	9.171	9.691	9.993	10.294	10.792	11.264	12.511	
$'t'(\hat{\beta}_1)$	−0.010	1.019	−2.384	−1.674	−1.319	−0.694	−0.015	0.667	1.279	1.664	2.430	
$\hat{\beta}_2$	0.500	0.066	0.328	0.394	0.422	0.462	0.500	0.536	0.576	0.608	0.678	10.196
$'t'(\hat{\beta}_2)$	−0.003	1.018	−2.352	−1.664	−1.295	−0.687	−0.005	0.669	1.304	1.677	2.408	
$'t'$ value	0.000		−2.406	−1.677	−1.299	−0.680	0.000	0.680	1.299	1.677	2.406	
Sample size $T = 100$												
$\hat{\beta}_1$	10.000	0.435	8.713	9.348	9.571	9.831	10.001	10.166	10.426	10.666	11.304	
$'t'(\hat{\beta}_1)$	0.003	1.007	−2.343	−1.665	−1.273	−0.670	0.005	0.672	1.296	1.664	2.355	
$\hat{\beta}_2$	0.500	0.033	0.413	0.446	0.461	0.481	0.500	0.518	0.538	0.552	0.585	10.184
$'t'(\hat{\beta}_2)$	−0.009	1.007	−2.364	−1.682	−1.298	−0.682	−0.009	0.675	1.272	1.642	2.353	
$'t'$ value	0.000		−2.365	−1.660	−1.290	−0.677	0.000	0.677	1.290	1.660	2.365	
Sample size $T = 500$												
$\hat{\beta}_1$	10.000	0.111	9.693	9.828	9.882	9.946	10.000	10.052	10.117	10.174	10.319	
$'t'(\hat{\beta}_1)$	−0.003	0.994	−2.307	−1.640	−1.282	−0.661	0.000	0.660	1.267	1.640	2.349	
$\hat{\beta}_2$	0.500	0.006	0.483	0.489	0.492	0.496	0.500	0.504	0.508	0.510	0.517	9.924
$'t'(\hat{\beta}_2)$	−0.004	0.995	−2.328	−1.635	−1.276	−0.674	−0.009	0.658	1.274	1.640	2.304	
$'t'$ value	0.000		−2.333	−1.645	−1.282	−0.675	0.000	0.675	1.282	1.645	2.333	

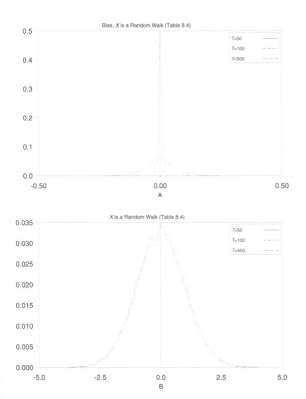

Figure 8.4 A – Distribution of bias of OLS estimator of slope. B – Distribution of 't' statistic for slope

particular this means that there are no dynamics in the cointegrating relationship and that there is no contemporaneous connection between ω_t and ε_t. This assumption is relaxed in the models introduced in the next chapter.

The Monte Carlo results are reported in Table 8.4 and Figures 8.4A and 8.4B. With only minor qualifications, note that the OLS estimators are again unbiased and the distributions of the 't' statistics are close to those in the previous tables and, hence, close to the theoretical 't' distributions. Comparing Tables 8.3 and 8.4 we see that there is a further increase in the concentration of the distribution of $\hat{\beta}_2$. For example, for $T = 500$ the estimated standard deviation of the distribution of $\hat{\beta}_2$ is reduced further from 0.009 to 0.006. Again this concentration is particularly noticeable in the empirical distribution of (the bias of) $\hat{\beta}_2$ shown in Figure 8.4A. As the sample size increases there is a very marked increase in the concentration of the distribution. The % rejections at the 10% nominal significance level for $T = 50$, 100 and 500 are 10.196%, 10.184% and 9.924%, respectively; all, again, very close to the 10% size of the test.

8.2.4 A spurious regression

The next situation we consider is where both Y_t and X_t are random walks but, in contrast to the previous experiment, are not cointegrated. This is an interesting variation because it mimics a situation of practical relevance: suppose Y_t and X_t are unrelated, integrated variables but the researcher mistakenly believes there is a relationship between these variables, will this lack of a relationship be discovered using standard techniques? This example is usually referred to as a *spurious regression* since Y_t and X_t are unrelated. Thus, the set-up of the simulations is that $Y_t = Y_{t-1} + \varepsilon_t$ and $X_t = X_{t-1} + \omega_t$ with ω_t and ε_t each normal white noise and uncorrelated. Yule (1926) first drew attention to the situation that arises with unrelated nonstationary variables. Granger and Newbold (1974) drew attention to the problem in econometrics and their article led to a greater awareness of the issue of spurious regressions in econometrics. Phillips (1986) gave a theoretical explanation of the implications of spurious regressions.

The Monte Carlo results are reported in Table 8.5 and Figures 8.5A and 8.5B. First note that the bias for both coefficients is slight for all sample sizes (remember that the true values of β_1 and β_2 are zero). The largest difference between the results in this table and the previous tables is in the distribution of the estimates and their 't' statistics. Throughout the different sample sizes the range of estimates has considerably increased; for example, for $\hat{\beta}_2$ and $T = 50$, the central 98% of the distribution lies between -1.580 and $+1.641$ and for $\hat{\beta}_1$, the central 98% of the distribution lies between -36.392 and 35.485. The first implications of a spurious regression are apparent and listed below.

- The chance of getting a nonzero estimate, even though the true values are zero, is substantial.
- The estimated regression coefficients can be quite misleading as to whether there is a relationship between the variables.

- The distribution of the 't' statistics is also quite unlike the other cases we have considered. For example, in the case of the 't' statistic for $\hat{\beta}_2$ with $T = 50$, the lower 5% critical value is -8.377 and the upper 5% critical value is 8.368.

Using the critical values from the 't' distribution or from the empirical distributions from the previous tables would be very misleading. For example, the lower and upper 5% critical values from the theoretical 't' distribution are ±1.677 for $T = 50$, so an estimate of, say, 3.00 would be judged as highly significant from these critical values. However, reference to Table 8.5 shows that this is close to the upper 25% critical value (that is 25% of the empirical distribution is above 3.136); and hence is nowhere near as significant as incorrectly using the critical values of the theoretical 't' distribution would suggest. If the critical values of ±1.677 of the theoretical 't' distribution for $T = 50$, for the 10% significance level and a two-sided test, were used the null hypothesis of no relationship would be rejected in 17,947 of the 25,000 cases generated here. That is the actual rejection percentage is 71.788% and not 10% as one might mistakenly believe from use of the 't' distribution. Further this situation is not improved as the sample size increases, indeed it gets worse! With a sample size of $T = 100$ the actual rejection rate using the critical values from the 't' distribution is 79.972%, and for $T = 500$, 91.132%.

The problem is apparent: if Y_t and X_t are I(1) but unrelated then it will be unsafe to use critical values from the 't' distribution. The obvious question is then: when will this situation occur?

- First, note that it occurs with I(1) variables, so initially establishing whether a series is consistent with an I(1) process will be useful.
- Second, if two series, Y_t and X_t, are cointegrated then a regression of Y_t on X_t will not be a spurious regression.

Table 8.5   OLS estimators with Y_t and X_t unrelated random walks

	Mean	$\hat{\sigma}$	1%	5%	10%	25%	50%	75%	90%	95%	99%	% rejection at 10% level
Sample size $T = 50$												
$\hat{\beta}_1$	−0.080	14.856	−36.392	−24.355	−18.511	−9.682	−0.040	9.528	18.499	24.076	35.485	
$'t'(\hat{\beta}_1)$	0.021	22.643	−68.410	−33.967	−21.527	−8.239	−0.024	8.243	21.788	34.318	60.000	
$\hat{\beta}_2$	0.002	0.632	−1.580	−1.025	−0.763	−0.378	0.002	0.382	0.767	1.025	1.641	71.788
$'t'(\hat{\beta}_2)$	0.018	5.117	−12.867	−8.377	−6.236	−3.101	0.017	3.136	6.316	8.368	12.739	
$'t'$ value	0.000		−2.406	−1.677	−1.299	−0.680	0.000	0.680	1.299	1.677	2.406	
Sample size $T = 100$												
$\hat{\beta}_1$	0.013	15.313	−36.996	−24.686	−18.765	−9.861	−0.040	9.923	19.137	24.930	37.27	
$'t'(\hat{\beta}_1)$	0.245	26.552	−75.623	−40.658	−26.869	−10.976	−0.045	11.017	27.474	42.859	81.972	
$\hat{\beta}_2$	0.000	0.628	−1.618	−1.041	−0.763	−0.379	0.002	0.380	0.760	1.017	1.571	79.972
$'t'(\hat{\beta}_2)$	0.056	7.299	−18.367	−11.817	−8.820	−4.376	0.023	4.540	8.946	11.943	18.362	
$'t'$ value	0.000		−2.365	−1.660	−1.290	−0.677	0.000	0.677	1.290	1.660	2.365	
Sample size $T = 500$												
$\hat{\beta}_1$	−0.080	17.887	−44.044	−29.031	−22.504	−11.649	0.065	11.515	22.401	28.866	42.826	
$'t'(\hat{\beta}_1)$	−0.007	38.328	−103.943	−63.100	−43.687	−19.710	0.107	19.779	43.755	61.925	105.257	
$\hat{\beta}_2$	−0.003	0.630	−1.560	−1.038	−0.780	−0.386	−0.002	0.382	0.769	1.029	1.606	91.132
$'t'(\hat{\beta}_2)$	−0.100	16.715	−42.372	−27.611	−70.755	−10.212	−0.053	10.115	20.306	27.328	40.745	
$'t'$ value	0.000		−2.333	−1.645	−1.282	−0.675	0.000	0.675	1.282	1.645	2.333	

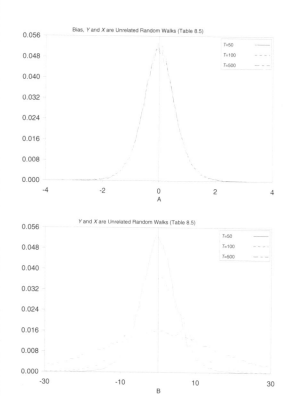

Figure 8.5   A – Distribution of bias of OLS estimator of slope. B – Distribution of 't' statistic for slope

Hence, the next step will be to establish whether Y_t and X_t are cointegrated variables. If Y_t and X_t are I(1), but unrelated, then the residuals from the regression of Y_t on X_t or vice versa will be consistent with an I(1) process, not the I(0) process that would occur if Y_t and X_t are cointegrated. This is considered further in section **8.3.2**.

In an important study Granger and Newbold (1974) drew attention to the problem of misleading inference when Y_t and X_t are unrelated random walks, and we briefly consider how their results relate to those reported here. Granger and Newbold used $T = 50$ and generated 100 replications of Y_t and X_t as unrelated random walks. They found the distribution of the estimated 't' statistic for $\hat{\beta}_2$ was asymmetric and differed substantially from the theoretical 't' distribution. They suggested that instead of using a 't' value of approximately 2.0 at the 5% significance level, a value of 11.2 should be used, the multiplying factor relating the two being 5.6.

Using the same number of replications we found that the results were too variable to come to firm conclusions on the distribution of 't'

Statistics for the distribution of 't'(β_2)

Experiment 1 (100 replications)											
mean	skewness	kurtosis	1%	5%	10%	25%	50%	75%	90%	95%	99%
0.024	−0.060	0.602	−9.758	−6.934	−6.050	−2.575	0.387	2.446	6.321	7.028	10.792
[0.958]	[0.808]	[0.235]									
Experiment 2 (100 replications)											
−0.522	−0.600	0.188	−15.580	−11.513	−8.483	−3.756	0.343	2.768	6.801	7.795	9.889
[0.361]	[0.016]	[0.710]									

Notes: The table entries for skewness and excess kurtosis are test statistics that indicate whether the distribution is skew (=0 for a symmetric distribution) and whether there is excess kurtosis relative to the normal distribution (=0 for a normal distribution). Marginal significance levels are given in parentheses [.].

statistic for $\hat{\beta}_2$. The results from two experiments each with 100 replications are given above.

In experiment (sample) 1 we find evidence to suggest that the distribution of the 't' statistic for $\hat{\beta}_2$ is symmetric with a zero mean (the msl in each case is well above 5%); however, in the second replication we find the skewness coefficient is significant with a marginal significance level of 1.6%. In both cases though we find no similarity with the theoretical 't' distribution. A better guide to the distribution is found from Table 8.5 where 25,000 replications were used. In that case the relevant statistics indicate that the distribution is symmetric (skewness coefficient = −0.005 with a marginal significant level of 73%) and a zero mean (estimated mean = 0.0002 with a marginal significance level of 99%). However, there is excess kurtosis (kurtosis coefficient = 0.942 with marginal significance level of 0%).

Using 25,000 replications, for $T = 100$ the critical values for a 10% significance level, with 5% either side, are approximately −11.82 and 11.94 to be compared with the corresponding values of ±1.66 from the theoretical 't' distribution. The factor of multiplication is about 7.1, but this varies with the quantiles being compared.

8.2.5 The distribution of R^2

Chapter 4 introduced the concept of R^2, which is often used as a measure of the goodness of fit of a regression equation. To recap briefly, if there is a constant in the regression equation then the definition of (sample) R^2 is:

$$R^2 = \text{ESS}/\text{TSS}$$
$$= 1 - \text{RSS}/\text{TSS}$$

where

ESS is the explained sum of squares

$$= \sum_{t=1}^{T} (\hat{y}_t - \bar{y})^2$$

RSS is the residual sum of squares

$$= \sum_{t=1}^{T} \hat{\varepsilon}_t^2$$

TSS is the total sum of squares

$$= \sum_{t=1}^{T} (y_t - \bar{y})^2$$

The limits of R^2 are 0 and +1. The conventional interpretation of this goodness of fit statistic is that it measures the proportion of variation in the dependent variable accounted for – or explained – by the regressors. However, this interpretation is not valid if the dependent variable is nonstationary.

In Table 8.6 and Figures 8.6A and 8.6B, the distribution of R^2 is reported for two opposite

Table 8.6 *Distribution of* R^2

| | **Y_t and X_t unrelated white noise** | | | | | | | | | | |
	Mean	$\hat{\sigma}$	1%	5%	10%	25%	50%	75%	90%	95%	99%
$T = 50$	0.020	0.028	0	0	0	0.001	0.005	0.013	0.027	0.038	0.005
$T = 100$	0.010	0.014	0	0	0	0.001	0.005	0.013	0.027	0.038	0.065
$T = 500$	0.002	0.003	0	0	0	0	0.001	0.002	0.005	0.008	0.013
	Y_t and X_t unrelated random walks										
	Mean	$\hat{\sigma}$	1%	5%	10%	25%	50%	75%	90%	95%	99%
$T = 50$	0.245	0.230	0	0.002	0.007	0.044	0.176	0.404	0.602	0.703	0.824
$T = 100$	0.241	0.226	0	0.002	0.007	0.044	0.173	0.392	0.596	0.693	0.827
$T = 500$	0.241	0.227	0	0.002	0.007	0.044	0.170	0.393	0.598	0.695	0.821

cases. In both cases Y_t and X_t are unrelated so that the true values of the coefficients are $\beta_1 = \beta_2 = 0$, but in the first case Y_t and X_t are stationary and, in particular, are white noise, whereas in the second case, as in Table 8.5, Y_t and X_t are random walks. The second case is

obviously another aspect of a spurious regression and it turns out that not only are the conventional 't' statistics misleading in such a case, so is R^2.

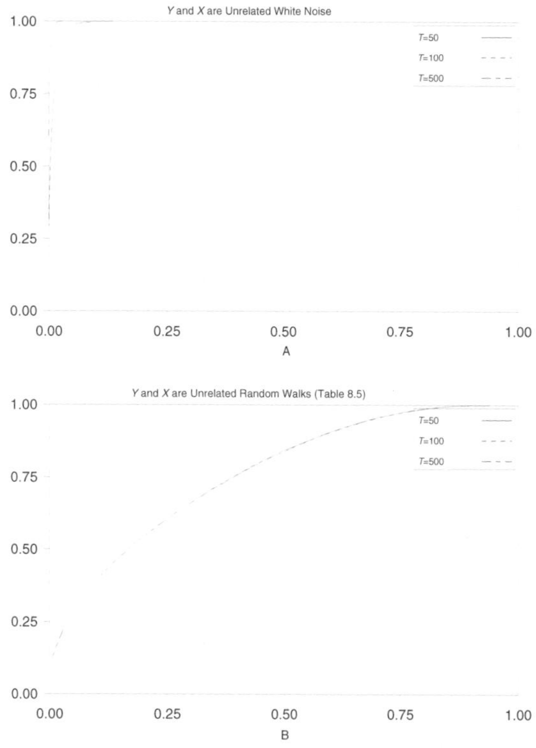

For the stationary case refer to Table 8.6 and Figure 8.6A. R^2, which is shown on the horizontal axis, is effectively zero throughout its distribution, and this is what we would expect from the conventional interpretation that R^2 should be zero if the dependent variable is unrelated to the regressor(s). Note that in Figure 8.6A (and 8.6B) the cumulative distribution is plotted so that the vertical axis refers to the cumulative relative frequency of the values on the horizontal axis. For example, for $T = 100$, 99% of the distribution of R^2 is below 0.065, and for $T = 500$ this falls to 0.013. Now contrast this situation with Y_t and X_t unrelated random walks. The mean value of R^2 is now about 0.24, and there is a 10% chance of obtaining an R^2 value, which exceeds about 0.6 even though Y_t and X_t are unrelated! Note also that the distribution of R^2 is reasonably stable for all three sample sizes considered here. Also, as the standard deviation of the distribution indicates, the distribution does not become more concentrated as the sample size increases, so the problem of high R^2 for unrelated nonstationary variables is *not* a problem associated with a small sample size: R^2 is a *random variable for nonstationary variables.*

Figure 8.6 A and B – *Cumulative distribution of* R^2

8.3 Cointegration

It is clear from the results of sections **8.2.3**–**8.2.4** that being able to distinguish between spurious and cointegrating regressions is vital in the context of nonstationary variables. This section and the next consider the details of this distinction. The central concept of cointegration is considered first in section **8.3.1**, for simplicity, in a bivariate framework and then, in section **8.4.4**, in the more realistic case involving more than two variables. The widely used version of the Dickey–Fuller test for (non)cointegration, due to Engle and Granger (1987), is described in section **8.4**. This is the first stage of what is known as the two-stage Engle–Granger procedure. The critical values for the test statistic, as in the parallel case in testing for a unit root in a single series, are obtained by simulation. However, MacKinnon (1991) has provided a set of response surfaces to obtain the critical values for any sample size, and these are described in section **8.4.3**. (These response surfaces also apply to the univariate case described in Chapter 6 but, unlike the Cheung–Lai response surfaces, do not make an adjustment for the number, p, of lags in the ADF test statistic.) The test procedure is illustrated with cointegrated variables in section **8.4.5** and noncointegrated variables in section **8.4.6**.

Testing for cointegration is only one part of a strategy for model building. If there is cointegration we are justified in going further and estimating not only the cointegrating – or equilibrium – relationship but also the dynamic relationship that incorporates both the equilibrium and how short-run adjustments to that equilibrium are made. This is the second stage of the Engle–Granger two-stage procedure, in which an error (or more precisely) equilibrium correction model is estimated. The links between cointegration and error correction models are described in section **8.5**. Given the close link between cointegration and error correction modelling, a modified Dickey–Fuller test statistic for (non) cointegration, taking this link into account, is derived in section **8.5.2**.

8.3.1 Cointegration: basic concepts

Initially consider two variables, Y_t and X_t, which have been generated by I(1) time series processes; then, in general, a linear combination of these variables, say $Y_t - \varphi_2 X_t = \zeta_t$, will also be I(1). Similarly if Y_t and X_t were each I(2) then a linear combination of them would, in general, be I(2). To fix ideas we stay with the I(1) case. Suppose that Y_t and X_t share the same stochastic trend so they are tied together in the long run; wherever Y_t goes X_t goes and vice versa at least given time for adjustment to short-run changes. Then it is possible that although Y_t and X_t are each I(1) a linear combination of them is I(0); that is the order of integration of the linear combination is one less than the common order of integration of each series. When this happens Y_t and X_t are said to be cointegrated. The cointegrating coefficients are the weights in the linear combination which reduce the variables to stationarity. In this case they are 1 and $-\varphi_2$, or any scalar multiple of these; that is if $Y_t - \varphi_2 X_t = \zeta_t$ is stationary then so is $\kappa(Y_t - \varphi_2 X_t) = \kappa \zeta_t$ for $\kappa \neq 0$. Similarly subtracting a constant from the linear combination does not alter its integration properties.

The cointegrating vector is usually 'normalised' on one of the variables. As an example of a normalisation suppose the linear combination $0.9Y_t - 0.45X_t = \zeta_t$ is stationary, then so is the simple transformation obtained by dividing through by 0.9 to give a coefficient of 1 on Y_t; that is $Y_t - 0.5X_t = \zeta_t/0.9$. This cointegrating combination has been normalised on Y_t. To normalise on X_t divide through by -0.45 to obtain $-2Y_t + X_t = -\zeta_t/0.45$. All that matters for cointegration is the relative weights. Also notice that adding a constant to the cointegrating combination does not alter the cointegrating property. While normalisation aids an interpretation of the cointegrating combination there is no presumption in cointegration analysis that any one variable has a different status from the others. When the cointegrating coefficients – or weights – are put into a vector it is known as the cointegrating vector. For example, with the coefficients normalised on Y_t the cointegrating vector is $(1, -\varphi_2)$; hence

$$(1, -\varphi_2)\begin{pmatrix} Y_t \\ X_t \end{pmatrix} = \zeta_t \sim I(0) \tag{8.2}$$

As we have seen the cointegrating vector is not unique, in the sense that any scalar multiple of a cointegrating vector is stationary, but it is unique in the sense that the weights must bear a certain ratio to each other. In principle, if there are more than two variables there can be more than one cointegrating vector. For the purposes of this chapter we assume there is only one cointegrating vector; the extension to more than one cointegrating vector is taken up in Chapters 14 and 15.

Suppose Y_t and X_t cointegrate then the normalised cointegrating combination $Y_t - \varphi_2 X_t = \zeta_t$ implies the cointegrating regression:

$$Y_t = \varphi_1 + \varphi_2 X_t + \xi_t \tag{8.3}$$

where $\xi_t = \zeta_t - \varphi_1$. A constant is included since cointegration does not imply that $Y_t = 0$ when $X_t = 0$, and adding or subtracting a constant from a cointegrating combination does not alter its properties. Usually we do not know whether Y_t and X_t cointegrate and the object of our analysis is to determine whether this is the case; nevertheless, although it generally needs qualification, the regression (8.3) is still usually referred to as the cointegrating regression with 'candidate' variables Y_t and X_t.

The concept of cointegration is easily extended to higher orders of integration and more variables. Suppose Y_t and X_t are each I(2) then, while it is generally the case that a linear combination of them will be I(2), it is also possible that the linear combination will be I(1) or even I(0).

A notation which is helpful in this context is to say that cointegrated series are CI(d, b), where d is the common order of integration of the candidate vari-

ables and b is the order of cointegration, that is the reduction relative to d in the order of integration of the linear combination of candidate variables.

I(1) variables that are reduced to stationarity are, therefore, CI(1, 1); I(2) variables that are reduced to I(1) in linear combination are CI(2, 1), and if reduced to I(0), they are CI(2, 2). The case with more than two variables is considered in section **8.4.4** below.

In Chapter 7 we considered the possibility that a univariate series with a seasonal pattern is integrated at the seasonal frequencies. For example, the unit root possibilities are: the (standard) long-run frequency, $I_0(1)$; semi-annual frequency, $I_{\frac{1}{2}}(1)$; and the quarterly frequency, $I_{\frac{1}{4}}(1)$, and all are possible in some combination. Alternatively the series could be stationary at all frequencies. Extending the number of series raises the possibility of cointegration at the seasonal frequencies. For example, consumption typically shows a strong seasonal pattern with a substantial increase in expenditure in the fourth quarter but in the United Kingdom, and possibly the United States as well, the quarterly pattern in income is not so marked. Using data for the United Kingdom, HEGY (1990) found evidence of unit roots at the zero, quarterly and semi-annual frequencies, that is $I_0(1)$, $I_{\frac{1}{4}}(1)$ and $I_{\frac{1}{2}}(1)$. For income they found unit roots at the zero frequency and semi-annual frequency but not at the quarterly frequency. Consumption and income could therefore potentially be cointegrated at the zero and semi-annual frequencies but not at the quarterly frequency. Using data from Japan, where there is an institutionalised pattern of end of year bonus payments to workers and a strong seasonal pattern in consumption, Engle, Granger, Hylleberg and Lee (1993) find evidence of cointegration at the quarterly frequency. The test statistic for non-cointegration at the semi-annual frequency has the same distribution as the standard unit root test, but the distribution for the test at a quarterly frequency has a different distribution. The reader is referred to Engle, Granger and Lee (*op. cit.*) for further details of the test procedure and the construction of appropriate error correction models.

8.3.2 Cointegrating versus spurious regressions

A cointegrating regression is not a *spurious* regression. A spurious regression occurs where there is no relationship between Y_t and X_t, in their joint generation through the DGP, but we wrongly conclude from a regression analysis that there is such a relationship. For example, many economic time series can be described as random walks (perhaps with drift), more generally they are I(1), so that they have stochastic trends and share a general pattern of increasing over time. A regression of Y_t on a constant and X_t may well be misleading as to whether a relationship does genuinely exist between the variables – see section **8.2.5**. The difference between a cointegrating regression and a spurious regression is whether a linear combination of I(1) candidate variables is reduced to stationarity. Given the development so far the natural focus of analysis will be on the properties of ξ_t; if ξ_t is I(0), given that Y_t and X_t are I(1), then (8.3) is a cointegrating regression; if ξ_t is I(1) then (8.3) is a spurious regression or, at least, a misspecified regression in the sense that it omits relevant I(1) variables.

We have already considered a case that is of relevance to this issue. In Table 8.5 we reported the Monte Carlo results for Y_t and X_t being unrelated random walks. Let us now reconsider and extend some of the previous results to see how they relate to the ideas of spurious regressions and cointegrating regressions.

8.4 Testing for noncointegration: the Engle–Granger (1987) approach

If Y_t and X_t are each I(1) and unrelated then the regression coefficient φ_2 in the cointegrating regression $Y_t = \varphi_1 + \varphi_2 X_t + \xi_t$ will equal zero, so

that $Y_t = \varphi_1 + \xi_t$ and the properties of ξ_t are just those of $Y_t - \varphi_1$. Thus if $Y_t \sim I(1)$ then $\xi_t \sim I(1)$. Alternatively suppose that the cointegrating regression should include a third variable Z_t so that the correct cointegrating regression is $Y_t = \varphi_1 + \varphi_2 X_t + \varphi_3 Z_t + \xi_t$, then the 'disturbance' in the bivariate model will actually be $\varphi_3 Z_t + \xi_t$, which is I(1) because, even though ξ_t is I(0), Z_t is I(1). Obviously this analysis could be extended so that more I(1) variables are incorrectly excluded from the regression model and, generally, incorrectly excluding I(1) variables will induce a disturbance which is I(1). The qualification 'generally' is required for situations like the following. Suppose the correct cointegrating regression is

$$Y_t = \varphi_1 + \varphi_2 X_t + \varphi_3 Z_t + \varphi_4 V_t + \xi_t \qquad (8.4)$$

but both Z_t and V_t are excluded; additionally suppose Z_t and V_t are each I(1) and cointegrate with $\varphi_3 = -\varphi_4$; a realistic example would be where Z_t is the nominal wage and V_t is the price level, so $Z_t - V_t$ is the real wage and is I(0) (all variables are in logs). If $\varphi_3 = 1$ then the omitted 'disturbance' in the bivariate regression between Y_t and X_t will be $Z_t - V_t + \xi_t$, which comprises the I(0) components $Z_t - V_t$ and ξ_t. Then even though Z_t and V_t are excluded from the analysis cointegration between just Y_t and X_t will occur.

8.4.1 The Engle–Granger (1987) approach (the bivariate case)

The procedure described in this section is due to Engle and Granger (1987), often referred to simply as EG, and is a test of *noncointegration*. This is first illustrated for the bivariate case involving just Y_t and X_t and then extended to many variables. The initial step is to assess the order of integration of each series using, for example, the Dickey–Fuller tests described in Chapter 6. We assume that each series is found to be consistent with the hypothesis that it is I(1). Hence, a necessary condition for the regression $Y_t = \varphi_1 + \varphi_2 X_t + \xi_t$ to be a cointegrating regression is met, namely that it is 'balanced' in the dominant time series properties of Y_t and X_t. The next step is to assess the properties of ξ_t; if it is I(1) the regression is not a cointegrating regression, whereas if it is I(0) it is a cointegrating regression (more precisely we should say: it is consistent with the hypothesis that it is a cointegrating regression). Since ξ_t is unobservable any tests will be based on an estimator of ξ_t. One possible estimator is provided by estimation of the cointegrating regression by OLS with residuals $\hat{\xi}_t$. That is

$$Y_t = \hat{\varphi}_1 + \hat{\varphi}_2 X_t + \hat{\xi}_t \qquad (8.5)$$

This is often referred to as the EG regression in the levels of the I(1) variables, sometimes this is called the 'static' or 'levels' because it ignores any dynamic adjustments that may be present in a complete model.

Stock (1987) has shown that the OLS estimators of the coefficients in a cointegrating regression have a desirable property known as superconsistency. As we saw in Chapter 4 consistency refers to the probability limit of an estimator; a consistent estimator is one whose probability limit is the same as the unknown coefficient being estimated. Another dimension of a consistent estimator is the 'speed' of its convergence to the population value – see Chapter 4. In this context the speed of a consistent estimator is indicated with reference to the sample size, T. For example, an estimator whose 'speed' is T^{-2} converges at a faster rate than one whose speed is T^{-1}. In the regression models considered in Chapter 4, the regression variables were assumed to be stationary; in this case a standard result is that the OLS estimator $\hat{\beta} = \beta + O_p(T^{-\frac{1}{2}})$, where $O_p(T^{-\frac{1}{2}})$ indicates terms that tend to 0 in probability as $T \to \infty$ but at the rate $T^{-\frac{1}{2}}$, hence $\text{plim}[\hat{\beta}] = \text{plim}[\beta + O_p(T^{-\frac{1}{2}})] = \beta$. If the regression variables are I(1) then $\hat{\beta} = \beta + O_p(T^{-1})$ so the rate of convergence to β is much faster. The OLS estimators are said to be superconsistent in this case. However, this does not mean that in finite

samples it is not possible to improve upon the OLS estimator as we shall see later in this chapter.

The next step is to assess whether the residuals, $\hat{\xi}_t$, are consistent with an I(1) process. By analogy with the Dickey–Fuller tests for a unit root, a test can be based on the regression

$$\hat{\xi}_t = \phi_1 \hat{\xi}_{t-1} + u_t \qquad (8.6)$$

with $\phi_1 = 1$ indicating noncointegration and $-1 < \phi_1 < 1$ indicating cointegration. A convenient reformulation of (8.6) is obtained by subtracting $\hat{\xi}_{t-1}$ from both sides to give

$$\Delta\hat{\xi}_t = \phi_1 \hat{\xi}_{t-1} + u_t \qquad (8.7)$$

where $\gamma = \phi_1 - 1$. As in the standard Dickey–Fuller regression, it may be necessary to augment the regression by p lagged values of $\Delta\hat{\xi}_t$ to ensure that the estimated u_t are free from serial correlation, in which case the maintained regression becomes

$$\Delta\hat{\xi}_t = \gamma\hat{\xi}_{t-1} + \sum_{i=1}^{p} \alpha_i \Delta\hat{\xi}_{t-i} + u_t \qquad (8.8)$$

This is referred to as the cointegrating ADF(p) regression (sometimes referred to as CRADF(p)). In both cases the test statistic is the estimated 't' statistic on γ, denoted $\hat{\tau}_\gamma$.

Note that in this case, unlike testing univariate series to see if they have a unit root, the regression will not usually contain a constant. The reason for this is that the mean of $\hat{\xi}_t$, over the sample used to estimate $\hat{\varphi}$ and $\hat{\varphi}_2$, will be zero (this is a property of OLS estimation when a constant is included in the original regression). The DF regression uses one less observation because $\hat{\xi}_t$ is lagged once and an augmented DF regression will use $p + 1$ fewer observations, but provided p is not large the mean of $\hat{\xi}_t$ will still be close to 0.

In obtaining the critical values of the DF test statistic note that the null hypothesis is $\phi_1 = 1$, i.e. $\gamma = 0$, and the alternative hypothesis is $\phi_1 < 1$, i.e. $\gamma < 0$. The reason for this is that $\phi_1 > 1$ implies an explosive, nonstationary process, whereas the alternative of interest is that the process is stationary. We are therefore only interested in the lower (that is left-hand) tail critical values.

To emphasise the linked decisions between the maintained regression and cointegration, in the EG procedure note the following summary.

- Nonrejection of the null hypothesis $\gamma = 0$, using the test statistic $\hat{\tau}_\gamma$, is nonrejection of the hypothesis that ξ_t is I(1). If ξ_t is I(1) then Y_t and X_t do not cointegrate.
- Rejection of the null hypothesis $\gamma = 0$, using the test statistic $\hat{\tau}_\gamma$, in the direction of the alternative hypothesis $\gamma < 0$ is rejection of the hypothesis that ξ_t has a unit root in favour of the hypothesis that ξ_t is I(0). If ξ_t is I(0) then Y_t and X_t cointegrate.

In effect the null hypothesis is of noncointegration rather than cointegration.

8.4.2 Critical values for the test statistic $\hat{\tau}_\gamma$: simulation

The distribution of the test statistic $\hat{\tau}_\gamma$ is nonstandard. It is not the same, and hence the critical values are not the same, as in the case of the ordinary Dickey–Fuller regression for a unit root in a univariate time series because it is based on regression residuals which first involve estimating the coefficients φ_1 and φ_2. However, if the regression coefficients are known, rather than estimated, for example suppose $\varphi_1 = 0$ and $\varphi_2 = 1$, then the Dickey–Fuller critical values are appropriate, in particular those for the test statistic $\hat{\tau}$ which is based on a maintained regression which does not contain a constant.

As in the standard Dickey–Fuller case the critical values are obtained by simulation. To illustrate, the data was generated by a Monte Carlo experiment with 25,000 replications according to the null hypothesis that both Y_t and X_t are random walks with uncorrelated sto-

Table 8.7 *Critical values of the DF test statistic, $\hat{\tau}_\gamma$, for noncointegration (bivariate case, no trend)*

		1%	5%	10%
$T = 50$	$\hat{\tau}_\gamma$	-4.085	-3.438	-3.094
$T = 100$	$\hat{\tau}_\gamma$	-4.048	-3.396	-3.091
$T = 500$	$\hat{\tau}_\gamma$	-3.908	-3.345	-3.048

chastic components. (Engle and Granger (1987) show that the same test statistic will be obtained even if the stochastic components are correlated.) We then carry out the two-stage procedure of estimating the regression of Y_t on a constant and X_t, saving the residuals, $\hat{\xi}_t$, and then estimate the maintained regression (8.5). $\hat{\tau}_\gamma$ is calculated for each replication and the distribution of $\hat{\tau}_\gamma$ across the 25,000 replications is recorded. For $T = 50$, 100 and 500 the critical values, shown in Table 8.7, were obtained.

These are larger negative values than for the corresponding DF test statistic in the standard univariate case. For example, the 5% critical value of $\hat{\tau}$, with $T = 100$, for the univariate case is -1.945, whereas for $\hat{\tau}_\gamma$ it is -3.396. Otherwise the procedure is as before and extensively outlined in Chapters 6 and 7.

A sample value more negative than the critical value leads to rejection of the null hypothesis of nonstationarity in the residuals and is, therefore, evidence in favour of the hypothesis of cointegration. For example, a sample value of -4.00 would lead to rejection of the null at the 5% significance level, and favour cointegration. A sample value less negative than the 5% critical value leads to nonrejection of the null hypothesis and hence rejection of cointegration. For example, a sample value of -3.00 would lead to nonrejection of the null hypothesis of nonstationarity at the 5% significance level, and would not favour cointegration.

In principle, application of the EG procedure could be with either variable as the 'dependent' variable in the cointegrating regression: the variables have equal or symmetric status. This is in keeping within the paradigm of the DGP as the probabilistic basis underlying our view of how the observed data has been generated. We start from the view that the relevant probability density function is the *joint* pdf although it may subsequently be valid to condition on one of the variables. OLS, which is the practical basis of the EG procedure is, however, a direction dependent method in the sense that reversing the roles of Y_t and X_t will not, generally, give the same results (because the residual sum of squares depends upon which variable is defined as the dependent variable). It is, therefore, theoretically possible to arrive at contradictory conclusions by switching the dependent variable. When R^2 is close to 1, whichever variable is chosen as the dependent variable, the results of the EG procedure will be robust. Difficulties arise when R^2 is not 'high', and in this context R^2 of 0.8 between stochastically trended variables is low, with the prospect of incompatible decisions. If this is the case then consideration should be given to reassessing the variables entering in the cointegration analysis.

8.4.3 MacKinnon's response surface for critical values

MacKinnon (1991) has provided what is known as a response surface for calculating the critical values for $\hat{\tau}_\gamma$, which is applicable whatever the sample size. The idea of a response surface is to capture the dependence of the critical values on one or two key parameters, in this case the sample size. We have already come across this idea in Chapter 6 with Cheung and Lai's response surface for testing for unit roots in the univariate case, which depends upon the sample size, and the lag length in the ADF regression. The general form of Mackinnon's response function is:

$$C(\alpha, T) = \kappa_\infty + \kappa_1/T + \kappa_2/T^2 \qquad (8.9)$$

where $C(\alpha, T)$ is the one-sided $\alpha\%$ critical value for a sample of size T. κ_∞ is the asymptotic

critical value which is modified in finite sample by terms which depend upon T^{-1} and T^{-2}.

MacKinnon gives a table of values for κ_∞, κ_1 and κ_2 – see Table A8.1 in the appendix – which depend upon T and the number of variables, N, in the cointegrating regression (this number is the total including the 'dependent' variable but not the constant). Two cases are distinguished depending on whether or not a time trend is included in the maintained regression; the cases are denoted 'no trend' and 'with trend'. For example, suppose $T = 50$ and $N = 2$, then the response function coefficients for the 5% critical value are obtained from the row headed $N = 2$, constant and no trend, size = 5%. These are $\kappa_\infty = -3.3377$, $\kappa_1 = -5.967$ and $\kappa_2 = -8.98$. The 5% critical value is then calculated as:

$$C(5\%, 50) = -3.3377 - 5.967/50 - 8.98/50^2$$
$$= -3.489$$

which compares well with our simulated value of -3.438. Some econometric programs, for example MICROFIT, include automatic calculation of the critical values for cointegrating regressions.

MacKinnon (1991) also provides critical values for the case when there is a deterministic trend in the cointegrating regression – this is the case described as 'constant and trend'. This situation could be of interest in two cases. First, suppose prior tests for integration, as outlined in Chapters 6 and 7, suggest that one or more of the variables contains a deterministic trend. If there is just one such variable then it is essential to include a deterministic trend in the cointegrating regression, otherwise it is not possible for the cointegrating regression to be balanced in terms of its time series properties. The introduction of the time trend in the cointegrating regression balances the time trend in one of the variables. If there is more than one variable which has a deterministic trend then it is possible that these cancel each other out; however, in order to allow for the possibility that this does not occur a time trend should be included in the cointegrating regression. Where a pair of variables each exhibits a deterministic trend then *deterministic cointegration* occurs when the time trends cancel each other out.

The second reason for including a time trend in the cointegrating regression is when there is doubt as to whether a constant should be included in the auxiliary regression given by (8.7) or (8.8). If a time trend is included it does not matter whether or not a constant is included in (8.7) or (8.8), provided that the appropriate distribution of the test statistic $\hat{\tau}_\gamma$ is used.

8.4.4   More than two variables

Typical situations in applied econometrics involve more than two candidate variables in the cointegrating regression; however, the concepts and procedure described above are easily modified to handle the general case.

First, consider the concept of cointegration. The simplest case with more than two variables is where each of, say, N variables is I(1). Then, in general, a linear combination of the N I(1) variables will be I(1). However, if a linear combination exists which is I(0), so the order of integration has been reduced by one, then the N variables are said to cointegrate CI(1, 1).

However, when there are more than two variables there are possibilities other than each variable has to be of the same order of integration. For example, suppose there are three candidate variables for cointegration Y_t, X_t and Z_t, then if these are all of the same order of integration nothing new is involved. If Y_t is I(1) and X_t and Z_t are each I(2) then in general a linear combination of the three variables will be I(2). For cointegration to be possible X_t and Z_t must first cointegrate, so that a linear combination of them is I(1), the simplest case is if the sum or difference of X_t and Z_t cointegrates; that cointegrating linear combination may then cointegrate with Y_t because it is of the same order of integration. An economic example is where

the candidate variables are, with all variables in logs, employment, E_t, which is I(1), and nominal wages, W_t, and prices, P_t, which are each I(2); then the difference between nominal wages and prices is the real wage, $W_t - P_t$, which we assume cointegrates, CI(2, 1). Given that the real wage is I(1) it may then cointegrate, CI(1, 1), with employment, E_t. As a further example, suppose Y_t is I(0), and X_t and Z_t are each I(1); then trivially the linear combination which assigns zero weights to X_t and Z_t is stationary. We should, therefore, separate I(0) variables from the cointegration analysis.

Let there be $N = (k + 1) \geq 2$ variables Y_t, $X_{t1}, \ldots, X_{tk}$, where the first subscript gives the observation number and the second the variable number. In the Engle–Granger, EG, procedure one of these variables, say Y_t, for convenience, is chosen as the dependent variable in an OLS regression (this will be referred to in Chapter 14 as a normalisation on Y_t). That is

$$Y_t = \varphi_1 + \sum_{j=1}^{k} \varphi_j X_{tj} + \xi_t \qquad (8.10)$$

with OLS estimators indicated by ∧, we can then define the residuals

$$\hat{\xi}_t = Y_t - \hat{\varphi} - \sum_{j=1}^{k} \hat{\varphi}_j X_{tj} \qquad (8.11)$$

By convention (8.10) is called the cointegrating regression even though the question of whether it is a stationary linear combination is the subject of the test procedure. The auxiliary regression required to test for a unit root is the same as equation (8.8).

Notice that (8.10) could also be written as

$$(1, -\varphi_1, \ldots, -\varphi_k) \begin{pmatrix} Y_t \\ X_{t1} \\ \vdots \\ X_{tk} \end{pmatrix} = \xi_t$$

giving rise to the terminology that the row vector $(1, -\varphi_1, \ldots, -\varphi_k)$ is the cointegrating vector.

As in the bivariate case the auxiliary regression (8.8) does not usually contain a constant, this is because, provided there is a constant in the original regression (8.10), the mean of $\hat{\xi}_t$ over the full sample will be zero. In (8.8), $p + 1$ observations are lost from the full sample because of the lagged values $\Delta\hat{\xi}_{t-1}$ to $\Delta\hat{\xi}_{t-p}$. However, in general, this will have a relatively minor effect on the mean of $\hat{\xi}_t$. The test could be rerun with any of the N variables being the left-hand side variable. The procedure for obtaining the critical values is as before with $N = 2, \ldots, 6$ in MacKinnon's table. For example, if $N = 6$ and $T = 200$, then for $\alpha = 5\%$ we find in the 'constant and no trend' case:

$$C(5\%, 200) = -4.7048 - 17.120/200$$
$$- 11.17/200^2$$
$$= -4.7906$$

At the 5% level of significance a sample value greater than -4.7906, for example -1.0, is consistent with the null hypothesis of noncointegration; a sample value less then -4.7906, for example -5.0, is not consistent with the null hypothesis of noncointegration.

8.4.5 An illustration of the testing procedure

The concepts of the previous section can be illustrated with the data used in the model of consumption in Chapter 5. In Figure 8.7A we again plot the time series for the log of real consumption expenditure and real personal disposable income, but here the emphasis is on the common trend in the two series. The series appear nonstationary but may well be linked together in the sense that they are cointegrated. In the context of consumption and income it is of interest to take the difference between the series; that is

$$\ln C_t - \ln Y_t = \ln(C_t/Y_t) = \ln(1 - S_t/Y_t)$$

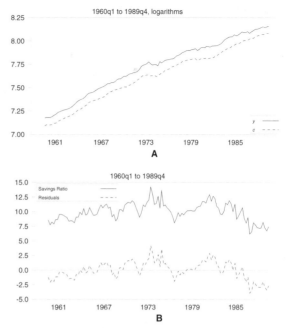

Figure 8.7 A – *US real income (y) and expenditure (c).* B – *US savings ratio (%)*

where $S_t = (Y_t - C_t)$ is savings, and

$$\ln(1 - S_t/Y_t) \approx -S_t/Y_t$$

So the log difference of consumption and income is approximately the negative of the savings ratio. *A priori* we expect the savings ratio to be stationary rather than nonstationary. The savings ratio is plotted in Figure 8.7B, there are two points suggested from this figure.

1. Although consumption and income have a clear trend the savings ratio is trendless.
2. While there are deviations from the mean these are suggestive of a long memory rather than a random walk.

These conclusions are based on a visual impression rather than more formal testing methods, which will be considered below.

The first step in the EG procedure is to assess the order of integration of each of the candidate

Table 8.8   Unit root tests: US c_t and y_t

Variable	Model	$\hat\tau$	Φ_1	$\hat\tau_\mu$	$\hat\mu$	$\hat\tau_\beta$	$\hat\beta$	Φ_3
			Test statistics for 2 unit roots					
c_t	ADF(1)	−4.771	16.068	−5.668	0.057	−5.960	−0.000	17.835
y_t	ADF(1)	−4.221	28.624	−7.566	0.008	−10.981	−0.000	60.295
Variable	Model	$\hat\tau$	Φ_1	$\hat\tau_\mu$	$\hat\mu$	$\hat\tau_\beta$	$\hat\beta$	Φ_3
			Test statistics for 1 unit root					
c_t	ADF(2)	4.629	13.743	−1.981	0.041	−2.280	0.000	4.140
y_t	ADF(1)	6.708	28.274	−2.603	0.076	−1.905	0.000	4.642

Notes: Sample period, 1961q2 to 1989q4; critical values for $\hat\tau_\mu$ and $\hat\tau_\beta$ calculated from Cheung and Lai's response surface coefficients:

	$\hat\tau_\mu$		$\hat\tau_\beta$	
	ADF(1)	ADF(2)	ADF(1)	ADF(2)
C(5%, 115)	−2.875	−2.869	−3.436	−3.427
C(10%, 115)	−2.573	−2.567	−3.140	−3.132

variables and Table 8.8 contains a number of test statistics to assist in this procedure. We use the convention that lower case letters denote logarithms. The test statistics unambiguously suggest rejection of the null hypothesis of two unit roots for both series. For example, Φ_3, for c_t, is 17.835 against a 5% critical value of 6.606 (for $T = 100$, the nearest entry in Table 6.7) and $\hat\tau_\beta = -5.960$ against a 5% critical value of −3.436 using Cheung and Lai's method – see Chapter 6. The null hypothesis of one unit root is not rejected. For example, Φ_3, for c_t, is 4.140 which is less than the 5% critical value, and $\hat\tau_\beta = -2.280$ which is also not significant. The testing sequence should end here: given that both c_t and y_t are trended, the question at issue is whether they are best described as difference stationary or trend stationary, so the maintained regression should include a deterministic time trend. If the sequence is continued the significant value of Φ_1 for each variable, that is 13.743 for c_t and 28.274 for y_t, is consistent with the view that both series have a unit root *with* drift. We conclude from these unit root tests that it is appropriate to move to the next stage of assessing whether c_t and y_t cointegrate, CI(1, 1).

As there is no presumption in cointegration analysis of a different status among the variables,

the cointegrating regression for the consumption–income example can be formulated with either variable as the 'dependent' variable. The cointegrating regressions estimated by OLS are:

$$\hat c_t = -0.082 + 0.998 y_t$$
$$(-2.161)(203.446)$$
$$R^2 = 0.997 \quad dw = 0.361 \quad (8.12)$$

$$\hat y_t = 0.104 + 0.999 c_t$$
$$(2.165)(203.426)$$
$$R^2 = 0.997 \quad dw = 0.361 \quad (8.13)$$

't' statistics in parentheses.
Sample period 1960q2 to 1989q4.

In both cases the estimated regression coefficient, on y_t in the first regression and on c_t in the second regression, is very close to 1 which accounts for the same (to 3 decimal places) values for R^2 and dw. The R^2 are impressive but spurious if consumption and income do not cointegrate. Because the estimated income elasticity in (8.12) is almost 1 the (negative of the) residuals will have virtually the same pattern as the savings ratio and this is borne out in Figure 8.7B.

The 't' statistics, reported beneath the estimated coefficients, are likely to be misleading because a complete empirical model of the relationship between consumption and income may involve lags of both variables and other variables; for the other variables to be validly excluded from a cointegrating regression they must be stationary. If stationary variables are excluded the 'disturbance' in the cointegrating regression is likely to be serially correlated and heteroscedastic and, hence, the estimated standard errors calculated according to the usual OLS formula are incorrect. Despite these likely characteristics of the cointegrating regression, the OLS estimators do have some desirable properties that are considered in section **8.7**.

The next step in the Engle–Granger (EG) procedure is to save the residuals from the cointegrating regressions and assess whether they are consistent with the hypothesis that disequilibrium is I(1), and hence c_t and y_t do not cointegrate. Equations (8.12) and (8.13) give the cointegrating regressions, the former is the regression of c_t on y_t and the latter is the reverse regression. To distinguish the residuals from these regressions the notation $\hat{\xi}_{1t}$ and $\hat{\xi}_{2t}$ is used. The auxiliary regressions are in the standard Dickey–Fuller form, see Table 8.9.

R^2 is close to 1 in the cointegrating regressions – see (8.12) and (8.13) – so the results from the Dickey–Fuller tests applied to the residuals using $\hat{\xi}_{1t}$ and $\hat{\xi}_{2t}$, respectively, are very

Table 8.9 DF tests: the consumption–income example

$\Delta\hat{\xi}_{1t} = -0.181\hat{\xi}_{1t-1} + \hat{u}_{1t}$ (-3.363)	$SC(4) = 6.571[0.160]$
$\Delta\hat{\xi}_{2t} = -0.183\hat{\xi}_{2t-1} + \hat{u}_{2t}$ (-3.412)	$SC(4) = 6.874[0.143]$

Notes: Sample period, 1961q2 to 1989q4; $T = 115$.
$\hat{\tau}_\gamma$ in parentheses.
The 5% and 10% critical values using MacKinnon's response function are:

$$C(5\%, T) = -3.3377 - 5.967/115 - 8.98/(115)^2$$
$$= -3.390$$
$$C(10\%, T) = -3.0462 - 4.069/115 - 5.73/(115)^2$$
$$= -3.082$$

close. There was no evidence of the need to augment the regressions; for example in the first regression the Lagrange-Multiplier test for serial correlation in its $\chi^2(4)$ version is 6.571, with an msl of 16%. $\hat{\tau}_\gamma$ is -3.363 from the first regression and -3.412 from the second regression, compared to 5% and 10% critical values of -3.390 and -3.082, respectively. The decision on whether or not to reject the null hypothesis is marginal at the 5% level but not at the 10% level where the null is rejected, suggesting the conclusion of cointegration between consumption and income. Some protection against the low power of unit root tests when ϕ_1 is close to 1 is offered by using a significance level rather larger than conventionally used. The conclusion is in line with the visual evidence in Figure 8.7B, which suggests a series with a long, but not infinite, memory. Also note that $\hat{\gamma} = -0.181$ implies $\hat{\phi}_1 = 1 - 0.181 = 0.819$, which is numerically quite a long way from 1, even if there is some ambiguity statistically, and lends support to stationarity of the residuals and, hence, cointegration.

Cointegration implies that there is a stationary long-run relationship among a set of variables, it does not model the short-run or dynamic adjustments which take place involving the cointegrating variables or others which, while excluded from the cointegrating regression, may have an important short-run role. Modelling the dynamic adjustments takes place in the second stage of the EG procedure, which is described in detail below. For the moment note that for short-run variables to be validly excluded they must be I(0) rather than I(1); if they are I(1) then they should have been candidate variables in the cointegrating regression.

With the concept of cointegration established it will be useful to briefly revisit the extended empirical example used in Chapter 5. The form of the model used there was:

$$\Delta c_t = \theta_0 + \theta_1 \Delta y_t + \theta_2 \Delta y_{t-1} + \theta_3 (c_t - y_t)_{-1}$$
$$+ \theta_4 \pi_t + \theta_5 \pi_{t-1} + \varepsilon_t \qquad (8.14)$$

We can now interpret this model in the following way. The cointegrating relationship is between c_t and y_t, with the static long run obtained by setting all I(0) variables to zero and ignoring lag subscripts, hence

$$0 = \theta_0 + \theta_3(c_t - y_t) \Rightarrow c_t = -\theta_0/\theta_3 + y_t$$

Taking the antilogarithm to express the relationship in the levels of the variables we obtain $C_t = AY_t$ where $A = \exp(-\theta_0/\theta_3)$. As C_t is consumers' expenditure on nondurable goods and services we anticipate $A < 1$. The I(0) variables, $\Delta y_t, \pi_t$ and their first lags, capture short-run adjustment to the long run. The regression is balanced because Δc_t on the left-hand side and $\Delta y_t, \Delta y_{t-1}, (c_t - y_t)_{-1}, \pi_t$ and π_{t-1} are all I(0).

8.4.6 An illustration of a spurious regression

Next we consider an example of a spurious regression in which consumption expenditure on nondurables and services is regressed on the price level. The data is quarterly, seasonally adjusted for the United Kingdom 1955q1 to 1993q2, a total of 154 observations. The variables are denoted CND_t and PC_t, where the latter is the implicit deflator for consumers' total expenditure. Such a regression might occur if it was thought that consumers were subject to money illusion – that is their decisions on a real variable, here consumption, were affected by the level of prices. For a related example using US data see Stock and Watson (1988).

The regression of CND_t on PC_t resulted in:

$$CND_t = 36377.9 + 38335.7PC_t + \hat{\xi}_t$$
$$(69.255) \quad (39.355)$$
$$R^2 = 0.911 \quad dw = 0.021$$
$$SC = 147.216[0.000] \qquad (8.15)$$

't' statistics in parentheses; sample 1955q1 to 1993q2.

The regression looks to have identified an important relationship between CND_t and PC_t.

The R^2 for the regression is 0.911 and the 't' statistic on the estimated coefficient on PC_t is 39.35, which on reference to standard 't' tables suggests that it is highly significant. However, this interpretation of the regression results ignores the stochastic properties of the variables. A hint that the regression is not adequate is provided by the Durbin–Watson statistic of 0.021.

If CND_t and PC_t are I(1) then the regression is at least 'balanced'. However, this is a necessary and not a sufficient condition for the regression to be sensible. For a regression in the levels of candidate variables, and with no dynamic structure, to make sense it must be interpreted as a possible cointegrating regression. There are, thus, two issues to be considered before the regression can be taken at face value. Are CND_t and PC_t separately I(1)? If so are CND_t and PC_t, CI(1, 1)?

A first step is to assess the nonstationarity of the two series. The data for CND_t is graphed in Figure 8.8A, with first and second differences in Figures 8.8B and 8.8C, respectively. The series is clearly trended, so the maintained regression for unit root testing should include a deterministic trend. Note that taking one difference appears sufficient to remove the trend and the first differenced series in Figure 8.8B looks stationary. The unit root test statistics for CND_t suggest that it is consistent with an I(1) process; for example, for two unit roots $\Phi_3 = 17.591$ compared to 5% and 10% critical values of (approximately) 6.5 and 5.5, respectively (interpolated from Table 6.7 between the entries for $T = 100$ and $T = 200$); and $\hat{\tau}_\beta = -5.931$ compared to a 5% critical value of -3.428 and a 10% critical value of -3.140. The corresponding test statistics for a single unit root are $\Phi_3 = 2.065$ and $\hat{\tau}_\beta = -1.875$, which suggest nonrejection of the null hypothesis.

Next we have to be alert to the possibility that PC_t is integrated of order 2, i.e. I(2). The visual evidence is reported in Figure 8.9A with the first and second differences of PC_t in Figures 8.9B and 8.9C, respectively. The graphical impression is of a possible I(2) series; PC_t increases smoothly with

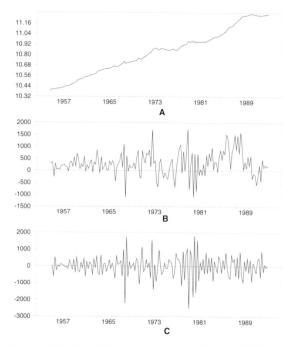

Figure 8.8 **A – UK consumers' expenditure (CND).**
B – First difference of CND. C – Second difference
of CND

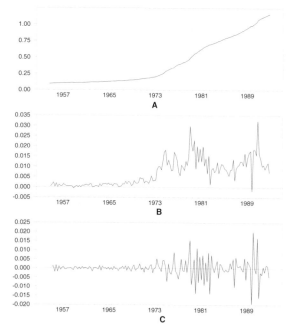

Figure 8.9 **A – UK consumer prices (PC). B – First**
difference of PC. C – Second difference of PC

almost no hint of variation about this pattern. However, the graph of the first difference of PC_t is suggestive of two points. First, a break in the pattern of the series around 1973, and, second, the possibility of a single unit root appears more likely after 1973. The second difference of PC_t, which is graphed in Figure 8.8C, emphasises a break in the series around 1973. Given the visual evidence of a break, the sample is split into two sub-periods, 1955q1 to 1973q4 and 1974q1 to 1993q2. A possible strategy is to move down a hierarchy of tests starting with the possibility that PC_t is I(3), then if that hypothesis is rejected consider the hypothesis that PC_t is I(2) and so on.

Starting with the first sub-period of 1955q1 to 1973q4 and testing for 3 unit roots, $\Phi_3 = 33.233$ and $\hat{\tau}_\beta = -8.099$. Both firmly indicate rejection of the null hypothesis of 3 unit roots; on testing for 2 unit roots $\Phi_3 = 2.68$ and $\hat{\tau}_\beta = -1.105$, hence neither support rejection of the null hypothesis of 2 unit roots. The testing sequence should end here. However, had the process incorrectly started with tests to assess whether PC_t is I(1), the results were $\Phi_3 = 13.451$ and $\hat{\tau}_\beta = 3.919$. It might be tempting to conclude either that, on the basis of a positive value of $\hat{\tau}_\beta$, PC_t was consistent with an I(1) process or that, on the basis of Φ_3, the null hypothesis of a unit root and no deterministic trend should be rejected in favour of the alternative of no unit root and a deterministic trend. Neither conclusion would have been correct; this illustration shows that the appropriate procedure is to test down if there is a suspicion that the series may contain more than 1 unit root.

The second period, 1974q1 to 1993q2, was then examined with the outcome of the tests indicating a different conclusion compared to the first period. In summary we can reject the hypothesis that PC_t is I(3) with $\Phi_3 = 43.328$ and $\hat{\tau}_\beta = -9.308$; and, in contrast to the earlier period, the hypothesis that PC_t is I(2) can be rejected with $\Phi_3 = 21.719$ and $\hat{\tau}_\beta = -6.585$. In this case we can legitimately move on to consider the hypothesis that PC_t is I(1); here we find that $\Phi_3 = 1.216$ and $\hat{\tau}_\beta = -1.536$, and the null hypothesis is not rejected.

The regression equation with CND_t as the dependent variable and PC_t as the explanatory variable is, therefore, in difficulty immediately through a lack of 'balance', at least in the first part of the sample, in terms of the time series properties of its variables. A consequence is that we would not expect to find that the residuals from this regression are stationary with the likely conclusion that the regression is 'unbalanced' and spurious. The results of the Dickey–Fuller tests on the residuals from the cointegrating regression are reported in Table 8.10.

It is evident from the whole sample or from either sub-sample that the hypothesis of non-cointegration between CND_t and PC_t cannot be rejected. For example, for the whole period $\hat{\tau}_\gamma = -2.286$ against a 5% critical value of -3.378 (using the coefficients from MacKinnon's table in the appendix). The corresponding test statistics for each sub-period are -0.961 and

-2.111, and both suggest that CND_t and PC_t do not cointegrate: the regression is spurious. Visual evidence supporting this conclusion is provided in Figure 8.9 which plots the residuals from the regression of CND_t on PC_t; the prolonged 'walks', especially in the first part of the sample, are strongly suggestive of a nonstationary series.

8.5 Links between cointegration and error correction models

Estimating the equilibrium relationship is, of course, only one part of the aim of empirical model building. Typically in a changing environment adjustment takes time and the adjustment also has to be modelled. For an interesting discussion of modelling strategies and how informative economic theory is about the long

Table 8.10 *DF tests: the consumption–price level example*

Overall period: 1955q1 to 1993q2 (before lagging)

$$\Delta\hat{\xi}_t = -0.025\hat{\xi}_{t-1} + 0.106\Delta\hat{\xi}_{t-1} + 0.336\Delta\hat{\xi}_{t-2} + 0.134\Delta\hat{\xi}_{t-3} + \hat{u}_t$$
$$\quad\;\;(-2.286)\quad\;\;(1.316)\qquad\;\;(4.394)\qquad\;\;(1.655)$$

$SC(4) = 8.370[0.078]$

First period: 1955q1 to 1973q4 (before lagging)

$$\Delta\hat{\xi}_t = -0.038\hat{\xi}_{t-1} + \hat{u}_t$$
$$\quad\;\;(-0.961)$$

$SC(4) = 4.632[0.327]$

Second period: 1974q1 to 1993q2 (before lagging)

$$\Delta\hat{\xi}_t = 0.047\hat{\xi}_{t-1} + 0.168\Delta\hat{\xi}_{t-1} + 0.304\Delta\hat{\xi}_{t-2} + \hat{u}_t$$
$$\quad\;(-2.111)\qquad(1.582)\qquad\;\;(3.583)$$

$SC(4) = 8.470[0.075]$

Notes: $\hat{\tau}_\gamma$ in parentheses for coefficient on $\hat{\xi}_{t-1}$; 't' statistics otherwise. The 5% and 10% critical values using MacKinnon's response function are:

$T = 150$:
$$C(5\%, T) = -3.3377 - 5.967/150 - 8.98/(150)^2 = -3.378$$
$$C(10\%, T) = -3.0462 - 4.069/150 - 5.73/(150)^2 = -3.074$$

$T = 75$:
$$C(5\%, T) = -3.3377 - 5.967/75 - 8.98/(75)^2 = -3.378$$
$$C(10\%, T) = -3.0462 - 4.069/75 - 5.73/(75)^2 = -3.074$$

run and the short run see Granger (1997) and Pesaran (1997). For our purposes this section draws out the link between cointegration and an error correction representation of the dynamic model. Recall that in its simplest form an ECM incorporates two key elements:

1. Adjustment to lagged disequilibrium so that, given no other change, equilibrium is gradually achieved.
2. Adjustment to contemporaneous changes in the variables that determine equilibrium.

Granger's representation theorem shows that there is an important link between the existence of cointegration and an error correction specification.

8.5.1 Engle and Granger's two-stage estimation method

In this section we first recap the basic features of a simple error correction model and link that to Engle–Granger's two-stage method of estimation.

We have already come across a simple ECM in the context of the consumption function. That is:

$$c_t = \varphi_1 + \varphi_2 y_t + \xi_t \tag{8.16}$$

with equilibrium given by $\xi_t = 0$. Hence, disequilibrium is:

$$\xi_t = c_t - \varphi_1 - \varphi_2 y_t \tag{8.17}$$

with the interpretation that ξ_t is positive if actual consumption exceeds target and negative if actual consumption is below target. If c_t and y_t are each I(1) then we can say, equivalently, that c_t and y_t cointegrate, C(1, 1), and, hence, ξ_t is I(0). To model what happens we need to incorporate not only a response to disequilibrium, which we assume the consumer wants to eradicate, but also a response to the stimulus of

a change in the variables determining equilibrium. In its simplest form this would be:

$$\begin{aligned} \Delta c_t &= \theta_1 \Delta y_t + \theta_2 \xi_{t-1} + \varepsilon_t \\ &= \theta_0 + \theta_1 \Delta y_t \\ &\quad + \theta_2 (c_t - \varphi_2 y_t)_{-1} + \varepsilon_t \end{aligned} \tag{8.18}$$

where $\theta_0 = -\theta_2 \varphi_1$

The 'error' is the lagged disequilibrium term ξ_{t-1}, and the error correction (or adjustment) coefficient is θ_2. To interpret this coefficient initially assume that $\Delta y_t = 0$; then if at the perspective of time $= t$ the economic agent was not in equilibrium last period, that is $\xi_{t-1} \neq 0$, c_t will have to change, and so $\Delta c_t \neq 0$ to ensure that a movement is made towards equilibrium. θ_2 has the limits $-1 \leq \theta_2 < 0$. θ_2 is negative because if $\xi_{t-1} > 0$ then $c_{t-1} > k + y_{t-1}$, that is actual consumption exceeds the target, and to keep on target c_t must be reduced. The lower limit on θ_2 of -1 implies complete eradication of last period's disequilibrium. The absolute size of θ_2 indicates how quickly the disequilibrium will be removed with equilibrium regained more quickly the larger is the absolute value of θ_2. For example, if $\theta_2 = -0.10$ then 10% of the disequilibrium at $t-1$ is removed in period t; whereas if $\theta_2 = -0.5$, 50% of the disequilibrium is removed.

To interpret θ_1 note that in the equilibrium specification c_t depends linearly on y_t, hence if y_t changes then, *ceteris paribus*, c_t should also change. Therefore, in deciding whether to change c_t in period t, the economic agent should consider not only whether he/she was in equilibrium last period but also whether $\Delta y_t \neq 0$. θ_1 will take the sign of φ_2. So that if, for example, $c_t = 0.5 + 1.0 y_t$ then if $\Delta y_t > 0$, Δc_t will also be positive. The limits of θ_1 are $0 \leq \theta_1 \leq \varphi_2$ for $\varphi_2 > 0$ and $0 \geq \theta_1 \geq \varphi_2$ for $\varphi_2 < 0$. If $\theta_1 = 0$ adjustment to disequilibrium takes place entirely through the error correction coefficient. Generally though we would expect $\theta_1 \neq 0$ and, *ceteris paribus*, this keeps the agent closer to a moving equilibrium. The limit $\theta_1 = \varphi_2$ is motivated from the specification of equilibrium in which the full adjustment of y_t to a unit change is φ_2. For example, if $\varphi_2 > 0$ then $\theta_1 > \varphi_2$ implies there is overadjustment to the change in y_t.

A popular method of estimating equations like (8.18) is to use a two-stage estimator due to Engle and Granger (1987). It is assumed in applying this method that there is only one cointegrating vector. In the first stage:

- estimate the 'levels' (or 'static') regression (8.16) by OLS to obtain estimates of the long-run coefficients φ_1 and φ_2; this is referred to as OLSEG estimation;
- from this regression form the residuals $\hat{\xi}_t$ and test for noncointegration.

In the second stage:

- if the null hypothesis of noncointegration is rejected in the first stage, replace the unknown ξ_{t-1} in (8.18) by $\hat{\xi}_{t-1}$ and estimate the remaining coefficients by OLS.

Stock (1987) has shown that: the first stage estimator of the long-run coefficients is super-consistent but not (generally) normally distributed even asymptotically; and the second stage estimator of the remaining I(0) coefficients is consistent and asymptotically normally distributed. Inference on the long-run coefficients using standard tables is, therefore, invalid, whereas it is asymptotically justified for the I(0) coefficients. A method for obtaining 't' statistics that are asymptotically normally distributed is described in Chapter 9. There are no substantive complications arising from more than two variables provided there is just one cointegrating vector; the only difference will be that both the levels regression and the ECM will involve more variables.

If there are N variables there are, in principle, N equations in the error correction model; this accords with the idea that the variables in a cointegration analysis have equal status. So even in the simple example given above there should

be a second equation to determine Δy_t which could, in principle, be of the same form as the equation for Δy_t.

$$\Delta y_t = \theta_{y1}\Delta c_t + \theta_{y2}\xi_{t-1} + \varepsilon_{yt} \qquad (8.19)$$

A y subscript has been added to the coefficients to indicate that they are not the same as those in the consumption equation. There can, though, only be one disequilibrium between two variables. If $\theta_{y2} \neq 0$ then there is a connection between the income and consumption equations as both involve the coefficient φ_2. These ECM equations could be generalised by including more I(0) terms. That is Δc_t and its lags, as well as lags of Δy_t, may be included in the consumption equation, and Δy_t and its lags as well as lags of Δc_t may be included in the income equation.

It may, in some circumstances, be possible to reduce the number of variables explicitly modelled. First, some variables may be deterministic. For example, a time trend and seasonal or special event dummy variables that have entries which 0 or 1 are variations on that theme, and it is legitimate to 'condition' on those variables – that is they are treated as determined outside the system of error correction equations. Second, some variables may be stochastic but uninformative about the parameters of interest; this is the idea of weak exogeneity, which is explored in detail in Chapters 9 and 15. For now we note that it is legitimate to condition on, that is not explicitly model, weakly exogenous stochastic variables. If a single equation error correction model is to be valid then $N - 1$ variables must fall into the category of conditioning variables. Often in single equation analysis this is taken as a matter of faith rather a subject of explicit testing; it is achieved in the classical linear regression model by assuming either that the regressors are fixed in repeated samples or, if stochastic, uncorrelated with the 'disturbance' term. In this chapter we will assume that it is legitimate to consider a single error correction equation.

The description of a simple error correction model given in the last paragraph refers to a *structural* equation in the sense that, in a system of several equations, simultaneous links are possible through the contemporaneous changes of the other variables. For example, suppose in a system determining c_t and y_t, the ECM for Δc_t includes terms in Δy_t and Δy_{t-1}, while the ECM for Δy_t includes terms in Δc_t and Δc_{t-1}, then the equations are linked through the simultaneous adjustments captured in the contemporaneous changes. Sometimes an ECM is defined with just lagged changes in the other variables (in addition to a lagged disequilibrium term). In this case the equations are in *reduced* form in the sense that the simultaneous adjustments have been solved out. Several examples of these models are given in Chapter 15.

There is a link between cointegration and error correction models, known as Granger's representation theorem, due to Granger and Weiss (1983), Engle and Granger (1987) and see also Granger (1991) and Engle and Yoo (1991). To fix ideas this theorem will be illustrated with the consumption and income example. If c_t and y_t are both I(1) and cointegrated CI(1, 1) (and neither has a trend in the mean) then there always exist an error correction representation of the form:

$$\Delta c_t = \text{lagged}(\Delta c_t, \Delta y_t)$$
$$+ \theta_{2c}\xi_{t-1} + v_{1t} \qquad (8.20a)$$

$$\Delta y_t = \text{lagged}(\Delta c_t, \Delta y_t)$$
$$+ \theta_{2y}\xi_{t-1} + v_{2t} \qquad (8.20b)$$

where $\xi_t = (c_t - \varphi_1 - \varphi_2 y_t)$, $v_{1t} = \omega(L)\varepsilon_{1t}$ and $v_{2t} = \omega(L)\varepsilon_{2t}$; $\omega(L)$ is a finite polynomial in the lag operator L and the ε_{it} are white noise. A condition on the error correction coefficients, $|\theta_{2y}| + |\theta_{2c}| \neq 0$, ensures that lagged disequilibrium, ξ_{t-1}, occurs in at least one of the equations. The specification of v_{it} allows for the possibility that they are serially correlated.

This representation is a reduced form error correction model with lagged values of Δc_t and Δy_t and lagged disequilibrium. If c_t and y_t are I(1) then the lagged Δc_t and Δy_t are I(0); also if c_t and y_t are cointegrated then ξ_t is I(0); hence, all the variables in (8.20) are I(0) and the time series properties of the right- and left-hand sides of each equation are balanced. If c_t and y_t are not cointegrated, ξ_t is I(1) and should not be present given that Δc_t and Δy_t are I(0); hence, the error correction representation does not exist if c_t and y_t do not cointegrate. If c_t and y_t are I(1) and cointegrated then knowledge of one variable helps forecast the other at least in one direction; that is either or both $c_t \Rightarrow y_t$ and $y_t \Rightarrow c_t$. This is the idea of Granger causality where a forecast of, for example, c_t can be improved (in a mean squared error sense) by using the link between c_t and y_t. These links between cointegration and error correction models mean that having established cointegration as a long-run property of the data it is natural to think of an ECM as an appropriate way of capturing dynamic adjustments to the long run.

8.5.2 Cointegration and error correction: an alternative test statistic for cointegration

The link between cointegration and the error correction representation also suggests another way of testing for cointegration. If c_t and y_t are I(1) and cointegrated then at least one of θ_{2y} and θ_{2c} should be nonzero, hence a test of cointegration could be based on the significance of these coefficients. As we are dealing with a single equation framework the test turns out to be very simple. We suppose that a single equation analysis of (just) the equation for Δc_t is valid. This requires that y_t is weakly exogenous for c_t, a concept that is considered in greater detail in Chapters 9 and 15. Here it amounts to the assumption that $\theta_{2y} = 0$ in (8.20b). Then a test for cointegration is a test that the error correction coefficient θ_{2c} is not equal to zero. The null hypothesis is $H_0: \theta_{2c} = 0$ and corresponds to noncointegration; the alternative hypothesis is formulated as H_a: $\theta_{2c} < 0$, since the negative rather than the positive direction corresponds to cointegration. $\theta_{2c} > 0$ implies that Δc_t moves in the wrong direction to correct for disequilibrium. Thus, rejection of $\theta_{2c} = 0$ against $\theta_{2c} < 0$ is evidence in favour of cointegration. The test statistic is the standard 't' statistic in the structural error correction equation but, as usual, its distribution is nonstandard.

8.5.2a   Known cointegration coefficients

The framework for this test, together with the distribution of the test statistic under the null hypothesis, is provided by Banerjee *et al.* (1986) and Kremers, Ericsson and Dolado (1992), hereafter KED. The procedure is initially illustrated in the bivariate case with the general notation of section **8.3.1**; it is then easily generalised. (It should be fairly easy for the reader to make the translation to the consumption–income example with the assumption of weak exogeneity of income.) We assume it is valid to consider the single error correction equation given by:

$$\Delta Y_t = \theta_0 + \theta_1 \Delta X_t$$
$$+ \theta_2 (Y_t - X_t)_{-1} + \varepsilon_t \qquad (8.21)$$

X_t is weakly exogenous in the sense that in the analogous equation for ΔX_t the error correction coefficient is zero. Hence, there is no ambiguity, only one subscript is needed on θ_2. X_t is generated by the I(1) process $\Delta X_t = \omega_t$. The relevant variances are $\text{Var}(\varepsilon_t) = \sigma_\varepsilon^2$ and $\text{Var}(\omega_t) = \sigma_\omega^2$. The null and alternative hypotheses are $\theta_2 = 0$ and $\theta_2 < 0$, and the test statistic is the 't' statistic on $\hat{\theta}_2$, that is:

$$t_{\text{ecm}} = \hat{\theta}_2 / \hat{\sigma}(\hat{\theta}_2) \qquad (8.22)$$

where $\hat{\sigma}(\hat{\theta}_2)$ is the estimated standard error of $\hat{\theta}_2$, with large negative values of t_{ecm} leading to rejection of the null hypothesis. Estimation is by OLS.

In order to carry out the test it is necessary to know the appropriate critical values of the distribution of t_{ecm}. KED (*op. cit.*) show that the distribution of t_{ecm} under the null of no cointegration differs from but is related to the DF distribution. For example, in this set-up when $\theta_1 = 1$ the asymptotic distribution of t_{ecm} is the same as the asymptotic distribution of the DF statistic $\hat{\tau}$, otherwise they differ. The extent of the difference can be characterised by a parameter q interpreted as the 'signal-to-noise' ratio: $q = -(\theta_1 - 1)\sigma_\omega/\sigma_\varepsilon$ and $q^2 = (\theta_1 - 1)^2 \sigma_\omega^2 / \sigma_\varepsilon^2$ which is the variance of $(\theta_1 - 1)\Delta X_t$ relative to the variance of ε_t. Given θ_1, and $0 < \theta_1 < 1$, q will increase as the variance of ω_t increases relative to the variance of ε_t. As q increases the distribution of t_{ecm} shifts from the DF distribution for $\hat{\tau}$ to a standard normal distribution – see KED (*op. cit.*, p. 330). When nothing is known about q a conservative procedure is to use the critical values from the DF distribution for $\hat{\tau}$.

The t_{ecm} test has a theoretical advantage over not just the DF test used as a test for noncointegration, but other tests based purely on the residuals from a first stage Engle–Granger regression. Other tests of the same genre include analogues of the Phillips semi-parametric unit root tests – see Chapter 7 – applied to cointegration testing. To see the connection consider the simple cointegrating regression given by:

$$Y_t = \varphi_2 X_t + \xi_t \qquad (8.23)$$

The argument is simpler if we first assume $\varphi_2 = 1$, so this becomes

$$Y_t = X_t + \xi_t \qquad (8.24)$$

First stage EG estimation serves to define disequilibrium

$$\xi_t = Y_t - X_t \qquad (8.25)$$

and the test regression for (non)cointegration is

$$\Delta \xi_t = \gamma \xi_{t-1} + u_t \qquad (8.26)$$

which on substitution for ξ_t gives

$$\Delta(Y_t - X_t) = \gamma(Y_{t-1} - X_{t-1}) + u_t$$
$$\Rightarrow \Delta Y_t = \Delta X_t + \gamma(Y_{t-1} - X_{t-1}) + u_t$$
$$(8.27)$$

The regressions (8.26) and (8.27) give identical results provided a coefficient of 1 is imposed on ΔX_t.

The regression (8.27) is interesting because it is a restricted version of the simple ECM:

$$\Delta Y_t = \theta_1 \Delta X_t + \theta_2(Y_{t-1} - X_{t-1}) + \varepsilon_t \quad (8.28)$$

with $\theta_1 = 1$, $\theta_2 = \gamma$. Hence if the restriction $\theta_1 = 1$ is not valid the DF regression is incorrectly based on a false restriction.

As the restriction $\theta_1 = 1$ is unlikely to have general validity, since it imposes equality between the short- and long-run elasticities, here both are set equal to 1, it should be possible to improve upon the DF test by not imposing the restriction. Since several other tests are based on the residuals ξ_t, the argument also applies to them. This argument is general in the sense that restricting φ_2 to unity and not including a constant or trend is not material to the conclusion.

KED (*op. cit.*) report a Monte Carlo simulation where they find that using t_{ecm} is more powerful than using $\hat{\tau}$ with the residuals from the first stage EG regression of Y_t on X_t. Specifically, with $T = 25$ and $\theta_2 = -0.05$, so Y_t and X_t are cointegrated but with a rather slow adjustment process, KED find that using the 5% DF critical value of -1.95, the power of $\hat{\tau}$ is about 9% irrespective of the size of q. In contrast using the same DF critical value, t_{ecm} gives power of about 10% for $q = 0$ but 92% for $q = 8$. Using the 5% critical value, -1.645, from the standard normal distribution is not recommended for small T, as in this experiment, because it leads to a distortion between the actual size of the tests, which is nearly 10% for $q = 0$, and the nominal size of 5%. This distortion diminishes as q increases, for example the actual size is 6.4% if $q = 8$.

To illustrate an application of the procedure using t_{ecm} we return to the empirical results reported in Chapter 5 for equation (8.21), where c_t is the log of consumption and y_t is the log of income (both in real terms). The estimated equation for the simplest version of the model was, in the notation of Chapter 5 and section **8.4.5**:

$$\Delta c_t = 0.00003 + 0.338\Delta y_t$$
$$(0.007) \quad (5.322)$$
$$- 0.055(c_t - y_t)_{-1} + \hat{\varepsilon}_t$$
$$(-1.356) \quad (8.29)$$

't' statistics in parentheses.

The 't' statistic on $\hat{\theta}_2$, t_{ecm}, is -1.356. Assuming nothing is known about q we use the DF 5% critical value of -1.95 and, therefore, do not reject the null hypothesis of no cointegration since $-1.95 < -1.356$. This is contrary to what we anticipate from the suggestion in section **8.4.5** that c_t and y_t do cointegrate; however, this difference serves to highlight an important lesson. Just as in any inferential procedure care has to be exercised in ensuring that the statistical model is adequate. In Chapter 5 we reported evidence that the simple ECM was not adequate and needed to be amended. In particular a development of the model was suggested which included inflation as a short-run variable. The resulting re-estimated model is reported below:

$$\Delta c_t = -0.0009 + 0.250\Delta y_t + 0.099\Delta y_{t-1}$$
$$(-0.257) \quad (4.286) \quad (1.786)$$
$$- 0.101(c_t - y_t)_{-1} + 0.002\pi_t$$
$$(-2.631) \quad (2.027)$$
$$- 0.005\pi_{t-1} + \hat{\varepsilon}_2$$
$$(-4.455) \quad (8.30)$$

't' statistics in parentheses.

The 't' statistic on $\hat{\theta}_2$, t_{ecm}, is now -2.631 which is significant even using the conservative DF 5% critical value of -1.95. Hence, we do not reject the hypothesis that c_t and y_t cointegrate.

In view of the results on the power of the two tests, where a decision is marginal using the DF $\hat{\tau}$ statistic it would be justified to move to the second stage of estimating an ECM, and use the more powerful t_{ecm} to assess cointegration.

8.5.2b   Unknown cointegration coefficients

There are some details of the procedure, outlined so far, for using t_{ecm} which now require emphasis. First, the cointegrating vector was assumed to be known. This means that the comparison is between t_{ecm} and the DF $\hat{\tau}$ statistic, where the latter is appropriate for unit root testing for a single variable or a potentially cointegrating combination when the coefficients are known and so a 'single' variable can be constructed. KED (*op. cit.*) give an application where the coefficients are estimated rather than assumed known. In their example the cointegrating relationship was between real money, real income, inflation, the 3-month local authority interest rate and the (learning adjusted) retail sight deposit rate with a constant included. The calculated t_{ecm} from an ECM including these variables is then compared with a critical value from MacKinnon's response surface using the 'constant and no trend' case, but KED (*op. cit.*, p. 341) note 'the appropriateness of MacKinnon's tables for this t_{ecm} (that is using an estimated cointegrating vector) is as yet a conjecture, albeit a natural one'. (My clarification in parentheses.)

(i) The modified t_{ecm} test
When the cointegrating coefficients are not known there are two possible approaches. To illustrate consider the bivariate model with the general notation Y_t, X_t. Suppose the potentially cointegrating combination, normalised on Y_t, is $Y_t - \varphi_2 X_t$, but φ_2 is unknown. Then the ECM is:

$$\Delta Y_t = \theta_0 + \theta_1 \Delta X_t$$
$$+ \theta_2(Y_t - \varphi_2 X_t)_{-1} + \varepsilon_t \qquad (8.31a)$$
$$= \theta_0 + \theta_1 \Delta X_t$$
$$+ \theta_2(Y_{t-1} - (1 + \varphi_2 - 1)X_{t-1}) + \varepsilon_t$$

$$= \theta_0 + \theta_1 \Delta X_t + \theta_2(Y_{t-1} - X_{t-1})$$
$$- \theta_2(\varphi_2 - 1)X_{t-1} + \varepsilon_t$$
$$= \theta_0 + \theta_1 \Delta X_t + \theta_2(Y_{t-1} - X_{t-1})$$
$$+ \theta_3 X_{t-1} + \varepsilon_t \qquad (8.31b)$$

where $\theta_3 = -\theta_2(\varphi_2 - 1)$. To complete the model we add two assumptions:

(i) $\Delta X_t = \omega_t$ with $\text{Var}(\omega_t) = \sigma_\omega^2$, that is X_t is a random walk; (8.32a)

(ii) ε_t and ω_t are uncorrelated white noise. (8.32b)

This way of writing the ECM separates out the possibility of $\varphi_2 \neq 1$; with the implication that $\theta_3 = 0$, and X_{t-1} is redundant, if $\varphi_2 = 1$. The regression (8.31b) should be used if the cointegrating vector is unknown. The test statistic is as before in the sense that it is a 't' test on the 'error correction coefficient' θ_2. Provided X_t is strongly exogenous for Y_t, the critical values for t_{ecm} do not depend upon the precise values of θ_1 and σ_ω – see Kiviet and Phillips (1992) and Hendry (1995, p. 299). Strong exogeneity means that the error correction term $(Y_t - \varphi_2 X_t)_{-1}$ only enters the ΔX_t equation and there is no feedback from lagged Y_t to current X_t (that is weak exogeneity plus an absence of Granger-Causality from Y_t to current X_t). This assumption is satisfied in the specification comprising (8.31b), (8.32a) and (8.32b). Banerjee et al. (1993) provide some critical values of t_{ecm}.

(ii) The modified Dickey–Fuller test
Another approach is to modify the DF regression so that it allows for the possibility that the restriction(s) are incorrect. To see how this works first return to the simple example (8.28) where φ_2 is known to be 1. Then:

$$\Delta Y_t = \theta_1 \Delta X_t$$
$$+ \theta_2(Y_{t-1} - X_{t-1}) + \varepsilon_t \qquad (8.28 \text{ again})$$

Which can be rewritten as:

$$\Delta Y_t - \Delta X_t = \theta_2(Y_{t-1} - X_{t-1}) + \varepsilon_t$$
$$+ (\theta_1 - 1)\Delta X_t \qquad (8.33)$$

that is

$$\Delta \xi_t = \theta_2 \xi_{t-1} + u_t \qquad (8.34)$$

Note from (8.24) that $Y_t = X_t + \xi_t$ implies that $\Delta Y_t - \Delta X_t = \Delta \xi_t$; and u_t in (8.34), which looks like a simple DF regression, is actually $\varepsilon_t + (\theta_1 - 1)\Delta X_t$. This observation suggests that modifying the standard DF regression by including ΔX_t as a regressor would correct for the possibly invalid restriction of $\theta_1 = 1$. If $\theta_1 = 1$ the original DF regression is valid and the coefficient on ΔX_t is zero. In this example φ_2 was assumed known, and equal to 1 in this case. We relax this assumption in two parts, first assume that $\varphi_2 \neq 1$. Now

$$\xi_t = Y_t - \varphi_2 X_t \qquad (8.35)$$

and the modified DF regression is

$$\Delta \xi_t = \gamma \xi_{t-1} + u_t \qquad (8.36)$$

$$\Rightarrow \Delta(Y_t - \varphi_2 X_t) = \gamma(Y_t - \varphi_2 X_t)_{-1} + u_t$$
$$\Rightarrow \qquad \Delta Y_t = \varphi_2 \Delta X_t$$
$$+ \gamma(Y_t - \varphi_2 X_t)_{-1} + u_t$$
$$(8.37)$$

Hence the restriction implicit in the standard DF regression is that the coefficient on ΔX_t is the same as the long-run coefficient φ_2. Equation (8.37) is a version of the ECM given by:

$$\Delta Y_t = \theta_1 \Delta X_t + \theta_2(Y_t - \varphi_2 X_t)_{-1} + \varepsilon_t$$

with restriction $\theta_1 = \varphi_2$. The unrestricted ECM can be rewritten as:

$$\Delta Y_t = \varphi_2 \Delta X_t + \theta_2(Y_t - \varphi_2 X_t)_{-1}$$
$$+ \varepsilon_t + (\theta_1 - \varphi_2)\Delta X_t \qquad (8.38a)$$

$$\Rightarrow \Delta(Y_t - \varphi_2 X_t)$$
$$= \theta_2(Y_t - \varphi_2 X_t)_{-1} + \varepsilon_t$$
$$+ (\theta_1 - \varphi_2)\Delta X_t \qquad (8.38b)$$
$$\Rightarrow \Delta \xi_t = \theta_2 \xi_{t-1} + u_t$$

where $u_t = \varepsilon_t + (\theta_1 - \varphi_2)\Delta X_t$, so if the restriction is valid the last term vanishes. Hence, to correct the standard DF regression add ΔX_t to the right-hand side, that is

$$\Delta \xi_t = \delta \Delta X_t + \gamma \xi_{t-1} + \varepsilon_t \qquad (8.39)$$

where $\delta = (\theta_1 - \varphi_2)$ and $\gamma = \theta_2$. Then (8.38b) and (8.39) are identical.

In practice ξ_t is replaced with $\hat{\xi}_t = Y_t - \hat{\varphi}_2 X_t$ where $\hat{\varphi}_2$ is the OLSEG, or another consistent estimator, of φ_2 (also a constant is usually included in the regression of Y_t on X_t). The test statistic is the 't' type statistic on γ with, as before, large negative values leading to rejection of the null hypothesis; the test procedure will be referred to as modified Dickey–Fuller – or MDF – with test statistic $m\hat{t}_\gamma$.

The procedure is easily generalised to more than two variables and to more dynamic models. In the first case if there are k 'regressors' X_{t2} to X_{tk} then

$$\hat{\xi}_t = Y_t - \sum_{j=2}^{k} \hat{\varphi}_{2j} X_{tj} \qquad (8.40)$$

and the modified DF regression is

$$\Delta \hat{\xi}_t = \sum_{j=2}^{k} \delta_j \Delta X_{tj} + \gamma \hat{\xi}_{t-1} + \varepsilon_t^* \qquad (8.41)$$

where ε_t^* differs from ε_t because $\hat{\xi}_t$ differs from $\hat{\xi}_t$.

The second case of a more dynamic ECM is best illustrated with an example. Suppose there are lags on both ΔY_t and ΔX_t, then:

$$(1 - \gamma_1 L)\Delta Y_t = (\phi_1 + \phi_2 L)\Delta X_t$$
$$+ \theta_2(Y_t - \varphi_2 X_t)_{-1} + \varepsilon_t$$
$$(8.42)$$

Now subtract $(1 - \gamma_1 L)\varphi_2 \Delta X_t$ from both sides and rearrange to obtain:

$$\Rightarrow (1 - \gamma_1 L)\Delta(Y_t - \varphi_2 X_t)$$
$$= \theta_2(Y_t - \varphi_2 X_t)_{-1} + \varepsilon_t + [(\phi_1 + \phi_2 L)$$
$$- (1 - \gamma_1 L)\varphi_2]\Delta X_t \qquad (8.43a)$$

$$\Rightarrow (1 - \gamma_1 L)\Delta\xi_t = \theta_2\xi_{t-1} + u_t$$
$$\Rightarrow \qquad \Delta\xi_t = \theta_2\xi_{t-1}$$
$$+ \gamma_1\Delta\xi_{t-1} + u_t \qquad (8.43b)$$

This looks like an ADF(1) regression, but note that:

$$u_t = \varepsilon_t + [(\phi_1 + \phi_2 L) - (1 - \gamma_1 L)\varphi_2]\Delta X_t$$
$$= \varepsilon_t + (\phi_1 - \varphi_2)\Delta X_t$$
$$+ (\phi_2 + \gamma_1\varphi_2)\Delta X_{t-1} \qquad (8.44)$$

Hence the modified ADF(1) regression is

$$\Delta\xi_t = \delta_1\Delta X_t + \delta_2\Delta X_{t-1} + \gamma\xi_{t-1}$$
$$+ \gamma_1\Delta\xi_{t-1} + \varepsilon_t \qquad (8.45)$$

where $\delta_1 = (\phi_1 - \varphi_2)$, $\delta_2 = (\phi_2 + \gamma_1\varphi_2)$ and $\gamma = \theta_2$. So ΔX_t and its lag are added to the ADF(1) regression. For the modified ADF(1) regression to reduce to the standard ADF(1) regression the following are required: $\phi_1 = \varphi_2$ and $\phi_2 = -\gamma_1\varphi_2$. In practice $\Delta\hat{\xi}_t$ replaces $\Delta\xi_t$, and the need for ΔX_t and its lags can be assessed by standard significance tests.

The general result is due to KED (*op. cit.*). First, define: $\gamma(L) = (1 - \sum_{i=1}^{p}\gamma_i L^i)$, $\phi_j(L) =$

$\sum_{s=0}^{q_j}\phi_{js}L^s$ for $j = 1, \ldots, k$; then the general ECM in k weakly exogenous regressors is

$$\gamma(L)\Delta Y_t = \sum_{j=1}^{k}\phi_j(L)\Delta X_{tj}$$
$$+ \theta_2\left(Y_t - \sum_{j=1}^{k}\varphi_{2j}X_{tj}\right)_{-1} + \varepsilon_t$$
$$(8.46)$$

Subtract $\gamma(L)\sum_{j=1}^{k}\varphi_{2j}\Delta X_{tj}$ from both sides

$$\gamma(L)\Delta\left(Y_t - \sum_{j=1}^{k}\varphi_{2j}X_{tj}\right)$$
$$= \sum_{j=1}^{k}\phi_j(L)\Delta X_{tj} + \theta_2\left(Y_t - \sum_{j=1}^{k}\varphi_{2j}X_{tj}\right)_{-1}$$
$$+ \varepsilon_t - \gamma(L)\sum_{j=1}^{k}\varphi_{2j}\Delta X_{tj}$$
$$= \theta_2\left(Y_t - \sum_{j=1}^{k}\varphi_{2j}X_{tj}\right)_{-1} + \varepsilon_t$$
$$+ \left[\sum_{j=1}^{k}\phi_j(L) - \gamma(L)\sum_{j=1}^{k}\varphi_{2j}\right]\Delta X_{tj}$$
$$(8.47a)$$

Table 8.11 *Critical values for the modified DF test for noncointegration (constant and no trend case)*

α	10%	5%	1%	α	10%	5%	1%
$N = 2$				$N = 5$			
$T = 50$	−2.956	−3.299	−4.000	$T = 50$	−3.884	−4.276	−5.004
100	−2.926	−3.244	−3.884	100	−3.761	−4.105	−4.811
200	−2.916	−3.255	−3.835	200	−3.709	−4.057	−4.637
500	−2.906	−3.299	−3.753	500	−3.681	−4.015	−4.636
$N = 3$				$N = 6$			
$T = 50$	−3.320	−3.675	−4.403	$T = 50$	−4.120	−4.519	−5.290
100	−3.246	−3.577	−4.232	100	−3.978	−4.339	−5.005
200	−3.217	−3.566	−4.176	200	−3.922	−4.257	−4.892
500	−3.210	−3.527	−4.089	500	−3.887	−4.208	−4.802
$N = 4$				$N = 7$			
$T = 50$	−3.599	−3.975	−4.732	$T = 50$	−4.372	−4.769	−5.596
100	−3.538	−3.864	−4.507	100	−4.213	−4.568	−5.267
200	−3.485	−3.817	−4.410	200	−4.161	−4.506	−5.154
500	−3.437	−3.758	−4.352	500	−4.089	−4.405	−5.072

$$\Rightarrow \Delta\xi_t = \theta_2\xi_{t-1} + \sum_{i=1}^{p} \gamma\Delta\xi_{t-i} + u_t$$

using $\quad \xi_t = \left(Y_t - \sum_{j=1}^{k} \varphi_{2j}X_{tj} \right) \qquad (8.47b)$

where $\quad u_t = \eta(L)\Delta X_{tj}$

and $\quad \eta(L) = \left[\sum_{j=1}^{k} \phi_j(L) - \gamma(L)\sum_{j=1}^{k} \varphi_{2j} \right]$

The modified ADF(p) regression will, in general, include ΔX_{tj} and its lags to the highest order in $\eta(L)$. If $\sum_{j=1}^{k} \phi_j(L) = \gamma(L)\sum_{j=1}^{k} \varphi_{2j}$, no such terms are needed and the modified and standard Dickey–Fuller maintained regressions coincide.

The critical values for the MDF test are obtained by simulation and depend upon N. For the simulations, the $N = k + 1$ variables were generated as unrelated random walks with $N(0, 1)$ shocks; the first stage regression, including a constant, served to define $\hat{\xi}_t$ which was then used in the modified DF regression. The critical values in Table 8.11 are analogues of the 'constant and no trend' case in MacKinnon's (1991) tables. Twenty-five thousand replications were used with $T = 50, 100, 200, 500$ and $N = 2, \ldots, 7$.

The critical values are slightly smaller in absolute value than for the standard DF test; for example, for $T = 50$ and $N = 2$, the comparison is $-2.956 : -3.127$, $-3.299 : -3.461$, $-4.000 : -4.123$ for the 10%, 5% and 1% significance levels, respectively, where the standard DF critical values were calculated using MacKinnon's response surface coefficients.

8.6 Alternative representations of the long-run relationship

There are two characteristics of an error correction model that are of interest. First, an ECM is dynamic in the sense that it involves lags of the dependent and explanatory variables, it thus captures short-run adjustments to changes, in particular adjustments to past disequilibria and contemporaneous changes in the explanatory variables. Second, the ECM is transparent in displaying the cointegrating relationship between or among the variables. There are several alternative ways of formulating these two aspects. One is the autoregressive distributed lag – or ADL – model, which represents the dynamics in a different way from the ECM and captures the equilibrium relationship in an implicit rather than explicit way. As one would expect all the information in an ECM is contained in the ADL version and vice versa, it is just a matter of how that information is parameterised and interpreted. Nevertheless it is useful to draw out the connections, partly because the ADL approach offers an alternative way of assessing whether the candidate variables do cointegrate. Another way of representing the information is the Bewley transformation – see Bewley (1979) – which is often useful in the context of direct estimation of the long-run coefficients and their (asymptotically) valid 't' statistics. Sections **8.6.1** and **8.6.2** consider these alternative ways of representing the short-run dynamics and the long run.

8.6.1 The ADL model and the ECM (the two variable case)

The ADL(p, q) in the two variables Y_t and X_t model was introduced in Chapter 2. Specifically,

$$Y_t = \alpha_0 + \sum_{j=0}^{q} \beta_j L^j X_t$$

$$+ \sum_{i=1}^{p} \gamma_i L^i Y_t + \varepsilon_t \qquad (8.48)$$

where L is the lag operator, $L^j \equiv X_{t-j}$. (8.48) is a dynamic model in the levels of the variables and their lags. It will be helpful to start with the ADL(1, 1) model in the variables Y_t and X_t given by

$$Y_t = \alpha_0 + \beta_0 X_t + \beta_1 X_{t-1}$$

$$+ \gamma_1 Y_{t-1} + \varepsilon_t \qquad (8.49)$$

At first sight given the existence of (8.49) estimating a cointegrating regression involving just Y_t and X_t would seem to involve omitting important information. However, when Y_t and X_t are nonstationary their properties dominate the regression results. To see this we first need to develop a few new 'tools' of analysis.

In contrast to the ECM approach, the long-run or equilibrium relationship between Y_t and X_t is implicit in the ADL model where it corresponds to the solution resulting when there is no incentive to change. Y_t will have then settled to an equilibrium value from which it will change only if there is a change in X_t. The defining characteristics of equilibrium are, therefore, $X_t = X_{t-1} = X_{t-2}, \ldots$, and $Y_t = Y_{t-1} = Y_{t-2}, \ldots$, using these conditions in (8.49) we can solve for the implicit equilibrium:

$$Y_t = \alpha_0 + \beta_0 X_t + \beta_1 X_t + \gamma_1 Y_t + \varepsilon_t$$

$$\Rightarrow (1 - \gamma_1)Y_t = \alpha_0 + (\beta_0 + \beta_1)X_t + \varepsilon_t$$

$$\Rightarrow \qquad Y_t = \frac{\alpha_0}{(1 - \gamma_1)} + \frac{(\beta_0 + \beta_1)}{(1 - \gamma)} X_t$$

$$+ \frac{\varepsilon_t}{(1 - \gamma_1)} \qquad (8.50)$$

Also in defining the equilibrium we assume that ε_t takes its expected value of 0, hence in equilibrium:

$$Y_t = \varphi_1 + \varphi_2 X_t \qquad (8.51)$$

where $\varphi_1 = \alpha_0/(1 - \gamma_1)$ and $\varphi_2 = (\beta_0 + \beta_1)/(1 - \gamma_1)$. The same notation has been used for the coefficients here as in the cointegration approach because the correspondence is exact. If Y_t and X_t cointegrate the difference between Y_t and $(\varphi_1 + \varphi_2 X_t)$ will be a stationary error, ξ_t, which we can interpret as disequilibrium. Cointegration implies that there are dynamic forces implicit in the ADL that will return Y_t to its equilibrium value following a change in X_t.

The ADL can also be formulated in its error correction form. For example, the ADL(1, 1) model given by

$$Y_t = \alpha_0 + \beta_0 X_t + \beta_1 X_{t-1}$$
$$+ \gamma_1 Y_{t-1} + \varepsilon_t \qquad (8.49 \text{ again})$$

with implicit long run

$$Y_t = \varphi_1 + \varphi_2 X_t \quad \text{where } \varphi_1 = \alpha_0/(1 - \gamma_1)$$
$$\text{and} \quad \varphi_2 = (\beta_0 + \beta_1)/(1 - \gamma_1)$$

can be rewritten as

$$\Delta Y_t = \theta_0 + \theta_1 \Delta X_t$$
$$+ \theta_2 (Y_t - \varphi_2 X_t)_{-1} + \varepsilon_t \qquad (8.52)$$

In the form (8.52), the model can be interpreted as an equilibrium correction model. To see that this correspondence holds, first subtract Y_{t-1} from both sides of (8.49) and add and subtract $\beta_0 X_{t-1}$ from the right-hand side of (8.49), this gives

$$Y_t - Y_{t-1} = \alpha_0 + \beta_0 X_t - \beta_0 X_{t-1} + \beta_0 X_{t-1}$$
$$+ \beta_1 X_{t-1} - (1 - \gamma_1)Y_{t-1} + \varepsilon_t$$
$$= \alpha_0 + \beta_0 \Delta X_t + (\beta_0 + \beta_1)X_{t-1}$$
$$- (1 - \gamma_1)Y_{t-1} + \varepsilon_1 \qquad (8.53)$$

Then multiply and divide the term in X_{t-1} by $(1 - \gamma_1)$ and collect terms

$$\Delta Y_t = \alpha_0 + \beta_0 \Delta X_t + (1 - \gamma_1)$$
$$\times [(\beta_0 + \beta_1)/(1 - \gamma_1)]X_{t-1}$$
$$- (1 - \gamma_1)Y_{t-1} + \varepsilon_t$$
$$= \alpha_0 + \beta_0 \Delta X_t - (1 - \gamma_1)$$
$$\times [Y_t - (\beta_0 + \beta_1)/(1 - \gamma_1)X_t]_{-1} + \varepsilon_t$$
$$= \beta_0 \Delta X_t - (1 - \gamma_1)[Y_t - \alpha_0/(1 - \gamma_1)$$
$$- (\beta_0 + \beta_1)/(1 - \gamma_1)X_t]_{-1} + \varepsilon_t \quad (8.54)$$

On comparison with (8.52) this gives the following correspondences:

$$\theta_0 = \alpha_0, \quad \theta_1 = \beta_0, \quad \theta_2 = -(1 - \gamma_1)$$
$$\varphi_2 = (\beta_0 + \beta_1)/(1 - \gamma_1)$$

and note that $\varphi_1 = \alpha_0/(1 - \gamma_1)$. Whether we choose to parameterise the information in the regression as an ADL model or an ECM is a matter of convenience and interpretation: (8.49) and (8.52) are equivalent.

8.6.2 The Bewley transformation

A second way of representing the information in an ADL model is through what is known as the Bewley transformation – see Bewley (1979), Inder (1993) and Banerjee *et al.* (1993). In particular, (8.49) can be expressed in terms of the equilibrium solution, involving nonstationary variables, and additional stationary variables.

First rewrite (8.49) as

$$Y_t - \gamma_1 Y_{t-1} = \alpha_0 + \beta_0 X_t + \beta_1 X_{t-1} + \varepsilon_t$$

then note that

$$\begin{aligned}\beta_0 X_t + \beta_1 X_{t-1} &= (\beta_0 + \beta_1)X_t - \beta_1(X_t - X_{t-1}) \\ &= (\beta_0 + \beta_1)X_t - \beta_1 \Delta X_t\end{aligned}$$

$$\begin{aligned}\text{and} \quad Y_t - \gamma_1 Y_{t-1} &= (1 - \gamma_1)Y_t + \gamma_1(Y_t - Y_{t-1}) \\ &= (1 - \gamma_1)Y_t + \gamma_1 \Delta Y_t\end{aligned}$$

Next use these two expressions in (8.49) and simplify to give:

$$Y_t = \frac{\alpha_0}{1 - \gamma_1} + \frac{(\beta_0 + \beta_1)}{1 - \gamma_1}X_t - \frac{\beta_1}{1 - \gamma_1}\Delta X_t$$

$$- \frac{\gamma_1}{1 - \gamma_1}\Delta Y_t + \frac{1}{1 - \gamma_1}\varepsilon_t \tag{8.55}$$

Note that

$$\varphi_1 = \alpha_0/(1 - \gamma_1), \quad \varphi_2 = (\beta_0 + \beta_1)/(1 - \gamma_1)$$

and define $\beta_1^* = -\beta_1/(1 - \gamma_1)$, $\gamma_1^* = -\gamma_1/(1 - \gamma_1)$, $\varepsilon_t^* = \varepsilon_t/(1 - \gamma_1)$; then

$$Y_t = \varphi_1 + \varphi_2 X_t + \beta_1^* \Delta X_t + \gamma_1^* \Delta Y_t + \varepsilon_t^* \tag{8.56}$$

which implies

$$\varepsilon_t^* = Y_t - (\varphi_1 + \varphi_2 X_t + \beta_1^* \Delta X_t + \gamma_1^* \Delta Y_t) \tag{8.57}$$

Equation (8.56) demonstrates that the dynamic equation (8.49) can be reformulated, using the Bewley transformation, to separate out the I(1) and I(0) variables. Thus we have:

- The long-run solution in levels of the I(1) variables, that is $Y_t = \varphi_1 + \varphi_2 X_t$.
- The I(0) terms in ΔX_t and ΔY_t.

If Y_t and X_t are I(1) then ΔY_t and ΔX_t are I(0) variables. Cointegration ensures that the linear combination $Y_t - (\varphi_1 + \varphi_2 X_t)$ is I(0), hence (8.56) is balanced in its time series properties and ε_t^* is I(0). Given (8.56) it is now possible to reinterpret the first step of the Engle–Granger approach, which involves a regression of Y_t on a constant and X_t. It is apparent that the cointegrating regression ignores the terms ΔX_t and ΔY_t. Consistency of the OLS estimators of the cointegrating coefficients occurs because the I(1) properties of Y_t and X_t dominate the I(0) properties of ΔX_t and ΔY_t – see Stock (1987). Nevertheless (8.56) is useful because it offers an alternative way of estimating the cointegrating coefficients, which may have some finite sample advantages over the Engle–Granger approach. It seems likely that including as much information as possible in the regression is likely to give the resulting estimators better properties, a result suggested by the simulations reported in Inder (1993). A summary of the three ways of writing the model is provided in Table 8.12.

The ECM with φ_2 unknown is nonlinear in the parameters because θ_2 and φ_2 are multiplied

Table 8.12 *An example of equivalent ways of representing a simple error correction model*

ADL(1, 1)
$Y_t = \alpha_0 + \beta_0 X_t + \beta_1 X_{t-1} + \gamma_1 Y_{t-1} + \varepsilon_t$
Bewley transformation
$Y_t = \varphi_1 + \varphi_2 X_t + \beta_1^* \Delta X_t + \gamma_1^* \Delta Y_t + \varepsilon_t^*$
ECM: nonlinear in the coefficients
$\Delta Y_t = \theta_0 + \theta_1 \Delta X_t + \theta_2(Y_t - \varphi_2 X_t)_{-1} + \varepsilon_t$

together; estimation therefore requires a nonlinear routine such as the nonlinear least squares routines programmed into TSP, RATS and MICROFIT. If φ_2 is known, for example a unit long-run elasticity, then the ECM becomes linear. The ECM parameterises the information in the ADL in a different form giving another interpretation of simple transformations of the ADL coefficients. The Bewley transformation offers another interpretation which isolates the long-run coefficients while keeping the model linear in a transformed set of coefficients.

8.6.3 A numerical example

It may be helpful to have a simple numerical example of the alternative representations of the same model. Returning to the connection between the autoregressive distributed lag and ECM representations suppose in:

$$Y_t = \alpha_0 + \beta_0 X_t + \beta_1 X_{t-1} \\ + \gamma_1 Y_{t-1} + \varepsilon_t \qquad \text{(8.49 again)}$$

the coefficients take the following values: $\alpha_0 = 5$, $\beta_0 = 0.15$, $\beta_1 = 0.10$, $\gamma_1 = 0.5$. The ECM representation of this model is:

$$\Delta Y_t = 0.15\Delta X_t \\ - 0.5(Y_{t-1} - 10 - 0.5X_{t-1}) + \varepsilon_t$$

or taking the constant out of disequilibrium

$$\Delta Y_t = 5 + 0.15\Delta X_t \\ - 0.5(Y_{t-1} - 0.5X_{t-1}) + \varepsilon_t \qquad \text{(8.58)}$$

The ECM coefficients are $\theta_0 = 5$, $\theta_1 = 0.15$, $\theta_2 = -0.5$, $\varphi_1 = 10$ and $\varphi_2 = 0.5$. These are interpreted as follows: from $\theta_2 = -0.5$ there is a 50% adjustment in period t to the disequilibrium in period $t - 1$. This implies a reasonably fast, but not instantaneous, adjustment. For example, assuming no further changes, after one more period 75% $(=(0.5 + 0.5 \times 0.5)\%)$ of the disequilibrium has been removed. From $\theta_1 = 0.15$ if X_t changes between $t - 1$ and t then there will

be a contemporaneous adjustment of $0.15\Delta X_t$. Here θ_1 is 30% $(=(0.15/0.5)\%)$ of the eventual long-run response of $\varphi_2 = 0.5$.

The ECM representation of an autoregressive distributed lag model is often an attractive one because the coefficients have a direct interpretation. Also note that where Y_t and X_t are nonstationary then, following Granger's representation theorem, for the ECM to exist they must cointegrate. The ECM is then balanced in terms of its time series properties. For example, suppose Y_t and X_t are each I(1), then ΔY_t is I(0) as is ΔX_t. Further if Y_t and X_t cointegrate, ξ_t is I(0) and the ECM is balanced as it is specified entirely in terms of I(0) variables.

The Bewley transformation of the ADL model is

$$Y_t = 10 + 0.5X_t - 0.2\Delta X_t \\ - 1.0\Delta Y_t + 2\varepsilon_t \qquad \text{(8.59)}$$

The long-run solution, obtained on setting $\Delta X_t = \Delta Y_t = \varepsilon_t = 0$, is $Y_t = 10 + 0.5X_t$. Again this is balanced equation since, by hypothesis, $Y_t - (10 + 0.5X_t)$ is stationary and ΔX_t, ΔY_t and ε_t are I(0). However, as noted below the Bewley transformation requires an instrumental variables estimation method.

8.6.4 The more general ADL model: alternative representations

The illustrative examples in the preceding sections have concerned the ADL(1, 1) model, it will be useful, therefore, to include, for reference, a brief extension to cover the more general model. This section could be omitted on a first reading. Generalisations can occur in two directions: first, keeping to two variables more lags may be involved, so the extension is to an ADL(p, q) model; second, more variables and more lags could be involved. We derive the first case in detail for the Bewley transformation and the ECM, and indicate how the second generalisation is achieved. It is useful to start with the Bewley transformation as it involves some derivations which are of use in obtaining the

ECM. Deriving the links between the different representations involves an attention to detail but is tedious rather than complex (and it should also become evident why important lessons on estimation and inference are usually illustrated with the simplest of models!).

(i) Bewley transformation
Consider the ADL(p, q) model:

$$Y_t = \alpha_0 + \sum_{j=0}^{q} \beta_j L^j X_t$$

$$+ \sum_{i=1}^{p} \gamma_i L^i Y_t + \varepsilon_t \qquad (8.60)$$

rewritten as:

$$\left(1 - \sum_{i=1}^{p} \gamma_i L^i\right) Y_t$$

$$= \alpha_0 + \sum_{j=0}^{q} \beta_j L^j X_t + \varepsilon_t \qquad (8.61)$$

Note that

$$\left(1 - \sum_{i=1}^{p} \gamma_i L^i\right) Y_t$$

$$= \left(1 - \sum_{i=1}^{p} \gamma_i\right) Y_t + \sum_{i=1}^{p} \gamma_i \Delta Y_t$$

$$+ \sum_{i=2}^{p} \gamma_i \Delta Y_{t-1} + \sum_{i=3}^{p} \gamma_i \Delta Y_{t-2} + \cdots$$

$$+ \gamma_p \Delta Y_{t-p+1} \qquad (8.62)$$

and

$$\sum_{j=0}^{q} \beta_j L^j X_t$$

$$= \sum_{j=0}^{q} \beta_j X_t - \sum_{j=1}^{q} \beta_j \Delta X_t - \sum_{j=2}^{q} \beta_j \Delta X_{t-1}$$

$$- \sum_{j=3}^{q} \beta_j \Delta X_{t-2} - \cdots - \beta_q \Delta X_{t-q+1}$$

$$\qquad (8.63)$$

For convenience define:

$$\Gamma_1 \equiv \sum_{i=1}^{p} \gamma_i; \quad \Gamma_2 \equiv \sum_{i=2}^{p} \gamma_i; \ldots; \Gamma_p \equiv \gamma_p$$

$$B_0 \equiv \sum_{j=0}^{q} \beta_j; \quad B_1 \equiv \sum_{j=1}^{q} \beta_j;$$

$$B_2 \equiv \sum_{j=2}^{q} \beta_j; \ldots; B_q \equiv \beta_q$$

Then

$$\left(1 - \sum_{i=1}^{p} \gamma_i L^i\right) Y_t$$

$$= (1 - \Gamma_1)Y_t + \Gamma_1 \Delta Y_t + \Gamma_2 \Delta Y_{t-1}$$

$$+ \Gamma_3 \Delta Y_{t-2} + \cdots + \Gamma_p \Delta Y_{t-p+1}$$

$$= (1 - \Gamma_1)Y_t + \sum_{i=1}^{p} \Gamma_i \Delta Y_{t-i+1} \qquad (8.64)$$

and

$$\sum_{j=0}^{q} \beta_j L^j X_t = B_0 X_t - B_1 \Delta X_t - B_2 \Delta X_{t-1}$$

$$- B_3 \Delta X_{t-3} - \cdots - B_q \Delta X_{t-q+1}$$

$$= B_0 X_t - \sum_{j=1}^{q} B_j \Delta X_{t-j+1} \qquad (8.65)$$

Using these expressions the ADL(p, q) model, (8.61), can be rewritten as

$$(1 - \Gamma_1)Y_t + \sum_{i=1}^{p} \Gamma_i \Delta Y_{t-i+1}$$

$$= \alpha_0 + B_0 X_t - \sum_{j=1}^{q} B_j \Delta X_{t-j+1} + \varepsilon_t \quad (8.66a)$$

$$\Rightarrow (1 - \Gamma_1)Y_t = \alpha_0 + B_0 X_t - \sum_{j=1}^{q} B_j \Delta X_{t-j+1}$$

$$- \sum_{i=1}^{p} \Gamma_i \Delta Y_{t-i+1} + \varepsilon_t \quad (8.66b)$$

$$\Rightarrow Y_t = \alpha_0/(1 - \Gamma_1) + [B_0/(1 - \Gamma_1)]X_t$$

$$- \left[\sum_{j=1}^{q} B_j/(1 - \Gamma_1) \right] \Delta X_{t-j+1}$$

$$- \left[\sum_{i=1}^{p} \Gamma_i/(1 - \Gamma_1) \right] \Delta Y_{t-i+1}$$

$$+ \varepsilon_t/(1 - \Gamma_1) \qquad (8.66c)$$

Notice that the long-run coefficients $\alpha_0/(1 - \Gamma_1)$ and $[B_0/(1 - \Gamma_1)]$ are now isolated, and the remaining coefficients are on the I(0) variables. This transformation is particularly useful for Y_t and $X_t \sim I(1)$; however, it is also valid when Y_t and $X_t \sim I(0)$.

As in the simpler case, considered in the previous section, estimation should use Y_{t-1} as an instrument for ΔY_t and X_{t-1} as an instrument for ΔX_t (although ΔX_t is perfectly valid if X_t is not endogenous). The extension to many variables is straightforward: regress Y_t on a constant, the levels of each of the explanatory variables and the differences and lagged differences of the variables; use Y_{t-1} as an instrument for ΔY_t.

(ii) ECM
Again consider the ADL(p, q) model:

$$Y_t = \alpha_0 + \sum_{j=0}^{q} \beta_j L^j X_t$$

$$+ \sum_{i=1}^{p} \gamma_i L^i Y_t + \varepsilon_t \qquad (8.60 \text{ again})$$

The aim is to show that this can be transformed into an error correction model which separates out lagged disequilibrium, ξ_{t-1}, and changes in X_t and Y_t. We need two results used in the Bewley transformation. Subtracting Y_t from both sides of (8.64) and changing sign note that

$$\sum_{i=1}^{p} \gamma_i L^i Y_t = \Gamma_1 Y_t - \Gamma_1 \Delta Y_t - \Gamma_2 \Delta Y_{t-1}$$

$$- \Gamma_2 \Delta Y_{t-2} - \cdots - \Gamma_p \Delta Y_{t-p+1}$$

$$= \Gamma_1 Y_{t-1} - \Gamma_2 \Delta Y_{t-1}$$

$$- \Gamma_3 \Delta Y_{t-2} - \cdots - \Gamma_p \Delta Y_{t-p+1}$$

$$= \Gamma_1 Y_{t-1} - \sum_{i=1}^{p} \Gamma_i \Delta Y_{t-i+1} \qquad (8.67)$$

Also (8.65) can be rearranged to suit our present purposes:

$$\sum_{j=0}^{q} \beta_j L^j X_t$$

$$= B_0 X_t - B_1 \Delta X_t - B_2 \Delta X_{t-1}$$

$$- B_3 \Delta X_{t-3} - \cdots - B_q \Delta X_{t-q+1}$$

$$= (B_0 - B_1)X_t + B_1 X_{t-1} - B_2 \Delta X_{t-1}$$

$$- B_3 \Delta X_{t-3} - \cdots - B_q \Delta X_{t-q+1}$$

$$= (B_0 - B_1)\Delta X_t + (B_1 + B_0 - B_1)X_{t-1}$$

$$- B_2 \Delta X_{t-1} - B_3 \Delta X_{t-3} - \cdots$$

$$- B_q \Delta X_{t-q+1}$$

$$= (B_0 - B_1)\Delta X_t + B_0 X_{t-1} - B_2 \Delta X_{t-1}$$

$$- B_3 \Delta X_{t-3} - \cdots - B_q \Delta X_{t-q+1}$$

$$= B_0 X_{t-1} + \beta_0 \Delta X_t - B_2 \Delta X_{t-1}$$

$$- B_3 \Delta X_{t-2} - \cdots - B_q \Delta X_{t-q+1}$$

using $B_0 - B_1 = \beta_0$

$$= B_0 X_{t-1} + \beta_0 \Delta X_t - \sum_{j=2}^{q} B_j \Delta X_{t-j+1} \qquad (8.68)$$

Now use (8.67) and (8.68) in the ADL model (8.60):

$$Y_t = \alpha_0 + B_0 X_{t-1} + \beta_0 \Delta X_t - \sum_{j=2}^{q} B_j \Delta X_{t-j+1}$$

$$+ \Gamma_1 Y_{t-1} - \sum_{i=1}^{p} \Gamma_i \Delta Y_{t-i+1} + \varepsilon_t \qquad (8.69)$$

and subtract Y_{t-1} from both sides

$$Y_t - Y_{t-1} = \alpha_0 + B_0 X_{t-1} + \beta_0 \Delta X_t$$

$$- \sum_{j=2}^{q} B_j \Delta X_{t-j+1} - (1 - \Gamma_1)Y_{t-1}$$

$$- \sum_{i=1}^{p} \Gamma_i \Delta Y_{t-i+1} + \varepsilon_t$$

$$= (1 - \Gamma_1)[\alpha_0/(1 - \Gamma_1)]$$
$$+ (1 - \Gamma_1)[B_0/(1 - \Gamma_1)]X_{t-1}$$
$$+ \beta_0 \Delta X_t - \sum_{j=2}^{q} B_j \Delta X_{t-j+1}$$
$$- (1 - \Gamma_1)Y_{t-1}$$
$$- \sum_{i=1}^{p} \Gamma_i \Delta Y_{t-i+1} + \varepsilon_t$$

$$= \beta_0 \Delta X_t - \sum_{j=2}^{q} B_j \Delta X_{t-j+1}$$
$$- \sum_{i=1}^{p} \Gamma_i \Delta Y_{t-i+1} + (\Gamma_1 - 1)$$
$$\times \{Y_{t-1} - \alpha_0/(1 - \Gamma_1)$$
$$- [\beta_0/(1 - \Gamma_1)]X_{t-1}\} + \varepsilon_t$$

$$= \beta_0 \Delta X_t - \sum_{j=2}^{q} B_j \Delta X_{t-j+1}$$
$$- \sum_{i=1}^{p} \Gamma_i \Delta Y_{t-i+1}$$
$$+ (\Gamma_1 - 1)\xi_{t-1} + \varepsilon_t \qquad (8.70)$$

where

$$\xi_{t-1} = Y_{t-1} - \alpha_0/(1 - \Gamma_1) - [\beta_0/(1 - \Gamma_1)]X_{t-1}$$

The equation (8.70) is an ECM with error correction coefficient $(\Gamma_1 - 1) = \sum_{i=1}^{p} \gamma_i - 1$ on the lagged disequilibrium error, and the other variables are expressed in current or lagged differences. The relationship between an ADL model and the corresponding ECM is easily extended to more than one explanatory variable: the disequilibrium term is redefined to include additional variables; and current and lagged differences of the additional variables are also included. Unless the γ_i coefficients are known, estimation is by nonlinear least squares, but no new problems of estimation are introduced in departing from the simpler model considered in the previous section.

8.7 Estimation, inference and simulation

This section is concerned with estimation, inference and simulation in the different formulations of the error correction model. In principle the three ways, ADL, ECM and Bewley transformation, of writing the model are equivalent. However, in practice estimation will deliver identical estimates of the coefficients for OLS estimation of the ADL and instrumental variables estimation of the Bewley transformation. However, there may be some minor differences between the numerical estimates obtained from these two methods and nonlinear estimation of the ECM, because the latter requires specification of a convergence criterion and nonlinear optimisation routine. Instrumental variables estimation of the Bewley transformation is necessary because the ΔY_t regressor will be correlated with the disturbance term ε_t. The reason for this is that since $\Delta Y_t = Y_t - Y_{t-1}$, then as Y_t depends, in part, upon ε_t, ΔY_t and ε_t must be correlated. Although this does not matter asymptotically if Y_t and X_t are I(1) variables, since their properties dominate the I(0) properties of ΔY_t and ε_t, the finite sample properties of the estimator are likely to be improved by using instrumental variables. In addition asymptotically valid 't' statistics will result from the IV method. The endogeneity of ΔY_t can be solved by using Y_{t-1} as its instrument, since Y_{t-1} is uncorrelated with ε_t, and X_{t-1} as an instrument for ΔX_t.

Assuming cointegration Stock (1987) shows that the nonlinear least squares estimator of the ECM has the following properties:

(i) It is a superconsistent estimator of the long-run coefficients.

(ii) It is a consistent and asymptotically normally distributed estimator of the coefficients on the I(0) terms.

The Bewley transformation adopts a similar distinction between the long-run coefficients and coefficients on I(0) variables and, provided it is estimated by instrumental variables to account for the endogeneity of ΔY_t, the resulting estimator, denoted IVB, will also have properties (i) and (ii). The implied estimator of the long-run coefficient from the ADL model is identical to the IV estimator of the Bewley transformation and will also be superconsistent.

The Engle–Granger procedure consists of two stages: first, estimate the cointegrating coefficients from a 'levels' regression and hence estimate the lagged disequilibrium – or error – $\hat{\xi}_{t-1}$; second, use $\hat{\xi}_{t-1}$ in place of ξ_{t-1} in the ECM, which, therefore, becomes linear, and estimate the remaining coefficients by OLS. Stock (1987) shows that the Engle–Granger two-stage estimator also has properties (i) and (ii). The two estimators (OLSEG and ECM/ADL) of the coefficients on the I(0) variables are asymptotically equivalent; but the two estimators of the long-run coefficients – the cointegrating vector – are not asymptotically equivalent. Stock (*op. cit.*, pp. 1043 *et seq.*) also notes a contrast between the nonlinear ECM estimator (or by implication its IVB and ADL equivalents) and the two-stage Engle–Granger procedure. The latter is likely to result in a greater finite sample bias, whereas the former may show a greater spread in its distribution.

8.7.1 A comparison of alternative ways of estimating the cointegrating coefficients

The EG procedure has been predominant in the single-equation approach to estimating cointegrating relationships. Nevertheless, alternative single-equation approaches, which incorporate more information can be based on the ADL model either by estimating it directly and solving for the implied long run – see (8.50); by estimating the Bewley transformation – see (8.55); or by nonlinear estimation of the ECM. To examine some of the issues involved we draw on a Monte Carlo study by Inder (1993) and a simulation study undertaken here. Chapter 9

also includes a simulation study, which shows that a key parameter is the speed of adjustment in the error correction model (equivalently the coefficient of the lagged dependent variable in the ADL formulation).

8.7.1a Simulation set-up

The simulation framework is as follows: Y_t and X_t are stochastic variables generated according to

$$Y_t = \alpha_0 + \beta_0 X_t + \beta_1 X_{t-1} + \gamma_1 Y_{t-1} + \varepsilon_t \qquad (8.49\,\text{again})$$

and

$$X_t = \phi_1 X_{t-1} + \omega_t, \quad |\phi_1| \leq 1 \qquad (8.71)$$

ω_t and ε_t are generated as uncorrelated, standardised, normal white noise. Setting $\phi_1 = 0$ corresponds to X_t having the properties of ω_t, and if $\phi_1 = 1$ then X_t is a pure random walk. Before describing the simulation results it will be helpful to summarise some relevant theoretical results.

(i) No dynamics

We first consider the simplest case with no dynamics: $\beta_1 = \gamma_1 = 0$, and ε_t and ω_t uncorrelated white noise. Then, with $X_t \sim I(1)$, the cointegrating regression, and the regression model to be estimated, is $Y_t = \alpha_0 + \beta_0 X_t + \varepsilon_t$. The cointegrating coefficients in this case are $\varphi_1 = \alpha_0$ and $\varphi_2 = \beta_0$, and the OLS/OLSEG estimators of these are superconsistent (Stock 1987). As there are no omitted I(0) terms, the 't' statistic for $\hat{\varphi}_2$ ($=\hat{\beta}_0$) is asymptotically normal. This case has already been simulated – see section **8.2.3**. It should be emphasised that this is a very special case as it assumes there are no dynamics in the process generating Y_t. Also the property of superconsistency can be quite misleading as an indication of bias in finite samples. While the convergence of the OLS estimator is at a faster rate than if the regressor was stationary, if there is a large finite sample bias, removal of the bias can still be quite slow – see Banerjee, Hendry and Smith (1986) for simulation evidence of substantial bias in finite samples.

(ii) Dynamics

We relax the assumption that the DGP for Y_t has no dynamics, so now β_1 and γ_1 are nonzero. Ignoring the dynamic terms and estimating the 'levels' regression of Y_t and X_t by OLS, this is the first stage of the EG procedure, still results in superconsistent estimators. However, the omitted dynamics are effectively captured in the residual in the static cointegrating regression inducing serial correlation and, possibly, heteroscedasticity, and inference using standard normal tables will not now be valid – even asymptotically.

Again superconsistency may not actually offer much comfort. In a simulation study reported in Banerjee et al. (1993, pp. 222), the DGP was dynamic as in (8.49) and (8.71) with $\phi_1 = 1$; the bias in estimating the long-run coefficient from a static regression varied from −39% to −21% for $T = 25$ and from −4% to −2% for $T = 400$, depending upon the design parameters in the DGP. The biases from estimating the ADL by OLS are not reported but described as 'negligible'. The ADL model, which includes dynamic effects, captures the serial correlation missed in the static regression by directly including the variables from which it arises. Finally, estimation of the nonlinear parameterisation of the ECM also results in superconsistent estimators of the long-run coefficients.

The distribution of the OLS estimators of the coefficients in the ADL model is established using results due to Sims, Stock and Watson (1990), hereafter SSW, and for a good exposition of their results see Banerjee et al. (1993, Chapter 6). In particular SSW show that if there is a linear transformation of integrated regressors that is stationary, then the OLS estimators of the parameters in the transformed model are asymptotically normally distributed. As the transformation is linear, which preserves the distribution, the original estimators are also asymp-

totically normally distributed. As emphasised in Banerjee (op. cit.) it is not actually necessary to undertake the transformation, estimate the parameters, then carry out the inverse of the transformation; all that is needed is that, in principle, such a linear transformation to stationarity exists.

The ADL(1, 1) specification models in the space of the I(1) variables Y_t, Y_{t-1}, X_t and X_{t-1}; however, cointegration ensures that a (nonunique) linear transformation to stationarity exists. For example, subtract Y_{t-1} from both sides of (8.49) and add and subtract $\beta_0 X_{t-1}$ to the right-hand side to give:

$$\Delta Y_t = \alpha_0 + \beta_0 \Delta X_t + (\beta_0 + \beta_1)X_{t-1} \\ + (\gamma_1 - 1)Y_{t-1} + \varepsilon_t \tag{8.72}$$

Cointegration ensures that $\xi_t = Y_t - \varphi - \varphi_2 X_t$ is stationary, where $\varphi_1 = \alpha_0/(1 - \gamma_1)$ and $\varphi_2 = (\beta_0 + \beta_1)/(1 - \gamma_1)$; hence, the following is also stationary

$$(\gamma_1 - 1)\xi_{t-1} = \alpha_0 + (\beta_0 + \beta_1)X_{t-1} \\ + (\gamma_1 - 1)Y_{t-1} \tag{8.73}$$

Also ΔX_t is stationary; hence the ADL can be rewritten entirely in terms of stationary variables, that is:

$$\Delta Y_t = \beta_0 \Delta X_t + (\gamma_1 - 1)\xi_{t-1} + \varepsilon_t \tag{8.74}$$

This is, of course, just the ECM representation which models in I(0) space; its relevance here is that it shows that there exists a linear transformation of integrated regressors which is stationary and, therefore, the OLS estimators of the coefficients of the integrated regressors in the original model are asymptotically normally distributed – *providing there is cointegration*. Hence, if this condition is satisfied inference in the ADL model with integrated regressors, using standard normal tables, is asymptotically justified. Because of the equivalence of the derived estimators of the long-run coefficients using OLS on the ADL model and instrumental variables estimation of the Bewley transformation, the estimators of the long-run coefficients in the latter case are also asymptotically normally distributed.

8.7.2 Simulation results

The data for the simulations reported in this chapter was generated by the following DGP:

$$Y_t = 5 + 0.15X_t + 0.10X_{t-1}$$
$$+ 0.5Y_{t-1} + \varepsilon_t \tag{8.75}$$

where X_t is a random walk, $X_t = X_{t-1} + w_t$. w_t and ε_t are uncorrelated, normal white noise, that is $w_t \sim N(0, 1)$ and $\varepsilon_t \sim N(0, 1)$. All results are based on 25,000 replications.

The implied long-run relationship is:

$$Y_t = 10 + 0.5X_t + u_t \tag{8.76}$$

In this context (8.76) is the cointegrating regression but, in contrast to the situation in Table 8.4 and section **8.2.3**, u_t is not white noise. In the set-up considered here this latter assumption is invalid because the disturbance term in the cointegrating regression is $u_t = -0.20\Delta X_t - \Delta Y_t + 2\varepsilon_t$.

The (single-equation) estimation methods considered here are:

1. The first stage of the procedure suggested by Engle and Granger (1987); that is, OLS estimation of $Y_t = \varphi_1 + \varphi_2 X_t + u_t$; this is denoted OLSEG.
2. OLS estimation of the Bewley transformation (8.56), denoted OLSB:

$$Y_t = \varphi_1 + \varphi_2 X_t + \beta_1^* \Delta X_t$$
$$+ \gamma_1^* \Delta Y_t + \varepsilon_t^* \tag{8.56 again}$$

3. Instrumental variables estimation of the Bewley transformation, denoted IVB. X_{t-1} is an instrument for ΔX_t and Y_{t-1} is an instru-

ment for ΔY_t; this gives the same result as OLS estimation of the ADL model

$$Y_t = \alpha_0 + \beta_0 X_t + \beta_1 X_{t-1} + \gamma_1 Y_{t-1} + \varepsilon_t$$

which is then solved for the implicit long run,

$$Y_t = \alpha_0/(1 - \gamma_1) + [(\beta_0 + \beta_1)/(1 - \gamma_1)]X_t$$

Estimation is undertaken with three specifications that are described further below. Briefly, 3a is the 'correct specification' and assumes no difference between the DGP and the estimated model; 3b is 'overspecified' and assumes the inclusion of an irrelevant dynamic term; and 3c is 'underspecified' and assumes the exclusion of a relevant dynamic term.

Method 1 is straightforward and requires no further comment at the moment; it is referred to as OLSEG, for OLS estimation of the cointegrating regression in the first stage of the Engle–Granger procedure. The second and third methods, referred to as OLSB and IVB, respectively, relate to estimation of (8.56) first by OLS and then by instrumental variables. If the implications of nonstationarity are put to one side, caution would normally be expressed against OLS estimation of (8.56) because the ΔY_t regressor will be correlated with the disturbance term ε_t. However, when it comes to estimating the coefficients of the long-run relationship between Y_t and X_t this does not matter! The nonstationary properties of Y_t and X_t dominate the stationary properties of ΔX_t and ΔY_t, resulting in consistent estimators of the long-run coefficients. The relevance of this method is to see if it improves upon the Engle–Granger first step by including the omitted dynamics in ΔX_t and ΔY_t, while still estimating by OLS. The problem with methods 1 and 2 is that the 't' statistics on the long-run coefficients do not have the 't' distribution even asymptotically, and hence are not valid for inference; and in method 2, OLSB, the estimators of the coefficients on the stationary variables are asymptotically biased.

To solve both these problems the instrumental variables version of Bewley's procedure is used. The endogeneity of ΔY_t can be solved by using Y_{t-1} as its instrument. This IVB method will give estimators of the long-run coefficients φ_1 and φ_2 which are identical to the derived estimators from the ADL method using OLS, and has the advantage of providing 't' statistics which are valid for inference on both the long-run coefficients and the coefficients on ΔX_t and ΔY_t. It should be emphasised that here IV is just a computationally convenient device equivalent to, but easier to use, than OLS on the dynamic model and then solving for the long run or estimating the implied ECM parameterisation by nonlinear least squares.

8.7.2a   Estimating the coefficients

The results of the simulations are reported in Table 8.13. In addition Figures 8.10 to 8.19 are presented which show the empirical distributions of $\hat{\varphi}_1$ and $\hat{\varphi}_2$ and their 't' statistics,

$(\hat{\varphi}_i - \varphi_i)/\hat{\sigma}(\hat{\varphi}_i)$. In each figure the top panel shows the distribution of the estimated coefficient minus the true value, and the lower panel shows the distribution of the 't' statistic. For each estimation method, or variation, there is one graph for the estimated constant and one for the estimated slope, each shown as the bias in estimating these coefficients.

It is evident, in contrast to the results reported in Table 8.4, that there is a finite sample bias to OLS estimation of the static regression. The relevant row is headed OLSEG. For example, at $T = 50$ the mean of the OLS estimates of $\hat{\varphi}_2$ is 0.436, which is a -12.80% bias (that is $100(0.436 - 0.5)/(0.5)$). At $T = 100$ the mean of the OLS estimates is 0.466 giving a bias of -6.82%; and at $T = 500$ there is a bias of -1.44%. The evidence here suggests a bias reducing as the sample size increases, but which could be important in the kind of samples available to economists.

Method 2, referred to as OLSB in Table 8.13, is estimation of equation (8.56) by OLS including the terms ΔX_t and ΔY_t; a small sample bias is expected because of the correlation between one

Table 8.13   % bias of different estimation methods for long-run coefficients. Long-run equation: $Y_t = 10 + 0.5X_t + u_t$ and $X_t = X_{t-1} + \omega_t$

			$\hat{\varphi}_1$	$\hat{\varphi}_2$
		$T = 50$		
Method 1:	OLSEG	Figures 8.10, 8.11	0.014	−12.800
Method 2:	OLSB	Figures 8.12, 8.13	0.020	−9.200
Method 3a:	IVB: correct specification	Figures 8.14, 8.15	−0.060	−1.112
Method 3b:	IVB: overspecified	Figures 8.16, 8.17	−0.073	−1.516
Method 3c:	IVB: underspecified	Figures 8.18, 8.19	−0.046	−4.240
		$T = 100$		
Method 1:	OLSEG	Figures 8.10, 8.11	−0.070	−6.820
Method 2:	OLSB	Figures 8.12, 8.13	−0.040	−5.000
Method 3a:	IVB: correct specification	Figures 8.14, 8.15	−0.040	−0.160
Method 3b:	IVB: overspecified	Figures 8.16, 8.17	0.002	−0.345
Method 3c:	IVB: underspecified	Figures 8.18, 8.19	−0.001	−1.720
		$T = 500$		
Method 1:	OLSEG	Figures 8.10, 8.11	0.002	−1.448
Method 2:	OLSB	Figures 8.12, 8.13	0.000	−1.200
Method 3a:	IVB: correct specification	Figures 8.14, 8.15	0.009	0.016
Method 3b:	IVB: overspecified	Figures 8.16, 8.17	0.080	0.008
Method 3c:	IVB: underspecified	Figures 8.18, 8.19	0.080	−0.280

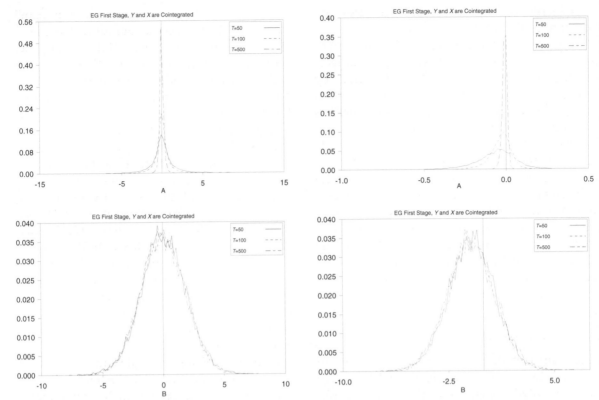

Figure 8.10 A – *Distribution of bias of OLSEG estimator of constant*. B – *Distribution of OLSEG 't' statistic for constant*

Figure 8.11 A – *Distribution of bias of OLSEG estimator of slope*. B – *Distribution of OLSEG 't' statistic for slope*

of the regressors, ΔY_t, and the disturbance term. The results in Table 8.13 show that despite this endogeneity there is an improvement over OLSEG estimation of the cointegrating relationship. For $T = 50$, the bias of $\hat{\varphi}_2$ is now -9.2%, and for $T = 100$, the bias is down to -5%. There is, however, almost no difference at $T = 500$, so the gain in including ΔY_t and ΔX_t is a small sample one.

A further improvement in the finite sample bias is achieved by using Bewley's instrumental variables method of estimation or, equivalently, estimating the ADL by OLS and solving for the long run. This is method 3, denoted IVB for instrumental variables estimation using Bewley's specification, in Table 8.13. The percentage bias for $\hat{\varphi}_2$ for the different sample sizes is now

-1.11% for $T = 50$, -0.16% for $T = 100$ and 0.016 for $T = 500$. Thus, the bias is slight for $T = 50$ and negligible for even the moderately sized sample of 100. This method shows the smallest bias for each of the sample sizes, and the reduction in the bias of estimating φ_2 is, in this example, quite substantial, especially compared to the often used first method, OLSEG. The evidence from this simulation suggests that using all the information in the dynamic model leads to an improvement in estimation of the cointegrating relationship.

Although IVB does very well in this set-up and substantially better than the simpler method of OLSEG, there are other considerations that might lead to use of the latter method. IVB does well here because the estimating equation and

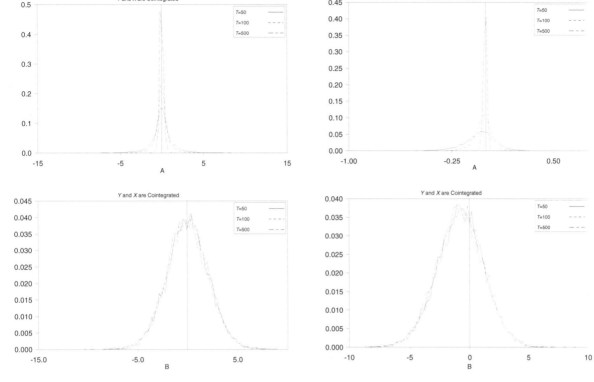

Figure 8.12 **A – *Distribution of bias of OLSB estimator of constant*. B – *Distribution of OLSB 't' statistic for constant***

Figure 8.13 **A – *Distribution of bias of OLSB estimator of slope*. B – *Distribution of OLSB 't' statistic for slope***

the data generating process coincide. In practice this is knowledge that we will not generally have. We are unlikely to be sure that the equation we estimate coincides with the DGP, in which case the effects of the misspecification may carry through to estimation of the long-run coefficients.

There are two kinds of error that can be committed in specifying the estimating equation. Dynamics may be included which are not present in the DGP; an example here would be if, say, Y_{t-2} was included in the estimating equation. Alternatively dynamics may be omitted which are present in the DGP, as, for example, in this case if X_{t-1} was omitted from the regression. The first is an error of overspecification and the second an error of underspecification.

In both cases OLS estimation of the cointegrating regression, OLSEG, is robust to such misspecification as it does not depend on the dynamics of equation. This may help to explain why OLS estimation of the cointegrating relationship is still a frequently used single-equation technique.

In the overspecified case, an irrelevant dynamic term is included and the problem that arises is in picking up this irrelevance in finite samples. In the underspecified case, a dynamic term is incorrectly omitted from the estimating equation, and we might anticipate that the OLS estimator of φ_2 will exhibit a bias on the grounds that removing X_{t-1} from the equation also removes β_1 and, as $\varphi_2 = (\beta_0 + \beta_1)/(1 - \gamma_1)$, the derived estimator of φ_2 will be biased. However,

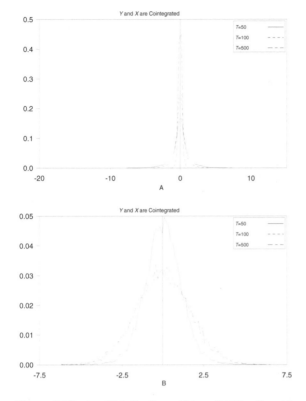

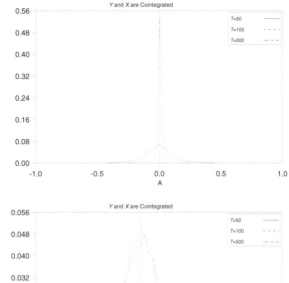

Figure 8.14 A – *Distribution of bias of IVB estimator of constant. B – Distribution of IVB 't' statistic for constant*

Figure 8.15 A – *Distribution of bias of IVB estimator of slope. B – Distribution of IVB 't' statistic for slope*

note that $X_t = X_{t-1} + \omega_t$ so $X_{t-1} = X_t - \omega_t$ and substituting for X_{t-1} in (8.49) we have:

$$Y_t = \alpha_0 + \beta_0 X_t + \beta_1(X_t - \omega_t)$$
$$+ \gamma_1 Y_{t-1} + \varepsilon_t \qquad (8.77a)$$
$$= \alpha_0 + (\beta_0 + \beta_1)X_t + \gamma_1 Y_{t-1}$$
$$+ \varepsilon_t - \beta_1 \omega_t \qquad (8.77b)$$

Thus, OLS estimation of the coefficient on X_t will now give an estimate of $(\beta_0 + \beta_1)$ not just β_0; therefore, the estimated coefficient on X_t divided by 1 minus the estimated coefficient on Y_{t-1} still provides a consistent estimator of φ_2. There will, however, be a bias in this estimator which arises from the correlation between X_t and the composite disturbance term $v_t = \varepsilon_t - \beta_1 \omega_t$.

To illustrate the issues in an empirical way we summarise some of the results from estimating using IVB (equivalently OLS on the ADL and solving for the long run) when (i) Y_{t-2} is erroneously included in the estimating equation and (ii) X_{t-1} is incorrectly excluded from the estimated equation. These results are reported as rows 3b and 3c, respectively, in Table 8.13. In both cases the DGP is as before – see equation (8.75). We concentrate on the results of estimating φ_2 as the bias in estimating φ_1 is negligible at all sample sizes considered here. For $T = 50$ the bias is -1.52% for the overspecification and -4.24% for underspecification. While slightly worse than when the ADL model is correctly specified there is still a substantial improvement over OLSEG. The picture is similar for $T = 100$ where the bias is -0.34% for the

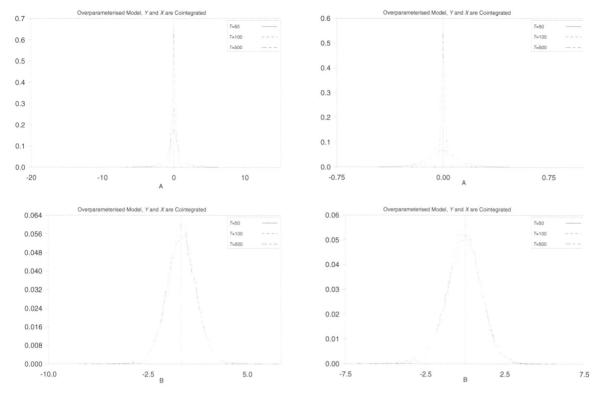

Figure 8.16 A – *Distribution of bias of IVB estimator of constant.* B – *Distribution of IVB 't' statistic for constant*

Figure 8.17 A – *Distribution of bias of IVB estimator of slope.* B – *Distribution of IVB 't' statistic for slope*

overspecification and −1.72% for the under-specification; at $T = 500$ there is a small negative bias of −0.28% for the underspecification and no bias for the overspecification. In all cases including an irrelevant variable results in a smaller bias than omitting a relevant variable.

Because of the limited nature of this experiment we can only draw tentative conclusions. However, it does seem warranted to suggest that estimating the long run from the ADL model is a serious alternative to the first stage of the widely used Engle–Granger procedure. The errors of overspecification, that is including irrelevant variables, are less serious, as far as bias is concerned, than the errors of underspecification. It would, therefore, seem wise to start with a potentially profligate ADL, since even with moderate sample sizes the irrelevant

variables have a limited impact on the finite sample bias of the estimate of the long run. This is another argument for adopting 'good' practice econometrics, in the sense of ensuring that the empirical ADL model passes tests for no misspecification – in particular no serial correlation, which could be proxying omitted lagged variables. Once the long run has been estimated, either by IVB or derived from the ADL model, it can be assessed for stationarity in the same way that the residuals from the first stage of the Engle–Granger procedure are used; for example, by using the DF procedure, the 't' statistic, t_{ecm}, on the error correction term or Boswijk's (1994) Wald test.

The first stage of the Engle–Granger procedure has the merit of simplicity, since all it requires, having established the order of integration of the

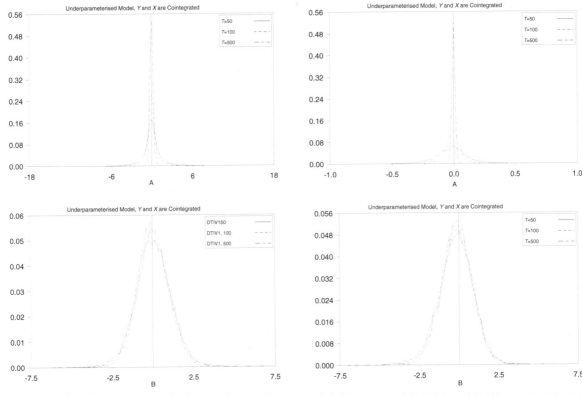

Figure 8.18   A – *Distribution of bias of IVB estimator of constant*. B – *Distribution of IVB 't' statistic for constant*

Figure 8.19   A – *Distribution of bias of IVB estimator of slope*. B – *Distribution of IVB 't' statistic for slope*

candidate variables, is a simple 'levels' regression and an assessment of whether the residuals are consistent with an I(1) or an I(0) process. If this test is passed it is then sensible to proceed to the second stage of incorporating the estimated disequilibrium in a dynamic error correction model. In a given economic context there may be some doubt over which variables should be included in the cointegrating regression, but such doubt is easily dealt with in the first stage of the EG procedure by estimating different levels regressions. The EG approach is economical and easily allows some experimentation with different candidate variables without building a complete dynamic model. Only when a cointegrating regression is found will it be necessary to estimate a dynamic model.

8.7.2b   Distribution of the 't' statistics

Another aspect on which the simulations are informative is the empirical distribution of the 't' statistics, especially that on $\hat{\varphi}_2$ and those on the dynamic terms ΔX_t and ΔY_t in the IVB specification. Using the 10% two-sided critical values from the 't' distribution, for example -1.6755 and $+1.6755$ for $T = 50$ the % of times the calculated 't' statistic fell outside this region (called the rejection region) was recorded. This empirical proportion should be close to the nominal size of 10%, and be equally distributed on the negative and positive side of the mean if the test statistic has a 't' distribution. (A further comparison with variations on the DGP is undertaken in Chapter 9, see especially section **9.5.1** and Table 9.3.)

The results are summarised in Table 8.14 where we have concentrated on the OLSEG and IVB (correct specification) estimators. The empirical distributions of the 't' statistics on $\hat{\varphi}_2$ are illustrated graphically for all methods in Figures 8.10 to 8.15. The first point to note confirms the prior theoretical view that the 't' statistic on $\hat{\varphi}_2$ using OLSEG does not have the 't' distribution – see, for example, Durlauf and

Table 8.14 *Proportion of times the 't' statistic falls in the rejection region using a two-sided nominal 10% size ($X_t \sim I(1)$)*

	$\hat{\varphi}_1$	$\hat{\varphi}_2$	ΔX_t	ΔY_t
df = 50				
OLSEG	10.009	0.437	n.a.	n.a.
't'% − ve	18.365	30.890	n.a.	n.a.
't'% + ve	18.650	6.115	n.a.	n.a.
IVB	10.008	0.495	−0.220	−0.845
't'% − ve	6.950	8.325	6.260	0
't'% + ve	7.095	5.735	1.775	21.370
df = 100				
OLSEG	9.996	0.466	n.a.	n.a.
't'% − ve	18.260	31.580	n.a.	n.a.
't'% + ve	18.93	6.525	n.a.	n.a.
IVB	10.006	0.499	−0.213	−0.917
't'% − ve	6.115	6.625	6.430	0.165
't'% + ve	6.190	5.435	2.615	16.525
df = 500				
OLSEG	9.998	0.493	n.a.	n.a.
't'% − ve	18.225	31.985	n.a.	n.a.
't'% + ve	17.765	7.050	n.a.	n.a.
IVB	9.999	0.500	−0.203	−0.983
't'% − ve	5.485	5.455	6.135	2.115
't'% + ve	5.135	5.065	4.115	9.460

Notes: Table entries are the estimated means of the coefficients over the simulation; numbers in the second and third lines of each set are the percentage of times that the associated 't' statistic fell outside the range given by $-t_{0.05}(df)$ and $+t_{0}.05(df)$, respectively; n.a. indicates not applicable; DGP for X_t is $X_t = \phi_1 X_{t-1} + \omega_t$ and DGP for Y_t is $Y_t = 5 + 0.15 X_t + 0.1 X_{t-1} + 0.5 Y_{t-1} + \varepsilon_t$, or in Bewley form $Y_t = 10 + 0.5 X_t - 0.2\Delta X_t + \Delta Y_t + 2\varepsilon_t$; ε_t and ω_t are uncorrelated, normal white noise with zero mean and unit variance. A test statistic is oversized if the table entry is greater than 5% and undersized if it is less than 5%. Table entries extracted from Chapter 9, Table 9.3.

Phillips (1988). Inference should not, therefore, be based on this standard test statistic when the underlying DGP is dynamic. Second, the 't' statistic on $\hat{\varphi}_2$ using IVB is oversized for $T = 50$ and $T = 100$, at about 14% for the former and 12% for the latter. Hence, if the true value of φ_2 is zero, carrying out a 10% two-sided test using the critical values from the 't' distribution would too often lead to rejection of the null hypothesis; the critical values should be slightly larger to negate the oversizing. At $T = 500$, when the 't' and normal distributions coincide, the empirical size of 10.520% is close to the nominal size of 10%. Of course, it is not just a matter of whether the overall size is close to the nominal size in total that is of interest, we also need to know whether there is approximately 5% in each side of the test. The slight negative bias in the IVB estimator of $\hat{\varphi}_2$ – see Table 8.13 – implies that oversizing is coming from the negative side; for example, for $T = 100$, 6.625% for 't' − ve, compared to 5.435% for 't' + ve.

In summary, the simulation evidence confirms that the distribution of the 't' statistic on $\hat{\varphi}_2$ using IVB is asymptotically normal; however, in finite samples the null hypothesis would be rejected too often using critical values from the 't' distribution. (Other results, not reported in the table, showed that overspecification led to slightly greater oversizing, whereas underspecification tends to correct the oversizing).

Using IVB there is a distinction between the 't' statistics on the coefficients of ΔX_t and ΔY_t. Consider the former first. Overall, the 't' test is slightly undersized at 8.035% for $T = 50$ and 9.045% for $T = 100$, but almost exactly sized at 10.25% for $T = 500$. However, these totals hide the asymmetry on the negative and positive sides. There is oversizing for 't'% − ve and undersizing for 't'% + ve, for example at $T = 100$, 6.430% and 2.615%, respectively.

We now consider the 't' statistic on the coefficient on ΔY_t. This is noticeably oversized at 21.370%, all on the positive side, for $T = 50$ and 16.69%, mostly on the positive side, for $T = 100$. Although at $T = 500$ the empirical size of 11.575% is getting close to the nominal size of 10%, this is still worrying because most of this (9.46%) is on the positive side. The oversizing in the smaller but quite reasonable sample sizes from the perspective of what is available to economists is worrying. Translating these results back to the ADL version of the model, these results follow because there is a negative finite sample bias in estimating the coefficient on Y_{t-1}, which is only slowly removed as the sample size increases, resulting in the 't' statistic being knocked 'off-centre'. A review question considers the bias and distribution of the 't' statistics further.

Overspecification of the dynamics alters the detail rather than the substance of these conclusions. The reader might like to note that the results for OLSB (not reported in Table 8.14) are simple to summarise since neither 't' statistic, on the coefficients of the dynamic variables ΔX_t and ΔY_t, is normally distributed in finite samples or asymptotically.

8.8　Concluding remarks

The OLS estimation method and hypothesis testing with use of critical values obtained from the 't' distributions are of central importance in applied econometrics. It is, therefore, vital to know when these methods can be applied and when they should not be applied. The standard textbook model assumes that the regressors are deterministic variables ('fixed in repeated samples') or if stochastic that they are stationary. Two further assumptions usually made are relevant here: (i) the disturbance terms are serially uncorrelated; and (ii) the disturbance terms are uncorrelated with the regressors. If both assumptions are valid then OLS is consistent – indeed it is unbiased – and the 't' and F distributions are valid for inference (provided also there is no heteroscedasticity). If (i) does not hold, and the serial correlation does not arise from misspecification of the model, then OLS is consistent but the usual 't' and F distributions

should not be used. If the disturbance terms are correlated with the regressors, as arises in simultaneous equation models and errors in variable models, OLS is not consistent and the 't' and F distributions do not apply. If the regressors are stationary random variables these results continue to hold provided neither assumptions (i) nor (ii) are invalid.

Turning to the case where some (or all) of the variables in the regression model are nonstationary – the situation most likely to occur for much economic data – the first distinction to be made is whether there is a cointegrating relationship among the variables. If there is not, the OLS estimators (and R^2) converge to random variables and consistency is not an appropriate concept in this case. As far as the estimators are concerned the results in Table 8.5 are of interest. They show, for example, that the distribution of $\hat{\beta}_2$ does not become more concentrated as the sample size increases. The standard deviation of the distribution is 0.632 for $T = 50$, 0.628 for $T = 100$ and 0.630 for $T = 500$; however, the mean is not significantly different from zero in all three cases.

Distinguishing between a cointegrating regression and a spurious regression with I(1) variables is important for the results on estimation and inference. In a spurious regression there is no relation between Y_t and X_t but it appears from OLS estimation and inference using the theoretical 't' distribution that there is a relation with significant coefficients. When $T = 500$ we found that using standard critical values for a two-sided test at the 10% significance level, with Y_t and X_t unrelated random walks, led to rejection of the null hypothesis of no relation in 91.132% of the cases!

If there is no cointegrating relationship the usual 't' and F distributions do not apply. Indeed we have shown that application of critical values from the conventional 't' distribution is very misleading, suggesting there is a relationship between the variables when there is not. For $T = 50$ the true critical values were underestimated by a factor of about 5. However, as shown in Table 8.5, this factor of under-estimation is not constant but varies positively with the sample size.

The remaining case is where there is a cointegrating relationship among the nonstationary variables. In addition to the nonstationary variables there may also be stationary variables and it may be possible to take linear combinations of the nonstationary variables which are stationary. One of the nonstationary variables is designated as the dependent variable in an OLS regression. The OLS estimators of the regression coefficients are consistent even if one or both of assumptions (i) and (ii) do not hold. This is in contrast to the case where, in the standard textbook model, the regressors are deterministic or stationary random variables. In this sense it is an advantage to have a regression with nonstationary variables provided these latter cointegrate. In general though the usual 't' and F distributions will not apply. If, however, assumptions (i) and (ii) remain valid as, for example in the illustration used in Table 8.4, the 't' (and F) distribution(s) continue to provide a good approximation even in relatively small samples. It should, however, be emphasised that this is a special case; in a more realistic situation the DGP for Y_t will be dynamic and OLS estimation ignoring the dynamic terms has a cost in terms of rendering invalid the usual 't' statistics.

In the dynamic model results due to SSW (1990) show that what is necessary for inference using standard 't' and F tables is that there exists a linear transformation of integrated regressors which is stationary. In that case the OLS estimators of the parameters in the transformed model are asymptotically normally distributed. It is not necessary to carry out the transformation because the original estimators will also be asymptotically normally distributed. Cointegration ensures that there is a linear transformation of integrated variables which is stationary.

The concept of cointegration provides a way of avoiding the misleading inference associated with a spurious regression. If Y_t and X_t are random walks and cointegrate then the regression of Y_t on X_t or X_t on Y_t is not a spurious regression. A necessary condition in building an empirical model with I(1) variables is, therefore, that of cointegration. A widely used test of cointegration due to Engle and Granger (1987) is actually set up with the null hypothesis that Y_t and X_t do not cointegrate; rejection of the null hypothesis is then desirable to avoid spurious regressions. The residuals from the EG first-stage estimation of a static regression are used in a Dickey–Fuller regression but, because the residuals are estimated, the critical values are not the same as for unit root testing of a single series. MacKinnon (1991) has provided a way of calculating the critical values for any sample size. There are many other tests for cointegration since, in principle, any of the tests for a unit root can be adapted to test for noncointegration. One test derived from the connection between cointegration and the existence of an error correction model – Granger's representation theorem – is the 't' test on the error correction term in an ECM. The same link also suggests a simple modification of the DF or ADF test, denoted here the MDF/MADF test.

When applying standard unit root tests and tests for noncointegration it is important to combine these with a graphical analysis of the data. The latter may well reveal that the properties of the time series are not uniform throughout the sample, and 'blind' application of tests for unit roots or noncointegration could be potentially misleading. There may well be structural breaks, which should be taken into account.

The chapter concludes with a simulation study designed to emphasise some key conclusions about the use, in particular, of OLS estimation of a static levels regression – designated the OLSEG estimator – compared to estimation of a dynamic model. While OLSEG delivers a super-consistent estimator this can be potentially misleading if the estimator starts with a large bias in small samples. Including the omitted dynamic terms does have benefits in finite samples: while the I(0) terms are not important asymptotically they are important in the kind of samples typically available to economists. This reinforces the conclusions of Inder (1993) and Banerjee *et al.* (1993). A simple transformation of the ADL model, known as the Bewley transformation, allows asymptotically valid inference using the '*t*' statistic on the long-run coefficient(s).

However, the simulations served to show, at least for one set of design parameters, that the asymptotic results are only a guide to what happens in finite samples. For example, with $T = 50$ the empirical size of the '*t*' statistic on $\hat{\varphi}_2$ when estimated by IVB, or an equivalent alternative, was about 14% for a 10% nominal size. Further, the slow convergence of consistent estimators, especially when estimating the coefficient on the lagged dependent variable in the ADL model (equivalently the coefficient on ΔY_t in the IVB specification) means that the '*t*' statistic is still off-centre for quite large sample sizes.

The following chapter takes up an important issue not addressed in this chapter. In particular we have assumed throughout that we can concentrate on just the equation for Y_t and that there is no loss in estimation or inference in doing this. Chapter 9 starts the move away from this assumption, a move which is continued in Chapters 14 and 15.

Review

1. A distinguishing feature of regression analysis concerns the time series properties of the dependent variable and the regressors.
2. This chapter has examined the finite sample distribution of the OLS estimator and its corresponding '*t*' statistic in the bivariate regression model where three cases were distinguished.
   (i) X_t is fixed in repeated samples;
   (ii) Y_t and X_t are stationary, stochastic variables;
   (iii) Y_t and X_t are nonstationary, stochastic variables.

3. A Monte Carlo, or simulation, experiment was set up with 25,000 replications for each case of interest. When X_t is 'fixed in repeated samples', the OLS estimators in the regression model are unbiased irrespective of the sample size.
4. When X_t is stochastic but white noise, and so stationary, there is a negligible bias in the OLS estimators for small and large samples.
5. When X_t is serially correlated with $X_t = 0.99X_{t-1} + \omega_t$, with ω_t white noise, the OLS estimators are (empirically) unbiased; when the sample size is increased the distribution of the OLS estimators becomes more concentrated on the population values.
6. When Y_t and X_t are uncorrelated random walks the OLS estimators are still (virtually) unbiased, but the distribution of the corresponding '*t*' statistic is no longer that of the theoretical '*t*' distribution. Using critical values from the theoretical '*t*' distribution when Y_t and X_t are unrelated random walks will, therefore, be very misleading.
7. Even if Y_t and X_t are unrelated random walks, the R^2 from a regression of Y_t on X_t (or X_t on Y_t) is likely to be nonzero. We found that there was a 10% chance of exceeding 0.6 even if Y_t and X_t were unrelated.
8. These ideas gave rise to the possibility of a spurious regression: that is one in which the estimated coefficients were apparently significant and the R^2 was greater than zero even though Y_t and X_t were unrelated.
9. The concept of cointegration helps to distinguish between genuine and spurious regressions. If Y_t and X_t cointegrate the regression is not spurious.
10. A test for cointegration – or more precisely noncointegration – due to Engle and Granger (1987) – is based on the Dickey–Fuller test statistic using the residuals from a first-stage 'levels' regression. Large negative values of the test statistic lead to rejection of the null hypothesis of noncointegration.

11. An alternative test statistic is the 't' statistic on the error correction term in an error correction model.
12. A simple modification of the DF/ADF test statistics avoids the (common factor) restrictions implicit in the standard DF/ADF tests. Critical values were obtained by simulation.
13. Granger's representation theorem provides a link between cointegration and the existence of an error correction model.
14. There are several alternative ways of representing the information in an ECM. The ECM can be seen as a transformation of an ADL model, and the ADL model can be transformed using the Bewley transformation to isolate the long-run coefficients.
15. A second set of simulations illustrated some of the key findings about the finite sample properties of two leading single-equation estimators with I(1) variables in a dynamic regression.
16. While the OLSEG estimator is superconsistent, with or without dynamics in the generating equation, this is of little comfort if it starts with a substantial small sample bias.
17. Confirming the results in Inder (1993) and Banerjee *et al.* (1993) we found that it was important to include the dynamic terms in obtaining an estimator of the long-run coefficients. In small samples, for example $T = 50$, $T = 100$, there were substantial reductions in bias in using an estimator based on the ADL model.
18. The omitted dynamics in a static levels regression are effectively captured in the residuals of cointegrating regression, generally rendering inference using standard normal tables invalid – even asymptotically.
19. The distribution of the OLS estimators of the coefficients in the ADL model is established using results due to Sims, Stock and Watson (1990):
    (i) if there is a *linear* transformation of integrated regressors which is stationary, then the OLS estimators of the parameters in the transformed model are asymptotically normally distributed;
    (ii) since the transformation is linear, which preserves the distribution, the original estimators are also asymptotically normally distributed.
20. The OLSEG procedure could have value as an initial diagnostic tool, especially if used with the modified DF/ADF test statistics. Given a set of candidate cointegrating variables it is simple to run some initial regressions to see if there is a 'suggestion' of cointegration and if so go on to the next stage of estimating a dynamic model.

Review questions

1. Standard textbooks often refer to a linear regression model in which the regressors are 'fixed in repeated samples'. What is meant by this term? Can you give some examples where this would be a reasonable assumption?
2. Refer to Table 8.1 and compare the simulated distributions for 't'$(\hat{\beta}_2)$ with the theoretical 't' distribution. For $T = 100$, what is the interquartile range (that is the middle 50%) of the simulated distribution of (i) $\hat{\beta}_2$ and (ii) 't'$(\hat{\beta}_2)$? What are the critical values of the 't'$(\hat{\beta}_2)$ distribution which cut off 5% in each tail?
3. Refer to Table 8.2 and comment on what is happening to the distributions of $\hat{\beta}_1$ and $\hat{\beta}_2$ as the sample size increases.
4. Refer to Tables 8.2 and 8.3 and compare the concentration of the distributions of $\hat{\beta}_1$ and $\hat{\beta}_2$, for like sample sizes, as the sample size increases. What do you conclude from this comparison?
5. (i) Refer to Table 8.4 and, as with question 4 above, comment on the distribution of $\hat{\beta}_1$ and $\hat{\beta}_2$ as the sample size increases; and compare the distributions of $\hat{\beta}_1$ and $\hat{\beta}_2$ in this case with those in Tables 8.2 and 8.3.

(ii) Compare the percentiles of the distributions of $'t'(\hat{\beta}_1)$ and $'t'(\hat{\beta}_2)$ with those in Table 8.1. What multiple (approximately) relates the percentiles in these two tables.

6. Suppose Y_t and X_t are random walks, are the correct critical values for a 10% two-sided test of the null hypothesis of no relation between the variables, with $T = 50$, ± 8.50 or ± 1.675?

7. Y_t and X_t are I(1) variables.
   (i) A student reports that the R^2 from his regression of Y_t on X_t is 0.6, that is '60% of the variation in the dependent variable is accounted for by the explanatory variable' and, therefore, he asserts that he has found an important determinant of Y_t. Is he right?
   (ii) If there is no relationship between the random walks Y_t and X_t, what is the probability that the R^2 from a regression of Y_t on X_t will exceed 0.7? (Assume $T = 50$.)

8. If Y_t and X_t are each I(1) then, in general, is the linear combination $Y_t - \varphi_2 X_t = \zeta_t$ stationary or nonstationary?

9. Explain why if $Y_t - \varphi_2 X_t = \zeta_t$ is stationary then so is $\kappa(Y_t - \varphi_2 X_t) = \kappa\zeta_t$ for $\kappa \neq 0$.

10. Suppose $\hat{u}_t$ are the residuals from a bivariate regression of Y_t on X_t and you are interested in testing whether Y_t and X_t cointegrate. Explain the testing procedure that uses the residuals $\hat{u}_t$ in an auxiliary regression and tests for a unit root.

11. Why would you not normally include a constant in the auxiliary regression referred to in question 10?

12. In testing for cointegration do you think it is sensible to set up the null hypothesis as that of no cointegration rather than cointegration between the variables? Why is this done?

13. Explain how a 'response surface' is obtained from Monte Carlo replications.

14. Refer to MacKinnon's (1991) table and obtain the 5% and 10% critical values for

$T = 40$ with $N = 4$, for the no trend and with trend case (in both cases a constant is included).

15. Explain how MacKinnon's response surface coefficients can be used to obtain the critical values for the Dickey–Fuller tests for a unit root in a univariate series.

16. When would you include a trend in the cointegrating regression?

17. Consider the simple ECM given by

$$\Delta Y_t = \theta_1 \Delta X_t + \theta_2 (Y_t - X_t)_{-1} + \varepsilon_t$$

   (i) Explain how to carry out the t_{ecm} test.
   (ii) Suppose $\hat{\theta}_2 = -0.1$ with a $'t'$ statistic of -3.0; if $T = 100$ do Y_t and X_t cointegrate?

18. (i) Consider the ECM given by:

$$(1 - \gamma_1 L - \gamma_2 L^2)\Delta Y_t$$
$$= (\phi_{11} + \phi_{12}L)\Delta X_{1t}$$
$$\quad + (\phi_{21} + \phi_{22}L)\Delta X_{2t}$$
$$\quad + \theta_2(Y_t - \varphi_{21}X_{1t} - \varphi_{22}X_{2t})_{-1} + \varepsilon_t$$

Where, for convenience, we have adopted the convention that X_{it} refers to the t–th obervation on variable X_i. Confirm that the test regression for the modified ADF, MADF, for this model is

$$\Rightarrow \Delta\xi_t = \theta_2\xi_{t-1} + \gamma_1\Delta\xi_{t-1} + \gamma_2\Delta\xi_{t-2}$$
$$\quad + \delta_{11}\Delta X_{1t} + \delta_{12}\Delta X_{1t-1}$$
$$\quad + \delta_{13}\Delta X_{1t-2} + \delta_{21}\Delta X_{2t}$$
$$\quad + \delta_{22}\Delta X_{2t-1} + \delta_{23}\Delta X_{2t-2} + \varepsilon_t$$

where:

$$\delta_{11} = (\phi_{11} - \varphi_{21}), \qquad \delta_{21} = (\phi_{21} - \varphi_{22})$$
$$\delta_{12} = (\phi_{12} + \gamma_1\varphi_{21}), \quad \delta_{22} = (\phi_{22} + \gamma_1\varphi_{22})$$
$$\delta_{13} = \gamma_2\varphi_{21}, \qquad\qquad \delta_{23} = \gamma_2\varphi_{22}$$

and $\xi_t = L(Y_t - \varphi_{21}X_{1t} - \varphi_{22}X_{2t})$. (Note the convention here to write X_{2t} rather than X_{t2} in order to facilitate writing the lags; for example X_{2t-1}.)

(ii) Hence confirm that the following restrictions must hold for the standard ADF test to be valid:

$$\phi_{11} = \varphi_{21} \qquad \phi_{21} = \varphi_{21}$$
$$\phi_{12} = -\gamma_1\varphi_{21} \qquad \phi_{22} = -\gamma_1\varphi_{21}$$
$$\gamma_1\varphi_{21} = 0 \qquad \gamma_2\varphi_{22} = 0$$

(iii) Why are restrictions like this called 'common factor' restrictions?

19. Consider the ECM given by:

$$\Delta Y_t = \theta_0 + \theta_1\Delta X_t + \theta_2(Y_t - \varphi_2 X_t)_{-1} + \varepsilon_t$$

(i) Show that this can be rewritten as

$$\Delta Y_t = \theta_0 + \theta_1\Delta X_t + \theta_2 Y_{t-1} - \phi X_{t-1} + \varepsilon_t$$

where $\phi = -\theta_2\varphi_2$. Justify the following.

(ii) If φ_2 is known then the null hypothesis of no cointegration is simply a test on θ_2; if $\theta_2 = 0$, then there is no cointegration.

(iii) When φ_2 is not known the null hypothesis of no cointegration should be formulated as the *joint* hypothesis H_0: $\theta_2 = 0$ and $\varphi_2 = 0$.

(iv) What is the restricted model under the joint null hypothesis?

(v) Suggest a test statistic based on the difference between the residual sum of squares from the restricted and unrestricted models – see Boswijk (1994).

20. Consider the ADL model in the three variables Y_t, X_{1t} and X_{2t}:

$$Y_t = \alpha_0 + \beta_{01}X_{1t} + \beta_{11}X_{1t-1} + \beta_{02}X_{2t}$$
$$+ \beta_{12}X_{2t-1} + \gamma_1 Y_{t-1} + \varepsilon_t$$

(i) Reformulate and interpret this model into an ECM.

(iia) Transform the ADL model using the Bewley transformation.

(iib) Interpret the transformed model.

(iic) Explain how to estimate it using the method of instrumental variables.

21. (i) Show that in the set-up of equations (8.77a) and (8.77b), reproduced below

$$Y_t = \alpha_0 + \beta_0 X_t + \beta_1(X_t - \omega_t)$$
$$+ \gamma_1 Y_{t-1} + \varepsilon_t \qquad (8.77a)$$
$$= \alpha_0 + (\beta_0 + \beta_1)X_t + \gamma_1 Y_{t-1}$$
$$+ \varepsilon_t - \beta_1\omega_t \qquad (8.77b)$$

there is a correlation between X_t and the composite disturbance term $v_t = \varepsilon_t - \beta_1\omega_t$.

(ii) Why is this correlation not important if Y_t and X_t are each I(1) and cointegrated?

22. The DGP of section **8.7** formulated as an ADL(1, 1), that is

$$Y_t = 5 + 0.15X_t + 0.10X_{t-1}$$
$$+ 0.5Y_{t-1} + \varepsilon_t \qquad (8.75)$$

was also estimated during the simulations reported in Tables 8.13 and 8.14. For $T = 100$ and T= 5,000 the simulation results are summarised below.

$T = 100$

true value	$\alpha_0 = 5$	$\beta_1 = 0.15$	$\beta_2 = 0.10$	$\gamma_1 = 0.5$
mean estimate	5.336	0.153	0.113	0.466
%'t' − ve	2.300	3.500	3.500	8.250
%'t' + ve	7.650	5.050	4.950	1.900

$T = 5,000$

true value	$\alpha_0 = 5$	$\beta_1 = 0.15$	$\beta_2 = 0.10$	$\gamma_1 = 0.5$
mean estimate	5.008	0.150	0.100	0.499
%'t' − ve	4.117	4.575	4.808	5.575
%'t' + ve	5.358	4.825	4.850	4.210

Interpret these results.

Appendix

Table A8.1 *MacKinnon's (1991) critical values for cointegration tests*

N	Variant	Size (%)	κ_∞	κ_1	κ_2
		Response surface estimates			
1	No constant or trend	1	−2.5658	−1.960	−10.04
		5	−1.9393	−0.398	0.0
		10	−1.6156	−0.181	0.0
1	Constant, no trend	1	−3.4335	−5.999	−29.25
		5	−2.8621	−2.738	−8.36
		10	−2.5671	−1.438	−4.48
1	Constant and trend	1	−3.9638	−8.353	−47.44
		5	−3.4126	−4.039	−17.83
		10	−3.1279	−2.418	−7.58
2	Constant, no trend	1	−3.9001	−10.534	−30.03
		5	−3.3377	−5.967	−8.98
		10	−3.0462	−4.069	−5.73
2	Constant and trend	1	−4.3266	−15.531	−34.03
		5	−3.7809	−9.421	−15.06
		10	−3.4959	−7.203	−4.01
3	Constant, no trend	1	−4.2981	−13.790	−46.37
		5	−3.7429	−8.352	−13.41
		10	−3.4518	−6.241	−2.79
3	Constant and trend	1	−4.6676	−18.492	−49.35
		5	−4.1193	−12.024	−13.13
		10	−3.8344	−9.188	−4.85
4	Constant, no trend	1	−4.6493	−17.188	−59.20
		5	−4.1000	−10.745	−21.57
		10	−3.8110	−8.317	−5.19
4	Constant and trend	1	−4.9695	−22.504	−50.22
		5	−4.4294	−14.501	−19.54
		10	−4.1474	−11.165	−9.88
5	Constant, no trend	1	−4.9587	−22.140	−37.29
		5	−4.4185	−13.641	−21.16
		10	−4.1327	−10.638	−5.48
5	Constant and trend	1	−5.2497	−26.606	−49.56
		5	−4.7154	−17.432	−16.50
		10	−4.4345	−13.654	−5.77
6	Constant, no trend	1	−5.2400	−26.278	−41.65
		5	−4.7048	−17.120	−11.17
		10	−4.4242	−13.347	0.0
6	Constant and trend	1	−5.5127	−30.735	−52.50
		5	−4.9767	−20.883	−9.05
		10	−4.6999	−16.445	0.0

Source: Reprinted from *Long Run Economic Relationships*, edited by R.F. Engle and C.W.J. Granger (1991), by permission, and copyright © Oxford University Press.

Notes: $N = k + 1$ is the total number of variables; k is the number of regressors excluding the constant. Table entries for $N = 1$ are appropriate for univariate unit root tests *or* cointegration tests with *known* cointegration coefficients. Table entries for $N > 1$ are appropriate for cointegration tests with residuals from a first-stage OLS regression. The table entries are coefficients in the following response surface:

$$C(\alpha, T) = \kappa_\infty + \kappa_1/T + \kappa_2/T^2$$

Where $C(\alpha, T)$ is the one-sided α% critical value for a sample of size T. κ_∞ is the asymptotic critical value which is modified in finite sample by terms that depend upon T^{-1} and T^{-2}. For example, the 5% critical value in a cointegrating regression with $N = 4$, a constant and no trend, is: $C(0.05, 100) = -4.100 - 10.745/100 - 21.57/10000 = -4.209$. A sample value more negative than this, for example -4.3, is evidence against the null hypothesis of no cointegration.

CHAPTER 9

Endogeneity and the fully modified OLS estimator

9.1 Introduction

This chapter links to the preceding one in the following way. The message so far is that whether or not I(1) variables cointegrate is an important aspect of an empirical enquiry. First, motivated by considerations of economic theory cointegration implies an equilibrium relationship among a set of variables. Second, econometric theory tells us that cointegration reduces a set of I(1) variables to stationarity and is essential in determining whether inference can be based on standard normal tables (at least asymptotically). However, there are a number of issues that have yet to be considered and which are of practical importance. The first of these comes under the general heading of endogeneity. The discussion of this topic comes in two parts. In this chapter we maintain the assumption of the last chapter that there is a single cointegrating vector – that is a single equilibrium relationship. The second part of the discussion comes in Chapters 14 and 15 where more than one cointegrating vector is allowed.

Approached from the viewpoint of the theory of stationary variables the existence of just one equilibrium relationship would rule out more than one endogenous variable; in conventional terms the number of equilibrium relationships matches the number of endogenous variables; a simultaneous equation model involves N equations in N endogenous and G exogenous variables, of which there will be $\leq G$ stochastic exogenous variables uncorrelated with the regression 'disturbances'. However, in the context of I(1) variables this paradigm is inappropriate. We might well have one cointegrating vector but N variables that are not (weakly) exogenous for the parameters of interest – which are usually, but not always, the long-run coefficients. This lack of exogeneity comes from between equation links involving the parameters of interest. This idea can be simply illustrated with a bivariate ECM such as the consumption function ECM used in the previous chapter. There it was implicitly assumed that lagged disequilibrium, ξ_{t-1}, only entered the consumption equation; so the consumption error corrected on ξ_{t-1} but income did not. If this is not the case the long-run coefficients which define ξ_t are present in both error correction equations and analysing one only misses information in the other. In addition we assumed that there was not a contemporaneous link between the disturbances in each equation.

The implications of endogeneity are far reaching. It imparts a bias to the OLSEG estimator (which because it is still consistent is termed a second order bias) and, *inter alia*, prevents the associated 't' statistic from having an asymptotically normal distribution centred about the true value. Phillips (1988) and Phillips and Hansen (1990) have shown how the OLSEG estimator can be modified so that it can be used for inference with standard normal tables. Essential to an understanding of endogeneity with I(1) variables is the distinction between the short-run – or conditional – variance matrix and the long-run variance matrix, a distinction that arises because of the essentially dynamic nature of the processes generating the stochastic variables.

The differences among the following variance matrices (throughout variance is shorthand for variance–covariance) are considered in section **9.2.1**: the conditional (or short-run) variance matrix, denoted Φ; the unconditional variance matrix, denoted Ψ; and the long-run variance matrix, denoted Ω. The distinctions are illustrated with some low order MA and AR processes in **9.2.1a** and **9.2.1b** and a decomposition of the long-run variance matrix is given in section **9.2.1c**. The discussion of endogeneity is started in section **9.3** (and continued in Chapters 14 and 15) where contemporaneity and failure of weak exogeneity are distinguished. Section **9.4** outlines the fully modified OLS, FMOLS, estimator due to Phillips and Hansen (1990), which adjusts the OLSEG estimator for bias, section **9.4.1a**, and endogeneity, section **9.4.1b**; a semi-parametric approach to estimating the corrections is described in section **9.4.1c**. Situations where there is an asymptotic equivalence between the FMOLS estimator and estimation of a dynamic single-equation model by OLS are considered in section **9.4.2**, and two applications, to consumption and income, and to the long rate and the short rate, are reported in section **9.4.3**. Simulation findings on whether the asymptotic gains from the FMOLS estimator are realised in finite samples are summarised in section **9.4.4**. A small simulation study is reported in section **9.5**, the idea being to see whether the very different implications of endogeneity for regression models with (clearly) stationary variables and nonstationary variables suggest that nearly integrated variables behave more like the former or the latter. This section also underlines the sensitivity of the simulation results to the magnitude of the coefficient which captures the speed with which disequilibrium is eradicated. Section **9.6** contains some concluding remarks and outlines the plan of the next four chapters. Finally, note that this is a relatively technical chapter and the reader interested in applications might profit from reading Chapters 10 to 13 first, and then returning to this chapter.

9.2 Distinguishing variance matrices

The discussion so far has had little to say about X_t (or more generally the regressors) apart from that, like Y_t, X_t is I(1). This needs to be rectified and the way to do this is to explicitly introduce an equation for X_t together with an appropriate specification of the stochastic links between Y_t and X_t. In a related issue, it is not generally the case that the 't' statistics which result from OLSEG estimation of the static levels regression are valid for inference; so, as yet, it is not possible to test hypotheses of interest, for example that the cointegrating coefficient in the regression of consumption on income is unity. It turns out that these two problems are intimately related, and that understanding the solution to them involves highlighting what is meant by endogeneity and its implications for estimation and inference.

Phillips and Hansen (1990) solved the problem of obtaining valid 't' statistics for the coefficients in the static levels regression which is the basis of OLSEG estimation. In so doing they obtain what is described as a fully modified OLS estimator, which has several desirable properties; in particular it is asymptotically normally distributed with an associated, suitably defined, 't' statistic which has a standard normal distribution asymptotically. The development necessary to understand this estimator provides an interesting and useful tour of what is meant by endogeneity in the context of I(1) cointegrating variables; of fundamental importance in this context is the distinction between the short-run, or conditional, variance and the long-run variance. Hence it is necessary to explain this distinction before obtaining the fully modified estimator, and this is done in section **9.2.1**.

9.2.1 Conditional, unconditional and long-run variance matrices

The purpose of this section is to distinguish the following variance matrices: the conditional variance matrix, also referred to as the contemporaneous or short-run variance matrix; the unconditional variance matrix; and the long-run variance matrix. The term variance matrix is used here as something of a shorthand. Consider two random variables ε_t and ω_t for $t = 1, \ldots, T$, each with zero mean and constant variance, and define the 2×1 vector $u_t = (\varepsilon_t, \omega_t)'$. Then the variance matrix defined by $E\{u_t u_t'\}$ has variances on the diagonals and covariances on the off-diagonals; it is a symmetric matrix. The variance matrix defined by $E\{u_t u_{t+k}'\}$ has the k-period (own) autocovariances, $E\{\varepsilon_t \varepsilon_{t+k}\}$ and $E\{\omega_t \omega_{t+k}\}$ on the diagonals, and the cross-(auto) covariances $E\{\varepsilon_t \omega_{t+k}\}$ and $E\{\omega_t \varepsilon_{t+k}\}$ on the off-diagonals; this is not (necessarily) a symmetric matrix because the first of these is the covariance of ω_t with the k-period *lag* of ε_t (note that assuming stationarity $E\{\varepsilon_t \omega_{t+k}\} = E\{\varepsilon_{t-k} \omega_t\}$) and the second is the covariance of ω_t with the k-period *lead* of ε_t.

We start with a simple example. Suppose the data is generated by

$$Y_t = \varphi_2 X_t + \varepsilon_t \tag{9.1}$$

$$X_t = X_{t-1} + \omega_t \tag{9.2}$$

Initially assume that ε_t and ω_t are uncorrelated white noise with variances σ_ε^2 and σ_ω^2; then the covariance matrix for $u_t = (\varepsilon_t, \omega_t)'$ is

$$\Phi = \begin{bmatrix} \sigma_\varepsilon^2 & 0 \\ 0 & \sigma_\omega^2 \end{bmatrix} \tag{9.3}$$

Although it seems redundant at the moment, write the errors ε_t and ω_t as

$$\varepsilon_t = \varepsilon_t \tag{9.4}$$

$$\omega_t = \omega_t \tag{9.5}$$

This emphasises that there is no structure, either in a correlation between components or temporal dependence within or between components, to the equation errors. There is no distinction between what happens in the short run, referring to the impact effect of a shock, and the long run, referring to the situation when all adjustment has taken place: in this simple structure they are the same. Hence, in this special case, Φ is also the long-run variance matrix.

9.2.1a Autoregressive processes

Now suppose ω_t is generated by the first order autoregressive process

$$\omega_t = \gamma \omega_{t-1} + v_t, \quad |\gamma| < 1 \tag{9.6}$$

where v_t is white noise, with variance σ_v^2, uncorrelated with ε_t; σ_v^2 is the variance of v_t and the variance of ω_t conditional on ω_{t-1}, that is $\text{Var}(\omega_t \mid \omega_{t-1}) = \sigma_v^2$. As we have seen, in Chapter 6, there is a distinction between the short-run – or conditional – variance, σ_v^2, which takes all variables in the function as fixed, and the unconditional variance, σ_ω^2.

The unconditional variance for the AR(1) process is:

$$\text{Var}(\omega_t) = \text{Var}(\gamma \omega_{t-1} + v_t)$$
$$= \gamma^2 \text{Var}(\omega_{t-1}) + \text{Var}(v_t)$$
$$\sigma_\omega^2 = \gamma^2 \sigma_\omega^2 + \sigma_v^2$$

$$\text{using } \text{Var}(\omega_t) = \text{Var}(\omega_{t-1}) \equiv \sigma_\omega^2$$
$$\text{and } \text{Var}(v_t) \equiv \sigma_v^2$$

hence

$$(1 - \gamma^2)\sigma_\omega^2 = \sigma_v^2$$
$$\Rightarrow \qquad \sigma_\omega^2 = \sigma_v^2/(1 - \gamma^2) \tag{9.7}$$

Notice that the unconditional variance takes into account the variance of ω_{t-1}; however, the long-run variance takes into account the implicit dependence of ω_t on *all* past values of ω_t. This could be seen explicitly by repeated back substitution of the lagged term in $w_t = \gamma w_{t-1} + v_t$ as in Chapter 6. However, it is convenient to approach this by first using the lag operator so that $w_t = (1 - \gamma L)^{-1} v_t$ and then the long-run variance is defined as $\text{Var}(w_t \mid L = 1)$, where we are using the trick that $L = 1$ defines the long run in a distributed lag function. In this simple example:

$$\text{Var}(w_t \mid L = 1)$$
$$= ((1 - \gamma L)^{-2} \sigma_v^2 \mid L = 1)$$
$$\text{treating } (1 - \gamma L)^{-1} \text{ as a constant}$$
$$= (1 - \gamma)^{-2} \sigma_v^2 \quad \text{using } L = 1 \tag{9.8}$$

Notice that for the interesting range of γ, that is $0 < \gamma < 1$, then the variance increases as we move from the short-run (that is conditional) variance to the long-run variance and the disparity increases with the dependence of w_t on its past as measured by γ:

$$\sigma_v^2 < \sigma_v^2/(1 - \gamma^2) < \sigma_v^2/(1 - \gamma)^2$$

Assuming that $\Phi = I$, the long-run variance matrix, Ω, for $u_t = (\varepsilon_t, w_t)'$ is now:

$$\Omega = \begin{bmatrix} \sigma_\varepsilon^2 & 0 \\ 0 & \sigma_v^2/(1 - \gamma)^2 \end{bmatrix} \tag{9.9}$$

If, as in the more realistic case, Φ is not diagonal, say

$$\Phi = \begin{bmatrix} \sigma_\varepsilon^2 & \sigma_{\varepsilon v} \\ \sigma_{\varepsilon v} & \sigma_v^2 \end{bmatrix} \tag{9.10}$$

then

$$\Omega = \begin{bmatrix} \sigma_\varepsilon^2 & \sigma_{\varepsilon v}/(1 - \gamma) \\ \sigma_{\varepsilon v}/(1 - \gamma) & \sigma_v^2/(1 - \gamma)^2 \end{bmatrix} \tag{9.11}$$

For an easy way to derive this matrix see (9.16) below.

The extension to allow ε_t to follow an AR process is straightforward. We now have:

$$\varepsilon_t = \gamma_\varepsilon \varepsilon_{t-1} + \zeta_t, \quad |\gamma_\varepsilon| < 1 \tag{9.12a}$$

$$w_t = \gamma_w w_{t-1} + v_t, \quad |\gamma_w| < 1 \tag{9.12b}$$

It is convenient to write this as

$$\begin{pmatrix} \varepsilon_t \\ w_t \end{pmatrix} = \begin{bmatrix} \gamma_\varepsilon & 0 \\ 0 & \gamma_w \end{bmatrix} \begin{pmatrix} \varepsilon_{t-1} \\ w_{t-1} \end{pmatrix} + \begin{pmatrix} \zeta_t \\ v_t \end{pmatrix}$$

Say

$$u_t = A u_{t-1} + \eta_t \tag{9.13}$$

where $u_t = (\varepsilon_t, w_t)'$ and $\eta_t = (\zeta_t, v_t)'$. The conditional variance of u_t is Φ, which is just the variance of η_t. The unconditional variance, Ψ, is:

$$E\{u_t u_t'\} = E\{(A u_{t-1} + \eta_t)(A u_{t-1} + \eta_t)'\}$$
$$= E\{A u_{t-1} u_{t-1}' A'\} + E\{\eta_t \eta_t\}'$$
$$\text{using } E\{u_{t-1} \eta_t'\} = 0$$
$$= A E\{u_{t-1} u_{t-1}'\} A' + \Phi$$

So

$$\Psi = A \Psi A' + \Phi \tag{9.14}$$

To obtain the long-run variance matrix it is convenient to use the lag operator, so that (9.13) is:

$$(I - AL) u_t = \eta_t$$
$$\Rightarrow \quad u_t = (I - AL)^{-1} \eta_t \tag{9.15}$$

and

$$\Omega = E\{u_t u_t' \mid L = 1\}$$
$$= E\{(I - AL)^{-1} \eta_t \eta_t'(I - A'L)^{-1} \mid L = 1\}$$
$$= [(I - AL)^{-1} E\{\eta_t \eta_t'\}(I - A'L)^{-1} \mid L = 1]$$
$$= [(I - AL)^{-1} \Phi (I - A'L)^{-1} \mid L = 1]$$
$$= (I - A)^{-1} \Phi (I - A')^{-1} \tag{9.16}$$

Inter-equation serial correlation, that is correlation between ε_t and w_t, is easily allowed for in this set-up. Continuing the first order AR example we have:

$$\varepsilon_t = \gamma_\varepsilon \varepsilon_{t-1} + \gamma_{\varepsilon w} w_{t-1} + \zeta_t \tag{9.17a}$$

$$w_t = \gamma_w w_{t-1} + \gamma_{w\varepsilon} \varepsilon_{t-1} v_t \tag{9.17b}$$

As a first order system in matrix notation this is

$$\begin{pmatrix} \varepsilon_t \\ w_t \end{pmatrix} = \begin{bmatrix} \gamma_\varepsilon & \gamma_{\varepsilon w} \\ \gamma_{w\varepsilon} & \gamma_w \end{bmatrix} \begin{pmatrix} \varepsilon_{t-1} \\ w_{t-1} \end{pmatrix} + \begin{pmatrix} \zeta_t \\ v_t \end{pmatrix} \tag{9.18}$$

With a suitable reinterpretation of the A matrix the long-run variance is as before.

The next interesting complication is to allow ε_t and w_t to be contemporaneously correlated. The simplest way to do this is to allow ζ_t and v_t to have a nonzero covariance $\sigma_{\zeta v} \neq 0$, so that the short-run conditional covariance matrix is

$$\Phi = \begin{bmatrix} \sigma_\zeta^2 & \sigma_{\zeta v} \\ \sigma_{\zeta v} & \sigma_v^2 \end{bmatrix} \tag{9.19}$$

A numerical example may help to fix ideas. Consider the first order system which has within and between equation serial correlation:

$$\varepsilon_t = 0.2\varepsilon_{t-1} + 0.1w_{t-1} + \zeta_t$$
$$w_t = 0.5\varepsilon_{t-1} + 0.4w_{t-1} + v_t$$

that is

$$u_t = \begin{bmatrix} 0.2 & 0.1 \\ 0.5 & 0.4 \end{bmatrix} u_{t-1} + \eta_t \quad \text{where}$$

$$u_t = (\varepsilon_t, w_t)' \quad \text{and} \quad \eta_t = (\zeta_t, v_t)' \tag{9.20}$$

where ζ_t and v_t have zero means and for convenience have unit variances, and covariance $\sigma_{\zeta v}$. The variances of ε_t and w_t conditional on ε_{t-1} and w_{t-1} are just the variances of ζ_t and v_t, respectively.

The long-run variance matrix is

$$\Omega = (I - A)^{-1} \Phi (I - A')^{-1}$$

For $\Phi = I$, that is $\sigma_{\zeta v} = 0$ and $\sigma_\zeta^2 = \sigma_v^2 = 1$, the calculations are:

$$A = \begin{bmatrix} 0.2 & 0.1 \\ 0.5 & 0.4 \end{bmatrix}$$

$$(I - A)^{-1} = \begin{bmatrix} 1 & 0 \\ 0 & 1 \end{bmatrix} - \begin{bmatrix} 0.2 & 0.1 \\ 0.5 & 0.4 \end{bmatrix} \Big]^{-1}$$

$$= \begin{bmatrix} 0.8 & -0.1 \\ -0.5 & 0.6 \end{bmatrix}^{-1}$$

and $\Omega = \begin{bmatrix} 2.001 & 2.055 \\ 2.055 & 4.813 \end{bmatrix}$

Note that although, in this example, the contemporaneous covariance, $\sigma_{\zeta v}$ is zero, there are nonzero covariances in the long run.

Another example is provided by a nondiagonal Φ.

If $\Phi = \begin{bmatrix} 1 & 0.5 \\ 0.5 & 1 \end{bmatrix}$ then $\Omega = \begin{bmatrix} 2.326 & 3.488 \\ 3.488 & 6.977 \end{bmatrix}$

and the existence of a positive contemporaneous covariance between the equations serves to amplify the long-run variances.

9.2.1b First order moving average process

An alternative specification of the contemporaneous and temporal connections between the stochastic components of (9.1) and (9.2) is to specify a moving average scheme. Now the system is:

$$Y_t = \varphi_2 X_t + \varepsilon_t \tag{9.1 again}$$

$$X_t = X_{t-1} + w_t \tag{9.2 again}$$

$$\varepsilon_t = \zeta_t + \theta_{11}\zeta_{t-1} + \theta_{12}v_{t-1}$$
$$w_t = v_t + \theta_{21}\zeta_{t-1} + \theta_{22}v_{t-1} \tag{9.21}$$

with $\text{Var}(\zeta_t, v_t)' = \Phi$.
In matrix form this is:

$$\begin{pmatrix} \varepsilon_t \\ w_t \end{pmatrix} = \begin{bmatrix} 1 & 0 \\ 0 & 1 \end{bmatrix} \begin{pmatrix} \zeta_t \\ v_1 \end{pmatrix}$$

$$+ \begin{bmatrix} \theta_{11} & \theta_{12} \\ \theta_{21} & \theta_{22} \end{bmatrix} \begin{pmatrix} \zeta_{t-1} \\ v_{t-1} \end{pmatrix} \tag{9.22}$$

which is succinctly written as:

$$u_t = \eta_t + \theta_1 \eta_{t-1}$$
$$= (I + \theta_1 L)\eta_t \tag{9.23}$$

where $u_t = (\varepsilon_t, \omega_t)'$, $\eta_t = (\zeta_t, v_t)'$ and θ_1 is defined by reference to (9.22). The unconditional variance matrix, Ψ, is:

$$
\begin{aligned}
\Psi &= E\{u_t u_t'\} \\
&= E\{(\eta_t + \theta_1 \eta_{t-1})(\eta_t' + \eta_{t-1}' \theta_1')\} \\
&= E\{\eta_t \eta_t'\} + \theta_1 E\{\eta_{t-1} \eta_{t-1}'\} \theta_1' \\
&\quad \text{using } E\{\eta_t \eta_{t-1}'\} = 0 \\
&= \Phi + \theta_1 \Phi \theta_1' \\
&\quad \text{using } E\{\eta_t \eta_t'\} = E\{\eta_{t-1} \eta_{t-1}'\} = \Phi
\end{aligned}
$$

(9.24)

and the long-run variance matrix, Ω, is:

$$
\begin{aligned}
\Omega &= E\{u_t u_t' \mid L = 1\} \\
&= E\{(I + \theta_1 L)\eta_t \eta_t'(I + \theta_1 L)' \mid L = 1\} \\
&= ((I + \theta_1 L)E\{\eta_t \eta_t'\}(I + \theta_1' L) \mid L = 1) \\
&= ((I + \theta_1 L)\Phi(I + \theta_1' L) \mid L = 1) \\
&= (I + \theta_1)\Phi(I + \theta_1') \quad \text{using } L = 1 \\
&= \Psi + \Phi\theta_1' + \theta_1\Phi \quad \text{using } \Psi = \Phi + \theta_1\Phi\theta_1' \\
&= \Psi + \Lambda + \Lambda' \quad \text{defining } \Lambda \equiv \Phi\theta_1' \quad (9.25)
\end{aligned}
$$

Again a numerical example may help to fix ideas. Consider the first order moving average process:

$$
\varepsilon_t = \zeta_t + 0.2\zeta_{t-1} + 0.3v_{t-1}
$$
$$
\omega_t = v_t + 0.1\zeta_{t-1} + 0.4v_{t-1}
$$

That is

$$
\begin{pmatrix} \varepsilon_t \\ \omega_t \end{pmatrix} = \begin{bmatrix} 1 & 0 \\ 0 & 1 \end{bmatrix} \begin{pmatrix} \zeta_t \\ v_t \end{pmatrix}
$$
$$
+ \begin{bmatrix} 0.2 & 0.3 \\ 0.1 & 0.4 \end{bmatrix} \begin{pmatrix} \zeta_{t-1} \\ v_{t-1} \end{pmatrix}
$$

(9.26)

Initially assume that $\Phi = I$, then

$$
\Psi = I + \theta_1 \theta_1' = \begin{bmatrix} 1.13 & 0.14 \\ 0.14 & 1.17 \end{bmatrix}
$$

and

$$
\Omega = (I + \theta_1)(I + \theta_1') = \begin{bmatrix} 1.53 & 0.54 \\ 0.54 & 1.17 \end{bmatrix}
$$

As in the case of an AR(1) process note that although the short-run variance matrix has a zero contemporaneous covariance, the unconditional and long-run covariances are nonzero.

Finally, we give another numerical example with $\Phi \neq I$.

If $\Phi = \begin{bmatrix} 1 & 0.5 \\ 0.5 & 1 \end{bmatrix}$ $\Psi = \begin{bmatrix} 1.19 & 0.67 \\ 0.67 & 1.21 \end{bmatrix}$ and

$$
\Omega = \begin{bmatrix} 1.89 & 1.40 \\ 1.40 & 2.11 \end{bmatrix}
$$

The effect of a nonzero contemporaneous covariance is to amplify the variances and covariances in the long run.

9.2.1c Decomposition of the long-run variance matrix

There is another very useful way of illustrating the decomposition of the long-run variance (matrix) which can be shown simply with the MA(1) process, but also holds more generally. We have already obtained the unconditional variance matrix $E\{u_t u_t'\}$, now consider the first order autocovariance: $E\{u_t u_{t+1}'\}$; in the MA(1) case this is

$$
\begin{aligned}
E\{u_t u_{t+1}'\} &= E\{(\eta_t + \theta_1 \eta_{t-1})(\eta_{t+1}' + \eta_t' \theta_1')\} \\
&= E\{\eta_t \eta_t'\} \theta_1' \\
&= \Phi \theta_1'
\end{aligned}
$$

(9.27)

The second line follows because all terms involving different subscripts have zero expectation; and all higher order autocovariances are zero for the same reason. Thus the serial correlation structure of an MA(1) process is particularly simple, with a cut-off at zero for $E\{u_t u_{t+s}'\}$ when $s > 1$. Now notice that $E\{u_t u_{t+1}'\} = \Lambda = \Phi\theta_1'$ as defined in (9.25), so that the long-run variance matrix is just the sum of the unconditional variance matrix, the first order autocovariance matrix and its transpose. If u_t was an MA(2) process we would need to add in the second order autocovariance matrix and its transpose; this sequence is easily generalised for MA(q) processes. If u_t was generated by an AR(p) process then there is not a cut-off point; the autocovariances die out slowly and, in principle, we would need to allow for an infinite sum of the autocovariance matrices and their transposes, even for $p = 1$.

9.2.2 A general result

We can summarise this discussion with the following general result. The long-run variance matrix can be obtained as follows:

$$\Omega = E\{u_0 u_0'\} + E\{u_0 u_1'\} + E\{u_0 u_2'\} + \cdots$$
$$+ (E\{u_0 u_1'\})' + (E\{u_0 u_2'\})' + \cdots$$

$$= E\{u_0 u_0'\} + \sum_{k=1}^{\infty} E\{u_0 u_k'\}$$

$$+ \sum_{k=1}^{\infty} E\{u_0 u_k'\}' \qquad (9.28a)$$

$$= \Psi + \Lambda + \Lambda' \qquad (9.28b)$$

where $E\{u_0 u_0'\} = \Psi$, $\Lambda = \sum_{k=1}^{\infty} E\{u_0 u_k'\}$, $\Lambda' = \sum_{k=1}^{\infty} E\{u_0 u_k'\}'$; and for future reference define $\Gamma \equiv \Psi + \Lambda$.

The u_t process is assumed to be stationary implying $E\{u_t u_t'\} = E\{u_{t-r} u_{t-r}'\} = \Psi$ for $r \neq 0$, and in particular $E\{u_0 u_0'\} = E\{u_t u_t'\}$, and $E\{u_0 u_k'\} = E\{u_{t-r} u_{t-r+k}'\}$ for arbitrary r and k. It will be useful for later purposes to look at the particular elements of Λ; in our example $u_t = (\varepsilon_t, \omega_t)'$, so $E\{u_t u_{t+k}'\}$ is the following

$$E\left\{ \begin{pmatrix} \varepsilon_t \\ \omega_t \end{pmatrix} (\varepsilon_{t+k}, \omega_{t+k}) \right\}$$

$$= \begin{bmatrix} E\{\varepsilon_t \varepsilon_{t+k}\} & E\{\varepsilon_t \omega_{t+k}\} \\ E\{\omega_t \varepsilon_{t+k}\} & E\{\omega_t \omega_{t+k}\} \end{bmatrix} \qquad (9.29)$$

And Λ is constructed as the sum of these elements. The relevant matrices followed by their elements are given below.

$$\Lambda = \sum_{k=1}^{\infty} E\{u_0 u_k'\} = \sum_{k=1}^{\infty} E\{u_t u_{t+k}'\} \qquad (9.30)$$

$$\begin{bmatrix} \Lambda_{11} & \Lambda_{12} \\ \Lambda_{21} & \Lambda_{22} \end{bmatrix}$$

$$= \begin{bmatrix} \sum_{k=1}^{\infty} E\{\varepsilon_t \varepsilon_{t+k}\} & \sum_{k=1}^{\infty} E\{\varepsilon_t \omega_{t+k}\} \\ \sum_{k=1}^{\infty} E\{\omega_t \varepsilon_{t+k}\} & \sum_{k=1}^{\infty} E\{\omega_t \omega_{t+k}\} \end{bmatrix}$$

$$\Lambda' = \sum_{k=1}^{\infty} E\{u_0 u_k'\}' = \sum_{k=1}^{\infty} E\{u_t u_{t+k}'\}'$$

$$\begin{bmatrix} \Lambda_{11} & \Lambda_{21} \\ \Lambda_{12} & \Lambda_{22} \end{bmatrix}$$

$$= \begin{bmatrix} \sum_{k=1}^{\infty} E\{\varepsilon_t \varepsilon_{t+k}\} & \sum_{k=1}^{\infty} E\{\omega_t \varepsilon_{t+k}\} \\ \sum_{k=1}^{\infty} E\{\varepsilon_t \omega_{t+k}\} & \sum_{k=1}^{\infty} E\{\omega_t \omega_{t+k}\} \end{bmatrix}$$

$$\Gamma = \sum_{k=0}^{\infty} E\{u_0 u_k'\} = \sum_{k=0}^{\infty} E\{u_t u_{t+k}'\} \qquad (9.31)$$

$$\begin{bmatrix} \Gamma_{11} & \Gamma_{12} \\ \Gamma_{21} & \Gamma_{22} \end{bmatrix}$$

$$= \begin{bmatrix} \sum_{k=0}^{\infty} E\{\varepsilon_t \varepsilon_{t+k}\} & \sum_{k=0}^{\infty} E\{\varepsilon_t \omega_{t+k}\} \\ \sum_{k=0}^{\infty} E\{\omega_t \varepsilon_{t+k}\} & \sum_{k=0}^{\infty} E\{\omega_t \omega_{t+k}\} \end{bmatrix}$$

Note that Γ is not a symmetric matrix. The long-run variance matrix is:

$$\Omega = \sum_{k=0}^{\infty} E\{u_0 u_k'\} + \sum_{k=1}^{\infty} E\{u_0 u_k'\}'$$

$$= \sum_{k=0}^{\infty} E\{u_t u_{t+k}'\} + \sum_{k=1}^{\infty} E\{u_t u_{t+k}'\}' \qquad (9.32)$$

$$\begin{bmatrix} \Omega_{11} & \Omega_{12} \\ \Omega_{21} & \Omega_{22} \end{bmatrix}$$

$$= \begin{bmatrix} \sum_{k=0}^{\infty} E\{\varepsilon_t \varepsilon_{t+k}\} + \sum_{k=1}^{\infty} E\{\varepsilon_t \varepsilon_{t+k}\} \\ \sum_{k=0}^{\infty} E\{\omega_t \varepsilon_{t+k}\} + \sum_{k=1}^{\infty} E\{\varepsilon_t \omega_{t+k}\} \end{bmatrix}$$

$$\begin{matrix} \sum_{k=0}^{\infty} E\{\varepsilon_t \omega_{t+k}\} + \sum_{k=1}^{\infty} E\{\omega_t \varepsilon_{t+k}\} \\ \sum_{k=0}^{\infty} E\{\omega_t \omega_{t+k}\} + \sum_{k=1}^{\infty} E\{\omega_t \omega_{t+k}\} \end{matrix}$$

Note that Ω is a symmetric matrix.

9.2.2a MA(1) example

It will be instructive to look at the elements in $E\{u_t u'_{t+1}\}$ for the following MA(1) process:

$$\begin{pmatrix} \varepsilon_t \\ \omega_t \end{pmatrix} = \begin{bmatrix} 1 & 0 \\ 0 & 1 \end{bmatrix} \begin{pmatrix} \zeta_t \\ v_t \end{pmatrix} + \begin{bmatrix} \theta_{11} & 0 \\ \theta_{21} & \theta_{22} \end{bmatrix} \begin{pmatrix} \zeta_{t-1} \\ v_{t-1} \end{pmatrix}$$

Then

$$\Phi = \begin{bmatrix} \sigma_\zeta^2 & \sigma_{\zeta v} \\ \sigma_{\zeta v} & \sigma_v^2 \end{bmatrix} \tag{9.33}$$

and

$$\begin{aligned} E\{\varepsilon_t \varepsilon_{t+1}\} &= E\{(\zeta_t + \theta_{11}\zeta_{t-1})(\zeta_{t+1} + \theta_{11}\zeta_t)\} \\ &= E\{\theta_{11}\zeta_t^2\} \\ &= \theta_{11}\sigma_\zeta^2 \end{aligned} \tag{9.34}$$

$$\begin{aligned} E\{\varepsilon_t \omega_{t+1}\} &= E\{(\zeta_t + \theta_{11}\zeta_{t-1}) \\ &\quad \times (v_{t+1} + \theta_{21}\zeta_t + \theta_{22}v_t)\} \\ &= E\{\theta_{21}\zeta_t\zeta_t + \theta_{22}\zeta_t v_t\} \\ &= \theta_{21}\sigma_\zeta^2 + \theta_{22}\sigma_{\zeta v} \end{aligned} \tag{9.35}$$

$$\begin{aligned} E\{\omega_t \varepsilon_{t+1}\} &= E\{(v_t + \theta_{21}\zeta_{t-1} + \theta_{22}v_{t-1}) \\ &\quad \times (\zeta_{t+1} + \theta_{11}\zeta_t)\} \\ &= E\{\theta_{11}v_t\zeta_t\} \\ &= \theta_{11}\sigma_{\zeta v} \end{aligned} \tag{9.36}$$

$$\begin{aligned} E\{\omega_t \omega_{t+1}\} &= E\{(v_t + \theta_{21}\zeta_{t-1} + \theta_{22}v_{t-1}) \\ &\quad \times (v_{t+1} + \theta_{21}\zeta_t + \theta_{22}v_t)\} \\ &= E\{\theta_{22}v_t^2 + \theta_{21}\zeta_t v_t\} \\ &= \theta_{22}\sigma_v^2 + \theta_{21}\sigma_{\zeta v} \end{aligned} \tag{9.37}$$

In each case the second line follows because all terms with different subscripts have zero expectation. Therefore,

$$\Lambda = \begin{bmatrix} \theta_{11}\sigma_\zeta^2 & \theta_{21}\sigma_\zeta^2 + \theta_{22}\sigma_{\zeta v} \\ \theta_{11}\sigma_{\zeta v} & \theta_{22}\sigma_v^2 + \theta_{21}\sigma_{\zeta v} \end{bmatrix} \tag{9.38}$$

and

$$\Lambda' = \begin{bmatrix} \theta_{11}\sigma_\zeta^2 & \theta_{11}\sigma_{\zeta v} \\ \theta_{21}\sigma_\zeta^2 + \theta_{22}\sigma_{\zeta v} & \theta_{22}\sigma_v^2 + \theta_{21}\sigma_{\zeta v} \end{bmatrix} \tag{9.39}$$

This example is illustrative since for an MA(1) process it is easier to use the result given above that $\Lambda \equiv \Phi\theta'_1$ for the particular specification of θ_1 with $\theta_{12} = 0$.

9.2.2b AR(1) example

We now take an example used earlier involving an AR(1) process for ω_t, which will also be used in a later analysis of the effects of endogeneity; specifically

$$\varepsilon_t = \varepsilon_t$$
$$\omega_t = \gamma\omega_{t-1} + v_t, \quad |\gamma| < 1$$

then $u_t = (\varepsilon_t, \omega_t)'$ and we are interested in the following matrices: Ψ, Λ, Γ and Ω.

$$\Psi \equiv E\{u_0 u'_0) = E\{u_t u'_t)$$
assuming stationarity; that is

$$\Psi = \begin{bmatrix} E\{\varepsilon_t^2\} & E\{\varepsilon_t\omega_t\} \\ E\{\omega_t\varepsilon_t\} & E\{\omega_t^2\} \end{bmatrix}$$

$$= \begin{bmatrix} \sigma_\varepsilon^2 & \sigma_{\varepsilon v} \\ \sigma_{\varepsilon v} & \sigma_v^2/(1-\gamma^2) \end{bmatrix} \tag{9.40}$$

Now consider each element of Γ in turn – see (9.31) – starting with the elements in the first diagonal: $E\{\varepsilon_t\varepsilon_t\} = \sigma_\varepsilon^2$; $\sum_{k=1}^{\infty} E\{\varepsilon_t\varepsilon_{t+k}\} = 0$ because ε_t is not serially correlated so $\Lambda_{11} = 0$ and $\Gamma_{11} = \sigma_\varepsilon^2$. Taking $E\{\varepsilon_t\omega_{t+1}\}$ from the upper diagonal element then

$$E\{\varepsilon_t\omega_{t+1}\} = E\{\varepsilon_t(\gamma\omega_t + \upsilon_{t+1})\}$$
$$= E\{\varepsilon_t(\gamma(\gamma\omega_{t-1} + \upsilon_t) + \upsilon_{t+1})\}$$
$$= \gamma\sigma_{\varepsilon\upsilon} \qquad (9.41)$$

and by a similar argument

$$E\{\varepsilon_t\omega_{t+2}\}$$
$$= E\{\varepsilon_t(\gamma\omega_{t+1} + \upsilon_{t+2})\}$$
$$= E\{\varepsilon_t(\gamma^2(\gamma\omega_{t-1} + \upsilon_t) + \gamma\upsilon_{t+1} + \upsilon_{t+2})\}$$
$$= \gamma^2\sigma_{\varepsilon\upsilon} \qquad (9.42)$$

and

$$E\{\varepsilon_t\omega_{t+k}\} = \gamma^k\sigma_{\varepsilon\upsilon} \qquad (9.43)$$

So ε_t is correlated with leads of ω_t (equivalently ω_t is correlated with lags of ε_t). Hence

$$\Lambda_{12} = \sum_{k=1}^{\infty} E\{\varepsilon_t\omega_{t+k}\}$$
$$= \sigma_{\varepsilon\upsilon}(\gamma + \gamma^2 + \cdots + \gamma^k + \cdots)$$
$$= \sigma_{\varepsilon\upsilon}\left(\frac{1}{1-\gamma} - 1\right)$$
$$= \sigma_{\varepsilon\upsilon}\left(\frac{\gamma}{1-\gamma}\right) \qquad (9.44)$$

and

$$\Gamma_{12} = \sum_{k=0}^{\infty} E\{\varepsilon_t\omega_{t+k}\}$$
$$= \sigma_{\varepsilon\upsilon}(1 + \gamma + \gamma^2 + \cdots + \gamma^k + \cdots)$$
$$= \sigma_{\varepsilon\upsilon}\left(\frac{1}{1-\gamma}\right) \qquad (9.45)$$

Taking $E\{\omega_t\varepsilon_{t+1}\}$ and $E\{\omega_t\varepsilon_{t+2}\}$ as illustrations from the lower off-diagonal element then:

$$E\{\omega_t\varepsilon_{t+1}\} = E\{(\gamma\omega_{t-1} + \upsilon_t)\varepsilon_{t+1}\} = 0$$
$$\text{because } \upsilon_t \text{ is uncorrelated}$$
$$\text{with leads of } \varepsilon_t$$

$$E\{\omega_t\varepsilon_{t+2}\} = E\{(\gamma\omega_{t-1} + \upsilon_t)\varepsilon_{t+2}\} = 0$$
$$\text{because } \upsilon_t \text{ is uncorrelated}$$
$$\text{with leads of } \varepsilon_t$$

and in general $E\{\omega_t\varepsilon_{t+k}\} = 0$ for $k > 0$; so ω_t is uncorrelated with leads of ε_t. Hence $\Lambda_{21} = 0$ and $\Gamma_{21} = \sigma_{\varepsilon\upsilon}$.

Lastly we need the lower diagonal elements. These are easily obtained by substitution. For example,

$$E\{\omega_t\omega_{t+1}\} = E\{\omega_t(\gamma\omega_t + \upsilon_{t+1})\}$$
$$= \gamma E\{\omega_t^2\}$$
$$= \gamma\frac{\sigma_\upsilon^2}{(1-\gamma^2)} \qquad (9.46)$$

Note that the last line uses the result that the unconditional variance of ω_t, σ_ω^2, is just σ_υ^2. Continuing:

$$E\{\omega_t\omega_{t+2}\} = E\{\omega_t(\gamma\omega_{t+1} + \upsilon_{t+1})\}$$
$$= E\{\omega_t(\gamma(\gamma\omega_t + \upsilon_{t+1}) + \upsilon_{t+2})\}$$
$$= \gamma^2 E\{\omega_t^2\}$$
$$= \gamma^2\frac{\sigma_\upsilon^2}{(1-\gamma^2)} \qquad (9.47)$$

and

$$E\{\omega_t\omega_{t+k}\} = \gamma^k\frac{\sigma_\upsilon^2}{(1-\gamma^2)} \qquad (9.48)$$

Hence,

$$\Lambda_{22} = \sum_{k=1}^{\infty} E\{\omega_t\omega_{t+k}\}$$
$$= \frac{\sigma_\upsilon^2}{(1-\gamma^2)}[\gamma + \gamma^2 + \cdots + \gamma^k + \cdots]$$

$$= \frac{\sigma_v^2}{(1-\gamma^2)} \left(\frac{1}{1-\gamma} - 1 \right)$$

$$= \gamma \frac{\sigma_v^2}{(1-\gamma^2)(1-\gamma)} \tag{9.49}$$

and

$$\Gamma_{22} = \Psi_{22} + \Lambda_{22}$$

$$= \sum_{k=0}^{\infty} E\{\omega_t \omega_{t+k}\}$$

$$= \frac{\sigma_v^2}{(1-\gamma^2)} [1 + \gamma + \gamma^2 + \cdots + \gamma^k + \cdots]$$

$$= \frac{\sigma_v^2}{(1-\gamma^2)(1-\gamma)} \tag{9.50}$$

and

$$\Omega_{22} = \Psi_{22} + 2\Lambda_{22}$$

$$= \frac{\sigma_v^2}{(1-\gamma^2)} \left(1 + \frac{2\gamma}{(1-\gamma)} \right)$$

$$= \frac{\sigma_v^2}{(1-\gamma^2)} \left(\frac{(1+\gamma)}{(1-\gamma)} \right)$$

$$= \sigma_v^2 \frac{(1+\gamma)(1-\gamma)}{(1-\gamma^2)(1-\gamma)^2}$$

$$= \sigma_v^2 \frac{1}{(1-\gamma)^2} \tag{9.51}$$

Bringing these various elements together we have:

$$\Lambda = \begin{bmatrix} \Lambda_{11} & \Lambda_{12} \\ \Lambda_{21} & \Lambda_{22} \end{bmatrix}$$

$$= \begin{bmatrix} 0 & \gamma \dfrac{\sigma_{\varepsilon v}}{(1-\gamma)} \\ 0 & \gamma \dfrac{\sigma_{\varepsilon v}}{(1-\gamma^2)(1-\gamma)} \end{bmatrix} \tag{9.52}$$

$$\Lambda' = \begin{bmatrix} \Lambda_{11} & \Lambda_{21} \\ \Lambda_{12} & \Lambda_{22} \end{bmatrix}$$

$$= \begin{bmatrix} 0 & 0 \\ \gamma \dfrac{\sigma_{\varepsilon v}}{(1-\gamma)} & \gamma \dfrac{\sigma_v^2}{(1-\gamma^2)(1-\gamma)} \end{bmatrix} \tag{9.53}$$

$$\Gamma = \begin{bmatrix} \Gamma_{11} & \Gamma_{12} \\ \Gamma_{21} & \Gamma_{22} \end{bmatrix}$$

$$= \begin{bmatrix} \sigma_\varepsilon^2 & \sigma_{\varepsilon v} \dfrac{1}{(1-\gamma)} \\ \sigma_{\varepsilon v} & \sigma_v^2 \dfrac{1}{(1-\gamma^2)(1-\gamma)} \end{bmatrix} \tag{9.54}$$

$$\Omega = \begin{bmatrix} \Omega_{11} & \Omega_{12} \\ \Omega_{21} & \Omega_{22} \end{bmatrix}$$

$$= \begin{bmatrix} \sigma_\varepsilon^2 & \sigma_{\varepsilon v} \dfrac{1}{(1-\gamma)} \\ \sigma_{\varepsilon v} \dfrac{1}{(1-\gamma)} & \sigma_v^2 \dfrac{1}{(1-\gamma^2)} \end{bmatrix} \tag{9.55}$$

If the structure in u_t is known, as assumed in these examples, a consistent estimator of the elements of $E\{u_t u'_{t-1}\}$ could be obtained by first estimating ε_t from (9.1), to obtain OLS residuals, $\hat{\varepsilon}_t$, and ω_t from $\omega_t = \Delta X_t$, and then estimating the moving average process. Alternatively, in the more likely case that the precise parameterisation of u_t is unknown, all that is required are consistent estimators of $E\{u_t u'_t\}$ and $E\{u_t u'_{t+k}\}$ which can be based on $\hat{\varepsilon}_t$, and ω_t, and their lags and leads.

9.3 Endogeneity

In a series of papers Phillips and his co-workers – see especially Park and Phillips (1988), Phillips and Hansen (1990) and Hansen and Phillips (1990) – show that a modified OLSEG estimator is (super)consistent, asymptotically unbiased, asymptotically normally distributed and, provided a modified standard error is used, has an associated 't' statistic which is asymptotically normally distributed permitting inference using standard tables. In contrast, in general, the unmodified OLSEG estimator while superconsistent is not asymptotically unbiased or asymptotically normally distributed.

The development of the fully modified estimator is particularly useful in understanding the effects of endogeneity on estimation and inference. The discussion proceeds by first considering the key concept of endogeneity and then describing the Phillips–Hansen adjustments to the OLSEG estimator.

9.3.1 Preliminaries

The discussion is motivated by example using the following cointegrated system:

$$Y_t = \varphi_2 X_t + \varepsilon_t \qquad (9.1 \text{ again})$$

$$X_t = X_{t-1} + \omega_t \qquad (9.2 \text{ again})$$

with conditional, unconditional and long-run variance matrices for the process $u_t = (\varepsilon_t, \omega_t)$ given by Φ, Ψ and Ω, respectively. For example, for the MA(1) process the variance matrices are given by:

$$\Phi \qquad\qquad \text{conditional} \quad (9.56a)$$

$$\Psi = \Phi + \theta_1 \Phi \theta_1' \qquad \text{unconditional} \quad (9.56b)$$

$$\Omega = \Psi + \Phi\theta_1' + \theta_1\Phi \quad \text{long-run}$$
$$\text{using } \Psi = \Phi + \theta_1\Phi\theta_1' \qquad (9.56c)$$

For reference from the general definition of Γ, note that in this case

$$\Gamma \equiv \Psi + \Phi\theta_1' \qquad (9.57)$$

In this example Ω, the long-run variance matrix, and Γ are 2×2 matrices with elements

$$\Omega = \begin{bmatrix} \omega_{11} & \omega_{21} \\ \omega_{21} & \omega_{22} \end{bmatrix} \quad \Gamma = \begin{bmatrix} \gamma_{11} & \gamma_{12} \\ \gamma_{21} & \gamma_{22} \end{bmatrix} \quad (9.58)$$

We will also need the reduced form of the cointegrated system obtained by substituting for X_t in (9.2) from $X_t = X_{t-1} + \omega_t$; that is

$$Y_t = \varphi_2 X_{t-1} + v_t$$
$$\text{where } v_t = \varepsilon_t + \varphi_2\omega_t \qquad (9.59)$$

$$X_t = X_{t-1} + \omega_t \qquad (9.60)$$

$$g_t \equiv (v_t, \omega_t)'$$

Φ^*, Ψ^* and Ω^* are the corresponding conditional, unconditional and long-run variance matrices for g_t.

This simple system facilitates a discussion of the concept of endogeneity which is based on the references to Phillips' work cited above and also Banerjee *et al.* (1993) and Hendry (1995), and is rather more complex than in the case of stationary variables. Endogeneity here refers to two distinct conceptual issues: simultaneity – or contemporaneity – as suggested by Hendry (*op. cit.*, p. 182); and the failure of weak exogeneity.

Contemporaneity is a useful description when the conditional variance matrix, Φ, is not diagonal: there is a contemporaneous link between ε_t and ω_t which implies that X_t and ε_t are contemporaneously correlated (because ω_t is 'part' of X_t, recall $\omega_t = \Delta X_t$). In the context of stationary variables this would be described as 'simultaneity bias', whereas for I(1) variables it is described as contemporaneity. Weak exogeneity of X_t will be defined more precisely below, for the moment note that the failure of weak exogeneity means that the equation for X_t contains information which should be used in estimating the parameter of interest φ_2. While endogeneity does not affect the consistency of the OLSEG and IVB (or equivalently, for example, OLS on the ADL model) estimators of φ_2, the distribution of the 't' statistic for φ_2 is no longer asymptotically normal.

9.3.1a Contemporaneity

If Φ is nondiagonal and there is no structure in the u_t process the endogeneity arises purely from contemporaneity. In the example this specification is:

$$Y_t = \varphi_2 X_t + \varepsilon_t$$
$$X_t = X_{t-1} + \omega_t$$
$$\varepsilon_t = \varepsilon_t; \quad \omega_t = \omega_t$$
$$u_t = (\varepsilon_t, \omega_t)'$$
$$E\{u_t u_t'\} \equiv \Psi = \Phi; \quad \Omega = \Phi$$

The equations for ε_t and ω_t are obviously redundant but they serve to make the point that there is no structure in the u_t process; in this case the conditional and unconditional variance matrices are equal, that is $\Phi = \Psi$.

9.3.1b Weak exogeneity

An example of the failure of weak exogeneity
Even if Φ is diagonal, so there is no contemporaneity, the serial correlation structure in u_t generates nonzero off-diagonal elements in Ω which may, in turn, induce long-run dependence and so a failure of weak exogeneity. Consider the following specification

$$Y_t = \varphi_2 X_t + \varepsilon_t \qquad (9.1 \text{ again})$$

$$X_t = X_{t-1} + \omega_t \qquad (9.2 \text{ again})$$

$$\varepsilon_t = \zeta_t$$

$$\omega_t = v_t + 0.3\zeta_{t-1}; \quad \eta_t = (\zeta_t, v_t)'; \quad \text{Var}(\eta_t) = \Phi$$

This is a simple example of an MA(1) process.

$$\begin{pmatrix} \varepsilon_t \\ \omega_t \end{pmatrix} = \begin{bmatrix} 1 & 0 \\ 0 & 1 \end{bmatrix} \begin{pmatrix} \zeta_t \\ v_t \end{pmatrix} + \begin{bmatrix} 0.0 & 0.0 \\ 0.3 & 0.0 \end{bmatrix} \begin{pmatrix} \zeta_{t-1} \\ v_{t-1} \end{pmatrix}$$

$$\text{with } \Phi = \begin{bmatrix} \sigma_\zeta^2 & \sigma_{\zeta v} \\ \sigma_{\zeta v} & \sigma_v^2 \end{bmatrix} \qquad (9.61)$$

Substituting for $\varepsilon_t = \zeta_t$ in ω_t using (9.1),

$$v_t + 0.3\varepsilon_{t-1} = v_t + 0.3(Y_{t-1} - \varphi_2 X_{t-1})$$
$$\text{where } \varepsilon_{t-1} = Y_{t-1} - \varphi_2 X_{t-1}$$

then (9.2) can be written:

$$X_t - X_{t-1} = 0.3(Y_{t-1} - \varphi_2 X_{t-1}) + v_t \qquad (9.62)$$

Now it is clear that X_t depends upon the cointegrating combination with cointegrating coefficient φ_2, so X_t cannot be weakly exogenous for φ_2 in (9.1); and this is so whether or not $\text{Var}(\eta_t) = \sigma^2 I$.

Another way of looking at this dependence is to note that ω_t depends upon the history of the innovations ζ_t which, in turn, determine $Y_t - \varphi_2 X_t$, so there is a connection between the equations – see Phillips (1988, p. 356). This example could be developed further. However, it turns out that even if the other MA parameters are nonzero so

$$\begin{pmatrix} \varepsilon_t \\ \omega_t \end{pmatrix} = \begin{bmatrix} 1 & 0 \\ 0 & 1 \end{bmatrix} + \begin{bmatrix} \theta_{11} & \theta_{12} \\ \theta_{21} & \theta_{22} \end{bmatrix} \begin{pmatrix} \zeta_{t-1} \\ v_{t-1} \end{pmatrix} \qquad (9.63)$$

the crucial parameter is θ_{21} because of the link it provides to the first equation. Phillips (*op. cit.*) shows that $\theta_{21} \neq 0$ is responsible for the limiting distribution of $T(\hat{\varphi}_2 - \varphi_2)$ being asymmetric and not centred on zero, which means that inference cannot be based on standard normal tables even asymptotically.

In (9.63) there is an MA structure to the errors ε_t and ω_t; however, similar problems arise if there is an AR structure with a link between ω_t and lagged values of ε_t. Consider the AR(1) process

$$\begin{pmatrix} \varepsilon_t \\ \omega_t \end{pmatrix} = \begin{bmatrix} \rho_{11} & \rho_{12} \\ \rho_{21} & \rho_{22} \end{bmatrix} \begin{pmatrix} \varepsilon_{t-1} \\ \omega_{t-1} \end{pmatrix} + \begin{pmatrix} \zeta_t \\ v_t \end{pmatrix} \qquad (9.64)$$

If $\rho_{21} \neq 0$ there is a link between ω_t and lagged values of ε_t which should be taken into account when estimating and making inferences on φ_2.

Taking the discussion of weak exogeneity further requires the development of the conditional expectation function, a concept familiar from Chapter 4, extended to bivariate normally distributed but correlated variables.

9.3.2 The regression (or conditional expectation) function and weak exogeneity

To understand weak exogeneity further some developments are required involving the conditional distribution using a result given in Chapter 4, see (4.20). Recall that if two variables

Y_t and X_t are jointly normally distributed with parameters $\mu_Y, \mu_X, \sigma_Y^2, \sigma_X^2, \rho_{XY}$, being the means, variances and correlation coefficient, respectively, then the conditional distribution of Y given X is

$$E\{Y_t \mid X_t\} = E\{Y_t\} + \rho_{XY}(\sigma_Y/\sigma_X)$$
$$\times [X_t - E\{X_t\}] \qquad (9.65)$$

The conditional expectation differs from the unconditional mean of Y_t by a term that depends upon the correlation between Y_t and X_t.

We apply this result to the reduced form of the simple cointegrated system:

$$Y_t = \varphi_2 X_t + \varepsilon_t$$
$$X_t = X_{t-1} + \omega_t$$

where ε_t and ω_t are correlated white noise with variance matrix

$$\Phi = \begin{bmatrix} \sigma_\varepsilon^2 & \sigma_{\varepsilon\omega} \\ \sigma_{\varepsilon\omega} & \sigma_\omega^2 \end{bmatrix} \qquad (9.66)$$

Substituting for X_t in (9.1) from (9.2) gives the 'reduced' form of Y_t; that is

$$Y_t = \varphi_2 X_{t-1} + \varepsilon_t + \varphi_2 \omega_t$$
$$= \varphi_2 X_{t-1} + v_t \quad \text{where } v_t = \varepsilon_t + \varphi_2 \omega_t \qquad (9.67)$$

with, as before,

$$X_t = X_{t-1} + \omega_t$$

Define $z_t \equiv (v_t, \omega_t)'$ and $\text{Var}(z_t) \equiv \Xi$; in this case

$$\Xi = \begin{bmatrix} \text{Var}(v_t) & \text{Cov}(v_t, \omega_t) \\ \text{Cov}(v_t, \omega_t) & \text{Var}(\omega_t) \end{bmatrix}$$

$$= \begin{bmatrix} \text{Var}(\varepsilon_t + \varphi_2 \omega_t) & \text{Cov}(\varepsilon_t + \varphi_2 \omega_t, \omega_t) \\ \text{Cov}(\varepsilon_t + \varphi_2 \omega_t, \omega_t) & \text{Var}(\omega_t) \end{bmatrix}$$

$$= \begin{bmatrix} \sigma_\varepsilon^2 + \varphi^2 \sigma_\omega^2 & \sigma_{\varepsilon\omega} + \varphi_2 \sigma_\omega^2 \\ \sigma_{\varepsilon\omega} + \varphi_2 \sigma_\omega^2 & \sigma_\omega^2 \end{bmatrix}$$

say

$$= \begin{bmatrix} \sigma_{11} & \sigma_{12} \\ \sigma_{21} & \sigma_{22} \end{bmatrix} \quad \text{note } \sigma_{22} = \sigma_\omega^2$$

and $\sigma_{12} = \sigma_{21}$

In order to obtain the expectation of Y_t conditional on X_t note the following. The relevant unconditional expectations are $E\{Y_t\} = \varphi_2 X_{t-1}$, because $E\{\varepsilon_t + \varphi_2 \omega_t\} = 0$ and $E\{X_t\} = X_{t-1}$ because $E\{\omega_t\} = 0$. $\sigma_Y^2 = \sigma_{11}$; $\sigma_X^2 = \sigma_{22}$ and $\rho_{XY} = \sigma_{21}/(\sigma_{11}\sigma_{22})^{\frac{1}{2}}$. Using these correspondences:

$$E\{Y_t \mid X_t\} = \varphi_2 X_{t-1} + [\sigma_{21}/(\sigma_{11}\sigma_{22})^{\frac{1}{2}}]$$
$$\times (\sigma_{11}/\sigma_{22})^{\frac{1}{2}}[X_t - X_{t-1}]$$
$$= \varphi_2 X_{t-1} + (\sigma_{21}/\sigma_{22})$$
$$\times [X_t - X_{t-1}] \qquad (9.68)$$

and, therefore, $\varsigma_t \equiv Y_t - E\{Y_t \mid X_t\}$ is an innovation relative to the information in X_t (see Chapter 4). Notice that if $\sigma_{\varepsilon\omega} = 0$ then $(\sigma_{21}/\sigma_{22}) = \varphi_2$, and (9.68) reduces to:

$$E\{Y_t \mid X_t\} = \varphi_2 X_{t-1} + \varphi_2[X_t - X_{t-1}]$$
$$= \varphi_2 X_t \qquad (9.69)$$

This is as anticipated and emphasises that it is the nonzero value of $\sigma_{\varepsilon\omega}$ that is crucial to $E\{Y_t \mid X_t\}$.

Substituting for $E\{Y_t \mid X_t\}$ from (9.68) in the definition of ς_t gives:

$$\varsigma_t \equiv Y_t - E\{Y_t \mid X_t\} \qquad (9.70a)$$
$$= (Y_t - \varphi_2 X_{t-1}) - (\sigma_{21}/\sigma_{22})[X_t - X_{t-1}]$$
$$= Y_t - \varphi_2 X_{t-1} - (\sigma_{21}/\sigma_{22})\omega_t$$
$$\text{using } X_t - X_{t-1} = \omega_t$$
$$= \varepsilon_t + \varphi_2 \omega_t - ((\sigma_{\varepsilon\omega} + \varphi_2 \sigma_\omega^2)/\sigma_\omega^2)\omega_t$$
$$\text{using } \sigma_{22} = \sigma_\omega^2$$
$$\text{and } Y_2 - \varphi_2 X_{t-1} = \varepsilon_t + \varphi_2 \omega_t$$
$$= \varepsilon_t - (\sigma_{\varepsilon\omega}/\sigma_\omega^2)\omega_t \qquad (9.70b)$$

For future reference note that:

$$\begin{aligned}
\text{Var}(\varsigma_t) &= \text{Var}(\varepsilon_t - (\sigma_{\varepsilon\omega}/\sigma_\omega^2)\omega_t) \\
&= \text{Var}(\varepsilon_t) + (\sigma_{\varepsilon\omega}/\sigma_\omega^2)^2 \, \text{Var}(\omega_t) \\
&\quad - 2(\sigma_{\varepsilon\omega}/\sigma_\omega^2) \, \text{Cov}(\varepsilon_t, \omega_t) \\
&= \sigma_\varepsilon^2 + \sigma_{\varepsilon\omega}^2/\sigma_\omega^2 - 2(\sigma_{\varepsilon\omega}^2/\sigma_\omega^2) \\
&= \sigma_\varepsilon^2 - (\sigma_{\varepsilon\omega}^2/\sigma_\omega^2)
\end{aligned} \tag{9.71}$$

and

$$\begin{aligned}
\text{Cov}(\varsigma_t, \omega_t) &= \text{Cov}([\varepsilon_t - (\sigma_{\varepsilon\omega}/\sigma_\omega^2)\omega_t]\omega_t) \\
&= \text{Cov}(\varepsilon_t, \omega_t) - (\sigma_{\varepsilon\omega}/\sigma_\omega^2) \, \text{Var}(\omega_t) \\
&= \sigma_{\varepsilon\omega} - (\sigma_{\varepsilon\omega}/\sigma_\omega^2)\sigma_\omega^2 \\
&= 0
\end{aligned} \tag{9.72}$$

The 'complete' regression model can now be written:

$$Y_t = \varphi_2 X_{t-1} + (\sigma_{21}/\sigma_{22})$$
$$\times [X_t - X_{t-1}] + \varsigma_t \tag{9.73}$$

$$X_t = X_{t-1} + \omega_t \tag{9.74}$$

$$g_t \equiv (\eta_t, \omega_t)'$$

$$\text{Var}(g_t) \equiv \Phi^* = \begin{bmatrix} \sigma_\varepsilon^2 - (\sigma_{\varepsilon\omega}^2/\sigma_\omega^2) & 0 \\ 0 & \sigma_\omega^2 \end{bmatrix} \tag{9.75}$$

For future reference note that by subtracting Y_{t-1} from both sides of (9.73) the regression equation can be put in an error correction form:

$$\Delta Y_t = -(Y_{t-1} - \varphi_2 X_{t-1})$$
$$+ (\sigma_{21}/\sigma_{22})[X_t - X_{t-1}] + \varsigma_t \tag{9.76}$$

The key question for the purposes of defining weak exogeneity of X_t for the parameter of interest φ_2 is whether the regression function (9.73), or equivalently (9.76), defined by the conditional expectation of Y_t, can be analysed without loss just by reference to the regression function (9.73) alone. For this purpose we will need to look at the structure of the variance matrices for $g_t = (\varsigma_t, \omega_t)'$. Since ς_t comprises the white noise components ε_t and ω_t, which are without temporal dependence, the short-run and long-run variance matrices will be the same;

further, they are diagonal so there is no information loss in basing estimation and inference on (9.73) alone. *The diagonality of the long-run variance matrix of g_t means that X_t is weakly exogenous for the parameter of interest φ_2.*

Failure of weak exogeneity occurs if the long-run variance matrix of g_t is not diagonal. We have already seen in section **9.3.1b** an example of the failure of weak exogeneity when u_t has an MA(1) structure with $\theta_{21} \neq 0$, then the off-diagonal elements in the long-run variance matrix are $\theta_{21}(\sigma_\varsigma^2 - \sigma_{\varsigma v}^2/\sigma_v^2)$ – see also Phillips (*op. cit.*, p. 356).

9.4 The fully modified (Phillips–Hansen) OLS estimator

The fully modified estimator of Phillips and Hansen makes two corrections to the simple OLS estimator and, accordingly, we introduce these adjustments in two steps.

9.4.1 Corrections for bias and endogeneity

9.4.1a A bias correction

The first adjustment arises from noting that endogeneity induces what is referred to as a second order bias in the OLS estimator; that is while the consistency of the estimator is unaffected, it is still superconsistent, its limiting distribution is 'knocked' off-centre by the presence of a nonzero value of Γ_{21}. Since Γ_{21} can be consistently estimated the bias can be removed. This leads to the 'bias-corrected' OLS estimator:

$$\begin{aligned}
\hat{\varphi}_2^* &= \left(\sum X_t Y_t - T\hat{\Gamma}_{21}\right)/\sum X_t^2 \\
&= \left(\sum X_t Y_t\right)/\sum X_t^2 - T\hat{\Gamma}_{21}/\sum X_t^2 \\
&= \hat{\varphi}_2 - T\left(\hat{\Gamma}_{21}/\sum X_t^2\right)
\end{aligned} \tag{9.77}$$

The bias correction to the simple OLS estimator is $T(\hat{\Gamma}_{21}/\sum X_t^2)$, where $\hat{\Gamma}_{21}$ is a consistent estimator of the appropriate element of $\Gamma = \Psi + \Lambda$. Γ_{21} will be zero if there is no contemporaneity, so Φ is diagonal, and no serial correlation structure in the error process, $u_t = (\varepsilon_t, \omega_t)'$, so Γ is null. This correction results in an estimator which is consistent and asymptotically unbiased; however, the bias correction is not sufficient to ensure that the corresponding 't' statistic is asymptotically normally distributed.

9.4.1b An endogeneity correction

A further correction is needed for the long-run endogeneity of the regressors. The nature of the adjustment or correction is as follows. Instead of using Y_t use adjusted Y_t defined as:

$$Y_t^+ = Y_t - (\hat{\Omega}_{21}/\hat{\Omega}_{22})\Delta X_t$$
$$= Y_t - \hat{\rho}\Delta X_t \quad \text{where } \hat{\rho} \equiv \hat{\Omega}_{21}/\hat{\Omega}_{22}$$

$$(9.78)$$

Where a hat indicates a consistent estimator of the corresponding parameter. (Also, in general, $\hat{\Omega}_{22}$ is a matrix and, therefore, $\hat{\Omega}_{22}^{-1}$ is used.) If $\hat{\Omega}_{21} = 0$ there is no endogeneity correction. The correction does not make a difference to the consistency property of the estimator. Bringing both corrections together results in the Phillips–Hansen 'fully modified' estimator, $\hat{\varphi}_2^+$, which is (super)consistent, asymptotically unbiased and has a 't' statistic which, provided the adjusted standard error given below is used, is asymptotically normally distributed. As the estimator is a modified version of OLS we refer to it as the FMOLS estimator.

$$\hat{\varphi}_2^+ = \left(\sum X_t Y_t^+ - T\hat{\Gamma}_{21}^+ \right) / \sum X_t^2$$
$$= \left[\sum X_t (Y_t - \hat{\rho}\Delta X_t) - T\hat{\Gamma}_{21}^+ \right] / \sum X_t^2$$
$$= \sum X_t Y_t / \sum X_t^2$$
$$\quad - \sum X_t \hat{\rho}\Delta X_t / \sum X_t^2 - T\hat{\Gamma}_{21}^+ / \sum X_t^2$$
$$= \hat{\varphi}_2 - \hat{\rho} \left(\sum X_t \Delta X_t / \sum X_t^2 \right)$$
$$\quad - T\left(\hat{\Gamma}_{21}^+ / \sum X_t^2 \right) \quad (9.79)$$

where $\hat{\Gamma}_{21}^+ = \hat{\Gamma}_{21} - \hat{\rho}\hat{\Gamma}_{22}$. Sometimes this bias correction is written in a slightly different but equivalent way. Define the second row of $\hat{\Gamma}$ as $\hat{\Gamma}_2 = (\hat{\Gamma}_{21}, \hat{\Gamma}_{22})$, then

$$\hat{\Gamma}_{21}^+ = \hat{\Gamma}_2^+ \begin{pmatrix} 1 \\ -\hat{\rho} \end{pmatrix} \quad (9.80)$$

In place of the conventional standard error in the calculation of the 't' statistic, the adjusted long-run standard error should be used; this is calculated as

$$\hat{\Omega}_{11}^+ = \hat{\Omega}_{11} - \hat{\Omega}_{21}^2 \hat{\Omega}_{22}^{-1} \quad (9.81)$$

So the 't' statistic for the null hypothesis that $\varphi_2 = 0$ is

$$'t'^+(\varphi_2 = 0) = \hat{\varphi}_2^+ / (\hat{\Omega}_{11}^+ \sum X_t^2)^{\frac{1}{2}} \quad (9.82)$$

A development of the MA(1) numerical example used above may help to fix ideas. In this example,

$$\begin{pmatrix} \varepsilon_t \\ \omega_t \end{pmatrix} = \begin{bmatrix} 1 & 0 \\ 0 & 1 \end{bmatrix} \begin{pmatrix} \zeta_t \\ v_t \end{pmatrix}$$
$$+ \begin{bmatrix} 0.2 & 0.0 \\ 0.3 & 0.4 \end{bmatrix} \begin{pmatrix} \zeta_{t-1} \\ v_{t-1} \end{pmatrix} \quad (9.83)$$

with, to illustrate, two different specifications of Φ:

$$\Phi = \begin{bmatrix} 1 & 0 \\ 0 & 1 \end{bmatrix} \quad \Phi = \begin{bmatrix} 1 & 0.5 \\ 0.5 & 1 \end{bmatrix}$$

Hence, Ω and Γ are:

$$\Omega = \begin{bmatrix} 1.44 & 0.36 \\ 0.36 & 1.96 \end{bmatrix} \quad \Omega = \begin{bmatrix} 1.44 & 1.20 \\ 1.20 & 2.47 \end{bmatrix}$$

$$\Gamma = \begin{bmatrix} 1.24 & 0.36 \\ 0.06 & 1.65 \end{bmatrix} \quad \Gamma = \begin{bmatrix} 1.24 & 1.10 \\ 0.70 & 1.92 \end{bmatrix}$$

so that $\rho = \Omega_{21}/\Omega_{22} = 0.36/1.96 = 0.184$ or $1.20/2.47 = 0.485$, respectively; then

$$\Gamma_{21}^+ = \Gamma_{21} - \rho\Gamma_{22}$$
$$= 0.06 - 0.184(1.65)$$
$$= -0.244$$
$$\Gamma_{21}^+ = \Gamma_{21} - \rho\Gamma_{22}$$
$$= 0.70 - 0.485(1.92)$$
$$= -0.231$$

The endogeneity corrections to Y_t are, respectively,

$$Y_t^+ = Y_t - 0.184\Delta X_t \quad \text{or} \quad Y_t^+ = Y_t - 0.485\Delta X_t$$

Notice that in the first case an endogeneity correction is generated even though there is no contemporaneity ($\Phi = I$). The fully modified estimator is:

$$\hat{\varphi}_2^+ = \hat{\varphi}_2 - 0.184\left(\sum X_t\Delta X_t / \sum X_t^2\right)$$
$$- (-0.244)T\left(\sum X_t / \sum X_t^2\right)$$

or

$$\hat{\varphi}_2^+ = \hat{\varphi}_2 - 0.485\left(\sum X_t\Delta X_t / \sum X_t^2\right)$$
$$- (-0.231)\left(T\sum X_t / \sum X_t^2\right)$$

In practice the process generating $u_t = (\varepsilon_t, \omega_t)'$ is unlikely to be known so that Γ_{21} has to be estimated. First, note that consistent estimators of ε_t and ω_t can be obtained from OLS estimation of (9.1) and (9.2). The equation for X_t may need to be modified if there is a trend in the data, in which case it is appropriate to add drift to (9.2), which becomes

$$X_t = X_{t-1} + \mu + \omega_t \quad (9.84)$$

with $\hat{\omega}_t = \Delta X_t - \hat{\mu}$ and $\hat{\mu} = \sum_{t=2}^{T}\Delta X_t/(T-1)$.

Also X_t may be I(1) but not a simple random walk with drift. More generally $a(L)X_t = \mu + \omega_t$ with $a(L)$ a pth order polynomial in L with $a(L) = (1-L)a^*(L)$, so $a(L)$ contains a

(single) unit root. For example, suppose $a^*(L) = 1 + 0.15L + 0.1L^2$ then

$$(1 - L)(1 + 0.15L + 0.1L^2)X_t$$
$$= \mu + \omega_t$$
$$\Rightarrow X_t = \mu + 0.85X_{t-1} + 0.05X_{t-2}$$
$$+ 0.1X_{t-3} + \omega_t \quad (9.85)$$

It is also likely that a constant will be needed in the cointegration space, hence (9.1) and (9.2) become

$$Y_t = \varphi_2 + \varphi_2 X_t + \varepsilon_t$$
$$\Rightarrow \hat{\varepsilon}_t = Y_t - \hat{\varphi}_1 - \hat{\varphi}_2 X_t$$
$$a(L)X_t = \mu + \omega_t \Rightarrow \hat{\omega}_t = \hat{a}(L)X_t - \hat{\mu}$$

where a hat indicates any consistent estimator, for example the OLS estimator, of the corresponding coefficient(s). The next step depends upon whether a parametric or nonparametric approach is taken. In the former a view needs to be taken about the structure generating the $u_t = (\varepsilon_t, \omega_t)'$ process; for example, is it MA or AR, and of what order? Once the structure is determined, for example an MA(1) process, then it can be estimated and the relevant calculations made in order to obtain the Phillips–Hansen adjustment parameters.

9.4.1c A semi-parametric approach to estimating the corrections

An alternative to estimating a particular structure for the errors is known as the semi-parametric approach. Recall that the bias correction requires an estimator of the appropriate element of

$$\Gamma = \Psi + \Lambda = E\{u_0u_0'\} + \sum_{k=1}^{\infty} E\{u_0u_k'\}$$

and with stationarity $E\{u_0u_0'\} = E\{u_tu_t'\}$ and $E\{u_0u_k'\} = E\{u_tu_{t+k}'\}$. For later convenience define $H_k \equiv E\{u_tu_{t+k}'\}$. If there is just one regressor the relevant element of Γ is Γ_{21} which is

$$\sum_{k=0}^{\infty} E\{\omega_t\varepsilon_{t+k}\} = E\{\omega_t\varepsilon_t\} + \sum_{k=1}^{\infty} E\{\omega_t\varepsilon_{t+k}\}$$

In practice the summation is assumed to be truncated at a point l. The semi-parametric approach does not model the structure of the generating process for u_t but estimates the covariances and autocovariances in

$$\sum_{k=0}^{l} E\{\omega_t \varepsilon_{t+k}\}$$

and then uses these estimates to form an estimate of Γ_{21}. For example,

$$\sum_{t=2}^{T} \{\hat{\omega}_t \hat{\varepsilon}_t\}/(T-1)$$

is an estimator of $E\{\omega_t \varepsilon_t\}$; the summation starts from $t = 2$ because one observation (at least) is lost from the sample in forming the estimate of $\hat{\omega}_t$. $\sum_{t=2}^{T-k} \{\hat{\omega}_t \hat{\varepsilon}_{t+k}\}/(T-k-1)$ is an estimator of $E\{\omega_t \varepsilon_{t+k}\}$. (Note that

$$\sum_{t=2}^{T-k} \hat{\omega}_t \hat{\varepsilon}_{t+k} = \sum_{t=k+2}^{T} \hat{\omega}_{t-k} \hat{\varepsilon}_t$$

and the autocovariances are sometimes presented in the latter form.)

In the present example $\hat{\varepsilon}_t$ is the residual from (9.1) and $\hat{\omega}_t$ is the residual from a suitably generalised version (9.2); in the simplest case $\hat{\omega}_t = \Delta X_t$, and

$$\hat{\Gamma}_{21} = \sum_{k=0}^{l} \left[\sum_{t=k+2}^{T} \hat{\omega}_{t-k} \hat{\varepsilon}_t/(T-k-1) \right]$$

$$= \sum_{k=0}^{l} \left[\sum_{t=k+2}^{T} \Delta X_{t-k} \hat{\varepsilon}_t/(T-k-1) \right]$$

$$(9.86)$$

For the fully modified estimator it is necessary to obtain the elements of the long-run variance matrix; however, this is straightforward since $\Omega = \Gamma + \Lambda'$, so no information is needed other than that already used in calculating Λ. A variation on this theme is to introduce a weighting scheme which attaches weights w_k to the autocovariances so that

$$\hat{\Lambda} = \sum_{k=1}^{l} w_k \hat{H}_k \qquad (9.87)$$

setting $w_k = 1$ for all k, sometimes called the uniform window, reproduces the initial choice of unweighted elements in Λ. The Bartlett window is $w_k = 1 - k/(l+1)$; for example, if $l = 4$ then the weights are: $w_1 = 0.8$, $w_2 = 0.6$, $w_3 = 0.4$, $w_4 = 0.2$. This choice of weighting scheme removes the problem that the estimated variances in Ω may be negative. MICROFIT also allows a choice of the Tukey window and the Parzen window – Pesaran and Pesaran (1997, p. 392).

9.4.2 Variations on a theme: when OLS on the ADL model is optimal

The development of the fully modified estimator of Phillips and Hansen (1990) shows that estimation of the ADL model will not in general lead to asymptotically unbiased estimators with standard normal distributions for the 't' statistics. However, there are some interesting special cases which link the methodology of estimating a dynamic model to optimal estimation and inference. The 'general-to-specific' methodology starts with a potentially profligate single-equation dynamic model which might be formulated in an ECM format with lagged disequilibrium and I(0) dynamic terms; the profligacy is removed by sequentially testing for redundant regressors to determine a 'parsimonious' empirical model which should (only) contain significant regressors. An alternative methodology is to assume that, as in the Phillips–Hansen framework, an equilibrium relationship is complicated by serially correlated errors which are potentially correlated with some of the cointegrating variables. These dependencies generally imply that optimal estimation and inference cannot be conducted in a single-equation framework. However, Phillips (1988) has shown that in some nontrivial cases these two methodologies produce the same results. This section outlines some examples of this coincidence.

Suppose there are no explicit dynamics in the DGP for Y_t and the endogeneity arises from contemporaneity alone. This case has been considered in section **9.3.1a**. The model upon which this discussion is based is from that section, and is a simplification of an example due to Phillips (1988) – and see also Banerjee *et al.* (1993, p. 245). The relevant equations are:

$$Y_t = \varphi_2 X_2 + \varepsilon_t \qquad \text{(9.1 again)}$$

$$X_t = X_{t-1} + \omega_t \qquad \text{(9.2 again)}$$

We now assume that the covariance between ε_t and ω_t is nonzero; the conditional variance matrix is

$$\Phi = \begin{bmatrix} \sigma_\varepsilon^2 & \sigma_{\varepsilon\omega} \\ \sigma_{\varepsilon\omega} & \sigma_\omega^2 \end{bmatrix}$$

Since there is no dynamic structure in ε_t and ω_t the short-run and long-run variance matrices are the same, $\Phi = \Omega$ and since $\Lambda = 0$ then $\Gamma = \Phi$. This structure means that there is no bias correction in the FMOLS estimator:

$$\Gamma_{21}^+ = \Gamma_{21} - \Omega_{21}\Omega_{22}^{-1}\Gamma_{22}$$
$$= \sigma_{\varepsilon\omega} - (\sigma_{\varepsilon\omega}/\sigma_\omega^2)\sigma_\omega^2$$
$$= 0$$

but there is an endogeneity correction

$$Y_t^+ = Y_t - \Omega_{21}\Omega_{22}^{-1}\Delta X_t$$
$$= Y_t - (\sigma_{\varepsilon\omega}/\sigma_\omega^2)\Delta X_t$$

The FMOLS estimator is asymptotically normally distributed, and has an associated 't' statistic, suitably defined, which has a standard normal distribution asymptotically. The superconsistency property of the OLSEG estimator is retained in the presence of endogeneity; however, as noted in section **9.3**, the OLSEG

estimator of φ_2 is not asymptotically normally distributed about the true value (potentially) giving rise to a problem with inference.

An asymptotically equivalent approach leads to a dynamic model which directly includes the endogeneity correction – see the development leading to (9.73). Substituting for X_t from (9.2) in (9.1) results in the 'reduced form' for Y_t; that is

$$Y_t = \varphi_2 X_{t-1} + \varepsilon_t + \varphi_2 \omega_t$$

Now subtracting Y_{t-1} from both sides to put the equation in ECM form:

$$\Delta Y_t = -(Y_{t-1} - \varphi_2 X_{t-1}) + v_t$$
$$\text{with } v_t = \varepsilon_t + \varphi_2 \omega_t$$

This model is not a regression function and so will not correct for endogeneity (more precisely contemporaneity in this case). The regression function has already been given as (9.76), reproduced here for convenience:

$$\Delta Y_t = -(Y_{t-1} - \varphi_2 X_{t-1}) + \delta \Delta X_t + \eta_t$$

where $\delta = \sigma_{21}/\sigma_{22}$. This equation may now be interpreted as embodying the endogeneity correction. The OLS estimator of φ_2 will be asymptotically unbiased and standard normal tables can be used for inference, at least asymptotically. See Banerjee *et al.* (*op. cit.*, p. 246) for an elaboration of this example. Thus, even though the original model was not cast in the form of a dynamic ECM, estimation of such a model provides an estimator with desirable properties. As a consequence Phillips (1988) makes the point that in some cases the methodology associated with Hendry – see Hendry and Richard (1982, 1983) – of simplifying a 'general' dynamic regression formulated as an ECM, leads to (asymptotically) optimal estimation and inference as it will pick up dynamic terms which are correcting the OLS estimator for bias and endogeneity.

Consider another simple example:

$$Y_t = \varphi_2 X_t + \varepsilon_t$$
$$X_t = X_{t-1} + \omega_t$$
$$\varepsilon_t = \varepsilon_t$$
$$\omega_t = \gamma\omega_{t-1} + \upsilon_t$$

ε_t and υ_t are assumed to be correlated white noise with covariance $\sigma_{\varepsilon\upsilon}$. In this example ω_t is an AR(1) process, a property which is likely to characterise many economic time series with a unit root. The long-run variance matrix for this set-up has already been derived – see section **9.2.1a**.

$$\Gamma = \begin{bmatrix} \Gamma_{11} & \Gamma_{12} \\ \Gamma_{21} & \Gamma_{22} \end{bmatrix}$$

$$= \begin{bmatrix} \sigma_\varepsilon^2 & \sigma_{\varepsilon\upsilon}/(1-\gamma) \\ \sigma_{\varepsilon\upsilon} & \sigma_\upsilon^2/[(1-\gamma^2)(1-\gamma)] \end{bmatrix} \quad (9.88)$$

$$\Omega = \begin{bmatrix} \Omega_{11} & \Omega_{12} \\ \Omega_{21} & \Omega_{22} \end{bmatrix}$$

$$= \begin{bmatrix} \sigma_\varepsilon^2 & \sigma_{\varepsilon\upsilon}/(1-\gamma) \\ \sigma_{\varepsilon\upsilon}/(1-\gamma) & \sigma_\upsilon^2/(1-\gamma)^2 \end{bmatrix} \quad (9.89)$$

The endogeneity correction is

$$Y_t^+ = Y_t - \Omega_{21}\Omega_{22}^{-1}\Delta X_t$$

in this case

$$\Omega_{21}\Omega_{22}^{-1} = \left(\frac{\sigma_{\varepsilon\upsilon}/(1-\gamma)}{\sigma_\upsilon^2/(1-\gamma)^2} \right)$$

$$= \left(\frac{\sigma_{\varepsilon\upsilon}(1-\gamma)}{\sigma_\upsilon^2} \right) \quad (9.90)$$

and the bias correction is:

$$\Gamma_{21}^+ = \Gamma_{21} - \Omega_{21}\Omega_{22}^{-1}\Gamma_{22}$$

$$= \sigma_{\varepsilon\upsilon} - \left(\frac{\sigma_{\varepsilon\upsilon}(1-\gamma)}{\sigma_\upsilon^2} \right) \left(\frac{\sigma_\upsilon^2}{(1-\gamma^2)(1-\gamma)} \right)$$

$$= \sigma_{\varepsilon\upsilon} - \left(\frac{\sigma_{\varepsilon\upsilon}}{(1-\gamma^2)} \right)$$

$$= \sigma_{\varepsilon\upsilon}\left(1 - \frac{1}{(1-\gamma^2)} \right)$$

$$= -\left(\frac{\gamma^2\sigma_{\varepsilon\upsilon}}{(1-\gamma)^2} \right) \quad (9.91)$$

These corrections should be used in the FMOLS estimator.

Alternatively Phillips (1988), and see also Banerjee *et al.* (1993), shows that a procedure asymptotically equivalent to FMOLS is to include ΔX_t *and* ΔX_{t-1} in the ECM form, which becomes

$$\Delta Y_t = -(Y_{t-1} - \varphi_2 X_{t-1}) + (\lambda + \varphi_2)\Delta X_t$$
$$\quad - \gamma\lambda\Delta X_{t-1} + \eta_t \quad \text{where } \lambda = \sigma_{\varepsilon\upsilon}/\sigma_\upsilon^2$$
$$\quad (9.92)$$

say

$$\Delta Y_t = \theta_1(Y_{t-1} - \varphi_2 X_{t-1}) + \theta_2\Delta X_t$$
$$\quad + \theta_3\Delta X_{t-1} + \eta_t \quad (9.93)$$

where $\theta_1 = -1$, $\theta_2 = (\lambda + \varphi_2)$ and $\theta_3 = -\gamma\lambda$. OLS applied to this regression will result in an estimator of φ_2 with the same limiting properties as FMOLS. Again this provides some justification for an empirical methodology which seeks to reduce an initially potentially overparameterised dynamic model; for example, working down by deleting insignificant variables should stop at ΔX_{t-1} in the above case, resulting in a estimator with desirable properties.

Including additional dynamic terms will not always be sufficient to ensure that the resulting estimator is the same as the FMOLS estimator and, hence, asymptotically equivalent to estimating the full set of equations. As noted in section **9.3.1**, generally, if ω_t is linked to past values of ε_t through either an MA or AR process, then X_t is not weakly exogenous for φ_2 and the optimum procedure is to jointly estimate the equations for Y_t and X_t.

9.4.3 Examples of FMOLS estimation

Two examples are used to illustrate the Phillips–Hansen estimator. First, we revisit the consumption–income example used in Chapters 5 and 8; and, second, estimate the relationship between the long-run and short-run rates of interest.

9.4.3a The consumption–income example

Briefly, recall that the data is real consumption and disposable income for the United States, and that OLS estimation of a static levels regression in the logs of consumption and income resulted in

$$\hat{c}_t = -0.082 + 0.998y_t$$
$$(-2.161)(203.446)$$
$$R^2 = 0.997 \quad SC(4) = 79.905[0.000] \quad (9.94)$$

The 't' statistics, in parentheses, are not valid for inference, so it will be of interest to re-estimate the equation using the Phillips–Hansen fully modified estimator.

If c_t and y_t are I(1), φ_1 and φ_2 are consistently estimated by OLS, but, given the absence of any dynamic structure in the estimated equation and the likely endogeneity of Y_t, the 't' statistics cannot be taken at face value. What we do next depends upon the generation of y_t. Since y_t is trended a drift is essential so that

$$\Delta y_t = \mu + \omega_t$$

Although not a formal check, estimation of an AR(1) model for y_t resulted in

$$y_t = 0.057 + 0.994y_{t-1} + \hat{\omega}_t \quad (9.95)$$

which suggested that the random walk with drift model was a close approximation.

There are two choice parameters in the practical implementation of the Phillips–Hansen estimator. First, there is the lag order, l, in the autocovariances; second, there is a choice of whether to choose a weighting scheme and if so which one. The cross-correlations at lag k defined by

$$\hat{\rho}_{\omega(-k)\varepsilon} = \sum_{t=k+2}^{T} \hat{\omega}_{t-k}\hat{\varepsilon}_t \bigg/ \left(\sum_{t=k+2}^{T} \hat{\omega}_{t-k} \sum_{t=k+2}^{T} \hat{\varepsilon}_t \right)^{0.5}$$
$$(9.96)$$

Table 9.1 *Cross-correlations and fully modified (Phillips–Hansen) estimates*

$k =$	-4	-3	-2	-1	0	1	2	3	4
$\rho_{\hat{\omega}(-k)\hat{\varepsilon}}$	0.154	0.152	0.169	0.316	-0.126	-0.024	0.025	-0.005	-0.005

			FMOLS estimates		
lag truncation l	0	1	2	3	4
$\hat{\varphi}_1^+$		-0.072	-0.090	-0.102	-0.107	-0.113
$\hat{\varphi}_1^+$ BW		-0.072	-0.082	-0.085	-0.087	-0.097
't'$^+$		(-1.941)	(-1.485)	(-1.372)	(-1.255)	(-1.225)
't'$^+$ BW		(-1.941)	(-1.631)	(-1.428)	(-1.295)	(-1.342)
$\hat{\varphi}_2^+$		0.996	0.999	1.000	1.000	1.002
$\hat{\varphi}_2^+$ BW		0.996	0.998	0.998	0.998	1.000
't'$^+$		(207.4)	(127.5)	(103.6)	(91.2)	(84.0)
't'$^+$ BW		(207.4)	(153.0)	(129.0)	(114.9)	(106.1)

Notes: Table entries are the fully modified (Phillips–Hansen) estimates of the cointegrating coefficients, $\hat{\varphi}_1^+$ and $\hat{\varphi}_2^+$, and the FMOLS 't' statistics, 't'$^+$, for $\varphi_1 = 0$ or $\varphi_2 = 0$; BW indicates estimates obtained using the Bartlett window weights.

can be helpful in choosing the lag order. (In some programs, for example RATS, the denominator is defined as $(\sum_{t=2}^{T} \hat{\omega}_t \sum_{t=2}^{T} \hat{\varepsilon}_t)^{0.5}$ with no degrees of freedom correction.) As to the second choice the Bartlett window weights are a popular choice and constrain $\hat{\Omega}$ to be positive definite.

The cross-correlations for $\hat{\rho}_{\omega(-k)\varepsilon}$, $k = -4, \ldots,$ $0, \ldots, 4$, in this case are reported in Table 9.1; these tend to be more noticeable for negative k, that is for the covariance of $\hat{\varepsilon}_t$ with leads of $\hat{\omega}_t$ and are, therefore, contributing to the Λ_{12} element in Λ and to the Ω_{21} element in Ω. There is a suggestion of a correlation between $\hat{\omega}_t$ and $\hat{\varepsilon}_t$, indicating some contemporaneity between the consumption and income equations; the cross-correlations of $\hat{\varepsilon}_t$ with lags of $\hat{\omega}_t$ are slight for $k = 1, 2$, and effectively zero for $k = 3, 4$. The FMOLS estimates for $l = 0, \ldots, 4$ are also reported in Table 9.1.

The adjustments result in slight changes to the coefficients. The estimate of $\hat{\varphi}_2$ moves closer to 1 for $l = 1$ and $l = 2$ compared to the OLSEG estimate of 0.998. At $l = 2$ the 't' statistic is 103.6 implying a 95% (asymptotic) confidence interval of $[0.981, 1.019]$, which could be taken as firm evidence of nonrejection of the hypothesis of a unit income elasticity. If the Bartlett window weights are used the changes to the estimates of $\hat{\varphi}_2$ are even less marked.

9.4.3b Long and short interest rates

In this second example the difference between the OLSEG and FMOLS estimates is more substantial. Here we consider a long-term and a short-term interest rate, specifically the former is the yield on 10-year US Treasury Bonds and the latter is the yield on 1-month US Treasury bills, denoted Y_t and X_t, respectively; both are comparable zero coupon financial instruments which are alike in all respects apart from their term to maturity. The data, which is due to McCulloch (1990) and updates, covers the period 1946m12 to 1991m2, and some theories underlying the relationship between financial instruments of different maturities, is examined

in greater detail in Chapter 11. For now we note that an interesting hypothesis is that if the long rate and short rate are each I(1) then they should be cointegrated with cointegrating vector $(1, -1)$, otherwise the spread which this cointegrating vector defines, that is $Y_t - X_t$, is nonstationary and implies that the long rate and the short rate are not tied together in the long run.

The model for the relationship between the long rate and the short rate is:

$$Y_t = \varphi_2 + \varphi_2 X_t + \varepsilon_t$$
$$X_t = X_{t-1} + \omega_t$$

A constant is initially included in the equation for Y_t to allow for a (constant) term premium between the short and long rates. Drift is not included in the equation for X_t. Estimation by OLS resulted in

$$Y_t = 1.668 + 0.931 X_t$$
$$(18.459)(59.601)$$

$$R^2 = 0.870 \quad SC(12) = 432.408[0.000]$$

$$(9.97)$$

't' statistics in parentheses.
Sample period: 1946m12 to 1991m2.

The estimated OLS 't' statistics in parentheses are not valid for inference on φ_1 and φ_2 given the significant LM statistic for serial correlation, $SC(12) = 432.408$, and the possibility of endogeneity between the variables – at the least we expect contemporaneity between the short and long rates.

The cross-correlations between $\Delta X_{t-k} = \omega_{t-k}$ and the residuals from the cointegrating regression, $\hat{\varepsilon}_t$, for $k = -12$ to $+12$ are reported in Table 9.2. Here the pattern is different from the consumption–income example. The cross-correlations for negative values of k tend to be smaller (in absolute value) than for positive values of k. Beyond $k = -1$ most correlations barely exceed 0; whereas for $k = 1, 2, 3$ the correlations are: -0.257, -0.243 and -0.174. Remember that negative values of k refer to

Table 9.2 *Cross-correlations and fully modified (Phillips–Hansen) estimates*

$k=$	-12	-11	-10	-9	-8	-7	-6	-5	-4	-3	-2	-1
$\rho_{\hat{\omega}(-k)\hat{\varepsilon}}$	0.047	0.064	0.050	0.057	-0.012	0.002	0.044	0.043	-0.085	0.081	0.056	0.011

$k=$	0	1	2	3	4	5	6	7	8	9	10	11	12
$\rho_{\hat{\omega}(-k)\hat{\varepsilon}}$	-0.271	-0.257	-0.243	-0.174	-0.133	-0.104	-0.092	-0.045	-0.098	-0.103	-0.108	-0.081	-0.080

FMOLS estimates

lag truncation $l=$	1	5	10
$\hat{\varphi}_1^+$	1.572	1.450	1.366
't'$^+$	(10.679)	(5.862)	(4.405)
$\hat{\varphi}_2^+$	0.952	0.982	1.001
't'$^+$	(37.346)	(22.968)	(18.682)

correlations between $\hat{\varepsilon}_t$ and leads of ω_t, that is ε_t and ω_{t+k}, whereas positive values of k refer to correlations between $\hat{\varepsilon}_t$ and lags of ω_t, that is $\hat{\varepsilon}_t$ and ω_{t-k}. Contemporaneity is suggested by a correlation of -0.271 between $\hat{\varepsilon}_t$ and ω_t. To illustrate the effect of varying the lag length l, the FMOLS estimates are reported in Table 9.2 for $l = 1, 5, 10$.

The estimates of φ_2 change from 0.931, for OLSEG estimation, to very close to the theoretically predicted value of 1 when $l = 10$. Assuming drift in the X_t process barely changes this estimate from 1.001 to 1.011 for $l = 10$. The 95% confidence interval for φ_2 is [0.896, 1.106], and while large would clearly not now lead to rejection of the null hypothesis that the spread is stationary.

9.4.4 Simulation findings

The Monte Carlo evidence about whether the fully modified OLS estimator offers a finite sample gain relative to estimation based on the ADL model (for example, direct OLS estimation, nonlinear estimation of the ECM or IVB estimation) is mixed. The results of three simulation studies are summarised below.

9.4.4a Simulation results: Phillips and Hansen (1990)

Phillips and Hansen (1990) specified the DGP as the simple cointegrated system given by (9.1) and (9.2) together with a first order MA process for the errors.

$$Y_t = \varphi_2 X_t + \varepsilon_t$$
$$X_t = X_{t-1} + \omega_t$$
$$\varepsilon_t = \zeta_t + 0.3\zeta_{t-1} - 0.4\upsilon_{t-1}$$
$$\omega_t = \upsilon_t + \theta_{21}\zeta_{t-1} + 0.6\upsilon_{t-1}$$
$$\Phi = \begin{bmatrix} 1 & \sigma_{\zeta\upsilon} \\ \sigma_{\zeta\upsilon} & 1 \end{bmatrix}$$

The design varied θ_{21} for a failure of weak exogeneity and varied $\sigma_{\zeta\upsilon}$ for contemporaneity. Three estimation methods were used: OLSEG, OLSADL with the model specified in ECM format, which is described as the Hendry method, and FMOLS. ΔY_t, ΔY_{t-1}, ΔY_{t-2}, ΔX_{t-1} and ΔX_{t-2} were included as additional regressors in the Hendry method and lags -5 to $+5$ were used in a Bartlett window for the FMOLS estimator. 30,000 replications were used with sample size of $T = 50$.

As far as bias is concerned, OLSEG was dominated by the Hendry method and FMOLS for all design parameter variations, but in important areas of the parameter space the differences were not great; for example, for $\theta_{21} = 0.4$ and $\sigma_{\zeta\upsilon} = 0.4$ the % biases were -1%, -0.95% and -0.6%, respectively. The greatest difference was with $\sigma_{\zeta\upsilon} = -0.8$ and $\theta_{21} = 0.8$, with % biases of -6.85%, 3.1% and 1.25%, respectively. For a given value of $\sigma_{\zeta\upsilon}$ the bias in all estimators increased with θ_{21} (varied from 0.0, 0.4, 0.8). For a given value of θ_{21} the bias increased with $\sigma_{\zeta\upsilon}$ (varied from -0.8, -0.4, $+0.4$ $+0.8$).

If the asymptotic results are a good guide, the mean of the 't' statistic for $\hat{\varphi}_2 - \varphi_2$ should be closer to 0 for FMOLS than the other methods. This was the case in seven out of 12 parameter variations and in three cases for the Hendry method; however, the differences were not as marked as this suggests because in three of the seven cases the FMOLS method was just dominant. Inder (1993) argues that the Phillips–Hansen procedure favoured the FMOLS method because the DGP for Y_t was not dynamic. Phillips and Hansen (*op. cit.*) acknowledged that the inclusion of a fixed number of lags of ΔY_t and ΔX_t in the Hendry method would not happen in practice, as these would be chosen according to a general-to-specific search strategy. Nevertheless, the message is that while there are some regions of the parameter space where FMOLS is dominant, even under the constraints imposed the Hendry method is a close second.

9.4.4b Simulation results: Hansen and Phillips (1990)

In a further simulation study Hansen and Phillips (1990) used the design

$$Y_t = 2X_t + u_t$$
$$X_t = Z_t + u_t$$
$$u_t = \lambda u_{t-1} + \varepsilon_{1t}$$
$$Z_t = Z_{t-1} + \varepsilon_{2t}$$

with $\quad \mathrm{Var}(\varepsilon_{1t}, \varepsilon_{2t}) = \begin{bmatrix} 1 & \theta\sigma \\ \theta\sigma & \sigma^2 \end{bmatrix}$

The rationale for this design is that Y_t and X_t are cointegrated with a serially correlated error, and X_t is 'driven' by the random walk, Z_t. The design parameters are: λ (serial correlation); θ (contemporaneity); σ^2 (signal-to-noise ratio). Two thousand replications for a sample of $T = 100$ were used. Hansen and Phillips (*op. cit.*) addressed a number of issues, one of concern here is the effect of the bias and endogeneity corrections. Without these OLSEG displayed noticeable bias for small signal-to-noise ratios;

for example, a bias of 27.25% and 12.05% for $\sigma = 0.5$ and 1.0, respectively (with $\theta = 0$, $\lambda = 0.7$, but these biases were typical for variations of these parameters). As the signal-to-noise ratio increased the bias decreased, for example to 0.15% for $\sigma = 10.0$. Hansen and Phillips then made the fully modified corrections, first assuming that the true coefficients were known; in practice this would be an unusual situation but indicates the best that the corrections could do. FMOLS does well in these circumstances with the bias reduced to -0.85% (from 27.25%) and -0.3% (from 12.05%) for $\sigma = 0.5$ and 1.0, respectively (with $\theta = 0$, $\lambda = 0.7$, but again these biases were typical).

Basing the residuals on prior first stage estimation, for example OLS estimation of $Y_t = \varphi_2 X_t + u_t$, to make FMOLS feasible, reduced its advantage over OLSEG. The biases were now 22.75% and 8.54% for $\sigma = 0.5$ and 1.0, respectively (with $\theta = 0$, $\lambda = 0.7$), and, in broad terms, the feasible FMOLS estimator effected a reduction of about 20% in the bias of the unmodified estimator. This is, perhaps, not surprising since we have already reported that the OLSEG estimates display substantial bias for low values of σ, so using them to provide estimates of the residuals for the second stage is likely to cause problems. Hansen and Phillips (*op. cit.*, p. 240) note: 'In general, feasible fully modified OLS performs better than unadjusted OLS, but not by much. When compared to the fully modified OLS estimates using the true coefficients ... we see that the use of first-stage regression coefficients significantly reduces the effectiveness of the modifications.' However, feasible FMOLS was still the best feasible estimation method considered by Hansen and Phillips (*op. cit.*) but, unlike the Phillips and Hansen (1990) study, the Hendry method was not included in this simulation study.

Hansen and Phillips (*op. cit.*) also considered the distribution of the OLSEG bias (only) corrected and fully modified 't' statistics; 8,000 replications were used, with $T = 100$. Here the results were more encouraging for the fully modified method. The OLSEG 't' statistic displayed substantial bias even for large σ, while the fully modified 't' statistic was closest to the normal $(0, 1)$ distribution. Bias correcting by itself did not lead to much of an improvement over OLSEG; the best gain was in using the fully modified 't' statistic.

9.4.4c   Simulation results: Inder (1993)

Inder (1993) re-examined some of the results of Phillips and Hansen (1990) in the light of his point that restricting the design so that there are no dynamics in the cointegrating regression is likely to favour OLSEG and FMOLS. Inder's design is an ADL$(1, 1)$ model for Y_t

$$Y_t = \alpha_0 + \beta_0 X_t + \beta_1 X_{t-1} + \gamma_1 Y_{t-1} + \varepsilon_t$$
$$X_t = X_{t-1} + \omega_t$$
$$\varepsilon_t = \rho_{11}\eta_t$$
$$\omega_t = \rho_{21}\eta_t + \rho_{22}\upsilon_t + \theta_{21}\eta_{t-1}$$

Where η_t and υ_t are uncorrelated, standard normal variables. FMOLS is used in its 'feasible' form; that is first stage regressions are required to obtain the residuals needed to form estimates of Γ and Ω.

Inder's results contrast with those of Phillips and Hansen (*op. cit.*). He notes:

(i)   In most cases *feasible* FMOLS yields no finite sample improvement on OLSEG.

(ii)   The Hendry method (that is estimating the ADL in ECM form) performs very well offering a 'huge' improvement in precision over OLSEG and feasible FMOLS when the DGP for Y_t is dynamic. 'The I(0) terms play a vital role in the precision of estimators in finite samples.' (Inder *op. cit.*, p. 61)

(iii)   Even when the dynamics are overspecified, as when $\beta_1 = \gamma_1 = 0$, the Hendry method does as well as the better of OLSEG and feasible FMOLS; and when $\theta_{21} = 0.5$, so there is a lack of weak exogeneity, the Hendry method is best with no substantial bias.

(iv)   It is also possible to apply the Phillips–Hansen modifications to the estimator based on the ADL model, which is called by Inder the modified ECM estimator. However, Inder (*op. cit.*, p. 64) concludes: '...the present evidence suggests that it may be unnecessary to use the modified ECM estimator: the standard unrestricted ECM estimator (the Hendry/ADL) method performs as well, if not better.' (My clarification in parentheses.)

It could be argued that Inder's design might favour the Hendry method because, apart from when $\beta_1 = \gamma_1 = 0$, it is the right model given the DGP. In practice the lag length in the ADL is also a matter for estimation but then so is the lag truncation parameter in the Phillips–Hansen procedure, so an element of choice is required in both methods. Despite these qualifications the weight of the simulation evidence suggests that while FMOLS with semi-parametric corrections, made using the true residuals, is likely to yield an advantage over OLSEG and IVB estimation (or its ADL/ECM equivalents), the need to estimate the residuals by a prior OLSEG regression, to make the method feasible, generally results in a loss of the clear-cut advantage. It is perhaps surprising that better estimation of the first stage from the IVB estimator, as in the modified ECM estimator, does not correct this problem. A secondary issue is whether using the (estimated) residuals in parametric second stage modelling, for example identifying an MA(q) or AR(p) or combined ARMA(p, q) process, would lead to an improvement in the finite sample performance of the Phillips–Hansen corrections.

9.5   Complications: nearly integrated processes and endogeneity

An issue raised in Chapter 7 concerned whether a time series generated by a nearly integrated but stationary process was better treated as a non-stationary process for purposes of estimation and inference. We return to this issue now in the following context. There is a sharp contrast in the implications of endogeneity for estimation depending on whether stationary or nonstationary variables are involved: from the theory of stationary variables we know that endogeneity implies estimator inconsistency; whereas the property of consistency is retained for nonstationary variables. So what happens for 'nearly' integrated variables? This section describes some illustrative simulations to get a feeling for the kind of differences involved. In so doing it allows, *en passant*, a discussion of some of the properties of different estimation methods.

The simulation set-up here is an extension of that in Chapter 8. Specifically the DGP is a variant of the ADL(1, 1) model

$$Y_t = 5 + 0.15X_t + 0.10X_{t-1}$$
$$+ 0.5Y_{t-1} + \varepsilon_t \qquad (9.98)$$

implying the long-run relationship

$$Y_t = 10 + 0.5X_t + u_t \qquad (9.99)$$

The generating process for X_t is

$$X_t = \phi_1 X_{t-1} + \omega_t \qquad (9.100)$$

In this context (9.99) is the cointegrating regression but, in contrast to the situation in Table 8.4, u_t is not white noise if the DGP for Y_t is dynamic.

Endogeneity is governed by the specification of the structure of ε_t and ω_t and the properties of X_t by the value of ϕ_1. For a random walk $\phi_1 = 1$. In the set-up of Chapter 8, ε_t and ω_t are uncorrelated, standardised white noise; here different specifications correspond to the presence of contemporaneity and lack of weak exogeneity.

9.5.1 X_t integrated/nearly integrated, no endogeneity

To establish a baseline we first assume no endogeneity and compare integrated and 'nearly'

integrated processes. This is an issue of practical importance because of the low power of tests for a unit root when the root is close to 1. The cointegration analysis so far, based on the work of Engle and Granger (1987), assumes that Y_t and X_t are nonstationary and integrated of order 1. But what if, because of the low power of unit root tests, we mistakenly conclude, for example, that X_t is I(1) when it is I(0) but with a root very close to 1? An argument considered in Chapter 7, suggested that, in finite samples, it may be better to treat stationary but 'nearly' integrated series as integrated for purposes of estimation and inference, rather than assume that the distribution theory associated with stationary processes is appropriate. To help assess this issue X_t was generated according to the 'nearly' integrated process $X_t = 0.975X_{t-1} + \omega_t$. As in Chapter 8, ε_t and ω_t are initially uncorrelated, standardised white noise but this assumption is relaxed below. As a reference point X_t was also generated as pure white noise so $\phi_1 = 0$.

The simulation results for estimating the long-run coefficients in the case of the OLSEG estimator and the long-run and short-run coefficients for the IVB (ADL/ECM) estimator, for three cases, pure stationarity, 'nearly' integrated, and integrated, are reported in Table 9.3. The two numbers in parentheses shown beneath the average coefficient estimate are the percentage of times that the associated 't' statistic fell outside the range given by $-t_{0.05}(\text{df})$ and $+t_{0.05}(\text{df})$, respectively. This gives an indication of the symmetry of the empirical distribution of the 't' statistic, and whether the empirical distribution of the 't' statistic is close to the theoretical distribution; if it is these percentages should be close to 5%. In interpreting the results note that the true values of the short-run coefficients are -0.2 for the coefficient on ΔX_t and -1.0 for the coefficient on ΔY_t.

When $\phi_1 = 0$ then, as expected, OLSEG performs badly because the omitted variables are of the same order in probability as the included variables, resulting in a very substantial bias in the estimator of φ_2. This is a straightforward case

Table 9.3　Mean of $\hat\varphi_2$ for OLSEG and IVB estimators; X_t 'exogenous' with different DGPs

	Pure stationarity $\phi_1 = 0$ coefficients on:				Nearly integrated $\phi_1 = 0.975$ coefficients on:				Integrated $\phi_1 = 1$ coefficients on:			
	$\hat\varphi_1$	$\hat\varphi_2$	ΔX_t	ΔY_t	$\hat\varphi_1$	$\hat\varphi_2$	ΔX_t	ΔY_t	$\hat\varphi_1$	$\hat\varphi_2$	ΔX_t	ΔY_t
df = 50												
OLSEG	10.002	0.143	n.a	n.a	10.001	0.427	n.a	n.a	10.009	0.437	n.a	n.a
't'% − ve	16.815	69.895	n.a	n.a	17.820	32.345	n.a	n.a	18.365	30.890	n.a	n.a
't'% + ve	17.375	0.005	n.a	n.a	18.175	5.530	n.a	n.a	18.650	6.115	n.a	n.a
IVB	10.003	0.487	−0.117	−0.938	10.008	0.495	−0.217	−0.851	10.008	0.495	−0.220	−0.845
't'% − ve	6.325	7.035	3.730	−0.000	6.880	8.165	6.305	0.000	6.950	8.325	6.260	0
't'% + ve	6.695	2.835	4.155	16.240	7.150	5.745	2.010	21.440	7.095	5.735	1.775	21.370
df = 100												
OLSEG	10.000	0.147	n.a	n.a	10.001	0.454	n.a	n.a	9.996	0.466	n.a	n.a
't'% − ve	17.200	91.040	n.a	n.a	18.078	34.725	n.a	n.a	18.260	31.580	n.a	n.a
't'% + ve	16.945	0.000	n.a	n.a	18.005	5.155	n.a	n.a	18.93	6.525	n.a	n.a
IVB	10.000	0.493	−0.199	−0.963	10.003	0.499	−0.210	−0.924	10.006	0.499	−0.213	−0.917
't'% − ve	5.975	6.320	4.205	0.195	6.205	6.940	6.245	0.195	6.115	6.625	6.430	0.165
't'% + ve	5.945	3.580	4.710	13.245	6.395	5.515	2.790	15.715	6.190	5.435	2.615	16.525
df = 500												
OLSEG	9.998	0.150	n.a	n.a	10.001	0.477	n.a	n.a	9.998	0.493	n.a	n.a
't'% − ve	18.200	100	n.a	n.a	17.420	49.120	n.a	n.a	18.225	31.985	n.a	n.a
't'% + ve	15.450	0	n.a	n.a	18.065	2.410	n.a	n.a	17.765	7.050	n.a	n.a
IVB	9.999	0.501	−0.201	−0.989	10.001	0.500	−0.202	−0.983	9.999	0.500	−0.203	−0.983
't'% − ve	5.250	5.600	4.650	1.850	5.280	5.460	5.765	1.980	5.485	5.455	6.135	2.115
't'% + ve	5.200	4.500	5.550	7.850	5.465	4.795	3.805	9.370	5.135	5.065	4.115	9.460

Notes: Table entries are the estimated means of the coefficients over the simulation; numbers in the second and third lines of each set are the percentage of times that the associated 't' statistic fell outside the range given by $-t_{0.05}(\text{df})$ and $+t_{0.05}(\text{df})$, respectively; n.a. indicates not applicable; DGP for X_t is $X_t = \phi_1 X_{t-1} + \omega_t$ and DGP for Y_t is $Y_t = 5 + 0.15X_t + 0.1X_{t-1} + 0.5Y_{t-1} + \varepsilon_t$, or in Bewley form $Y_t = 10 + 0.5X_t - 0.2\Delta X_t - \Delta Y_t + 2\varepsilon_t$; ε_t and ω_t are uncorrelated, normal white noise with zero mean and unit variance.

of omitted variables bias in a regression with stationary variables; the estimator of φ_2 is biased and the 't' statistics should not be used for inference. Of particular interest in this context is whether, when X_t is stationary but nearly integrated, the OLSEG estimator is close to the case when X_t is integrated. This is the case: the OLSEG estimator is substantially less biased than when $\phi_1 = 0$ and close to the case when $\phi_1 = 1$.

Note that IVB dominates OLSEG in terms of lack of bias for the three values of ϕ_1. The point of particular interest here though is the performance of the IVB estimator in the 'nearly' integrated case. Here the difference in results is much less marked than for the OLSEG estimator;

nevertheless, for the smaller sample sizes considered, the IVB estimator of φ_2 is less biased for $\phi_1 = 0.975$ compared to $\phi_1 = 0$, and closer to the case where $\phi_1 = 1$. Note also that the negative bias in the IVB estimator of φ_2, which is more noticeable for $\phi_1 = 0$, causes some problems for the distribution of its 't' statistic; there is more of the distribution in the negative tail, even though the overall empirical size comes out approximately right at 10%. The reduction in the bias shown with $\phi_1 = 0.975$ helps to alleviate this problem and, in terms of the agreement of the empirical size in each tail with the nominal size of the test, it is better for the X_t process to be integrated rather than purely stationary.

Of note, throughout the values of ϕ_1, is the relatively slow convergence of the coefficient on ΔY_t and the consequential effect of this on its 't' statistic. (In the OLS estimator of the ADL model equivalent, this will show up in the coefficient on the lagged dependent variable.) For df $= 500$ the biases are 1.1% ($\phi_1 = 0$), 1.7% ($\phi_1 = 0.975$) and 1.7% ($\phi_1 = 1$); there is then too much of the empirical distribution of the 't' statistic in the positive tail – for example, 7.85% for $\phi_1 = 0$. (*Note*: The bias is positive because the true coefficient value is -1; for example, for df $= 50$, the bias is $-0.989 - (-1) = +0.011$.)

The results in this simulation (which assume no endogeneity), although limited, tend to confirm that, in contrast to the theoretical results, there is not a finite sample dichotomy between integrated and stationary processes. There is, rather, a continuum of finite sample distributions; for practical purposes it may be better to treat a nearly integrated process as an integrated process rather than as a stationary process. Hence, the low power of unit root tests when the root is close to 1 may be telling us what the finite sample distributions of the estimators subsequently indicate.

9.5.2 X_t integrated/nearly integrated and endogenous

Does endogeneity of the 'forcing' variable X_t materially alter the conclusions above? We know from Stock (1987) and Phillips and Hansen (*op. cit.*) that endogeneity does not affect the consistency of the OLSEG estimator; however, the limiting distribution of $T(\hat{\varphi}_2 - \varphi_2)$ is not centred on zero and this is referred to as second order bias. The extent of the bias depends upon Γ_{21} and, in general, the IVB estimator of φ_2 suffers from the same problem.

9.5.2a Contemporaneity

As the discussion of endogeneity in section **9.3** indicated we distinguish between contempor-

aneity and a failure of weak exogeneity. Contemporaneity, which we consider in this section, is achieved in the simulations by setting $\lambda \neq 0$ in $X_t = \phi_1 X_{t-1} + \omega_t$ where $\omega_t = \nu_t + \lambda \varepsilon_t$ with ν_t and ε_t uncorrelated, normal white noise.

Guidance from established theory is as follows. If X_t is stationary, which in this model corresponds to $|\phi_1| < 1$, the OLSEG estimator of φ_2 will lack consistency since plim$(X_t \varepsilon_t) \neq 0$ and will be biased since $E\{X_t \varepsilon_t\} = \lambda \sigma_\varepsilon \neq 0$. The superconsistency result of Stock (1987) applies to processes which are I(d), $d \geq 1$, and this is not applicable for $d = 0$, the stationary case. IVB lacks consistency since it is computationally equivalent to OLS on the ADL model and does not, therefore, avoid the problem of the correlation of X_t with ε_t. Where the expectation of the estimator exists, it is biased in finite samples and asymptotically. The 't' statistic for the estimator of φ_2 will not have a normal distribution asymptotically.

If X_t is I(1), contemporaneity does not affect the consistency of the estimators of φ_2 using OLSEG and IVB. However, there is a second order bias and, as a result, the 't' statistic on the IVB estimator of φ_2 does not have a standard 't' distribution. The OLSEG 't' statistic on φ_2 will not have a standard 't' distribution because of variables omitted from the levels regression (the DGP for Y_t is dynamic) and the second order bias.

With contemporaneity the DGP is now:

$$Y_t = 5 + 0.15X_t + 0.10X_{t-1} + 0.5Y_{t-1} + \varepsilon_t \qquad (9.101a)$$

$$X_t = \phi_1 X_{t-1} + \omega_t \qquad (9.101b)$$

$$\omega_t = \nu_t + \lambda \varepsilon_t \quad \lambda = 0.5 \qquad (9.101c)$$

The (conditional) variance matrix of $(\varepsilon_t, \omega_t)$ is

$$\Phi = \begin{bmatrix} \sigma_\varepsilon^2 & \sigma_{\varepsilon\omega} \\ \sigma_{\varepsilon\omega} & \sigma_\omega^2 \end{bmatrix}$$

where
$$\sigma_{\varepsilon\omega} = E\{\varepsilon_t(\nu_t + \lambda\varepsilon_t)\}$$
$$= \lambda\sigma_\varepsilon^2 \quad \text{using } E\{\varepsilon_t\nu_t\} = 0$$

and
$$\sigma_\omega^2 = E\{(\nu_t + \lambda\varepsilon_t)^2\}$$
$$= \sigma_\nu^2 + \lambda^2\sigma_\varepsilon^2$$

In the simulations $\sigma_\nu^2 = \sigma_\varepsilon^2 = 1$ and $\lambda = 0.5$ so

$$\Phi = \begin{bmatrix} 1 & 0.5 \\ 0.5 & 1.25 \end{bmatrix} \qquad (9.102)$$

As before three cases were distinguished: $\phi_1 = [0, 0.975, 1]$. To highlight the issues we concentrate on estimation by OLSEG and IVB (correct specification). Table 9.4 presents a summary of the main results.

Starting with the results for $\phi_1 = 0$, so X_t is clearly stationary, note that 'simultaneous equations bias' is evident in the IVB estimates of the long-run coefficient φ_2 (recall that in this set-up IVB is equivalent to OLS estimation of the dynamic model). The mean estimates for the three sample sizes are 1.282, 1.291 and 1.297, respectively, whereas the true value is 0.5. OLSEG does better than this, with a mean of about 0.54, even though it omits the dynamic terms from

Table 9.4 *Mean of $\hat{\varphi}_2$ for OLSEG and IVB estimators; X_t endogenous with different DGPs*

| | | | | | **Contemporaneity** | | | | | | | |
| | Pure stationarity $\phi_1=0,\ \lambda=0.5$ coefficients on: | | | | Nearly integrated $\phi_1=0.975,\ \lambda=0.5$ coefficients on: | | | | Integrated $\phi_1=1,\ \lambda=0.5$ coefficients on: | | | |
	$\hat{\varphi}_1$	$\hat{\varphi}_2$	ΔX_t	ΔY_t	$\hat{\varphi}_1$	$\hat{\varphi}_2$	ΔX_t	ΔY_t	$\hat{\varphi}_1$	$\hat{\varphi}_2$	ΔX_t	ΔY_t
df = 50												
OLSEG	10.000	0.537	n.a	n.a	9.997	0.526	n.a	n.a	9.987	0.509	n.a	n.a
't'% − ve	17.150	3.025	n.a	n.a	16.445	9.470	n.a	n.a	16.250	13.570	n.a	n.a
't'% + ve	17.065	7.670	n.a	n.a	16.460	24.220	n.a	n.a	16.285	18.270	n.a	n.a
IVB	10.000	1.282	−0.209	−0.945	9.998	0.521	0.489	−0.836	9.995	0.501	0.509	−0.836
't'% − ve	6.355	0	6.975	0.020	7.395	4.650	0	0	7.155	6.720	0	0
't'% + ve	6.390	73.765	1.285	15.420	7.235	10.710	80.95	22.375	7.150	7.190	83.355	22.58
df = 100												
OLSEG	10.000	0.543	n.a	n.a	9.997	0.525	n.a	n.a	9.993	0.505	n.a	n.a
't'% − ve	17.080	1.885	n.a	n.a	16.710	6.890	n.a	n.a	16.935	14.090	n.a	n.a
't'% + ve	17.220	10.475	n.a	n.a	16.920	30.900	n.a	n.a	16.455	19.110	n.a	n.a
IVB	10.000	1.291	−0.206	−0.970	10.000	0.521	0.534	−0.914	9.990	0.500	0.550	−0.910
't'% − ve	5.395	0	6.610	0.365	6.015	2.675	0	0.110	6.43	6.275	0	0.075
't'% + ve	5.755	95.470	2.425	12.195	6.190	12.965	99.350	16.735	6.295	6.520	99.590	16.985
df = 500												
OLSEG	10.000	0.548	n.a	n.a	10.003	0.522	n.a	n.a	10.00	0.501	n.a	n.a
't'% − ve	16.955	0.240	n.a	n.a	17.200	1.255	n.a	n.a	16.890	14.650	n.a	n.a
't'% + ve	17.040	27.390	4.155	17.130	62.315	n.a	n.a		17.260	19.150	n.a	n.a
IVB	10.000	1.297	−0.201	−0.992	10.000	0.520	0.569	−0.981	9.999	0.500	0.590	−0.981
't'% − ve	5.045	0	5.950	2.330	5.320	0.400	1.805	5.340	5.095	0	1.730	0
't'% + ve	5.210	100.00	3.915	8.505	5.515	31.845	100		5.260	5.290	100	9.358

Notes: Table entries are the estimated means of the coefficients over the simulation; numbers in the second and third lines of each set are the percentage of times that the associated 't' statistic fell outside the range given by $-t_{0.05}(\text{df})$ and $+t_{0.05}(\text{df})$, respectively; n.a. indicates not applicable; DGP for X_t is $X_t = \phi_1 X_{t-1} + \omega_t$ and DGP for Y_t is $Y_t = 5 + 0.15X_t + 0.1X_{t-1} + 0.5Y_{t-1} + \varepsilon_t$, or in Bewley form $Y_t = 10 + 0.5X_t - 0.2\Delta X_t - \Delta Y_t + 2\varepsilon_t$; $\omega_t = \nu_t + \lambda\varepsilon_t$, $\lambda = 0.5$; ε_t and ν_t are uncorrelated, normal white noise with zero mean and unit variance.

the estimating equation (but note that the bias increases with the sample size).

The 't' statistics on the OLSEG estimators of the long-run coefficients clearly do not have the 't' distribution because of the omitted dynamics and contemporaneity. (Recall that in order for an OLS estimator of the levels regression to deliver estimators with 't' distributions it is necessary, in general, to use the Phillips–Hansen FMOLS estimator – see section **9.4**.) The 't' statistic on the IVB estimator of φ_2 also does not have the 't' distribution.

The IVB estimator of the coefficient on ΔX_t is virtually unbiased (because X_{t-1} is not correlated with ε_t); for example, with df $= 500$, the mean of the estimates is -0.201. The estimator of the coefficient on ΔY_t converges more slowly with a slight bias, of -0.8%, at df $= 500$. Although at df $= 500$ the overall actual size associated with the 't' statistics on these two coefficients is close to the nominal size of 10%, this hides a skewness in each empirical distribution, with too much in the left tail for the coefficient on ΔX_t and too much in the right tail for the coefficient on ΔY_t.

It is convenient now to look at the results for the case $\phi_1 = 1$, so X_t is I(1). The OLSEG estimator although consistent is expected to be asymptotically biased. However, the empirical bias is slight – indeed it is less than when there is no endogeneity; for df $= 500$ the mean of the estimates of φ_2 is 0.501, a bias of 0.2%. The IVB estimator of φ_2 is effectively unbiased even for df $= 100$. There is thus a clear contrast between the results comparing $\phi_1 = 0$ and $\phi_1 = 1$. A second contrast is that the actual size of the 't' statistic on the IVB estimator of φ_2, at 10.38%, is very close to the nominal size of 10% for df $= 500$, with no evidence of asymmetry. A third contrast is that the estimator of the coefficient on ΔX_t is biased; with df $= 500$ the mean estimate is 0.59 compared to the true value of -0.2. (Note that this also contrasts with the no contemporaneity case – see Table 9.3.) This finding is then reflected in the 't' statistic

of the estimated coefficient on ΔX_t, which is not centred about the true value of the coefficient and has a rejection rate approaching 100%. In effect the simultaneous equations bias has been transferred to the stationary endogenous variable when $\phi_1 = 1$.

As IVB estimation is equivalent to OLS estimation of the ADL model and direct estimation of the nonlinear ECM, the consequences of endogeneity with an I(1) regressor are that while the long run remains consistently estimated, the coefficients on ΔX_t and ΔY_t are not consistently estimated. Whereas with contemporaneity (simultaneity) and an I(0) regressor, the long run is not consistently estimated although the coefficients on ΔX_t and ΔY_t are consistently estimated.

(Note that endogeneity does make a difference. The reduction in the bias of OLSEG is noticeable throughout the range of sample sizes; for example, with df $= 100$ the bias in estimating φ_2 is only 0.972% compared to 6.820% without endogeneity; and while IVB is still the superior of the alternative methods there is much less to choose between them.)

The three contrasts form a basis for assessing whether, when X_t is generated by a nearly integrated process, guidance as to estimation and inference better comes from the stationary or nonstationary case.

We consider bias first. When $\phi_1 = 0.975$, the bias in the OLSEG estimator of φ_2 is about 5% and, in contrast to $\phi_1 = 0$, the bias decreases slowly with the sample size which, at least in terms of direction, is like the nonstationary case. The IVB estimator of φ_2 is also biased, the mean of the estimates coming out at around 0.52 for df $= 500$, compared to the true value of 0.5. For the purposes of this comparison, note that the IVB estimates of φ_2, for the nearly integrated X_t process, are much closer to those from the integrated case than the pure stationarity case. For example, with df $= 500$ the means of the estimates of φ_2 for the three cases, $\phi_1 = 0, 0.975$ and 1.0, are 1.297, 0.520 and 0.500, respectively.

Even though the empirical bias is slight when $\phi_1 = 0.975$, for example 4% for df = 500, it is enough to throw the distribution of the 't' statistic off-centre with 31.845% rejections coming from the right-hand tail and only 0.4% from the left-hand tail for a nominal size of 10%. The third point of comparison is with the estimated coefficient on ΔX_t. Here the 'nearly' integrated case is much like the integrated case. The bias is substantial; for example, for df = 500 the mean estimated coefficient on ΔX_t is 0.569 compared to -0.201 for $\phi_1 = 0$ and 0.590 for $\phi_1 = 1$.

Overall, for estimation purposes, although the nearly integrated process, $X_t = 0.975X_{t-1} + \omega_t$, is a stationary process, it has effects much like the integrated process. Certainly using the theory of stationary processes as guidance would be misleading for IVB estimation (and hence any of the equivalent formulations). These results again suggest that the dichotomy in the theoretical distributions which depends upon whether $\phi_1 = 1$ or $|\phi_1| < 1$ is misleading for finite samples. However, care has to be taken in assuming that a 'nearly' integrated process can be treated in all respects like an integrated process; we have seen that this is not so for the distribution of the 't' statistics for the long-run coefficient, φ_2; the small bias present results in the associated 't' statistic not being centred on the true value.

Before considering the failure of weak exogeneity it is worth noting some other aspects of the simulation results. The finite sample biases of both OLSEG and IVB are not substantial when X_t is integrated; for df = 500 both methods deliver essentially unbiased estimates of φ_2 *despite* contemporaneity. While this is in line with Inder's (*op. cit.*) findings, here we find that IVB is not so dominant over OLSEG; in addition we find that the bias in the estimates of the short-run coefficient, on the stationary 'endogenous' variable ΔX_t, could be of concern. A possible route for improvement is to recognise the endogeneity of ΔX_t and use an instrumental variable approach. (In terms of what is happening in OLS estimation of the ADL model, the estimator of the short-run coefficient on X_t is biased,

but this bias is not translated into the estimator of the long-run coefficient.)

9.5.2b Failure of weak exogeneity

Failure of weak exogeneity occurs when the variance matrix for the system comprising the reduced form for Y_t and the marginal process for X_t is not diagonal – see section **9.3.2**. Assuming X_t is I(1), weak exogeneity will fail when X_t is correlated with lagged values of ε_t. This correlation could arise from a moving average process – see Phillips (1988) – or an autoregressive process – see Banerjee *et al.* (1993). We illustrate the results with an AR process. If X_t is I(1) then, as with contemporaneity, the OLSEG and IVB estimators will remain superconsistent but will have a second order bias which depends upon Γ_{21}. The 't' statistics for the OLSEG estimator will not have a standard 't' distribution because the levels regression omits variables (of lower order in probability) and because of endogeneity; the 't' statistic for the IVB estimator will just suffer from the latter problem. If X_t is I(0) then, in contrast to contemporaneity (or 'simultaneous equations bias') the IVB estimator of all the coefficients should be consistent and asymptotically unbiased.

The DGP is now:

$$Y_t = 5 + 0.15X_t + 0.10X_{t-1} + 0.5Y_{t-1} + \varepsilon_t \tag{9.103a}$$

$$X_t = \phi_1 X_{t-1} + \omega_t \tag{9.103b}$$

$$\omega_t = \theta_{21}\varepsilon_{t-1} + \nu_t \quad \theta_{21} = 0.5 \tag{9.103c}$$

A nonzero value of θ_{21} ensures long-run endogeneity through the failure of weak exogeneity. To ensure that the focus is on this aspect of endogeneity, ε_t and ν_t have a zero covariance, so there is no contemporaneity.

As before, to establish a point of reference we first consider the simulation results for $\phi_1 = 0$. The OLSEG estimator of φ_2 is biased for the three sample sizes considered here because the

Table 9.5 *Mean of $\hat{\varphi}_2$ for OLSEG and IVB estimators; X_t endogenous with different DGPs*

| | \multicolumn{12}{c}{**Failure of weak exogeneity**} |
| | \multicolumn{4}{c}{Pure stationarity $\phi_1 = 0$, $\theta_{21} = 0.5$ coefficients on:} | \multicolumn{4}{c}{Nearly integrated $\phi_1 = 0.975$, $\theta_{21} = 0.5$ coefficients on:} | \multicolumn{4}{c}{Integrated $\phi_1 = 1$, $\theta_{21} = 0.5$ coefficients on:} |
	$\hat{\varphi}_1$	$\hat{\varphi}_2$	ΔX_t	ΔY_t	$\hat{\varphi}_1$	$\hat{\varphi}_2$	ΔX_t	ΔY_t	$\hat{\varphi}_1$	$\hat{\varphi}_2$	ΔX_t	ΔY_t
df $= 50$												
OLSEG	9.998	0.332	n.a	n.a	10.000	0.439	n.a	n.a	10.013	0.437	n.a	n.a
't'% $-$ve	17.975	34.185	n.a	n.a	18.105	29.790	n.a	n.a	18.485	33.880	n.a	n.a
't'% $+$ve	17.525	0.660	n.a	n.a	18.040	5.260	n.a	n.a	18.615	4.165	n.a	n.a
IVB	9.997	0.447	-0.169	-0.936	10.002	0.427	-0.175	-0.859	10.002	0.426	-0.182	-0.869
't'% $-$ve	6.725	3.835	3.830	0.020	8.760	14.600	2.165	0	9.295	17.260	1.940	0
't'% $+$ve	6.405	4.800	2.890	15.420	8.605	2.155	5.845	22.130	9.150	1.570	5.715	21.815
df $= 100$												
OLSEG	10.000	0.342	n.a	n.a	10.000	0.470	n.a	n.a	10.008	0.464	n.a	n.a
't'% $-$ve	17.850	46.145	n.a	n.a	17.715	28.180	n.a	n.a	18.830	34.760	n.a	n.a
't'% $+$ve	18.030	0.265	n.a	n.a	18.040	17.365	n.a	n.a	18.760	4.390	n.a	n.a
IVB	10.000	0.476	-0.185	-0.970	10.000	0.463	-0.187	-0.922	10.010	0.459	-0.190	-0.920
't'% $-$ve	6.050	4.000	4.500	0.085	7.485	12.960	3.070	0.020	8.95	17.165	3.065	0.010
't'% $+$ve	5.755	5.065	3.885	13.460	7.650	2.145	6.055	16.570	8.935	1.400	5.475	16.790
df $= 500$												
OLSEG	10.000	0.348	n.a	n.a	9.999	0.496	n.a	n.a	9.999	0.493	n.a	n.a
't'% $-$ve	16.955	0.240	n.a	n.a	16.970	19.615	n.a	n.a	18.540	35.110	n.a	n.a
't'% $+$ve	17.040	27.390	n.a	n.a	17.445	13.305	n.a	n.a	18.100	4.700	n.a	n.a
IVB	10.000	0.496	-0.198	-0.993	9.999	0.493	-0.197	-0.984	9.999	0.492	-0.198	-0.984
't'% $-$ve	5.185	4.785	5.130	2.030	5.875	8.555	4.155	1.785	8.375	16.260	4.125	1.825
't'% $+$ve	5.210	5.290	4.630	8.605	5.635	3.270	5.585	9.655	8.375	0.995	5.365	9.485

Notes: Table entries are the estimated means of the coefficients over the simulation; numbers in the second and third lines of each set are the percentage of times that the associated 't' statistic fell outside the range given by $-t_{0.05}(df)$ and $+t_{0.05}(df)$, respectively; n.a. indicates not applicable; DGP for X_t is $X_t = \phi_1 X_{t-1} + \omega_t$ and DGP for Y_t is $Y_t = 5 + 0.15X_t + 0.1X_{t-1} + 0.5Y_{t-1} + \varepsilon_t$, or in Bewley form $Y_t = 10 + 0.5X_t - 0.2\Delta X_t - \Delta Y_t + 2\varepsilon_t$; $\omega_t = 0.5\varepsilon_{t-1} + \nu_t$, ν_t and ε_t are uncorrelated, normal white noise with zero mean and unit variance.

omitted variables are of the same order as the included variables. The results for IVB estimation are interesting and contrast with endogeneity parameterised as contemporaneity. The IVB estimators show small empirical biases; for example, for df $= 500$ the bias is 0.82% for the estimator of φ_2, and 1% and 0.75% for the coefficients on ΔX_t and ΔY_t, respectively. What matters for estimation, if X_t is undoubtedly stationary, is conventional simultaneous equations bias (contemporaneity) *not* long-run endogeneity. The actual size of the 't' statistics is close to their theoretical size, apart from the coefficient on ΔY_t where convergence is much slower.

Again it is convenient now to look at the results for $\phi_1 = 1$. First, note that the OLSEG estimator of φ_2, which is consistent when $\phi_1 = 1$, is better behaved because the omitted variables from the levels regression are of a lower order in probability than the included variables. There is a finite sample bias, which declines with the sample size, of -1.4% for df $= 500$. The IVB estimator of φ_2 also exhibits a bias and, in this simulation set-up, is not as close to the true value as the OLSEG estimator; for example, the bias at df $= 500$ is -1.7%. The mean of the estimates of the coefficient on ΔX_t is close to the case where $\phi_1 = 0$, with a bias of 1% for df $= 500$;

the estimated coefficient on ΔY_t is also biased – for example, 1.6% at df $= 500$, about double that for $\phi_1 = 0$. Compared to contemporaneity, the failure of weak exogeneity results in a noticeable bias in the IVB estimator of φ_2, but the estimated coefficient on ΔX_t does not suffer from such large biases. A second contrast with the contemporaneity case is that the empirical distributions of the 't' statistics for the IVB estimators of φ_2 (and φ_1) are not close to standard 't' distributions. The negative bias in the estimates of φ_2 is reflected in too much of the distribution in the left-hand tail.

What happens for the 'nearly' integrated process? The OLSEG estimator of φ_2 is very close to that for the nonstationarity case – for example, with df $= 50$ the mean estimate is 0.439 compared to 0.437 for $\phi_1 = 1$ and 0.332 for $\phi_1 = 0$. This picture is similar although not so marked for the IVB estimator. The lack of such a noticeable difference arises because, inference aside, there is not a marked contrast between any of the estimated coefficients in the two processes. For example, with df $= 500$ the mean IVB estimates of φ_2 are: 0.496 ($\phi_1 = 0$), 0.493 ($\phi_1 = 0.975$) and 0.492 ($\phi_1 = 1$). For $\phi_1 = 0$ the 't' statistic on φ_2 has an empirical size close to the nominal size; however, as the bias in estimating φ_2 increases with ϕ_1, the empirical distribution of the 't' statistic moves away from zero with too much of the distribution in the left-hand tail. Thus, although not so marked as in the case of contemporaneity, the 'nearly' integrated process has effects on estimation like an integrated process. As far as inference is concerned, the 't' statistic on ϕ_1 looks like that in the pure stationarity case, but the 't' statistic on φ_2 is affected by the bias in estimating φ_2 and moves in the direction of the nonstationary process.

9.5.2c Summary

A brief summary of the various results arising from the complications introduced in this section might be useful.

1. If X_t is 'exogenous' and generated by a nearly integrated process with a root 'close' to unity, then it mimics an integrated process both in estimation (by OLSEG or IVB) and inference

2. Endogeneity in the form of contemporaneity leads to the same conclusion unequivocally for IVB estimation. There was a clear contrast between the polar cases of pure stationarity, $\phi_1 = 0$, and nonstationarity, $\phi_1 = 1$. In the former case, the simulations illustrated the classical result of 'simultaneous equations bias' on the IVB estimator of φ_2; in the latter case the IVB estimator of φ_2 was empirically unbiased but the estimator of the coefficient on the stationary variable, ΔX_t, was biased. In IVB estimation the 'nearly' integrated process was very close to the integrated process. With OLSEG estimation the differences were not so marked; the OLSEG estimator, which is based on a regression with incorrectly omitted variables, was biased with $\phi_1 = 0$ and (almost) unbiased with $\phi_1 = 1$; the nearly integrated process was broadly in between with a moderate bias (of about 5% whatever the sample size).

3. The effects of endogeneity in the form of a failure of weak exogeneity (FOWE) can be distinguished from contemporaneity. When $\phi_1 = 1$, FOWE is more destructive than contemporaneity; however, when $\phi_1 = 0$ contemporaneity is more destructive than FOWE. With either FOWE or contemporaneity, IVB estimation with a nearly integrated process 'looks like' estimation with an integrated process. This is also the case for OLSEG estimation with FOWE; however, the differences are less marked for OLSEG estimation with contemporaneity.

4. Apparently small biases in estimating φ_2 can lead to 't' statistics which are not centred on the true value so inference with nearly integrated processes is not straightforward. For example, consider df $= 500$ with contemporaneity and IVB estimation of φ_2; then when $\phi_1 = 1$ the mean estimate is 0.5 and the overall empirical size of the 't' statistic

is 10.34%, split as 5.095%/5.29% in the left- and right-hand tails, very close to the nominal size of 10% suggesting that standard tables can be used for inference in large samples. When $\phi_1 = 0.975$ the mean IVB estimate is 0.52, a 'moderate' 4% bias; however, the overall size of the 't' statistic is 32.245% split as 0.4%/31.845% in the left- and right-hand tails and, hence, standard tables should not be used.

9.5.3 Sensitivity to changes in the design parameters: slow adjustment

Previous simulation studies suggest that a design parameter of particular importance is the coefficient, γ_1, on the lagged dependent variable in the ADL model; equivalently – see section **8.6.1** – the coefficient on the error correction term, $-(1 - \gamma_1)$ in the ECM representation. Adjustment to past disequilibria becomes slower as γ_1 moves closer to 1; hence, the time taken to adjust to a shock to equilibrium will be longer the closer γ_1 is to 1. This is likely to have an impact on estimators designed to 'discover' the long run where the long run has been 'contaminated' by I(0) adjustment dynamics. Intuitively the faster the adjustment to the long run the better will be the finite sample performance of estimators of the long run. In the simulations reported here (in section **9.5**) and section **8.7.2**, $\gamma_1 = 0.5$, so that in an ECM context 50% of adjustment to a disequilibrium takes place in one period and 75% in two periods. This is relatively fast adjustment, so it is important to assess whether any of the key results in this and the previous chapter depend upon this design parameter. The study by Inder (*op. cit.*) and a follow-up study by Montalvo (1995), which uses the same design, suggests that the magnitude of γ_1 is important. For example, Montalvo (*op. cit.*) finds a bias of -32.44% when $\gamma_1 = 0.8$, with $T = 50$ (no other sample sizes are considered) for the OLSEG estimator of φ_2, compared to a bias of -9.52% when $\gamma_1 = 0.8$. This is an exam-

ple of where superconsistency ensures faster than normal convergence but this is of little comfort if the starting point is a large finite sample bias.

The DGP for Y_t used in this and the previous chapter was revised to briefly assess the significance of the magnitude of γ_1. While keeping the same long-run solution, γ_1 was increased from 0.5 to 0.9, a typical value in empirical studies, implying an error correction coefficient of -0.1. The DGP for Y_t and X_t was: $Y_t = 1 + 0.03X_t + 0.02X_{t-1} + 0.9Y_{t-1} + \varepsilon_t$; and $X_t = X_{t-1} + \omega_t$. Three cases were distinguished according to the properties of ε_t and ω_t. In the first case, as in Chapter 8, X_t was 'exogenous', ε_t and ω_t were uncorrelated, standardised, normal white noise; in the second case contemporaneity was imposed as in section **9.5.2a**; and in the third case there was a FOWE as in section **9.5.2b**. To keep the comparison focused we concentrate on the effects of this change on the mean estimates of the long-run coefficients φ_1 and φ_2; these are summarised in Table 9.6. (A more complete table of results is the subject of a review question.)

We first consider the case where X_t is 'exogenous'. It is evident that increasing γ_1, which is equivalent to slowing down the response to past disequilibria in the ECM format, has profound effects on the OLSEG estimator. Even for a moderately sized sample with df $= 100$ the bias in estimating φ_2 is unacceptably large at -32.2%; and with df $= 500$ the bias is still quite large at -9.2%; these are increases (in absolute value) from -6.8% and -1.4% compared to when $\gamma_1 = 0.5$. In contrast, although the IVB estimator is empirically biased, and suffers relative to when $\gamma_1 = 0.5$, because it has a better starting point the impact of the increase in bias is numerically less important. For example, with df $= 100$ and 500 the biases are now -5.6% and 0.4% compared to -0.2% and 0%, respectively, when $\gamma_1 = 0.5$.

The next set of columns in the table refer to contemporaneity. Again the OLSEG estimator suffers more than the IVB estimator from the

Table 9.6 *The effect on the mean estimated long-run coefficients of increasing γ_1*

	X_t 'exogenous'		Contemporaneity		FOWE	
	$\hat{\varphi}_1$	$\hat{\varphi}_2$	$\hat{\varphi}_1$	$\hat{\varphi}_2$	$\hat{\varphi}_1$	$\hat{\varphi}_2$
df = 50						
OLSEG	10.070	0.259(0.437)	9.961	0.463(0.509)	9.993	0.324(0.437)
IVB	9.819	0.450(0.495)	10.330	0.522(0.501)	9.811	0.315(0.426)
df = 100						
OLSEG	9.995	0.339(0.466)	10.000	0.476(0.505)	10.009	0.352(0.464)
IVB	10.041	0.472(0.499)	10.027	0.495(0.500)	10.010	0.355(0.459)
df = 500						
OLSEG	9.992	0.454(0.493)	10.016	0.493(0.501)	10.000	0.382(0.493)
IVB	9.994	0.498(0.500)	10.020	0.499(0.500)	10.000	0.476(0.492)

Coefficients in parentheses are mean estimates when $\gamma_1 = 0.5$; main entries are for $\gamma_1 = 0.9$.
The DGP for Y_t is: $Y_t = 1 + 0.03X_t + 0.02X_{t-1} + 0.9Y_{t-1} + \varepsilon_t$. The Bewley form is $Y_t = 10 + 0.5X_t - 0.2\Delta X_t - 9\Delta Y_t + 10\varepsilon_t$. The DGP for X_t is: $X_t = X_{t-1} + \omega_t$. X_t 'exogenous' is where ε_t and ω_t are uncorrelated, standardised, normal white noise; with contemporaneity $\omega_t = 0.5\varepsilon_t + v_t$ where ε_t and v_t are uncorrelated, standardised, normal white noise; with FOWE $\omega_t = 0.5\varepsilon_{t-1} + v_t$ where v_t and ε_t are uncorrelated, standardised, normal white noise.

increase in γ_1 from 0.5 to 0.9. For example, with df = 100 the bias in estimating φ_2 by OLSEG increases from +1% to −4.8%; whereas for the IVB estimator the increase in absolute value is from 0% to −1%. The final set of columns refers to a failure of weak exogeneity. Here the changes for both estimators are quite marked, especially for the smaller sample sizes. For example, with df = 100 the biases increase from 7.2% to 29.6% for the OLSEG estimator and from 8.2% to 29% for the IVB estimator. The situation improves for the IVB estimator with df = 500 but not for the OLSEG estimator; for the latter the bias increases from 1.4% to 23.6% and for the former the bias increases from 1.6% to 4.8%.

These results are likely to be of empirical importance. Typical sample sizes with nonfinancial data are relatively small. For example, 25 years of observations with quarterly data give a sample of 100 observations, and even with a 'complete' set of post-war data the sample is unlikely to exceed 160 observations. In addition there is substantial evidence from studies of consumers' expenditure and the demand for money, that agents adjust to past disequilibria quite slowly, so that a value for γ_1, with quarterly data, of 0.9 is in the relevant range. The simulation results here indicate that, in general, great

care should be taken in using OLSEG rather than a method that takes into account the I(0) dynamics.

Most destructive to the finite sample properties of OLSEG is the combination of slow adjustment and a failure of weak exogeneity. Other simulation studies – see section **9.4.4** – suggest that while the FMOLS estimator is an improvement on OLSEG, when the true residuals are known, feasible FMOLS, which first estimates the residuals using OLSEG, is not dominant overestimation of the dynamic model (for example, using IVB or nonlinear estimation of an ECM). It is clear from the results in Table 9.6 that FOWE is potentially destructive not only to OLSEG but also to estimators based on a dynamic model. A sensible starting point where FOWE is likely to be present is to consider a system of equations and construct a test of whether weak exogeneity can be maintained. Johansen's (1992b) approach to this problem is described in Chapters 14 and 15.

9.6 Concluding remarks

Although simulation studies have not provided compelling practical reasons for using Phillips and Hansen's fully modified OLS estimator over the OLS estimator applied to a dynamic model, the framework provided by the motivation for this estimator is invaluable in understanding, at least theoretically, several important issues – especially the distinction between the short-run and the long-run variance. There is though support in the simulation studies for use of the 't' statistics associated with the FMOLS estimator of the long-run coefficients.

As Phillips (1988, p. 357) notes the methodology, associated with David Hendry, of simplifying an initially potentially overparameterised dynamic model by sequentially removing redundant variables '... comes remarkably close to achieving an optimal inference procedure. In some case it actually does so and in other cases it can be further modified to achieve it, as the Phillips–Hansen corrections indicate.' This is an important theoretical finding, which has implications for empirical research. It often seems beyond credibility that in a single-equation context there is no endogeneity, either in the form of contemporaneity or a lack of weak exogeneity (for the long-run parameters). The Phillips examples show how a dynamic equation might implicitly correct for endogeneity by including sufficient I(0) terms. However, this should not be taken as a prescription for just single-equation estimation in empirical research. There are gains, conceptually and potentially empirically, in explicit consideration of the full set of equations, particularly if there is more than one cointegrating vector and if more than one equation contains the cointegrating vector(s). This topic is developed further in Chapters 14 and 15.

There are also other single-equation OLS estimators which have been found to perform well in simulation studies. For example, in a development of the Hendry–Phillips approach Stock and Watson (1993) suggest an OLS estimator in a single-equation model which includes lagged I(0) terms, ΔX_t, as in (9.76) or (9.93), *and* leads; in effect they introduce a two-sided lag function on ΔX_t (assuming, for

simplicity, a single regressor), the idea being that this eliminates the asymptotic bias due to endogeneity or serial correlation. Montalvo (1995), in an extension of Inder's (*op. cit.*) study, reports simulation results which indicate that the two-sided dynamic OLS estimator is worthwhile in terms of the reduction of bias relative to both the OLSEG estimator and a canonical cointegration regression method due to Park (1992). While the one-sided (lag) dynamic OLS approach is not included in Montalvo's study, an earlier study by Stock and Watson (1993) suggested that the two-sided approach could have benefits relative to the lag-only approach.

Montalvo's (*op. cit.*) simulation results indicated that endogeneity, either in the form of contemporaneity or failure of weak exogeneity, leads to a reduction in empirical bias. This is so even for the OLSEG estimator, which makes no attempt at an endogeneity correction. In this sense endogeneity is good for estimator performance whether or not a corrected estimator is used. The results in this chapter, summarised in Tables 9.4 and 9.5, suggest that while contemporaneity has this beneficial effect, failure of weak exogeneity does not.

The plan of the remaining chapters is as follows. While previous chapters have included empirical examples, these have been illustrative of particular aspects of technique rather than substantive applications. The next four chapters consider four areas of application: the demand for money; the term structure of interest rates; the Phillips curve; and the exchange rate and purchasing power parity. Each chapter outlines a theoretical background and considers how econometric techniques are used in an empirical enquiry. These applications are essentially single-equation applications; this choice is partly governed by a desire to show that interesting results can be obtained in this limited context. A multi-equation setting, which builds directly upon the ideas introduced in this chapter, is used in Chapters 14 and 15.

Review

1. This chapter has taken the first step to focusing on the joint determination of all the variables in a (potentially) cointegrating relationship.
2. The distinction among the conditional, unconditional and long-run variance matrices is crucial to understanding whether a single equation can be considered without loss of information for the parameters of interest.
3. Throughout a simple prototypical example was used to motivate the distinction and its implications. In particular the data is assumed to be generated by

$$Y_t = \varphi_2 X_t + \varepsilon_t$$
$$X_t = X_{t-1} + \omega_t$$

Then the links between the equations were captured in the structure of ε_t and ω_t, especially in the variance–covariance matrix for $u_t = (\varepsilon_t, \omega_t)'$.
4. If ε_t has no structure and $\omega_t = \gamma \omega_{t-1} + v_t$, $|\gamma| < 1$ then the conditional variance of ω_t is σ_v^2; the unconditional variance is $\sigma_v^2/(1 - \gamma^2)$ and the long-run variance is $\sigma_v^2/(1 - \gamma)^2$.
5. The notation for the three variance matrices is: Φ, the conditional, or short-run, variance matrix; Ψ, the unconditional variance matrix; Ω, the long-run variance matrix.
6. The first extension of the set-up used in Chapter 8 is to allow ε_t and ω_t to be contemporaneously correlated; thus ε_t and $X_t = X_{t-1} + \omega_t$ are correlated. If X_t was stationary this would give rise to the classical problem of simultaneous equations bias in the OLS estimator of φ_2. In an I(1) context we refer to this as contemporaneity.
7. If there is contemporaneity but otherwise no structure in the process generating ε_t and ω_t then Φ has nonzero off-diagonal elements and $\Phi = \Psi = \Omega$.
8. A second extension is to allow a structure to the process generating ε_t and ω_t; for example, an AR process with intra- and inter-

equation serial correlation or an MA process with similar properties. In this case, in general, $\Phi \neq \Psi \neq \Omega$; and even if there is no contemporaneity the off-diagonal elements of Ψ and Ω are nonzero.
9. The long-run variance matrix can be decomposed in the following way:

$$\Omega = E\{u_0 u_0'\} + \sum_{k=1}^{\infty} E\{u_0 u_k'\}$$

$$+ \sum_{k=1}^{\infty} E\{u_0 u_k'\}'$$

$$= \Psi + \Lambda + \Lambda'$$

where $E\{u_0 u_0'\} = \Psi$, $\Lambda = \sum_{k=1}^{\infty} E\{u_0 u_k'\}$, $\Lambda' = \sum_{k=1}^{\infty} E\{u_0 u_k'\}'$.
10. Assuming stationarity: $E\{u_0 u_0'\} = E\{u_t u_t'\}$ and $E\{u_t u_k'\} = E\{u_{t-r} u_{t-r+k}'\}$.
11. An important matrix in the development of the Phillips–Hansen corrections to the OLSEG estimator is: $\Gamma \equiv \Psi + \Lambda$.
12. Estimating Γ and Ω can be done either by identifying a particular parameterisation of the structure of ε_t and ω_t, for example an MA, AR or ARMA specification, or by obtaining consistent estimators of $E\{u_t u_t'\}$ and $E\{u_t u_{t-k}'\}$ without detailed knowledge of the underlying structure; the latter approach is referred to as semi-parametric.
13. The distinction among the different variance matrices is crucial to an understanding of the meaning and implications of *endogeneity*.
14. Endogeneity arises either from contemporaneity or the failure of weak exogeneity, FOWE. The first of these is a relatively simple concept – see point 6 above; FOWE is more complex, and is not an absolute concept in the sense that it is defined with respect to particular parameters of interest, usually the long-run coefficients.
15. A simple example of FOWE was given by a first order MA process for ε_t and ω_t, this resulted in an equation for X_t in ECM form, which also involved the long-run coefficient, φ_2. Hence X_t was not weakly exogenous for φ_2.

16. Weak exogeneity will not fail in every case that the long-run variance matrix is not diagonal. Generally, problems arise when there are links, either MA or AR, between ω_t and lagged values of ε_t because past ε_t depend upon past $Y_t - \varphi_2 X_t$.

17. In general an innovation is defined by $\eta_t \equiv Y_t - E\{Y_t \mid X_t\}$ where $E\{Y_t \mid X_t\}$ is the conditional expectation function, CEF. Define $g_t = (\eta_t, \omega_t)'$ and conditional and long-run variance matrices Φ^* and Ω^*, then if Ω^* is diagonal X_t is weakly exogenous for the parameter of interest φ_2.

18. While endogeneity and serial correlation do not affect the superconsistency of OLSEG and IVB (or equivalently, for example, OLS on the ADL model) estimators of the long-run coefficients, the 't' statistics do not have standard normal distributions even asymptotically.

19. Phillips and Hansen (1990) show that a modified OLSEG estimator, which takes account of endogeneity and serial correlation, is superconsistent, asymptotically unbiased, asymptotically normally distributed and, provided a modified standard error is used, has an associated 't' statistic which is asymptotically normally distributed permitting inference using standard tables.

20. The fully modified OLS, FMOLS, estimator of Phillips and Hansen makes two corrections to the simple OLS estimator, one for bias and one for endogeneity.

21. The resulting FMOLS estimator of φ_2 in the prototypical system is:

$$\hat{\varphi}_2^+ = (\Sigma X_t Y_t^+ - T\hat{\Gamma}_{21}^+)/\Sigma X_t^2$$

where the endogeneity correction is

$$Y_t^+ = Y_t - (\hat{\Omega}_{21}\hat{\Omega}_{22}^{-1})\Delta Y_t$$

and the bias correction is

$$\hat{\Gamma}_{21}^+ = \hat{\Gamma}_{21} - \hat{\Omega}_{21}\hat{\Omega}_{22}^{-1}\hat{\Gamma}_{22}$$

22. The fully modified 't' statistic for the null hypothesis that $\varphi_2 = 0$ is

$$'t'^+(\varphi_2 = 0) = \hat{\varphi}_2^+/(\hat{\Omega}_{11}^+ \Sigma X_t^2)^{\frac{1}{2}}$$

where the adjusted long-run variance is

$$\hat{\Omega}_{11}^+ = \hat{\Omega}_{11} - \hat{\Omega}_{21}^2 \hat{\Omega}_{22}^{-1}$$

23. Consistent estimators of ε_t and ω_t can be obtained from OLS estimation of the equations for Y_t and X_t where the latter are extended, if necessary, to include a constant in the cointegrating equation and drift in the X_t equation.

24. Then a parametric or semi-parametric approach could be taken to form $\hat{\Gamma}_{21}$, $\hat{\Gamma}_{22}$, $\hat{\Omega}_{21}$ and $\hat{\Omega}_{22}$. Either a parametric structure is estimated for the $u_t = (\varepsilon_t, \omega_t)'$ process or semi-parametric estimates are obtained. Phillips and Hansen (1990) suggest the latter.

25. The bias correction requires an estimator of the appropriate element of

$$\Gamma = \Psi + \Lambda = E\{u_0 u_0'\} + \sum_{k=1}^{\infty} E\{u_0 u_k'\}$$

$$= E\{u_t u_t'\} + \sum_{k=1}^{\infty} E\{u_t u_{t+k}'\}$$

assuming stationarity. The infinite summation is truncated at a point l.

26. For the fully modified estimator it is necessary to obtain the elements of the long-run variance matrix; however, this is straightforward since $\Omega = \Gamma + \Lambda'$, so no information is needed other than that already used in calculating Λ.

27. Phillips (1988) shows that despite contemporaneity and/or serial correlation in the ω_t process, there are some cases where optimal estimation and inference will be obtained from OLS estimation of a single equation provided the cointegrating relationship is augmented by lag(s) of ΔX_t. These results provide a link between the

dynamic single-equation modelling methodology associated with David Hendry and an optimal approach.

28. Two examples were used to illustrate the Phillips–Hansen, FMOLS, estimator. The first was the consumption–income example used in Chapter 8 and Chapter 5; and, second, the relationship between the long-run and short-run rates of interest.

29. The results from several simulation studies provide somewhat mixed evidence for whether the FMOLS dominates other single-equation estimators in finite samples. The problem is that the corrections require prior estimation of the appropriate elements of Γ and Ω, and these are based on the first-stage estimation using OLSEG, which has rather poor properties.

30. A study by Inder (1993) suggested that, even with contemporaneity and FOWE, the OLS estimator from a single-equation dynamic model (which is equivalent to IVB estimation) was usually the best estimator.

31. The simulation evidence seems somewhat stronger on the distribution of the modified 't' statistic being closer to being correctly distributed in finite samples than some other 't' statistics.

32. The differences between the implications of endogeneity, especially contemporaneity, for regressions involving I(0) variables compared to I(1) variables offers the opportunity to assess whether regressions involving stationary but nearly integrated variables behave like the former or the latter.

33. From the theory of stationary variables contemporaneity implies estimator inconsistency; whereas the property of consistency is retained for nonstationary variables.

34. While the simulation results reported in section **9.5** are only illustrative, they did suggest some interesting tentative conclusions. The key parameter was ϕ_1 in $X_t = \phi_1 X_{t-1} + \omega_t$, with $\phi_1 = 0, 0.975, 1$.

35. A benchmark simulation set-up with no endogeneity showed that the OLSEG estimator performed very poorly when $\phi_1 = 0$ but when $\phi_1 = 0.975$ was close to the results obtained when $\phi_1 = 1$.

36. Endogeneity was distinguished by contemporaneity or FOWE. In the former case when $\phi_1 = 0$, so X_t is clearly stationary, 'simultaneous equations bias' was evident in the IVB estimates of the long-run coefficient while the IVB estimator of the coefficient on ΔX_t was virtually unbiased.

37. When $\phi_1 = 1$, in contrast to when $\phi_1 = 0$, the IVB estimator of the long-run coefficient was empirically unbiased but the estimator of the coefficient on ΔX_t was biased In effect the simultaneous equations bias has been transferred to the stationary endogenous variable when $\phi_1 = 1$.

38. When $\phi_1 = 0.975$ the IVB estimator of φ_2 was biased but much closer to the case when $\phi_1 = 1$ than $\phi_1 = 0$, and similar results held for the estimated coefficient on ΔX_t. Here the 'nearly' integrated case is much like the integrated case despite the fact it is stationary.

39. These results again suggest that the dichotomy in the theoretical distributions which depends upon whether $\phi_1 = 1$ or $|\phi_1| < 1$ is misleading for finite samples; but a 'nearly' integrated process cannot be treated in all respects like an integrated process. Because there is still a bias, albeit small, when $\phi_1 = 0.975$, the 't' statistic for φ_2 is not centred on the true value.

40. The simulation then modelled a FOWE through an MA(1) process linking X_t to past values of ε_t. For the 'nearly' integrated process the OLSEG estimator of φ_2 is very close to that for the nonstationarity case; for example, with df $= 50$ the mean estimate is 0.439 compared to 0.437 for $\phi_1 = 1$ and 0.332 for $\phi_1 = 0$.

41. This picture is similar although not so marked for the IVB estimator where there is a lack of marked differences among the estimates for the different values of ϕ_1. For example, with df $= 500$ the mean IVB

estimates of φ_2 are: 0.496 ($\phi_1 = 0$), 0.493 ($\phi_1 = 0.975$) and 0.492 ($\phi_1 = 1$).

42. Although not so marked as in the case of contemporaneity, with FOWE the 'nearly' integrated process has effects on estimation like an integrated process.

43. In conclusion, the evidence from simulation studies is that for the full benefit of the Phillips–Hansen corrections the true 'residuals', ε_t and ω_t, have to be known; replacing these with relatively poor estimates from first-stage OLSEG estimation quickly removes the benefit of FMOLS over other single-equation methods.

44. Nevertheless, the conceptual basis involved in defining the Phillips–Hansen corrections has considerable benefit in extending the single-equation framework to a more realistic multi-equation paradigm; a theme which is taken up again in Chapters 14 and 15.

Review questions

1. Why do the conditional, unconditional and long-run variance matrices differ?

2. (i) Given the following structure confirm the long-run variance matrix:

$$Y_t = \varphi_2 X_t + \varepsilon_t$$
$$X_t = X_{t-1} + \omega_t$$

$$\begin{pmatrix} \varepsilon_t \\ \omega_t \end{pmatrix} = \begin{bmatrix} 1 & 0 \\ 0 & 1 \end{bmatrix} \begin{pmatrix} \zeta_t \\ \upsilon_t \end{pmatrix}$$
$$+ \begin{bmatrix} 0.2 & 0.3 \\ 0.0 & 0.4 \end{bmatrix} \begin{pmatrix} \zeta_{t-1} \\ \upsilon_{t-1} \end{pmatrix}$$

with $\Phi = I$, generates

$$\Omega = \begin{bmatrix} 1.53 & 0.42 \\ 0.42 & 1.96 \end{bmatrix}$$

$$\begin{pmatrix} \varepsilon_t \\ \omega_t \end{pmatrix} = \begin{bmatrix} 1 & 0 \\ 0 & 1 \end{bmatrix} \begin{pmatrix} \zeta_t \\ \upsilon_t \end{pmatrix}$$
$$+ \begin{bmatrix} 0.2 & 0.0 \\ 0.3 & 0.4 \end{bmatrix} \begin{pmatrix} \zeta_{t-1} \\ \upsilon_{t-1} \end{pmatrix}$$

with $\Phi = I$, generates

$$\Omega = \begin{bmatrix} 1.44 & 0.36 \\ 0.36 & 1.96 \end{bmatrix}$$

(ii) Explain why Ω is nondiagonal even though $\Phi = I$.

(iii) Suppose $\Phi = \begin{bmatrix} 1 & 0.5 \\ 0.5 & 1 \end{bmatrix}$

derive and interpret Ω and compare it with the case when $\Phi = I$.

3. As before suppose that

$$Y_t = \varphi_2 X_t + \varepsilon_t$$
$$X_t = X_{t-1} + \omega_t$$

but ε_t and ω_t follow the MA(1) process:

$$\begin{pmatrix} \varepsilon_t \\ \omega_t \end{pmatrix} = \begin{bmatrix} 1 & 0 \\ 0 & 1 \end{bmatrix} \begin{pmatrix} \zeta_t \\ \upsilon_t \end{pmatrix}$$
$$+ \begin{bmatrix} \theta_{11} & \theta_{12} \\ \theta_{21} & \theta_{22} \end{bmatrix} \begin{pmatrix} \zeta_{t-1} \\ \upsilon_{t-1} \end{pmatrix}$$

where

$$\Phi = \begin{bmatrix} \sigma_\zeta^2 & \sigma_{\zeta\upsilon} \\ \sigma_{\zeta\upsilon} & \sigma_\upsilon^2 \end{bmatrix}$$

Obtain and interpret $\Gamma = \Psi + \Lambda$ and Ω.

4. (i) Given $u_t = A u_{t-1} + \eta_t$ as in the text, with $E\{\eta_t\} = 0$ for all t, show by successive backsubstitution that

$$u_t = A^{j+1} u_{t-(j+1)} + \sum_{i=0}^{j} A^i \eta_{t-i}$$

(ii) Note that $A^{j+1} \to 0$ as $j \to \infty$ so, in the limit – or long run in this context – the first term can be ignored leaving

$$u_t = \sum_{i=0}^{\infty} A^i \eta_{t-i}$$

Confirm that u_t has a zero mean.

(iii) Using the result that $\sum_{i=0}^{j} A^i \rightarrow (I - A)^{-1}$ as $j \rightarrow \infty$ – see, for example, Lutkepohl (1991, p. 10) – confirm that the long-run variance matrix for $u_t = \sum_{i=0}^{\infty} A^i \eta_{t-1}$ is

$$\Omega = (I - A)^{-1} \Phi (I - A')^{-1}$$

5. In the next example, the simple cointegrated system is extended to add a third variable:

$$Y_t = \varphi_1 + \varphi_2 X_t + \varphi_3 Z_t + \varepsilon_t$$
$$X_t = \mu_X + X_{t-1} + \omega_t$$
$$Z_t = \mu_Z + Z_{t-1} + \bar{\omega}_t$$
$$h_t \equiv (\varepsilon_t, \omega_t, \bar{\omega}_t)'$$

(i) Write the conditional variance matrix, Φ, for h_t assuming contemporaneity.

(ii) Assuming no structure for h_t other than contemporaneity explain how you would estimate Φ and hence Ω.

(iii) What condition(s) ensure weak exogeneity of X_t and Z_t for the parameters φ_1, φ_2 and φ_3?

(iv) Rewrite the equation for Y_t in error correction format.

6. (i) Explain the semi-parametric approach to estimating Γ and Ω.

(ii) What choice parameters are involved in the semi-parametric approach and how are these chosen?

(iii) Explain the parametric approach to estimating Γ and Ω.

(iv) What elements of choice are involved in the parametric approach?

7. (i) Explain why the covariance of ε_t with lags of ω_t is relevant for adjustments to the OLSEG estimator just based on Γ, whereas the covariance of ε_t with leads of ω_t is also relevant for adjustments based on Γ and Ω.

(ii) Is $E\{\varepsilon_t\varepsilon_{t-k}\} = E\{\varepsilon_t\varepsilon_{t+k}\}$? Explain your answer.

(iii) Is $E\{\varepsilon_t\omega_{t-k}\} = E\{\varepsilon_t\omega_{t+k}\}$? Explain your answer.

8. (i) Discuss the following statement: 'As the true residuals are rarely available, the feasible FMOLS estimator loses much of its theoretical advantage over the OLSEG estimator in finite samples.'

(ii) Suggest a method that has the potential to improve over feasible FMOLS (when the latter is based on prior estimation by OLSEG).

9. Discuss the following statement: 'Feasible FMOLS is a realistic alternative to OLS estimation of a dynamic model, because it is robust to the unknown dynamic structure.'

10. Distinguish between the effects of contemporaneity on regressions involving (a) clearly stationary variables and (b) I(1) variables.

11. Suppose the DGP for Y_t in a simulation study is:

$$Y_t = \alpha_0 + \beta_0 X_t + \beta_0 X_{t-1} + \gamma_1 Y_{t-1} + \varepsilon_t$$
$$X_t = X_{t-1} + \omega_t$$

Which design parameters are likely to be important in determining the results of the simulation?

Part III
Applications

CHAPTER 10

The demand for money

10.1 Introduction

One of the most important areas for the development and application of statistical and quantitative techniques has been in studying the demand for money. In this chapter we take two historical episodes and undertake an empirical analysis using the concepts of integration and cointegration introduced in earlier chapters. The historical periods considered are quite different and serve to illustrate the flexibility of the concepts and empirical tools. The first period, covering the months from 1921 through to the end of 1923, is short but justification for consideration of such a short sample is provided by the substantial academic interest in that period. It refers to a particularly interesting time after the First World War in Germany in which inflation was high enough to lead to it being described as *hyperinflation*. The justification for using a fairly small sample period corresponds in part to the difficulty in obtaining a consistent dataset for a longer period, but also to the idea that this hyperinflationary episode had some special characteristics which distinguished it from adjacent historical periods. The second dataset we consider brings us up to date in looking at a recent sample of monthly data for the United States; we apply the same techniques and find some interesting results.

In this chapter section **10.2** is concerned with some general theoretical principles which underpin many empirical studies of the demand for money. Subsections outline the transactions, precautionary and speculative motives for holding money. Section **10.3** is concerned with an application to the hyperinflationary period in post-First World War Germany. This section includes subsections on the historical background and the influential article by Cagan (1956) which specifies a demand for money function for hyperinflationary situations. Non-stationarity is assessed and possible cointegrating specifications are estimated. Section **10.4** switches to a more contemporaneous time period: the United States for the period 1974 to 1993. Even though the time period and country change the general principles find considerable support. Section **10.5** draws some together concluding remarks.

10.2 The demand for money

10.2.1 A definition of money

An empirical study of the demand for money presupposes that we are able to define 'money'. In practice there are a number of official, statistical definitions of money, which we try and match to the chosen conceptual measure of money deriving from the functions that money performs. Presently, official sources – the Federal Reserve Board in the United States and the Bank of England in the United Kingdom – define money at its least inclusive to include currency (notes and coins), demand deposits at commercial banks and other checkable deposits (that is deposits against which checks can be written), and at its most extensive to include time deposits in commercial banks and thrift institutions in the United States and building societies in the United Kingdom. (The differences between the two countries are matters of detail rather than substance.)

Much empirical work on the demand for money has concentrated on money in its liquid form measured as currency in circulation plus demand deposits at commercial banks; together these were known as M1. However, in the 1980s this definition of money had to respond to institutional changes such as the introduction in the United States of NOW (negotiable order of withdrawal) accounts by thrift institutions, which are in liquidity and function – that of enabling transactions – just like commercial bank checkable deposits. This led to a redefinition of M1 to include not only demand deposits at commercial banks but also 'other checkable deposits'. Initially data on two narrowly defined monetary aggregates known as M-1A = currency + demand deposits at commercial banks and M-1B = M-1A + other checkable deposits, was published in the Federal Reserve Bulletin (Monetary Aggregates, Table A13) but in January 1982, M-1B was retitled as M1 and M-1A was not separately distinguished.

In matching a conceptual measure of money to an empirical measure we require a framework which motivates the former. Such a framework was provided by Keynes (1936) and is still relevant today. Keynes distinguished three motives for holding money: the transactions motive; the precautionary motive; and the speculative motive. We deal with these in turn in the next and subsequent sections.

10.2.2 The transactions motive

The demand for money for transactions purposes is perhaps the one that comes most immediately to mind because it is closely linked to the original function of money. That of facilitating the exchange of goods and services while avoiding barter, and since it is one that faces almost all households and corporations on a frequent basis. Money is held to facilitate trans-

actions because income and expenditure have very different time profiles; income is, generally, much 'lumpier' than expenditure. Wages, salaries and benefits all tend to be paid on a regular once a week or once a month basis, whereas expenditure needs usually have to be met on a daily basis. There is an imperfect synchronisation between the pattern of receipts and the pattern of expenditures whether taken on a monthly basis or a seasonal basis (for example, in smoothing over the exceptional expenditure associated with Christmas). How can we ensure that we have sufficient money on hand to meet expenditure needs, which occur more frequently than income receipts or are otherwise imperfectly synchronised with them, even when both are known with certainty? One possibility is simply to convert income into money (the means of transactions) immediately on its receipt. However, this is potentially a costly approach as has been pointed out by a number of authors – see especially Baumol (1952), Tobin (1956) and Barro (1976), upon which the following analysis is based. (For a development of the Baumol model see Karni (1973).)

Suppose, for simplicity that the only money available is currency while the nearest alternative in terms of liquidity – that is ease of access – is a thrift (building society) savings account which has a nominal interest rate, R, of 10% p.a. and that a typical individual has a monthly salary of $3,000. Then placing the salary on deposit would earn $0.1(\$3,000)/12 = \$25$ interest per month; but the flaw with this strategy is that it would leave the individual no means of payment! A more practical suggestion is to spread the transfers of income to money across the month to meet anticipated expenditure; if, for simplicity, we assume that expenditure is evenly spread across the month then the individual could make n transfers of $1/n$ of his income. For example, if $n = 2$ the individual transfers half his income immediately on its receipt and then transfers the remaining half halfway through the month. Let Y_m denote nominal, monthly income then the average monthly balance, M, is $(\frac{1}{2}Y_m/n)$ with a monthly interest cost of $R_m[\frac{1}{2}(Y_m/n)]$ where $R_m = R/12$; now it is clear that the opportunity cost of holding money goes to zero as $n \to \infty$, that is the number of transfers tends to infinity, with the implication that the average money balance tends to zero. We do not observe such a situation because transfers themselves have an opportunity cost which we capture in the function $c = c(n, b, Y_m)$, where b is the fixed cost of a transfer; in practice the nature of the transfer costs depends upon the alternative asset to money. For transfers between near money, for example a no access penalty thrift or building society account and money, the costs tend to be psychological rather than actual in nature. Where the alternative is a T-Bond or an access penalty thrift or building society account, with R_m likely to be higher, transfer costs take a physical form in a broker's fee or interest related penalty. The individual is assumed to minimise total costs, TC, which are the sum of transfer costs and the opportunity cost of holding money balances. To simplify the analysis assume that one transfer a month is essential so that $n \geq 1$, this can be justified by assuming either that income is first paid into the savings account and then has to be transferred into cash, Dornbusch and Fischer (1981), or that each time income is received it is necessary to 'go to the bank', Barro (1976).

The objective is to minimise $TC = c(n, b, Y_m) + R_m[\frac{1}{2}(Y_m/n)]$. The usual suggestion for the transfer cost function is simply $c(n, b, Y_m) = nb$, that is each transaction carries a fixed cost b. Minimising TC with respect to n, the number of transfers, we obtain:

$$\frac{\partial TC}{\partial n} = \frac{\partial\{nb + R_m[\frac{1}{2}(Y_m/n)]\}}{\partial n}$$

$$= b - R_m Y_m/2n^2 \qquad (10.1)$$

and

$$\frac{\partial^2 TC}{\partial n^2} = \frac{R_m Y_m}{n^3} > 0 \quad \text{for } n > 0$$

Setting the first derivative to zero is a necessary condition for a minimum (noting that the second derivative with respect to n is positive for $n > 0$ as required for a minimum), and solving for n, with the optimum denoted n^*, we find

$$n^* = (R_m Y_m/2b)^{0.5} \qquad (10.2)$$

The optimal number of transfers increases with the nominal interest rate and nominal income and decreases with the broker's fee. To find the optimal average holding of money we substitute n^* into $M = (\frac{1}{2})Y_m/n$ to obtain

$$M^* = (bY_m/2R_m)^{0.5} \qquad (10.3)$$

where M^* is the optimal money balance. This expression shows that the income and interest rate elasticities of M^* and R_m are equal but opposite in sign at 0.5 and -0.5, respectively; this is the famous 'square root' rule of optimal money balances viewed as an inventory to hold against *known* expenditure needs.

An income elasticity of 0.5 implies that money balances increase less than in proportion to an increase in income; another way of putting this is to say that there are economies of scale in money holdings. This feature arises because the cost function is simplified to $c(n, b, Y_m) = nb$ and so, specifically, there is a fixed cost per transaction independent of the scale of the transaction and of income. It could be argued that this is rather unrealistic of transaction costs in two respects. First, the fee, whether it is a broker's fee or penalty cost, is likely to be related to the scale of the withdrawal or transfer; second, where no broker's fees are formally incurred, as in the transfer from one 'near money' asset to money, the time and trouble in making the transfer is likely to have an implicit opportunity cost – or shadow price – related to income. To explore the implications of this last suggestion we alter the cost function to $c(n, b, Y_m) = naY_m$ so that each transaction carries the cost aY_m and total transaction costs are naY_m, then we find that optimal money balances are

$$M^* = (a/2R_m)^{0.5}Y_m \qquad (10.4)$$

Now, while maintaining the interest elasticity at -0.5 the income elasticity has increased to 1.

Another argument which suggests that the income elasticity may be greater than 0.5 is due to Barro (1976), and see also Dornbusch and Fischer (1981). Barro noted that there is a need to constrain the optimal n to be an integer since an individual agent or corporation could not make, say, 1.29 transfers. To illustrate the importance of this point, we return to the original 'square root' formulation with cost function given by (10.1). Now consider an individual with a monthly salary of $3,000 with the nominal rate on 'near money' at 3% p.a., then we first derive the value of b which corresponds to $n^* = 1$, that is just one transfer per month with a corresponding average cash balance of $3,000/2 = $1,500. From (10.2) we find $b = $3.75, a moderate enough sum to suggest that the sort of calculations here are likely to be reasonable. Now with this value of b, what would Y_m have to be to induce a second transfer given that a noninteger number of transfers are not possible? (Recall that we are assuming that one transfer per month is necessary.)

The answer to this question is due to Barro (1976). First note that the second derivative of (10.1) with respect to n is positive for all $n \geq 0$, so that there is a single trough in $TC(n)$ corresponding to the unconstrained optimum, n^*. Let int(n^*) be the integer part of n^* and let n_I denote the optimal n constrained to be an integer, then n_I will be adjacent to n^* being either int(n^*) or int(n^*) + 1. n_I must satisfy the following criterion

$$TC(n_I - 1) \geq TC(n_I) \leq TC(n_I + 1) \qquad (10.5)$$

That is shifting n_I by one either way must not reduce costs. Substituting for TC from (10.1) and rearranging we obtain

$$[n_I(n_I - 1)]^{0.5} \leq n^* \leq [n_I(n_I + 1)]^{0.5}$$
$$\text{for } n_I \geq 1 \qquad (10.6)$$

For example, if n^* is between 0 and $2^{0.5} = 1.414$, then $n_I = 1$; if n^* is between $2^{0.5} = 1.414$ and

$6^{0.5} = 2.449$, then $n_I = 2$; if n^* is between $6^{0.5} = 2.449$ and $12^{0.5} = 3.464$, then $n_I = 3$; and so on.

Returning to the question posed above we see that the switchover point from $n_I = 1$ to $n_I = 2$ is $n^* = 2^{0.5}$; substituting this value into (10.2) and solving for Y_m we find the corresponding switchover point for monthly income is $Y_m = 4b/R_m = $6,000 for $b = 3.75$ and $R_m = 0.03/12$. That is monthly income has to double, from $3,000 to $6,000, before the number of transfers switches from 1 to 2. Hence for increases in income which raise the monthly salary to below the switchover limit, all of the increase in income is held in cash balances. For example, if income increases from $3,000 to $4,500, then the increase of $1,500 is added to cash balances increasing them from $1,500 to $1,500 + $1,500/2 = $2,250, so that the proportionate increase in cash balances exactly matches the proportionate increase in income; in this situation the income elasticity of money is +1 not +0.5.

By a similar line of reasoning the interest rate elasticity will not be as large, in absolute value, as the -0.5 given by (10.3). The integer constraint means that in order for changes in the nominal rate of interest to have an effect they have to be sufficient to induce a move to the next integer number of transfers; therefore, for some individuals interest rate changes will not induce any response in money demand and so, taking into account integer constraints, money demand will not be as interest elastic as suggested by (10.3).

The move to electronic transfers between accounts in the 1980s is likely to have reduced both the actual and psychological costs of transfers. In the context of (10.3) this implies that, *ceteris paribus*, n^* increases and M^* declines. However, if the trend of easier transfers is correlated with a trend increase in income then, without explicit recognition of these factors in an empirical demand for money function, the decline in equilibrium cash balances from this cause will reduce the estimated income elasticity.

The above analysis assumed that 'money' was not interest bearing so that an appropriate measure of the opportunity cost was the rate on a 'near' money alternative. However, in the United States NOW accounts, automatic transfers from savings, ATS, credit union share-draft balances and demand deposits at thrift institutions, all of which are included in the definition of M1, are interest earning checkable deposits. In principle such developments in a transaction-based measure of money can easily be taken into account with R, or R_m in (10.1), now defined as the spread between the 'own' rate on money and the money alternative. In practice where these components are a small proportion of the total the overall return, which is a weighted sum of zero and the product of the proportion of interest bearing assets times their rate of interest, may well still be sufficiently close to zero to warrant the usual practice in studies of the demand for M1 to take the own rate as zero. This assumption though should be under regular review. For example, in December 1980, other checkable deposits were just under 7% of M1 whereas in December 1995 they were just over 31% of M1.

10.2.3   The precautionary motive

While the transactions motive relates to smoothing the pattern of known expenditure needs given lumpy income, Keynes (1936, p. 196) suggested that precautionary money is held 'to provide for contingencies requiring sudden expenditure and for unforeseen opportunities of advantageous purchases, and also to hold an asset of which the value is fixed in terms of money to meet a subsequent liability in terms of money'.

Whalen (1966) suggested an extension and a qualification to this motive as expressed by Keynes. As to the extension he noted that the financial embarrassment of illiquidity could result from uncertainty as to the timing of receipts as well as sudden expenditure. The qualification is to note that if an asset is held to meet a subsequent liability and the date of payment is known, holding money for this purpose falls into the transactions rather than the precautionary motive. In essence the precautionary motive applies because net disbursements are uncertain.

Whalen (*op. cit.*) suggests that three factors affect the optimal size of precautionary cash balances (which we refer too simply as money): the cost of illiquidity; the opportunity cost of holding precautionary money; and the average volume and variability of receipts and disbursements. In an analysis, which is very similar to that for transactions balances, the individual, or corporation, can be viewed as minimising the cost of holding precautionary money. The objective function is

$$PC = p(d)c(d) + R_m M_p \qquad (10.7)$$

where $p(d)$ is the probability of financial 'distress', which occurs when required net disbursements are greater than precautionary money; $c(d)$ is a cost function which depends upon financial distress, thus $p(d)c(d)$ is the expected cost of each occurrence of financial distress arising from illiquidity; and, analogous to the term occurring in the transactions cost function, $R_m M_p$ is the opportunity cost, in terms of foregone interest, in holding precautionary money. For simplicity we assume that $c(d)$ is a constant, c, which is the cost of suffering financial distress; for a specification of $c(d)$ which takes into account variable costs see Whalen (*op. cit.*).

We assume that the distribution of net disbursements has a zero mean, so on average receipts equal expenditure, and standard deviation σ. The cost function, PC, captures the following trade-off. At one extreme an individual could hold no precautionary money, thus setting to zero the opportunity cost element; however, with $\sigma > 0$ there is a positive probability that required expenditure exceeds actual receipts and the individual suffers financial distress incurring a cost $c(d)$. For example, suppose the distribution of net disbursements is symmetric about a zero mean, then the probability of distress is 0.5. To reduce this probability the individual holds a positive M_p. Suppose, to illustrate the calculations, the distribution of net disbursements is normal and the individual holds precautionary money equal to $k\sigma$, then the probability of distress is the probability that required net disbursements are greater than $k\sigma$ from the mean (here equal to zero); for example, with precautionary money holdings of $2,000 and $\sigma = \$1,000$, so $k = 2$, and from tables of the normal distribution we see there is a 2.28% chance of financial distress; increasing k reduces the probability of financial distress but at the cost of increasing foregone interest, whether it is worth doing this depends upon the cost of financial distress. Suppose, to continue the example, the individual decides to wipe out the probability of distress and doubles M_p to $4,000, then $k = 4$ and consulting standard normal tables we see that $p(z \geq 4)$ is effectively zero; his aim has been achieved but at an overall cost of $R_m(\$4,000)$. These extremes suggest that, depending on the cost of distress, there is a holding of M_p that minimises PC.

To obtain a solution for optimal M_p requires some information about $p(d)$ and specifying the distribution of net disbursements will be sufficient. However, even without specification of the distribution Whalen (*op. cit.*) shows that some progress can be made. He uses Chebycheff's inequality – see Kendall and Stuart (1977, p. 90) – which states that $p(|x - \mu| \geq k\sigma) \leq 1/k^2$, that is the probability that a random variable x exceeds its mean, μ, by more than $k\sigma$ on either side is at most $1/k^2$; standardising the expression in brackets does not affect the inequality so that $p(|z| \geq k) \leq 1/k^2$ where $z = (x - \mu)/\sigma$. We can now apply this result to the problem of choosing optimal M_p.

The probability we seek is the probability that the random variable net disbursements, suitably standardised, will exceed $+k$ where $k = M_p/\sigma$, since when net disbursements exceed this value of k there is financial distress. We assume that

the distribution of net disbursements is symmetric otherwise, from Chebycheff's inequality, we cannot assign a probability to a positive deviation of k in the standardised distribution or $k\sigma$ in the unstandardised distribution. The required probability is at most

$$0.5(1/k^2) = 0.5/(M_p/\sigma)^2 = 0.5(\sigma/M_p)^2$$

for example, if $M_p = \$4,000$ and $\sigma = \$1,000$ then $k = 4$ and $0.5(1/k^2) = 0.03125$; that is, at most, the probability of required net disbursements exceeding $4,000 is 3.125%. As we saw above knowledge of the actual distribution usually allows a much tighter bound on this probability. With nothing else known about the distribution of net disbursements, and adopting a conservative money management policy, we take the upper bound of the probability as relevant and the total cost function becomes

$$PC = 0.5(\sigma/M_p)^2 c + R_m M_p \qquad (10.8)$$

with

$$\frac{\partial PC}{\partial M_p} = -c(\sigma^2/M_p^3) + R_m \qquad (10.9)$$

and

$$\frac{\partial^2 PC}{\partial (M_p)^2} = 3c(\sigma^2/M_p^4) \qquad (10.10)$$

Setting (10.9) to zero and solving for optimal M_p, denoted M_p^*, and noting that the derivative in (10.10) is positive as required for a minimum for positive values of c, σ^2, and M_p, we obtain:

$$M_p^* = [c\sigma^2/R_m]^{\frac{1}{3}} \qquad (10.11)$$

It is evident from (10.11) that optimal precautionary money increases with the cost of financial distress, increases with the uncertainty in the distribution of net disbursements and decreases with R_m with an interest rate elasticity of $-\frac{1}{3}$. (Whalen (*op. cit.*, p. 318) derives

$M_p^* = [2c\sigma^2/R_m]^{\frac{1}{3}}$, in our notation, the difference arises because he takes the probability of distress as, at most, $(1/k^2)$; however, this is the (two-sided) probability of $|x - \mu| \geq k\sigma$ not $x - \mu \geq k\sigma$; financial distress occurs when re-quired net disbursements, defined as required expenditure minus actual receipts, are positive; negative required net disbursements imply that actual receipts exceed required expenditure which does not cause financial distress.)

10.2.4   The speculative motive

For Keynes (1936) it was the speculative motive, rather than the transactions and precautionary motives, that provided the basis of monetary management and the link between money and the rate of interest.

> In normal circumstances the amount of money required to satisfy the transactions-motive and the precautionary-motive is mainly a resultant of the general activity of the economic system and of the level of money income. But it is by playing on the speculative-motive that monetary management … is brought to bear on the economic system … whereas experience indicates that the aggregate demand for money to satisfy the speculative-motive usually shows a continuous response to gradual changes in the rate of interest. (Keynes *op. cit.*, pp. 196–197).

As we have seen a number of authors after Keynes suggested that the transactions and precautionary motives for holding money would be sensitive to the interest rate. Nevertheless if Keynes is right about the speculative motive his argument reinforces the link between money and the interest rate.

For Keynes (*op. cit.*, p. 170) the speculative motive arose from the 'object of securing profit from knowing better than the market what the future will bring forth', and 'that *uncertainty* as to the future course of the rate of interest is the sole intelligible explanation of the type of liquidity-preference L_2 which leads to the holding of cash M_2' (*op. cit.*, p. 170 and p. 201; M_2 is money held to satisfy the speculative motive, italics in original). Keynes elaborated that what mattered for M_2 was not the level of the interest rate but its divergence from a 'fairly safe level', but added two reasons for anticipating that a fall in the market rate, given expectations of the safe level, would be associated with an increase in M_2. First, if the safe level of R is unchanged, a change in the market rate increases the risk of illiquidity – where illiquidity arises from the holding of bonds and financial assets other than money (for simplicity we refer to these illiquid assets just as bonds). The risk of illiquidity arises because bonds are capital-uncertain; for example, investing \$1 in a consol buys an annual income of \$R$ in perpetuity; the capital value P of this consol is $1/R$ and so variations in R directly and inversely affect its value. If $R < R^s$, where R^s is the 'safe' value, then $P = 1/R > P^s = 1/R^s$, and the capital loss if the consol is bought at P and sold at P^s is $g = (P^s - P)/P = (R/R^s) - 1$; for example, if $R = 0.05$ and $R^s = 0.10$, then the capital loss is $g = (10 - 20)/20 = -0.5$. On this argument the size of the possible capital loss increases as R falls below R^s so, given the latter, there will be a disincentive to holding consols rather than cash. This argument applies to bonds more generally although it is simplest to illustrate with consols. Second, a reduction in R reduces the earnings from illiquid assets which as Keynes puts it 'are available as a sort of insurance premium to offset the risk of loss on capital account' (*op. cit.*, p. 202). Hence on two counts the attractions to holding bonds rather than cash have diminished by the fall in the interest rate below the safe level.

A number of authors after Keynes were critical of an important assumption in his analysis of the effects of a reduction in the market rate of interest relative to the safe rate – see, for example, Leontief (1947) and Fellner (1946). In the passage from which the quotations above are taken it was assumed that movements in R did not affect R^s: the safe level is completely inelastic with respect to the current rate. Now this may – or may not – be the case. For example, consider the first of Keynes' arguments but with the difference that any movement in R is exactly matched by a movement in R^s; then there is no risk of illiquidity from the reduction in R and no disincentive to holding bonds, and hence moving to money.

An alternative justification for a negative relation between money held for speculative reasons and the interest rate is due to Tobin (1958) in a famous paper entitled 'Liquidity Preference as Behaviour Towards Risk'. (And see also Feige and Parkin (1971) on the trade-off between money and bonds, and Chang, Hamberg and Mirata. (1983) for a critical view of the role of liquidity preference.) In Tobin's model for the individual, the future rate of interest on consols, R_{t+1}, is not certain so that holding consols involves the risk of capital gains or losses as well as a return R_t. In the simplest case money ('cash') and consols are held in a portfolio in proportions A_{1t} and A_{2t}, and the expected return at time t on the portfolio, $E_t\{r\}$, assuming for simplicity that money is not interest bearing, is

$$E_t\{r\} = E_t\{A_{2t}(R_t + g_{t+1})\} \qquad (10.12)$$

R_t is the current rate on consols and g_{t+1} is the one period (rate of) capital gain or loss given by $g_{t+1} = (R_t/R_{t+1}) - 1$. g_{t+1} is the only random variable in (10.12). If $E\{g_{t+1}\} = 0$ then

$$E_t\{r\} \equiv \mu_r$$
$$= A_{2t}R_t \qquad (10.13)$$

The risk attached to the portfolio is measured by the standard deviation of r, σ_r, which since A_{2t} and R_t are regarded as fixed at time t is $A_{2t}\sigma_g$ where σ_g is the standard deviation of capital gains; that is

$$\sigma_r = A_{2t}\sigma_g \qquad (10.14)$$

Substituting for $A_{2t} = \sigma_r/\sigma_g$ in (10.13) we obtain

$$\mu_r = (R_t/\sigma_g)\sigma_r \qquad (10.15)$$

This is the equation of an *opportunity locus* between the expected return μ_r, and the risk σ_r, with slope given by R_t/σ_g. The locus summarises the relationship between the expected return and risk; as the slope is positive, an increase in expected return can only be obtained with an increased risk. Tobin assumes that the investor has preferences between μ_r and σ_r; which can be represented as a field of indifference curves. Combining these indifference curves with the opportunity locus yields a solution, the nature of which depends upon the type of investor as characterised by the shape of the indifference curves. If the indifference curves are concave upward investors are known as *diversifiers* who will only accept more risk if it is coupled with a higher expected return. In such a case an interior solution is a possible with positive holdings of both consols and cash.

An increase in the interest rate increases the slope of the opportunity locus; hence, with positively sloped indifference curves, the substitution effect (which is obtained at the point of tangency of the original indifference curve with the slope of the new opportunity locus) moves the investor to a portfolio with more risk, so decreasing cash holdings in favour of consols. However, the income effect of the increase in the interest rate moves the investor back in favour of cash since the increase enables the possibility of both a higher return *and* a lower risk. The new position will depend upon the relative strengths of the substitution and income effects. In some cases, for example a utility function quadratic in the rate of return, Tobin was able to rule out the possibility of the income effect overcoming the substitution effect with the result that, as in Keynes' analysis, money and the interest rate are negatively related.

One other aspect of Tobin's mean-variance analysis is relevant for the demand for money. The analysis presupposes a two-stage or possibly multi-stage budgeting process which takes as given a prior allocation of total wealth, W, into monetary and nonmonetary assets. The decision on the allocation of monetary assets between bonds and cash is assumed to be separable from the decision on the allocation of total wealth, although the general principles introduced by Tobin are also applicable to the first stage decision. Tobin's explicit contribution was to analyse the allocation of a fixed monetary wealth into money ('cash') and alternative monetary assets giving rise to proportions A_1 of (speculative) money and A_2 of consols. To obtain actual holdings we need to multiply these proportions by the size of the portfolio, say W_m. An implication of this approach is that the proportions are independent of the scale of W_m, implying that the portfolio demands for (speculative) money and bonds each have a unit elasticity with respect to 'expenditure' on monetary assets, W_m. For example, suppose $A_1 = 0.1$, $A_2 = 0.9$ and $W_m = 1,000$ so that holdings of money and consols are 100 and 900, respectively; then if W_m increases by 1% to 1,010, money and consols also increase by 1% to 101 and 909, respectively, maintaining the proportions 0.1 and 0.9.

Even if there is a scale dependency, we do not expect money to be an inferior good with respect to W_m; accordingly, we anticipate that the demand for money arising from portfolio allocation will depend positively upon W_m, or more generally W. Note also that the reference here is to money held, in Tobin's terms, for investment balances or, in Keynes' terms, arising from the speculative motive. For present purposes we denote this quantity as M_1 (not to be confused with the M1 definition of money – see section **10.2.1**) and 'other' money as M_2 and define $M \equiv M_1 + M_2$, with $M_1 = A_1 W_m$ where A_1 is a function of R, σ_g and the parameters of the utility function. The elasticity of M, total money, with respect to W_m is

$$\frac{\partial M}{\partial W_m} \frac{W_m}{M} = \frac{M_1}{M} \leq 1 \qquad (10.16)$$

(we have assumed that M_2 is not a function of W_m). From (10.16) we see that the elasticity of total money with respect to W_m is likely to be substantially less than 1.

10.2.5　Bringing the motives together

Taken together the transactions, precautionary and speculative motives suggest that the demand for nominal money will depend, *inter alia*, upon: the price level; nominal income; payment and expenditure arrangements with regard both to disbursements which can be foreseen with certainty and those which are uncertain; the availability and cost of facilities for transfers between money and other monetary assets; the spread between the return on money (usually, but not always advisedly, taken to be zero for a narrow measure of money) and a 'near money' alternative; and a measure of wealth.

As a broad indication, the inventory theory of the transaction's demand for money, with a fixed cost per transfer, suggests an income elasticity of 0.5 and an interest rate elasticity of -0.5; however, taking into account integer constraints on the number of transactions and relating the cost of transfers to income suggest that the income elasticity may be greater than 0.5 while the interest elasticity may be closer to 0. A simple analysis of the precautionary demand for money suggested an interest elasticity of about $-1/3$, while that for the speculative motive, based on Tobin's mean-variance portfolio analysis, could not be made that precise without specification of the utility function underlying the indifference curves in the space of μ_r and σ_r. Nevertheless a negative relationship between money and the rate of interest seems likely to arise from this source and a positive relationship between money and wealth.

A summary way of representing the primary determinants of the demand for money is to write the functional relationship as

$$M = f(Y, P, R, W, Z) \qquad (10.17)$$

where M is the demand for nominal money, Y is nominal income, P is the price level, R is the nominal interest rate on a 'near money' alternative or the spread if money is interest bearing, W is nominal wealth and Z is a set of variables representing other factors such as the timing of income payments, the cost of transfers, the cost of illiquidity and so on. A conventional shorthand, if the variables in Z are constant, is to omit them from the functional relationship but bear in mind that if this assumption is invalid it could lead to problems such as predictive failure in the empirical representation. Adopting this convention

$$M = F(Y, P, R, W) \qquad (10.18)$$

An important property of demand for money functions is their homogeneity with respect to the price level. Suppose that the price level, P, increases by the factor μ and income Y and wealth W, which are in nominal terms, also increased by the same factor; then if the resulting value of M, say M^+, is

$$M^+ = \mu^h F(Y, P, R, W) \qquad (10.19)$$

the function is said to be homogeneous of degree h. There are two important cases that arise in many different economic contexts. These are $h = 0$ and $h = 1$, which we refer to as homogeneity of degree zero and homogeneity of degree 1, respectively. In the former case the changes in P, Y and W have no effect on M, that is $M = M^+$ because $\mu^0 = 1$, and in the latter case M^+ changes exactly in proportion to the factor μ.

Consider the effect on the demand for nominal money of, to fix ideas, a doubling of the price level and, consequently, a doubling of nominal income, Y, and wealth, W, which are measured in current prices. In a very important sense nothing has changed. Real income and real wealth, which are the ratios of income and wealth in current prices to the price level, are unchanged and so it would seem unlikely that the demand for real money will change. If the demand for real money is unchanged that must imply that the demand for nominal money has doubled to exactly compensate the doubling of the price level. In this case the demand for nominal money is homogeneous of degree one in the

price level, and the demand for real money is homogeneous of degree zero in the price level.

Suppose the particular functional relationship is

$$\ln M = \alpha_1 \ln Y + \alpha_2 \ln W$$
$$+ \alpha_3 \ln P + \alpha_4 R \qquad (10.20)$$

What value of α_3 will ensure that the function is homogeneous of degree one in the price level and can, therefore, be formulated in real terms? Working backwards the function in real terms is

$$\ln M - \ln P = \alpha_1 (\ln Y - \ln P)$$
$$+ \alpha_2 (\ln W - \ln P)$$
$$+ \alpha_4 R \qquad (10.21)$$

Comparing (10.20) and (10.21), for equality we require $\alpha_3 = 1 - \alpha_1 - \alpha_2$. For example, if $\alpha_1 = 0.5$ and $\alpha_2 = 0.1$, then for homogeneity of degree 1 we require $\alpha_3 = 0.4$. Bearing in mind that $\ln M - \ln P = \ln(M/P)$, $\ln Y - \ln P = \ln(Y/P)$ and $\ln W - \ln P = \ln(W/P)$, then (10.21) is specified in terms of real money (M/P), real income, (Y/P), and real wealth, (W/P) so that the function for real money is homogeneous of degree zero in the price level. The function is said to be free from money or price illusion. There is now considerable evidence – see, for example, Baba, Hendry and Starr (1992) and Johansen and Juselius (1990) – that this is a property of demand for money functions and, following Hoffman and Rasche (1991), in the empirical work reported below, we specify the demand for money function in terms of the real variables.

10.2.6 Some variations on a theme: the velocity of circulation

The velocity of circulation is the number of times a unit of currency has to *circulate during period t* in order to finance the overall level of transactions. For example, suppose the value of income in current prices for period t is 100 units and the stock of money is 25 units then, on average, each unit of money has to circulate 4 times over the period to service the income flow. The smaller is the stock of money relative to transactions then the more times does a unit of currency have to circulate. Y_t/M_t, which is the ratio of nominal income to nominal money, is the *velocity of circulation* of the money stock and M_t/Y_t is the *inverse velocity of circulation*. Letting lower case letters denote logarithms of the corresponding upper case letters then $y_t - m_t$ and $m_t - y_t$ are the logs of the velocity of circulation and the inverse velocity of circulation, respectively.

Given a demand for money function we can always rearrange it into an inverse velocity of circulation function. For example consider the demand function of (10.21) but with the wealth term omitted for simplicity, that is

$$\ln M_t - \ln P_t = \alpha_1(\ln Y_t - \ln P_t)$$
$$+ \alpha_4 R_t \qquad (10.22)$$

Subtracting $\ln Y_t$ from both sides and rearranging we get the log of the inverse velocity of circulation

$$\ln M_t - \ln Y_t = \alpha_1(\ln Y_t - \ln P_t)$$
$$- (\ln Y_t - \ln P_t) + \alpha_4 R_t$$
$$= (\alpha_1 - 1)(\ln Y_t - \ln P_t)$$
$$+ \alpha_4 R_t \qquad (10.23)$$

If the income elasticity, α_1, is equal to 1 the log of the inverse velocity is just a function of R_t otherwise, as, for example, implied by the square root formulation of equation (10.3), inverse velocity, and hence velocity, is a function of income.

Another approach to the velocity of circulation arises from what is known as the Cambridge cash-balances equation which, given the background of sections **10.2.2** to **10.2.4**, we recognise as a demand for money equation with the specification that the income elasticity is constrained to 1. Specifically the Cambridge cash-balances equation asserts that real cash balances

remain proportional to real income under given conditions. That is

$$M_t/P_t = K_t(Y_t/P_t)$$

The 'under given conditions' term is captured by the idea that K_t is a constant $= K$, but in any event we can view it as representing the terms other than income in the more general formulation given by equation (10.17). Taking logs of both sides and letting lower case letters denote logarithms results in

$$m_t - p_t = k_t + y_t - p_t$$

Cancelling p_t on both sides of the equation and rearranging results in a simple log inverse velocity equation

$$m_t - y_t = k_t$$

Whether or not this is a valid specification of the demand for cash balances depends upon the income elasticity and this is a matter to which we return in the empirical sections below.

10.3 The demand for money during the German hyperinflation

The theoretical background to the demand for money outlined in section **10.2** is a fairly common framework for empirical demand for money studies, although there may be variation as to the detail between different studies. To illustrate some of the considerations, which lead to variations, we first report on the demand for money during hyperinflation in Germany just after the First World War. Cagan's (1956) seminal study of hyperinflation in several countries created considerable interest in this topic, and his approach has remained influential (see, for example, Abel, Dornbusch, Huizinga and Marcus (1979), Goodfriend (1982), Christiano (1987), Phylaktis and Taylor (1993) and Engsted (1993)).

10.3.1 Historical background

A historical episode that has fascinated economists is the period following the First World War, particularly the effects on the German economy of reparations to the Allies' and the French occupation of the Ruhr – a heavily industrialised region of Germany – in January 1923. Reparations to the Allies from Germany took the form of deliveries in kind, beginning in August 1919, suspended in June 1922 and formally ending in November 1923, and monetary payments that continued until August 1924. In marked contrast to the general pattern of reasonably stable growth and readjustment, which followed the Second World War, the German economy after the First World War experienced dramatic changes in monetary and real variables. For example, between December 1920 and November 1923 the index of wholesale prices increased by a factor of 66,342,065,000 and, over the same period, the nominal money supply, measured as the quantity of authorised bank notes in circulation, increased by a factor of 5,817,280,000 and this figure does not take account of illegal currencies that were circulating. It is clear from the scale of price increases that the German economy was subject to considerable and unique inflation. In a classic article entitled 'The Monetary Dynamics of Hyperinflation', Cagan (1956) suggested that such an increase in prices be termed a *hyperinflation*, which he defined as 'beginning in the month the rise in prices exceeds 50 per cent and as ending in the month before the monthly rise in prices drops below that amount and stays below for at least a year' (*op. cit.*, p. 25). Cagan noted that his definition was arbitrary but it served to identify particularly turbulent periods in monetary history.

Cagan (*op. cit.*) also suggested that in hyperinflations the fall in real income and real output tends to be small compared with the typical rise in prices. He cited an index of output, due to Graham (1930), based on 1913 = 100, calculated as a simple average of indices of industrial production, agricultural output and commercial transportation, which took the following values and tend to confirm this view:

Index of Output for Germany
1920: 66; 1921: 73; 1922: 80; 1923: 61.

However, Cagan is able to separate out the index for the period Sept.–Dec. 1923, which takes a value of 42 rather than the average for the year, which was 61. So although the decline in real output on this average index is not as dramatic as the increase in prices it is nevertheless substantial. This latter view is supported by evidence used in a study by Michael, Nobay and Peel (1994), hereafter referred to as MNP (1994), who report that an index of Aggregate Real Income of the German Industrial Population, also due to Graham (1930), took the following range of values:

Index of Aggregate Real Income
1920: 60 to 85; 1921: 75 to 105; 1922: 70 to 90; 1923(Jan.–Aug.): 58 to 76; 1923(Nov): 36 to 47.

Dramatic changes in economic variables such as those illustrated above provide a challenge to economists: are they able to provide an explanation of the movements in these variables especially, as in Cagan's work, the remarkable increase in the demand for money?

10.3.2 Cagan's specification of the demand for money function: background

The starting point for Cagan in his specification of the demand for real cash balances falls broadly within the framework outlined in section **10.2** above. In Cagan's own words:

Because money balances serve as a reserve of ready purchasing power for contingencies, the *nominal* amount of money that individuals want to hold at any moment depends primarily on the value of money, or the absolute price level. Their desired *real* cash balances depend in turn on numerous variables. The main variables that affect an individual's desired cash balances are (1) his wealth in real terms; (2) his current real income; and (3) the expected returns from each form in which wealth can be held, including money. (Cagan *op. cit.*, p. 29, italics in original)

While accepting that the demand for real cash balances is likely to be a function of these three sets of variables, Cagan argues that in hyperinflations, wealth and income in real terms are relatively stable compared to the large fluctuations in real cash balances and prices, and, therefore, the focus of attention should be on expected returns in explaining the variation in real cash balances.

As we have seen, holding cash balances involves an opportunity cost which will be the difference between the expected return on holding an alternative asset and holding cash. The alternatives to cash are fixed-return assets, variable-return assets such as stocks and shares, and consumers' durable goods. The money return on hand-to-hand currency (cash), which is Cagan's measure of money, was zero so the opportunity cost will be the return on the alternative asset. Cagan argues that while in normal times the expected return on these different assets will be dominated by interest rates, the price of shares and, perhaps, the physical depreciation of durable goods, in times of hyperinflation these variables are unimportant compared to the change in the real value of a given nominal cash balance. Consider, for example, holding a bank deposit account of 1,000 Deutschmarks which pays a nominal interest rate of 10% per annum at a price level of $P = 1.00$. At the end of one year you receive an interest payment of $100 = 1,000 \times 0.1$ but your overall return will depend upon what has happened to the price level. Suppose at the end of the year $P = 1.10$, then the real value of your bank deposit is $909.09 = 1,000/1.10$. Thus, while you have received interest of 100

Deutschmarks, you have to balance this against the loss in the *real* value of your bank deposit.

Cagan argues that for this historical period it is the loss due to the change in the price level which is the dominant factor in expected returns. Indeed he states:

> The only cost of holding cash balances that seems to fluctuate widely enough to account for the drastic changes in real cash balances during hyperinflation is the rate of depreciation in the value of money or, equivalently, the rate of change of prices. (*op. cit.*, p. 31).

This is an early expression of the idea that both sides of a regression equation should be balanced. Cagan argues that it is reasonable to assume that other variables are approximately constant during hyperinflations, and that the crucial variable is what is expected to happen to the rate of change of prices. If this is positive the real value of cash balances is falling and individuals will seek to reduce their holdings of an asset, which is depreciating in value in real terms. He attributes some forward looking behaviour to individuals in suggesting that it is the 'expected rate of change of prices' which is important as an influence on current cash balances, although for practical purposes it is likely that, in order to model an 'expected' rate, some dependence on current and past rates will be introduced.

Cagan is aware that to focus on one variable alone, that is the expected rate of change of prices is misleading unless the effects of other variables, such as real income or real output, wealth and interest rates, are negligible. Whether he was right to do so is a matter to which we return below. We first consider the basic Cagan specification.

10.3.3 Cagan's demand for money function: basic specification

The starting point for the demand for real cash balances ('money') in the German hyperinflation is the following equation, see Cagan (*op. cit.*, p. 35, equation (2)),

$$m_t - p_t = \delta - \alpha pi_t + v_t \qquad (10.24)$$

where m_t is the log of the nominal value of notes and coins in circulation, M_t; p_t is the log of the price level, P_t, practically this is taken to be the index of wholesale prices; pi_t is the expected rate of inflation and v_t is an innovation. Remember that $\ln M_t - \ln P_t = \ln(M_t/P_t)$, so that the dependent variable is the (natural) logarithm of real cash balances. The individual seeks to reduce the losses that are signalled by an expected rate of inflation, pi_t, which is positive; hence, we anticipate that α will be positive so that $-\alpha$ is negative: as expected inflation increases, the demand for real money declines as agents seek to divest themselves of an asset whose value is declining in real terms.

Note that $-\alpha$ is the semi-elasticity of real money balances with respect to the expected inflation rate: it gives the effect of a 1 percentage point increase or decrease in the inflation rate – for example, from 3% per month to 4% per month. In order to obtain the elasticity we need to multiply $-\alpha$ by pi_t. (Taking the anti-logarithm of (10.24) and setting the innovation to zero we have $M_t/P_t = \exp\{\delta - \alpha pi_t\}$, hence $\partial(M_t/P_t)/\partial pi_t = -\alpha M_t/P_t$ and the elasticity is $(-\alpha M_t/P_t)pi_t/(M_t/P_t) = -\alpha pi_t$.) Cagan's decision for the elasticity to vary with pi_t is a deliberate one, he wanted to allow the possibility that agents 'reduce their holdings by an increasing proportion of each successive rise in the expected rate' (Cagan *op. cit.*, p. 88). Thus, a varying inflation elasticity, in particular one which increases with the increase in inflation, is an important part of the empirical specification to explain why agents do not immediately take 'extreme flight' when currency is issued on such a grand scale, rather they have 'lingering confidence in its future value' – but this confidence erodes with increases in the expected rate of inflation.

There are two immediate problems with the specification (10.24). The first is that a series on expected inflation is not available and has to be constructed and, therefore, a replacement variable has to be found for pi_t. Second, it omits a number of variables, especially one that captures the scale of economic transactions.

The absence of a directly observed series on expected inflation can be overcome by considering whether we can replace pi_t by a variable that is observed. Cagan (*op. cit.*, p. 39) suggested calculating pi_t as a weighted average of current and past inflation. However, this method can be problematical with variables that are not stationary, and there is evidence, as we show below, that inflation is I(1). An alternative solution to the problem that expected inflation is an unobservable variable, and the one adopted here, is due to MNP (1994) (and for alternative approaches see Christiano (1987) and Engsted (1993)). In essence it amounts to substituting the observable actual change in (the log of) prices, Δp_t, plus a stationary residual for the unobservable, expected inflation rate, pi_t. Define the difference between these two series as the random variable η_{1t}, that is

$$\eta_{1t} = \Delta p_t - pi_t \qquad (10.25)$$

A reasonable property to expect η_{1t} to have is that it is stationary. Suppose it is not, then that implies that expected inflation consistently misses actual inflation, a situation which seems unlikely as if this were to occur, even temporarily, individuals would revise the way in which they were forming their expectations.

A related way of looking at the relationship, summarised by (10.25), between actual and expected inflation is to say that they are cointegrated – they move together rather than wandering away. Two series that are cointegrated must have an I(0) residual; and instead of using the unobservable variable pi_t we replace it by $\Delta p_t - \eta_{1t}$, from which it differs by an I(0) component, in equation (10.24) to obtain

$$m_t - p_t = \delta - \alpha \Delta p_t + u_t \qquad (10.26)$$

where $u_t = v_t + \alpha \eta_{1t}$, which comprises stationary components.

The second omission raised above concerns whether Cagan was right not to include an income or wealth variable (or both) in his empirical equation. MNP (*op. cit.*) suggest adding the log of real income, $(y_t - p_t)$, to equation (10.26) which becomes

$$m_t - p_t = \delta - \alpha \Delta p_t$$
$$+ \theta(y_t - p_t) + u_t \qquad (10.27)$$

However, a measure of real income is not available for the German hyperinflationary period, and MNP (*op. cit.*) use as a proxy an index of skilled public workers' real wages, X_t/P_{xt}, where a subscript on the price index allows for the possibility that the deflator may differ from P_t. The minimal condition they hope this proxy will satisfy is that

$$\eta_{2t} = (x_t - p_{Xt}) - (y_t - p_t)$$
$$\text{and} \quad \eta_{2t} \text{ is } I(0) \qquad (10.28)$$

where x_t is the log of X_t. This condition assumes that $(x_t - p_{Xt})$ and $(y_t - p_t)$ have a common trend so that their difference is a stationary variable. Replacing the unobservable variable real income variable using (10.28), then (10.27) becomes

$$m_t - p_t = \delta - \alpha \Delta p_t$$
$$+ \theta(x_t - p_{Xt}) = \xi_t \qquad (10.29)$$

with $\xi_t = u_t - \theta \eta_{2t}$. If $\theta = 1$ in (10.29) the equation can be rearranged as an inverse velocity function; that is

$$m_t - p_t - (x_t - p_{Xt}) = \delta - \alpha \Delta p_t + \xi_t \qquad (10.30)$$

As $\xi_t = v_t + \alpha \eta_{1t} - \theta \eta_{2t}$, a finding that ξ_t is I(1) could arise from one of three causes: $m_t - p_t$ does not cointegrate with pi_t and $y_t - p_t$ in (10.27); Δp_t is a poor proxy for pi_t; and $x_t - p_{Xt}$ is a poor proxy for $y_t - p_t$. It is often the case in empirical economics that the cause of a breakdown in a model is not uniquely identified.

In summary there are three variants to be estimated based on the work of Cagan (1956) and MNP (1994). These are the basic specification (10.26) which relates the demand for real cash balances to a proxy for expected inflation; an extension of this specification in (10.29) which adds a proxy for real income; and, if the income elasticity is 1, the inverse velocity equation given by (10.30).

10.3.4   A graphical analysis of the data

Before moving on to the estimation results, a first step in the empirical analysis is to assess whether the equations are *balanced* in terms of their time series properties. In this context a graphical analysis can be a useful initial step. Figure 10.1 brings together time series plots of (the log of) real money, $m_t - p_t$, with values indicated on the left-hand side axis, and (negative) inflation with values indicated as % per month (p.m.) on the right-hand scale. Negative inflation has been used in this figure because the relationship between real money and inflation is hypothesised to be negative and so this plot makes it easier to see the relationship between the two variables. The visual impression is quite striking. Note how the dramatic increase in inflation (which will be a fall in Figure 10.1) from 1923m6 to the end of the period is

Figure 10.1 *The German hyperinflation, real money and negative inflation*

associated with a large decline in the holdings of real money. Overall, while there is a distinct tendency for the two series to move together though there is a suspicion that inflation may be insufficient by itself to explain all of the movement in real money over the hyperinflationary period.

Cagan suggested a negative linear relationship between real money and (expected) inflation. A useful graphical device that complements the time series plots is a scatter diagram with real money plotted against inflation – see Figure 10.2. In that figure we see that there is a definite impression of a negative relationship with a decrease in the holdings of real money associated with an increase in inflation. There is a suspicion, however, that while a linear relationship seems to fit quite well for some of the observations a nonlinear relationship might also be considered.

Two further figures, Figures 10.3 and 10.4, consider the same issues but using the (log of the) inverse velocity of circulation, $m_t - p_t - (x_t - p_{xt})$, rather than real money. The time series plots in Figure 10.3 suggest a broad relationship between inverse velocity and negative inflation, one which is particularly noticeable at the beginning and end of the sample period. The scatter diagram, Figure 10.4, again

Figure 10.3 *The German hyperinflation, inverse velocity and negative inflation*

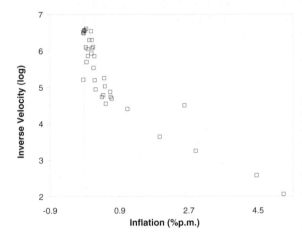

Figure 10.4 *The German hyperinflation, inverse velocity and inflation*

shows a negative relationship between the two variables but, as with Figure 10.2, the pattern is suggestive of a nonlinear relationship – a possibility that appears to have been overlooked in previous empirical work. (A review question suggests further work in this area.) For the purposes of this section we note that the visual impression is favourable to the view that $m_t - p_t$ and Δp_t, and $m_t - p_t - (x_t - p_{xt})$ and Δp_t have similar time series properties.

10.3.5 Testing for nonstationarity

A more formal analysis of the time series properties of the data is based on determining

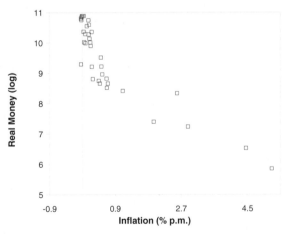

Figure 10.2 *The German hyperinflation, real money and inflation*

whether the variables are integrated of the same order and, if so, whether there is a cointegrating relationship between the variables. Although there has been considerable interest in explaining the German hyperinflation, this has been confined to a period limited in terms of the number of observations. Here even the full sample only runs from 1920m12 to 1923m11, a total of 36 observations, and within this total MNP (*op. cit.*) distinguish what they describe as the 'conventional period' of analysis of 1921m1 to 1923m6, which is a sample of 30 observations. Even if adjustment to change during this period is very fast, so that the long run is short in calendar time, inference may well be quite fragile and unit root tests subject to problems of low power. Nevertheless, this is an interesting period and will serve to illustrate some of difficulties of interpreting the various test statistics. For comparability with MNP we report, in Table 10.1, the results of the unit root test statistics for the conventional period.

We start with tests for the order of integration of the series and, in particular given the dramatic movements in the data, initially consider whether the series are I(2). That is test the hypothesis of 2 unit roots, moving on to the hypothesis of a single unit root if the data is not consistent with the I(2) hypothesis. One possible area of fragility arises in determining the appropriate empirical model on which to base inference. Generally a minimum requirement is that the estimated maintained regression should be free from serial correlation, although that aspect of testing is limited by the short sample. Here we look at the Lagrange-Multipler test for serial correlation in either or both its χ^2 or F form – see Chapter 5 for details – and denoted SC(i) as a test for ith order serial correlation using $i = 1, \ldots, 4$ in its χ^2 form. For convenience where the msl is not given approximate critical values for the 5% and 10% significance levels for the relevant test statistics are also given in the table.

Table 10.1   *The German hyperinflation: unit root tests*

Variable	Model	Test statistics for 2 unit roots						
		$\hat{\tau}$	Φ_1	$\hat{\tau}_\mu$	$\hat{\mu}$	$\hat{\tau}_\beta$	$\hat{\beta}$	Φ_3
$m_t - p_t$	ADF(3)	−2.297	6.956	−3.651	−0.098	−3.706	−0.004	7.151
$x_t - p_{Xt}$	DF	−6.403	19.931	−6.313	−0.011	−6.194	−0.001	19.244
$m_t - p_t - (x_t - p_{Xt})$	DF	−3.133	6.090	−3.347	−0.053	−3.449	−0.003	6.204
Δp_t	ADF(3)	−2.961	5.696	−3.272	0.048	−2.911	0.002	5.285

Variable	Model	Test statistics for 1 unit root						
		$\hat{\tau}$	Φ_1	$\hat{\tau}_\mu$	$\hat{\mu}$	$\hat{\tau}_\beta$	$\hat{\beta}$	Φ_3
$m_t - p_t$	ADF(4)	−2.600	3.450	0.373	−0.274	−2.443	−0.051	3.445
$x_t - p_{Xt}$	DF	−0.404	2.749	−2.321	1.412	−3.439	0.009	5.924
$m_t - p_t - (x_t - p_{Xt})$	ADF(1)	−1.515	1.136	−0.430	0.079	−2.895	−0.031	4.420
Δp_t	ADF(4)	0.895	1.139	−0.468	0.070	−2.372	0.023	2.974

Effective sample period: 1921m2 to 1923m6 for DF; 1921m3 to 1923m6 for ADF(1) and so on.
Critical values

	$\hat{\tau}$	$\hat{\tau}_\mu$	$\hat{\tau}_\beta$	Φ_1	Φ_3
5%	−1.968	−2.949	−3.554	5.140	7.223
10%	−1.613	−2.605	−3.205	4.064	5.906

Critical values of $\hat{\tau}$, $\hat{\tau}_\mu$ and $\hat{\tau}_\beta$ obtained using Cheung–Lai response surface coefficients for $T = 30$ and $p = 1$; critical values of Φ_1 and Φ_3 obtained by simulation for $T = 25$ – see Chapter 6.

First, a general point is apparent from the relevant part of Table 10.1 concerning which maintained regression model is appropriate for inference. Although the full set of statistics is reported it is evident throughout that the deterministic time trend is not necessary; the 't' statistics are nowhere significant – see Table 6.10 for relevant critical values extracted from Dickey and Fuller (1981). Since it is rarely evident in general that the second difference of a variable is trended, this is part of a typical pattern when testing for two unit roots. If the data, here the second difference, is not trended a significant constant will most likely indicate that there is not a (second) unit root, otherwise the drift imparted by the constant will show up as a trend in the data implying a contradiction.

There is also no empirical role for a constant in the maintained regressions as indicated by the 't' statistics, which are all well below relevant critical values – again see Table 6.10. The 10% critical value of Φ_1 is 4.064 – see Table 6.5 – so all sample values of this test statistic are significant indicating rejection of the joint null that the constant is equal to zero together with a (second) unit root. Together these point to rejection of the (second) unit root. A typical 5% critical value for $\hat{\tau}$ using Cheung and Lai's response surface for $p = 1$ and $T = 30$ is -1.968, and all sample values of the test statistics are larger negative than this value. With one possible qualification this set of inferences does not appear fragile; the qualification is that the maintained regressions without the time trend were generally more robust to the impact of minor changes to the lag length p, in the ADF(p) model, on the absence of serial correlation than when the time trend was included. However, as noted above a reasonable presumption is that the time trend is not needed when testing for 2 unit roots.

The next step is to test for a single unit root in the various series. In this case there is no general presumption that the time trend should be absent. Indeed, for data series that are evidently trended an essential part of the testing strategy is

to allow for the possibility of a deterministic time trend under the alternative, otherwise there is no mechanism to account for the characteristics of the series other than a unit root with drift. Here the results are generally more fragile than when testing for 2 unit roots and are likely to suffer from the low power problems associated with unit root tests.

Real money, $m_t - p_t$.
The test results for $m_t - p_t$ are as follows:

an ADF(4) maintained regression is required to ensure a clean profile of SC(i) test statistics;

$\Phi_3 = 3.445$ which is below the 10% critical value of approximately 5.91 suggesting non-rejection of the joint null of a unit root and no time trend;

the 't' statistic on the time trend coefficient is -2.590 compared to, say, the 10% critical value, under the null of a unit root, of -2.85 implying nonrejection of the null that the time trend coefficient is 0;

omitting the time trend, $\Phi_1 = 3.450$ which is below the 10% critical value of approximately 4.06, implying nonrejection of the joint null that the constant equals 0 together with a unit root;

$\hat{\tau}_\mu = 0.373$, which is wrong signed for rejection of the null of a unit root;

the 't' statistic on the constant is -0.596 suggesting that it could be omitted without loss;

when the constant is omitted $\hat{\tau} = -2.600$, with $\hat{\gamma} = -0.010$, suggesting rejection of the null of a unit root since the 5% critical value is -1.968.

MNP (*op. cit.*) resolve the problem of a significant value of $\hat{\tau}$ by referring to the insignificant value of Φ_1 and conclude that $m_t - p_t$ is I(1).

Proxy for real income, $x_t - p_{Xt}$.
The test results for $x_t - p_{Xt}$ are as follows:

the sample value of Φ_3 is 5.924, which is close to the 10% critical value of approximately 5.91 suggesting rejection of the joint null of no time trend together with a unit root;

however, on the null of a unit root the 't' statistic of -2.356, for the coefficient on the time trend, is not significant;

omitting the time trend gives $\Phi_1 = 2.749$ which is below the 5% critical value suggesting nonrejection of the joint null that the constant equals 0 together with a unit root;

the sample value of $\hat{\tau}_\mu$ is -2.321 compared to a 5% critical value of approximately -2.95, suggesting nonrejection of the null of a unit root;

the 't' statistic on $\hat{\mu}$ is 2.304 whereas the 10% critical value is approximately 2.61 assuming a unit root;

omitting the constant gives an unambiguous result since $\hat{\tau} = -0.404$, with $\hat{\gamma} = -0.003$, well below the 5% critical value of approximately -1.968.

Inverse velocity, $m_t - p_t - (x_t - p_{Xt})$.
The test results for $m_t - p_t - (x_t - p_{Xt})$ are as follows:

an ADF(1) model is preferred on the basis of the SC(i), $i = 1, \ldots 4$, statistics for serial correlation;

$\Phi_3 = 4.420$, suggesting nonrejection of the associated joint null;

the 't' statistic on the time trend coefficient is -2.932 which is significant at the 10% level but not the 5% level; the critical values under the null of a unit root being approximately ± 3.25 and ± 2.85, respectively;

the maintained model with a time trend was not estimated by MNP (*op. cit.*) so this possibility was not considered;

if the time trend is excluded $\Phi_1 = 1.136$, which is well below the usual critical values;

$\hat{\tau}_\mu = -0.430$, indicating nonrejection of the null, and the constant is not significant with a 't' statistic of 0.247;

omitting the constant $\hat{\tau} = -1.515$, $\hat{\gamma} = -0.010$, also suggesting nonrejection of the null of a unit root.

The most crucial step in this sequence is the decision to omit the time trend. A test statistic relevant to this case, but usually rarely used, is Dickey and Fuller's (1981) Φ_2 for testing the joint null comprising: a unit root, no constant and no time trend, that is $\mu = 0$, $\gamma = 0$ and $\beta = 0$. Like Φ_3 it is an F type test with a nonstandard distribution under the null, with critical values tabulated by simulation in Dickey and Fuller (*op. cit.*); the sample value of Φ_2 is 4.026 compared to a 10% critical value of 4.67 (for $T = 25$ from Dickey and Fuller (*op. cit.*)) suggesting nonrejection of the null.

Inflation, Δp_t.
The test results for Δp_t are as follows:

an ADF(1) model is preferred on the basis of the SC(i), $i = 11, \ldots 4$, statistics for serial correlation;

$\Phi_3 = 2.974$ suggesting nonrejection of the associated joint null;

the 't' statistic on the time trend coefficient is -2.382 which is not significant at the 10% level under the null of a unit root;

when the time trend is excluded $\Phi_1 = 1.139$, which is well below the usual critical values;

$\hat{\tau}_\mu = -0.468$, indicating nonrejection of the null, and the constant is not significant with a 't' statistic of 1.208;

omitting the constant $\hat{\tau} = 0.895$, $\hat{\gamma} = 0.100$, which is wrong signed for rejection of the unit root null.

In general these results indicate the following aspect of unit root testing noted in Chapter 5: if the data has a nonzero mean, as in this case, then once the constant is omitted (the maintained regression already having been reduced by the deletion of the time trend), the finding of a unit root is *almost inevitable* since it alone can account for the characteristics of the time series.

10.3.6 Cointegration

At this stage we tentatively conclude that the time series properties of equations (10.26), (10.29) and (10.30) are balanced in terms of their orders of integration. This is a necessary but not sufficient condition for a sensible regression and is less certain than in usual applications because of the low power likely with a small sample. The next stage in the empirical analysis is to estimate these equations and assess whether the following cointegrate: from (10.26), $m_t - p_t$ and Δp_t; from (10.29), $m_t - p_t$, Δp_t and $x_t - p_{Xt}$; and from (10.30), $m_t - p_t - (x_t - p_{Xt})$ and Δp_t.

MNP (*op. cit.*) found no evidence of cointegration using OLSEG estimation among combinations of $m_t - p_t$, $x_t - p_{Xt}$ and Δp_t over the conventional period, 1921m1 to 1923m6, and further regressions, undertaken by the author, for the full sample period also suggested no cointegration. Some of the results for the 'conventional period' used by MNP (*op. cit.*) are reported in Table 10.2. We consider the basic Cagan specification to show how the results are interpreted. The estimated equation is $m_t - p_t = 10.505 - 2.522\Delta p_t + \hat{\xi}_t$, note that the significant values of SC(1) and SC(4) prevent inference using the 't' statistics. The standard Engle–Granger test for noncointegration uses the equation residuals, with the auxiliary regression $\Delta\hat{\xi}_t = -0.293\hat{\xi}_{t-1} + 0.424\Delta\hat{\xi}_{t-1}$, this model being adequate judged by the SC(i) statistics; the test statistic is $\hat{\tau}_\gamma = -2.299$. Using MacKinnon's response surface coefficients – see Chapter 8 – the 5% and 10% critical values are −3.554 and −3.193, leading to the conclusion of nonrejec-

tion of the null of a unit root and hence no cointegration. The paradigm of unit root testing leads to this conclusion; however, while −0.293 is not statistically different from zero it is large enough to suggest that there could be a problem with the low power of the unit root test.

We take the opportunity with this example to illustrate an application of the modified ADF test procedure of section **8.5.2**, which is based on the ECM. Specifically to avoid the common factor restriction implicit in DF tests for cointegration it is necessary to add changes in the rhs variables of the cointegrating regression to the auxiliary regression. The estimated auxiliary regression is, extracting from Table 10.2,

$$\Delta\hat{\xi}_t = 1.563\Delta\Delta p_t - 1.358\Delta\Delta p_{t-1}$$
$$- 0.029\hat{\xi}_{t-1} + 0.616\Delta\hat{\xi}_{t-1} + \hat{u}_t$$

as in the standard ADF test, the test statistic is the 't' statistic of the coefficient on $\hat{\xi}_{t-1}$, in this case $\hat{\tau}_\gamma = -0.978$ which is clearly not significant – the critical values are obtained from Table 8.11. These results confirm the visual impression gained from Figure 10.1 that while some part of the variation in $m_t - p_t$ is accounted for by Δp_t, we are unable to say that $m_t - p_t$ and Δp_t cointegrate. The results are improved, but not markedly, if the proxy for the log of real income, $x_t - p_{Xt}$ is included in the regression which corresponds to equation (10.29); also imposing an income elasticity of unity, so that the equation can be respecified as an inverse velocity equation does not offer an improvement. It is still the case that the null hypothesis of a nonstationary residual cannot be rejected with an ADF(1) test statistic of −2.168 and a modified ADF statistic of −1.953.

MNP (*op. cit.*) curtail the sample period to focus on the period of hyperinflation, which they suggest starts in 1922m7 and ends in 1923m9. This severely shortens the sample and, in general, it is not recommended practice to use such a limited number of observations. The results are, therefore, reported here as

Table 10.2 *The German hyperinflation: cointegrating regressions*

Sample period: 1921m1 to 1923m6 (the conventional period)

Demand for money (equation (10.26))

$$m_t - p_t = 10.505 - 2.522\Delta p_t + \hat{\xi}_t$$
$$\quad\quad (84.505)(-7.679)$$

$\hat{\sigma} = 0.490$
dw $= 0.452$
SC(1) $= 17.864[0.000]$
SC(4) $= 18.643[0.000]$

$$\Delta\hat{\xi}_t = -0.293\hat{\xi}_{t-1} + 0.424\Delta\hat{\xi}_{t-1}$$
$$\quad (-2.299)\quad\quad (2.115)$$

SC(1) $= 1.051[0.305]$
SC(4) $= 8.141[0.086]$

$$\Delta\hat{\xi}_t = 1.563\Delta\Delta p_t - 1.358\Delta\Delta p_{t-1} - 0.029\hat{\xi}_{t-1} + 0.616\Delta\hat{\xi}_{t-1}$$
$$\quad (21.459)\quad\quad (-7.896)\quad\quad (-0.978)\quad\quad (5.663)$$

SC(1) $= 0.249[0.618]$
SC(4) $= 5.573[0.233]$

Demand for money (equation (10.29), adds real income proxy)

$$m_t - p_t = 3.054 - 1.947\Delta p_t + 1.749(x_t - p_{Xt}) + \hat{\xi}_t$$
$$\quad\quad (1.534)(-6.246)\quad\quad (3.746)$$

$\hat{\sigma} = 0.405$
dw $= 0.922$
SC(1) $= 15.370[0.000]$
SC(4) $= 11.670[0.020]$

$$\Delta\hat{\xi}_t = -0.463\hat{\xi}_{t-1}$$
$$\quad (-2.808)$$

SC(1) $= 0.826[0.363]$
SC(4) $= 4.058[0.394]$

$$\Delta\hat{\xi}_t = 0.996\Delta\Delta p_t - 1.000\Delta\Delta p_{t-1} - 1.608\Delta(x_t - p_{Xt}) + 1.161\Delta(x_t - p_{Xt})_{-1}$$
$$\quad (11.826)\quad\quad (-6.988)\quad\quad (-17.328)\quad\quad\quad (5.502)$$

$$\quad\quad -0.022\hat{\xi}_{t-1} + 0.688\Delta\hat{\xi}_{t-1}$$
$$\quad\quad (-0.358)\quad\quad (5.777)$$

SC(1) $= 0.037[0.847]$
SC(4) $= 2.582[0.630]$

Inverse velocity (equation (10.30))

$$m_t - p_t - (x_t - p_{Xt}) = 6.245 - 2.193\Delta p_t + \hat{\xi}_t$$
$$\quad\quad (53.177)(-7.863)$$

$\hat{\sigma} = 0.416$
dw $= 0.654$
SC(1) $= 13.584[0.000]$
SC(4) $= 13.674[0.008]$

$$\Delta\hat{\xi}_t = -0.318\hat{\xi}_{t-1}$$
$$\quad (-2.168)$$

SC(1) $= 1.487[0.222]$
SC(4) $= 5.473[0.242]$

$$\Delta\hat{\xi}_t = 1.447\Delta\Delta p_t - 0.152\hat{\xi}_{t-1}$$
$$\quad (8.821)\quad\quad (-1.953)$$

SC(1) $= 0.661[0.416]$
SC(4) $= 3.301[0.509]$

Sample period: 1922m7 to 1923m9 (the hyperinflation period)

Demand for money (equation (10.26))

$$m_t - p_t = 9.214 - 0.659\Delta p_t + \hat{\xi}_t$$
$$\quad\quad (90.430)(-10.027)$$

$\hat{\sigma} = 0.295$
dw $= 0.762$
SC(1) $= 5.287[0.021]$
SC(4) $= 6.218[0.183]$

$$\Delta\hat{\xi}_t = -0.562\hat{\xi}_{t-1}$$
$$\quad (-2.885)$$

SC(1) $= 2.614[0.106]$
SC(4) $= 2.137[0.710]$

$$\Delta\hat{\xi}_t = 0.033\Delta\Delta p_t - 0.551\hat{\xi}_{t-1}$$
$$\quad (0.342)\quad\quad (-2.695)$$

SC(1) $= 2.525[0.112]$
SC(4) $= 2.152[0.707]$

Demand for money (equation (10.29), adds real income proxy)

$$m_t - p_t = 4.129 - 0.615\Delta p_t + 1.256(x_t - p_{Xt}) + \hat{\xi}_t$$
$$\quad\quad (3.197)(-13.196)\quad\quad (3.944)$$

$\hat{\sigma} = 0.209$
dw $= 1.467$
SC(1) $= 2.299[0.129]$
SC(4) $= 10.127[0.038]$

(*continued*)

Table 10.2 *continued*

Demand for money (equation (10.29), adds real income proxy) (*continued*)

$\Delta\hat{\xi}_t = -0.879\hat{\xi}_{t-1}$
$\quad\quad(-3.541)$

$\quad\quad\quad\quad\quad\quad\quad\quad\quad\quad\quad\quad$ SC(1) = 3.611[0.057]
$\quad\quad\quad\quad\quad\quad\quad\quad\quad\quad\quad\quad$ SC(4) = 7.107[0.130]

$\Delta\hat{\xi}_t = 0.018\Delta\Delta p_t - 0.273\Delta(x_t - p_{Xt}) - 0.757\hat{\xi}_{t-1}$
$\quad\quad(0.223)\quad\quad\quad(-1.053)\quad\quad\quad\quad\quad(-2.672)$

$\quad\quad\quad\quad\quad\quad\quad\quad\quad\quad\quad\quad$ SC(1) = 8.316[0.080]
$\quad\quad\quad\quad\quad\quad\quad\quad\quad\quad\quad\quad$ SC(4) = 8.135[0.004]

Inverse velocity (equation (10.30))

$m_t - p_t - (x_t - p_{Xt}) = 5.166 - 0.624\Delta p_t + \hat{\xi}_t$
$\quad\quad\quad\quad\quad\quad\quad\quad\quad(74.849)(-14.006)$

$\quad\quad\quad\quad\quad\quad\quad\quad\quad\quad\quad\quad$ $\hat{\sigma} = 0.200$
$\quad\quad\quad\quad\quad\quad\quad\quad\quad\quad\quad\quad$ dw = 1.196
$\quad\quad\quad\quad\quad\quad\quad\quad\quad\quad\quad\quad$ SC(1) = 5.289(0.021)
$\quad\quad\quad\quad\quad\quad\quad\quad\quad\quad\quad\quad$ SC(4) = 8.207(0.084)

$\Delta\hat{\xi}_t = -1.192\hat{\xi}_{t-1} + 0.498\Delta\hat{\xi}_{t-1}$
$\quad\quad(-4.257)\quad\quad(3.288)$

$\quad\quad\quad\quad\quad\quad\quad\quad\quad\quad\quad\quad$ SC(1) = 0.608[0.403]
$\quad\quad\quad\quad\quad\quad\quad\quad\quad\quad\quad\quad$ SC(4) = 5.637[0.228]

$\Delta\hat{\xi}_t = 0.161\Delta\Delta p_t - 0.255\Delta\Delta p_{t-1} - 1.228\hat{\xi}_{t-1} + 0.560\Delta\hat{\xi}_{t-1}$
$\quad\quad(1.400)\quad\quad\quad(-1.560)\quad\quad\quad\quad(-4.209)\quad\quad(2.580)$

$\quad\quad\quad\quad\quad\quad\quad\quad\quad\quad\quad\quad$ SC(1) = 0.818[0.366]
$\quad\quad\quad\quad\quad\quad\quad\quad\quad\quad\quad\quad$ SC(4) = 5.113[0.275]

Approximate critical values for $\hat{\tau}_\gamma$:

$N = 2$ (no trend)

$C(5\%, 29) = -3.3377 - 5.967/29 - 8.98/29^2 = -3.554$
$C(10\%, 29) = -3.0462 - 4.069/29 - 5.73/29^2 = -3.193$
$C(5\%, 15) = -3.3377 - 5.967/15 - 8.98/15^2 = -3.775$
$C(10\%, 15) = -3.0462 - 4.069/15 - 5.73/15^2 = -3.343$

$N = 3$ (no trend)

$-3.7429 - 8.352/29 - 13.41/29^2 = -4.047$
$-3.4518 - 6.241/29 - 2.79/29^2 = -3.670$
$-3.7429 - 8.352/15 - 13.41/15^2 = -4.359$
$-3.4518 - 6.241/15 - 2.79/15^2 = -3.880$

---

illustrative. The estimation results using this shortened sample period are summarised in the lower half of Table 10.2. The evidence for cointegration appears more favourable whether real money, $m_t - p_t$, or inverse velocity, $m_t - x_t$, is used as the dependent variable.

In the basic Cagan specification, equation (10.26), the DF test statistic improves to -2.885; adding real income, equation (10.29), gives a DF test statistic of -3.541 (which improves to -4.256 in an ADF(1) regression (not reported)). For the inverse velocity specification, equation (10.30), the ADF(1) test statistic is -4.257. The 5% and 10% critical values, obtained using MacKinnon's procedure, are -3.775 and -3.343, respectively, for equations (10.26) and (10.30), and -4.359 and -3.880, respectively, for equation (10.29). (Incidentally, MNP (*op. cit.*) use critical values for $T = 50$ from Engle and Yoo (1987).) On the basis of these test statistics the equations with real income fare slightly better than the basic specification, and there is evidence of cointegration between $m_t - p_t$, Δp_t and $x_t - p_{Xt}$, and $m_t - p_t - (x_t - p_{Xt})$ and Δp_t.

The modified ADF test statistics also improve and are now -2.695, -2.672 and -4.209 for equations (10.26), (10.29) and (10.30), respectively; the modified auxiliary regression for testing cointegration in (10.29) is not entirely satisfactory, in particular SC(4) is significant, but could not be improved without running out of degrees of freedom. Nevertheless, it is clear that the additional terms in the modified auxiliary regressions are not generally significant, and the standard and modified test statistics are, therefore, much closer than for the longer sample period. Of the three regressions, the test statistics are most favourable when an income elasticity of 1 is imposed and the regression is formulated as an inverse velocity equation.

The estimated income elasticity from the curtailed sample period is 1.256 and 1.749 from the longer sample. The 't' statistics in the cointegrating regressions are not valid for inference; however, this is an opportunity to use the Phillips–Hansen FMOLS estimator which enables inference using standard tables. A summary of the results using the Bartlett

Table 10.3 *FMOLS estimation of* $m_t - p_t = \delta - \alpha\Delta p_t + \theta(x_t - p_{Xt}) + \xi_t$

Bartlett window truncation lag	Coefficient estimates		
	$\hat{\delta}$	$\hat{\alpha}$	$\hat{\theta}$
$l=0$	3.610	−0.616	1.383
$'t'^+$	(3.253)	(−15.386)	(5.052/1.400)
$l=1$	3.377	−0.614	1.445
$'t'^+$	(2.779)	(−14.010)	(4.819/1.484)
$l=2$	3.209	−0.613	1.491
$'t'^+$	(3.251)	(17.204)	(6.119/2.055)
$l=3$	3.650	−0.613	1.379
$'t'^+$	(3.898)	(18.147)	(5.970/1.641)

Notes: Main entries are the FMOLS estimates of the coefficients; $'t'^+$ is the associated fully modified $'t'$ statistic for the null that the true coefficient value is zero, except the entry following / is for the null that the income elasticity is 1.

Figure 10.5 A and B – *The German hyperinflation, one step ahead forecasts*

window is provided in Table 10.3. The estimates assume no drift in the regressors, as suggested by the unit root tests; however, the results are little changed if drift is assumed. The estimates of the coefficients on Δp_t and $x_t - p_{Xt}$ show minor variations with the truncation lag, the latter estimates being somewhat more variable. Both coefficients are significantly different from zero; however, of particular interest is whether the null hypothesis of a unit income elasticity is consistent with the data. Generally this is the case, the least consistent being a truncation lag of 2, although even this is not significant at the 5% level.

Additionally we note that on the basis of the stationarity of the regression residuals there is very little to choose between the regression with an unrestricted income elasticity, equation (10.29), and the regression which imposes a unit income elasticity, equation (10.30), corresponding to an inverse velocity specification. Accordingly in Figure 10.5A we use the estimated equation with the income elasticity restricted to unity to illustrate the goodness of fit of equation (10.30) to the data on $m_t - p_t$. The estimated values are indicated as 'CI Regression' and are obtained from equation (10.30),

reported in the lower part of Table 10.2, with forecasts made for 1923m10 and m11 and backcasts for the months preceding 1922m7 (but note that these are indistinguishable from the restricted ECM – see **10.3.7**). The equation fits the data quite well within the sample and in forecasting the final two months; however, the earlier part of the sample is not well fitted by the cointegrating regression. In the next section we examine the question of whether dynamics can add anything to the cointegrating regression.

In section **10.3.3**, reference was made to Cagan's preference for a functional form which enabled the elasticity of cash balances with respect to the inflation rate to vary with the inflation rate, the idea being that individuals would not take flight from the currency immediately but would increase their flight as the inflation rate increased. The semi-elasticity is

$-\alpha$, whereas the elasticity is $-\alpha\Delta p_t$, and the elasticity will thus vary with Δp_t; for example, taking the estimate of α as 0.624, from the inverse velocity equation reported in the lower half of Table 10.2, the estimated elasticity is -0.105 for 1921m7 with an inflation rate of just under 17% per month whereas it is -2.785 for 1923m9 when inflation was about 446% per month.

10.3.7 Dynamic models

We give some consideration here to whether the (static) cointegrating regression can be successfully augmented by terms that allow for a dynamic model. In view of the short sample period preferred by MNP (op. cit.), a dynamic model needs to be simple to avoid using up the few degrees of freedom left for estimation. The reported model is a simple error correction mechanism, ECM, of the form used in previous chapters – see especially Chapter 8. The long run for $m_t - p_t$ is defined from the empirical version of equation (10.30) which imposes an income elasticity of 1 – see the lower half of Table 10.2 – as the evidence was there most favourable to cointegration. The error correction term is, therefore,

$$ecm_t = m_t - p_t - (5.166 - 0.624\Delta p_t$$
$$+ (x_t - p_{Xt})) \tag{10.31}$$

This is incorporated into the following dynamic model:

$$\Delta(m_t - p_t) = \theta_0 + \theta_1\Delta(\Delta p_t)$$
$$+ \theta_2\Delta(x_t - p_{Xt})$$
$$+ \theta_3 ecm_{t-1} + \varepsilon_t \tag{10.32}$$

The anticipated signs of the coefficients are: $\theta_1 < 0$, as the inflation rate increases agents want to reduce their holdings of real cash; $\theta_2 > 0$, an increase in real income implies, ceteris paribus, an increase in the demand for money; and $\theta_3 < 0$, a positive value for ecm_t implies that actual real cash exceeds equilibrium holdings,

with the consequence that the former should be decreased to reduce the difference between actual and equilibrium. Adjustment towards equilibrium will be faster the larger, in absolute value, is $\theta_3 < 0$.

Estimation details of equation (10.32) are reported in Table 10.4. The coefficient signs are as anticipated and significant subject to the qualification that the residuals are not entirely free from serial correlation as indicated by the SC(1) statistic which is significant, although SC(4) is not significant at the 5% level; these statistics are also reported here in their F versions; however, the degrees of freedom adjustments do not alter these conclusions.

One hypothesis of interest in the context of the dynamic model concerns the speed of adjustment of real money to past disequilibrium; the unconstrained estimate is -0.725, implying 72.5% of disequilibrium is removed in one month, an alternative would be that all past disequilibrium is removed and, therefore, $\theta_3 = -1$. An F test of this hypothesis against the two-sided alternative gives $F = 1.119$ with an msl of 31.2%, indicating nonrejection of the null. Imposing the restriction results in a much cleaner profile for the SC(i) statistics, with neither the χ^2 or F versions of SC(1) or SC(4) significant, giving some confidence in the consistency of the restriction with the data.

The restricted regression is also reported in Table 10.4. An interesting point to note about the coefficients in this regression, and to a lesser extent in the unrestricted regression, is how close the estimates of θ_1 and θ_2 are to their long-run coefficients. That is $\hat{\theta}_1 = -0.619$ compared to -0.624, and $\hat{\theta}_2 = 0.915$ compared to 1; together with an ecm coefficient of $\theta_3 = -1$, they indicate agents keeping in (almost) perfect step by eradicating past disequilibrium and making dynamic adjustments which take account of changes between periods $t - 1$ and t. If adjustment was absolutely perfect, there would be no distinction between the short run and the long run: agents would always be in equilibrium. The coefficient estimates give some comfort in using

Table 10.4 *The German hyperinflation: dynamic models*

Sample period: 1922m8 to 1923m9

Demand for money with real income proxy

$$\Delta(m_t - p_t) = -0.598\Delta\Delta p_t + 0.872\Delta(x_t - p_{Xt}) - 0.725ecm_{t-1} + \hat{\varepsilon}_t$$
$$\quad\quad\quad (-7.391) \quad\quad (3.577) \quad\quad\quad (-2.789)$$

$\hat{\sigma} = 0.171$
$dw = 1.543$
$SC(1) = 8.031[0.005]; F(1,9) = 14.317[0.004]$
$SC(4) = 8.379[0.079]; F(4,3) = 3.466[0.167]$
$FF(1) = 0.020[0.886]; JB(2) = 0.852[0.653];$
$HS(1) = 1.695[0.193]$

$$ecm_t = m_t - p_t - (5.166 - 0.624\Delta p_t + (x_t - p_{Xt}))$$

from Table 10.2

ecm coefficient restricted to -1

$$\Delta(m_t - p_t) = -0.619\Delta\Delta p_t + 0.915\Delta(x_t - p_{Xt}) - 1.000ecm_{t-1} + \hat{\varepsilon}_t$$
$$\quad\quad\quad (-7.852) \quad\quad (3.794) \quad\quad\quad (-2.789)$$

$\hat{\sigma} = 0.172$
$dw = 1.477$
$SC(1) = 0.485[0.486]; F(1,10) = 0.378[0.552]$
$SC(4) = 7.392[0.117]; F(4,4) = 2.784[0.172]$
$FF(1) = 0.071[0.790]; JB(2) = 0.204[0.903];$
$HS(1) = 2.084[0.149]$

Sample period: 1921m1 to 1923m9

Demand for money with real income proxy

$$\Delta(m_t - p_t) = 0.368\Delta(m_t - p_t) - 0.522\Delta\Delta p_t + 1.098\Delta(x_t - p_{Xt}) - 1.040dv\Delta(x_t - p_{Xt}) - 1.167ecm_{t-1}$$
$$\quad\quad (4.689) \quad\quad\quad (-10.268) \quad\quad (7.369) \quad\quad\quad (-4.293) \quad\quad\quad\quad (-5.710)$$
$$\text{Robust 't'} \quad \{5.184\} \quad\quad \{-11.034\} \quad\quad \{6.124\} \quad\quad\quad \{-4.735\} \quad\quad\quad\quad \{-4.636\}$$

$$+ 1.140dvecm_{t-1} + \hat{\varepsilon}_t$$
$$(5.514)$$
$$\{4.485\}$$

$\hat{\sigma} = 0.099$
$dw = 1.874$
$SC(1) = 0.152[0.696]; F(1,23) = 0.0113[0.740]$
$SC(4) = 9.662[0.050]; F(4,17) = 1.948[0.149]$
$FF(1) = 1.906[0.167]; JB(2) = 2.649[0.266];$
$HS(1) = 8.207[0.004]$

$$ecm_t = m_t - p_t - (5.166 - 0.624\Delta p_t + (x_t - p_{Xt}))$$

from Table 10.2

't' statistics in (.) parentheses;
robust 't' statistics in {.} parentheses.

the methodology of unit root testing and co-integration with such a small sample; although the sample is small by conventional standards, adjustment is fast as agents keep close to equilibrium.

Because there is very fast adjustment to past disequilibria and contemporaneous changes, there is very little difference between the forecast values from either of the dynamic regressions in Table 10.4 and the static coin-tegrating regression. The one step ahead fore-casts and backcasts shown in Figure 10.5A, denoted 'CI Regression' and 'Restricted ECM', respectively, are virtually indistinguishable.

To see where some of the problems arise in the early part of the sample, multiplicative dummy variables were defined for the period prior to 1922m7. First define dv_t as 1 for 1921m1 to 1922m7 and 0 for 1922m8 to 1923m9; then multiply each explanatory variable by dv_t, that is $dv_t\Delta\Delta p_t = dv_t$ times $\Delta\Delta p_t$, $dv\Delta(x_t - p_{Xt}) = dv_t$ times $\Delta(x_t - p_{Xt})$ and $dvecm_t = dv_t$ times ecm_t. These multiplicative dummy variables are then included in the regression: their coefficients indicate the difference from the base period coefficients estimated over 1922m8 to 1923m9, and the 't' statistics indicate whether these differences are (individually) different from zero. The ecm_t term is as defined for the shorter period, as there was some evidence of stationarity in that case. The equation is reported in the lower part of Table 10.4, and the one step ahead forecasts and backcasts are shown in Figure 10.5B and denoted 'Full Sample ECM'. The significant multiplicative dummy variables were $dv\Delta(x_t - p_{Xt})$ and $dvecm_{t-1}$, there being relative minor variation in the coefficient on $\Delta\Delta p_t$ so the dummy variable was omitted. There was one cautionary diagnostic statistic, namely HS(1) was significant so care has to be taken in interpreting standard errors and hypothesis tests. To see if the results were robust to heteroscedasticity, heteroscedastic consistent standard errors – see Chapter 5 – were calculated, and the robust 't' statistics are shown in {.} parentheses. The differences relative to the usual 't' statistics are slight. The significant dummy variables indicate marked changes in the coefficients on ecm_{t-1} and $\Delta(x_t - p_{Xt})$; in the former case the estimate of θ_3 is -1.167 for the base period but $-1.167 + 1.140 = -0.027$ otherwise; in the latter case the estimate of θ_2 is 1.098 for the base period but $1.098 - 1.040 = 0.058$ otherwise.

It is evident from Figure 10.5B that the period preceding 1922m7 can be fitted quite well by allowing changes in the key coefficients, indicating a marked change in regime. It is apparent then that not all is yet resolved when the 'conventional period' is considered – but this is part of the essence of a progressive research strategy which can convey the potential for further improvements in estimation and understanding.

10.4 The demand for M1: a study using recent US data

In this section we assess whether the general principles, outlined in section **10.2**, for the formulation of demand for money functions meet with success when applied to a relatively recent period in the United States. The motivation for the choice of this period was twofold. First, it provides a contrast to the hyperinflationary period in Germany after the First World War. The sample period for this section is 1974m1 to 1993m12, which, while a period of relative stability compared to the 1920s, still contains sufficient movement in the key variables – money, prices, income and interest rates – to offer a challenge for empirical modelling. The number of observations also provides a contrast, which, in this section, is more representative of the kind of sample sizes commonly available. Second, a study by Hoffman and Rasche (1991), hereafter HR (1991), over a slightly different sample period, addresses several issues of importance and provides a general motivation for this choice of country and sample. (For a critical review of the demand for money in the United States, see Lucas (1988).) HR (1991) use integration and cointegration techniques to examine the demand for money using monthly data; their model has the usual elements found in a large number of studies of the demand for money which concentrate on the transactions demand for money. That is a narrow definition of money such as M1 is specified as a function of income and a nominal interest rate which captures the opportunity cost of holding narrow money rather than an alternative interest paying asset. If the stock of money is measured in nominal terms, then the price level should be included as a determinant of the demand for money. While HR's econometric techniques are more advanced than those used here, in the sense that they use the multivariate cointegration procedure due to Johansen (1988), and see Chapters 14 and 15, their results suggest the existence of just one cointegrating vector among the variables real money, real income and an interest rate. Hence, a single-equation analysis is (potentially) valid. (We would also need to find that the chosen right-hand side variables were weakly exogenous for the parameters of interest.)

10.4.1   Model specification

The specification we adopt here is broadly that of sections **10.2** and **10.3** which dealt with the determinants of the demand for money and an application, following Cagan (1956) and MNP (1994), to the German hyperinflationary period after the First World War. In turn, this provided an application of the modelling strategy introduced in Chapter 8, which led to the construction of a dynamic model incorporating a cointegrating – or   equilibrium – relationship. As to the latter in the context of the present study we start with the following specification, which has been adopted in a number of previous studies – see HR (1991) and references therein:

$$m_t - p_t = \beta_0 + \beta_1(y_t - p_t)$$
$$+ \beta_2 f(R_t) + \xi_t \qquad (10.33)$$

Where, as before $m_t - p_t$, is the log of real money, a particular definition of which is considered in greater detail below; $(y_t - p_t)$ is real income (note that here we use y_t rather than x_t as the notation for nominal income, the latter previously being used as a proxy for income); R_t is the spread between the own rate on m_t and a 'near money' alternative, again we consider this in greater detail below, and $f(R_t)$ indicates a function of R_t which, in practice, is usually taken to be either R_t or the logarithm of R_t – in the

former case β_2 is the semi-elasticity whereas in the latter case it is the elasticity.

The first step in the modelling strategy is to establish whether the regression in (10.33) is balanced in its time series properties. This is the subject of sections **10.4.3** and **10.4.4** below. For example, if $m_t - p_t$ is integrated of order 1, I(1), then the following will meet the necessary condition for a balanced regression: either or both $y_t - p_t$ and R_t (or $\ln R_t$) are I(1), if just one of these is I(1) then the other must be I(0); in principle, a balance could also be achieved if $y_t - p_t$ and R_t (or $\ln R_t$) were each of the same but higher order of integration, for example I(2), but they cointegrated on a pairwise basis to be I(1). The balance of an equation is, as we have seen, not a sufficient condition in a modelling strategy; that requires the existence of a cointegrating vector among the three variables $m_t - p_t$, $y_t - p_t$ and R_t (or $\ln R_t$) so that ξ_t is I(0). We consider this issue in section **10.4.5**. Given a stationary innovation, ξ_t, the next step in the modelling strategy is to allow for short-term dynamics as well as the long run, or equilibrium, given by the cointegrating relationship, this is considered in section **10.4.6**. Section **10.4.2** defines the data.

10.4.2   Data definitions

In defining the data to be used in the empirical study, two of the key issues are which measurement concept of money most closely matches the theoretical concept and the related issue of how to measure the 'own' rate of return or, if relevant, spread which captures the opportunity cost associated with the money definition.

The definition of money. The following definitions of money are published on a monthly basis in the Federal Reserve Bulletin: M1, M2, M3 and L. M1 is the monetary aggregate usually associated with 'transactions' money, it is currently defined as currency (notes and coins), traveller's cheques, demand deposits at commercial banks and other checkable deposits (OCDs) consisting of negotiable order of withdrawal (NOW) and automatic transfer service (ATS) accounts, credit union share draft accounts, and demand deposits at thrift institutions. In short M1 is currency, traveller's cheques, demand deposits and OCDs, all of which are capable of financing transactions and hence are at the most liquid end of the spectrum of monetary assets. Prior to 1980 M1 did not include OCDs but as the data prior to 1980 reveal the redefinition was essentially a matter of anticipating monetary developments rather than correcting for past developments. For example, in December 1980 OCDs were 6.73% of M1, whereas in December 1994 they were 35% of M1. For further details of the redefinition of the monetary aggregates see the Federal Reserve Bulletin, Simpson (1980).

M2 is M1 plus savings and small time deposits (plus some minor technical adjustments); the difference between M2 and M1 is termed the nontransaction component in the Federal Reserve Bulletin tables. In December 1980 M2 was 1,669.4 compared to 415.6 for M1, with savings and small time deposits of 1,149.8. In December 1994 the corresponding figures were M2 = 3,509.4, M1 = 1,124.8, with savings and small time deposits of 1,972.5 (all figures are seasonally adjusted, billions US$, sources Federal Reserve Bulletin, January 1982, Table A13, May 1996, Table A14). M3 adds to M2 large (>$100,000) time deposits at all depository institutions plus term repurchase liabilities issued by commercial banks and savings and loans associations. In December 1980 M3 = 1,965.1 with large time deposits of 256.8 and in December 1994 M3 = 4,319.7 with large time deposits of 363.5. A further published measure is known as L, which is intended as a broad measure of liquid assets. It adds to M3 the non-bank public holdings of US savings bonds, short-term Treasury securities, commercial paper, and bankers' acceptances, net of money market fund holdings of these assets. In December 1980, L was 2,378.4 and in December 1994, 5,303.7.

Following HR (1991), the transactions measure of money, M1, was chosen for this study.

For a related study using cross-section data and an M1 concept of money see Bomberger (1993), and an excellent, but somewhat advanced, review of modelling issues in the context of the demand for M1 is provided by Baba, Hendry and Starr (1992), hereafter referred to as BHS (1992). For an approach similar to HR (1991), but applied to M2, see Mehra (1993). For simplicity we denote the nominal stock of M1 at the end of period t as M_t; M_t/P_t is the real stock of M1, where P_t is the price level which we take to be the US Consumer Price Index. In logs these variables are m_t, $m_t - p_t$ and p_t.

We take Y_t to be personal income and Y_t/P_t is, therefore, real personal income, but note that other choices of a variable to capture the scale of economic transactions are possible. For example, BHS (1992) use GNP and Elyasiani and Nasseh (1994) compare scale measures based alternately on consumers' expenditure, income and wealth. In logs, nominal income and real income are y_t and $y_t - p_t$.

The specification of R_t, the opportunity cost variable in (10.35), should be linked to the choice, and characteristics, of the monetary aggregate. In the Baumol/Barro framework outlined in section **10.2.2**, for simplicity money is assumed not to be explicitly interest bearing and there is assumed to be a single 'alternative financial asset' with interest rate R_t. When money is just currency this framework can be justified and R_t is the appropriate opportunity cost. However, in practice there are two problems. First, money is usually defined to include checking deposits that may either implicitly or explicitly include a return; and, second, there is a wide range of alternative financial instruments yielding different returns.

As to the former the inclusion of interest bearing other checkable deposits in M1 implies that a weighted average of the returns on the noninterest bearing and interest bearing components of M1 would be nonzero. This is perhaps not so important where the dominant part of the sample period does not relate to the take-off in the interest bearing component of

M1; and as HR (*op. cit.*, p. 668) note there is anyway 'difficulty in measuring an own rate for transaction balances'. In this study we follow the standard practice of assuming that the own rate is zero for our sample period. However, we note the important work by BHS (1992), which constructs a weighted average of the yield on interest bearing OCDs with weights given by an exponential learning curve that takes full effect 5 years after introduction of the asset.

As to the second of the problems, that is the existence of a wide range of alternative financial assets, different authors have, in practice, made different choices. BHS (*op. cit.*) suggest reference to nontransactions M2 with the alternative rate given by the maximum (learning adjusted) yield in that category. HR (*op. cit.*) alternately try a short rate – the 90-day Treasury Bill rate- and a long rate – the 10-year Government Bond rate. We also experiment with two different rates, in our case the 90-day Treasury Bill rate and the 3-year Treasury Bond rate; we refer to these as SR_t and LR_t, respectively. In practice the choice of an interest rate may not be too crucial if the different rates are nonstationary and cointegrated. For example, suppose R_{1t} and R_{2t} are alternative interest rates and both are I(1) and, as seems plausible, they are also cointegrated with coefficients $+1$ and -1 so that their difference, known as the spread, is stationary. Then even if the 'wrong' choice is made it should have little impact on the estimates in the cointegrating regression since their difference is I(0) by assumption. Indeed on reference to HR (1991, p. 669, Table 3) for their sample of 1953m4 to 1988m12, which captures the period most likely to indicate nonstationarity, we find that the estimates of the coefficients on their alternate interest rates are identical to 3 decimal places.

Finally, we also note that there is not a consensus on whether to enter the chosen interest rate as R_t or $\ln R_t$. As we have seen Cagan (*op. cit.*) preferred the variable elasticity approach associated with the former, as did BHS (*op. cit.*); on the other hand, Goldfeld (1976) and HR (*op. cit.*) opt for the constant elasticity

formulation implied by the latter specification. Our preference is for the variable elasticity formulation associated with using R_t.

The data on M_t, P_t, Y_t, SR_t and LR_t is monthly, and seasonally adjusted with the exception of the interest rate data; the overall sample period, before any lags are taken, is 1974m1 to 1993m12.

10.4.3 A graphical analysis of the data

The first step in the empirical analysis is to gather a visual impression of the data followed by more formal testing of the order of integration of the variables. In Figure 10.6 we graph real money, $m_t - p_t$, and real income, $y_t - p_t$. We note that while both share the same upward trend the series for real money is more variable with noticeable dips in the early 1980s and the early 1990s. There is also a noticeable dip in real income in the early 1980s but not in the early 1990s. In Figure 10.7 we make use of a dual scale graph with real money indicated on the left-hand scale and interest rates (short rate and long rate) on the right-hand scale. The dip in real money in the 1980s corresponds to increasing interest rates during that period; similarly, although the timing is not so clear, the dip in the early 1990s shows some correspondence with

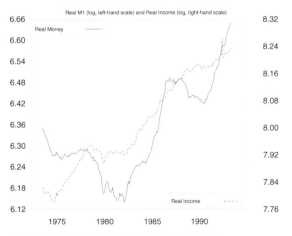

Figure 10.6 *US real M1 and real income*

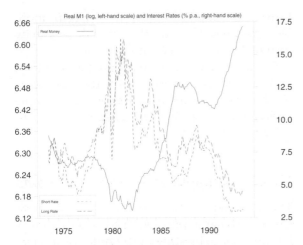

Figure 10.7 *US real M1 and interest rates*

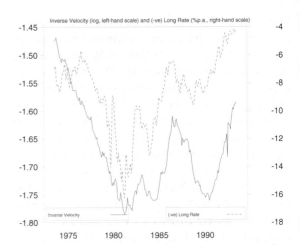

Figure 10.9 *US inverse velocity and the (−ve) long rate*

slightly earlier increases in interest rates. The general correspondence between real money and interest rates is easier to see in Figure 10.8 where, since the expected association is negative, we graph real money and the *negative* of the interest rate variables. Finally, in Figure 10.9 we graph inverse velocity $m_t - y_t$ against the negative of the long rate (either rate would do here as they share the same broad pattern). The similarity in overall pattern between real money and the interest rate is noticeable – and, therefore, hopeful in the more formal analysis to which we now turn.

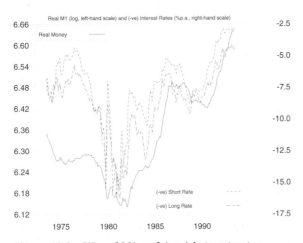

Figure 10.8 *US real M1 and (−ve) interest rates*

10.4.4   Testing for nonstationarity

The test results for the order of integration of the candidate variables are reported in Table 10.5; in the first half of the table we consider whether the data is consistent with the hypothesis that 2 unit roots are present. The general point made earlier, in connection with testing for 2 unit roots with the German data, is relevant here also. Although the complete range of test statistics is presented, it is usually the case the alternative of 1 unit root and a deterministic time trend can be quickly dispensed with, so the sample values of Φ_3 and $\hat{\tau}_\beta$ are not usually the focus of attention.

The evidence seems firmly against the hypothesis of 2 unit roots. This conclusion is illustrated with the log of real money, $m_t - p_t$; in this case $\Phi_3 = 6.379$, compared with 5% and 10% critical values of 6.397 and 5.433, respectively, for $T = 200$ from Table 6.7. We are, therefore, on the margin of rejecting the null hypothesis at the 5% level, with definite rejection at the 10% level. As $\hat{\beta}$ is zero to 4 decimal places (and zero to 2 decimal places when divided by the equation standard error), and insignificant, the time trend is excluded; in this case we obtain $\hat{\tau}_\mu = -3.278$, and $\hat{\mu} = 0.000$, compared to the 5% critical value of (approximately) -2.850 suggesting rejection of the null hypothesis. The sample value of Φ_1 at 5.458 is

Table 10.5   US demand for money: unit root tests

Variable	Model	$\hat{\tau}$	$\hat{\Phi}_1$	$\hat{\tau}_\mu$	$\hat{\mu}$	$\hat{\tau}_\beta$	$\hat{\beta}$	Φ_3
			Test statistics for 2 unit roots					
$m_t - p_t$	ADF(6)	−3.317	5.458	−3.278	0.000	−3.562	0.000	6.379
$y_t - p_t$	ADF(1)	−10.169	65.219	−11.419	0.002	−11.395	0.000	64.954
$m_t - y_t$	ADF(2)	−6.610	21.977	−6.629	0.000	−7.410	0.000	27.459
SR_t	ADF(4)	−3.874	7.506	−3.860	−0.010	−4.028	0.000	8.146
LR_t	ADF(5)	−7.289	26.622	−7.296	−0.015	−7.379	0.000	27.255
			Test statistics for 1 unit root					
$m_t - p_t$	ADF(8)	6.462	0.876	−0.340	0.007	−1.698	0.000	2.057
$y_t - p_t$	ADF(1)	4.616	10.609	0.083	0.000	−1.871	0.000	1.854
$m_t - y_t$	ADF(5)	−0.847	2.372	−2.147	−0.025	−1.215	0.000	3.628
SR_t	ADF(15)	−0.704	1.074	−1.441	0.160	−1.825	−0.001	2.323
LR_t	ADF(6)	−0.771	0.598	−0.956	0.086	−1.282	−0.001	1.435

Overall sample period (before lagging): 1974m1 to 1993m12.
(Typical) critical values

	$\hat{\tau}$	$\hat{\tau}_\mu$	$\hat{\tau}_\beta$	Φ_1	Φ_3
5%	1.927	2.850	3.399	4.696	6.397
10%	1.602	2.555	3.111	3.835	5.433

Critical values of $\hat{\tau}$, $\hat{\tau}_\mu$ and $\hat{\tau}_\beta$ obtained using Cheung–Lai response surface coefficients for $T = 235$ and $p = 6$; critical values of Φ_1 and Φ_3 obtained by simulation for $T = 200$ – see Chapter 6.

significant (the 5% critical value for $T = 200$ is 4.696) leading to rejection of the joint null hypothesis of a (marginal) second root and no constant. The estimated constant is zero to 3 decimal places; if it is omitted (so the rejection at Φ_1 is attributed to the rejection of a second unit root), we obtain $\hat{\tau} = -3.317$ compared to the 5% critical value of (approximately) −1.927, and the null hypothesis of 2 unit roots is again rejected. The conclusion is the same for the other series with the test statistics even more pronounced in their rejection of the null hypothesis of 2 unit roots.

Turning now to the tests for 1 unit root the results are, again, reasonably uniform and rather than going through each on a repetitive basis we illustrate the results for $m_t - p_t$.

In this case we obtain $\Phi_3 = 2.057$ which is well below the 5% critical value of 6.397 indicating nonrejection of the null hypothesis

of a unit root. The estimate of β is zero to 3 decimal places and insignificant; with the time trend excluded, $\hat{\tau}_\mu = -0.340$ which is well below (in absolute value) the 5% critical value of (approximately) −2.850 implying nonrejection of the null hypothesis of a unit root. The sample value of $\Phi_1 = 0.876$ is considerably below the 5% critical value of (approximately) 4.696 and suggests $m_t - p_t$ is a driftless unit root process. If the constant is omitted, $\hat{\tau} = 6.462$, which is wrong signed for rejection of the null hypothesis. This conclusion applies equally, but with some nuances, to the other four series: we cannot reject the hypothesis that each series is I(1), the necessary condition for the balance of equation (10.33) is satisfied and it would be valid to move to the next step to assess whether $m_t - p_t$, $y_t - p_t$ and either SR_t or LR_t cointegrate. A nuance for real income, $y_t - p_t$, is the value of $\Phi_1 = 10.609$, which is significant. This sample value is greater than the 5% critical value, and hence suggests rejection of the joint null of a unit root and no constant; however, what this is indicating is that in the context of a unit root model for real income, drift should be included. Imposing the null, the estimated constant is 0.002 and significant with a 't' statistic of 4.615; although this estimate seems numerically negligible, this is not correct: it represents *annual* growth of about 2.5%, which is plausible. As noted in Chapter 6, when a series is trended removal of the deterministic trend from the maintained ADF regression is likely to lead to the conclusion of a unit root process with drift.

10.4.5 Cointegration

As noted the unit root test results suggest that it would be sensible to consider a cointegration analysis of the data. We first try out the basic specification of the long-run demand for money function, (10.33), in which $m_t - p_t$ is specified as a function of $y_t - p_t$ and a measure of the opportunity cost of holding money. For the latter we try as alternatives the short rate, SR_t, and the long rate, LR_t.

To illustrate the results of Chapter 8 we report in Table 10.6 details of estimating the cointegrating regressions by: (a) the first step of Engle–Granger, EG, estimation; and (b) by estimation of an autoregressive distributed lag, ADL, model which is then solved for the implicit long-run solution. The first set of results is for the regression with the short rate and the second with the long rate. In the former case the estimated long-run income elasticity is 0.617 from EG estimation but rather higher at 0.765 from ADL estimation. This result supports the illustrative Monte Carlo simulation results reported in Chapter 8, where the EG estimates of the long-run coefficients in a similar situation tended to be lower than the ADL estimates. The estimated coefficient on the short rate is −0.021 from EG estimation and −0.030 from ADL estimation.

With each estimation method the residuals were saved and used in an ADF regression to assess the null hypothesis of noncointegration. For EG estimation an ADF(4) regression was necessary with a test statistic, $\hat{\tau}_\gamma$, of −3.371, and with ADL estimation an ADF(6) gave a test statistic of −3.068. The test statistics are, therefore, slightly below (in absolute value) the 10% critical value of −3.426 but close enough to suggest that a cointegrating relationship is a realistic possibility.

The next set of regressions in Table 10.6 uses the long rate rather than the short rate with broadly similar results, which confirms the supposition above that the choice of an interest rate among a nonstationary set of alternatives may not be too critical to the results. The marginal differences are that the EG estimate of the income elasticity is 0.606 compared to 0.617 with the short rate, and the ADL estimate of the income elasticity is 0.772 compared to 0.765 using the short rate. The estimated coefficient on the long rate is −0.026 from EG estimation and −0.030 from ADL estimation.

The ADL models were chosen to ensure that there was no evidence of serial correlation in the residuals. For example, for the short-rate model an ADL with 4 lags of the variables gave an SC(12) statistic of 17.10 with a marginal significance level of just under 15%. For the long-rate model an ADL with 5 lags of the variables gave an SC(12) statistic of 11.39 with a marginal significance level of just under 50%.

On the basis of the results so far it is worth going to the next step in Engle–Granger estimation of constructing a dynamic model of the US demand for money and hence also of considering further the (dynamic) ADL model. However, before moving to this stage the long-run coefficients are considered in greater detail. The estimated coefficients on the interest rate variables from ADL estimation are the same at −0.030 (to 3 decimal places) whether the short rate or the long rate is used. In interpreting this value it is useful to calculate the elasticity of the demand for money with respect to the interest

Table 10.6 *US demand for money: estimation of the long run*

Using the short rate
OLSEG
$$m_t - p_t = 1.557 + 0.617(y_t - p_t) - 0.021SR_t + \hat{\xi}_t$$
$$\quad(7.912)(25.531)\quad\quad(-18.292))$$

$$\Delta\hat{\xi}_t = -0.064\hat{\xi}_{t-1}$$
$$\quad(-3.069)$$

$$\Delta\hat{\xi}_t = -0.0764\hat{\xi}_{t-1} + \sum_{i=1}^{4}\hat{\alpha}_i\Delta\hat{\xi}_{t-i}$$
$$\quad(-3.371)$$

$\hat{\sigma} = 0.047$
dw = 0.160
SC(12) = 204.00[0.000]
SC(12) = 50.940[0.000]

SC(12) = 21.068[0.050]

ADL
$$m_t - p_t = 0.0442 + 0.765(y_t - p_t) - 0.030SR_t + \hat{\xi}_t$$
$$\Delta\hat{\xi}_t = -0.074\hat{\xi}_{t-1}$$
$$\quad(-3.378)$$

$$\Delta\hat{\xi}_t = -0.0072\hat{\xi}_{t-1} + \sum_{i=1}^{6}\hat{\alpha}_i\Delta\hat{\xi}_{t-i}$$
$$\quad(-3.068)$$

ADL(4): SC(12) = 17.102[0.146]
SC(12) = 55.063[0.000]

SC(12) = 8.706[0.728]

Using the long rate
EG
$$m_t - p_t = 1.708 + 0.606(y_t - p_t) - 0.026LR_t + \hat{\xi}_t$$
$$\quad(10.473)(30.413)\quad\quad(-24.402)$$

$$\Delta\hat{\xi}_t = -0.073\hat{\xi}_{t-1}$$
$$\quad(-3.057)$$

$$\Delta\hat{\xi}_t = -0.082\hat{\xi}_{t-1} + \sum_{i=1}^{6}\hat{\alpha}_i\Delta\hat{\xi}_{t-i}$$
$$\quad(-3.104)$$

$\hat{\sigma} = 0.039$
dw = 0.140
SC(12) = 199.83[0.000]
SC(12) = 55.910[0.000]

SC(12) = 20.96[0.051]

ADL
$$m_t - p_t = 0.434 + 0.772(y_t - p_t) - 0.030LR_t + \hat{\xi}_t$$
$$\Delta\hat{\xi}_t = -0.061\hat{\xi}_{t-1}$$
$$\quad(-2.899)$$

$$\Delta\hat{\xi}_t = -0.0067\hat{\xi}_{t-1} + \sum_{i=1}^{5}\hat{\alpha}_i\Delta\hat{\xi}_{t-i}$$
$$\quad(-3.054)$$

ADL(5): SC(12) = 11.388[0.496]
SC(12) = 51.930[0.000]

SC(12) = 20.930[0.051]

Using inflation rather than an interest rate
EG
$$m_t - p_t = 0.093 + 0.780(y_t - p_t) - 0.002\Delta p_t + \hat{\xi}_t$$
$$\quad(0.293)(19.864)\quad\quad(-0.139)$$

$$\Delta\hat{\xi}_t = -0.010\hat{\xi}_{t-1} + \sum_{i=1}^{3}\hat{\alpha}_i\Delta\hat{\xi}_{t-i}$$
$$\quad(-1.529)$$

$\hat{\sigma} = 0.073$
dw = 0.010
SC(12) = 225.77[0.000]
SC(12) = 19.885[0.070]

Sample period: 1974m1 to 1993m12 for OLSEG equations; 1974m5 to 1993m12 for ADL equations.
The 5% and 10% critical values for $\hat{\tau}_\gamma$ calculated from MacKinnon's response surface coefficients are:

$$C(5\%, 239) = -3.7429 - 8.352/239 - 13.41/239^2 = -3.777$$
$$C(10\%, 239) = -3.4518 - 6.241/239 - 2.79/239^2 = -3.426.$$

rate which, because the estimated coefficient is a semi-elasticity, will vary with the interest rate. Specifically $e_R = -0.030R$ (where R will be either the short rate or the long rate); hence, in order to evaluate e_R we need to choose a representative value for the interest rate, or if there has been a good deal of variation over the sample period, choose a set of typical values and calculate the corresponding values of the elasticity. The means of SR and LR over the sample period are 7.465% p.a. and 8.700% p.a., respectively, with associated standard deviations of 2.871% p.a. and 2.600% p.a. For illustrative purposes e_{SR} and e_{LR} are calculated for the mean and $\pm$ one standard deviation – see Table 10.7.

The elasticity varies being larger, in absolute value, the higher the interest rate. At the higher end of the range the estimated elasticities are broadly what we would expect from sections **10.2.2** and **10.2.3** on the transactions and precautionary motives for holding money. These elasticities have the usual interpretation giving the (estimated) effect on real M1 of a 1% change in the interest rate, for example an increase in R from 8% to 8.08% p.a. However, in this case this may not be as easy to interpret as asking: what is the effect on the demand for money of a 1 percentage point increase in the interest rate, for example from 8% p.a. to 9% p.a.? The answer to this question is provided directly by the semi-elasticity, which is just the estimated coefficient on the interest rate. So if there is an increase in R from 8% p.a. to 9% p.a., the estimated long-run effect of this change will be a decline in the demand for money balances of 0.03%.

Table 10.7 *US demand for money, estimated long-run interest elasticities*

	mean -1 s.d.	mean	mean $+1$ s.d.
SR =	4.593	7.465	10.337
e_{SR} =	-0.138	-0.224	-0.310
LR =	6.100	8.700	11.300
e_{SR} =	-0.183	-0.260	-0.337

Note: Calculations use estimated semi-elasticity of -0.030 from unrestricted ADL estimation.

Earlier in this section we mentioned that some authors – for example, HR (1991) – have preferred to use the log of the interest rate rather than its level as used here. This issue is briefly considered here to show that the alternative specification does not lead to an improvement in the results. As before lower case letters denote logs. First, the hypothesis of 2 unit roots was easily rejected for both sr_t and lr_t; for example, $\hat{\tau}_\mu = -6.570(\text{ADF}(1))$ and $-11.730(\text{ADF}(6))$, respectively; and the hypothesis of 1 unit root was not rejected with $\hat{\tau}_\mu = -2.013(\text{ADF}(16))$ and $-0.716(\text{ADF}(2))$, respectively. Second, regressions of the form (10.33) but with sr_t or lr_t, estimated by OLS (that is the first stage of Engle–Granger) resulted in:

$$m_t - p_t = 1.917 + 0.591(y_t - p_t)$$
$$- 0.160sr_t + \hat{\xi}_t$$
$$\hat{\sigma} = 0.047;\ \text{dw} = 0.072$$
$$\text{SC}(12) = 18.412[0.104]$$

$$\Delta\hat{\xi}_t = -0.055\hat{\xi}_{t-1} - 0.254\Delta\hat{\xi}_t$$
$$(-3.247)$$

$$m_t - p_t = 2.140 + 0.585(y_t - p_t)$$
$$- 0.223lr_t + \hat{\xi}_t$$
$$\hat{\sigma} = 0.039;\ \text{dw} = 0.122$$
$$\text{SC}(12) = 18.840[0.093]$$

$$\Delta\hat{\xi}_t = -0.077\hat{\xi}_{t-1} + \sum_{i=1}^{8} \hat{\alpha}_i\Delta\hat{\xi}_{t-i}$$
$$(-3.094)$$

The test statistics from the ADF regressions are very similar to those in Table 10.6, which use interest rate levels. For example, $\hat{\tau}_\gamma = -3.371$ with SR_t and $\hat{\tau}_\gamma = -3.247$ for sr_t; and $\hat{\tau}_\gamma = -3.104$ with LR_t and $\hat{\tau}_\gamma = -3.094$ with lr_t. The estimated equation standard errors are almost identical at 0.047 with the short rate and 0.039 with the long rate, in either version. The estimated elasticities are comparable at the sample mean. Using the EG estimate from Table 10.6, with the short rate, at the sample mean we obtain an estimated elasticity of -0.157, compared to the constant elasticity estimate of -0.160 with sr_t; and with the long rate the estimated elasticity from OLSEG estimation, evaluated at the sample mean, is identical to 3 decimal places with the constant elasticity estimate of -0.223.

Returning to the equations reported in Table 10.6, we turn now to the estimated coefficient on real income. From ADL estimation this is about 0.77 whichever interest rate is used, which is similar to the estimate obtained by HR (1991) who reported a value of 0.79 over a sample period of 1953m1 to 1988m12; they also considered the hypothesis that the income elasticity is unity. As we saw earlier if this is the case the demand for money function can be reformulated as an equation for the inverse velocity of

Table 10.8 *US inverse velocity: estimation of the long run*

Short rate
EG
$$m_t - y_t = 1.564 - 0.0144SR_t + \hat{\xi}_t$$
$$\qquad (127.50)\ (-9.404)$$

$\hat{\sigma} = 0.068$
$dw = 0.032$
$SC(12) = 218.16[0.000]$
$SC(12) = 23.344[0.025]$

$$\Delta\hat{\xi}_t = -0.034\hat{\xi}_{t-1}$$
$$\qquad (-2.992)$$

$$\Delta\hat{\xi}_t = -0.038\hat{\xi}_{t-1} + \sum_{i=1}^{2} \hat{\alpha}_i \Delta\hat{\xi}_{t-i}$$
$$\qquad (-3.281)$$

$SC(12) = 16.331[0.177]$

ADL
$$m_t - y_t = -1.484 - 0.027SR_t + \hat{\xi}_t$$
$$\Delta\hat{\xi}_t = -0.047\hat{\xi}_{t-1}$$
$$\qquad (-2.978)$$

ADL(4): $SC(12) = 12.185[0.430]$
$SC(12) = 46.649[0.000]$

$$\Delta\hat{\xi}_t = -0.0054\hat{\xi}_{t-1} + \sum_{i=1}^{7} \hat{\alpha}_i \Delta\hat{\xi}_{t-i}$$
$$\qquad (-3.210)$$

$SC(12) = 7.803[0.800]$

Long rate
EG
$$m_t - y_t = 1.512 - 0.018LR_t + \hat{\xi}_t$$
$$\qquad (-104.71)(-11.493)$$

$\hat{\sigma} = 0.064$
$dw = 0.038$
$SC(12) = 217.30[0.000]$
$SC(12) = 26.689[0.009]$

$$\Delta\hat{\xi}_t = -0.033\hat{\xi}_{t-1}$$
$$\qquad (-2.639)$$

$$\Delta\hat{\xi}_t = -0.038\hat{\xi}_{t-1} + \sum_{i=1}^{3} \hat{\alpha}_i \Delta\hat{\xi}_{t-i}$$
$$\qquad (-3.022)$$

$SC(12) = 16.396[0.0174]$

ADL
$$m_t - y_t = 1.484 - 0.027LR_t + \hat{\xi}_t$$
$$\Delta\hat{\xi}_t = -0.047\hat{\xi}_{t-1}$$
$$\qquad (-2.978)$$

ADL(4): $SC(12) = 12.185[0.430]$
$SC(12) = 46.649[0.000]$

$$\Delta\hat{\xi}_t = -0.0054\hat{\xi}_{t-1} + \sum_{i=1}^{7} \hat{\alpha}_i \Delta\hat{\xi}_{t-i}$$
$$\qquad (-3.210)$$

$SC(12) = 7.803[0.800]$

Note: Sample period 1974m1 to 1993m12.

circulation. That is if the long-run demand for money function is

$$m_t - p_t = \beta_0 + \beta_1(y_t - p_t) + \beta_2 R_t + \xi_t$$

$$(10.34)$$

then if $\beta_1 = 1$ this becomes

$$m_t - p_t - (y_t - p_t) = \beta_0 + \beta_2 R_t + \xi_t \quad (10.35)$$

that is, if the deflators for the money stock and nominal income are identical,

$$m_t - y_t = \beta_0 + \beta_2 R_t + \xi_t \quad (10.36)$$

which is the log of the inverse velocity of circulation. In this example, there is no ambiguity over the price deflator, which is the same for money and income. If $\beta_1 = 1$, and $\beta_2 < 0$, the inverse velocity is a negative function of the interest rate. Alternatively we can say that the velocity of money is positively related to the rate of interest: as the interest rate increases agents economise on their cash balances, holding a smaller stock with which to undertake a given level of transactions and the velocity of money increases as on average each unit of money has to finance more transactions. We saw in Figure 10.9 that there was a distinct visual impression of the inverse velocity being negatively related to the interest rate.

In order to see whether an income elasticity of 1 can be supported by our dataset we consider the (log of) the inverse velocity, $m_t - y_t$. Recall from Table 10.5 that the null hypothesis that $m_t - y_t$ is I(1) was not rejected by the data. It is, therefore, valid in terms of the balance of the cointegrating regression, to reformulate the dependent variable so that it is the inverse velocity of circulation. Comparative estimation details are reported in Table 10.8 on the previous page alternatively using the short-rate and the long-rate, and Engle–Granger and ADL estimation. Slightly better results are obtained using the short rate. With OLSEG estimation $\hat{\tau}_\gamma = -3.281$, using an ADF(2) model, and with ADL estimation $\hat{\tau}_\gamma = -3.210$, using an ADF(7) model,

both are close enough to the 10% critical value to suggest that the specification of a dynamic inverse velocity equation would be worthwhile. If the long rate is used, OLSEG estimation gives $\hat{\tau}_\gamma = -3.022(\text{ADF}(3))$ and $\hat{\tau}_\gamma = -3.210(\text{ADF}(7))$ for ADL estimation.

10.4.6 Dynamic models

The next stage in estimation is to incorporate the equilibrium, defined by the cointegrating regression, in a dynamic model of (a) money demand and (b) the inverse velocity of circulation. We will concentrate on the specification using the short rate as there is little variation using the long-rate; and compare the results using the second stage of the Engle–Granger procedure with estimation of an ADL model.

The results of first-stage estimation using the Engle–Granger method were reported in Table 10.6. The first stage serves to define (an estimated) equilibrium by:

$$ecm_t = m_t - p_t - \{1.557 + 0.617(y_t - p_t) \\ - 0.021 SR_t\} \quad (10.37)$$

This definition has an unrestricted income elasticity.

In the dynamic model the dependent variable is $\Delta(m_t - p_t)$, which is regressed on the lagged ecm_t, lags of the dependent variable and changes in the variables, $y_t - p_t$ and SR_t, which determine equilibrium. Starting from a general specification in which the maximum lag length was set at 4, and then simplifying, the preferred equation using the EG first stage is the first in Table 10.9. The diagnostic test statistics are satisfactory with one exception detailed below: SC(12) is acceptable with a sample value of 17.899 and msl = 12%; FF(1), which is Ramsey's RESET test, is acceptable at 0.820 and msl = 36.5%; JB(2), the test for normality, is acceptable at 2.058 with msl = 35.7%. The one exception is HS(1), the 'standard' test for heteroscedasticity, which at 6.328 has an msl = 1.2%. The coefficients are well determined, judged by the significance of the 't' statistics; however, in view

Table 10.9 US money demand: dynamic equations

EG second stage estimation

$$\Delta(m_t - p_t) = 0.271\Delta(m_t - p_t)_{-1} + 0.322\Delta(m_t - p_t)_{-3} + 0.173\Delta(y_t - p_t) + 0.107\Delta(y_t - p_t)_{-1}$$

$$\begin{array}{llll}(4.678) & (5.958) & (3.766) & (2.253)\\ \{4.266\} & \{6.446\} & \{3.177\} & \{2.439\}\end{array}$$

$$-0.105\Delta(y_t - p_t)_{-4} - 0.002\Delta SR_t - 0.002\Delta SR_{t-1} - 0.002\Delta SR_{t-2} - 0.025ecm_{t-1} + \hat{u}_t$$

$$\begin{array}{lllll}(-2.365) & (-3.955) & (-3.738) & (-3.776) & (-3.094)\\ \{-1.770\} & \{-3.385\} & \{-3.016\} & \{-3.946\} & \{-3.043\}\end{array}$$

$\hat{\sigma} = 0.0048;\ dw = 2.049;$
$SC(12) = 17.899[0.120];\ FF(1) = 0.820[0.365];$
$JB(2) = 2.058[0.357];\ HS(1) = 6.328\{0.012]$

$$\Delta(m_t - p_t) = 0.277\Delta(m_t - p_t)_{-1} + 0.317\Delta(m_t - p_t)_{-3} + 0.174\Delta(y_t - p_t) + 0.106\Delta(y_t - p_t)_{-1}$$

$$\begin{array}{llll}(5.264) & (6.222) & (3.810) & (2.257)\\ \{4.511\} & \{6.500\} & \{3.203\} & \{2.410\}\end{array}$$

$$-0.108\Delta(y_t - p_t)_{-4} - 0.006A\Delta SR_t - 0.026ecm_{t-1} + \hat{u}_t$$

$$\begin{array}{lll}(-2.439) & (-7.692) & (-3.190)\\ \{-1.840\} & \{-6.737\} & \{-3.114\}\end{array}$$

$\hat{\sigma} = 0.0048;\ dw = 2.057;$
$SC(12) = 17.920[0.118];\ FF(1) = 0.825[0.364];$
$JB(2) = 2.006[0.367];\ HS(1) = 6.240[0.012]$

$$A\Delta SR_t \equiv \tfrac{1}{3}(\Delta SR_t + \Delta SR_{t-1} + \Delta SR_{t-2})$$
$$ecm_t = m_t - p_t - \{1.557 + 0.617(y_t - p_t) - 0.021SR_t\}$$

ADL estimation

$$\Delta(m_t - p_t) = 0.022 + 0.203\Delta(m_t - p_t)_{-1} + 0.247\Delta(m_t - p_t)_{-3} + 0.161\Delta(y_t - p_t) + 0.089\Delta(y_t - p_t)_{-1}$$

$$\begin{array}{lllll}(0.972) & (3.393) & (4.335) & (3.375) & (1.819)\\ \{1.033\} & \{3.023\} & \{4.785\} & \{2.840\} & \{2.224\}\end{array}$$

$$-0.118\Delta(y_t - p_t)_{-4} - 0.002\Delta SR_t - 0.002\Delta SR_{t-1} - 0.002\Delta SR_{t-2}$$

$$\begin{array}{llll}(-2.611) & (-3.729) & (-3.084) & (-2.930)\\ \{-2.419\} & \{-3.429\} & \{-2.561\} & \{-2.967\}\end{array}$$

$$-0.036\{(m_t - p_t) - (0.742(y_t - p_t) - 0.031SR_t)\}_{-1} + \hat{u}_t$$

$$\begin{array}{lll}(-4.203) & (10.174) & (-8.112)\\ \{-4.218\} & \{11.232\} & \{-7.953\}\end{array}$$

$\hat{\sigma} = 0.0047;\ dw = 1.986;$
$SC(12) = 18.711[0.100];\ FF(1) = 2.845[0.092];$
$JB(2) = 3.315[0.191];\ HS(1) = 0.856\{0.354]$

$$\Delta(m_t - p_t) = 0.021 + 0.200\Delta(m_t - p_t)_{-1} + 0.250\Delta(m_t - p_t)_{-3} + 0.161\Delta(y_t - p_t) + 0.089\Delta(y_t - p_t)_{-1}$$

$$\begin{array}{lllll}(0.938) & (3.548) & (4.696) & (3.397) & (1.840)\\ \{0.981\} & \{3.006\} & \{5.228\} & \{2.846\} & \{2.215\}\end{array}$$

$$-0.117\Delta(y_t - p_t)_{-4} - 0.005A\Delta SR_t - 0.036\{(m_t - p_t) - (0.746(y_t - p_t) - 0.031SR_t)\}_{-1} + \hat{u}_t$$

$$\begin{array}{llll}(-2.627) & (-6.361) & (-4.260) & (10.206) & (-8.045)\\ \{-2.420\} & \{-6.002\} & \{-4.304\} & \{11.055\} & \{-7.855\}\end{array}$$

$\hat{\sigma} = 0.0047;\ dw = 1.987;$
$SC(12) = 16.496[0.170];\ FF(1) = 2.835[0.093];$
$JB(2) = 3.200[0.202];\ HS(1) = 0.844\{0.358]$

't' statistics in (.) parentheses;
robust 't' statistics in {.} parentheses.

Note: Sample period 1974m5 to 1993m12.

of the suggestion of heteroscedasticity, to be sure of this aspect robust standard errors and robust 't' statistics were also calculated with the latter shown in {.} parentheses in Table 10.9. The differences between the standard and robust 't' statistics are slight and do not alter the conclusions.

Of particular interest in the first equation is the coefficient on the lagged ecm: this has the correct sign ($-$ve) and is significant; an estimate of -0.025 indicates that 2.5% of the preceding month's disequilibrium is eliminated in the current month. However, this is not the complete story as far as adjustment to disequilibrium is concerned as the presence of terms in the lagged dependent variable implies that the adjustment process is enforced by reactions to past changes in ($m_t - p_t$).

The second equation in Table 10.9 is a further simplification that arises from noting that the estimated coefficients on ΔSR_t, ΔSR_{t-1} and ΔSR_{t-2} are almost identical. Hence, a 3-period moving average of changes in interest rates was defined:

$$A\Delta SR_t = \tfrac{1}{3}(\Delta SR_t + \Delta SR_{t-1} + \Delta SR_{t-2})$$

This simplifies the equation and is consistent with the data. Otherwise the equations are almost the same.

In the second half of Table 10.9 we report ADL estimation of the dynamic model. To understand how these estimates are obtained, first recall that the cointegrating equations reported in the second part of Table 10.6 were obtained by solving for equilibrium in an ADL model with 4 lags on each of the variables. Second, recall from Chapter 8 that an ADL model can be reformulated – or reparameterised – into a dynamic ECM. We therefore take the ADL underlying the results in Table 10.6 and reformulate it as a dynamic ECM. Given that in this version of the estimated model there has been no attempt at simplification by deleting insignificant variables, we carry out one further step in estimation by considering a more parsimonious specification guided by the insignificance of some of the

coefficients in the first model. The simplified model has almost the same equilibrium specification but slightly fewer variables. The diagnostic statistics are all now acceptable including the test for heteroscedasticity, and the estimated standard error is smaller than the second-stage EG equation.

The estimated long-run income elasticity is 0.742 with a standard error of 0.073, hence the 't' statistic for the null that the income elasticity is 1 is $(0.742 - 1)/0.073 = -3.534$, which is significant. Adjustment to past disequilibria is faster according to this equation, with an estimate of -0.036, or 3.6% per month; this is then enforced by further reactions to past changes in real money. *Ceteris paribus*, if there is a 1% change in current real income there will be a contemporaneous change of 0.161% in real money; in the next period this is enforced both by the past change in real money and the positive coefficient of 0.089 on $\Delta(y_t - p_t)_{-1}$. The dynamic responses to disequilibrium and changes in income are thus quite complex. The picture is similar, although of course with the opposite signed response, to changes in the interest rate.

The second ADL equation simplifies the first by using the moving average term for changes in the short rate; this results in a slightly smaller estimated standard error (which is now 0.466%) while still maintaining the acceptable diagnostics and relatively unchanged estimated coefficients. This is the preferred equation from Table 10.9. There is evidence again that first stage OLSEG estimation tends to result in a lower estimate of the income elasticity, perhaps reflecting a larger finite sample bias compared to ADL estimation.

By way of comparison, dynamic ECM equations were estimated with the income elasticity restricted to unity, which then have the interpretation of dynamic equations for the inverse velocity of circulation. The estimation details are reported in Table 10.10. The first equation, with ecm_{t-1} defined from first stage EG estimation, is an attempt to match the fit of the first equation in Table 10.9 where the latter does not have a

Table 10.10 *US inverse velocity of money: dynamic equations*

EG second stage estimation

$$\Delta(m_t - y_t) = -0.159\Delta(m_t - y_t)_{-1} + 0.120\Delta(m_t - y_t)_{-2} + 0.121\Delta(m_t - y_t)_{-3} + 0.124\Delta(m_t - y_t)_{-4}$$
$$\qquad\quad (-2.479) \qquad\qquad (1.883) \qquad\qquad\quad (1.958) \qquad\qquad\quad (2.006)$$
$$\qquad\quad \{-0.938\} \qquad\qquad \{1.977\} \qquad\qquad\quad \{1.713\} \qquad\qquad\quad \{1.827\}$$

$$\qquad -0.001\Delta SR_t - 0.003\Delta SR_{t-1} - 0.001\Delta SR_{t-2} - 0.001\Delta SR_{t-3} - 0.029 ecm_{t-1} + \hat{u}_t$$
$$\qquad (-1.039) \quad (-3.408) \qquad (-1.441) \qquad\quad (-1.903) \qquad\quad (-3.449)$$
$$\qquad \{-1.311\} \quad \{-3.391\} \qquad \{-1.206\} \qquad\quad \{-2.441\} \qquad\quad \{-3.636\}$$

$$\hat{\sigma} = 0.0075; \text{ dw} = 2.041;$$
$$\text{SC}(12) = 16.570[0.166]; \text{ FF}(1) = 0.847[0.357];$$
$$\text{JB}(2) = 1562.9[0.000]; \text{ HS}(1) = 7.8048[0.005]$$

$$\Delta(m_t - y_t) = 0.168\Delta(m_t - p_t)_{-3} + 0.297\Delta(y_t - p_t)_{-1} - 0.007 A\Delta SR_t - 0.027 ecm_{t-1} + \hat{u}_t$$
$$\qquad\quad (2.330) \qquad\qquad\quad (4.336) \qquad\qquad (-5.193) \qquad\quad (-3.259)$$
$$\qquad\quad \{2.106\} \qquad\qquad\quad \{1.559\} \qquad\qquad \{-5.833\} \qquad\quad \{-4.462\}$$

$$\hat{\sigma} = 0.0073; \text{ dw} = 1.942;$$
$$\text{SC}(12) = 22.410[0.033]; \text{ FF}(1) = 7.111[0.008];$$
$$\text{JB}(2) = 855.28[0.000]; \text{ HS}(1) = 36.321\{0.000\}$$

$$A\Delta RS_t \equiv 0.25(\Delta SR_t + \Delta SR_{t-1} + \Delta SR_{t-2} + \Delta SR_{t-3})$$
$$ecm_t = m_t - y_t - 1.564 - 0.014 SR_t$$

ADL estimation

$$\Delta(m_t - y_t) = 0.053 \; - \; 0.017\Delta(m_t - y_t)_{-1} + 0.105\Delta(m_t - y_t)_{-2} + 0.081\Delta(m_t - y_t)_{-3} - 0.001\Delta SR_t$$
$$\qquad\quad (-4.145)\;(-2.655) \qquad\quad (1.644) \qquad\qquad\quad (1.284) \qquad\qquad\quad (-1.246)$$
$$\qquad\quad \{-4.107\}\{-0.999\} \qquad \{1.793\} \qquad\qquad\quad \{1.000\} \qquad\qquad\quad \{-1.672\}$$

$$\qquad -0.002\Delta SR_{t-1} - 0.001\Delta SR_{t-2} - 0.001\Delta SR_{t-3} - 0.036\{m_t - y_t - (-0.027 SR_t)\}_{-1} + \hat{u}_t$$
$$\qquad (-2.835) \qquad\quad (-1.263) \qquad\quad (-1.381) \qquad\quad (-4.322) \qquad\qquad (-4.916)$$
$$\qquad \{-3.124\} \qquad\quad \{-1.159\} \qquad\quad \{-1.986\} \qquad\quad \{-3.927\} \qquad\qquad \{-4.917\}$$

$$\hat{\sigma} = 0.0075; \text{ dw} = 2.022;$$
$$\text{SC}(12) = 18.046[0.114]; \text{ FF}(1) = 0.621[0.431];$$
$$\text{JB}(2) = 1256.4[0.000]; \text{ HS}(1) = 0.161[0.688]$$

$$\Delta(m_t - y_t) = -0.041 + 0.175\Delta(m_t - p_t)_{-3} + 0.332\Delta(y_t - p_t)_{-1} - 0.007 A\Delta SR_t$$
$$\qquad\quad (-3.331)\;(2.209) \qquad\qquad (4.803) \qquad\qquad\quad (-4.956)$$
$$\qquad\quad \{-4.538\}\{2.366\} \qquad\qquad \{1.685\} \qquad\qquad\quad \{-5.797\}$$

$$\qquad -0.026\{m_t - y_t - (-0.022 SR_t)\}_{-1} + \hat{u}_t$$
$$\qquad (-3.269) \qquad\qquad (-3.138)$$
$$\qquad \{-4.395\} \qquad\qquad \{-3.170\}$$

$$A\Delta SR_t \equiv 0.25(\Delta SR_t + \Delta SR_{t-1} + \Delta SR_{t-2} + \Delta SR_{t-3})$$

$$\hat{\sigma} = 0.0072; \text{ dw} = 1.975;$$
$$\text{SC}(12) = 15.605[0.210]; \text{ FF}(1) = 0.529[0.468];$$
$$\text{JB}(2) = 862.908[0.000]; \text{ HS}(1) = 0.259[0.610]$$

'*t*' statistics in (.) parentheses;
robust '*t*' statistics in {.} parentheses.

Note: Sample period 1974m5 to 1993m12.

restricted long-run income elasticity. Although it was possible to obtain an empirical equation with similar diagnostics for serial correlation and functional form, the fit of the equation, measured by $\hat{\sigma}$%, deteriorated from 0.48% to 0.75%, and there were indications of nonnormality and heteroscedasticity which needed to be explored further.

The second equation in Table 10.10 is motivated from the first in the following ways. It uses a moving average of changes in the short rate, here defined as a 4-period moving average; second, it separates the components of the change in inverse velocity and enters their lags separately. To understand this point note that $\Delta(m_t - y_t) = \Delta(m_t - p_t) - \Delta(y_t - p_t)$, so that, for example,

$$0.5\Delta(m_t - y_t)_{-1} = 0.5\Delta(m_t - p_t)_{-1}$$
$$- 0.5\Delta(y_t - p_t)_{-1}$$

and $\Delta(m_t - p_t)_{-1}$ and $\Delta(y_t - p_t)_{-1}$, therefore, enter with coefficients which are equal but of opposite sign; entering the lags separately relaxes this constraint. However, neither of these options resulted in a marked improvement. Although the equation is parsimonious, $\hat{\sigma}\%$ is reduced but only to 0.73%, and so still does not compete with the dynamic equation with an unrestricted long-run income elasticity. In particular the problems of nonnormality and heteroscedasticity remain. Inspection of the residuals revealed a problem specific to 1992m12, which results in a substantial 'outlier' and hence a significant JB test statistic and it is also likely to be contributing to the significant HS(1) test statistic. We consider this problem and its cause further below.

Table 10.10 also includes corresponding equations using ADL estimation. Earlier we found rejection of the hypothesis that the long-run income elasticity was unity from unrestricted ADL estimation, it should not, therefore, be a surprise to find the fit of the equation deteriorates with the restriction imposed. The estimated interest rate semi-elasticity declines (in absolute value) as does the adjustment speed. In the EG and ADL dynamic equations there are indications of nonnormality from the JB statistic; these are due to an exceptional increase in real income in 1992m12, which the restricted equations, in contrast to the unrestricted equations, cannot track. If the sample is curtailed to 1992m11, there is no evidence against normality in the residuals.

10.4.7 Out of sample performance

As we have seen comparison of the within sample goodness of fit statistics of the dynamic models, with and without the restriction that the long-run income elasticity is unity, favours the unrestricted model. For example, comparing the preferred equations in Tables 10.9 and 10.10 we see that the former has $\hat{\sigma} = 0.0047$ against $\hat{\sigma} = 0.0072$, so that the estimated standard error for the dynamic inverse velocity equation is about 1.5 times that of the dynamic demand for money equation.

As a final comparison we consider the out of sample performance of forecasts of the log of real money. The dynamic equations, with and without the restriction on the long-run income elasticity are estimated through to 1989m12, and then the series of one step ahead forecasts and corresponding forecast errors for 1990m1 to

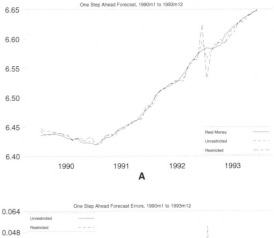

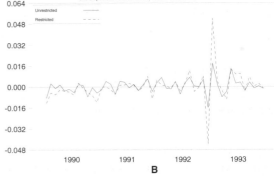

Figure 10.10 A – US real money (logs): one step ahead forecasts. B – US real money: forecasting errors

1993m12 are computed. The forecasts are 'one step' because the lagged values of the dependent variable are taken to be the actual values throughout the forecast period. The forecast errors are plotted in Figure 10.10. Apart from the exceptional forecast error for the restricted model in 1992m12 and the subsequent months, the unrestricted model fits better. The exceptional forecast error for the restricted model can be traced to an exceptional increase in real personal income in 1992m12. Some summary statistics for the two models are reported in Table 10.11. The root mean squared error, rmse, is a standard measure of out of sample equation performance. If the equation stays 'on track' this should not be dissimilar to the estimated percentage standard error, $\hat{\sigma}\%$, of the equation. In addition Hendry's forecast test, HF(F), is calculated, with large values relative to $\chi^2(F)$ indicating a deterioration in forecast performance relative to the in-sample performance. In order that the restricted model is not hampered by the exceptional increase in income, the summary statistics are also presented for 1990m1 to 1992m11.

It is apparent from Table 10.11, as indicated by rmse and HF(48), that the dynamic model without the long-run income elasticity restricted fares well even given the exceptional increase in income; rmse is close to the in-sample $\hat{\sigma}\%$ and HF(48) is not significant. This is not so when the income elasticity is restricted to unity, where the rmse is over double that for the unrestricted case and HF(48) is significant. Curtailing the forecast period to end in 1992m11 helps the restricted model, now HF(35) is not significant, but the rmse is still substantially larger than in the unrestricted case, although smaller than the corresponding in-sample $\hat{\sigma}\%$. Note that in the HF test, and the Chow tests, the standard of comparison is relative to the variance in the sample period, hence a lack of significance should not be interpreted as providing a better model: the unrestricted model fits better both within and out of sample.

10.4.8 A brief comparison with Hoffman and Rasche (1991) and Baba, Hendry and Starr (1992)

We conclude this section with a brief comparison of our results with those in two other studies to which reference has been made. Using an overall sample period of 1953m1 to 1988m12, HR (1991) found a single cointegrating vector with the variables real M1, real income and an interest rate, the better results being obtained

Table 10.11 *Dynamic equation one step ahead forecast errors*

Forecast period	1990m1 to 1993m12 ($F=48$)		1990m1 to 1992m11 ($F=35$)	
	mean error	rmse	mean error	rmse
Unrestricted long-run income elasticity	−0.0005	0.484	−0.0012	0.377
HF(F)	48.940[0.435]		21.555[0.963]	
Restricted long-run income elasticity	0.0011	1.150	0.0004	0.494
HF(F)	184.161[0.000]		24.796[0.900]	

Where: mean error $= \sum_{f=1}^{F}(\text{error}_f)/F$

$\text{error}_f = (m_f \widehat{- p_f}) - (m_f - p_f)$ and $m_f \widehat{- p_f}$ is the one step ahead forecast.

rmse is the root mean squared error defined as: rmse $= 100 \sum_{f=1}^{F}\{(\text{error}_f)^2/F\}^{\frac{1}{2}}$

with the 90-day Treasury Bill rate rather than a 10-year rate. In a double log specification they obtained estimated nominal interest rate and real income elasticities of -0.408 and 0.793, respectively. While HR (*op. cit.*) did not reject the null hypothesis that the income elasticity was unity, their published dynamic models defined the error correction term using the unrestricted income elasticity. Their dynamic equation for the log of real money had an estimated equation standard error, $\hat{\sigma}$, of 0.005.

Our results are in line with those of HR, with some exceptions, which we note below. In broad agreement, we find the estimates of the real income elasticity in the range 0.742 to 0.772 (ADL estimates). Following Cagan (*op. cit.*) and BHS (1992) we preferred to allow the interest rate elasticity to vary; even so within our study there was little to choose between the cointegrating regressions with the level or log of the interest rate. However, our estimates were somewhat smaller in absolute value than those reported by HR. Specifically, at the sample mean we obtained an estimated short rate elasticity of -0.228, and -0.316 at the sample mean plus one standard deviation (using the ADL estimate of -0.031 from the preferred equation in Table 10.9). The estimated equation standard error of our preferred dynamic model for real money at 0.0047 was slightly lower than the 0.0050 of HR, but not much weight can be placed on this relatively small difference. Restricting the income elasticity to unity led to an increase in the estimated equation standard error to about 0.0075 and a deterioration in the out of sample performance. In contrast to HR our preferred specification would, therefore, not impose a long-run unit income elasticity.

This last finding is in line with the more complex study by BHS (*op. cit.*), who obtained a long-run 'income' elasticity of 0.51 using GNP as the scale variable and the multivariate cointegration technique due to Johansen (1988), and 0.574 from solving a single-equation ADL model. BHS found a single cointegrating vector with the following extended set of six variables:

real money; real income proxied by GNP; an opportunity cost variable based on a short rate less the own rate on M1, R_{1t}^*; inflation, Δp_t; the spread between the yield on a 20-year Treasury Bond and a 1-month Treasury Bill, S_t; and a measure of the risk associated with holding bonds, V_t. Specifically, the BHS estimated equilibrium relationship was:

$$
\begin{aligned}
m_t - p_t = {} & 0.51(y_t - p_t) - 0.039R_{1t}^* \\
& - 0.014\Delta p_t - 0.066S_t \\
& + 0.037V_t
\end{aligned} \tag{10.38}
$$

(Note that in comparing numerical estimates of the coefficients with the BHS article, therein all rates, except inflation, are expressed as decimal fractions whereas % points at an annual rate are used here; hence, a coefficient of 3.9 in BHS is scaled by 1/100 to 0.039 to be comparable with the estimates presented here; in addition Δp_t in BHS is a quarterly rate whereas here all rates are annual, so the BHS coefficient on quarterly Δp_t as a decimal fraction was 400 times -0.014.) In addition to the empirical findings reported in this section, the BHS results suggest the following: inflation exerts a separate negative influence on real money, this could arise because nominal interest rates do not fully adjust to inflation rates; an increase in the spread has a negative influence on real money separate from either the long or the short rate; and an increase in the risk of holding bonds increases the demand for real money. BHS present a number of dynamic equations with estimated standard errors of around 0.039 suggesting that their extra variables are a useful addition to the 'standard' set of demand for money variables.

10.5 Concluding remarks

The demand for money has been an active area of study for empirical economists for a number of decades with early interest engendered by the seminal works of Keynes (1936), Baumol (1952), Cagan (1956), Friedman (1956) and Tobin (1956, 1958). This chapter has reported results for two very different historical periods, the first relating to the post-First World War period of hyperinflation in Germany and, by way of contrast, the second to a relative stable period in recent US history. These different periods though share an intense interest by empirical economists in studying the determinants of the demand for money.

Further research on the German post-war period is warranted. Even though there is evidence that there is a very fast adjustment of money balances, in response to large changes in inflation and lesser changes in real income, there remains a concern that there has to be a very selective approach to the sample period in order to obtain satisfactory results. The resulting difficulties are theoretical and practical. At a theoretical level if there was a change in regime with the onset of 'hyperinflation', can the nature of the structural change be modelled? For example, are the ECM coefficients themselves functions of the (hyper)inflation rate? In an unexplored suggestion, but one prompted by a graphical analysis of the data, the possibility of a nonlinear, rather than linear, relationship between real money (or inverse velocity) and inflation seems worth further research – see Ashworth and Evans (1996). At a practical level, estimation with 14 or 15 observations is not generally to be encouraged because of the difficulty of exploring dynamic models and estimating diagnostic statistics to establish a statistically adequate model for inference. Hence, there remains the goal of achieving a theoretical and empirical explanation of the complete post-war period rather than a selective period. It is possible to model the demand for money over long periods. For example, Taylor (1995a) estimates the demand for broad money for the United Kingdom for the period 1871–1913, and Ericsson, Hendry and Prestwich's (1998) estimate the demand for broad money for the United Kingdom over the period 1878–1993. Although whether anything like this can be done for an economy with more turbulent periods remains to be seen.

From the study of the US demand for money our results suggest, along with recent results reported by Baba, Hendry and Starr (1992), but in contrast to the results of Hoffman and Rasche (1991), that the estimated income elasticity is too far from unity to sustain the view that demand for money equations can be reformulated as inverse velocity equations.

A number of important theoretical contributions inform the background of these empirical studies. The framework suggested by Keynes – especially the distinction among the transaction, precautionary and speculative motives – has proved to be an enduring one, providing stimulation to further theoretical work and insights for empirical research. Early work on the demand for money for transactions purposes with a fixed cost per transfer from income to money, suggested interest rate and income elasticities equal but opposite in sign at -0.5 and 0.5, which is Baumol's 'square root' rule. Extensions of that work to allow for integer constraints in the number of monthly transfers, which is typically quite small, and transfer costs which are related to income, tend to move the interest elasticity to be lower in absolute value and the income elasticity to be higher. This is, broadly, what we find with estimates of the interest rate elasticity between about -0.25 and -0.4 and unrestricted estimates of the income elasticity above 0.5 but probably not greater than 0.8. Recent work by BHS (*op. cit.*) has suggested other variables that are relevant to the demand for transactions money. In particular they found a role for inflation separately from the nominal interest rate, the spread between a long-term rate and a short-term rate, and a measure of the riskiness associated with holding bonds.

Some studies of the demand for money define money to be broader than M1. Modelling broad measures of money means that it is necessary to make a distinction between rates of return on the assets included in the monetary aggregate, the inside return, and rates of return on assets outside the monetary aggregate, the outside return. An increase in the inside return increases the demand for money (as defined in the aggregate), whereas an increase in an outside return decreases the demand for money. Otherwise the general approach is similar to that taken here.

Review

1. In this chapter we considered some theoretical aspects of the demand for money coupled with an empirical analysis of two contrasting historical periods, Germany after the First World War and the United States from 1970 through to the early 1990s.

2. An empirical study of the demand for money presupposes that we are able to define 'money'. Much empirical work on the demand for money has concentrated on money in its liquid form as currency in circulation plus demand deposits and other checkable deposits; together these are known as M1.

3. A framework for discussing the motives for holding money due to Keynes (1936) is still relevant today. Keynes distinguished three motives for holding money: the transactions motive; the precautionary motive; and the speculative motive.

4. Money is held to facilitate transactions because income and expenditure have very different time profiles. There is an imperfect synchronisation between the pattern of receipts and the pattern of expenditures even when both are known with certainty.

5. A practical suggestion is to spread the transfers of income to money across the month to meet anticipated expenditure; if, for simplicity, we assume that expenditure is evenly spread across the month then the individual could make n transfers of $1/n$ of his income.

6. Let Y_m denote nominal, monthly income then the average monthly balance, M, is $\frac{1}{2}(Y_m/n)$ with a monthly interest cost of $R_m[(\frac{1}{2}Y_m/n)]$ where $R_m = R/12$. Transfers themselves have an opportunity cost which we capture in the function $c = c(n, b, Y_m)$, where b is the fixed cost of a transfer. Suppose $c(n, b, Y_m) = nb$, that is each transaction carries a fixed cost b then by minimising total costs, the optimal number of transfers is $n = (R_m Y_m/2b)^{0.5}$.

7. The optimal stock of transactions money is $M^* = (bY_m/2R_m)^{0.5}$. The income and interest rate elasticities of M^* and R_m are equal but opposite in sign at 0.5 and -0.5, receptively; this is the famous 'square root ' rule for optimal money balances.

8. An income elasticity of 0.5 arises because the cost function is simplified to $c(n, b, Y_m) = nb$; if we alter the cost function to $c(n, b, Y_m) = naY_m$ so that each transaction carries the cost aY_m and total transaction costs are naY_m, then we find that optimal money balances are $M^* = (a/2R_m)^{0.5}Y_m$. Now, while maintaining the interest elasticity at -0.5, the income elasticity has increased to 1.

9. Another argument that suggests that the income elasticity may be greater than 0.5 is due to Barro (1976) who noted that there is a need to constrain the optimal n to be an integer. In that case there are situations where a proportionate increase in cash balances exactly matches the proportionate increase in income; in this situation the income elasticity of money is $+1$ not $+0.5$.

10. The integer constraint means that in order for changes in the nominal rate of interest to have an effect they have to be sufficient to induce a move to the next integer number of transfers; and so, taking into account integer constraints, the interest elasticity of money demand will not be as elastic as -0.5.

11. So far we assumed that 'money' was not interest bearing so that an appropriate measure of the opportunity cost was the rate on a 'near' money alternative. However, developments in the 1980s led to interest bearing checkable accounts so the

opportunity cost should, in principle, be defined as the spread between the 'own' rate on money and the money alternative.

12. Keynes (1936) suggested that precautionary money is held 'to provide for contingencies requiring sudden expenditure and for unforeseen opportunities of advantageous purchases'.

13. Whalen (1966) suggested that the financial embarrassment of illiquidity can result from uncertainty as to the timing of receipts as well as sudden expenditure. In essence the precautionary motive applies because net disbursements are uncertain.

14. In an analysis which is very similar to that for transactions balances the individual, or corporation, can be viewed as minimising the cost of holding precautionary money. The objective function is $PC = p(d)c(d) + R_m M_p$ where $p(d)$ is the probability of financial 'distress', $c(d)$ is a cost function which depends upon financial distress and $R_m M_p$ is the opportunity cost, in terms of forgone interest, in holding precautionary money.

15. We assume that the distribution of net disbursements has a zero mean, so on average receipts equal expenditure, and standard deviation σ. Suppose the distribution of net disbursements is symmetric about a zero mean, then the probability of distress is 0.5. To reduce this probability the individual holds a positive M_p. Depending on the cost of distress, there is a holding of M_p, which minimises PC.

16. To obtain a solution for optimal M_p requires some information about $p(d)$ and specifying the distribution of net disbursements will be sufficient. However, even without specification of the distribution we can derive optimal precautionary money balances, $M_p^* = (c\sigma^2/R_m)^{\frac{1}{3}}$.

17. Optimal precautionary money increases with the cost of financial distress, increases with the uncertainty in the distribution of net disbursements and decreases with R_m with an interest rate elasticity of $-1/3$.

18. For Keynes (*op. cit.*, p. 170) the key reason for the speculative motive arose from *uncertainty* as to the future course of the rate of interest and in particular its divergence from a 'fairly safe level'. If the safe level of R, R^s, is unchanged a change in the market rate increases the risk of illiquidity which arises because bonds are capital-uncertain. The size of the possible capital loss increases as R falls below R^s so, given the latter, there will be a disincentive to holding consols rather than cash.

19. A reduction in R reduces the earnings from illiquid assets which as Keynes puts it 'are available as a sort of insurance premium to offset the risk of loss on capital account' (*op. cit.*, p. 202). Hence on two counts the attractions to holding bonds rather than cash have diminished by the fall in the interest rate below the safe level.

20. An alternative justification for a negative relation between money held for speculative reasons and the interest rate is due to Tobin (1958). In Tobin's asset-portfolio model the expected return at time t on the portfolio, $E_t\{r\}$, assuming for simplicity that money is not interest bearing, is

$$E_t\{r\} = E_t\{A_{2t}(R_t + g_{t+1})\} = A_{2t}R_t$$

if $E\{g_{t+1}\} = 0$ where R_t is the current rate on consols and g_{t+1} is the one-period (rate of) capital gain or loss.

21. The risk attached to the portfolio is measured by the standard deviation of r, that is $\sigma_r = A_{2t}\sigma_g$ where σ_g is the standard deviation of capital gains. The equation of an *opportunity locus* between the expected return μ_r, and the risk σ_r, is $\mu_r = (R_t/\sigma_g)\sigma_r$; if the slope is positive then an increase in expected return can only be obtained with an increased risk. If the indifference curves are concave upward then investors are known as *diversifiers* who will only accept more risk if it is coupled with a higher expected return. In such a case an interior solution is possible with positive holdings of both consols and cash.

22. An increase in the interest rate increases the slope of the opportunity locus and the new position will depend upon the relative strengths of the substitution and income effects. In some cases Tobin was able to rule out the possibility of the income effect overcoming the substitution effect with the result that, as in Keynes' analysis, money and the interest rate are negatively related.

23. Taken together the transaction, precautionary and speculative motives suggest that the demand for nominal money will depend, *inter alia*, upon: the price level, nominal income, payment and expenditure arrangements, the availability and cost of facilities for transfers between money and other monetary assets, the spread between the return on money and a 'near money' alternative, and a measure of wealth.

24. A summary way of representing the primary determinants of the demand for money is to write the functional relationship as $M = f(Y, P, R, W, Z)$ where M is the demand for nominal money, Y is nominal income, P is the price level, R is the nominal interest rate on a 'near money' alternative or the spread if money is interest bearing, W is nominal wealth and Z is a set of variables representing other factors such as the timing of income payments, the cost of transfers, the cost of illiquidity and so on.

25. Suppose that the price level, P, increases by the factor μ and income and wealth, which are in nominal terms, also increased by the same factor; then if the resulting value of M, say M^+, is $M^+ = \mu^h F(Y, P, R, W)$ the function is said to be homogeneous of degree h. Two important cases are $h = 0$ and $h = 1$, which we refer to as homogeneity of degree zero and homogeneity of degree one, respectively. We anticipate that the demand for *nominal money* is homogeneous of degree one in the price level, and the demand for *real money* is homogeneous of degree zero in the price level.

26. The velocity of circulation is the number of times a unit of currency has to *circulate during period t* in order to finance the overall level of transactions. Y_t/M_t, is the *velocity of circulation* of the money stock and M_t/Y_t is the *inverse velocity of circulation*.

27. Given a demand for money function we can always rearrange it into an inverse velocity of circulation function. For example, if the demand function is $\ln M_t - \ln P_t = \alpha_1(\ln Y_t - \ln P_t) + \alpha_4 R_t$ then subtracting $\ln Y_t$ from both sides and rearranging we get the log of the inverse velocity of circulation $\ln M_t - \ln Y_t = (\alpha_1 - 1)(\ln Y_t - \ln P_t) + \alpha_4 R_t$.

28. The hyperinflationary period following the First World War was a historical episode, which has fascinated economists. A seminal work on the demand for money during this period was Cagan (1956).

29. Cagan argued that in hyperinflations wealth and income, in real terms, are relatively stable compared to the large fluctuations in real cash balances and these changes were primarily due to expected inflation.

30. Cagan's basic equation is $m_t - p_t = \delta - \alpha pi_t + v_t$ where pi_t is the expected rate of inflation; $-\alpha$ is the semi-elasticity of real money balances with respect to the expected inflation rate: it gives the effect of a 1 percentage point increase or decrease in the inflation rate – for example, from 3% per month to 4% per month. In order to obtain the elasticity we need to multiply $-\alpha$ by pi_t.

31. Cagan suggested calculating the unobservable pi_t as a weighted average of current and past inflation. An alternative solution to the problem due to Michael, Nobay and Peel (MNP (1994)) is to substitute the observable actual change in (the log of) prices, Δp_t, plus a stationary residual for the expected inflation rate, pi_t.

32. Instead of using the unobservable variable pi_t it is replaced by $\Delta p_t - \eta_{1t}$, from which it differs by an I(0) component to obtain $m_t - p_t = \delta - \alpha \Delta p_t + u_t$ where $u_t = v_t + \alpha \eta_{1t}$ which comprises stationary components.

33. MNP suggest adding the log of real income, $(y_t - p_t)$, to obtain

$$m_t - p_t = \delta - \alpha \Delta p_t + \theta(y_t - p_t) + u_t$$

use as a proxy an index of skilled public workers real wages, X_t/P_{Xt}. Replacing the unobservable variable $y_t - p_t$ using $y_t - p_t = x_t - p_{Xt} - \eta_{2t}$, the equation to be estimated becomes $m_t - p_t = \delta - \alpha \Delta p_t + \theta(x_t - p_t) + \xi_t$ with $\xi_t = u_t - \theta \eta_{2t}$.

34. The first step in the empirical analysis is to assess whether the equations are *balanced* in terms of their time series properties. ADF tests for the order of integration of the series led to rejection of the hypothesis of 2 unit roots not nonrejection of the hypothesis of 1 unit root.

35. The next stage in the empirical analysis is to estimate these equations and assess whether the following cointegrate: $m_t - p_t$ and Δp_t; $m_t - p_t$, Δp_t and $x_t - p_{Xt}$; and $m_t - p_t - (x_t - p_{Xt})$ and Δp_t.

36. MNP suggest two periods of estimation: the conventional period, 1921m1 to 1923m6, for which there is no evidence of cointegration and the hyperinflation period for which there is some evidence of cointegration.

37. Cagan's specification implies that the interest rate elasticity is variable, increasing with the inflation rate. The estimates from the inverse velocity equation over the hyperinflation period varies from -0.105 for 1921m7, with an inflation rate of just under 17% per month, to -2.785 for 1923m9, when inflation was about 446% per month.

38. The estimated income elasticity from the hyperinflation period is 1.256 which differs from the estimate of 1.749 for the longer period; the 't' statistics and estimated standard errors from the cointegrating regression are not valid for inference. To test the restriction of a unit income elasticity the Phillips–Hansen FMOLS method was used and the restriction was consistent with the data at the 5% significance level.

39. Some simple dynamic models in the form of ECMs were estimated to see if they could improve upon the static, cointegrating regressions using error correction mechanisms. The error correction term was defined as

$$ecm_t = m_t - p_t$$
$$- (5.166 - 0.624\Delta p_t + (x_t - p_{Xt}))$$

40. The error correction term was incorporated in the following ECM

$$\Delta(m_t - p_t) = \theta_1 \Delta(\Delta p_t) + \theta_2 \Delta(x_t - p_t)$$
$$+ \theta_3 ecm_{t-1} + u_t$$

41. The restriction of complete adjustment to disequilibrium within the period, that is $\theta_3 = -1$, was consistent with the data; further the estimated values of θ_1 and θ_2 were very close to their estimated equilibrium values suggesting very fast adjustment to the changes during the hyprinflationary period.

42. To provide a contrast to the hyperinflationary period in Germany after the First World War, the second empirical study was of the demand for money in the United States with a sample period of 1974m1 to 1993m12. A study by Hoffman and Rasche (1991), HR (1991), addressed several issues of importance to us and provided a general motivation for this choice of country and sample.

43. HR (1991) results suggest the existence of just one cointegrating vector among the variables: real money (M1), real income and an interest rate. Hence a single equation analysis is valid with the long run specified as $m_t - p_t = \beta_0 + \beta_1(y_t - p_t) + \beta_2 R_t + \varepsilon_t$.

44. We also experimented with two nominal interest rates, the 90-day Treasury Bill rate and the 3-year Treasury Bond rate, referred to as SR_t and LR_t, respectively. In practice the choice of an interest rate may not be too crucial if the different rates are nonstationary and cointegrated.

45. In an initial analysis of the time series properties of $m_t - p_t$, $y_t - p_t$, $m_t - y_t$ and either SR_t or LR_t, the evidence seems firmly against the hypothesis that 2 unit roots are present. However, we cannot reject the hypothesis that each series is I(1) and so the necessary condition for the balance of the long-run equation is satisfied. The next step is to assess whether $m_t - p_t$, $y_t - p_t$ and either SR_t or LR_t cointegrate.

46. We estimated the cointegrating regressions by: (a) the first step of Engle–Granger, EG, estimation, that is an OLS regression on the long run; and (b) by estimation of an autoregressive distributed lag, ADL, model which is then solved for the implicit long-run solution.

47. With the long rate the EG estimate of the income elasticity is 0.606 compared to 0.617 with the short rate, and the ADL estimate of the income elasticity is 0.772 compared to 0.765 using the short rate. The estimated coefficient on the long rate is −0.026 from EG estimation compared to −0.021 with the short rate and −0.030 from ADL estimation whichever rate is used.

48. The estimated coefficient on the interest rate is a semi-elasticity, the elasticity is, from the ADL estimates, $e_R = -0.030R$ which at the sample means of SR_t and LR_t is −0.235 and −0.258, respectively.

49. Some authors have preferred to use the log of the interest rate rather than its level as used here. This specification did not lead to an improvement in the results in this case; and the estimated interest rate elasticities were similar to the levels formulation evaluated at the sample mean.

50. With each estimation method the residuals were saved and used in an ADF regression to assess the null hypothesis of noncointegration. With both estimation methods the test statistics were slightly below (in absolute value) the 10% critical value but close enough to suggest that a cointegrating relationship is a realistic possibility.

51. The hypothesis that the income elasticity is unity was also considered. If this is the case then the demand for money function can be reformulated as an equation for the inverse velocity of circulation; that is, in logs, $m_t - y_t = \beta_0 + \beta_2 R_t + \varepsilon_t$. We obtained ADF test statistics close enough to the 10% critical value to suggest this could be a cointegrating relationship. Using a more formal test, HR (op. cit.) concluded that a unit real income elasticity cannot be rejected by the data at conventional significance levels. (See review question 36 for FMOLS estimates for the US data used here.)

52. The next step in Engle–Granger estimation is to construct a dynamic model of the US demand for money in the form of an ECM, and for comparison the ADL was rearranged into the same form.

53. Using the short rate the OLS EG estimate of equilibrium is

$$ecm_t = m_t - p_t - (1.557 + 0.617(y_t - p_t) - 0.021SR_t)$$

which is incorporated in an ECM of the form

$$\begin{aligned} \Delta(m_t - p_t) = \theta_0 &+ \varphi_1(L)\Delta(y_t - p_t) \\ &+ \varphi_2(L)\Delta SR_t \\ &+ \varphi_3(L)\Delta(m_t - p_t) \\ &+ \theta_1 ecm_{t-1} + u_t \end{aligned}$$

where $\varphi_i(L)$ is a lag polynomial.

54. The ECM coefficients, whether from EG estimation or from the ADL reformulation, are well determined and correctly signed. In particular, the coefficient on ecm_{t-1} has the correct sign (−ve) and is significant.

55. We also estimated dynamic ECM equations with the income elasticity restricted to unity, which then have the interpretation of dynamic equations for the inverse velocity of circulation. These equations do not fit as well as when the income elasticity is unrestricted, the estimated standard error

is 0.007 compared to just under 0.005 for the corresponding equation with an unrestricted income elasticity.

56. As a final comparison we consider the out of sample performance of forecasts of the log of real money. The dynamic model without the long-run income elasticity restricted fares well and substantially better than with the restriction of a unit income elasticity.

57. These results are broadly in line with those of HR (1991) with one major exception. In agreement, our ADL estimates of the income elasticity were in the range 0.742 to 0.772 compared to 0.793 for HR. The estimated equation standard error of our preferred dynamic model for real money at 0.0047 was slightly lower than the 0.0050 of HR. In contrast to HR our preferred specification would not impose a long-run unit income elasticity due to the deterioration of within and out of sample performance.

58. BHS (*op. cit.*) obtained a long-run 'income' elasticity of 0.51 using GNP as the scale variable and the multivariate cointegration technique due to Johansen (1988), and 0.574 from solving a single-equation ADL model.

59. BHS found a *single* cointegrating vector with an extended set of six variables: real money; real income proxied by GNP; an opportunity cost variable based on a short rate less the own rate on M1, R_{1t}^*; inflation, Δp_t; the spread between the yield on a 20-year Treasury Bond and a 1-month Treasury Bill, S_t; and a measure of the risk associated with holding bonds, V_t.

Review questions

1. What is money and what are its functions?
2. What are the main motives for holding money rather than interest bearing alternatives?
3. What is liquidity preference?

4. What are the differences among M1, M2 and M3?
5. What is the transactions motive for holding money?
6. What are 'other checkable deposits' and what impact have they had on transactions money?
7. Confirm that minimising

$$TC = nb + R_m[\tfrac{1}{2}(Y_m/n)]$$

with respect to n, with the optimum denoted, n^*, yields $n^* = (R_m Y_m/2b)^{0.5}$ and optimal money balances of

$$M^* = (bY_m/2R_m)^{0.5}$$

8. Alter the cost function to $c(n, b, Y_m) = naY_m$ and derive n^* and M^* and comment on the income elasticity.
9. Consider an individual with a monthly salary of $Y_m = \$5,000$ and a nominal rate on 'near money' of 10% p.a., and assume that transfer costs are nb:
   (i)   Derive the value of b which corresponds to $n^* = 1$.
   (ii) What is the average holding of money in this case?
   (iii) With this value of b, what would Y_m have to be to induce a second transfer given that a noninteger number of transfers is not possible? (Recall that we are assuming that one transfer per month is necessary.)
10. Explain why integer constraints on the number of transfers are likely to increase the income elasticity and reduce (in absolute value) the interest elasticity.
11. How does the precautionary motive for holding money differ from the transactions motive?
12. Suppose the distribution of net disbursements is normal and the individual holds precautionary money equal to 1.5σ with $\sigma = \$2,000$, what is the probability of financial distress, $p(d)$? What is $p(d)$ if M_p increases to $\$4,000$?

13. Explain how Chebycheff's inequality,

$$p(|x - \mu| \geq k\sigma) \leq 1/k^2$$

can be used to provide an upper bound for the probability of distress. Formulate the precautionary cost function as

$$PC = 0.5(\sigma/M_p)^2 c + R_m M_p$$

and show that the solution for optimal precautionary money is $M_p^* = (c\sigma^2/R_m)^{\frac{1}{3}}$.

14. What is the role of the 'safe rate' in Keynes' explanation of the effect of an increase or decrease in the market rate of interest?

15. Using Tobin's asset-portfolio approach derive the equation of an *opportunity locus* between the expected return μ_r, and the risk σ_r; hence, examine the conditions when an increase in the interest rate reduces cash holdings.

16. Explain what is meant by saying that the demand for nominal money is homogeneous of degree one in the price level but the demand for real money is homogeneous of degree zero in the price level.

17. Show that if the demand for *nominal* cash balances is homogeneous of degree one with respect to the price level it can be reformulated as a demand for *real* cash balances.

18. Suppose the particular functional relationship is

$$\ln M = \alpha_1 \ln Y + \alpha_2 \ln W$$
$$+ \alpha_3 \ln P + \alpha_4 R$$

what value of α_3 will ensure that the function is homogeneous of degree one in the price level? How would you test whether this property was data consistent?

19. What is the velocity of circulation? What is the inverse velocity of circulation?

20. Show that if the demand for nominal cash balances is homogeneous of degree one with respect to the price level, and the real income elasticity is unity then it can be re-

formulated as an inverse velocity of circulation function.

21. Do you agree with Cagan (1956) that: 'The only cost of holding cash balances that seems to fluctuate widely enough to account for the drastic changes in real cash balances during (the German) hyperinflation is the rate of depreciation in the value of money or, equivalently, the rate of change of prices' (*op. cit.*, p. 31)?

22. Do you agree with Cagan (1956) that changes in output or real income during the hyperinflationary period in post-First World War Germany were relatively slight compared to changes in the price level and changes in the amount of money in circulation?

23. In the context of the specification of a demand for money function explain the difference between a semi-elasticity and an elasticity.

24. Consider the basic Cagan specification

$$m_t - p_t = \delta - \alpha p i_t + v_t$$

and show that this entails a varying inflation; in particular with $-\alpha = -0.6$ calculate the inflation rate elasticity with $pi_t = 5\%$ per month and 100% per month.

25. Replacing pi_t by Δp_t entails introducing a measurement error of η_{1t}; that is (1) $\Delta p_t = pi_t + \eta_{1t}$ or (2) $pi_t = \Delta p_t - \eta_{1t}$, substituting from (2) into $m_t - p_t = \delta - \alpha p i_t + v_t$ we obtain $m_t - p_t = \delta - \alpha \Delta p_t + v_t + \alpha \eta_{1t}$, and from (1) we see that this introduces a correlation between the observable regressor Δp_t and a component of the disturbance, that is η_{1t}. Explain the conditions for obtaining a consistent estimator of α.

26. Do you think Cagan (1956) and MNP (1994) should have used a nominal interest rate rather than the actual inflation rate in their demand or money equations?

27. There follows an extract from Table 10.1. What do you conclude from these test statistics?

Variable	Model	$\hat{\tau}$	Φ_1	$\hat{\tau}_\mu$	$\hat{\mu}$	$\hat{\tau}_\beta$	$\hat{\beta}$	Φ_3
			Test statistics for 2 unit roots					
$m_t - p_t$	ADF(3)	−2.297	6.956	−3.651	−0.098	−3.706	−0.004	7.151
			Test statistics for 1 unit root					
$m_t - p_t$	ADF(4)	−2.600	3.450	0.373	−0.274	−2.443	−0.051	3.445

28. In the context of the Geman hyperinflation do the following cointegrate: $m_t - p_t$ and Δp_t; $m_t - p_t$, Δp_t and $x_t - p_{Xt}$ and $m_t - p_t - (x_t - p_{Xt})$ and Δp_t?

29. What signs and magnitudes would you expect the coefficients to take in the following ECMs:

$$\Delta(m_t - p_t) = \theta_1(\Delta p_t) + \theta_2 ecm_{t-1} + \varepsilon_t$$

and

$$\Delta(m_t - p_t) = \theta_1 \Delta(\Delta p_t) + \theta_2 \Delta(x_t - p_{Xt}) + \theta_3 ecm_{t-1} + \varepsilon_t$$

30. Suppose the variables in MNP's extension of Cagan's demand for money function are actually I(0) rather than I(1) (but the low power of unit root tests in general and the small sample size prevent us from finding this), what are the implications for the consistency of the coefficient estimates on the proxy variables Δp_t and p_{Xt}?

31. Another problem with small sample sizes is the bias in the OLSEG estimates. As an alternative, estimation of an ADL for the 'hyperinflation period', 1922m7 to 1923m9, resulted in:

$$m_t - p_t = 2.585 + 0.501(m_t - p_t)_{-1} \\ - 0.562\Delta p_t - 0.266\Delta p_{t-1} \\ + 0.784(x_t - p_{Xt}) \\ - 0.298(x_t - p_{Xt})_{-1}$$

   (i) Derive the implied long run and explain how you would assess the stationarity of the residuals.

   (ii) Assess the sensitivity of the long-run estimates to lengthening the ADL lags.

32. Carry out the following two-stage EG procedure: Estimate the cointegrating regression for $m_t - p_t - (x_t - p_{Xt})$ over the full sample period, 1921m1 to 1923m11; then define a corresponding ecm_t term and estimate the dynamic model regressing

$$\Delta\{m_t - p_t - (x_t - p_{Xt})\}$$

on Δp_t, $\Delta\{m_t - p_t - (x_t - p_{Xt})\}_{-1}$ and ecm_{t-1}. Comment on the resulting equation; obtain one step ahead forecasts of $m_t - p_t$ and compare these with $m_t - p_t$. Although these forecasts fit the data well, even before 1922m7, why is the model not yet satisfactory?

33. Explain how the ADL estimates in Table 10.9 are obtained and comment on any differences from the EG estimates.

34. Show how an ADL model can be reparameterised into an ECM.

35. Consider the results reported for the US demand for money, do you think that a short-term or a long-term interest rate is a better measure of the opportunity cost of holding noninterest bearing bank deposits and cash?

36. The following estimates are of the cointegrating regression for the United States with unrestricted income elasticity, using the Phillips–Hansen FMOLS estimator with the Bartlett window lags:

Truncation lag:	0	1	6	9	12
constant	1.552	1.603	1.869	1.957	2.008
	(0.182)	(0.249)	(0.408)	(0.459)	(0.501)
$y_t - p_t$	0.618	0.613	0.584	0.574	0.568
	(0.022)	(0.030)	(0.050)	(0.056)	(0.061)
SR_t	−0.022	−0.0023	−0.027	−0.029	−0.029
	(−0.001)	(−0.001)	(−0.002)	(−0.003)	(−0.003)

Note: Estimated standard errors in parentheses; dependent variable $\Delta(m_t - p_t)$.

Compare these estimates with those in the text. Would you reject the hypothesis that the long-run income elasticity is 1?

37. Do you think there is a role for the interest rate spread, $LR_t - SR_t$, in the demand for money function?

38. A possible long-run relation between the nominal interest rate, R_t, and the inflation rate is summarised by the Fisher hypothesis where,

$$R_t = r_t + \Delta p_t$$

where r_t is the real interest rate and Δp_t is the inflation rate. If the Fisher hypothesis does not hold in the short run is there any merit in including both a nominal interest rate and the inflation rate in the demand for money equation?

39. Interpret the estimated coefficients on the dynamic equations in Tables 10.9 and 10.10.

40. Suppose we wrongly conclude that short-term and long-term interest rates are I(1), whereas they are I(0). Modify the OLSEG and ADL methods to take this into account.

41. What are the main contributions of BHS to modelling the demand for M1?

CHAPTER 11

The term structure of interest rates

11.1 Introduction

Interest rates are a familiar theoretical and practical concept. For example, if you place funds into your thrift institution (building society in the United Kingdom, savings and loans association in the United States) you expect to receive a payment for making those funds available to someone else. The payment is usually expressed in the form of an annual interest rate, $R(t)$; for example, if $100 (the principal) is placed it will attract $R(t)$ times $100 as interest on that account in one year.

Larger personal investors and institutional investors have many other options open to them, although some of the considerations motivating the placement of their funds will be similar to those of smaller investors. Pension funds will be concerned that they can service the current and future flow of pension payments and will plan an investment strategy with this in mind. The need to consider the future raises the question of whether to invest in an asset with exactly the maturity (that is the time to payment of the principal) which matches the payment flow, or to successively invest in a sequence of shorter period assets which ends up at the same point in the future. For reference a long maturity asset is referred to as an n-period asset, and a shorter period asset is referred to as an m-period asset. The first strategy involves investing 'long', the second is a strategy which 'rolls over' a sequence of shorter-term, m-period, assets. The first strategy minimises the uncertainty to the pension fund, since it is possible to contract now to buy an n-period asset with a known return,

whereas the second strategy involves a sequence of assets whose future returns will, generally, be uncertain. What is of importance to the pension fund is the relationship between the n-period rate and the sequence of m-period rates, and hence what is known as the 'spread' or difference between the long period rate and the short period rate.

Similarly, suppliers of debt will also be concerned with the relative cost of offering debt of different maturities. A major supplier of debt is the government that issues bonds through its treasury; these bonds are assets to investors and liabilities to the government. Bonds can take several forms, the simplest kind being a (pure) discount bond, which is a promise by the government, or issuer, to pay a 'principal', which is a single fixed payment, with no other payments, at a specified date; at that date the bond is said to be 'redeemed' at maturity, and the time or 'term to maturity' is the elapse time before redemption. Discount bonds are so called because in order to persuade investors to buy them they have to be offered at a discount price relative to the principal that is paid on maturity. Investors are buying the 'promise' of payment of a fixed amount, the price they are willing to pay will depend, *ceteris paribus*, on the length of time they have to wait for the promise to be fulfilled. From the discount price and principal it is possible to calculate an implicit 'yield', or put more simply 'rate of interest', on the discount bond. Bonds can be more complicated than discount bonds. If the term to maturity is greater than 12 months, bonds may also come with an annual payment until maturity, known as the 'coupon', and are known as coupon bonds. In this case a comparison of the cost of issuing debt will need to take into account the coupon as well as the discount price relative to the principal.

The term structure of interest rates is concerned with the relationship between the interest rate and the term to maturity, and the 'yield curve' is the graphical representation of this relationship. Pure discount bonds, especially those issued by government treasuries, are important in this context because the only respect in which they differ is their term to maturity. In particular, risk of default, that is failure to honour the 'promise', is controlled (and usually zero), so like is compared with like apart from term to maturity. It is possible to work with coupon rather than discount bonds but the relevant mathematical expressions are more complicated without adding anything to the theory. By issuing bonds of particular maturities, governments lock themselves into particular payment profiles and redemption costs and it will also be their concern to get the profile right to meet future commitments.

The term structure of interest rates has attracted a great deal of research, both theoretical and empirical. The leading theory is the combination of the expectations model and the rational expectations hypothesis. Important work includes Campbell and Shiller (1987, 1991), Shiller (1979, 1981), Shiller, Campbell and Schoenholtz (1983), Campbell (1996) and for an earlier summary see Dodds and Ford (1974). In addition to the empirical work included in these references, the following is a brief selection of empirical contributions: Cuthbertson (1996b), Cuthbertson, Hayes and Nitzsche (1996), Evans and Lewis (1994), Hall, Anderson and Granger (1992), Johnson (1994), Hardouvelis (1994), Mankiw and Miron (1986), Mills (1991), Shea (1992) and Taylor (1992). Excellent summaries are provided by Shiller (1990) and Cuthbertson (1996a), which also contains a useful set of references; and Campbell and Kracaw (1993) is an excellent source for

the language of financial instruments for those unfamiliar with this area.

In this chapter section **11.2** deals with the underlying concepts of the term structure in greater detail. Section **11.3** describes the components of the expectations model and some of the implications which follow from the assumption that expectations are formed rationally. Section **11.4** focuses on three ways of assessing the expectations model using a dataset on the yields of US Government securities due to McCulloch (1990). Section **11.5** extends **11.4** in the sense of drawing together other methods of assessment and empirical evidence from some other studies, and also considers alternative models which develop the expectations model to account for: the possibility of time varying risk premium; overreaction of the spread to changes in the short rate; and market segmentation. As usual, the final section provides some concluding remarks.

The notation in this chapter is a departure from the subscript notation generally used elsewhere. One of the key aspects of the expectations model of term structure of interest rates is its implications for what is known as the spread, that is the difference between yields with different maturities. This requires the use of three distinguishing features: time, maturity, n, of the 'long' bond and maturity, m, of the 'short' bond. We use the notation $R(t, n, m)$. Alternatives found in the literature include $R_t^{n,m}$ and $R_{t,n,m}$, which are notationally more complex.

11.2 Term structure of interest rates

This section lays out the basic building blocks, which lead to the term structure of interest rates. These are the original term to maturity, the yield, pure discount securities and the yield curve.

11.2.1 Term to maturity

At a national level an important borrower and lender is the government through its Treasury, which has a special characteristic which will help to explain the term structure of interest rates. That characteristic is that funds placed with the Treasury are as close as you can get to a *risk-free* investment. An important distinguishing feature of the range of financial instruments offered by the Treasury is the differing terms to maturity on offer. For example, it is possible to lend 'short' by buying a 3-month Treasury Bill (sometimes referred to as a 3-month T-Bill); or lend 'long' by buying a 10-year Treasury Bond. The difference here is the *term to maturity* of the financial instrument: in one case 3 months, in the other 10 years. (By convention a T-Bill has less than 12 months to maturity, whereas a T-Bond has a longer maturity.) For a more detailed description of US Treasury operations see Campbell and Kracaw (1993). The terms to maturity here are the *original* terms as a market exists for 'secondhand' T-Bills and Bonds. That is an agent could hold a 3-month T-Bill for 1 month and then sell it on the secondary market, in this case the 3-month T-Bill has effectively become a 2-month T-Bill.

The term to maturity of a bill or a bond is the length of time before it will be redeemed by the original issuer; and as noted above there is an *original* maturity which is usually incorporated in the title of the bill or bond. The existence of secondary markets that will buy and sell existing T-Bills with different actual, as compared to original, terms to maturity means that there is a spectrum of terms to maturity ranging from the very short term, measured in days, through to the long term, measured in years.

11.2.2 The discount rate, the interest rate and continuous compounding

It will help to concentrate on the characteristics of bills and bonds somewhat further. The nature of the T-Bill market is unusual compared to the way in which domestic lenders structure their loans to household customers. For example, if

the Government needs to raise funds to finance its spending programme and decides to raise part of these funds through borrowing (rather than taxation) it sells T-Bills (or bonds) to individuals, financial institutions and corporations. To simplify suppose that the Treasury decides to raise $1,000,000 to be paid back in 12 months' time. Rather than issue a single $1,000,000 12-month T-Bill it decides to issue 10,000, $100 12-month T-Bills. This is the face value of the bill, sometimes referred to as the redemption price of the bill. Each one of these is a promise by the Treasury to pay (or redeem) the stated sum in 12 months' time. Because the Treasury will have use of the money paid for the T-Bill for 12 months, a potential buyer will not pay $100 for this bill. The bill, therefore, will have to be sold at a *discount* with a discount price relative to the face value and an implied discount rate. For example, suppose a buyer is willing to pay $95 now in order to receive $100 in 12 months' time. In effect the $100 12-month T-Bill is being sold at a discount, with the *discount rate* given implicitly by

$$95 = (1 - r_d)100$$

which solves for $r_d = 0.05$, where r_d is the 12-month discount rate. This rate is different from the *simple interest rate r*, defined by the following equation

$$r = \frac{P_1}{P_0} - 1 \quad \text{which implies } P_1 = P_0(1 + r)$$

$$(11.1)$$

where P_1 is the (redemption) value of the bill at the end of one annual period and P_0 is the initial value of the bill, that is the price paid now (at the beginning of the year). In this case $P_0 = \$95$ and $P_1 = \$100$, so the simple interest rate is

$$r = \frac{100}{95} - 1 = 0.05263 \text{ or } 5.263\% \text{ p.a.}$$

The difference between r_d and r arises because the discount rate is worked out as a discount on

P_1, whereas the actual amount lent is P_0. Note $(1 + r) = 1/(1 - r_d)$. It is conventional to express discount rates and interest rates on a % p.a. basis.

The interest rate is simple in the sense that interest is assumed to be calculated just once and 'paid' at the end of the period, so $95 invested for 12 months at an annual interest rate of 5.263% gives $100: the calculation is $95.00(1 + 0.05263) = 100$. To illustrate an alternative conceptualisation suppose interest was viewed as being applied monthly with an annual rate $r^{(12)}$. The notation uses superfluous brackets on r to indicate that it is the annual rate corresponding to interest compounded monthly. After 1 month the discount price is $95(1 + r^{(12)}/12)$, after 2 months

$$95(1 + r^{(12)}/12)(1 + r^{(12)}/12)$$
$$= 95(1 + r^{(12)}/12)^2$$

and after 12 months $95(1 + r^{(12)}/12)^{12}$. The interest rate, $r^{(12)}$, is given as the solution to:

$$95(1 + r^{(12)}/12)^{12} = 100$$

which solves for $r = 5.1403\%$; this is less than the simple interest rate because interest builds up on a monthly basis. In this example interest is said to be compounded monthly. To extend the example suppose interest is assumed to be compounded even more frequently than monthly. The interest rate is $r^{(m)}$, where m indicates the number of times (with a uniform interval) interest is compounded. In this example $r^{(m)}$ is solved from

$$95(1 + r^{(m)}/m)^m = 100$$

As $m \to \infty$, $(1 + r^{(m)}/m)^m \to \exp\{r^{(m)}\}$; and note for later use that after n periods as $m \to \infty$, $[(1 + r^{(m)}/m)^m]^n \to \exp\{r^{(m)}n\}$. To simplify the notation, define the continuously compounded interest rate as $R \equiv r^{(m)}$ as $m \to \infty$. Then using this relationship $95(\exp\{R\}) = 100$ solves for $R = \ln(100/95) = 0.05129$, that is 5.129% p.a., which is less than the simple interest rate and

less than $r^{(12)}$ because compounding is more frequent than in either case.

Given a simple interest rate it is possible to obtain the implied equivalent continuously compounded rate and vice versa. Investing A for n years at the rate $r^{(m)}$ has a terminal value, $TV(n)$, of $A[(1 + r^{(m)}/m)^m]^n$; if compounding was continuous then for an identical terminal value this must equal $A[\exp\{Rn\}]$, hence

$$\exp\{Rn\} = [(1 + r^{(m)}/m)^m]^n \quad \text{and, therefore,}$$
$$R = m[\ln(1 + r^{(m)}/m)]$$

In the example above the simple interest rate is 0.05263 so $R = \ln(1 + 0.05263) = 0.05129$; using the monthly interest rate gives the same answer,

$$R = 12[\ln(1 + 0.05134/12)] = 0.05129$$

and these confirm the earlier direct calculation. Cuthbertson (1996a, Chapter 1) contains an excellent review of different kinds of interest rates.

A clear definition of the yield to maturity is needed in order to understand the construction of a yield curve and the term structure of interest rates. The yield to maturity is the return, expressed as a rate or fraction, obtained by holding the instrument until it matures; the length of time the instrument is held is the holding period. Yield curves may be constructed on the basis of simple interest rates or assuming a continuously compounded interest rate. An example of the latter case is the dataset on US Treasury Bills and Bonds due to McCulloch (1990), elements of which are used for the empirical study reported later in this chapter. McCulloch (op. cit.) infers the yield curve from the prices of securities for a range of maturities from 1 month through to 25 years. As noted by McCulloch, bond yields are quoted in the press and elsewhere on a semi-annual compounding basis that, as we have seen, gives higher yields than continuous compounding. Nevertheless, provided the same basis of compounding is used throughout the maturity range, and other factors are also constant, the plot of yield against maturity is still valid.

To get a clear picture of the yield curve (and so term structure) it is useful to obtain observations on as many maturities as possible provided the market is active at those maturities. This will mean using observations from the secondary market where terms differ from those of original maturity. We have already seen how to calculate the yield, either as a simple interest rate, a semi-annual rate or a continuously compounded rate, where the holding period matches the original term to maturity of 12 months.

$$\text{yield to maturity} = \frac{P_1}{P_0} - 1 = r$$

This calculation is more complicated if the 12-month T-Bill has less than 12 months to maturity. For example, suppose a 12-month T-Bill is halfway through its term, that is it has 6 months to maturity, and a dealer offers to sell this T-Bill for $97.50, what is (a) its discount rate and (b) its yield to maturity if the bill is purchased for $97.50? By convention the discount rate is expressed as an annual rate but here there are 6 months to maturity so the calculation is

$$97.50 = 100(1 - 0.5r_d)$$

therefore, $r_d = 0.05$ or 5% p.a.

On paying $97.50 for a 12-month T-Bill with 6 months to maturity and receiving $100 on redemption, the simple interest rate is:

simple interest rate

$$= \left(\frac{100}{97.50} - 1\right)\frac{12}{6}$$

$$= 0.05128 \text{ or } 5.128\% \text{ p.a.}$$

The expression in brackets is 0.0256, which is the simple interest rate, 2.56%, on a half-year basis; multiplying by $12/6 = 2$ gives the annual rate of 5.128% p.a. A 12-month T-Bill with

2 months to maturity would have the weight $12/2 = 6$. To obtain the equivalent continuously compounded rate we can use $R = c[\ln(1 + r^{(c)}/c)]$ with $r^{(1)} = 0.05128$, which implies $R = \ln(1 + 0.05128) = 0.050008$, so the equivalent continuously compounded interest rate is 5.0008% p.a.

11.2.3   The yield curve

The kind of bill referred to in the last section is known as a zero coupon, or pure discount, bill because it pays out nothing in the interim between purchase and redemption. There are other bills and bonds which pay a regular fixed amount usually annually, known as the *coupon*, between purchase and redemption; but for the moment the simplest case is the zero-coupon bill or bond and this case is useful in describing how to construct a *yield curve* for financial instruments with different terms to maturity. The yield curve is a graphical representation of the term structure of interest rates. That is the relationship between the term to maturity of a financial instrument and its yield. The instruments, which form the basis of the yield curve, should be alike in all respects apart from their term to maturity. They should, for example, have the same risk of default, the same tax treatment, and the same transaction costs, the same coupon and so on. If they do not some part of the yield may be due to differences in these factors. For this reason empirical studies of the yield curve usually use data on risk-free, zero-coupon financial instruments – often Treasury Bills and Bonds – because these are generally homogeneous across different maturities. To summarise: 'The yield curve shows the yield-to-maturity prevailing at a given point in time for bonds that differ only by maturity.' (Campbell and Kracaw, 1993, p. 74.)

To abstract from the problems that arise with coupon bonds the financial instruments considered here are assumed to be zero-coupon bills and bonds. For an extension to coupon bonds see Shiller (1990) and Cuthbertson (1996a, Chapters 9 and 10).

11.3 The expectations model of the term structure

A leading model of the term structure is the expectations model – see, for example, Shiller (1979) and Campbell and Shiller (1987). The essence of the model is quite simple. The long rate is a weighted average of expected future short rates over the lifetime of the long asset, plus a risk premium; this implies that the spread, that is the difference between the long rate and the short rate, is a weighted average of expected changes in future short rates, plus a function of the risk premium. If the interest rates are those on pure discount bonds, the weights relating the long rate to expected future short rates are equal. If the bonds carry coupons then the weights are geometrically declining with expected short-term rates in the near future having more weight than those in the distant future (Shiller 1979, p. 1194). While reference is made to coupon bearing bonds the central case considered in this section is pure discount bonds.

11.3.1 The yield to maturity and the forward rate

A leading theory of the term structure of interest rates is the expectations model. In order to understand this the following notation is used: let $R(t, m)$ be the yield to maturity of an m period pure discount (that is zero-coupon) bond as at time t, expressed as an annual rate. n is reserved to indicate the longest maturity bond; and, because of the need here to distinguish the time index from the maturity index, we depart from the convention in previous chapters of using subscripts to indicate the time or observation index. For example, with $m = 1$, $R(t, 1)$ is the yield to maturity of a one period bond; with $m = 2$, $R(t, 2)$ is the yield to maturity of a bond with two periods to maturity and so on. As a variation on this notation $R(t + 1, 1)$ is the yield to maturity on a one period bond held at

time $t + 1$, and hence maturing in time $t + 2$. $R(t + n - 1, 1)$ is the yield to maturity of a one period bond held at time $t + n - 1$, and hence maturing in $t + n - 1 + 1 = t + n$; and $R(t + i, m)$ is the yield to maturity on an m period bond held at time $t + i$ and hence maturing in $t + i + m$. For simplicity, in this and subsequent sections, it is assumed that $(n/m) \equiv k$ is an integer; that is k is the integer number of short periods in the longest period. For example, if $n = 20$ and $m = 4$ then $k = 5$, if $m = 1$ and $n = 20$ and $n = k = 20$. Quite often it is useful to illustrate the results with some simple cases and $m = 1$ is chosen for this purpose.

Now suppose that at time t you wish to invest in such a way that your funds are available to you n periods hence. A simple strategy is to contract now to buy an n period bond. This strategy reduces the unknowns to a minimum: the actual return, which is $R(t, n)$, can be contracted *now*. However, there are a number of alternative strategies open to you. One possibility is to 'roll over' a sequence of n one period bonds. That is a time t rather than buying an n period bond you buy a one period bond with an actual yield of $R(t, 1)$. Then, also at time t, you undertake a series of contracts in a 'forward' market. That is you agree now to buy a one period bond in $t + 1$ that matures at the end of that period. That rolls over the first period and the rate at which you fix for that contract is denoted $F(t + 1, 1)$; this is one period *forward* rate contracted at t for $t + 1$. Your next contract will be to buy a one period bond in $t + 2$ that matures at the end of that period and the rate which you fix for that contract is denoted $F(t + 2, 1)$. The alternative strategy should be clear now. Altogether there will be n contracts with rates given by the sequence: $R(t, 1)$, $F(t + 1, 1)$, $F(t + 2, 1), \ldots, F(t + n - 1, 1)$. The notation $F(t + j, 1)$ is reserved for the one period forward rate. The notation $R(t + j, 1)$ is reserved for the *actual* rate or yield and it may – or may not – be the case that $F(t + j, 1) = R(t + j, 1)$ for $j > 0$. It is, of course, trivially true that $F(t, 1) = R(t, 1)$. If you rolled over a sequence of m period bonds, the sequence of rates would be: $R(t, m)$, $F(t + m, m)$, $F(t + 2m, m), \ldots, F(t + (k - 1)m, m)$; thus, in general there will be k contracts involving m period bonds.

To illustrate further take $n = 5$ and $m = 1$ and consider two strategies. In strategy A, $\$A$ is invested in a 5 period bond held to maturity with terminal value TV_{ak} given by:

$$TV_{ak} = \$A[1 + R(t, 5)]^5 \qquad (11.2)$$

In the roll-over sequence, called strategy B, $\$A$ invested at time t will have a terminal value TV_{bk} in k periods of (all interim interest is reinvested for comparability with holding a k period bond to maturity):

$$\begin{aligned}
TV_{bk} = \ &\$A[1 + R(t, 1)][1 + F(t + 1, 1)] \\
&\times [1 + F(t + 2, 1)][1 + F(t + 3, 1)] \\
&\times [1 + F(t + 4, 1)] \qquad (11.3)
\end{aligned}$$

In an efficient market an investor will be indifferent between these two strategies and, since both are contracted at the beginning of period t, this requires:

$$TV_{ak} = TV_{bk}, \text{ which implies}$$

$$\begin{aligned}
[1 + R(t, 5)]^5 = \ &[1 + R(t, 1)][1 + F(t + 1, 1)] \\
&\times [1 + F(t + 2, 1)] \\
&\times [1 + F(t + 3, 1)] \\
&\times [1 + F(t + 4, 1)] \qquad (11.4)
\end{aligned}$$

Taking logs of both sides of (11.4):

$$\begin{aligned}
5 \ln&[1 + R(t, 5)] \\
= \ &\ln[1 + R(t, 1)] + \ln[1 + F(t + 1, 1)] \\
&+ \ln[1 + F(t + 2, 1)] \\
&+ \ln[1 + F(t + 3, 1)] \\
&+ \ln[1 + F(t + 4, 1)]
\end{aligned}$$

To a good approximation for 'small' R, $\ln[1 + R] = R$; using this approximation and dividing both sides of equation (11.4) by 5 gives the following:

$$\begin{aligned}
R(t, 5) = \tfrac{1}{5} [&R(t, 1) + F(t + 1, 1) + F(t + 2, 1) \\
&+ F(t + 3, 1) + F(t + 4, 1)] \qquad (11.5)
\end{aligned}$$

This is the relationship between the actual yield to maturity on the 5 period bond bought now, i.e. $R(t, 5)$, and the sequence of one period forward rates. In words, the actual yield to maturity of a 5 period bond bought at time t is equal to the arithmetic average of the actual yield to maturity on a one period bond and the subsequent sequence of four one period forward rates.

In general for n an integer multiple, k, of m, this is:

$$R(t, n) = \frac{1}{k} \left[\sum_{i=1}^{k} F(t + (i - 1)m, m) \right] \quad (11.6)$$

and for $m = 1$ (so $n = k$)

$$R(t, n) = \frac{1}{k} \left[\sum_{i=1}^{k} F(t + (i - 1), 1) \right] \quad (11.6a)$$

The insight behind this relationship is as follows. An efficient market will ensure that the alternatives of (a) buying an n period bond at time t and (b) buying a sequence of shorter period bonds will not yield the expectation of a profit. If it does it will be arbitraged away by the (efficient) market.

The next step in the expectations model is the relationship between the sequence of forward rates and corresponding sequence of actual rates. A forward rate is the rate for a future loan and is likely to be related to the anticipated actual rate. For example, a possibility is

$$F(t + j, m) = E_t[R(t + j, m)] + \tau(t + j, m) \quad (11.7)$$

with $m = 1$ this is

$$F(t + j, 1) = E_t[R(t + j, 1)] + \tau(t + j, 1) \quad (11.7a)$$

That is the one period forward rate for $t + j$ is equal to the expected actual one period rate for that period plus an additional factor $\tau(t + j, m)$, which is known as the risk or term premium. This premium could have a number of justifications. For example, it could arise because the future path of interest rates is uncertain and there is, therefore, inevitably a risk associated with making a forward contract. In what has become known as the 'pure expectations hypothesis' – or PEH – term premia are zero; in the 'expectations hypothesis' – or EH – the term premia are nonzero but constant; and in the 'liquidity preference hypothesis' – or LPH – the term premium increases with the period to maturity and hence is not a constant across different maturities – see Cuthbertson (*op. cit.*, Table 9.1) for further details.

Substituting the expression for $F(t + j, m)$ into that for $R(t, n)$ gives:

$$R(t, n) = \frac{1}{k}\left[\sum_{i=1}^{k} E_t\{R(t + (i - 1)m, m)\}\right]$$
$$+ L(t, m) \tag{11.8}$$

$$\text{where} \quad L(t, m) = \frac{1}{k}\left[\sum_{i=1}^{k} \tau(t + i, m)\right] \tag{11.9}$$

The expression (11.8) might be regarded as the 'fundamental relationship' of the expectations model. It states that the long rate is a weighted average, with equal weights summing to 1 for pure discount securities, of current and expected future short rates. To illustrate the interpretation of this relationship between the yield on an n period bond (a long rate) and the yield on a sequence of short-term rates take $n = 2$ and $m = 1$. Then

$$R(t, 2) = \tfrac{1}{2}[E_t R(t, 1) + E_t R(t + 1, 1)] + L(t, 1)$$
$$= \tfrac{1}{2}R(t, 1) + \tfrac{1}{2}E_t R(t + 1, 1) + L(t, 1)$$
$$\tag{11.10}$$

Since $R(t, 1)$ is known at time t then $E_t R(t, 1)$ is identically equal to $R(t, 1)$. The two period bond rate is, therefore, the simple arithmetic average of the actual one period rate and the expected one period rate for $t + 1$, plus a risk premium. Thus, *ceteris paribus*, if the one period forward rate increases, driven by an anticipation that the actual rate will increase, then the 'long' bond rate will also increase. Thus, an anticipation that short-term rates will increase leads to an increase in the long rate. Of course if the term or risk premia are not constant the expectations model loses much of its content, unless the variation can itself be modelled. For present purposes it is assumed that the term premia do not vary over time – that is they are 'time invariant'.

If the bonds are coupon bearing the weights in (11.8) change, in particular the long rate is no longer a simple average of expected future short rates. The appropriate relationship is

$$R(t, n) = \frac{1 - \gamma}{1 - \gamma^k}\sum_{i=0}^{k-1} \gamma^i E_t\{R(t + im, m)\}$$
$$+ L(t, m)$$

The weights are now exponentially (or geometrically) declining, truncated to the number of short periods, m, in the long period, n, and scaled by $(1 - \gamma^k)$ to ensure they sum to 1. The interpretational change this makes to (11.8) is that expected rates in the near future receive a larger weight than expected rates in the distant future. Shiller (1979) suggests setting $\gamma = \bar{R}(t, n)$, that is the average long bond rate, which is appropriate for consols with $n = \infty$ and for coupon bearing bonds which are selling near par. A bond whose current price equals the principal paid at maturity is said to be selling 'at par'. For fixed m as $n \to \infty$, $k = (n/m) \to \infty$ and, therefore, $(1 - \gamma^k) \to 1$ for $0 \leq \gamma < 1$, so the weights simplify to those of an infinite geometrically declining lag distribution scaled to sum to 1; note that $\sum_{i=0}^{\infty} \gamma^i = 1/(1 - \gamma)$, hence $(1 - \gamma)\sum_{i=0}^{\infty} \gamma^i = 1$.

11.3.2 The spread

Subtracting $R(t, 1)$ from both sides of (11.10) gives:

$$R(t, 2) - R(t, 1) = \tfrac{1}{2}E_t[R(t + 1, 1) - R(t, 1)] + L(t, 1) \qquad (11.11)$$

The left-hand side of this expression is the 'spread' between the two period and the one period bond rate. The notation $S(t, 2, 1)$ is used for the spread in the above equation; this indicates the difference between the two period rate and the one period rate at time t. The right-hand side comprises the term premium, $L(t, 1)$, and one-half the expected change in the one period rate between t and $t + 1$. This last term has the interpretation of the expected change in the short-term rate. If this is zero then the only reason for a nonzero spread is the existence of a term premium. An important prediction from this equation is that the long-term rate, and hence the spread, will increase if the short-term rate is expected to increase.

A spread can be defined for the difference between any two bonds with different maturities. If the longest maturity bond has a maturity of n periods and 1 is the shortest maturity then $S(t, n, 1)$ is the long–short spread. In general the spread is $S(t, n, m)$. This can also be expressed in an informative way as:

$$S(t, n, m) = \sum_{i=1}^{k-1} \left(\frac{k - i}{k} \right) E_t\{\Delta R(t + im, m)\} + L(t, m) \qquad (11.12)$$

where

$$\Delta R(t + im, m) = R(t + im, m) - R(t + (i - 1)m, m) \qquad (11.13)$$

For $m = 1$ (and so $n = k$), (11.12) is:

$$S(t, k, 1) = \sum_{i=1}^{k-1} \left(\frac{k - i}{k} \right) E_t\{\Delta R(t + i, 1)\} + L(t, k) \qquad (11.12a)$$

and for $m = 1$, (11.13) is

$$\Delta R(t + i, 1) = R(t + i, 1) - R(t + (i - 1), 1) \qquad (11.13a)$$

According to (11.12) a spread between the yield on the n period and m period bonds occurs because, apart from the liquidity premium, expected changes in the short rate over the horizon of the long bond are nonzero. If there are no expected changes the long bond yield and the short bond yield should just differ by the liquidity premium.

If $n = 5$ and $m = 1$, as in the earlier example, then

$$S(t, 5, 1) = 0.8E_t\{\Delta R(t + 1, 1)\} + 0.6E_t\{\Delta R(t + 2, 1)\} + 0.4E_t\{\Delta R(t + 3, 1)\} + 0.2E_t\{\Delta R(t + 4, 1)\} + L(t, 1) \qquad (11.14)$$

So the long–short spread is the weighted sum of the sequence of expected changes in the short rate, plus a liquidity premium, with *expected changes in the short rate close to t receiving a greater weight than expected changes further away in time.*

Another insight as to why a spread occurs follows from identifying the 'perfect foresight spread' in (11.12) for the n and m period bonds; at time t this is:

$$PFS(t, n, m) = \sum_{i=1}^{k-1} \left(\frac{k - i}{k} \right) \Delta R(t + im, m) \qquad (11.15)$$

and for future reference define $w_i = 1 - i/k$ for $i = 1, \ldots, k - 1$. The perfect foresight spread is just what its description suggests: it is 'the spread that would obtain, given the model, if there were perfect foresight about future interest rates' (Campbell and Shiller 1991, p. 498 and see Cuthbertson *et al.* 1996, p. 399). Rewriting (11.12) with this definition then:

$$S(t, n, m) = E_t\{PFS(t, n, m)\} + L(t, m)$$

If expectations of future rates on one period bonds are formed according to the rational expectations hypothesis (REH) then

$$R(t + im, m) = E_t\{R(t + im, m)\}$$
$$+ \varepsilon(t + im, m) \quad \text{for } i \geq 1$$
$$R(t, m) = E_t\{R(t, m)\} \quad \text{for } i = 0$$
(11.16)

That is the difference between the outturn in $t + i$ and the rate expected at time t for $t + i$ is a stationary error with $E_t\{\varepsilon(t + im, m)\} = 0$. For $i = 0$, $R(t, m) = E_t\{R(t, m)\}$ with $\varepsilon(t, m) = 0$. In (11.16) $E_t\{R(t + im, m)\}$ is (according to the REH) the optimal predictor of $R(t + im, m)$; from Chapter 4 this can be recognised as the conditional expectation of $R(t + im, m)$. This expression is important because (11.16) can be used to substitute for $E_t\{\Delta R(t + im)\}$ in (11.12). That is from (11.16)

$$E_t\{R(t + im, m)\}$$
$$= R(t + im, m) - \varepsilon(t + im, m)$$

Lagging this expression once gives:

$$E_t\{R(t + (i - 1)m, m)\}$$
$$= R(t + (i - 1)m, m) - \varepsilon(t + (i - 1)m, m)$$

Hence

$$E_t\{R(t + im, m)\} - E_t\{R(t + (i - 1)m, m)\}$$
$$\equiv E_t\{\Delta R(t + im, m)\}$$
$$= \Delta R(t + im, m) - \Delta\varepsilon(t + im, m)$$
(11.17)

Substituting for $E_t\{\Delta R(t + im, m)\}$ in (11.12) using (11.17) gives:

$$S(t, n, m) = \sum_{i=1}^{k-1} w_i \Delta R(t + im, m)$$
$$+ \varphi(t, m) + L(t, m) \quad (11.18)$$

where $\varphi(t, m) = \sum_{i=1}^{k-1} w_i^* \varepsilon(t + im, m)$ and $w_i^* = w_{i+1} - w_i$ for $i = 1, \ldots, k - 2$ and $w_{k-1}^* = -w_{k-1}$;

note that there is no term in $\varepsilon(t, m)$ because $E_t\{R(t, m)\} = R(t, m)$. In (11.18) the spread between the n period and one period bond rate is expressed as a function of the observable changes in the one period rates for $t + m$ through to $t + (k - 1)m$, these can be thought of as 'driving' the spread. In addition there are two other terms. One, $L(t, m)$, represents term premia (or transaction costs in implementing a 'rollover' strategy); and the other, $\varphi(t, m)$, is a composite stochastic term which is a weighted average of the expectation errors which are, by assumption, stationary. $L(t, k)$ is assumed to be stationary which is consistent with a number of models: in the PEH term premia are zero; in the EH they are constant and the same for all maturities; in the liquidity preference hypothesis, LPH, they are constant but vary with the period to maturity; and in the time varying risk hypothesis, TVRH, they vary over time and with the period to maturity but are usually regarded as stationary.

11.3.3 Implications for economic policy

The expectations model carries with it some important implications for economic policy, particularly the operation of monetary policy. Decisions on the 'real' side of the economy, for example those on investment by industry and expenditure on durable goods by consumers, are generally thought to be related to long-term rather than short-term rates of interest, primarily because such decisions involve evaluating the returns to investment and the returns from consumer durables over a relatively long period of time. One alternative – and opportunity cost, therefore – of tying up funds in physical goods is to buy an equivalent term financial asset. Thus, in order to influence 'real' activity the government will need to influence long-term rates. However, the government (or its brokers the central bank) is usually able to exert greater influence over short-term rates because of its dominance in the market for short-term assets (primarily T-Bills). If the term structure is as described by the expectations model it can influence the long-term rate by influencing the appropriate sequence of current and expected short-term rates.

11.4 Assessing the expectations model

The empirical support for the expectations model of the term structure can be assessed in three ways from equation (11.18), these are summarised below together with a brief discussion of some of the estimation problems that arise in each case. Other ways of assessing the expectations model are considered in section **11.5**.

11.4.1 Three implications of the expectations model

(1) *Are the spreads stationary given that yields are nonstationary?* There is substantial empirical evidence that (zero-coupon) T-Bill and T-Bond rates are consistent with I(1) processes. Thus, in particular, if $R(t + im, m)$ is I(1), then $\Delta R(t + im, m)$ will be I(0); and a linear combination of I(0) variables, as on the right-hand side of equation (11.18), will be I(0). The spread, therefore, must be I(0) so that the left- and right-hand sides of the equation are balanced in terms of their time series properties. The requirement that the spread be I(0) if the sequence of $\Delta R(t + im, m)$, and $\varphi(t, m)$ and $L(t, m)$, are I(0) is a necessary rather than a sufficient condition for the expectations model to be consistent with the data. RE is not essential to this procedure as it will be valid for any expectations process which generates I(0) errors.

(2) *Do the lead weights correspond to the theoretical pattern:* $w_i = 1 - i/k$? Provided the data on rates corresponds to zero-coupon bills or bonds, the weights which combine the sequence of

terms in $\Delta R(t + im, m)$ should be $(k - i)/k = 1 - i/k$ for $i = 1, \ldots, k - 1$. However, estimation of the lead weights from (11.18) is not straightforward and requires an instrumental variables procedure. The reason for this is that in (11.18), $\varphi(t, m)$ and $PFS(t, n, m) = \sum_{i=1}^{k-1} w_i \Delta R (t + im, m)$ are correlated, with the implication that the OLS estimators of the lead weights will be inconsistent.

From (11.16) observe that a shock to the innovation, $\varepsilon(t + im, m)$, is translated directly into a shock to $R(t + im, m)$, resulting in a positive correlation. The chosen instruments should in principle be uncorrelated with $\varepsilon(t + im, m)$. A conventional procedure of choosing the instruments as lagged values of the regressors is not followed here because this is expensive in terms of lost degrees of freedom. This 'expense' arises because $\varphi(t, m)$ is a weighted sum of $k - 1$ terms with an overall temporal distance of $n - m$ periods and will exhibit a moving average of order $[(n - m) - 1]$. Intuitively this arises because of the temporal overlap between $\varphi(t + m, m)$ and $\varphi(t, m)$ which have $[(n - m) - 1]$ terms in common. To avoid serial correlation between the instruments and the composite disturbance error, $\varphi(t, m)$, the instruments must be lagged at least $[(n - m) - 1] + 1$ times. At least as many instruments as regressors are then required; for example, in the case of $n = 120$ and $m = 1$, $[(120 - 1) - 1] + 1 = 119$ and candidate instruments are the lagged regressors: $\Delta R(t, 120, 1)$ for $\Delta R(t + 119, 120, 1)$, $\Delta R(t - 1, 120, 1)$ for $\Delta R(t + 118, 120, 1)$ and so on with the last being $\Delta R(t - 118, 120, 1)$ for $\Delta R(t + 1, 120, 1)$. Lagging the data removes 118 observations from the beginning of the sample, and leading the data removes 119 observations from the end of the sample. Hence, a total of 337 observations in the overall sample cannot be used in the estimation for this choice of instruments.

An alternative choice is to use the yield on a maturity adjacent to $R(t, n, 1)$ as an instrument, and adjacent to $R(t, n, 1)$ in the general case. This should satisfy the criterion of being correlated with the regressor while not being directly correlated with $\varepsilon(t, n, 1)$, or $\varepsilon(t, n, m)$ in general. For example, use $R(t, 120, 2)$ as an instrument for $R(t, 120, 1)$.

In order to calculate consistent test statistics we have to take into account the moving average process in $\varphi(t, m)$. Following Hansen and Hodrick (1980) and Newey and West (1987) 'robust' standard errors and test statistics are calculated – see Chapter 5 for details.

(3) *Does the actual spread forecast the perfect foresight spread?* A third way of assessing the data consistency of (11.18) first requires some minor rearrangement. Substitute in (11.18) for the definition of the perfect foresight spread from (11.15) to obtain:

$$S(t, n, m) = PFS(t, n, m) + \varphi(t, m) + L(t, m)$$
$$(11.19)$$

Suppose, for simplicity, that the term premia are constant so that $L(t, m) = \alpha_{m0}$ for all t, then (11.19) can be interpreted as either:

$$S(t, n, m) = \alpha_{m0} + \alpha_{m1} PFS(t, n, m) + \varphi(t, m)$$
$$(11.20)$$

with $\alpha_{m1} = 1$ according to EH + REH; or

$$PFS(t, n, m) = \beta_{m0} + \beta_{m1} S(t, n, m) + \varphi^*(t, m)$$
$$(11.21)$$

with $\beta_{m1} = 1$. Even if $L(t, m)$ is not a constant, provided it is stationary and cannot itself be modelled, for example as a function of other variables, the bivariate regression interpretation of (11.20) and (11.21) can be maintained. Campbell and Shiller (1991), Cuthbertson (1996b) and Cuthberston et al. (1996) estimate (11.21) rather than (11.20) in testing whether $\beta_{m1} = 1$. The reason for this is that as noted above $\varphi(t, m)$ and $PFS(t, n, m)$ are correlated, with the implication that the OLS estimator of α_{m1} in (11.20) will be inconsistent. Equation (11.21) is a CEF whereas (11.20) is not. In (11.21)

the spread $S(t, n, m)$ is a variable dated at t which is uncorrelated with future innovations (expectations errors) and OLS is consistent. As in estimating the lead weights, the standard errors and test statistics are robust, calculated using Newey and West's (1987) correction for a moving average process of order $[(n - m) - 1]$.

The differences and connections between the tests in (2) and (3) are as follows. The test in (2) involves $k - 1$ restrictions and completely specifies the lead weights according to the null hypothesis $w_i = 1 - i/k$. If this null hypothesis is consistent with the data then (11.20) and (11.21) are satisfied with $\alpha_{m1} = \beta_{m1} = 1$. The alternative hypothesis in this set-up is $H_a: w_i \neq 1 - i/k$ for at least one value of i. The test statistic will be distributed as χ^2 with $k - 1$ degrees of freedom (equal to the number of restrictions) under the null hypothesis. The test in (3) is a 1 degree of freedom test in which the null hypothesis is $\beta_{m1} = 1$ and the alternative hypothesis is $\beta_{m1} \neq 1$. If the null hypothesis is consistent with the data then the implication is that $w_i = 1 - i/k$ is consistent with the data. The alternative hypothesis in (3) is 1 rather than $k - 1$ dimensional, it only allows the lead weights to differ from $w_i = 1 - i/k$ by a scale factor, while maintaining the linear pattern. Hence, it will be more powerful than the test in (2) if that is indeed the direction in which the alternative departs from the null, and given a sufficiently large sample this should be detected by the test in (3).

Since the alternative hypothesis in (3) maintains the linear pattern it is actually a constrained version of $w_i = a_{m0} + a_{m1}i$, with $a_{m0} = \alpha_{m1}$ and $a_{m1} = -\alpha_{m1}/k$. To see this note that the pattern $w_i = 1 - i/k$ corresponds to $a_{m0} = 1$ and $a_{m1} = -1/k$, hence if the lead weights are scaled by α_{m1} then $a_0 = \alpha_{m1}$ and $a_{m1} = -\alpha_{m1}/k$. For example, suppose with $k = 3$ the lead weights are 0.5 and 0.25, rather than the 2/3 and 1/3 as required by the expectations model, then $\alpha_{m1} = 0.75$, $\beta_{m1} = 4/3$, $a_{m0} = 0.75$ and $a_{m1} = -0.25$, and given a sufficiently large sample this should be detected by the test in (3). The alternative hypothesis in (3) maintains the linear pattern but differs in the scale factor. In the example the test in (2) has $k - 1 = 3 - 1 = 2$, rather than 1, degrees of freedom because it *also* allows the lead weights to differ from the linear pattern. When $k - 1 = 1$, that is when $k = 2$, the null and alternative hypotheses in tests (2) and (3) are identical and just reformulations of each other. However, in a particular empirical situation the test statistics are likely to differ because estimation of (11.18) requires an instrumental variables procedure while (11.21) can be consistently estimated by OLS.

The subsequent sections deal in turn with the data (**11.4.2**), its definition and characteristics (**11.4.3**); unit root tests on the yields (**11.4.4**); a graphical analysis of the spreads (**11.4.5**) and unit root tests on the spreads (**11.4.6**); estimation of the expectations model and hypothesis testing (**11.4.7**); and estimation of the bivariate regression of the perfect foresight spread on the actual spread (**11.4.8**).

11.4.2   The data

Chapter 1 emphasised the need to match the theoretical constructs of a particular economic model with corresponding empirical variables. This is particularly relevant in this case. The development of the expectations model of the term structure (and this will also be true for other models) makes central reference to bills or bonds that are alike except in one respect: that is their term to maturity. It is important, therefore, to use data that matches this concept. Further, the yield curve, that is the relationship between the rates of return on bills or bonds which differ only in their maturity, has been constructed here on the basis of bills or bonds with a zero coupon. It is important not to mix data on yields where those yields relate to financial instruments that differ in characteristics, apart from their maturity. Thus, it would be incorrect to assess models of the term structure using rates from a mixture of financial instruments some of which are zero-coupon bonds and some of which pay a coupon (coupon bearing).

The data used here is due to McCulloch (1990 and unpublished updates) and measures the yield on zero-coupon (that is pure discount) US T-Bills and T-Bonds. The complete dataset comprises maturities of 1, 2, 3, 4, 5, 6 and 9 and 12 months, and 2, 3, 4, 5 and 10 years, although only a subset of that data is used here. It is important to note that this data is appropriate for an empirical assessment of the expectations model of the yield curve as it relates to bills and bonds which only differ in their maturity.

To illustrate the shape of the yield curve Figure 11.1 graphs the yield curves for 1950m1, 1960m1, 1990m1 and, in addition, the average yield curve for the complete sample of 1946m12 through to 1991m2. The average yield curve demonstrates that yields tend to increase the longer the term to maturity. Particular yield curves do not always display this pattern; for example, that for 1960m1 shows a decline in yields with the longer dated maturities, and the yield curve is downward sloping in the latter part of its range. However, the yield curves for 1950m1 and 1990m1 do conform to the average pattern. The question being addressed to this chapter is whether an expectations model of the term structure can account for the slope of

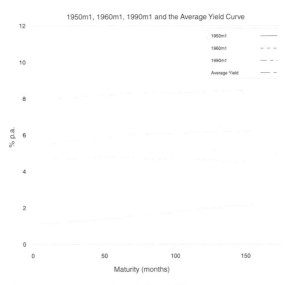

Figure 11.1   *Examples of the yield curve*

the yield curve. There are several aspects to this assessment which are now considered.

11.4.3 A graphical analysis of the data: yields

The first stage in our empirical assessment is to consider the order of integration of the yield series. A useful preliminary analysis and 'feel' for the properties of the data can be obtained by plotting the time series. The sample period is December 1946 through to February 1991 and the frequency of the data is monthly so that

there are 531 observations in the full sample. The dataset for this study comprises the yields on T-Bills of 1-, 6- and 12-month maturities and the yields on T-Bonds of 5- and 10-year maturities. The time series characteristics of the data are illustrated in Figures 11.2A to 11.2D with the yields of the four shorter maturities plotted alongside the yield on the 10-year T-Bond. All the series share the same general pattern of trending upwards until about 1985 with a broad decline thereafter. Overall the pattern is consistent with each of the processes exhibiting a stochastic trend. There are some differences

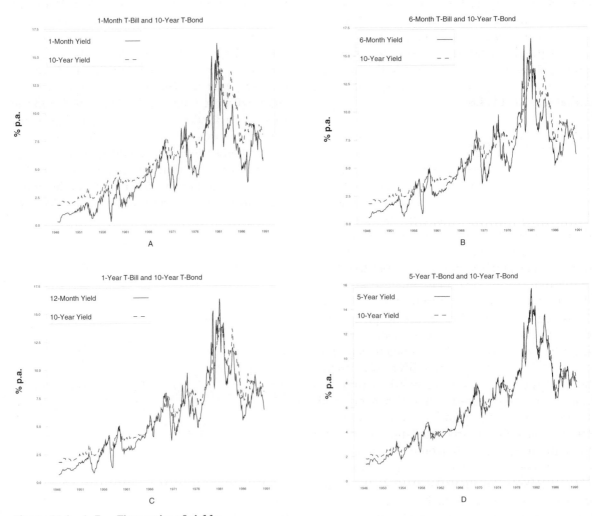

Figure 11.2 A–D – *Time series of yields*

though among the series that can be seen on the figures; for example, the yields on the shorter-term maturities tend to be more volatile than those on the longer-term maturities.

A process with a stochastic trend will contain at least 1 unit root – see Chapter 6; if there is just 1 unit root in a series the first difference of that series should not show any stochastic trend – or random walk behaviour. To examine this for the yield series, the first differences are graphed in Figures 11.3A to 11.3D, plotting each of the shorter maturities alongside the first difference of the yield on the 10-year T-Bond. The figures

show a very clear pattern of mean reversion for each series; that is there is no tendency for the first differences of the yields to wander in a random walk pattern; on the contrary there is a frequent crossing of the mean which is a pattern consistent with I(0) series. Examining the standard set of statistical tests assesses these conclusions more formally.

11.4.4 Unit root tests on the yields

The standard set of test statistics to determine the number of unit roots in the yield series is

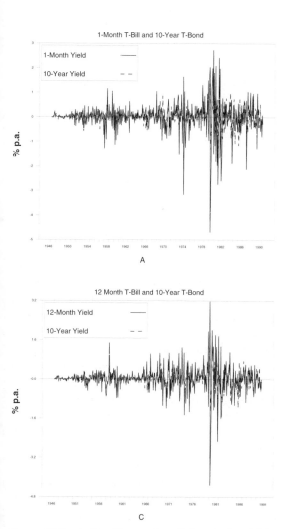

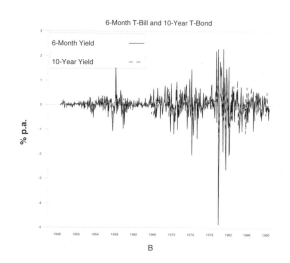

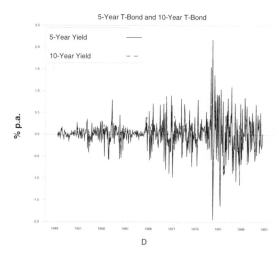

Figure 11.3 A–D – *Time series of changes in yields*

Table 11.1 *Unit root tests for yields*

Variable	Model	$\hat{\tau}$	Test statistics for 2 unit roots Φ_1	$\hat{\tau}_\mu$	$\hat{\mu}$	$\hat{\tau}_\beta$	$\hat{\beta}$	Φ_3
$R(t, 1)$	ADF(21)	-8.742	38.222	-8.751	0.013	-8.761	0.000	38.394
$R(t, 6)$	ADF(19)	-4.959	12.346	-4.972	0.010	-4.997	0.000	12.514
$R(t, 12)$	ADF(11)	-6.385	21.656	-6.586	0.011	-6.606	0.000	21.832
$R(t, 60)$	ADF(1)	-17.192	147.673	-17.202	0.012	-17.204	0.000	147.989
$R(t, 120)$	ADF(1)	-16.513	136.473	-16.536	0.012	-16.538	0.000	136.761

Variable	Model	$\hat{\tau}$	Test statistics for 1 unit uoot Φ_1	$\hat{\tau}_\mu$	$\hat{\mu}$	$\hat{\tau}_\beta$	$\hat{\beta}$	Φ_3
$R(t, 1)$	ADF(21)	-0.441	1.731	-1.772	0.091	-2.682	0.000	3.714
$R(t, 6)$	ADF(19)	-0.643	2.165	-2.033	0.090	-3.041	0.000	4.800
$R(t, 12)$	ADF(11)	-0.547	1.930	-1.905	0.081	-2.761	0.000	3.985
$R(t, 60)$	ADF(1)	-0.197	1.670	-1.689	0.059	-2.533	0.000	3.374
$R(t, 120)$	ADF(1)	0.098	1.444	-1.461	0.047	-2.110	0.000	2.400

Critical values		$T = 570$	$p = 20$			$T = 570$	$p = 1$		
	$\hat{\tau}$	$\hat{\tau}_\mu$	$\hat{\tau}_\beta$	Φ_1	Φ_3	$\hat{\tau}$	$\hat{\tau}_\mu$	$\hat{\tau}_\beta$	Φ_1	Φ_3
5%	-1.921	-2.837	-3.379	4.464	6.238	-1.933	-2.860	-3.412	4.464	6.238
10%	-1.599	-2.546	-3.096	3.803	5.321	-1.609	-2.567	-3.125	3.803	5.321

Critical values of $\hat{\tau}$, $\hat{\tau}_\mu$ and $\hat{\tau}_\beta$ obtained using Cheng-Lai response surface coefficients; critical values of Φ_1 and Φ_3 obtained by simulation for $T = 500$ – see Chapter 6.

reported in Table 11.1. The unit root tests indicate a uniform rejection of the null hypothesis that the yield series are I(2). Although the complete set of test statistics is reported for 2 unit roots, the estimates of $\hat{\beta}$ are uniformly insignificant and numerically virtually zero (even when normalised by the equation standard error). Anyway, the sample values of Φ_3 and $\hat{\tau}_\beta$ firmly indicate rejection of the null of 2 unit roots for all series. For example, for $R(t, 1)$, $\Phi_3 = 38.394$, compared to a 5% critical value of approximately 6.238, and $\hat{\tau}_\beta = -8.761$ compared to a 5% critical value of approximately -3.379. Dropping the time trend does not alter these conclusions. The sample values of $\hat{\tau}_\mu$ are significant; for example, for $R(t, 1)$, $\hat{\tau}_\mu = -8.751$ compared to the 5% critical value of approximately -2.837. There is again no ambiguity in rejecting the null hypothesis of 2 unit roots. In each case the estimated constant, $\hat{\mu}$, is not significant, whether evaluated under the null (that is imposing the unit root) or in the maintained regression;

coupled with the significant values of Φ_1, this suggests rejection of the (second) unit root. Finally, in this context, note that dropping the time trend and then the constant leaves the test statistics virtually unaltered, suggesting that the inclusion of a trend and/or constant is not necessary. The unit root test statistics point to rejection of the null of 2 unit roots, so it is now appropriate to turn to testing the null hypothesis of 1 unit root.

The test statistics for 1 unit root are straightforward: the results are consistent with each of the series having 1 unit root. First note that again there is no suggestion that a deterministic time trend is needed. In passing note that the sample values of Φ_3 and $\hat{\tau}_\beta$ are not significant. Neither are the sample values of $\hat{\tau}_\mu$ and Φ_1 significant, and they are generally well below (in absolute value) the 5% critical values. For example, for $R(t, 1)$, $\hat{\tau}_\mu = -1.772$, with $\hat{\mu} = 0.091$, compared to a 5% critical value of approximately -2.837; and $\Phi_1 = 1.731$ compared to a 5%

critical value of approximately 4.464. The values of Φ_1 suggest that there is a unit root and $\hat{\mu}$ is not significantly different from 0. We would not expect to find drift in one of the yields and not the others; drift is likely to impart a sustained direction to the yield series, which would be an uncomfortable, and counterfactual, implication over a long period.

In evaluating test statistics for a unit root, it may be tempting just to look at the test statistics; however, it is also of interest to know whether the root is numerically close to 1 – see Harvey (1997). To illustrate in this case, the maintained regressions for $R(t, 60)$ are:

$$\Delta R(t, 60) = 0.059 - 0.008R(t - 1, 60)$$
$$(1.817)(-1.689)$$

$$+ 0.078\Delta R(t - 1, 60) + \hat{u}(t, 60)$$
$$(1.816)$$

'*t*' statistics in parentheses.

and with the null of a unit root imposed,

$$\Delta R(t, 60) = 0.011 + 0.076\Delta R(t - 1, 60)$$
$$(0.696) \quad (1.745)$$

$$+ \hat{u}(t, 60)$$

'*t*' statistics in parentheses.

From the first of these regressions note that $\hat{\gamma} = -0.008$, which is not numerically large; imposing the null of a unit root gives the second regression where the constant is clearly not significant.

11.4.5 A graphical analysis of the data: spreads

The next stage in an empirical evaluation of the expectations model is to consider the order of integration of the spreads. The longest spread which can be defined from the dataset is that between the 10-year bond rate and the 1-month

bill rate; denoting each, respectively, as $R(t, 120)$ and $R(t, 1)$, the spread for this long–short comparison is, therefore, denoted $S(t, 120, 1)$. The notation $S(t, 120, 6)$ is the spread between the 10-year bond rate and the 6-month rate. Thus, taking the long rate as $R(t, 120)$ the following four spreads can be defined:

$$S(t, 120, 1) \equiv R(t, 120) - R(t, 1)$$
$$S(t, 120, 6) \equiv R(t, 120) - R(t, 6)$$
$$S(t, 120, 12) \equiv R(t, 120) - R(t, 12)$$
$$S(t, 120, 60) \equiv R(t, 120) - R(t, 60)$$

Taking the long rate as $R(t, 60)$ then three spreads can be defined:

$$S(t, 60, 1) \equiv R(t, 60) - R(t, 1)$$
$$S(t, 60, 6) \equiv R(t, 60) - R(t, 6)$$
$$S(t, 60, 12) \equiv R(t, 60) - R(t, 12)$$

Taking the long rate as $R(t, 12)$, two spreads can be defined:

$$S(t, 12, 1) \equiv R(t, 12) - R(t, 1)$$
$$S(t, 12, 6) \equiv R(t, 12) - R(t, 6)$$

And, finally, taking the long rate as $R(t, 6)$, one spread can be defined:

$$S(t, 6, 1) \equiv R(t, 6) - R(t, 1)$$

In all 10 spreads can be defined from this data.

If each of these spreads is consistent with an I(0) process, this is evidence in favour of the expectations hypothesis given that the earlier tests suggested that each of the yields is consistent with an I(1) process.

A first step in this analysis is to graph the 10 spreads in Figures 11.4 and 11.5. In each case there are sufficient crossings of their respective means to suggest that the series are not I(1). This is so even though for some relative short sample periods there is some 'local' wandering. This

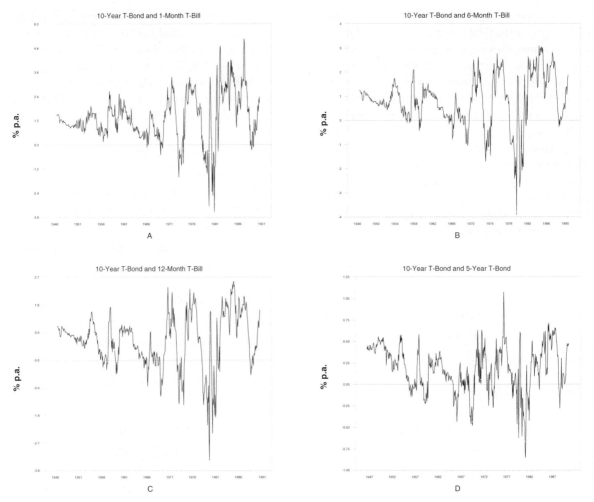

Figure 11.4 **A–D – *Time series of spreads (relative to 10-year rate)***

conclusion can be assessed more formally by considering the standard set of tests for the number of unit roots in a series.

11.4.6 Unit root tests on the spreads

The test statistics to determine the number of unit roots in the spread series are reported in Table 11.2. Starting with the tests for 2 unit roots, there is a very firm rejection of the null hypothesis that the spread series are I(2). Details of these results are brief given that the inter-

pretation of these tables should by now be quite straightforward. Taking the spread between the 10-year yield and the 1-month yield, $S(t, 120, 1)$, as an example, then $\Phi_3 = 66.939$ and $\hat{\tau}_\beta = -11.570$, both firmly rejecting the null hypothesis that the series is I(2). Omitting the insignificant time trend, then $\hat{\tau}_\mu = -11.579$ with $\hat{\mu}$ not significant; then $\hat{\tau} = -11.590$, which confirms this conclusion. The picture is similar for the other spread series.

Turning to the test statistics for 1 unit root, in each case the hypothesis that the spreads are I(1) is rejected. Taking $S(t, 120, 1)$ as an example,

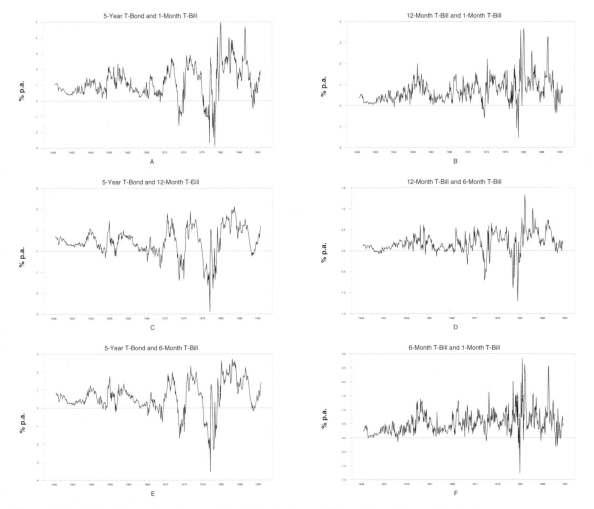

Figure 11.5 A–F – *Time series of spreads (relative to 5-year, 12-month and 6-month rates)*

$\Phi_3 = 9.586$ and $\hat{\tau}_\beta = -4.376$ compared to the 5% critical values of (approximately) 6.238 and -3.379, respectively; both indicate rejection. Then $\hat{\tau}_\mu = 4.109$, and $\hat{\mu} = 0.145$ with a 't' statistic of -3.457; the size, and significance, of $\hat{\mu}$ seems implausible as an estimate of drift, since there is not a sustained trend in the spread series. It is, however, consistent with a constant in a stationary process. To avoid repetition not all of the test statistics are evaluated here. It is evident from the table that the conclusion is the same for the other spread series, with differences being ones of degree rather than kind.

11.4.7 Estimation of the spread equations

So far the empirical evidence is in favour of the view that each of the yields is consistent with an I(1) process, and further that each of the spreads is consistent with an I(0) process. This is support for the expectations view of the term structure; but two more stringent tests were outlined in Section **11.4.1**. The first of these is given by an empirical assessment of the precise way in which each spread is related to the expected change in the short rate. It might be helpful to

Table 11.2 *Unit root tests for spreads*

Variable	Model	$\hat{\tau}$	Φ_1	$\hat{\tau}_\mu$	$\hat{\mu}$	$\hat{\tau}_\beta$	$\hat{\beta}$	Φ_3
			Test statistics for 2 unit roots					
$S(t, 6, 1)$	ADF(21)	−8.662	32.430	−8.654	0.002	−8.687	0.000	37.737
$S(t, 12, 1)$	ADF(19)	−8.179	33.390	−8.171	0.002	−8.182	0.000	33.472
$S(t, 60, 1)$	ADF(6)	−11.815	69.677	−11.803	0.002	−11.792	0.000	69.539
$S(t, 120, 1)$	ADF(6)	−11.590	66.913	−11.579	0.001	−11.570	0.000	66.939
$S(t, 12, 6)$	ADF(9)	−9.762	47.561	−9.752	0.000	−9.743	0.000	47.470
$S(t, 60, 6)$	ADF(21)	−5.691	16.169	−5.685	0.001	−5.694	0.000	16.254
$S(t, 120, 6)$	ADF(19)	−5.816	16.855	−5.809	0.001	−5.805	0.000	16.899
$S(t, 60, 12)$	ADF(19)	−5.507	15.139	−5.500	0.001	−5.496	0.000	15.150
$S(t, 120, 12)$	ADF(8)	−8.940	39.811	−8.932	0.002	−8.930	0.000	39.878
$S(t, 120, 60)$	ADF(6)	−11.296	63.558	−11.285	0.000	−11.286	0.000	63.689
			Test statistics for 1 unit root					
$S(t, 6, 1)$	ADF(17)	−1.513	7.751	−3.934	0.124	−4.840	0.000	11.823
$S(t, 12, 1)$	ADF(12)	−6.847	10.063	−4.485	0.139	−5.337	0.000	14.269
$S(t, 60, 1)$	ADF(18)	−2.198	9.162	−4.278	0.150	−4.726	0.000	11.168
$S(t, 120, 1)$	ADF(14)	−2.200	8.451	−4.109	0.145	−4.376	0.000	9.586
$S(t, 12, 6)$	ADF(16)	−3.213	9.442	−4.345	0.030	−4.717	0.000	11.129
$S(t, 60, 6)$	ADF(20)	−2.726	7.885	−3.970	0.059	−4.167	0.000	8.712
$S(t, 120, 6)$	ADF(19)	−2.978	9.867	−4.441	0.081	−4.572	0.000	10.512
$S(t, 60, 12)$	ADF(17)	−3.577	11.799	−4.850	0.049	−4.958	0.000	12.342
$S(t, 120, 12)$	ADF(17)	−3.247	10.395	−4.558	0.065	−4.606	0.000	10.684
$S(t, 120, 60)$	ADF(3)	−3.945	12.807	−4.961	0.021	−4.945	0.000	12.299

Note: For critical values see Table 11.1.

recap some relevant details here with a simple example. The long and short rates are taken, respectively, as those on the 10-year T-Bond and the 1-year T-Bill; then the spread between these rates, working in units of months, should be,

$$S(t, 120, 12) = 0.9E_t\{\Delta R(t + 12, 12)\}$$
$$+ 0.8E_t\{\Delta R(t + 24, 12)\}$$
$$+ 0.7E_t\{\Delta R(t + 36, 12)\}$$
$$+ 0.6E_t\{\Delta R(t + 48, 12)\}$$
$$+ 0.5E_t\{\Delta R(t + 60, 12)\}$$
$$+ 0.4E_t\{\Delta R(t + 72, 12)\}$$
$$+ 0.3E_t\{\Delta R(t + 84, 12)\}$$
$$+ 0.2E_t\{\Delta R(t + 96, 12)\}$$
$$+ 0.1E_t\{\Delta R(t + 108, 12)\}$$
$$+ L(t, 12) \qquad (11.22)$$

where

$$\Delta R(t + 12, 12) \equiv R(t + 12, 12) - R(t, 12)$$
$$\Delta R(t + 24, 12) \equiv R(t + 24, 12)$$
$$- R(t + 12, 12)$$

and so on. This equation says that the spread is a particular weighted combination of the lead changes in the short rate. The weights decline linearly from 0.9 on the nearest change to 0.1 on the most distant change. Replacing $E_t\{\Delta R(t + 12i, 12)\}$ with $\Delta R(t + 12i, 12)$ using the rational expectations hypothesis of equation (11.16) adds in the composite weighted average error $\varphi(t, m)$ and (11.22) becomes:

$$S(t, 120, 12) = 0.9\Delta R(t + 12, 12)$$
$$+ 0.8\Delta R(t + 24, 12)$$
$$+ 0.7\Delta R(t + 36, 12)$$

$$+ 0.6\Delta R(t + 48, 12)$$
$$+ 0.5\Delta R(t + 60, 12)$$
$$+ 0.4\Delta R(t + 72, 12)$$
$$+ 0.3\Delta R(t + 84, 12)$$
$$+ 0.2\Delta R(t + 96, 12)$$
$$+ 0.1\Delta R(t + 108, 12)$$
$$+ \varphi(t, 12) + L(t, 12) \quad (11.23)$$

There are really two hypotheses embodied in the constraints that the lead weights are generated according to the expectations model. The first is that the weights decline linearly; that is plotting the weights against time would reveal that they lie exactly on a straight line. To model this general possibility set:

$$w_i = a_0 + a_1 i \quad \text{for } i = 1, \ldots, k - 1$$

which imposes a linear pattern in the lead weights. In this scheme there are just two coefficients, a_0 and a_1, to be estimated compared to the $k - 1$ coefficients when the lead weights are freely estimated. The linear pattern, therefore, imposes $(k - 1) - 2 = k - 3$ restrictions which can be tested with a χ^2 test with $k - 3$ degrees of freedom in the usual way. The second hypothesis is that given that the weights decline linearly then their pattern of decline is: $w_1 = 1 - (1/k)$, $w_2 = 1 - (2/k)$, $w_3 = 1 - (3/k)$, $\ldots, w_{k-1} = 1/k$, where k is the maturity of the long-rate bond as a multiple of the maturity of the short-rate bond. This pattern completely specifies the $k - 1$ lead weights and hence imposes $k - 1$ restrictions on the freely estimated model, which can be tested with a χ^2 test with $k - 1$ degrees of freedom.

To assess the empirical support for this aspect of the expectations theory of the term structure all possible combinations in the sample were estimated with $n/m \equiv k$ an integer. This gave rise to the following spread combinations: $S(t, 6, 1)$, $S(t, 12, 1)$, $S(t, 60, 1)$ and $S(t, 120, 1)$; $S(t, 12, 6)$, $S(t, 60, 6)$, and $S(t, 120, 6)$; $S(t, 60, 12)$ and $S(t, 120, 12)$; and finally $S(t, 120, 60)$. These were each estimated as a linear combination of

the lead changes in the respective short rates. The first stage of estimation is simply to estimate without any restrictions on the lead weights: these are the 'freely estimated' coefficients. We then restrict the lead weights, first according to the pattern $w_i = a_0 + a_1 i$; and then according to the pattern $w_i = 1 - i/k$, at each stage calculating an appropriate test statistic.

In the first stage an appropriate null hypothesis is that the $k - 1$ lead weights are simultaneously equal to zero, the alternative being that they are not equal to zero. In the second stage the null hypothesis $w_i = a_0 + a_1 i$ can be assessed against the alternative that the lead weights are unrestricted. To see whether this null hypothesis is consistent with the data a $\chi^2(k - 3)$ test statistic is calculated for each case. For example, in the case of the spread equation $S(t, 120, 12)$ the χ^2 statistic will have $10 - 3$ degrees of freedom. The next test statistic is for the null hypothesis $w_i = 1 - i/k$, against the alternative that the lead weights are unrestricted. In this case the χ^2 statistic will have $k - 1$ degrees of freedom, so that apart from a constant the regression is completely specified under the null hypothesis.

The spread equations are estimated using an instrumental variables procedure and the robust standard errors option to take account of the moving average error. Recall from section **11.4.1** and equation (11.19) that $\varphi(t, m)$ and

$$PFS(t, n, m) = \sum_{i=1}^{k-1} w_i \Delta R(t + im, m)$$

are correlated, with the implication that the OLS estimators of the lead weights will be inconsistent. The chosen instruments were adjacent yields: $\Delta R(t, 2)$ for $\Delta R(t, 1)$; $\Delta R(t, 5)$ for $\Delta R(t, 6)$; $\Delta R(t, 11)$ for $\Delta R(t, 12)$; and $\Delta R(t, 12)$ for $\Delta R(t, 60)$.

The freely estimated coefficients from the spread equations $S(t, 120, 1)$, $S(t, 120, 6)$ and $S(t, 120, 12)$ are graphed in Figures 11.6A to 11.6C; those for $S(t, 60, 1)$, $S(t, 60, 6)$ and $S(t, 60, 12)$ in Figures 11.7A to 11.7C; and those for $S(t, 12, 1)$ and $S(t, 6, 1)$ in Figures 11.8A

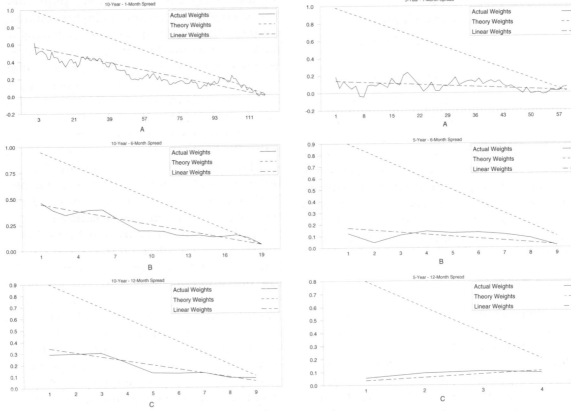

Figure 11.6 A–C – *Lead weights from the spread equation (relative to 10-year rate)*

Figure 11.7 A–C – *Lead weights from the spread equation (relative to 5-year rate)*

and 11.8B. In each case the theoretical weights $w_i = 1 - i/k$, $i = 1, \ldots, k - 1$, are also plotted as well as the linearly restricted weights, $w_i = a_0 + a_1 i$. Considering Figure 11.6 first, the freely estimated weights decline in a roughly monotonic way, a pattern which is more closely conformed to for $S(t, 120, 6)$ and $S(t, 120, 12)$, although they are usually below the theoretical weights. Generally, the lead weights decline linearly, but not in the way predicted by the expectations theory. Turning to Figure 11.7, observe that the freely estimated coefficients are below the theory weights, and substantially so in most cases. In Figures 11.7B and 11.7C the freely estimated coefficients and linearly restricted weights appear reasonably close. The picture is much the same in Figures 11.8A and

11.8B, where there is little similarity in the pattern of theory weights and the freely estimated coefficients.

The test statistics for the hypotheses are reported in Table 11.3. In the top half of the table the values of the $\chi^2(k - 1)$ test statistics are reported, with a large value of the test statistic leading to rejection of the null hypothesis: $w_i = 1 - i/k$. In all 10 cases this is rejected without qualification; for example, the χ^2 statistic for the spread equation $S(t, 120, 1)$ is $\chi^2(119) = 267{,}678$ which has a marginal significance level of zero. The conclusion is unequivocally the same for the other nine equations.

In the lower half of Table 11.3 the $\chi^2(k - 3)$ test statistics are reported, with a large value of the test statistic leading to rejection of the null

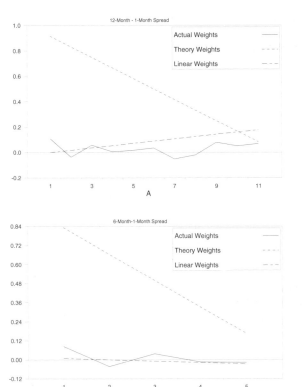

Figure 11.8   A and B – *Lead weights from the spread equation (relative to 12-month rate)*

hypothesis $w_0 = a_0 + a_i i$. (Note that since $k = 2$ in the equations for $S(t, 12, 6)$ and $S(t, 120, 60)$, there are no restrictions to be tested in these cases.) First, consider the spread equations with the 1-month short rate. That is the first column of results in this part of the table. The null hypothesis is not rejected at the 5% level for the spread $S(t, 6, 1)$ with the msl of the test statistic equal to 6.5%, whereas it is rejected for the 12-, 60- and 120-month long rates. Taking the 6-month rate as the short rate the null hypothesis is not rejected for $S(t, 60, 6)$ with the msl of the test statistic equal to 16.1%, but the null is rejected when the long rate is the 120-month rate with a test statistic of 77.286. The results for the case with the 12-month rate as the short rate are given in the final column. In both cases the null hypothesis is not rejected. The test statistics are 0.444, with msl = 80%, and 9.094,

with msl = 24.6%, where the long rate is 60 and 120 months, respectively.

In summary, on the basis of these test statistics there is no evidence to support the null hypothesis that the lead weights decline according to the pattern $w_i = 1 - i/k$. If this hypothesis is weakened to allow the weights to decline linearly there is some support from the following spreads: $S(t, 6, 1)$, $S(t, 60, 6)$, $S(t, 60, 12)$ and $S(t, 120, 12)$.

Given that there is no evidence to support the strong implication from the REH model concerning the pattern of the lead weights, what evidence is there for the weaker implication that future changes in the short rates are, at least, significant determinants of the spread? To assess this question Table 11.4 summarises some of the regression details, giving the $\bar{R}^2$ and the number of significant coefficients, judged at the 5% significance level against the one-sided alternative $w_i > 0$, expressed as a ratio of the total number of estimated lead weights.

The evidence summarised in Table 11.4 suggests that where the long rate used in defining the spread is for a relatively short maturity as with the 6- and 12-month rates, there is little evidence of a significant relationship between the spread and future changes in the short rate. For example, in the spread equation $S(t, 6, 1)$ none of the estimated coefficients are significant and $\bar{R}^2 = 0.039$. Lengthening the period of maturity of the long rate leads to improvements in $\bar{R}^2$ and in the number of significant coefficients. For example, in the equation for $S(t, 120, 1)$, $\bar{R}^2 = 0.683$ and all but the last four of the estimated lead weights are significant. The largest estimated lead weight is the first with a decline in the lead weights which although not monotonic or linear is quite regular. This suggests support for a connection between the long rate and successive short rates, even if the lead weights do not follow the predicted pattern. In the equation for $S(t, 120, 6)$ all but one of the estimated lead weights are significant at conventional significance levels, and the decline in the lead weights is regular even though it does

Table 11.3 χ^2 *tests for hypotheses on the lead weights*

| | χ^2 **test statistics**
 Theory weights: $H_0, w_i = 1 - i/k, i = 1, \ldots, k-1$ | | | |
| | | Spread equation
 Short rate | | |
$m =$ long rate	1	6	12	60
$n = 6$	$\chi^2(5) = 682$ [0.000]	–	–	–
$n = 12$	$\chi^2(11) = 1{,}003$ [0.000]	$\chi^2(1) = 715$ [0.000]	–	–
$n = 60$	$\chi^2(59) = 7{,}325$ [0.000]	$\chi^2(9) = 226$ [0.000]	$\chi^2(4) = 228$ [0.000]	–
$n = 120$	$\chi^2(119) = 267{,}678$ [0.000]	$\chi^2(19) = 5{,}450$ [0.000]	$\chi^2(9) = 1{,}120$ [0.000]	$\chi^2(1) = 1{,}664$ [0.000]
	Test statistics **Linear weights:** $H_0, w_i = a_0 + a_i i, i = 1, \ldots, k-1$			
		Spread equation Short rate		
$m =$ long rate	1	6	12	60
$n = 6$	$\chi^2(3) = 7.214$ [0.065]	–	–	–
$n = 12$	$\chi^2(9) = 21.130$ [0.000]	–	–	–
$n = 60$	$\chi^2(57) = 379.33$ [0.000]	$\chi^2(7) = 10.524$ [0.161]	$\chi^2(2) = 0.444$ [0.800]	–
$n = 120$	$\chi^2(117) = 3{,}405$ [0.000]	$\chi^2(17) = 77.286$ [0.000]	$\chi^2(7) = 9.094$ [0.246]	–

Notes: Leading the data shortens the sample period, estimation periods were as follows: $S(t, 6, 1)$, 1952m2 to 1990m9; $S(t, 12, 1)$, 1952m2 to 1990m3; $S(t, 60, 1)$, 1952m2 to 1986m3; $S(t, 120, 1)$, 1952m2 to 1981m3; $S(t, 12, 6)$, 1952m2 to 1990m8; $S(t, 60, 6)$, 1952m2 to 1986m8; $S(t, 120, 6)$, 1952m2 to 1981m8; $S(t, 60, 12)$, 1952m2 to 1987m2; $S(t, 120, 12)$ 1952m2 to 1982m2; $S(t, 120, 60)$, 1952m2 to 1986m2. Estimation method was instrumental variables using the following instruments: $\Delta R(t, 2)$ for $\Delta R(t, 1)$; $\Delta R(t, 5)$ for $\Delta R(t, 6)$; $R(t, 11)$ for $\Delta R(t, 12)$ and $\Delta R(t, 12)$ for $\Delta R(t, 60)$. All equations were estimated using the Hansen/Newey and West method of correcting the standard errors for heteroscedasticity and moving average innovation of order $n - m - 1$.

not conform to the pattern suggested by the expectations model. The picture is similar in the equation for $S(t, 120, 12)$, where all the estimated coefficients are significant. The equation is reported in Table 11.5. Notice that while the estimated lead weights are significant, the pattern is much flatter than that suggested by the expectations model with the first three weights very close to each other rather than declining monotonically – see Figure 11.6.

The last spread equation to be considered is $S(t, 120, 60)$, and if the expectations model is correct the estimated coefficient on $\Delta R(t + 60, 0)$ should be significant at around 0.5. In fact while

Table 11.4 *Estimated spread equations: summary details, $\bar{R}^2$ and the number of significant coefficients/total number of coefficients*

	Short rate			
$m =$	1	6	12	60
$n = 6$				
$\bar{R}^2$	0.039	–	–	–
significant coefficients	0/5			
$n = 12$				
$\bar{R}^2$	0.033	−0.002	–	–
significant coefficients	2/11	0/1		
$n = 60$				
$\bar{R}^2$	−0.006	0.121	0.107	–
significant coefficients	10/59	3/9	1/4	
$n = 120$				
$\bar{R}^2$	0.683	0.729	0.576	0.168
significant coefficients	115/119	18/19	9/9	1/1

Notes: Table entries for significant coefficients are: number significant/total number; significance judged at the 5% level.

Table 11.5 *Unrestricted estimation of the spread equation, S(t, 120, 12)*

Constant	$\Delta R(t + 12, 12)$	$\Delta R(t + 12, 24)$	$\Delta R(t + 12, 36)$	$\Delta R(t + 12, 48)$	$\Delta R(t + 12, 60)$
0.030	0.291	0.298	0.303	0.219	0.130
{0.257}	{5.549}	{5.945}	{7.539}	{5.468}	{3.497}
	$\Delta R(t + 12, 72)$	$\Delta R(t + 12, 84)$	$\Delta R(t + 12, 96)$	$\Delta R(t + 12, 108)$	
	0.126	0.128	0.084	0.079	
	{4.038}	{4.143}	{2.438}	{2.027}	

$\bar{R}^2 = 0.576$; $\hat{\sigma} = 0.573$.

Note: Sample period, 1952m2 to 1982m2; instrumental variables estimation; robust 't' statistics in {.} parentheses, with moving average error of order $120 - 12 - 1 = 107$.

the estimated coefficient is significant, with a robust 't' statistic of 12.717, at 0.049 it is a long way from its theoretical value so there is little support for the expectations model from this spread equation.

11.4.8 Bivariate regressions: the perfect foresight spread

The third way of assessing the expectations model, detailed in section **11.4.1**, is to estimate the bivariate regression in which the perfect foresight spread is regressed on a constant and the yield spread. Such a regression is possible for combinations of n and m in the dataset where n is an integer multiple of m, where n is the 'long' rate and m is the 'short' rate in the spread $S(t, n, m)$. Campbell and Shiller (1991) present a detailed table with results for all possible combinations available in the McCulloch dataset using a shorter sample period than the one we use. Here the regression results are reported

Table 11.6 *Regression of perfect foresight spread, PFS(t, n, m), on actual spread, S(t, n, m) for selected values of n and m. (Estimates from Campbell and Shiller's data period in column (i); longer data period in column (ii))*

| | m | | | | | | | |
| | 1 | | 6 | | 12 | | 60 | |
	(i)	(ii)	(i)	(ii)	(i)	(ii)	(i)	(ii)
$n = 6$								
constant	−0.109	−0.155						
robust s.e.	{0.077}	{0.070}						
slope	0.235	0.320						
robust s.e.	{0.166}	{0.146}						
R^2	0.015	0.032						
$H_0 : \beta_{m1} = 1$								
$\chi^2(1)$	21.080							
[msl]	[0.000]							
$n = 12$								
constant	−0.066	−0.140	0.021	0.015				
robust s.e.	{0.148}	{0.135}	{0.085}	{0.081}				
slope	0.161	0.272	0.037	0.093				
robust s.e.	{0.227}	{0.208}	{0.330}	{0.303}				
R^2	0.007	0.024	0.000	0.001				
$H_0 : \beta_{m1} = 1$								
$\chi^2(1)$	13.545	12.218	8.524	8.935				
[msl]	[0.000]	[0.000]	[0.000]	[0.000]				
$n = 60$								
constant	−0.617	−0.270	−0.032	−0.041	0.121	0.083		
robust s.e.	{0.136}	{0.094}	{0.171}	{0.151}	{0.403}	{0.229}		
slope	1.233	0.511	1.244	0.612	1.128	0.558		
robust s.e.	{0.182}	{0.411}	{0.161}	{0.383}	{0.167}	{0.302}		
R^2	0.363	0.078	0.318	0.090	0.228	0.061		
$H_0 : \beta_{m1} = 1$								
$\chi^2(1)$	1.643	1.414	2.287	1.018	0.586	2.138		
[msl]	[0.200]	[0.334]	[0.130]	[0.312]	[0.444]	[0.144]		
$n = 120$								
constant	0.040	−0.352	0.600	0.253	0.726	0.345	0.335	0.111
robust s.e.	{0.228}	{0.232}	{0.282}	{0.214}	{0.276}	{0.212}	{0.199}	{0.384}
slope	1.157	1.402	1.227	1.567	1.273	1.618	2.794	2.289
robust s.e.	{0.094}	{0.146}	{0.100}	{0.167}	{0.114}	{0.195}	{0.961}	{1.003}
R^2	0.649	0.691	0.619	0.688	0.556	0.551	0.370	0.197
$H_0 : \beta_{m1} = 1$								
$\chi^2(1)$	2.824	7.499	5.109	11.552	5.776	10.098	3.487	2.252
[msl]	[0.093]	[0.006]	[0.028]	[0.000]	[0.016]	[0.001]	[0.062]	[0.112]

continued

for all the possible combinations relevant to the sub-set of the McCulloch data; these combinations serve to illustrate the general principles involved in estimation, testing and evaluation. To ensure comparability, estimates for Campbell and Shiller's (*op. cit.*) data period of 1952m1 to 1987m2 are also reported in the columns labelled (i) in Table 11.6, as well as, in the columns labelled (ii), the longer sample period used here that adds a further 4 years of data. For

Table 11.6 *(continued)*

	Summary of rejections, ×, and nonrejections, ✓							
				m				
	1		6		12		60	
	(i)	(ii)	(i)	(ii)	(i)	(ii)	(i)	(ii)
$n = 6$	×	×						
$n = 12$	×	×	×	×				
$n = 60$	✓	✓	✓	✓	✓	✓		
$n = 120$	✓	×	×	×	×	×	×	✓

Notes: robust standard errors are given in {.} parentheses beneath coefficients rather than 't' statistics (because we are interested in the null hypothesis $\beta_{m1} = 1$); estimation assumes a moving average error of order $n - m - 1$, see Chapter 5 and Campbell and Shiller (1991), Cuthbertson *et al.* (1996) and Hansen and Hodrick (1980). Marginal significance levels of test statistic $\chi^2(1)$ for $H_0 : \beta_{m1} = 1$ given in [.]. The last month of the shorter sample period, that is (i), allowing for leads with all samples starting in 1952m1 was: 1977m3 for $S(t, 120, 1)$, 1977m9 for $S(t, 120, 6)$, 1978m1 for $S(t, 120, 12)$ and 1982m1 for $S(t, 120, 60)$; 1982m3 for $S(t, 60, 1)$, 1982m8 for $S(t, 60, 6)$, and 1983m12 for $S(t, 60, 12)$; 1986m3 for $S(t, 12, 1)$ and 1986m8 for $S(t, 12, 6)$; and 1986m10 for $S(t, 6, 1)$. The longer sample period, indicated as (ii) in the table, added 4 years of data to each sample.
  × and ✓ *judged at 5% significance level.*

convenience the relevant regression equation is reproduced below:

$$PFS(t, n, m) = \beta_{m0} + \beta_{m1} S(t, n, m) + \varphi^*(t, m) \tag{11.24}$$

For the shorter sample period the estimates of β_{m1} are very close to those reported in Campbell and Shiller (1991, Table 2). While there are some changes in the estimated coefficients between the two sample periods the same broad conclusion, although with an exception which is noted below, emerges in both cases. Judging by the $\chi^2(1)$ test statistics for the hypothesis that $\beta_{m1} = 1$ against the two-sided alternative, there is no evidence, using the short maturities of 6 months and 12 months to define the yield spread, that $\beta_{m1} = 1$ as required by the REH model of the term structure. For convenience a summary table follows the main table in which the null hypothesis is judged at the 5% significance level, a tick, ✓, indicating nonrejection and a cross, ×, rejection of the null hypothesis. The picture is similar if the longest rate in the sample, the 10-year rate, is used to define the yield spread. In the longer sample, with the

spread between the 10-year and 5-year yields, there is some evidence in favour of the REH view at these maturities. In that case while the test statistic is not significant the estimate of β_{m1} is 2.289, which is a long way from 1, and the hypothesis that $\beta_{m1} = 1$ is effectively rescued by a large standard error.

The spread, which appears to find some favour with the REH view, is where the long rate is the 5-year rate. In all such cases, $S(t, 60, 1)$, $S(t, 60, 6)$ and $S(t, 60, 12)$, the null hypothesis is not rejected at the 5% level or better. However, even here, for the longer sample, the nonrejection of $\beta_{m1} = 1$ has to be qualified: in each case the estimate of β_{m1} is less than 2 standard errors away from 0. The estimates are too imprecise relative to their standard errors to offer convincing evidence either way, although they are closer to 1 than to unity.

Note from Table 11.6 that estimates of β_{m1} for the yield spreads with the 12-month rate as the long rate tend to be below 1, whereas when the 10-year rate is used the estimates tend to be above 1. Broadly speaking the switch point tends to be when the 5-year rate is used as the long rate.

Although, comparing the two sample periods, the broad conclusion is the same there is a difference worth mentioning. The forecast power of the spread for changes in the short rates taking the 5-year rate as the long rate, the case most favourable to the EH + REH view, is much less for the longer sample period. For example, whereas with $n = 60$ and $m = 1$ the estimated slope coefficient is 1.233 for the shorter sample period, this estimate falls to 0.511 when 4 years of data are added.

11.5 Other studies and other methods of testing the expectations model

There have been a number of studies concerned with assessing theories of the term structure of interest rates. Recently, in large part due to the work of Shiller (1979, 1989) and Campbell and Shiller (1987, 1991), the dominant hypothesis has been the combination of the expectations hypothesis and the rational expectations hypothesis, denoted EH + REH. With different conclusions emerging from different empirical studies, and sometimes differences within a study depending on the method of evaluation. It should be clear from the discussion in section **11.4.1** that there is more than one way of evaluating the EH + REH view of the term structure. The purpose of section **11.5.1** is to summarise the methods of section **11.4.1,** and add to them the results and methods of other studies; and in section **11.5.2** suggest some explanations where the expectations model has not been found to be consistent with the data.

11.5.1 Methods and results

(1) *If the rates* R(t, m) *for* m = 1, . . . , n *are* I(1) *then the spreads* S(t, n, m) *should be* I(0). This is a necessary but not sufficient condition for the EH + REH to be valid. There are two methods of assessing this implication depending on

whether the spreads are considered separately (a univariate approach) or jointly (a multivariate approach). In this chapter each spread was assessed separately using the standard augmented Dickey–Fuller (univariate) techniques of Chapter 6; alternatively, using more advanced techniques due to Johansen (1988), see Chapters 14 and 15, the spreads can be assessed jointly.

Using separate tests MacDonald and Speight (1988) with UK data on 5-, 10- and 20-year government bonds found that they could not reject the hypothesis that the spreads were I(0); similarly Taylor (1992) with UK data on 3-month Treasury Bills and Treasury Bonds of 10, 15 and 20 years' maturity rejected the hypothesis that the spreads were I(1) in favour of the hypothesis that they were I(0). In contrast, using multivariate techniques Hall *et al.* (1992) with data on US Treasury Bills with 1 to 11 months to maturity found that they could reject the null hypothesis that the spreads were I(0). Two possible explanations for this rejection were offered: not all but some of the spreads are I(0); rejection of the I(0) hypothesis is caused by changes in monetary regimes over the sample period (1970m3 to 1988m12). The sample period includes the possible change in regime period of October 1979 to September 1982 when the Federal Reserve's 'new operating procedures' led to increased volatility in short-term rates, a feature that is evident in Figure 11.2. As to the first explanation Hall *et al.* (*op. cit.*) found that the evidence is most favourable when only pairs of interest rates are considered separately; for example, using the 1-month rate as the short rate and, successively, the 2- through to the 11-month rate as the long rate in defining the spread, Hall *et al.* (*op. cit.*) found in favour of I(0) for seven out of ten cases. As to the explanation that regime changes lead to rejection, using the four shortest rates Hall *et al.* (*op. cit.*) found that in the two sample periods either side of the October 1979 regime change there was nonrejection of the null hypothesis that the spreads were I(0); however, there was rejection for the sample period 1979m10 to 1982m9.

(2)   *The spread predicts future changes in the short rates.* Regressions of the perfect foresight spread on the actual spread, that is:

$$PFS(t, n, m) = \beta_{m0} + \beta_{m1}S(t, n, m) + \varphi^*(t, m)$$

where

$$PFS(t, n, m) = \sum_{i=1}^{k-1} w_i R(t + im, m)$$

should give an estimate of β_{m1} not significantly different from 1. Campbell and Shiller's results for the sample period 1952m1 to 1987m2 led them to the conclusion that 'At this short end of the term structure (where the longer-term bond is below 3 or 4 years), asymptotic standard errors imply rejection of the expectations theory at conventional significance levels. At the long end of the term structure, the regression coefficients are very close to one and the expectations theory is not rejected' (Campbell and Shiller *op. cit.*, p. 505, my clarification in parentheses).

At variance to this quotation there are rejections of the hypothesis $\beta_{m1} = 1$ for $S(t, 120, 6)$, $S(t, 120, 12)$ and $S(t, 120, 60)$ but not for $S(t, 120,$ 1); and only for $S(t, 48, m)$, for $m = 1, 2, 3, 4, 6,$ 12, 24, and $S(t, 60, m)$, for $m = 1, 2, 3, 4, 6, 12,$ are there uniform nonrejections of the hypothesis $\beta_{m1} = 1$. On the basis of the (asymptotic) standard errors it is in the medium-term maturities, not the long end, where this regression evidence supports the EH + REH view. Adding 4 years of data does not materially alter these conclusions.

Cuthbertson (1996b) and Cuthbertson *et al.* (1996) report estimation of the perfect foresight spread regression using two datasets for the United Kingdom. The first is London Inter-Bank (offer), LIBO, rates for maturities of 1, 4, 13, 26 and 52 weeks' duration, with weekly data for the period January 1981 to February 1992 ($T = 580$ observations). The second is Sterling Certificates of Deposit, SCD, rates for maturities of 4, 12, 24, 39 and 52 weeks with weekly data over the period October 1975 to October 1992 ($T = 890$ observations), respectively. The estimates of β_{m1} together with the marginal significance level of the test of $\beta_{m1} = 1$ for the various spreads are reported in Table 11.7. The estimates of β_{m1} from these regressions vary from 0.73 for $S(t, 4, 1)$ to 1.32 for $S(t, 52, 26)$ for LIBO rates and 0.65 for $S(t, 39, 13)$ to 0.96 for $S(t, 52, 4)$ for

Table 11.7   *Perfect foresight spread regressions, London Interbank Rates and Sterling Certificates of Deposit*

$$PFS(t, n, m) = \beta_{m0} + \beta_{m1}S(t, n, m) + \varphi^*(t, m)$$

$S(t, n, m)$ for choices of n and m in months

London Interbank rates

$n =$	4	13	26	52	52	26	52	52
$m =$	1	1	1	1	4	13	13	26
β_{m1}	0.73	0.98	1.02	1.09	1.17	0.97	1.22	1.32
s.e.	0.06	0.07	0.10	0.15	0.21	0.23	0.30	0.44
$\beta_{m1} = 1$ [msl]	0.000	0.82	0.86	0.54	0.42	0.88	0.46	0.47

Sterling Certificates of Deposit rates

n	52	52	26	52	39
m	13	26	13	4	13
β_{m1}	0.80	0.67	0.73	0.96	0.65
s.e.	0.25	0.31	0.23	0.19	0.34
$\beta_{m1} = 1$ [msl]	0.43	0.28	0.26	0.82	0.13

Source: Extracted from Cuthbertson (1996b), Cuthbertson *et al.* (1996).

SCD rates. Because of the relatively large standard errors only in the case of LIBO $S(t, 4, 1)$ is the null hypothesis $\beta_{m1} = 1$ formally rejected with an msl virtually zero; for example, with LIBO $S(t, 52, 26)$ although the estimate of β_{m1} is 1.32 the estimated standard error is 0.44, hence the null $\beta_{m1} = 1$ is not rejected, the msl of the test being 47%. The estimates of β_{m1} are numerically closer to 1 for the LIBO rates compared to the SCD rates; in the latter case although the hypothesis $\beta_{m1} = 1$ is not rejected only the estimate of β_{m1} for $S(t, 52, 4)$ at 0.96 is near 1, the others being 0.80 or below.

(3) *The spread predicts changes in long rates.* Another implication, due to Campbell and Shiller (1991), of what might be regarded as the fundamental equation of the expectations hypothesis is that the spread predicts changes in the long rate. Recall that expectations hypothesis implies

$$R(t, n) = \frac{1}{k}\left[\sum_{i=1}^{k} E_t\{R(t + (i-1)m, m)\}\right] + L(t, m) \qquad \text{(11.8) again}$$

The yield on an n period bond at time t being the weighted sum, with weights $1/k$, of expected rates on the m ($m < n$) period bond over the lifetime of the n period bond plus a predictable excess return. As time shifts by one period the n period bond becomes an $n - 1$ period bond with a rate $R(t + 1, n - 1)$; shifting time by m periods the n period bond becomes an $n - m$ period bond with rate $R(t + m, n - m)$. The change in the n period rate over m periods is, therefore, $R(t + m, n - m) - R(t, n)$, this is the m period change in the long rate and $E_t\{R(t + m, n - m)\} - R(t, n)$ is the expected m period change in the long rate. A manipulation of the fundamental equation, (11.8), shows that (omitting constant terms for simplicity):

$$[m/(n-m)]S(t, n, m) = E_t\{R(t + m, n - m)\} - R(t, n) \qquad \text{(11.25)}$$

See Cuthbertson (1996a, pp. 226 *et seq.*) for details. A multiple, $m/(n - m)$, of the spread equals the expected m period change in the n period rate. For example, if $n = 12$ and $m = 1$ then (11.25) is:

$$[1/11]S(t, 12, 1) = E_t\{R(t + 1, 11)\} - R(t, 12)$$

This equation says that the expected one period change in the 12 period rate should equal 1/11 of the spread at time t between the 12 period and 1 period rates. For example, if the spread is positive, that is $R(t, 12) > R(t, 1)$, then $E_t\{R(t + 1, 11)\} - R(t, 12)$ must be > 0 so that the rate on the 12 period bond is expected to increase from t to $t + 1$; hence, the spread predicts changes in the long rate.

Assuming rational expectations

$$E_t\{R(t + im, n - m)\} = R(t + m, n - m) - \varepsilon(t + m, n - m)$$

substituting into (11.25) and rearranging gives:

$$\begin{aligned} R(t + m, n - m) &- R(t, n) \\ &= [m/(n - m)]S(t, n, m) + \varepsilon(t + m, n - m) \end{aligned} \qquad \text{(11.26)}$$

which says that the m period change in the n period rate should equal a multiple of the spread plus a stationary error. The equation (11.26), therefore, provides another means of testing the EH + REH by a simple regression: the regression of $R(t + m, n - m) - R(t, n)$ on $[m/(n - m)]S(t, n, m)$ should give a slope coefficient of 1.

Campbell and Shiller (*op. cit.*) report regressions of this kind using the McCulloch (1990) monthly dataset. Cuthbertson *et al.* (1996) also report such regressions using SCD rates. A summary of the results in Campbell and Shiller (*op. cit.*), for the maturities considered in this chapter, and Cuthbertson *et al.* (*op. cit.*) is given in Table 11.8.

It is starkly evident from the results in Table 11.8 for the US Treasury rates that this aspect of the EH + REH is rejected; the spread does not

Table 11.8 *Does the spread predict changes in the long rates?*

US Treasury rates, Campbell and Shiller (1991) Short rate				
$m =$	1	6	12	60
Long rate				
$n = 6$	-1.029	–	–	–
robust s.e.	\{0.537\}			
$n = 12$	-1.381	-0.913	–	–
robust s.e.	\{0.683\}	\{0.657\}		
$n = 60$	-3.099	-1.750	-2.022	–
robust s.e.	\{1.749\}	\{1.096\}	\{1.205\}	
$n = 120$	-5.024	-3.198	n.a.	4.575
robust s.e.	\{2.316\}	\{1.673\}		\{1.926\}
Sterling Certificate of Deposit Rates, Cuthbertson *et al.* (1996) Short rate			
$m =$	13	26	39
Long rate			
$n = 26$	0.48	–	–
robust s.e.	\{0.47\}		
$n = 39$	n.a.	0.002	–
robust s.e.		\{0.54\}	
$n = 52$	n.a.	0.34	0.13
robust s.e.		\{0.62\}	\{0.69\}

Notes: n.a means not available in original source; the first table entry for each (n, m) pair is the estimated coefficient in the regression of $R(t + m, n - m) - R(t, n)$ on $[m/(n - m)]S(t, n, m)$ and a constant; the second table entry, in parentheses \{.\}, is the robust standard error.

predict changes in the long rate with the estimated coefficients, apart from 1, of the wrong sign. The results using SCD rates are a little more encouraging with the estimated coefficients of the right sign. The large standard errors mean that the null hypothesis that the regression coefficient is unity is not rejected at conventional significance levels, but they also mean that the null hypothesis that the regression coefficient is 0 is not rejected. Hence, not much comfort can be taken from this result.

(4) *The actual and theoretical spreads should be 'close'.* Campbell and Shiller (*op. cit.*) note some disadvantages of the single-equation regression approach described in (2) above. First, the regressions involve 'overlapping' errors. We saw this explicitly in (11.18) where a moving average error of order $n - m - 1$ was induced in the perfect foresight spread. Apart from the econometric problems that may arise in such cases, the need to lead the data can have a substantial effect on the sample size. For example, an overall dataset of 1952m1 to 1987m2 translates into a usable sample of 1952m1 to 1977m3 for $S(t, 120, 1)$ so 120 observations are lost from the sample. Second, the regressions do not indicate the similarity of the movements in the actual spread to those predicted by the expectations theory.

This latter point leads into an alternative methodology for evaluating the EH + REH view of the term structure. For the moment assume that we have an expression for the theoretical spread denoted $S'(t, n, m)$ based on a vector autoregressive model, VAR (see Chapter 2 for an introduction to the VAR and Chapters 14 and 15 for a more extensive discussion). The theoretical spread and the actual spread can then be compared, and if the expectations theory is true, the two should be the same. The comparison between $S'(t, n, m)$ and $S(t, n, m)$ could be in terms of the levels of each, in which case the simple correlation coefficient, R, provides an indication of the degree of linear association between the two variables; in addition the variability – or volatility – can be compared by forming the ratio of the standard deviation of $S'(t, n, m)$ to the standard deviation of $S(t, n, m)$. A standard deviations ratio, σ_{re}/σ_a, below 1 indicates that the actual spread is too volatile relative to the expectations model. The missing link here is how to form the theoretical spread.

The underlying point of departure is the perfect foresight spread – see equation (11.15). The VAR includes an equation for the one period change in the m period interest rate, that is $\Delta R(t, m)$ so that given the estimated VAR coefficients it is possible to compute optimal forecasts of $\Delta R(t, m)$ for any forecast horizon. At a minimum the VAR equation for $\Delta R(t, m)$ should include lagged values of $\Delta R(t, m)$ and lagged values of the spread $S(t, n, m)$; to complete the model there is a VAR equation for $S(t, n, m)$ with the same set of lagged values. The optimal forecasts of $\Delta R(t + im, m)$, for $i = 1, \ldots, k - 1$, can then be used to compute the perfect foresight spread which is $S'(t, n, m)$.

In addition to the correlation coefficient and standard deviation comparisons it is also possible to test a set of nonlinear restrictions which ensure that the actual and theoretical spreads are equal. For later purposes the test statistic constructed for this purpose will be referred to as W. A departure from the null hypothesis may be statistically significant but not of economic significance; assessing this difference may be difficult in practice but the suggestion is that a formal rejection using W may be overridden if the correlation coefficient R and σ_{re}/σ_a are close to 1.

There have been a number of studies reporting these three aspects (the correlation coefficient, the standard deviation ratio, and testing the nonlinear restrictions) of testing the expectations model. Table 11.9 extracts results from Campbell and Shiller (1991) for the maturities used in this chapter, presenting the correlation coefficient, R, and the ratio of the standard deviation of the theoretical spread to the actual spread, σ_{re}/σ_a. The correlation coefficient is positive and tends to increase with the term to maturity of the long bond. For example, with $m = 1$ and $n = 6$, $R = 0.486$, but with $n = 60$, $R = 0.912$ and $n = 120$ gives $R = 0.979$. Also the estimated standard error tends to be smaller as n increases; for example, with $m = 1$ and $n = 6$ the s.e. of R is 0.373, so an R of 0.486 is not significantly different from 0 at conventional significance levels. But with $n = 120$, the s.e. $= 0.045$ so $R = 0.979$ is significantly different from 0 but not significantly different from 1. Also reported in Table 11.9 are the values of σ_{re}/σ_a, recall that this ratio is 1 if the EH + REH view is correct; if it is below 1, the actual spread is 'too volatile', and this is what the reported numbers indicate. For example, with $m = 1$ and $n = 6$,

Table 11.9 Correlation coefficients, R, and ratio of standard deviations of theoretical to actual spreads, σ_{re}/σ_a

US Treasury rates, Campbell and Shiller (1991) Short rate				
$m =$	1	6	12	60
Long rate $n = 6$				
R	0.486	–	–	–
s.e.	(0.373)			
σ_{re}/σ_a	0.501	–	–	–
s.e.	(0.145)			
$n = 12$				
R	0.391	−0.111	–	–
s.e.	(0.468)	(1.494)		
σ_{re}/σ_a	0.382	0.332	–	–
s.e.	(0.119)	(0.155)		
$n = 60$				
R	0.912	0.939	0.893	–
s.e.	(0.218)	(0.209)	(0.375)	
σ_{re}/σ_a	0.357	0.353	0.340	–
s.e.	(0.291)	(0.476)	(0.450)	
$n = 120$				
R	0.979	0.984	0.975	0.990
s.e.	(0.045)	(0.038)	(0.062)	(0.020)
σ_{re}/σ_a	0.474	0.485	0.478	0.552
s.e.	(0.285)	(0.398)	(0.383)	(0.385)

Sterling Certificate of Deposit rates, Cuthbertson et al. (1996) Short rate			
$m =$	4	13	26
Long rate $n = 6$			
W	–	38.92	–
cv		(15.51)	
R	–	0.987	–
s.e.		(0.011)	
σ_{re}/σ_a		(0.225)	
s.e.		(0.225)	
$n = 39$			
W	–	11.48	–
cv		(9.49)	
R	–	0.992	–
s.e.		(0.010)	
σ_{re}/σ_a	–	0.581	–
s.e.		(0.216)	
$n = 52$			
W	13.65	13.44	33.68
cv	(26.30)	(9.49)	(12.59)
R	0.997	0.997	0.987
s.e.	(0.008)	(0.004)	(0.013)
σ_{re}/σ_a	0.883	0.762	0.557
s.e.	(0.252)	(0.247)	(0.355)

$\sigma_{re}/\sigma_a = 0.501$; with an estimated standard error (s.e.) of 0.145 this is significantly different from 1. The situation does not improve as n increases, with $m = 1$ and $n = 120$, $\sigma_{re}/\sigma_a = 0.474$ with s.e. $= 0.285$.

Table 11.9 also reports Cuthbertson *et al.* (1996) results for R and σ_{re}/σ_a using UK SCD rates and the test statistic, W, with the appropriate 5% critical value, cv, for the restrictions that would impose equality on the theoretical and actual spreads. If $W > cv$ then the restrictions are not consistent with the data at the 5% level. The correlation coefficients, R, are statistically and numerically close to one, and hence support the EH + REH view of the term structure at least as far as like movements in the levels of the theoretical and actual spreads. However, on the basis of the ratio of standard deviations, actual spreads are too volatile, that is $\sigma_{re} < \sigma_a$ for all maturities in the text, but large standard errors rescue the hypothesis that this ratio is 1 at conventional significance levels. In only one case, for the spread $S(t, 52, 4)$, are the restrictions not rejected using the test statistic W. On this basis the evidence is rather mixed, some test results are for and some against EH + REH; even with the rejections there is greater support for the expectations hypothesis using UK SCD rates compared to US Government securities.

Taylor (1992) also reports a number of tests of the expectations hypothesis using weekly data on 3-month UK Treasury Bills and 10-, 15- and 20-year UK Treasury Bonds over the period January 1985 to November 1989 ($T = 253$ observations). He finds the series nonstationary in the levels, and the three spreads, relative to the short rate, stationary. However, the standard deviations ratio, σ_{re}/σ_a, is significantly below 1 at 0.66 for $S(t, 120, 1)$, 0.593 for $S(t, 160, 1)$ and 0.569 for $S(t, 240, 1)$, all indicating excess volatility. The test statistics, W, for equality of the theoretical and actual spreads indicate a very firm rejection of the restrictions, so the evidence points unequivocally in the direction that formal rejection is due to economically important departures from the expectations model.

In contrast MacDonald and Speight (1988) using data similar to Taylor (*op. cit.*), that is 3-month UK Treasury Bills and 10-, 15- and 20-year UK Treasury Bonds, but quarterly over the period 1963q1 to 1987q1, find firmly in favour of nonrejection of EH + REH using the W test statistic. However, this is qualified to the extent that the standard deviations ratio is only 0.725 for each of the three long-short spreads. The differences between these two studies may be attributable to the higher frequency and perhaps better quality data used by Taylor (*op. cit.*) as well as the different sample periods.

11.5.2 Why do tests of EH + REH tend to indicate rejection?

It is not enough to know that, on various datasets, a number of authors have found evidence which does not support the EH + REH view of the term structure. That would be a rather destructive end; what are the constructive possibilities that have arisen from these negative results? Some suggestions which have been put forward are as follows.

(1) *The existence of 'noise traders' who follow fads.* A simple modification to the central relationship, (11.8), offers an interesting interpretation of results which are at variance to EH + REH. Add a stochastic 'noise' term $N(t)$ to the left-hand side of (11.8) that becomes:

$$R(n, m) = \frac{1}{k}\left[\sum_{i=0}^{k-1} E_t\{R(t + im, m)\}\right] + L(t, m) + N(t) \qquad (11.27)$$

Similarly the equation (11.12) for the spread becomes:

$$S(t, n, m) = E_t\{PFS_t\} + L(t, m) + N(t) \qquad (11.27a)$$

where $N(t)$ has a zero mean and is unrelated (orthogonal) to $E_t\{PFS_t\}$. $N(t)$ could be viewed just as an econometric disturbance to the otherwise 'exact' rational expectations model, as a time varying term premium, or, as in Cuthbertson *et al.* (1996), as capturing the existence of 'noise traders'. The latter are to be contrasted with 'smart money' whose expectations are represented in (11.8); noise traders follow fads for which $S(t, n, m) = E_t\{PFS_t\} + L(t, m)$ does not hold, their existence means that smart money cannot arbitrage away price differentials from alternative investment strategies.

The econometric implications of $N(t)$ are as follows.

(a) In the regression

$$R(t + m, n - m) - R(t, n)$$
$$= \theta_0 + \theta_1 s\{t, n, m\} + \varepsilon(t + m, n - m)$$

(11.28)

where $s(t, n, m) = [m/(n - m)]S(t, n, m)$, the OLS estimate of θ_1 can be negative even if θ_1 is positive. Potentially this explains the 'wrong sign' results in Table 11.8.

(b) In the regression of the perfect foresight spread on the actual spread, that is:

$$PFS(t, n, m) = \beta_{m0} + \beta_{m1} S(t, n, m) + \varphi^*(t, m)$$

the OLS estimator of β_{m1} has a probability limit less than 1, so that estimates of $\beta_{m1} < 1$ will be typical. The following hold – see Campbell and Shiller (1991, p. 511) and Cuthbertson (1996b, p. 410):

regression coefficient:
plim $\beta_{m1} = 1/(1 + v)$ ≤ 1 for $v \geq 0$

ratio of standard deviations:
$\sigma_{re}/\sigma_a = 1/(1 + v)^{0.5}$ ≤ 1 for $v \geq 0$

correlation coefficient:
$R[S'(t, n, m), S(t, n, m)] = 1/(1 + v)^{0.5}$
≤ 1 for $v \geq 0$

where $v = \sigma^2(N)/\sigma^2(PFS)$ is the ratio of the variance of $N(t)$ to the variance of the perfect foresight spread, $PFS(t, n, m)$.

At least potentially, the existence of noise traders explains some of the results reported in Tables 11.7 to 11.9, that is negative estimates of θ_1, and estimates of β_{m1}, σ_{re}/σ_a and R less than 1. However, note that in Table 11.9, and especially with Campbell and Shiller's results, as the maturity of the long bond increases R *does* tend to 1, whereas σ_{re}/σ_a does not, so the explanation is not complete.

(2) *An overreaction model (Campbell and Shiller op. cit., pp. 510 et seq.).* In the over-/under-reaction model, (11.8) is modified as follows:

$$S(t, n, m) = hE_t\{PFS(t, n, m)\} + L(t, n, m)$$

(11.29)

where $h > 1$ for the overreaction model and $h < 1$ for the underreaction model. A regression of the perfect foresight spread on the actual spread will give an estimate of the slope coefficient $1/h$ which is less than 1 for $h > 1$. The standard deviations ratio, σ_{re}/σ_a, will be $1/h$, which is less than 1 for $h > 1$, whereas $R[S'(t, n, m), S(t, n, m)] = 1$; these implications are consistent with Campbell and Shiller's results and Cuthbertson's (1996b) results for SCD rates.

For $h > 1$ the model of (11.29) states that the spread overreacts in the following sense: '... the long rate differs from the short rate in the direction implied by the expectations theory; however, the spread between the two rates is larger than can be justified by rational expectations of future short rate changes' (Campbell and Shiller *op. cit.*, p. 513). Two possible explanations are first that there are time varying risk premia correlated with expected increases in future short-term rates; the actual spread takes these into account but the regression model does not, hence a reconciliation is through $h > 1$.

The second explanation is more complex. To illustrate take $m = 1$ and $k = n = 5$ in (11.8), assume for simplicity that there is perfect foresight so $E_t\{R(t + (i - 1), 1)\} = R(t + (i - 1), 1)$ for

$i > 1$, and rearrange to make $R(t, 1)$ explicit. That is:

$$R(t, n) = (1/5)R(t, 1)$$

$$+ (1/5) \sum_{i=2}^{5} R(t + (i - 1), 1) + L(t, 1)$$

$$(11.30a)$$

Then

$$R(t, n) - R(t, 1) = -(4/5)R(t, 1)$$

$$+ (1/5) \sum_{i=2}^{5} R(t + (i - 1), 1)$$

$$+ L(t, 1) \qquad (11.30b)$$

On this interpretation the spread is a distributed lag on the current short rate and future short rates, with the weight on $R(t, 1)$ equal to the negative of the sum of the remaining weights so that the overall sum is 0. For example, a one-off 1 percentage point (p.p.) increase in $R(t, 1)$ should result in a temporary increase of 0.2 in the long rate and a decrease of 0.8 p.p. in the spread. The long rate is said to be sluggish if it increases less than predicted; for example, if in this case it increased by say 0.1 p.p. and so the spread decreases more than expected, in this case 0.9 p.p.

If the increase in short rates is sustained then according to (11.30a) and (11.30b) the long rate should increase by 1 p.p. so that the spread is unchanged. If the long rate is sluggish in the face of a sustained change in short rates the spread has to overreact to future changes in the short rates, otherwise the spread differential will not be maintained. In this example the long rate must increase by 1 p.p. But having increased by only 0.1 in response to the change in the current short rate it must now increase by 0.9 not 0.8 as the weights in (11.30b) suggest; hence, a factor of $0.9/0.8 = 1.125$ needs to be applied to future short rates to ensure an unchanged spread.

Campbell and Shiller (1984) suggest that sluggishness of the long rate with respect to the current level of the short rate is a characteristic of interest rates, combined with weights larger than expected for the future short rates, so maintaining the unit sum overall. In a sense the later weights overreact to catch up for the initial sluggish response ensuring that the right spread according to (11.30b) is maintained. Somewhat confusingly this sluggishness characteristic is described as the *underreaction* of the long rate to the current level of the short rate.

(3) *A market segmentation/preferred habitat model (Modigliani and Sutch 1966 and Taylor op. cit., p. 526 et seq.).* The essence of the expectations model is that if expectations are realised then the return from a rollover sequence over n periods is the same as from the one-off purchase of an n period bond. Otherwise an efficient market will arbitrage away potential profits. The existence of nonzero term premia negates this implication. One possible explanation of term premia is the market segmentation/preferred habitat model. In this model the market splits into 'segments' with investors and dealers working in their 'preferred habitat' as far as maturity is concerned and not, generally, operating in the other segments. In this case excess returns between segments are not arbitraged away, as that requires traders buying or selling outside their preferred habitat. A possible segmentation is a long–short divide with pension funds dominating the long end of the market.

Compared to tests of the expectations model there have been relatively few tests of the market segmentation approach. However, one of interest is due to Taylor (1992) who noted that over his sample period the UK Government was using the budget surplus to redeem fixed interest debt (that is of a fairly long maturity), hence reducing the stock of debt of that maturity. For reference we refer to this as g period debt. Redeeming the debt is likely to have increased g period bond prices, so reducing the return to holding such debt. This return is known as the holding period return. For example, suppose the holding period is 3 months, then the return to holding a bond with g periods to maturity for 3 months is a combination of the coupon payment, which is typically paid on bonds (that is with an original maturity greater than 12 months), plus any capital gain or loss on selling the bond 3 months hence. The 3-month holding period return for a g period bond is denoted $H(t+3,g)$. One alternative to holding the g period bond for 3 months is to buy a 3-month Treasury Bill at a known discount rate $R(t,3)$. A predictable difference between these two returns, that is a premium, is suggestive of a market segmentation model where excess returns are not arbitraged away.

In Taylor's model the excess return

$$H(t+3,g) - R(t,3)$$

is a function of the stock of g period debt, $K(t,g)$ and the total stock of debt of all maturities, $K(t,\Sigma)$, that is

$$H(t+3,g) - R(t,3)$$
$$= \kappa_0 + \kappa_1 \ln[K(t,g)/K(t,\Sigma)] + \zeta(t+3)$$
$$(11.31)$$

In a market segmentation model κ_1 is expected to be positive: a reduction in the relative amount of g period debt $K(t,g)/K(t,\Sigma)$ increases the current g period bond price and so decreases

Table 11.10 *Estimates of the market segmentation model, Taylor (1992)*

$H(t+3,g) - R(t,3) =$ $\kappa_0 + \kappa_1 \ln[K(t,g)/K(t,\Sigma)] + \zeta(t+3)$			
g	κ_0	κ_1	R^2
120	0.029	0.049	0.55
s.e.	{0.008}	{0.005}	
180	0.026	0.054	0.52
s.e.	{0.004}	{0.005}	
240	0.019	0.036	0.32
s.e.	{0.004}	{0.003}	

Note: Estimation method is OLS with robust standard errors in parentheses {.}.

the holding period return. Taylor used data on maturities of $g = 120, 180, 240$ to estimate this model with the results summarised in Table 11.10.

Estimates of κ_1 are positive, consistent with the market segmentation model, and highly significant.

11.6 Concluding remarks

The term structure of interest rates has attracted a great deal of attention with a large theoretical and empirical literature. This chapter has focused on the expectations theory of the term structure combined with the rational expectations hypothesis. The central relationship of this view is that long rates are a weighted sum of expected short rates over the duration of the long bond, with expectations formed rationally in the sense that actual and expected short rates differ only by an unpredictable error. A further implication of this view is that the spread between the long and short rate is a weighted sum of expected changes in the short rate over the duration of the long bond. Thus what drives the long rate is expectations (formed at t) of future short rates, and what opens up a wedge between the current long and short rates is the expectation of change in future short rates. The theory is attractive: it seems unlikely that long rates are unrelated to expected changes in future short rates. However, the empirical evidence is mixed. Even in well-developed financial markets, for example for Government securities, some of the implications of EH + REH have been found to be at variance with the data. (Campbell and Shiller (1991) and Shea (1992) for the United States and Taylor (1992) for the United Kingdom)). Cuthbertson (1996a) finds some, but not unequivocal, support for EH + REH using London Interbank rates.

To complicate the assessment there are, as this chapter has shown, a number of methods, rather than a single method, of evaluating the expectations model. If the yield data is I(1) a minimum requirement is that the spreads are I(0). This implication is generally found to be consistent with the data used in various studies. However, this implication is not unique to the EH + REH model since any expectations process generating I(0) forecasting errors should satisfy this condition.

With pure discount bonds the weights on expected changes in future short rates should equal $w_i = 1 - i/k$, and this implication forms the basis of two tests. First, a direct test using REH to substitute in for the unknown expectations variables and, second, the construction of what is known as the perfect foresight spread, PFS, and the regression of the PFS on the actual spread with a slope coefficient of one. In both cases the expectations model starts to fault here. The estimated weights are not as expected and estimates of the slope coefficient typically come out below one.

The spread should also predict changes in the long rate but regressions typically deliver an estimated regression coefficient of the wrong sign. The regression-based tests may find a statistically significant result even though the departure from the expectations model may not be of economic significance, hence an alternative set of evidence relates to more informal evidence concerning the 'similarity' of the theoretical spread, $S'(t, n, m)$, and the actual spread, $S(t, n, m)$; and the evidence which often comes closest to the expectations model is that on the correlation coefficient, R, between the $S'(t, n, m)$ and $S(t, n, m)$, especially as the maturity of the long bond increases. Typically, however, the ratio of standard deviations of $S'(t, n, m)$ and $S(t, n, m)$ is below 1, suggesting that the actual spread is 'too volatile' compared to the spread predicted by the expectations model. (Contrary evidence in this respect is rather minimal, but some is provided by Cuthbertson's study of LIBO rates for particular maturities considered in that study.)

Also, as Shiller (1979) notes, the long rate, which according to the expectations model is a weighted average of expected future short rates, is too volatile compared to the long rate predicted by the expectations model. Even though the empirical evidence on the expectations model is mixed, that model provides a useful baseline for developments which in due course may provide an explanation of the long rate and the term structure. Alternative models have to improve upon the expectations model. These developments include the overreaction model, and market segmentation or preferred habitat model both described briefly in section **11.5.2**.

Another possible explanation for the failure of the expectations model is the existence of a time varying risk premium. This extension is motivated by two observations. First, the 'excess volatility' of the spread/long rate relative to the expectations model suggests a need to explain that volatility. Second, in the data on US securities used in this chapter, although not picked up formally in the unit root tests reported in section **11.4.4**, the variance (as an indication of volatility) of the actual spread does seem to have increased from about 1978/9 onwards, and so the spread might more adequately be modelled to take this feature into account. For example, Engle, Lilien and Robins (1987) on US data and Taylor (1992) on UK data, modelled the excess return, that is the holding period return on a long bond minus the safe return, as a function of the unanticipated variability of the holding period return. The latter was modelled using a scheme known as autoregressive conditional heteroscedasticity, or ARCH, in which the variance of the holding period return depends upon its own past values. This approach is described in greater detail in Chapter 16.

Review

1. Financial instruments take many different forms. Thrift institutions (building societies), banks, private and public corporations all issue financial instruments of varying kinds. An important class of financial

instruments comprises those issued by the US Treasury known as Treasury Bills and Treasury Bonds.

2. Financial instruments differ in a number of ways. Two important distinguishing characteristics are the term to maturity and the yield.

3. The term to maturity is the length of time before a financial instrument will be redeemed by the original issuer. For example, if a 3-month T-Bill is bought, at its time of issue its term to maturity is 3 months; however, if it is bought on the secondary market 1 month after its issue then its term to maturity is 2 months.

4. In order to understand what is meant by the yield on a financial instrument consider the (simple) interest rate and the rate of discount. Let P_0 be the initial value of a bond and P_1 be the value of the bond after one annual period, then the annual interest rate is $r = (P_1/P_0) - 1$. This is also the yield if the bond is bought at P_0 and then held to redemption. Markets for government securities usually quote the discount rate on an annual basis which is given by $rd = 1 - (P_0/P_1)$, so $r = rd/(1 - rd)$.

5. A particularly important kind of financial instrument is a bill or a bond with a zero coupon. The coupon is the amount, usually paid on a regular basis, between the issue and redemption of a bond. For example, if a 10-year bond paid $10 at the end of each year from year 1 through to year 10, then $10 would be the coupon on the bond. A zero-coupon instrument is, therefore, one which does not pay any coupon between issue and redemption. These are usually known as pure discount instruments.

6. The yield curve shows the yield to maturity for financial instruments that differ only in their term to maturity, and is usually illustrated with yields from zero-coupon (pure discount) financial instruments.

7. The term structure of interest rates is the relationship between the yield and maturity

of a class of financial instruments that are alike in all other characteristics. The yield curve and term structure is often studied for Treasury securities.

8. A forward market is where it is possible to arrange for a loan to begin in the future; this is known as a forward loan. Forward rates correspond to the rates of interest which are payable on forward loans.

9. The Fisher–Hicks formula states that the yield to maturity at time t on a k period zero-coupon bond is: the arithmetic average of the actual yield at time t on a one period zero-coupon bond and the subsequent sequence of $k - 1$ forward rates for the corresponding zero-coupon bonds.

10. According to the expectations model of the term structure of interest rates, forward rates may be replaced by the corresponding expected rate; for example, $E_t\{R(t + j, 1)\}$ for $F(t + j, 1)$ and the two expressions will only differ by a term premium which is either zero or a stationary stochastic process.

11. The expectations model of the term structure predicts that the yield on an n period bond is the arithmetic average of the sequence of expected values of the yield on one period bonds over the duration of the long bond, plus a term premium.

12. The spread between two bonds of different maturities is the difference between their corresponding yields. The spread between the one and n period bonds at time is denoted $S(t, n, 1)$.

13. Where bonds differ only in their term to maturity then, according to the expectations model of the term structure, the spread is a weighted sum of the expected changes in the short rate plus a term premium.

14. In a dataset comprising the yields on zero-coupon US Treasury Bills and bonds the yields were consistent with I(1) processes, indicating that first differences of the yields were I(0).

15. The spreads between the 10-year T-Bond and, respectively, the 1-month, 6-month,

12-month T-Bills and the 5-year T-Bond, were stationary, i.e. I(0). This aspect of the expectations theory of the term structure was, therefore, consistent with the dataset used here.

16. The difference between the expected and actual changes in the yields should be stationary if expectations are formed rationally and the levels are I(1).

17. Substituting the actual changes in the yields for the expected changes allows a further and more stringent test of the expectations theory of the term structure. The spread should be a weighted sum of the actual changes in yields with weights which decline linearly according to the pattern $w_i = 1 - i/k$.

18. The 'perfect foresight spread' is:

$$PFS(t, n, m) = \sum_{i=1}^{k-1} \left(\frac{k - i}{k} \right) \Delta R(t + im, m)$$

which is the spread that would obtain, given the expectations model, if there were perfect foresight about future interest rates.

19. According to the expectations model the actual spread should forecast the perfect foresight spread, with a regression coefficient of 1.

20. The concepts and tests described were illustrated with a selection of yields from McCulloch's dataset on the yields of US Treasury Bills and Bonds.

21. Selected regressions of the spreads on the sequence of changes in the corresponding short rate, with instrumental variables estimation, gave some limited support for the expectations model. Generally the short rates were significant as predicted by the model; however, while the lead weights declined they did not do so according to the pattern suggested by the model.

22. In the case of the 10-year–1-year spread the hypothesis that the lead weights declined linearly according to the linear pattern $w_i = a_0 + a_1 i$ was consistent with the data.

23. With the McCulloch data regressions of the perfect foresight spread, PFS, on the actual spread typically give an estimated coefficient below 1 where the 'long' rate is at the short end of the spectrum (for example, 12 months), above 1 where the 'long' rate is long (for example, 10 years) and about 1 when the 'long' rate is at the medium maturities (for example, 5 years).

24. Cuthbertson (1996b) and Cuthbertson *et al.* (1996) provide some evidence on PFS regressions using London Interbank rates and Sterling Certificate of Deposit rates. For the former there is support for the expectations model with the regression coefficients, generally, numerically close to 1 and only one significantly different from 1. With SCD rates the estimates are below, but not significantly different from, 1.

25. Another implication of the expectations model is that the spread predicts changes in long-rates so that a regression of

$$R(t + m, n - m) - R(t, n)$$

on $[m(n - m)]S(t, n, m)$ should give a slope coefficient of 1.

26. Using the McCulloch dataset Campbell and Shiller (1991) find that such regressions give wrong-signed coefficients. Cuthbertson *et al.* (1996) find positive coefficients, but these are not significantly different from 0.

27. Three other tests arise from the idea that the actual and theoretical spreads, $S'(t, n, m)$, should be the same if the expectations model is correct. The measures of 'closeness' are: the correlation coefficient, R, between $S'(t, n, m)$ and $S(t, n, m)$; the ratio of the standard deviation of $S'(t, n, m)$ to the standard deviation of $S(t, n, m)$, σ_{re}/σ_a; a test statistic, W, based on the restrictions imposed by the expectations hypothesis on a VAR model.

28. To stylise the evidence, most support for the expectations model comes from R which tends to be close to 1 as the maturity of the

long bond increases. Typically σ_{re}/σ_a is less than 1 indicating that the actual spread is too volatile relative to $S'(t, n, m)$; and the test statistic W often indicates statistical rejection of the expectation restrictions.

29. Several possible explanations of the expectations model have been suggested. Among these are the following: the market comprises 'smart money' and 'noise traders', with the latter leading to a mispricing of bonds relative to the arbitrage which would occur with the former; and 'overreacters' who scale up the expected perfect foresight spread by a factor $h > 1$, so that the spread is larger than can be justified by rational expectations of future short-rate changes.

30. Also of interest is the market segmentation/preferred habitat model with investors and dealers working in just a segment of the spectrum of maturities. One test of this model is due to Taylor (1992) who regressed the excess (holding period) return on the ratio of the stock of g period debt, $K(t, g)$ to the total stock of debt of all maturities with an anticipated positive regression coefficient. A result that was confirmed with data on UK Treasury Bill and Bond rates.

31. The term structure of interest rates is a topic of central importance in financial economics. While, on balance, the evidence is against the expectations model it provides a baseline from which other models can be developed.

Review questions

1. What are pure discount securities and how do they differ from coupon bearing bonds?
2. What is the difference between the (simple) rate of interest and the rate of discount?
3. What is the difference between the simple rate of interest and the continuously compounded rate of interest?

4. The discount price of a 12-month T-Bill with a par of $100 is $90, what is its yield to maturity alternately using:
   (i) the simple rate of interest?
   (ii) semi-annual compounding?
   (iii) continuous compounding?
5. Assume that the 12-month T-Bill of question 4 has 3 months to maturity and its price is $97, what is its yield to maturity using:
   (i) the simple rate of interest?
   (ii) monthly compounding?
   (iii) continuous compounding?
6. What is the yield curve?
7. Summarise the expectations theory of the term structure.
8. (i) What is a risk premium?
   (ii) What sign do you expect the risk premium to take?
9. Suppose $n = 72$ (months) and $m = 12$, what are the weights in the spread $S(t, 72, 12)$ as a function of expected short rates over the horizon of the 72-month bond when the bond:
   (i) carries no coupon?
   (ii) is coupon bearing?
10. What is the perfect foresight spread?
11. (i) Suppose $R(t, m)$, $m > 1$, is a pure random walk and so $I(1)$, what are the integration and serial correlation properties of

$$\Delta R(t + im, m)$$
$$= R(t + im, m) - R(t + (i - 1)m, m)$$

   and hence what are the integration properties of the perfect foresight spread?
   (ii) How does your answer change if $m = 1$?
12. If the yields of an n period bond and a j period bond are $I(1)$, what order of integration will $S(t, n, j)$ be, according to the expectations theory of the term structure?
13. If $S(t, n, 12)$ is $I(0)$ and $S(t, 12, 1)$ is $I(0)$ what order of integration is $S(t, n, 1)$?
14. Suppose

$$E_t\{\Delta R(t + i, 1)\}$$
$$\equiv \Delta R(t + i, 1) + \varepsilon(t + i, 1)$$

but $\varepsilon(t+i,1)$ is I(1) rather than I(0) as assumed in the text, do you think that expectations are being formed in a sensible way?

15. Write an equation for $S(t,120,60)$ in terms of expected changes in yields.

16. Show that another implication of the expectations model is:

$$[m/(n-m)]S(t,n,m)$$
$$= E_t\{R(t+m,n-m)\} - R(t,n)$$

and assuming rational expectations then, in the regression,

$$R(t+m,n-m) - R(t,n)$$
$$= \theta_0 + \theta_1 s(t,n,m) + \varepsilon(t+m,n-m)$$

where $s(t,n,m) = [m/(n-m)]S(t,n,m)$, the estimate of θ_1 should not be significantly different from 1.

17. A linear equation can be completely characterised by two constants. For example, if the lead weights w_i have a linear pattern then:

$$w_i = a_0 + a_1 i, \quad i = 1,\ldots,k-1$$

Suppose $w_i = 1 - i/k$, what are a_0 and a_1?

18. Does a finding that the spreads are I(0) necessarily imply that they have been generated by the expectations model plus rational expectations?

19. Explain what is meant by the theoretical spread, and how is this formed using a VAR model?

20. When the standard deviations ratio, σ_{re}/σ_a, is less than 1 the actual spread is said to be exessively volatile, explain what is meant by this, and what evidence is there that this is the case?

21. Prove that if a noise term, $N(t)$, is introduced into the 'fundamental' relationship of the expectations model, that is:

$$R(t,n)$$
$$= \frac{1}{k}\left[\sum_{i=0}^{k-1} E_t\{R(t+im,m)\}\right] + L(t,m)$$

then in the regression of the perfect foresight spread on the actual spread, the following hold:

$$PFS(t,n,m) = \beta_{m0} + \beta_{m1}S(t,n,m)$$
$$+ \varphi^*(t,m)$$

(i) plim $\beta_{m1} = 1(1+\nu) \quad \leq 1$ for $\nu \geq 0$
(ii) $\sigma_{re}/\sigma_a = 1/(1+\nu)^{0.5} \quad \leq 1$ for $\nu \geq 0$
(iii) $R[S'(t,n,m), S(t,n,m)] = 1/(1+\nu)^{0.5}$
≤ 1 for $\nu \geq 0$

where $\nu = \sigma^2(N)/\sigma^2(PFS)$ is the ratio of the variance of $N(t)$ to the variance of the perfect foresight spread, $PFS(t,n,m)$.

22. Show that in the overreaction model

$$S(t,n,m) = hE_t\{PFS(t,n,m)\} + L(t,n,m)$$

then in a regression of the perfect foresight spread on the actual spread the following will hold:

(i) the slope coefficient will be an estimate of $1/h$, which is less than 1 for $h > 1$;
(ii) the standard deviations ratio, σ_{re}/σ_a, will be $1/h$, which is less than 1 for $h > 1$;
(iii) the correlation coefficient $R[S'(t,n,m), S(t,n,m)]$ will be 1.

23. What justifies an overreaction coefficient, that is $h > 1$?

24. Explain what is meant by the GARCH model of the risk premium – see Engle, Lilien and Robins (1987), Taylor (1992) and Chapter 16.

CHAPTER 12
The Phillips curve

12.1   Introduction

When the demand for a commodity or service is high relatively to the supply of it we expect the price to rise, the rate of rise being greater the greater the excess demand. Conversely when the demand is low relatively to the supply we expect the price to fall, the rate of fall being greater the greater the deficiency of demand. It seems plausible that this principle should operate as one of the factors determining the rate of change of money wage rates. (Phillips 1958, p. 283)

Phillips' analysis seems very persuasive and obvious, yet it is utterly fallacious. It is fallacious because no economic theorist has ever asserted that the demand and supply of labour were functions of the *nominal* wage rate (i.e. wage rate expressed in £s). (Friedman 1975, p. 15, emphasis in original)

The first quotation is the opening sentence of one of the most famous articles in quantitative and empirical economics. It heralded decades of research in many different countries into the relationship between wage or price inflation on the one hand and unemployment on the other. It gave rise to 'The Phillips curve' which in its original form was a graph of the relationship between the rate of change of money wage rates – that is wage inflation – and unemployment. The second quotation comes from one of Phillips' most persistent critics, who in turn offered an alternative interpretation of the phenomena observed by Phillips and an explanation of how *in his view* it was that Phillips came to make what might be seen as an

elementary confusion between nominal wages and real wages (Friedman *op. cit.*, pp. 16–18).

The debate over the validity of the Phillips curve proved to be a stimulus not only to further research into the relationship between inflation and unemployment but also to the development of the modelling of expectations. Indeed influential papers by Lucas (1972) and Sargent (1973), which arose out of the inflation/unemployment debate, led to profound changes in how economists and econometricians perceived the formation and modelling of expectations more generally; they led to the dominant paradigm changing from one of adaptive expectations, or some variant thereof, to rational expectations.

Consideration of the inflation/unemployment trade-off provides an interesting opportunity to illustrate the historical development of economic ideas as they relate to a particular body of empirical evidence, and how the same general phenomena are capable of different interpretations. That is the motivation for this chapter. As Desai (1984, p. 253) noted: 'The bewildering course of the debate is a quintessential example in the history of econometrics of the interaction of economic theory, the nature of the data, the specification of the equation and the estimation and testing of the econometric equation.'

In section **12.2** Phillips' estimation techniques and results are re-examined. Phillips' original paper contained some interesting ideas on how to use simple nonlinear functions in empirical modelling and this section provides a baseline from which to judge further developments. In section **12.3** a number of criticisms of the original Phillips formulation of the inflation/unemployment trade-off are considered. These include an important prior article by Fisher (1926), rediscovered in the 1970s, which placed the causation from inflation to unemployment rather than, on the usual interpretation of the Phillips curve, from unemployment to inflation. Fisher (1926) also suggested that the trade-off was likely to be of a temporary nature. Friedman (*op. cit.*) was critical of the Phillips curve because, in his view, it ignored the distinction between nominal and real wages and gave no role to expectations of inflation. Desai's view, that it is Friedman rather than Phillips who is mistaken, especially in the context of nominal versus real wages, is also considered in this section. In section **12.4**, the difficult issue of how to model expectations in greater detail is considered. Initially the adaptive expectations hypothesis, which had proved so popular in a number of empirical applications, is considered. This approach was criticised by Lucas and Sargent who developed the idea of rational expectations, an approach which had been suggested in a different context by Muth (1961). An expectations augmented version of the Phillips curve is estimated using the (weakly) rational expectations method suggested by McCallum (1976). All of the different models in these sections are estimated with the same UK dataset used originally by Phillips (*op. cit.*) – a strategy which should make transparent how different assumptions lead to different estimation results. In section **12.5**, another data set is used, that for the US for 1972–1995, to illustrate a different approach to the relationship between unemployment and inflation. Section **12.6** contains some concluding remarks. We caution now though that, as indicated in the above quotation by Desai, this is one of the most controversial areas in the history of econometrics. Here we can only give an outline of some of the issues that have been raised in what is a voluminous and controversial literature. This chapter will have succeeded in its aim if it motivates the reader to find out more about the debate.

12.2 The Phillips curve

In this section a number of issues are considered arising from Phillips' formulation of the empirical relationship between wage inflation and unemployment. The original numerical estimates of the Phillips curve are reported and the 'menu of choice' interpretation that was given to these estimates is discussed. We note that some authors interpreted the relationship between money wages and unemployment in the US as providing evidence for a Phillips curve. The original dataset for the period 1861–1913 used by Phillips is analysed together with re-estimation of the Phillips curve.

12.2.1 Basic ideas

In this section the key concepts associated with the Phillips curve are summarised; a critique both as to its exegesis and interpretation is left to section **12.3**. The Phillips curve captured a trade-off that appeared to exist between wage inflation and unemployment. Ideally a situation in which decreases in unemployment – which are generally regarded as good – were not associated with increases in wage inflation would be preferable for an economy over a situation where decreases in unemployment could only be 'bought' at the expense of an increase in wage inflation. In the latter case there would be an inflation – unemployment trade-off: a lower unemployment rate would be associated with a higher rate of wage inflation and, conversely, a higher unemployment rate would be associated with a lower rate of wage inflation. This trade-off is represented graphically as a negatively sloping curve with, by convention, wage inflation on the vertical axis and unemployment of the horizontal axis. Figure 12.1 reproduces Phillips' original scatter diagram using annual data on these two variables for the United Kingdom over the period 1861–1913. Phillips has drawn in a curve, which he views as capturing the central features of the scatter of pairs of observations. This curve is

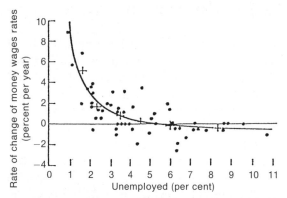

Figure 12.1 *The original Phillips curve for the UK, 1861–1913. (Source: reprinted from Phillips (1958) by permission of Blackwell Publishers; copyright © the London School of Economics.)*

negatively sloping and nonlinear in the following sense. Consider an initial position on the curve, for example 2% unemployment is associated with wage inflation of 2.77% p.a., now consider the rate of wage inflation associated with a decrease in unemployment to 1% and, alternately, an increase to 3%. In the first case the associated rate of wage inflation is around 8.74% p.a. – an increase of nearly 6% points. In the second case the associated rate of wage inflation is 1.186, a decrease of just 1.59% points. Phillips thus suggested that further decreases in unemployment would be associated with increases in wage inflation which would themselves be increasing to achieve the same reduction in unemployment.

Phillips also observed that wage inflation at any given level of unemployment seemed to be related to whether unemployment was decreasing or increasing. If unemployment was decreasing wage inflation tended to be higher than if there was no change in unemployment or if unemployment was increasing. The reasoning behind this idea was that 'employers will be bidding more vigorously for the services of labour than they would be in a year during which the average percentage unemployment was the same but the demand for labour was not increasing' (Phillips *op. cit.*, p. 284). Conversely if unemployment was increasing wage inflation

tended to be lower than if there was no change in unemployment or if unemployment was decreasing. These arguments suggested that not only should wage inflation be specified as a negative function of unemployment it should also be a negative function of the rate of change of unemployment. The latter term would capture the effect that if unemployment was decreasing, so that the change in unemployment was negative, then wage inflation would be positive.

12.2.2 Phillips' original estimates and interpretation

Notice on Figure 12.1 that some observations from the years 1861 to 1913 are distinguished by +. It is these that Phillips used to fit a simple nonlinear equation of the following form:

$$\pi_{wt} + a = bu_t^c \tag{12.1}$$

or taking logarithms of both sides

$$\log(\pi_{wt} + a) = \log b + c \log(u_t) \tag{12.2}$$

where π_{wt} is the rate of change of wage rates and u_t is the unemployment rate. The resulting parameter estimates gave

$$\pi_{wt} + 0.9 = 9.638 u_t^{-1.394} \tag{12.3}$$

so that $a = 0.9$, $b = 9.638$ and $c = -1.394$; in logs this is

$$\log(\pi_{wt} + 0.9) = 0.984 - 1.394(\log(u_t)) \tag{12.4}$$

Apart from the constant, equal to 0.9, this is a double-log or linear in the logs specification (where here, following Phillips, log refers to logs to the base 10 rather than e).

Following the idea that the rate of change of money wage rates should also be related to whether unemployment was increasing or decreasing, Phillips suggested that an equation of the form

$$\pi_{wt} + a = bu_t^c + h\left(\frac{du_t/dt}{u_t^m}\right) \qquad (12.5)$$

would probably be suitable, where h and m are parameters.

Phillips' estimation procedure has been the subject of some debate that has a bearing on the substantive issue of the methodological nature of the Phillips curve. To understand this we need some more detail of Phillips' computational method. First, the crosses on Phillips' figure are those pairs of observations on average values of π_{wt} and u_t for the following 6 intervals for unemployment: 0–2, 2–3, 3–4, 4–5, 5–7, 7–11. Phillips (*op. cit.*, p. 248) notes: 'Since each interval includes years in which unemployment was increasing and years in which it was decreasing the effect of changing unemployment on the rate of change of wage rates tends to be cancelled out by this averaging, so that each cross gives an approximation to the rate of change of wages which would be associated with the indicated level of unemployment if unemployment were held constant at that level.' The coefficients b and c were estimated by least squares using the 4 observations corresponding to the first 4 intervals, then a was chosen by trial and error to make the curve pass as close as possible to the remaining 2 pairs of observations. Phillips noted that provided u_t is a trend free variable, u_t^c is uncorrelated with $(du_t/dt)/u_t^m$ so omitting the latter term will not bias the remaining coefficients.

Gilbert (1976) views this procedure as one of computational convenience, rather than a methodological issue, which should be simply related to the difficulty at the time of estimating a nonlinear relationship. Support for this view could come from Phillips' (*op. cit.*, p. 249) note that 'At first sight it might appear preferable to carry out a multiple regression of y on the variables x and dx/dt. However, owing to the particular form of the relation between y and x in the present case it is not easy to find a suitable multiple linear regression equation.' (Phillips uses y for wage inflation and x for unemployment.) The implication being that if the computational means had existed in 1957, Phillips would have used them and all of the sample observations to estimate his preferred multiple regression.

A contrary opinion is taken by Desai (*op. cit.*), who views equation (12.1) as arising from steady state equilibrium defined by constant unemployment, say $u_t = u^*$ which implies $\Delta u_t = 0$, and constant wage inflation, say $\pi_{wt} = \pi_w^*$. In Desai's view the crosses on Phillips' diagram represent a static steady state equilibrium:

$$\pi_{wt}^* - \Delta q_t = a + f(u_t^*)$$

where Δq_t is productivity growth, and Phillips estimates this steady state relationship. Desai views the Phillips' procedure as approximating a cycle-free measure of u_t and π_{wt} with the preferred multiple regression arising by adding to the equilibrium the 'short-run' cyclical factor du_t/u_t. The problem with this explanation is that within each of Phillips' 6 intervals average $\Delta u_t = 0$ but u_t is not constant across the intervals, ranging from around 1.5% to 8.5%; with annual data, removing the cyclical effect should leave the trend, and if u_t is trend free this should be constant. While I am not convinced by this aspect of Desai's interpretation of Phillips, on balance preferring Gilbert's explanation, his views are relevant to section **12.3** below when we come to consider Friedman's critique of the Phillips curve.

12.2.3 The Phillips curve: a menu of choice?

Phillips suggested a further use of his estimated relationship between wage inflation and unemployment. The relationship could be used in reverse to find the level of unemployment associated with particular rates of wage inflation that might be thought desirable. For example, the level of unemployment associated with stable wage rates – or zero wage inflation – can be found by solving for u_t in

$$0 + 0.9 = 9.638u_t^{-1.394}$$

where $\pi_{wt} = 0$, which gives a value of u_t equal to 5.47%. As an alternative Phillips calculated the level of employment associated with a stable level of product prices assuming an increase in productivity of 2% p.a. In this case, assuming that the increase in productivity is paid out in full to employees, wage inflation of 2% p.a. will imply zero (product) price inflation. To obtain the corresponding value of u_t solve

$$2 + 0.9 = 9.638u_t^{-1.394}$$

to obtain $u_t = 2.36\%$.

It appeared, from the Phillips curve, that there was a menu of inflation–unemployment choices; high inflation and low unemployment through to low inflation and high unemployment.

12.2.4 The Phillips curve in the United States: an early view

There were several studies of interest, which followed that of Phillips, which seemed to support his view. Samuelson and Solow (1960) examined data for the United States from the 1890s through the late 1950s (surprisingly no precise sample period is given in their article). Their scatter diagram, with the percent increase in hourly earnings in manufacturing, as a proxy for wage inflation more generally, plotted against unemployment, is reproduced here as Figure 12.2. Samuelson and Solow (1960) observed:

> ... the bulk of the observations – the period between the turn of the century and the first war, the decade between the end of that war, and the Great Depression, and the most recent ten or twelve

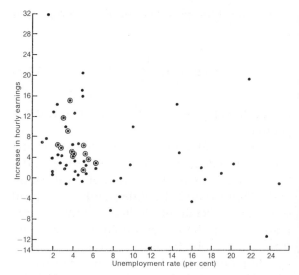

Figure 12.2 *Phillips scatter diagram for the United States – the circled points are for recent years. (Source: reprinted from Samuelson and Solow (1960) by permission, and copyright ©, of the American Economic Association.)*

years – all show a rather consistent pattern. Wage rates do tend to rise when the labour market is tight, and the tighter the faster. ... Manufacturing wages seem to stabilise absolutely when 4 or 5 per cent of the labour force is unemployed; and wage increases equal to the productivity increase of 2 to 3 per cent per year is the normal pattern at about 3 per cent unemployment. This is not so terribly different from Phillips' results for the UK....

Within this general pattern Samuelson and Solow note that the US Phillips curve seems to have shifted upward slightly in the 1940s and 1950s; and on the basis of this more recent data concludes that if wage inflation is to match the 2.5% p.a. productivity growth characteristic of the post-Second World War US economy then unemployment would have to be between 5 and 6% of the civilian labour force. This would give price stability. If the target level of unemployment was lower at, say, 3%, then price inflation would have to be higher at 4 to 5% p.a. and, with productivity growth of 2.5% p.a., this would imply wage inflation of 6.5 to 7.5% p.a. What seemed to be on offer was a 'menu of choice' and

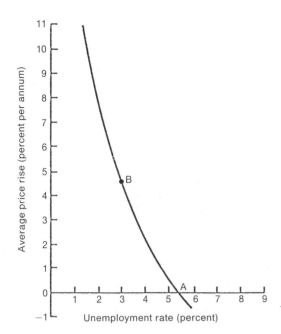

Figure 12.3 *Modified Phillips curve for the United States – a menu of choice? (Source: reprinted from Samuelson and Solow (1960) by permission, and copyright ©, of the American Economic Association.)*

Samuelson and Solow (1960) represented this in their Figure 2, which is reproduced here as Figure 12.3. The vertical axis is now (product) price inflation rather than wage inflation, but with constant productivity increases that were fully passed on, the translation between the two axes was simply the rate of productivity growth (that is price inflation of 0% p.a. would be associated with wage inflation of 2.5% p.a. and so on).

Although the menu seemed to characterise real choices available, Samuelson and Solow (1960) cautioned that their US Phillips curve would not necessarily maintain its shape in the longer run when it might be shifted down: '... it might be that the low pressure demand would so act upon wage and other expectations as to shift the curve downward in the longer run ...'. However, they continue: 'But also the opposite is conceivable. A low-pressure economy might build up within itself over the years larger and

larger amounts of structural unemployment.... The result would be an upward shift of our menu of choice ...'.

The 'menu of choice' view of the Phillips curve prevailed through much of the 1960s, but it was increasingly being questioned by economists. A number of the central criticisms are summarised in section **12.3** below. To provide a baseline to interpret subsequent developments we first analyse and re-estimate the Phillips curve using Phillips' original dataset for the United Kingdom for 1861–1913. As in previous chapters we start by assessing the time series properties of the data, first graphically in section **12.2.5** and then in section **12.2.6** using more formal statistical tests.

12.2.5   A graphical analysis of Phillips' data for 1861–1913

Given the considerable historical interest in the Phillips curve the first part of this chapter concentrated on reporting estimates using Phillips' own approach. However, in general, what we advocate is that there first be an assessment of the time series properties of the data as these have an important bearing on interpreting subsequent estimation results. In the case, where there are just two series, the data can be plotted on a scatter diagram – as in the original Phillips curve – and, in addition, use can be made of the device of plotting both series as time series using the left-hand scale for one variable and the right-hand scale for the other. Where the relationship between the two variables is thought to be negative a pattern may be easier to distinguish if the negative of one of the variables is used. In Figure 12.4 wage inflation (left-hand scale) is plotted against unemployment (right-hand scale), and in Figure 12.5 wage inflation is plotted against negative unemployment. The pattern between the two variables is brought out more clearly in Figure 12.5 where there is a broad, although not perfect, coincidence between the peaks and troughs in the two series.

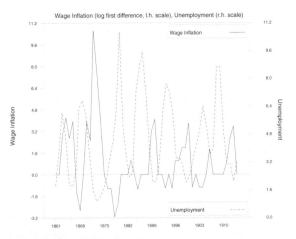

Figure 12.4 *Wage inflation and unemployment, United Kingdom 1861–1913*

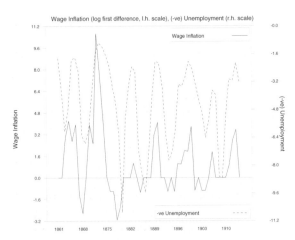

Figure 12.5 *Wage inflation and (−ve) unemployment, United Kingdom 1861–1913*

There are three points of note from these figures:

1. there is evidence of a negative correlation between the two series – wage inflation tends to be high when unemployment is low and vice versa;
2. given that the scales on the left- and right-hand axes are broadly the same, it is apparent that the unemployment series tends to display more variability than the wage inflation series, particularly after about 1880;

3. both series have a tendency to revert to their respective means (of 0.99% p.a. for wage inflation and 4.41% p.a. for unemployment) suggesting they are stationary to at least the first order. On this basis there is, therefore, something in Phillips' assertion of a negative relationship between wage inflation and unemployment over the period 1861–1913.

The next step in the analysis is to assess the stationarity of wage inflation and unemployment more formally, but first note an issue raised by Gilbert (1976) in his re-estimation of the Phillips curve which is concerned with how to approximate rates of change. Phillips defined the rate of wage inflation as the centred first difference, that is

$$\pi_{wt}^{+} \equiv 100(W_{t+1} - W_{t-1})/2W_t$$

where W_t is the money wage rate. An alternative approximation to the wage inflation rate, and one preferred by many writers since Phillips and used by Gilbert (*op. cit.*) in his re-estimation of the Phillips curve, is the log first difference (using natural logarithms, ln),

$$\pi_{wt} \equiv 100[\ln(W_t/W_{t-1})]$$

with logs taken to the base e. In addition Gilbert (*op. cit.*) also suggests that u_t^c should be approximated by $0.5(u_t^c + u_{t-1}^c)$. In the next section the results are compared using these alternative definitions of wage inflation and unemployment.

12.2.6 Testing for nonstationarity

The standard set of unit root tests is reported in Table 12.1. We first take Phillips' definition of the rate of change of money wage rates as the centred first difference, π_{wt}^{+}. In this case the results are quite surprising as they contrast with the visual impression from Figure 12.4. Formally $\Phi_3 = 3.106$ is not significant and neither is the $\hat{\tau}_{\beta}$ statistic of -2.462; both suggest a unit root; but the point estimate of β is close to zero, and

Table 12.1   *Unit root tests*

Variable	Model	$\hat{\tau}$	Φ_1	$\hat{\tau}_\mu$	$\hat{\mu}$	$\hat{\tau}_\beta$	$\hat{\beta}$	Φ_3
				Tests for 1 unit root				
π_{wt}^+	ADF(4)	−2.100	2.997	−2.421	0.221	−2.462	−0.007	3.106
π_{wt}	ADF(0)	−3.219	6.477	−3.591	0.463	−3.600	−0.010	6.489
u_t^{-1}	ADF(1)	−1.940	13.304	−5.177	0.136	−5.500	−0.002	15.129
u_t^c	ADF(1)	−2.510	11.954	−4.909	0.100	−5.228	−0.002	13.667
u_t	ADF(1)	−2.144	14.481	−5.381	2.499	−5.456	0.014	14.889
π_t	ADF(0)	−4.796	11.275	−4.745	0.004	−4.787	0.019	11.473

Notes: Sample period (before lags) 1861–1913.
π_{wt}^+ is the centred first difference of money wage rates, that is $\pi_{wt}^+ \equiv 100(W_{t+1} - W_{t-1})/2W_t$;
$\pi_{wt} \equiv 100[\ln(W_t/W_{t-1})]$; $u_t^{-1} \equiv 1/u_t$; $u_t^c \equiv u_t^{-1.324}$; $\pi_t \equiv 100[\ln(P_t/P_{t-1})]$.
Critical values

	$\hat{\tau}$	$\hat{\tau}_\mu$	$\hat{\tau}_\beta$	Φ_1	Φ_3
5%	−1.951	−2.903	−3.480	4.809	6.776
10%	−1.610	−2.584	−3.166	3.917	5.667

Critical values of $\hat{\tau}$, $\hat{\tau}_\mu$ and $\hat{\tau}_\beta$ obtained using Cheung–Lai response surface coefficients for $T = 52$ and $p = 1$; critical values of Φ_1 and Φ_3 obtained by simulation for $T = 50$ – see Chapter 6.

not significant; excluding the time trend we obtain $\hat{\tau}_\mu = -2.421$ with $\hat{\mu} = 0.221$. It might be tempting now to use Table 6.6 with a nonzero value for μ; however, the time series plot does not suggest a unit root process with drift, so some care has to be taken in interpreting these results. $\hat{\mu}$ is not significant with a 't' statistic of 1.236, or −0.304 if a unit root is imposed. If the constant is omitted then $\hat{\tau} = -2.100$ which is significant, the 5% critical value being approximately −1.951. Hence, rejection of the null hypothesis of a unit root is the conclusion, providing the power of the test is improved by basing inference on the most parsimonious model consistent with the data.

There is less ambiguity when the more usual definition of the rate of change of money wage rates as the first difference of the logarithm is used, but care still has to be taken. Although $\Phi_3 = 6.489$ is between the 5% and 10% critical values, the point estimate of β is again very close to zero and not significant, whether or not the unit root is imposed. With the time trend excluded $\hat{\tau}_\mu = -3.591$ which exceeds, in absolute value, the 5% critical value of (approximately) −2.903. Note that $\hat{\mu} = 0.463$ and, again,

with $\hat{\mu}$ so large, there must be doubt over the unit root hypothesis because there is no indication of drift in the time series. However, $\hat{\mu}$ is not significant, with a 't' statistic of 1.524 or 0.216 if the unit root is imposed. Omitting the constant $\hat{\tau} = -3.219$, which is also significant; and note that $\Phi_1 = 6.477$, which is significant.

The next two variables in Table 12.1 are motivated from Phillips' suggestion that the relationship between wage inflation and the unemployment rate is nonlinear. Candidate variables being u_t^{-1} and u_t^c where $c = -1.324$, this value of c is suggested by re-estimation of the Phillips curve – see Table 12.2 below. In both cases the null hypothesis of a unit root is firmly rejected. For example, for $u_t^c = u_t^{-1.324}$, $\Phi_3 = 13.667$, $\hat{\tau}_\beta = -5.228$, $\Phi_1 = 11.954$ and $\hat{\tau}_\mu = -4.909$, and all suggest rejection of the null hypothesis of a unit root. For later reference, also included in Table 12.1 are test statistics for u_t and price inflation, $\pi_t = 100 \ln(P_t/P_{t-1})$, where P_t is price of final products (the series published in Phelps-Brown and Hopkins (1950)). The case of u_t has already been considered in section **7.9.2** so we can be brief here. All the test statistics strongly suggest rejection of the unit root hypothesis.

Table 12.2 *Re-estimation of the Phillips curve*

Centred first difference

1. Phillips' original estimates

$$\hat{\pi}_{wt}^{+} = -0.9 + 9.638u_t^{-1.394}$$

2. Re-estimation using all data

$$\hat{\pi}_{wt}^{+} = -0.883 + 8.938u_t^{-1.384(-4.350)}$$
$$(-1.499)\ (9.466)$$

$\hat{\sigma} = 1.322$
dw $= 0.777$
SC(1) $= 26.859[0.000]$

Log difference

3. $\hat{\pi}_{wt} = -1.408 + 10.833u_t^{-1.324(-5.271)}$
$(-2.308)\ (11.883)$

$\hat{\sigma} = 1.279$
dw $= 1.853$
SC(1) $= 0.262[0.610]$

4. $\hat{\pi}_{wt} = -2.323 + 10.925(1/u_t)$
$(-6.978)\ (11.749)$

$\hat{\sigma} = 1.287$
dw $= 1.885$
SC(1) $= 0.152[0.697]$

5. $\hat{\pi}_{wt} = -1.018 + 10.613(0.5u_t^{-1.549(-3.800)} + 0.5u_{t-1}^{-1.549(-3.800)})$
$(-1.343)\quad (8.381)$

$\hat{\sigma} = 1.592$
dw $= 1.342$
SC(1) $= 6.140[0.013]$

6. $\hat{\pi}_{wt} = -1.092 + 10.526(u_t^{-1.447(-4.452)} + u_{t-1}^{-1.447(-4.452)})$
$(-1.746)\ (10.410)$

$\quad - 0.063(100/(1 - 1.951))(u_t^{(1-1.951)(5.041)} - u_{t-1}^{(1-1.951)(5.041)})$
$(-2.516)\qquad\quad (5.041)$

$\hat{\sigma} = 1.297$
dw $= 1.977$
SC(1) $= 0.001[0.970]$

7. $\hat{\pi}_{wt} = -0.661 + 9.838u_t^{-1.572(-4.833)} - 0.011(100)(0.5(\Delta u_t/u_{t-1}) + (\Delta u_{t-1}/u_{t-2}))$
$(-1.746)\ (9.418)\qquad\qquad (-1.900)$

$\hat{\sigma} = 1.269$
dw $= 1.883$
SC(1) $= 0.000[0.977]$

Notes: Sample period (before lags): 1861–1913.
't' statistics in parentheses (.); marginal significance level in parentheses [.].

For example, $\Phi_3 = 14.889$ is considerably in excess of the 5% critical value of 6.776; similarly $\hat{\tau}_\beta$, $\hat{\tau}_\mu$ and $\hat{\tau}$ all suggest rejection of the unit root. In the case of π_t, the unit root hypothesis is also firmly rejected: $\Phi_3 = 11.473$, $\hat{\tau}_\beta = -4.787$, $\Phi_1 = 11.275$ and $\hat{\tau}_\mu = -4.745$, and all indicate rejection of the null hypothesis.

The test statistics for a unit root should be accompanied by an assessment of the maintained regression from which they come. The order of the ADF(p) regression has to be determined to ensure that the residuals are free from serial correlation; generally, this is done in combination with deleting insignificant lagged dependent variables. Also of interest is how far numerically, rather than statistically which is what the DF test statistics assess, $\hat{\gamma}$ is from 0; equivalently how close is $\sum_{i=1}^{p+1} \hat{\phi}_i$ to 1? To illustrate both of these issues consider the process for assessing π_{wt}. Starting from an ADF(4) maintained regression, the LM test statistic for serial correlation was SC(4) $= 7.916$ with msl $= 9.4\%$ and marginal 't' statistic $= 1.389$ with msl $= 17.2\%$. Reducing to an ADF(3), SC(4) $= 6.666$

with msl = 15.5%, and marginal 't' statistic = 1.414 with msl = 16.4%. Reducing further to an ADF(2), SC(4) = 7.266 with msl = 12.2% and marginal 't' statistic = 1.689 with msl = 9.83%; as two variables have been deleted an F test is now possible and gives $F(2, 44) = 1.182$ with msl = 17.5%. Reducing to an ADF(1), SC(4) = 9.649 with msl = 4.7%, and marginal 't' statistic of 0.867 with msl = 39.1%; the F test gave $F(3, 43) = 1.906$ with msl = 14.3%. The value of SC(4) is closest yet to stopping the reduction process, but if the regression is reduced to ADF(0), SC(4) = 3.844 with msl = 42.7%, which is satisfactory; further, the F test gave $F(4, 42) = 1.943$ with msl = 12.1% – again satisfactory against the 'general' model. The F and marginal 't' tests will not always give the same results in this 'general-to-specific' strategy, and on occasion judgement, together with an evaluation of the serial correlation test statistics, will be necessary. In multiple tests is usual to use a lower msl to stop the reduction process and to control the overall type one error. The resulting preferred regression is:

$$\Delta \hat{\pi}_{wt} = 0.463 - 0.419 \pi_{wt-1}$$
$$(1.524)(-3.591)$$

Note that $\hat{\gamma} = -0.419$ which implies $\hat{\phi}_1 = 0.581$. This seems sufficiently far from the unit root *not* to worry about whether the process generating π_{wt} is close to a nonstationary process.

12.2.7   Re-estimation of the Phillips curve, 1861–1913

Estimation of Phillips' original equation and some variants are reported in Table 12.2. Apart from regression 1, which reports Phillips' original coefficients, the equations use all the data in the sample period. When the centred first difference is used Phillips' original estimates are quite close to those resulting from (nonlinear) estimation using all the data – compare regressions 1 and 2. For example, Phillips' estimate of the exponent on the unemployment rate is −1.394

compared to −1.384 from the full sample. One aspect of this regression which Gilbert (1976) drew attention to is the serial correlation in the residuals. In regression 2 the dw statistic is low, and the SC(1) statistic is firmly in favour of (at least) first order serial correlation.

In regression 3 the centred first difference of wage rates is replaced with the log difference. As in regression 2 the estimates are significant, but in regression 3 there is no evidence of (first) order serial correlation with a dw statistic of 1.853 and an SC(1) statistic of 0.262 with an msl of 61%. The estimate of c is −1.324 with an estimated standard error of 0.251, giving a 't' statistic of −5.271. The test statistic for the null hypothesis that $c = -1$ is $(-1.324 - (-1))/0.251 = -1.291$, which does not imply rejection of the null hypothesis at conventional significance levels. Imposing $c = -1$ leads to regression 4 which uses the reciprocal of the unemployment rate, with only minor differences in the goodness of fit, dw and SC statistics compared to the previous regression.

Regression 5 takes up the suggestion in Gilbert (*op. cit.*) of replacing u_t with $0.5(u_t^c + u_{t-1}^c)$, while also using the log difference of wage rates. There is, however, a deterioration in the goodness of fit comparing regressions 3 and 5, with an increase in the estimated standard error of about 25%, and some evidence of first order serial correlation from the SC statistic.

Regression 6 takes up Phillips' suggestion captured in equation (12.5), reproduced below for reference,

$$\pi_{wt} + a = bu_t^c + h\left(\frac{du_t/dt}{u_t^m}\right) \quad (12.6)$$

with the expected relationship between wage inflation and the rate of change of unemployment negative. Gilbert (*op. cit.*) approximates $(du_t/dt)/u_t^m$ by

$$[100/(1 - m)][u_t^{(1-m)} - u_{t-1}^{(1-m)}] \quad \text{for } m \neq 1$$

and

$$100[\ln(u_t) - \ln(u_{t-1})] \quad \text{for } m = 1$$
$$(12.7)$$

This approximation is used in regression 6 and, compared with regression 5, there are only minor changes to the estimated coefficients a, b and c. The estimate of h is -0.063 with a 't' statistic of -2.516, and the estimate of m is 1.951 with a 't' statistic of 5.041, both coefficients are significant and have the anticipated sign. The estimated standard error of the regression at 1.297 is still slightly larger than for regression 4, but it is a clear improvement over regression 5 which does not include an approximation to the rate of change of unemployment.

As a final variant regression 7 adds to regression 3 a simpler approximation to a variable capturing the rate of change of unemployment; specifically the simple moving average given by $0.5[(\Delta u_t/u_{t-1}) + (\Delta u_{t-1}/u_{t-2})]$ was used. This variable is significant (recall that the anticipated sign is negative so the alternative hypothesis is one sided) and the coefficient is negative, and there is a minor improvement in the goodness of fit.

In summary, re-estimation of the Phillips curve in regression 2, using all the sample data from 1861 to 1913 and Phillips' definition of wage inflation as the centred first difference, produced coefficient estimates remarkably similar to those originally published by Phillips who used just six observations based on an averaging procedure. There was, however, evidence of serial correlation in the residuals of this regression, which Gilbert (*op. cit.*) suggested may be an artefact of using the centred first difference. Re-estimation with the log first difference of money wage rates in regression 3 removed the serial correlation, and constraining c to equal -1 in regression 4 led only to a minor deterioration in the goodness of fit. Using the approximation to u_t^m suggested by Gilbert (*op. cit.*) did not lead to an improvement in either goodness of fit or the serial correlation statistics. In regression 6, following Gilbert (*op cit.*), a term was added to approximate the rate of change of unemployment; this improved regression 5 but showed no marked improvement over the simpler regression 3. The best fitting equation was regression 7, which used a simple moving average of the rate of change of unemployment to improve regression 3.

The apparent statistical success of the re-estimated Phillips curve(s) reported in Table 12.2 should not, however, rule out the possibility that their specification can be improved. In section **12.3** a number of issues are considered relating to whether or not the Phillips curve is misspecified.

12.3 Is the Phillips curve misspecified?

In this section we briefly recap Phillips' theoretical justification for the existence of a negative relationship between wage inflation and unemployment, this is so as to put in context criticisms and alternative justifications of the Phillips curve. In sections **12.3.1**, **12.3.2** and **12.3.3**, respectively, three alternative views of the correlation between wage or price inflation and unemployment are outlined due in turn to Fisher (1926), Friedman (1968, 1975, 1977) and a number of authors, especially Layard and Nickell (1985, 1986), who have developed an imperfect competition model which involves a Phillips curve. For an extensive critique of the early literature on the inflation–unemployment trade-off see Santomero and Seater (1978) and for a more recent discussion and assessment see King, Stock and Watson (1994a, b, 1995) and Evans (1994).

In section **12.3.4** we briefly consider a comparison between the Phillips curve and what, with some licence, are called the 'Fisher' and 'Friedman' curves. The alternative views suggest a point of agreement in the need to extend the Phillips curve to include expected price inflation, this is taken up in section **12.3.5**, and **12.3.6** indicates some of the difficulties in distinguishing between Phillips' interpretation of inflation and unemployment and the supply side interpretation.

First, note that Phillips has been criticised from both sides of the Atlantic for apparently failing to derive the theoretical basis of the negative relationship between wage inflation and unemployment. 'As is well known, Phillips nowhere derived from theoretical considerations the relationship that bears his name' (Gilbert 1976, p. 52). Phillips was also criticised for apparently getting wrong the theoretical justification he did give: 'Some of us were sceptical from the outset about the validity of a stable Phillips curve, primarily on theoretical rather than empirical grounds. What mattered for employment, we argued, was not wages in dollars or pounds or kroner but real wages' (Friedman 1977, p. 455). However these criticisms are rather harsh. In Phillips' model employers compete for the services of labour; if labour is in short supply relative to demand, as indicated by the state of unemployment, wage rates are bid up, tempting labour from other firms and industries. The change in money wage rates is positively related to the excess demand for labour, and excess demand is negatively related to unemployment; hence the negative relationship between wage inflation and unemployment. In addition, according to Phillips, when activity is increasing, as evidenced by an unemployment rate which is decreasing, employers bid more vigorously for labour. Employers and labour are aware of the real wage implications of increases in nominal wage rates particularly through cost of living adjustments. It could certainly be argued that this is not as sophisticated or complete an explanation as later theories, but Phillips is aware of the need to justify the relationship that bears his name.

12.3.1 Fisher (1926) and Phillips (1958)

In this section we consider two differences of specification between the Phillips curve and, what we might call, by analogy, the 'Fisher' curve arising from Fisher's 1926 article 'A Statistical Relation Between Unemployment and Price Changes'. This article predates Phillips by 50 years or so and was concerned with a negative correlation between price inflation and unemployment in the United States between 1915 and 1925. A scatter diagram that relates price, rather than wage, inflation to unemployment is what we designate as the Fisher curve. An illustration of this and comparison with the Phillips curve is given in section **12.3.4**. The differences referred to here relate to the direction of causation and the temporary nature of the inflation–unemployment trade-off.

It has already been noted that Phillips emphasised the causal relation as running from unemployment to wage inflation: 'when the demand for labour is high and there are very few unemployed we should expect employers to bid wage rates up quite rapidly' (Phillips *op. cit.*, p. 245). In contrast Fisher (1976, p. 498) suggested that the correlation arises due to causation the other way round. Inflation is a stimulus to employment which arises because 'when the price level is rising, a business man finds his receipts rising as fast, on the average, as this general rise of prices, but not his expenses, because his expenses consist, to large extent, of things which are contractually fixed', and as a result 'Employment is stimulated – *for a time at least*' (my emphasis). On this view a crucial distinction is that of contractual differences between output prices and input prices.

Friedman (1975, p. 12) describes the difference in causation as 'the truth of 1926 (Fisher) and the error of 1958 (Phillips)' (my notes in parentheses). Fisher is aware that the observed correlation might not be causal, that there might be some third influence affecting both inflation and employment but, notwithstanding this theoretical point, he concludes in favour of 'a genuine and straightforward casual relationship' (*op. cit.*, p. 502). We return to this point in the context of recent US data in section **12.5**.

This view of the origin of the correlation between price inflation and unemployment subsequently finds a formalisation in monetarist macroeconomic models – see, for example,

Anderson and Carlson (1972) – which include an aggregate supply curve of the form

$$u_t = \alpha_0 + \alpha_1 \pi_t + \varepsilon_{st} \tag{12.8}$$

where π_t is inflation, ε_{st} is a supply side shock and $\alpha_1 < 0$, which contrasts with Phillips' view that

$$\pi_t = \beta_0 + \beta_1 u_t + \varepsilon_{dt} \tag{12.9}$$

While models of the form (12.8) are also subject to the criticism that they do not distinguish between actual and anticipated inflation, an issue we take up below, the central point here is that Fisher's causation, and aggregate supply equations of the form (12.8), emphasise different economic mechanisms compared to Phillips' view. As equations (12.8) and (12.9) contain the same variables they are, without further restrictions, observationally equivalent; the question of whether it is possible to distinguish between these alternative models from an econometric point of view is a matter taken up by King and Watson (1987).

In addition to the difference on causation another substantive difference arises from the importance of Fisher's remark that employment is stimulated 'for a time at least'. This suggests that the inflation stimulus is temporary: there is not a permanent trade-off, since, with time, the contractually fixed items of expenses are renegotiated and catch up with the increase in prices to leave relative magnitudes unchanged.

(Fisher refers throughout to price rather than wage inflation and, to a considerable degree, this has led to a difference of terminology and tradition between studies based in the United States and the United Kingdom where, in the former, the 'Phillips correlation' is taken to refer to the correlation between price inflation and unemployment and in the latter wage inflation replaces price inflation. Friedman (*op. cit.*, p. 13) does not regard this as a substantive difference on the grounds that prices and wages tend to move together.)

Fisher's concern about the distinction between the short-run and the long-run trade-off anticipated a considerable amount of research which sought to establish whether the observed negative correlation between contemporaneous values of inflation and unemployment would be sustained in anything other than the short term. This subsequent research has, however, been primarily motivated by a distinction between nominal and real wages, which we consider in the next section. Fisher's point was different: he suggested that input prices were less flexible in the short run than output prices, but that in the long run renegotiations of contracts would not lead to short run differences persisting.

12.3.2 Friedman's model

Friedman (1968) argued that Phillips had made a fundamental mistake in failing to distinguish between *nominal* wages and *real* wages; and he further distinguished between anticipated and unanticipated variables. As to the first distinction:

> A lower level of unemployment is an indication that there is an excess demand for labour that will produce upward pressure on *real* wages. A higher level of unemployment is an indication that there is an excess supply of labour that will produce downward pressure on *real* wage rates. (My emphasis)

On this basis the Phillips curve which relates inflation in nominal wage rates to unemployment seems completely counter to economic intuition. Nevertheless, in the interim or adjustment period there may occur a negative short-run correlation between wage inflation and unemployment.

The essence of Friedman's model, which leads to short-run Phillips curves which are not vertical, is the misperception of workers as to whether real wages have increased following an increase in nominal wages. This takes place in an economy with perfectly competitive firms producing where the real wage is equal to the marginal product of labour. Suppose starting from a position in which the labour market clears there is an increase in aggregate nominal demand resulting in an increase in prices, following this employers are willing to pay higher nominal wages to attract additional workers (this part of the story is as in Phillips' competitive bidding). Now in order to produce extra output the employers' real wage, which is equated to the marginal product of labour, has to fall. Provided any consequent increase in money wages is less than the increase in prices, the real wage has fallen and there will be an increase in output.

Workers adjust their perception of prices more slowly than employers, because what matters to them is prices in general, on which information is costly to obtain or which is only available with a lag, rather than prices in particular. Friedman (1977, p. 466) notes: 'Price indexes are imperfect; they are only available with a lag and generally are applied to contract terms only with a further lag.' Workers therefore perceive an increase in nominal wages as an increase in real wages and offer more labour. The apparent contradiction of employers demanding more labour at a lower real wage and workers supplying it at a higher real wage than initially is resolved by their different perceptions of the real wage. As a result of the increase in demand, prices and money wages have increased and unemployment has decreased. There is a Phillips curve relationship between wage inflation and unemployment conditional on the workers' perception of price inflation.

But, as Friedman points out (1977, p. 457), this is temporary situation: in due course workers' perceptions catch up with reality and, therefore, as the relative price of labour has not changed employment returns to its original market clearing position and unemployment returns to its 'natural' rate given the labour force. This scenario could be rehearsed again for a different perceived rate of inflation, which would draw out another short-run relationship between wage inflation and price inflation. However, in Friedman's model only one long

run, the natural rate of unemployment, is sustainable since that is determined by real forces, and is compatible with any perceived rate of inflation. Hence there is a series of short-run Phillips curves each conditional on a perceived or expected rate of price inflation, but the long-run Phillips curve is vertical. To achieve a long-run trade-off between wage inflation and unemployment there must be a continuing acceleration in perceived price inflation, but even that assumes workers will not come to understand the nature of their continuing mistakes in the perception of inflation.

If one accepts the view that the long-run Phillips curve is vertical, at what Friedman has called the 'natural rate of unemployment', and that if a trade-off exists it is a purely temporary phenomenon, what led Phillips to suggest a relationship between changes in nominal wage rates and unemployment? Friedman (1975, p. 16 *et seq.*) has suggested that Phillips was working within a framework in which prices were regarded as stable, in which case changes in nominal wages are equal to changes in real wages. But this does not adequately answer the puzzle: it assumes that increases in wages are not passed on into the price level as would occur if output prices were set on a mark-up over cost basis. There is some room for wages to increase with no increase in prices if the difference is made up in productivity gains but, in general, this seems an inadequate key to the puzzle although it is part of it as we shall see.

The key to the puzzle lies, as Desai (*op. cit.*, p. 253) suggests, in a careful reading of Phillips' original article. Phillips (*op. cit.*, p. 246) was aware of the importance of price inflation to wage inflation and of the distinction between nominal and real wage rates: 'A third factor (apart from unemployment and its rate of change) which may affect the rate of change of money wage rates is the rate of change of retail prices, operating through cost of living adjustments in wage rates' (my clarification in parentheses). To understand the role of price inflation (the rate of change of retail prices) in

Phillips' analysis we have to understand his distinction between demand pull and cost push inflation. First, note that in Phillips' framework employers bid competitively for the services of labour, that is the pressure for money wage rates to increase or decrease from the demand side. Suppose money wage rates increase by 3% p.a. as a result of this competitive bidding and simultaneously retail prices increase by, say, 1% (resulting from, say, 3% price inflation less a 2% increase in productivity), then the 'demand pull' increase in money wage rates exceeds the 'cost push' increase in retail prices. Even though the 3% increase in money wage rates has arisen from competitive bidding it can be viewed as compensating for the increase in retail prices – no additional increase is needed.

So when is an increase in money wage rates pushed by the cost of living? Suppose employers' competitive bidding for labour creates no pressure on money wage rates to change, so there is no demand pull; import price inflation is 20% p.a. and import costs have a weight of 0.1 in the unit cost of output so that, *ceteris paribus*, final output prices will increase by 2% p.a. (=0.1 × 20%). If productivity growth is less than 2% p.a. a cost of living adjustment is required to ensure that real wages do not fall. In general a cost of living adjustment is needed when the increase in money wage rates due to competitive bidding is less than the deficiency in productivity growth relative to price inflation from the cost side. During the period 1861–1913 Phillips suggests that only in 1862 would the increase in import prices (of 12.5% p.a.) be sufficient to trigger a separate cost of living adjustment. It is not that Phillips is unaware of the importance of price inflation to wage inflation, as some authors have suggested, he argues that certain conditions have to be satisfied if it is to have a separate role and they were not generally satisfied during this period. It seems likely that if Phillips had been undertaking his empirical analysis with data from the 1970s and 1980s he would have explicitly included a price inflation term in his equation.

12.3.3 Imperfect competition

More recent explanations of the Phillips curve have stressed the importance of imperfect competition – see especially Layard and Nickell (1985, 1986) and for an excellent exposition Carlin and Soskice (1990) – in which wages are set through bargains between trade unions and employers. If claims to output by employers and workers exceed the total available then, given an accommodating monetary policy, competing (and inconsistent) claims result in inflation and unemployment. The natural rate of unemployment in Friedman's model is replaced with the nonaccelerating inflation rate of unemployment, usually referred to as the NAIRU. This is the rate at which the competing claims of labour and profits are reconciled and inflation is constant.

On the union side the bargained real wage, BRW, is a positive function of employment, that is, given a constant labour force, it is a negative function of unemployment; *ceteris paribus* an increase in unemployment weakens the bargaining strength of unions (and individuals in a nonunion context). Employers on the other hand are interested in the price-determined real wage, PDRW. For example, with normal cost pricing the labour cost per unit is marked up by a constant fraction μ, so that output price is $(1 + \mu)$ times labour cost per unit, say $P_t = (1 + \mu) W_t e_t / y_t$ where P_t is the per unit output price, W_t is the wage per unit of labour, e_t is employment and y_t output. Rearranging this expression to obtain W_t/P_t, the price-determined real wage is $(1 + \mu)^{-1} y_t / e_t$ where y_t/e_t is output per unit of labour – or labour productivity. With constant labour productivity the PDRW is constant. Combining this with the BRW, which is a positive function of employment, gives an equilibrium at their point of intersection, at which profit per unit plus labour cost per unit sum exactly to the output price: the competing claims are consistent. Given the labour force this determines an equilibrium rate of unemployment – the NAIRU. If unemployment is less than NAIRU unions bargain for a real wage greater than at equilibrium: money wages increase more than at the NAIRU, and so do product prices as employers respond to their potential loss of profit per unit of output by raising prices more than they had anticipated at the NAIRU. Lower unemployment is achieved but with higher wage and price inflation: there is a Phillips curve at least in the short run.

12.3.4 The Phillips, 'Fisher' and 'Friedman' curves

To engage in an interesting but hypothetical situation suppose some 40 years ago, following the arguments sketched above, you were aware of the following three possibilities: a negative relationship between wage inflation and unemployment (the Phillips curve); a negative relationship between price inflation and unemployment (the 'Fisher' curve); and a negative relationship between real wage inflation, that is $\pi_{wt} - \pi_t$, and unemployment (the 'Friedman' curve). Which of these three possibilities gets most support from the data when contemporaneous variables are taken together? Figure 12.6 plots these curves. The original Phillips curve which uses the centred first difference is Figure 12.6A and the log first difference is Figure 12.6B; the 'Fisher' curve is Figure 12.6C and the 'Friedman' curve is Figure 12.6D. It is evident from Figure 12.6 that the Phillips curve, with either the centred first difference or the log first difference, captures a stronger empirical relationship than either of the other relationships. In Figure 12.6C there is, perhaps, a weak and possibly negative, linear relationship between price inflation and unemployment; and in Figure 12.6D there is very little support for any clear relationship. To be fair to Fisher and Friedman, they both emphasised the importance of lags in their respective relationships. The former found the maximum correlation between price inflation and unemployment using US data for 1915 to 1925 at 6 months, and the latter suggested that workers' perception of prices

lagged behind actual prices. Nevertheless using annual data may well capture the lag within the frequency of a year. It is perhaps not surprising that the Phillips curve generated such interest: it was an empirical phenomenon prompting further research.

Scatter diagrams are limited to two dimensions and could be misleading if there is a need to condition wage inflation on a second variable in order to examine the marginal contribution of a third variable (or condition one variable on two others to examine the marginal contribution of a fourth variable, and so on). The criticisms of the Phillips curve contain a common element, to which we turn in the next section, the need to recognise the potential importance of expectations of inflation.

12.3.5 Expectations and the reformulation of the Phillips curve

Dissatisfaction with the theoretical basis of the Phillips curve led to a number of reformulations, especially to take into account the importance of real wages and expected prices – see Friedman (1968, 1975, 1977) and Phelps (1970). Suppose, in line with the Friedman critique, wage units are interested in their real wage rather than their nominal wage but at the time they bargain for increases in wages, future prices are generally unknown. For example, suppose the wage level, at time $t-1$ is low and the wage unit is bargaining for an increase in wages to last until the next wage round one year hence in period t. Suppose productivity growth is 2% p.a. so that, *ceteris paribus*, an increase in wages of 2% p.a. could be accommodated with no increase in prices. However, in anticipating prices over the period $t-1$ to t the wage unit expects an increase in the price level from 100 to 110, thus in order to gain a 2% p.a. increase in *real* wages the wage unit should bargain for an increase in wages of 12.2% to take it to 112.2. In terms of real wages the comparison is period

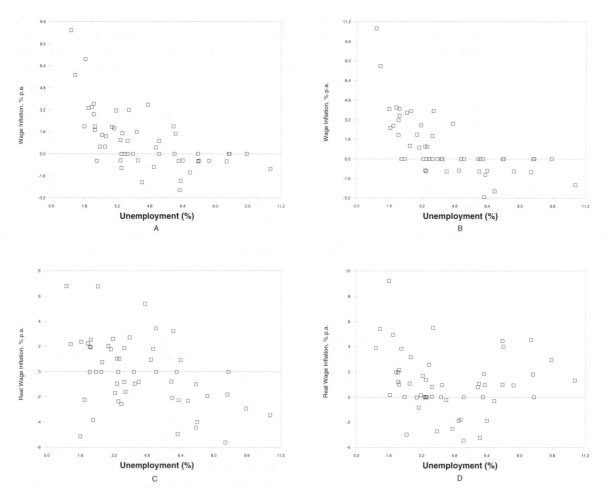

Figure 12.6   A – *The Phillips curve – wage inflation (centred first difference). B – The Phillips curve – wage inflation (log first difference). C – Price inflation and unemployment – the Fisher curve. D – Real wage inflation and unemployment – the Friedman curve*

$t - 1$, $W_{t-1}/P_{t-1} = (100/100) = 1$, to period t, $(W_t/P_t) = (112.2/110) = 1.02$. Hence, if inflation is correctly anticipated the wage unit receives its bargained for increase in real wages of 2%.

This suggests that the Phillips curve should be modified to add expected inflation to the right-hand side. That is,

$$\pi_{wt} = a + f(u_t) + \delta\pi_t^e + \eta_t \qquad (12.10)$$

where π_t^e is (price) inflation expected at $t - 1$ to prevail over period t, that is $E_{t-1}\{\pi_t\}$; and δ is a

coefficient reflecting the degree of adjustment of wage inflation to anticipated price inflation. We have also now made explicit a zero mean 'disturbance' term, η_t. The value of δ is critical in determining the trade-off between wage inflation and unemployment. If $\delta = 1$ then for a *given* level of unemployment, π_{wt} is greater by exactly the amount π_t^e; and in this case by taking π_t^e to the left-hand side (12.10) can be viewed as an equation determining wage inflation less expected price inflation, $\pi_{wt} - \pi_t^e$. Otherwise the vertical displacement in the Phillips curve is given by $\delta\pi_t^e$.

12.3.6 A supply side interpretation of the importance of inflation expectations

For another way of introducing expectations into the relationship between inflation and unemployment recall the aggregate supply interpretation of the Phillips correlation given by equation (12.8), that is $u_t = \alpha_0 + \alpha_1 \pi_t + \varepsilon_{st}$, but now with the modification that unemployment also depends upon expected inflation π_t^e,

$$u_t = \alpha_0 + \alpha_1 \pi_t + \alpha_2 \pi_t^e + \varepsilon_{st}$$

In the special case $\alpha_1 = -\alpha_2$ unemployment is a function of unexpected inflation $\pi_t - \pi_t^e$:

$$u_t = \alpha_0 + \alpha_1 (\pi_t - \pi_t^e) + \varepsilon_{st} \qquad (12.11)$$

so that when actual and expected inflation are equal then, apart from the stochastic term, unemployment is equal to a constant, sometimes referred to as the 'natural rate', and it is only when inflation is unexpected that there is an impact on unemployment.

A reinterpretation of a simple version of the Phillips curve results in the same observationally equivalent structure if bargaining is in terms of real wages, that is $\delta = 1$. Start with a linear version of the Phillips curve,

$$\pi_{wt} = a + b u_t + \delta \pi_t^e + \eta_t$$

with the assumption that wage inflation is equal to price inflation plus productivity growth, ρ, that is $\pi_{wt} = \pi_t + \rho$. Substituting for π_{wt} and rearranging we obtain:

$$u_t = a_1^* + a_2^* \pi_t + a_3^* \pi_t^e + \eta_t^* \qquad (12.12)$$

where $a_1^* = (\rho - a)/b$, $a_2^* = 1/b$, $a_3^* = -\delta/b$, $\eta_t^* = \eta_t/b$. This is observationally equivalent to (12.11) if $\delta = 1$, reducing to

$$u_t = a_1^* + a_2^* (\pi_t - \pi_t^e) + \eta_t^* \qquad (12.13)$$

So that in this linear case, unless further criteria are brought to bear, the supply side and price equation interpretations of the Philips correlation are identical.

12.4 Estimation of the expectations augmented Phillips curve (EAPC)

We now consider estimation of the original Phillips curve with the difference that the equation is augmented by expected price inflation; however, over the sample period there are no series available to directly measure expected inflation and so this problem has to be circumvented. Two solutions to this problem are considered as they appeared chronologically in the empirical literature; first, that of adaptive expectations and, second, rational expectations. In terms of the historical development of estimating the expectations augmented Phillips curve, adaptive expectations, or some close relative thereof, was the dominant framework until the critiques and assessments of Lucas (1972) and Sargent (1971) and the practical implementations of rational expectations methods by, for example, Lucas (1973), Sargent (1973) and McCallum (1976). We follow the historical development in this section to assess the impact of these ideas and methods using the original Phillips data for the period 1861–1913.

12.4.1 Timing of expectations

There is an ambiguity in the empirical literature concerning the timing of expectations on the price inflation variable in the augmented Phillips curve, (12.10). We alternatively find the expectation of inflation defined at $t - 1$ for t, or at t for $t + 1$; we denote these respectively as $_{t-1}\pi_t^e$ and $_t\pi_{t+1}^e$. The choice should be related back to what is an appropriate definition of the expected real wage for period t. For example, suppose the log of the wage rate, set at the end of period $t - 1$ to prevail through to the end of period t, is denoted w_t and at the beginning of period t the average price level for period t is unknown. Agents form an expectation of the log of the price level for t based on information at $t - 1$, say $E_{t-1}\{p_t\}$, and hence an expected (log) real wage for t: $w_t - E_{t-1}\{p_t\}$. This is one possible definition of the 'expected real wage'. Subtracting the log of the real wage at $t - 1$, $w_{t-1} - p_{t-1}$, we obtain the difference between wage inflation and expected price inflation: $\pi_{wt} - \{_{t-1}\pi_t^e\}$, where the following have been defined, $\pi_{wt} \equiv w_t - w_{t-1}$ and

$$_{t-1}\pi_t^e \equiv E_{t-1}\{p_t - p_{t-1}\} = E_{t-1}\{p_t\} - p_{t-1}$$

This development suggests that the standard Phillips curve should be augmented by $_{t-1}\pi_t^e$, so that the general form is

$$\pi_{wt} = a + f(u_t) + \delta(_{t-1}\pi_t^e) + \eta_t$$

This is the dating of inflation expectations preferred in this section and how we interpret equation (12.10) above. In order to justify the use of the alternative

$$_t\pi_{t+1}^e \equiv E_t\{p_{t+1} - p_t\} = E_t\{p_{t+1}\} - p_t$$

rather than $_{t-1}\pi_t^e$ we could return to the definition of the real wage and argue that this should be defined as $w_t - E_t\{p_{t+1}\}$. McCallum (1976) uses $_t\pi_{t+1}^e$ as his central case but notes (McCallum *op. cit.*, p. 46, fn 8) that the results are 'not too dissimilar'. The impact of choosing this alternative is considered in a review question.

12.4.2 The adaptive expectations hypothesis: formulation

The simplest adaptive expectations hypothesis, AEH, for price inflation is

$$\pi_t^e - \pi_{t-1}^e = \gamma(\pi_{t-1} - \pi_{t-1}^e) + \xi_1 \qquad (12.14a)$$

that is

$$\pi_t^e = \pi_{t-1}^e + \gamma(\pi_{t-1} - \pi_{t-1}^e) + \xi_t \qquad (12.14b)$$

where ξ_t is a zero mean disturbance term and $0 < \gamma \leq 1$. (In some formulations ξ_t is set identically to zero.) In this section there is no ambiguity in suppressing the first subscript on inflation expectations so we write π_t^e for $_{t-1}\pi_t^e$ and π_{t-1}^e for $_{t-2}\pi_{t-1}^e$. The idea is that the revision to expected inflation is a proportion, γ, of last periods error, $\pi_{t-1} - \pi_{t-1}^e$, in predicting inflation. The parameter γ governs the sensitivity, or speed of adjustment, of the learning mechanism; for example, a value of γ equal to 0.9 implies a much swifter adjustment to past errors than if $\gamma = 0.1$. If $\gamma = 1$ then the change in inflation expectations is set exactly equal to last period's error. For more on the properties of the AEH see Flemming (1976).

Muth (1961) showed that (with $\xi_t = 0$) the adaptive expectations scheme is an exponentially weighted forecast. Rearrange (12.14), with $\xi_t = 0$,

$$\pi_t^e = (1 - \gamma)\pi_{t-1}^e + \gamma\pi_{t-1} \qquad (12.15)$$

now lag once

$$\pi_{t-1}^e = (1 - \gamma)\pi_{t-2}^e + \gamma\pi_{t-2} \qquad (12.16)$$

and substitute back into (12.15) to obtain

$$\pi_t^e = (1 - \gamma)[(1 - \gamma)\pi_{t-2}^e + \gamma\pi_{t-2}] + \gamma\pi_{t-1}$$
$$= (1 - \gamma)^2\pi_{t-2}^e + (1 - \gamma)\gamma\pi_{t-2} + \gamma\pi_{t-1} \qquad (12.17)$$

Repeat this process to obtain

$$\pi_t^e = (1 - \gamma)^j\pi_{t-j}^e + \gamma\sum_{i=1}^{i=j}(1 - \gamma)^{i-1}\pi_{t-i} \qquad (12.18)$$

Now let $j \to \infty$, then $(1 - \gamma)^j \to 0$ for $0 \leq \gamma < 1$ and (12.18) becomes

$$\pi_t^e = \gamma\sum_{i=1}^{\infty}(1 - \gamma)^{i-1}\pi_{t-i} \qquad (12.19)$$

So that π_t^e is a weighted average of past inflation rates. Muth (*op. cit.*) then asked the question:

for what kind of time series process generating the actual values is the adaptive expectations scheme the optimal forecasting scheme? (Optimal being defined as minimising the average squared forecast error.) The answer to this question applied to the context of forecasting inflation is that the AEH is optimal if inflation is generated by

$$\pi_t = \psi_t + \gamma \sum_{i=1}^{\infty} \psi_{t-i} \tag{12.20}$$

where $[\psi_t]$ is a sequence of independent random shocks with zero mean and constant variance. Because the upper limit on the summation operator in (12.19) is infinity the effect of a shock is longlasting with magnitude depending upon γ where $0 < \gamma \leq 1$. Another way of viewing the process for which the AEH is the optimal predictor is to rewrite (12.20) as follows:

$$\pi_t = \psi_t + \gamma\psi_{t-1} + \gamma \sum_{i=2}^{\infty} \psi_{t-i} \tag{12.21}$$

and lagging (12.20) once,

$$\pi_{t-1} = \psi_{t-1} + \gamma \sum_{i=2}^{\infty} \psi_{t-i} \tag{12.22}$$

so

$$\pi_t - \pi_{t-1} = \psi_t + (\gamma - 1)\psi_{t-1} \tag{12.23}$$
$$(1 - L)\pi_t = \psi_t + (\gamma - 1)\psi_{t-1}$$

Now (12.24) is seen as a process with a unit root, that is integrated of order 1, and a first order moving average error. As γ approaches 1, the process in (12.24) comes closer to a pure random walk.

12.4.3 The AEH: estimation

In order to incorporate the AEH, (12.14), into the expectations augmented Phillips curve one modification is necessary which becomes relevant below when we consider the Lucas/Sargent critique of the usual method of identifying the

crucial coefficient δ. Note that rearranging (12.14) using the lag operator (see Chapter 2) we obtain

$$[1 - (1 - \gamma)L]\pi_t^e = \gamma L\pi_t + \xi_t \tag{12.24}$$

and, therefore,

$$\pi_t^e = \frac{\gamma L}{1 - (1 - \gamma)L} \pi_t + \xi_t^*$$
$$= \gamma^*(L)\pi_t + \xi_t^*$$

where $\gamma^*(L) = \gamma L/(1 - (1 - \gamma)L)$ and $\xi_t^* = \xi_t/(1 - (1 - \gamma)L)$. Incidentally the form of the lag function

$$\gamma^*(L) = \gamma L/(1 - (1 - \gamma)L)$$
$$= \gamma L \sum_{i=0}^{\infty} (1 - \gamma)^i L^i$$

immediately gives the correspondence with the infinite sequence of weights in (12.19). The AEH incorporates the restriction that the sum of the lag weights is 1; that is, setting ξ_t to its mean of zero:

$$\pi_t^e = \gamma^*(1)\pi_t \tag{12.25}$$
$$= [\gamma/(1 - (1 - \gamma))]\pi_t$$
$$= \pi_t$$

Where the notation $\gamma^*(1)$ indicates that the function $\gamma^*(L)$ is being evaluated by setting $L = 1$ (and assume $|\gamma| < 1$ so that the sum is convergent). To capture the possibility that $\gamma^*(1) \neq 1$ the AEH is modified so that the sum of the lag weights can differ from unity. To achieve this we allow the coefficient in the numerator of $\gamma^*(L)$ to differ from γ; that is

$$[1 - (1 - \gamma)L]\pi_t^e = \mu L\pi_t + \xi_t$$

so

$$\pi_t^e = \mu L[1 - (1 - \gamma)L]^{-1}\pi_t \tag{12.26}$$
$$+ [1 - (1 - \gamma)L]^{-1}\xi_t$$
$$= \mu(L)\pi_t + \xi_t^*$$

where $\mu(L) = \mu L[1 - (1 - \gamma)L]^{-1}$. In equation (12.26) the sum of the lag weights is $\mu(1) = \mu/\gamma$ which does not equal 1 unless $\mu = \gamma$. Substituting (12.26) into (12.10) gives:

$$\pi_{wt} = a + f(u_t) + \delta\{\mu L[1 - (1 - \gamma)L]^{-1}\}\pi_t + \eta_t^* \qquad (12.27)$$

where $\eta_t^* = \eta_t + \delta\xi_t^*$. Now define $\gamma(L) = 1 - (1 - \gamma)L$ and multiply (12.27) through by $\gamma(L)$ to obtain,

$$\gamma(L)\pi_{wt} = \gamma(L)[a + f(u_t)] + \delta\mu L\pi_t + \gamma(L)\eta_t^* \qquad (12.28)$$

Using the definition of $\gamma(L)$ we obtain,

$$\pi_{wt} = (1 - \gamma)\pi_{wt-1} + a + f(u_t) - (1 - \gamma)[a + f(u_{t-1})] + \delta\mu\pi_{t-1} + \gamma(L)\eta_t^* \qquad (12.29a)$$

which can be conveniently rearranged as follows,

$$\pi_{wt} = a + f(u_t) + (1 - \gamma)[\pi_{wt-1} - a - f(u_{t-1})] + \delta\mu\pi_{t-1} + \eta_t^+$$

where $\eta_t^+ = \gamma(L)\eta_t + \delta\xi_t$.

On substituting a specific form for $f(u_t)$, equation (12.29b) can now be estimated; however, without a further assumption δ cannot be separately identified. To illustrate this point for simplicity take $f(u_t) = bu_t$, then (12.29b) becomes:

$$\pi_{wt} = a + bu_t + (1 - \gamma)(\pi_{wt-1} - a - bu_{t-1}) + \delta\mu\pi_{t-1} + \eta_t^+ \qquad (12.30)$$

There are five coefficients in (12.30), a, b, γ, δ and μ, but only four variables, the constant, u_t, $(\pi_{wt-1} - a - bu_{t-1})$ and π_{t-1}: we cannot identify all the coefficients, in particular only the product of δ and μ can be determined. In order

to resolve this problem an assumption standard to the literature before the Lucas/Sargent critique was that $\mu = \gamma$, implying $\mu(L) = \gamma^*(L)$ and $\pi_t^e = \pi_t$ in the long run – see (12.25). For the moment we proceed as if $\mu = \gamma$ is a reasonable identifying restriction, returning to this issue in section **12.4.4** below.

The immediate aim of this section is to obtain a version of Phillips' original specification amended by modelling expectations using the AEH. To this end now substitute $f(u_t) = bu_t^c$, as in the original Phillips specification, into (12.29b), with the identifying restriction $\mu = \gamma$, to obtain the following equation:

$$\pi_{wt} = a + bu_t^c + (1 - \gamma)(\pi_{wt-1} - a - bu_{t-1}^c) + \delta\gamma\pi_{t-1} + \eta_t^+ \qquad (12.31)$$

The disturbance term in (12.31), $\eta_t^+ = \gamma(L)\eta_t + \delta\xi_t$, is a composite of the disturbance in the expectations augmented Phillips curve, η_t, and the disturbance in the adaptive learning scheme, ξ_t. (The AEH is usually presented with $\xi_t = 0$ and, in general, the contribution of ξ_t in (12.31) cannot be distinguished from η_t.) There are two potential problems that involve η_t^+, relating first to the possibility of serial correlation in η_t^+ and second to correlation between the lagged regressor π_{wt-1} and η_t^+. On the first of these note that the disturbances one period apart are:

$$\eta_t^+ = \eta_t - (1 - \gamma)\eta_{t-1} + \delta\xi_t \qquad (12.32)$$

and

$$\eta_{t-1}^+ = \eta_{t-1} - (1 - \gamma)\eta_{t-2} + \delta\xi_{t-1} \qquad (12.33)$$

Because of the common term η_{t-1}, η_t^+ and η_{t-1}^+ will, in general, be serial correlated with an MA(1) structure. In particular

$$E\{\eta_t^+ \eta_{t-1}^+\} = E\{[\eta_t - (1 - \gamma)\eta_{t-1} + \delta\xi_t] \\ \times [\eta_{t-1} - (1 - \gamma)\eta_{t-2} + \delta\xi_{t-1}]\} \\ = -E\{(1 - \gamma)\eta_{t-1}\eta_{t-1}\} \\ = -(1 - \gamma)\sigma_\eta^2 \qquad (12.34)$$

where $E\{\eta_{t-1}\eta_{t-1}\} = \sigma_{\eta}^2$. (In evaluating (12.34) the following assumptions have been used: $E\{\eta_t\eta_{t-1}\} = 0$, $E\{\xi_t\xi_{t-1}\} = 0$, $E\{\eta_t\xi_{t-1}\} = 0$ and $E\{\eta_{t-1}\xi_{t-1}\} = 0$; if $\xi_t \equiv 0$, only the first of these is needed.) If $\gamma = 1$, (12.32) and (12.33) reduce to $\eta_t^+ = \eta_t + \delta\xi_t$ and $\eta_{t-1}^+ = \eta_{t-1} + \delta\xi_{t-1}$, which are not serially correlated. To anticipate the estimation results reported in Table 12.4, we find $\hat{\gamma} \approx 1$ coupled with the absence of evidence of serial correlation in the residuals.

The second potential problem arises because π_{wt-1} is a regressor in (12.31). Lagging (12.31) once we see that π_{wt-1} depends in part upon η_{t-1}^+, a component of which is η_{t-1}; hence, unless $\gamma = 1$, there is a nonzero correlation between one of the regressors, π_{wt-1}, and the 'disturbance', η_t^+. A solution to this problem is to use an instrumental variables procedure. The instruments should include the other regressors in (12.31), u_t, u_{t-1} and π_{t-1}, and at least one other instrument, candidates being lags of π_{wt-1}, and further lags of u_t and π_t. The differences between the OLS and IV estimates will depend crucially on how close γ is to 1.

12.4.4 The Lucas/Sargent critique of the identifying assumption

Before reporting the results from re-estimation of the Phillips curve combined with the AEH, we need to consider the critique due to Lucas (1972) and Sargent (1971). In general terms the procedure so far outlined replaces the unobservable variable π_t^e with a weighted sum of past inflation rates. In the AEH this sum is infinite but in other applications it may be truncated to a finite maximum lag. Schematically we have

$$\pi_{wt} = a + f(u_t) + \delta\pi_t^e + \eta_t \qquad (12.35)$$

and

$$\pi_t^e = \sum_{i=1}^{m} w_i\pi_{t-i} \qquad (12.36)$$

$$= w(L)\pi_t$$

where the $\{w_i\}$ are a set of distributed lag weights, $w(L) = \sum_{i=1}^{m} w_iL^i$, and letting $m = \infty$ captures the infinite case associated with the AEH. Substitution of (12.36) into (12.35) provides the basis of a widely applied method. However, in order to obtain an estimate of δ from such a procedure an 'identifying' assumption is needed; that is there are m distributed lag coefficients in (12.36) to be estimated as well as δ, in all $m + 1$ coefficients arising from this part of the specification, but there are only m variables – the lags of π_t.

In order to identify δ from $\delta\sum_{i=1}^{m} w_i$ a common assumption (for future reference we shall call it the standard assumption) is that $\sum_{i=1}^{m} w_i = 1$, hence $\delta\sum_{i=1}^{m} w_i = \delta$, and δ is 'identified'. The AEH imposes $\sum_{i=1}^{m} w_i = 1$, which can be confirmed on reference to (12.25). As we have seen δ is a crucial coefficient upon which, on one interpretation, the existence of a short-run trade-off between wage inflation and unemployment depends – Sargent (op. cit., p. 721) calls it 'the notorious parameter'! Without an identifying assumption all that can be ascertained is the product of δ and $\sum_{i=1}^{m} w_i$; if this is significantly different from zero wage inflation depends upon price inflation but we are unable to say, for example, whether the estimates favour what is known as the 'accelerationist' hypothesis associated with $\delta = 1$.

The 'standard' identifying assumption is based on the idea that a sustained increase in inflation will eventually be fully anticipated so that $\pi_t^e = w(L)\pi_t$ with $w(1) = 1$. Sargent (op. cit.) questions the validity of this identifying assumption on the basis that the kind of expectations generator it is appropriate to use depends upon 'the actual behaviour of the inflation rate during the period being studied', and 'for the periods used in estimation, inflation was never as sustained as in the mental experiment (of sustained inflation)', (Sargent op. cit., p. 722, my clarification in parentheses). The Lucas/Sargent critique led to a re-evaluation of the modelling of expectations in general, with subsequent developments in the application of Muth's (1961)

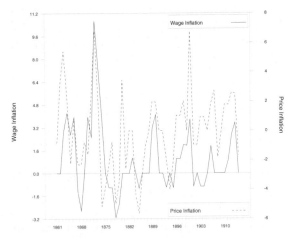

Figure 12.7 *Wage and price inflation, United Kingdom 1861–1913*

earlier idea of rational expectations – see, for example, Lucas (1973).

While Sargent was criticising post-war empirical studies his point has equal relevance for the Phillips period of 1861–1913, as in neither period is there evidence of permanent shocks in inflation. Price inflation for the United Kingdom over the period 1861–1913 is plotted in Figure 12.7 and we see a general tendency for mean reversion that is confirmed in more formal modelling. For example, two candidate models are reported in Table 12.3.

The time series models for the United Kingdom, 1861–1913, need only be quite simple to fit the data; there is a marginal preference for the MA(1) model over the AR(1), with AIC and SIC both indicating this choice (across a range of possibilities, not reported, allowing for up to

fourth order AR and MA terms separately and in combination). SIC and AIC are 'information' criteria designed to help select a model. In general the model which minimises these criteria over a range of parameter values is preferred – see section **12.5.3** below for an elaboration of those criteria. Neither model suggests a unit root – see also Table 12.2 which reports the standard set of unit root statistics. For comparison with (12.36) the MA(1) model can be put into an autoregressive form as follows. The MA(1) model is

$$\pi_t = \theta_0 + (1 + \theta_1 L)\varepsilon_t \tag{12.37}$$

and pre-multiplying by $(1 + \theta_1 L)^{-1}$ gives

$$(1 + \theta_1 L)^{-1}\pi_t = (1 + \theta_1 L)^{-1}\theta_0 + \varepsilon_t \tag{12.38}$$

Bearing in mind that for $|\theta_1| < 1$ the first order MA operator has an (infinite) autoregressive representation,

$$
\begin{aligned}
(1 + \theta_1 L)^{-1} &\equiv [1 - \theta_1 L(1 + \theta_1 L)^{-1}] \\
&= [1 + (-\theta_1 L) + (-\theta_1 L)^2 \\
&\quad + (-\theta_1 L)^3 \\
&\quad + (-\theta_1 L)^4 + \cdots]
\end{aligned}
$$

then (12.38) can be written as:

$$
\begin{aligned}
(1 + (-\theta_1 L) + (-\theta_1 L)^2 + (-\theta_1 L)^3 \\
+ (-\theta_1 L)^4 + \cdots)\pi_t = (1 + \theta_1 L)^{-1}\theta_0 + \varepsilon_t
\end{aligned}
\tag{12.39}
$$

Table 12.3 *Time series models for price inflation, United Kingdom 1861–1913*

AR(1)		
$\hat{\pi}_t = 0.006 + 0.371\pi_{t-1}$	$\hat{\sigma} = 2.643$	AIC $= 308.503$
$\quad\;\;(0.010)\;\;(2.802)$	dw $= 1.825$	SIC $= 312.406$
MA(1)		
$\hat{\pi}_t = 0.006 + \varepsilon_t + 0.459\varepsilon_{t-1}$	$\hat{\sigma} = 2.642$	AIC $= 306.448$
$\quad\;\;(0.012)\qquad\;(3.649)$	dw $= 1.973$	SIC $= 310.351$

Note: Sample period (before lagging): 1861–1913.

or explicitly as an infinite autoregression

$$\pi_t = (1 + \theta_1 L)^{-1}\theta_0 + \theta_1 L(1 + \theta_1 L)^{-1}\pi_t + \varepsilon_t$$
$$= (1 + \theta_1 L)^{-1}\theta_0 + \theta_1\pi_{t-1} - \theta_1^2\pi_{t-2}$$
$$+ \theta_1^3\pi_{t-3} - \theta_1^4\pi_{t-4} + \cdots + \varepsilon_t \qquad (12.40)$$

which is in the form (12.36). The sum of the weights on the lagged inflation rates is $\theta_1 L(1 + \theta_1 L)^{-1}$ evaluated at $L = 1$, that is $\theta_1(1 + \theta_1)^{-1}$; for $\theta_1 = 0.459$ from Table 12.3 the sum is 0.315, which is well below unity and tends to confirm the Lucas/Sargent critique in this case.

In the next section we report estimation details for the AEH version of the Phillips curve, and consider whether it makes a difference to the estimate of δ which identifying assumption is made.

12.4.5 Estimation results: adaptive expectations augmented Phillips curve

The OLS and IV estimates for the Phillips Curve augmented by the AEH are reported in Table 12.4; the IV estimates use $u_t, u_{t-1}, \pi_{wt-2}, \pi_{t-1}$ and π_{t-2} as instruments. The estimates obtained with the addition of a variable to capture the rate of change of unemployment effect are also reported in Table 12.4. Bearing in mind the results in Table 12.2, to capture this effect the simpler option of $0.5(\Delta u_t/u_{t-1} + \Delta u_{t-1}/u_{t-2})$ was chosen. In this case, therefore, the instruments also include u_{t-2}.

From Table 12.4 the results indicate that the estimated Phillips curve coefficients, a, b and c, remain in the region originally suggested by Phillips. For example, Phillips estimated a value of -1.394 for c, whereas with AEH the OLS and IV estimates of c are -1.380 and -1.361, respectively.

As noted above, identification of δ is on the basis that $\gamma^*(1) = 1$ – see (12.25); and different identification assumptions will lead to different estimates of δ. In the upper part of Table 12.4 the IV estimate of δ is 0.122, which is just significant at conventional significance levels

with a 't' statistic of 1.670. That is since we have in mind the one-sided alternative, $\delta > 0$, it is preferable to use a one-sided marginal significance level, which in this case is 5%.

Suppose, however, we adopt the following identification procedure for δ. Given Sargent's (*op. cit.*) suggestion of looking at the actual path of inflation, note that the time series models reported in Table 12.3 do not indicate any evidence in the sample period of permanent shocks as, for example, would be characterised by a unit root. The sum of the autoregressive coefficients found by inverting the preferred MA(1) model of inflation is 0.315; therefore, on reference back to (12.26), $\mu[1 - (1 - \gamma)]^{-1} = 0.315$ implying $\mu = 0.315\gamma$. The estimated coefficient on π_{t-1} is $\widehat{\delta\mu} = 0.130 = (0.122)(1.065)$; hence, $\hat{\delta} = 0.130/\hat{\mu} = 0.130/0.315\hat{\gamma} = 0.412$, for $\hat{\gamma} = 1.065$. Using this identification there is about a factor of three difference between the estimate of the crucial δ coefficient.

Whether the equation is estimated by OLS or IV, there is no evidence of serial correlation and the difference between the OLS and IV estimates is slight; together these findings indirectly support the view that $\gamma \approx 1$, and indeed this is what the direct estimates show with an IV estimate of 1.065 and estimated standard error of 0.183. This is significantly different from 0, but an equally interesting question is whether it is significantly different from 1? The appropriate 't' statistic for this hypothesis is $(1.065 - 1)/0.183 = 0.355$, which is well below the critical value for any reasonable significance level. As noted above a value of γ of 1 implies that the change in inflation expectations is set exactly equal to last period's error. Alternatively from (12.14) note that $\gamma = 1$ implies $\pi_t^e = \pi_{t-1}$, where we have ξ_t set equal to its expected value of zero; on the basis of the first two equations reported in Table 12.4 expected inflation is equal to lagged actual inflation.

If we now impose $\gamma = 1$ the augmented Phillips curve (12.31) reduces to

$$\pi_{wt} = a + bu_t^c + \delta\pi_{t-1} + \eta_t^+ \qquad (12.41)$$

Table 12.4 *Adaptive expectations augmented Phillips curve*

Model: $\pi_{wt} = a + bu_t^c + (1 - \gamma)\{\pi_{wt-1} - a - bu_{t-1}^c\} + \delta\gamma\pi_{t-1} + \eta_t^+$
Estimation method: OLS

$\hat{a}$	$\hat{b}$	$\hat{c}$	$\hat{\delta}$	$\hat{\gamma}$	$\hat{\sigma}$	dw	SC(1)
−1.127	10.127	−1.380	0.117	1.038	1.297	1.934	0.090[0.765]
(−1.815)	(10.053)	(−4.844)	(1.606)	(6.155)			

Estimation method: IV

$\hat{a}$	$\hat{b}$	$\hat{c}$	$\hat{\delta}$	$\hat{\gamma}$	$\hat{\sigma}$	dw	SC(1)
−1.129	9.970	−1.361	0.122	1.065	1.303	1.971	0.058[0.809]
(−1.803)	(9.419)	(−4.566)	(1.670)	(5.821)			

Estimation method: OLS, $\gamma = 1$ imposed

$\hat{a}$	$\hat{b}$	$\hat{c}$	$\hat{\delta}$	$\hat{\gamma}$	$\hat{\sigma}$	dw	SC(1)
−1.117	10.157	−1.388	0.112	1.000	1.284	1.994	0.101[0.750]
(−1.838)	(9.927)	(−4.992)	(1.532)	–			

Model: $\pi_{wt} = a + bu_t^c + (1 - \gamma)(\pi_{wt-1} - a - bu_{t-1}^c) + \delta\gamma\pi_{t-1} + 0.5h[100(\Delta u_t/u_{t-1} + \Delta u_{t-1}/u_{t-2})] + \eta_t^+$
Estimation method: IV

$\hat{a}$	$\hat{b}$	$\hat{c}$	$\hat{\delta}$	$\hat{\gamma}$	$\hat{h}$	$\hat{\sigma}$	dw	SC(1)
−0.495	9.039	−1.589	0.125	1.108	−0.010	1.274	2.090	0.559[0.455]
(−0.875)	(8.452)	(−4.358)	(1.797)	(5.988)	(−1.945)			

Estimation method: OLS, $\gamma = 1$ imposed

$\hat{a}$	$\hat{b}$	$\hat{c}$	$\hat{\delta}$	$\hat{\gamma}$	$\hat{h}$	$\hat{\sigma}$	dw	SC(1)
−0.416	9.220	−1.668	0.100	1.000	−0.011	1.250	2.108	0.604[0.437]
(−0.747)	(8.416)	(−4.668)	(1.557)	–	(−1.913)			

Notes: Sample period: 1863–1913; '*t*' statistics in parentheses.

and we anticipate that the estimates obtained will be statistically indistinguishable from the first two equations in Table 12.4. Such an equation can be consistently estimated by OLS because, when $\gamma = 1$, there are no problems with serial correlation or endogenous regressors. This is the third equation reported in Table 12.4 in which the estimated coefficients are, as anticipated, very similar to the previous equations.

Finally what difference does it make to add the rate of change variable, $(\Delta u_t/u_{t-1} + \Delta u_{t-1}/u_{t-2})$? There is a slight improvement in the estimated standard error, which falls from 1.303 to 1.274. The changes to the common coefficients are relatively minor; for example, the estimate of δ is 0.125 compared to 0.122 from IV estimation without the additional variable. The estimated value of h is −0.010 with a '*t*' statistic of −1.945, which is significant at the 5% level using a one-sided test – remember h is expected to be negative. The estimate of γ increases slightly to 1.108, compared to the IV estimate of 1.065 from Table 12.4, but with an estimated standard error of 0.185 this is not significantly different from 1. Hence, as before, we can impose $\gamma = 1$ and estimate by OLS, the results being reported as the last equation in Table 12.4. The estimate of δ falls slightly to 0.100 compared to the estimate of 0.125 from the previous equation; however, in general our supposition is confirmed and on the basis of these estimates using the AEH we can set $\pi_t^e = \pi_{t-1}$.

At one level the regressions reported in Table 12.4 are well specified – there is no evidence of serial correlation, the estimated coefficients are of the anticipated sign and are significant – so why not stop with these? The answer to this question is that the Lucas/Sargent critique of the standard identifying assumption had a greater impact than just on the narrow focus of identifying δ. Subsequent papers – especially Sargent (1973) – led to a replacement of the paradigm of adaptive expectations, or variants thereof, with that of rational expectations: 'This amounts to supposing that the public's expectations depend, in the proper way, on the things that economic theory says they ought to' (Sargent *op. cit.*, p. 431). The framework of the AEH rules out the possibility that, subject only to a zero mean error, $\pi_t^e = \pi_t$, which is just what the rational expectations approach allows. The next section illustrates the application of one possible rational expectations approach to the Phillips curve.

12.4.6 Rational expectations (RE): general principles

The expectation formed at time t of a variable in the future is said to be rational for a given information set Ω_t if it is the same as the conditional expectation of that variable. For example, at time t the rational expectation of inflation in period $t + 1$ given Ω_t is

$$_t\pi_{t+1}^e = E_t\{\pi_{t+1} \mid \Omega_t\} \qquad (12.42\text{a})$$

That is the expectation of inflation, formed at t, to prevail at $t + 1$ is the conditional expectation of π_{t+1} given the information set Ω_t. In this section the first subscript is important and is not suppressed, it indicates the date at which the expectation is formed. Expectations can be formed at different times and for more than one period hence. For example, the rational expectation, formed at $t - 1$, of inflation for period t is

$$_{t-1}\pi_t^e = E_{t-1}\{\pi_t \mid \Omega_{t-1}\} \qquad (12.42\text{b})$$

and the rational expectation of inflation formed at t for inflation h periods hence is

$$_t\pi_{t+h}^e = E_t\{\pi_{t+h} \mid \Omega_t\} \qquad (12.42\text{c})$$

The relation between the outturn and the rational expectation is a regression or condi-

tional expectation function (CEF) as defined in Chapter 4. For example, for (12.42a) this is

$$
\begin{aligned}
\pi_{t+1} &= E_t\{\pi_{t+1} \mid \Omega_t\} + \varepsilon_{t+1} \\
&= {}_t\pi_{t+1}^e + \varepsilon_{t+1}
\end{aligned} \qquad (12.43\text{a})
$$

and for (12.42b)

$$
\begin{aligned}
\pi_t &= E_{t-1}\{\pi_t \mid \Omega_{t-1}\} + \varepsilon_t \\
&= {}_{t-1}\pi_t^e + \varepsilon_t
\end{aligned} \qquad (12.43\text{b})
$$

It follows from the CEF interpretation that the innovation (or forecast error), ε_{t+1}, in (12.43a) has a zero mean and is uncorrelated (orthogonal) with all the components of the information set Ω_t whether taken separately or as a group; similarly ε_t has a zero mean and is orthogonal to Ω_{t-1}. In a sense the innovation is 'news' as far as the components of the information set are concerned. In principle (12.43) holds for any information set, but to give economic content to the idea of rational expectations, the (fully) rational information set consists of the variables which actually determine inflation. For example, assume that the CEF is linear and, to simplify the exposition, that π_t depends on a single variable, say x_t, its lagged values and lagged values of π_t, then the rational expectation, formed at time t, of inflation at $t + 1$ is:

$$
\begin{aligned}
_t\pi_{t+1}^e = {}&\alpha_{10}x_t + \alpha_{11}x_{t-1} + \cdots + \alpha_{1m}x_{t-m} \\
&+ \alpha_{21}\pi_{t-1} + \cdots + \alpha_{2n}\pi_{t-n} \quad (12.44\text{a})
\end{aligned}
$$

and the rational expectation, formed at time $t - 1$, of inflation at t is:

$$
\begin{aligned}
_{t-1}\pi_t^e = {}&\alpha_{10}x_{t-1} + \alpha_{11}x_{t-2} + \cdots + \alpha_{1m}x_{t-(m+1)} \\
&+ \alpha_{21}\pi_{t-2} + \cdots + \alpha_{2n}\pi_{t-(n+1)}
\end{aligned}
$$

$$(12.44\text{b})$$

12.4.7 Implementing rational expectations

There are a number of further issues which arise in the context of interpreting and applying rational expectations, but these are now best considered in the context of estimating the expectations augmented Phillips curve. As in the AEH the expected inflation variable is taken to be $_{t-1}\pi_t^e$.

The first step is to rearrange (12.43b) to obtain expected inflation:

$$_{t-1}\pi_t^e = \pi_t - \varepsilon_t \tag{12.45}$$

There is now a two-equation system comprising the augmented Phillips curve and the expectations equation:

$$\pi_{wt} = a + f(u_t) + \delta(_{t-1}\pi_t^e) + \eta_t \tag{12.46}$$
$$_{t-1}\pi_t^e = \pi_t - \varepsilon_t \tag{12.45 again}$$

An obvious approach to obtaining an estimator of the coefficients in (12.46) is to substitute (12.45) into (12.46) to obtain

$$\pi_{wt} = a + f(u_t) + \delta\pi_t + \upsilon_t \tag{12.47}$$

where

$$\upsilon_t = \eta_t - \delta\varepsilon_t \tag{12.48}$$

An econometric issue arising with the specification comprising (12.47) and (12.48) is that there is an errors in variables (EIV) problem: replacing $_{t-1}\pi_t^e$ by π_t has introduced the error of measurement ε_t, and from (12.43b) ε_t and π_t are correlated so (12.47) is not a CEF, and OLS estimation will not yield the parameters of interest. An alternative way of expressing this problem is to say that the OLS estimators of the coefficients in (12.47) will be inconsistent because of the correlation between ε_t and π_t. A solution to the estimation problem is to use an instrumental variables estimator. To simplify the discussion assume in (12.46) that $f(u_t) = bu_t$ and u_t is exogenous, then the problem is to obtain consistent estimators of a, b and δ in

$$\pi_{wt} = a + bu_t + \delta\pi_t + \upsilon_t \tag{12.49}$$

The general principle of IV estimation requires that π_t is regressed on a set of instruments, which are correlated with $_{t-1}\pi_t^e$ but uncorrelated with ε_t. u_t must be included in the instrument set (or alternatively it can be regarded as a legitimate instrument for itself). Consideration of the rational expectations formulation (12.44b) in this simplified example suggests that the appropriate set of instruments, if Ω_{t-1} is known, is $x_{t-1}, \ldots, x_{t-(m+1)}$ and $\pi_{t-2}, \ldots, \pi_{t-(n+1)}$.

The IV procedure is, therefore, straightforward if Ω_{t-1} is known; but what if, in the more realistic situation, only a subset of Ω_{t-1}, say Ψ_{t-1}, is known? In the latter case it is still possible to obtain consistent estimators using Ψ_{t-1}, as noted by Sargent (1973) and McCallum (1976), who have suggested the term 'partly rational expectations' for such a situation. A leading case of partly rational expectations arises when just lagged values of the own variable are used as the information set, here that is $\pi_{t-2}, \ldots, \pi_{t-(n+1)}$; this situation is sometimes referred to as weakly rational expectations. The essential property on which consistency of the IV procedure relies is that the rational expectations forecast errors ε_t are orthogonal to each component of the information set term by term, so using a subset of the complete information set will still result in a consistent estimator – see McCallum (*op. cit.*, p. 45 and 50).

In using Ψ_{t-1} rather than Ω_{t-1} we can distinguish two cases which, while amounting to the same thing in practice, allow an important distinction. (i) Even though Ω_{t-1} is the relevant set of information on which π_t is actually determined, the 'market participants' only use Ψ_{t-1}. As Sargent (*op cit.*, p. 470) notes: 'One criticism that has been made of the kind of (rational expectations) model presented here is that it seems to require extraordinary amounts of wisdom and information...' (my clarification in parentheses). Thus, the partly rational expectations formulation counters this criticism; provided market participants use a subset of the correct information set they are doing the right thing according to the RE paradigm. (ii) Market participants use Ω_{t-1} but the econometrician has incomplete knowledge and uses

Ψ_{t-1}. As already noted this will result in consistent (but inefficient) estimators. McCallum (*op. cit.*, p. 50) suggests 'it might be desirable, in practice, to limit Z (the variables in Ω_t) to those variables that are 'most likely' to be considered by market participants. Lagged values of y (the variable on which expectations are formed) are probably the leading contenders...' (my clarification in parentheses).

12.4.8 Estimation results with (weakly) rational expectations

Table 12.5 reports estimation of equation (12.46) first by OLS and then by IV, in the latter case using the instrument set u_t, u_{t-1}, π_{wt-2}, π_{t-1}, and π_{t-2}. (No role could be found for a variable capturing the rate of change of unemployment in the EAPC + RE equations, compare Table 12.4, so none is reported here.) In terms of the earlier distinction a complete model of price determination has not been specified – for an illustration of that approach see Sargent (1973), McCallum (1976) – but the instruments have been chosen as an example of 'weakly rational' expectations, and are a plausible set of variables likely to influence inflation. We have already noted that π_t is consistent with an I(0) process and is, therefore, a valid regressor in the expectations augmented version of the Phillips curve.

If we put to one side the potential problems arising from the endogeneity of π_t, the OLS version of the modified Phillips curve, which is the first equation in Table 12.5, is an improvement over the original reported in Table 12.2 (regression 3). The estimated coefficient on π_t is 0.247 and is significant with a 't' statistic of 3.848. The estimated standard error is 0.064 so that the 't' statistic for the null hypothesis that $\delta = 1$ against the alternative $\delta \neq 1$ is $(0.247 - 1)/0.064 = -11.731$, which is overwhelmingly against the null hypothesis. Note also that the estimates of the remaining coefficients are remarkably close to Phillips' original estimates and the re-estimates reported in Table 12.2, and there is no evidence of serial correlation in the residuals.

Turning to the second equation in Table 12.5, which is estimated by IV, note that while there are some differences in the coefficient estimates compared to the OLS estimates, the broad picture is the same. The estimate of δ is slightly higher at 0.311 with an estimated standard error of 0.132 giving a conventional 't' statistic of 2.355, and a 't' statistic for the null hypothesis that $\delta = 1$ of 5.217, both leading to rejection of the respective null hypotheses at conventional significance levels. The IV estimate of c is -1.488 with an estimated standard error of 0.734 and conventional 't' statistic of -2.026, which is significant. Against the null hypothesis that $c = 1$ the 't' statistic is 0.664, which is not significant. According to either set of estimates there was a trade-off between wage inflation and unemployment during this period, with the position of the trade-off depending upon the magnitude of price inflation.

Table 12.5 *(Weakly) rational expectations augmented Phillips curve*

Model: $\pi_{wt} = a + bu_t^c + \delta\pi_t + v_t$ Estimation method: OLS						
$\hat{a}$	$\hat{b}$	$\hat{c}$	$\hat{\delta}$	$\hat{\sigma}$	dw	SC(1)
-0.865	9.387	-1.431	0.247	1.148	1.939	0.008[0.927]
(-1.850)	(10.793)	(-5.325)	(3.848)			
Estimation method: IV						
$\hat{a}$	$\hat{b}$	$\hat{c}$	$\hat{\delta}$	$\hat{\sigma}$	dw	SC(1)
-0.644	8.756	-1.488	0.311	1.161	1.914	0.017[0.895]
(-0.716)	(4.676)	(-2.026)	(2.355)			

Notes: Sample period: 1863–1913; 't' statistics in parentheses.

Comparing the estimated adaptive expectations model in Table 12.4 with the rational expectations model in Table 12.5, first recall that in the former the estimate of γ at 1.065 with a standard error of 0.183 was statistically indistinguishable from 1, with the implication that $\pi_t^e = \pi_{t-1}$. Hence, the difference between the two specifications turns on whether expected inflation is specified as π_{t-1}(adaptive) or π_t(rational). The goodness of fit statistics, for example $\hat{\sigma} = 1.284$(adaptive) and $\hat{\sigma} = 1.161$(rational), which can be taken at face value here because we are dealing with stationary variables, suggest a preference for the rational expectations version of the augmented Phillips curve.

The estimates reported in Table 12.5 suggest there is a difference between the short-run and long-run Phillips curves for the period 1863–1913, with the IV estimate of $\delta = 0.311$. For example, consider a situation in which expected inflation is zero then, taking the IV equation in Table 12.5, the estimated values of π_{wt} are given by

$$\hat{\pi}_{wt} = -0.644 + 8.756 u_t^{-1.488}$$

This is the curve shown in Figure 12.8 for 0% price inflation. Now if expected inflation increases to 5% the Phillips curve shifts up vertically by $5(0.311) = 1.555\%$ p.a., where 0.311 is the coefficient on π_t^e in the estimated equation. This is the curve shown in Figure 12.8 for 5% price inflation. So for a given level of unemployment, wage inflation is everywhere increased but not by as much as the increase in expected inflation. Similarly if anticipated inflation increases to 10% the Phillips curve again shifts up, in this case displaced by $10(0.311) = 3.11\%$ p.a. compared to the situation of zero expected price inflation.

There is now an answer to the question posed at the end of section **12.4.5**: why not stop with the AEH version of the Phillips curve when the equation appears well specified? White noise residuals and significant coefficients, as in the regression models of Table 12.4, are necessary but not by themselves sufficient conditions for

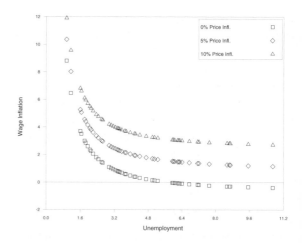

Figure 12.8 *Expectations augmented Phillips curves*

a satisfactory empirical model. Similarly it is likely that the equations in Table 12.5 can be improved upon; they can only be tentatively adequate. One possibility which we have not explored here is to develop a 'fully' rational approach in the sense of making explicit the links between the equations determining labour supply, labour demand, output, and wage and price inflation. For an approach along these lines see McCallum (1973, 1974, 1976).

12.5 The Phillips correlation

The difference of view between Fisher (1926) and Phillips (1958) as to the appropriate direction of causation between inflation and unemployment was mentioned earlier – see section **12.3.1** – with the former of the view that causation runs from price inflation to unemployment and the latter that the causation runs from unemployment to wage inflation (and hence to price inflation). This issue was taken up by Friedman (1975) who regarded Fisher's view as correct.

The purpose of this section is to see if statistical causation tests can throw any light on this debate. First, note that the Fisher–Phillips dichotomy comprises just two out of the list of possibilities. More exhaustively we have: (a) $\pi_t \Rightarrow u_t$; (b) $u_t \Rightarrow \pi_t$; (c) $\pi_t \nRightarrow u_t$; (d) $u_t \nRightarrow \pi_t$;

(e) $u_t \Leftrightarrow \pi_t$. The symbols are interpreted as follows: $\Rightarrow$ indicates one way causation; $\nRightarrow$ indicates no causation; and $\Leftrightarrow$ indicates mutual causation. Cases (a)–(d) are straightforward, and case (e) follows from the mutual satisfaction of both (a) and (b). An operational definition of causation is required to assess these opposing points of view, and the approach illustrated here, which has become quite influential, is due to Granger (1969) who suggested tests for what has become known as Granger-causality.

12.5.1   Granger-causation tests

To simplify the analysis assume there are two time series of interest, which are denoted y_{1t} and y_{2t}. The central idea is that y_{1t} is not Granger caused by y_{2t} if the optimal predictor of y_{1t} does not use information from y_{2t} (Lütkepohl 1991, p. 36). In applications of this idea the predictor is usually restricted to be an optimal *linear* predictor and optimality is defined as minimising the mean squared error of the h-step predictor of y_{1t}.

To be specific suppose y_{1t} and y_{2t} have a vector autoregressive representation (VAR) in which y_{1t} depends upon lags of itself and lags of y_{2t} and symmetrically y_{2t} depends upon lags of itself and lags of y_{1t}. The VAR model is considered in greater detail in Chapters 14 and 15. For notational simplicity a common lag length of p is assumed, but this is not necessary in an empirical application.

$$y_{1t} = \mu_{10} + \pi_{11.1}y_{1t-1} + \cdots$$
$$+ \pi_{11.p}y_{1t-p} + \pi_{12.1}y_{2t-1} + \cdots$$
$$+ \pi_{12.p}y_{2t-p} + \varepsilon_{1t} \qquad (12.50a)$$

$$y_{2t} = \mu_{20} + \pi_{21.1}y_{1t-1} + \cdots$$
$$+ \pi_{21.p}y_{1t-p} + \pi_{22.1}y_{2t-1} + \cdots$$
$$+ \pi_{22.p}y_{2t-p} + \varepsilon_{2t} \qquad (12.50b)$$

Note that we are adopting the convention that the first subscript denotes the variable and the second denotes the observation index. This is a two variable, or bivariate, pth order VAR. The

processes for y_{1t} and y_{2t} are a system of two equations and the errors ε_{1t} and ε_{2t} may be contemporaneously correlated, so that a shock to one of the equations has a 'ripple' effect on the other equation. The specification of the ε_{it}, $i = 1, 2$, is as follows. As in the single-equation case each equation is assumed to have an innovation with zero mean, constant variance and no serial correlation, that is $E\{\varepsilon_{it}\} = 0$ and $E\{\varepsilon_{it}^2\} = \sigma_i^2$, for $i = 1, 2$ and $E\{\varepsilon_{it}\varepsilon_{is}\} = 0$ for $t \neq s$ and $i = 1, 2$. In addition there is assumed to be no serial correlation between equations, that is $E\{\varepsilon_{1t}, \varepsilon_{2s}\} = 0$, for $t \neq s$. The 'ripple' effect is captured by the covariance between ε_{1t} and ε_{2t}, denoted σ_{12}, which is assumed to be constant. Thus, for all t the error variance matrix for the VAR with p lags is:

$$\Omega(\varepsilon, p) \equiv E \begin{pmatrix} \varepsilon_{1t} \\ \varepsilon_{2t} \end{pmatrix} (\varepsilon_{1t} \varepsilon_{2t})$$

$$= \begin{bmatrix} \sigma_1^2 & \sigma_{12} \\ \sigma_{12} & \sigma_2^2 \end{bmatrix} \qquad (12.51)$$

Equations (12.50a) and (12.50b) can be written in matrix form in two ways. They may be written so as to emphasise either the lag length or, alternatively, the component variables. In the former case this is:

$$\begin{pmatrix} y_{1t} \\ y_{2t} \end{pmatrix} = \begin{pmatrix} \mu_{10} \\ \mu_{20} \end{pmatrix} + \begin{bmatrix} \pi_{11.1} & \pi_{12.1} \\ \pi_{21.1} & \pi_{22.1} \end{bmatrix} \begin{pmatrix} y_{1t-1} \\ y_{2t-1} \end{pmatrix}$$

$$+ \cdots + \begin{bmatrix} \pi_{11.p} & \pi_{12.p} \\ \pi_{21.p} & \pi_{22.p} \end{bmatrix} \begin{pmatrix} y_{1t-p} \\ y_{2t-p} \end{pmatrix}$$

$$+ \begin{pmatrix} \varepsilon_{1t} \\ \varepsilon_{2t} \end{pmatrix} \qquad (12.52)$$

A third subscript is necessary on the coefficients to distinguish the lag length which runs from 1 through to p. A simple way of writing this VAR, used extensively in the following chapters, is:

$$y_t = \mu + \Pi_1 y_{t-1} + \cdots + \Pi_p y_{t-p} + \varepsilon_t \qquad (12.53)$$

where $y_t' = (y_{1t}, y_{2t})$, $\mu' = (\mu_{10}, \mu_{20})$, $\varepsilon_t' = (\varepsilon_{1t}, \varepsilon_{2t})$ and the Π_i are 2×2 matrices defined by reference to (12.52). The notation in equations

(12.52) and (12.53) is reasonably standard in this area; however, in the context of this chapter the notation π_t has been used for inflation so the reader should be alert to the difference in meaning between π_t and, for example, $\pi_{11.1}$, which is a VAR coefficient.

An alternative formulation, which separates out the variables, is more useful in the present context; that is:

$$
\begin{pmatrix} y_{1t} \\ y_{2t} \end{pmatrix} = \begin{bmatrix} 1 & y_{1t-1} & \cdots & y_{1t-p} & y_{2t-1} & \cdots & y_{2t-p} & 0 & 0 & \cdots & 0 & 0 & \cdots & 0 \\ 0 & 0 & \cdots & 0 & 0 & \cdots & 0 & 1 & y_{1t-1} & \cdots & y_{1t-p} & y_{2t-1} & \cdots & y_{2t-p} \end{bmatrix} \begin{pmatrix} \mu_{10} \\ \pi_{11.1} \\ \vdots \\ \pi_{11.p} \\ \pi_{12.1} \\ \vdots \\ \pi_{12.p} \\ \mu_{20} \\ \pi_{21.1} \\ \vdots \\ \pi_{21.p} \\ \pi_{22.1} \\ \vdots \\ \pi_{22.p} \end{pmatrix} + \begin{pmatrix} \varepsilon_{1t} \\ \varepsilon_{2t} \end{pmatrix}
$$

$$(12.54)$$

This can be represented more conveniently as:

$$y_t = Z_t \alpha + \varepsilon_t \tag{12.55}$$

where Z_t and α are defined by reference to (12.54). The vector y_t is of dimension 2×1, Z_t is $2 \times (2 + 4p)$; α, the vector which brings together the coefficients in the two equations, is of dimension $(2 + 4p) \times 1$ and ε_t is 2×1.

At t the optimal 1 step and h step ahead predictors of the y_{1t} and y_{2t} processes are:

$$\hat{y}_{1t+1|t} = \mu_{10} + \pi_{11.1} y_{1t} + \cdots + \pi_{11.p} y_{1t-p+1} + \pi_{12.1} y_{2t} + \cdots + \pi_{12.p} y_{2t-p+1} \tag{12.56a}$$

$$\vdots \qquad \vdots \qquad \qquad \vdots \qquad \qquad \vdots \qquad \qquad \vdots$$

$$\hat{y}_{1t+h|t} = \mu_{10} + \pi_{11.1} \hat{y}_{1t+h-1|t} + \cdots + \pi_{11.p} \hat{y}_{1t-p+h} + \pi_{12.1} \hat{y}_{2t+h-1|t} + \cdots + \pi_{12.p} \hat{y}_{2t-p+h} \tag{12.56b}$$

$$\hat{y}_{2t+1|t} = \mu_{20} + \pi_{21.1} y_{1t} + \cdots + \pi_{21.p} y_{t-p+1} + \pi_{22.1} y_{2t} + \cdots + \pi_{22.p} y_{2t-p+1} \tag{12.56c}$$

$$\vdots \qquad \vdots \qquad \qquad \vdots \qquad \qquad \vdots \qquad \qquad \vdots$$

$$\hat{y}_{2t+h|t} = \mu_{20} + \pi_{21.1} \hat{y}_{1t+h-1|t} + \cdots + \pi_{21.p} \hat{y}_{1t-p+h} + \pi_{22.1} \hat{y}_{2t+h-1|t} + \cdots + \pi_{22.p} \hat{y}_{2t-p+h} \tag{12.56d}$$

In writing these predictors it has been assumed that $h > p$; if $h \leq p$ then, for example, y_{1t-p+h} and y_{2t-p+h} are still available and their actual values are used in the prediction formula. The h step ahead mean squared prediction error for y_{1t} over the sample period $T_1 + 1$ to T_2 is:

$$\text{mse}[y_{1t}(h)] = \sum_{h=T_1+1}^{T} (y_{1t+h} - \hat{y}_{1t+h|t})^2 / (T_2 - T_1) \tag{12.57}$$

Let $y_{1t}(h \mid \{y_{1s}, y_{2s} \mid s \le t\})$ denote the optimal h-step predictor, (12.56b), of y_{1t} given information on present and past y_{1t} and y_{2t}, and let $y_{1t}(h \mid \{y_{1s} \mid s \le t\})$ denote the optimal h-step predictor of y_{1t} which excludes information on y_{2t}. Then y_{2t} is said to be Granger-noncausal for y_{1t} if removing the information on y_{2t} does not change the optimal predictor, that is:

$$y_{1t}(h \mid \{y_{1s}, y_{2s} \mid s \le t\}) = y_{1t}(h \mid \{y_{1s} \mid s \le t\}) \tag{12.58}$$

In the linear model this follows if and only if: $\pi_{12.1} = \cdots = \pi_{12.p} = 0$; that is the coefficients on lagged y_{2t} in (12.56b) are all zero (Lütkepohl 1991, p. 39). If any of the $\pi_{12.i}$ are nonzero, y_{2t} Granger-causes y_{1t}. By reversing the roles of y_{1t} and y_{2t} we conclude that y_{1t} is Granger-noncausal for y_{2t} if and only if $\pi_{21.1} = \cdots = \pi_{21.p} = 0$; and if any of the $\pi_{21.i}$ are nonzero y_{1t} Granger-causes y_{2t}. If y_{2t} Granger-causes y_{1t} and y_{1t} Granger-causes y_{2t}, that is at least one each of the $\pi_{12.i}$ and $\pi_{21.i}$ is nonzero, the system is said to be a 'feedback' system. Table 12.6 summarises the different possibilities.

12.5.2 Estimation and hypothesis tests

The hypothesis tests associated with each of the propositions in Table 12.6 are straightforward. For example, the null hypothesis of Granger-noncausality of y_{2t} for y_{1t} is $\pi_{12.i} = \cdots = \pi_{12.p} = 0$ and the alternative is that at least one $\pi_{12.i} \ne 0$. The null hypothesis can be expressed as a set of restrictions on the coefficient vector α:

$$
\begin{bmatrix}
0 & 0 & \cdots & 0 & 1 & 0 & \cdots & 0 & 0 & 0 & \cdots & 0 & 0 & \cdots & 0 \\
0 & 0 & \cdots & 0 & 0 & 1 & \cdots & 0 & 0 & 0 & \cdots & 0 & 0 & \cdots & 0 \\
\vdots & \vdots & & \vdots & \vdots & \vdots & & \vdots & \vdots & \vdots & \vdots & & \vdots & \vdots & & \vdots \\
0 & 0 & \cdots & 0 & 0 & 0 & \cdots & 1 & 0 & 0 & \cdots & 0 & 0 & \cdots & 0
\end{bmatrix}
\alpha =
\begin{pmatrix} 0 \\ 0 \\ \vdots \\ 0 \end{pmatrix}
\tag{12.59}
$$

Table 12.6 *Granger-causality in a bivariate system*

y_{2t} does not Granger-cause y_{1t}; $y_{2t} \nRightarrow y_{1t}$
$\pi_{12.1} = \cdots = \pi_{12.p} = 0$
y_{2t} Granger-causes y_{1t}; $y_{2t} \Rightarrow y_{1t}$
At least one $\pi_{12.i} \ne 0$
y_{1t} does not Granger-cause y_{2t}; $y_{1t} \nRightarrow y_{2t}$
$\pi_{21.1} = \cdots = \pi_{21.p} = 0$
y_{1t} Granger-causes y_{2t}; $y_{1t} \Rightarrow y_{2t}$
At least one $\pi_{21.i} \ne 0$
y_{2t} does not Granger-cause y_{1t} and y_{1t} does not Granger-cause y_{2t}; $y_{2t} \nRightarrow y_{1t}$ and $y_{1t} \nRightarrow y_{2t}$
$\pi_{12.1} = \cdots = \pi_{12.p} = 0$ and $\pi_{21.1} = \cdots = \pi_{21.p} = 0$
y_{2t} Granger-causes y_{1t} and y_{1t} Granger-causes y_{2t}; $y_{2t} \Leftrightarrow y_{2t}$
At least one $\pi_{12.i} \ne 0$ and at least one $\pi_{21.i} \ne 0$

Say $R\alpha = \underline{0}$ where R is a $p \times (2 + 4p)$ matrix with 0 entries apart from a 1 placed against each $\pi_{12.i}$, $i = 1, \ldots p$, coefficient and $\underline{0}$ is the right-hand side $p \times 1$ vector of zeros in (12.59). The alternative hypothesis is $R\alpha \neq \underline{0}$.

The principle of hypothesis testing is as straightforward as in the case of a single equation: a test statistic is constructed, large values of which are evidence against the null hypothesis. There is, however, a complication to be taken into account which makes the test statistic somewhat more complex than in the single equation case. As noted above the contemporaneous variance–covariance matrix for the errors will not necessarily have zeros on the off-diagonals, so the test statistic must take this into account. The $2 + 4p$ coefficients in the α vector can be estimated by OLS in the usual way on an equation by equation basis. That is estimate (12.50a) by running the regression of y_{1t} on a constant, p lags of y_{1t} and p lags of y_{2t}; then estimate (12.50b) by running the regression of y_{2t} on the same set of explanatory variables. This gives the OLS estimator $\hat{\alpha}$ of α. Then $\Omega(\varepsilon, p)$ can be consistently estimated from the OLS residuals. Let $\hat{\varepsilon}_{it}$ be the OLS residual based on a regression with T observations (after lags have been taken) then a consistent estimator of $\Omega(\varepsilon, p)$, referred to below as the residual variance matrix, is given by:

$$\tilde{\Omega}(\varepsilon, p) = \begin{bmatrix} \tilde{\sigma}_1^2 & \tilde{\sigma}_{12} \\ \tilde{\sigma}_{12} & \tilde{\sigma}_2^2 \end{bmatrix} \qquad (12.60)$$

where $\tilde{\sigma}_i^2 = \Sigma \hat{\varepsilon}_{it}^2 / T$ and $\tilde{\sigma}_{12} = \Sigma \hat{\varepsilon}_{1t} \hat{\varepsilon}_{2t} / T$. As each regression is based on $T - 2p - 1$ degrees of freedom, a small sample adjustment to $\tilde{\Omega}(\varepsilon, p)$ suggested by Lütkepohl (*op. cit.*, p. 68) is:

$$\hat{\Omega}(\varepsilon, p) = \tilde{\Omega}(\varepsilon, p)[T/(T - 2p - 1)] \qquad (12.61)$$

Construction of a test statistic requires the distribution of $\hat{\alpha}$ to establish whether deviations from the restrictions, that is $R(\hat{\alpha} - \alpha)$, have occurred by 'chance'. In general only the asymptotic distribution of $\hat{\alpha}$ is known. The following (Wald) statistic is asymptotically distributed as χ^2 with p degrees of freedom under the null hypothesis:

$$\lambda_w = (R\hat{\alpha})'[R\hat{\Phi}R']^{-1}R\hat{\alpha} \qquad (12.62)$$

where $\hat{\Phi}$ is the estimated variance (–covariance) matrix of $\hat{\alpha}$ which depends upon the data matrices and a consistent estimator of $\Omega(\varepsilon, p)$. A more extensive derivation is given in Lütkepohl (*op. cit.*) who suggests that an F version of this test statistic is obtained as

$$\lambda_F = \lambda_w / p \qquad (12.63)$$

which is approximately distributed as $F(f_1, f_2)$ where f_1 and f_2 are the numerator and denominator degrees of freedom, respectively. In the present case $f_1 = p$, although the testing principle obviously applies more generally where f_1 is the number of independent restrictions in the null hypothesis; and, analogous to the standard regression case, f_2 is the number of degrees of freedom in the regression equal to $2T - (2 + 4p)$ or, in general, $kT - (k + k^2 p)$ where k is the number of equations in the VAR. Lütkepohl (*op. cit.*, p. 94) suggests cancelling out the common k in f_2 as it is simpler to use $F(f_1, f_2/k)$ which is approximately equal to $F(f_1, f_2)$.

12.5.3 Practical problems

There are some important practical problems in implementing Granger-causation tests. The first is in establishing the lag length p, which can be done in two ways: on an equation by equation basis without the constraint that the lag length is the same in both equations; or on a system basis either with or without a common value of p. In the example below the alternatives are illustrated; whichever way, a criterion or criteria are required to choose the lag length. Two commonly used criteria are the Akaike (1974) Information Criterion, and the Schwarz (1978) Information Criterion, usually referred to as AIC and SIC, respectively, and both can be used in a single-equation (see Chapter 6) or multi-equation setting (see Chapter 14). These criteria work on the basis of penalising additional lagged values of y_{1t} and y_{2t}. In a single-equation context the AIC and SIC are:

$$\text{AIC}(m) = T \ln \hat{\sigma}^2(m) + 2m \qquad (12.64a)$$

$$\text{SIC}(m) = T \ln \hat{\sigma}^2(m) + m(\ln T) \qquad (12.64b)$$

where T is the number of observations (after lagging), m is the number of regressors in a single regression $\hat{\sigma}^2(m) = \text{RSS}(m)/T$ where $\text{RSS}(m)$ is the residual sum of squares from a regression with m regressors. The procedure is to calculate the criterion over the range of m being considered, the model with the smaller value being preferred. For example, consider the AIC and a regression with $p = 2$, then $m = 5$ as there are two lagged values each of y_{1t} and y_{2t} and a constant. Now increasing p to 3 cannot lead to an increase in RSS (because OLS minimises the RSS, it can always set the coefficients on the additional lagged values to zero and achieve the previous RSS); hence, on the first part of the criterion there is a reduction (or at least not an increase), but in the case of the AIC the second part has increased from 10 for $p = 2$ to 14 for $p = 3$. Whether AIC decreases depends on the balance of these two terms. The principle is similar for SIC although the penalty factor is $m(\ln T)$ rather than $2m$. Because of the different penalty functions AIC and SIC can result in different choices of lag length. In particular AIC tends to overparameterise in the sense of asymptotically overestimating the true lag order with positive probability, whereas this is not a proerty of SIC. In addition their use does not guarantee that other desirable features of an empirical model are met, such as residuals which are consistent with a white noise process. As a practical matter choosing the smallest AIC (or SIC) value subject to nonrejection of the null hypothesis of white noise innovations is a commonly used procedure.

If the two, and in general k, equations are considered together the detail of the information criteria changes but not the principle. The AIC and SIC become

$$\text{AIC}(m) = T \ln |\hat{\Omega}(\varepsilon, p)| + 2m \qquad (12.65a)$$

$$\text{SIC}(m) = T \ln |\hat{\Omega}(\varepsilon, p)| + m(\ln T) \qquad (12.65b)$$

where $m = pk^2 + k$; $|\hat{\Omega}(\varepsilon, p)|$ is the determinant of the residual variance matrix (estimated by maximum likelihood or OLS without the degrees of freedom correction); p is the lag length of the VAR; k is the number of equations in the VAR; and T is the number of observations (after lags have been taken) in a single series. According to the criteria the lag length is chosen which minimises $\text{AIC}(m)$ or $\text{SIC}(m)$, although as in the single-equation case there may be a difference as to which order is chosen.

Besides the practical problem of choosing the lag length a number of authors have pointed out problems with Granger-causation tests – see, for example, Lütkepohl (op. cit., pp. 41 et seq.) and Hendry (1995, p. 176). In principle the optimal predictor should be based on all possible information not just a part of it. For example, the optimal predictor for y_{1t} may depend on y_{2t} and y_{3t}; excluding y_{3t} to analyse a bivariate system is a misspecification that may lead to incorrect inferences. The researcher can guard against this possibility by undertaking the usual set of diagnostic tests designed to detect misspecification not only as to potentially excluded variables but also of nonlinearity of the system. In addition Johansen (1995a, p. 21) suggests that in his experience if a long lag length is needed to get white noise residuals it often pays to consider extending the information set. While useful this advice has to be coupled with some guidance as to what is a 'long' lag length. In the examples of applications to quarterly data on the demand for money and the exchange rate given in Johansen (op. cit., pp. 23 et seq.) lag lengths of 2 are adequate, and a possible guide is that lag lengths longer than the annual number of observations might be an informal indicator of the need to extend the information set. Although imprecise this advice suggests guarding against mechanically increasing the lag length until white noise residuals are obtained.

12.5.4 Granger-causation tests: wage/price inflation and unemployment, United Kingdom

The abstract discussion of the previous sections is put into context with applications from two datasets. First, reported in this section, the existence of Granger-causation is assessed for the Phillips' data for the United Kingdom comprising unemployment, u_t, and wage inflation, π_{wt} (this example is extended to include price inflation in a review question). A second dataset, reported in the next section, comprising recent data for the United States provides an interesting contrast to the historical data set of Phillips.

In both cases the hypotheses of interest are H_{01}: wage/price inflation causes unemployment (Fisher) and H_{02}: unemployment causes wage/price inflation (Phillips). In addition there may

be no causation in the Granger sense or mutual causation, that is a feedback system. The hypotheses are tested in the context of (a statistically adequate) VAR of the form given by (12.50); the VAR is modelled in stationary variables so that the test statistics have standard distributions. (This is a sufficient condition for inference using standard distributions – for a complete statement of necessary and sufficient conditions see Sims, Stock and Watson (1991).) A first step is, therefore, to assess the order of integration of u_t and π_{wt}.

In the case of the UK data set, test statistics for a unit root have already been reported in Table 12.1, with the conclusion that u_t and π_{wt} are I(0). The information criteria, AIC and SIC, for choosing the order of the VAR are reported in Table 12.7 together with the SC test statistics for serial correlation. Looking at the single-equation criteria, for the u_t equation AIC and SIC both have a minimum at lag 2; and a lag of 2 is necessary for the SC test statistic to be satisfactory. In the case of the π_{wt} equation AIC has a minimum at lag 2 whereas SIC has a minimum at lag 1. However, at lag 1 there are indications of serial correlation with SC(4) = 9.354[0.0] but

Table 12.7 VAR order selection: information criteria and LM test for serial correlation, UK dataset

Lag order	Single-equation criteria: u_t			
	1	2	3	4
AIC	60.726	**44.991**	45.450	48.321
SIC	66.402	**54.450**	58.693	65.348
SC(4)	17.954	3.060	2.756	2.960
msl	[0.000]	[0.547]	[0.600]	[0.564]

Lag order	Single-equation criteria: π_{wt}			
	1	2	3	4
AIC	73.919	**71.444**	71.346	73.881
SIC	**79.587**	80.903	84.588	90.907
SC(4)	9.354	3.616	6.582	8.610
msl	[0.052]	[0.460]	[0.160]	[0.072]

Lag order	System criteria			
	1	2	3	4
AIC	117.347	**105.052**	106.298	111.064
SIC	124.914	**120.106**	128.999	141.333

Notes: All entries are calculated using a common sample period of 1865 to 1913; bold entries indicate the minimum.

Table 12.8   *Test statistics for Granger-causality, UK dataset*

H_{01}: does (wage) inflation Granger-cause unemployment?			
Lag order	1	2	3	4
F test	3.931	3.051	2.455	2.015
[msl]	[0.053]	[0.057]	[0.076]	[0.110]

H_{02}: does unemployment Granger-cause (wage) inflation?			
Lag order	1	2	3	4
F test	0.468	2.920	1.869	1.177
[msl]	[0.497]	[0.064]	[0.150]	[0.336]

at lag 2, SC(4) = 3.616 with an msl of 46%; hence lag 2 is preferred for both equations. This is confirmed with the system versions of AIC and SIC which again suggest a lag of 2. For completeness, the test statistics for Granger-causation with lags 1 to 4 are reported in Table 12.8.

The test statistics for Granger-causation are reported in Table 12.8. At the preferred lag of 2 the F statistic for H_{01}: wage/price inflation causes unemployment (Fisher) is 3.051 with an msl of 5.7% and the F statistic for H_{02}: unemployment causes wage/price inflation (Phillips) is 2.920 with an msl of 6.4%. These marginal significance levels are fairly small, suggesting mutual causation: $\pi_{wt} \Leftrightarrow u_t$. The maintained model for these test statistics is a VAR which is linear in the variables, hence this result does not carry over immediately to the nonlinear framework of the Phillips curve, nevertheless they are indicative – or suggestive – of a feedback system of the kind proposed by Lipsey (1960), which is consistent with the instrumental variables approach reported in section **12.4.7**.

12.5.5   Granger-causation tests: wage/price inflation and unemployment, United States

The dataset used in this section comprises monthly (seasonally adjusted) data for the United States, for the period 1972m1 to 1995m2 (before lags are taken) on the unemployment rate, u_t, and price inflation, π_t, measured as the log difference of the consumer price index. Test statistics to assess the order of integration of u_t, and price inflation, π_t, are

Table 12.9   *Unit root tests for unemployment and inflation*

Variable	Model	$\hat{\tau}$	Φ_1	$\hat{\tau}_\mu$	$\hat{\mu}$	$\hat{\tau}_\beta$	$\hat{\beta}$	Φ_3
				Test statistics for 2 unit roots				
u_t	ADF(3)	−4.814	11.553	−4.805	−0.002	−4.907	−0.000	12.125
π_t	ADF(5)	−11.472	65.558	−11.450	−0.007	−14.449	−0.001	65.548
				Test statistics for 1 unit root				
u_t	ADF(4)	−0.410	4.629	−3.039	0.186	−3.145	−0.000	5.539
π_t	ADF(6)	−1.178	2.935	−2.423	0.788	−3.510	−0.000	6.354

Sample: 1972m1 to 1995m2 (before lags).
Critical values

	$\hat{\tau}$	$\hat{\tau}_\mu$	$\hat{\tau}_\beta$	Φ_1	Φ_3
5%	−1.928	−2.851	−3.400	4.696	6.397
10%	−1.603	−2.556	−3.113	3.835	5.433

Critical values of $\hat{\tau}$, $\hat{\tau}_\mu$ and $\hat{\tau}_\beta$ obtained using Cheung–Lai response surface coefficients for $T = 270$ and $p = 6$; critical values of Φ_1 and Φ_3 obtained by simulation for $T = 2000$ – see Chapter 6.

reported in Table 12.9 – see also section **7.9.3** where unit root test statistics were reported for US unemployment. For related work see Samavati, Dilts and Deitsch (1994).

It is clear from the test statistics in the upper part of the table that the null hypothesis of 2 unit roots for both series should be rejected. Turning to the lower part of the table the null hypothesis of a single unit root is also rejected, but this conclusion is less straightforward. Φ_3 for u_t is 5.539, which is close to the 10% critical value of 5.433 for $T = 200$ (critical values from Table 6.7) but the estimate of the trend coefficient is effectively zero and omitting it we obtain $\hat{\tau}_\mu = -3.039$, with $\hat{\mu} = 0.186$ and 't' statistic of 3.014. The magnitude of $\hat{\mu}$, and the significance of its 't' statistic, suggests that a unit root is unlikely; there is no suggestion in the data of drift of this size – the constant is providing the basis of the estimate of long-term unemployment. The (approximate) 5% and 10% critical values for $\hat{\tau}_\mu$ are -2.851 and -2.556, and here, guarding against the low power of unit roots tests, we opt for rejection of the null hypothesis. Support for this conclusion comes from the marked change in the test statistic in the maintained regression without a constant and see also Chapter 7, where the US unemploy-

ment rate was used as an illustrative example of unit root testing.

A similar pattern is followed for π_t. First, $\Phi_3 = 6.354$, which is just below the 5% critical value, with the estimate of β zero to 3 decimal places and not significant (and note, anyway, that $\hat{\tau}_\beta = -3.510$ is significant); omitting the time trend we find $\hat{\tau}_\mu = -2.423$ which is close to the 10% critical value of (approximately) -2.556. The estimated constant is again large, $\hat{\mu} = 0.788$, with a 't' statistic of 2.112. Altogether this suggests a stationary series with a root close to unity.

The preliminary tests for a unit root suggest series with similar characteristics: each appears to be I(0), but with a root close to unity that is problematic for the standard unit root tests. Conditional on this conclusion we can move to the next step of determining the order of the VAR. The information criteria, AIC and SIC, for choosing the order of the VAR are reported in Table 12.10 together with the LM test statistics for serial correlation (denoted SC(12)). Considering the u_t equation first, the single-equation AIC and SIC lead to lag lengths of 7 and 5, respectively, and both choices are associated with insignificant values of the SC(12) statistic for serial correlation. The system versions of AIC

Table 12.10 *US Phillips and Fisher correlations: model selection criteria*

					Single-equation criteria							
						u_t						
Lag =	1	2	3	4	5	6	7	8	9	10	11	12
AIC	−860.80	−863.35	−879.46	−891.95	−899.19	−899.95	**−900.08**	896.36	−894.72	−892.01	−889.10	−888.32
SIC	−850.06	−845.45	−854.40	−859.73	**−859.82**	−853.42	−846.39	−835.51	−826.70	−816.84	−806.77	−798.82
SC(12)	38.487	39.034	33.515	19.877	13.901	14.056	11.604	13.995	19.909	17.511	27.547	21.706
[msl]	[0.000]	[0.000]	[0.000]	[0.069]	[0.307]	[0.297]	[0.478]	[0.300]	[0.068]	0.131]	[0.006]	[0.040]
						π_t						
Lag =	1	2	3	4	5	6	7	8	9	10	11	12
AIC	634.51	598.02	600.42	600.02	597.96	597.09	578.55	578.90	**566.47**	569.11	572.71	574.15
SIC	645.26	**615.92**	625.48	632.24	637.34	643.63	632.25	639.75	634.49	644.28	655.05	663.65
SC(12)	61.392	42.702	50.224	42.771	50.749	51.621	35.003	32.595	17.951	21.362	22.186	20.197
[msl]	[0.000]	[0.000]	[0.000]	[0.000]	[0.000]	[0.000]	[0.000]	[0.001]	[0.117]	[0.045]	[0.035]	[0.063]
					System criteria							
Lag =	1	2	3	4	5	6	7	8	9	10	11	12
AIC	−232.81	−273.77	−288.88	−301.91	−312.30	−312.87	**−330.55**	−326.38	−337.63	−332.77	−326.23	−322.35
SIC	−218.47	−245.10	**−245.88**	−244.57	−240.64	−226.86	−230.21	−211.71	−208.62	−189.43	−168.55	−150.53

Notes: All entries are calculated using a common sample period of 1973m1 to 1995m2; bold entries indicate the minimum.

Table 12.11   *US Phillips and Fisher correlations: F test statistics for Granger-causality*

						Does inflation Granger-cause unemployment?						
Lag =	1	2	3	4	5	6	7	8	9	10	11	12
F test	14.116	6.345	4.096	4.292	3.712	3.834	3.801	3.331	3.162	2.939	2.745	2.547
[msl]	[0.000]	[0.002]	[0.007]	[0.002]	[0.003]	[0.001]	[0.000]	[0.001]	[0.001]	[0.002]	[0.002]	[0.003]
						Does unemployment Granger-cause inflation?						
Lag =	1	2	3	4	5	6	7	8	9	10	11	12
F test	5.124	1.927	1.329	1.572	1.799	1.945	3.510	3.458	4.0167	3.764	3.407	3.301
[msl]	[0.024]	[0.147]	[0.265]	[0.182]	[0.113]	[0.074]	[0.001]	[0.000]	[0.000]	[0.000]	[0.000]	[0.000]

and SIC suggest 7 and 3, respectively; however, the latter choice leads to a large and significant value of the SC(12) statistic, so the longer lag is preferred. Bearing in mind Johansen's informal advice, a lag of 7 months does not seem excessively long given the use of monthly data. Turning to Table 12.11 it transpires that whatever the choice of lag length in this range, the outcome of the F test is unaffected: there is a clear rejection of Granger-noncausality, the test statistic is significant, inflation Granger-causes unemployment. For example, with a lag of 7 the F statistic is 3.801 with an msl of zero.

The situation is more problematical with the π_t equation. There is a noticeable difference between the single-equation information criteria, with AIC suggesting a lag length of 9 and SIC having a minimum at a lag of 2; these contrast with the system AIC and SIC which suggest 7 and 3, respectively. A lag of 9 seems preferable as it is only then that the SC(12) test statistic is not significant at conventional levels. With this lag length the null hypothesis that unemployment is Granger-noncausal for inflation is rejected. The choice of lag length *does* turn out to be critical in assessing the null hypothesis, as at lag lengths 2 to 6 the null hypothesis would not be rejected at the 5% level. However, the serial correlation at these shorter lag lengths is quite marked, with marginal significance levels virtually zero, and inference is unlikely to be sound. Thus, in common with the UK dataset, the conclusion suggested by the data is one of mutual causation, that is a feedback system involving π_t and u_t.

The reader should, however, be aware of some limitations of this kind of testing procedure for causation. VARs are linear in the variables, even if these are transformations of the original variables, so nonlinearities may well be missed if present in the DGP. In common with estimation more generally, omission of relevant variables can bias the results; thus, if in a bivariate application, a relevant third variable is omitted only in exceptional circumstances will the bivariate results remain robust to this specification error. If the variables are nonstationary, say I(1), it might be tempting to difference the variables to make them I(0) and then use the differenced variables in a VAR; if, however, the I(1) variables are cointegrated, there will be loss of important information, tying the variables together in the long run, in a VAR in first differences. Chapters 14 and 15 show an appropriate procedure in the context of I(1) variables.

This conclusion leads on to the subject matter of Chapters 14 and 15, which deal explicitly with a systems approach to model formulation and estimation.

12.6   Concluding remarks

In an article which subsequently generated an extensive and sometimes quite hostile debate Phillips (1958), using nearly a century (1861–1957) of UK data, suggested that 'the rate of change of money wage rates can be explained by the level of employment and the rate of change of unemployment, except in or immediately after those years in which there is a sufficiently rapid rise in import prices to offset the tendency for increased productivity to reduce the cost of living'. As a result the term 'Phillips curve', describing a negative and nonlinear relationship between wage inflation and unemployment, was introduced into the economists' vocabulary. Subsequent articles apparently found evidence of a Phillips curve using data from countries other than the United Kingdom. This was not, though, the first time that evidence had been reported of a negative correlation between inflation and unemployment. Much earlier, using US data, Fisher (1926) had suggested a relationship between price (rather than wage) inflation and unemployment, although his emphasis was on the reverse line of causation compared to Phillips.

This chapter has sought to give a historical perspective to some of the developments in interpreting and estimating the Phillips curve, starting with Phillips' own estimates. Phillips originally obtained estimates of his famous curve from a relatively small number of data points in his sample period of 1861–1913. Re-estimation using all the sample observations and modern methods of obtaining nonlinear least squares estimates, with Phillips' original specification, suggested that the original estimates were quite close to those obtained when the complete sample is used – see also Gilbert (1976). Further, the resulting regression equation seemed well-specified with, for example, significant coefficients of the anticipated sign and no evidence of serial correlation in the residuals.

A number of rationalisations for the existence of a negative relationship between wage inflation and unemployment have been given in the literature. First, note that Phillips has been criticised from both sides of the Atlantic for failing to derive the theoretical basis of this negative relationship. However, these criticisms are rather harsh. In Phillips' model employers compete for the services of labour; if labour is in short supply relative to demand wage rates are bid up, tempting labour from other firms and industries. The change in money wage rates is positively related to the excess demand for labour, and excess demand is negatively related to unemployment; hence, the negative relationship between wage inflation and unemployment. In addition, according to Phillips, when activity is increasing, as evidenced by an unemployment rate that is decreasing, employers bid more vigorously for labour. Employers and labour are aware of the real wage implications of increases in nominal wage rates particularly through cost of living adjustments. It could certainly be argued that this is not as sophisticated or complete an explanation as later theories but Phillips is aware of the need to justify the relationship that bears his name.

In an alternative model, due to Friedman, short-run Phillips curves, which are not vertical, arise due to the misperception of workers as to whether real wages have increased following an increase in nominal wages. This takes place in an economy with perfectly competitive firms that produce where the real wage is equal to the marginal product of labour. Suppose starting from a position in which the labour market clears there is an increase in aggregate nominal demand resulting in an increase in prices, following this employers are willing to pay higher nominal wages to attract additional workers (this part of the story is as in Phillips' competitive bidding). Now in order to produce extra output the employers' real wage, which is equated to the marginal product of labour, has to fall. Provided any consequent increase in money wages is less than the increase in prices there will be an increase in output. Workers adjust their perception of prices more slowly than employers, because what matters to them is prices in general on which information is costly to obtain, or which is only available with a lag, rather than prices in particular. Workers therefore perceive an increase in nominal wages as an increase in real wages and offer more labour. The apparent contradiction of employers demanding more labour at a lower real wage and workers supplying it at a higher real wage than initially is resolved by their different perceptions of the real wage. As a result of the increase in demand, prices and money wages have increased and unemployment has decreased. There is a Phillips curve relationship between wage inflation and unemployment conditional on the workers' perception of price inflation. But, as Friedman points out (1977, p. 457), this is a temporary situation: in due course workers' perceptions catch up with reality and, therefore, as the relative price of labour has not changed employment returns to its original market clearing position and unemployment returns to its 'natural' rate given the labour force. This scenario could be rehearsed again for a different perceived rate of inflation, which would draw out another short-run relationship between wage inflation and price inflation.

In Friedman's model only one long run, the natural rate of unemployment, is sustainable since that is determined by real forces, and is compatible with any perceived rate of inflation. Hence, there is a series of short-run Phillips curves each conditional on a perceived or expected rate of price inflation, but the long-run Phillips curve is vertical. To achieve a long-run trade-off between wage inflation and unemployment there must be a continuing acceleration in perceived price inflation, but even that assumes workers will not come to understand the nature of their continuing mistakes in the perception of inflation.

More recent explanations of the Phillips curve have stressed the importance of imperfect competition – see especially Layard and Nickell (1985, 1986) and Carlin and Soskice (1990) – in which wages are set through bargains between trade unions and employers. If claims to output by employers and workers exceed the total available then, given an accommodating monetary policy, competing (and inconsistent) claims result in inflation and unemployment. The natural rate of unemployment in Friedman's model is replaced with the nonaccelerating inflation rate of unemployment, usually referred to as the NAIRU. This is the rate at which the competing claims of labour and profits are reconciled and inflation is constant. On the union side the bargained real wage, BRW, is a positive function of employment, that is given a constant labour force it is a negative function of unemployment; *ceteris paribus* an increase in unemployment weakens the bargaining strength of unions (and individuals in a nonunion context). Employers on the other hand are interested in the price-determined real wage, PRW. With constant labour productivity the PRW is constant. Combining this with the BRW, which is a positive function of employment, gives an equilibrium at their point of intersection, at which profit per unit plus labour cost per unit sum exactly to the output price: the competing claims are consistent. Given the labour force this determines an equilibrium rate of unemployment – the NAIRU. If unemployment is less than NAIRU unions bargain for a wage greater than at equilibrium: money wages increase more than at the NAIRU, and so do product prices as employers respond to their potential loss of profit per unit of output. Lower unemployment is associated with higher wage and price inflation: there is a Phillips curve at least in the short run.

The development of empirical (rather than purely theoretical) attempts at improving Phillips' original approach centred on whether he had confused money wages with real wages and whether he had failed to distinguish the role of expected inflation. This led to the formulation of an expectations augmented Phillips curve of the general form $\pi_{wt} = a + f(u_t) + \delta\pi_t^e + \eta_t$. A crucial role was attributed to the coefficient δ, which enabled a distinction between the short run and the long run. A δ of 0 implied that there was complete money illusion in the wage bargaining process – it was money wages rather than real wages that mattered. A δ of 1 implied that the appropriate dependent variable in the modified Phillips curve was $\pi_{wt} - \pi_t^e$: there was no long-run trade-off between wage inflation and unemployment, the Phillips curve was vertical in the long run. A value of δ between 0 and 1 implied that the long-run Phillips curve was not vertical. Such was the critical nature of the debate that Sargent (1972) described δ as the 'notorious parameter'.

In this chapter an expectations augmented Phillips curve was estimated for 1861–1913, one of the data periods used by Phillips (*op. cit.*), assuming expectations were generated by the adaptive expectations hypothesis, section **12.4.2**, and rational expectations, section **12.4.8**. As to the former, interpretation of the coefficient on expected inflation depends on what assumption is used to identify δ. Sargent was critical of the standard assumption that in the context of modelling π_t^e as a distributed lag function of lagged inflation, $\pi_t^e = w(L)\pi_t$, it was sensible to maintain the hypothesis that $\pi_t^e = w(L = 1)\pi_t = \pi_t$. On the standard assumption our estimate of δ was about 0.12 depending on the estimation method. However, looking at the historical behaviour of actual inflation led to an estimate of δ of 0.41, whereas using a weakly rational approach to specification of the expectations variable led to an estimate of δ of 0.31.

The Phillips curve, with or without expected inflation, is an example of a reduced form equation. Specification of the underlying structural equations, for example for labour demand and labour supply, output and price determination may be a preferable approach and would enable implementation of a 'fully' rational expectations estimator. A systems approach to model building and estimation is taken up in Chapters 14 and 15.

Part of the debate about the Phillips curve involved a disagreement about whether unemployment causes inflation or inflation causes unemployment. While that question cannot be definitively resolved here, it served to motivate the use of Granger-causation tests on two datasets comprising the Phillips UK data and US data on price inflation and unemployment. On the basis of the F tests for Granger-causation unemployment and inflation comprise a feedback system. However, note that these tests assume a linear rather than a nonlinear relationship and

the results, for the United Kingdom, are sensitive to small changes in the significance level used in evaluating the test statistics.

Review

1. The Phillips curve captured a negative, nonlinear trade-off that appeared to exist between wage inflation and unemployment using UK data over the period 1861–1957. Phillips' (1958) microeconomic model to account for this relationship involved competitive bidding by employers for the services of labour.

2. Phillips also observed that wage inflation at any given level of unemployment seemed to be related to whether unemployment was decreasing or increasing. If unemployment was decreasing wage inflation tended to be higher than if there was no change in unemployment or if unemployment was increasing.

3. Using data for 1861–1913, Phillips fitted a simple nonlinear equation of the following form using six data points that were averages of π_{wt} and u_t:

$$\pi_{wt} + 0.9 = 9.638 u_t^{-1.394}$$

where π_{wt} is the rate of change of wage rates and u_t is the unemployment rate.

4. Phillips also suggested adding the term $h(\Delta u_t / u_t^m)$ to capture the cyclical effect of increasing and decreasing unemployment.

5. Phillips did not expect his empirical relationship to explain wage inflation 'in those years in which there was a very rapid rise in import prices'; however, he omitted a price term from his equation because in very few years had there been a sufficient increase in import prices.

6. It appeared, from the Phillips curve, that there was a menu of inflation–unemployment choices; high inflation and low unemployment through to low inflation and high unemployment.

7. Samuelson and Solow (1960) examined data for the United States from the 1890s through the late 1950s and found that their results were 'not so terribly different from Phillips' results for the United Kingdom'.

8. To provide a baseline to interpret subsequent developments we re-estimated the Phillips curve using Phillips' original dataset for the United Kingdom for 1861–1913. Two prior issues before estimation concerned how to measure rates of change and whether the time series are stationary.

9. Phillips defined π_{wt}^+ as the centred first difference, that is $\pi_{wt}^+ \equiv 100(W_{t+1} - W_{t-1})/2W_t$ where W_t is the money wage rate. An alternative approximation is the log first difference, $\pi_{wt} \equiv 100[\ln(W_t/W_{t-1})]$.

10. A prior analysis of the data suggested that wage inflation, measured as the log first difference, and unemployment were stationary. When the centred first difference was used there was some ambiguity in the test results for a unit root.

11. With the centred first difference we see that Phillips' original estimates were quite close to those resulting from nonlinear estimation using all the data.

12. Re-estimation of the Phillips curve using all the sample data from 1861 to 1913, and Phillips' definition of wage inflation as the centred first difference, produced coefficient estimates remarkably similar to those originally published by Phillips who used just 6 observations based on an averaging procedure.

13. There was, however, evidence of serial correlation in the residuals of this regression which Gilbert (*op. cit.*) suggested may be an artefact of using the centred first difference. Re-estimation with the log first difference of money wage rates removed the serial correlation.

14. The apparent statistical success of the re-estimated Phillips curve should not, however, rule out the possibility that its specification could be criticised and improved.

15. Phillips emphasised the causal relation as running from unemployment to wage inflation. In contrast Fisher (1976, p. 498) suggested that the correlation arises due to causation the other way round and is temporary.

16. Friedman (1968) argued that Phillips had made three mistakes: (i) he failed to distinguish between nominal wages and real wages and (ii) ignored temporary and permanent trade-offs; and (iii) he did not assign a role to expected inflation.

17. These criticisms led to the 'expectations augmented Phillips curve', EAPC:

$$\pi_{wt} = a + f(u_t) + \delta\pi_t^e + \eta_t$$

where π_t^e is expected inflation. The value of δ is critical in determining the trade-off between wage inflation and unemployment. For a given increase in expected inflation the vertical displacement in the Phillips curve is given by $\delta\pi_t^e$.

18. How to model expectations has been the subject of considerable debate. One of the simplest schemes is the adaptive expectations hypothesis, AEH, given by:

$$\pi_t^e - \pi_{t-1}^e = \gamma(\pi_{t-1} - \pi_{t-1}^e) + \xi_t$$

Muth showed that (with $\xi_t = 0$) the adaptive expectations scheme is an exponentially weighted forecast where π_t^e is a weighted average of past inflation rates:

$$\pi_t^e = \gamma \sum_{i=1}^{\infty} (1 - \gamma)^{i-1} \pi_{t-i}$$

19. The AEH incorporates the restriction that the sum of the lag weights is 1, that is,

$$\pi_t^e = \gamma^*(L = 1)\pi_t$$
$$= [\gamma/(1 - (1 - \gamma))]\pi_t = \pi_t$$

20. The AEH can be modified so that the sum of the lag weights differs from unity by allowing the coefficient in the numerator of $\gamma^*(L)$

to differ from γ; that is $\pi_t^e = \mu(L)\pi_t$ where $\mu(L) = \mu L[1 - (1 - \gamma)L]^{-1}$. Now the sum of the lag weights is $\mu(1) = \mu/\gamma$.

21. The EAPC combined with the AEH leads to the following model:

$$\pi_{wt} = a + f(u_t) + (1 - \gamma)[\pi_{wt} - a - f(u_{t-1})] + \delta\mu\pi_{t-1} + \eta_{lt}^+$$

However, we can only determine the product of δ and μ unless we make an assumption about μ. If we assume $\mu = \gamma$ (the 'standard' assumption), that is $\pi_t^e = \pi_t$ in the long run, δ is identified.

22. Estimation of the EAPC + AEH has to take into consideration a potential moving average error and correlation between the lagged dependent variable and the contemporaneous error. The results indicate that the estimated Phillips curve coefficients, a, b and c, remain in the region originally suggested by Phillips.

23. Different identification assumptions lead to different estimates of δ. Using the standard assumption, the IV estimate of δ is 0.122 but allowing for the time series properties of actual inflation the estimate of the crucial δ coefficient is 0.412.

24. The IV estimate of γ is 1.065, which is not significantly different from 1, implying that if the AEH is used expected inflation is equal to lagged actual inflation.

25. The Lucas/Sargent critique of the standard identifying assumption had a greater impact than just on the narrow focus of identifying δ. Subsequent papers – especially Sargent (1973) – led to a replacement of the paradigm of adaptive expectations, or variants thereof, with that of rational expectations.

26. The expectation formed at time t of a variable in the future is said to be rational for a given information set Ω_t if it is the same as the conditional expectation of that variable. The rational expectation of inflation, formed at $t - 1$, to prevail at t is the con-

ditional expectation of π_t given the information set Ω_{t-1}: $_{t-1}\pi_t^e = E_{t-1}\{\pi_t \mid \Omega_{t-1}\}$.

27. The relation between the outturn and the rational expectation is

$$\pi_t = E_{t-1}\{\pi_t \mid \Omega_{t-1}\} + \varepsilon_t = _{t-1}\pi_t^e + \varepsilon_t$$

where ε_t has a zero mean and is orthogonal to Ω_{t-1}.

28. We now have a two-equation system comprising the EAPC and the rational expectations hypothesis, REH:

$$\pi_{wt} = a + f(u_t) + \delta(_{t-1}\pi_t^e) + \eta_t$$
$$_{t-1}\pi_t^e = \pi_t - \varepsilon_t$$

resulting in:

$$\pi_{wt} = a + f(u_t) + \delta\pi_t + \upsilon_t$$

where $\upsilon_t = \eta_t - \delta\varepsilon_t$.

29. There is an errors in variables (EIV) problem in the EAPC + REH: replacing $_{t-1}\pi_t^e$ by π_t has introduced the error of measurement ε_t which is correlated with π_t.

30. A consistent estimator can be obtained by using the method of IV. If only a subset of Ω_{t-1}, say Ψ_{t-1}, is known then it is still possible to obtain consistent estimators using Ψ_{t-1}, as noted by Sargent (1973) and McCallum (1976).

31. For Phillips' original data, 1861–1913, using a 'weakly' rational choice of instruments, the estimate of δ is 0.311 with a 't' statistic for $\delta = 0$ of 2.355 and for $\delta = 1$ of 5.217.

32. Comparing the estimated adaptive expectations and rational expectations models the goodness of fit statistics suggest a preference for the rational expectations version of the augmented Phillips curve.

33. While the AEH version of the Phillips curve appeared to be well specified it did not dominate the RE version using a weakly rational information set. The comparison of models shows that white noise residuals and significant coefficients are necessary but not by themselves sufficient conditions for a

satisfactory empirical model. By the same logic the RE version of the EAPC is only tentatively adequate.

34. In section **12.5** we illustrated the use of tests of Granger-causality to see if they could inform the debate about the direction of causation between inflation and unemployment. u_t is said to be Granger-noncausal for π_t if removing the information on u_t does not change the optimal (linear) predictor of π_t.

35. Granger-causality (G-c) tests are usually applied in the context of a linear model known as a vector autoregressive model – or VAR – although the conceptual basis of such tests is not limited to linear models.

36. Within the G-c framework causation can run from u_t to π_t, from π_t to u_t or there can be mutual causation in which case the system is said to exhibit 'feedback'.

37. In principle the test is easy to apply, its usual form being an F test. For example, in the (auto)regression of π_t on lagged own values and lags of u_t, u_t is said to be noncausal for π_t if the coefficients on the lagged u_t are jointly not significant.

38. The following (Wald) statistic is asymptotically distributed as χ^2 with p (=the number of lags in the VAR) degrees of freedom under the null hypothesis:

$$\lambda_W = (R\hat{\alpha})'[R\hat{\Phi}R']^{-1}R\hat{\alpha}$$

where $\hat{\Phi}$ is a consistent estimator of the variance–covariance matrix of the VAR coefficients, $\hat{\alpha}$. An F version of this test statistic is obtained as $\lambda_F = \lambda_W/p$.

39. There are some important practical problems with Granger-causation tests although, they are not separate from the usual problems associated with obtaining a statistically adequate model. For example, two variables may be part of a larger system, which cannot be reduced without loss of information, and the choice of lag length p can be crucial to the results.

40. The G-c tests were illustrated with data with Phillips' original variables and with data on π_t and u_t for the United States for the period 1972m1 to 1995m2. On balance, in both cases, the test statistics were interpreted as providing evidence of a feedback system for unemployment and inflation.

Review questions

1. Suppose Phillips' original estimates do summarise a trade-off between unemployment and wage inflation, then what is the elasticity of the trade-off?

2. Consider equation (12.5) in the text, what is the effect on the Phillips curve of adding the term $(du_t/dt)/u_t^m$?

3. What are the arguments against interpreting the Phillips curve as a 'menu of choice' between unemployment and wage inflation?

4. Suppose W_t, the nominal wage rate, is normally distributed with a zero mean, constant variance and is serially uncorrelated, is the variable defined by the centred first difference, $\pi_{wt}^+ = 100(W_{t+1}W_{t-1})/W_t$, serially uncorrelated?

5. Consider the estimates reported in Table 12.2, is the exponent on u_t in regression 3 significantly different from 1?

6. Re-estimate the equations in Table 12.2 with allowance for a dummy variable, which takes the value 1 in 1870, and 0 elsewhere. Confirm that none of the coefficient estimates are materially altered by the inclusion of this dummy variable. Why should such a dummy variable be considered for 1870 on (a) statistical and (b) economic grounds?

7. Summarise the argument for including anticipated price inflation in the Phillips curve with a coefficient δ. What is the importance of $\delta = 1$?

8. Why is the learning scheme for inflation expectations given by equation (12.14) described as an adaptive process?

9. What is your interpretation of the adaptive learning scheme when $\gamma = 1$?

10. Derive the first order autocorrelation coefficient for η_t^+ in (12.29b); what happens to this when $\gamma = 1$?

11. Show that the implied set of lag weights in the MA(1) model, $\pi_t = \theta_0 + (1 + \theta_1)\varepsilon_t$, has the sum $\theta_1/(1 + \theta_1)$.

12. Consider the estimates reported in the first equation in Table 12.4, interpret the estimated coefficient on π_{t-1}.

13. Explain the method of instrumental variables (IV) estimation reported in Table 12.4. Why is IV estimation necessary?

14. Explain what is meant by rational expectations.

15. What is the problem with OLS estimation of equation (12.47) reproduced below?

$$\pi_{wt} = a + f(u_t) + \delta\pi_t + v_t$$
$$v_t = \eta_t - \delta\varepsilon_t$$

16. Summarise the difference of view between Phillips and Fisher as to the direction of causation between inflation and unemployment.

17. (i) Write a second order VAR in the three variables, y_{1t}, y_{2t}, and y_{3t}.
    (ii) Specify the necessary and sufficient conditions for:
    (a) y_{3t} to be Granger-noncausal (G-nc) for y_{1t};
    (b) y_{2t} and y_{3t} to be G-nc for y_{1t};
    (c) y_{1t} and y_{3t} to be G-nc for y_{2t}.

18. The bivariate VAR in the variables π_{wt} and u_t of section **12.5.4** was extended to include price inflation, π_t, and estimated for the period 1861–1913 (excluding lags). The system AIC suggested a lag length of 2, whereas the system SIC suggested a lag length of 1; however, in the latter case there was evidence of serial correlation so the test statistics are for a lag of 2. The F test statistics for the exclusion of lags of the row variable from the equation for the column variable are shown in Table 12.12 below.

Table 12.12 F test statistics for exclusion of lags of the row variable from the equation for the column variable

	Equation			
	π_{wt}	u_t	π_t	π_t
Exclude				
π_{wt}	4.052	2.440	0.634	0.142
[msl]	[0.024]	[0.099]	[0.535]	[0.934]
u_t	2.494	14.563	0.915	2.996
[msl]	[0.094]	[0.000]	[0.409]	[0.042]
π_t	0.093	0.167	0.784	1.767
[msl]	[0.911]	[0.846]	[0.463]	[0.169]

Notes: Main entries are for a lag length of 2; italicised entries are for a lag length of 3; estimation period 1865–1913.

(i) Using an msl of 10% summarise the evidence for Granger-causation among the three variables.

(ii) On the basis of these results is it valid to consider the bivariate system between π_{wt} and u_t?

(iii) Why might the results in the last column be considered a little surprising? The single-equation AIC had a minimum at lag 3 for this equation; with this lag length, the column of revised F test statistics is shown in italics. Reconsider your answers to the last two questions.

19. Collect data for a more recent historical period and assess the evidence for a modified version of the Phillips curve.

CHAPTER 13

The exchange rate and purchasing power parity

13.1 Introduction

What determines the exchange rate? This is one of the most important questions in economics. The central concern of this chapter is one possible answer to this question, that is purchasing power parity or PPP for short. Whether by itself or in combination with other equilibrium conditions, for example uncovered interest parity, UIP, purchasing power parity is an almost invariable ingredient of (macroeconomic) models of the exchange rate. While theoretically attractive, the empirical support for PPP is mixed; slight variations in data definitions, sample periods, test statistics and estimation methods have all had marked effects on the results and, hence, conclusions. Some authors find in favour of PPP, others do not. The research on PPP is extensive, a flavour of the results can be obtained from Adler and Lehman (1983), Balassa (1964), Bilson (1978), Engel (1993), Frenkel (1981), Hakkio (1984), Richardson (1978), Taylor (1995b) and Rogoff (1996). That so much research has been reported on this subject indicates, in part, a reluctance to accept that PPP does not hold, at least in the long run.

An outline of the basic theory of PPP is presented in section **13.2**. We recognise that the empirical implementation and testing of PPP, which in its simplest form relates to the comparable price of a single homogeneous good or basket of homogeneous goods, is likely to be complicated by a number of practical considerations. Essential to PPP is the idea of international commodity arbitrage. This is the mechanism by which, according to the theory, pricing deviations from PPP are rectified. Recognition of this element of PPP necessarily introduces time as an important practical consideration and allows us to draw a distinction between the possibility of short-run deviations from PPP while maintaining a long-run tendency for PPP to hold. Complications and distinctions between the short run and long run and the nominal exchange rate and the real exchange rate are dealt with in various subsections.

As in Chapters 10 to 12 there is something to be learnt not just from reporting the results of other studies but also in following through the details and complications using a particular dataset. Thus, section **13.3** considers some aspects of the support, or lack of it, for PPP using monthly data for the post-1973 period of floating exchange rates for the following four bilateral rates against the US dollar: the Canadian dollar, the German Deutschmark (DM), the Japanese yen and the UK pound sterling. Graphing the data and its differences and autocorrelations are a useful initial step which is followed by application of the standard set of unit roots tests.

Section **13.4** focuses on the real exchange rate with estimates of the persistence of shocks; this is important because one implication of a unit root in the real exchange rate process is that shocks have an infinite life. Since it is known that the OLS estimator of coefficients in an autoregressive model are generally biased it may be important to bias adjust the coefficients to avoid a misleading estimate of the persistence of shocks. This section also considers a potentially more powerful technique due to Abuaf and Jorion (1990), which pools the separate country data into a 'panel' of data and applies a generalised least squares estimator.

Section **13.5** reports some simple models and tests for cointegration. The first step is to relax the assumption that if a cointegrating vector exists for the nominal exchange rate and relative prices it should have the coefficients $+1$ and -1. Other subsections report OLSEG estimates and the modified ADF test.

Section **13.6** considers some variations on the PPP theme illustrating a model of the 'fundamentals' of exchange rates, in this case the flexible price monetary model, FPMM. Section **13.7** contains some concluding remarks.

13.2 Purchasing power parity

Consider a simple example in which there are just two countries, say the United States with the dollar as its currency unit and the United Kingdom with the pound sterling as its currency unit. We can express the exchange rate as either the number of dollars per pound, or its reciprocal the number of pounds per dollar. For example, suppose that the exchange rate, viewed as the number of dollars it takes to buy one pound, is 2; then the reciprocal exchange rate is that one dollar is worth 0.5 pounds. To develop the example we will choose one of the countries as the domestic country, in this case the United States, and the other, that is the United Kingdom, as the overseas country. We define the exchange rate here as the number of domestic currency units it takes to buy one unit of foreign currency; in our example this is 2 dollars for one

pound, $2 : £1$. This is sometimes referred to as the domestic price of foreign currency. Now, for simplicity, we assume that there is just one good which has a price of \$100 in the United States; if that good has a price of £50 in the United Kingdom then the PPP exchange rate is $2 : £1$. If the actual exchange rate deviates from this then PPP does not hold. At a microeconomic level PPP is also known as the law of one price, LOOP, and it has a very simple rationale: the price of the same good in different countries with their own currencies should be the same when the domestic price of the good is converted to a common currency.

If the UK price of the good changes, say to £80, then if PPP holds the exchange rate should make an exactly compensating movement; in this case from the ratio of 100 over 50 which equals 2 to 100 over 80 which equals 1.25, or in exchange rate terms from $2 : £1$ to $1.25 : £1$. The dollar has appreciated relative to the pound as it takes fewer dollars to buy one pound, and conversely the pound has depreciated relative to the dollar. Thus, in this simple example, we can see that if PPP holds, the foreign price of the good converted to the same currency unit as in the domestic country will be the same as the domestic price of the good. The key to why PPP is an attractive theory of the exchange rate is what is known as arbitrage in goods – or commodities. Suppose in their own currency units, the price of the (single) good is \$100 in the United States and £50 in the United Kingdom, and the exchange rate is $1.80 : £1$; then at that exchange rate the good could be bought for £50 in the United Kingdom and imported into the United States at a price which when converted into dollars at the going exchange rate would be \$90 ($=50 \times 1.80$), some \$10 less than the domestic price. In this case there are profitable arbitrage opportunities with the result that there is pressure on the exchange rate to adjust to reflect the relative price of the good in the two countries. That is, it should adjust to $2 : £1$ to rule out a profit from arbitrage. In this example, for simplicity, we have assumed that there are no transportation costs; however, even if this is the case profitable arbitrage opportunities may still exist. For example, if the unit cost of importation is £2, which equals $3.60 at the going exchange rate, the good is still $6.40 per unit cheaper when imported.

13.2.1 Complications for PPP

According to the simplest form of PPP with a single homogeneous good (or common basket of goods), the exchange rate should equal the ratio of the domestic price of the good to the foreign price of the good when both are expressed in the same currency unit. There are, though, a number of complications in practice and we now highlight six of these.

1 Transportation costs

The presence of transportation costs will, as we saw above, rule out a simple comparison of relative prices. However, PPP theory can easily be adjusted to take account of these costs and we consider this aspect below in section **13.5.1**.

2 Multiple goods

In practice there is a large number of goods available, not a single good with a single price. This raises the problem of how the theory of PPP applies in this more complex but realistic case. The approach taken is to compare the domestic and foreign price levels using an aggregate index number of the many prices in each country. For example, suppose there are now two goods X_1 and X_2 with corresponding prices of P_1 and P_2 in the domestic country; then a simple form of price index would be $P = w_1P_1 + w_2P_2$ with $w_1 + w_2 = 1$. If P_1 and P_2 increase in the same proportion, say by $x\%$, then P will also increase by $x\%$; if P_1 and P_2 increase in different proportions then the effect on P will depend on the relative weights w_1 and w_2. We denote the foreign price index as $P^* = w_1^*P_1^* + w_2^*P_2^*$. When there are multiple goods PPP states that the nominal exchange rate at time t, E_t, should be equal to the ratio of the domestic price level, as

measured by the index P_t, to the foreign price level, as measured by the index P_t^*. We can express this as

$$E_t = A(P_t/P_t^*) \qquad (13.1)$$

With $A = 1$ this is known as the absolute version of PPP and if A is not equal to 1 then this is the relative version of PPP, RPPP. Differences in the way that index numbers are constructed in the domestic and foreign countries will generally rule out the possibility of testing the absolute version of PPP, as will the convention of setting the price index to some convenient number such as 1 or 100 in a particular base year. Thus we could find $A \neq 1$ simply because of different statistical conventions and this finding would have no bearing on whether PPP is valid.

The relative version of PPP applies irrespective of the value of A (provided it is a constant) and states that an $\alpha\%$ change in the relative price level, P_t/P_t^*, will have an $\alpha\%$ effect on the nominal exchange rate. Another way of putting this is to note that the elasticity of the nominal exchange rate with respect to relative prices is unity. For example, suppose initially $P_t = 100$ and $P_t^* = 100$ with $A = 2$, then the nominal exchange rate is $2:£1$. Now if P_t increases to 110, which is a 10% increase in the domestic price level and a 10% increase in the relative price level from 1.0 to 1.1, then, according to relative PPP, there will be a 10% change in the nominal exchange rate. It will now take $2.2 dollars to buy one pound. This is a depreciation in the dollar relative to the pound.

3 Tradable and nontradable goods

The mechanism behind PPP, which makes it an attractive theory, is the idea that differences in the price of the same good in different countries, when converted to a common currency unit, will open up the prospect of profits to be made by buying the good in one country and selling it in others. That is deviations from PPP represent profitable commodity arbitrage opportunities.

This is fine for goods – or commodities – such as motor cars, food, cereals, video games and so on can be traded internationally but the presence of many nontraded goods can complicate testing PPP. If a good is not traded then there is no international market in which it can be bought and sold and it does not contribute to the demand for, or supply of, foreign currency. According to this view, at a practical level, this means that the price indices which are used in testing PPP should be constructed from the prices of traded goods and wholesale price indices are usually chosen.

An alternative view can, however, be taken in which the exchange rate is the relative price of national monies; currency is held as an asset which can if necessary, and like other forms of wealth, be converted into purchasing power over tradable and nontradable goods. Hence, a consumer price index, which includes the prices of nontraded as well as traded goods, is appropriate. At a rather casual level taking a foreign holiday involves demanding currency as an asset and taking a view on national monies: what matters is the relative price of domestic currency to the overseas (holiday destination) currency.

4   Barriers to trade

As the essence of PPP is the pressure exerted by the possibility of profitable commodity arbitrage opportunities, the presence of barriers to trade, which principally come in the form of tariffs and quotas, will effectively frustrate this mechanism and allow deviations from PPP to be sustained.

5   Fixed exchange rates

The theory of PPP assumes that exchange rates can adjust to reflect changing relative prices; however, for a large part of the post-Second World War period a number of industrialised countries operated fixed exchange rates, thus preventing movements in exchange rates as a result of changing price levels at home and abroad. Indeed, the operation of fixed exchange rates suggests that the causation implied by PPP is reversed with the domestic price level adjust-

ing to the fixed exchange rate and (largely) exogenous overseas price levels. Of course, this assumes that PPP is the relevant theory; if this is not the case, or PPP is only part of the story, then other factors will also be important.

6   Pricing-to-market

The idea captured by pricing-to-market, PTM, is that there are some kinds of tradable goods for which arbitrage across national frontiers is difficult or impossible. A leading example is where a producer with some monopoly power, which might arise from product differentiation and strong brand identification, can price discriminate across different export destinations, so that prices are set to be 'market-specific'. They are not the result of taking a single uniform domestic price and converting that price into the currency units of the destination country at the going exchange rate. The implication is that the producer's mark-up over marginal cost is not constant for different export destinations with differing price elasticities of demand for the product. The producer is effectively exploiting the price leverage available from monopoly power. While this power may arise from genuine monopolies, an important aspect of PTM seems to arise from the establishment of branded goods which distinguish otherwise similar products and allow the producer some power in price discrimination.

13.2.2   Short-run and long-run considerations

In what is rather characteristic of economics, the theory of PPP is timeless in the sense that the passage of time is not accorded an essential role in the theory. However, if PPP is a correct description of how exchange rates are determined in a freely floating system, are any deviations from PPP allowed? The answer depends very much on how fast any exchange rate deviations from PPP can be corrected. In principle PPP requires instantaneous adjustment of bilateral exchange rates to the domestic and relevant overseas price levels, otherwise PPP does not hold. However, even if there are inherent tendencies for arbitrage in commodities to correct for an 'unbalanced' exchange rate, adjustment may not be instantaneous; information about profitabie arbitrage opportunities may take time to be come available. This view leads to the suggestion that while PPP does not hold in the short run, it may hold in the long run. Therefore, at any particular point in time we may observe short-run deviations from PPP even though there is a long run tendency for PPP to hold.

13.2.3 The nominal exchange rate, E_t, and the real exchange rate, RE_t

A distinction often made by economists is between the nominal exchange rate and the real exchange rate; and sometimes the adjective 'nominal' is omitted and reference is made simply to the exchange rate. The nominal exchange rate – or simply the exchange rate – is the rate we have been referring to so far. The real exchange rate is the ratio of the price level of the overseas country to that in the domestic country expressed in the same currency. That is let RE_t denote the real exchange rate then

$$RE_t = E_t P_t^*/P_t \qquad (13.2)$$

Consider the numerator of this expression P_t^*. is the overseas price level in units of the foreign currency and E_t is the nominal exchange rate, that is the domestic price of a unit of foreign currency; multiplying P_t^* by E_t serves to convert the overseas price level into domestic currency units which is then directly comparable to the domestic price level P_t. If PPP holds then this ratio – that is the real exchange rate – will be 1. For example, suppose $P_t = 200$ in US\$ and $P_t^* = 100$ in UK£, then absolute PPP implies a (nominal) exchange rate of $E_t = 2$, that is \$2 : £1 and a real exchange rate of $RE_t = 1$. If PPP is regarded as the equilibrium tendency of the nominal exchange rate, then deviations of RE_t

from 1 indicate disequilibrium and a relatively undervalued or overvalued currency. We now consider these two possibilities.

The first possibility is:

$$RE_t > 1, \quad \text{that is } E_t > P_t/P_t^*$$

In this case the dollar is undervalued and the pound is overvalued. An example may help here. Suppose $P_t = 200$ and $P_t^* = 100$ implying a PPP nominal exchange rate of \$2 : £1, but the actual nominal exchange rate is \$3 : £1 then the dollar cost of the pound is 50% higher than implied by PPP. According to a PPP interpretation, the cost of a UK pound is too high. The real exchange rate is $3 \times 0.5 = 1.5 > 1$, the dollar is undervalued and the pound is overvalued.

The second possibility is:

$$RE_t < 1, \quad \text{that is } E_t < P_t/P_t^*$$

In this case the dollar is overvalued and the pound is undervalued. Now the position is reversed and, relative to a PPP interpretation, the dollar cost of a pound is lower than that implied by PPP.

If absolute PPP (APPP) holds then deviations of the real exchange rate from unity offer profitable commodity arbitrage opportunities. However, we saw above that APPP is not in general a testable proposition especially because P_t and P_t^* are price indices rather than the price of a single good. This means that the implied equilibrium real exchange rate is not necessarily one; indeed a simple manipulation of the expression for PPP using price indices shows that

$$RE_t = E_t(P_t^*/P_t) = A \qquad (13.3)$$

and A is not necessarily equal to unity if P_t and P_t^* are price indices. Taking the logarithm of RE_t we obtain

$$\ln RE_t = \ln E_t + \ln P_t^* - \ln P_t$$
$$= \ln A \qquad (13.4)$$

and following our convention of letting lower case letters denote the (natural) logarithm of the corresponding upper case letter we can write this as

$$re_t = e_t + p_t^* - p_t$$
$$= a \qquad (13.5)$$

where $a = \ln A$. If APPP holds then the log of the real exchange rate equals zero (recall that $\ln(1) = 0$).

To examine the implications of relative PPP (RPPP) for the real exchange rate we take the first difference of re_t that is:

$$\Delta re_t = \Delta e_t + \Delta p_t^* - \Delta p_t \qquad (13.6)$$

Recall that the first difference of the logarithm of a variable is a very good approximation to the rate of growth in that variable. Thus (13.6) says that the rate of change of the real exchange rate is equal to the rate of change of the nominal exchange rate plus inflation in the overseas price minus domestic inflation. Now, according to RPPP, the right-hand side of Δre_t should equal zero. That is the nominal exchange rate moves to exactly compensate the relative growth in foreign and domestic price indices. To the extent that this does not happen Δre_t will be nonzero. For example, suppose there is 10% increase in the overseas price index and a 5% increase in the domestic price index, then according to RPPP the nominal exchange rate should decrease by 5%. If it does not then there is a change in the real exchange rate. In this example if there is, say, just a -4% change in E_t then $\Delta re_t = -0.04 + 0.10 - 0.05 = 0.01$ and there is a relative appreciation in the real exchange rate of 1%.

13.2.4　A strategy for testing RPPP

If RPPP holds at every point in time then $E_t = AP_t/P_t^*$ and taking logs of both sides we obtain

$$e_t = a + p_t - p_t^* \qquad (13.7)$$

which implies

$$e_t - p_t + p_t^* = a \qquad (13.8)$$

The left-hand side of this last expression is the real exchange rate, so RPPP, with multiple goods (and, therefore, the use of price indices), implies that the real exchange rate is constant. We can allow for the possibility of random deviations from RPPP by adding a stochastic 'shock', ξ_t, to the right-hand side of this expression, that is:

$$e_t - p_t + p_t^* = a + \xi_t \qquad (13.9)$$

The properties of ξ_t are important if RPPP is to hold. It should be stationary and in particular have a constant mean, otherwise the mean value of the real exchange rate will depend in some way on t. It should not exhibit random walk behaviour. If it does there will be no tendency for e_t and $-p_t + p_t^*$ to be tied together in the long run. That is we can view the real exchange rate as being comprised of the nominal exchange rate and the relative price of the domestic and foreign goods. To emphasise this point we re-write the last expression as

$$e_t - (p_t - p_t^*) = a + \xi_t \qquad (13.10)$$

where the term in brackets is the logarithm of the relative price. To avoid random walk behaviour in ξ_t then e_t and $(p_t - p_t^*)$ should be cointegrated.

These observations suggest the following testing strategy for the RPPP hypothesis.

1. First assess the time series properties of the (logs of the) nominal exchange rate and the relative price variables, in particular examine whether each is consistent with an I(1) process.
2. If e_t and $p_t - p_t^*$ are I(1) assess whether the real exchange rate is I(0).
3. If the real exchange rate is I(0) the evidence is supportive of the view that there is a long-run tendency for RPPP to hold; whereas if the real

exchange rate is I(1) it exhibits random walk behaviour and e_t and $p_t - p_t^*$ are not cointegrated. This suggests that RPPP does not hold in the long run.

4. If step 3 does not support RPPP, consider whether there are further factors to be taken into account in testing the RPPP hypothesis.

13.3 Assessing the evidence for PPP

The evidence, which has been used to assess PPP, can be distinguished according to whether it is microeconomic or macroeconomic in origin. In the former case the emphasis is on whether the law of one price (LOOP) holds for specific goods or categories of goods, and the data used is, therefore, at a disaggregated level, sometimes disaggregated to individual products. See, for example, De Gregorio, Giovannini and Kreuger (1994), De Gregorio, Giovannini and Wolf (1994), Kasa (1992) and Knetter (1989, 1993). Using macroeconomic evidence the emphasis is largely on the time series properties of the nominal exchange rate, relative prices and the real exchange rate; and, where the components of the real exchange rate or relative prices are distinguished, the price levels used are aggregate, rather than disaggregated, price indices.

13.3.1 The nature of the evidence

In the studies using disaggregated data, changes in the nominal exchange rate are taken as exogenous. As Knetter (1989, p. 198) notes: 'The simple, integrated, competitive market model predicts that local currency prices should change in proportion to the nominal exchange rate for a country too small to influence world prices.' According to LOOP there should be a one-to-one proportional relationship between import prices and nominal exchange rates. If following a change in the nominal exchange rate, import prices change to reflect no change in the real exchange rate, the 'pass-through' of the change

in the nominal exchange rate is said to be complete. If the local currency price of the imported good is unchanged then there is no pass-through of the change in the nominal exchange rate. In this situation exporters are implicitly adjusting their profit margins, following a change in the nominal exchange rate, to achieve local currency price stability.

In evaluating LOOP from studies using disaggregated data Rogoff (1996, p. 654) concludes that: 'Overall, it is hard to read the empirical evidence without concluding that outside a fairly small range of various homogeneous goods, short-run international arbitrage has only a limited effect on equating international goods market prices.'

This conclusion is based on a number of studies, using disaggregated data, which indicate that there are substantial and persistent deviations from LOOP. Isard (1977) found substantial deviations from LOOP using disaggregated data on highly traded goods such as clothing, industrial chemicals, and paper and glass products. Giovannini (1988) found large differences between the export and domestic prices of homogeneous Japanese manufactured goods including ball bearings, screws, nuts and bolts. Gagnon and Knetter (1991) report a pass-through of only approximately 30% on Japanese car export prices. More generally, in assessing the extent of pass-through in a wide range of goods, Knetter (1993, p. 479) reports, 'The surprising finding is that pricing-to-market is an important phenomenon in relatively homogeneous chemical-product categories, rather than being confined to differentiated durable goods.'

However, Knetter (1993) also found some evidence of complete pass-through in, for example, US exports of cars with engines over 6 cylinders, cigarettes and bourbon whiskey. (In these three cases the estimated pass-through coefficient was not significantly different from the value associated with complete pass-through.)

Further evidence suggests that the magnitude and persistence from LOOP at an international level is of a different order of magnitude from domestic deviations from LOOP. It is likely that you will have observed differences in the prices of homogeneous goods at different domestic retail outlets; for example, the price of the same grade of petrol at different garages (gas stations) within a well-defined geographical area. Hence, a possible modification to LOOP applied across national borders, which can be assessed using disaggregated data, is that deviations from one price should be no more volatile or persistent than those observed domestically. However, studies that examine this proposition – see Engel (1993) and Rogers and Jenkins (1995) – find evidence of a 'border' effect on relative prices and relative price volatility. That is comparing two cities in the same country with two cities in different countries at broadly the same distance apart, the relative price of the same good is more volatile in the cross-border comparison.

Studies at a macroeconomic level have largely concentrated on assessing whether, using time series data, the real exchange rate follows a random walk or, more generally, has a unit root. We noted in Chapter 6 that if a time series process follows a random walk it has an infinite memory to one-off shocks. Thus, if the real exchange rate does follow a random walk, deviations from PPP are persistent rather than self-correcting: there is no mechanism which ensures that even if PPP held in one historical period then, following a perturbation, it would continue to hold. A random walk real exchange rate does not revert to a constant mean – in the terminology of the time series/exchange rate literature it is not 'mean reverting'. Put another way a random walk real exchange rate implies that currency appreciations or depreciations are not offsetting inflation differentials. A perturbation to either the nominal exchange rate or relative prices is carried through into the real exchange rate with lasting effect.

Rogoff (1996) contains a useful summary of time series tests of the random walk model – see also Rogoff (1992). The conclusions from these studies are by no means uniform and depend, *inter alia*, upon: the frequency of the data and the length of the sample period; the countries included in the sample; and the econometric techniques used to evaluate the random walk hypothesis. Broadly tests which have used monthly data for the post-1973 period of floating exchange have failed to reject the random walk hypothesis. However, the strength of this conclusion has to be mitigated by recent studies – see Abuaf and Jorion (1990) and Mac-Donald (1996) – which construct a panel of data comprising time series observations on a group of countries, and find some evidence against the random walk, real exchange rate hypothesis. Generally studies that use long runs of annual data find some evidence of mean reversion – see, for example, Lothian and Taylor (1996). However, a problem with using these long runs of data is that they encompass very different fixed and floating exchange rate regimes and, for this reason, some authors have preferred not to mix data from different regimes.

The next subsections illustrate some of the issues and techniques involved in testing for PPP using macroeconomic, monthly data for the post-1973 period of floating exchange rates for four bilateral rates of the US dollar against the Canadian dollar, the German Deutschmark (DM), the Japanese yen, and the UK pound sterling.

13.3.2 Measuring the real exchange rate

The data used here was obtained from International Financial Statistics (IFS) published by the International Monetary Fund. In IFS the UK exchange rate is published as 'US dollars per pound', which is as required. (The definition of the nominal exchange rate is the domestic price of foreign currency and, for illustrative purposes, the United States is the domestic country). The exchange rates for the other currencies are the inverse of what is required. The entry for Canada is in terms of 'Canadian dollars per US dollar', that for Germany is 'Deutschmark per US dollar' and for Japan we find 'yen per US dollar'. It is a simple matter to convert these last three currencies into our required form. For convenience of scale we measure the $US:yen rate as the dollar price of 100 yen.

The corresponding real exchange rates depend upon relative prices. Here we take the wholesale price index for each country as a measure of the price level and calculate the four real exchange rates. Because we are dealing with price indices rather than the price of a single good we cannot assume that the real exchange rates will tend to unity if PPP holds. What we can say in this situation is that if relative PPP holds then the % change in the real exchange rate should be zero.

13.3.3   Visual impression of the data

The first step in assessing the empirical evidence is to graph the data. Figures 13.1A to 13.1D show the four bilateral nominal exchange rates, with the left-hand scale being relevant here. The relative wholesale price level is also shown on the same graph expressed as P_t^*/P_t. The reason for this device is that if RPPP holds there should be parallel movements in E_t and P_t^*/P_t. The right-hand scale is relevant for the relative price level. The frequency of the data is monthly and for E_t relates to the average for each month. As each of the exchange rates has been defined as the dollar cost of a unit of foreign currency,

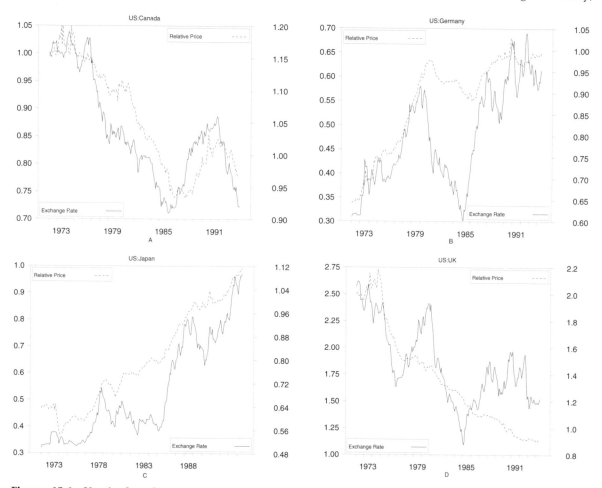

Figure 13.1 Nominal exchange rates and relative prices. A – US/Canada. B – US/Germany. C – US/Japan. D – US/UK

an upward movement in the relevant figure represents a depreciation in the nominal exchange rate, that is the cost of obtaining a unit of foreign currency has increased; and a downward movement is an appreciation in the nominal exchange rate.

Over the sample period the US dollar has generally appreciated against the Canadian dollar and the UK pound, but depreciated against the German DM and Japanese yen. In all four cases there is no tendency for the series to revert to a constant mean. At this stage the visual impression of the nominal exchange rate in each case

being consistent with random walk and hence, an I(1) process.

The autocorrelations of the four nominal exchange rates are presented in Figures 13.2A to 13.2D. These indicate series with, at the least, a very long memory, the most pronounced being the exchange rates for the United States and Canada, and the United States and Japan. In the other two countries the autocorrelations do show a tendency to die out but only at very long lags. The autocorrelations of the first differences of the nominal exchange rates are shown in Figures 13.3A to 13.3D. In general these

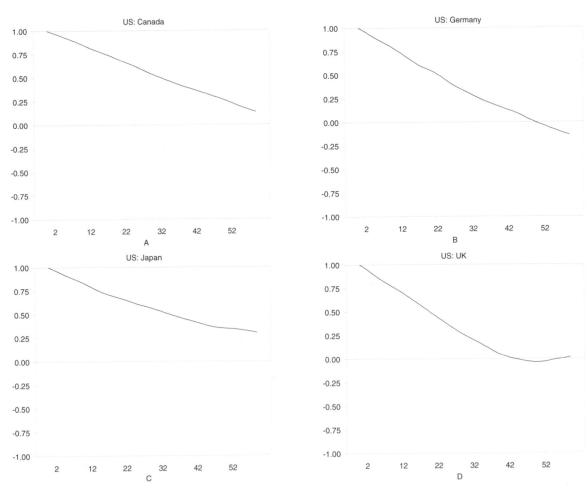

Figure 13.2 *Nominal exchange rates (autocorrelations of level). A – US/Canada. B – US/Germany. C – US/Japan. D – US/UK*

approach the zero axis quickly, although they do not die out completely even at fairly long lags. They do indicate though that taking the first difference of the nominal exchange rate results in a series which is much closer to an I(0) process than for the series in levels.

Returning to Figures 13.1A to 13.1D we now look at the pattern of relative prices. The first visual impression is that the exchange rates tend to be more variable than relative prices, indicating that movements in the latter can only hope to explain the general tendency of movements in the exchange rate. The closest agreement

between movements in the series is for the United States and Canada, and for the United States and the United Kingdom. For both the United States and Japan and the United States and Germany there is a substantial block of observations in the 1980s where the exchange rate and relative prices diverge.

The autocorrelations of the four relative prices are shown in Figures 13.4A to 13.4D. These are indicative of series with very long memories and possibly, therefore, consistent with I(1) processes. The graphical evidence here seems stronger than is the case for the nominal exchange

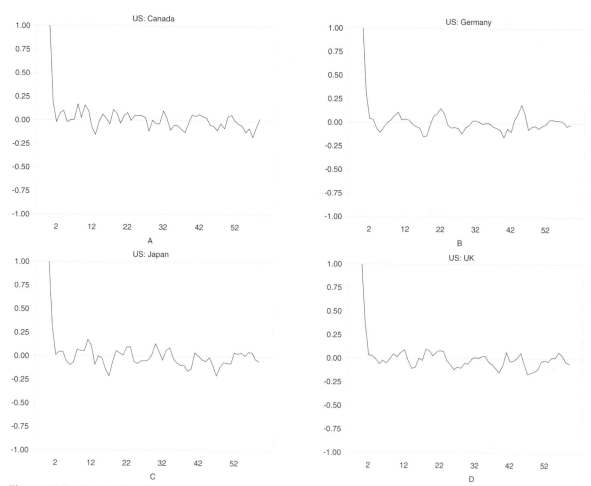

Figure 13.3 *Nominal exchange rates (autocorrelations of first difference). A – US/Canada. B – US/Germany. C – US/Japan. D – US/UK*

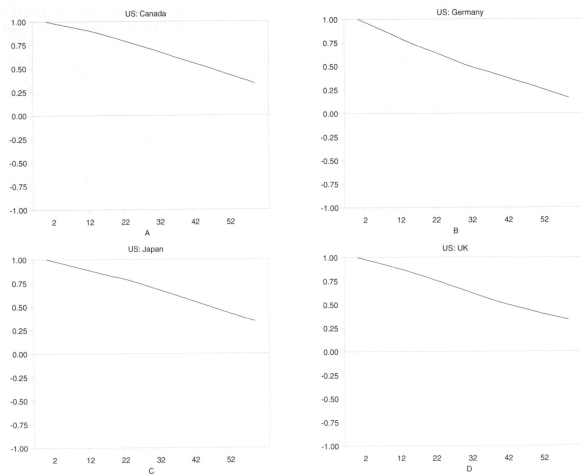

Figure 13.4 *Relative prices (autocorrelations of level).* **A – US/Canada. B – US/Germany. C – US/Japan. D – US/UK**

rates that the time series are I(1). The autocorrelations of the first differences of the series are shown in Figures 13.5A to 13.5D. The zero axis is approached quickly for all four countries, although with the United Kingdom some of the nonzero autocorrelations are noticeable.

The real exchange rates are shown in Figures 13.6A to 13.6D with the autocorrelations of the levels in Figures 13.7A to 13.7D and autocorrelations of the first differences in Figures 13.8A to 13.8D. Each of the real exchange rates is normalised to equal 1 in 1972m1. Considering first the real exchange rates notice that there is some wandering in each series consistent with

a random walk, and this pattern is most pronounced for the United States and Canada and least pronounced in the case of United States and Germany. The autocorrelations of the levels indicate series with a long memory, whereas the autocorrelations of the first differences approach zero relatively quickly. This pattern is consistent with the real exchange rate in each case being an I(1) process, and hence taking the first difference results in an I(0) process. However, there may be some practical difficulty in distinguishing between an I(1) process and an I(0) process with a very long – but not infinite – memory.

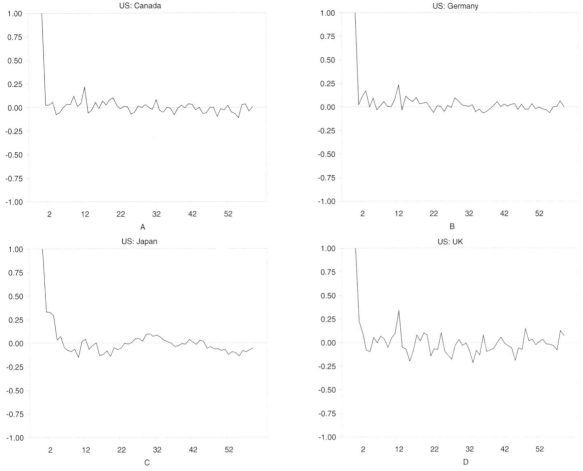

Figure 13.5 *Relative prices (autocorrelations of first difference).* **A – US/Canada. B – US/Germany. C – US/Japan. D – US/UK**

In summary, the figures presented here indicate two features which do no support the view that, at least in the short run, currency appreciations and depreciations and inflation differentials are offsetting, as they would have to be to ensure a constant real exchange rate and hence RPPP. First, there are substantial periods when there is divergence between the nominal exchange rate and relative prices – see, especially, the United States and Germany and the United States and Japan between 1979 and 1987 and the United States and the United Kingdom after 1986. Second, nominal exchange rates are,

in general, far more volatile than relative prices, the exception being for the US : UK comparison.

Table 13.1 on page 568 reports the coefficient of variation (cv) and the standard deviation of the logarithm of the nominal exchange rate, relative prices and the real exchange rate. For example, for the United States and Germany and the United States and Japan the cv for the nominal exchange rate is about 70% larger than that for relative prices. Even where the variation in the nominal exchange rate and relative prices is broadly matched by these measures, as in the case of the United States : United Kingdom, these

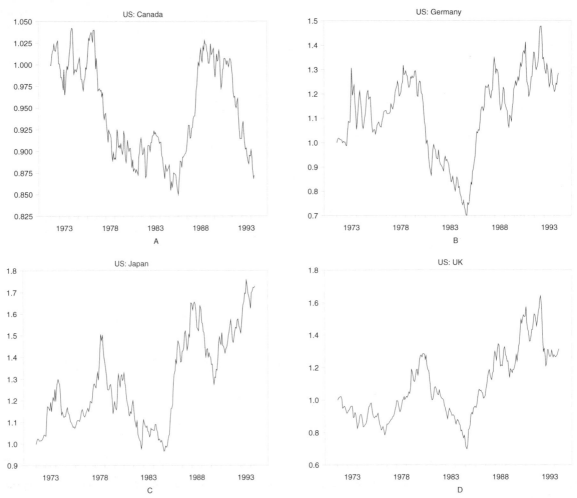

Figure 13.6 *Real exchange rates.* **A** – *US/Canada.* **B** – *US/Germany.* **C** – *US/Japan.* **D** – *US/UK*

variations are not offsetting as indicated by a cv for the real exchange rate which is 85% of that for the nominal exchange rate.

13.3.4 Dickey–Fuller unit root tests

In this section we report the standard set of Dickey–Fuller test statistics designed to assess the evidence against the unit root null hypothesis. In a later section – see **13.4.2** – we consider an alternative procedure due to Abuaf and Jorion (1990), which results in a modified Dickey–Fuller test statistic.

The results for the five countries, and hence four bilateral rates, considered here are reported in Table 13.2 on page 569, with further regression details for the ADF regression model with a constant given in Table 13.3; and a review question looks at the test statistics for 2 unit roots, details of which are given in Table 13.10. It is likely to be useful, however, first to concentrate on one bilateral rate to illustrate in detail the test statistics and conclusions, and the rate we choose is the US dollar : Canadian dollar rate. If RPPP is a reasonable guide to the determination of exchange rates then considering two

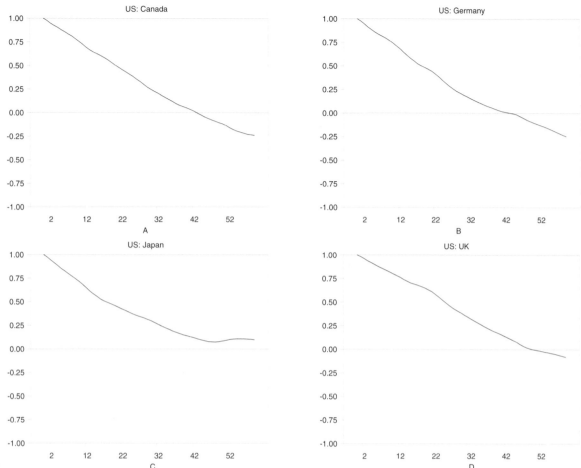

Figure 13.7   *Real exchange rates (autocorrelations of level). A – US/Canada. B – US/Germany. C – US/Japan.* D – US/UK

adjacent countries, which minimises complications arising from transportation costs, should provide a favourable arena for the theory to be data consistent.

For each country we need to assess whether the following variables have a unit root: the log of the nominal exchange rate; the log of relative prices; and the log of the real exchange rate.

Canada

We follow the testing strategy outlined in Chapter 6, which is now illustrated with the log of the nominal exchange rate for the United States and Canada – see Table 13.2A. Starting with an ADF regression including a deterministic time trend it was necessary to use an ADF(8) version which gave an SC(12) statistic for serial correlation of 18.76 with a marginal significance level, msl, of just under 10%; higher orders of lag augmentation increased the msl without changing the results. The Φ_3 test of the null hypothesis $\gamma = 0$ and $\beta = 0$ gave a sample value of 2.014; the 5% and 10% critical values, for $T = 200$, are 6.397 and 5.433, respectively. We conclude, therefore, that the null hypothesis is not rejected. This is also the conclusion from $\hat{\tau}_\beta = -0.617$, which is well below (in absolute value) the 5% critical value. The estimate of β was zero to 4 decimal places and insignificant,

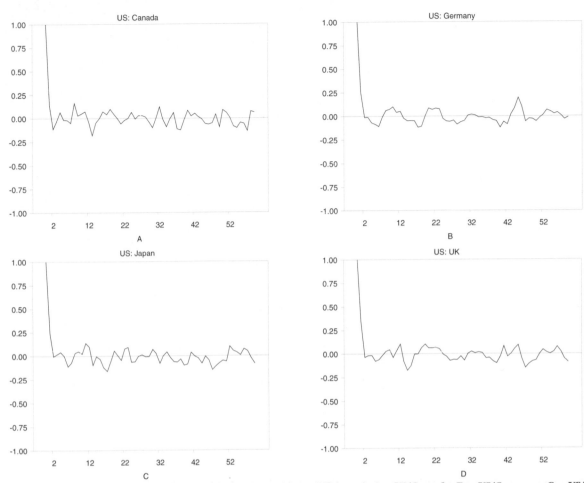

Figure 13.8 Real exchange rates (autocorrelations of first difference). A – US/Canada. B – US/Germany. C – US/ Japan. D – US/UK

Table 13.1 *Measures of variation*

Coefficient of variation				
	US : Canada	US : Germany	US : Japan	US : UK
E_t	0.107	0.175	0.291	0.183
RP_t	0.076	0.103	0.172	0.191
RE_t	0.058	0.149	0.142	0.156
Standard deviation of the logarithm				
e_t	0.105	0.760	0.270	0.185
rp_t	0.076	0.099	0.172	0.200
re_t	0.058	0.159	0.139	0.156

Notes: The coefficient of variation is the standard deviation/mean; sample period, 1974m1 to 1990m6.

Table 13.2 *Test statistics for one unit root*

				A US : Canada				
Variable	Model	$\hat{\tau}$	Φ_1	$\hat{\tau}_\mu$	$\hat{\mu}$	$\hat{\tau}_\beta$	$\hat{\beta}$	Φ_3
e_t	ADF(8)	-0.288	2.175	-1.926	-0.003	-0.617	0.000	2.014
rp_t	ADF(0)	-2.211	3.306	-1.122	0.000	-0.616	0.000	0.676
re_t	ADF(4)	-0.231	1.401	-1.662	-0.005	-1.282	0.000	2.933

				B US : Germany				
Variable	Model	$\hat{\tau}$	Φ_1	$\hat{\tau}_\mu$	$\hat{\mu}$	$\hat{\tau}_\beta$	$\hat{\beta}$	Φ_3
e_t	ADF(1)	-1.319	1.609	-1.470	-0.011	-1.565	0.000	1.225
rp_t	ADF(13)	-1.956	2.234	-1.924	0.000	-2.179	0.000	2.685
re_t	ADF(4)	-0.426	1.221	-1.561	-0.012	-1.429	0.000	1.443

				C US : Japan				
Variable	Model	$\hat{\tau}$	Φ_1	$\hat{\tau}_\mu$	$\hat{\mu}$	$\hat{\tau}_\beta$	$\hat{\beta}$	Φ_3
e_t	ADF(1)	-1.554	1.395	-1.099	-0.003	-1.852	0.000	1.723
rp_t	ADF(3)	-3.049	4.825	-1.212	0.005	-3.326	0.001	5.768
re_t	ADF(1)	-0.696	1.577	-1.763	-0.010	-1.953	0.000	1.906

				D US : UK				
Variable	Model	$\hat{\tau}$	Φ_1	$\hat{\tau}_\mu$	$\hat{\mu}$	$\hat{\tau}_\beta$	$\hat{\beta}$	Φ_3
e_t	ADF(1)	-0.914	1.462	-1.655	0.008	-1.659	0.000	1.542
rp_t	ADF(16)	-2.326	3.634	-0.905	-0.001	-3.533	0.000	6.313
re_t	ADF(1)	0.016	1.709	-1.581	-0.007	-1.973	0.000	1.974

e_t is the log of the nominal exchange rate; rp_t is the log of the relative prices; re_t is the log of the real exchange rate. Sample period (before lagging) 1974m1 to 1990m6.
Critical values:

	$\hat{\tau}$	$\hat{\tau}_\mu$	$\hat{\tau}_\beta$	Φ_1	Φ_3
5%	-1.930	-2.856	-3.408	4.696	6.397
10%	-1.604	-2.559	-3.119	3.835	5.433

Critical values of $\hat{\tau}$, $\hat{\tau}_\mu$ and $\hat{\tau}_\beta$ obtained using Cheung–Lai response surface coefficients for $T = 190$ and $p = 4$; critical values of Φ_1 and Φ_3 obtained by simulation for $T = 200$ – see Chapter 6.

so the time trend was dropped resulting in $\hat{\tau}_\mu = -1.926$ which is not significant compared to the 5% critical value of (approximately) -2.856; note from Table 13.3 that $\hat{\mu} = -0.003$ with a 't' statistic of -2.065 which is not significant at the 10% level – see Table 6.10 for critical values. If the constant is excluded then $\hat{\tau} = -0.288$ which, compared to the 5% critical value of (approximately) -1.930, strongly indicates nonrejection of the null hypothesis of one unit root. Also note that $\Phi_1 = 2.175$, which is below the 10% critical value of (approximately) 3.835.

We follow the same strategy for the log of relative prices for Canada. Starting with the maintained regression with a time trend $\Phi_3 = 0.676$, and $\hat{\tau}_\beta = -0.616$, both suggest nonrejection of the null hypothesis. The coefficient on the time trend is not significant and dropping

the time trend we obtain $\hat{\tau}_\mu = -1.122$. From Table 13.3 note that $\hat{\mu} = -0.000$, with a 't' statistic, $t(\mu)$, of -1.306 which is not significant; however, if the constant is omitted $\hat{\tau} = -2.211$ which is larger negative than the 5% critical value of (approximately) -1.930. Directly testing the joint hypothesis of a unit root and no constant using Φ_1 we obtain a test statistic of 3.306, which is below the 5% critical value of (approximately) 3.835, so the balance of evidence points to nonrejection of the null hypothesis of a unit root.

There is no ambiguity for the real exchange rate – see the last part of Table 13.2A. The test statistics are: $\Phi_3 = 2.933$, $\hat{\tau}_\beta = -1.282$, $\hat{\tau}_\mu = -1.662$, $\Phi_1 = 1.401$ and $\hat{\tau} = -0.231$; all of which suggest nonrejection of the null hypothesis.

Table 13.3 *Regression details for ADF test statistics $\hat{\tau}_\mu$ (no trend case)*

	Constant	y_{t-1}	ADF	dw	SC(12)
Nominal exchange rate					
Canada	−0.003 (−2.065)	−0.014 (**−1.926**)	8	1.979	19.042 [0.090]
Germany	−0.011 (−1.216)	−0.015 (**−1.470**)	1	1.949	6.753 [0.873]
Japan	−0.003 (−0.616)	−0.007 (**−1.099**)	1	1.874	14.730 [0.256]
UK	0.008 (1.443)	−0.015 (**−1.655**)	1	1.897	9.404 [0.668]
Relative prices					
	Constant	y_{t-1}	ADF	dw	SC(12)
Canada	−0.000 (−1.306)	−0.006 (**−1.122**)	0	1.839	14.232 [0.286]
Germany	−0.000 (−0.805)	−0.007 (**−1.924**)	13	2.017	13.634 [0.400]
Japan	−0.001 (−0.616)	−0.003 (**−1.212**)	3	2.066	20.328 [0.061]
UK	0.001 (1.353)	−0.003 (**−0.905**)	16	1.981	21.988 [0.144]
Real exchange rates					
	Constant	y_{t-1}	ADF	dw	SC(12)
Canada	−0.004 (−1.657)	−0.022 (**−1.662**)	4	2.003	19.236 [0.083]
Germany	−0.012 (−1.503)	−0.018 (**−1.561**)	4	2.004	8.268 [0.764]
Japan	−0.010 (−0.632)	−0.022 (**−1.763**)	1	1.860	16.498 [0.169]
UK	0.007 (1.849)	−0.019 (**−1.581**)	1	1.883	11.338 [0.500]

Note: Sample period: 1974m1 to 1990m6; $\hat{\tau}_\mu$ indicated in bold in parentheses beneath estimated coefficients; the maintained regression is: $\Delta y_t = \mu + \gamma y_{t-1} + \sum_{i=1}^{p} \alpha_i \Delta y_{t-i} + \varepsilon_t$ where y_t is a generic notation for the nominal exchange rate, the relative price and the real exchange rate for each bilateral comparison.

We can now put all these results together. In particular the finding that the nominal exchange rate and relative prices are each I(1) but that the real exchange rate is also I(1) is not consistent with RPPP. It implies that the nominal exchange rate and relative prices do not cointegrate. That is the linear combination given by $e_t − (p_t − p_t^*)$ is not stationary. Another way of expressing this result is to say that, from

the standard Dickey–Fuller tests reported here for the United States and Canada, the nominal exchange rate and relative prices are not tied together in the long run.

Germany

The results for the United States and Germany – see Table 13.2B – are relatively straightforward and suggest that each of the three series is consistent with a unit root process. To avoid repetition we can be brief on the details. Note that in each case the coefficient on the time trend is zero to (at least) three decimal places and insignificant, hence consideration can be focused on the models without a time trend. Further, note that the sample values of Φ_1 are not significant suggesting nonrejection of the joint null hypothesis for a unit root and no drift; this conclusion finds confirmatory evidence from Table 13.3 where the constants are individually not significantly different from zero. Again there is no evidence from these test statistics to support RPPP for the United States and Germany.

Japan

In the case of Japan, the results for the nominal exchange rate and the real exchange rate are straightforward: all the test statistics point unambiguously to nonrejection of the null hypothesis of a unit root.

There is, however, some ambiguity in the case of relative prices. Note first that $\Phi_3 = 5.768$ is close to the 10% critical value of (approximately) 5.433 and $\hat{\tau}_\beta = -3.326$ is larger negative than the 10% critical value of (approximately) -3.119. The coefficient on the time trend is 0.00015 with a 't' statistic, $t(\beta)$, of 3.162; the estimated constant is -0.034, and -5.23 when standardised by $\hat{\sigma}$, with a 't' statistic, $t(\mu)_\beta$, of -3.095. Table 6.10 gives the critical values for $t(\mu)_\beta$ and $t(\beta)$ assuming a unit root; for $T = 250$, the nearest row entry to the present sample size, the 5% and 10% two-sided critical values for $t(\mu)_\beta$ are ± 3.39 and ± 3.09, suggesting the constant has an msl of about 10%. The 5% and 10% critical values for $t(\beta)$ depend upon (standardised) μ; for $\mu = 0$ they are (approximately) ± 3.12 and ± 2.79. The nearest value of μ to the estimated value is $\mu = 1$, which gives right-hand tail values of 3.69 and 3.43 for 5% and 10% significance levels, respectively, so formally the time trend is not significant; however, given the approximations involved, there is a lack of robustness about this conclusion.

If the trend is dropped we obtain $\hat{\tau}_\mu = -1.212$ and an insignificant constant – but dropping the constant leads to $\hat{\tau} = -3.049$, which is significant, suggesting no unit root. Further, $\Phi_1 = 4.825$ which is just above the 5% critical value of (approximately) 4.696. However, the estimate of γ at -0.003, shown in Table 13.3, is numerically closer to zero than for either Germany or Japan, and closer to zero than for any of the nominal exchange rates. Reference back to Figure 13.1C shows a definite positive trend in relative prices; if the deterministic trend is absent then this must be accounted for by drift in the unit root process. The choice is between a trend stationary process or a unit root process with drift.

However, whatever the conclusion, the evidence for Japan does not favour RPPP. If the nominal exchange rate and relative prices are each I(1), then RPPP requires the real exchange rate to be I(0), and there is no support for this conclusion at conventional significance levels. If the nominal exchange rate is I(1) and relative prices are I(0), then the real exchange rate, which is a linear (in logs) combination of these two, must also be I(1) since cointegration is not now possible, and hence is not constant or mean reverting.

United Kingdom

The pattern of test statistics for the United Kingdom is similar to that for Japan. There is no ambiguity for either the nominal or real exchange rates, both are consistent with unit root processes.

In the case of relative prices $\Phi_3 = 6.313$ is close to the 5% critical value of approximately 6.397. Further, in contrast to the situation for Canada and Germany, the coefficient on the time trend although small at -0.0002, or -0.033 when standardised by the estimated equation standard error, has a 't' statistic, $t(\beta)$, of -3.428 which is large; reference to Table 6.10 shows that the 10% two-sided critical values for $t(\beta)$ are ± 2.79, assuming $\mu = 0$. Here the estimate of μ is 0.046 with a 't' statistic of 3.324 which is significant at the 10% level – see Table 6.10 (upper panel) for critical values of $t(\mu)_\beta$. When $\mu \neq 0$, different critical values apply to $t(\beta)$, dividing $\hat{\mu} = 0.046$ by $\hat{\sigma} = 0.0063$ gives a standardised value of 7.3. The nearest entry in Table 5.10 is for $\mu = 1.0$, and with $T = 250$ the 10% two-sided critical values for $t(\beta)$ are 0.92/3.43, so there is still the suggestion that the time trend is significant and a trend stationary process seems a clear possibility. With this in mind $\hat{\tau}_\beta = -3.533$ is a relevant test statistic. Taking $\beta = 0.05$ as the nearest entry in Table 6.8, the 5% and 10% critical values are -1.729 and -1.377, and the null hypothesis of a unit root is firmly rejected. Thus with the nominal exchange rate I(1), but relative prices I(0), the real exchange rate must be I(1), and cointegration, with a $(1, -1)$ cointegrating vector, is not possible.

Summary

In summary, the Dickey–Fuller test statistics do not lead to rejection of the following null hypotheses (for the logarithms of the relevant variables) for the bilateral comparison of the United States with Canada and Germany:

(i)   the nominal exchange rate is I(1);
(ii) relative prices are I(1);
(iii) the real exchange rate is I(1).

Taken together these results imply that the simple linear combination of the nominal exchange rate and the negative of relative prices is not cointegrated; a finding which is not consistent with the version of RPPP represented by equation (13.10).

For the bilateral comparison of the United States with Japan and the United Kingdom, the reasoning is slightly different but the conclusion the same. The following null hypotheses are not rejected at conventional significance levels:

(i)   the nominal exchange rate is I(1);
(ii) the real exchange rate is I(1); however,
(iia) there is some evidence, more so with the United Kingdom than with Japan, that

relative prices are consistent with a trend stationary, that is I(0), process rather than an I(1) process.

The reasoning for rejection of RPPP is now that the real exchange rate, which is a linear combination of an I(1) and an I(0) process, must be I(1) and hence not mean reverting.

In the following two sections some further related issues are addressed. It is known that standard Dickey–Fuller tests have low power for alternatives close to 1, a more powerful procedure and a further assessment of the persistence of shocks to the real exchange rate is considered in section **13.4**. In section **13.5** we assess whether relaxing the view that the appropriate cointegrating coefficients for the nominal exchange rate and relative prices are $+1$ and -1 leads to any greater support for PPP.

13.4   The real exchange rate: some more considerations and tests

In the context of PPP the hypothesis that the real exchange rate follows a random walk, or more generally is an AR(p) process with a unit root, is a particularly striking example of a *sharp* hypothesis. According to this hypothesis shocks to the real exchange rate are never reversed, so PPP does not hold even in the long run. In contrast even if the (largest) root of the AR(p) process is fractionally below one, shocks to the real exchange rate are reversed – the process eventually reverts to its PPP mean although it may take a considerable period of time to do so. For an assessment of the 'long memory' in exchange rates and the implications for mean reversion of the real exchange rate, see Cheung (1993), Cheung and Lai (1994) and Sarno and Taylor (1998). For an interesting historical perspective on the behaviour of real exchange rates under the Gold Standard see Diebold, Husted and Rush (1991).

13.4.1 An example of the persistence of shocks

Suppose that the (log of the) real exchange rate follows a near unit root process, which for illustrative purposes we take to be

$$re_t = \phi_0 + \phi_1 re_{t-1} + \varepsilon_t \qquad (13.11)$$

with ε_t a zero mean stationary innovation and ϕ_1 is close to, but less than, one. Setting ε_t to its mean value of zero, the implied long run is

$$re^0 = \phi_0/(1 - \phi_1) \qquad (13.12)$$

Note that we do not expect $\phi_0 = 0$, which implies $re^0 = 0$ and $RE^0 = 1$, for reasons outlined earlier in this chapter relating to the use of price indices in formulating the relative version of PPP. While for $\phi_1 = 1$, re^0 is not defined, for $\phi_1 = 0.995$ re^0 is defined, but shocks to the real exchange rate decline very slowly. We can summarise the speed of response to a perturbation by the $\frac{1}{4}$, $\frac{1}{2}$ and $\frac{3}{4}$ lives of the shock, which in this simple model can be calculated analytically as $\ln(0.75)/\ln \phi_1$, $\ln(0.5)/\ln \phi_1$ and $\ln(0.25)/\ln \phi_1$, respectively. The interpretation of these fractional lives is straightforward; for example, the half-life tells us how long it takes for a unit shock to reduce to 0.5. The sensitivity of $\frac{1}{4}$, $\frac{1}{2}$ and $\frac{3}{4}$ lives to variations in ϕ_1 is shown in Table 13.4.

The table entries illustrate how apparently small changes in ϕ_1 imply substantial changes in the response time to a perturbation. For example, the half-life of a shock with $\phi_1 = 0.99$ is 69 periods, which is over five times that for $\phi_1 = 0.95$. If, as suggested by the estimates reported below in Table 13.5, the relevant parameter governing the speed of response is of the order of 0.994 then, with monthly data, the half-life of a shock is between 11 and 12 years, and 25% of the adjustment back to the long run is still to take place after 23 years.

These considerations suggest an additional agenda in assessing the macroeconomic evidence on whether the real exchange rate has a unit root. First, can we improve the power of the ADF test procedure since it is known that this is low for alternatives close to but less than unity? In section **13.4.2** we follow a suggestion made by Abuaf and Jorion (1990) to pool the time series observations for individual countries into a group or 'panel' of observations which increases the power of the ADF procedure. Second, do the numerical estimates of the coefficients that govern the speed of response suggest that shocks take a very long time to die out? We consider this issue in section **13.4.3**.

13.4.2 Pooling observations: a panel unit root test

If the real exchange rate has a 'near' unit root, it is statistically very difficult to distinguish the correct alternative from the false null. Recall that the ability of a test to distinguish in this case is known as the power of the test, and the power of the ADF test is known to be low for alternatives close to the unit root. One suggestion, due to Abuaf and Jorion (1990), to increase the power of the test that the real exchange rate has a unit root is to pool the observations of the bilateral real exchange rates of the individual countries into a cross-section of time series; this creates a 'panel' of data distinguished not just by

Table 13.4 $\frac{1}{4}$, $\frac{1}{2}$ and $\frac{3}{4}$ lives of a shock in the AR(1) model

$\phi_1 =$	0.90	0.95	0.975	0.985	0.99	0.995
$\frac{1}{4}$-life	2.730	5.608	11.362	19.034	28.624	57.392
$\frac{1}{2}$-life	6.679	13.513	27.378	45.862	68.967	138.282
$\frac{3}{4}$-life	13.157	27.026	54.755	91.724	137.935	276.565

the observation number (the row reference) but also by the country indicator (the column reference). With T observations on each of N countries there are TN observations in all in the panel. In our case with a common sample period of 1974m1 to 1990m6, $T = 198$ and $N = 4$ so $TN = 792$. This increase in the number of observations used for the test procedure should result in a more powerful procedure; that is, one which, for a given significance level, is more likely to identify a false null hypothesis.

To accommodate the use of a panel of data we need to make some changes to the way that the unit root test is carried out. For convenience we denote the individual countries in our sample as $i = 1, 2, 3, 4$ for, respectively, the US bilateral real exchange rate against: Canada, Germany, Japan and the United Kingdom. Then the set of ADF regressions is

$$\Delta re_{it} = \gamma_{i0} + \gamma_{i1} re_{it-1} + \sum_{j=1}^{p_i} \alpha_{ij} \Delta re_{it-j} + \varepsilon_{it}$$

$$\text{for} \quad i = 1, \ldots, 4 \quad \text{and} \quad t = 1, \ldots, T$$

$$(13.13)$$

To estimate these equations we use generalised least squares, GLS, for seemingly unrelated equations, SURE. GLS takes into account the following features of the four equations viewed as a set of equations: while it may be reasonable to assume that each country has a homoscedastic error, it is not reasonable to assume that the constant variance for each country is the same for different countries. That is while we assume $E\{\varepsilon_{it}^2\} = \sigma_i^2$ for $i = 1, \ldots, 4$ we allow for the possibility that $\sigma_1^2 \neq \sigma_2^2 \neq \sigma_3^2 \neq \sigma_4^2$; considered as a group, partitioned by country, the errors are potentially heteroscedastic. Second, although there are no explicit connections among the four equations, in the sense that the real exchange rate for country i does not enter the equation for country j, there may be an indirect linkage through a 'ripple' effect from shocks to the errors being transmitted from one country to another. A ripple effect is captured by allowing

the covariance between ε_{it} and ε_{jt} for $i \neq j$ to be nonzero. Zellner (1962) suggested that equations of this form be termed seemingly unrelated regression equations, SURE, to distinguish them from simultaneous equations. GLS applied to SURE is a modification of OLS which allows for partitioned heteroscedasticity and errors which have nonzero contemporaneous covariances. The GLS procedure is described in greater detail in Chapter 5.

In the context of the system of equations (13.13) the null hypothesis is that there is a unit root in each real exchange rate. That is

$$H_0: \gamma_{11} = \gamma_{21} = \gamma_{31} = \gamma_{41} = 0$$

There are two possible hypotheses of interest which are alternatives to this null hypothesis. Abuaf and Jorion (1990) suggest the following procedure. First, restrict the γ_{i1} to be equal across the countries, on the basis that if the null hypothesis is correct then the γ_{i1} are equal, but allow for the possibility that this common value, say γ_1, is less than zero. A potential problem with this approach is that if the real exchange rates do not have a unit root there is no reason to impose the same coefficient across different countries. It is useful to think of the Abuaf and Jorion procedure as comprising two hypotheses:

$$H_{a1}: \gamma_{11} = \gamma_{21} = \gamma_{31} = \gamma_{41} = \gamma_1$$

and

$$H_{a2}: \gamma_1 < 0$$

If H_{a1} is consistent with the data imposing the restriction will make the most of pooling the data into a panel, and then a test of H_{a2} is very easy to implement. Testing proceeds by estimating the model by GLS with the restriction that $\gamma_{11} = \gamma_{21} = \gamma_{31} = \gamma_{41} = \gamma_1$ imposed; we refer to this as restricted GLS, RGLS. Then calculate the (pseudo) 't' statistic on γ_1, say $\tilde{\tau}_\gamma$ with critical values obtained by simulation, as in the case of the standard ADF test statistic. In the simulations the DGP is as specified according to the null

Table 13.5 *OLS, GLS and RGLS estimates of the real exchange rate equations*

Model: $\Delta re_{it} = \gamma_{i0} + \gamma_{i1} re_{it-1} + \sum_{j=1}^{p_i} \alpha_{ij} \Delta re_{it-j} + \varepsilon_{it}$

		γ_{i0}	γ_{i1}	ADF order
Canada	OLS	−0.004	−0.017	4
	$'t'/\hat{\tau}_\mu$	(−1.275)	(−1.338)	
	GLS	−0.003	−0.016	4
	$'t'/\hat{\tau}_\mu$	(−1.306)	(−1.378)	
	5% cv		−3.068	
	10% cv		−2.730	
	RGLS	−0.004	−0.021	4
	$'t'/\tilde{\tau}_\gamma$	(−2.974)	(−3.425)	
	5% cv		−4.236	
	10% cv		−3.913	
Germany	OLS	−0.012	−0.019	1
	$'t'/\hat{\tau}_\mu$	(−1.511)	(−1.605)	
	GLS	−0.016	−0.026	1
	$'t'/\hat{\tau}_\mu$	(−2.792)	(−3.004)	
	5% cv		−3.474	
	10% cv		−3.186	
	RGLS	−0.013	−0.021	1
	$'t'/\tilde{\tau}_\gamma$	(−3.035)	(−3.425)	
	5% cv		−4.236	
	10% cv		−3.913	
Japan	OLS	−0.010	−0.022	1
	$'t'/\hat{\tau}_\mu$	(−1.654)	(−1.737)	
	GLS	−0.014	−0.029	1
	$'t'/\hat{\tau}_\mu$	(−2.668)	(−2.857)	
	5% cv		−3.378	
	10% cv		−3.035	
	RGLS	−0.010	−0.021	1
	$'t'/\tilde{\tau}_\gamma$	(−2.915)	(−3.425)	
	5% cv		−4.236	
	10% cv		−3.913	
UK	OLS	0.006	−0.018	1
	$'t'/\hat{\tau}_\mu$	(1.702)	(−1.486)	
	GLS	0.005	−0.014	1
	$'t'/\hat{\tau}_\mu$	(1.697)	(−1.492)	
	5% cv		−3.440	
	10% cv		−3.126	
	RGLS	0.007	−0.021	1
	$'t'/\tilde{\tau}_\gamma$	(−2.856)	(−3.425)	
	5% cv		−4.236	
	10% cv		−3.913	

Notes: All estimation is over the common sample period, after lagging, of 1974m1 to 1990m6.

hypothesis but taking into account the RGLS estimates of the constants for each equation, $\hat{\gamma}_{i0}$, and the RGLS estimate of the covariance matrix of the residuals.

An alternative procedure is not to restrict the γ_{i1} to be equal across countries. Then separate the components of H_0, that is

$$H_{01}: \gamma_{11} = 0; \quad H_{02}: \gamma_{21} = 0$$
$$H_{03}: \gamma_{31} = 0; \quad H_{04}: \gamma_{41} = 0$$

with alternative hypotheses

$$H_{a1}: \gamma_{11} < 0; \quad H_{a2}: \gamma_{21} < 0$$
$$H_{a3}: \gamma_{31} < 0; \quad H_{a4}: \gamma_{41} < 0$$

In this procedure there is a test statistic for each of the countries, as in the standard approach, and, therefore, the possibility of rejection or nonrejection for each country rather than for the group of countries as a whole.

The estimation results for the common sample period 1974m1 to 1990m6 are reported in Table 13.5. For reference we first report the OLS estimates (the minor differences from the results reported in Table 13.2 are due to the use of a common sample period here for all estimation methods); next we report the unrestricted GLS estimates and then the RGLS estimates. The GLS and OLS estimates of the test statistic are virtually unchanged for Canada and the United Kingdom but are noticeably larger, in absolute value, for Germany and Japan. However, whether this change is a statistically important one depends upon the critical values for the GLS estimates. From simulation we find that the 5% and 10% critical values for Germany are -3.474 and -3.186, and the test statistic of -3.004 has an msl of about 13%. For Japan the 5% and 10% critical values are -3.378 and -3.035, and the test statistic of -2.857 has an msl of about 12.5%. There is, therefore, some evidence, with an msl of around 12% to 13% in both cases, against the unit root real exchange rate hypothesis for these two countries.

Before commenting on the RGLS estimates note that a standard test statistic for the null hypothesis that the γ_{i1} are equal, which is distributed as $\chi^2(3)$, gives a sample value of 2.010 with an msl of 57%, from which we take the view that the restrictions in the Abuaf and Jorion procedure can be imposed here. However, nonrejection of a joint test is compatible with a mixture of insignificant and significant results of the constituent individual tests. With the restrictions imposed across all countries the 5% and 10% critical values of the test statistic $\tilde{\tau}_\gamma$ are -4.236 and -3.913, and the sample value of -3.425 has an msl of about 24%; so with conventional significance levels we would not reject the null hypothesis of a unit root for all four countries. However, while the restrictions in the Abuaf and Jorion procedure are here consistent with the data, imposing them tends to mask the individual country results reported in the previous paragraph.

13.4.3 Estimating the speed of response to a shock to the real exchange rate

Besides assessing the ADF test statistics for different methods of estimation there are two other issues which have a bearing on assessing the PPP hypothesis. While the ADF statistics are designed to assess whether, in a statistical sense, the data is consistent with the hypothesis of a unit root we are also interested in how close, in a numerical sense, the root is to unity. Second, another related aspect of the unit root conjecture is that shocks – or perturbations – have a permanent effect if there is a unit root, with no reversion to a constant mean, but if the root is even fractionally below unity there is mean reversion, although the process of adjustment may be very slow indeed

The ADF regressions indicated that the AR(1) model, which corresponds to an unaugmented DF regression, was inadequate so we start here with an AR($p + 1$) model to match up with the ADF(p) regressions reported in Table 13.2. That is

$$re_t = \phi_0 + \sum_{j=1}^{p+1} \phi_j re_{t-j} + \varepsilon_t \qquad (13.14)$$

then the implied long run for this equation – see Chapter 2 – setting ε_t to zero in the long run, is

$$re_t^0 = \phi_0 \left/ \left(1 - \sum_{j=1}^{p+1} \phi_j\right)\right. \qquad (13.15)$$

Recall that in the AR(1) case this was just $\phi_0/(1 - \phi_1)$, and if $\phi_1 = 1$ there is a unit root and the long run is not defined. More generally a necessary condition for a unit root is $\Sigma\phi_j = 1$, which is the null hypothesis in the ADF test. Also note that in the ADF(p) model

$$\Delta re_t = \mu + \gamma re_{t-1} + \sum_{j=1}^{p} \alpha_j \Delta re_{t-j} + \varepsilon_t \qquad (13.16)$$

$\mu = \phi_0$ and $\gamma = \sum_{j=1}^{p+1} \phi_j - 1$, from the latter we see that $\hat{\gamma}$ from the estimated regression indicates the estimated distance from the unit root; alternatively we can calculate $\Sigma\hat{\phi}_j = 1 + \hat{\gamma}$.

A problem which is true to some degree whether the OLS or GLS estimators are used is that these estimators are biased in small samples; if, however, the bias was known or approximated a bias correction could be made to the point estimates. Shaman and Stine (1988) and Stine and Shaman (1989) have obtained the 'first order' bias – or bias to order T – for the OLS estimators for any order of AR model. (See also Marriott and Pope (1954), and for an alternative methodology to deal with the same problem, see Andrews (1993).) In an AR(1) model, with estimated constant, the first order bias is

$$\begin{aligned} \text{bias}(\hat{\phi}_1) &\equiv E\{\hat{\phi}_1\} - \phi_1 \\ &= -(1 + 3\phi_1)/T \end{aligned} \qquad (13.17)$$

The bias to order T captures the dependence of the bias on the level of the sample size, T, but ignores the bias which depends upon higher order terms in T such as T^2. For $\phi_1 = 0.95$ the first order bias is $-3.85/T$; for moderate T this adjustment could be quite critical.

Because ϕ_1 is unknown the first order bias expression is not strictly operational; however, following Orcutt and Winokur (1969), we can substitute $\hat{\phi}_1$ for $E\{\hat{\phi}_1\}$ and solve for the resulting value of ϕ_1 which we denote $\hat{\hat{\phi}}_1$. In the AR(1) model this results in

$$\hat{\hat{\phi}}_1 = \hat{\phi}_1 T/(T-3) + 1/(T-3) \qquad (13.18)$$

Reference to Table 13.2 shows that we need to extend the AR model to AR(2) $\equiv$ ADF(1) for Germany, Japan and the United Kingdom, and AR(5) $\equiv$ ADF(4) for Canada. We illustrate the bias correction for the AR(2) case. From Shaman and Stine (1988) and Stine and Shaman (1989) we find that the first order biases for $\hat{\phi}_1$ and $\hat{\phi}_2$ are

$$\text{bias}(\hat{\phi}_1) = -(1 + \phi_1 + \phi_2)/T$$

and

$$\text{bias}(\hat{\phi}_2) = -(2 + 4\phi_2)/T$$

and so for $\Sigma\hat{\phi}_j$ the first order bias is

$$\text{bias}(\Sigma\hat{\phi}_j) = -(3 + \phi_1 + 5\phi_2)/T$$

Following the Orcutt and Winokur procedure of substituting $\hat{\phi}_j$ for $E\{\hat{\phi}_j\}$, we can solve for first order unbiased estimators, distinguished by a double hat, to obtain

$$\hat{\hat{\phi}}_1 = \hat{\phi}_1 T/(T-1) + 1/(T-1) + \hat{\phi}_2/(T-1)$$

where

$$\hat{\hat{\phi}}_2 = \hat{\phi}_2 T/(T-4) + 2/(T-4)$$

(The detail of the bias adjustments for the AR(5) model are arithmetically more complicated and

Table 13.6 *OLS, $\hat{\phi}_j$, and first order unbiased estimates, $\hat{\tilde{\phi}}_j$*

OLS	$\hat{\phi}_1$	$\hat{\phi}_2$	$\hat{\phi}_3$	$\hat{\phi}_4$	$\hat{\phi}_5$	$\Sigma\hat{\phi}_j$
First order unbiased	$\hat{\tilde{\phi}}_1$	$\hat{\tilde{\phi}}_2$	$\hat{\tilde{\phi}}_3$	$\hat{\tilde{\phi}}_4$	$\hat{\tilde{\phi}}_5$	$\Sigma\hat{\tilde{\phi}}_j$
Canada	1.177	−0.325	0.130	0.098	-0.098	0.983
	1.183	−0.326	0.136	0.105	-0.098	1.000
Germany	1.322	−0.341	–	–	–	0.981
	1.332	−0.337	–	–	–	0.994
Japan	1.268	−0.285	–	–	–	0.978
	1.273	−0.281	–	–	–	0.992
UK	1.341	−0.360	–	–	–	0.982
	1.351	−0.357	–	–	–	0.994

Notes: $\Sigma\hat{\phi}_j$ and $\Sigma\hat{\tilde{\phi}}_j$ may not equal the sum of the components in the table due to rounding; for each country the first entry is $\hat{\phi}_i$ and the second entry is $\hat{\tilde{\phi}}_i$.

are left to a review question.) The results of applying the first order bias adjustments are reported in Table 13.6. The uniform picture is that the estimate of the sum of the coefficients moves closer to 1 and in one case, that of Canada, the estimate is now marginally above one. For the remaining countries the sum of coefficients is now remarkably similar at between 0.992 and 0.994. Although we have here just considered the OLS estimates similar adjustments could, in principle, be made to the GLS estimates; however, to the author's knowledge the analytical results of Stine and Shamon (1989) have not yet been extended to the GLS estimator, but a simple guide could be obtained by simulating the bias. There seems little doubt though that if the GLS estimates were used a qualitatively similar result – of the estimated

sum of the coefficients moving closer to 1 – would be obtained.

We now consider the estimated response time to a perturbation in the real exchange rate using the bias adjusted OLS estimates. The $\frac{1}{4}$-, $\frac{1}{2}$- and $\frac{3}{4}$-life responses are reported in Table 13.7, and the pattern of response is shown in Figure 13.9. In the case of Canada the implication of $\Sigma\hat{\tilde{\phi}}_j \geq 1$ is that there is no return to the pre-shock real exchange rate; otherwise the initial response is to magnify the shock and then, but only very slowly, the impact of the shock dies out. The

Table 13.7 *Estimated response times to a perturbation (bias adjusted OLS estimates)*

	Canada	Germany	Japan	UK
$\frac{1}{4}$-life	∞	83	57	87
$\frac{1}{2}$-life	∞	130	93	134
$\frac{3}{4}$-life	∞	200	156	205

Note: Table entries are the estimated response times in months (rounded to the nearest month).

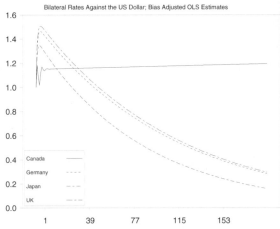

Figure 13.9 *Response to a shock to the real exchange rate*

estimated response times in Table 13.7 illustrate the difficulty in deciding whether or not there is a unit root in the process driving the real exchange rate. For Germany and the United Kingdom the half-life of the shock is estimated to be around 11 years and for Japan around 8 years.

13.5   Simple tests for noncointegration

This section considers some variations on the PPP theme that there should be a link between the nominal exchange rate and relative prices in the long run. In section **13.5.1** the assumption that the cointegrating vector is $(1, -1)$ is relaxed. Section **13.5.2** reports the results of first stage OLSEG estimation of (potentially) cointegrating regressions. Section **13.5.3** uses this application to illustrate the connection between an error correction model and the modified ADF regression. Despite these relaxations PPP fares little better than reported in section **13.3**.

13.5.1   Relaxing the $(1, -1)$ cointegrating vector

The sample evidence summarised in section **13.3.4** was against PPP, given that the four real exchange rates considered were found to be consistent with I(1) processes rather than I(0) processes. On the other hand, as reported in section **13.4.2,** using the Abuaf and Jorion procedure of pooling the observations but allowing individual countries to differ, there was some evidence that the unit root hypothesis for the real exchange rate could be rejected for Germany and Japan. To examine the evidence further we follow a suggestion made by Taylor (1988) who considered the stationarity of the linear combination given by

$$e_t - \beta(p_t - p_t^*) \qquad (13.19)$$

Instead of imposing $\beta = 1$, as in the definition of the real exchange rate, the suggestion is to allow

β to differ from 1 if that improves the chance of finding a stationary linear combination. Thus PPP is weakened to symmetry rather than proportionality; in this case a 1% increase in the relative price ratio implies a β% long-run depreciation of the exchange rate. (For an empirical study using a similar methodology applied to some Pacific Rim currencies, see Cooper (1994).)

Some motivation for $\beta \neq 1$ is provided by considering the role of transportation costs which lead to a 'wedge' between the domestic price of tradable goods and their overseas prices. For example, letting the United States be the home country, suppose a domestically produced tradable good sells for P_t and in the overseas country, say the United Kingdom, the same good domestically produced sells for P_t^*. If there were no transportation costs then arbitrage in this good would be profitable if the cost in US dollars of the UK produced good, that is $E_t P_t^*$, was less than the US price of that good, P_t. However, if there are costs of transporting the UK produced goods into the United States these have to be taken into account in working out whether arbitrage is profitable. For simplicity say that transportation costs are related to the price of the good with the total price of the imported good from the United Kingdom given by $P_t^{*\kappa}$, or κp_t^* where a lower case letter indicates the log of the variable, with $\kappa > 1$. Then an 'implicit' exchange rate $E_t^{(1)}$ on this good is defined by

$$E_t^{(1)} = P_t/P_t^{*\kappa} \quad \text{or in logs } e_t^{(1)} = p_t - \kappa p_t^*$$

$$(13.20)$$

What this 'implicit' exchange rate tells us is the rate at which arbitrage, taking into account transportation costs, is not profitable by importing the good from the United Kingdom into the United States. $E_t^{(1)}$ may not equal the actual exchange rate E_t hence using E_t rather than $E_t^{(1)}$ to assess PPP is likely to be misleading.

Conversely, we can consider the position by reversing the roles of the countries. That is, when is arbitrage profitable by importing US produced goods into the United Kindgom? Allowing again for transportation costs and assuming for simplicity they are the same whichever the direction of importation, we define a second 'implicit' exchange rate $E_t^{(2)}$ as

$$E_t^{(2)} = P_t^\kappa / P_t^* \quad \text{or in logs } e_t^{(2)} = \kappa p_t - p_t^*$$
$$(13.21)$$

This tells us the exchange rate at which arbitrage is not profitable by importing the good into the United Kingdom from the United States. As before $E_t^{(2)}$ may not equal the actual exchange rate, E_t.

If, following Taylor (*op. cit.*), we assume that the actual exchange rate E_t is the geometric average of the two implicit rates, that is, $E_t = (E_t^{(1)})(E_t^{(2)})^{0.5}$ so that $e_t = 0.5(e_t^{(1)} + e_t^{(2)})$, then on substituting for $e_t^{(1)}$ and $e_t^{(2)}$ we obtain:

$$e_t = 0.5(p_t - \kappa p_t^* + \kappa p_t - p_t^*)$$
$$= 0.5(\kappa + 1)(p_t - p_t^*)$$
$$= \beta(p_t - p_t^*) \quad (13.22)$$

where $\beta = 0.5(\kappa + 1)$; and as $\kappa > 1$ then $\beta > 1$.

13.5.2 OLSEG estimation of the cointegrating regressions

In this development of PPP the coefficient β may differ from unity. Practically this means computing the regression of the log of the nominal exchange rate e_t on a constant and the log of relative prices, and then assessing whether this is a cointegrating regression. There is one qualifying comment here. The results of the Dickey–Fuller tests in section **13.3.4** suggested that for the United Kingdom, and to a lesser extent for Japan, relative prices could have been generated by a trend stationary rather than a difference stationary process, whereas there was no ambiguity for the nominal exchange rate. If this is so the cointegrating regression is not balanced and, *a priori*, we should find noncointegration even

allowing $\beta \neq 1$. We keep the US : UK comparison in the sample to see if this implication follows through in the test results. These considerations also suggest that there may be a role for a time trend in the cointegrating regressions.

The regressions involving the nominal exchange rate and relative prices, and in the alternative a time trend, are reported in the first part of Table 13.8. For example, for Canada the estimated equations are:

$$\hat{\xi}_t = -0.223 + 1.162(p_t - p_t^*) \quad (13.23a)$$

and with a time trend

$$\hat{\xi}_t = -0.287 + 1.453(p_t - p_t^*)$$
$$+ 0.0004t \quad (13.23b)$$

In this case the estimate of β is 1.162 or 1.453 if a trend is included. However, not all of the estimates are above unity. For Germany the estimates of β are 0.789 and 0.849 with a trend in the regression, respectively; and for the United Kingdom the estimate of β switches from 0.622 without a trend to 1.260 with a trend.

These regressions are potentially misleading for I(1) variables unless a stationary linear combination is defined by the regression. In order to assess this we turn to the second part of Table 13.8. Here we report the auxiliary regressions for assessing whether the residual, $\hat{\xi}_t$, from the first regression is consistent with the null hypothesis of a unit root. Rejection of this null hypothesis is evidence in favour of stationarity. The 5% and 10% critical values are obtained from MacKinnon's (1991) procedure for the 'Constant and no trend' and 'Constant and trend' cases, respectively. See Chapter 8 for details. For $T = 198$ these are $-3.368/-3.067$ and $-3.829/-3.532$, respectively.

In no case do we reject the null hypothesis of a unit root and hence noncointegration. For example, the sample value of the test statistic for Canada is -1.450 without a trend in the cointegrating regression and -1.485 with a trend. There are only relatively minor differences between the test statistics with and without a

Table 13.8 *Cointegrating regressions*

Dependent variable: e_t	Constant	$p_t - p_t^*$	trend	$\hat{\sigma}$	dw
Canada	−0.223	1.162	–	0.057	0.036
	(−46.00)	(21.750)	–		
	−0.287	1.453	0.0004	0.057	0.040
	(−7.319)	(7.893)	(1.651)		
Germany	−0.693	0.789	–	0.158	0.029
	(−38.04)	(6.928)	–		
	−0.670	0.849	−0.001	0.158	0.029
	(−9.816)	(4.105)	(−0.348)		
Japan	−0.358	1.403	–	0.121	0.045
	(−21.48)	(28.060)	–		
	1.003	3.45	−0.006	0.104	0.075
	(6.114)	(13.815)	(−8.333)		
UK	0.379	0.622	–	0.137	0.039
	(21.01)	(12.760)	–		
	−0.101	1.260	0.002	0.134	0.048
	(−0.648)	(5.958)	(3.095)		

Dependent variable: $\Delta\hat{\xi}_t$	Constant	$\hat{\xi}_{t-1}$	ADF(p)	SC(12)
Canada				
No trend	−0.000	−0.020	4	17.823
	(−0.090)	(−1.450)		[0.121]
With trend	−0.000	−0.022	2	20.200
	(−0.101)	(−1.485)		[0.063]
Germany				
No trend	0.000	−0.017	1	7.166
	(0.355)	(−1.528)		[0.846]
With trend	0.000	−0.018	1	7.172
	(0.359)	(−1.523)		[0.845]
Japan				
No trend	−0.000	−0.032	1	16.756
	(−0.443)	(−2.235)		[0.159]
With trend	−0.000	−0.054	2	21.232
	(−0.449)	(−2.872)		[0.047]
UK				
No trend	0.000	−0.024	1	10.846
	(0.325)	(−1.816)		[0.542]
With trend	0.001	−0.030	1	12.803
	(0.379)	(−2.056)		[0.384]

Sample period: 1974m1 to 1990m6. 't' statistics in parentheses.
Critical values, calculated from MacKinnon's response surface:

$\hat{\tau}_\gamma$	Constant and no trend	Constant and trend
5%	−3.368	−3.829
10%	−3.067	−3.532

trend. The closest we come to rejecting the null hypothesis, although even that is some way off, is with Japan where the test statistic is -2.235 without a trend compared to the 10% critical value of -3.067, and -2.872 with a trend compared to the 10% critical value of -3.532.

13.5.3 An illustration of the modified ADF test statistic

We take the opportunity here to illustrate the modified ADF test of section **8.3.8b**. Recall that an alternative approach to testing for cointegration is based upon the link between an error correction model and the maintained regression for the Dickey–Fuller test. In the notation of Chapter 8 suppose the ECM is

$$(1 - \gamma_1 L)\Delta Y_t$$
$$= (\phi_1 + \phi_2 L)\Delta X_t + \theta_2 (Y_t - \varphi_2 X_t)_{-1} + \varepsilon_t \quad (13.24)$$

then the modified ADF(1) regression is

$$\Delta \xi_t = \delta_1 \Delta X_t + \delta_2 \Delta X_{t-1} + \gamma \xi_{t-1}$$
$$+ \gamma_1 \Delta \xi_{t-1} + \varepsilon_t \quad (13.25)$$

where $\delta_1 = (\phi_1 - \varphi_2)$, $\delta_2 = (\phi_2 + \gamma_1 \varphi_2)$ and $\gamma = \theta_2$. The modified ADF(1) regression differs from the standard ADF(1) by the addition of ΔX_t and its lag; there is no difference if $\phi_1 = \varphi_2$ and $\phi_2 = -\gamma_1 \varphi_2$. In practice $\hat{\xi}_t$ from the first stage levels regression replaces ξ_t. Critical values are given in Table 8.11.

In the present context Y_t is the log of the nominal exchange rate and X_t is the log of relative prices. The results are illustrated for the US : Germany comparison. Estimation of the ECM gave (with 't' statistics in parentheses):

$$\Delta e_t = 0.356\Delta e_{t-1} + 0.761\Delta(p_t - p_t^*)$$
$$(4.794) \qquad (2.274)$$

$$- 0.847\Delta(p_t - p_t^*)_{-1} - 0.009\hat{\xi}_{t-1} + \hat{u}_t$$
$$(-2.549) \qquad (-0.696)$$

$$SC(12) = 6.867[0.866]$$

where $\hat{\xi}_t = e_t - \{-0.693 + 0.789(p_t - p_t^*)\}$. Estimation of the modified ADF(1) regression gave:

$$\Delta \hat{\xi}_t = -0.009\hat{\xi}_{t-1} + 0.326\Delta \hat{\xi}_{t-1}$$
$$(-0.696) \qquad (4.794)$$

$$- 0.028\Delta(p_t - p_t^*)$$
$$(-0.083)$$

$$- 0.590\Delta(p_t - p_t^*)_{-1} + \hat{u}_t$$
$$(-1.763)$$

$$SC(12) = 6.867[0.866]$$

These regressions are, of course, identical: they are just reformulations of each other. As noted in Chapter 8, for the modified and standard ADF(1) regressions to coincide requires $\delta_1 = (\phi_1 - \varphi_2) = 0$ and $\delta_2 = (\phi_2 + \gamma_1 \varphi_2) = 0$. In this case $\hat{\delta}_1 = -0.028$ indicating that $\phi_1 \approx \varphi_2$; however, $\hat{\delta} = -0.590$ suggesting that $\phi_2 \neq -\gamma_1 \varphi_2$, and, therefore, the common factor restriction of the standard ADF test is likely to be invalid. However, this does not rescue RPPP since the modified ADF test statistic is -0.696 compared to the 10% critical value of -2.916 from Table 8.11, so rejection of RPPP is even more pronounced.

13.5.4 (Very) 'weak' form PPP

Some authors have reported evidence in favour of a weaker form of PPP than that considered here. For example, MacDonald (1993) and Chen (1995) use multivariate techniques due to Johansen (1988), considered in detail in Chapters 14 and 15, to examine the following regression,

$$e_t = \beta_0 + \beta_1 p_t - \beta_2 p_t^* + \varepsilon_t \quad (13.26)$$

This reduces to the regression corresponding to the simplest form of RPPP if $\beta_1 = \beta_2 = 1$ (proportionality); alternatively if $\beta_1 = \beta_2$ (symmetry) but $\neq 1$ we obtain the variation considered in section **13.5.2** of this chapter. A weak form of PPP is when β_1 and β_2 are neither equal to one nor equal to each other but, to give the theory some substance, there is a stationary linear combination of e_t, p_t and p_t^*. That is normalised on e_t the cointegrating vector is $(1, -\beta_1, \beta_2)$. In this case the nominal exchange rate, and the domestic and overseas price levels are tied together in the long run but with the implication that 1% increases in domestic and overseas inflation are not completely offsetting in their effect on the nominal exchange rate. To see this and judge its implications for e_t rewrite (13.26) as

$$e_t = \beta_0 + \beta_1(p_t - p_t^*)$$
$$+ (\beta_1 - \beta_2)p_t^* + \varepsilon_t \qquad (13.27)$$

so that

$$\Delta e_t = \beta_1\Delta(p_t - p_t^*)$$
$$+ (\beta_1 - \beta_2)\Delta p_t^* + \Delta\varepsilon_t \qquad (13.28)$$

Now, from (13.28), we see that even if domestic and overseas inflation, Δp_t and Δp_t^*, respectively, are identical so that $\Delta(p_t - p_t^*) = 0$, e_t will still be affected by a nonzero value of Δp_t^*. This seems a fairly uncomfortable implication of the empirical analysis and will require further research before such findings can be regarded as providing definitive support for PPP.

13.6 Other models of the exchange rate

PPP by itself may be insufficient to explain the exchange rate. It focuses on equilibrium in the goods market while more 'fundamentalist' models incorporate this as one of several equilibrium relationships including, for example, equilibrium in money and asset markets. A popular model in this respect is the flexible price monetary model which is outlined in the next section, **13.6.1**, and then illustrated with the US : UK comparison in section **13.6.2**.

13.6.1 The flexible price monetary model

The flexible price monetary model can be regarded as a development of purchasing power parity – see Hallwood and MacDonald (1994) and Cuthbertson (1996a); and for an application involving rational expectations see Diebold, Husted and Rush (1993). The starting point is the familiar PPP condition:

$$e_t = a + (p_t - p_t^*) \qquad (13.29)$$

This can be regarded as the equilibrium condition in the market for tradable goods. In addition we consider the conditions for monetary equilibria in the domestic and overseas country. In each case monetary equilibrium is achieved with the equality of the demand and supply of money. The demand for money is given by functions of the form considered in Chapter 10 (where an * indicates the overseas country).

For the domestic country:

$$m_t^d - p_t = \alpha_1(y_t - p_t) + \alpha_2 R_t \qquad (13.30a)$$

and for the overseas country:

$$m_t^{d*} - p_t^* = \alpha_1^*(y_t^* - p_t^*) + \alpha_2^* R_t^* \qquad (13.30b)$$

where $m_t^d - p_t$ is the demand for real money, $y_t - p_t$ is real income and R_t is the nominal interest rate.

In addition the money supply, m_t^s, is assumed to be exogenously determined by the monetary authorities and the money market is always in equilibrium so that $m_t^s = m_t^d = m_t$. Using this assumption, monetary equilibrium in each country is given by

$$m_t - p_t = \alpha_1(y_t - p_t) + \alpha_2 R_t \qquad (13.31a)$$

$$m_t^* - p_t^* = \alpha_1^*(y_t^* - p_t^*) + \alpha_2^* R_t^* \qquad (13.31b)$$

Subtracting (13.31b) from (13.31a) and rearranging in terms of the price differential $p_t - p_t^*$ we obtain:

$$
\begin{aligned}
&m_t - p_t - (m_t^* - p_t^*) \\
&\quad = \alpha_1(y_t - p_t) + \alpha_2 R_t \\
&\qquad - \{\alpha_1^*(y_t^* - p_t^*) + \alpha_2^* R_t^*\} \\
&m_t - m_t^* - (p_t - p_t^*) \\
&\quad = \alpha_1(y_t - p_t) - \alpha_1^*(y_t^* - p_t^*) + \alpha_2 R_t \\
&\qquad - \alpha_2^* R_t^* \\
&\Rightarrow (p_t - p_t^*) \\
&\quad = m_t - m_t^* - \alpha_1(y_t - p_t) + \alpha_1^*(y_t^* - p_t^*) \\
&\qquad - \alpha_2 R_t + \alpha_2^* R_t^* \qquad (13.32)
\end{aligned}
$$

Bearing in mind the anticipated negative sign for α_2 the sign of $-\alpha_2$ is anticipated to be positive. The economic argument behind (13.32) is that given exogenously determined interest rates, the equilibrating mechanism in the money market is the price level (not the interest rate); (13.31a) and (13.31b) can, therefore, be regarded as determining the price level. In each case the price level is 'flexible' as is the outcome of equilibrating money supply and money demand. In effect, for example, (13.31a) is rearranged with p_t as the dependent variable implying that money, real income and the nominal interest rate are being regarded as exogenous.

A condition known as uncovered interest parity, UIP, is also assumed to hold. Consider like assets, called 'bonds', issued by the Treasuries of the domestic and overseas countries with rates of interest R_t and R_t^*, and assume, for sake of argument, that these assets have one period to maturity. Then from the domestic point of view an investment of principal A_t may be made at time t giving a total return of $A_t(1 + R_t)$ in $t + 1$; alternatively the principal can be converted at an exchange rate of E_t to purchase an overseas bond which will then be converted back into domestic currency at the end of period $t + 1$, a process known as 'round-tripping'. At an exchange rate of E_t, A_t units of domestic currency will buy A_t/E_t units of foreign currency; this will then have a value of $(A_t/E_t)(1 + R_t^*)$ units of for-

eign currency at the end of period $t + 1$, which is then converted back to units of domestic currency using the exchange rate E_{t+1}. As the exchange rate at $t + 1$ is unknown, in evaluating this 'round trip' the expected exchange rate is used. At t the expected value of the alternative strategy is $(A_t/E_t)(1 + R_t^*)_t E_{t+1}^e$, where the exchange rate expected at t to prevail at $t + 1$ is denoted $_t E_{t+1}^e$. If no return is required for the risk of an uncertain future exchange rate then equalisation of the returns from the two strategies requires:

$$
A_t(1 + R_t) = (A_t/E_t)(1 + R_t^*)_t E_{t+1}^e \qquad (13.33)
$$

which implies $_t E_{t+1}^e / E_t = (1 + R_t)/(1 + R_t^*)$, or in logarithms $_t e_{t+1}^e - e_t \approx R_t - R_t^*$, using

$$
\log(1 + R_t) \approx R_t
$$

This is the UIP condition which will hold given perfect mobility of capital and risk neutral investors. The role of UIP in the FPMM is to provide for equilibrium on the capital market.

The FPMM then consists of: equilibrium on the money markets, (13.31), equilibrium on the capital markets, (13.33) and equilibrium on the traded goods market (13.29); in addition output is assumed to be determined at the full employment level. Substituting (13.32) into the PPP condition gives the flexible price monetary model, FPMM, of the exchange rate:

$$
\begin{aligned}
e_t &= a + (p_t - p_t^*) \\
&= a + (m_t - m_t^*) - \alpha_1(y_t - p_t) \\
&\quad + \alpha_1^*(y_t^* - p_t^*) - \alpha_2 R_t + \alpha_2^* R_t^* \qquad (13.34)
\end{aligned}
$$

If $\alpha_1 = \alpha_1^*$ and $\alpha_2 = \alpha_2^*$ this reduces to:

$$
\begin{aligned}
e_t &= a + m_t - m_t^* - \alpha_1\{(y_t - p_t) - (y_t^* - p_t^*)\} \\
&\quad - \alpha_2(R_t - R_t^*) \qquad (13.35)
\end{aligned}
$$

with the interpretation that the exchange rate depends upon relative money supplies, $m_t - m_t^*$, relative real income, $(y_t - p_t) - (y_t^* - p_t^*)$, and the interest rate differential, $R_t - R_t^*$. These differentials affect relative prices and, hence, through the PPP condition the exchange rate. For an elaboration of the implied transmission mechanism see Cuthbertson (*op. cit.*, Chapter 13). As with the PPP relationship between the nominal exchange rate and relative prices, (13.34) is interpreted in econometric terms as the long-run or equilibrium relationship. According to the FPMM, if e_t is I(1), (13.34) is a linear combination of the three cointegrating relationships given by the PPP condition, (13.29), and (what should be) two further cointegrating relationships given by domestic and overseas demand for money, (13.31a) and (13.31b). In the short run there are deviations from FPMM equilibrium but it provides the tendency to which the exchange rate should return.

There have been a number of empirical studies of the FPMM – see, for example, Kearney and MacDonald (1990), MacDonald and Taylor (1994) and Meese (1990), and for earlier studies Bilson (1978), Hodrick (1978) and Putnam and Woodbury (1980). Our purpose here is to see whether equations such as (13.34) or (13.35) offer an improvement over direct testing of the PPP relationship given by (13.29). The results are illustrated for the US : UK comparison.

13.6.2 An illustration of the FPMM with US : UK quarterly data

One difficulty facing testing of the FPMM arises from the need for a precise empirical definition of 'money', coupled with the limitations imposed by data availability. Some motivation for the determination of the price level using (13.31) can be provided from viewing the demand for money function as an implementation of the quantity theory of money – see Friedman (1956) – which favours a narrow definition of money. This would suggest using M0, which is primarily high-powered money comprising notes and coin in circulation. Practically, a bilateral comparison between the United States and the United Kingdom is limited by what is available. For the period of interest, the time series available for the United

Kingdom are M0 and M4, where the latter is the most extensive definition of money, which primarily comprises notes and coin and sterling deposits at banks and building societies (thrift institutions). In logarithms these are denoted $m0^*$ and $m4^*$. For the United States time series are available on 'currency', effectively M0, and M1 through M2 and M3 to L, which is effectively M4; in logarithms the first and last of these are denoted $m0$ and $m4$. The interest rates are the rates on 3-month US and UK Treasury bills, denoted R_t and R_t^*. The income series, in logarithms denoted $y_t - p_t$ and $y_t^* - p_t^*$, are for real personal income, but because the UK series is only available on a quarterly rather than a monthly frequency, the sample period becomes 1974q1 to 1990q2.

There are some important features of the data that warrant comment and may be relevant to the subsequent empirical analysis. First, note that the FPMM must explain steady appreciation in the dollar relative to sterling; while £1 cost about US\$2.28 in 1974q1 this fell to US\$1.67 in 1990q2. (Recall that the US\$ is the 'domestic' country.) By itself differential growth of M0 will not explain this development and points to the opposite conclusion – that, *ceteris paribus*, the £ should have appreciated not the US\$. In the United States, M0 grew by a factor of about 3.75 over the period, while in the United Kingdom there was an increase in M0 of 3.30. While other factors are important this feature of the data may well be strong enough to result in a wrong sign on the domestic money supply in the regression (13.34); further, US wholesale prices increased by a factor of about 2.33 over the period but UK wholesale prices quintupled, which is not suggested by the relative growth in M0 alone. With growth in consumer prices of about 2.75 in the United States and 4.50 in the United Kingdom it is evident that while there was growth in real M0 for the United States, in the United Kingdom the stock of real M0 declined. This prior reasoning suggests that, unless there are strong offsetting movements in relative real income and interest rates, M0 may not be the appropriate measure of money for the United Kingdom. The alternative is M4, a much broader measure of money, which underwent a 9-fold increase in the United Kingdom compared to a 4-fold increase for the United States, between 1974q1 and 1990q2. To see how these considerations bear on the empirical results, we first give brief consideration to a summary of the results of the unit root tests. All variables are in logarithms apart from the interest rate variables.

As there are eight variables to consider we will just report extracts from the set of standard unit root test statistics. The conclusion that a series 'is I(1)', means that the relevant test statistic has not led to rejection of the null hypothesis of a unit root at the 5% significance level. Other considerations in deciding whether to reject or not reject the null are briefly noted. First, note that since the series for nominal money and real income are trended the alternative models are either stationary with a deterministic trend (trend stationary) or I(1) with drift (difference stationary); the simplest testing strategy in such a case is to use $\hat{\tau}_\beta$ which protects against the unknown value of μ.

The unit root tests indicate the following. For the United States:

(i) $m0_t$ is I(1) with drift. $\hat{\tau}_\beta = -1.509(ADF(1))$, which is not significant.

(ii) $m4_t$ is I(1) with drift. Arguing as for $m0_t$ we obtain $\hat{\tau}_\beta = 1.712(ADF(1))$, which is wrong signed for rejection of the null hypothesis (but there was no evidence of two unit roots).

(iii) $y_t - p_t$ is I(1) with drift. $\hat{\tau}_\beta = -1.588(ADF(1))$ which is not significant.

(iv) R_t is probably I(1), $\hat{\tau} = -0.049$. A serious alternative in this case is that the series is stationary with a nonzero mean; moving to the maintained model without a constant relies upon interpreting $\hat{\mu} = 1.083$ with $t(\mu) = 2.436$, in the model with a constant, as not significant; $\Phi_1 = 3.071$ tends to confirm this interpretation. A similar situation arises with the UK interest rate.

For the United Kingdom:

(i) $m0_t^*$ is probably I(1) with drift. In the maintained model with a time trend $\hat{\tau}_\beta = -2.644(ADF(1))$ which is not significant if $\beta = 0$; the trend coefficient is insignificant with $t(\beta) = 1.564$; together these suggest an I(1) series. However, this contrasts with $\Phi_3 = 9.254$, which is significant. If the trend is omitted then $\hat{\tau}_\mu = -3.963$, which is significant, but $\hat{\gamma} = -0.015$ which is numerically close to zero. Rejecting the unit root *and* the earlier rejection of the deterministic time trend means that there is no mechanism to account for the upward drift in the (nominal) series. Consistency with the visual pattern suggests sticking with $\hat{\tau}_\beta$ and tentatively interpreting the results as an I(1) series with drift.

(ii) $m4_t^*$ is I(1) with drift. $\hat{\tau}_\beta = -2.172(ADF(1))$, which is not significant.

(iii) $y_t^* - p_t^*$ is I(1) with drift, $\hat{\tau}_\mu = -2.036$ $(ADF(1))$, which is not significant.

(iv) R_t^* is probably I(1), $\hat{\tau} = -0.214$; but, as with R_t, this rests upon interpreting $\mu = 1.814$ with $t(\mu) = 2.211$ as not significant; $\Phi_1 = 2.471$ tends to confirm this interpretation.

The nominal exchange rate, e_t, is I(1) without drift; the relevant test statistics being $\hat{\tau}_\mu = -1.803(ADF(1))$ and $\Phi_1 = 1.714$, neither of which is significant, and $\hat{\tau} = -1.146$ which is not significant.

There are two further points to note about these test results. First, as noted in Chapter 6, the finding of I(1) for an interest rate is likely to be a 'local' property. I(1) *with* drift is an unlikely characterisation of interest rates over the calendar long run, but the alternative of I(1) *without* drift is also unlikely as it allows the possibility of negative interest rates. Second, a point to remember in interpreting the cointegrating regressions, reported in Table 13.9, is that while not formally significant there was some evidence in the faster growing series, for example both M4 series and both real income

Table 13.9 *EG estimates of the FPMM for the US:UK comparison – see equation (13.34)*

constant	$m0_t$	$m0_t^*$	$y_t - p_t$	$y_t^* - p_t^*$	R_t	R_t^*	trend	$\hat{\sigma}$	dw	$\hat{\tau}_\gamma$
-31.849	-1.855	0.777	-0.568	3.450	0.017	-0.013	$-$	0.093	0.716	-3.726
-31.186	-2.091	0.816	-0.595	3.436	0.017	-0.013	0.004	0.094	0.718	-3.732

constant	$m0_t$	$m4_t^*$	$y_t - p_t$	$y_t^* - p_t^*$	R_t	R_t^*	trend	$\hat{\sigma}$	dw	$\hat{\tau}_\gamma$
-25.342	-0.285	-0.548	-0.304	3.224	0.024	-0.008	$-$	0.097	0.634	-3.474
-35.505	0.874	0.141	0.042	3.138	0.019	-0.006	-0.049	0.097	0.604	-3.401

Note: Sample period: 1974q1 to 1990q2. The dependent variable is e_t.

series, of the time trend contributing something to the regressions.

Some illustrative regressions estimated by the first stage Engle–Granger procedure are reported in Table 13.9. The first regression does not include a trend and uses the M0 definition of money for the United States and the United Kingdom; however, this results in wrong signs on domestic and overseas money. For consistency with the FPMM model, the coefficients on domestic and overseas money should be 1 and -1, respectively. This problem was alluded to earlier because of the relatively slow growth in UK M0 given the depreciation of the £ and the increase in UK prices relative to the United States. An alternative is to use M4, the broadest measure of money. All pairings were tried but the only combination to give some support to the FPMM was to use US M0 with UK M4, and a trend in the cointegrating regression; this is the last equation in Table 13.9. The trend can be justified from the earlier unit root tests where there was some evidence that UK M4 and both income series were close to the margin of including a trend. Even so the estimates provide little comfort to a strict interpretation of the FPMM; while the coefficient on $m0_t$ is positive, the coefficient on $m4_t$ is also positive whereas it should be negative. A Dickey–Fuller test on the residuals from this regression resulted in $\hat{\tau}_\gamma = -3.401$. Although this was not formally significant, for example the 10% critical value is -4.949, the estimate of γ is -0.305 so the estimated root, 0.695, is numerically a long way from 1.

These results are disappointing for the FPMM. They cannot be attributed to the finite sample biases in EG estimation; since the alternatives of FMOLS and ADL estimation methods (not reported here) did not lead to materially different conclusions. It could be argued that a different interest rate should be used when M4 is used. The 3-month rate is appropriate when a narrow definition of money is used, but broadening money means that the 3-month rate no longer captures the margin of substitution which has been internalised as far as M0 in M4 is concerned. However, this seems unlikely to rescue the results for the FPMM since interest rates for different maturities are likely to be cointegrated; and the only coefficients to consistently have the correct signs, that is plus for the domestic interest rate and minus for the overseas interest rate, in the cointegrating regressions are those on the interest rate variables. A more promising objection is that neither M0 nor M4 are appropriate, especially for the United Kingdom where the behaviour of these two aggregates is much at odds with what has been happening in the United States, and is in need of explanation. In the United Kingdom real M0 has fallen while real M4 has grown by a factor of 2 over the sample period.

In one development of the FPMM, prices are assumed to be sticky in the short run but PPP holds in the long run. This is the sticky-price monetary model, SPMM, which ties in with the econometric distinction between the cointegrating relationship which models the long-run relationship, here PPP and flexible prices, and the dynamic adjustment model which captures short-run changes. Since the FPMM and the SPMM have the same long run this development is unlikely to offer an explanation of why support for the FPMM is limited.

13.7 Concluding remarks

Purchasing power parity is an attractive theory of the exchange rate in the sense that it has a substantial commonsense appeal. In essence it compares the common currency price of identical goods produced in different countries. If there is a difference then arbitrage should remove the difference in the common currency price by adjustments in the nominal exchange rate to leave the real exchange rate unchanged. The emphasis in this approach is on tradable goods. Alternatively the nominal exchange rate can be viewed as the relative price of different monies, which includes the purchasing power over nontradable as well as tradable goods. Whichever view is taken then as Rogoff (1996, p. 647) puts it:

> While few empirically literate economists take PPP seriously as a short-term proposition, most instinctively believe in some variant of purchasing power parity as an anchor for long-run real exchange rates. Warm, fuzzy feelings about PPP are not, of course, a substitute for hard evidence.

One of the aims of this chapter was to see whether there was 'hard evidence' using the techniques introduced in earlier chapters. In this context a central implication of PPP is that the real exchange rate should be 'mean reverting', for without that property shocks to the real exchange rate do not die out; thus if, for example, by historical coincidence the real exchange rate was at its PPP level, then a shock would move the actual rate away from the PPP rate to which it would not return.

However, evaluating the hard evidence is not a straightforward matter. While it seems clear from the microeconomic evidence reported elsewhere – see, for example, Knetter (1989, 1993) – and the macroeconomic evidence detailed in this chapter, that PPP does not hold in the short run, assessing the long-run situation is more problematical. One of the problems that was evident from section **13.4.3** is that point estimates of the key parameter, which governs the speed of response of perturbations to the real exchange rate and the existence of a unit root, are very close to unity. With a finite sample of observations it is going to be very difficult for any statistical techniques to identify an alternative so close to the null hypothesis. Nevertheless, one might argue that in such a case since the estimated adjustment time to a perturbation is so long it really makes very little difference in practice whether we conclude in favour of rejecting PPP or not rejecting it with the qualification that the process has a very long, if not infinite, memory.

The econometric results reported here are mixed on whether the real exchange rate is mean reverting. The EG estimates point uniformly to nonrejection of the null of a unit root. However, it is well known that tests based on this procedure suffer from very poor power characteristics when the root is close to unity. Increasing the power by pooling the data on exchange rates, as suggested initially by Abuaf and Jorion (1990), and distinguishing among the various countries, does offer some contradictions to the EG-based results; now, over the sample period considered here, the real exchange rates for Germany and Japan may be mean reverting. In a further development of this procedure Sarno and Taylor (1998), with data for the period 1973m1 to 1996m12, find evidence in favour of mean reversion for bilateral comparisons against the US dollar for sterling, the French franc, the Deutschmark and the yen; and Snell (1996) finds evidence of mean reversion for nine OECD countries.

Enders (1988) estimates autoregressive models with a unit root, which also allow moving average errors (these are called ARIMA, that is autoregressive, integrated, moving average models) for the real exchange rate for the United States against Canada, Germany and Japan using monthly data for 1960–1971 and 1973–1986. He finds some mixed support for RPPP. The ARIMA models are convergent with point estimates of the roots less than unity *but* the largest root is not statistically different from unity; so while these estimates favour mean reversion they are not statistically far enough away from the null. Enders (*op. cit.*) notes that even the fastest adjustment to deviations from PPP is slow – a half-life of 15 months for Japan in the period 1973–1986. Standardising the real exchange rate to equal unity at the beginning of each period allows a test of whether reversion is to a mean of one, so favouring RPPP. Enders (*op. cit.*) notes that all estimated means are within two standard deviations of one.

Cheung and Lai (1993) use a cointegration approach which allows a more general conclusion than that the residual from a cointegrating regression is an integer usually either 0 or 1. They regress the log of $E_t P_t^*$ on a constant and the log of P_t and assess the residual for fractional integration; that is, consider the operator $(1 - L)^d \hat{\xi}_t$, where $\hat{\xi}_t$ is the residual from the cointegrating regression, then $d = 1$ corresponds to a unit root in $\hat{\xi}_t$; but if, for example, $0 < d < 1$ then d is fractional. Using annual data for exchange rates and consumer prices for 1914–1989 and bilateral rates against the US dollar for Canada, France, Italy, the United Kingdom and Japan, and relaxing proportionality, Cheung and Lai (*op. cit.*) find evidence for PPP for the first three countries but not for the last two.

Whether or not real exchange rates mean revert is only part of the story. If they do, what are the mechanisms by which this happens? PPP is part of the story reflecting equilibrium in the (international) goods market. Models of the 'fundamentals' attempt to complete the picture by integrating the goods market with money and asset markets. However, generally, the jury, in the form of the weight of empirical evidence

seems to have come out against models of 'fundamentals' like the FPMM and SPMM – see, for example, Meese (1986, 1990) and Kearney and MacDonald (1990), and for a summary of exchange rate models and empirical results see Taylor (1995b). Cuthbertson (*op. cit.*, p. 307) comments: 'At present it would appear to be the case that *formal* tests of the various models lead one to reject them' (italics in original).

There is though limited support in patches. MacDonald and Taylor (1991, 1993) report some support for the FPMM. For example, MacDonald and Taylor (1993) use monthly data for the period 1976m1 to 1990m12 for the United States (the 'home' country), Germany, Japan and the United Kingdom, with an M1 measure of money, industrial production used as a proxy for real income and long-term interest rates; all variables in logs apart from the interest rates and they use the cointegration approach due to Johansen (1988) to estimate the cointegrating vectors. In a bilateral comparison with the United States they find evidence of one cointegrating vector for Germany, two cointegrating vectors for the United Kingdom and three cointegrating vectors for Japan. MacDonald and Taylor (*op. cit.*) also conduct tests of the FPMM in which: the coefficients on home and overseas money are equal to +1 and −1, respectively; the coefficients on home and overseas 'income' are equal but opposite in sign; and the coefficients on home and overseas interest rates are equal but opposite in sign. At the 5% level they find nonrejection of all these hypotheses for US : Germany; rejection of all these hypotheses for US : UK; and rejection of all except the restriction on the income coefficients for US : Japan.

Johansen and Juselius (1992) model the structure rather than the reduced form of the central relationships in PPP and UIP. In their study PPP and UIP are equilibrium relationships which serve to define two error correction mechanisms, ecm_{1t} and ecm_{2t}, in a multivariate error correction model of five equations. The model comprises equations for: domestic prices, overseas prices; the nominal exchange rate; the domestic interest rate; and the overseas interest rate. All of these depend, in principle, upon both error correction mechanisms defined as follows: $ecm_{1t} = (p_t - p_t^*) - e_t$ and $ecm_{2t} = e_{t+1} - e_t - (R_t - R_t^*)$. Note that on comparison with the derivation of the logarithmic specification of the UIP relation following (13.33), e_{t+1} replaces $_t e_{t+1}^e$ on the assumption that the difference between the outturn and the expected exchange rate is stationary. Note that this analysis is testing for the existence of two cointegrating vectors among the five variables: $(p_t, p_t^*, e_t, R_t, R_t^*)$; the first cointegrating vector normalised on p_t should be: $(1, -1, -1, 0, 0)$ and the second cointegrating vector normalised on R_t should be $(0, 0, 0, 1, -1)$. Using quarterly data over the period 1972q1 to 1987q2 and the UK effective exchange rate, Johansen and Juselius (*op. cit.*) find some evidence in support of PPP and UIP. The techniques they, and MacDonald and Taylor (1993), use are described in detail in Chapters 14 and 15.

In a similar vein MacDonald and Marsh (1996, 1997) suggest combining the PPP and UIP conditions; departures from the former determine the current account balance, ca_t, while departures from the latter determine the capital account balance, ck_t. These departures are $\xi_{1t} = e_t - (p_t - p_t^*)$ and $\xi_{2t} = _t e_{t+k}^e - e_t - (R_t - R_t^*)$, respectively; apart from a change in sign ξ_{1t} is ecm_{1t} in Johansen and Juselius (*op. cit.*). The equilibrium condition is

$$ca_t + ck_t = \delta_1 \xi_{1t} + \delta_2 \xi_{2t} = 0$$

'Solving' for the exchange rate gives

$$e_t = (p_t - p_t^*) + (\delta_2/\delta_1)(R_t - R_t^* - \Delta e_{t+k}^e)$$

where $\Delta e_{t+k}^e \equiv _t e_{t+k}^e - e_t$. ($R_t$ is here the yield on a k period bond; the 'solution' for e_t assumes it is valid to condition on Δe_{t+k}^e.) Using Johansen's multivariate cointegrating techniques, Mac-Donald and Marsh (1997) find some

evidence for proportionality if interest rates are allowed to enter the cointegrating vector in an unrestricted way for the US:UK and US:Japan comparisons and with equal but opposite signed coefficients, as UIP suggests, for the US:Germany comparison.

The next two chapters describe one approach to the possibility of more than one cointegrating vector. Chapter 14 is primarily concerned with basic techniques while Chapter 15 presents several illustrations of applications of the techniques and interpretation of the results.

Review

1. Purchasing power parity – or PPP for short – has been an influential theory of the determination of the exchange rate. This chapter reviews the theory, some of its developments and some empirical evidence.

2. PPP states that the price of the same good in different countries with their own currencies should be the same when the domestic price of the good is converted to a common currency.

3. The nominal exchange rate is simply the domestic price of a unit of foreign currency; quite often this is just referred to as the exchange rate. In this chapter the United States. is the 'home' country, so all currencies have been expressed relative to the US$.

4. PPP is viewed as a theory of the exchange rate. If the domestic price of a commodity changes then, if PPP holds, the exchange rate should make an exactly compensating movement. If the exchange rate is fixed PPP could be viewed as a theory of price determination whereby there is disequilibrium in the home and overseas price levels until they form the ratio given by the exchange rate.

5. The key to why PPP is an attractive theory of the exchange rate is arbitrage in commodities. According to PPP if an imported

commodity, identical to one produced domestically, can be bought at a price which, when converted into units of domestic currency, is cheaper than the domestically produced commodity then it is possible to make a profit by trading in that good.

6. PPP may not hold for a number of reasons:
   (a) Transportation costs create a 'wedge' between domestic and overseas prices.
   (b) Multiple goods means using relative price indices rather than the simple price comparisons.
   (c) The presence of nontradable goods, which are included in price indices but for which no arbitrage is possible, will tend to misleading price changes.
   (d) Barriers to trade may prevent arbitrage in commodities.
   (e) Fixed or pegged exchange rates prevent the movement that PPP would require.
   (f) Adjustment to the PPP exchanges rate may take time, thus PPP may hold in the long run but not in the short run.

7. If there was just one internationally traded good with domestic and overseas prices given by P_{1t} and P_{1t}^* then the PPP exchange rate would be $E_t = P_{1t}/P_{1t}^*$. This is the absolute version of PPP, denoted APPP. With multiple goods and the use of price indices, P_t and P_t^*, this is modified to $E_t = AP_t/P_t^*$; in general, $A \neq 1$. In place of APPP we have relative purchasing power parity, denoted RPPP: a 1% change in the ratio of price indices in the home and overseas countries will lead to a 1% change in the nominal exchange rate.

8. The real exchange rate is $RE_t = E_t P_t^*/P_t$, which is the ratio of the overseas price level, converted to domestic currency units, to the domestic price level.

9. If there is a single good and APPP holds the equilibrium value of the real exchange rate is 1; otherwise, with the use of price indices, it is a constant $\neq 1$.

10. Assuming APPP, if $RE_t > 1$ the domestic currency is undervalued; if $RE_t < 1$ the domestic currency is overvalued. In the RPPP case the real exchange rate is constant and any changes in domestic and overseas price levels must be matched by an exactly compensating movement in the nominal exchange rate.

11. To a good approximation the % change in the real exchange rate equals the % change in the nominal exchange rate plus overseas inflation minus domestic inflation. Hence, if overseas and domestic inflation differ there will be pressure on the nominal exchange rate if the real exchange rate is to remain unchanged.

12. The evidence from a number of studies using microeconomic data indicates that there are substantial and persistent deviations from PPP interpreted as the law of one price (LOOP). There is evidence that homogeneous goods are priced differently for different markets – a phenomenon referred to as 'pricing-to-market'.

13. There is also evidence that disparities in the price of the same good across international boundaries, adjusted to be in common currency units, are much greater than intra-country disparities. This gives rise to what is known as a 'border effect'.

14. If RPPP holds, then the log of the nominal exchange rate, e_t, and the log of the price ratio, $p_t - p_t^*$, should be cointegrated with a cointegrating vector $(1, -1)$.

15. A test of RPPP, which can be applied using macroeconomic data, comprises first assessing whether the logs of the nominal exchange rate, e_t, and relative prices, $p_t - p_t^*$, are I(1); if they are, then RPPP implies that the log of the real exchange rate, $e_t - (p_t - p_t^*)$, should be I(0).

16. The graphical evidence supported the view of 'long memory' in the nominal exchange rates, relative prices and the real exchange rate. For example, the autocorrelations of the levels of these series died out very slowly.

17. While there were some parallels between the movements in nominal exchange rates and

relative prices there were some periods, especially for the United States and Germany and the United States and Japan, when there were marked divergences.

18. Table 13.1 also indicated that not only were there short-term divergences between the nominal exchange rates and relative prices, but that variations in these two series were not offsetting.

19. Standard DF tests failed to provide support for RPPP.

20. If PPP holds then the linear combination $e_t - \beta(p_t - p_t^*)$ should be stationary with $\beta = 1$ (proportionality). However, transportation costs and other factors suggest $\beta \neq 1$ (symmetry but not proportionality) but even allowing for this relaxation of the cointegrating vector, simple cointegration tests did not provide support for PPP.

21. The power of standard DF tests is low when the alternative is that of a 'near' unit root; to alleviate this problem we followed a suggestion by Abuaf and Jorion (1990) to pool the observations on the separate countries to create a 'panel', that is a time series of cross-sectional observations, of data on which to conduct unit root tests.

22. The estimation method in the Abuaf and Jorion procedure is an application of generalised least squares, GLS, to seemingly unrelated regression equations, SURE. GLS differs from OLS in taking into account the possibility of: (i) different error variances across countries, and (ii) nonzero error covariances among countries.

23. (i) The regression model and null hypothesis in this procedure are:

$$\Delta re_{it} = \gamma_{i0} + \gamma_{i1} re_{it-1}$$

$$+ \sum_{j=1}^{p_i} \alpha_{ij} \Delta re_{it-j} + \varepsilon_{it}$$

for $i = 1, \ldots, 4$ and

$t = 1, \ldots, T$

and $H_0: \gamma_{11} = \gamma_{21} = \gamma_{31} = \gamma_{41} = 0$

with the alternative hypothesis:

$H_a: \gamma_{11} = \gamma_{21} = \gamma_{31} = \gamma_{41} = \gamma_1 < 0$

(ii) This implies a single test statistic $\tilde{\tau}_\gamma$ in a regression estimated by GLS with the restriction that the coefficients are equal; these estimates were denoted RGLS. Critical values for $\tilde{\tau}_\gamma$ are obtained by simulation.

(iii) Alternately the null hypotheses can be formulated as

$H_{01}: \gamma_{11} = 0; \quad H_{02}: \gamma_{21} = 0$
$H_{31}: \gamma_{31} = 0; \quad H_{41}: \gamma_{41} = 0$

with alternatives

$H_{a1}: \gamma_{11} < 0; \quad H_{a2}: \gamma_{21} < 0$
$H_{a3}: \gamma_{31} < 0; \quad H_{a4}: \gamma_{41} < 0$

(iv) This set-up implies four separate test statistics, allowing the possibility that we may obtain rejection for some countries but nonrejection for others. Again the test statistics are obtained by simulation.

24. With GLS estimation there was very little change, compared to OLS, to the test statistics for Canada and the United Kingdom, but those for Germany and Japan moved closer to rejection of the null hypothesis of a unit root with a marginal significance level of between 12 and 13%.

25. The restriction that the γ_{i1} coefficients are equal was consistent with the data. RGLS estimation gave a test statistic $\tilde{\tau}_\mu$ of -3.425 with a marginal significance level of about 24%.

26. Mean reversion in the AR(1) model of the real exchange rate given by

$$re_t = \phi_0 + \phi_1 re_{t-1} + \varepsilon_t$$

requires that $|\phi_1| < 1$; if this condition is satisfied the (long-run) mean is

$$re^0 = \phi_0/(1 - \phi_1)$$

The numerical estimate of the mean is very sensitive to the value of ϕ_1 or $\Sigma\phi_j$ in the more general AR model.

27. Another interesting aspect of estimating AR models for the real exchange rate is the response time to a perturbation or shock to the equation. A unit root implies no return to the pre-shock position, whereas even if the root is only slightly below unity there will be 'mean reversion'.

28. In evaluating the estimated response time we must take account of the known bias in least squares estimators of the coefficients in an autoregressive model. Following Shaman and Stine (1988) and Stine and Shaman (1989) the OLS estimates were bias adjusted, which invariably moved the key parameter $\Sigma\hat{\phi}_j$ closer to unity, and in the case of Canada $\Sigma\hat{\phi}_j$ was marginally above unity implying no mean reversion.

29. The shortest estimated response time was for Japan with a half-life of the shock of about just under 8 years, whereas the estimated half-life was about 11 years for Germany and the United Kingdom. It is perhaps not surprising that with such long estimated responses it is very difficult statistically to distinguish between a unit root and a near unit root, and that practically there is very little difference if the alternative is so close to unity.

30. Some authors using more advanced statistical techniques – see MacDonald (1993) and Chen (1995) – and working with a modified version of PPP have reported favourable results. However, one approach which leads to the following exchange rate equation,

$$e_t = a + \beta_1(p_t - p_t^*) + (\beta_1 - \beta_2)p_t^* + \varepsilon_t$$

suggests only a very weak form of PPP.

31. The flexible price monetary model, FPMM, is a model of 'fundamentals' in the sense that it is a macroeconomic model of the underlying economic relationships. It combines PPP with equilibrium in the money and capital markets, to obtain a reduced form equation for the exchange rate.

32. An illustrative application of the FPMM to the US:UK comparison revealed a number of difficulties suggesting little support for the FPMM.

33. Although this chapter has reported largely negative results as far as PPP is concerned there are some studies that have found support either for PPP alone or in the context of a model of fundamentals.

34. The evidence most favourable to PPP comes from recent studies which use long runs of annual data – see, especially, Glen (1992) and Lothian and Taylor (1996). Also see MacDonald and Taylor (1991) for support for a model of 'fundamentals' and Sarno and Taylor (1998) for a further development and application of the Abuaf and Jorion procedure which is favourable to mean reversion in real exchange rates.

Review questions

1. Suppose there is a single good with domestic and overseas prices given by 100 US$ and 300 Deutschmarks (DM) respectively, what is the PPP exchange rate viewed (a) from the domestic country and (b) from the overseas country?

2. Explain what is meant by arbitrage in commodities and why it is an important part of the theory of PPP.

3. Suppose, to continue the example in question 1, transportation costs of 10% of the selling price are added to the dollar price of goods imported into Germany. If the dollar:DM exchange rate is 0.3636 is it worthwhile to import the good from the United States into Germany?

4. (i) Consider the case of two goods with prices of US$100 and US$200 in the United States and DM300 and DM600

in Germany. Suppose a price index is
formed with weights in both countries
given by $w_1 = 0.25$ and $w_2 = 0.75$. What
is the exchange rate?

(ii) Suppose the weights of the US price
index are as in 4(i) but the weights in the
German price index are 0.5 and 0.5.
What is the PPP exchange rate?

5. Revert to the weights given in question 4(i).
Consider two periods with first period prices
as in 4(i) and with second period prices
given by US$150 and US$300 in the United
States and DM450 and DM900 in Germany.
Suppose the US statisticians base their price
index with the first period price, P, set to 1,
whereas the German statisticians set the first
period price to 100. What is the PPP
exchange rate in each period?

6. Give some examples of nontradable goods,
and explain why their inclusion in a price
index, which was used to test the implications of PPP, would not be appropriate.

7. (i) What is the difference between the
nominal exchange rate and the real
exchange rate?

(ii) If PPP holds and there is a 4% increase
in the overseas price index and a 3%
increase in the domestic price index
what will happen to the nominal exchange rate?

8. Consider one bilateral rate of your choice
and on reference to Figures 13.1A to 13.1D
and 13.2A to 13.2D describe the salient
properties the data with particular reference to:

(i) periods of depreciation and appreciation
of the nominal and real exchanges rates;

(ii) the existence of long memory in the
data and whether the data appears nonstationary.

9. In Table 13.10 we report test statistics for
2 unit roots. Adopt an appropriate testing
strategy to draw conclusions from this table
about whether any of the series are I(2).

Table 13.10 Test statistics for 2 unit roots

Variable	Model	$\hat{\tau}$	$\hat{\tau}_\mu$	$\hat{\mu}$	$\hat{\tau}_\beta$	$\hat{\beta}$	Φ_3
			US : Canada				
e_t	ADF(6)	−4.789	−4.900	0.000	−6.009	0.000	18.126
rp_t	ADF(0)	−12.642	−12.923	0.000	−12.950	0.000	83.858
re_t	ADF(1)	−10.696	−8.442	0.000	−10.841	0.000	58.774
			US : Germany				
e_t	ADF(0)	−10.272	−10.302	0.002	−10.277	0.000	52.832
rp_t	ADF(12)	−3.703	−2.512	0.000	−2.522	0.000	3.251
re_t	ADF(0)	−10.008	−9.987	−0.000	−9.985	0.000	49.875
			US : Japan				
e_t	ADF(0)	−10.051	−10.112	0.002	−10.088	0.000	50.886
rp_t	ADF(0)	−10.112	−11.086	0.002	−11.031	0.000	61.385
re_t	ADF(0)	−10.678	−10.651	0.000	−10.629	0.000	56.510
			US : UK				
e_t	ADF(0)	−9.550	−9.545	0.000	9.559	0.000	45.689
rp_t	ADF(16)	−2.252	−3.344	−0.002	−3.108	0.000	5.621
re_t	ADF(0)	−9.777	−9.802	0.001	−9.790	0.000	47.932

Note: e_t is the log of the nominal exchange rate; rp_t is the log of the relative prices; re_t is the log of the real exchange rate. Sample period (before lagging) 1974m1 to 1990m6.

What complications arise for PPP if any of the variables are I(2)?

10. (i) What is meant by 'mean reversion'?

(ii) Why is it that a series with a unit root does not exhibit mean reversion?

(iii) What is the half-life of a shock to the real exchange rate if the latter has a unit root?

(iv) If the real exchange rate shows mean reversion, what is the mean to which it will revert according to PPP?

11. (i) Show that in the simple AR(1) model of equation (13.16), the response to a one- off 1 unit shock to ε_t is a decline provided $|\phi_1| < 1$. When is the decline monotonic?

(ii) Show that if the 1 unit shock is sustained then re_t is eventually permanently higher by $1/(1 - \phi_1)$.

12. (i) Summarise the evidence for and against the FPMM.

(ii) Explain why some authors find that the data supports the FPMM but others have found this not to be the case.

Part IV
Extensions

CHAPTER 14
Multivariate models and cointegration

14.1 Introduction

In previous chapters we have concentrated on a single equation, with one variable designated the dependent variable explained conditionally on a vector of other variables, which are implicitly assumed to be (weakly) exogenous for the parameters of interest. This framework was relaxed somewhat in Chapter 9 where endogeneity was allowed, but the approach was restricted in the sense that it was assumed that there was just one equilibrium relationship which, in general, is unrealistic. In this chapter we extend the analysis to cover multivariate regression models. These are models which have several endogenous, that is jointly determined, variables which characterises much of economic analysis; for example, in the elementary model of demand and supply two variables – price and quantity – are determined; in the IS/LM model four variables – investment, savings, money and the interest rate – are determined.

Another important aspect of multivariate models is that like univariate models they are often dynamic involving lags of both the endogenous and exogenous variables. Adjustment to equilibrium following a shock takes time, which means that an empirical model is likely to need two distinct characteristics: it will need to capture the equilibrium relationships among the variables; and it will need to capture the adjustment to equilibrium following a shock. Also, modelling endogenous variables can take place by modelling the structure of the behavioural relations suggested by economic theory, for example the simultaneous pair given by the demand function and the supply function plus market clearing, or modelling the solution of the simultaneous relationships in the reduced form. Whichever route is taken the combination of modelling equilibrium and dynamic adjustment is likely to be empirically important.

We examine conditions for the stability and stationarity of the VAR and show how the presence of nonstationary variables is potentially useful in providing information about the long-run relationships. A key aspect in this approach is in isolating and identifying the r cointegrating combinations among a set of k integrated variables and incorporating them into an empirical model. In some places the development is necessarily technical since the extension to multivariate modelling raises new and quite complex questions. Some technical concepts, such as the eigenvalues of the characteristic polynomial, occur at different places in the development of the modelling framework and it is essential to have a firm understanding of such concepts. However, the general emphasis in this chapter is on illustrating rather than proving results. For those interested in the more technical side there are excellent books by Lütkepohl (1991) and Johansen (1995a) to which reference can be made.

The aim of this chapter is to introduce a number of key concepts related to VARs and cointegration in the context of some simple models. For example, the bivariate model is used extensively to motivate some general concepts, such as deriving the eigenvalues and cointegrating rank; and occasionally a third variable is introduced to illustrate how generality can be achieved. The idea is that a firm understanding of the basic concepts is essential before it is possible to understand and evaluate empirical work, which often involves more than three variables. While the concentration in this chapter is on basic concepts, the next chapter picks up the baton of how these form the fundamental tools of empirical analysis and illustrates their use in a number of studies. These include the following topics: purchasing power parity and uncovered interest parity, the cointegration of real wages, the demand for money, the structure of IS/LM models and the demand for imports.

The plan of this chapter is as follows. Section **14.2** introduces some basic concepts. In particular the vector autoregressive model – or more simply VAR – is introduced in subsection **14.2.1** and other subsections consider the related concepts of stability, stationarity and eigenvalues. A simple multivariate error correction model, ECM, is introduced in section **14.3**, and forms the basis for understanding the concept of the cointegrating rank of a VAR. How to test for the cointegrating rank is the subject of section **14.4** and conditions for the identification of cointegrating vectors are presented in section **14.5**. Also considered in section **14.5** is the distinction between a structural error correction model and a reduced form error correction model, and whether it is possible to identify the short-run structure. Concluding remarks are presented in section **14.6**.

14.2 Some basic concepts

This section introduces the vector autoregressive model as a framework for modelling multivariate relationships and the multivariate version of the error correction model. Stability and stationarity in the VAR are considered and the importance of calculating the eigenvalues of what is known as the companion matrix is emphasised. As in the single-equation case nonstationarity turns out to be an important aspect of model development. The main aim in this section is to introduce some basic but key concepts, which are developed at length in subsequent sections.

14.2.1 The VAR

A linear model, which arises frequently in modelling multivariate relationships, is the vector autoregressive model, or VAR, which was introduced in Chapter 2. It can be viewed as an extension of the autoregressive univariate model in the following way. Suppose economic theory suggests a relationship between two variables, y_{1t} and y_{2t}, modelling each series separately might, for example, involve an autoregression of y_{1t} on lagged values of y_{1t}, and autoregression of y_{2t} on lagged values of y_{2t}. However, such a separate approach would not capture any interactions between the variables that might be present. For example, suppose y_{1t} is consumption and y_{2t} is income, then it is likely that y_{1t} and y_{2t} are related and modelling these variables should take place in a multivariate (here bivariate) framework. In a VAR y_{1t} is related not just to its own lagged values but also those of y_{2t}, and similarly y_{2t} is related to its own lagged values and those of y_{1t}. A VAR has two dimensions: the length, or order, p of the longest lag in the autoregression; and the number, k, of variables being jointly modelled. For example, a first order, $p = 1$, bivariate, $k = 2$, VAR is

$$\begin{pmatrix} y_{1t} \\ y_{2t} \end{pmatrix} = \begin{pmatrix} \mu_1 \\ \mu_2 \end{pmatrix} + \begin{bmatrix} \pi_{11.1} & \pi_{12.1} \\ \pi_{21.1} & \pi_{22.1} \end{bmatrix} \begin{pmatrix} y_{1t-1} \\ y_{2t-1} \end{pmatrix} \tag{14.1a}$$

$$+ \begin{pmatrix} \varepsilon_{1t} \\ \varepsilon_{2t} \end{pmatrix} \tag{14.1b}$$

Say

$$y_t = \mu + \Pi_1 y_{t-1} + \varepsilon_t \tag{14.2}$$

where $\mu' = (\mu_1, \mu_2)$ is the vector of constants usually known as drifts; and $\varepsilon'_t = (\varepsilon_{1t}, \varepsilon_{2t})$ are innovations relative to the information set

$y'_{t-1} = (y_{1t-1}, y_{2t-1})$. A pth order VAR in k variables is given by

$$y_t = \mu + \Pi_1 y_{t-1} + \Pi_2 y_{t-2} + \cdots$$
$$+ \Pi_p y_{t-p} + \varepsilon_t \qquad (14.3)$$

where $y'_t = (y_{1t}, y_{2t}, \ldots, y_{kt})$, $\varepsilon'_t = (\varepsilon_{1t}, \varepsilon_{2t}, \ldots, \varepsilon_{kt})$ and

$$\Pi_j = \begin{bmatrix} \pi_{11.j} & \pi_{12.j} & \cdots & \pi_{1k.j} \\ \pi_{21.j} & \pi_{22.j} & \cdots & \pi_{2k.j} \\ \vdots & \vdots & \cdots & \vdots \\ \pi_{k1.j} & \pi_{k2.j} & \cdots & \pi_{kk.j} \end{bmatrix}$$

When the VAR is first order, the third subscript can be omitted without loss. This form of the VAR is a *reduced form* in the sense that no current dated values of the k variables appear in any of the equations. The genesis of the reduced form VAR could be as the solution of a dynamic simultaneous equation model. For example, in the bivariate case consider

$$y_{1t} = \kappa_1 + \gamma_{11} y_{2t} + \varphi_{11} y_{1t-1}$$
$$+ \varphi_{12} y_{2t-1} + \zeta_{1t} \qquad (14.4a)$$

$$y_{2t} = \kappa_2 + \gamma_{21} y_{1t} + \varphi_{21} y_{1t-1}$$
$$+ \varphi_{22} y_{2t-1} + \zeta_{2t} \qquad (14.4b)$$

These equations are sometimes termed structural in the sense that they directly represent the behavioural relationships, for example demand and supply functions, in the structure of the economy, rather than the interaction of such relationships. In this specification the endogeneities, that is y_{2t} in the equation for y_{1t} and y_{1t} in the equation for y_{2t}, are explicit. These can be solved out either by direct substitution, for example substitute y_{2t} from the second equation into the first equation, or by first rewriting the two equations so that the endogenous variables are on the left-hand side

$$\begin{bmatrix} 1 & -\gamma_{11} \\ -\gamma_{21} & 1 \end{bmatrix} \begin{pmatrix} y_{1t} \\ y_{2t} \end{pmatrix}$$
$$= \begin{pmatrix} \kappa_1 \\ \kappa_2 \end{pmatrix} + \begin{bmatrix} \varphi_{11} & \varphi_{12} \\ \varphi_{21} & \varphi_{22} \end{bmatrix} \begin{pmatrix} y_{1t-1} \\ y_{2t-1} \end{pmatrix} + \begin{pmatrix} \zeta_{1t} \\ \zeta_{2t} \end{pmatrix}$$

and then pre-multiplying by the inverse of the matrix of coefficients on the endogenous variables to obtain the reduced form,

$$\begin{pmatrix} y_{1t} \\ y_{2t} \end{pmatrix} = \begin{bmatrix} 1 & -\gamma_{11} \\ -\gamma_{21} & 1 \end{bmatrix}^{-1} \begin{pmatrix} \kappa_1 \\ \kappa_2 \end{pmatrix}$$
$$+ \begin{bmatrix} 1 & -\gamma_{11} \\ -\gamma_{21} & 1 \end{bmatrix}^{-1} \begin{bmatrix} \varphi_{11} & \varphi_{12} \\ \varphi_{21} & \varphi_{22} \end{bmatrix}$$
$$\times \begin{pmatrix} y_{1t-1} \\ y_{2t-1} \end{pmatrix} + \begin{bmatrix} 1 & -\gamma_{11} \\ -\gamma_{21} & 1 \end{bmatrix}^{-1} \begin{pmatrix} \zeta_{1t} \\ \zeta_{2t} \end{pmatrix}$$
$$(14.5)$$

A comparison between (14.4) and (14.5) gives the connection between the coefficients in the reduced form and how they originated from the structural form. Whether, given the reduced form coefficients, we can retrieve the structural coefficients, which are likely to have an economic interpretation, is the issue of identification to which we return in section **14.5** below.

14.2.2 Stability and stationarity in the VAR

This section is concerned with the stability of a VAR and provides an introduction to the modelling of nonstationary variables. Broadly speaking stability is concerned with the following question. Consider the impact of a shock to the innovation in one of the equations of a VAR; does the response to this shock (eventually) die out as we get further away in time from the date of the shock? If the answer is yes the model is stable; if not the model is unstable. A stable VAR is stationary, that is it has first and second moments that are time-invariant. We know from our analysis of univariate models – see Chapter 6 – that some models have an infinite memory to shocks, whose effect is, therefore, persistent, and that these models have a unit root in the autoregressive polynomial. In the same way we can expect VAR models which have a unit root to be unstable; and a VAR which is unstable through a unit root is nonstationary. While if there is just one unit root a stable process might be obtained by modelling in first differences, and hence in stationary variables, this is not necessarily the best solution for this kind of nonstationarity.

A particularly important class of models arises if nonstationary variables are cointegrated; then linear combinations of nonstationary variables are reduced to stationarity. For example, it is likely that the time series processes generating consumption and income for the United States are I(1), and hence contain a unit root. A VAR model in the levels of these variables would be nonstationary and one alternative is to define new variables as the first difference of consumption and income, which are I(0), and model the VAR using these stationary variables. This option is unsatisfactory if there is cointegration between consumption and income, as the linear cointegrating combination links the variables in the long run and is I(0); together with the I(0) first differences this provides a set of stationary variables which can be modelled. Omitting the cointegrating combination is a specification error in a VAR in first differences and, in addition, such a VAR provides no information about the long run which is often of considerable interest to economists.

Consider the first order VAR

$$y_t = \mu + \Pi_1 y_{t-1} + \varepsilon_t \tag{14.6}$$

then, as in the univariate case, by repeatedly substituting in for y_{t-1}, this can be viewed as the weighted cumulative sum of past observations. In particular imagine the process starting in period 1 with y_0 given:

$$y_1 = \mu + \Pi_1 y_0 + \varepsilon_1$$
$$y_2 = \mu + \Pi_1(\mu + \Pi_1 y_0 + \varepsilon_1) + \varepsilon_2$$
$$= (I + \Pi_1)\mu + \Pi_1^2 y_0 + \Pi_1 \varepsilon_1 + \varepsilon_2$$
$$y_3 = \mu + \Pi_1[(I + \Pi_1)\mu$$
$$+ \Pi_1^2 y_0 + \Pi_1 \varepsilon_1 + \varepsilon_2] + \varepsilon_3$$

$$= (I + \Pi_1 + \Pi_1^2)\mu + \Pi_1^3 y_0$$
$$+ \Pi_1^2 \varepsilon_1 + \Pi_1 \varepsilon_2 + \varepsilon_3$$

$$\vdots$$

$$y_t = (I + \Pi_1 + \Pi_1^2 \cdots + \Pi_1^{t-1})\mu$$
$$+ \Pi_1^t y_0 + \sum_{i=0}^{t-1} \Pi_1^i \varepsilon_{t-i} \tag{14.7}$$

(In the last term note that $\Pi_1^0 \equiv I$.) Now y_t is expressed as a function of the drift, μ, the initial value, y_0, and current and past innovations, ε_{t-i}. Stability concerns the eventual impact of a shock or perturbation from any of these three sources. If the model is stable then there are four important implications:

(i) suppose there is a one unit change in the drift in period 1 then the effect in period t is $(I + \Pi_1 + \Pi_1^2 \cdots + \Pi_1^{t-1})$, and this sequence has a finite limit as $t \to \infty$, equal to $(I - \Pi_1)^{-1}$;

(ii) suppose there is a one unit change to y_0, the effect t periods hence is Π_1^t, and as $t \to \infty$, $\Pi_1^t \to 0$ so the effect of the shock dies out;

(iii) the matrix of long-run multipliers exists and is $(I - \Pi_1)^{-1}$;

(iv) the VAR is stationary.

The condition which ensures that the model is stable is that all eigenvalues of Π_1 have modulus less than one (Lütkepohl 1991, p. 460) – the meaning of this condition is explained in section **14.2.4** below. A stable model is thus well behaved in the sense that the impact of shocks is calculable and finite. This is particularly important in the context of what is known as multiplier analysis. To illustrate, suppose we have a two-equation first order VAR in the variables wage inflation, y_{1t}, and unemployment, y_{2t}: what is the effect of a one unit change in the innovation to unemployment on wage inflation? In answering this question we can distinguish three timescales: the immediate effect of the shock, that is the impact response or multiplier; the interim effect for $0 < s < \infty$ giving the interim responses or multipliers; the eventual effect as $s \to \infty$, this is the long-run response or multiplier.

The bivariate, first order VAR is:

$$\begin{pmatrix} y_{1t} \\ y_{2t} \end{pmatrix} = \begin{pmatrix} \mu_1 \\ \mu_2 \end{pmatrix} + \begin{bmatrix} \pi_{11} & \pi_{12} \\ \pi_{21} & \pi_{22} \end{bmatrix} \begin{pmatrix} y_{1t-1} \\ y_{2t-1} \end{pmatrix}$$
$$+ \begin{pmatrix} \varepsilon_{1t} \\ \varepsilon_{2t} \end{pmatrix} \qquad (14.8)$$

As there is no ambiguity in the first order case, we have adopted an economy of notation where, comparing (14.1) and (14.8), $\pi_{11} \equiv \pi_{11.1}$, $\pi_{12} \equiv \pi_{12.1}$, $\pi_{21} \equiv \pi_{21.1}$ and $\pi_{22} \equiv \pi_{22.1}$. To concentrate on isolating the required effects the following simplifying assumptions are made: zero drift; the starting values, y_{10} and y_{20} are zero and y_{10} is then subjected to a one unit shock; all other innovations are set to zero. Tracing out the effects of this shock we find:

starting values:

$$y_0 = \begin{pmatrix} y_{10} \\ y_{20} \end{pmatrix} = \begin{pmatrix} 1 \\ 0 \end{pmatrix} \begin{matrix} \leftarrow \text{the first variable.} \\ \leftarrow \text{No shock to the} \\ \text{second variable.} \end{matrix}$$

A one unit shock to the first variable.

$t = 1$

$$\begin{pmatrix} y_{11} \\ y_{21} \end{pmatrix} = \Pi_1 \begin{pmatrix} y_{10} \\ y_{20} \end{pmatrix} = \begin{bmatrix} \pi_{11} & \pi_{12} \\ \pi_{21} & \pi_{22} \end{bmatrix} \begin{pmatrix} 1 \\ 0 \end{pmatrix}$$
$$= \begin{pmatrix} \pi_{11} \\ \pi_{21} \end{pmatrix} \equiv \Pi_{1.1} \leftarrow \begin{matrix} \text{The first} \\ \text{column of } \Pi_1. \end{matrix}$$

$t = 2$

$$\begin{pmatrix} y_{12} \\ y_{22} \end{pmatrix} = \Pi_1 \begin{pmatrix} y_{11} \\ y_{21} \end{pmatrix} = \begin{bmatrix} \pi_{11} & \pi_{12} \\ \pi_{21} & \pi_{22} \end{bmatrix} \begin{bmatrix} \pi_{11} + 0 \\ \pi_{21} + 0 \end{bmatrix}$$
$$= \begin{bmatrix} \pi_{11}^2 + \pi_{12}\pi_{21} \\ \pi_{21}\pi_{11} + \pi_{22}\pi_{21} \end{bmatrix}$$
$$= \Pi_{1.1}^2 \leftarrow \text{The first column of } \Pi_1^2.$$

$t = 3$

$$\begin{pmatrix} y_{13} \\ y_{23} \end{pmatrix} = \Pi_{1.1}^3$$

and, generally, for $t = s$

$$\begin{pmatrix} y_{1s} \\ y_{2s} \end{pmatrix} = \Pi_{1.1}^s \leftarrow \text{The first column of } \Pi_1^s.$$
$$(14.9)$$

The effects of the unit shock to the first variable are traced out in the first column, $\Pi_{1.1}^s$, of Π_1^s. After s periods the effect of the shock to the first variable on the second variable is the element in the second row and first column of Π_1^s; the 'own' effect is the element in the first row and first column. If the second rather than the first variable was shocked the responses are obtained from $\Pi_{1.2}^s$, which is the second column of Π_1^s. The matrix Π_1^s therefore gives the complete set of s period responses or multipliers for one unit shocks to the component variables of the VAR. It follows from implication (ii) of a stable model that as $s \to \infty$, $\Pi_1^s \to 0$; that is the multipliers eventually die out.

Also of interest are the cumulative multipliers obtained by taking the (partial) sum of the responses from 0 to period s. The initial response is just the identity matrix, I, since $(1, 0)'$ is the shock to the first variable and $(0, 1)'$ is the shock to the second variable. Thereafter the responses are $\Pi_1, \Pi_1^2, \ldots, \Pi_1^s$; the cumulative sum is $I + \Pi_1 + \Pi_1^2 + \cdots + \Pi_1^s$ which converges to $(I - \Pi_1)^{-1}$, as $s \to \infty$, for a stable model. The matrix $(I - \Pi_1)^{-1}$ gives the total (cumulative) multipliers; the ijth element is the total cumulative response of variable i to a one unit shock to variable j.

Stability is sufficient, but not necessary, for stationarity; however, while this means that some unstable models will be stationary these are not generally of interest. The unstable models of primary interest are those which contain a unit root in the autoregressive polynomial, and these are nonstationary. In order to check whether a particular model is stable we need to calculate the eigenvalues of Π_1, and this is considered in section **14.2.4** after a brief reminder in the next section on stability in a univariate model.

14.2.3 Stability and roots in the univariate model

We start with some reminders of relevant concepts in a univariate model and then generalise them to a multivariate model in the next section. The univariate model considered is a second order autoregression in y_t, which is here a scalar variable:

$$y_t = \phi_1 y_{t-1} + \phi_2 y_{t-2} + \varepsilon_t$$
$$= (\phi_1 L + \phi_2 L^2) y_t + \varepsilon_t \quad (14.10)$$

That is

$$(1 - \phi_1 L - \phi_2 L^2) y_t = \varepsilon_t$$

say

$$\phi(L) y_t = \varepsilon_t$$

Stability of this model requires that both roots of the polynomial $\phi(L)$ have modulus greater than one. If $\phi(L)$ has a unit root, two consequences follow: first, $\phi(L = 1) = 0$; second, the unit root polynomial, $1 - L$, can be factored out of $\phi(L)$ and the model can be reformulated into first differences. To illustrate suppose $\phi_1 = 3/4$ and $\phi_2 = 1/4$ then the model is

$$(1 - 3/4L - 1/4L^2) y_t = \varepsilon_t \quad (14.11)$$

and notice that $\phi(L = 1) = (1 - 3/4 - 1/4) = 0$. The polynomial $\phi(L)$ factors into $(1 - L)$ $(1 + 1/4L)$ which has roots of $+1$ and -4; that is there is a unit root; and once the unit root has been extracted the model will be stable (because the other root is -4, so $|-4| > 1$). Using this factorisation the model can be written as:

$$(1 + 1/4L)(1 - L) y_t = \varepsilon_t \quad (14.12)$$

that is

$$\Delta y_t = -1/4 \Delta y_{t-1} + \varepsilon_t \quad (14.13)$$

A model with a unit root, which is reformulated into first differences, will not necessarily be a stable model, whether that is the case depends upon the other root having modulus greater than 1. In this example the other root is -4 so the model in first differences is stable.

As a second example consider the univariate model given by:

$$(1 + 3L - 4L^2) y_t = \varepsilon_t \quad (14.14)$$

The lag polynomial factors into

$$(1 + 4L)(1 - L) y_t = \varepsilon_t$$

and so $\Delta y_t = 4\Delta y_{t-1} + \varepsilon_t$. The roots of $\phi(L)$ are $+1$ and $-1/4$ indicating that neither the model in levels nor first differences is stable.

14.2.4 Eigenvalues and roots: the multivariate model

The necessary and sufficient condition for stability in a first order VAR is that all the eigenvalues of Π_1 have modulus less than 1. This section explains what is meant by an eigenvalue and how it is related to the root of a polynomial, starting with a first order system and then generalising to a pth order lag. The first order VAR, for simplicity without drift, is:

$$y_t = \Pi_1 y_{t-1} + \varepsilon_t \quad (14.15)$$

that is

$$A(L) y_t = \varepsilon_t \quad (14.16)$$

where $A(L) = I - \Pi_1 L$ is the autoregressive polynomial. The eigenvalues of Π_1 are the roots of the kth order characteristic polynomial $|\Pi_1 - vI|$ obtained by solving the characteristic equation:

$$|\Pi_1 - vI| = 0 \quad (14.17)$$

where $|B|$ indicates the determinant of the matrix B. The *reverse* characteristic polynomial is $|I - \rho\Pi_1|$ with roots obtained by solving

$$|I - \rho\Pi_1| = 0 \qquad (14.18)$$

The condition for stability of the VAR can be stated in terms of the roots of either polynomial and can be confusing if it is not clear which polynomial is being referred to. In terms of the characteristic polynomial (14.17) the stability condition is that all eigenvalues (roots) have modulus less than 1. In the case of complex roots, say $v_j = v_j^r + v_j^i i$, where v_j^r and v_j^i are the real and imaginary parts of v_j, the modulus is defined as $\mathrm{mod}(v_j) = [(v_j^r)^2 + (v_j^i)^2]^{0.5}$. In terms of the *reverse* characteristic polynomial (14.18) the stability condition is that *none* of its roots has modulus less than 1. Part of the potential confusion arises from the convention that the conditions for stability in a univariate model are usually stated in terms of the reverse characteristic polynomial, whereas for a multivariate model the stability conditions are usually stated in terms of the characteristic polynomial.

Some examples illustrate these ideas. First consider

$$\Pi_1 = \begin{bmatrix} 5/8 & 1/2 \\ 1/4 & 5/8 \end{bmatrix} \qquad (14.19)$$

then the eigenvalues of Π_1 are obtained as the roots of

$$\begin{aligned} |\Pi_1 - vI| &= \left| \begin{bmatrix} 5/8 & 1/2 \\ 1/4 & 5/8 \end{bmatrix} - \begin{bmatrix} v & 0 \\ 0 & v \end{bmatrix} \right| \\ &= \begin{bmatrix} 5/8 - v & 1/2 \\ 1/4 & 5/8 - v \end{bmatrix} \\ &= (5/8 - v)^2 - 1/8 \\ &= (0.978 - v)(0.271 - v) \quad (14.20) \end{aligned}$$

with roots of $v_1 = 0.978$ and $v_2 = 0.271$ (that is setting v to either of these values results in $|\Pi_1 - vI| = 0$); 0.978 and 0.271 are thus the eigenvalues of Π_1. A VAR with this Π_1 is stable as the eigenvalues are less than 1.

The reverse characteristic polynomial is

$$\begin{aligned} |I - \rho\Pi_1| &= \left| \begin{bmatrix} 1 & 0 \\ 0 & 1 \end{bmatrix} - \begin{bmatrix} 5/8\rho & 1/2\rho \\ 1/4\rho & 5/8\rho \end{bmatrix} \right| \\ &= \left| \begin{bmatrix} 1 - 5/8\rho & -1/2\rho \\ -1/4\rho & 1 - 5/8\rho \end{bmatrix} \right| \\ &= (1 - 5/8\rho)^2 - 1/8\rho^2 \\ &= (1 - 0.978\rho)(1 - 0.271\rho) \end{aligned}$$

$$(14.21)$$

with roots of $\rho_1 = 1/0.978 = 1.022$ and $\rho_1 = 1/0.271 = 3.690$, which are the reciprocals of the roots of the characteristic polynomial and greater than 1, and hence the model is stable. One point to note about the roots is that one of them is quite close to unity and so on the borderline of instability.

In the second example there is a minor change to one of the elements of Π_1, which is now

$$\Pi_1 = \begin{bmatrix} 5/8 & 1/2 \\ 1/4 & 2/3 \end{bmatrix} \qquad (14.22)$$

with the eigenvalues obtained as the roots of

$$\begin{aligned} |\Pi_1 - vI| &= (5/8 - v)(2/3 - v) - 1/8 \\ &= 7/24 - 31/24v + v^2 \\ &= (1 - v)(7/24 - v) \quad (14.23) \end{aligned}$$

The eigenvalues are $v_1 = 1$ and $v_2 = 7/24$. Π_1 has a unit root and with this specification the VAR is unstable. (The roots of the reverse polynomial are 1 and 24/7.)

The reverse characteristic polynomial arises quite naturally in the context of a VAR model because it is just the determinant of $A(L) = I - \Pi_1 L$, with L taking the role of the artificial variable ρ. Hence, the condition for stability could equally be stated as the roots of $|A(L)|$ have modulus greater than 1.

In assessing stability it turns out to be sufficient to look at the first order VAR, as a pth order

VAR, $p > 1$, can always be reformulated as a first order system by putting it in what is known as the companion form. Consider the pth order VAR given by

$$y_t = \mu + \Pi_1 y_{t-1} + \Pi_2 y_{t-2} + \cdots$$
$$+ \Pi_p y_{t-p} + \varepsilon_t \qquad (14.24)$$

The companion form is:

$$Y_t = A_0 + A_1 Y_{t-1} + E_t$$

which can be written as

$$A(L)Y_t = A_0 + E_t \qquad (14.25)$$

where $A(L) = I_{kp} - A_1 L$ and I_{kp} is the identity matrix of order $kp \times kp$; $Y_t = (y_t, y_{t-1}, \ldots, y_{t-p+1})'$, $A_0 = (\mu, 0, \ldots, 0)'$, $E_t = (\varepsilon_t, 0, \ldots, 0)'$ and

$$A_1 = \begin{bmatrix} \Pi_1 & \Pi_2 & \cdots & \Pi_{p-1} & \Pi_p \\ I & 0 & \cdots & 0 & 0 \\ 0 & I & \cdots & 0 & 0 \\ 0 & 0 & \cdots & 0 & 0 \\ \vdots & \vdots & \cdots & \vdots & \vdots \\ 0 & & \cdots & I & 0 \end{bmatrix}$$

For $p = 2$ we obtain:

$$\begin{pmatrix} y_t \\ y_{t-1} \end{pmatrix} = \begin{pmatrix} \mu \\ 0 \end{pmatrix} + \begin{bmatrix} \Pi_1 & \Pi_2 \\ I & 0 \end{bmatrix} \begin{pmatrix} y_{t-1} \\ y_{t-2} \end{pmatrix}$$
$$+ \begin{pmatrix} \varepsilon_t \\ 0 \end{pmatrix}$$

For $p = 3$ we obtain:

$$\begin{pmatrix} y_t \\ y_{t-1} \\ y_{t-2} \end{pmatrix} = \begin{pmatrix} \mu \\ 0 \\ 0 \end{pmatrix} + \begin{bmatrix} \Pi_1 & \Pi_2 & \Pi_3 \\ I & 0 & 0 \\ 0 & I & 0 \end{bmatrix} \begin{pmatrix} y_{t-1} \\ y_{t-2} \\ y_{t-3} \end{pmatrix}$$
$$+ \begin{pmatrix} \varepsilon_t \\ 0 \\ 0 \end{pmatrix}$$

Stability requires the eigenvalues of A_1 to have modulus less than 1; equivalently in terms of the

reverse characteristic polynomial, the roots of $A(\rho) = I_{kp} - A_1 \rho$ have modulus greater than 1. The roots of $A(\rho)$ are obtained as the solution of

$$|I_{kp} - \rho A_1| = 0$$

which is identical to

$$|I - \rho \Pi_1 - \rho^2 \Pi_2 \cdots - \rho^p \Pi_p| = 0$$

see Lütkepohl (1991, p. 12). Practically a number of econometric software packages, for example RATS and TSP, have routines to calculate the eigenvalues of a matrix, so the condition in terms of the eigenvalues of A_1 is easier to check.

Consider the second order system in two variables (that is $k = 2$) defined by the following matrices:

$$\Pi_1 L = \begin{bmatrix} 5/8L & 5/16L \\ 3/4L & 3/16L \end{bmatrix}$$

and

$$\Pi_2 L^2 = \begin{bmatrix} -1/8L^2 & -1/4L^2 \\ -1/4L^2 & 3/4L^2 \end{bmatrix} \qquad (14.26)$$

Then in companion form this is:

$$\begin{pmatrix} y_{1t} \\ y_{2t} \\ y_{1t-1} \\ y_{2t-1} \end{pmatrix} = \begin{pmatrix} \mu_1 \\ \mu_2 \\ 0 \\ 0 \end{pmatrix}$$

$$+ \begin{bmatrix} 5/8 & 5/16 & -1/8 & -1/4 \\ 3/4 & 3/16 & -1/4 & 3/4 \\ 1 & 0 & 0 & 0 \\ 0 & 1 & 0 & 0 \end{bmatrix} \begin{pmatrix} y_{1t-1} \\ y_{2t-1} \\ y_{1t-2} \\ y_{2t-2} \end{pmatrix}$$

$$+ \begin{pmatrix} \varepsilon_t \\ 0 \\ 0 \\ 0 \end{pmatrix} \qquad (14.27)$$

To assess stability we need to obtain the eigenvalues of A_1, known as the eigenvalues of the companion matrix. As the determinant polynomial is fourth order there are four roots:

Root:	v_1	v_2	v_3	v_4
Real	1.0	−0.947	0.380	0.380
Imaginary	0	−0	−0.144	0.144
Modulus	1.0	−0.947	−0.406	0.406

Although three of the roots have modulus less than 1, the first root is a unit root and the stability condition is not satisfied.

14.2.5 What to do if there is a unit root

As noted in section **14.2.2** one possible response to a unit root is to formulate the VAR in the first differences of the variables; that is define $\Delta y_{it} \equiv y_{it} - y_{it-1}$ and $\Delta y_t \equiv (\Delta y_{1t}, \Delta y_{2t}, \ldots, \Delta y_{kt})'$ and estimate

$$\Delta y_t = \mu^* + \Pi_1^* \Delta y_{t-1} + \varepsilon_t^* \qquad (14.28)$$

(One might want to set $\mu^* = 0$ in this model on the grounds that if $\Delta y_t = \Delta y_{t-1} = 0$ is sustained the equation is inconsistent unless $\mu^* = 0$.) However, such a formulation provides no information on the relationship between the levels of the variables in the VAR, and it is this aspect on which economic theory is usually most informative. This option is not, therefore, generally satisfactory even though the VAR in differences models in stationary variables and would be acceptable from a statistical point of view.

A satisfactory alternative arises when the variables in y_t are cointegrated. Suppose the variables in y_t are nonstationary but on differencing once they become stationary, that is they are I(1) and so modelling them using a VAR in levels would reveal a unit root in the autoregressive polynomial. We know from Chapter 8 that a linear combination of I(1) variables can be I(0), a situation summarised with the shorthand CI(1, 1) to indicate that I(1) variables are reduced by one order of integration in a linear combination. In this case the candidate I(0) variables are,

therefore, not just the first differences but also the cointegrating combination(s) formed from the I(1) variables. Note the use of the plural here: when $k > 2$ there may be more than one linear combination of the k I(1) variables which is stationary, each of which is a candidate regressor. Hence a more promising way forward is to formulate models which capture short-run responses and the long-run relationships as represented in the cointegrating combinations. A result due to Engle and Granger (1987), which is part of what is known as the Granger Representation Theorem (implication 4), is of relevance here; it states that if the $k \times 1$ vector of variables y_t is CI(1, 1) then there exists an error correction representation of the general form:

$$\Delta y_t = \alpha z_{t-1} + \Gamma_1 \Delta y_{t-1} + \Gamma_2 \Delta y_{t-2} + \cdots$$
$$+ \Gamma_{p-1} \Delta y_{t-(p-1)} + \vartheta(L)\varepsilon_t \qquad (14.29)$$

where $z_{t-1} = \beta' y_{t-1}$ are the r linear, cointegrating combinations among the k variables, with β the $k \times r$ matrix of r cointegrating vectors. There may be a moving average 'disturbance', $\vartheta(L)\varepsilon_t$, with $\vartheta(L)$ a lag polynomial, but often for practical purposes $\vartheta(L)$ is degenerate, that is the identity matrix which is an assumption we will adopt for the remainder of this chapter. (On estimating VARs with moving average terms see Lütkepohl (1991, part III).)

The interpretation of the error correction representation is appealing: the long-run or equilibrium relationships among the levels of the variables are captured by the cointegrating combinations, $z_{t-1} = \beta' y_{t-1}$; nonzero values of z_{t-1} indicate (lagged) disequilibria which are eradicated through the adjustment coefficients in α, a $k \times r$ matrix of coefficients, with each column associated with one of the r stationary cointegrating combinations; short-run dynamic adjustments are captured by nonzero values for the elements in Γ_i. The error correction representation thus models entirely in the space (that is 'with') I(0) variables: $\beta' y_{t-1}$ is I(0) through cointegration and Δy_t is I(0) by differencing. The remainder of this chapter is concerned with some of the many aspects of the specification of error correction models. In particular, the next section starts with a very simple error correction model to develop some of the key ideas.

14.3 Simple multivariate (vector) error correction models

This is an important section. Through a series of simple numerical examples it develops some key ideas related to the specification and interpretation of error correction models. For a discussion of the connection between cointegration and error correction models see Hylleberg and Mizon (1989b).

14.3.1 A bivariate model

It will be useful in motivating some of the general ideas to consider first a simple numerical example – Example 1 – which involves just two variables y_{1t} and y_{2t} which are treated symmetrically in the sense of modelling both variables. At this stage a 'closed' system is considered: no variables other than y_{1t} and y_{2t} are specified. A simple ECM for y_{1t} and y_{2t} is:

Example 1

$$\Delta y_{1t} = -1/2(y_{1t-1} - 1/8y_{2t-1}) + \varepsilon_{1t}$$
$$\Delta y_{2t} = 1/2(y_{1t-1} - 1/8y_{2t-1}) + \varepsilon_{2t} \quad (14.30)$$

First, note that on setting $\Delta y_{1t} = \Delta y_{1t-1} = \cdots = 0$, $\Delta y_{2t} = \Delta y_{2t-1} = \cdots = 0$, and ε_{1t} and ε_{2t} to their expected values of zero, the implied static steady state or equilibrium is obtained: $y_{1t} - 1/8y_{2t} = 0$. Define $\xi_t = y_{1t} - 1/8y_{2t}$, then to the extent that $\xi_{t-1} \neq 0$ there is disequilibrium last period causing Δy_{1t} and Δy_{2t} to change and correct the disequilibrium. The adjustment coefficients are those on the disequilibrium terms in the two equations; in the Δy_{1t} equation the adjustment coefficient is negative, here it is

$-1/2$ because $\xi_t > 0 \Rightarrow y_{1t-1} > 1/8y_{2t-1}$, so that y_{1t} should decrease to move towards equilibrium; conversely $\xi_t < 0 \Rightarrow y_{1t-1} < 1/8y_{2t-1}$ so that y_{1t} should increase to move towards equilibrium. The adjustment coefficient in the Δy_{2t} equation is positive, here it is $+1/2$; again this helps to correct the disequilibrium, for example if $\xi_t > 0$ then $\Delta y_{2t} > 0$ ensures a movement closer to equilibrium. Alternatively note that $1/2(y_{1t-1} - 1/8y_{2t-1}) = -1/16(y_{2t-1} - 8y_{1t-1})$ so the second equation could be written as

$$\Delta y_{2t} = -1/16(y_{2t-1} - 8y_{1t-1}) + \varepsilon_{2t} \quad (14.31)$$

and Δy_{2t} can be regarded as correcting on its own disequilibrium. Which way we choose to write the equilibrium is arbitrary at this stage since y_{1t} and y_{2t} are treated symmetrically. Notice, however, that with two variables at most one equilibrium relationship can be defined even though it can be transformed – or reparameterised – in an infinite number of ways.

This numerical example can be explained further if it is written in matrix–vector form.

$$\begin{pmatrix} \Delta y_{1t} \\ \Delta y_{2t} \end{pmatrix} = \begin{bmatrix} -1/2, & 1/16 \\ 1/2, & -1/16 \end{bmatrix} \begin{pmatrix} y_{1t-1} \\ y_{2t-1} \end{pmatrix}$$
$$+ \begin{pmatrix} \varepsilon_{1t} \\ \varepsilon_{2t} \end{pmatrix} \quad (14.32)$$

Say

$$\Delta y_t = \Pi y_{t-1} + \varepsilon_t \quad \text{where } y_t = \begin{pmatrix} y_{1t} \\ y_{2t} \end{pmatrix},$$

$$\Pi = \begin{bmatrix} -1/2 & 1/16 \\ 1/2 & -1/16 \end{bmatrix} \quad \text{and}$$

$$\varepsilon_t = \begin{pmatrix} \varepsilon_{1t} \\ \varepsilon_{2t} \end{pmatrix} \quad (14.33)$$

An interesting way of rewriting the coefficient matrix is to separate out the adjustment coefficients and the equilibrium coefficients, these are denoted α and β, respectively; in the numerical example $\alpha' = (-1/2, 1/2)$ and $\beta' = (1, -1/8)$.

Note that the equilibrium combination is $\beta'y_t = \xi_t$, and $\Pi = \alpha\beta'$, so the following are equivalent ways of writing this example:

$$\Delta y_t = \Pi y_{t-1} + \varepsilon_t \quad \Delta y_t = \alpha(\beta'y_{t-1}) + \varepsilon_t$$

$$(14.34)$$

In the numerical example:

$$\begin{pmatrix} \Delta y_{1t} \\ \Delta y_{2t} \end{pmatrix} = \begin{bmatrix} -1/2 & 1/16 \\ 1/2 & -1/16 \end{bmatrix} \begin{pmatrix} y_{1t-1} \\ y_{2t-1} \end{pmatrix} + \begin{pmatrix} \varepsilon_{1t} \\ \varepsilon_{2t} \end{pmatrix}$$

which is the same as

$$\begin{pmatrix} \Delta y_{1t} \\ \Delta y_{2t} \end{pmatrix} = \begin{bmatrix} -1/2 & (1, -1/8) \\ 1/2 & \end{bmatrix} \begin{pmatrix} y_{1t-1} \\ y_{2t-1} \end{pmatrix} + \begin{pmatrix} \varepsilon_{1t} \\ \varepsilon_{2t} \end{pmatrix}$$

The second way is useful because it emphasises the concepts of adjustment through the α coefficients and (dis)equilibrium through the linear combination $\beta'y_{t-1}$.

This decomposition is even more useful when we consider the time series properties of the data. Suppose y_{1t} and y_{2t} are I(1) then Δy_{1t} and Δy_{2t} are I(0); in order to balance this time series property on the left-hand side of the equation the right-hand side must also be I(0). However, at first sight there seems to be a contradiction because the lagged levels of y_{1t} and y_{2t} appear on the r.h.s., but the levels are I(1) and a linear combination of I(1) variables is, in general, I(1). (Remember that ε_{1t} and ε_{2t} are I(0) by assumption.) So what can solve this puzzle? As we have seen – see section **14.2.5** – the solution lies in whether there is a linear combination of I(1) variables which is I(0), if so the equation is balanced in its time series properties and when this occurs y_{1t} and y_{2t} are said to be *cointegrated*. In the numerical example the cointegrating combination is

$$\beta'y_{t-1} = (1, -1/8)y_{t-1} = y_{1t-1} - 1/8y_{2t-1}$$

and β' is the *cointegrating vector*; although note that any scalar multiple of this linear combination is also a cointegrating combination. We will show how to check the stationarity of this combination directly in a moment; but before doing this it will be useful to write the ECM in its VAR form, that is in the levels and lags of y_{1t} and y_{2t}. Again consider Example 1 which can be written in the following, VAR, form:

$$y_{1t} = 1/2y_{1t-1} + 1/16y_{2t-1} + \varepsilon_{1t}$$
$$y_{2t} = 1/2y_{1t-1} + 15/16y_{2t-1} + \varepsilon_{2t} \quad (14.35)$$

or more simply

VAR form	ECM form
$y_t = \Pi_1 y_{t-1} + \varepsilon_t$	$\Delta y_t = \Pi y_{t-1} + \varepsilon_t$
	where $\Pi = \Pi_1 - I$

where I is the identity matrix of the same order as the number of variables in y_t. Note that the ECM form is easily obtained by subtracting

$$y_{t-1} = \begin{bmatrix} 1 & 0 \\ 0 & 1 \end{bmatrix} y_{t-1}$$

from both sides of the VAR. In the numerical example the coefficient matrices are:

$$\Pi_1 = \begin{bmatrix} 1/2 & 1/16 \\ 1/2 & 15/16 \end{bmatrix} \quad \Pi = \begin{bmatrix} -1/2 & 1/16 \\ 1/2 & -1/16 \end{bmatrix}$$

Now check that the linear combination

$$(1, -1/8)y_{t-1} = y_{1t-1} - 1/8y_{2t-1}$$

is indeed a cointegrating combination. To do this first move the time subscript forward one period, then write the cointegrating combination substituting for y_{1t} and y_{2t} from the VAR:

$$y_{1t} - 1/8y_{2t} = 1/2y_{1t-1} + 1/16y_{2t-1}$$
$$+ \varepsilon_{1t} - 1/8(1/2y_{1t-1}$$
$$+ 15/16y_{2t-1} + \varepsilon_{2t})$$
$$= 7/16(y_{1t-1} - 1/8y_{2t-1})$$
$$+ \varepsilon_{1t} - 1/8\varepsilon_{2t} \quad (14.36)$$

From earlier $\xi_t \equiv (y_{1t} - 1/8y_{2t})$, therefore the last line is:

$$\xi_t = 7/16\xi_{t-1} + \varepsilon_t^*$$

where $\varepsilon_t^* = \varepsilon_{1t} - 1/8\varepsilon_{2t}$. As $|7/16| < 1$, ξ_t is a stationary process. Notice that it would have made no difference here if the cointegrating vector had been scaled by, say, 100 since if the linear combination $(1, -1/8)y_{t-1}$ is a stationary combination then so is $100(1, -1/8)y_{t-1}$. Indeed, as the scaling factor of 100 was chosen arbitrarily to illustrate the point, we know that scaling ξ_t by $\kappa \neq 0$ will result in a stationary combination. We can get an important point from this illustration: what has been done in defining ξ_t is to normalise the cointegrating vector $\beta' = (\beta_{11}, \beta_{21})$ so that the first element, that is β_{11}, is equal to 1. This normalisation is not unique but it is often helpful to think of the equilibrium as determining a particular variable, for example $y_{1t} = 1/8y_{2t} + \xi_t$.

Of course since $\Pi = \alpha\beta'$, if β' is scaled by κ, α must be scaled by κ^{-1} to ensure that Π is unchanged; that is $\Pi = \alpha\kappa^{-1}\kappa\beta' = \alpha\beta'$. In general κ is an $r \times r$ matrix, where r is the number of cointegrating vectors. In the numerical example $r = 1$ and taking $\kappa = 100$ the scaling results in:

$$\begin{pmatrix} -1/2 \\ 1/2 \end{pmatrix}((1/100)100(1, -1/8))$$

$$= \begin{pmatrix} -1/200 \\ 1/200 \end{pmatrix}(100, -12.5)$$

What these examples show is that while the error correction and equilibrium coefficients cannot be uniquely determined, a normalisation can be chosen which helps their interpretation in an economic context. Technically the cointegration 'space' can be isolated but not *the* cointegrating vector(s); this is discussed in greater detail below. The standard assumption in this chapter is that where there are r cointegrating vectors, each cointegrating vector is normalised

on a different variable, with the coefficient on the normalising variable taking the value 1. For more on the role of normalisation see Phillips (1991) and Boswijk (1996).

14.3.2   The eigenvalues of Π and the existence of cointegrating vectors

So will it always be the case that a cointegrating vector exists? Intuition suggests that this cannot be the case. Suppose y_{1t} is unrelated to y_{2t} or y_{1t} and y_{2t} are part of a larger system, then we should not be able to find a cointegrating vector for y_{1t} and y_{2t}. This prompts the question: what particular features of the set-up so far alert us to the existence of a cointegrating vector? Notice that the first row of Π in (14.32) can be obtained from the second row by multiplying by -1, or the first column can be obtained from the second by multiplying by -8; Π is an example of a matrix which does not have independent rows or columns. Technically Π is a matrix with less than full rank; in this case its rank is 1, that is there is only 1 independent row or column in Π even though it is a 2×2 matrix. Π is said to have *reduced* or deficient rank.

There are related characteristics of Π which alert us to its deficient rank. Notice that its determinant is 0: $|\Pi| = (-1/2)(-1/16) - (1/2)(1/16) = 0$ and one of the eigenvalues of Π is zero. From section **14.2.4** to obtain the eigenvalues, v, of Π it is necessary to solve the characteristic equation given by:

$$|\Pi - vI| = 0 \quad \text{where } v \text{ is a scalar}$$

In this example:

$$\Pi - vI = \begin{bmatrix} -1/2 & 1/16 \\ 1/2 & -1/16 \end{bmatrix} - \begin{bmatrix} v & 0 \\ 0 & v \end{bmatrix}$$

$$= \begin{bmatrix} -1/2 - v & 1/16 \\ 1/2 & -1/16 - v \end{bmatrix} \quad (14.37)$$

therefore

$$|\Pi - \nu I| = (1/2 + \nu)(1/16 + \nu)$$
$$- (1/2)(1/16) = 0$$
$$= 1/32 + 9/16\nu + \nu^2 - 1/32 = 0$$
$$= \nu^2 + 9/16\nu = 0$$
$$= \nu(\nu + 9/16) = 0$$

Hence, this quadratic equation is satisfied by the roots $\nu_1 = 0$ and $\nu_2 = -9/16$; that is there are two eigenvalues obtained as the solutions to the characteristic equation. The zero value for one of the eigenvalues alerts us to the deficient rank of Π. In general the number of nonzero eigenvalues of Π is its rank.

Π can only be completely deficient in rank, that is rank$(\Pi) = 0$, if it is the zero matrix. However, in the sense of looking for a cointegrating vector, this order of deficiency is too much, for if $\Pi = 0$ then $\Delta y_t = \Pi y_{t-1} + \varepsilon_t \Rightarrow \Delta y_t = \varepsilon_t$ so that the VAR is stationary in first differences (so the components of y_t each have a unit root) but there is no cointegrating vector.

The basic model is now generalised in two directions in order to make it more relevant for empirical analysis. In the first generalisation it is extended to more than two variables in the VAR, which allows the possibility of more than one cointegrating vector; and in the second generalisation it is extended to allow longer lags.

14.3.3   More than one cointegrating vector

Consider the ECM in the three variables y_{1t}, y_{2t} and y_{3t}, given in Example 2 below.

Example 2

ECM	Equilibrium

$$\Delta y_{1t} = -1/2\xi_{1t-1} \qquad \xi_{1t} = y_{1t} - 1/8y_{2t}$$
$$+ 1/4\xi_{2t-1} + \varepsilon_{1t}$$
$$\Delta y_{2t} = 1/8\xi_{1t-1} \qquad \xi_{2t} = y_{2t} - 1/4y_{3t}$$
$$- 5/8\xi_{2t-1} + \varepsilon_{2t}$$
$$\Delta y_{3t} = 1/4\xi_{1t-1}$$
$$+ 3/8\xi_{2t-1} + \varepsilon_{3t} \qquad (14.38)$$

Matrix form

$$\begin{pmatrix} \Delta y_{1t} \\ \Delta y_{2t} \\ \Delta y_{3t} \end{pmatrix} = \begin{bmatrix} -1/2 & 1/4 \\ 1/8 & -5/8 \\ 1/4 & 3/8 \end{bmatrix} \begin{pmatrix} \xi_{1t-1} \\ \xi_{2t-1} \end{pmatrix}$$
$$+ \begin{pmatrix} \varepsilon_{1t} \\ \varepsilon_{2t} \\ \varepsilon_{3t} \end{pmatrix}$$

$$= \begin{bmatrix} -1/2 & 1/4 \\ 1/8 & -5/8 \\ 1/4 & 3/8 \end{bmatrix}$$

$$\times \begin{bmatrix} 1 & -1/8 & 0 \\ 0 & 1 & -1/4 \end{bmatrix} \begin{pmatrix} y_{1t-1} \\ y_{2t-1} \\ y_{3t-1} \end{pmatrix}$$

$$+ \begin{pmatrix} \varepsilon_{1t} \\ \varepsilon_{2t} \\ \varepsilon_{3t} \end{pmatrix}$$

Eigenvalues: $(-0.7928, -0.4416, 0)$

$$\Pi = \begin{bmatrix} -1/2 & 5/16 & -1/16 \\ 1/8 & -41/64 & 5/32 \\ 1/4 & -11/32 & -3/32 \end{bmatrix}$$

Adjustment Coefficients

$$\alpha = \begin{bmatrix} -1/2 & 1/4 \\ 1/8 & -5/8 \\ 1/4 & 3/8 \end{bmatrix}$$

Cointegrating Vectors

$$\beta' = \begin{bmatrix} 1 & -1/8 & 0 \\ 0 & 1 & -1/4 \end{bmatrix}$$

An interpretation of the ECM in three variables is a straightforward extension of the two variable case. With three variables it is possible to define up to two independent equilibrium relationships; this example illustrates a choice of two with definitions given by ξ_{1t} and ξ_{2t}, where these have been normalised on y_{1t} and y_{2t}, respectively. The fact that some restrictions have been imposed on the coefficients in the cointegrating vectors is important. Note that ξ_{1t} specifies a zero restriction on y_{3t} and ξ_{2t} specifies a zero restriction on y_{1t}, this is to ensure that the two equilibria are distinguishable or 'identified'; this is discussed further below. The own adjustment coefficients are $-1/2$ for ξ_{1t-1} in the y_{1t} equation and $-5/8$ for ξ_{2t-1} in the y_{2t} equation.

The rank of Π is 2 indicating that the full rank is reduced by 1 and there are, therefore, two cointegrating vectors. Suppose the rank of Π is not known beforehand (and the number of cointegrating or equilibrium relationships was not known) and the problem was to try and infer it; then when Π has more than two columns it is quite difficult to infer its rank simply by examining the rows or columns for redundancies – another method is needed. While calculating the determinant helps, a matrix with any deficient rank has a zero determinant, so that would not tell us the extent of the reduced rank. One solution to this problem is to calculate the eigenvalues of the Π matrix, then the number of nonzero eigenvalues is the rank of the matrix. In this case the eigenvalues for the Π matrix are $(-0.7928, -0.4416, 0)$; two of these are nonzero and one is zero, confirming the existence of two cointegrating vectors. Suppose the example is reworked with only one cointegrating vector which we choose to be ξ_{1t}, so all terms (including the adjustment coefficients) involving ξ_{2t-1} are set to zero; Π is still a 3×3 matrix but it can only be of rank 1 because α is 3×1 and β' is 1×3. The eigenvalues are now $(-0.5156, 0, 0)$, confirming that Π is rank 1 and there is only one cointegrating vector.

14.3.4 Longer lags

The other direction in which the model needs to be generalised is to allow for longer lags. For example, in the bivariate case suppose the ECM is:

Example 3

$$\Delta y_{1t} = -1/2(y_{1t-1} - 1/8y_{2t-1})$$
$$+ 1/8\Delta y_{1t-1} + 1/4\Delta y_{2t-1} + \varepsilon_{1t}$$
$$\Delta y_{2t} = 1/2(y_{1t-1} - 1/8y_{2t-1})$$
$$+ 1/4\Delta y_{1t-1} - 3/4\Delta y_{2t-1} + \varepsilon_{2t}$$

$$(14.39)$$

Matrix form

$$\Delta y_t = \Pi y_{t-1} + \Gamma_1 \Delta y_{t-1} + \varepsilon_t$$

where

$$\Pi = \alpha\beta' = \begin{pmatrix} -1/2 \\ 1/2 \end{pmatrix}(1, \ -1/8)$$

$$= \begin{bmatrix} -1/2 & 1/16 \\ 1/2 & -1/16 \end{bmatrix}$$

and

$$\Gamma_1 = \begin{bmatrix} 1/8 & 1/4 \\ 1/4 & -3/4 \end{bmatrix}$$

The addition of lags in Δy_{1t} and Δy_{2t} could, for example, be justified by the need to ensure that ε_{1t} and ε_{2t} are white noise and their omission distorts the dynamic (short-run) pattern of response. On the assumption that y_{1t} and y_{2t} are I(1), Δy_{1t} and Δy_{2t} are I(0) so the time series balance of the ECM is maintained provided $y_{1t} - 1/8y_{2t}$ is a cointegrating combination. The VAR corresponding to this extended model is:

$$y_{1t} = 5/8y_{1t-1} + 5/16y_{2t-1} - 1/8y_{1t-2}$$
$$- 1/4y_{2t-2} + \varepsilon_{1t}$$
$$y_{2t} = 3/4y_{1t-1} + 3/16y_{2t-1} - 1/4y_{1t-2}$$
$$+ 3/4y_{2t-2} + \varepsilon_{2t} \qquad (14.40)$$

That is

$$y_t = \Pi_1 y_{t-1} + \Pi_2 y_{t-2} + \varepsilon_t$$

where

$$\Pi_1 = \begin{bmatrix} 5/8 & 5/16 \\ 3/4 & 3/16 \end{bmatrix}$$

and

$$\Pi_2 = \begin{bmatrix} -1/8 & -1/4 \\ -1/4 & 3/4 \end{bmatrix}$$

The relationship between the coefficients in the VAR and in the ECM is

$$\Pi = \Pi_1 + \Pi_2 - I \quad \text{and} \quad \Gamma_1 = -\Pi_2$$

More generally if the VAR is a pth order autoregression given by

$$y_t = \Pi_1 y_{t-1} + \Pi_2 y_{t-2} + \cdots + \Pi_p y_{t-p} + \varepsilon_t$$

$$(14.41)$$

then the ECM is

$$\Delta y_t = \Pi y_{t-1} + \Gamma_1 \Delta y_{t-1} + \Gamma_2 \Delta y_{t-2} + \cdots$$
$$+ \Gamma_{p-1} \Delta y_{t-(p-1)} + \varepsilon_t \quad (14.42)$$

with $\Pi = \Pi_1 + \Pi_2 \cdots + \Pi_p - I$ and $\Gamma_i = -(\Pi_{i+1} + \Pi_{i+2} + \cdots + \Pi_p)$ for $i = 1, \ldots, p-1$.

The extension to include more lags does not alter the analysis of the number of cointegrating vectors. The numerical example has been constructed to have one cointegrating vector and, just as in the two previous examples, this can be checked by calculating the eigenvalues of Π; of course for Π in this example these have already calculated as $\upsilon = (0, -9/16)$. The rank of $\Pi = \alpha\beta'$ is equal to the number of cointegrating vectors; denote this rank as r, then r is the column dimension of α and the column dimension of β (that is the row dimension of β').

14.3.5 The multivariate model: the existence of a unit root and reduced rank of Π

In this section we show the connection between the existence of a unit root and the reduced rank of Π in the multivariate model. It provides a link with section **14.2.4**, which was concerned with the role of the eigenvalues of Π_1 in assessing the stability and stationarity of a VAR.

To emphasise the link between the existence of a unit root and reduced rank of Π the first order VAR is considered:

$$y_t = \Pi_1 y_{t-1} + \varepsilon_t$$

which has an equivalent ECM representation as $\Delta y_t = \Pi y_{t-1} + \varepsilon_t$. This VAR can also be written as:

$$(I - \Pi_1 L)y_t = \varepsilon_t$$

say

$$A(L)y_t = \varepsilon_t \quad \text{where} \quad A(L) = (I - \Pi_1 L)$$

Now consider what is meant by the existence of a unit root in the time series process determining y_t. Recall that in the case of the first order univariate process $y_t = \phi_1 y_{t-1} + \varepsilon_t$ stability required $|\phi_1| < 1$. If $\phi_1 \geq 1$ the impact of a shock to ε_t would either be persistent, $\phi_1 = 1$, or explosive, $\phi_1 > 1$. In the case of a first order VAR the condition for stability is that all eigenvalues of Π_1 have modulus less than 1 or, equivalently, that the roots of the reverse characteristic polynomial have modulus greater than 1, sometimes expressed as the roots lie outside the unit circle. Consider a graph with real numbers, h, on the horizontal axis and imaginary numbers, v times i, on the vertical axis, where $i \equiv \sqrt{-1}$; the unit circle is a circle of radius 1 with origin 0 on this graph. The unit circle, therefore, cuts these axes at $+1$ and -1 on the real line and $+1$ and -1 on the line of imaginary numbers. For stability the roots of the reverse characteristic polynomial lie outside the unit circle, whereas the corresponding eigenvalues lie inside the unit circle. (In Example 1 the eigenvalues are $+1$ and $+7/16$, so the roots of the reverse polynomial are 1 and 16/7 and, hence, because one of the roots is $+1$ the condition for stability is not met.)

Recall from elementary matrix algebra that for a square matrix A, $A^{-1} = \text{adj}[A]/|A|$ and hence $|A|A^{-1} = \text{adj}[A]$, where $\text{adj}[A]$ is the adjoint matrix, that is the transpose of the matrix of cofactors of A – see, for example, Sydsaeter and

Hammond (1995). Premultiplying $A(L)$ by its adjoint we obtain:

$$|A(L)|A(L)^{-1}A(L)y_t = \text{adj}[A(L)]\varepsilon_t$$

that is

$$|A(L)|y_t = \text{adj}[A(L)]\varepsilon_t \qquad (14.43)$$

Now $|A(L)|$ is a kth order (scalar) polynomial in the lag operator L which is applied to each component of y_t. If y_t is I(1) then $|A(L)|$ can be factored into the unit root operator $(1-L)$ and a polynomial of one lower order, say $A^*(L)$. The unit root operator applies to each variable in y_t. Notice that in order to determine the number of cointegrating vectors in the ECM version of the VAR we assessed the rank of $\Pi = \sum \Pi_i - I$, with the number of nonzero eigenvalues giving the rank of Π and cointegration implying reduced rank. Now in order to assess whether there is a unit root in the process generating y_t we evaluate $|A(L)| = |I - \sum \Pi_i(L)|$, and note that the existence of a unit root implies $|A(1)| = |I - \sum \Pi_i| = -|\Pi| = 0$. Hence if there is a unit root in the VAR, Π will be of reduced rank implying that there is at least one cointegrating vector.

It may be easier to see what is happening here if Example 1 is used to illustrate the ideas. To recap, in this case the VAR is

$$y_t = \Pi_1 y_{t-1} + \varepsilon_t \quad \text{where}$$
$$\Pi_1 = \begin{bmatrix} 1/2 & 1/16 \\ 1/2 & 15/16 \end{bmatrix} \qquad (14.44)$$

and

$$A(L) = I - \Pi_1 L$$
$$= \begin{bmatrix} 1 & 0 \\ 0 & 1 \end{bmatrix} - \begin{bmatrix} 1/2L & 1/16L \\ 1/2L & 15/16L \end{bmatrix}$$

therefore

$$|A(L)| = 1 - (23/16)L + (7/16)L^2$$

with roots of $+1$ and $+16/7$; the existence of a unit root means we can factor

$$|A(L)| = |A^*(L)(1-L)|$$
$$= (1 - 7/16L)(1-L)$$

where $A^*(L) = (1 - 7/16L)$. Notice that $|A(1)| = 0$, which is analogous to the univariate case when a unit root exists. On the left-hand side of (14.43) we have in this case,

$$(1 - 7/16L)(1-L)y_t$$

that is

$$(1 - 7/16L)\begin{pmatrix} \Delta y_{1t} \\ \Delta y_{2t} \end{pmatrix}$$

Evidently a unit root can be factored out for each variable in the VAR. On the right-hand side we have $\text{adj}[A(L)]\varepsilon_t$, explicitly in this case,

$$\begin{bmatrix} 1 - 15/16L & 1/16L \\ 1/2L & 1 - 1/2L \end{bmatrix}\begin{pmatrix} \varepsilon_{1t} \\ \varepsilon_{2t} \end{pmatrix}$$
$$= \begin{pmatrix} (1 - 15/16L)\varepsilon_{1t} + (1/16L)\varepsilon_{2t} \\ (1/2L)\varepsilon_{1t} + (1 - 1/2L)\varepsilon_{2t} \end{pmatrix}$$
$$\qquad (14.45)$$

Bringing both sides of the VAR together we see that the model in the first difference, Δy_t, is stable:

$$\Delta y_{1t} = 7/16\Delta y_{1t-1} + \varepsilon_{1t}^*$$
$$\Delta y_{2t} = 7/16\Delta y_{2t-1} + \varepsilon_{2t}^* \qquad (14.46)$$

where

$$\varepsilon_{1t}^* = \varepsilon_{1t} - 15/16\varepsilon_{1t-1} + 1/16\varepsilon_{2t-1}$$
$$\varepsilon_{2t}^* = 1/2\varepsilon_{1t} + \varepsilon_{2t} - 1/2\varepsilon_{2t-1} \qquad (14.47)$$

In this case there are two roots one of which, $+16/7$, satisfies the condition for stability but the other, $+1$, does not; in such a situation the model in first differences, which corresponds to factoring out the unit root, is stable.

14.4 Testing for cointegration

In general the number of cointegrating relations among a set of k variables is not known. The limits are 0 and k, and while economic theory should provide a guide to the number of equilibrium relationships there remains the problem of determining the number in practice. There are several tests for cointegration rank – see, for example, Watson (1994) for a summary – the one we describe here, due to Johansen (1988, 1992a), is the most popular and is widely programmed in econometric software – see, for example CATS (Cointegration Analysis of Time Series) by Hansen and Juselius (1995) in RATS (Regression Analysis of Time Series) by Doan (1996).

14.4.1 Establishing a firm base for inference on the cointegrating rank

In the Johansen framework the first step is the estimation of a congruent, unrestricted, closed, pth order VAR in k variables. We first explain, or recap, the meaning of these terms. Suppose that economic theory, and perhaps previous empirical work, suggests the existence of equilibrium relationships among k stochastic variables. Linearity of the relationships is assumed, perhaps in the logs of the variables. A modelling framework, which distinguishes between equilibrium and dynamic adjustment to equilibrium, is the multivariate ECM, which in turn is just a reparameterisation of a VAR. That is the VAR in the $k \times 1$ vector y_t is:

$$y_t = \Pi_1 y_{t-1} + \Pi_2 y_{t-2} + \cdots$$
$$+ \Pi_p y_{t-p} + \Psi D_t + \varepsilon_t \qquad (14.48)$$

which can be reparameterised as an ECM

$$\Delta y_t = \Pi y_{t-1} + \Gamma_1 \Delta y_{t-1} + \Gamma_2 y_{t-2} + \cdots$$
$$+ \Gamma_{p-1} \Delta y_{t-(p-1)} + \Psi D_t + \varepsilon_t \qquad (14.49)$$

All terms have so far been explained with the exception of ΨD_t. D_t is a $d \times 1$ vector of deterministic terms, typical elements would be a 1 to capture the constant, previously designated μ_{i0}, in each equation, the time trend t and centred seasonal dummy variables, should they be needed, and other 'intervention' dummy variables which will depend upon the particular circumstances of the empirical application. Centred seasonal dummies sum to zero over four/twelve consecutive quarters/months if the data is quarterly/monthly and only $(sf - 1)$ seasonal dummy variables are needed if a constant is included, where sf is the seasonal frequency of the data. Ψ is the associated $k \times d$ matrix of coefficients on these deterministic variables, with one row for each equation.

The VAR is pth order in the sense that the longest lag is of length p, which translates into a lag of $p - 1$ on Δy_t in the ECM. There are k equations in the VAR/ECM so the system is closed, no variables are left unexplained, apart from conditioning on the deterministic variables in D_t; further no current dated, stochastic variables appear in the VAR/ECM, so the model is a reduced form rather than a 'conditional' model. All conditioning on the stochastic variables has been solved out (see section **14.5.1** below for more on this distinction). The lag length and information set – that is the choice of the variables in y_t and D_t – need to be determined in a practical application.

The central model design criteria are captured in the congruency of the estimated model. Constituents of this criteria include: equation residuals which are not serially correlated; residuals which are not heteroscedastic conditional on the information set $\{ y_{t-1}, \ldots, y_{t-p}, D_t \}$; residuals which are consistent with the hypothesis that the innovations are normally distributed (although Johansen (1995a, p. 20) relaxes this last requirement so the residuals 'do not deviate too much from Gaussian white noise'). Ideally we would also add that the parameters, at least the long-run parameters, are constant. Tests are available for each of these criteria.

The key decision variable is often the lag length p, for which a common practice is to choose p by an information criteria, such as AIC or SIC, subject to that choice passing a test, for example the Lagrange-Multiplier test, for the absence of serial correlation. Intervention dummy variables of the 0, 1 form may be needed for exceptional events to remove 'outliers' which contribute to evidence of nonnormality and heteroscedasticity – see Clements and Mizon (1991) – or it may be necessary to introduce conditioning variables *ex post* as in Johansen and Juselius (1992), who used the growth rate in the world price of oil in real terms in an analysis of purchasing power parity and uncovered interest rate parity. The use of such 'intervention' variables is not generally to be encouraged, although it may be practically necessary in some circumstances to maintain the congruency of the estimated model.

Finally, the VAR/ECM is unrestricted in the following sense: no prior imposition or assumption is made about the rank of Π; initially in the decomposition $\Pi = \alpha\beta'$, α and β are $k \times k$ matrices and what is established by means of a series of hypothesis tests is whether any columns of β, that is rows of β', are statistically indistinguishable from zero vectors. We have seen that the existence of r cointegrating vectors reduces the rank of Π by $k - r$, the extent of this reduced rank being indicated by the number of zero eigenvalues, and allowing the decomposition $\Pi = \alpha\beta'$, where α and β are now $k \times r$ matrices. If this information is imposed the VAR is restricted.

14.4.2 Estimation of the UVAR and test statistics for testing the cointegrating rank (optional)

This section sets out the basic framework of Johansen's formulation and solution of the problem of how to estimate the cointegrating rank of Π and obtain estimators of the long-run and short-run parameters. The references for this section are Johansen (1988), Johansen and

Juselius (1990) and Johansen (1995a); other important contributions have been made by Velu and Reinsel (1987), Ahn and Reinsel (1988, 1990) and Reinsel and Ahn (1992). This section is optional in that it contains material that is at a more advanced level than the rest of the book (but even then it leaves much to be discovered in the references!). It is included to give an idea of how the test statistics, and sequence of tests, in section **14.4.3** are motivated. It can be omitted, although not without loss; the omission will not affect the self-contained nature of the remaining sections.

The multivariate VAR reparameterised in ECM form is

$$\Delta y_t = \Pi y_{t-1} + \Gamma_1 \Delta y_{t-1} + \Gamma_2 \Delta y_{t-2} + \cdots$$
$$+ \Gamma_{p-1} \Delta y_{t-(p-1)} + \Psi D_t + \varepsilon_t$$

$$(14.49 \text{ again})$$

with ε_t independent and identically distributed as multivariate normal with variance–covariance matrix Λ. First, it is convenient to establish the following notation: $Z_{0t} = \Delta y_t$; $Z_{1t} = y_{t-1}$;

$$Z_{2t} = (\Delta y_{t-1}, \dots, \Delta y_{t-(p-1)}, D_t)'$$

$\Gamma = (\Gamma_1, \dots, \Gamma_{p-1}, \Psi)$, with dimensions $k \times 1$, $k \times 1$, $[k(p-1)+d] \times 1$, and $k \times [k(p-1)+d]$, respectively. In this notation the ECM becomes:

$$Z_{0t} = \Pi Z_{1t} + \Gamma Z_{2t} + \varepsilon_t$$

Under the decomposition $\Pi = \alpha\beta'$ this model is

$$Z_{0t} = \alpha\beta' Z_{1t} + \Gamma Z_{2t} + \varepsilon_t \qquad (14.50)$$

This model is nonlinear in that it involves the product of α and β, and also involves the cross-equation restrictions that the ith row of β' is the same whichever equation it appears in. Maximising the log likelihood function $\ln L(\alpha, \beta, \Gamma, \Lambda)$, the first order conditions for estimating Γ are:

$$\sum_{t=1}^{T} (Z_{0t} - \alpha\beta' Z_{1t} - \hat{\Gamma} Z_{2t}) Z_{2t}' = 0 \qquad (14.51)$$

that is, where $\hat{\Gamma}$ is an estimate of Γ,

$$\sum_{t=1}^{T} Z_{0t}Z_{2t}' = \alpha\beta' \sum_{t=1}^{T} Z_{1t}Z_{2t}'$$

$$+ \hat{\Gamma} \sum_{t=1}^{T} Z_{2t}Z_{2t}'$$

In a simpler notation (and dividing by T)

$$M_{02} = \alpha\beta' M_{12} + \hat{\Gamma}M_{22} \qquad (14.52)$$

where the following are defined:

$$M_{ij} = \sum_{t=1}^{T} Z_{it}Z_{jt}'/T \quad \text{for } i, j = 0, 1, 2$$

Postmultiplying (14.52) by M_{22}^{-1} and solving for $\hat{\Gamma}$ as a function of α and β then

$$\hat{\Gamma} = M_{02}M_{22}^{-1} - \alpha\beta' M_{12}M_{22}^{-1} \qquad (14.53)$$

Consider also the following regressions:

$$Z_{0t} = \Omega_{02}Z_{2t} + \eta_t \qquad (14.54)$$

which is the regression of Δy_t on $(\Delta y_{t-1}, \ldots, \Delta y_{t-(p-1)}, D_t)'$, with residual

$$R_{0t} = Z_{0t} - M_{02}M_{22}^{-1}Z_{2t} \qquad (14.55)$$

and

$$Z_{1t} = \Omega_{12}Z_{2t} + \nu_t \qquad (14.56)$$

which is the regression of y_{t-1} on $(\Delta y_{t-1}, \ldots, \Delta y_{t-(p-1)}, D_t)'$ with residual

$$R_{1t} = Z_{1t} - M_{12}M_{22}^{-1}Z_{2t} \qquad (14.57)$$

Note from (14.50) that $\varepsilon_t = Z_{0t} - \alpha\beta'Z_{1t} - \Gamma Z_{2t}$ and, for Γ replaced by its estimator in (14.53), the residual $\hat{\varepsilon}_t$ is:

$$\hat{\varepsilon}_t = Z_{0t} - \alpha\beta'Z_{1t}$$
$$- (M_{02}M_{22}^{-1} - \alpha\beta'M_{12}M_{22}^{-1})Z_{2t}$$
$$= Z_{0t} - M_{02}M_{22}^{-1}Z_{2t}$$
$$- \alpha\beta'(Z_{1t} - M_{12}M_{22}^{-1}Z_{2t})$$
$$= R_{0t} - \alpha\beta'R_{1t} \qquad (14.58)$$

a simple rearrangement of the last line gives

$$R_{0t} = \alpha\beta'R_{1t} + \hat{\varepsilon}_t \qquad (14.59)$$

which is a regression of the residuals R_{0t} on the residuals R_{1t}. Comparing this with (14.50) observe that Z_{2t} has been eliminated by the two preliminary regressions leaving the same parameters $\alpha\beta'$. For given β', (14.59) can be estimated to provide an estimator of α; that is from

$$R_{0t} = \alpha(\beta'R_{1t}) + \hat{\varepsilon}_t \qquad (14.60)$$

The OLS estimator $\hat{\alpha}$ is:

$$\hat{\alpha} = \sum_{t=1}^{T} R_{0t}(\beta'R_{1t})' \left[\sum_{t=1}^{T} (\beta'R_{1t})(\beta'R_{1t})' \right]^{-1}$$

$$\text{for given } \beta$$

$$= \sum_{t=1}^{T} R_{0t}R_{1t}'\beta \left[\beta' \sum_{t=1}^{T} R_{1t}R_{1t}'\beta \right]^{-1}$$

$$= S_{01}\beta(\beta'S_{11}\beta)^{-1} \qquad (14.61)$$

where

$$S_{ij} = \sum_{t=1}^{T} R_{it}R_{jt}'/T$$

for $i, j = 0, 1$ and note that $S_{ji} = S_{ji}'$; and, for below, define the estimated values of R_{0t}, $\hat{R}_{0t} \equiv \hat{\alpha}(\beta'R_{1t})$.

An estimator of Λ, the variance–covariance matrix of ε_t, for fixed β, is given by:

$$\hat{\Lambda} = \left(\sum [R_{0t} - \hat{\alpha}(\beta'R_{1t})] \right.$$
$$\left. \times [R_{0t} - \hat{\alpha}(\beta'R_{1t})]' \right) / T$$
$$= \left(\sum R_{0t}R_{0t}' - \sum \hat{\alpha}(\beta'R_{1t})R_{0t}' \right.$$
$$- \sum R_{0t}R_{1t}'\beta\hat{\alpha}'$$
$$\left. + \sum \hat{\alpha}(\beta'R_{1t})R_{1t}'\beta\hat{\alpha}' \right) / T$$
$$= S_{00} - \hat{\alpha}\beta'S_{11}\beta\hat{\alpha}'$$

$$= S_{00} - S_{01}\beta(\beta'S_{11}\beta)^{-1}\beta'S_{11}\beta$$
$$\times (S_{01}\beta(\beta'S_{11}\beta)^{-1})' \quad \text{substituting for } \hat{\alpha}'$$
$$= S_{00} - S_{01}\beta(\beta'S_{11}\beta)^{-1}\beta'S_{10} \qquad (14.62)$$

where $S_{10} = S_{01}'$, all summations are over $t = 1, \ldots, T$ and in going from the second to the third line we have used

$$\sum \hat{\alpha}(\beta'R_{1t})R_{1t}'\beta\hat{\alpha}' = \sum \hat{\alpha}(\beta'R_{1t})R_{0t}'$$
$$\sum \hat{\alpha}(\beta'R_{1t})[R_{1t}'\beta\hat{\alpha}' - R_{0t}'] = 0$$
$$\sum \hat{R}_{0t}[\hat{R}_{0t}' - R_{0t}'] = 0$$
$$\sum \hat{R}_{0t}\hat{\varepsilon}_t' = 0 \qquad (14.63)$$

the last line follows because, from the normal equations, the residuals, $\hat{\varepsilon}_t'$, from an OLS regression are orthogonal to the fitted values, $\hat{R}_{0t}$.

The estimator of $\hat{\Lambda}$ is a function of β, to denote this explicitly write $\hat{\Lambda}(\beta)$, and apart from a constant, the likelihood function to be maximised is now:

$$L(\beta) = |\hat{\Lambda}(\beta)|$$
$$= |S_{00} - S_{01}\beta(\beta'S_{11}\beta)^{-1}\beta'S_{10}| \qquad (14.64)$$

Johansen (1995a, p.92) shows that the maximum of $L(\beta)$ is obtained by solving the following eigenvalue problem

$$|\lambda S_{11} - (S_{11} - S_{10}S_{00}^{-1}S_{01})| = 0 \qquad (14.65)$$

for the k solutions $\lambda_1, \ldots, \lambda_k$ with corresponding eigenvectors $v_1, \ldots, v_k$; each λ_i is a scalar and each v_i is a $k \times 1$ vector. The λ_i are ordered such that $\lambda_1 > \lambda_2 > \lambda_3 \cdots > \lambda_k$. The space spanned by the eigenvectors corresponding to the r largest eigenvalues is the r-dimensional cointegrating space; hence, we choose $\hat{\beta}$, of dimension $k \times r$, as the first r eigenvectors. For example, if $r = 1$, $\hat{\beta}$ is $k \times 1$ and is the eigenvector corresponding to

the largest eigenvalue; if $r = 2$, $\hat{\beta}$ is $k \times 2$, the first column is as for $r = 1$ and the second column is the eigenvector corresponding to the second largest eigenvalue; this pattern continues, the last being $r = k$, in which case $\hat{\beta}$ is $k \times k$ and comprises all the eigenvectors which are ordered by decreasing size of the eigenvalues. The only case not dealt with is $r = 0$, but then we know that $\Pi = 0$ (so that no long run is defined) and all the eigenvalues are zero. Hence, in one set of calculations all cases from $r = 0$ through to $r = k$ have been dealt with in Johansen's formulation; all the calculations take place with the sample moment matrices defined from the 'firm base' model referred to above in **14.4.1** – hence the importance of getting that model 'right'. The eigenvalues and eigenvectors, which solve this problem, are distinguished as $\hat{\lambda}_i$ and $\hat{\beta}$, respectively. Given $\hat{\beta}$, the equation for the estimator of α in (14.61) is operational.

With this choice of $\hat{\beta}$ the resulting value of the maximised likelihood is:

$$L(H(r)) = |S_{00}| \prod_{i=1}^{r} (1 - \hat{\lambda}_i) \qquad (14.66)$$

Where $H(r)$ denotes the hypothesis that the rank of Π is r. The likelihood ratio test statistic for $H(r)$ against $H(k)$ is

$$LR(r \mid k) = L(H(r))/L(H(k))$$
$$= |S_{00}| \prod_{i=1}^{r} (1 - \hat{\lambda}_i)/|S_{00}| \prod_{i=1}^{k} (1 - \hat{\lambda}_i) \qquad (14.67)$$

Notice that $|S_{00}|$ cancels in $LR(r \mid k)$ as do the common values, $i = 1, \ldots, r$, of $(1 - \hat{\lambda}_i)$ in the products. Johansen's trace test statistic is $-2 \ln [(LR(r \mid k)]$:

$$\text{trace}(r \mid k) = -2 \ln[LR(r \mid k)]$$
$$= -T \sum_{i=r+1}^{k} \ln(1 - \hat{\lambda}_i) \qquad (14.68)$$

A 'large' value of trace($r \mid k$) is evidence against $H(r)$: the cointegrating rank is greater than r; a 'small' value of trace($r \mid k$) is not evidence against $H(r)$: the cointegrating rank is less than or equal to r. By itself then comparison of trace($r \mid k$) with the appropriate critical value does not pin down the precise rank; however, Johansen has suggested a test sequence – see section **14.4.3** below – which does this. An alternative comparison can be made between a cointegrating rank of r against a cointegrating rank of $r + 1$, resulting in the λ_{max} test statistic:

$$\lambda_{max} = -2\ln[LR(r \mid r + 1)]$$

$$= -T\ln(1 - \hat{\lambda}_{r+1}) \qquad (14.69)$$

For both test statistics the asymptotic distribution is, generally, nonstandard and depends upon the deterministic terms included in D_t. Otherwise the asymptotic distributions depend upon $k - r$ and have been tabulated from simulations undertaken by Johansen (1988), Johansen and Juselius (1990), Osterwald-Lenum (1992) and Hansen and Juselius (1995); and see Hansen (1992) for estimation and testing in the presence of deterministic trends. More detail on the appropriate tables and sequence of tests is provided in the next two sections.

14.4.3 Hypothesis tests on the cointegrating rank

Having established a well-designed empirical model the next stage is to determine the cointegrating rank corresponding to the number of equilibrium relationships among the variables in the VAR. Further stages involve assessing whether the cointegrating vectors are identified, and estimating the cointegrating vectors and adjustment coefficients in the model restricted by the reduced rank. As a reminder the implications of a particular cointegrating rank are summarised below:

Cointegrating rank	Implications
$r = k$ (maximum)	VAR is stationary in the levels
$1 \leq r \leq k - 1$	r cointegrating vectors (r stationary linear combinations)
$r = 0$	VAR can be reformulated entirely in first differences (no implied long run)

The procedure for assessing the cointegrating rank is an application of the general hypothesis testing procedure: formulate the null and alternative hypotheses and a test statistic whose distribution is tabulated, in this case by simulation, assuming the null hypothesis to be correct. A 'large' value of the test statistic is evidence against the null hypothesis; 'large' being determined by reference to a table of critical values which show the probability that a value of the test statistic greater than or equal to the observed value would have occurred if the null hypothesis is true. There are some complications relative to, say, the simple procedure involved in testing whether a single regression coefficient differs from zero. In particular a sequence of tests is necessary to establish the cointegrating rank and the tables of critical values are nonstandard and depend in a crucial way on the deterministic terms (for example, constant and trend) included in the regression – see (14.49) above. The testing sequence is dealt with in this section and the role of deterministic terms is dealt with in section **14.4.5**.

Johansen formulates the process for determining the cointegration rank as follows. The context is an unrestricted pth order VAR in k variables, formulated as an ECM, and referred to here as $H(k)$. Let $H(r)$ denote the hypothesis that the rank of Π in $H(k)$ is $\leq r$; for example, $H(0)$ states that the rank of Π is 0, $H(1)$ states that the rank of Π is 0 or 1. Now associate with each $H(r)$ a test statistic Q_r and a critical value, c_{k-r}, for a given confidence level where the critical values are obtained by simulation and tabulated in several sources – see below. If the sample value of Q_r exceeds c_{k-r} then reject $H(r)$; if the sample value of Q_r is less than c_{k-r} then do not reject $H(r)$, so the data evidence is consistent with the hypothesis that the cointegrating rank is $\leq r$. In order to determine the cointegrating rank, rather than simply that it is $\leq r$, construct the following sequence of tests.

1. First test $H(0)$ in $H(k)$, if $H(0)$ is not rejected the sequence stops, conclude that $r = 0$ is consistent with the data; if $H(0)$ is rejected move on to test $H(1)$ in $H(k)$.
2. If $H(1)$ is not rejected the sequence stops, conclude that $r \leq 1$ and further, given that $r = 0$ was rejected, conclude that $r = 1$ is consistent with the data; if $H(1)$ was rejected move on to test $H(2)$ in $H(k)$.
3. If $H(2)$ is not rejected the sequence stops, conclude that $r \leq 2$ and further given that $r \leq 1$ was rejected conclude that $r = 2$; if $H(2)$ was rejected move on to test $H(3)$ in $H(k)$.
4. Continue this process. The last possibility is testing $H(k - 1)$ in $H(k)$; if $H(k - 1)$ is not rejected conclude that $r = k - 1$; if $H(k - 1)$ is rejected conclude $r = k$.

As noted in section **14.4.2** Johansen suggests two test statistics to determine the cointegration rank. The first of these is known as the trace statistic

$$\text{trace}(r_0 \mid k) = -T \sum_{i=r_0+1}^{k} \ln(1 - \hat{\lambda}_i)$$

where $\hat{\lambda}_i$ are the ordered (estimated) eigenvalues $\lambda_1 > \lambda_2 \cdots > \lambda_k$ and r_0 ranges from 0 to $k - 1$ depending upon the stage in the sequence. This is the relevant test statistic for the null hypothesis $r \leq r_0$ against the alternative $r \geq r_0 + 1$. Following steps 1 to 4 above, the testing sequence is as follows.

In the first test set $r_0 = 0$, and hence $r_0 + 1 = 1$, then the first test statistic is

$$\text{trace}(0 \mid k) = -T \sum_{i=1}^{k} \ln(1 - \hat{\lambda}_i)$$

if $\text{trace}(0 \mid k) > c_k$, then reject $H(0)$ and move onto testing $H(1)$, otherwise stop. For the second test statistic set $r_0 = 1$ and calculate

$$\text{trace}(1 \mid k) = -T \sum_{i=2}^{k} \ln(1 - \hat{\lambda}_i)$$

if $\text{trace}(1 \mid k) > c_{k-1}$, then reject $H(1)$ and move onto testing $H(2)$. If necessary continue the sequence until $H(k - 1)$ with

$$\text{trace}(k - 1 \mid k) = \ln(1 - \hat{\lambda}_k)$$

if $\text{trace}(k - 1 \mid k) > c_1$ then reject $H(k - 1)$ in favour of $H(k)$.

The second test statistic is the maximum eigenvalue test known as $\lambda_{\max}$: for consistency with previous notation this test statistic is referred to as $\lambda_{\max}(r_0)$. This is closely related to the trace statistic but arises from changing the alternative hypothesis from $r \geq r_0 + 1$ to $r = r_0 + 1$. The idea is to try and improve the power of the test by limiting the alternative to a cointegration rank just one more than under the null hypothesis. The $\lambda_{\max}$ test statistic is $\lambda_{\max}(r_0) = -T \ln(1 - \hat{\lambda}_i)$ for $i = r_0 + 1$. This difference implies a slight change to the test sequence: start with $H(0)$ but test it in $H(1)$; if $H(0)$ is not rejected stop the sequence, but if $H(0)$ is rejected move onto $H(1)$ testing it against $H(2)$; if necessary continue in this fashion until the last test which is $H(k - 1)$ in $H(k)$, with the test statistic in this case coinciding with the last trace test statistic, that is

$$\lambda_{\max}(k - 1) = \text{trace}(k - 1 \mid k)$$
$$= -T \ln(1 - \hat{\lambda}_k)$$

The sequence of test statistics in shown in Table 14.1. (Note that this table is ordered according to the logical sequence of hypothesis tests; the tables of critical values are, however, usually ordered in the reverse sequence). A convenient notation to indicate which hypothesis is being tested against which alternative is $H(r \mid k)$ for the trace test and $H(r \mid r + 1)$ for the $\lambda_{\max}$ test.

Table 14.1 *Structure of hypothesis tests for cointegrating rank*

λ_{max} tests			Trace tests		
Null	Alternative	λ_{max} test statistic	Null	Alternative	Trace test statistic
$r = 0$	$r = 1$	$-T\ln(1 - \hat{\lambda}_1)$	$r = 0$	$r \geq 1$	$-T\sum_{i=1}^{k}\ln(1 - \hat{\lambda}_i)$
$r \leq 1$	$r = 2$	$-T\ln(1 - \hat{\lambda}_2)$	$r \leq 1$	$r \geq 2$	$-T\sum_{i=2}^{k}\ln(1 - \hat{\lambda}_i)$
$r \leq 2$	$r = 3$	$-T\ln(1 - \hat{\lambda}_3)$	$r \leq 2$	$r \geq 3$	$-T\sum_{i=3}^{k}\ln(1 - \hat{\lambda}_i)$
$\vdots$	$\vdots$	$\vdots$	$\vdots$	$\vdots$	$\vdots$
$r \leq k - 1$	$r = k$	$-T\ln(1 - \hat{\lambda}_k)$	$r \leq k - 1$	$r = k$	$-T\ln(1 - \lambda_k)$

To get a feel for how the trace and λ_{max} tests work consider two simple examples with $k = 3$, $T = 100$, and suppose that in the first instance $\hat{\lambda}_1 = 0.9$ and $\hat{\lambda}_2 = \hat{\lambda}_3 = 0$, then the cointegration rank is 1 and this is what we would like the test statistics to indicate. Using the trace statistic for the null $r = 0$ against the alternative $r \geq 1$ then:

$$\text{trace}(0 \mid 3) = -T([\ln(1 - 0.9)]$$
$$+ [\ln(1 - 0.0)] + [\ln(1 - 0.0)])$$
$$= -100(-2.302 + 0 + 0)$$
$$= 230.2$$

Bearing in mind that $\ln(1) = 0$, when $\hat{\lambda}_i$ is close to 0, and so $1 - \hat{\lambda}_i$ is close to 1, this term will contribute little to the test statistic, whereas $\hat{\lambda}_i$ close to 1 makes the test statistic large. This is as we would want. The calculated value of the test statistic is then compared to the critical values that have been tabulated, for some significance levels, by Johansen (1988, 1992a), Johansen and Juselius (1992), Osterwald-Lenum (1992) and Hansen and Juselius (1995). Use of these tables depends upon the specification of the deterministic terms in the VAR; for the purpose of the example we will extract the relevant table entries from the case with a constant in the cointegrating relationship – see Osterwald-Lenum (*op. cit.*, Table 1*) – deferring detailed consideration until later. The 95% quantiles (that is

critical values corresponding to the 5% significance level) for the trace test are: $r = 0$ against $r \geq 1$, 34.91; $r \leq 1$ against $r \geq 2$, 19.96; $r \leq 2$ against $r = 3$, 9.24. Thus a test value of $230.2 > 34.91$ leads to rejection of $H(0)$, and on to the next stage in the sequence. For the null $r \leq 1$ against the alternative $r \geq 2$ the test statistic is:

$$\text{trace}(1 \mid 3) = -100([\ln(1 - 0)] + [\ln(1 - 0)])$$
$$= -100(0 + 0)$$
$$= 0 < 19.96$$

This value leads to nonrejection of $H(1)$, hence conclude $r = 1$. For completeness $\text{trace}(2 \mid 3)$, for the null $r \leq 2$ against $r = 3$, is

$$-100[\ln(1 - 0)] = 0 < 9.24$$

The sequence of λ_{max} statistics and 95% quantiles is:

$$\lambda_{max}(0 \mid 1) = -T[\ln(1 - 0.9)]$$
$$= -100[\ln(0.1)]$$
$$= 230.2 > 22.00;$$

$$\lambda_{max}(1 \mid 2) = -T[\ln(1 - 0.0)]$$
$$= -100[\ln(1.0)]$$
$$= 0 < 15.67;$$

$$\lambda_{max}(2 \mid 3) = -T[\ln(1 - 0.0)]$$
$$= -100[\ln(1.0)]$$
$$= 0 < 9.24$$

The large value of $\lambda_{max}(0 \mid 1) = 230.2$ leads to rejection of $H(0)$ in $H(1)$; at the next step the zero value of $\lambda_{max}(1 \mid 2)$ does not lead to rejection of $H(1)$ in $H(2)$. Having rejected the null, $r = 0$, but not rejected the null $r = 1$, further analysis would be conditional on a cointegration rank of 1.

In a second example suppose the estimates of λ_i are: $\hat{\lambda}_1 = 0.9$, $\hat{\lambda}_2 = 0.5$ and $\hat{\lambda}_3 = 0.04$ (hence the cointegrating rank is likely to be found to be 2). The sequence of trace statistics is:

$$\begin{aligned}
trace(0 \mid 3) = &-100([\ln(1 - 0.9)] \\
&+ [\ln(1 - 0.5)] \\
&+ [\ln(1 - 0.04)]) \\
= &-100(-2.302 - 0.693 - 0.041) \\
= &\ 303.6 > 34.91;
\end{aligned}$$

$$\begin{aligned}
trace(1 \mid 3) = &-100([\ln(1 - 0.5)] \\
&+ [\ln(1 - 0.04)]) \\
= &-100(-0.693 - 0.041) \\
= &\ 73.3 > 19.96;
\end{aligned}$$

$$\begin{aligned}
trace(2 \mid 3) = &-100[\ln(1 - 0.04)] \\
= &\ 4.082 < 9.24
\end{aligned}$$

The sequence is: reject $H(0)$; reject $H(1)$; do not reject $H(2)$; conclude $r = 2$.

The sequence of λ_{max} statistics is:

$$\begin{aligned}
\lambda_{max}(0 \mid 1) = &-100[\ln(1 - 0.9)] \\
= &\ 230.2 > 22.00;
\end{aligned}$$

$$\begin{aligned}
\lambda_{max}(1 \mid 2) = &-100[\ln(1 - 0.5)] \\
= &\ 69.3 > 15.67;
\end{aligned}$$

$$\begin{aligned}
\lambda_{max}(2 \mid 3) = &-100[\ln(1 - 0.04)] \\
= &\ 4.082 < 9.24
\end{aligned}$$

Again the conclusion is $r = 2$.

Although they do not in these examples, it is possible for the trace and λ_{max} statistics to lead to different conclusions. A further example will illustrate the kind of situation which gives rise to this possibility. Suppose the estimates of λ_i are: $\hat{\lambda}_1 = 0.9$, $\hat{\lambda}_2 = 0.15$ and $\hat{\lambda}_3 = 0$, again with a sample size of $T = 100$, then while the cointegration rank is 2, the problem will be whether, with $\hat{\lambda}_2$ relatively close to 0 and $\hat{\lambda}_3$ equal to 0, the trace statistic will be powerful enough to detect $r = 2$. The sequence of trace statistics is:

$$trace(0 \mid 3) = 246.5 > 34.91;$$
$$trace(1 \mid 3) = 16.25 < 19.96;$$
$$trace(2 \mid 3) = 0 < 9.24$$

As $trace(1 \mid 3)$ is less than the 95% quantile, conclude $r = 1$ rather than $r = 2$. The sequence of λ_{max} statistics is:

$$\lambda_{max}(0 \mid 1) = 230.25 > 22.00;$$
$$\lambda_{max}(1 \mid 2) = 16.25 > 15.67;$$
$$\lambda_{max}(2 \mid 3) = 0 < 9.24$$

Here the conclusion is $r = 2$. The difference arises because of the combination of a relatively small eigenvalue, 0.15, and very small (here zero) eigenvalue. To guard against this possibility the usual practice is to compute both test statistics and, if the λ_{max} test indicates a higher cointegration rank, condition further analysis on the higher rank coupled with the concern of being able to identify all the cointegrating vectors. (Identification is dealt with below in section **14.5.2.**)

Reimers (1992) and Cheung and Lai (1993) have examined the finite sample performance of Johansen's two tests. They find that the finite sample bias is a function of $T/(T - pk)$, with the implication that in finite samples the test statistics too often indicate cointegration. Reimers (*op. cit.*) suggests scaling the test statistics down by $(T - pk)/T$; equivalently Cheung and Lai (*op. cit.*) suggest scaling up the Johansen critical values by $T/(T - pk)$. Either way, the result will be that marginal values of the test statistics in finite samples will not be indicating cointegration whereas they would without the adjustment.

14.4.4 An alternative method of selecting the cointegrating rank

A key element in the specification of the VAR, which forms the basis of inference for the cointegrating rank, is the lag length or order. Usually this is chosen either or both on the basis that the equation residuals should be free from serial correlation, as assessed by, say, an appropriate Lagrange-Multiplier test, and one of the information criteria. Of the latter, three are routinely programmed in commercially available econometric software: the Akaike information criterion, AIC, Hannan–Quinn, HQIC, and the Schwarz information criterion, SIC. These are given by:

$$\text{AIC} = \ln|\hat{\Lambda}(r,p)| + (2/T)m$$

$$\text{HQIC} = \ln|\hat{\Lambda}(r,p)| + [2\ln(\ln T)/T]m$$

$$\text{SIC} = \ln|\hat{\Lambda}(r,p)| + (\ln T/T)m$$

where m is the number of freely estimated parameters in a VAR model of lag $= p$ and cointegrating rank $= r$, and

$$\hat{\Lambda}(r,p) = \hat{\varepsilon}_t\hat{\varepsilon}_t'/T$$

where $\hat{\varepsilon}_t$ is the residual vector in the restricted rank VAR. (Note that there is a slight, but not material, difference of definition compared to (12.65), which uses T times the expressions given here; any monotonic transformation will give the same result.)

The dependence on p and r is now made explicit. First, the estimator of the innovation variance-covariance matrix, $\hat{\Lambda}(r,p)$, depends upon the cointegrating rank imposed in the pth order VAR model. Second, the number of freely estimated parameters also depends on the cointegrating rank. In the initial stage of the Johansen procedure an unrestricted pth order VAR in k variables is estimated so the number of freely estimated parameters is simply $pk^2 + k$, that is there are p coefficient matrices each with

k^2 coefficients and k constants. The dominant practice is to choose p using one of the information criteria plus the requirement that there should be no evidence of serial correlation; and then switch to the Johansen procedure for determining the cointegrating rank. However, the information criteria could be used to simultaneously choose lag length and cointegrating rank by constructing a two-dimensional grid with p and r as the different dimensions; the minimum on the preferred criterion indicates the choice of lag length and cointegrating rank. Lütkepohl (1991, p. 202) suggests this for stationary, reduced rank VARs, Reimers (1992) reports some Monte Carlo evidence on this and other selection criteria for nonstationary VARs and Pesaran and Pesaran (1997) incorporate the information criteria-based selection procedure into their MICROFIT program.

Although design dependency is a factor in the conclusions from a Monte Carlo study the evidence reported in Reimers (*op. cit.*) is certainly of interest. With the null hypothesis of no cointegration in a three- ($k = 3$) dimensional process, with data generated by three independent random walks ($p = 1$), Reimers found that for $T = 50$, the percentage of replications with the correct lag order identified was: AIC, 85.9%; HQIC, 98.1%; SIC, 100%. AIC does not perform as well as HQIC or SIC but its performance is not grossly inferior. However, the fraction with the correct order *and* rank was: AIC, 13.9%; HQIC, 48.1%; SIC, 90.4%; hence the AIC fell badly in this design in determining both the order and rank. This problem is not solved by increasing the sample size. With $T = 200$ the fraction with the correct order *and* rank was: AIC, 17.6%; HQIC, 77.4%; SIC, 99.5%. It is evident that AIC does not penalise additional parameters sufficiently enough; for example, with $T = 200$ although AIC correctly identifies the lag order in 93.3% of cases, it suggests a rank of 3, rather than 0, 21.8% of the time. The dominance of SIC is not so clear when the Monte Carlo design is changed. With data generated by a three variable system with $p = 2$

and $r = 2$, an additional design parameter is the strength of cointegration; with weak cointegration SIC only chooses the right lag length 16.3% of the time although it chooses the correct cointegrating rank 89.9% of the time; corresponding figures for AIC are 82.9% and 25.5%. With strong cointegration AIC and SIC choose the correct order 92.8% and 82.9% of the time and the correct order *and* rank 37.9% and 61.2%, respectively. Cheung and Lai (1993) find in their simulation experiments that when the DGP is a second order VAR, AIC and SIC choose the correct lag length nearly all of the time (99.86% for AIC and 99.96% for SIC).

On the basis of these experiments two possible practical procedures are: (i) use an information criterion to determine the order, then use the Johansen procedure to estimate the cointegrating rank; (ii) of the information criteria use SIC to simultaneously estimate order and cointegrating rank. Related to the first suggested strategy, Reimers (*op. cit.*) finds that the Reinsel and Ahn (1988) small sample correction to the maximum likelihood trace test brings the actual size of the test closer to its nominal size; that is a test which should result in, say, 5% rejections when the null hypothesis is correct because the 5% (=95% quantile) critical value being used actually results in close to 5% rejections in the Monte Carlo experiment. The small sample adjusted trace test statistic is $(T - pk)/T$ times the usual trace statistic; however, despite the Monte Carlo evidence in Reimers (*op. cit.*), and indeed perhaps because of the potential difference the adjustment can make to inference for relatively small T and large p, the adjustment is not in widespread use.

Using an information criterion to simultaneously select order and rank requires calculation of the number of freely estimated parameters. For simplicity assume $\Psi = 0$, then in a reduced rank VAR there are $k^2(p-1)$ due to the $p-1$ coefficient matrices $\Gamma_1, \Gamma_2, \ldots, \Gamma_{p-1}$; and in $\Pi = \alpha\beta'$, α and β are each $k \times r$, giving $2kr$ coefficients but with r^2 restrictions; so the total number of freely estimated parameters, m, is

$$m = k^2(p-1) + (2kr - r^2) = k^2p - k^2$$
$$+ (2kr - r^2) = k^2p - (k-r)^2$$

That is the number of parameters in the full rank model minus the number of restrictions due to the reduction in the rank, $k - r$, of Π. For given p this varies between $k^2(p-1)$ when $r = 0$ and k^2p when $r = k$. A grid of the information criteria over r and feasible p provides the basis of choosing rank and lag length simultaneously. An example of the application of these criteria is provided in section **15.3**. (If $\Psi \neq 0$, then while m increases by the number of nonzero coefficients in Ψ, the basis of the grid search over r and p does not change.)

14.4.5 Intercepts and trends in the VAR for the trace and $\lambda_{\max}$ statistics

Which table of critical values to use depends upon whether deterministic terms in the form of an intercept or trend have been included in the VAR/ECM. At first the seemingly large number of tables of critical values can seem very confusing; however, in practice one or two dominant cases tend to arise and the situation is much simpler than it seems at first.

To illustrate the possibilities return to Example 1, which is reproduced here for convenience.

$$\begin{pmatrix} \Delta y_{1t} \\ \Delta y_{2t} \end{pmatrix} = \begin{bmatrix} -1/2, & 1/16 \\ 1/2, & -1/16 \end{bmatrix} \begin{pmatrix} y_{1t-1} \\ y_{2t-1} \end{pmatrix}$$
$$+ \begin{pmatrix} \varepsilon_{1t} \\ \varepsilon_{2t} \end{pmatrix}$$

which is the same as

$$\begin{pmatrix} \Delta y_{1t} \\ \Delta y_{2t} \end{pmatrix} = \begin{bmatrix} -1/2, & (1, -1/8) \\ 1/2 & \end{bmatrix} \begin{pmatrix} y_{1t-1} \\ y_{2t-1} \end{pmatrix}$$
$$+ \begin{pmatrix} \varepsilon_{1t} \\ \varepsilon_{2t} \end{pmatrix} \tag{14.70}$$

Equilibrium, normalised on y_{1t}, is $y_{1t} = 1/8y_{2t}$. Now this is modified by introducing a constant $= 1/10$ into the equilibrium, that is

$y_{1t} = 1/8y_{2t} + 1/10$, so the ECM becomes

$$\begin{pmatrix} \Delta y_{1t} \\ \Delta y_{2t} \end{pmatrix} = \begin{bmatrix} -1/2 & (1, -1/8, -1/10) \\ 1/2 & \end{bmatrix}$$

$$\times \begin{pmatrix} y_{1t-1} \\ y_{2t-1} \\ 1 \end{pmatrix} + \begin{pmatrix} \varepsilon_{1t} \\ \varepsilon_{2t} \end{pmatrix} \qquad (14.71)$$

corresponding to the following VAR:

$$y_{1t} = 1/20 + 1/2y_{1t-1} + 1/16y_{2t-1} + \varepsilon_{1t}$$
$$y_{2t} = -1/20 + 1/2y_{1t-1} + 15/16y_{2t-1} + \varepsilon_{2t}$$

$$(14.72)$$

Now looking at the VAR representation without knowing that the constant had arisen purely because of its inclusion in the cointegrating relationship – sometimes referred to as the 'cointegrating space' – there is a dilemma. The constant in the VAR could be generated from two sources: as seen here it could come from the cointegration space; however, and/or it could be generated within the VAR but not in the cointegration space. This latter case will be justified in a moment, for now we are effectively using the restriction that the constant comes just from the cointegration space to 'map' the constants of 1/20 and −1/20 in the y_{1t} and y_{2t} equations back into the cointegrating combination and vice versa.

Introducing a constant for each equation, the VAR model becomes

$$y_t = \mu + \Pi_1 y_{t-1} + \varepsilon_t \quad \text{where } \mu = \begin{pmatrix} \mu_{10} \\ \mu_{20} \end{pmatrix}$$

$$(14.73)$$

In the example (14.71) we are saying that μ belongs entirely to the cointegration space; that is we can write the vector of constants as

$$\mu = \alpha\mu_1 \qquad (14.74)$$

where μ_1 is the constant in the cointegrating combination; in the numerical example $\mu_1 = -1/10$ so

$$\mu = \alpha\mu_1 = \begin{pmatrix} \mu_{10} \\ \mu_{20} \end{pmatrix}$$

$$= \begin{pmatrix} -1/2 \\ 1/2 \end{pmatrix}(-1/10) = \begin{pmatrix} 1/20 \\ -1/20 \end{pmatrix}$$

$$(14.75)$$

We can go from the VAR to the ECM because we know that the constant arises just from the cointegration space:

VAR

$$y_t = \mu + \Pi_1 y_{t-1} + \varepsilon_t \quad \text{with } \mu = \alpha\mu_1 \Leftrightarrow$$

ECM with constant in the cointegration space

$$\Delta y_t = \alpha\mu_1 + \alpha\beta' y_{t-1} + \varepsilon_t$$

$$= \alpha(\beta', \mu_1)\begin{pmatrix} y_{t-1} \\ 1 \end{pmatrix} + \varepsilon_t \qquad (14.76)$$

Including a constant in the cointegrating combination – the cointegration space – is usually a sensible procedure. In linear models we would generally want to allow for a nonzero intercept so that the relationship between the cointegrating variables is not forced through the origin. In loglinear models the relationship usually involves a 'scale' factor; for example, in the Cobb–Douglas production function $Q_t = AL_t^\eta K_t^\varphi$, the scale factor is A and in logs, $\ln(Q_t) = \ln(A) + \eta\ln(L_t) + \varphi\ln(K_t)$; and in the consumption function $C_t = KY_t^\theta$ so $\ln(C_t) = \ln(K) + \theta\ln(Y_t)$ where K, the scale factor, has the interpretation of the average propensity to consume for $\theta = 1$.

We now have to consider whether apart from the cointegration space there should be a constant in the VAR and what conditions are necessary to be able to separate out the contributions of both constants should they be present. To illustrate some of the issues reconsider the first order VAR with I(1) variables in the following form:

$$y_t = \mu + \Pi_1 y_{t-1} + \varepsilon_t$$

so

$$A(L)y_t = \mu + \varepsilon_t \quad \text{where } A(L) = (I - \Pi_1 L)$$

and (see also (14.43))

$$|A(L)|y_t = \text{adj}[A(L)]\mu + \text{adj}[A(L)]\varepsilon_t$$

In the numerical example (14.72), $|A(L)| = (1 - 7/16L)(1 - L)$, so there is a unit root; we have

$$\Delta y_{1t} = 7/16\Delta y_{1t-1} + \mu_{10}^* + \varepsilon_{1t}^*$$
$$\Delta y_{2t} = 7/16\Delta y_{2t-1} + \mu_{20}^* + \varepsilon_{2t}^* \qquad (14.77)$$

where (see also (14.45))

$$\text{adj}[A(L)]\mu = \begin{bmatrix} 1 - 15/16L & 1/16L \\ 1/2L & 1 - 1/2L \end{bmatrix} \begin{pmatrix} \mu_{10} \\ \mu_{20} \end{pmatrix}$$

$$= \begin{pmatrix} (1 - 15/16)\mu_{10} + 1/16\mu_{20} \\ (1/2\mu_{10} + (1 - 1/2)\mu_{20}) \end{pmatrix}$$

$$= \begin{pmatrix} 1/16(\mu_{10} + \mu_{20}) \\ 1/2(\mu_{10} + \mu_{20}) \end{pmatrix}$$

$$(14.78)$$

bearing in mind that lagging a constant leaves it unchanged ($L\mu_{10} = \mu_{10}$ and $L\mu_{20} = \mu_{20}$). If we assume for simplicity of interpretation that y_{1t} and y_{2t} are in logs then Δy_{1t} and Δy_{2t} are rates of growth and according to (14.77) the constant μ_{10}^* is the autonomous 'drift' or constant growth per period in y_{1t}. This gives rise to a linear deterministic trend in the level of y_{1t} as the constant growth cumulates into the level. It is important to bear this connection in mind when deciding whether to include a constant in the VAR which is not in the cointegrating space; if the VAR consists entirely of I(1) variables the presence of a constant implies that at least some of these variables also have a linear trend. To distinguish this role of the constant from the constant in the cointegration space we refer to the former as generating *linear trends in the data*.

The next question to be considered in this context is how we can distinguish not only the role but also the (numerical) contribution of

the constant in the cointegration space from that in the data. If only the latter is present then $\mu = \alpha\mu_1$, and the constant is confined to the cointegration space. Note the dimension of these matrices/vectors: μ is $k \times 1$, α is $k \times r$ and μ_1 is $r \times 1$ so that there is one constant for each of the cointegrating relationships; and, for below, define μ_2 a $(k - r) \times 1$ vector. Now define a full rank matrix $\alpha_\perp$ of dimension $k \times (k - r)$ which has the following property: $\alpha'\alpha_\perp = 0$; because of this property $\alpha_\perp$ is said to be orthogonal to α. The purpose of defining $\alpha_\perp$ is that we seek a partition of μ into two unrelated parts: the constant(s) from the cointegration space and the constant(s) from the data; choosing $\alpha_\perp$ ensures an orthogonal (unrelated) partition. This partition is:

$$\mu = \alpha\mu_1 \qquad + \qquad \alpha_\perp\mu_2 \qquad (14.79)$$
$$\downarrow \qquad\qquad\qquad \downarrow$$

Constants in   Linear trends
the cointegration   in the data
space

So if the constant is just in the cointegration space then $\mu = \alpha\mu_1$ because $\alpha_\perp\mu_2 = 0$; and if the constant is not in the cointegration space but rather generates linear trends in the data then

$$\alpha\mu_1 = 0 \quad \text{and} \quad \mu = \alpha_\perp\mu_2$$

Given μ and α we can obtain μ_1 as follows: premultiply μ by $(\alpha'\alpha)^{-1}\alpha'$ and use $\alpha'\alpha_\perp = 0$ to obtain,

$$(\alpha'\alpha)^{-1}\alpha'\mu = \mu_1 \qquad (14.80)$$

Then in similar fashion premultiply μ by $(\alpha'_\perp\alpha_\perp)^{-1}\alpha'_\perp$ to obtain,

$$(\alpha'_\perp\alpha_\perp)^{-1}\alpha'_\perp\mu = \mu_2 \qquad (14.81)$$

This partition is illustrated with the following calculations from Example 1 amended with the constants $-3/40$ in the y_{1t} equation and $1/40$ in the y_{2t} equation:

$$y_{1t} = -3/40 + 1/2y_{1t-1} + 1/16y_{2t-1} + \varepsilon_{1t}$$
$$y_{2t} = 1/40 + 1/2y_{1t-1} + 15/16y_{2t-1} + \varepsilon_{2t}$$
$$(14.82)$$

by construction it is known that

$$\alpha = \begin{pmatrix} -1/2 \\ 1/2 \end{pmatrix}$$

and, hence, we can easily calculate

$$\alpha_\perp = \begin{pmatrix} -1/2 \\ -1/2 \end{pmatrix}$$

and check

$$\alpha'\alpha_\perp = (-1/2, 1/2)\begin{pmatrix} -1/2 \\ -1/2 \end{pmatrix}$$
$$= (1/4 - 1/4) = 0$$

From these we obtain

$$\mu_1 = (\alpha'\alpha)^{-1}\alpha'\mu = \left[(-1/2, 1/2)\begin{pmatrix} -1/2 \\ 1/2 \end{pmatrix}\right]^{-1}$$
$$\times (-1/2, 1/2)\begin{pmatrix} -3/40 \\ 1/40 \end{pmatrix} = 1/10$$
$$(14.83)$$

and hence the constants in the cointegration space are

$$\alpha\mu_1 = \begin{pmatrix} -1/2 \\ 1/2 \end{pmatrix}1/10 = \begin{pmatrix} -1/20 \\ 1/20 \end{pmatrix} \quad (14.84)$$

Also

$$\mu_2 = (\alpha'_\perp\alpha_\perp)^{-1}\alpha_\perp\mu$$
$$= \left[(-1/2, -1/2)\begin{pmatrix} -1/2 \\ -1/2 \end{pmatrix}\right]^{-1}$$
$$\times (-1/2, -1/2)\begin{pmatrix} -3/40 \\ 1/40 \end{pmatrix} = 1/20$$
$$(14.85)$$

and hence the constants that give rise to linear trends in the data are

$$\alpha_\perp\mu_2 = \begin{pmatrix} -1/2 \\ -1/2 \end{pmatrix}1/20 = \begin{pmatrix} -1/40 \\ -1/40 \end{pmatrix} \quad (14.86)$$

With this decomposition of the constants the VAR in ECM form is:

$$\begin{pmatrix} \Delta y_{1t} \\ \Delta y_{2t} \end{pmatrix} = \begin{pmatrix} -1/40 \\ -1/40 \end{pmatrix}$$
$$+ \left[\begin{matrix} -1/2 & (1, -1/8, -1/10) \\ 1/2 & \end{matrix}\right]$$
$$\times \begin{pmatrix} y_{1t-1} \\ y_{2t-1} \\ 1 \end{pmatrix} + \begin{pmatrix} \varepsilon_{1t} \\ \varepsilon_{2t} \end{pmatrix} \quad (14.87)$$

In deciding whether to include a constant in the VAR/ECM it is important to remember that confining the constant to the cointegration space is relevant for data which show no evidence of having a linear trend component.

The next complication arises in an analogous way in deciding whether to include a linear trend directly in the VAR/ECM. The discussion parallels that of whether to include a constant in the VAR and so can be briefer. The first order VAR with a constant and a trend is

$$y_t = \mu + \Pi_1 y_{t-1} + \delta t + \varepsilon_t \quad (14.88)$$

where t is the time trend incrementing by 1 each period and δ is a $k \times 1$ vector of 'trend' coefficients. The trend could arise because it is in the cointegration space and/or there are *quadratic* trends in the data. To illustrate the former consider Example 1 now with the linear trend $\delta t = \alpha\delta_1 t$ in the cointegration space where

$$\alpha\delta_1 = \begin{pmatrix} -1/2 \\ 1/2 \end{pmatrix}1/20 = \begin{pmatrix} -1/40 \\ 1/40 \end{pmatrix} \quad (14.89)$$

so $\xi_{1t} = y_{1t} - 1/8y_{2t} - 1/10 - 1/20t$. The ECM is

$$\begin{pmatrix} \Delta y_{1t} \\ \Delta y_{2t} \end{pmatrix} = \begin{pmatrix} -1/40 \\ -1/40 \end{pmatrix}$$

$$+ \begin{bmatrix} -1/2 & (1, -1/8, -1/10, -1/20) \\ 1/2 \end{bmatrix}$$

$$\times \begin{pmatrix} y_{1t-1} \\ y_{2t-1} \\ 1 \\ t \end{pmatrix} + \begin{pmatrix} \varepsilon_{1t} \\ \varepsilon_{2t} \end{pmatrix} \qquad (14.90)$$

In this example the trend is confined to the cointegration space. In effect while the vector $(1, -1/8)$ reduces the I(1) variables y_{1t} and y_{2t} to an I(0) combination, the resulting cointegrating combination still contains a linear trend which is taken out with the term $\delta_1 t = (-1/20)t$. A complementary interpretation is that where individual data series contain a linear trend, if these linear trends do not cancel it is necessary to include a linear trend in the cointegrating combination. By analogy with the definition of cointegration with I(1) variables we could say that if y_{1t} and y_{2t} contain linear trends then they are deterministically cointegrated (that is the linear trend is 'annihilated') if there is no linear trend in the cointegrating combination.

As in the case of a constant in the VAR the role played by the linear trend δt differs by one level if it is in the VAR but not in the cointegration space. A constant in the VAR but not in the cointegration space leads to a linear trend in the data; a linear trend in the VAR but not in the cointegration space leads to quadratic trends in the data; a quadratic trend in the VAR but not in the cointegration space leads to cubic trends in the data and so on. Analogous to the case of a constant the total linear trend can be partitioned into that in the cointegration space and that responsible for quadratic trends in the data:

$$\begin{array}{ccc} \delta = \alpha \delta_1 & + & \alpha_\perp \delta_2 \qquad (14.91) \\ \downarrow & & \downarrow \\ \text{Linear trends in} & & \text{Quadratic trends} \\ \text{the cointegration} & & \text{in the data} \\ \text{space} & & \end{array}$$

In general δ_1 is an $r \times 1$ vector, with one trend coefficient for each cointegrating vector; and δ_2 is $(k - r) \times 1$, with one coefficient for each underlying quadratic trend. With this partition, and including a constant, the first order VAR is

$$y_t = \alpha \mu_1 + \alpha_\perp \mu_2 + \Pi_1 y_{t-1} \\ + \alpha \delta_1 t + \alpha_\perp \delta_2 t + \varepsilon_t \qquad (14.92)$$

and the ECM is

$$\Delta y_t = \alpha(\beta', \mu_1, \delta_1) \begin{pmatrix} y_{t-1} \\ 1 \\ t \end{pmatrix}$$

$$+ \alpha_\perp(\mu_2, \delta_2) \begin{pmatrix} 1 \\ t \end{pmatrix} + \varepsilon_t \qquad (14.93)$$

Table 14.2 provides a summary of the possible situations and reference to the appropriate table of critical values to be used for testing cointegrating rank.

The question of which model and hence which table of critical values in testing for cointegrating rank can seem quite confusing with such a range of possibilities. In this context it will help to mention the models which tend to arise most often in practice. Some models can usually be ruled out *a priori*. First, the most restricted model (Model 1, critical values: Table 14.3) has μ and δ equal to zero and is unlikely to find general use because, at the least, a constant will usually be included in the cointegration space. The least restricted model (Model 5, critical values: Table 14.7), with $\mu \neq 0$ and $\delta \neq 0$, allows for quadratic trends in the data which occur relatively infrequently; Hansen and Juselius (1995) suggest investigating the causes of the quadratic growth, replacing the quadratic trend term with variables accounting for that feature in the data. The choice between Models 2 and 3 rests upon whether there is a need to allow for the possibility of linear trends in the data, a preliminary graphing of the data is often helpful

Table 14.2 *Deterministic terms: guide to tables of critical values*

$\mu = \alpha\mu_1 + \alpha_\perp\mu_2$	$\delta = \alpha\delta_1 + \alpha_\perp\delta_2$

Model 1

	$\mu = 0$		$\delta = 0$
Cointegration space	*Data space*	*Cointegration space*	*Data space*
No constant	No linear trend	No linear trend	No quadratic trend
	$\mu = 0; \delta = 0$	**Critical values: Table 14.3**	

(Table 0, Osterwald-Lenum (1992); Table B1, Hansen and Juselius (1995))

Model 2

	$\mu \neq 0$		$\delta = 0$
Cointegration space	*Data space*	*Cointegration space*	*Data space*
Constant	No linear trend	No linear trend	No quadratic trend
$\alpha\mu_1 \neq 0$	$\alpha_\perp\mu_2 = 0$	$\alpha\delta_1 = 0$	$\alpha_\perp\delta_2 = 0$
	$\mu_1 \neq 0; \mu_2 = 0; \delta = 0$	**Critical values: Table 14.4**	

(Table 1*, Osterwald-Lenum (1992); Table B2, Hansen and Juselius (1995))

Model 3

	$\mu \neq 0$		$\delta = 0$
Cointegration space	*Data space*	*Cointegration space*	*Data space*
Constant	Linear trend	No linear trend	No quadratic trend
$\alpha\mu_1 \neq 0$	$\alpha_\perp\mu_2 \neq 0$	$\alpha\delta_1 = 0$	$\alpha_\perp\delta_2 = 0$
	$\mu_1 \neq 0, \mu_2 \neq 0; \delta = 0$	**Critical values: Table 14.5**	

(Table 1, Osterwald-Lenum (1992); Table B3, Hansen and Juselius (1995))

Model 4

	$\mu \neq 0$		$\delta \neq 0$
Cointegration space	*Data space*	*Cointegration space*	*Data space*
Constant	Linear trend	Linear trend	No quadratic trend
$\alpha\mu_1 \neq 0$	$\alpha_\perp\mu_2 \neq 0$	$\alpha\delta_1 \neq 0$	$\alpha_\perp\delta_2 = 0$
	$\mu_1 \neq 0, \mu_2 \neq 0; \delta_1 \neq 0, \delta_2 = 0$	**Critical values: Table 14.6**	

(Table 2*, Osterwald-Lenum (1992); Table B4, Hansen and Juselius (1995))

Model 5

	$\mu \neq 0$		$\delta \neq 0$
Cointegration space	*Data space*	*Cointegration space*	*Data space*
Constant	Linear trend	Linear trend	Quadratic trend
$\alpha\mu_1 \neq 0$	$\alpha_\perp\mu_2 \neq 0$	$\alpha\delta_1 \neq 0$	$\alpha_\perp\delta_2 \neq 0$
	$\mu_1 \neq 0, \mu_2 \neq 0; \delta_1 \neq 0, \delta_2 \neq 0$	**Critical values: Table 14.7**	

(Table 2, Osterwald-Lenum (1992); Table B5, Hansen and Juselius (1995))

Quick reference for tables of critical values

Model 1	$\mu = 0; \delta = 0$ Critical values: **Table 14.3**	No constants or trends in the CI space and/or data.
Model 2	$\mu_1 \neq 0, \mu_2 = 0; \delta = 0$ Critical values: **Table 14.4**	Constant in the CI space.
Model 3	$\mu_1 \neq 0, \mu_2 \neq 0; \delta = 0$ Critical values: **Table 14.5**	Constant in the CI space, linear trend in the data.
Model 4	$\mu_1 \neq 0, \mu_2 \neq 0; \delta_1 \neq 0, \delta_2 = 0$ Critical values: **Table 14.6**	Constant in the CI space, linear trend in the data; linear trend in the CI space.
Model 5	$\mu_1 \neq 0, \mu_2 \neq 0; \delta_1 \neq 0, \delta_2 \neq 0$ Critical values: **Table 14.7**	Constant in the CI space; linear trend in the CI space, linear and quadratic trends in the data.

Table 14.3 *Model 1 critical values*

Model 1: $\mu = 0$, $\delta = 0$. No constants or trends in the CI space and/or data			
$k - r$	90%	95%	99%
		λ_{max}	
1	2.86	3.84	6.51
2	9.52	11.44	15.69
3	15.59	17.89	22.99
4	21.58	23.80	28.82
5	27.62	30.04	35.17
6	33.62	36.36	41.00
7	38.98	41.51	47.15
8	44.99	47.99	53.90
9	50.65	53.69	59.78
10	56.09	59.06	65.21
11	61.96	65.30	72.36
		Trace	
1	2.86	3.84	6.51
2	10.47	12.53	16.31
3	21.63	24.31	29.75
4	36.58	39.89	45.58
5	55.44	59.46	66.52
6	78.36	82.49	90.45
7	104.77	109.99	119.80
8	135.24	141.20	152.32
9	169.45	175.77	187.31
10	206.05	212.67	226.40
11	248.45	255.27	269.81

Notes: Critical values for Tables 14.3 to 14.7 extracted from Osterwald-Lenum (1992) by permission of Blackwell Publishers; copyright © Blackwell Publishers/Institute of Economics and Statistics, University of Oxford.

Table 14.4 *Model 2 critical values*

Model 2: $\mu_1 \neq 0$, $\mu_2 = 0$, $\delta = 0$. Constants in the CI space			
$k - r$	90%	95%	99%
		λ_{max}	
1	7.52	9.24	12.97
2	13.75	15.67	20.20
3	19.77	22.00	26.81
4	25.56	28.14	33.24
5	31.66	34.40	39.79
6	37.45	40.30	46.82
7	43.25	46.45	51.91
8	48.91	52.00	57.95
9	54.35	57.42	63.71
10	60.25	63.57	69.94
11	66.02	69.74	76.63
		Trace	
1	7.52	9.24	12.97
2	17.85	19.96	24.60
3	32.00	34.91	41.07
4	49.65	53.12	60.16
5	71.86	76.07	84.45
6	97.18	102.14	111.01
7	126.58	131.70	143.09
8	159.48	165.58	177.20
9	196.37	202.92	215.74
10	236.54	244.15	257.68
11	282.45	291.40	307.64

practice the dominant models will be Models 3 and 2, in that order.

14.4.6 Separating I(1) and I(0) variables

The aim of the cointegration tests is to assess whether a linear combination of 'candidate' I(1) variables reduces to stationarity, that is becomes I(0). If it does there is cointegration, or rather the hypothesis of cointegration is not rejected. Suppose an I(0) variable is inadvertently included among the initial group of otherwise I(1) candidate variables, then the linear combination which assigns a zero weight to the I(1) variables and a nonzero weight to the I(0) variable will be stationary. But this is not cointegration in the sense used here, hence I(0) variables should be separated from I(1) variables in testing for cointegrating rank and

in this respect. If Model 3 is preferred to Model 2 only then does Model 4 need to be considered since the data has to have a linear trend if we are to consider allowing a trend in the cointegration space. Again, while there are formal methods for testing among these possibilities, a graphical analysis is likely to prove useful; this time, graph the cointegrating combinations estimated from Model 3 (that is without a linear trend in the cointegration space), for example ξ_{1t} and ξ_{2t}, against time and see if they 'hug' the origin or need to be accounted for by adding a deterministic trend. There is perhaps a presumption that variables which are (stochastically) cointegrated are also deterministically cointegrated, so that in

Table 14.5 *Model 3 critical values*

Model 3: $\mu_1 \neq 0$, $\mu_2 \neq 0$, $\delta = 0$. Constants in the CI space, linear trends in the data			
$k - r$	90%	95%	99%
		λ_{max}	
1	2.69	3.76	6.65
2	12.07	14.07	18.63
3	18.60	20.97	25.52
4	24.73	27.07	32.24
5	30.90	33.46	38.77
6	36.76	39.37	45.10
7	42.32	45.28	51.57
8	48.33	51.42	57.69
9	53.98	57.12	62.80
10	59.62	62.81	69.09
11	65.38	68.83	75.95
		Trace	
1	2.69	3.76	6.65
2	13.33	15.41	20.04
3	26.79	29.68	35.65
4	43.95	47.21	54.46
5	64.84	68.52	76.07
6	89.48	94.15	103.18
7	118.50	124.24	133.57
8	150.53	156.00	168.36
9	186.39	192.89	204.95
10	225.85	233.13	247.18
11	269.96	277.71	293.44

Table 14.6 *Model 4 critical values*

Model 4: $\mu_1 \neq 0$, $\mu_2 \neq 0$, $\delta_1 \neq 0$, $\delta_2 = 0$. Constants in the CI space, linear trends in the data, linear trends in the CI space			
$k - r$	90%	95%	99%
		λ_{max}	
1	10.49	12.25	16.26
2	16.85	18.96	23.65
3	23.11	25.54	30.34
4	29.12	31.46	36.65
5	34.75	37.52	42.36
6	40.91	43.97	49.51
7	46.32	49.42	54.71
8	52.16	55.50	62.46
9	57.87	61.29	67.88
10	63.18	66.23	73.73
11	69.26	72.72	79.23
		Trace	
1	10.49	12.25	16.26
2	22.76	25.32	30.45
3	39.06	42.44	48.45
4	59.14	62.99	70.05
5	83.20	87.31	96.58
6	110.42	114.90	124.75
7	141.01	146.76	158.49
8	176.67	182.82	196.08
9	215.17	222.21	234.41
10	256.72	263.42	279.07
11	303.13	310.81	327.45

some programs, for example MICROFIT, build this into their testing procedure.

This observation can also be used constructively. The Johansen trace and λ_{max} test statistics could be used as a test for a unit root with the null hypothesis of stationarity rather than non-stationarity as with the DF test statistics. For example, suppose that there is some doubt as to whether a particular variable is I(1) or I(0), then one possibility is to include it in the cointegration analysis. If it is I(0) then one of the cointegrating vectors could be normalised on the I(0) variable with close to zero weights (normalised cointegrating coefficients) on the remaining variables. For example, suppose there are three variables in the analysis with the I(0) variable appearing first, then one of the cointerating vectors should be proportional to $(1, 0, 0)$.

If this is so, then the first variable should be removed from the I(1) analysis.

14.5 Identification

An empirical analysis is usually concerned to provide estimates of both the long-run structure and short-run dynamics. That is not only do we want to know the underlying equilibrium tendency among a set of variables, we also want to know how, given a shock, the variables react and adjust on the path to equilibrium. Is adjustment slow or fast, do some variables react more quickly and in response to different disequilibria? These dynamic interactions can often be very important and insightful in a policy context. For example, suppose exchange rates are

Table 14.7 *Model 5 critical values*

Model 5: $\mu_1 \neq 0$, $\mu_2 \neq 0$, $\delta_1 \neq 0$, $\delta_2 \neq 0$. Constants in the CI space, linear trends in the CI space, linear and quadratic trends in the data			
$k - r$	90%	95%	99%
		$\lambda_{\max}$	
1	2.57	3.74	6.40
2	14.84	16.87	21.47
3	21.53	23.78	28.83
4	27.76	30.33	35.68
5	33.74	36.41	41.58
6	39.50	42.48	48.17
7	45.49	48.45	54.48
8	51.14	54.25	60.81
9	57.01	60.29	66.91
10	62.69	66.10	72.96
11	68.22	71.68	78.51
		Trace	
1	2.57	3.74	6.40
2	16.06	18.17	23.46
3	31.42	34.55	40.49
4	50.74	54.64	61.24
5	73.40	77.74	85.78
6	100.14	104.94	114.36
7	130.84	136.61	146.99
8	164.34	170.80	182.51
9	201.95	208.97	222.46
10	244.12	250.84	263.94
11	288.08	295.99	312.58

determined by the relative price of tradable goods, that is purchasing power parity holds, and that the domestic (wholesale) price level is 'shocked', for example by a tax on fuel, does the exchange rate react quickly and is much competitiveness lost before equilibrium is regained? Generally, economic theory has more to offer on the determination of equilibrium than on the nature of dynamic adjustments. Nevertheless both are usually of interest – see Pesaran (1997) – but the lack of theory on dynamic adjustment often leads to a greater reliance on the information in the data to suggest, for example, restrictions which are needed to identify the short-run adjustment coefficients.

This section is in three parts. In the first, a distinction is drawn between the structural and reduced form error correction models. In the second, identification of the long-run structure, that is the cointegrating vectors, is considered and with that problem solved we consider, in the third section, when it is possible to determine the short-run structure.

14.5.1 Structural and reduced form error correction models

There are several senses in which the word structural has been used in the context of an econometric model. Here, as in section **14.2.1**, it is used in the sense of a simultaneous model that represents behavioural economic relationships. It captures the structure in the sense of imposing restrictions derived from economic theory upon the relationships among the variables. For example, consider the demand for and supply of an agricultural good; demand will be a function of the own (relative) price, the (relative) prices of substitutes and complements and real income; while supply is also likely to be a function of the own price it will be distinguished from demand by excluding real income but including agricultural considerations such as the weather, fertiliser used and land fertility. Thus economic theory suggests a distinction in the 'structure' of the demand and supply relationships which serves to separate them.

To simplify the example suppose demand is a function of the own (relative) price and income, and supply is a function of the own (relative) price and fertiliser, and transactions take place when the market for this good clears, that is when demand equals supply. Market clearing on, for example, successive days generates a series of observations corresponding to the respective equilibria, that is to the solution of a pair of simultaneous equations representing demand and supply. These solutions give price and quantity as a function of real income and fertiliser; they are the reduced form of the corresponding structure. To represent this system algebraically it is convenient to rearrange the supply function with price as the dependent variable, that is view this as what is known as the 'inverse-supply' or price equation. The variables are: z_t^d, quantity demand; z_t^s, quantity supply; x_t, supply price; inc_t, real income; and f_t, fertiliser. If these behavioural functions are assumed to be linear, then the structure, or *structural form*, of the model is:

the demand function

$$z_t^d = \mu_{10} + \beta_{11}x_t + b_{12}inc_t + \zeta_{1t}$$

the inverse supply function

$$x_t = \mu_{20} + \beta_{21}z_t^s + b_{23}f_t + \zeta_{2t}$$

(14.94)

market clearing

$$z_t^d = z_t^s(=z_t)$$

The third equation of the structural form is the market clearing equation, which equates quantity demand with quantity supply.

The *reduced form* is obtained by solving for the values of z_t and x_t conditional on inc_t and f_t. As we saw in Chapter 4 the reduced form can be obtained by substituting in the first equation for x_t from the second equation, and then substituting for z_t in the second equation. Alternatively, and more conveniently for present purposes, we first put the structural form into a matrix representation distinguishing between endogenous and exogenous variables, z_t, x_t and inc_t, f_t, respectively:

$$\begin{bmatrix} 1 & -\beta_{11} \\ -\beta_{21} & 1 \end{bmatrix} \begin{pmatrix} z_t \\ x_t \end{pmatrix}$$

$$= \begin{pmatrix} \mu_{10} \\ \mu_{20} \end{pmatrix} + \begin{bmatrix} b_{12} & 0 \\ 0 & b_{23} \end{bmatrix} \begin{pmatrix} inc_t \\ f_t \end{pmatrix}$$

$$+ \begin{pmatrix} \zeta_{1t} \\ \zeta_{2t} \end{pmatrix}$$

(14.95)

say

$$\beta y_t = \mu_0 + Bw_t + \zeta_t$$

where $y_t = (z_t, x_t)'$, $w_t = (inc_t, f_t)'$ and so on. Then the reduced form is obtained on premultiplication by β^{-1}:

$$y_t = \beta^{-1}\mu_0 + \beta^{-1}Bw_t + \beta^{-1}\zeta_t$$

(14.96)

The coefficients on the exogenous variables in the reduced form are functions of the structural form coefficients. In this example the system is 'open' rather than 'closed': nothing has been said about the determination of real income and fertiliser, both the structural and reduced form are conditional on these two variables which, for the purpose of this analysis, are exogenous to this system. In practice this may – or may not – be the case, it is not something that can be taken for granted and we would certainly want to allow the possibility of including their determination in our analysis and testing the exogeneity assumption.

The problem with 'opening' the system is that the number of equations can become unmanageable in the sense of driving down the degrees of freedom in an empirical analysis. This is considered further in Chapter 15. This consideration aside, to close the system sufficient structural equations are needed to determine all the variables. If this is so there are k equations for the k stochastic variables. In the closed system w_t is empty (null), although this is a somewhat unusual feature from the perspective of a standard textbook approach assuming stationary variables. With a suitable reinterpretation of the dimensions of the various matrices and vectors the structural and reduced forms are now:

$$\beta y_t = \mu_0 + \zeta_t$$

(14.97)

and

$$y_t = \beta^{-1}\mu_0 + \beta^{-1}\zeta_t$$

(14.98)

The reduced form in (14.98) is useful in showing how shocks to ζ_t, for example to the first element, ζ_{1t}, are distributed across all the variables (assuming β is not diagonal) but, otherwise, together with the structural form, would seem strange in the context of I(0) variables. However, in the context of models with I(1) variables the structure in (14.97) describes the equilibrium, or cointegrating, relationships, with β less than full rank (if β is of full rank, y_t is a vector of stationary variables), and to capture the dynamics of short-run adjustment these are embedded in an error correction model which, therefore, models both the long run and short run.

In a structural error correction model, SECM, there are simultaneities in the long run, as in (14.97), and in the dynamic adjustment as represented by Δy_t terms. Specifically an example of an SECM is given by:

$$\Phi \Delta y_t = \Gamma_1^+ \Delta y_{t-1} + a\beta' y_{t-1} + \zeta_t \qquad (14.99)$$

where Φ is *not* the identity matrix. The variables in y_t are now assumed to be I(1), so β' is an $r \times k$ matrix of r cointegrating vectors and $\beta' y_{t-1}$ is an $r \times 1$ vector of lagged disequilibrium terms. a is a $k \times r$ matrix of adjustment coefficients, the ith row of which relates to the ith equation in y_t and a_{ij} refers to the jth cointegrating vector; these coefficients are sometimes referred to as the (structural) error correction coefficients. The 'own' error correction coefficient is often of particular interest; that is suppose the jth column of β, denoted β_j, is normalised on the ith element so $\beta_{ij} = 1$, corresponding to the interpretation that $\beta_j' y_{t-1}$ is an equation for the ith variable, then α_{ij} is the own error correction coefficient with Δy_{it} correcting directly on $\beta_j' y_{t-1}$ by the coefficient α_{ij}. In general, we expect $\alpha_{ij} < 0$, a positive (negative) disequilibrium being corrected by $\Delta y_{it} < 0$ (>0). For convenience of interpretation the variables can be rearranged so that the own error correction coefficients are α_{ii}, for $i = 1, \ldots, r$.

Note though that a just captures the direct effects of adjustment, whether own or cross-equation, due to disequilibrium. Indirect effects are present whenever the off-diagonal elements of Φ are nonzero; in this case an adjustment in the ith equation takes place due to adjustment in the jth equation if the ijth element of Φ is nonzero. Adjustments are generally distributed throughout the system even if they originate in one equation. This has led to some suggestions on the structure of a and Φ. For example, in an open system of m equations with $s = k - m$ exogenous variables and $m = r$ cointegrating vectors, a is a square matrix; in this case, Boswijk

(1994) suggests a class of models where a is diagonal, so that in the structure y_{it} only corrects directly on its own equilibrium (and see also Ericsson (1995)). Also if Φ is (upper) triangular, with some reordering of variables if necessary, there is an order to the causation of the contemporaneous effects with the first in the chain being Δy_{kt} which feeds through to $\Delta y_{(k-1)t}$, in turn these jointly feed through to $\Delta y_{(k-2)t}$ and so on (strictly for this interpretation to hold the covariance matrix of ζ_t must also be diagonal). At this stage, however, no assumptions on the structure of a and Φ are made. Solving out the contemporaneous adjustments represented by the nonzero off-diagonal elements in Φ is easily done by premultiplying throughout by Φ^{-1} to obtain:

$$\begin{aligned} \Delta y_t &= \Phi^{-1} \Gamma_1^+ \Delta y_{t-1} \\ &\quad + \Phi^{-1} a\beta' y_{t-1} + \Phi^{-1} \zeta_t \\ &= \Gamma_1 \Delta y_{t-1} + \alpha\beta' y_{t-1} + \varepsilon_t \qquad (14.100) \end{aligned}$$

where $\Gamma_1 = \Phi^{-1} \Gamma_1^+$, $\alpha = \Phi^{-1} a$ and $\varepsilon_t = \Phi^{-1} \zeta_t$. This representation is the reduced form error correction model, usually referred to without qualification as *the* error correction model. Only the long-run relationship, $\beta' y_{t-1}$, is the same in the structural and reduced form error correction models. The adjustment coefficients are functions of the error correction coefficients: $\alpha = \Phi^{-1} a$ and, in general, the impact of multiplying through by Φ^{-1} is to distribute the error correction through all the equations.

The following is an example of an (unrestricted) SECM in the two variables y_{1t} and y_{2t}:

$$\begin{aligned} & \begin{bmatrix} 1 & -\phi_{12} \\ -\phi_{21} & 1 \end{bmatrix} \begin{pmatrix} \Delta y_{1t} \\ \Delta y_{2t} \end{pmatrix} \\ &= \begin{bmatrix} \Gamma_{11}^+ & \Gamma_{12}^+ \\ \Gamma_{21}^+ & \Gamma_{22}^+ \end{bmatrix} \begin{pmatrix} \Delta y_{1t-1} \\ \Delta y_{2t-1} \end{pmatrix} \\ &\quad + \begin{bmatrix} a_{11} & a_{12} \\ a_{21} & a_{22} \end{bmatrix} \begin{bmatrix} \beta_{11} & \beta_{21} \\ \beta_{12} & \beta_{22} \end{bmatrix} \begin{pmatrix} y_{1t-1} \\ y_{2t-1} \end{pmatrix} \\ &\quad + \begin{pmatrix} \zeta_{1t} \\ \zeta_{2t} \end{pmatrix} \qquad (14.101) \end{aligned}$$

Then the reduced form ECM is:

$$\begin{pmatrix} \Delta y_{1t} \\ \Delta y_{2t} \end{pmatrix} = \begin{bmatrix} \Gamma_{11} & \Gamma_{12} \\ \Gamma_{21} & \Gamma_{22} \end{bmatrix} \begin{pmatrix} \Delta y_{1t-1} \\ \Delta y_{1t-1} \end{pmatrix}$$

$$+ \begin{bmatrix} \pi_{11} & \pi_{12} \\ \pi_{21} & \pi_{22} \end{bmatrix} \begin{pmatrix} y_{1t-1} \\ y_{2t-1} \end{pmatrix} + \begin{pmatrix} \varepsilon_{1t} \\ \varepsilon_{2t} \end{pmatrix}$$

$$(14.102)$$

where

$$\begin{bmatrix} \pi_{11} & \pi_{12} \\ \pi_{21} & \pi_{22} \end{bmatrix} = \begin{bmatrix} \alpha_{11} & \alpha_{12} \\ \alpha_{21} & \alpha_{22} \end{bmatrix} \begin{bmatrix} \beta_{11} & \beta_{21} \\ \beta_{12} & \beta_{22} \end{bmatrix}$$

and

$$\Gamma_{11} = (\Gamma_{11}^+ + \phi_{12}\Gamma_{21}^+)/\delta$$
$$\Gamma_{12} = (\Gamma_{12}^+ + \phi_{12}\Gamma_{22}^+)/\delta$$
$$\Gamma_{21} = (\Gamma_{21}^+ + \phi_{21}\Gamma_{11}^+)/\delta$$
$$\Gamma_{22} = (\Gamma_{22}^+ + \phi_{21}\Gamma_{12}^+)/\delta$$
$$\delta = 1/(1 - \phi_{12}\phi_{21})$$
$$\alpha_{11} = (a_{11} + \phi_{12}a_{21})/\delta$$
$$\alpha_{12} = (a_{12} + \phi_{12}a_{22})/\delta$$
$$\alpha_{21} = (a_{21} + \phi_{21}a_{11})/\delta$$
$$\alpha_{22} = (a_{22} + \phi_{21}a_{12})/\delta$$

This SECM is unrestricted in the sense that: none of the off-diagonal elements in Φ are zero; none of the elements of Γ_1^+ are zero; lagged disequilibria $\beta'y_{t-1}$ enter both equations; and none of the elements of β' are zero. In a specific example some of these coefficients will be zero.

Identification is concerned with whether there is sufficient *a priori* information to relate a reduced form to a particular structural form. We want to be aware of situations where no matter what the size of our sample we cannot do this. The information available relates to: the statistical properties of the time series; restrictions from economic theory concerning the structure of the cointegrating vectors – in the economic example above that fertiliser does not

enter demand function and income does not enter the supply function; and restrictions on the structure of the short-run adjustments where these may be informed both by economic theory and the statistical information in the data. An example of the first of these is when y_{1t} and y_{2t} are I(1), then there can be at most one cointegrating vector; assuming one then β_{12} and β_{22} can be set to zero and hence α_{12} and α_{22} also to zero; thus this information reduces the number of unknown coefficients. Economic theory should reduce the number of unknowns further, whether that is sufficient to establish a mapping from the reduced form coefficients $(\Gamma_1, \ldots, \Gamma_p, \Pi)$ to the structural form coefficients $(\Phi, \Gamma_1^+, \ldots, \Gamma_p^+, a, \beta)$ is considered in the following sections. Subsequently we distinguish between: identification of the cointegrating vectors, β; and identification of the coefficients, $(\Phi, \Gamma_1^+, \ldots, \Gamma_p^+, a)$, which capture dynamic adjustment.

14.5.2 Identification of the cointegrating vectors

This section introduces the concept of generic identification of cointegrating vectors. The development here draws upon Johansen and Juselius (1994) and Johansen (1995a, b) and see also Boswijk (1996) and Davidson (1994).

To get a feel for the problem which this section addresses consider Example 2 given in section **14.3.3** above, which involved two cointegrating vectors. For convenience the relevant details are reproduced here:

$$\begin{pmatrix} \Delta y_{1t} \\ \Delta y_{2t} \\ \Delta y_{3t} \end{pmatrix} = \begin{bmatrix} -1/2 & 1/4 \\ 1/8 & -5/8 \\ 1/4 & 3/8 \end{bmatrix} \begin{pmatrix} \xi_{1t-1} \\ \xi_{2t-1} \end{pmatrix}$$

$$+ \begin{pmatrix} \varepsilon_{1t} \\ \varepsilon_{2t} \\ \varepsilon_{3t} \end{pmatrix}$$

where

$$\xi_{1t} = y_{1t} - 1/8y_{2t}$$

$$\xi_{2t} = y_{2t} - 1/4y_{3t}$$

That is

$$
\begin{pmatrix} \Delta y_{1t} \\ \Delta y_{2t} \\ \Delta y_{3t} \end{pmatrix} = \begin{bmatrix} -1/2 & 1/4 \\ 1/8 & -5/8 \\ 1/4 & 3/8 \end{bmatrix}
$$

$$
\times \begin{bmatrix} 1 & -1/8 & 0 \\ 0 & 1 & -1/4 \end{bmatrix} \begin{pmatrix} y_{1t-1} \\ y_{2t-1} \\ y_{3t-1} \end{pmatrix}
$$

$$
+ \begin{pmatrix} \varepsilon_{1t} \\ \varepsilon_{2t} \\ \varepsilon_{3t} \end{pmatrix} \tag{14.103}
$$

It is apparent that β', which is here a 2×3 matrix with one row for each cointegrating combination, has some elements which are set to zero. Why is this? Consider ξ_{1t}, the omission of y_{3t} distinguishes this linear combination from ξ_{2t}; variations in y_{3t} leave ξ_{1t} unaffected while changing ξ_{2t}. Similarly the omission of y_{2t} from ξ_{2t} distinguishes it from ξ_{1t}: variations in y_{2t} leave ξ_{2t} unaffected while changing ξ_{1t}. In this way ξ_{1t} and ξ_{2t} can be distinguished from each other; more technically they are said to be 'identified'. Moreover since a linear combination of stationary variables is also stationary we could, for example, replace ξ_{2t} by $\xi_{2t}^* = \eta \xi_{1t} + (1 - \eta)\xi_{2t}$ which will be a linear combination of y_{1t}, y_{2t} and y_{3t}, but ξ_{1t} can be distinguished from ξ_{2t}^* because it omits y_{3t}. These restrictions on ξ_{1t} and ξ_{2t} are in the nature of *zero* or *exclusion* restrictions – they specify the absence of certain variables from the cointegrating relationships – however, identifying restrictions may be of a different form. For example, if $\xi_{1t} = y_{1t} - 1/8(y_{2t} - y_{3t})$ with ξ_{2t} as before, then ξ_{1t} and ξ_{2t} are still identified because of the restriction that changing y_{2t} and y_{3t} by one unit will have an offsetting effect on ξ_{1t} but ξ_{2t} will change by 3/4. These restrictions are formalised

as follows, referring to them as cases 1 and 2, respectively.

Case 1

Exclusion restrictions only

First cointegrating vector

$$
(0 \quad 0 \quad 1) \begin{pmatrix} \beta_{11} \\ \beta_{21} \\ \beta_{31} \end{pmatrix} = 0
$$

that is $\beta_{31} = 0$

Second cointegrating vector

$$
(1 \quad 0 \quad 0) \begin{pmatrix} \beta_{12} \\ \beta_{22} \\ \beta_{32} \end{pmatrix} = 0
$$

that is $\beta_{12} = 0$

Case 2

Equality and exclusion restrictions

First cointegrating vector

$$
(0 \quad 1 \quad 1) \begin{pmatrix} \beta_{11} \\ \beta_{21} \\ \beta_{31} \end{pmatrix} = 0
$$

that is $\beta_{21} + \beta_{31} = 0$

Second cointegrating vector

$$
(1 \quad 0 \quad 0) \begin{pmatrix} \beta_{12} \\ \beta_{22} \\ \beta_{32} \end{pmatrix} = 0
$$

that is $\beta_{12} = 0$

It is evident in these simple examples that the restrictions serve to distinguish the cointegrating vectors from each other and so to 'identify' them one from the other.

In the way just presented the restrictions do not rely on particular numerical values of the β_{ij} coefficients, we are asking whether *in general* the restrictions – whether exclusion or equality – will identify the parameter values and hence the cointegrating vectors. Such an approach is referred to as *generic* identification. It is possible to specify conditions that ensure generic identification purely in terms of an algebraic condition, which does not depend upon empirical values of the coefficients. While this approach does not relate in principle to a particular set of estimated values it is likely, in practice, to require the empirical specification of the number of cointegrating vectors, since the conditions for generic identification are conditional upon this quantity.

Empirical identification focuses on whether multiple cointegrating vectors are empirically distinguishable from each other. For example, suppose generic identification of a particular cointegrating vector rested upon a certain coefficient having a value of $+1$, as in the demand for money example given below, but the data did not support this hypothesis; then the model would not be *empirically* identified. Similar examples could be given where generic identification was based on an equality restriction that was not supported by the data, hence in such a case the model would lack empirical identification. Normalisation is also important here, since an invalid normalisation arises if the variable on which the cointegrating relation is normalised has a zero coefficient – see Boswijk (1996).

To consider the more general case we will need some notation and a set of conditions that can be checked for particular values of r, the number of cointegrating vectors. As to notation denote the ith column of β as β_i, a $k \times 1$ vector, and the vector/matrix of restrictions on β_i as R_i, of dimension $g_i \times k$, then cases 1 and 2 are special cases of $R_i\beta_i = c_i$, where c_i is a $g_i \times 1$ vector of constants, with R_1 and R_2 each 1×3 vectors and c_1 and c_2 equal to 0. There are no redundant restrictions in R_i which, therefore, has rank g_i. R_1 and R_2 in cases 1 and 2 each have rank 1. With this notation we can state the following condition for identification of the cointegrating combinations.

Suppose there are r cointegrating vectors and that a normalisation has already been imposed, for example that one element in each β_i has been normalised to 1, then for generic identification: there must be at least $r - 1$ independent restrictions of the form $R_i\beta_i = 0$ placed on each cointegrating vector, $i = 1, \ldots, r$.

It, therefore, follows that since R_i is $g_i \times k$ it is necessary for identification of the ith cointegrating vector that $g_i \geq r - 1$. That is the number of restrictions, g_i, on the ith cointegrating vector must be at least $r - 1$. Certainly if $g_i < r - 1$ the ith cointegrating vector cannot be identified. As this condition entails counting up the restrictions and comparing them to $r - 1$, it is sometimes called the counting or order condition for identification. In the examples opening this section $r = 2$ and so $r - 1 = 1$, which motivated the exclusion or equality restrictions. Note also that the condition is necessary but not sufficient since it says nothing of the relationship between the restrictions, that is the R_i matrices. For example, suppose $g_1 = g_2 = r - 1$, but the same restrictions were imposed on β_1 and β_2, then while R_1 and R_2 each have rank $r - 1$, β_1 and β_2 cannot be distinguished from each other: the condition is necessary but not sufficient. We must add a condition, for example for β_1, that no linear combination of the remaining β_i vectors could be mistaken for β_1.

While the general statement (and proof) is quite complex a necessary and sufficient condition can be stated which is simple to apply for $r \leq 3$. First, define the vector of 'hyperparameters' φ_i associated with each cointegrating vector β_i. Note that as β_i is a $k \times 1$ vector of 'free' parameters, imposing g_i restrictions effectively reduces the number of free parameters to $k - g_i$, these are the hyperparameters φ_i; therefore to each β_i vector and set of restrictions R_i, we can associate a $(k - g_i) \times 1$ vector φ_i with typical element φ_{fi}. When the R_i define zero or exclusion restrictions the hyperparameters are easily related back to the nonzero elements of β_i.

For each R_i define $H_i \equiv R_{i\perp}$ where H_i is of full rank; that is H_i is orthogonal to R_i so that $R_i H_i = 0$. R_i is of dimension $g_i \times k$ and H_i is of dimension $k \times (k - g_i)$. Then $\beta_i = H_i \varphi_i$ and $R_i \beta_i = R_i H_i \varphi_i = 0$ because $R_i H_i = 0$, and the restrictions are satisfied. H_i is often easy to obtain by inspection for exclusion restrictions; for example, if, as in case 1 above, $R_1 = (0, 0, 1)$ and $R_2 = (1, 0, 0)$, which are 1×3 vectors, then

$$H_1 = \begin{bmatrix} 1 & 0 \\ 0 & 1 \\ 0 & 0 \end{bmatrix} \quad \text{and} \quad H_2 = \begin{bmatrix} 0 & 0 \\ 1 & 0 \\ 0 & 1 \end{bmatrix}$$

with

$$R_1 H_1 = 0 \quad \text{and} \quad R_2 H_2 = 0$$

Obviously H_1 and H_2 are not unique (all that is required in this example is that the last row of H_1 is 0 and the first row of H_2 is zero) and hence neither are φ_1 and φ_2 unique, but that does not affect any of the results on identification; choosing elements of an orthogonal basis (as in this case where the transpose of the first column times the second column is zero) often aids interpretation of the hyperparameters. Notice that the requirement that the rank of $H_i = 2$, in this case, rules out a simple replication of the first column since that would result in a matrix of less than full row rank.

The following necessary and sufficient conditions for identification for $r = 2$ and $r = 3$ can now be stated:

$$r = 2$$
$$\text{rank}(R_1 H_2) \geq 1 \quad \text{and} \quad \text{rank}(R_2 H_1) \geq 1$$
$$r = 3 \qquad (14.104)$$
$$\text{rank}(R_1 H_2) \geq 1, \text{rank}(R_1 H_3) \geq 1,$$
$$\text{rank}(R_2 H_1) \geq 1$$
$$\text{rank}(R_2 H_3) \geq 1, \text{rank}(R_3 H_1) \geq 1,$$
$$\text{rank}(R_3 H_2) \geq 1$$
$$\text{rank}(R_1(H_2, H_3)) \geq 2, \text{rank}(R_2(H_1, H_3)) \geq 2,$$
$$\text{rank}(R_3(H_1, H_2)) \geq 2\}$$
$$(14.105)$$

Consider the example with $r = 2$ and exclusion restrictions, that is case 1, then the rank condition is satisfied as follows:

$$\text{rank}(R_1 H_2) = \text{rank}(0, 0, 1) \begin{bmatrix} 0 & 0 \\ 1 & 0 \\ 0 & 1 \end{bmatrix}$$
$$= \text{rank}(0, 1) = 1$$

$$\text{rank}(R_2 H_1) = \text{rank}(1, 0, 0) \begin{bmatrix} 1 & 0 \\ 0 & 1 \\ 0 & 0 \end{bmatrix}$$
$$= \text{rank}(1, 0) = 1$$

Similarly with exclusion and equality restrictions:

$$R_1 = (0, 1, 1) \quad \text{and} \quad H_1 = \begin{bmatrix} 0 & 1 \\ 1 & 0 \\ -1 & 0 \end{bmatrix}$$

with R_2 and H_2 as before. The conditions to check are:

$$\text{rank}(R_1 H_2) = \text{rank}(0, 1, 1) \begin{bmatrix} 0 & 0 \\ 1 & 0 \\ 0 & 1 \end{bmatrix}$$
$$= \text{rank}(1, 1) = 1$$

$$\text{rank}(R_2 H_1) = \text{rank}(1, 0, 0) \begin{bmatrix} 0 & 1 \\ 1 & 0 \\ -1 & 0 \end{bmatrix}$$
$$= \text{rank}(0, 1) = 1$$

Both rank conditions are satisfied.

A rather more complex example is provided here based on Johansen and Juselius (1994) who consider the following vector of variables in order to determine the number of cointegrating relationships: $(m_t, inc_t, p_t, r_t^s, r_t^b, t)$, where m_t is the log of a measure of (nominal) M3, inc_t is the log of real GDP, p_t is the log of the implicit deflator of GDP, r_t^s is a short-term interest rate (the 3-month commercial bill rate), r_t^b is the 10-year bond rate and t is a time trend (and so a time trend is allowed in the cointegrating space). Johansen and Juselius (*op. cit.*) find evidence that $r = 3$, that is 3 cointegrating vectors, so in $\Pi = \alpha\beta'$, α is 5×3, that is there is one equation for each of the variables apart from the time trend and β is 6×3, thus there are three columns in β one for each cointegrating relationship. These columns are indicated below:

Columns of β:

$$
\beta =
\begin{bmatrix}
\beta_{11} & \beta_{12} & \beta_{13} \\
\beta_{21} & \beta_{22} & \beta_{23} \\
\beta_{31} & \beta_{32} & \beta_{33} \\
\beta_{41} & \beta_{42} & \beta_{43} \\
\beta_{51} & \beta_{52} & \beta_{53} \\
\beta_{61} & \beta_{62} & \beta_{63}
\end{bmatrix}
$$

$$
\begin{matrix}
\beta_1 & \beta_2 & \beta_3
\end{matrix}
$$

Given $r = 3$, a possible set of economic relationships of interest for a just-identified system is:

(i) A demand for (real) money relationship characterised by coefficients on m_t and p_t of equal but opposite sign so that we may form the log of real money, $m_t - p_t$, as a function of real income, the short-term interest rate and (possibly) a trend; the bond rate, r_t^b, is assumed to have a zero coefficient. Thus there are 2 restrictions imposed on the first cointegrating vector. In terms of the R_i and H_i matrices these are:

$$
R_1\beta_1 = 0
$$

$$
\begin{bmatrix}
1 & 0 & 1 & 0 & 0 & 0 \\
0 & 0 & 0 & 0 & 1 & 0
\end{bmatrix}
\begin{pmatrix}
\beta_{11} \\
\beta_{21} \\
\beta_{31} \\
\beta_{41} \\
\beta_{51} \\
\beta_{61}
\end{pmatrix}
=
\begin{pmatrix}
0 \\
0
\end{pmatrix}
$$

and

$$
R_1 H_1 = 0
$$

$$
\begin{bmatrix}
1 & 0 & 1 & 0 & 0 & 0 \\
0 & 0 & 0 & 0 & 1 & 0
\end{bmatrix}
\begin{bmatrix}
1 & 0 & 0 & 0 \\
0 & 1 & 0 & 0 \\
-1 & 0 & 0 & 0 \\
0 & 0 & 1 & 0 \\
0 & 0 & 0 & 0 \\
0 & 0 & 0 & 1
\end{bmatrix}
$$

$$
=
\begin{bmatrix}
0 & 0 & 0 & 0 \\
0 & 0 & 0 & 0
\end{bmatrix}
$$

(ii) The second cointegrating vector could be interpreted as determining the interest rate differential, $r_t^s - r_t^b$, with a zero coefficient for the trend. The interest rate coefficients thus have equal but opposite signs; otherwise nonzero coefficients on m_t, inc_t and p_t are possible (although these are further restricted to zero in an example used by Johansen to illustrate overidentification). In terms of the R_i and H_i matrices these are:

$$
R_2\beta_2 = 0
$$

$$
\begin{bmatrix}
0 & 0 & 0 & 0 & 0 & 1 \\
0 & 0 & 0 & 1 & 1 & 0
\end{bmatrix}
\begin{pmatrix}
\beta_{12} \\
\beta_{22} \\
\beta_{32} \\
\beta_{42} \\
\beta_{52} \\
\beta_{62}
\end{pmatrix}
=
\begin{pmatrix}
0 \\
0
\end{pmatrix}
$$

and

$$
R_2 H_2 = 0
$$

$$
\begin{bmatrix}
0 & 0 & 0 & 0 & 0 & 1 \\
0 & 0 & 0 & 1 & 1 & 0
\end{bmatrix}
\begin{bmatrix}
0 & 0 & 0 & 1 \\
1 & 0 & 0 & 0 \\
0 & 1 & 0 & 0 \\
0 & 0 & 1 & 0 \\
0 & 0 & -1 & 0 \\
0 & 0 & 0 & 0
\end{bmatrix}
$$

$$
=
\begin{bmatrix}
0 & 0 & 0 & 0 \\
0 & 0 & 0 & 0
\end{bmatrix}
$$

(iii) The third cointegrating vector could be viewed as determining the bond rate as a function of p_t, m_t and the trend with, therefore, zero restrictions on inc_t and r_t^s. In terms of the R_i and H_i matrices we have:

$$R_3\beta_3 = 0$$

$$\begin{bmatrix} 0 & 1 & 0 & 0 & 0 & 0 \\ 0 & 0 & 0 & 1 & 0 & 0 \end{bmatrix} \begin{pmatrix} \beta_{13} \\ \beta_{23} \\ \beta_{33} \\ \beta_{43} \\ \beta_{53} \\ \beta_{63} \end{pmatrix} = \begin{pmatrix} 0 \\ 0 \end{pmatrix}$$

and

$$R_3 H_3 = 0$$

$$\begin{bmatrix} 0 & 1 & 0 & 0 & 0 & 0 \\ 0 & 0 & 0 & 1 & 0 & 0 \end{bmatrix} \begin{bmatrix} 1 & 0 & 0 & 0 \\ 0 & 0 & 0 & 0 \\ 0 & 1 & 0 & 0 \\ 0 & 0 & 0 & 0 \\ 0 & 0 & 1 & 0 \\ 0 & 0 & 0 & 1 \end{bmatrix}$$

$$= \begin{bmatrix} 0 & 0 & 0 & 0 \\ 0 & 0 & 0 & 0 \end{bmatrix}$$

Although many normalisations are possible, economists usually find that the interpretation of the cointegrating vectors suggests that one of the coefficients in each vector should be set equal to 1. For example, the interpretation of the first cointegrating vector as a demand for money relationship suggests dividing through each β_{1j} by β_{11} so that the first coefficient, that on m_t, is 1 thus facilitating the economic interpretation with money as the dependent variable. The cointegrating vector is said to have been normalised on the first coefficient. The second cointegrating vector is normalised on β_{42}, the coefficient on r_t^s, and the third cointegrating vector is normalised on β_{53}, the coefficient on r_t^b.

The necessary condition for identification is satisfied since each of the R_i matrices is of rank 2, that is there are two restrictions on each cointegrating vector. We now turn to checking the complete set of conditions which are set out in (14.105) for the case of $r = 3$.

$$\text{rank}(R_1 H_2) = \text{rank} \begin{bmatrix} 0 & 1 & 0 & 1 \\ 0 & 0 & -1 & 0 \end{bmatrix} = 2$$

$$\text{rank}(R_1 H_3) = \text{rank} \begin{bmatrix} 1 & 1 & 0 & 0 \\ 0 & 0 & 1 & 0 \end{bmatrix} = 2$$

$$\text{rank}(R_2 H_1) = \text{rank} \begin{bmatrix} 0 & 0 & 0 & 1 \\ 0 & 0 & 1 & 0 \end{bmatrix} = 2$$

$$\text{rank}(R_2 H_3) = \text{rank} \begin{bmatrix} 0 & 0 & 0 & 1 \\ 0 & 0 & 1 & 0 \end{bmatrix} = 2$$

$$\text{rank}(R_3 H_1) = \text{rank} \begin{bmatrix} 0 & 1 & 0 & 0 \\ 0 & 0 & 1 & 0 \end{bmatrix} = 2$$

$$\text{rank}(R_3 H_2) = \text{rank} \begin{bmatrix} 1 & 0 & 0 & 0 \\ 0 & 0 & 1 & 0 \end{bmatrix} = 2$$

We also need

$$\text{rank}(R_1(H_2, H_3))$$
$$= \text{rank} \begin{bmatrix} 0 & 1 & 0 & 1 & 1 & 1 & 0 & 0 \\ 0 & 0 & -1 & 0 & 0 & 0 & 1 & 0 \end{bmatrix} = 2$$

$$\text{rank}(R_2(H_1, H_3))$$
$$= \text{rank} \begin{bmatrix} 0 & 0 & 0 & 1 & 0 & 0 & 0 & 1 \\ 0 & 0 & 1 & 0 & 0 & 0 & 1 & 0 \end{bmatrix} = 2$$

$$\text{rank}(R_3(H_1, H_2))$$
$$= \text{rank} \begin{bmatrix} 0 & 1 & 0 & 0 & 1 & 0 & 0 & 0 \\ 0 & 0 & 1 & 0 & 0 & 0 & 1 & 0 \end{bmatrix} = 2$$

This set of restrictions satisfies the rank conditions and they are, therefore, generically identifying.

To illustrate what happens in the case where restrictions are overidentifying rather than just-identifying, return to the first cointegrating vector and add the restriction that the coefficient on income is 1 so that the equation can be specified as an inverse velocity equation in $m_t - inc_t - p_t \equiv m_t - i_t^n$ where i_t^n is (the log of) nominal income, $i_t^n - p_t = inc_t$. This is an 'overidentifying' restriction in the sense that the first cointegrating vector is already distinguishable from the other cointegrating vectors. $R_1 \beta_1$ and $R_1 H_1$ are now:

$$R_1 \beta_1 = 0$$

$$\begin{bmatrix} 1 & 0 & 1 & 0 & 0 & 0 \\ 0 & 0 & 0 & 0 & 1 & 0 \\ 1 & 1 & 0 & 0 & 0 & 0 \end{bmatrix} \begin{pmatrix} \beta_{11} \\ \beta_{21} \\ \beta_{31} \\ \beta_{41} \\ \beta_{51} \\ \beta_{61} \end{pmatrix} = \begin{pmatrix} 0 \\ 0 \end{pmatrix}$$

and

$$R_1 H_1 = 0$$

$$\begin{bmatrix} 1 & 0 & 1 & 0 & 0 & 0 \\ 0 & 0 & 0 & 0 & 1 & 0 \\ 1 & 1 & 0 & 0 & 0 & 0 \end{bmatrix} \begin{bmatrix} 1 & 0 & 0 \\ -1 & 0 & 0 \\ -1 & 0 & 0 \\ 0 & 1 & 0 \\ 0 & 0 & 0 \\ 0 & 0 & 1 \end{bmatrix}$$

$$= \begin{bmatrix} 0 & 0 & 0 \\ 0 & 0 & 0 \end{bmatrix}$$

The addition of the third restriction means that there is one less coefficient in φ_1, which is now 3×1. The rank conditions, which need to be checked, are:

$$\text{rank}(R_1 H_2) = \text{rank} \begin{bmatrix} 0 & 1 & 0 & 1 \\ 0 & 0 & -1 & 0 \\ 1 & 0 & 0 & 1 \end{bmatrix} = 3$$

$$\text{rank}(R_1 H_3) = \text{rank} \begin{bmatrix} 1 & 1 & 0 & 0 \\ 0 & 0 & 1 & 0 \\ 1 & 0 & 0 & 0 \end{bmatrix} = 3$$

$$\text{rank}(R_2 H_1) = \text{rank} \begin{bmatrix} 0 & 0 & 1 \\ 0 & 1 & 0 \end{bmatrix} = 2$$

$$\text{rank}(R_3 H_1) = \text{rank} \begin{bmatrix} -1 & 0 & 0 \\ 0 & 1 & 0 \end{bmatrix} = 2$$

with $R_2 H_3$ and $R_3 H_2$ as before. Also needed are:

$$\text{rank}(R_1(H_2, H_3))$$
$$= \text{rank} \begin{bmatrix} 0 & 1 & 0 & 1 & 1 & 1 & 0 & 0 \\ 0 & 0 & -1 & 0 & 0 & 0 & 1 & 0 \\ 1 & 0 & 0 & 1 & 1 & 0 & 0 & 0 \end{bmatrix} = 3$$

$$\text{rank}(R_2(H_1, H_3))$$
$$= \text{rank} \begin{bmatrix} 0 & 0 & 1 & 0 & 0 & 0 & 1 \\ 0 & 1 & 0 & 0 & 0 & 1 & 1 \end{bmatrix} = 2$$

$$\text{rank}(R_3(H_1, H_2))$$
$$= \text{rank} \begin{bmatrix} -1 & 0 & 0 & 0 & 1 & 0 & 0 \\ 0 & 1 & 0 & 0 & 0 & 1 & 0 \end{bmatrix} = 2$$

As rank $(R_1(H_2, H_3)) = 3 > 2 = r - 1$, the restrictions on the first cointegrating vector are 'overidentifying'.

14.5.3 Testing overidentifying restrictions on the cointegrating vectors

When restrictions placed on the cointegrating vectors are overidentifying, it is possible to test whether the restrictions are consistent with the data by a standard χ^2 test with degrees of freedom equal to the number of overidentifying restrictions – see Johansen and Juselius (1994). (We assume that none of the normalisations is invalid see Boswijk (1996).) To determine the degrees of freedom of the test note that there are k coefficients in each column, β_i, of β but that it is necessary for just-identification that $r - 1$ restrictions are placed on each column, implying that the maximum number of freely estimated coefficients for each column is $k - (r - 1)$. If the number of freely estimated coefficients, s_i, is less than this, it must arise because further, that is overidentifying, restrictions have been imposed. Hence the total number, v, of overidentifying restrictions (relative to the number required for just-identification) is:

$$v = \sum_{i=1}^{r} [k - (r - 1) - s_i]$$

$$= r(k + 1 - r) - \sum_{i=1}^{r} s_i \qquad (14.106)$$

A 'large' value of $\chi^2(v)$ indicates that the over-identifying restrictions are not consistent with the data.

An empirical test of overidentifying restrictions is provided in the example in the previous section due to Johansen and Juselius (1994). The restrictions placed on the cointegrating vectors are as follows.

(i)   On β_1: the vector is normalised on inc_t, with coefficients on m_t and p_t equal but opposite in sign and zero restrictions on the two interest rates; this equilibrium relationship is interpreted as a proxy for aggregate demand around a linear trend with positive effects from real money.

(ii) On β_2: all coefficients are zero except those on the two interest rates which are equal but opposite in sign; normalising on one of these, the interpretation is that the interest rate differential is stationary.

(iii) On β_3: the coefficients on m_t, inc_t and r_t^s are zero, with nonzero coefficients on p_t and t; normalising on r_t^b, the interpretation is of an equation determining the bond rate as a function of prices and a time trend.

The number of restrictions, g_i, and freely estimated coefficients, s_i, on each vector and the corresponding R_i and H_i matrices is as follows:

$$g_1 = 3 \qquad\qquad s_1 = 3$$
$$R_1 \qquad\qquad H_1$$

$$\begin{bmatrix} 1 & 0 & 1 & 0 & 0 & 0 \\ 0 & 0 & 0 & 1 & 0 & 0 \\ 0 & 0 & 0 & 0 & 1 & 0 \end{bmatrix} \begin{bmatrix} 1 & 0 & 0 \\ 0 & 1 & 0 \\ -1 & 0 & 0 \\ 0 & 0 & 0 \\ 0 & 0 & 0 \\ 0 & 0 & 1 \end{bmatrix}$$

$$g_2 = 5 \qquad\qquad s_2 = 1$$
$$R_2 \qquad\qquad H_2$$

$$\begin{bmatrix} 1 & 0 & 0 & 0 & 0 & 0 \\ 0 & 1 & 0 & 0 & 0 & 0 \\ 0 & 0 & 1 & 0 & 0 & 0 \\ 0 & 0 & 0 & 1 & 1 & 0 \\ 0 & 0 & 0 & 0 & 0 & 1 \end{bmatrix} \begin{pmatrix} 0 \\ 0 \\ 0 \\ 1 \\ -1 \\ 0 \end{pmatrix}$$

$$g_3 = 3 \qquad\qquad s_3 = 3$$
$$R_3 \qquad\qquad H_3$$

$$\begin{bmatrix} 1 & 0 & 0 & 0 & 0 & 0 \\ 0 & 1 & 0 & 0 & 0 & 0 \\ 0 & 0 & 0 & 1 & 0 & 0 \end{bmatrix} \begin{bmatrix} 0 & 0 & 0 \\ 0 & 0 & 0 \\ 1 & 0 & 0 \\ 0 & 0 & 0 \\ 0 & 1 & 0 \\ 0 & 0 & 1 \end{bmatrix}$$

Hence, the number of degrees of freedom of the test is:

$$v = [6 - (3 - 1) - 3] + [6 - (3 - 1) - 1]$$
$$+ [6 - (3 - 1) - 3]$$
$$= 1 + 3 + 1$$
$$= 5$$

Johansen and Juselius (*op. cit.*, p. 26) calculate the test statistic for these overidentifying restrictions as 3.5, which is distributed as $\chi^2(5)$ under the null hypothesis. The 95% quantile of $\chi^2(5)$ is 11.07, so the null hypothesis is not rejected. However, this example illustrates that nonrejection of a set of restrictions does not imply acceptance since it is possible to formulate several different sets of overidentifying restrictions. Whether this particular set is acceptable rests upon at least two other considerations. First, does estimation imposing the restrictions result in economically meaningful coefficient estimates? That is the structure is economically identified. Second, are the adjustment coefficients, α_{ij}, economically meaningful?

14.5.4   Identification of the short-run structure

The short-run structure refers to the error correction coefficients, a, the simultaneous structure represented in the off-diagonal elements of Φ, and the lagged dynamic adjustments from the Γ_i coefficients (for simplicity these dynamics are restricted to Γ_1). Assuming that the cointegrating vectors have been identified the SECM can be written:

$$(\Phi, -\Gamma_1^+, -a)\begin{pmatrix} \Delta y_t \\ \Delta y_{t-1} \\ \beta' y_{t-1} \end{pmatrix} = \zeta_t \qquad (14.107)$$

say

$$A'X_t = \zeta_t \qquad (14.108)$$

where X_t is a vector of stationary variables. Each row of A', that is each column of A, relates to a particular equation. As in the case of identifying the cointegrating vectors, restrictions are required on the columns of A to ensure identification (restrictions on the covariance matrix of innovations can also be identifying). The argument is analogous to the previous discussion on identifying the long-run structure so it can be fairly brief. A necessary condition for identification is that each equation in the k equation system should have $k - 1$ coefficient restrictions.

Let $A_1, \ldots, A_k$ denote the k columns of A, then the restrictions can be formulated either in the form $R_i A_i = 0$ or by mapping the coefficients into a lower dimensional space as in $A_i = H_i \varphi_i$, where $R_i H_i = 0$. If there are more than $k - 1$ restrictions on a particular equation that equation is overidentified by the order condition in its short-run structure. As before it is possible to check whether the necessary conditions are sufficient by reference to the rank condition.

The two-equation example (14.101) used in section **14.5.1** is used here with the difference that the restriction of one cointegrating vector has been imposed.

$$\begin{bmatrix} 1 & -\phi_{12} \\ -\phi_{21} & 1 \end{bmatrix}\begin{pmatrix} \Delta y_{1t} \\ \Delta y_{2t} \end{pmatrix}$$
$$= \begin{bmatrix} \Gamma_{11}^+ & \Gamma_{12}^+ \\ \Gamma_{21}^+ & \Gamma_{22}^+ \end{bmatrix}\begin{pmatrix} \Delta y_{1t-1} \\ \Delta y_{2t-1} \end{pmatrix}$$
$$+ \begin{pmatrix} a_{11} \\ a_{21} \end{pmatrix}(\beta_{11} \quad \beta_{21})\begin{pmatrix} y_{1t-1} \\ y_{2t-1} \end{pmatrix} + \begin{pmatrix} \zeta_{1t} \\ \zeta_{2t} \end{pmatrix}$$
$$(14.109)$$

Application of the necessary condition shows that neither equation is identified in its short-run structure. The columns of A are:

$$\begin{matrix} A_1 & A_2 \end{matrix}$$
$$\begin{bmatrix} 1 & -\phi_{21} \\ -\phi_{12} & 1 \\ -\Gamma_{11}^+ & -\Gamma_{21}^+ \\ -\Gamma_{12}^+ & -\Gamma_{22}^+ \\ -a_{11} & -a_{21} \end{bmatrix}$$

and as $k = 2$, at least $2 - 1 = 1$ restriction(s) is (are) required on each column of A_i and none are presently imposed. A recursive structure would correspond to either ϕ_{21} or $\phi_{12} = 0$, but not both since Φ is the identity matrix in which case the structural and reduced forms coincide. In contrast to identification of the cointegrating vectors, identification of the short-run structure may rely more on the statistical information in the data, or at least ideas suggested by the empirical pattern of adjustments, rather than strong *a priori* reasoning – see Johansen and Juselius (1994, p. 31) but for a contrasting view see Pesaran (1997). Overparameterisation in the short-run structure often occurs in practice since the VAR(p) model includes all lags up to the pth whereas not all may be needed to achieve a similar degree of explanation of the data.

14.6 Concluding remarks

This chapter and the next should be seamless in the sense that while this chapter is concerned with techniques and the next with applications, understanding either requires an understanding of both. Hence, if possible, on a first reading it would make sense to go straight to the next chapter after this conclusion and *then* review both chapters and attempt the review questions together. Perhaps even more so than with single-equation techniques and applications, the methods of this chapter gain much from the repetition of examples and solution of practical problems.

Econometric techniques are not always driven by the need to solve practical problems. There is a place for theorising and for what might be regarded as pure theory, but application driven theoretical solutions have a greater immediacy and are tested by the increase in understanding they bring to empirical problems. The techniques of this chapter due, as the references have indicated, to Johansen and his coworkers, are very much in the vein of solving practical problems. Of his collaboration with Juselius, Johansen (1995a) notes in the preface to his book: '... we have worked on developing the theory in close contact with the applications, and the results we have obtained have been driven by the need to understand the variation of economic data. Thus the theory has been forced upon us by the applications, and the

theory has suggested new questions that could be asked in practice.'

The revolution in applied econometric methodology following Davidson *et al.* (1978) and Engle and Granger (1987) was faced with the problem of how to deal with multiple cointegrating vectors, and the sense that the balance of applications of econometrics had shifted uncomfortably in the direction of single-equation estimation because OLS estimation of a single cointegrating vector produced superconsistent estimators even in the presence of endogenous regressors (Stock 1987). Whereas, previously, good econometric practice used the concepts and methods of simultaneous equation specification and estimation, although with hindsight sometimes incorrectly applied to nonstationary variables, the dominant empirical methodology was in danger of providing lip service only to such considerations. Johansen and others responded to the need to integrate these previously important conceptual building blocks into an applicable methodology. They placed the concept of simultaneous equilibrium into the methodology of modelling nonstationary time series; and they linked and extended the concept of identification in simultaneous systems to the identification of the long-run and short-run structure in multivariate error correction models. As a result the development of applicable econometric techniques seems less like a series of step changes and more like a progressive strategy which encompasses previous developments (Hendry 1995).

Another important link in the methodology of empirical econometrics has been the development of a research strategy to cope with the practical considerations involved in multivariate systems – see, for example, Hendry and Mizon (1993) and Johansen and Juselius (1994). It is not generally sufficient just to determine the number of cointegrating relations among k variables; the final aim is usually an empirical model of the long-run and short-run structure in order to gain a better understanding of how the economy works. Like the Engle–Granger two-stage methodology applied to a single equation, identified cointegrating vectors estimated by Johansen's maximum likelihood method form a first stage defining error correction mechanisms for inclusion in the second stage of estimating a structural model which is parsimonious compared to the original VAR. The final empirical model should be congruent with the data (including, for example, no serial correlation in the residuals, homoscedastic innovations and constant parameters) and lose nothing in explanatory power compared to the VAR: it should encompass the VAR. This technique is illustrated in the next chapter.

The methodology of the VAR approach is not, though, without its criticisms. We note four here.

1. The move from a single-equation to a VAR-based, multi-equation system inevitable faces the compromise forced by a trade-off between the number of variables to be included in the VAR and the number of degrees of freedom left in the sample. If a variable is to be included in the analysis it is included up to the maximum lag order in *every* equation of the VAR, with the result that the criterion of data congruency often leads to the introduction of 'special effect' dummy variables, rather than an extension of the information set for the VAR model. Sims (1991) suggests that the introduction of such dummies can 'disconnect' the fitted model and the real world interpretation, constituting a list of exceptions that flaw the model. The 'manageable number' criterion is sometimes invoked to limit the number of variables in the empirical analysis. These issues are also discussed further in the next chapter.

2. The I(1) nonstationary paradigm may be used as a straightjacket for some variables. A variable may be treated as nonstationary for the convenience of the analysis rather than because it is inherently nonstationary. Two examples in this vein are the unem-

ployment rate and the nominal interest rate. While nonstationarity can take many forms, the paradigm that the nonstationarity is of the form that can be removed by differencing may not be appropriate for some variables. An I(1) variable can wander without bound and, indeed, this is a data consistent characteristic for some economic times series but the unemployment rate is bounded theoretically and historically. If we find it to be I(1) that could simply reflect the lack of power of the unit root test and, as is taught from first principles in texts on introductory statistics, nonrejection of an hypothesis does not imply its acceptance. An unemployment rate could be nonstationary without being I(1). An argument with the same thrust could be made, but perhaps with slightly less force, about the nominal interest rate and certainly about the real interest rate. I(0) variables can and should be separated from I(1) variables in the VAR.

3. The sequence of formal and informal tests associated with assessing the stationarity/nonstationarity of the data and reducing a VAR to manageable proportions involves 'pre-test' bias 3(a) and builds up type 1 errors 3(b).

3(a) Pre-testing occurs in many practical applications of econometrics and refers to the practice of conditioning a subsequent stage on the outcome of a test in a previous stage. For example, suppose in the standard, single-equation, linear regression model, $y = X\beta + u$, the objective is to obtain an estimator of β and the restrictions $R\beta = s$ are thought to hold. A pre-test determines whether the restrictions are data consistent at a particular significance level, and if they are the restricted OLS estimator b_r is used; if they are not the unrestricted OLS estimator, b, is used. The pre-test estimator is a combination of b and b_r as a function of the significance level used in the pre-test. Define $R\beta - s = c$, then depending on c, the risk (=mean square error) of the pre-test may exceed the risk of either b, b_r or both – see, for example, Judge *et al.* (1985, p. 75).

3(b) The methodology of this and the next chapter involves a number of steps that illustrate the role of interpretation of data and statistical tests, and the build-up of type 1 errors. The first step, establishing what was described in section **14.4.1** as a firm base for inference, while guided by economic theory and past empirical work, also calls heavily on what is found to be consistent with the data by a series of statistical tests – for example, for serial correlation, nonnormality or heteroscedasticity of the residuals. Each of these has a probability of false rejection of a true null hypothesis (that is a type 1 error). Responses to rejection of a null hypothesis may involve the addition of further variables, so that the framework previously thought general enough proves inadequate, and a further round of misspecification tests. The second step involves determining the data consistent cointegrating rank through a sequence of hypothesis tests – see section **14.4.3**; in the third step there may be tests on the cointegrating vectors to see whether they are overidentifying; in the fourth step, conditional on the cointegrating vectors, the short-run structure of the SECM is identified and if overidentified the restrictions are tested for data consistency. This last step will also involve ensuring that the final structure is not misspecified and is a valid simplification relative to the VAR in the first step. All in all a large number of tests are likely to be applied in a particular empirical study. Whether this seems alien depends in part on the results of applying the methodology; has there been a contribution to our understanding of the economic structure? And whether on this criterion an alternative methodology is superior.

4. The sequence of formal and informal tests referred to in 3 above and can also lead to irreproducibility of results. The argument here is that since the final empirical model depends to a great extent on what is 'discovered' in the data by the individual researcher, this creates a path or route, which is potentially different for different researchers. It is undoubtedly the case that there are a number of data analytic steps in constructing an error correction model, whether in structural or reduced form. In a typical analysis economic theory is informative about a candidate set of variables which are linked in equilibrium but not so informative about the nature of short-run adjustments to ensure equilibrium. Further there are likely to be aspects of the theory which have proved in past studies to be disputable and on which perhaps different datasets have delivered different answers or different techniques on the same dataset have delivered different answers. For example, in the theory of purchasing power parity domestic and overseas price levels should have equal but opposite elasticities. Some studies have suggested this is the case, some have suggested it is not. A methodology, which relies upon information in the data at various stages, is open to the criticism that the final model is 'researcher path dependent', since interpretation of test results will not necessarily be uniform among researchers.

Review

1. Multivariate regression models are those which have several endogenous variables; these are usually more efficiently considered as a system rather than separately as single equations.

2. Modelling endogenous variables can take place by modelling the structure of the

behavioural relations suggested by economic theory or by modelling the solution of the simultaneous relationships in the reduced form.

3. The vector autoregressive model – or VAR – is a multivariate extension of the univariate autoregressive model. For example, consider two variables y_{1t} and y_{2t}, in a VAR y_{1t} is related to its own lagged values and those of y_{2t}, and similarly y_{2t} is related to its own lagged values and those of y_{1t}.

4. A VAR has two dimensions: the length, or order, p of the longest lag in the autoregression; and the number, k, of variables being jointly modelled.

5. A pth order VAR in k variables is written

$$y_t = \mu + \Pi_1 y_{t-1} + \Pi_2 y_{t-2} + \cdots$$
$$+ \Pi_p y_{t-p} + \varepsilon_t \quad \text{or} \quad A(L)y_t = \mu + \varepsilon_t$$

where $A(L) = I - \Pi_1 L - \cdots - \Pi_p L$ and the Π_i are $k \times k$ coefficient matrices.

6. A stable VAR is stationary, that is has first and second moments which are time invariant. For a first order VAR the condition which ensures that the model is stable is that all eigenvalues of Π_1 have modulus less than one.

7. In a first order VAR, the eigenvalues of Π_1 are the roots of the kth order characteristic polynomial $|\Pi_1 - vI|$ obtained by solving the characteristic equation: $|\Pi_1 - vI| = 0$. The reverse characteristic polynomial is $|I - \rho\Pi_1|$ with roots obtained by solving: $|I - \rho\Pi_1| = 0$.

8. The condition for stability of the VAR can be stated in terms of the roots of either polynomial. In terms of the characteristic polynomial the stability condition is that all eigenvalues (roots) have modulus less than 1. In terms of the reverse characteristic polynomial the stability condition is that none of its roots has modulus less than 1.

9. A pth order VAR, $p > 1$, can always be reformulated as a first order system by putting it in what is known as the companion form. Say:

$$Y_t = A_0 + A_1 Y_{t-1} + E_t$$

or

$$A(L)Y_t = A_0 + E_t$$

where $A(L) = I_{kp} - A_1 L$ and I_{kp} is the identity matrix of order $kp \times kp$;

$$Y_t = (y_t, y_{t-1}, \ldots, y_{t-p+1})'$$
$$A_0 = (\mu, 0, \ldots, 0)'$$
$$E_t = (\varepsilon_0, 0, \ldots, 0)'$$

10. Stability requires the eigenvalues of A_1 to have modulus less than 1; equivalently in terms of the reverse characteristic polynomial we require that the roots of $A(\rho) = I_{kp} - A_1\rho$ to have modulus greater than 1.

11. The variables in the VAR should be stationary for standard inference techniques to be valid. However, suppose the variables in the VAR, y_{1t}, are I(1) so $\Delta y_{it} \sim$ I(0) then one possible response is to formulate the VAR in the first differences of the variables, say

$$\Delta y_t = \mu^* + \Pi_1^* \Delta y_{t-1} + \varepsilon_t^*$$

12. Modelling entirely in first differences provides no information on the relationship between the levels of the variables in the VAR and is not, therefore, generally satisfactory even though the VAR in differences models in stationary variables and, therefore, appears to be statistically satisfactory. A satisfactory alternative arises when the variables in y_{1t} are cointegrated, so that a linear combination of I(1) variables is I(0).

13. The Granger Representation Theorem (implication 4) tells us that if the vector of variables y_t is CI(1, 1) then there exists an error correction representation of the general form:

$$\Delta y_t = \alpha z_{t-1} + \Gamma_1 \Delta y_{t-1} + \Gamma_2 \Delta y_{t-2} + \cdots$$
$$+ \Gamma_{p-1} \Delta y_{t-(p-1)} + \vartheta(L)\varepsilon_t$$

where $z_{t-1} = \beta' y_{t-1}$ are the r linear, cointegrating combinations among the k variables, with β the $k \times r$ matrix of r cointegrating vectors. A matrix of particular importance is $\Pi = \alpha\beta'$.

14. The equilibrium relationships among the levels of the variables are captured by the cointegrating combinations, $z_{t-1} = \beta' y_{t-1}$; nonzero values of z_{t-1} indicate (lagged) disequilibria which are eradicated through the adjustment coefficients in α, a $k \times r$ matrix of coefficients with each column associated with one of the r stationary cointegrating combinations; short-run dynamic adjustments are captured by nonzero values for the elements in Γ_i. β is a $k \times r$ matrix of r cointegrating vectors.

15. With two variables, at most one equilibrium relationship can be defined even though it can be transformed – or reparameterised – in an infinite number of ways. Any scalar multiple of a cointegrating vector is also a cointegrating vector so that only the cointegration 'space' not the cointegrating vector can be isolated.

16. The number of cointegrating vectors, r, where $0 \le r \le k$, is the rank of Π, which also equals the number of nonzero eigenvalues of Π. If rank$(\Pi) = 0$, $r = 0$ and Π is the zero matrix, the VAR is in first differences only. If rank$(\Pi) = k$, $r = k$ and the VAR is stationary in the levels of y_{1t} so contradicting the assumption that $y_{1t} \sim \mathrm{I}(1)$. Since by assumption $y_{1t} \sim \mathrm{I}(1)$, if there is cointegration $1 \le r \le k - 1$.

17. The VAR can be written as $A(L)y_t = \varepsilon_t$, where for convenience the drift, μ, has been set equal to zero, for example in the first order case $A(L) = I - \Pi_1 L$; multiplying by the adjoint of $A(L)$ leads to:

$$|A(L)|y_t = \mathrm{adj}[A(L)]\varepsilon_t$$

Where $|A(L)|$ is a kth order (scalar) polynomial in the lag operator L which is applied to each component of y_t.

18. If y_t is $\mathrm{I}(1)$ then $|A(L)|$ can be factored into the unit root operator $(1 - L)$ and a polynomial of one lower order, say $A^*(L)$.

19. The framework for estimation and inference of this chapter is due to Johansen. The first step is the estimation of a congruent, unrestricted, closed, pth order VAR in k variables. Let $H(r)$ denote the hypothesis that the rank of Π is r then the likelihood ratio test statistic for $H(r)$ against $H(k)$ is known as the trace test statistic:

$$\mathrm{trace}(r \mid k) = -2\ln[LR(r \mid k)]$$

$$= -T \sum_{i=r+1}^{k} \ln(1 - \hat{\lambda}_i)$$

A 'large' value of trace$(r \mid k)$ is evidence against $H(r)$: the cointegrating rank is greater than r; a 'small' value of trace$(r \mid k)$ is not evidence against $H(r)$: the cointegrating rank is less than or equal to r.

20. A test statistic for the null that the cointegrating rank is r against the alternative that the rank is $r + 1$ is known as the $\lambda_{\max}$ test statistic:

$$\lambda_{\max} = -2\ln[LR(r \mid r + 1)]$$
$$= -T\ln(1 - \hat{\lambda}_{r+1})$$

21. For both test statistics the asymptotic distribution is, generally, nonstandard and depends on the deterministic terms included in the VAR although it is invariant to centred seasonal dummy variables.

22. To determine the cointegrating rank a sequence of test statistics starts with $H(0)$ in $H(k)$ for the trace test and $H(0)$ in $H(1)$ for the $\lambda_{\max}$ test. The cointegrating rank is estimated as the smallest r in the sequence that is not rejected at a given level of significance (Johansen 1992b, p. 318).

23. Which table of critical values to use depends upon whether deterministic terms in the form of an intercept or trend have been included in the VAR/ECM. The constant

in the VAR can be partitioned into the co-integration space and linear trends in the data. Confining the constant to the cointegration space is relevant for data that shows no evidence of having a linear trend component.

24. Analogous to the case of a constant the total linear trend can be partitioned into that in the cointegration space and that responsible for quadratic trends in the data.

25. Table 14.2 contains a typology of models. Those most likely to arise in practice are Model 2 which confines the constant to the cointegration space, Model 3 which allows linear trends in the data and, perhaps to a lesser extent, Model 4 which allows a linear trend in the cointegration space.

26. The lag length of the VAR and the cointegrating rank can be estimated simultaneously using an information criterion. Some Monte Carlo experiments reported by Reimers (*op. cit.*) suggest that the SIC performs well in this context.

27. A VAR can be specified in structural form where equations contain current dated regressors or in reduced form when only lagged values are present.

28. A first order ECM in structural form – the SECM – is written as:

$$\Phi \Delta y_t = \Gamma_1^+ \Delta y_{t-1} + a\beta' y_{t-1} + \zeta_t$$

where Φ contains the simultaneities – an identity matrix indicating none; Γ_1^+ are short-run adjustments coefficients and a is a $k \times r$ matrix of error correction coefficients; β' is as before. The 'own' error correction coefficients are often of particular interest. Indirect effects of disequilibrium are present in the structure whenever the off-diagonal elements of Φ are nonzero.

29. For identification of the cointegrating vectors there must be at least $r - 1$ independent restrictions of the form $R_i\beta_i = 0$, where R_i is $g_i \times k$ of rank g_i, placed on each cointegrating vector, $i = 1, \ldots, r$. Hence it is necessary

for identification of the ith cointegrating vector that $g_i \geq r - 1$.

30. Imposing g_i restrictions effectively reduces the number of free parameters to $k - g_i$, these are the hyperparameters φ_i. For each R_i define $H_i = R_{i\perp}$ where H_i is of full rank; that is H_i is orthogonal to R_i so that $R_iH_i = 0$. Then $\beta_i = H_i\varphi_i$ and $R_i\beta_i = R_iH_i\varphi_i = 0$.

31. Overidentifying restrictions on the cointegrating vectors can be tested by a standard χ^2 test with degrees of freedom equal to the number of overidentifying restrictions. The total number, v, of overidentifying restrictions (relative to the number required for just-identification) is:

$$v = \sum_{i=r}^{r} [k - (r - 1) - s_i]$$

$$= r(k + 1 - r) - \sum_{i=1}^{r} s_i$$

A 'large' value of $\chi^2(v)$ indicates that the overidentifying restrictions are not consistent with the data.

32. A necessary condition for identification of the short-run structure is that each equation in the k equation SECM should have $k - 1$ coefficient restrictions. As before a check of whether the necessary conditions are sufficient can be made by reference to the rank condition.

33. Overparameterisation in the short-run structure often occurs in practice since the VAR(p) model includes all lags up to the pth whereas not all may be needed to achieve a similar degree of explanation of the data. This links in with parsimonious encompassing, a concept introduced in the next chapter.

34. In the Johansen framework the concepts of simultaneous equilibrium and identification once again have a central place in econometric methodology.

35. It is not generally sufficient just to determine the number of cointegrating relations

among k variables; the final aim is usually an empirical model of the long-run and short-run structure in order to gain a better understanding of how the economy works.

36. The methodology of the VAR approach is not, though, without its criticisms, included in these are:

 (i) the nonstationary paradigm, whereby nonstationarity has to be removed by differencing, is a straightjacket for some variables;

 (ii) the sequence of formal and informal tests associated with reducing a VAR to manageable proportions and finally estimating a SECM is likely to involve pre-test bias and builds up type 1 errors;

 (iii) there can be 'researcher dependence' of results;

 (iv) the trade-off between the number of variables to be included in the VAR and the number of degrees of freedom left in the sample.

Review questions

1. (i) Obtain the eigenvalues of:

$$\Pi_1 = \begin{bmatrix} 2 & 1.5 \\ 0 & 3 \end{bmatrix}$$

 (ii) Specify the reverse characteristic polynomial and obtain its roots.

 (ii) Is a first order ECM with this Π_1 either stable or stationary?

2. Consider the second order system in two variables (that is $k = 2$), used in section **14.2.4**, defined by the following matrices:

$$\Pi_1 L = \begin{bmatrix} 5/8L & 5/16L \\ 3/4L & 3/16L \end{bmatrix}$$

and

$$\Pi_2 L^2 = \begin{bmatrix} -1/8L^2 & -1/4L^2 \\ -1/4L^2 & 3/4L^2 \end{bmatrix}$$

 (i) Show that the reverse characteristic polynomial of this example is:

$$\begin{bmatrix} 1 & 0 \\ 0 & 1 \end{bmatrix} - \begin{bmatrix} 5/8\rho & 5/16\rho \\ 3/4\rho & 3/16\rho \end{bmatrix}$$
$$- \begin{bmatrix} -1/8\rho^2 & -1/4\rho^2 \\ -1/4\rho^2 & 3/4\rho^2 \end{bmatrix}$$
$$= \begin{bmatrix} 1 - 5/8\rho + 1/8\rho^2, -5/16\rho + 1/4\rho^2 \\ -3/4\rho + 1/4\rho^2, 1 - 3/16\rho - 3/4\rho^2 \end{bmatrix}$$

 (ii) Obtain the roots of this polynomial and assess the stability of the model.

 (iii) Explain how you would obtain the eigenvalues of the associated companion matrix.

 (iv) Put a fourth order VAR in three variables into companion form.

3. Consider $\Delta y_t = \Pi y_{t-1} + \varepsilon_t$ where

$$y_t = \begin{pmatrix} y_{1t} \\ y_{2t} \end{pmatrix} \quad \text{and} \quad \Pi = \begin{bmatrix} -1/8 & 1/32 \\ 1/2 & -1/8 \end{bmatrix}$$

and

$$\varepsilon_t = \begin{pmatrix} \varepsilon_{1t} \\ \varepsilon_{2t} \end{pmatrix}$$

 (i) Obtain the eigenvalues of Π.

 (ii) What is the rank of Π?

 (iii) How many cointegrating vectors are there in this case?

 (iv) Obtain the cointegrating vector(s) and normalise on y_{1t}.

 (v) Show that the normalisation in (iii) is not unique.

 (vi) Obtain the VAR in levels corresponding to this ECM.

4. (i) Explain the difference between the alternative hypotheses for the λ_{max} and trace statistics.

 (ii) Explain how to estimate the cointegrating rank using the λ_{max} and trace statistics.

 (iii) How is it possible for the λ_{max} and trace statistics to suggest different cointegrating ranks? What would you do in such a case?

5. In the following example there are four variables: consumers' expenditure, M1, disposable income and the rate on 3-month Treasury Bills; apart from the latter all variables are measured in constant prices and logs are taken; data is for the United States with a sample period, before lags are taken, of 1963m1 to 1991m12. The estimated eigenvalues from a second order VAR, which includes an unrestricted constant, are: 0.2811. 0.1184, 0.0598, 0.0053.

   (i) Construct a table of the form of Table 14.1 with the $\lambda_{\max}$ and trace test statistics together with their 90% and 95% quantiles.

   (ii) From the table you have constructed, estimate the cointegrating rank.

6. This example is from Clements and Mizon (1991) who define five variables in their analysis: earnings per hour worked, e; the consumer price index, r; productivity measured as output per person, p; average hours worked, h; and the unemployment rate, u; all variables are in logs for the United Kingdom. The vector y_t is specified as: $(e - r)_t$, Δr_t, $(p - h)_t$, h_t, u_t. A fifth order unrestricted VAR was estimated over the period 1966q3 to 1989q3 (which is the sample period *after* lags have been taken) and resulted in the following ordered eigenvalues: 0.5832, 0.3924, 0.1995, 0.1247, 0.0418. Clements and Mizon (1991) describe their VAR as 'A constant was allowed to enter the VAR unrestrictedly, thus implying a linear trend in the system for the levels of the variables being modelled.'

   (i) Bearing this description in mind, construct a table of the form suggested by Table 14.1 including the $\lambda_{\max}$ and trace test statistics and their 95% quantiles.

   (ii) Estimate the number of cointegrating vectors.

   (iii) Assume, for illustrative purposes, that the cointegrating rank is $r = 2$. Suppose

   $$\beta_1' = (1, 0, -1, \beta_{41}, \beta_{51})$$

   and

   $$\beta_2' = (\beta_{12}, 0, \beta_{12}, 1, \beta_{52})$$

   where β_{ij} indicates an unrestricted coefficient. Formulate the restrictions on β_1' and β_2' in the form $R_i \beta_i = 0$ and $\beta_i = H_i \varphi_i$.

   (iv) Are the cointegrating vectors generically identified by the necessary condition?

   (v) Check the rank condition for identification.

   (vi) Now assume that the cointegrating rank is $r = 3$ and in addition to the specification in (iii)

   $$\beta_3' = (\beta_{13}, -1, -\beta_{13}, \beta_{43}, \beta_{53})$$

   are the cointegrating vectors generically identified?

   (vii) The following estimated β and corresponding α vectors are reported by Clements and Mizon (*op. cit.*, Table 4) (see table below).

   (viii) Discuss and interpret these vectors. Clements and Mizon (*op. cit.*, Table 7) report the following estimated SECM,

	β_1	β_2	β_3	α_1	α_2	α_3
$(e - r)_t$	1.000	0.368	0.100	0.167	-1.327	-0.298
Δr_t	0	0	-1.000	0.005	0.127	-0.339
$(p - h)_t$	-1.000	0.368	-0.100	-0.229	1.369	0.021
h_t	5.983	1.000	-0.050	0.086	-0.339	-0.404
u_t	0.112	0.0001	-0.009	-0.913	6.218	1.360

apart from dummy variables, which have been omitted for simplicity:

$$\Delta(e - r)_t = -0.693\Delta r_t$$
$$-0.572\Delta h_t + 0.273\Delta r_{t-1}$$
$$-0.074ecm_{t-1}$$

$$\Delta r_t = 0.244\Delta(e - r)_{t-1}$$
$$+0.158\Delta(e - r)_{t-2}$$
$$-0.312\Delta(p - h)_{t-2}$$
$$+0.591\Delta r_{t-1}$$
$$+0.482\Delta r_{t-4}$$
$$-0.258\Delta r_{t-5}$$

$$\Delta(p - h)_t = 0.042\Delta u_t$$
$$-0.175\Delta(p - h)_{t-1}$$
$$+0.122h_{t-1} + 0.041\Delta u_{t-4}$$

$$\Delta h_t = -0.161\Delta(e - r)_{t-1}$$
$$-0.129\Delta(p - h)_{t-4}$$
$$-0.164\Delta r_{t-1} - 0.079h_{t-1}$$
$$-0.170\Delta h_{t-1}$$

$$\Delta u_t = -2.468\Delta h_t - 2.027\Delta h_{t-1}$$
$$+0.407\Delta r_{t-1}$$
$$-2.027\Delta h_{t-1}$$
$$-0.356h_{t-1} + 0.589\Delta u_{t-1}$$
$$-0.823\Delta(p - h)_{t-2}$$
$$+0.078\Delta u_{t-4}$$

where

$$ecm_t = (e - r)_t - (p - h)_t + 0.112u_t$$

(ix) Arrange these estimates into the form of the SECM given in section **14.5.4**.

(x) Is the short-run structure identified?

(xi) Derive the implied reduced form from these estimates and compare the direct and derived estimates of the adjustment coefficients (α).

(xii) By interchanging Δu_t and Δh_t show that Φ becomes triangular; interpret the triangular Φ (Sims 1991, p. 924).

(xiii) Why is $5.983h_t$ not included in the definition of the error correction term?

7. Consider the estimated eigenvectors and weights relating to the example of over-identifying restrictions given in section **14.5.2**. The variables are: ($m_t, inc_t, p_t, r_t^s, r_t^b, t$), where m_t is the log of a measure of (nominal) M3, inc_t is the log of real GDP, p_t is the log of the implicit deflator of GDP, r_t^s is a short-term interest rate (the 3-month commercial bill rate), r_t^b is the 10-year bond rate and t is a time trend.

	$\hat{\beta}_i$			$\hat{\alpha}_i$		
m_t	−0.193	0.000	0.000	0.030	0.159	−0.569
inc_t	1.000	0.000	0.000	−0.458	−0.001	0.405
p_t	0.193	0.000	−0.488	0.325	−0.039	0.054
r_t^s	0.000	−1.000	0.000	0.337	−0.308	−0.168
r_t^b	0.000	−1.000	1.000	0.109	0.023	−0.213
t	−0.005	0.000	0.009			

Source: Johansen and Juselius (1994, Table 6).

(i) Confirm that the three cointegrating vectors are generically identified.

(ii) Explain what the test for overidentification reported in the text is testing for.

(iii) Do the estimated values of the β and α coefficients sustain the structural interpretation of the first cointegrating vectors as a domestic demand relationship, the second as a stationary interest rate differential and the third as determining the real bond rate (see Johansen and Juselius *op. cit.*, p. 25)?

CHAPTER 15

Applications of multivariate models involving cointegration

15.1   Introduction

In this chapter we link up with the concepts and examples of the previous chapter. In particular the aim is to provide some extended illustrations of the practical issues arising in applying the concepts associated with cointegration, first based on published empirical work and second on a dataset used in a previous chapter. In places we also need to extend the theoretical background to cope with problems which arise in practice. For example, an issue for empirical researchers adopting a multivariate framework is where to draw the line in terms of the number of variables to be included in the VAR analysis. With a little imagination even a study with a limited aim runs into problems of which variables to exclude completely (marginalising) and which to include but not explain (conditioning). For example, the simplest version of purchasing power parity, PPP, suggests an equilibrium relationship between the nominal exchange rate, E_t, the domestic price level, P_t, and the overseas price level, P_t^*. A VAR in these three variables, however, may well be inadequate to produce a congruent model; for example, domestic and overseas interest rates are also likely to influence the exchange rate through a condition known as uncovered interest parity, UIP. Including these extends the dimension of the VAR from three

to five variables, and also raises the question of whether the interest rates can be adequately explained in the VAR by the other variables, especially since there is an absence of variables one would expect in a policy reaction function. Further, domestic and overseas wage levels, which are likely to influence price levels, are excluded. Their inclusion increases the number of variables in the VAR to seven, and also raises the question of whether these new variables can be adequately explained in the (revised) VAR. The dimension of the VAR could easily grow in this manner to risk exhausting the observations available, hence some decisions have to be made on exclusion and conditioning. Section **15.6** considers some of the key issues in this area.

Several examples are given of estimating structural error correction mechanisms, SECMs, and the link between the SECM coefficients and reduced form VAR coefficients. Also in this context we introduce the concept of parsimonious encompassing due to Hendry and his coworkers – see, for example, Hendry and Mizon (1993). Since the SECM can be viewed as a reduction of the VAR, it is nested, that is contained as a special case, in the VAR. The VAR encompasses the SECM in the sense that by imposition of the appropriate restrictions it can reproduce the results of the SECM. The VAR is assumed to be congruent otherwise it is not an appropriate starting point for statistical inference. If the VAR is congruent then the question naturally arises as to whether the reduction to the SECM is valid: is the SECM also congruent? Provided it is, then the SECM being a simpler model, in the sense of being of smaller dimension than the VAR, is said to parsimoniously encompass the VAR.

The following examples are used in this chapter. Building upon Chapter 13, which illustrated single-equation approaches to the PPP theory of the exchange rate, the first example in section **15.2**, due to Johansen and Juselius (1992) and Juselius (1995), is a multivariate approach to the long-run existence of PPP and uncovered interest parity, UIP. Next, in section **15.3**, we consider the cointegration of real wages in the US manufacturing sector, a topic considered by Dickey and Rossana (1994). In section **15.4** the estimation of an IS/LM model, suggested in Johansen and Juselius (1994), provides an illustration of identification of the short-run structure and estimation of a structural error correction model. An example due to Hendry and Mizon (1993) continues this theme in section **15.5** in the context of the UK demand for money. Further examples require development of the concept of weak exogeneity, and related concepts of joint, conditional and marginal models, which is taken up in section **15.6**. In section **15.7** Urbain's analysis of Belgian imports and PPP provides the framework for an extended illustration of most of the concepts associated with the multivariate cointegration approach. Finally, in section **15.8**, we revisit the US demand for money example of Chapter 10 to compare the single-equation and multi-equation approaches; as the dataset for this example is provided through the website the reader is given an opportunity to confirm the results reported in this chapter and, perhaps, improve upon the reported SECM.

After the section headings for sections **15.2** to **15.5** an indication (shown in italics) is given of the purpose of the example together with brief, relevant extracts from Chapter 14.

15.2 Purchasing power parity and uncovered interest parity, Johansen and Juselius (1992); *establishing a firm base for inference; identification of the cointegrating vectors; using the λ_{max} and trace test statistics*

*There must be at least $r - 1$ independent restrictions of the form $R_i\beta_i = 0$ placed on each cointegrating vector, $i = 1, \ldots, r$. For each R_i define $H_i = R_{i\perp}$ where H_i is of full rank; that is H_i is orthogonal to R_i so that $R_iH_i = 0$. R_i is of dimension $g_i \times k$ and H_i is of dimension $k \times (k - g_i)$. Then $\beta_i = H_i\varphi_i$ and $R_i\beta_i = R_iH_i\varphi_i = 0$ because $R_iH_i = 0$, and the restrictions are satisfied. Section **14.5.2**.*

*In the Johansen framework the first step is the estimation of a congruent, unrestricted, closed, pth order VAR in k variables. Section **14.4.1**.*

*Having established a well-designed empirical model the next stage is to determine the cointegrating rank which tells us how many equilibrium relationships there are among the variables in the VAR. Section **14.4.3**.*

Johansen and Juselius (1992) analysed the long-run foreign transmission effects between the United Kingdom and the rest of the world and Juselius (1995) considered similar issues for Denmark and Germany; both focused on the long-run relations of purchasing power parity, PPP, and uncovered interest parity, UIP. Since the purpose of this example is illustrative only brief details of the underlying theory are necessary here; and Chapter 13 provides a detailed introduction to PPP.

15.2.1 An outline of PPP and UIP

PPP is based on the attractive idea that the same internationally traded good produced in different countries should have an identical price when converted to units of a common currency. If this is not the case there is room for profitable arbitrage in that good; however, if the exchange rate is free to adjust and there are no impediments to trade, the potential for profitable arbitrage should be removed by movements in the exchange rate such that the PPP condition holds. In practice this adjustment may take time, so that PPP may hold in the long run but not in the short run. Letting P_t and P_t^* denote the domestic and overseas prices and E_t the nominal exchange rate, measured as the domestic price of a unit of foreign currency, then at its simplest PPP implies $E_t = P_t/P_t^*$. So, with lower case letters denoting logarithms, the long-run relationship between these variables is given by $p_t - p_t^* - e_t = \xi_{1t}$, where ξ_{1t} is a stationary, zero mean, random variable which allows for the possibility of short-run deviations from the 'fundamental' PPP equilibrium characterised by $\xi_{1t} = 0$.

While PPP concentrates on the goods market we may also expect a capital market condition known as uncovered interest parity, UIP, to hold. Suppose that in addition to the domestically produced good, each country also has a financial asset which, like the good, we assume to be the same (in terms of, for example, maturity and risk) apart from the country of origin; for simplicity we will call this asset a bond, with domestic and overseas interest rates on this bond denoted r_t and r_t^*, respectively. Arbitrage on the capital market creates pressure on the exchange rate ensuring that an interest rate differential is only associated with a difference between the exchange rate expected at t for $t+1$ and the current (spot) rate. In summary $r_t - r_t^* = \xi_{2t}$, where $\xi_{2t} = E_t\{e_{t+1}\} - e_t$ is a stationary, random variable and $E_t\{e_{t+1}\}$ is the expected value at time t of the exchange rate in period $t+1$.

15.2.2 Generic identification of the cointegrating relationships

If PPP and UIP hold then we expect to find two cointegrating relationships among the following

five variables: $p_t, p_t^*, e_t, r_t, r_t^*$; corresponding to PPP and UIP, respectively, the following should be cointegrating vectors: $(1, -1, -1, 0, 0)$ and $(0, 0, 0, 1, -1)$. It is easy to verify that these are generically identified for $r = 2$. While this assessment could be approached formally with the rank conditions given above, note that the PPP relationship does not involve the interest rates and the UIP relationship does not involve the PPP variables, hence the PPP and UIP relationships are distinguishable (identified) from each other. With $r = 2$ the necessary condition for identification is that there should be $2 - 1 = 1$ restriction on each vector, whereas there are 4 restrictions on the first vector comprising 2 exclusions and 2 equality restrictions and 4 restrictions on the second vector comprising 3 exclusions and 1 equality restriction, and hence each is overidentified. The R_i and H_i of section **14.5.2** are summarised below.

Identifying restrictions: PPP and UIP

First cointegrating vector: PPP, other coefficients equal to zero.

$$R_1\beta_1 = 0$$

$$\begin{bmatrix} 1 & 1 & 0 & 0 & 0 \\ 1 & 0 & 1 & 0 & 0 \\ 0 & 0 & 0 & 1 & 0 \\ 0 & 0 & 0 & 0 & 1 \end{bmatrix} \begin{pmatrix} \beta_{11} \\ \beta_{21} \\ \beta_{31} \\ \beta_{41} \\ \beta_{51} \end{pmatrix} = 0$$

$$\beta_1 = H_1\varphi_{11}$$

$$\begin{pmatrix} \beta_{11} \\ \beta_{21} \\ \beta_{31} \\ \beta_{41} \\ \beta_{51} \end{pmatrix} = \begin{pmatrix} 1 \\ -1 \\ -1 \\ 0 \\ 0 \end{pmatrix} \varphi_{11} \quad (15.1)$$

Second cointegrating vector: UIP, other coefficients equal to zero.

$$R_2\beta_2 = 0$$

$$\begin{bmatrix} 1 & 0 & 0 & 0 & 0 \\ 0 & 1 & 0 & 0 & 0 \\ 0 & 0 & 1 & 0 & 0 \\ 0 & 0 & 0 & 1 & 1 \end{bmatrix} \begin{pmatrix} \beta_{12} \\ \beta_{22} \\ \beta_{32} \\ \beta_{42} \\ \beta_{52} \end{pmatrix} = 0$$

$$\beta_1 = H_2\varphi_{12}$$

$$\begin{pmatrix} \beta_{12} \\ \beta_{22} \\ \beta_{32} \\ \beta_{42} \\ \beta_{52} \end{pmatrix} = \begin{pmatrix} 0 \\ 0 \\ 0 \\ 1 \\ -1 \end{pmatrix} \varphi_{12} \qquad (15.2)$$

Less restrictive but still overidentifying is that the first vector contains the PPP relationship but the other coefficients are unrestricted. In this case there are 2 restrictions given by the first two rows of R_1 and a suitably amended H_1 matrix, that is:

Identifying restrictions: PPP and UIP

PPP, no restrictions on other coefficients.

$$R_1\beta_1 = 0$$

$$\begin{bmatrix} 1 & 1 & 0 & 0 & 0 \\ 1 & 0 & 1 & 0 & 0 \end{bmatrix} \begin{pmatrix} \beta_{11} \\ \beta_{21} \\ \beta_{31} \\ \beta_{41} \\ \beta_{51} \end{pmatrix} = 0$$

$$\beta_1 = H_1\varphi_1$$

$$\begin{pmatrix} \beta_{11} \\ \beta_{21} \\ \beta_{31} \\ \beta_{41} \\ \beta_{51} \end{pmatrix} = \begin{bmatrix} 1 & 0 & 0 \\ -1 & 0 & 0 \\ -1 & 0 & 0 \\ 0 & 1 & 0 \\ 0 & 0 & 1 \end{bmatrix} \begin{pmatrix} \varphi_{11} \\ \varphi_{21} \\ \varphi_{31} \end{pmatrix} \qquad (15.3)$$

Similarly a less restrictive version of UIP is to enforce the equality restriction but otherwise

leave the coefficients unconstrained; note that now $g_2 = 1$ so the cointegrating vector is just identified (by the necessary condition). The amended restriction matrices are:

UIP, no restrictions on other coefficients.

$$R_2\beta_2 = 0$$

$$\begin{bmatrix} 0 & 0 & 0 & 1 & 1 \end{bmatrix} \begin{pmatrix} \beta_{12} \\ \beta_{22} \\ \beta_{32} \\ \beta_{42} \\ \beta_{52} \end{pmatrix} = 0$$

$$\beta_1 = H_2\varphi_2$$

$$\begin{pmatrix} \beta_{12} \\ \beta_{22} \\ \beta_{32} \\ \beta_{42} \\ \beta_{52} \end{pmatrix} = \begin{pmatrix} 1 & 0 & 0 & 0 \\ 0 & 1 & 0 & 0 \\ 0 & 0 & 1 & 0 \\ 0 & 0 & 0 & 1 \\ 0 & 0 & 0 & -1 \end{pmatrix} \begin{pmatrix} \varphi_{12} \\ \varphi_{22} \\ \varphi_{32} \\ \varphi_{42} \end{pmatrix} \qquad (15.4)$$

Note that the rank conditions are met with these revised restrictions since rank$(R_1H_2) = 2 \geq 1$ and rank$(R_2H_1) = 1$. Having established that the PPP and UIP relations in different forms are generically identified the next stage is to see if there is empirical confirmation of these structural relations in the data. The first step of the next stage is to assess the number of cointegrating vectors consistent with the data.

15.2.3 Estimating the cointegrating rank

The following variables were defined by Johansen and Juselius (1992) for the United Kingdom using quarterly data for the sample period 1972q1 to 1987q2: P_t, the UK wholesale price index; P_t^*, trade weighted foreign wholesale price index; E_t, UK effective exchange rate; r_t, 3-month Treasury Bill rate; r_t^*, 3-month Euro-dollar rate. Logs of variables were used, indicated

Table 15.1   *Residual misspecification test statistics: second order VAR with oil prices*

Equation	Standard deviation	Skewness	Excess kurtosis	Normality test, $\chi^2(2)$	Serial correlation $\chi^2(20)$
p_t	0.007	0.29	1.27	4.84	6.09
p_t^*	0.007	0.28	2.16	**12.44**	9.59
e_t	0.030	0.30	0.17	0.95	13.54
r_t	0.011	0.58	0.25	3.55	9.11
r_t^*	0.013	−0.51	3.76	**37.95**	16.41

Source: Johansen and Juselius (*op. cit.*, Table 1, p. 220). 5% critical values: $\chi^2(2) = 5.99$, $\chi^2(20) = 31.41$. Bold entries indicate significant values.

by lower case letters, except for the interest rates. The vector y_t is defined as follows:

$$y_t = (p_t, p_t^*, e_t, r_t, r_t^*)$$

On inspecting graphs of the data Johansen and Juselius (*op. cit.*) concluded that the price series have a linear trend and so the appropriate model should have an unrestricted constant (that is Model 3 of Table 14.2) to allow linear trends in the data. Initially a second order VAR in y_t was estimated, but there was evidence of nonnormality from excess kurtosis and Johansen and Juselius (*op. cit.*, p. 219) were not satisfied with this model as a firm base for inference (see section **14.4.1**). The nonstationarity in

the variance was accounted for by including the growth in world oil prices, Δy_{6t} and Δy_{6t-1} where y_{6t} is the world oil price, in the second order VAR. The misspecification test statistics for this model are reported in Table 15.1. The serial correlation test is passed for all equations, but the equations for p_t^* and r_t^* still show signs of residual nonnormality; however, Johansen and Juselius (*op. cit.*) note that the importance of the deviation from normality is lessened to the extent that subsequent tests indicate that p_t^* and r_t^* are (weakly) exogenous for the parameters of interest (see section **15.6** below for a detailed explanation of these terms). The cointegration rank tests are based on this model.

Table 15.2   *Test statistics for cointegrating rank, Johansen and Juselius (1992)*

Null	Alt.	$\hat{\lambda}_i$	λ_{max} statistic	95% quantile	Null	Alt.	Trace statistic	95% quantile
$r = 0$	$r = 1$	0.407	$-T\ln(1 - \hat{\lambda}_1) = 31.33 < 33.46$		$r = 0$	$r \geq 1$	$T\sum_{i=1}^{k}\ln(1 - \hat{\lambda}_i) = \mathbf{80.75} > \mathbf{68.52}$	
$r \leq 1$	$r = 2$	0.285	$-T\ln(1 - \hat{\lambda}_2) = 20.16 < 27.07$		$r \leq 1$	$r \geq 2$	$-T\sum_{i=2}^{k}\ln(1 - \hat{\lambda}_i) = \mathbf{49.42} > \mathbf{47.21}$	
$r \leq 2$	$r = 3$	0.254	$-T\ln(1 - \hat{\lambda}_3) = 17.59 < 20.97$		$r \leq 2$	$r \geq 3$	$-T\sum_{i=3}^{k}\ln(1 - \hat{\lambda}_i) = 29.26 \approx 29.68$	
$r \leq 3$	$r = 4$	0.102	$-T\ln(1 - \hat{\lambda}_4) = 6.48 < 14.07$		$r \leq 3$	$r \geq 4$	$-T\sum_{i=4}^{k}\ln(1 - \hat{\lambda}_i) = 11.67 < 15.14$	
$r \leq 4$	$r = 5$	0.083	$-T\ln(1 - \hat{\lambda}_5) = 5.19 > 3.76$		$r \leq 4$	$r = 5$	$-T\ln(1 - \hat{\lambda}_5) = 5.19 > 3.76$	

Source: Johansen and Juselius (1992, Table 2); critical values are from Table 14.5 corresponding to Table 1 of Osterwald-Lenum (1992); these differ slightly from the critical values presented by Johansen and Juselius (*op. cit.*) due to stochastic variability in the simulations. $k = 5$.

The inclusion of an unrestricted constant in the VAR indicates that the estimated equations correspond to Model 3 in Table 14.2 of Chapter 14, so that $\mu_1 \neq 0$, $\mu_2 \neq 0$ and $\delta = 0$; there is a constant in the CI space and a linear trend in the data with critical values obtained from Table 14.5. The test statistics obtained by Johansen and Juselius (1992, Table 2) are reported in Table 15.2.

The first three estimated eigenvalues, $\hat{\lambda}_i$, at 0.407, 0.285 and 0.254 suggest the distinct possibility of 3 cointegrating vectors, so what do the formal test statistics indicate? Starting with the λ_{max} test and $H(0 \mid 1)$ we find nonrejection of the null that $r = 0$; however, that is a fairly marginal decision since the 90% quantile is 30.90 and, hence, at the 10% significance level we would reject $r = 0$. Moving to test $H(1 \mid 2)$ we again find nonrejection using the 95% quantile since $20.16 < 27.07$, and this is also the case if we use the 80% quantile which is 21.98, although this is now quite a marginal decision. Even though the formal testing sequence should stop with nonrejection, it is informative to continue since the null $H(2 \mid 3)$ is again quite close to the margin of rejection with $17.59 < 20.97$ but

$17.59 \approx 18.60$ (90% quantile), whereas we would definitely conclude $r < 4$.

With the trace statistic we find rejection of $H(0 \mid 5)$ since $80.75 > 68.52$, and rejection of $H(1 \mid 5)$ since $49.42 > 47.21$; the next null hypothesis $H(2 \mid 5)$ is on the borderline of rejection since $29.26 \approx 29.68$, whereas $H(3 \mid 5)$ is not rejected. Hence the evidence from the trace test is in favour of $r = 3$.

15.2.4 Interpreting the unrestricted cointegrating vectors

Johansen and Juselius (*op. cit.*) suggest looking at the estimated coefficients and possible stationary combinations to resolve the ambiguity in the formal testing procedure. In the (unrestricted) VAR in which testing is based, α and β are 5×5 matrices with each column, β_i, potentially a cointegrating vector. The unrestricted estimated values are given in Table 15.3.

Johansen and Juselius (*op. cit.*) have normalised the β_i vectors by inspection of the unnormalised coefficients with the PPP and UIP structural relations in mind. For PPP we expect the coefficients on p_t^* and e_t to be equal but

Table 15.3 *Unrestricted estimates of the cointegrating vectors and adjustment coefficients*

	Estimated β_i vectors (the eigenvectors)				
	β_1	β_2	β_3	β_4	β_5
Variable					
p_t	1.00	0.03	0.36	1.00	1.00
p_t^*	−0.91	0.03	−0.46	−2.40	−1.45
e_t	−0.93	−0.10	0.41	1.12	−0.48
r_t	−3.38	1.00	1.00	−0.41	2.28
r_t^*	−1.89	−0.93	−1.03	2.98	0.76
	Estimated α_i vectors (the adjustment coefficients)				
	α_1	α_2	α_3	α_4	α_5
Equation					
p_t	**−0.07**	0.04	−0.01	**0.00**	**−0.01**
p_t^*	−0.02	0.00	−0.04	0.01	0.01
e_t	0.10	−0.01	−0.15	−0.04	−0.05
r_t	0.03	**−0.15**	**0.03**	0.01	−0.02
r_t^*	0.06	0.29	0.01	0.03	−0.01

Source: Johansen and Juselius (*op. cit.*, Table 3). 'Own' adjustment coefficients (conditional on the normalisation in β) are indicated in bold.

opposite in sign to the coefficient on p_t; and for UIP the coefficients on r_t and r_t^* should be equal but opposite in sign. On this basis the first vector corresponds to the PPP relationship since neither the second nor the third vectors have the same sign on p_t^* and e_t. Both the second and third vectors meet the basic UIP condition of opposite signs on the coefficients on r_t and r_t^*; Johansen and Juselius (*op. cit.*) prefer to interpret the second vector as the UIP relationship partly because the remaining coefficients are closer to zero and the time series graph of implied equilibrium, $\beta_3' y_t$, is less convincing as a stationary relationship compared to $\beta_2' y_t$. Also the α matrix is of interest in this context. We have seen that neither α nor β are unique but if, given a particular normalisation of β, α is interpretable that will support the choice of normalisation. In this case the own adjustment coefficients are indicated in bold in the table, with those in the first and second columns negative but that in the third column positive, this supports the interpretation of the first vector as capturing the PPP relationship and the second the UIP relationship which is the conclusion of Johansen and Juselius (*op. cit.*, p. 222).

15.3 Wage differentials in the United States, Dickey and Rossana (1994); *using the λ_{max} and trace test statistics; identification of cointegrating vectors; distinguishing identifying and nonidentifying restrictions*

Using univariate tests on real wage data for particular manufacturing industries in the US

manufacturing sector Rossana and Seater (1992) find that a unit root null hypothesis cannot be rejected. However, Dickey and Rossana (1994) suggest that the finding of independent unit root processes for different industries is counterintuitive. As we saw in Chapter 6 a random shock to a univariate time series process with a unit root permanently changes the level of the series. Hence, on this basis wage differentials between industries could be permanently changed by random shocks, suggesting that competitive forces do not work to restore an equilibrium differential. If, however, real wages among industries are cointegrated an optimal wage differential can be maintained in the long run despite the presence of a unit root in the individual series.

15.3.1 Estimating the cointegrating rank

To test this proposition Dickey and Rossana (*op. cit.*) used a monthly data set, for the period 1958m1 to 1988m2, comprising (nominal) average hourly earnings for production workers for 4 manufacturing industries within the sector producing paper and allied products, and the consumer price index for all urban workers. In natural logarithms these variables are denoted $w_{it}, i = 1, \ldots, 4$ and p_t, respectively; and define the 6×1 vector $y_t = (w_{1t}, w_{2t}, w_{3t}, w_{4t}, p_t, 1)'$. Seasonality in the data required the use of centred seasonal dummy variables in the VAR. The VAR model used by Dickey and Rossana (*op. cit.*) includes a constant restricted to the cointegration space. The λ_{max} and trace statistics are reported in Table 15.4.

It seems unlikely that *nominal* wage rates do not contain a trend, hence there must be some doubt about the model used here, which, in the typology of Chapter 14, Table 14.2 is Model 2. This model restricts the constant to the cointegration space and hence does not allow linear trends in the data space. It would have been useful to graph the data and start with Model 3,

Table 15.4 *Test statistics for cointegrating rank, Dickey and Rossana (1994)*

Null	Alt.	$\lambda_{\max}$ statistic		95% quantile	Null	Alt.	Trace statistic		95% quantile
$r = 0$	$r = 1$	**107.32**	>	**34.40**	$r = 0$	$r \geq 1$	**182.19**	>	**76.07**
$r \leq 1$	$r = 2$	**39.63**	>	**28.14**	$r \leq 1$	$r \geq 2$	**74.87**	>	**53.12**
$r \leq 2$	$r = 3$	19.03	<	22.00	$r \leq 2$	$r \geq 3$	**35.24**	>	**34.91**
$r \leq 3$	$r = 4$	n.g.		15.67	$r \leq 3$	$r \geq 4$	n.g.		19.96
$r \leq 4$	$r = 5$	n.g.		9.24	$r \leq 4$	$r = 5$	n.g.		9.24

Source: Entries for test statistics, Dickey and Rossana (*op. cit.*, Table 1, p. 347); n.g. means not given in the source. Critical values from Table 14.4 corresponding to Table 1* of Osterwald-Lenum (1992). Bold entries indicate significant values.

which includes trends in the data, or Model 4, which allows a trend in the cointegration space and then determine the appropriate model along with the cointegrating rank.

If the Dickey–Rossana hypothesis is correct and there are n industries there should be $n - 1$ cointegrating vectors. As 4 industries are included in the study we would expect to find 3 cointegrating vectors under the null hypothesis; if so we can interpret this as 1 common trend driving wages in the 4 industries. A finding of 2 cointegrating vectors implies 2 common trends.

Consider first the $\lambda_{\max}$ test statistics. The null of $r = 0$ is rejected against $r = 1$ as $107.32 > 34.40$; then the null of $r = 1$ is rejected against $r = 2$ as $39.63 > 28.14$; however, with $19.03 < 22.00$ the null of $r = 2$ is not rejected against $r = 3$, but note that the 90% quantile is 19.77 so the decision here is marginal. Using the trace

test and the 95% quantile leads to the conclusion that $r = 3$. Dickey and Rossana choose $r = 2$ although there is theoretical and empirical support from the trace test that $r = 3$.

With $r = 2$, Dickey and Rossana (*op. cit.*) report the following estimates of α and β – see Table 15.5.

The estimates of β_1 and β_2 in Table 15.5 are normalised on the first element in each case. However, given the symmetric way in which wage rates enter the analysis, the estimates could have been normalised on any of the first 4 coefficients. Indeed the possibility that p_t depends upon wage rates in the manufacturing sector would not rule out normalisation on the coefficient of p_t. A structure to enable interpretation of the cointegrating vectors and their associated adjustment coefficients is outlined in section **15.3.3** below. The latter also pose some problems of interpretation; they are numerically very small, indeed in the case of the second cointegrating vector all the coefficients are virtually zero. All the coefficients in α_1 are positive hindering an interpretation of an 'own' adjustment coefficient, which we would expect to be negative (although, of course, simultaneities in the SECM can transform negative error correction coefficients into positive adjustment coefficients).The lack of structure is not surprising as the cointegrating vectors are not yet identified, an issue which we consider further in section **15.3.3**. Restrictions associated with whether real

Table 15.5 *Estimates of the eigenvectors, β, and adjustment coefficients, α*

	β_1	β_2	α_1	α_2
w_{1t}	1.000	1.000	0.0023	−0.0003
w_{2t}	1.032	−1.185	0.0019	−0.0003
w_{3t}	0.852	0.320	0.0014	−0.0003
w_{4t}	−3.429	0.049	0.0013	−0.0003
p_t	0.236	−0.161	0.0005	0.0000
1	−0.720	0.439		

wage rates cointegrate, which we consider next, apply to each cointegrating vector and are not, therefore, identifying.

15.3.2 Cointegration of real wages

The hypothesis that real wages are cointegrated can be seen easily by first considering just two wage series w_{1t} and w_{2t} and the price index p_t; then the cointegrating vector should be of the form $(\beta_{11}, \beta_{21}, -[\beta_{11} + \beta_{21}])$. The coefficient on price is the negative of the sum of the coefficients on the wage terms, so the cointegrating relation is

$$
\begin{aligned}
ecm_{1t} &= \beta_{11}w_{1t} + \beta_{21}w_{2t} - (\beta_{11}p_t + \beta_{21}p_t) \\
&= \beta_{11}(w_{1t} - p_t) + \beta_{21}(w_{2t} - p_t) \quad (15.5)
\end{aligned}
$$

To represent this restriction we can either formulate the indirect or the direct parameterisation, that is:

indirect

$$
(1 \quad 1 \quad 1)\begin{pmatrix} \beta_{11} \\ \beta_{21} \\ \beta_{31} \end{pmatrix} = 0 \quad \text{or}
$$

direct

$$
\begin{pmatrix} \beta_{11} \\ \beta_{21} \\ \beta_{31} \end{pmatrix} = \begin{bmatrix} 1 & 0 \\ 0 & 1 \\ -1 & -1 \end{bmatrix}\begin{pmatrix} \varphi_{11} \\ \varphi_{21} \end{pmatrix} \quad (15.6)
$$

The direct parameterisation is not unique, in this case it has been formulated for ease of interpretation so that

$$
\begin{aligned}
&\beta_{11} = \varphi_{11}, \quad \beta_{21} = \varphi_{21} \quad \text{and} \\
&\beta_{31} = -(\varphi_{11} + \varphi_{21}) = -(\beta_{11} + \beta_{21})
\end{aligned}
$$

Now extending to n industries the null hypothesis of no divergence in wage rates implies $n - 1$ cointegrating vectors, so for $n = 4$ there should be a restriction of the form $\sum_{i=1}^{4} \beta_{ij} = -\beta_{5j}$ for each of the $j = n - 1$ cointegrating vectors. The

direct parameterisation is:

$$
\begin{pmatrix} \beta_{1j} \\ \beta_{2j} \\ \beta_{3j} \\ \beta_{4j} \\ \beta_{5j} \\ \beta_{6j} \end{pmatrix} = \begin{bmatrix} 1 & 0 & 0 & 0 & 0 \\ 0 & 1 & 0 & 0 & 0 \\ 0 & 0 & 1 & 0 & 0 \\ 0 & 0 & 0 & 1 & 0 \\ -1 & -1 & -1 & -1 & 0 \\ 0 & 0 & 0 & 0 & 1 \end{bmatrix}\begin{pmatrix} \varphi_{1j} \\ \varphi_{2j} \\ \varphi_{3j} \\ \varphi_{4j} \\ \varphi_{5j} \end{pmatrix}
$$

$$(15.7)$$

This is now simple to interpret since $\beta_{ij} = \varphi_{ij}$ for $i = 1, \ldots, 4$, $\beta_{5j} = -(\varphi_{1j} + \varphi_{2j} + \varphi_{3j} + \varphi_{4j})$ and $\beta_{6j} = \varphi_{5j}$, where the last coefficient is the constant in the cointegration space.

Dickey and Rossana test the null hypothesis $H_0: \sum_{i=1}^{4} \beta_{ij} = -\beta_{5j}$ for each of the $j = 1, 2$ cointegrating vectors. The test statistic is

$$
T \ln([1 - \hat{\lambda}_1^*][1 - \hat{\lambda}_2^*]/[1 - \hat{\lambda}_1][1 - \hat{\lambda}_2])
$$

which is distributed as $\chi^2(2)$ under the null hypothesis. $\hat{\lambda}_i^*$ are the estimated eigenvalues imposing the restrictions under H_0; and the degrees of freedom follows from the imposition of 1 restriction on each of the 2 cointegrating vectors. In general this is $r(k - s)$ where s is the number of free parameters in the indirect parameterisation not including the constant. The test statistic is 82.7 compared with the 5% critical value for $\chi^2(2)$ of 5.99, hence rejection is definite. An alternative methodology is first to consider restrictions which enable the cointegrating vectors to be identified, which gives a structure to the interpretation of the estimated eigenvectors and adjustment coefficients, and then test the real wage hypothesis.

15.3.3 Identification of the cointegrating vectors

Recall that identification of the cointegrating vectors requires that there must be at least $r - 1$ independent restrictions of the form $R_i\beta_i = 0$ placed on each cointegrating vector, $i = 1, \ldots, r$. How many this is depends on whether we take

$r = n - 1 = 3$, which finds support from the trace test and from the theoretical background for the study, or $r = 2$ as suggested by Dickey and Rossana (*op. cit.*, p. 349) from the λ_{max} test. In the former case identification requires $3 - 1 = 2$ restrictions and in the latter case $2 - 1 = 1$ restriction.

As a reminder, in the indirect parameterisation $R_i \beta_i = 0$, R_i is $g_i \times k$ with g_i the number of restrictions and it is necessary for identification of the ith cointegrating vector that $g_i \geq r - 1$; certainly if $g_i < r - 1$ the ith cointegrating vector cannot be identified. The necessary and sufficient conditions for identification for $r = 2$ are rank$(R_1 H_2) \geq 1$ and rank$(R_2 H_1) \geq 1$. The restriction that real wages cointegrate, $\sum_{i=1}^{4} \beta_{ij} = -\beta_{5j}$, is the same for each cointegrating vector, hence it cannot be identifying, formally rank$(R_1 H_2) = 0$ and rank$(R_2 H_1) = 0$, and no other identifying restrictions are offered. Thus, although the statistical analysis suggests at least 2 cointegrating vectors, without further information no generic or economic identification is possible. For example, although Dickey and Rossana motivate their study with the absence of divergent wage differentials, there could be a relationship in which the price level depends upon industry price levels, hence the lack of identification for particular cointegrating vectors.

Suppose just 2 industries were used in the statistical analysis then with 1 cointegrating vector among w_{1t}, w_{2t} and p_t no restrictions are required for generic identification; the cointegrating vector is saying that a linear combination of the 2 wage rates and prices is stationary. With 1 cointegrating vector further restrictions are overidentifying and testable. In this special case the hypothesis that real wages cointegrate with coefficients $(\beta_{11}, \beta_{21}, -[\beta_{11} + \beta_{21}])$ does impose 1 overidentifying restriction on the single cointegrating vector. A further restriction is that the wage differential is stationary in the long run obtained by setting $\beta_{21} = -\beta_{11}$, which implies $[\beta_{11} + \beta_{21}] = 0$ resulting in the restricted cointegrating vector $(\beta_{11}, -\beta_{11}, 0)$, which, for simplicity of interpretation, normal-

ised on the first variable, is $(1, -1, 0)$; altogether 2 restrictions are now imposed. Inclusion of a constant in the cointegration space is seen to be an important point since it allows for a constant wage differential rather than equality of wages; that is

$$ecm_{1t} = w_{1t} - w_{2t} + \beta_{10} \Rightarrow$$
$$ECM_{1t} = B_{10} W_{1t}/W_{2t}$$

where $B_{10} = \exp(\beta_{10})$, in levels, and might seem desirable *a priori* rather than impose $B_{10} = 1$ and so $\beta_{10} = 0$.

Increasing the number of industries to 3 suggests 2 cointegrating vectors and, therefore, a minimum of 1 independent restriction on each is needed for identification. One possibility is to consider constant long-run wage differentials across industries; the constant in the cointegration space capturing the differential, with particular cointegrating vectors isolating the pairwise connection between industries. With $y_t = (w_{1t}, w_{2t}, w_{3t}, p_t, 1)$ and $r = 2$ the suggested identifying restrictions are given in Table 15.6.

For example, in R_1 the first row sets $\beta_{11} + \beta_{21} = 0$ and the second row excludes w_{3t} by setting $\beta_{31} = 0$. It is easy to establish rank $R_1 H_2 = 1$ and rank $R_2 H_1 = 1$, hence these conditions are sufficient. As 2 restrictions are imposed on each cointegrating vector, whereas only 1 is necessary, these restrictions are overidentifying.

When there are 4 industries $y_t = (w_{1t}, w_{2t}, w_{3t}, w_{4t}, p_t, 1)$, and if $r = 3$, then a minimum of 2 independent restrictions on each cointegrating vector is required for identification. Continuing the idea of each cointegrating vector capturing a pairwise constant long-run wage differential we can add exclusion restrictions for the other wage rates – see Table 15.7. Now, in the case of R_1, the third row excludes w_{4t} by setting $\beta_{41} = 0$.

As a final point note that the restriction that real wages cointegrate appears not to be the same for different cointegrating vectors; for example, with $n = 3$ and $r = 2$ for the first cointegrating vector we require $\beta_{11} + \beta_{21} + \beta_{41} = 0$ and

Table 15.6 *Identifying restrictions for 3 industries*

$$R_1\beta_1 = 0 \qquad\qquad \beta_1 = H_1\varphi_1$$

$$\begin{bmatrix} 1 & 1 & 0 & 0 & 0 \\ 0 & 0 & 1 & 0 & 0 \end{bmatrix} \begin{pmatrix} \beta_{11} \\ \beta_{21} \\ \beta_{31} \\ \beta_{41} \\ \beta_{51} \end{pmatrix} = \begin{pmatrix} 0 \\ 0 \end{pmatrix} \qquad \begin{pmatrix} \beta_{11} \\ \beta_{21} \\ \beta_{31} \\ \beta_{41} \\ \beta_{51} \end{pmatrix} = \begin{bmatrix} 1 & 0 & 0 \\ -1 & 0 & 0 \\ 0 & 0 & 0 \\ 0 & 1 & 0 \\ 0 & 0 & 1 \end{bmatrix} \begin{pmatrix} \varphi_{11} \\ \varphi_{21} \\ \varphi_{31} \end{pmatrix} \qquad (15.8)$$

$$R_2\beta_2 = 0 \qquad\qquad \beta_2 = H_2\varphi_2$$

$$\begin{bmatrix} 1 & 0 & 1 & 0 & 0 \\ 0 & 1 & 0 & 0 & 0 \end{bmatrix} \begin{pmatrix} \beta_{12} \\ \beta_{22} \\ \beta_{32} \\ \beta_{42} \\ \beta_{52} \end{pmatrix} = \begin{pmatrix} 0 \\ 0 \end{pmatrix} \qquad \begin{pmatrix} \beta_{12} \\ \beta_{22} \\ \beta_{32} \\ \beta_{42} \\ \beta_{52} \end{pmatrix} = \begin{bmatrix} 1 & 0 & 0 \\ 0 & 0 & 0 \\ -1 & 0 & 0 \\ 0 & 1 & 0 \\ 0 & 0 & 1 \end{bmatrix} \begin{pmatrix} \varphi_{12} \\ \varphi_{22} \\ \varphi_{32} \end{pmatrix} \qquad (15.9)$$

for the second $\beta_{12} + \beta_{32} + \beta_{42} = 0$. The revised restriction matrices are given in Table 15.8. However, substituting in the first restriction in each case, that is $\beta_{11} + \beta_{21} = 0$ and $\beta_{12} + \beta_{32} = 0$, respectively, shows that the restrictions are just

$\beta_{41} = 0$ and $\beta_{42} = 0$; that is the coefficient on price in each cointegrating vector is zero. A hint that this is the case is given by the rank of, for example, R_1H_2, which has not been increased by this restriction; these restrictions do not,

Table 15.7 *Identifying restrictions for 4 industries*

$$R_1\beta_1 = 0 \qquad\qquad \beta_1 = H_1\varphi_1$$

$$\begin{bmatrix} 1 & 1 & 0 & 0 & 0 & 0 \\ 0 & 0 & 1 & 0 & 0 & 0 \\ 0 & 0 & 0 & 1 & 0 & 0 \end{bmatrix} \begin{pmatrix} \beta_{11} \\ \beta_{21} \\ \beta_{31} \\ \beta_{41} \\ \beta_{51} \\ \beta_{61} \end{pmatrix} = \begin{pmatrix} 0 \\ 0 \\ 0 \end{pmatrix} \qquad \begin{pmatrix} \beta_{11} \\ \beta_{21} \\ \beta_{31} \\ \beta_{41} \\ \beta_{51} \\ \beta_{61} \end{pmatrix} = \begin{bmatrix} 1 & 0 & 0 \\ -1 & 0 & 0 \\ 0 & 0 & 0 \\ 0 & 0 & 0 \\ 0 & 1 & 0 \\ 0 & 0 & 1 \end{bmatrix} \begin{pmatrix} \varphi_{11} \\ \varphi_{21} \\ \varphi_{31} \end{pmatrix} \qquad (15.10)$$

$$R_2\beta_2 = 0 \qquad\qquad \beta_2 = H_2\varphi_2$$

$$\begin{bmatrix} 1 & 0 & 1 & 0 & 0 & 0 \\ 0 & 1 & 0 & 0 & 0 & 0 \\ 0 & 0 & 0 & 1 & 0 & 0 \end{bmatrix} \begin{pmatrix} \beta_{12} \\ \beta_{22} \\ \beta_{32} \\ \beta_{42} \\ \beta_{52} \\ \beta_{62} \end{pmatrix} = \begin{pmatrix} 0 \\ 0 \\ 0 \end{pmatrix} \qquad \begin{pmatrix} \beta_{12} \\ \beta_{22} \\ \beta_{32} \\ \beta_{42} \\ \beta_{52} \\ \beta_{62} \end{pmatrix} = \begin{bmatrix} 1 & 0 & 0 \\ 0 & 0 & 0 \\ -1 & 0 & 0 \\ 0 & 0 & 0 \\ 0 & 1 & 0 \\ 0 & 0 & 1 \end{bmatrix} \begin{pmatrix} \varphi_{12} \\ \varphi_{22} \\ \varphi_{32} \end{pmatrix} \qquad (15.11)$$

$$R_3\beta_3 = 0 \qquad\qquad \beta_3 = H_3\varphi_3$$

$$\begin{bmatrix} 1 & 0 & 0 & 1 & 0 & 0 \\ 0 & 1 & 0 & 0 & 0 & 0 \\ 0 & 0 & 1 & 0 & 0 & 0 \end{bmatrix} \begin{pmatrix} \beta_{13} \\ \beta_{23} \\ \beta_{33} \\ \beta_{43} \\ \beta_{53} \\ \beta_{63} \end{pmatrix} = \begin{pmatrix} 0 \\ 0 \\ 0 \end{pmatrix} \qquad \begin{pmatrix} \beta_{13} \\ \beta_{23} \\ \beta_{33} \\ \beta_{43} \\ \beta_{53} \\ \beta_{63} \end{pmatrix} = \begin{bmatrix} 1 & 0 & 0 \\ 0 & 0 & 0 \\ 0 & 0 & 0 \\ -1 & 0 & 0 \\ 0 & 1 & 0 \\ 0 & 0 & 1 \end{bmatrix} \begin{pmatrix} \varphi_{13} \\ \varphi_{23} \\ \varphi_{33} \end{pmatrix} \qquad (15.12)$$

Table 15.8 *Identifying restrictions for 3 industries and restriction that real wages cointegrate*

$$R_1\beta_1 = 0 \qquad\qquad\qquad \beta_1 = H_1\varphi_1$$

$$\begin{bmatrix} 1 & 1 & 0 & 0 & 0 \\ 0 & 0 & 1 & 0 & 0 \\ 1 & 1 & 0 & 1 & 0 \end{bmatrix} \begin{pmatrix} \beta_{11} \\ \beta_{21} \\ \beta_{31} \\ \beta_{41} \\ \beta_{51} \end{pmatrix} = 0 \qquad \begin{pmatrix} \beta_{11} \\ \beta_{21} \\ \beta_{31} \\ \beta_{41} \\ \beta_{51} \end{pmatrix} = \begin{bmatrix} 1 & 0 \\ -1 & 0 \\ 0 & 0 \\ 0 & 0 \\ 0 & 1 \end{bmatrix} \begin{pmatrix} \varphi_{11} \\ \varphi_{21} \end{pmatrix} \qquad (15.13)$$

$$R_2\beta_2 = 0 \qquad\qquad\qquad \beta_2 = H_2\varphi_2$$

$$\begin{bmatrix} 1 & 0 & 1 & 0 & 0 \\ 0 & 1 & 0 & 0 & 0 \\ 1 & 0 & 1 & 1 & 0 \end{bmatrix} \begin{pmatrix} \beta_{12} \\ \beta_{22} \\ \beta_{32} \\ \beta_{42} \\ \beta_{52} \end{pmatrix} = 0 \qquad \begin{pmatrix} \beta_{12} \\ \beta_{22} \\ \beta_{32} \\ \beta_{42} \\ \beta_{52} \end{pmatrix} = \begin{bmatrix} 1 & 0 \\ 0 & 0 \\ -1 & 0 \\ 0 & 0 \\ 0 & 1 \end{bmatrix} \begin{pmatrix} \varphi_{12} \\ \varphi_{22} \end{pmatrix} \qquad (15.14)$$

therefore, identify or overidentify the cointegrating vectors.

A structure has been suggested here to overcome the problem of the lack of interpretability of the unrestricted eigenvectors – a problem that occurs in many areas of application of these techniques. In particular identification requires bringing prior reasoning to bear to distinguish linear combinations of variables that would otherwise look like each other. Where overidentifying restrictions are specified they can be tested along with other restrictions, such as those associated with the cointegration of real wages, which affect all cointegrating vectors (and hence are not themselves identifying except in special circumstances).

15.4 The IS/LM model, Johansen and Juselius (1994); *identification of the short-run structure and estimation of a structural ECM (SECM)*

A necessary condition for identification (of the short-run structure) is that each equation in the k equation system should have k − 1 coefficient

restrictions. Let $A_1, \ldots, A_k$ denote the k columns of A, then we can formulate the restrictions either in the form $R_iA_i = 0$ or by mapping the coefficients into a lower dimensional space as in $A_i = H_i\varphi_i$ where $R_iH_i = 0$. If there are more than $k - 1$ restrictions on a particular equation that equation is overidentified (by the order condition) in its short-run structure. As before we can check whether the necessary conditions are sufficient by reference to the rank condition. Section **14.5.4**.

An example of identification of the short-run structure is provided in the article by Johansen and Juselius (1994), which was also used in section **14.5.2** to illustrate the identification of co-integrating vectors with the conclusion that 3 cointegrating vectors were identified. As a reminder there are five variables in the analysis: $y'_t = (m_t, inc_t, p_t, r^s_t, r^b_t)'$, where m_t is the log of a measure of (nominal) M3, inc_t is the log of real GDP, p_t is the log of the implicit deflator of GDP, r^s_t is a short-term interest rate (the 3-month commercial bill rate), r^b_t is the 10-year bond rate; and a time trend, t, is allowed in the cointegrating space. The contemporaneous sample covariances, s_{ij}, between the first differences of these variables, standardised by the product of the standard deviations to give the sample correlation coefficient, $R = s_{ij}/(s_{ii}s_{jj})^{0.5}$, are given in Table 15.9.

Table 15.9 *Sample correlation coefficient, R*

	Δm_t	Δinc_t	Δp_t	Δr_t^s	Δr_t^b
Δm_t	1	0.29	0.20	−0.10	−0.10
Δinc_t	0.29	1	0.35	−0.18	0.00
Δp_t	0.20	0.35	1	−0.12	−0.10
Δr_t^s	−0.10	−0.18	−0.12	1	0.65
Δr_t^b	−0.10	0.00	−0.10	0.65	1

Source: Johansen and Juselius (*op. cit.*, Table 7).

The pattern of these correlations suggests the possibility of two simultaneous blocks, one comprising Δm_t, Δinc_t, Δp_t and the other Δr_t^s and Δr_t^b; it therefore seems worth considering the simultaneous structure among the variables.

15.4.1 Identifying the short-run structure

The short-run structure refers to the error correction coefficients, a, the simultaneous structure represented in the off-diagonal elements of Φ, and the lagged dynamic adjustments from the Γ_i^+ coefficients. Assuming that $r = 3$ cointegrating vectors have been identified in a second order VAR, the SECM can be written:

$$(\Phi, -\Gamma_1^+, -a) \begin{pmatrix} \Delta y_t \\ \Delta y_{t-1} \\ \beta' y_{t-1} \end{pmatrix} = u_t \qquad (15.15)$$

Say

$$A'X_t = u_t \qquad (15.16)$$

where $\beta' y_{t-1}$ is the 3×1 vector corresponding to the 3 cointegrating vectors.

The maximum number of nonzero coefficients in each equation (=row) is 4 from Φ (remember that Φ is normalised so the diagonal elements are unity), 5 from Γ_1^+ and 3 from a, giving a total of 12. A just-identified system for the short-run structure imposes exactly $5 - 1 = 4$ restrictions on each column of A (that

is each equation). The restrictions initially tried by Johansen and Juselius (*op. cit.*, Table 8) were:

Equation	Zero coefficients imposed (just-identified)				Number of zero restrictions
Δm_t	Δr_t^s	Δinc_t	Δr_t^b	Δinc_{t-1}	4
Δinc_t	Δr_t^s	Δp_t	Δr_t^b	Δr_{t-1}^b	4
Δp_t	Δr_t^b	Δp_{t-1}	Δr_{t-1}^s	Δr_{t-1}^b	4
Δr_t^s	Δr_{t-1}^s	Δinc_{t-1}	Δp_{t-1}	Δr_{t-1}^b	4
Δr_t^b	Δinc_t	Δm_t	Δp_t	Δr_{t-1}^b	4

These restrictions are imposed on the model which is estimated in the simultaneous form given in section **14.5.4** above; for example, the equation for Δm_t includes Δp_t, Δp_{t-1}, Δm_{t-1}, Δr_{t-1}^s and Δr_{t-1}^b, and the three identified cointegrating combinations $ecm_{it-1} \equiv \beta_i' y_{t-1}$ from the VAR restricted by $r = 3$, and *excludes* Δr_t^s, Δinc_t, Δr_t^b and Δinc_{t-1}. This is an example of two-stage estimation with the cointegrating relations determined from the first stage VAR; in a sense this is a multivariate analogue of the Engle–Granger single-equation procedure. However, although these restrictions were generically identifying, the estimated model revealed a lack of empirical identification with only a few 't' statistics significant. Further analysis by Johansen and Juselius (*op. cit.*) suggested that while various choices of restrictions were generically identifying, it proved difficult to determine an empirically identified system for all five variables. As a result the system was partitioned into two blocks, the first a simultaneous system of Δm_t, Δinc_t, and Δr_t^s, and the second the reduced form equations for Δp_t and Δr_t^b. Nineteen zero restrictions were imposed on the first block which now contains three variables, so there are $19 - (3 - 1)3 = 13$ overidentifying restrictions. The final estimates are given in Table 15.10.

The estimated coefficients are now generally significant and the (over)identified model is empirically identified. A χ^2 test of the overidentifying restrictions with 13 degrees of freedom had

Table 15.10 *Estimation of the overidentified SECM for Δm_t, Δinc_t and Δr_t^s and reduced form for Δp_t and Δr_t^b*

Structural ECM

$\Delta m_t = 0.35\Delta p_t + 0.31\Delta m_{t-1} + 0.41\Delta p_{t-1} + 0.20ecm_{2t-1} - 0.55ecm_{3t-1}$
    (2.6)   (2.9)   (3.4)   (2.3)   (−3.6)

$\Delta inc_t = 0.25\Delta m_t + 0.31\Delta p_t + 0.17\Delta r_{t-1}^s - 0.44ecm_{1t-1} + 0.28ecm_{3t-1}$
     (1.1)   (2.0)   (1.3)   (−4.1)   (1.3)

$\Delta r_t^s = 1.10\Delta r_t^b + 0.34\Delta r_{t-1}^s + 0.21\Delta m_{t-1} - 0.24\Delta p_{t-1} - 0.45\Delta r_{t-1}^s + 0.19ecm_{1t-1} - 0.28ecm_{2t-1}$
     (6.5)   (3.2)   (3.0)   (−2.8)   (−2.1)   (2.8)   (−4.7)

Reduced form ECM

$\Delta p_t = -0.08\Delta m_{t-1} - 0.13\Delta p_{t-1} + 0.20ecm_{1t-1} - 0.12ecm_{2t-1} + 0.48ecm_{3t-1}$
    (0.8)   (1.0)   (2.2)   (1.4)   (3.4)

$\Delta r_t^b = 0.08\Delta m_{t-1} + 0.12ecm_{1t-1} - 0.09ecm_{3t-1}$
    (1.7)   (3.0)   (1.3)

Cointegrating vectors

$ecm_{1t-1} = inc_{t-1} - 0.19(m_{t-1} - p_{t-1}) - 0.005t - 0.027D84_t - 8.43$
$ecm_{2t-1} = r_{t-1}^s - r_{t-1}^b + 0.010D84_t + 0.03$
$ecm_{3t-1} = r_{t-1}^b - 0.49(p_{t-1} - 0.02t) - 0.008D84_t - 0.52$

Source: Johansen and Juselius (*op. cit.*, Tables 6 and 9); '*t*' statistics in parentheses; $D84_t$ is a dummy variable which takes the value 1 in 1984q1 to 1991q1 and 0 elsewhere; t is a time trend.

a sample value of 4.82 compared with the 95% quantile of 22.36, so the restrictions are not rejected. Given that the first and second cointegrating vectors have been normalised on inc_t and r_t^s, of particular interest are the estimates of the 'own' error correction coefficients; these are −0.44 and −0.28, respectively, with signs as anticipated and significant.

$$\Phi^{-1} = \begin{bmatrix} 1 & 0 & 0 & 0.35 & 0 \\ 0.25 & 1 & 0 & 0.40 & 0 \\ 0 & 0 & 1 & 0 & 1.1 \\ 0 & 0 & 0 & 1 & 0 \\ 0 & 0 & 0 & 0 & 1 \end{bmatrix}$$

$$a = \begin{bmatrix} 0 & 0.2 & -0.55 \\ -0.44 & 0 & 0.28 \\ 0.19 & -0.28 & 0 \\ 0.20 & -0.12 & 0.48 \\ 0.12 & 0 & -0.09 \end{bmatrix}$$

15.4.2 The simultaneous structure

The simultaneous structure is now very sparse. The Φ matrix, its inverse, the error correction coefficients, a, and the derived adjustment coefficients, $\alpha = \Phi^{-1}a$, are given below:

$$\Phi = \begin{bmatrix} 1 & 0 & 0 & -0.35 & 0 \\ -0.25 & 1 & 0 & -0.31 & 0 \\ 0 & 0 & 1 & 0 & -1.1 \\ 0 & 0 & 0 & 1 & 0 \\ 0 & 0 & 0 & 0 & 1 \end{bmatrix}$$

Derived adjustment coefficients
$\alpha = \Phi^{-1}a$

Equation	α_1	α_2	α_3
Δm_t	0.070	0.158	−0.382
Δinc_t	−0.360	0.002	0.333
Δr_t^s	0.322	−0.280	−0.100
Δp_t	0.200	−0.120	0.480
Δr_t^b	0.120	0.000	−0.090

Although not pronounced here because Φ, and hence Φ^{-1}, is sparse, the zeros in the upper 3×3 block of a, which relate to the simultaneous part of the system, become nonzeros in α showing how the disequilibrium effects are transmitted to all variables in the reduced form.

15.5 The demand for money in the United Kingdom, Hendry and Mizon (1993); *using the λ_{max} and trace test statistics; identification of the cointegrating vectors; identification of the short-run structure and estimation of a structural ECM (SECM)*

Hendry and Mizon (1993) model the demand for M1 in the United Kingdom using seasonally adjusted data over the period 1963q1 to 1984q4. The data used were: nominal M1, M_t; constant price total final expenditure, EXP_t; the implicit deflator for EXP_t, P_t; the 3-month local authority interest rate, R_t; the inflation rate, $\Delta \ln P_t$; and a trend denoted t. Logs were taken of all variables except the trend, and lower case letters denote logs. As there was evidence that m_t and p_t were I(2) but their difference, $m_t - p_t$, which is 'real money', was I(1), the vector of variables for the cointegration analysis was $y'_t = (m_t - p_t, exp_t, \Delta p_t, r_t, t)'$. The estimated VAR included 4 lags of each variable. The constant and trend were specified as in Model 4 of Table 14.2 – corresponding to $\mu_1 \neq 0, \mu_2 \neq 0; \delta_1 \neq 0, \delta_2 = 0$; that is a constant in the CI space, linear trend in the data and linear trend in the CI space.

15.5.1 Estimating the cointegrating rank

If we accept that $m_t - p_t$, exp_t, Δp_t and r_t are I(1), the minimum possible number of cointegrating vectors is 0 and the maximum is 4. The test statistics and critical values are given in Table 15.11.

Starting with the λ_{max} test we find that the null of $r = 0$ against the alternative of $r = 1$, that is $H(0 \mid 1)$, is rejected with a test statistic of 45.01 which is greater than the 95% quantile of 30.33: hence reject $r = 0$. Moving on to the null of $r = 1$ against the alternative of $r = 2$, $H(1 \mid 2)$, the test statistic is 25.70 which is again greater than the 95% quantile of 23.78: hence reject

Table 15.11 *Test statistics for cointegrating rank, Hendry and Mizon (1993)*

Null	Alt.	$\hat{\lambda}_i$	λ_{max} statistic	95% quantile	Null	Alt.	Trace statistic	95% quantile
$r = 0$	$r = 1$	0.419	$-T\ln(1-\hat{\lambda}_1) = \mathbf{45.01} > \mathbf{30.33}$		$r = 0$	$r \geq 1$	$-T\sum_{i=1}^{k}\ln(1-\hat{\lambda}_i) = \mathbf{77.20} > \mathbf{54.64}$	
$r \leq 1$	$r = 2$	0.266	$-T\ln(1-\hat{\lambda}_2) = \mathbf{25.70} > \mathbf{23.78}$		$r \leq 1$	$r \geq 2$	$-T\sum_{i=2}^{k}\ln(1-\hat{\lambda}_i) = 32.19 < 34.55$	
$r \leq 2$	$r = 3$	0.072	$-T\ln(1-\hat{\lambda}_3) = 6.17 < 16.87$		$r \leq 2$	$r \geq 3$	$-T\sum_{i=3}^{k}\ln(1-\hat{\lambda}_i) = 6.49 < 18.17$	
$r \leq 3$	$r = 4$	0.004	$-T\ln(1-\hat{\lambda}_4) = 0.32 < 3.74$		$r \leq 3$	$r = 4$	$-T\ln(1-\hat{\lambda}_4) = 0.32 < 3.74$	

Notes: Test values are taken from Hendry and Mizon (1993, Table 18.2). Critical values are taken from Table 14.6 and correspond to Table 2 of Osterwald-Lenum (1992, p. 470) and Table B4 of Hansen and Juselius (1995); bold entries show significant entries at the 5% significance level (=test statistic > 95% quantile). $k = 4$.

$r = 1$. For the null of $r = 2$ against the alternative $r = 3$, $H(2 \mid 3)$, the test statistic of 6.17 is less than the 95% quantile, hence do not reject $r = 2$. We conclude $r = 2$ and the sequence ends.

There is a slight difference when the trace test statistics are used. Starting with the null of $r = 0$ against $r \geq 1$, $H(0 \mid 4)$, we reject the null with a test statistic of 77.20, which is greater than the 95% quantile of 54.64. Moving on to the null of $r \leq 1$ against $r \geq 2$, $H(1 \mid 4)$, the test statistic of 32.19 is just below the 95% quantile of 34.55; formally, this leads to nonrejection of the null, but since the rejection is 'only just' and the $\lambda_{\max}$ test indicates $r = 2$, the analysis proceeds on the basis of 2 cointegrating vectors. Notice also that the estimated eigenvalues, $\hat{\lambda}_i$, suggest a dichotomy of 2 eigenvalues close to zero and 2 nonzero values.

15.5.2 Unrestricted estimates of the cointegrating vectors and adjustment coefficients

The unrestricted estimates of α and β are given in Table 15.12. Given that the test statistics for the cointegration rank indicate $r = 2$, Hendry and Mizon (*op. cit.*) suggest the following inter-

Table 15.12 *Unrestricted estimates of the cointegrating vectors, β, normalised on:* $m_t - p_t$, Δp_t, r_t *and* exp_t*; and the adjustment coefficients, α*

Estimated β_i vectors (the normalised eigenvectors)			
β_1	β_2	β_3	β_4
Variable			
$m_t - p_t$ 1.000	0.011	−3.430	−0.480
Δp_t 5.940	1.000	−25.300	−0.900
r_t 0.966	0.003	1.000	−0.005
exp_t −0.648	−0.283	1.140	1.000
Estimated α_i vectors (the adjustment coefficients)			
α_1	α_2	α_3	α_4
Equation			
$m_t - p_t$ −0.102	0.017	0.008	−0.013
Δp_t 0.025	−0.540	−0.001	−0.002
r_t −0.016	−3.010	−0.098	0.089
exp_t 0.017	0.390	−0.002	−0.029

Source: Hendry and Mizon (*op. cit.*, Tables 18.3 and 18.4).

pretation of the first two β_i vectors. The first is a demand for real money relationship in which $m_t - p_t$ is a function of Δp_t, r_t and exp_t and, in addition, one might want to impose a coefficient of -1 on exp_t in the cointegrating vector; the second is an inflation relationship that depends upon the deviation of income from trend. Alternatively since a linear combination of cointegrating vectors is also a cointegrating vector they suggest considering the sum of β_1 and β_2, which is $(1.011, 6.94, 0.969, -0.931)$; normalising on the first element gives $(1.000, 6.864, 0.958, -0.921)$ corresponding to the coefficients on $m_t - p_t$, Δp_t, r_t and exp_t, the possible advantage of this combination is that the expenditure coefficient at -0.921 is closer to the hypothesized value.

15.5.3 Identification of the cointegrating vectors

Can the suggested cointegrating relationships be generically identified given $r = 2$? A necessary (but not sufficient) condition is that not less than $r - 1$ restrictions are imposed on each cointegrating vector and in this case $r - 1 = 1$. In the first case this is simply that the trend has a zero coefficient. If the unit expenditure elasticity is also imposed the cointegrating vector is overidentified as 2 restrictions are imposed. In the second cointegrating vector zero restrictions are placed on $m_t - p_t$ and r_t, so that this equation is overidentified by the necessary condition. Other identifying restrictions are possible. For example, Boswijk (1994) suggests that to obtain a just-identified model the trend is included in the first cointegrating vector and the expenditure coefficient is restricted to unity. As to the second cointegrating vector, exclude real money, $m_t - p_t$, and include the interest rate. In this case one restriction is placed on each of the cointegrating vectors. This makes the point that generic identification does not lead to a unique set of restrictions.

For illustrative purposes we consider Hendry and Mizon's (*op. cit.*) identification restrictions with the first cointegrating vector normalised on real money and the second on inflation. The estimated cointegrating vectors for the next stage of the empirical analysis, that of constructing an SECM, were based on the unrestricted estimates in Table 15.12 in the following sense. In the second cointegrating vector the coefficients on $m_t - p_t$ and r_t are empirically quite close to 0 at 0.011 and 0.003, respectively; Hendry and Mizon (*op. cit.*, p. 290) set these coefficients to 0 and keep the coefficient of -0.283 on exp_t. As to the first cointegrating vector Hendry and Mizon (*op. cit.*) impose a unit expenditure coefficient, reduce (in absolute value) the interest elasticity from -0.97 to -0.7 and increase (in absolute value) the coefficient on Δp_t to -7.0. They comment on the interest rate elasticity that despite the cointegration evidence the larger elasticity did not prove data coherent in estimating their SECM. The equilibrium relationships used in the next stage of estimation are given in Table 15.13.

It might be helpful if the cointegrating vectors are explicitly written as equations in real money and inflation, with associated error correction mechanisms ecm_{1t} and ecm_{2t}:

$$m_t - p_t = -7.0\Delta p_t - 0.7r_t + exp_t$$
$$\Rightarrow ecm_{1t} \equiv m_t - p_t + 7.0\Delta p_t + 0.7r_t - exp_t$$
$$(15.17)$$
$$\Delta p_t = 0.28exp_t - 0.0014t$$
$$= 0.28(exp_t - 0.005t)$$
$$\Rightarrow ecm_{2t} \equiv \Delta p_t - 0.28exp_t + 0.0014t$$
$$= \Delta p_t - 0.28(exp_t - 0.005t)$$
$$(15.18)$$

Note the last equation sustains the interpretation that inflation is a positive function of the deviation of expenditure from trend, with a quarterly coefficient of 0.005 corresponding to an annual trend of $(1 + 0.005)^4 - 1 \approx 0.02$, that is 2% p.a., which is consistent with observed growth in real expenditure over the sample period.

15.5.4 Estimating an SECM

These estimates of the cointegrating vectors were incorporated in a structural ECM – defined in section **14.5.1** – with current dated regressors. Hendry and Mizon (*op. cit.*) also added two dummy variables: $DOUT_t$, which was equal to 1 in 1972q4, 1973q1 and 1979q2 and 0 elsewhere; and $DOIL_t$ which was equal to 1 in 1973q3, 1973q4 and 1979q3 and 0 elsewhere. The estimated model is reported in Tables 15.14a and 15.14b.

The estimates in Table 15.14a result from a simplification process: there are only 2 cointegrating vectors; the cointegrating vectors are identified; the cointegrating vectors only enter certain equations; and the dynamic structure is simplified by deleting redundant (insignificant) regressors. According to these estimates a positive disequilibrium in money ('excess money') lowers next period's demand for money with an error correction coefficient of just below 10% ($\hat{a}_{11} = -0.095$); a positive disequilibrium in inflation lowers next period's inflation with adjustment which is much faster than in the money equation ($\hat{a}_{22} = -0.235$). Next period expenditure grows faster than trend with an adjustment coefficient of 0.338 which, in turn,

Table 15.13 *Generically and economically identified cointegrating vectors*

$$
\begin{array}{cc}
\text{Generically identified} & \text{Economically identified} \\[4pt]
\begin{bmatrix} 1 & \beta_{21} & \beta_{31} & \beta_{41} & 0 \\ 0 & 1 & 0 & \beta_{42} & \beta_{52} \end{bmatrix}
\begin{pmatrix} m_t - p_t \\ \Delta p_t \\ r_t \\ exp_t \\ t \end{pmatrix}
&
\begin{bmatrix} 1 & 7.0 & 0.7 & -1 & 0 \\ 0 & 1 & 0 & -0.28 & 0.0014 \end{bmatrix}
\begin{pmatrix} m_t - p_t \\ \Delta p_t \\ r_t \\ exp_t \\ t \end{pmatrix}
\end{array}
$$

Source: Economically identified estimates, Hendry and Mizon (*op. cit.*, Table 18.7).

Table 15.14a *SECM for real money, inflation, the nominal interest rate and real expenditure*

$$\Delta(m_t - p_t) = -0.095ecm_{1t-1} - 0.520\Delta(\Delta p_t) - 0.082\Delta r_t - 0.195\Delta(m_t - p_t)_{-1} + 0.195\Delta exp_{t-1} - 0.196$$
$$\qquad\qquad (-10.555)\qquad (-1.534)\qquad (-3.037)\quad (-2.708)\qquad\qquad\qquad (2.708)\qquad (-10.889)$$

$$\Delta(\Delta p_t) = -0.235ecm_{2t-1} - 0.236\Delta(\Delta p_t)_{-1} + 0.018DOIL_t - 0.707$$
$$\qquad\qquad (-3.615)\qquad (-2.744)\qquad\qquad (4.500)\qquad (-3.607)$$

$$\Delta r_t = 7.630\Delta(\Delta p_t) + 2.400\Delta p_{t-1} + 0.162\Delta r_{t-1} + 1.550\Delta exp_{t-1} - 0.141r_{t-2} - 0.395$$
$$\quad\;\; (2.847)\qquad\;\; (2.069)\qquad\;\; (1.687)\qquad\;\; (1.782)\qquad (-3.065)\quad (-3.085)$$

$$\Delta exp_t = 0.338ecm_{2t-1} - 0.0448\Delta(\Delta p_t)_{-1} - 0.184\Delta exp_{t-1} + 0.262\Delta(m_t - p_t)_{-2} - 0.300\Delta p_{t-4}$$
$$\qquad\quad (2.112)\qquad\;\; (-2.748)\qquad\qquad (-2.115)\qquad\;\; (4.517)\qquad\qquad\;\; (-3.225)$$

$$\qquad\quad + 0.043DOUT_t + 1.030$$
$$\qquad\qquad (7.166)\qquad\;\; (2.191)$$

Note: '*t*' statistics in parentheses.

Table 15.14b *Simultaneities, error correction and adjustment coefficients*

Simultaneities

$$\Phi = \begin{bmatrix} 1 & 0.520 & 0.082 & 0 \\ 0 & 1 & 0 & 0 \\ 0 & -7.63 & 1 & 0 \\ 0 & 0 & 0 & 1 \end{bmatrix} \qquad \Phi^{-1} = \begin{bmatrix} 1 & -1.146 & -0.082 & 0 \\ 0 & 1 & 0 & 0 \\ 0 & 7.630 & 1 & 0 \\ 0 & 0 & 0 & 1 \end{bmatrix}$$

variable	Error correction coefficients a		derived $\alpha = \Phi^{-1}a$		Adjustment coefficients unrestricted α			
$m_t - p_t$	-0.095	0	-0.095	0.270	-0.102	0.017	0.008	-0.013
Δp_t	0	-0.235	0	-0.235	0.025	-0.540	-0.001	-0.002
r_t	0	0	0	-1.793	-0.016	-3.010	-0.098	0.089
exp_t	0	0.338	0	0.338	0.017	0.390	-0.002	-0.029

Source: Estimation results, Hendry and Mizon (*op. cit.*, Table 18.7). Unrestricted α estimates from the same source, Table 18.4.

will reduce disequilibrium in inflation through the term $-0.28(exp_t - 0.005t)$ in ecm_{2t}; thus inflation above equilibrium implies $\Delta exp_t > 0$, which could be interpreted as inflation 'buying' a temporary increase in real income/output. To these effects there are added some I(0) dynamics. The simultaneous I(0) links are from the growth of inflation and the nominal interest rate in the demand for money equation, and the growth in inflation in the nominal interest rate equation. Generally, though, the simultaneous structure is sparse as indicated by the estimated Φ which has a predominance of zeros (if $\Phi = I$ the structural and reduced form error correction models are identical) and the short-run dynamics are largely represented by lagged I(0) terms.

15.5.5 Identification of the short-run structure

Is the short-run structure identified? Assuming that 2 cointegrating vectors have been identified and that the system is fourth order, as in the unrestricted VAR estimated by Hendry and Mizon (*op. cit.*), the SECM can be written:

$$(\Phi,\; -\Gamma_1^+,\; -\Gamma_2^+,\; -\Gamma_3^+, -a) \begin{pmatrix} \Delta y_t \\ \Delta y_{t-1} \\ \Delta y_{t-2} \\ \Delta y_{t-3} \\ \beta' y_{t-1} \end{pmatrix} = u_t$$

$$(15.19)$$

The maximum number of nonzero coefficients in each equation is 3 from Φ, 4 each from Γ_i^+, $i = 1, \ldots, 3$, and 2 from a, giving a total of 17. Recall that the necessary condition for identification of the short-run structure – see section **14.5.4** – is that each equation in the k equation system should have $k - 1$ coefficient restrictions. In this case $k = 4$, hence $k - 1 = 3$. For example, in the first equation, of the current dated variables Δexp_t is excluded; of the once lagged variables ecm_{2t-1} and Δr_{t-1} are excluded and the coefficients on $\Delta(m_t - p_t)_{-1}$ and Δexp_{t-1} are imposed equal but of opposite sign; there are no other lagged variables in the first equation. There are 4 unrestricted coefficients, hence there are 13 restrictions and the first equation is over-identified. Similarly the other three equations are also overidentified on this criterion.

With this example we can also illustrate the connection between the error correction coefficients, a, and the adjustment coefficients, α. Recall that each row of a or α refers to a particular equation, that is why there are four rows in this example, and each column of a particular row of a or α refers to the weight given to the corresponding error correction mechanism. From section **14.5.4** we know that $\alpha = \Phi^{-1}a$, and that zeros in the coefficient vector a will not necessarily carry through into the reduced form coefficients α. However, in this case because Φ is sparse the derived adjustment coefficients – see the lower part of Table 15.14b – generally show a similar pattern in the structural and reduced forms. In particular $\hat{a}_{11} = \hat{\alpha}_{11} = -0.095$, and $\hat{a}_{1j} = \hat{\alpha}_{1j} = 0$ for $j = 2, 3, 4$. So as we shall see – see section **15.6** below – inflation, the nominal interest rate and expenditure are weakly exogenous for the long-run parameters of the demand for money cointegrating vector. It is the second column of $\hat{\alpha}$ which demonstrates how a simultaneity – that is a nonzero element of Φ, in this case the coefficient of 7.63 on $\Delta(\Delta p_t)$ in the interest rate equation – can transmit a disequilibrium from one equation throughout the system. Notice that in the reduced form the second error correction mechanism, ecm_{2t-1}, does enter

the real money equation with an estimated coefficient, $\hat{\alpha}_{12}$, of 0.270, although it does not enter the SECM. Also noticeable is $\hat{\alpha}_{23} = -1.793$, the adjustment coefficient on ecm_{2t-1} in the nominal interest rate equation, which was absent in the SECM.

The decomposition of $\Pi = \alpha\beta'$ using the restricted coefficients estimated by Hendry and Mizon (op. cit., Table 18.7) is shown in Table 15.15 (the coefficients on the trend are not given in the source, apart from the one in the second cointegrating vector, and are assumed to be negligible).

15.6 Weak exogeneity: when is it valid to model the partial system?

Often it is more convenient to model the detail of one, or a few, rather than many economic relationships. For example, if the focus is the demand for money a multivariate approach forces a wider analysis, which must include an analysis of the determinants of the demand for money. If, as in the simplest approach, the demand for money is specified as a function of the price level, real income, and a variable or variables capturing the opportunity cost of holding money, then a system approach requires consideration of how these variables are determined with, most likely, additional explanatory variables which themselves need further specification of their determinants. The system might be in danger of growing to exceed the number of observations available!

It might be possible, in some cases, to find proxy or reduced form variables that alleviate the problem. For example, in the demand for money example of section **15.5** one of the cointegrating relationships was interpreted as determining inflation as a positive function of the deviation of income from *trend*. Now it is likely that inflation is actually a more complex

Table 15.15 *The decomposition of* $\Pi = \alpha\beta'$*: unrestricted and restricted estimates*

Unrestricted estimates

Equation	α				β'					Π Variable				
										$m_t - p_t$	Δp_t	r_t	exp_t	trend
$m_t - p_t$	-0.102	0.017	0.008	-0.013	1.000	5.940	0.966	-0.648	0.000	-0.128	-0.789	-0.091	0.067	0.000
Δp_t	0.025	-0.540	-0.001	-0.002	0.011	1.000	0.003	-0.283	0.001	0.023	-0.364	0.021	0.133	0.000
r_t	-0.016	-3.010	-0.098	0.089	-3.430	-25.300	1.000	1.140	0.000	0.244	-0.706	-0.123	0.840	0.000
exp_t	0.017	0.390	-0.002	-0.029	-0.048	-0.900	-0.005	1.000	0.000	0.042	0.568	0.016	-0.153	0.000

Restricted estimates

Equation	α		β'					Π Variable				
								$m_t - p_t$	Δp_t	r_t	exp_t	trend
$m_t - p_t$	-0.095	0.270	1.000	7.000	0.700	-1.000	0.000	-0.095	-0.396	-0.067	0.019	0.000
Δp_t	0.000	-0.235	0.000	1.000	0.000	-0.280	0.0014	0.000	-0.235	0.000	0.066	0.000
r_t	0.000	-1.793						0.000	-1.793	0.000	0.502	0.000
exp_t	0.000	0.338						0.000	0.338	0.000	-0.095	0.000

process than suggested by this simple formulation, and the trend is a proxy for the interaction of a number of economic relationships, but the deviation from trend interpretation serves to limit the variables in the analysis to a manageable number. The trend serves another purpose as Hendry and Mizon (*op. cit.*, p. 283) note: '... to account for the level of *exp_t*, a linear trend was used as a proxy for the combined effects of input growth and technical progress, although this is not a very satisfactory resolution of a difficult problem'. (Note to avoid confusion we have used our notation exp_t for the expenditure measure which Hendry and Mizon denote y_t.) Modelling input growth and technical progress would require a marked extension of the information set.

15.6.1 Containing the number of variables in the VAR

Containing the number of variables to a manageable number is a pragmatic if not theoretically justified procedure. For example, Clements and Mizon (1991) analyse the determination of earnings and prices in the United Kingdom choosing the following five variables to include in a system approach: earnings per hour, the consumer price index, output per person, average hours and the unemployment rate; all variables are in logarithms. However, they note that previous work has suggested that, *inter alia*, the exchange rate, expected inflation, the retention ratio and a measure of strike activity may also be relevant to the analysis. Practically they chose 'to model the dynamic behaviour of the five variables listed above in a systems context, and this leaves too few degrees of freedom to make an extension of the list feasible'. Clements and Mizon (*op. cit.*) used a fifth order VAR with a sample of 93 usable observations; with five variables and a fifth order VAR there are 25 coefficients in each equation in addition to a constant and 'special effects' dummy variables.

An alternative would have been to 'condition' on variables that were not part of the VAR

system. That is rather than extend the VAR by adding further variables to the system, some variables are viewed as being determined outside the system – so we condition on them in explaining the remaining variables. The variables in the VAR are 'endogenous' and the conditioning variables are 'exogenous'. Neither approach is, generally, free from criticism – see the discussion and criticism of the 'manageable size' criterion by Kirchgässner (1991) and Sims (1991) following Clements and Mizon (1991). In order to achieve a statistically adequate VAR model, in their five chosen variables, Clements and Mizon (*op. cit.*) introduce ten 'special effect' dummy variables which may, in part, be capturing effects which could otherwise be accounted for by omitted behavioural variables; the dummy variables could be taken as an indication that some variables have been incorrectly 'marginalised' (omitted) from the analysis. However, conditioning on variables that are not in fact exogenous, generally, leads to problems of inconsistent estimators and incorrect inference, so adding 'conditioning' variables is not necessarily a simple solution.

Valid conditioning variables should be weakly exogenous for the parameters of interest, where, generally, the latter are the equilibrium, or long-run, coefficients β, and the adjustment coefficients α. Johansen (1992b and 1995a) has suggested a conceptual framework and testing procedure in order to establish weak exogeneity of subsets of variables in this context. In what might be regarded as a drawback of this approach the testing takes place within the extended system. That is suppose the 'complete' vector of variables is y_t which we partition into $y_t = (y_{1t}, y_{2t}, D_t)$ where y_{1t} contains m variables and y_{2t} contains $k - m$ variables and D_t contains deterministic variables such as seasonal dummy variables; and the hypothesis of interest is that the subset y_{2t} contains only weakly exogenous variables – that is we may legitimately condition on y_{2t} where the parameters of interest are α and β. A 'closed' VAR determines the complete set of k stochastic variables. Let $H(k)$ denote the closed VAR system with all k variables and let $H(m)$ denote the VAR with $k - m \equiv s$ weakly exogenous variables. An 'open' VAR is one in which $s > 0$, where y_{2t} is the set of conditioning variables. In the Johansen procedure hypotheses on weak exogeneity, $H(m)$, are tested within $H(k)$, so that the extended model has to be estimated. This may not be such a drawback as it seems in, say, the context of the 'manageable size' criterion. First, Johansen (1995a) has suggested that VARs with long lags may arise because the information set rather than the lag length needs to be extended, so there may well be a trade-off between lags and variables. Second, often we are not interested in the detail of the unrestricted VAR, rather it forms a basis, if congruent with the data, from which to assess the consistency of hypotheses of interest which are often of a simplifying nature; hence, if such hypotheses are consistent with the data, the unrestricted VAR is not the stopping point in the sequence of model construction.

15.6.2 Closed or open systems?

What then are the circumstances when the analysis can legitimately be limited, without loss of efficiency, to an open rather than a closed system? The answer to this question will include the important special case where a single equation with a designated dependent variable is the subject of analysis. The Johansen procedure comprises two stages: hypothesis testing; and model (re)formulation. The first of these is often of interest in its own right and will not necessarily lead to the second stage.

The framework for this discussion will be variants of the familiar first order reduced form ECM:

$$\Delta y_t = \Pi y_{t-1} + \Gamma_1 \Delta y_{t-1} + \varepsilon_t$$

parameterised as

$$\Delta y_t = \alpha(\beta' y_{t-1}) + \Gamma_1 \Delta y_{t-1} + \varepsilon_t \qquad (15.20)$$

To introduce some important aspects of when it is legitimate to consider the partial rather than

the complete system it will be useful first to consider a two-equation system. In error correction form with one cointegrating vector this is:

$$
\begin{pmatrix} \Delta y_{1t} \\ \Delta y_{2t} \end{pmatrix} = \begin{bmatrix} \pi_{11} & \pi_{12} \\ \pi_{21} & \pi_{22} \end{bmatrix} \begin{pmatrix} y_{1t-1} \\ y_{2t-1} \end{pmatrix}
$$
$$
+ \begin{bmatrix} \Gamma_{11} & \Gamma_{12} \\ \Gamma_{21} & \Gamma_{22} \end{bmatrix} \begin{bmatrix} \Delta y_{1t-1} \\ \Delta y_{2t-1} \end{bmatrix}
$$
$$
+ \begin{pmatrix} \varepsilon_{1t} \\ \varepsilon_{2t} \end{pmatrix} \qquad (15.21)
$$

Making the cointegrating vector explicit we have:

$$\Delta y_{1t} = \alpha_{11}(y_{1t-1} + \beta_{21}y_{2t-1}) + \Gamma_{11}\Delta y_{1t-1}$$
$$+ \Gamma_{12}\Delta y_{2t-1} + \varepsilon_{1t}$$
$$\Delta y_{2t} = \alpha_{21}(y_{1t-1} + \beta_{21}y_{2t-1}) + \Gamma_{21}\Delta y_{1t-1}$$
$$+ \Gamma_{22}\Delta y_{2t-1} + \varepsilon_{2t} \qquad (15.22)$$

Suppose the parameters of interest are those in $\beta' = (1, \beta_{21})$, where we have normalised on the first coefficient, and $\alpha = (\alpha_{11}, \alpha_{21})'$, then when is the second equation uninformative about these parameters? The answer is that if $\alpha_{21} = 0$, estimation of the first equation alone will be efficient for β' and α_{11}. Setting $\alpha_{21} = 0$ we see that the error correction term drops out of the second equation which, thus, conveys no information about the equilibrium coefficients. In this case we say that y_{2t} is weakly exogenous for the parameters of interest α_{11} and β. A convenient, although sometimes misleading, terminology is to say that y_{2t} is (weakly) exogenous in the first equation. If in addition to $\alpha_{21} = 0$, $\Gamma_{21} = 0$, that is y_{2t} does not depend upon lagged values of y_{1t}, then y_{2t} is said to be strongly exogenous for β and α_{11}. The models in these two cases are summarised below.

Weak exogeneity of y_{2t} for β_{21} and α_{11}: y_{2t} unaffected by lagged disequilibrium

$$\Delta y_{1t} = \alpha_{11}(y_{1t-1} + \beta_{21}y_{2t-1})$$
$$+ \Gamma_{11}\Delta y_{1t-1} + \Gamma_{12}\Delta y_{2t-1} + \varepsilon_{1t}$$
$$\Delta y_{2t} = \Gamma_{21}\Delta y_{1t-1} + \Gamma_{22}\Delta y_{2t-1} + \varepsilon_{2t}$$
$$(15.23)$$

Strong exogeneity of y_{2t} for β_{21} and α_{11}: y_{2t} unaffected by lagged disequilibrium and no feedback from y_{1t} to y_{2t}.

$$\Delta y_{1t} = \alpha_{11}(y_{1t-1} + \beta_{21}y_{2t-1})$$
$$\qquad + \Gamma_{11}\Delta y_{1t-1} + \Gamma_{12}\Delta y_{2t-1} + \varepsilon_{1t}$$
$$\Delta y_{2t} = \qquad\qquad \Gamma_{22}\Delta y_{2t-1} + \varepsilon_{2t}$$

$$(15.24)$$

The first equation in each case is nonlinear in the coefficients because α_{11} and β_{21} enter multiplicatively. If your econometric software has a nonlinear OLS option the equation may be estimated directly. Alternatively the equation can be estimated simply by applying OLS in one step to

$$\Delta y_{1t} = \alpha_{11}y_{1t-1} + \delta_{11}y_{2t-1} + \Gamma_{11}\Delta y_{1t-1}$$
$$\qquad + \Gamma_{12}\Delta y_{2t-1} + \varepsilon_{1t} \qquad (15.25)$$

where $\delta_{11} \equiv \alpha_{11}\beta_{21}$, and an estimate of β_{21} can be obtained by dividing the estimate of δ_{11} by the estimate of α_{11}. Alternatively the Engle–Granger two-step method can be used first to run a regression in the levels of y_{1t} and y_{2t} to obtain an estimate of β_{21} and then, conditional on this value, estimate the remaining coefficients by OLS.

To develop the example further suppose that a third variable y_{3t} should be included in the analysis, although we still maintain the assumption that there is one cointegrating vector, so $r = 1$. Then in error correction form the VAR is:

$$\Delta y_{1t} = \alpha_{11}(y_{1t-1} + \beta_{21}y_{2t-1} + \beta_{31}y_{3t-1})$$
$$\qquad + \Gamma_{11}\Delta y_{1t-1} + \Gamma_{12}\Delta y_{2t-1}$$
$$\qquad + \Gamma_{13}\Delta y_{3t-1} + \varepsilon_{1t}$$
$$\Delta y_{2t} = \alpha_{21}(y_{1t-1} + \beta_{21}y_{2t-1} + \beta_{31}y_{3t-1})$$
$$\qquad + \Gamma_{21}\Delta y_{1t-1} + \Gamma_{22}\Delta y_{2t-1}$$
$$\qquad + \Gamma_{23}\Delta y_{3t-1} + \varepsilon_{2t}$$
$$\Delta y_{3t} = \alpha_{31}(y_{1t-1} + \beta_{21}y_{2t-1} + \beta_{31}y_{3t-1})$$
$$\qquad + \Gamma_{31}\Delta y_{1t-1} + \Gamma_{32}\Delta y_{2t-1}$$
$$\qquad + \Gamma_{33}\Delta y_{3t-1} + \varepsilon_{3t} \qquad (15.26)$$

Now analysis of the first equation alone requires both y_{2t} and y_{3t} to be weakly exogenous for the parameters of interest α and β. As written the equations for y_{2t} and y_{3t} contain information about β through the lagged cointegrating combination. However, if both $\alpha_{21} = 0$ and $\alpha_{31} = 0$ then the second and third equations are uninformative in this respect, and y_{2t} and y_{3t} are weakly exogenous for $\alpha' = (\alpha_{11}, 0, 0)$ and $\beta' = (1, \beta_{21}, \beta_{31})$.

The situation is more complicated if there is more than one cointegrating vector. Suppose in the previous example with three variables $r = 2$, so that the complete system (now in matrix notation for simplicity) is:

$$\begin{pmatrix} \Delta y_{1t} \\ \Delta y_{2t} \\ \Delta y_{3t} \end{pmatrix} = \begin{bmatrix} \alpha_{11} & \alpha_{12} \\ \alpha_{21} & \alpha_{22} \\ \alpha_{31} & \alpha_{32} \end{bmatrix} \begin{bmatrix} 1 & \beta_{21} & 0 \\ 0 & 1 & \beta_{32} \end{bmatrix} \begin{pmatrix} y_{1t-1} \\ y_{2t-1} \\ y_{3t-1} \end{pmatrix}$$

$$\begin{bmatrix} \Gamma_{11} & \Gamma_{12} & \Gamma_{13} \\ \Gamma_{21} & \Gamma_{22} & \Gamma_{23} \\ \Gamma_{31} & \Gamma_{32} & \Gamma_{33} \end{bmatrix} \begin{pmatrix} \Delta y_{1t-1} \\ \Delta y_{2t-1} \\ \Delta y_{3t-1} \end{pmatrix}$$

$$+ \begin{pmatrix} \varepsilon_{1t} \\ \varepsilon_{2t} \\ \varepsilon_{3t} \end{pmatrix} \qquad (15.27)$$

The cointegrating vectors have been normalised on y_{1t} and y_{2t}, respectively, and each is assumed to be identified by a simple exclusion restriction. The normalisation suggests that y_{1t} and y_{2t} are being regarded as endogenous with y_{3t} possibly weakly exogenous. By a straightforward extension of the previous argument, for y_{3t} to be weakly exogenous for the parameters in α and β, both α_{31} and α_{32} must be zero otherwise the equation for y_{3t} is informative about the parameters of interest. If y_{3t} is weakly exogenous we can consider the two-equation system and so ignore the (marginal) model for y_{3t}. The first two equations can be estimated by maximum likelihood or nonlinear least squares imposing the restrictions that the equilibrium coefficients are the same in both equations:

$$\Delta y_{1t} = \alpha_{11}(y_{1t-1} + \beta_{21}y_{2t-1})$$
$$+ \alpha_{12}(y_{2t-1} + \beta_{32}y_{3t-1}) + \Gamma_{11}\Delta y_{1t-1}$$
$$+ \Gamma_{12}\Delta y_{2t-1} + \Gamma_{13}\Delta y_{3t-1} + \varepsilon_{1t}$$

$$(15.28a)$$

$$\Delta y_{t2} = \alpha_{21}(y_{1t-1} + \beta_{21}y_{2t-1})$$
$$+ \alpha_{22}(y_{2t-1} + \beta_{32}y_{3t-1}) + \Gamma_{21}\Delta y_{1t-1}$$
$$+ \Gamma_{22}\Delta y_{2t-1} + \Gamma_{23}\Delta y_{3t-1} + \varepsilon_{2t}$$

$$(15.28b)$$

Weak exogeneity can also be applied to subsets of the parameters of interest. Suppose the α matrix in the demand for money example of section **15.5.4** took the following form:

Equation	α restricted		
$\begin{pmatrix} m_t - p_t \\ \Delta p_t \\ r_t \\ exp_t \end{pmatrix}$	$\begin{bmatrix} \alpha_{11} & 0 \\ 0 & \alpha_{22} \\ 0 & 0 \\ 0 & \alpha_{42} \end{bmatrix}$		

The zeros in the third row of α indicate that r_t is weakly exogenous for β, that is the cointegrating coefficients in ecm_{1t} and ecm_{2t}, and the remaining nonzero coefficients in α. The other zeros in the first column of α are also of interest; they indicate that while, for example, Δp_t and exp_t are not weakly exogenous for all the parameters of interest they are weakly exogenous for the first column of β, that is the cointegrating coefficients of the money demand relationship.

15.6.3 Joint, conditional and marginal models

Johansen (1992c, 1995a) shows that an alternative way of representing the VAR system is as a conditional model and a marginal model. Specifically in the two-equation model of the last section we could model the distribution of y_{1t} conditional on the current value of y_{2t} and lagged values of y_{1t} and y_{2t}, and the distribution of y_{2t} conditional just on lagged values of y_{1t} and y_{2t}. Using the results in Johansen (1992c) we can formulate the first equation as a conditional error correction model and the second as a marginal (or reduced form) error correction model:

$$\Delta y_{1t} = \omega\Delta y_{2t} + \alpha_{11}^*(y_{1t-1} + \beta_{21}y_{2t-1})$$
$$+ \Gamma_{11}^*\Delta y_{1t-1} + \Gamma_{12}^*\Delta y_{2t-1} + \varepsilon_{1t}^*$$

$$(15.29a)$$

$$\Delta y_{2t} = \alpha_{21}(y_{1t-1} + \beta_{21}y_{2t-1})$$
$$+ \Gamma_{21}\Delta y_{1t-1} + \Gamma_{22}\Delta y_{2t-1} + \varepsilon_{2t}$$

$$(15.29b)$$

where $E\{\varepsilon_{2t}^2\} = \sigma_{22}, E\{\varepsilon_{1t}, \varepsilon_{2t}\} = \sigma_{12}, \omega = \sigma_{12}/\sigma_{22}, \alpha_{11}^* = \alpha_{11} - \omega\alpha_{21}, \Gamma_{11}^* = \Gamma_{11} - \omega\Gamma_{21}, \Gamma_{12}^* = \Gamma_{12} - \omega\Gamma_{22}$, and $\varepsilon_{1t}^* = \varepsilon_{1t} - \omega\varepsilon_{2t}$.

In the first equation Δy_{1t} is modelled as a function of the current value of Δy_{2t} as well as the lagged values which are familiar from previous way of writing the VAR. The coefficients have changed and are now dependent on the ratio of covariance of ε_{1t} and ε_{2t} and the variance of ε_{2t}. The first equation is said to be a conditional (on y_{2t}) model. The point of writing the system in this way is that there are many equations like the first reported in the empirical literature, often analysed without reference to the remaining equations. For a famous example, where consumption is analysed conditional on income, see Davidson et al. (1978). This framework allows us to determine when such a single-equation analysis is legitimate. Notice that the 'error correction coefficient' in the first equation is $\alpha_{11}^* = \alpha_{11} - \omega\alpha_{21}$ which depends upon α_{21}, and that the cointegrating coefficients, here just β_{21}, enter the first and second equations. The equations are 'intertwined' and, in general, one should not be analysed, for example estimated, without the other. However, if $\alpha_{21} = 0$, this linking between the equations is broken: the first equation can be analysed without reference to the second; and the second equation does not contain any cointegration. As we have seen this is just the condition for weak exogeneity of y_{2t} with respect to α_{21} and β_{21}.

15.6.4 Hypothesis testing and weak exogeneity

The hypothesis of weak exogeneity of the subset y_{2t} in the set y_t, for the parameters of interest (α, β), can be formulated as the hypothesis that the block of α coefficients corresponding to the error correction (VAR) equations for y_{2t} is zero. Then:

$$\text{weak exogeneity of } y_{2t} \Leftrightarrow \alpha_2 = 0$$

where α_2 is the corresponding block of coefficients in α. To test this hypothesis let $\hat{\lambda}_i$ be the estimated eigenvalues from the unrestricted model and $\hat{\lambda}_i^*$ be the estimated eigenvalues when the model is restricted by $\alpha_2 = 0$, then the following test statistic (weak exogeneity test statistic – WETS) is relevant:

$$\text{WETS} \equiv T \sum_{i=1}^{r} \ln[(1 - \hat{\lambda}_i^*)/(1 - \hat{\lambda}_i)] \quad (15.30)$$

WETS is asymptotically distributed as χ^2 with $(r.s)$ degrees of freedom where s is the number of weakly exogenous variables under the null hypothesis; note that $r.s$ is the number of zeros in the α matrix.

The simplest case is that there is just one variable in the subset, for convenience say the last, y_{kt}, then the null hypothesis is:

$$H_0: (\alpha_{k1}, \alpha_{k2}, \ldots, \alpha_{kr}) = 0$$

that is the kth row of α is zero; and now WETS has r degrees of freedom under the null hypothesis.

15.6.5 Examples of testing for weak exogeneity

Johansen (1992b) provides the following example of testing for weak exogeneity. Based on the study of the demand for money by Hendry and Mizon (1990), Johansen estimates a fifth order VAR in. nominal money M1, M_t; constant price total final expenditure, EXP_t; the implicit deflator, P_t, of EXP_t; and the opportunity cost of holding money, R_t, measured as the 3-month local authority interest rate minus the learning adjusted sight-deposit interest rate. Logarithms were taken of the first three variables denoted here by lower case letters. The data are quarterly, seasonally adjusted from 1963q1 to 1989q2 which, after lagging, gave a usable sample of 100 observations. The unrestricted VAR in ECM form was estimated and a cointegration analysis suggested at least one but not more than two cointegrating vectors. Choosing $r = 1$, each variable was first tested individually for weak exogeneity with respect to the parameters of

Table 15.16 *Tests of weak exogeneity*

WETS: individual tests of weak exogeneity for variable indicated			
	m_t	exp_t	p_t	R_t
WETS =	$24.82 > 3.84$	$4.21 > 3.84$	$0.11 < 3.84$	$1.89 < 3.84$

95% quantile: $\chi^2(1) = 3.84$

WETS: joint test, the set (exp_t, p_t, R_t) is weakly exogenous

WETS = $4.85 < 7.81$

95% quantile: $\chi^2(3) = 7.81$

Source: Johansen (1992b, pp. 323–324).

interest, β, and those coefficients in α not set to zero in the null hypothesis. Johansen (1992b, pp. 323–324) obtained the results in Table 15.16.

Considering the individual tests of weak exogeneity, Johansen (*op. cit.*) found rejection of the null hypothesis of weak exogeneity for money and expenditure, but nonrejection for the price level and the opportunity cost of money. Hence, it would be valid to condition an analysis of money and expenditure on prices and the opportunity cost of money, but a single-equation analysis of money conditional on exp_t, p_t and R_t is not justified by these results. It is possible that a small sample adjustment to the $\chi^2(1)$ critical value would mitigate the clear rejection. Also Johansen notes that the joint test of exp_t, p_t and R_t as a weakly exogenous group, which has $r.s = 3$ degrees of freedom, would not lead to rejection but that occurs because the clear nonrejection of p_t and R_t tends to mask the rejection of p_t. The results of the individual tests, which suggest that m_t and exp_t are not exogenous, in conjunction with the ambiguity concerning whether there are one or two cointegrating vectors, suggest that a re-analysis with $r = 2$ might have been fruitful in this case.

15.7 An extended illustration: Urbain's (1995) study of the demand for imports in Belgium

Urbain's (1995) study of the demand for imports in Belgium is a very useful illustration of a number of points which arise in practice. The starting point for the analysis is the stylised long-run import demand model:

$$im_t = f(inc_t, e_t, pmfc_t, pd_t) \tag{15.31}$$

where im_t is import volume, inc_t is real domestic income, e_t is the exchange rate expressed as the domestic price of a unit of foreign currency, $pmfc_t$ is the import price expressed in foreign currency, pd_t is the domestic price as measured by the wholesale price index. All variables are in natural logarithms with upper case letters indicating corresponding levels. The price of imports in units comparable to the domestic price is $PM_t = E_t$ times $PMFC_t$, in logs this is $pm_t = e_t + pmfc_t$; this emphasises that import prices in domestic currency can alter because the exchange rate alters or because the foreign currency price alters.

An interesting hypothesis suggested by Urbain (*op. cit.*) is that while in the long run the relevant import price is pm_t, so that the long-run coefficients on e_t and $pmfc_t$ are equal, short-run responses may differ depending on the source of the shock, with high frequency shocks from the exchange rate and low frequency shocks from foreign currency import prices. Another hypothesis of interest is that it is only the price of imports, pm_t, relative to the domestic price, pd_t, that matters so that in the long run the coefficients on pm_t and pd_t should be equal but opposite in sign, with the coefficient on pm_t negative if the hypothesised relationship is a demand function. This latter interpretation can be sustained by the assumption of an infinite supply elasticity, if this is not so an additional equation to capture the supply response is needed together with an assumption on how the market for import goods clears. One of the merits of a cointegration approach is that, at least in principle, it allows the question of the identification of different long-run structural relations to be determined; so, for example, if there is a supply function as well as a demand function we should find $r = 2$ (at least).

15.7.1 Estimating the cointegrating rank

Using the five variables in Urbain's analysis define

$$y_t = (im_t, inc_t, e_t, pmfc_t, pd_t)'$$

In the (closed) system approach the first step is to estimate an unrestricted VAR and ensure that it is congruent with the data. The sample period before lagging was 1970q2 to 1990q2 inclusive $= 85$ observations, with quarterly seasonally unadjusted data. In deciding the lag length Urbain considered:

(i)   the information criteria, SIC and AIC;
(ii) absence of serial correlation in the residuals;
(iii) the significance of the short-run coefficient estimates, with the joint null hypothesis that the jth column in the VAR is zero, that is $\Gamma_{ij} = 0$ for $i = 1, \ldots, k$.

Although the SIC and AIC suggested lag lengths of 2 and 3, criteria (ii) and (iii) suggested a lag of 4, which was used in the empirical analysis. Jarque and Bera's test for normality, distributed as $\chi^2(2)$ under the null, suggested rejection of normality for the pd_t equation and sequential Chow tests pointed to 'outliers' in the years 1973, 1979, 1982 and 1986. As in the Clements and Mizon (1991) study, Urbain was faced with the need either to extend the number of variables in the system or account for these outliers by dummy variables. To illustrate he chose the latter option with dummy variables augmenting the fourth order VAR. As the data series displayed trends an unrestricted constant was also included in the VAR; thus the relevant table of critical values is Table 14.5 corresponding to the specification of a constant in the CI space and linear trend in the data. The cointegration test statistics are presented in Table 15.17 and the estimated eigenvectors and adjustment coefficients in Table 15.18.

From Table 15.17 we conclude that the null hypothesis of no cointegrating vectors is easily rejected for the λ_{max} and trace test statistics; the null hypothesis of one cointegrating vector is also rejected, although now the rejection is marginal if the 5% significance level (95% quantile) is used; the null hypothesis of 2 cointegrating vectors is comfortably not rejected. Urbain's analysis is, therefore, based on $r = 2$.

An aid in deciding on an appropriate normalisation is that the import demand function is anticipated to have approximately equal coefficients on pm_t and e_t, which are opposite in sign to the coefficient on pd_t. On this basis the first cointegrating vector, reported in Table 15.18, is

Table 15.17   *Test statistics for cointegrating rank, Urbain (1995)*

Null	Alt.	$\hat{\lambda}_i$	λ_{max} statistic	95% quantile	Null	Alt.	Trace statistic	95% quantile
$r = 0$	$r = 1$	0.402	$-T\ln(1 - \hat{\lambda}_1) = \mathbf{39.53} > \mathbf{33.46}$		$r = 0$	$r \geq 1$	$-T\sum_{i=1}^{k}\ln(1 - \hat{\lambda}_i) = \mathbf{88.08} > \mathbf{68.52}$	
$r \leq 1$	$r = 2$	0.299	$-T\ln(1 - \hat{\lambda}_2) = \mathbf{27.30} > \mathbf{27.07}$		$r \leq 1$	$r \geq 2$	$-T\sum_{i=2}^{k}\ln(1 - \hat{\lambda}_i) = \mathbf{48.55} > \mathbf{47.21}$	
$r \leq 2$	$r = 3$	0.131	$-T\ln(1 - \hat{\lambda}_3) = 10.81 < 20.97$		$r \leq 2$	$r \geq 3$	$-T\sum_{i=3}^{k}\ln(1 - \hat{\lambda}_i) = 21.24 < 29.68$	
$r \leq 3$	$r = 4$	0.111	$-T\ln(1 - \hat{\lambda}_4) = 9.09 < 14.07$		$r \leq 3$	$r \geq 4$	$-T\sum_{i=4}^{k}\ln(1 - \hat{\lambda}_i) = 10.43 < 15.41$	
$r \leq 4$	$r = 5$	0.017	$-T\ln(1 - \hat{\lambda}_5) = 1.34 < 3.76$		$r \leq 4$	$r = 5$	$-T\ln(1 - \hat{\lambda}_5) = 1.34 < 3.76$	

Source: Urbain (1995, p. 191, Table 2); critical values are from Table 14.5 corresponding to Table 1 of Osterwald-Lenum (1992). Bold entries are significant using the 95% quantile. $k = 5$.

Table 15.18 *Unrestricted estimates of the eigenvectors vectors, β, and the adjustment coefficients α*

	Estimated β_i vectors (the normalised eigenvectors)				
	β_1	β_2	β_3	β_4	β_5
im_t	1.000	0.242	1.000	1.000	1.000
inc_t	−1.030	−0.444	17.443	−70.561	−0.629
pm_t	0.310	0.443	263.065	59.022	0.463
e_t	0.301	1.000	305.184	136.194	0.658
pd_t	−0.654	−0.581	409.612	75.561	−1.265
	Estimated α_i vectors (the adjustment coefficients)				
	α_1	α_2	α_3	α_4	α_5
im_t	−0.792	−0.439	0.000	0.000	−0.019
inc_t	−0.255	−0.611	0.000	0.000	−0.045
pm_t	−0.121	0.099	−0.001	0.000	0.002
e_t	0.105	−0.310	0.000	0.000	0.007
pd_t	−0.075	0.004	0.000	0.000	0.015

Source: Urbain (1995, *op. cit.*).

normalised on im_t which then has coefficients of 0.310 on pm_t, 0.301 on e_t and −0.654 on pd_t, and the own adjustment coefficient corresponding to this normalisation is −0.792. The second cointegrating vector is more difficult to interpret without identification restrictions, which are dealt with in the next section.

15.7.2 Identification of the cointegrating vectors

Generically identifying restrictions are suggested as follows to give two just-identified cointegrating vectors. For the first vector the coefficients on pm_t and e_t are constrained to be equal so that in the long run the effect of a shock to the import price is the same whether it comes from the exchange rate or the foreign currency price. As to the second vector Urbain suggests an exclusion restriction on income to interpret the relationship as a PPP relationship for the exchange rate modified by the inclusion of import volumes; in this case we expect approximately equal but oppositely signed coefficients on pm_t and pd_t, and the exchange rate to depreciate with an increase in import volume suggesting a positive sign on im_t. These considerations impose 1 restriction on each coin-

tegrating vector which are, thus, just identified by the order condition. Imposing these restrictions gives the estimated long-run relationships designated ecm_{1t} and ecm_{2t} and adjustment coefficients shown in Table 15.19:

$$ecm_{1t} = im_t - (1.030inc_t - 0.316(e_t + pm_t) + 0.661pd_t) \tag{15.32}$$

$$ecm_{2t} = e_t - (0.344pd_t - 0.356pm_t + 0.217im_t) \tag{15.33}$$

Finally, imposing a unit income elasticity on the first vector and equal but oppositely signed coefficients on pd_t and pm_t in the second vector gives an overidentified system (each vector now

Table 15.19 *Adjustment coefficients for the just-identified cointegrating vectors*

Adjustment coefficients, α, corresponding to just-identified (normalised) cointegrating vectors		
equation	α_1	α_2
$\begin{pmatrix} im_t \\ inc_t \\ pm_t \\ e_t \\ pd_t \end{pmatrix}$	$\begin{bmatrix} -0.978 \\ -0.009 \\ -0.078 \\ -0.029 \\ -0.073 \end{bmatrix}$	$\begin{bmatrix} -0.368 \\ -0.531 \\ -0.087 \\ -0.270 \\ 0.004 \end{bmatrix}$

Source: Urbain (*op. cit.*, p. 193, Table 3).

has 2 restrictions imposed whereas just-identification requires 1 restriction). One restriction has to be placed on each of the 2 cointegrating vectors for just-identification; any further restrictions serve to overidentify the structural relationships. In this case the R_i and H_i matrices are (where g_i is the number of restrictions on the ith cointegrating vector and s_i is the number of freely determined coefficients):

$$R_1\beta_1 = 0$$

$$\begin{bmatrix} 1 & 1 & 0 & 0 & 0 \\ 0 & 0 & 1 & -1 & 0 \end{bmatrix} \begin{pmatrix} \beta_{11} \\ \beta_{21} \\ \beta_{31} \\ \beta_{41} \\ \beta_{51} \end{pmatrix} = \begin{pmatrix} 0 \\ 0 \end{pmatrix}$$

$$g_1 = 2$$

$$\beta_1 = H_1\varphi_1$$

$$\begin{pmatrix} \beta_{11} \\ \beta_{21} \\ \beta_{31} \\ \beta_{41} \\ \beta_{51} \end{pmatrix} = \begin{bmatrix} 1 & 0 & 0 \\ -1 & 0 & 0 \\ 0 & 1 & 0 \\ 0 & 1 & 0 \\ 0 & 0 & 1 \end{bmatrix} \begin{pmatrix} \varphi_{11} \\ \varphi_{21} \\ \varphi_{31} \end{pmatrix}$$

$$s_1 = 3$$

$$R_2\beta_2 = 0$$

$$\begin{bmatrix} 0 & 1 & 0 & 0 & 0 \\ 0 & 0 & 1 & 0 & 1 \end{bmatrix} \begin{pmatrix} \beta_{12} \\ \beta_{22} \\ \beta_{32} \\ \beta_{42} \\ \beta_{52} \end{pmatrix} = \begin{pmatrix} 0 \\ 0 \end{pmatrix}$$

$$g_2 = 2$$

$$\beta_2 = H_2\varphi_2$$

$$\begin{pmatrix} \beta_{12} \\ \beta_{22} \\ \beta_{32} \\ \beta_{42} \\ \beta_{52} \end{pmatrix} = \begin{bmatrix} 0 & 0 & 1 \\ 0 & 0 & 0 \\ 0 & 1 & 0 \\ 1 & 0 & 0 \\ 0 & -1 & 0 \end{bmatrix} \begin{pmatrix} \varphi_{12} \\ \varphi_{22} \\ \varphi_{32} \end{pmatrix}$$

$$s_2 = 3$$

15.7.3 Testing restrictions

As noted in section **14.5.3** when restrictions placed on the cointegrating vectors are over-identifying it is possible to test whether these are consistent with the data by a standard χ^2 test with degrees of freedom equal to the number of overidentifying restrictions. The maximum number of freely estimated coefficients for each column is $k - (r - 1)$, here $5 - (2 - 1) = 4$. If the number of freely estimated coefficients, s_i, is less than this, it must arise because further, that is overidentifying, restrictions have been imposed. The total number, v, of overidentifying restrictions (relative to the number required for just-identification) is:

$$v = \sum_{i=1}^{r} [k - (r - 1) - s_i]$$

$$= r(k + 1 - r) - \sum_{i=1}^{r} s_i \qquad (15.34)$$

In this example the number of overidentifying restrictions is

$$v = [5 - (2 - 1) - 3] + [5 - (2 - 1) - 3]$$
$$= \qquad [1] \qquad + \qquad [1]$$
$$= 2$$

Urbain also suggested 5 restrictions on the α matrix – see Table 15.20 which reports the restricted α matrix – relating to the overidentified cointegrating vectors. Specifically, as the

Table 15.20 *Restricted adjustment coefficients for the overidentified cointegrating vectors*

Restricted adjustment coefficients, α		
Equation	α_1	α_2
$\begin{pmatrix} im_t \\ inc_t \\ pm_t \\ e_t \\ pd_t \end{pmatrix}$	$\begin{bmatrix} -0.821 \\ 0.000 \\ 0.000 \\ 0.000 \\ 0.000 \end{bmatrix}$	$\begin{matrix} 0.000 \\ -0.437 \\ 0.144 \\ -0.196 \\ 0.021 \end{matrix}$

Source: Urbain (*op. cit.*, p. 194, Table 5).

only sizeable coefficient in the first column of α is α_{11}, that is the own adjustment coefficient, then α_{i1}, $i = 2, 3, 4, 5$, could be set to zero with the interpretation that the first cointegrating vector only enters the import demand equation; the fifth restriction was that the second cointegrating vector does not enter the im_t equation. Given that its relative magnitude is the second largest (in absolute value) it might be advantageous to reconsider this restriction. If there is a positive disequilibrium the domestic currency needs to appreciate ($e_t\downarrow$) to restore equilibrium, a reduction in imports would encourage this movement by lessening the demand for foreign currency so the negative estimate of α_{42} accords with this interpretation.

With overidentifying restrictions the revised estimates of equilibrium are:

$$ecm_{1t} = im_t - (1.000inc_t - 0.259(e_t + pm_t) \\ + 0.587pd_t) \qquad (15.35a)$$

$$ecm_{2t} = e_t - (0.347(pd_t - pm_t) + 0.194im_t) \\ \qquad (15.35b)$$

A joint test of the 2 overidentifying restrictions and the 5 exclusion restrictions on α gave a test statistic of 10.125 distributed as $\chi^2(7)$ under the null hypothesis; with 95% quantile equal to 14.067 the joint null is not rejected. An alternative strategy is to split the hypothesis tests into their constituent parts, that is a test of the overidentifying restrictions and, separately, a test of the exclusion on α restrictions.

15.7.4 The parsimonious VAR, PVAR, and SECM

The next stage in the methodology is to estimate what is known as a parsimonious VAR – or PVAR. The rationale for this model is that the original unrestricted VAR may be quite profligate in its number of coefficients. For example, a fourth order UVAR in five variables implies 20 coefficients in each equation; in addition there are four special event dummy variables and a constant in each equation, a total of 25 coefficients and 125 overall in the VAR. Reduction of this UVAR is quite likely to be possible without loss of degree of fit or congruency with the data. The usual strategy in this reduction process is to delete variables where an insignificant test statistic is obtained for the joint null hypothesis that a *column* of coefficients in the VAR is zero; that is a particular lagged variable, or one of the dummy variables, does not enter *any* of the equations. This reduction takes as given the error correction mechanisms, ecm_{1t} and ecm_{2t}, defined in the earlier stages of determining just- or overidentified cointegrating vectors.

All of the variables in the PVAR are I(0), which is checked to ensure that it is congruent with the data, specifically that standard tests for parameter constancy, normality of the residuals and absence of serial correlation are not rejected. The PVAR is not reported in detail in Urbain (*op. cit.*), its role is to provide a base against which to compare the structural error correction model, SECM. The SECM again models in I(0) space but differs from the VARs in two central respects. First, the SECM will usually involve current dated regressors, that is it is a conditional model, and is guided by economic theory which relates to the structural rather than the reduced form. Second, it is likely to be parsimonious relative to the UVAR *and* the PVAR; for example, individual coefficients, rather than columns, may be tested for significance; also, although all dummy variables appear in all equations in the VAR it is usually possible to allocate them more precisely to particular equations in the SECM. The 125 coefficients in the UVAR are reduced to 86 in the PVAR and 37 in the SECM. There are 49 restrictions to get from the PVAR to the SECM; a χ^2 test of these restrictions with 49 degrees of freedom is not rejected with a test value of 48.1 compared to the 95% quantile of 66.3. (This is an example of what is known as a parsimonious encompassing test, considered in greater detail in sections **15.8.6**.)

So by a process of reduction, using a general-to-specific modelling approach, Urbain (*op. cit.*,

p. 195) is able to simplify the UVAR to a PVAR, which is congruent with the data, and then estimate an even more parsimonious SECM. Since current dated regressors appear in the SECM the estimation method has to take this into account and a system method (full information maximum likelihood, see Chapter 4, appendix) is used for estimation. The estimation results are presented in Table 15.21.

The import volume equation shows a fairly fast adjustment to equilibrium with a significant own error correction coefficient of -0.704, with simultaneous effects from income and domestic prices. Separating out the contributions from

Table 15.21 *SECM for import volume, income, import prices, exchange rate and domestic prices*

$$\Delta im_t = -0.704ecm_{1t-1} + 0.689\Delta inc_t + 1.435\Delta pd_t + 0.404\Delta inc_{t-3} - 1.086\Delta e_{t-3} - 0.475\Delta pm_{t-2}$$
$$\quad (7.822) \qquad\quad (3.000) \qquad\quad (-3.986) \qquad\quad (3.672) \qquad\quad (-3.745) \qquad\quad (-2.639)$$

$$\quad -0.174\Delta pm_{t-4} + 1.757\Delta pd_{t-3}$$
$$\quad (2.486) \qquad\quad (4.183)$$

$$\Delta inc_t = -0.260ecm_{2t-1} - 1.478\Delta pd_t - 0.333\Delta inc_{t-1} - 0.294\Delta inc_{t-3} + 0.070D82_t + 0.048D86_t$$
$$\quad (-3.250) \qquad\quad (-4.618) \qquad\quad (-3.700) \qquad\quad (-3.267) \qquad\quad (3.500) \qquad\quad (2.400)$$

$$\Delta pm_t = 0.140ecm_{2t-1} + 0.410\Delta e_t - 0.080\Delta im_{t-4} - 1.504\Delta e_{t-1} + 1.494\Delta pd_{t-1} + 0.260D73_t$$
$$\quad (2.333) \qquad\quad (2.158) \qquad (-2.000) \qquad\quad (-13.673) \qquad\quad (10.671) \qquad\quad (2.600)$$

$$\Delta e_t = -0.195ecm_{2t-1} - 0.587\Delta pd_t + -0.109\Delta im_{t-1} + 0.099\Delta im_{t-4} + 0.153\Delta pm_{t-1} - 0.135\Delta pm_{t-4}$$
$$\quad (-48.75) \qquad\quad (-4.515) \qquad\quad (-2.725) \qquad\quad (2.475) \qquad\quad (-3.825) \qquad\quad (-4.500)$$

$$\quad +0.223\Delta e_{t-1} - 0.039D82_t$$
$$\quad (2.788) \qquad\quad (-3.90)$$

$$\Delta pd_t = -0.092ecm_{2t-1} + 0.449\Delta pm_t + 0.102\Delta pm_{t-2} + 0.052\Delta pm_{t-4} + 0.581\Delta e_{t-1} - 0.390\Delta pd_{t-3}$$
$$\quad (-1.840) \qquad\quad (7.483) \qquad\quad (3.400) \qquad\quad (2.600) \qquad\quad (4.469) \qquad\quad (-3.545)$$

$$\quad +0.260D73_t - 0.048D86_t$$
$$\quad (43.333) \qquad\quad (-6.000)$$

Cointegrating vectors
$$ecm_{1t-1} = im_{t-1} - inc_{t-1} \qquad + 0.259(pm_{t-1} + e_{t-1}) - 0.587pd_{t-1}$$
$$ecm_{2t-1} = e_{t-1} \qquad - 0.194im_{t-1} + 0.347pm_{t-1} \qquad - 0.347pd_{t-1}$$

Simultaneities: Φ 　　　　　　　　　　　　　　　Φ^{-1}

$$\Phi = \begin{bmatrix} 1 & -0.689 & 0 & 0 & -1.435 \\ 0 & 1 & 0 & 0 & 1.478 \\ 0 & 0 & 1 & -0.410 & 0 \\ 0 & 0 & 0 & 1 & 0.587 \\ 0 & 0 & -0.449 & 0 & 1 \end{bmatrix} \qquad \Phi^{-1} = \begin{bmatrix} 1 & 0.689 & 0.169 & 0.069 & 0.376 \\ 0 & 1 & -0.599 & -0.246 & -1.334 \\ 0 & 0 & 0.903 & 0.370 & -0.217 \\ 0 & 0 & -0.238 & 0.903 & -0.530 \\ 0 & 0 & 0.405 & 0.166 & 0.903 \end{bmatrix}$$

Error correction coefficients: a 　　　Adjustment coefficients: $\alpha = \Phi^{-1}a$

$$a = \begin{bmatrix} -0.704 & 0 \\ 0 & -0.260 \\ 0 & 0.140 \\ 0 & -0.195 \\ 0 & -0.092 \end{bmatrix} \qquad \alpha = \begin{bmatrix} -0.704 & -0.204 \\ 0 & -0.173 \\ 0 & 0.074 \\ 0 & -0.160 \\ 0 & -0.059 \end{bmatrix}$$

Source: Estimation results, Urbain (*op. cit.*, Table 5 and p. 195); '*t*' statistics in parentheses beneath estimated coefficients.

import prices and the exchange rate is important in the short run as the latter has a more important effect than the former. The exchange rate shows a slower rate of adjustment to disequilibrium with an own error correction coefficient of -0.195. Simultaneous effects are more limited in the exchange rate equation and, overall, the Φ matrix is quite sparse – as in the earlier example from Johansen and Juselius (1994). The restriction that only the own disequilibrium, ecm_{1t-1} appears in the import equation in the SECM is not restrictive on the derived reduced form where $\alpha = \Phi^{-1}a$ and the coefficient on ecm_{2t-1} is -0.204; however, the assumption that ecm_{1t-1} does not enter any other equations turns out to be binding in the reduced form as well because of the absence of simultaneities involving Δim_t – that is the first column of Φ is zero apart from 1 in the first element.

Although the SECM encompasses the PVAR in the sense that the $\chi^2(49)$ test statistic at 48.13 is less than the 95% quantile, Urbain (*op. cit.*, p. 196) notes that the dummy variables which

are present in all but the import equation are necessary to this conclusion. This points to a problem, also encountered by Clements and Mizon (1991): there is a trade-off, in order to keep the VAR to manageable proportions some intervention dummies are necessary, but these are most likely suggesting that the information set needs to be extended.

15.8 Revisiting the demand for money in the United States

In this section we revisit the demand for M1 example used in Chapter 10. Recall that using monthly (seasonally adjusted) data for the United States, an error correction model was constructed in which the equilibrium specification, involving real M1, real income and a nominal interest rate, was alternatively estimated by (i) the first stage of the Engle–Granger (1987)

Table 15.22 *OLS estimation of the US demand for money (extracted from Table 10.9)*

EG second stage estimation
$$\Delta m1_t = \underset{(4.678)}{0.271}\Delta m1_{t-1} + \underset{(5.958)}{0.322}\Delta m1_{t-2} + \underset{(3.766)}{0.173}\Delta inc_t + \underset{(2.253)}{0.107}\Delta inc_{t-1} - \underset{(-2.365)}{0.105}\Delta inc_{t-4}$$
$$\{4.266\} \qquad \{6.446\} \qquad \{3.177\} \qquad \{2.439\} \qquad \{-1.770\}$$

$$\underset{(-3.955)}{-0.002}\Delta SR_t - \underset{(-3.738)}{0.002}\Delta SR_{t-1} - \underset{(-3.776)}{0.002}\Delta SR_{t-2} - \underset{(-3.094)}{0.025}ecm_{t-1} + \hat{u}_t$$
$$\{-3.385\} \qquad \{-3.016\} \qquad \{-3.946\} \qquad \{-3.043\}$$

$$\hat{\sigma} = 0.0048; \; dw = 2.049$$
$$SC(12) = 17.899[0.120]; \; FF(1) = 0.820[0.365]$$
$$JB(2) = 2.058[0.357]; \; HS(1) = 6.328[0.120]$$

ADL estimation
$$\Delta m1_t = \underset{(0.972)}{0.022} + \underset{(3.393)}{0.203}\Delta m1_{t-1} + \underset{(4.335)}{0.247}\Delta m1_{t-3} + \underset{(3.375)}{0.161}\Delta inc_t + \underset{(1.819)}{0.089}\Delta inc_{t-1} - \underset{(-2.611)}{0.118}\Delta inc_{t-4}$$
$$\{1.033\} \; \{3.023\} \qquad \{4.785\} \qquad \{2.840\} \qquad \{2.224\} \qquad \{-2.419\}$$

$$\underset{(-3.729)}{-0.002}\Delta SR_t - \underset{(-3.084)}{0.002}\Delta SR_{t-1} - \underset{(-2.930)}{0.002}\Delta SR_{t-2} - \underset{(-4.203)}{0.036}\{(m1_t) - (\underset{(10.174)}{0.742}inc_t - \underset{(-8.112)}{0.031}SR_t)\}_{-1} + \hat{u}_t$$
$$\{-3.429\} \qquad \{-2.561\} \qquad \{-2.967\} \qquad \{-4.218\} \qquad \{11.232\} \quad \{-7.953\}$$

$$\hat{\sigma} = 0.0047; \; dw = 1.986$$
$$SC(12) = 18.711[0.100]; \; FF(1) = 2.845[0.092];$$
$$JB(2) = 3.315[0.191]; \; HS(1) = 0.856[0.354]$$

Source: Table 10.9; '*t*' statistics in parentheses (.); robust '*t*' statistics in {.} and msl in [.].

two-stage procedure and (ii) a solved, single-equation autoregressive distributed lag, ADL, model. With real M1 in logs as the dependent variable the estimated error correction mechanisms were, apart from a constant,

Engle–Granger:
$$ecm_t^* = m1_t - (0.617inc_t - 0.021SR_t)$$

$$(15.36a)$$

ADL:
$$ecm_t^+ = m1_t - (0.742inc_t - 0.031SR_t)$$

$$(15.36b)$$

The notation is as follows: $m1_t \equiv m_t - p_t$ is the log of real money, inc_t is the log of real income (previously $y_t - p_t$) and, as before, SR_t is a short rate, here the US Treasury Bill 3-month rate – broadly similar results were obtained throughout with the 3-year rate – see Table 10.6. The differences between the estimates from the two methods are that the income elasticity is larger and the absolute value of the interest rate semi-elasticity is larger for the ADL method. Of the two methods of estimation the (limited) Monte Carlo results in Chapter 8 suggested a noticeable small-sample bias for the Engle–Granger method relative to the ADL method with correct specification of the lag length.

The second stage of estimation resulted in an empirically well-specified dynamic model of the demand for the log of real M1. For convenience these equations for the alternative methods are reproduced in Table 15.22 from Table 10.9.

15.8.1 A multivariate approach: choosing the lag length

It is now of interest to compare these results with those obtained using the methodology of this and the previous chapter, particularly the various aspects which arise from an explicitly multivariate approach. Questions of interest include: was it right to assume the existence of just one cointegrating vector? Can real income and the interest rate be regarded as weakly exogenous for the parameters of interest? How does the

dynamic money demand equation estimated within a multivariate framework compare to the single-equation approach?

From Table 10.5 note that the univariate time series processes for $m1_t$, inc_t and SR_t were all consistent with having a single unit root, with ADF test statistics of -0.340, 0.083 and -1.441, respectively, compared to 5% critical values of approximately -2.85; hence, we can legitimately consider an I(1) model as suggested by the Johansen approach. The latter is system based but can reduce to a single equation in some circumstances. The first stage is to estimate an unrestricted VAR in the three variables $m1_t$, inc_t and SR_t, a key factor being to determine the lag length of the VAR. Estimation uses the CATS in RATS program, Hansen and Juselius (1995), Doan (1996). Some details for choosing the lag length are reported in Table 15.23.

Note that the AIC and SIC are at a minimum at system lag lengths of 4 and 2, respectively; as expected the SIC suggests a shorter lag length compared to the AIC which does not penalise additional lags as heavily as the SIC. Another important factor in lag length determination is that the residuals should be free of serial correlation. Johansen's (1995, p. 22) system test for serial correlation, distributed as $\chi^2(4)$ under the null, is not significant at either of the lags suggested by the information criteria. The normality test statistics, distributed as $\chi^2(2)$, 5% critical value $= 3.84$ under the null, indicate rejection at all lag lengths considered for real income and the interest rate, but nonrejection at lag length 2 for $m1_t$. We will concentrate here on a system lag length of 2, with consideration of alternative lag lengths in sections **15.8.4**.

The nonnormality of the residuals for real income is to be expected from the earlier discussion in Chapter 10 of what seemed to be a substantial outlier in 1992; real income increased from 3,694 to 3,878 in 1992m12 returning to 3,666 in 1993m1 (all quantities in 1987 \$US billion). In logs this is an increase of 0.05, from 8.21 to 8.26, which is over 10 times the estimated standard deviation of the real

Table 15.23 *Choosing the lag length*

Lag length	AIC	SIC	System SC(4) $\sim \chi^2(4)$	Normality $\sim \chi^2(2)$		
				$m1_t$	inc_t	SR_t
1	−21.160	−20.981	10.179[0.34]	7.682	756.152	265.657
2	−21.496	**−21.180**	7.338[0.60]	3.528	531.786	165.978
3	−21.510	−21.057	9.601[0.38]	5.535	513.351	135.369
4	**−21.522**	−20.924	12.178[0.20]	9.354	521.208	122.345
5	−21.474	−20.743	16.978[0.05]	8.688	484.078	17.592
6	−21.479	−20.611	14.873[0.09]	8.438	509.433	105.495

Notes: Throughout all tables the common sample period is 1975m1 to 1993m12 = 228 observations. Minimum indicated in bold.

income equation in the VAR. In addition the tax cutting budget of 1975 led to an exceptional increase in real income in the second quarter. Problems relating to the nonnormality of the residuals from the interest rate equation may stem from the change in the operating policy of the Federal Reserve Board in the early 1980s, which led to much greater variability in nominal interest rates.

Two impulse dummy variables were introduced for 1975 and 1992/3 to account for the special effects on real income and one impulse dummy variable to capture the change in the FRB operating policy around 1980. (An impulse dummy variable has no long-run effect consisting of a combination of multiples of 0/1 entries.) These dummy variables can rightly be regarded as capturing 'special effects' in a very parsimonious way. In addition, even though normality of residuals in the real M1 equation was not formally rejected there were two 'outliers', of nearly four times the estimated equation standard error, in 1983m1 and 1986m12, for which two 0/1 dummy variables were introduced; while these are not so justified on 'special intervention' grounds it transpired that the results are not qualitatively affected by their omission. With these dummy variables the normality test statistics were 1.692, 3.845 and 181.253 for the equation residuals from $m1_t$, inc_t and SR_t, respectively; the nonnormality in the residuals from the interest rate equation

obviously remains despite the special intervention dummy variables. This heightens the concern over whether we can obtain a cointegrating vector interpretable as a demand for money relationship; and whether we can interpret the interest rate as weakly exogenous, and hence consider the analysis as conditional on the (nonnormal) interest rate.

In the context of a UK analysis of the demand for money, Hendry and Mizon (1993) used the log rather than the level of their interest rate variable because of the large increase in residual variance over the sample period. For different reasons, in Chapter 10 we noted the alternative use of the log of the interest rate – in the present context switching to logs did not materially alter the results, in particular the nonnormality remained. Adding the dummy variables did not affect the choice of lag length with AIC and SIC again indicating 4 and 2, respectively. In the context of testing for PPP and UIP between the United States and Australia, Johansen (1992d, 1995a) noted the nonnormality of the US interest rate but (fortunately) found it to be weakly exogenous for α and β.

15.8.2 A multivariate approach: estimating the cointegrating rank by the Johansen method

The $\lambda_{\max}$ and trace test statistics are reported in Table 15.24. The large sample distribution of the

Table 15.24   *Test statistics for cointegrating rank*

Lag length $= 2$								
Null	Alt.	$\hat{\lambda}_i$	λ_{max} statistic	95% quantile	Null	Alt.	Trace statistic	95% quantile
$r = 0$	$r = 1$	0.167	$-T\ln(1 - \hat{\lambda}_1) = \mathbf{41.22} > \mathbf{20.97}$		$r = 0$	$r \geq 1$	$-T\sum_{i=1}^{3}\ln(1 - \hat{\lambda}_i) = \mathbf{54.07} > \mathbf{29.68}$	
		(0.220)	(56.02)					(71.97)
$r \leq 1$	$r = 2$	0.055	$-T\ln(1 - \hat{\lambda}_2) = 12.70 < 14.07$		$r \leq 1$	$r \geq 2$	$-T\sum_{i=2}^{3}\ln(1 - \hat{\lambda}_i) = 12.84 < 15.41$	
		(0.067)	(15.69)					(15.95)
$r \leq 2$	$r = 3$	0.001	$-T\ln(1 - \hat{\lambda}_3) = 0.15 < 3.76$		$r \leq 2$	$r = 3$	$-T\ln(1 - \hat{\lambda}_3) = 0.15 < 3.76$	
		(0.001)	(0.26)					(0.26)

Roots of the companion matrix

real	complex	modulus
1.002	0	1.002
0.978	0	0.978
0.826	0	0.826
0.349	0.196	0.400
0.349	−0.196	0.400
−0.323	0	−0.323

Notes: Critical values are from Table 14.5 corresponding to Table 1 of Osterwald-Lenum (1992); italicised entries are for models with dummy variables. The dummy variables are specified as follows: $d831$, $d828$ and $d8612$ are simple dummy variables with zeros everywhere except for a one in 1983m1, 1982m8 and 1986m12, respectively; $d75$, $d80$ and $d92$ are linear combinations of simple dummy variables, specifically $d75 = d775 + d756 - d757$, $d80 = d803 - 0.75d804 - 1.5d805 + d809 + d8010 + d8011 + d8012 - d8011 - d813$ and $d92 = d9212 - d931 - 0.5d932$.

test statistics is known for the model with Gaussian (normal) variables and without dummy variables. The distribution is likely to be robust to departures from normality in large samples and Johansen (1995a, p. 29) notes that the asymptotic properties only require that the errors are iid rather than normal. Cheung and Lai (1993b) examine the issue of the importance of nonnormality in finite samples on Johansen's λ_{max} and trace tests through some simulation experiments with $T = 200$ (which is close to the sample size here). They find that the trace test is 'reasonably' robust to excess kurtosis and skewness, whereas although the λ_{max} test is 'reasonably' robust to excess kurtosis it is senstive to excess skewness. This suggests that where there is a conflict in test results in the presence of nonnormality, the trace test is to be preferred. The distribution of the test statistics is not known

when there are dummy variables, although Hansen and Juselius (1995) suggest that impulse dummy variables, that is those with no long-run effect, may not affect the distribution.

The test statistics in the model without dummy variables are considered first. Both the λ_{max} and trace test statistics suggest one cointegrating vector. The test statistics for the null of 0 against the alternatives of 1 (for λ_{max}) and greater than or equal to 1 (for trace) are both greater than the 95% quantile, whereas this is not the case for the next hypothesis in the sequence; this suggests that the cointegrating rank, r, is one. When the dummy variables are included the test statistics increase, which marginally affects the decision as to whether there are 2 cointegrating vectors if the same quantiles are used. Given the uncertainty about the distribution of the test statistics in this case

Table 15.25 *Unrestricted estimates of the eigenvectors, β, and the adjustment coefficients α*

	(Unnormalised) estimated β_i vectors (the eigenvectors)			Normalised β_i vectors		
	β_1	β_2	β_3	β_1	β_2	β_3
$m1_t$	−24.118	−5.347	−16.675	1.000	1.000	1.000
inc_t	17.719	11.307	8.223	−0.735	−2.115	−0.493
SR_t	−0.760	0.145	−0.161	0.032	0.027	0.009

Estimated α_i vectors (the adjustment coefficients after normalisation)

	α_1	α_2	α_3
$m1_t$	−0.055	0.000	0.000
inc_t	−0.013	0.007	0.001
SR_t	0.303	0.373	−0.236

Weak exogeneity restrictions on the adjustment coefficients

	Unrestricted	Income weakly exogenous	Interest rate weakly exogenous	Both weakly exogenous
	α_1	α_1	α_1	α_1
$m1_t$	−0.055(−6.647)	−0.054(−6.399)	−0.054(−6.593)	−0.053(−6.306)
inc_t	−0.013(−1.261)	0	−0.014(−1.320)	0
SR_t	0.303(0.300)	0.518(0.504)	0	0

Resulting estimated β_1 vectors and test statistics

	β_1	β_1	β_1	β_1
$m1_t$	1.000	1.000	1.000	1.000
inc_t	−0.735	−0.764	−0.730	−0.758
SR_t	0.032	0.030	0.032	0.030
Test statistic		$\chi^2(1)=1.19$ [0.28]	$\chi^2(1)=0.08$ [0.77]	$\chi^2(2)=1.43$ [0.49]

Note: Lag length of VAR = 2, 't' statistics in (.) parentheses; msl in [.] parentheses.

and that at other relevant lags (3 and 4) the evidence is for $r = 1$, the subsequent analysis is, therefore, conditioned on $r = 1$.

The unrestricted estimates of the eigenvectors are presented in Table 15.25. Normalising on the first element, corresponding to real M1, the first eigenvector can be interpreted as a long-run demand for money relationship with a real income elasticity of 0.735 and an interest rate semi-elasticity of −0.032, which defines the error correction mechanism

$$ecm_{1t} = m_t - (0.735inc_t - 0.032SR_t)$$

Including dummy variables in the VAR changes this specification only slightly, with an income elasticity of 0.731 and an interest rate semi-elasticity of −0.030. Figures 15.1–15.3 plot the

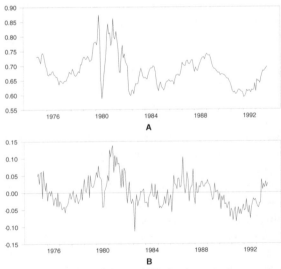

Figure 15.1 *The first estimated cointegrating vector.*
$\mathbf{A} - \hat{\beta}'_1\mathbf{y}_t$. $\mathbf{B} - \hat{\beta}'_1\mathbf{R}_{1t}$

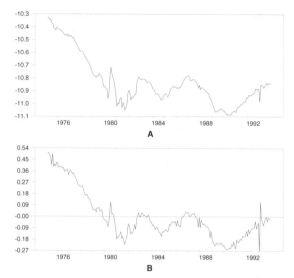

Figure 15.2 *The second estimated cointegrating vector.* $\mathbf{A} - \hat{\beta}_2' \mathbf{y_t}.$ $\mathbf{B} - \hat{\beta}_2' \mathbf{R}_{It}$

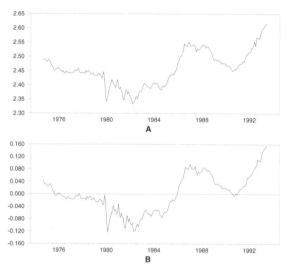

Figure 15.3 *The third estimated cointegrating vector.* $\mathbf{A} - \hat{\beta}_3' \mathbf{y_t}.$ $\mathbf{B} - \hat{\beta}_3' \mathbf{R}_{It}$

(potential) cointegrating relations corresponding to the three eigenvectors. For example, in Figure 15.1 the upper panel is the plot of $\hat{\beta}_1' y_t$, where $\hat{\beta}_1$ is the estimate of the first (normalised) cointegrating vector; $\hat{\beta}_1' y_t$ can be regarded as a direct estimate of the cointegrating relationship, motivated by its inclusion in the same form in the VAR – see, for example, (14.49). The lower

panel exploits a slightly different approach. Recall from section **14.4.2** that the residuals from the regression of y_{t-1} on $(\Delta y_{t-1}, \ldots, \Delta y_{t-(p-1)}, D_t)'$ are denoted R_{1t}, where this regression can be interpreted as 'purging' y_{t-1} of its short-run and deterministic components; and R_{0t} are the residuals from the regression of Δy_t on the same short-run and deterministic components. Hence, a regression of R_{0t} on R_{1t} isolates the 'purged' or pure long-run effects, this is regression (14.60), that is $R_{0t} = \alpha(\beta' R_{1t}) + \hat{\varepsilon}_t$; therefore, another estimate of the r equilibrium relationships is provided by $\beta_1' R_{1t}$. The first element of $\beta' R_{1t}$ with $\hat{\beta}_1$ replacing β_1, that is $\hat{\beta}_1' R_{1t}$, is shown in the lower panel of Figure 15.1, and is a typical output from CATS in RATS (Hansen and Juselius 1995). If the short-run and deterministic effects are slight these plots will not differ much from each other.

In the case of the first cointegrating vector – see Figure 15.1 – the visual evidence is for stationarity; this is perhaps more easily seen from the lower plot because the residual R_{1t} has a zero mean by construction and it is, therefore, easy to assess whether there is a frequent crossing of the mean: this is the case using the first eigenvector. Turning to Figures 15.2 and 15.3, it is apparent that there is now a wandering which becomes more noticeable as we move from the first to the second eigenvector (Figure 15.2) and then from the second to the third eigenvector (Figure 15.3). Visually the evidence is for just one cointegrating vector and hence $r = 1$.

Also of interest are the roots of the companion matrix which are given in the lower part of Table 15.24 (these are virtually unchanged by the inclusion of the dummy variables). Recall that a cointegrating rank of r implies $k - r$ unit roots; hence, in this case if $r = 1$ then we expect to find $3 - 1 = 2$ roots close to the unit circle. The largest roots at 1.002 and 0.978 are close to 1, and then there is a numerical break with the third root of 0.826 being some way from 1; hence, again the data points to a cointegrating rank of 1.

Conditional on the suggested normalisation the adjustment coefficients are given in the lower part of Table 15.25; these serve to re-inforce the conclusion that $r = 1$, with the first column indicating a negative own adjustment coefficient equal to -0.055. Conditional on the normalisation and $r = 1$ we obtain 't' statistics for the adjustment coefficients and, with the relevant coefficients, these are

$$\hat{\alpha}_{11} = -0.055(-6.647)$$
$$\hat{\alpha}_{21} = -0.013(-1.261)$$
$$\hat{\alpha}_{31} = 0.303(0.300)$$

The own adjustment coefficient is clearly significant but, with the estimates of α_{21} and α_{31} insignificant, it looks likely that we will find that real income and the interest rate are weakly exogenous for the parameters of interest (β_1 and α_{11}). The test statistics for real income weakly exogenous, $\alpha_{21} = 0$, the interest rate weakly exogenous, $\alpha_{31} = 0$, both individually and then jointly are given in the lower part of Table 15.25. They indicate nonrejection of the null of weak exogeneity for both real income and the interest rate; for example, the joint test statistic, distributed as $\chi^2(2)$ under the null, is 1.43 with a marginal significance level of 49%. Also of interest in this case are the estimated equilibrium coefficients and the adjustment coefficients, which under weak exogeneity are 0.758 and -0.030, and $\hat{\alpha}_{11} = -0.053(-6.306)$, $\hat{\alpha}_{21} = \hat{\alpha}_{31} = 0$. The finding of weak exogeneity, as noted by Johansen (1995a), suggests a conditional model is valid – the conditioning variables in this case being real income and the interest rate. Imposing a cointegrating rank of 1, and hence two roots of 1, and weak exogeneity for income and the interest rate leaves the third largest root of the companion matrix at 0.833, which is virtually unchanged compared to the unrestricted case (see Table 15.24) and below unity (in this case three unit roots would imply no cointegration). We can also test whether the null hypothesis of a unit income elasticity is consistent with the data within the Johansen framework; the test statistic, distributed as $\chi^2(1)$ under the null, is 10.35[0.000] (or with dummy variables $16.88[0.000]$), indicating a firm rejection of the null hypothesis.

15.8.3 A multivariate approach: estimating the cointegrating rank by the Schwarz Information Criterion (SIC)

As noted in section **14.4.4** an alternative method for estimating the cointegrating rank is to use an information criterion to simultaneously select the lag order of the VAR and the cointegrating rank. The basis of the criterion is that penalties are imposed on increasing the lag length and increasing the cointegrating rank, since both increase the overall number of coefficients to be estimated. The Monte Carlo evidence in Reimers (1992) suggests that while the differences among the AIC, HQIC and SIC are relatively minor in choosing the lag length, the SIC is dominant when simultaneously selecting lag length and cointegrating rank.

Following the practice in MICROFIT (Pesaran and Pesaran 1997) it is often easier to think of a function as being maximised, as with the log likelihood, rather than a negative one being

Table 15.26 *Simultaneous selection of the lag length, p, and cointegrating rank, r. Entries are (transformed) SIC for the (p, r) pair indicated*

	Cointegrating rank, r			
	$r = 0$	$r = 1$	$r = 2$	$r = 3$
$p = 1$	1,382.8	1,428.9	1,424.5	1,421.8
	1,492.5	*1,548.2*	*1,544.5*	*1,541.8*
$p = 2$	1,443.3	**1,451.0**	1,448.0	1,445.4
	1,545.0	***1,560.1***	*1,557.9*	*1,555.3*
$p = 3$	1,437.3	1,438.3	1,434.9	1,432.2
	1,546.9	*1,553.0*	*1,550.1*	*1,547.4*
$p = 4$	1,430.0	1,425.0	1,421.7	1,419.0
	1,540.5	*1,539.7*	*1,537.0*	*1,534.3*

Notes: Bold indicates a maximum; italicised entries are for the VAR with dummy variables.

minimised, so a simple transformation of the SIC as given in section **14.4.4** is reported in Table 15.26. That is since $LL(p, r) = $ constant $- (T/2)\ln|\hat{\Omega}(p, r)|$, where $LL(p, r)$ is the log likelihood for a pth order VAR with cointegrating rank r, then choosing p and r to minimise SIC is the same as choosing p and r to *maximise* $LL(p, r) - (\ln T/2)m$, where m is the number of freely estimated parameters. In Table 15.26 this transformed SIC is presented over the relevant range and the selected model is that which maximises this criterion. The maximum is at $p = 2$ and $r = 1$, whether or not the dummy variables are included, so confirming the two stage analysis of the previous section. This confirmation will not always occur, just as the results of the Johansen trace and λ_{max} tests can result in different choices. In the case of contradiction other criteria must be brought to bear; in the empirical literature examples can be found of reference to a graphical impression of the marginal cointegrating vector(s) or variation in the significance level of the tests. Further evaluation of the robustness of the specification is reported in the next section.

15.8.4   Robustness of specification

The practical specification of a VAR from which to estimate the cointegrating rank involves several elements of choice. Table 14.2 summarised the choice of deterministic components relating to the inclusion/exclusion of a constant/linear trend/quadratic trend in the VAR and the dependence of the critical values on this aspect of specification; and different model selection criteria can lead to different choices of the lag length. Both of these issues are considered in this section. In particular on the former this example is used to illustrate the procedure suggested by Hansen and Juselius (1995, p. 68) to determine the cointegrating rank jointly with the appropriate deterministic (not dummy) variables in the VAR. Another element of choice is which variables to include in the VAR. A review

question takes up the suggestion in Baba *et al.* (1992) that inflation should be included as well as an interest rate variable.

In Chapter 14, Table 14.2 summarised the alternative specification of the constant and trend in the VAR together with the implications of particular models. For example, the model upon which inference has so far been based is Model 3 of Table 14.2; that is since there are evidently linear trends in the data, most notably in (the log of) real income, an unrestricted constant is included in the VAR. Model 2 which confines the constant to the cointegration space would not be adequate given this observation on the characteristics of the data. Model 4 introduces a linear trend in the cointegration space, which is a specification preferred by Hendry and Mizon (1993) in their analysis of the UK demand for money. Hansen and Juselius (1995, p. 68) caution against routine use of a trend in the cointegration space, but as noted in section **15.6.1** use of a proxy variable such as time may be a reasonably practical measure in keeping the VAR to manageable dimensions.

The procedure suggested by Hansen and Juselius (*op. cit.*) is an application of the Dickey–Pantula principle (Dickey and Pantula 1987, Pantula 1989) of working out from a most restricted to a least restricted model, stopping at the first model which is not rejected. The first step in the procedure, which is programmed in CATS for RATS, is to delimit the acceptable models. Given the characteristics of the data these are Models 3 and 4. Now define M_{rs} as model rs where r is the cointegrating rank, in this case $r = 0, 1, 2, 3$, and s is the deterministic model specification, in this case $s = 3, 4$. The range of models is therefore M_{03}, M_{04}, to M_{33}, M_{34}. Then start by testing the most restrictive model M_{03} in the usual way; referring to Table 15.27 this is illustrated with the λ_{max} test statistics. For $r = 0$ the test statistic is $\lambda_{max} = 41.22$ in M_{03} against a 95% quantile of 20.97, therefore do not reject the null; moving on to M_{04} we obtain $\lambda_{max} = 52.74$ against a 95% quantile of 25.54, again the null hypothesis is

Table 15.27 *Determining the cointegrating rank and deterministic components*

		Model 3		Model 4		Model 3		Model 4	
r	$k-r$	λ_{max}	95% quantile	λ_{max}	95% quantile	Trace	95% quantile	Trace	95% quantile
0	3	41.22	20.97	52.74	25.54	54.07	29.68	75.49	42.44
1	2	12.70	14.07	13.26	18.96	12.84	15.41	22.75	25.32
2	1	0.15	3.76	19.49	12.25	0.15	3.76	0.15	9.49

not rejected. Continuing the sequence in M_{13}, $\lambda_{max} = 12.70$ against a 95% quantile of 14.07, so the alternative of $r = 2$ is rejected in favour of $r = 1$. The first rejection ends the sequence; if this was continued, then in M_{14} the test statistic $\lambda_{max} = 13.26$ against a 95% quantile of 18.96 leads to rejection. Application of this procedure, therefore, confirms the earlier choice of $r = 1$ in Model 3 (that is with an unrestricted constant and no trend in the cointegration space). Including the dummy variables and/or using the trace test statistics did not change this decision sequence. A review question considers the likelihood procedure for determining M_{rs} suggested in Johansen and Juselius (1990, p. 181), and whether the Dickey–Pantula principle is an application of general-to-specific or specific-to-general modelling strategy.

Another aspect of model specification is the lag length of the VAR. As noted above while the SIC was minimised at a system lag of 2, the AIC had a minimum at a lag of 4. To ensure that our results are robust we give a brief summary here, and in Table 15.28, using lags 3 and 4. With a lag of 3 we obtain λ_{max} and trace statistics of 28.12 and 40.87, respectively, for the null $r = 0$, both indicate rejection; we then do not reject the null of $r = 1$. With a lag of 4 the λ_{max} and trace statistics at 15.68 and 28.38 are below their respective 95% quantiles but the latter only marginally so; with the dummy variables in the VAR both lead to rejection of the null using the same 95% quantiles. Overall, there is nothing in these alternative lags to suggest that the previous conclusions are not robust. Weak exogeneity for income and the interest rate is also not rejected for lags 3 and 4 with test statistics of 0.91[0.64] and 1.21[0.55], respectively, distributed as $\chi^2(2)$ under the null with msl in [.]. The corresponding cointegrating vectors for lags 3 and 4 are (1, −0.770, 0.031) and (1, −0.774, 0.029), respectively, with adjustment coefficients of −0.047 ('t' = −5.133) and −0.035 ('t' = −3.675). The only marginal difference

Table 15.28 *λ_{max} and trace test statistics for alternative lags*

		Lag 3	Lag 4		Lag 3	Lag 4	
r	$k-r$	λ_{max}	λ_{max}	95% quantile	Trace	Trace	95% quantile
0	3	28.12 (39.12)	15.68 (25.34)	20.97	40.87 (54.20)	28.38 (40.09)	29.68
1	2	12.73 (15.03)	13.264 (14.74)	14.07	12.75 (15.08)	12.69 (14.76)	15.41
2	1	0.02 (0.05)	19.486 (0.02)	3.76	0.02 (0.05)	0.000 (0.02)	3.76

Note: Italicised entries are for the model with dummy variables.

compared to a lag of 2 is that the estimated speed of adjustment is somewhat slower for a lag of 4.

15.8.5 A comparison with the OLS results

At this stage the results of the previous sections can now be compared with those reported earlier in Chapter 10 (with some relevant details being reproduced above in Table 15.22). The single-equation analysis using OLS estimation of an ADL equation implicitly assumed weak exogeneity of real income and the interest rate, with estimated equilibrium coefficients of 0.742 and −0.031, which are very close in the case of the real income elasticity and almost identical in the case of the interest rate semi-elasticity to the estimates using the Johansen procedure. Including dummy variables in the VAR model does not alter this conclusion with estimated equilibrium coefficients of 0.731 and −0.030, or using the lag of 4 suggested by AIC the estimated coefficients are 0.774 and −0.029 (no dummy variables) and 0.772 and −0.026 (with dummy variables). These results, however, do combine to contrast with the first stage Engle–Granger estimates, reported in Chapter 10, of 0.617 and −0.021. The weight of the evidence here points towards an equilibrium real income elasticity of between 0.74 and 0.77 and an interest rate semi-elasticity of about −0.030. In turn the estimated income elasticity here is close to the estimate of 0.79 by Hoffman and Rasche (1991), who used data for the period 1953m1 to 1988m12. Thus, nowhere have we obtained an income elasticity as low as that from the first stage of the Engle–Granger procedure.

15.8.6 A structural error correction model and parsimonious encompassing

This section and the next are linked in that both consider aspects of an SECM for money, income and the interest rate. The concept of parsimo-

nious encompassing, which considers the SECM as a reduction of a VAR, is considered more formally in this section and estimation of an SECM and calculation of a parsimonious encompassing test statistic is reported in the next section.

By way of reminder an SECM in first order form is,

$$\Phi\Delta y_t = \Gamma_1^+ \Delta y_{t-1} + a\beta' y_{t-1} + \zeta_t \qquad (15.37)$$

The solution of which gives the restricted reduced form:

$$\Delta y_t = \Gamma_1 \Delta y_{t-1} + \alpha\beta' y_{t-1} + \Phi^{-1}\zeta_t \qquad (15.38)$$

where $\Gamma_1 = \Phi^{-1}\Gamma_1^+$ and $\alpha = \Phi^{-1}a$.

If the SECM is assumed to be identified, then this reduced form is restricted in the sense that the derived coefficients Γ_1 and α are given from the structural coefficients Φ, Γ_1^+ and a. This contrasts with the unrestricted VAR in the Johansen analysis where Γ_1 (or, more generally, Γ_i) and α are not restricted by the structural form. By virtue of the presence of restrictions the derived reduced form can, therefore, be seen as a special case of the unrestricted reduced form; the former is nested in the latter in the sense that it is a special case which can be obtained by imposition of the restrictions. In a terminology due to Hendry and his coworkers – see, for example, Hendry and Richard (1982, 1989), Hendry (1988) and Hendry and Mizon (1993) – the VAR is said to encompass the SECM since the former can account for the results of the latter simply by the imposition of the appropriate restrictions – the SECM is a reduction of the VAR. The question then arises as to whether the SECM is a valid reduction of the more general VAR: can the simpler model encompass the more general model?

In an extension of the general concept of encompassing Hendry and Mizon (1993) introduce the idea of parsimonious encompassing applied to multivariate models. If a simple model can account for the results of the more general model within which it is nested, for example the

SECM and the VAR, the simple model is said to parsimoniously encompass the more general model. To develop a test for parsimonious encompassing by way of example reconsider the second order, reduced form ECM:

$$\Delta y_t = \Pi y_{t-1} + \Gamma_1 \Delta y_{t-1} + \Gamma_2 \Delta y_{t-2} + \varepsilon_t \tag{15.39}$$

where $\Pi = \alpha\beta'$; it is useful to put this in the following form

$$\begin{pmatrix} \beta' y_{t-1} \\ \Delta y_t \\ \Delta y_{t-1} \\ \Delta y_{t-2} \end{pmatrix} = \begin{bmatrix} I & \beta' & 0 & 0 \\ \alpha & \alpha\beta' + \Gamma_1 & \Gamma_2 & 0 \\ 0 & I & 0 & 0 \\ 0 & 0 & I & 0 \end{bmatrix}$$
$$\times \begin{pmatrix} \beta' y_{t-2} \\ \Delta y_{t-1} \\ \Delta y_{t-2} \\ \Delta y_{t-3} \end{pmatrix} + \begin{pmatrix} 0 \\ \varepsilon_t \\ 0 \\ 0 \end{pmatrix} \tag{15.40}$$

say

$$X_t = \Lambda_1 X_{t-1} + \Psi_t \tag{15.41}$$

where $X_t = (\beta' y_{t-1}, \Delta y_t, \Delta y_{t-1}, \Delta y_{t-2})'$, and constants and trend terms are omitted for simplicity. This representation is assumed to be congruent and so a valid basis for inference. An SECM which embodies data-based and theory-based restrictions is a reduction relative to this VAR, and can also be expressed in terms of the vector X_t. Consider the second order SECM:

$$\Phi \Delta y_t = a\beta' y_{t-1} + \Gamma_1^+ \Delta y_{t-1} + \Gamma_2^+ \Delta y_{t-2} + \zeta_t$$

that is

$$[-a, \ \Phi, \ -\Gamma_1^+, \ -\Gamma_2^+]X_t = \zeta_t$$

say

$$\Theta X_t = \zeta_t \tag{15.42}$$

where

$$\Theta = [-a, \ \Phi, \ -\Gamma_1^+, \ -\Gamma_2^+]$$

The connection between the VAR and the SECM is established by premultiplying (15.41) by Θ, that is

$$\Theta X_t = \Theta \Lambda_1 X_{t-1} + \Theta \Psi_t$$
$$= \zeta_t \tag{15.43}$$

The last line follows from (15.42).

Using (15.41) consider the following two expectations. The first is $E\{\zeta_t X'_{t-1}\}$, which relates to the orthogonality, or lack of it, between ζ_t and X_{t-1}. The second is the first order autocovariance, $E\{\zeta_t \zeta'_{t-1}\}$, which, if equal to zero, is by way of example what is required for the absence of serial correlation.

(i) $E\{\zeta_t X'_{t-1}\} = E\{(\Theta\Lambda_1 X_{t-1} + \Theta\Psi_t)X'_{t-1}\}$
$$= \Theta\Lambda_1 \Sigma_X$$

where $\Sigma_X \equiv E\{X_{t-1}X'_{t-1}\}$ and $E\{\Psi_t X'_{t-1}\} = 0$ as (15.41) is a CEF.

(ii) $E\{\zeta_t \zeta'_{t-1}\} = E\{(\Theta\Lambda_1 X_{t-1} + \Theta\Psi_t)X'_{t-1}\Theta'\}$
$$= E\{\Theta\Lambda_1 X_{t-1}X'_{t-1}\Theta' + \Theta\Psi_t X'_{t-1}\Theta'\}$$
$$= E\{\Theta\Lambda_1 X_{t-1}X'_{t-1}\Theta'\}$$
$$= \Theta\Lambda_1 \Sigma_X \Theta'$$

The first expectation shows that $\Theta\Lambda_1 = 0$ is required for ζ_t to be an innovation relative to X'_{t-1}; and the second shows that unless $\Theta\Lambda_1 = 0$ the ζ_t are serially correlated (the first order example is easily generalised). If ζ_t is not an innovation something has been lost in the reduction process and the SECM cannot encompass the VAR (which is congruent by assumption). On the other hand, if ζ_t is an innovation, the SECM is a valid reduction of the VAR: in this case the SECM is said to parsimoniously encompass the VAR. If $\Theta\Lambda_1 \neq 0$, the SECM cannot encompass the VAR and is misspecified in its dynamics.

A test of parsimonious encompassing is a test of $\Theta\Lambda_1 = 0$. In principle, given an overidentified SECM (a just-identified model does not impose any restrictions) and a corresponding more general VAR, a test could be based on directly evaluating $H_0: \Theta\Lambda_1 = 0$. However, it is simpler to base a test on, for example, (minus twice) the difference between the log likelihoods of the SECM and the VAR, with degrees of freedom equal to the difference in the number of degrees of freedom in the two models. We will call such a test a parsimonious encompassing test, or PET, with large values of the test statistic interpreted as evidence against parsimonious encompassing. Hendry and Mizon (1993) illustrate a practical application of a PET with the demand for money in the United Kingdom, other aspects of their study being considered in section **15.5** above. They test their SECM against a PVAR which is itself a reduction of a more general model. This is a valid step because parsimonious encompassing, denoted ε_p, is transitive; that is if model C ε_p model B and model B ε_p model A, then model C ε_p model A. So for the test against the PVAR to be useful the PVAR must ε_p UVAR: the PVAR has to be a valid reduction of the corresponding UVAR.

15.8.7 An estimated SECM for money, income and the interest rate

In a sense there is no need to estimate a SECM for money, income and the interest rate. The weak exogeneity tests reported above – see section **15.8.2** – resulted in nonrejection of the null hypothesis of weak exogeneity for income and the interest rate. This implies that a conditional model for $\Delta m1_t$ is valid. However, this example is used to see whether this is borne out empirically: we estimate an SECM and obtain the parameters of interest (for which income and the interest rate are weakly exogenous), and then consider whether they differ from those in the original reduced form VAR.

An SECM was estimated by simplifying a third order model (equivalent to a fourth order VAR), deleting redundant regressors. The exception here was that the dummy variables $d831_t$ and $d8612_t$ in the $\Delta m1_t$ equation and $d828_t$ in the ΔSR_t equation were kept because even though statistically insignificant they were numerically

important. The estimated SECM is reported in Table 15.28; because of the potential simultaneity, full information maximum likelihood was the estimation method. A third order model was preferred as two of the second and third order lags were significant. The $\Delta m1_t$ equation is a simple error correction model including a significant error correction term, ecm_{1t-1}, with a negative coefficient, the contemporaneous and lagged changes in SR_t and two lags of $\Delta m1_t$. A 'classic' error correction model would also include Δinc_t, along the lines suggested by Davidson et al. (1978); however, this term was not significant individually or jointly with its lags – the test statistic for the joint hypothesis being 1.84 distributed as $\chi^2(4)$, 5% critical value = 9.49. Interestingly there were some (relatively small) simultaneous links in the real income equation with both the coefficients on $\Delta m1_t$ and ΔSR_t significant, otherwise only the first and second lags on Δinc_t were significant. The error correction mechanism was not significant in the equations for real income or the interest rate – as we shall see below this is not, however, sufficient for the corresponding adjustment coefficients to be zero, that is $a_{21} = a_{31} = 0$ does not imply $\alpha_{21} = \alpha_{31} = 0$. The significant variables in the interest rate equation were the first and second lags of ΔSR_t and $\Delta m1_t$.

The equation system is put into matrix–vector form (apart from the dummy variables, which are omitted for simplicity) in the lower part of Table 15.29. In this form it is easier to obtain the relevant parts of the derived reduced form, and of particular interest are the derived adjustment coefficients. Because $\hat{a}_{21}$ and $\hat{a}_{31}$ are zero, $\hat{\alpha}_{11} = \hat{a}_{11} = -0.053$, and this estimate is identical to three decimal places to the estimate obtained under weak exogeneity reported in Table 15.25; nonzeros in the second row of Φ ensure that $\hat{\alpha}_{21}$ is nonzero and at -0.014 is very close to the estimate of -0.013 reported in Table 15.25. Finally, $\hat{a}_{31} = 0$ and zeros in the first two places of the last row of Φ ensure that $\hat{\alpha}_{31} = 0$. Overall the derived adjustment coefficients are very close to those from the unrestricted reduced form.

Table 15.29 *SECM for $\Delta m1_t$, Δinc_t, and ΔSR_t*

$\Delta m1_t = 0.027 - 0.002\Delta SR_t + 0.273\Delta m1_{t-1} + 0.157\Delta m1_{t-3} - 0.001\Delta SR_{t-1} - 0.053ecm_{1t-1} - 0.017d831_t$
$\qquad$ (6.592)(−2.547)$\qquad$(4.507)$\qquad\qquad$(3.003)$\qquad\qquad$(−2.512)$\qquad\qquad$(−6.558)$\qquad\qquad$(−0.004)

$\qquad +0.0156d8612_t$
$\qquad\quad$(0.002)

$\Delta inc_t = 0.002 + 0.260\Delta m1_t + 0.001\Delta SR_t - 0.157\Delta inc_{t-1} + 0.096\Delta inc_{t-2} + 0.010d75_t + 0.045d92_t$
$\qquad$ (4.668) (3.654)$\qquad$(1.546)$\qquad$(−4.266)$\qquad\qquad$(2.636)$\qquad\qquad$(4.420)$\qquad$(15.128)

$\Delta SR_t = -0.010 + 17.201\Delta m1_{t-1} - 15.903\Delta m1_{t-2} + 0.317\Delta SR_{t-1} - 0.168\Delta SR_{t-2} + 1.783d80_t - 3.027d828_t$
$\qquad$ (−0.280)$\quad$(2.645)$\qquad\qquad$(−2.283)$\qquad\qquad$(7.826)$\qquad\qquad$(−4.502)$\qquad\qquad$(11.302)$\qquad$(−0.036)

'*t*' statistics in parentheses.

Matrix representation: $\hat{\Phi}\Delta y_t = \hat{\mu} + \hat{\Gamma}_1^+ \Delta y_{t-1} + \hat{\Gamma}_2^+ \Delta y_{t-2} + \hat{\Gamma}_3^+ \Delta y_{t-3} + \hat{a}(\beta' y_{t-1}) + \hat{\zeta}_t$

$$\begin{bmatrix} 1 & 0 & 0.002 \\ -0.260 & 1 & -0.001 \\ 0 & 0 & 1 \end{bmatrix}\begin{pmatrix} \Delta m1_t \\ \Delta inc_t \\ \Delta SR_t \end{pmatrix} = \begin{pmatrix} 0.027 \\ 0.002 \\ -0.010 \end{pmatrix} + \begin{bmatrix} 0.273 & 0 & -0.001 \\ 0 & -0.157 & 0 \\ 17.201 & 0 & 0.317 \end{bmatrix}\begin{pmatrix} \Delta m1_{t-1} \\ \Delta inc_{t-1} \\ \Delta SR_{t-1} \end{pmatrix}$$

$$+ \begin{bmatrix} 0 & 0 & 0 \\ 0 & 0.096 & 0 \\ -15.903 & 0 & -0.0168 \end{bmatrix}\begin{pmatrix} \Delta m1_{t-2} \\ \Delta inc_{t-2} \\ \Delta SR_{t-2} \end{pmatrix}$$

$$+ \begin{bmatrix} 0.157 & 0 & 0 \\ 0 & 0 & 0 \\ 0 & 0 & 0 \end{bmatrix}\begin{pmatrix} \Delta m1_{t-3} \\ \Delta inc_{t-3} \\ \Delta SR_{t-3} \end{pmatrix} + \begin{bmatrix} 0.053 & 0 & 0 \\ 0 & 0 & 0 \\ 0 & 0 & 0 \end{bmatrix}\begin{pmatrix} ecm_{1t-1} \\ ecm_{2t-1} \\ ecm_{3t-1} \end{pmatrix} + \begin{pmatrix} \hat{\zeta}_{1t} \\ \hat{\zeta}_{2t} \\ \hat{\zeta}_{3t} \end{pmatrix}$$

Error correction coefficients $\hat{a}$	Derived adjustment coefficients $\hat{\alpha} = \hat{\Phi}^{-1}\hat{a}$
−0.053	−0.053
0	−0.014
0	0.000

Finally, we consider some aspects of whether the reported SECM is a valid reduction of a congruent VAR – see the previous section and section **15.7.4** which used Urbain's study of the demand for imports as an example in the same context. Generally we expect the SECM to be parsimonious relative to the VARs that form the basis of inference of the cointegrating rank; the latter are likely to be profligate whereas the former embody data-based and theory-based exclusion restrictions. Suppose, as in the case considered here, the UVAR suggests $r = 1$ and hence one error correction mechanism (cointegrating vector), ecm_{1t}, is defined, then conditional on this a fourth order VAR, reparameterised into a third order reduced

form ECM will, at most, have in each equation: 9 coefficients due to the lags, 1 adjustment coefficient on the ecm, 1 constant and 6 coefficients for the dummy variables; a total of 17 coefficients and so 51 in the three-equation system. It may well be possible to reduce this potentially profligate number by estimating a PVAR which, while also conditioning on ecm_{1t-1}, deletes redundant regressors. As this is quite often a step in the empirical analysis which is not reported in published work, the details of one possible approach are reported for this example.

Starting with the most general model in this class the first stage is to assess whether the third lag of each variable can be deleted; initially this is done on an individual variable basis and the

Table 15.30   *Simplifying the UVAR (LL ≡ log likelihood)*

	Third order reduced form ECM: LL 1,683.18		
	Delete third lag		
Delete (individually)	$\Delta m1_{t-3}$	Δinc_{t-3}	ΔSR_{t-3}
LL	1,675.50	1,682.40	1,682.23
Test statistic	$\chi^2(3) = 15.36$	$\chi^2(3) = 1.56$	$\chi^2(3) = 1.90$
Delete (jointly)	Δinc_{t-3} and ΔSR_{t-3}		
LL	1,681.63		
Test statistic	$\chi^2(6) = 3.10$		
	Delete second lag		
Delete (individually)	$\Delta m1_{t-2}$	Δinc_{t-2}	ΔSR_{t-2}
LL	1,676.85	1,677.66	1,668.39
Test statistic	$\chi^2(3) = 9.56$	$\chi^2(3) = 7.94$	$\chi^2(3) = 26.48$
	Delete first lag		
Delete (individually)	$\Delta m1_{t-1}$	Δinc_{t-1}	ΔSR_{t-1}
LL	1,674.51	1,674.03	1,662.31
Test statistic	$\chi^2(3) = 14.24$	$\chi^2(3) = 15.20$	$\chi^2(3) = 38.64$

Critical values				
	10%	5%	2.5%	1%
$\chi^2(3)$	6.25	7.81	9.35	11.34
$\chi^2(6)$	10.64	12.59	14.45	16.81

results are reported in Table 15.30. The log likelihood of the general model is 1,683.18, which on deletion of $\Delta m1_{t-3}$, Δinc_{t-3} and ΔSR_{t-3} is reduced to 1,675.50, 1,682.40 and 1,682.23, respectively, resulting in likelihood ratio test statistics, distributed as $\chi^2(3)$ under the null, of 15.36, 1.56 and 1.90. The 5% critical value is 7.81 implying rejection of the first null but not of the second two, although it could be argued that a lower significance level should be used in a sequence of tests in order to control the overall type 1 error; however, at this stage this is not likely to make a difference since even with the 1% critical value of 11.34 the decision is the same. Also care has to be taken in that deleting variables often has implications for the properties of the residuals, so parallel testing for serial correlation should be maintained otherwise congruence could be lost in the reduction process. On testing whether the joint hypothesis that Δinc_{t-3} and ΔSR_{t-3} should be deleted we obtain a test statistic, distributed as $\chi^2(6)$ under the null, of 3.10, hence we reduce the model by excluding these variables.

We then assess whether the second lag of each variable can be deleted conditional on the deletion of Δinc_{t-3} and ΔSR_{t-3}. Now the size of the test becomes critical since for $\Delta m1_{t-2}$ and Δinc_{t-2}, individually, we reject the null at the 5% significance level but not the 1% level, and on balance we keep both variables. The rejection for ΔSR_{t-2} is unambiguous so the second lag is maintained throughout. Similarly the test statistics for the deletion of the first lag of each variable suggest each should be kept. Overall, therefore, the PVAR involves the deletion of six variables to leave $51 - 6 = 45$ coefficients. Relative to this the SECM has 22 coefficients and a log likelihood (LL) of 1,663.75, hence against the PVAR we obtain a test statistic of $-2(1663.75 - 1681.63) = 35.76$ compared to 5% and 2.5% critical values of 35.17 and 38.07; the first of these is just on the 5% margin. Against the more general model we obtain a test statistic of $-2(1663.75 - 1683.18) = 38.86$ compared to 5% and 2.5% critical values of $\chi^2(29) = 42.57$ and 45.72. Overall, while no doubt further improvements could be made, the relatively simple

SECM offers the potential to model the relationship between money, income and the interest rate in a much smaller dimensional, and more readily interpretable, space than the VAR. Other aspects of the relationship between the SECM and the reduced form VAR are suggested in a review question.

15.9 Concluding remarks

This and the previous chapter have used a number of examples to illustrate a methodological approach to specifying and estimating multivariate models. There is enough common ground in these empirical studies to suggest it would be useful to summarise in schematic form the key elements of this methodology, although not all aspects of the scheme are present in every study.

1. *Theoretical guidance and previous research*: economic theory and past empirical studies inform the choice of variables and functional form.
2. *Data investigation*: graph the data. What are its salient features? Are there linear trends? These inform the specification of the UVAR.
3. *Identification*: establish generic identification of possible cointegrating vectors (equilibrium relationships); undertake generic rank calculations.
4. *UVAR*: estimate an unrestricted VAR ensuring its congruency with the data (for example, that the residuals are consistent with the absence of serial correlation and heteroscedasticity). Are 'special effect' dummy variables needed? Is the information set adequate, should it be enlarged?
5. *Cointegrating rank*: determine the cointegrating rank using formal testing procedures (for example, Johansen λ_{max} and trace test statistics) and informal procedures such as graphing the potentially stationary linear combinations.

6. *Test overidentifying restrictions*: if the identifying restrictions are overidentifying test their consistency with the data.
7. *Weak exogeneity*: consider hypotheses on the weak exogeneity of subsets of the variables.
8. *RVAR*: estimate a restricted VAR which incorporates the restrictions imposed for (over)identification and, if relevant, weak exogeneity.
9. *PVAR*: define error correction mechanisms from the restricted VAR; by definition these will be I(0), as will Δy_{it-j} for $j = 0, \ldots, p - 1$. Estimate a parsimonious VAR in these I(0) variables using a general-to-specific methodology for the elimination of redundant variables judged by the significance of columns of the coefficient matrices.
10. *Roots of the companion matrix*: calculate the characteristic roots of the companion matrix both for the unrestricted and restricted VARs. Assess how close they are to the unit circle and whether the restrictions have a marked effect.
11. *SECM*: using a full information maximum likelihood or instrumental variables method estimate a structural error correction model, SECM, in I(0) variables using current dated regressors Δy_{it}, as well as lagged regressors, eliminating insignificant variables.
12. *Encompassing*: compare the PVAR and SECM by means of a test of the number of restrictions – this is a parsimonious encompassing test.

The emphasis throughout in the methodology is on linking theory, data and estimation in the context of potentially simultaneous economic relationships.

The conclusion to the previous chapter noted that the framework due to Johansen and Juselius, and Hendry and his co-authors was not without potential criticisms and four were enumerated there. Some other considerations follow distinguishing between technique and methodology.

By technique is meant the detailed methods, for example maximum likelihood analysis of the VAR in the Johansen approach, which form the basis of inference on the cointegrating rank and estimation of the cointegrating vectors. Stock and Watson (1988) suggest testing for what are known as the common trends which are, in a sense, complementary to the cointegrating vectors. Consider a univariate I(1) process then – see Chapter 6 – this can be viewed as being driven by the stochastic trend in the partial sum of cumulated 'disturbances'. In a k-dimensional vector of variables there is the possibility that the stochastic trends are common to several of the variables so if there are r cointegrating vectors in a k-dimensional set of variables there are $k - r$ common trends. As Stock and Watson (1988) note: '...the number of unit roots in a multiple time series may be less than the sum of the number of unit roots in the constituent univariate time series. Equivalently, although each univariate series might contain a stochastic trend, in a vector process these stochastic trends might be common to several of the variables.' In a bivariate case with variables which are individually I(1), for example consumption and income, but cointegrated there is one common trend. In a trivariate case, again with variables which are individually I(1) but cointegrated, there will be either two common trends corresponding to $r = 1$ or one common trend corresponding to $r = 2$. Stock and Watson's (1988) procedure is based on estimating the number of random walks in the vector y_t process.

There are also many discussions in the econometrics literature on different techniques of estimating the cointegrating rank see, for example, Kleibergen and van Dijk (1994), Watson (1994), and the references therein, and Boswijk (1994). Reimers (1992) has evaluated three methods (Johansen, information criteria and a method due to Phillips and Ouliaris (1988)) using Monte Carlo simulations with the conclusion: 'Altogether, the lag order is successfully estimated by the order selection criteria. For an empirical analysis we recommend first to estimate the lag order and then to specify the cointegration rank by different test procedures since no procedure dominates the others in all cases.'

An alternative methodology for multivariate models is due to Sims – see, for example, Sims (1988). Sims is critical of the data analytic steps involved in the specification search leading to a final empirical model. For example, Sims (1991) comments on the Clements and Mizon (1991) study:

> In the type of specification search engaged by Clements and Mizon, the restrictions imposed are in fact random variables, very much influenced by the observed data. Though treated formally as precise *a priori* knowledge, they are a main source of uncertainty about any application of the model. A Bayesian approach makes the source of uncertainty explicit and incorporates it into formal measures of uncertainty, like standard errors on coefficients or on conditional forecasts.

Sims prefers what has become known as a BVAR – that is Bayesian VAR with an explicit prior distribution on the coefficients which recognises the uncertainty, rather than precision, of prior information. A second issue arises from setting to unity roots which are not significantly different from unity. This has an important effect in assessing the impulse response function (IRF) of the VAR. This is the multivariate extension of the univariate procedure illustrated in Chapter 13 arising from shocking the innovation in a single equation and tracing out the response path. A system with a root numerically close to but not actually unity can exhibit a very different response path from one with a root of unity. *A fortiori* a root of, say, 0.85, but not significantly different from 1, will imply a very different response compared to a root of 0.99 which is also not significantly different from 1. The reader interested in this debate could usefully consult Doan, Litterman and Sims (1984) and Sims (1988).

The analysis of this and the previous chapter has assumed that the time series variables are not of higher order than I(1). However, in practice some variables are, at least, candidates for I(2) categorisation; for example, the level of (nominal) wages and prices often look smooth enough to be I(2). This problem may be solved by pairwise cointegration, as would be the case if I(2) wages and prices cointegrated to become I(1) real wages. For more on the treatment of I(2) variables see Johansen (1992d, e), Juselius (1994) and Hansen and Johansen (1998, especially Chapter 9). Granger (1997) is somewhat sceptical about the possibility of I(2) economic variables. To understand why this might be so, recall that in the simplest I(1) case given by the random walk $x_t = x_{t-1} + \varepsilon_t$, with ε_t white noise, starting the process at $t = 0$ and assuming, for simplicity, that all 'pre-sample' values are 0 then $x_t = \sum_{i=0}^{t} \varepsilon_i$. For present purposes note not only the persistence of shocks but also their equal weighting however distant the shocks; for example, the shock ε_s has the same impact on x_t as the shock ε_r for $s < r$. What happens if x_t is generated by a simple I(2) process? Consider $(1 - L)^2 x_t = \varepsilon_t$, that is $x_t = 2x_{t-1} - x_{t-2} + \varepsilon_t$, and, as in the I(1) case, starting the process at $t = 0$ with $x_0 = \varepsilon_0$ then

$$x_t = \varepsilon_t + 2\varepsilon_{t-1} + 3\varepsilon_{t-2} + 4\varepsilon_{t-3} + \cdots,$$

$$= \sum_{i=0}^{t} (i + 1)\varepsilon_{t-i}$$

In this case distant shocks have a greater weight than recent shocks. As Granger (*op. cit.*) notes this means that, for current x_t, a unit shock to the economy in the First World War has a bigger impact than a unit shock in the Second World War. Variables may appear to be I(2) because they are I(1) but with a deterministic trend which changes over the sample period, much as an apparently I(1) series could have been generated by an I(0) series with a shifting deterministic trend – see Chapter 7 and Perron (1989, 1997). However, this returns the debate about the generation of time series to whether it is sensible to base an explanation on a deterministic trend with the problems of interpretation which that entails, for an alternative view and references see, for example, Harvey (1997); and as a reminder of the problems of spurious deterministic trends see Nelson and Kang (1981).

Review

1. The aim of this chapter is to provide some extended illustrations of the practical issues which arise in applying the concepts associated with cointegration. A number of published studies are analysed as well as a re-examination of the demand for money example of Chapter 10.

2. Johansen and Juselius (1992) and Juselius (1995) show that if purchasing power parity, PPP, and uncovered interest parity, UIP, hold then we expect to find two cointegrating relationships among the following five variables: p_t, p_t^*, e_t, r_t, r_t^*; and corresponding to PPP and UIP, respectively, the following should be cointegrating vectors: $(1, -1, -1, 0, 0)$ and $(0, 0, 0, 1, -1)$.

3. On inspecting graphs of the data Johansen and Juselius (1992) concluded that the price series have a linear trend and so the appropriate model should have an unrestricted constant (that is Model 3 of Table 14.2) to allow linear trends in the data.

4. The estimated eigenvalues suggest the distinct possibility of 3 cointegrating vectors. The $\lambda_{\max}$ test led to rejection of $r = 0$ but nonrejection of $r = 1$; with the trace statistic the null hypothesis $H(2 \mid 5)$ is on the borderline of rejection since $29.26 \approx 29.68$, whereas $H(3 \mid 5)$ is not rejected. On balance the trace test favours $r = 3$.

5. Johansen and Juselius (*op. cit.*) suggest looking at the estimated coefficients and possible stationary combinations to resolve the ambiguity (is $r = 2$ or 3?) in the formal testing procedure. For PPP we expect the coefficients on p_t^* and e_t to be equal but

opposite in sign to the coefficient on p_t; and for UIP the coefficients on r_t and r_t^* should be equal but opposite in sign. On this basis Johansen and Juselius (*op. cit.*, p. 222) interpret the first vector as capturing the PPP relationship and the second the UIP relationship.

6. Using univariate tests on real wage data for particular manufacturing industries in the US manufacturing sector, Rossana and Seater (1992) find that a unit root null hypothesis cannot be rejected. However, Dickey and Rossana (1994) suggest that the finding of independent unit root processes for different industries is counter-intuitive as it suggests that long-run wage differentials can be divergent.

7. Using data on four manufacturing industries within the sector producing paper and allied products and the consumer price index for all urban workers, Dickey and Rossana considered the hypothesis that real wages are cointegrated. The VAR model used by Dickey and Rossana (*op. cit.*) includes a constant restricted to the cointegration space and centred seasonal dummy variables.

8. If the Dickey–Rossana hypothesis is correct and there are n industries there should be $n - 1$ cointegrating vectors. As four industries are included in the study we would expect to find 3 cointegrating vectors under the null hypothesis. The λ_{max} statistic sequence ended with nonrejection of $r = 2$ against $r = 3$ whereas the trace test led to the conclusion that $r = 3$. Dickey and Rossana choose $r = 2$ although there is theoretical and empirical support from the trace test that $r = 3$.

9. The hypothesis that real wages are cointegrated implies the restriction $\sum_{i=1}^{4} \beta_{ij} = -\beta_{5j}$ for each of the $j = n - 1$ cointegrating vectors. For $r = 2$ the test statistic is

$$T \ln([1 - \lambda_1^*][1 - \lambda_2^*]/[1 - \hat{\lambda}_1][1 - \hat{\lambda}_2])$$

which is distributed as $\chi^2(2)$ under the null hypothesis. The test statistic is 82.7 compared with the 5% critical value for $\chi^2(2)$ of 5.99, hence rejection is definite.

10. However, although $r = 2$, the estimated eigenvectors and adjustment coefficients lacked interpretability. The latter were numerically very small and in the case of the second cointegrating vector virtually zero.

11. An identifying structure was suggested to aid an interpretation of the cointegrating vectors. Identification of the cointegrating vectors requires that there must be at least $r - 1$ independent restrictions of the form $R_i \beta_i = 0$ placed on each cointegrating vector, $i = 1, \ldots, r$. The restriction that real wages cointegrate is the same for each cointegrating vector, hence it cannot be identifying.

12. Identification requires bringing prior reasoning to bear to distinguish linear combinations of variables which would otherwise look like each other. The suggested identification scheme was based on the idea of each cointegrating vector capturing a pairwise constant long-run wage differential with exclusion restrictions for the other wage rates.

13. An example of identification of the short-run structure is provided by Johansen and Juselius (1994) with five variables in the analysis: $(m_t, inc_t, p_t, r_t^s, r_t^b)$.

14. The short-run structure refers to the error correction coefficients, a, the simultaneous structure represented in the off-diagonal elements of Φ, and the lagged dynamic adjustments from the Γ_i^+ coefficients. A just-identified system for the short-run structure imposes exactly $5 - 1 = 4$ restrictions on each column of A (that is each equation).

15. While not pronounced in this example because Φ, and hence Φ^{-1}, is sparse the zeros in the upper 3×3 block of a, which relate to the simultaneous part of the system, become nonzeros in α showing how the disequilibrium effects are transmitted to all variables in the reduced form.

16. In an example which illustrated identification of the cointegrating vectors and short-run structure, Hendry and Mizon (1993) model the demand for M1 in the United Kingdom with the vector of variables $(m_t - p_t, exp_t, \Delta p_t, r_t, t)$. The constant and trend were specified as in Model 4 of Table 14.2 – corresponding to $\mu_1 \neq 0$, $\mu_2 \neq 0$; $\delta_1 \neq 0$, $\delta_2 = 0$; that is a constant in the CI space, linear trend in the data and linear trend in the CI space.

17. The analysis suggested 2 cointegrating vectors, one a demand for real money relationship in which $m_t - p_t$ is a function of Δp_t, r_t and exp_t, and the other an inflation relationship which depends upon the deviation of income from trend.

18. The cointegrating vectors were generically identified given $r = 2$. In the first vector the trend has a zero coefficient and a unit coefficient on expenditure, and so is overidentified as 2 restrictions are imposed. In the second cointegrating vector zero restrictions are placed on $m_t - p_t$ and r_t, which is, therefore, also overidentified.

19. The following error correction mechanisms were incorporated in (a) a PVAR and (b) an SECM:

$$ecm_{1t} \equiv m_t - p_t + 7.0\Delta p_t + 0.7r_t - exp_t$$
$$ecm_{2t} \equiv \Delta p_t - 0.28exp_t + 0.0014t$$

20. The necessary condition for identification of the short-run structure is that each equation in the k equation system should have $k - 1$ coefficient restrictions. In this case $k = 4$, hence $k - 1 = 3$ and the four equations in the SECM were overidentified on this criterion.

21. Estimation of the SECM illustrated how a simultaneity can transmit a disequilibrium from one equation throughout the system in the reduced form.

22. In what can be seen as a drawback to the VAR-based approach it is often quite difficult to contain the number of variables to a manageable number. If there is an equation in the VAR for each variable the VAR is said to be closed. An alternative to the closed VAR is to condition on variables which are not part of the VAR system – that is an open VAR.

23. Valid conditioning variables should be weakly exogenous for the parameters of interest, generally the latter are the equilibrium, or long-run, coefficients β, and the adjustment coefficients α.

24. Weak exogeneity of variable i requires that the ith row of α should be zero. That is there should be no cointegration in the ith equation of the reduced form ECM. To test this hypothesis let $\hat{\lambda}_i$ and $\hat{\lambda}_i^*$ be the estimated eigenvalues from the unrestricted model and restricted model, respectively, then

$$\text{WETS} \equiv T \sum_{i=1}^{r} \ln[(1 - \hat{\lambda}_i^*)/(1 - \hat{\lambda}_i)]$$

is asymptotically distributed as χ^2 with $(r.s)$ degrees of freedom where s is the number of weakly exogenous variables under the null hypothesis.

25. Weak exogeneity can also be applied to subsets of the parameters of interest, so $\alpha_{ij} = 0$ can be interpreted as variable i being weakly exogenous for the parameters of the jth cointegrating vector.

26. Urbain's (1995) study of the demand for imports in Belgium is a very useful illustration of a number of points that arise in practice. The starting point for the analysis is the stylised long-run import demand model: $im_t = f(inc_t, e_t, pmfc_t, pd_t)$.

27. Urbain's analysis is based on $r = 2$. For the first vector the coefficients on pm_t and e_t are constrained to be equal. As to the second vector Urbain suggests an exclusion restriction on income to interpret the relationship as a PPP relationship for the exchange rate modified by the inclusion of import volumes.

28. A joint test of the 2 overidentifying restrictions and the 5 exclusion restrictions on α

gave a test statistic of 10.125 distributed as $\chi^2(7)$ under the null hypothesis; with 95% quantile equal to 14.067 the joint null is not rejected.

29. The 125 coefficients in the UVAR were reduced to 86 in the PVAR and 37 in the SECM. A $\chi^2(49)$ test of the restrictions going from the PVAR to the SECM with 49 degrees of freedom was not rejected and, therefore, the SECM encompasses the PVAR.

30. Finally, we revisited the Chapter 10 example of the demand for M1 in the United States with estimates of the long run of Engle–Granger:

$$ecm_t = m1_t - (0.617inc_t - 0.021SR_t)$$

and ADL:

$$ecm_t = m1_t - (0.742inc_t - 0.031SR_t)$$

31. Estimating an unrestricted VAR, the AIC and SIC were at a minimum at system lag lengths of 4 and 2, respectively. There was evidence of nonnormality of the residuals for real income and the nominal interest rates.

32. The λ_{max} and trace statistics suggested a cointegrating rank of 1 which was consistent with the roots of the companion matrix, the two largest being 1.002 and 0.978 with the third 0.826.

33. The first eigenvector was interpreted as a long-run demand for money relationship with a real income elasticity of 0.735 and an interest rate semi-elasticity of −0.032.

34. The test statistics for the weak exogeneity of real income and the interest rate both individually and jointly indicated nonrejection. Under weak exogeneity the income and interest rate coefficients were 0.758 and −0.030, and

$$\hat{\alpha}_{11} = -0.053(-6.306)$$
$$\hat{\alpha}_{21} = \hat{\alpha}_{31} = 0$$

35. This example was also used to illustrate the procedure suggested by Hansen and Juselius (*op. cit.*) to determine the appropriate specification of the deterministic terms in the VAR. Application of this procedure confirmed the earlier choice of $r = 1$ in Model 3 (that is with an unrestricted constant and no trend in the cointegration space).

36. As another insight on the earlier weak exogeneity tests, which suggested that a model conditional on income and the interest rate would be valid, an SECM was also estimated. Confirming the implications of weak exogeneity, the coefficients of the cointegrating vector and the derived adjustment coefficients were virtually identical to those from the reduced form ECM.

37. An SECM which embodies data-based and theory-based restrictions is usually a reduction relative to a VAR. A test of parsimonious encompassing is a test of whether the simpler model (SECM) can encompass the more general model (VAR).

38. Parsimonious encompassing, denoted ε_p, is transitive; that is if model C ε_p model B and model B ε_p model A, then model C ε_p model A.

39. Although the technical and methodological details of the illustrative studies of this chapter are not identical, there is enough common ground to suggest that there is a paradigm of empirical analysis that can be associated with Johansen and Hendry and their co-authors.

Review questions

1. (i) Let H_1 be the hypothesis that the long-run matrix Π is unrestricted: how many free parameters are there in Π under H_1?

   (ii) Let $H_2(r)$ be the hypothesis that the cointegrating rank is r: how many free parameters are there in Π under $H_2(r)$? Hence how many restrictions does the hypothesis of cointegration impose on Π?

Let $H_2(r)$ be as before and with an unrestricted constant so there is a trend in the data space (Model 3 of Table 14.2); that is in the notation of Chapter 14 $\alpha\mu_1 \neq 0$ and $\alpha_\perp\mu_2 \neq 0$.

Let $H_2^*(r)$ be the hypothesis that the cointegrating rank is r in the model with a constant in the cointegration space but no linear trend in the data space (Model 2 of Table 14.2); that is in the notation of Chapter 14 $\alpha\mu_1 \neq 0$, $\alpha_\perp\mu_2 = 0$.

(iii) Show that $H_2^*(r) \subset H_2(r)$ (where $\subset$ means is nested in), and that:

$$H_2(0) \subset H_2(r) \ldots \subset H_2(k)$$

$$H_2^*(0) \subset H_2(0) \ldots$$

$$H_2^*(r) \subset H_2(r) \ldots$$

$$H_2^*(k) \subset H_2(k)$$

(Johansen 1995, p. 99).

(iv) Discuss Johansen's decision sequence: accept rank r and the presence of a trend if:
$H_1(0) \ldots H_1(r-1)$ are rejected, $H_1(r)$ is not rejected; and
$H_1^*(1) \ldots H_1^*(r-1)$, $H_1^*(r)$ are rejected. Accept rank r and no trend if:
$H_1(0) \ldots H_1(r-1)$ are rejected; and
$H_1^*(1) \ldots H_1^*(r-1)$ are rejected, $H_1^*(r)$ is not rejected.

(v) Relate this decision sequence to the Dickey–Pantula principle discussed in the text – see section **15.8.4**.

(vi) Is the Dickey–Pantula principle an application of a general-to-specific or specific-to-general modelling strategy?

2. With a dataset comprising Danish data on real M2, $m2_t$, real income, inc_t, both in natural logs, the bond rate, i_t^b and deposit rate i_t^d, Johansen and Juselius (1990, p. 182) and Johansen (1995a) report the following results, but the column of 95% quantiles has been left blank:

r	$\hat{\lambda}_{r+1}$	Trace	95% quantile
0	0.433	49.14	
1	0.178	19.06	
2	0.113	8.89	
3	0.043	2.35	

(i) Fill in the missing critical values bearing in mind Johansen's (1995, p. 112) description of his model: '... inspection of the plots indicates that the data have no deterministic trends ... In this model, the value 1 is appended to the data vector.'

(ii) Calculate the λ_{max} statistics and their 95% quantiles.

(iii) Using the λ_{max} and trace statistics estimate the cointegrating rank.

Johansen (*op. cit.*) reports the unnormalised estimates of the long-run parameters shown in Table 15.31:

(iv) Interpret these eigenvectors and, in particular, which one, or combination, lends itself to the interpretation of a demand for money function?

(v) Normalise the eigenvectors.

Table 15.31 *The unnormalised estimates of the long-run parameters β and adjustment coefficients α for the Danish data*

	β_1	β_2	β_3	β_4	β_5	α_1	α_2	α_3	α_4
$m2_t$	−21.97	14.66	7.95	1.02	11.36	9.69	−0.33	4.41	1.98
inc_t	22.70	−20.05	−25.64	−1.93	−7.20	−5.23	1.35	6.28	1.08
i_t^b	−114.42	3.56	4.28	25.00	19.20	−1.05	−0.72	0.44	−1.58
i_t^d	92.64	100.26	−44.88	−14.65	−21.53	−1.05	−0.72	0.44	−1.58
1	133.16	−62.59	62.75	−2.32	−91.28				

(vi) Formulate the following hypotheses on the cointegrating vector(s), both in the direct and indirect parameterisations (that is $\beta = H\varphi$ and $R\beta = 0$):

  (a) money and income have equal coefficients with opposite signs;

  (b) the opportunity cost of money can be measured as the bond rate minus the deposit rate.

Conditional on normalising each eigenvector on its first element Johansen obtains the following α matrix:

$m2_t$	-0.21	0.00	0.04	0.00	0.00
inc_t	0.12	0.02	0.05	0.00	0.00
i_t^b	0.02	-0.01	0.00	0.00	0.00
i_t^d	0.03	-0.03	0.00	0.00	0.00

(vii) Why isn't this matrix square?

(viii) Interpret these adjustment coefficients.

(ix) Based on these estimates, which variables would be candidates to test for weak exogeneity? (References: Johansen (1995a) and Johansen and Juselius (1990).)

3. Consider the demand for money study by Hendry and Mizon (1993), in particular the SECM reported in Table 15.14 (Table 18.7 of the original article).

  (i) Discuss the specification of each of the equations in the SECM. Should r_{t-2} and Δp_{t-1} be retained in the Δr_t equation?

  (ii) Explain the role of the following tests reported in Hendry and Mizon (*op. cit.*): sequential Chow tests on the equations from the PVAR; F test of parameter constancy of the SECM; the PETS of 22.87 distributed as $\chi^2(34)$ under the null.

4. In the following example there are four variables: consumers' expenditure, money measured as M1, disposable income and the rate on 3-month Treasury bills; apart from the latter all variables are measured in constant prices and logs are taken; data is for the US, sample period, before lags are taken, of 1963m1 to 1991m12.

(i) Given the following trace statistics determine the cointegrating rank and specification of the deterministic components.

		Model 3		Model 2	
Null	Alt.	Trace	90% quantile	Trace	90% quantile
$r = 0$	≥ 1	97.04	43.95	180.97	49.65
$r \leq 1$	≥ 2	46.75	26.79	66.80	32.00
$r \leq 2$	≥ 3	10.41	13.33	23.19	17.85
$r \leq 3$	$= 4$	0.13	2.69	1.85	7.53

Johansen and Juselius (1990) suggest the following likelihood ratio test statistic for the absence of a trend in the data:

$$T \sum_{i=r+1}^{k} \ln[(1 - \hat{\lambda}_i^*)/(1 - \hat{\lambda}_i)] \sim \chi^2(k - r)$$

where $\hat{\lambda}_i^*$ are the estimated eigenvalues from the model without a trend.

(ii) Show that this test statistic is the difference between the trace test statistics for Models 2 and 3; and calculate and interpret it for the numerical example of this question.

(iii) What are the merits of the following three strategies.

  (a) Test for the cointegrating rank in Model 2, then when r is determined check, by means of the LR test, that the trend should be absent. If the test indicates that the trend should be present switch to Model 3.

  (b) Test for the cointegrating rank in Model 3, then when r is determined check, by means of the LR test, that the trend should be present. If the test indicates that the trend should be absent switch to Model 2.

  (c) Apply the Dickey–Pantula principle.

5. Ahn and Reinsel (1988) suggest the following small sample adjusted trace statistic:

$$-(T - kp) \sum_{i=r_0+1}^{k} \ln(1 - \hat{\lambda}_i)$$

$$= [(T - kp)/T](\text{trace statistic})$$

where T is the estimation sample size (which equals T^+, the overall sample period before lagging, minus p). In the example from Urbain (1995), $T^+ = 85$ from 1970q2 to 1990q2 inclusive, $p = 4$ so $T = 85 - 4 = 81$ and $(T - kp)/T = (81 - 20)/81 = 0.753$.

(i)   Re-evaluate the results of this chapter using Ahn and Reinsel's small sample adjusted trace statistic.

(ii)   Consider the first line of Tables 14.5 and 14.7 and compare them with the corresponding quantiles of the $\chi^2(1)$ distribution. Explain your finding.

(iii)   Explain how the following information criteria due to Akaike, AIC, Hannan–Quinn, HQIC, and Schwarz, SIC, for a multivariate model, could be used to simultaneously select the lag order and cointegrating rank:

$$\text{AIC} = \ln|\hat{\Lambda}(r, p)| + (2/T)m$$

$$\text{HQIC} = \ln|\hat{\Lambda}(r, p)| + (2\ln(\ln T)/T)m$$

$$\text{SIC} = \ln|\hat{\Lambda}(r, p)| + (\ln T/T)m$$

where m is the number of freely estimated parameters in a VAR model of lag $= p$ and cointegrating rank $= r$ and

$$\hat{\Lambda}(r, p) = \hat{\varepsilon}_t \hat{\varepsilon}_t'/T$$

where $\hat{\varepsilon}_t$ is the residual vector in the restricted rank VAR.

6. Consider the first order reduced form ECM in the three variables

$$\Delta y_t = (\Delta y_{1t} \; \Delta y_{2t} \; \Delta y_{3t})' \quad \text{and}$$
$$\Delta y_t = \Pi y_{t-1} + \Gamma_1 \Delta y_{t-1} + \varepsilon_t$$

(i)   State and interpret the conditions for Δy_{2t} and Δy_{3t} to be weakly exogenous for the nonzero parameters in α and β.

(ii)   State and interpret the conditions for Δy_{2t} to be weakly exogenous and Δy_{3t} to be strongly exogenous for the nonzero parameters in α and β.

(iii)   Explain how you would test each of these statements about weak and strong exogeneity.

7. Now consider the structural ECM in the two variables $\Delta y_t = (\Delta y_{1t}, \Delta y_{2t})'$ so

$$\Phi = \begin{bmatrix} 1 & -\Phi_{12} \\ -\Phi_{21} & 1 \end{bmatrix}$$

(i)   Johansen's conditions for weak exogeneity are stated in terms of restrictions on α, explain in the context of this two variable model why a zero row in a does not necessarily translate into a zero row in α.

(ii)   Show that one set of sufficient conditions for weak exogeneity of y_{2t} is: $a_{21} = a_{22} = 0$ and $\Phi_{21} = 0$, which state no error correction and no simultaneity in the second equation. Why is the no simultaneity condition required?

(iii)   Can we state that no error correction in the second equation of the SECM implies weak exogeneity of y_{2t}?

(iv)   Extend the analysis to more than two equations and show that: for the ith row of α to be 0, implying weak exogeneity of the ith variable, a sufficient set of conditions is that the ith row of a is zero and the ith row of Φ is 0 apart from 1 in the iith element.

8. Cagan (1956) suggests that the demand for money is a function of (expected) inflation and Baba *et al.* (1992) include inflation as well as other interest rate-based measures of the opportunity cost of holding money.

(i)   What are the theoretical reasons for including inflation as well as the nominal interest rate in the demand for money function?

(ii) With the US dataset provided re-evaluate the model reported in this chapter including inflation as a separate variable.

9. The following questions concern the empirical study by Dickey and Rossana (1994) of wage differentials in the US manufacturing industry – see section **15.3**.

(i) Why did the VAR model used by Dickey and Rossana (*op. cit.*) include a constant restricted to the cointegration space?

(ii) How many cointegrating vectors would you expect to find?

(iii) Explain how you would test the hypothesis that real wages are cointegrated.

(iv) Formulate identifying restrictions for the case of six industries both as indirect and direct parameterisations.

(v) Why aren't the restrictions that real wages cointegrate identifying?

(vi) If there are four industries and $r = 2$, can wage differentials be constant in the long run?

(vii) Discuss how to extend the methodology of the Dickey–Rossana study.

10. Consider $(1 - L)^2 x_t = \varepsilon_t$ and show that

$$x_t = \varepsilon_t + 2\varepsilon_{t-1} + 3\varepsilon_{t-2} + 4\varepsilon_{t-3} + \cdots,$$

$$= \sum_{i=0}^{t} (i+1)\varepsilon_{t-i}$$

Hint: $x_0 = \varepsilon_0$ assuming $x_{-1} = x_{-2} = 0$, then

$$x_1 = 2x_0 + \varepsilon_1 = \varepsilon_1 + 2\varepsilon_0$$

$$x_2 = 2x_1 - x_0 + \varepsilon_2$$

$$= 2(\varepsilon_1 + 2\varepsilon_0) - \varepsilon_0 + \varepsilon_2$$

$$= \varepsilon_2 + 2\varepsilon_1 + 3\varepsilon_0$$

and so on.

11. (i) Discuss the following from Harvey (1997, p. 196). 'Testing for unit roots has become almost mandatory in applied economics. This is despite the fact that, much of the time, it is either unnecessary or misleading.'

(ii) Summarise and evaluate Harvey's structural time series models as an alternative to: (a) AR or ARIMA modelling for a univariate series; and (b) VAR or VECM, that is vector error correction mechanism, for multivariate series. (See the references in Harvey (1997).)

CHAPTER 16

Autoregressive conditional heteroscedasticity: modelling volatility

16.1 Introduction

An important distinction was made in Chapter 9 between the unconditional and conditional variance in a regression function. It might have seemed that this was a rather technical distinction of little practical importance. However, a specification, which draws on this distinction, has had an enormous empirical impact especially in financial econometrics and is the subject of this chapter.

For example, consider how stock prices are determined. One leading possibility is the rational valuation formula, RVF, which states that the price of a stock at time t, say P_t is the expected discounted present value of future dividend streams, that is

$$P_t = E_t \left\{ \sum_{j=1}^{\infty} \gamma_{t+j} D_{t+j} \right\}$$

Where D_{t+j} is the dividend in period $t + j$ and E_t is the expectation formed at time; γ_{t+j} is the factor that discounts dividends received at some future date back to the present. The discount factor is a function of the risk-free rate and a premium that captures the 'riskiness' of future returns – see Cuthbertson (1996a, Chapter 17). *Ceteris paribus*, an increase in perceived risk leads to a decline in the stock price so that the return,

R_t, defined as the proportionate change in price, declines. Perceptions of riskiness thus directly impact upon the price of the stock. One possibility for assessing risk is that it is related to the variance – or volatility – also assessed at time t (that is conditional on time t information), of forecast errors for returns: an increase in conditional variance leads to an increase in the risk premium and the stock price declines. Crucial to an empirical implementation of these ideas is a method of estimating the conditional variance of forecast errors. This framework is also relevant for other assets with risky returns such as bills and bonds (with time varying risk premia) and exchange rates.

The central econometric development in this area is due to Engle, who published an article in 1982 showing how to model the conditional variance. The essence of the method picks up on the often observed characteristic that large shocks to the unpredictable component of returns tend to occur in clusters (not necessarily of the same sign), and the histogram of shocks has fatter tails than would be expected if they had been generated from a normal distribution. The key feature is that there seems to be an autoregressive nature to the (squared) shocks so Engle's ARCH (for autoregressive conditional heteroscedasticity) process allows the conditional variance to vary over time driven by past shocks. This specification together with its generalisations has proved to be very popular, finding its primary area of application in financial econometrics, although it was originally applied to modelling the conditional variance of inflation.

Some areas of empirical application of the ARCH specification with illustrative references are noted below.

- A shock affects the variance of stock market returns, for example as measured by Standard and Poor's 500 index, or the FTSE index, at a particular point in time: this shock affects the market risk premium; for examples see French, Schwert and Stambaugh (1987), Noh, Engle and Kane (1994), Nelson (1991).
- An increase in the variance of excess returns on bonds, for example the return on a 6-month T-Bill relative to a 3-month T-Bill, causes the risk premium to increase – see Engle, Lilien and Robins (1987). Market volatility drives individual stock return volatility and predictable market volatility affects individual stock returns – see Engle, Ng and Rothschild (1990).
- US stock market volatility has a 'spillover' effect to the UK and Japanese stock markets see Hamao, Masulis and Ng (1990) and Susmel and Engle (1992).
- The deviations of the log difference of various nominal exchange rates, that is $\ln E_t - \ln E_{t-1}$, from a random walk may be uncorrelated, but there is a tendency for large (small) deviations to cluster together. Ballie and Bollerslev (1989), Bollerslev (1990) and Harvey, Ruiz and Shepherd (1994).

The basic concepts of conditional variance and the ARCH specification are elaborated in section **16.2**. If you are wondering what an ARCH effect looks like it may help to turn straight to section **16.2.4,** where ARCH effects are illustrated for prices from the New York and Japanese stock exchanges. Section **16.3** considers the stationarity and persistence of ARCH processes. Section

16.4 outlines the estimation problem in a relatively nontechnical way. This is taken up further in the appendix, which outlines the maximum likelihood method applied to the ARCH specification. Testing for ARCH effects is considered in section **16.5** and some popular variations on the ARCH theme are described in section **16.6**, including the extension which models the mean as a function of the conditional variance referred to as ARCH-M. Section **16.7** is devoted to asymmetric effects because of their particular importance in modelling stock market returns. A number of examples in section **16.8** show how the models are used in practice. Finally, section **16.9** contains some concluding remarks.

16.2 Basic concepts

The regression models prior to this chapter have focused on explaining the expected, or mean, value of a variable or variables of interest; hence the emphasis on the conditional expectation function (CEF). However, in the case of modelling volatility the conditional variance is also of equal interest, and the conditional variance may affect the conditional mean giving rise to a regression model for the mean that includes some function of the conditional variance. For example, in modelling the returns to holding a financial asset, the conditional variance is unlikely to remain constant over time; apart from a multitude of smaller shocks affecting particular industries, large events, like oil field discoveries, OPEC price fixing, the October 1987 stock market crash and changes of government, all potentially affect the volatility of returns. Given that volatility is unlikely to be constant over time, how could it be modelled so that it responds to time varying shocks? Engle's answer to this question is an ARCH process. There are literally hundreds of articles that have used ARCH processes to model volatility – see Bollerslev, Chou and Kroner (1992) for a survey, and

Engle (1995a) contains a very useful collection of articles on ARCH processes and applications.

This section starts in **16.2.1** with a reminder of the distinction between the conditional and unconditional variance in an AR(1) process for the mean, that is the regression function. This serves to show that the basic distinction is one we have already come across in Chapter 9, although its application here to an ARCH process involves some differences as the latter operates on the conditional variance. Engle's ARCH(q) process is defined in section **16.2.2** and generalised to GARCH models in section **16.2.3**.

16.2.1 Conditional and unconditional variances: a crucial distinction

As a reminder of the distinction between the conditional and unconditional variance we start with a simple AR(1) process:

$$y_t = \phi_0 + \phi_1 y_{t-1} + \varepsilon_t, \quad |\phi_1| < 1 \qquad (16.1)$$

where ε_t is white noise with $\text{Var}(\varepsilon_t) \equiv \sigma_\varepsilon^2$. In the terminology of Chapter 9, σ_ε^2 is also the variance of y_t conditional on y_{t-1}, $\text{Var}(y_t \mid y_{t-1})$; that is holding y_{t-1} fixed, the only source of variation is ε_t which has variance σ_ε^2. In short it is the conditional variance – see section **9.2.1a**. The assumption so far is that this variance is constant. The forecast of y_t, taken as the expected value of y_t, the forecast error and the forecast error variance, conditional on y_{t-1}, are, respectively:

$$E\{y_t \mid y_{t-1}\} = \phi_0 + \phi_1 y_{t-1}$$
$$\varepsilon_t \mid y_{t-1} = y_t - (\phi_0 + \phi_1 y_{t-1})$$
$$\text{Var}(y_t \mid y_{t-1}) = E\{\varepsilon_t^2 \mid y_{t-1}\}$$

If the conditional variance of ε_t, $t = 1, \ldots, T$, is constant, that is homoscedastic, then

$$\text{Var}(y_{t+1} \mid y_t) = \sigma_\varepsilon^2$$

and the same degree of uncertainty is attached to the (one step) ahead forecast whichever point in the sequence $[y_t]$ is being considered; in particular the (one step) ahead forecast variance is invariant to past values of ε_t or ε_t^2. The ARCH process described below relaxes this assumption.

The unconditional variance of y_t was derived in Chapter 9. To recap in the notation of this chapter, the unconditional variance is derived as follows.

$$\text{Var}(y_t) = \text{Var}(\phi_0 + \phi_1 y_{t-1} + \varepsilon_t)$$
$$= \phi_1^2 \text{Var}(y_{t-1}) + \text{Var}(\varepsilon_t)$$
$$\sigma_y^2 = \phi_1^2 \sigma_y^2 + \sigma_\varepsilon^2 \quad \text{using}$$
$$\text{Var}(y_t) = \text{Var}(y_{t-1}) \equiv \sigma_y^2 \quad \text{and}$$
$$\text{Var}(\varepsilon_t) \equiv \sigma_\varepsilon^2$$

hence

$$(1 - \phi_1^2)\sigma_y^2 = \sigma_\varepsilon^2$$
$$\Rightarrow \sigma_y^2 = \sigma_\varepsilon^2/(1 - \phi_1^2)$$

the unconditional variance
of y_t $\qquad (16.2)$

Where heteroscedasticity is suspected a standard approach – see section **5.5** – is to specify the heteroscedasticity as a function of another variable. For example, suppose

$$y_t = \varepsilon_t x_{t-1} \qquad (16.3)$$

where x_t is an exogenous variable. Then

$$\text{Var}(y_t \mid x_{t-1}) = x_{t-1}^2 \sigma_\varepsilon^2$$

which depends upon x_{t-1}^2. This approach depends upon knowledge of the causes of heteroscedasticity and, as Engle (1995b) notes, these are not usually known and hence rarely applied in time series analysis. The calculation of heteroscedasticity consistent standard errors, which does not require explicit specification of the variance scheme, is far more popular in this context.

16.2.2   ARCH(q)

Engle (*op. cit.*) suggested an alternative scheme where the heteroscedasticity depends upon past values of y_t. The simplest version is:

$$y_t = u_t \sigma_t \quad \text{and} \quad \sigma_t^2 = \alpha_0 + \alpha_1 y_{t-1}^2 \quad (16.4)$$

For convenience, since a normalisation can always achieve the same aim, we set $\text{Var}(u_t) = 1$; then $\text{Var}(y_t \mid y_{t-1}) = \text{Var}(u_t \sigma_t) = \text{Var}(u_t)\sigma_t^2 = \sigma_t^2$. Now the conditional variance of y_t, σ_t^2, depends upon past squared values of y_t as specified in the σ_t^2 function. As σ_t^2 is a variance it must be nonnegative and is usually positive, which imposes the following conditions on the coefficients α_0 and α_1:

(i) $\alpha_0 \geq 0$; if $\alpha_1 = 0$ then the conditional variance is α_0, hence this coefficient must be nonnegative and will usually be positive.

(ii) $\alpha_1 \geq 0$; y_{t-1}^2 is always nonnegative, hence for the product $\alpha_1 y_{t-1}^2$ to be nonnegative $\alpha_1 \geq 0$. If $\alpha_1 > 0$ then the conditional variance of y_t will increase with y_{t-1}^2.

(iii) $\alpha_1 < 1$; otherwise the process will not be covariance stationary (see also the discussion on stationarity in section **16.3** below).

(iv) $3\alpha_1^2 < 1$; for a finite fourth moment – see Engle (1982, theorem 1).

Engle's original notation was to use $h_t^{0.5}$ for σ_t and, hence, h_t for σ_t^2. Some subsequent authors have used the σ_t^2 notation – see, for example, Nelson (1990) and Engle and Chowdury (1992). The σ_t^2 notation is preferred here to provide consistency with the notation in Chapter 5.

The heteroscedasticity is autoregressive because it depends upon past values of y_t and is conditional on these values; hence the term autoregressive conditional heteroscedasticity – or ARCH. The simple scheme in (16.4) is relevant where a large (positive or negative) value of y_{t-1} leads to a large variance of y_t but there is no memory apart from this one period. Suppose y_t is inflation, then an ARCH(1) process

says high inflation last period leads to a large variance in inflation this period. Note that if $\alpha_1 = 0$ then $\sigma_t^2 = \alpha_0$, and there is no (conditional) heteroscedasticity, the variance is just $\alpha_0 > 0$.

Simple generalisations of the basic scheme are fairly obvious. The first is to include more lags of y_t. Thus, an ARCH(q) process is:

$$\sigma_t^2 = \alpha_0 + \alpha_1 y_{t-1}^2 + \cdots + \alpha_q y_{t-q}^2 \quad (16.5)$$

The next development is to extend the determination of the mean of y_t to a regression model, so that the ARCH process applies to the disturbance term. The model is as follows:

Specification of the mean (the regression function):

$$E\{y_t \mid X_t = x_t\} = x_t \beta$$

Specification of the conditional variance of y_t:

$$\text{Var}(y_t \mid X_t = x_t) = \sigma_t^2$$

Hence $y_t = x_t \beta + \varepsilon_t$ where

$$\varepsilon_t \equiv y_t - E\{y_t \mid X_t = x_t\} = y_t - x_t \beta$$

The heteroscedasticity function σ_t^2 is now a function of $\varepsilon_{t-1}^2, \ldots, \varepsilon_{t-q}^2$. The ARCH($q$) specification applied to the regression disturbance is:

$$\varepsilon_t = u_t \sigma_t \quad \text{where } u_t \text{ is white noise}$$
$$\text{with } \text{Var}(u_t) = 1$$
$$\sigma_t^2 = \alpha_0 + \alpha_1 \varepsilon_{t-1}^2 + \cdots + \alpha_q \varepsilon_{t-q}^2 \quad (16.6)$$

A simple case to interpret is the ARCH(1) process, which is

$$\sigma_t^2 = \alpha_0 + \alpha_1 \varepsilon_{t-1}^2 \quad (16.7)$$

Thus a large shock in period $t - 1$ leads to a large (conditional) variance in period t. The subsequent impact of this large conditional variance depends upon the structure of the conditional expectation function $E\{y_t \mid X_t = x_t\} = x_t \beta$. For example, if $y_t = \phi_0 + \phi_1 y_{t-1} + \varepsilon_t$, then a large shock in $t-1$ leads to a large conditional variance in t, its impact depending upon the magnitude of α_1. However, that is not the end of the effect. As y_{t+1} depends upon y_t, there will be an effect on y_{t+1}, which depends upon the magnitude of ϕ_1; by a simple extension of this argument y_{t+f}, $f > 0$ will be affected, but the effect dies out as $f \to \infty$.

The unconditional variance (which is also the long-run variance in this case) is denoted $_u\sigma_t^2$, and defined as $E\{\sigma_t^2\} \equiv E\{\text{Var}(\varepsilon_t \mid \varepsilon_{t-1}, \ldots, \varepsilon_{t-q})\}$. The t subscript on $_u\sigma_t^2$ allows for the possibility that this is time varying, but usually we will be interested in cases where it is constant and finite, say $_u\sigma^2$; this is satisfied if the process generating σ_t^2 is (covariance) stationary. Provided certain conditions are met – see section **16.3** – the unconditional variance of the ARCH(q) process is positive, finite and constant, that is $_u\sigma_t^2 = {}_u\sigma^2 > 0$, where:

$$_u\sigma^2 = \frac{\alpha_0}{\left(1 - \sum\limits_{i=1}^{q} \alpha_i\right)}$$

Although the proof of this statement is quite complex (see Engle 1982, appendix 1) it is easily motivated. Note that taking the expectation of (16.6)

$$E\{\sigma_t^2\} = E\{\alpha_0 + \alpha_1 \varepsilon_{t-1}^2 + \cdots + \alpha_q \varepsilon_{t-q}^2\}$$
$$= \alpha_0 + \alpha_1 E\{\varepsilon_{t-1}^2\} + \cdots + \alpha_q E\{\varepsilon_{t-q}^2\}$$
$$= \alpha_0 + \alpha_1 \sigma_{t-1}^2 + \cdots + \alpha_q \sigma_{t-q}^2$$
$$\text{using } E\{\varepsilon_{t-i}^2\} = \sigma_{t-i}^2$$
$$_u\sigma^2 = \alpha_0 + {}_u\sigma^2 \alpha_1 + \cdots + {}_u\sigma^2 \alpha_q \Rightarrow$$
$$_u\sigma^2 = \frac{\alpha_0}{\left(1 - \sum\limits_{i=1}^{q} \alpha_i\right)}$$

The last but one line assumes that in the long run the conditional variances are constant and equal to the long-run variance $_u\sigma^2$. (We have implicitly used the variance decomposition with

$$\text{Var}(E\{\varepsilon_t \mid \varepsilon_{t-1}, \ldots, \varepsilon_{t-q}\}) = 0$$

see section **16.4** below for an elaboration of this point in the ARCH(1) case.)

ARCH accounts for three stylised facts associated with time series of asset prices and associated returns.

- Conditional variances change over time, sometimes quite substantially.
- There is volatility clustering – large (small) changes in unpredictable returns tend to be followed by large (small) changes of either sign.
- The unconditional distribution of returns has 'fat' tails giving a relatively large probability of 'outliers' relative to the normal distribution.

Researchers before Engle's (1982) article were aware of the importance of these features – see, for example, Mandlebrot (1963) – but the methods used to capture them were rather *ad hoc*, for example using a moving variance (see Chapter 3) to capture the time variation in variances. Alternatives to ARCH have also been suggested since Engle (1982). For example, Hseih (1993) suggests an autoregressive volatility model based on the range estimator of the standard deviation. The range standard deviation is a constant times the log of the highest and lowest transaction price in a given period; this is then related by an autoregression to past values of the range standard deviation.

The fat tail property of ARCH models relates to the unconditional distribution of ε_t: the conditional distribution is assumed normal. To see that this is the case the kurtosis coefficient, κ, for the ARCH(1) model can be calculated from the fourth and second moments of the unconditional distribution of ε_t given by Engle (1982):

$$\kappa = \frac{E\{\varepsilon_t^4\}}{E\{\varepsilon_t^2\}^2} = 3\frac{(1 - \alpha_1^2)}{(1 - 3\alpha_1^2)} > 3$$

$$\text{for } 0 < \alpha_1 \quad \text{and} \quad 3\alpha_1^2 < 1$$

That is κ is the ratio of the fourth moment to the squared second moment, and $\kappa = 3$ for the normal distribution. In the ARCH(1) case $\kappa > 3$ indicating leptokurtosis and, hence, fat tails. The condition $3\alpha_1^2 < 1$ is required to ensure that the fourth moment is finite and implies $\alpha_1 < 0.577$. Notice that kurtosis increases nonlinearly with α_1; for example, $\kappa = 3.062$ for $\alpha_1 = 0.1$, $\kappa = 3.739$ for $\alpha_1 = 0.3$ and $\kappa = 9$ for $\alpha_1 = 0.5$.

16.2.3 GARCH(p, q)

Another possibility, analogous to an autoregressive distributed lag model, to avoid long lag lengths on y_t^2 in (16.5) or ε_t^2 in (16.6), is to include lags of σ_t^2, since, for example, σ_{t-1}^2 is implicitly an infinite lag on y_t^2 in (16.5) or ε_t^2 in (16.6). Taking (16.5) as an example, then

$$\sigma_t^2 = \alpha_0 + \alpha_1 y_{t-1}^2 + \beta_1 \sigma_{t-1}^2 \qquad (16.8)$$

This is an example of a generalised ARCH process, known as GARCH(p, q) where p refers to the lag on σ_t^2 and q to the lag on y_t^2 and is due to Bollerslev (1986); here $p = 1$ and $q = 1$. Note that for σ_t^2 to be interpreted as a (conditional) variance it must always be nonnegative; sufficient conditions are that the coefficients satisfy $\alpha_0 > 0$, $\alpha_1 \geq 0$, $\beta_1 \geq 0$. (Necessary conditions are given in Nelson and Cao 1992.) Stationarity of the unconditional variance imposes other conditions – see section **16.3** below. In addition assuming $0 \leq \beta_1 < 1$ then:

$$(1 - \beta_1 L)\sigma_t^2 = \alpha_0 + \alpha_1 y_{t-1}^2$$

$$\Rightarrow \sigma_t^2 = \frac{\alpha_0}{(1 - \beta_1)} + \frac{\alpha_1}{(1 - \beta_1 L)} y_{t-1}^2$$

$$\qquad (16.9)$$

Note that the distributed lag function is:

$$\frac{\alpha_1}{(1 - \beta_1 L)} = \alpha_1 + \alpha_1 \beta_1 L + \alpha_1 \beta_1^2 L^2$$

$$+ \alpha_1 \beta_1^3 L^3 + \cdots \qquad (16.10)$$

and is, therefore, an infinite distributed lag. Hence, writing this explicitly:

$$\sigma_t^2 = \frac{\alpha_0}{(1 - \beta_1)} + \alpha_1 \sum_{j=1}^{\infty} \beta_1^{j-1} y_{t-j}^2 \qquad (16.11)$$

Thus the GARCH model can be interpreted as an infinite distributed lag on past y_t^2 or past ε_t^2 for the regression model.

To illustrate further a GARCH(2, 1) process for the regression model is:

$$\sigma_t^2 = \alpha_0 + \alpha_1 \varepsilon_{t-1}^2 + \beta_1 \sigma_{t-1}^2 + \beta_2 \sigma_{t-2}^2 \quad (16.12)$$

In general the GARCH(p, q) specification for the regression model is:

Specification of the mean and conditional variance:

$$E\{y_t \mid X_t = x_t\} = x_t \beta; \ \mathrm{Var}(y_t \mid X_t = x_t) = \sigma_t^2$$

Specification of σ_t^2 as GARCH(p, q):

$$\sigma_t^2 = \alpha_0 + \sum_{i=1}^{q} \alpha_i \varepsilon_{t-i}^2 + \sum_{j=1}^{p} \beta_j \sigma_{t-j}^2$$

In practice the GARCH generalisation is particularly useful as only fairly small values of p and q are usually required.

Notice that the GARCH(p, q) process can be interpreted as an ARMA process but to do so is not quite as straightforward as identifying the AR part as p lags of σ_t^2 and the moving average as q lags of ε_{t-1}^2. The following interpretation is due to Bollerslev (1986) and see also Engle (1995b). To illustrate we use the GARCH (1, 1) process. There are three steps in the derivation:

$$\sigma_t^2 = \alpha_0 + \alpha_1 \varepsilon_{t-1}^2 + \beta_1 \sigma_{t-1}^2$$

$$\varepsilon_t^2 - \sigma_t^2 = \varepsilon_t^2 - (\alpha_0 + \alpha_1 \varepsilon_{t-1}^2 + \beta_1 \sigma_{t-1}^2)$$

$$= \varepsilon_t^2 - \alpha_0 - (\alpha_1 + \beta_1)\varepsilon_{t-1}^2$$

$$+ \beta_1(\varepsilon_{t-1}^2 - \sigma_{t-1}^2))$$

$$\varepsilon_t^2 = \alpha_0 + (\alpha_1 + \beta_1)\varepsilon_{t-1}^2 + (\varepsilon_t^2 - \sigma_t^2)$$

$$- \beta_1(\varepsilon_{t-1}^2 - \sigma_{t-1}^2)$$

The first line is GARCH(1, 1); then subtract σ_t^2 from ε_t^2 and add and subtract $\beta_1 \varepsilon_{t-1}^2$; finally, rearrange.

This is the ARMA representation because the AR component is the lag on ε_t^2 and the moving average components are the terms in $(\varepsilon_t^2 - \sigma_t^2)$ and its lag. What makes this the ARMA representation is that $(\varepsilon_t^2 - \sigma_t^2)$ has zero mean (whereas ε_{t-1}^2 in the GARCH(1, 1) does not have zero mean).

The unconditional variance for the GARCH process can be motivated in the same way as for the ARCH process, although its formal proof is quite complex – see Bollerslev (1986, theorem 1). For the GARCH(p, q) process the unconditional variance is:

$$_u\sigma^2 = \frac{\alpha_0}{\left(1 - \sum_{i=1}^{q} \alpha_i - \sum_{j=1}^{p} \beta_j\right)}$$

Conditions for $_u\sigma^2$ to be defined are given in section **16.3**.

As in the ARCH case the unconditional distribution of ε_t is leptokurtic even though the conditional distribution is normal. Specifically in the case of GARCH(1, 1), Bollerslev (1986) shows that

$$\kappa - 3 = 6 \frac{\alpha_1^2}{(1 - 3\alpha_1^2 - \beta_1^2 - 2\alpha_1\beta_1)} > 0$$

for $0 < \alpha_1$ and

$$3\alpha_1^2 + \beta_1^2 + 2\alpha_1\beta_1 < 1$$

16.2.4 What does data with an ARCH effect look like?

A graph more readily tells the story of ARCH effects, which are typically present in asset price data such as stock prices for individual corporations or indices of traded stocks, exchange rates and interest rates. This section illustrates what ARCH effects look like by using data for Standard and Poor's 500 index, S&P 500, for the New York stock exchange and the Nikkei–Dow index for the Japanese stock exchange. A formal testing procedure for ARCH effects is described in section **16.5** and its application to the S&P 500 is reported in section **16.8.4**. (As a matter of record test results for the series used here confirmed the presence of ARCH effects.)

To illustrate we first consider weekly data for the S&P 500 for the period 31 November 1987 to 22 June 1998. The sample period is started after the October 1987 crash simply to avoid the dimension of the crash, which makes it difficult to scale the graph to show the clustering typical of ARCH effects. The level of the index is graphed in Figure 16.1A and the weekly returns, measured as the first difference of the log of the level of the series, are graphed in Figure 16.1B. The level looks like an integrated series, which trends strongly up over the sample period. The weekly returns, however, look stationary. What is of interest for the ARCH effect is the squared weekly returns, which are a measure of the volatility of the series, graphed in Figure 16.1C. An ARCH effect is evident in that there are clusters of large positive squared residuals, for example in 1990 and 1997, and clusters of small positive squared residuals, as in 1993. This suggests serial correlation but in the squares of the series, here the weekly returns, and is suggestive of an ARCH effect. It is likely that a variation on equations (16.4) and (16.5), with $y_t =$ weekly returns minus the mean of the series, would find support with this data. The same picture – see Figure 16.1D – is evident if weekly returns are first regressed – or 'filtered' – on lags 1 to 4 of the series so that the ARCH effect is in the squared regression residuals as in equations (16.6) and (16.7). (In the literature on financial econometrics the residuals are often referred to as shocks.)

The second illustration is with the Nikkei–Dow index, which is graphed in Figures 16.2A to 16.2D. In contrast to the S&P 500, there is no strong upward trend in the level of the index. The weekly returns are shown in Figure 16.2B and look stationary, apart from a possible increase in variance after 1990. The ARCH effect is again present in the squared weekly returns – see Figure 16.2C – and in the filtered series – see Figure 16.2D. Graphically, apart

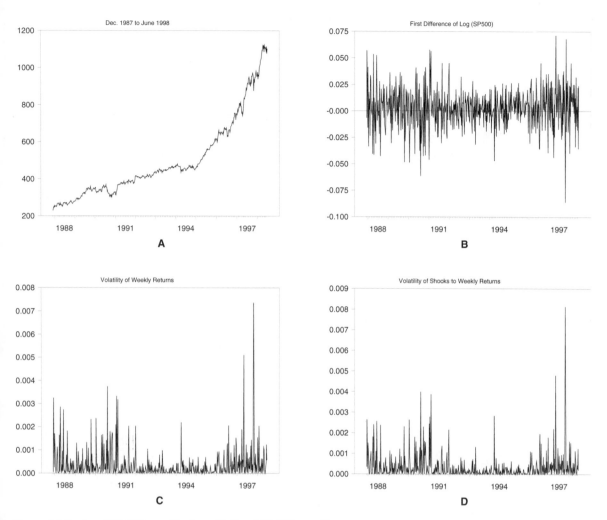

Figure 16.1 **A – S&P 500, weekly data. B–D – S&P 500, weekly returns**

from a two-year period after the 1987 crash, there seem to be fewer periods of relative tranquillity in the Nikkei–Dow index compared to the S&P 500.

16.3 Stationarity and persistence in some standard models

Stationarity of the ARCH(q) process imposes conditions on the α_i coefficients. We have already seen that in the ARCH(1) process for the regression disturbances. In that case the unconditional variance of ε_t is $_u\sigma^2 = \alpha_0/(1 - \alpha_1)$; but for this expression to make sense we must have $0 \leq \alpha_1 < 1$. If $\alpha_1 > 1$, the expression is negative which is not sensible for a variance, and if $\alpha_1 = 1$ the expression is not defined as $\alpha_0/(1 - \alpha_1) \to \infty$ as $\alpha_1 \to 1$; and $\alpha_1 \geq 0$ is required for nonnegativity of the conditional variance. (Use of the word 'stationarity' without qualification refers to second order – or covariance – stationarity; strict stationarity applied to ARCH type models is distinguished from covariance stationarity by Nelson (1990) and is

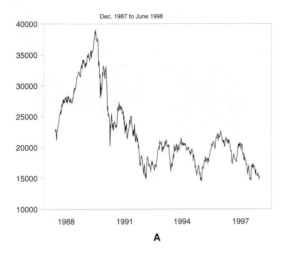

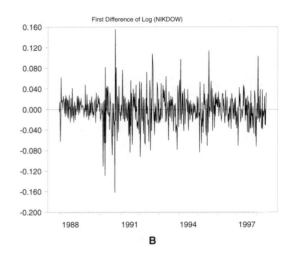

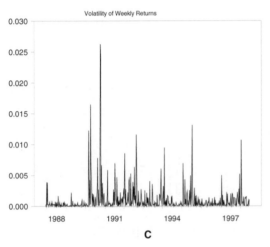

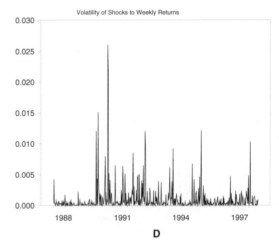

Figure 16.2   A – Nikkei–Dow, weekly data. B–D – Nikkei–Dow, weekly returns

mentioned below – see Chapter 3 for an explanation of the difference.)

16.3.1   ARCH(q)

In the ARCH(q) process:

$$\sigma_t^2 = \alpha_0 + \sum_{i=1}^{q} \alpha_i \varepsilon_{t-i}^2 \qquad (16.13)$$

$$_u\sigma^2 = \frac{\alpha_0}{\left(1 - \sum\limits_{i=1}^{q} \alpha_i\right)} \qquad (16.14)$$

For σ_t^2 to be nonnegative, whatever the values of ε_{t-i}^2, and $_u\sigma^2$ to be finite and nonnegative, we must have $\alpha_0 \geq 0$, $\alpha_i \geq 0$ and $0 \leq \sum_{i=1}^{q} \alpha_i < 1$.

16.3.2   GARCH(p, q)

Stationarity of the GARCH(p, q) process imposes conditions on the α_i and β_j coefficients. Specifically, write the GARCH(p, q) model as:

$$\sigma_t^2 = \alpha_0 + \sum_{i=1}^{q} \alpha_i \varepsilon_{t-i}^2 + \sum_{j=1}^{p} \beta_j \sigma_{t-j}^2 \qquad (16.15)$$

Then a necessary and sufficient condition for stationarity is $\sum_{i=1}^{q} \alpha_i + \sum_{j=1}^{p} \beta_j < 1$, this result is due to Bollerslev (1986, theorem 1). If $\alpha_0 \geq 0$, $\alpha_i \geq 0$, $\beta_i \geq 0$ and $0 \leq \sum_{i=1}^{q} \alpha_i + \sum_{j=1}^{p} \beta_j < 1$, then $_u\sigma^2$ is nonnegative and finite, and given by

$$_u\sigma^2 = \frac{\alpha_0}{\left(1 - \sum_{i=1}^{q} \alpha_i - \sum_{j=1}^{p} \beta_j\right)} \quad (16.16)$$

16.3.3 IGARCH(1, 1)

In some empirical applications, the condition $0 \leq \sum_{i=1}^{q} \alpha_i < 1$ for ARCH(q), or $0 \leq \sum_{i=1}^{q} \alpha_i + \sum_{j=1}^{p} \beta_j < 1$ for GARCH(p, q) models, is not met. To focus the discussion consider the widely applied GARCH(1, 1) model:

$$\sigma_t^2 = \alpha_0 + \alpha_1 \varepsilon_{t-1}^2 + \beta_1 \sigma_{t-1}^2 \quad (16.17)$$

Then estimation sometimes results in

$$\hat{\alpha}_1 + \hat{\beta}_1 \approx 1$$

or even $\hat{\alpha}_1 + \hat{\beta}_1 > 1$, where $\hat{\alpha}_1$ is the ML estimator of α_1 and so on. For example, Engle and Chowdury (1992) report the following estimated GARCH(1, 1) models for stock returns for IBM, Bethlehem Steel (BS) and Dow Chemicals (DC), for the period July 1962 to December 1985:

$$\text{IBM: } y_t = 0.00056 + \hat{\varepsilon}_{t-1}$$
$$\text{BS: } y_t = 0.00047 + \hat{\varepsilon}_{t-1}$$
$$\text{DC: } y_t = 0.00056 + \hat{\varepsilon}_{t-1}$$

$$\text{IBM: } \hat{\sigma}_t^2 = \hat{\alpha}_0 + 0.053\hat{\varepsilon}_{t-1}^2 + 0.953\hat{\sigma}_{t-1}^2$$
$$\text{BS: } \hat{\sigma}_t^2 = \hat{\alpha}_0 + 0.038\hat{\varepsilon}_{t-1}^2 + 0.965\hat{\sigma}_{t-1}^2$$
$$\text{DC: } \hat{\sigma}_t^2 = \hat{\alpha}_0 + 0.042\hat{\varepsilon}_{t-1}^2 + 0.962\hat{\sigma}_{t-1}^2$$

Note that in each case $\hat{\alpha}_1 + \hat{\beta}_1 \approx 1$.

Engle and Bollerslev (1986) show that if $\alpha_1 + \beta_1 \geq 1$, the conditional variance is persistent to shocks in the following sense. Conditional on information at t, consider the expected conditional variance at some time $t + f$, where t is the present and $t + f$ is the future ($f > 0$). Then:

$$E\{\sigma_{t+f}^2 \mid \sigma_t^2\} = \alpha_0 \left(\sum_{k=0}^{f-1} (\alpha_1 + \beta_1)^k\right)$$
$$+ (\alpha_1 + \beta_1)^f \sigma_t^2 \quad (16.18)$$

The detail of this derivation (with hints) is left to a review question. To interpret this expression, suppose there is a large positive shock to ε_{t-1} and so to ε_{t-1}^2, then the conditional variance σ_t^2 increases. This shock is always 'remembered' if $\alpha_1 + \beta_1 \geq 1$ because $(\alpha_1 + \beta_1)^f \geq 1$, but 'dies' out if $\alpha_1 + \beta_1 < 1$ because $(\alpha_1 + \beta_1)^f \to 0$ as $f \to \infty$. In this sense in the former case the shock is persistent, with the critical switch point being $\alpha_1 + \beta_1 = 1$.

From (16.18) note that:

$$E\{\sigma_{t+1}^2 \mid \sigma_t^2\} = \alpha_0 + (\alpha_1 + \beta_1)\sigma_t^2$$
$$E\{\sigma_{t+2}^2 \mid \sigma_t^2\} = \alpha_0 + \alpha_0(\alpha_1 + \beta_1)$$
$$+ (\alpha_1 + \beta_1)^2 \sigma_t^2$$
$$= \alpha_0 + (\alpha_1 + \beta_1)E\{\sigma_{t+1}^2 \mid \sigma_t^2\}$$
$$E\{\sigma_{t+3}^2 \mid \sigma_t^2\} = \alpha_0 + \alpha_0(\alpha_1 + \beta_1)$$
$$+ \alpha_0(\alpha_1 + \beta_1)^2 + (\alpha_1 + \beta_1)^3 \sigma_t^2$$
$$= \alpha_0 + (\alpha_1 + \beta_1)E\{\sigma_{t+2}^2 \mid \sigma_t^2\}$$
$$\vdots$$
$$E\{\sigma_{t+j}^2 \mid \sigma_t^2\} = \alpha_0 + (\alpha_1 + \beta_1)E\{\sigma_{t+j-1}^2 \mid \sigma_t^2\}$$
$$(16.19)$$

The conditional expectation therefore evolves recursively. If $\alpha_1 + \beta_1 = 1$ then:

$$E\{\sigma_{t+j}^2 \mid \sigma_t^2\} = \alpha_0 + E\{\sigma_{t+j-1}^2 \mid \sigma_t^2\} \quad (16.20)$$

which has the structure of a random walk with drift in the conditional expectation. Therefore, by analogy to standard unit root processes, when $\alpha_1 + \beta_1 = 1$ the GARCH(p, q) model is said to be integrated, and is referred to as IGARCH(p, q), with drift if $\alpha_0 > 0$. However, Nelson (1990, especially theorems 1 and 2) points out that the analogy with a random walk is not precise. In particular, and in contrast to a univariate random walk process, if $\alpha_1 + \beta_1 = 1$ and $\alpha_0 = 0$, the distribution of σ_{t+f}^2 becomes concentrated around 0 and σ_{t+f}^2 tends to 0 as $f \to \infty$. The more relevant case is $\alpha_0 > 0$, and in this case σ_{t+f}^2 tends to a constant long-run variance as $f \to \infty$. The important point is that even though there is persistence, in the sense defined by Engle and Bollerslev, there is stationarity in the sense that the conditional variance tends to the unconditional (long-run) variance despite $\alpha_1 + \beta_1 = 1$. (The critical difference of interpretation of persistence, is subtle: in the Engle and Bollerslev sense, the forecast *moments*, for example $E\{\sigma_{t+f}^2 \mid \sigma_t^2\}$, are persistent to shocks, the hint here being that the 'random walk' is in the conditional expectation, but shocks are not persistent in the forecast *distribution* – see Nelson (*op. cit.*) and also Engle and Bollerslev (1986), Engle and Chowdury (1992), Geweke (1986) and the discussion in Harvey, Ruiz and Shephard (1994); and refer to Chapter 3 for the distinction between covariance stationarity and complete or strict stationarity.)

16.3.4   Nonnegativity constraints in GARCH models

Another problem, which has occurred in the literature on empirical GARCH models, relates to whether the estimated coefficients satisfy conditions for the conditional variance to be nonnegative. That is since σ_t^2 is a variance, estimates of it should not be negative. A sufficient set of conditions was given above; that is α_0 and all the α_i and β_j coefficients should be nonnegative (these are referred to as Bollerslev's conditions). However, these constraints are sometimes not met in practice. For example, as Nelson and Cao

(1992) note, Engle, Ito and Lin (1990) estimate a GARCH(1, 4) for intra-daily data on the yen–dollar exchange rate and obtain:

$$
\begin{aligned}
\hat{\sigma}_t^2 = {}& 0.0006 + 0.1169 \hat{\varepsilon}_{t-1}^2 - 0.0627 \hat{\varepsilon}_{t-2}^2 \\
& - 0.0047 \hat{\varepsilon}_{t-3}^2 - 0.0181 \hat{\varepsilon}_{t-4}^2 \\
& + 0.9581 \hat{\sigma}_{t-1}^2
\end{aligned}
$$

Although the sum of the coefficients at 0.9895 is less than one, the estimates of the α_i, $i = 2, 3, 4$, are negative and so Bollerslev's conditions for nonnegativity are not met. However, as Nelson and Cao (*op. cit.*) show in GARCH(1, q) models with $q > 1$, the requirement that all the coefficients be nonnegative can be relaxed. Their theorem 1 gives necessary and sufficient conditions whereas in most cases Bollerslev's conditions are sufficient; 'most cases' refers to the exception of the GARCH(1, 1) model where the two sets of conditions are the same. We state and interpret Nelson and Cao's theorem 1 rather than prove it:

In the GARCH(1, q) model

$$
\sigma_t^2 = \alpha_0 + \sum_{i=1}^{q} \alpha_i \varepsilon_{t-i}^2 + \beta_1 \sigma_{t-1}^2
$$

Necessary and sufficient conditions for nonnegativity of σ_t^2 are:

(i) $\alpha_0 \geq 0$;

(ii) $\beta_1 \geq 0$;

(iii) $\omega_k \equiv \displaystyle\sum_{i=0}^{k} \alpha_{i+1} \beta_1^{k-i} \geq 0$

   for $k = 0, \ldots, q - 1$

The first two conditions are straightforward. To motivate the third condition, as noted above, a GARCH model can be viewed as an infinite distributed lag on past ε_t^2 and denote the coefficients in this distributed lag function ω_k, $k = 0, \ldots, \infty$, then the condition ensures that these coefficients are positive. These conditions assume $\beta_1 \neq 1$, otherwise the constant in the infinite distributed lag representation is not defined.

In the case of a GARCH(1, 1) model, the conditions are the same as Bollerslev's; in this case $k = q - 1 = 0$, so the third condition is just $\alpha_1 \beta_1^0 = \alpha_1 \geq 0$, which is as before. However, for $q > 1$ they are not so stringent. For example, for the GARCH(1, 2) model they are: (a) $\alpha_0 \geq 0$; (b) $0 \leq \beta_1 < 1$; (c) $\beta_1 \alpha_1 + \alpha_2 \geq 0$; and (d) $\alpha_1 \geq 0$. The condition (c) offers the relaxation in the sense that it is satisfied for some $\alpha_2 < 0$ provided $\beta_1 \alpha_1$ is large enough. A review question considers whether the estimated coefficients in the Engle, Ito and Lin example satisfy the necessary and sufficient conditions.

16.4   Estimation

Initially we consider estimation in the regression model with an ARCH(1) disturbance and no lagged dependent variables. The discussion in this section is not technical, focusing on why OLS is no longer optimal. An appendix presents the more technical maximum likelihood approach.

16.4.1   Specification

The specification is as follows:

(i)   Specification of the mean of y_t:

$$E\{y_t \mid X_t = x_t\} = x_t\beta$$

(ii)   Specification of the conditional variance of y_t: $\mathrm{Var}(y_t \mid X_t = x_t) = \sigma_t^2$.
(iii)   Specification of the conditional density as normal: $(y_t \mid X_t = x_t) \sim N(x_t\beta, \sigma_t^2)$.
(iv)   Definition of the 'disturbance':

$$\varepsilon_t \equiv y_t - E\{y_t \mid X_t = x_t\} = y_t - x_t\beta$$

(v)   Specification of the disturbance as ARCH(1):
(a) $\varepsilon_t = u_t\sigma_t$
with $E\{u_t\} = 0$ and $\mathrm{Var}(u_t) \equiv 1$
(b) $\sigma_t^2 = \alpha_0 + \alpha_1\varepsilon_{t-1}^2$.
(vi) X_t contains no lagged dependent variables.

This specification is relatively simple in that in practical applications X_t may contain lagged dependent variables.

Substituting (v)(b) into (v)(a), the disturbance is

$$\varepsilon_t = u_t(\alpha_0 + \alpha_1\varepsilon_{t-1}^2)^{\frac{1}{2}} \qquad (16.21)$$

For the purposes of assessing whether OLS estimation of β is BLUE, we need $E\{\varepsilon_t\}$, $\mathrm{Var}(\varepsilon_t)$ and $\mathrm{Cov}(\varepsilon_t, \varepsilon_s)$ for $t \neq s$. We derive the first two of these here, the third is left to a review question. To anticipate, the derivations show the following:

- $E\{\varepsilon_t\} = 0$
- $\mathrm{Var}(\varepsilon_t)$, the unconditional variance, is constant.
- $\mathrm{Cov}(\varepsilon_t, \varepsilon_s) = 0$ for $t \neq s$; the unconditional covariances are zero.

Hence the conditions of the Gauss–Markov theorem for OLS to be BLUE are met.

First note that the expectation of ε_t given ε_{t-1} is zero, that is:

$$\begin{aligned}
E\{\varepsilon_t \mid \varepsilon_{t-1}\} \\
= E\{u_t(\alpha_0 + \alpha_1\varepsilon_{t-1}^2)^{\frac{1}{2}} \mid \varepsilon_{t-1}\} \\
= (\alpha_0 + \alpha_1\varepsilon_{t-1}^2)^{\frac{1}{2}}E\{u_t \mid \varepsilon_{t-1}\} \\
\text{because } \alpha_0 + \alpha_1\varepsilon_{t-1}^2 \text{ is constant} \\
= 0 \quad \text{because } E\{u_t \mid \varepsilon_{t-1}\} = E\{u_t\} = 0
\end{aligned}$$

The unconditional expectation is

$$E\{\varepsilon_t\} = E\{E\{\varepsilon_t \mid \varepsilon_{t-1}\}\} = E\{0\} = 0$$

where the first expectation is taken over ε_{t-1} and the expectation of 0 is 0.

Next consider the conditional and unconditional variances of ε_t. The conditional variance of ε_t is:

$$\begin{aligned}
\mathrm{Var}(\varepsilon_t \mid \varepsilon_{t-1}) &= E\{\varepsilon_t^2 \mid \varepsilon_{t-1}\} \\
&= E\{(u_t^2)(\alpha_0 + \alpha_1 \varepsilon_{t-1}^2) \mid \varepsilon_{t-1}\} \\
&= \alpha_0 \,\mathrm{Var}(u_t) + \alpha_1 \varepsilon_{t-1}^2 \,\mathrm{Var}(u_t) \\
&\qquad \text{because } E\{u_t^2\} \equiv \mathrm{Var}(u_t) \\
&= \alpha_0 + \alpha_1 \varepsilon_{t-1}^2 \quad \text{because } \mathrm{Var}(u_t) = 1
\end{aligned}$$

We know this already because this is the ARCH(1) specification where $\mathrm{Var}(\varepsilon_t \mid \varepsilon_{t-1}) \equiv \sigma_t^2$. What we are really interested in for estimation by OLS is the unconditional variance, which does not take lagged values of ε_{t-1}, for example ε_{t-1}, as fixed. We use what is known as the variance decomposition (see section **3.4.8**),

$$\mathrm{Var}(\varepsilon_t) = E\{\mathrm{Var}(\varepsilon_t \mid \varepsilon_{t-1})\} + \mathrm{Var}(E\{\varepsilon_t \mid \varepsilon_{t-1}\})$$

where the first expectation is taken over ε_{t-1} (or more generally information dated $t-1$ or earlier). The second term in the variance decomposition is 0 because $E\{\varepsilon_t \mid \varepsilon_{t-1}\}$ does not vary, thus $\mathrm{Var}(\varepsilon_t) = E\{\mathrm{Var}(\varepsilon_t \mid \varepsilon_{t-1})\}$:

$$\begin{aligned}
\mathrm{Var}(\varepsilon_t) &= E\{\mathrm{Var}(\varepsilon_t \mid \varepsilon_{t-1})\} = E\{\alpha_0 + \alpha_1 \varepsilon_{t-1}^2\} \\
&= \alpha_0 + \alpha_1 E\{\varepsilon_{t-1}^2\} \\
&= \alpha_0 + \alpha_1 \,\mathrm{Var}(\varepsilon_{t-1}) \\
&= \alpha_0 + \alpha_1 \,\mathrm{Var}(\varepsilon_t)
\end{aligned}$$

The last line assumes $\mathrm{Var}(\varepsilon_t) = \mathrm{Var}(\varepsilon_{t-1})$, that is the unconditional variances are homoscedastic. In terms of the notation of section **16.2.2**, the unconditional variance, denoted $_u\sigma_t^2$, is defined as $E\{\sigma_t^2\} \equiv E\{\mathrm{Var}(\varepsilon_t \mid \varepsilon_{t-1})\}$, which is $_u\sigma^2$ when the unconditional variance is constant. Then following on from the last line we have:

$$\begin{aligned}
&\Rightarrow (1 - \alpha_1)_u\sigma^2 = \alpha_0 \\
&\qquad \Rightarrow {}_u\sigma^2 = \alpha_0/(1 - \alpha_1) \qquad (16.22)
\end{aligned}$$

provided $\alpha_1 \neq 1$. Stationarity and nonnegativity imply $0 \leq \alpha_1 < 1$.

The implication of these results is that OLS estimator of β is BLUE, and the usual estimator of the OLS coefficient variance matrix is unbiased (and consistent) provided there are no lagged dependent variables among the regressors. (By contrast OLS is just unbiased for the forms of heteroscedasticity described in Chapter 5, which also require heteroscedastic consistent standard errors.)

If lagged dependent variables are included in the regressors we know from Chapter 5 that OLS is consistent rather than unbiased; however, a complication if the disturbances follow an ARCH process is that the standard errors computed as the square roots of the diagonals of $\hat{\sigma}^2 (X'X)^{-1}$ are no longer consistent and should not, therefore, be used. The reason is that the variance matrix involves squares of the regressors, and as lagged dependent variables are included so are squares of the lagged dependent variables. However, the ARCH process involves squares of the disturbances, which are functions of the lagged dependent variables. The squares of the disturbances are, therefore, correlated with the squares of the lagged dependent variables. To ensure consistency White's heteroscedastic consistent standard errors should be used if the regression model includes lagged dependent variables and there is an ARCH (or GARCH) process for the disturbances.

16.4.2 A nonlinear estimator 'beats' the linear OLS estimator

If OLS is BLUE or at least consistent (if there are lagged dependent variables among the regressors) even if the regression model has an ARCH or GARCH process, then what advantage can be gained from recognising a conditionally heteroscedastic scheme? The answer is that the OLS estimator does not have minimum variance if we relax the class of estimators to include nonlinear rather than just linear estimators. In particular the maximum likelihood estimator is non-linear and asymptotically efficient. Engle (1982) shows that in the regression model with an ARCH(1) disturbance, the gain in using MLE rather than OLS, that is the relative efficiency, is a function of α_1 and the gain increases as α_1 approaches 1. The technical details of the derivation of the ML estimator are beyond the scope of this book – the details are given in Engle (1982) for the ARCH estimator and Bollerslev (1986) for the GARCH estimator. For a textbook exposition see Greene (1997). An important point to note is that because OLS is, at least, consistent the ML method can 'get started' by first estimating the substantive regression, that is $x_t\beta$, by OLS and then consistent estimators of the squared residuals are available as required in the ARCH/GARCH process. The ML estimator is programmed in most commercially available econometric software.

16.5 Testing for ARCH/GARCH effects

Testing for an ARCH or GARCH process could be undertaken using any one of the Lagrange–Multiplier, LM, likelihood ratio, LR, or Wald principles – see section **5.4.1** on the general issues. To illustrate we will first consider testing for an ARCH(q) process. It is sensible to consider the LM principle which just requires estimation under the null hypothesis and does not, therefore, initially require ML estimation.

16.5.1 LM test for ARCH effects

The null and alternative hypotheses are:

H_0: $\alpha_1 = \alpha_2 = \cdots = \alpha_q = 0$

H_a: at least one $\alpha_i \neq 0, i = 1, \ldots, q$

Under the null, OLS is consistent and efficient; whereas under the alternative OLS is consistent

but not efficient. The test statistic, assuming normality for the conditional distribution of y_t, is due to Engle (1982) and turns out to have the same form as suggested by Breusch and Pagan (1979) and Godfrey (1978a). The form of the test will be familiar from the LM test for serial correlation. There are three steps:

(i) Estimate $y_t = x_t\beta + \varepsilon_t$, obtain the OLS residuals $\hat{\varepsilon}_t$ and hence form $\hat{\varepsilon}_{t-i}^2$ for $i = 1, \ldots, q$.
(ii) In an auxiliary regression, regress $\hat{\varepsilon}_t^2$ on a constant and $\hat{\varepsilon}_{t-1}^2, \ldots, \hat{\varepsilon}_{t-q}^2$.
(iii) T times R^2 is asymptotically distributed as $\chi^2(q)$ when the null hypothesis is true; T is the number of observations in the auxiliary regression, and R^2 is the centred R^2 as the auxiliary regression contains a constant.

The usual testing procedure follows: ideally obtain the msl of the sample value of the test statistic; if the sample msl is below the reference significance level, for example 5%, then reject the null hypothesis. Alternatively, if the sample value of the test statistic exceeds the critical value for the reference significance level, reject the null hypothesis.

By analogy with the F version of the LM test for serial correlation, it is tempting to suggest an F version of this test, which might be useful if q is large and/or T is 'small'. That is in step (iii) denote the residual sum of squares as URSS, and RRSS as the residual sum of squares from the regression of $\hat{\varepsilon}_t^2$ just on a constant, then an F statistic can be formed in the usual way with $F(q, T - q - 1)$ degrees of freedom – see, in particular, section **5.4.2** and equation (5.26) – with large values leading to rejection of the null hypothesis. The use of the F distribution is likely to be approximate since the justification for the test in the TR^2 form, as given in steps (i) to (ii), is asymptotic. The $\chi^2(q)$ and $F(q, T - q - 1)$ test statistics are standard output in several econometric software programs.

Other hypotheses are also likely to be of interest. For example, if it is strongly suspected that an ARCH process is present but the order is not known then q could be set at, say, q^* and sequential tested for ARCH(q^*) against ARCH($q^* - 1$), that is $\alpha_q = 0$; and then ARCH($q^* - 1$) against ARCH($q^* - 2$) and so on, stopping at the first significant test statistic. The test statistic is the square of 't' statistic on the marginal coefficient, that is on α_q in the first step, α_{q-1} in the second step and so on, which is asymptotically distributed as $\chi^2(1)$ when the null hypothesis is true. As in the standard regression case a final check of the simplified model against the general model could be undertaken with an F test. Using the 't' statistic directly as the test statistic, rather than its square, and assuming it has the (small sample) 't' distribution involves an approximation, just as in using the F test above; however, it may have some advantage since for the ARCH process to result in a positive variance we require $\alpha_i \geq 0$, and therefore the one-sided positive alternative would maximise power.

16.5.2 GARCH(p, q)

There is a difficulty in testing directly for a GARCH process given the null hypothesis is that the process is ARCH(q) (and a special case is no ARCH, that is ARCH(0)). This is because the LM test statistic coincides even though the alternative hypotheses differ. (In a sense this is similar to the problem in the LM test for serial correlation, see Chapter 5, which is unable to distinguish between moving average or autoregressive serial correlation of the same order.) The LM test statistic for the ARCH(q) null H_0 is the same whether the alternative is ARCH($q + r$) or GARCH(r, q), which we denote as the alternatives H_{a1} and H_{a2}, respectively, below:

$$H_0: \ \sigma_t^2 = \alpha_0 + \alpha_1 \varepsilon_{t-1}^2 + \cdots$$
$$+ \alpha_q \varepsilon_{t-q}^2 \qquad \text{ARCH}(q)$$
$$H_{a1}: \sigma_t^2 = \alpha_0 + \alpha_1 \varepsilon_{t-1}^2 + \cdots$$
$$+ \alpha_q \varepsilon_{t-q}^2 + \cdots$$
$$+ \alpha_{q+r} \varepsilon_{t-(q+r)}^2 \qquad \text{ARCH}(q + r)$$

$$H_{a2}: \sigma_t^2 = \alpha_0 + \sum_{i=1}^{q} \alpha_i \varepsilon_{t-i}^2$$
$$+ \sum_{j=1}^{r} \beta_j \sigma_{t-j}^2 \qquad \text{GARCH}(r, q)$$

The LM test statistic for the null of no ARCH, that is $q = 0$, against ARCH(r), is the same as for GARCH($r, 0$); similarly ARCH(1) against ARCH($1 + r$) results in the same LM test statistic as for GARCH($r, 1$). This result does not mean that the LM test for ARCH effects should not be carried out! What it implies, from a practical viewpoint, is that a significant test statistic is indicative of either an ARCH or a GARCH process. A long lag in an ARCH(q) process is suggestive of a GARCH(p, q) process with $p > 0$ and q of low order; hence, the ARCH process may be more economically parameterised as a low order GARCH process. Typically, empirical studies have found $p = 1$ and $q = 1$, or $p = 2$ and $q = 1$ quite adequate.

(Other tests for ARCH effects have been suggested by Peguin-Feissolle (1999) and Hong and Sheradeh (1999).)

16.6 Variations on an ARCH/GARCH theme

There are a number of variations on the ARCH theme and we consider some of the more influential ones in this and the next section, **16.7**. In the first subsection, **16.6.1**, we consider two relatively popular extensions of ARCH, the ABSGARCH and EGARCH specifications, and in subsection **16.6.2** the extension to 'ARCH in mean' processes. In section **16.7** we concentrate on asymmetry and introduce the interesting graphical device of the 'news impact curve' together with some further asymmetric ARCH extensions.

16.6.1 ABSGARCH, EGARCH

If σ_t^2 is the conditional variance of ε_t given information at time t, it must be nonnegative with probability 1. This is ensured in ARCH/ GARCH models because, provided certain coefficient restrictions are met, see section **16.3**, a linear function of positive random variables, that is ε_{t-i}^2 and σ_{t-j}^2, is positive. There are at least two alternatives to this approach.

16.6.1a ABSGARCH

In the absolute ARCH/GARCH model, as the name suggests, the absolute values of the innovations $|\varepsilon_t|$ are used. The absolute ARCH model applied to the conditional variance was suggested in Engle's original article – see Engle (*op. cit.*, section 4) – although not taken up in detail there.

The GARCH(p, q) type specification can then be applied to the conditional variance, that is:

$$\sigma_t^2 = \alpha_0 + \sum_{i=1}^{q} \alpha_i |\varepsilon_{t-i}| + \sum_{j=1}^{p} \beta_j \sigma_{t-j}^2 \quad (16.23)$$

Comparison with the GARCH(p, q) model shows that $|\varepsilon_{t-i}|$ replaces ε_{t-i}^2, so that the relative impact of 'large' innovations is dampened by taking the absolute value rather than squaring the innovations.

Alternatively, as in MICROFIT (Pesaran and Pesaran 1997), the ARCH/GARCH(p, q) specification can be applied to the conditional standard error:

$$\sigma_t = \alpha_0 + \sum_{i=1}^{q} \alpha_i |\varepsilon_{t-i}| + \sum_{j=1}^{p} \beta_j \sigma_{t-j} \quad (16.24)$$

We refer to this as the absolute GARCH model, abbreviated to ABSGARCH, even if $p = 0$ in some applications.

16.6.1b EGARCH

A second alternative way of ensuring positivity is due to Nelson (1991), and known as EGARCH for exponential GARCH. Nelson's formulation has the advantage that it allows negative and positive shocks (innovations) to have differential effects, in contrast to the GARCH or

ABSGARCH specifications. Thus it allows financial markets to respond asymmetrically to 'bad news', a negative innovation, and 'good news', a positive innovation, even though the innovations are of the same absolute value. (Further consideration is given to this model in the next subsection.)

The EGARCH specification looks somewhat more complex than the previous GARCH models, but the components are straightforward. The EGARCH(p, q) model is:

$$\ln(\sigma_t^2) = \alpha_0 + \sum_{i=1}^{q} \alpha_i \left[\frac{\varepsilon_t}{\sigma_t} \right]_{-i} +$$

$$\sum_{i=1}^{q} \alpha_i^* \left[\left| \frac{\varepsilon_t}{\sigma_t} \right|_{-i} - \mu \right] + \sum_{j=1}^{p} \beta_j \ln(\sigma_{t-j}^2)$$

$$(16.25)$$

where $\mu = E\left\{ \left| \frac{\varepsilon_t}{\sigma_t} \right| \right\} = \left[\frac{2}{\pi} \right]^{0.5}$ if $\varepsilon_t \sim N(0, 1)$.

First note that specifying the function as the logarithm of σ_t^2 ensures positivity (so even if the product of a right-hand side variable and its coefficient are negative, the antilog must be positive). Dividing the innovations ε_t by the conditional standard deviation σ_t results in the *scaled* or *standardised* shocks. Thus, the effect of these terms depends upon their relative size. The second set of variables results from subtracting the mean from the absolute value of the scaled innovations. To see how an asymmetry is induced consider the simplest case with $q = 1$ and $p = 0$, then:

$$\ln(\sigma_t^2) = \alpha_0 + \alpha_1 v_{t-1} + \alpha_1^* [|v_{t-1}| - \mu]$$

$$(16.26)$$

For convenience we have defined

$$v_{t-1} \equiv \frac{\varepsilon_{t-1}}{\sigma_{t-1}}$$

Now consider a positive scaled shock and a negative scaled shock of the same absolute magnitude, say $+1.0$ and -1.0, and $\alpha_1 = 0.4$, $\alpha_1^* = 0.2$, then the impact of the former is

$$1.0\alpha_1 + \alpha_1^*(1.0 - \mu) = 0.4 + 0.2(1 - 0.798)$$
$$= 0.4404$$

whereas the impact of the latter is

$$-1.0\alpha + \alpha_1^*(1.0 - \mu)$$
$$= -0.4 + 0.2(1 - 0.798) = -0.3596$$

The positive shock has a greater impact in absolute terms. In the next example the sign of α_1 is changed so $\alpha_1 = -0.4$ and, as before, $\alpha_2^* = 0.2$. Then the impact of a $+1$ shock is -0.3596, whereas the impact of a -1 shock is 0.4404. Now the negative shock has a greater impact in absolute terms. The key coefficient is α_1, which allows the sign of the shock to have an impact over and above its magnitude. (If $\alpha_1 = 0$, then the impact of the shocks is the same because the absolute value function in the third term leads to the sign being ignored.) For more on the asymmetry of the EGARCH model, see section **16.7** below.

16.6.2 ARCH-M, GARCH-M, ABSGARCH-M, EGARCH-M

The next extension not only models the heteroscedasticity process, but also includes the resulting measure of 'volatility' in the regression or mean function. In some ways this is where the real benefit of ARCH modelling is to be found, since it allows a practical implementation of the theoretical result that, for example, the mean return on a financial asset is affected by the volatility of shocks to those returns.

At its simplest the square root of the conditional variance, that is the conditional standard deviation, is included in the regression function. That is:

$$y_t = x_t\beta + \delta\sigma_t + \varepsilon_t \tag{16.27}$$

In some applications the log of σ_t has been used. The notational convention is to add '-M' to the

ARCH type specification to indicate the 'in mean' specification. Thus ARCH-M stands for (simple) ARCH in the mean, and is due to Engle, Lilien and Robins, hereafter ELR (1987). An obvious extension to the ARCH-M model is to specify the heteroscedasticity as GARCH(p, q), and then add the conditional variance or some function of it to the specification of the mean function. The resulting model is known as GARCH-M.

ARCH-M models have found widespread application where a time varying measure of risk is required. In ELR's seminal article, described in greater detail below, the excess return on holding a long bond relative to a short bond is modelled as a function of the log of the conditional standard deviation of the innovations in the regression model. The interpretation of this variable is as a measure of the time varying risk premium.

As in the ARCH and GARCH cases, a measure of uncertainty based on the conditional variance of the innovations modelled by variations of the ARCH/GARCH process can be included in the mean function. These lead to the EGARCH-M and ABSGARCH-M models. (Note that the MICROFIT options for ARCH-M, GARCH-M, EGARCH-M and ABSGARCH-M automatically include the conditional variance in the mean function for the 'in mean' options.)

16.7 The importance of asymmetry in ARCH models

Asymmetry was introduced briefly in the EGARCH model; however, its importance in the literature on ARCH modelling and, especially, its use in financial econometrics, requires a separate treatment. This section deals with this topic more extensively motivated by the need to distinguish between 'good news' and 'bad news' and their impact on (predictable) volatility in financial markets. One reason for this distinction lies in the 'leverage' effect – see Black

(1976) and Christie (1982). Suppose there is bad news, which decreases the asset price in period t, this, in turn, decreases the equity value of the firm and so increases the debt-to-equity ratio. This makes the firm riskier causing an increase in future expected variance of returns. Asymmetry also has important implications for 'betas', that is the covariance between the return on an asset and the return on the market portfolio (the market return) divided by the variance of the market return – see Braun, Nelson and Sunier (1995).

16.7.1   The news impact curve

The news impact curve was introduced by Engle and Ng (1993) and summarises the effect of a shock, interpreted either as bad news (a negative shock) or good news (a positive shock), on the time varying conditional variance. The conditional variance of the return on a financial asset is the predictable volatility of the return (assuming the coefficients of the ARCH process are known).

The Engle and Ng (*op. cit.*) framework is as follows. Let:

y_t be the rate of return on a stock from time $t - 1$ to t;

Ω_{t-1} the information set containing realised values of all relevant variables up to $t - 1$;

$m_t \equiv E\{y_t \mid \Omega_{t-1}\}$ the conditional mean given information to $t - 1$;

$\sigma_t^2 \equiv \mathrm{Var}(y_t \mid \Omega_{t-1})$ the conditional variance given information to $t - 1$;

$\varepsilon_t \equiv y_t - m_t$ the unexpected return at time t.

m_t is the expected (predicted or forecast) return for t given information at time $t - 1$. The market for this stock is efficient in the following sense. No information available at the time of forming the expectation, summarised as Ω_{t-1}, can improve the forecast value of the return. ε_t is, therefore, 'news' relative to Ω_{t-1}. A positive ε_t is an unexpected increase in the price of the stock and is good news; conversely a negative ε_t is an

unexpected decrease in the price and bad news. In the ARCH(q) model the impact of news on the conditional variance is captured by the α_i, $i = 1, \dots, q$, coefficients; the impact of news one period ago is α_1, two periods ago α_2 and so on, with news $q + 1$ periods ago having no effect. The GARCH(p, q) model generalises this pattern of news impact. The GARCH(p, q) model can be interpreted as an infinite order ARCH, so news in the distant past continues to have an effect, for example in a GARCH(1, 1) model the effect of the news declines geometrically.

One problem with these models of volatility is that they impose particular effects on predictable volatility. A one unit shock, for example, whether it is good news, $\varepsilon_t = +1$, or bad news, $\varepsilon_t = -1$, has the same impact on the conditional variance. However, the market may react differently to good and bad news. It has been suggested that an unexpected fall in the price, which is bad news, increases predictable volatility more than a same size unexpected increase in price. It is important, therefore, to be able to test for and allow asymmetry in the ARCH type specification. We have already come across an asymmetric effect in the EGARCH model. For example, in the EGARCH(1, 1) model this is represented by $\alpha_1 v_{t-1}$, and α_1 is typically negative so that a negative shock has a greater effect on volatility than an equally sized positive shock. Further, an increase in the shock increases volatility at a rate proportional to the square of the shock, that is the relation between the size of the shock and volatility is quadratic. However, volatility may increase at a rate greater than the square of the shock ('big' news has a big impact!).

To assess the impact of good and bad news Engle and Ng (*op. cit.*) define the *news impact curve*. If information dated at $t - 2$ or earlier is held constant, and lagged conditional variances are evaluated at the level of the unconditional variance, then the news impact curve is the relation between news, ε_{t-1}, and volatility, σ_t^2, with variations of the former on the horizontal axis and the latter on the vertical axis.

16.7.2 Examples of the news impact curve

The simplest ARCH(1) model is a good starting point. That is $\sigma_t^2 = \alpha_0 + \alpha_1 \varepsilon_{t-1}^2$, then the news impact curve will be symmetric about $\varepsilon_{t-1} = 0$ with (constant) slope $\partial \sigma_t^2 / \partial \varepsilon_{t-1} = 2\alpha_1 \varepsilon_{t-1}$, so the strength of the effect on σ_t^2 is determined by α_1 and increases with ε_{t-1} (take the absolute value here as the slope will be negative for $\varepsilon_{t-1} < 0$). The GARCH$(1, 1)$ model is $\sigma_t^2 = \alpha_0 + \alpha_1 \varepsilon_{t-1}^2 + \beta_1 \sigma_{t-1}^2$. To evaluate the news impact curve set $\sigma_{t-1}^2 = {}_u\sigma^2$ (the unconditional variance), and graph $\sigma_t^2 = A + \alpha_1 \varepsilon_{t-1}^2$ against ε_{t-1}, where $A = (\alpha_0 + \beta_1({}_u\sigma^2))$. As in the ARCH case, this will be symmetric about $\varepsilon_{t-1} = 0$ with slope of $2\alpha_1 \varepsilon_{t-1}$. What is happening to the slope over the range of possible values of ε_{t-1} is also of interest, indicating what is happening to marginal news. An example of the ARCH(1)/GARCH$(1, 1)$ news curve and corresponding slope curve is shown on Figure 16.3.

The EGARCH$(1, 1)$ model is:

$$\ln(\sigma_t^2) = \alpha_0 + \alpha_1 \left[\frac{\varepsilon_{t-1}}{\sigma_{t-1}} \right] + \alpha_1^* \left[\left| \frac{\varepsilon_{t-1}}{\sigma_{t-1}} \right| - \mu \right]$$

$$+ \beta_1 \ln(\sigma_{t-1}^2) \qquad (16.28)$$

with the news impact curve obtained as follows. First set $\sigma_{t-1}^2 = {}_u\sigma^2$, collect terms not involving ε_{t-1}, then take the antilog to obtain σ_t^2 and note that the impact depends upon the sign of ε_{t-1}:

$$\ln(\sigma_t^2) = a + \alpha_1 \left[\frac{\varepsilon_{t-1}}{{}_u\sigma} \right] + \alpha_1^* \left[\left| \frac{\varepsilon_{t-1}}{{}_u\sigma} \right| \right]$$

where $a = \alpha_0 + \beta_1 \ln({}_u\sigma^2) - \alpha_1^* \mu$

$$\sigma_t^2 = A \exp\left(\left[\frac{\alpha_1 + \alpha_1^*}{{}_u\sigma} \right] \varepsilon_{t-1} \right)$$

for $\varepsilon_{t-1} > 0$

$$\sigma_t^2 = A \exp\left(\left[\frac{\alpha_1 - \alpha_1^*}{{}_u\sigma} \right] \varepsilon_{t-1} \right)$$

for $\varepsilon_{t-1} < 0$

where $A = ({}_u\sigma^2)^{\beta_1} \exp(\alpha_0 - \alpha_1^* \mu)$

(Note for comparison with the numerical example of asymmetry in the EGARCH given above – see (16.26) – that for a negative shock, of say -1, the relevant part of the term in parentheses in the news impact curve for $\varepsilon_{t-1} < 0$ is $(\alpha_1 - \alpha_1^*)(-1) = (\alpha_1^* - \alpha_1)$.)

The EGARCH news impact curve differs from the GARCH news impact curve in two ways.

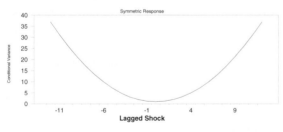

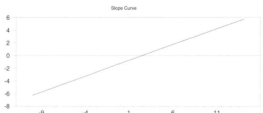

Figure 16.3 *News impact curve for ARCH/GARCH model*

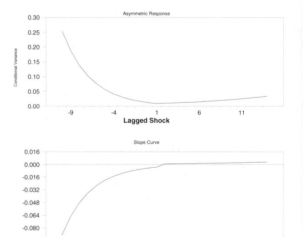

Figure 16.4 *News impact curve for EGARCH model*

First, it is not symmetric and, second, 'big' news can have a much greater impact than in the GARCH model. Nevertheless, typical patterns from EGARCH models tend to show a severe, and perhaps implausible, attenuation of effect on one side, for example, the positive side for negative values of α_1, so that good news may have very little effect compared to bad news. See Figure 16.4 for an illustration of an EGARCH news impact curve.

16.7.3 Asymmetry in more detail

Because of the potential importance of distinguishing between good and bad news in their effect on predictable volatility, a number of ARCH type models have been suggested which capture the following aspects of nonlinearity.

- Assuming that the conditional variance function has a single minimum and is monotonic either side of the minimum, then zero asymmetry occurs if the minimum is $\varepsilon_{t-1} = 0$; therefore, $\partial\sigma_t^2/\partial\varepsilon_{t-1} = 0$ for $\varepsilon_{t-1} = 0$. Conversely off-zero asymmetry occurs if $\partial\sigma_t^2/\partial\varepsilon_{t-1} \neq 0$ for $\varepsilon_{t-1} = 0$. The standard ARCH/GARCH models are symmetric about zero since $\partial\sigma_t^2/\partial\varepsilon_{t-1} = 0$ for $\varepsilon_{t-1} = 0$.
- Slope asymmetry about zero occurs if the absolute value of the slope $\partial\sigma_t^2/\partial\varepsilon_{t-1}$ is not equal for positive and negative values of ε_{t-1} that are equal apart from sign. The standard ARCH/GARCH models are slope symmetric about zero since $\partial\sigma_t^2/\partial\varepsilon_{t-1} = 2\alpha_1\varepsilon_{t-1}$.
- Slope asymmetry about the minimum occurs if the absolute value of the slope $\partial\sigma_t^2/\partial\varepsilon_{t-1}$ is not equal for positive and negative deviations from the minimum that are equal apart from sign. The standard ARCH/GARCH models are also slope symmetric about the minimum since $\partial\sigma_t^2/\partial\varepsilon_{t-1} = 2\alpha_1\varepsilon_{t-1}$.

16.7.3a The AGARCH and GJR asymmetric models

To see how these definitions work consider some suggested asymmetric models. First the AGARCH(1, 1) model – see Engle and Ng (*op. cit.*) – given by:

$$\sigma_t^2 = \alpha_0 + \alpha_1[\varepsilon_{t-1} + \gamma]^2 + \beta_1\sigma_{t-1}^2$$
$$\text{AGARCH}(1, 1) \quad (16.29)$$

Then $\partial\sigma_t^2/\partial\varepsilon_{t-1} = 2\alpha_1(\varepsilon_{t-1} + \gamma)$, which is 0 at $\varepsilon_{t-1} = -\gamma$, hence there is off-zero asymmetry. There is also slope asymmetry about zero; for $\gamma > 0$ the slope is steeper in absolute value for $\varepsilon_{t-1} > 0$ than for $\varepsilon_{t-1} < 0$. For example, with $\gamma = 0.5$, $\alpha_1 = 0.6$ then for $\varepsilon_{t-1} = +1$ the slope is $1.2(1 + 0.5) = 1.60$, whereas for $\varepsilon_{t-1} = -1$ it is $1.2(-1 + 0.5) = -0.6$. However, about the minimum of $\varepsilon_{t-1} = -\gamma$ the slope is symmetric. In sum AGARCH displaces the minimum from zero but is symmetric about this displacement. An example of an AGARCH news impact curve and the slope of the curve are shown in Figure 16.5. (The slope curves for the ARCH/GARCH and EGARCH models are also given in the lower panels of Figures 16.3 and 16.4, respectively.)

Asymmetry could also be introduced by distinguishing the sign of the shock and there are various ways to do this. One of the simplest is to separate the positive and negative shocks and

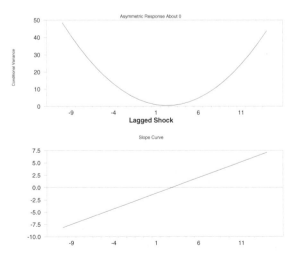

Figure 16.5 *News impact curve for AGARCH model*

allow them to have different coefficients in an ARCH or GARCH model. That is define:

$$\varepsilon_{t-1}^+ = \varepsilon_{t-1} \text{ for } \varepsilon_{t-1} \geq 0$$
$$\equiv 0 \text{ for } \varepsilon_{t-1} < 0; \text{ and}$$
$$\varepsilon_{t-1}^- = \varepsilon_{t-1} \text{ for } \varepsilon_{t-1} < 0$$
$$\equiv 0 \text{ for } \varepsilon_{t-1} \geq 0$$

Then, for example, a simple extension of the basic GARCH(p, q) model is given by:

$$\sigma_t^2 = \alpha_0 + \sum_{i=1}^{q} \alpha_i^+ (\varepsilon_{t-i}^+)^2 + \sum_{i=1}^{q} \alpha_i^- (\varepsilon_{t-i}^-)^2$$

$$+ \sum_{j=1}^{p} \beta_j \sigma_{t-j}^2 \qquad (16.30)$$

This reduces to the standard GARCH(p, q) model if $\alpha_i^+ = \alpha_i^-$ for $i = 1, \dots, q$, which are testable restrictions; if these conditions hold then the sign of the shock is not distinguished. An equivalent way of formulating this model is to keep the original GARCH(p, q) specification but add either (but not both) lags of ε_t^+ or ε_t^-. (Estimated versions of these two ways of writing the model may differ slightly because they may not converge to exactly the same numerical values.) ε_t^- is usually added because of the emphasis that negative shocks (bad news) have a greater impact on volatility than positive shocks (good news). This formulation is:

$$\sigma_t^2 = \alpha_0 + \sum_{i=1}^{q} \alpha_i^+ \varepsilon_{t-i}^2 + \sum_{i=1}^{q} \delta_i (\varepsilon_{t-i}^-)^2$$

$$+ \sum_{j=1}^{p} \beta_j \sigma_{t-j}^2 \qquad (16.31)$$

The hypothesis of interest for symmetry is that $\delta_i = 0$ for $i = 1, \dots, q$. In the popular GARCH(1, 1) case this is $\delta_1 = 0$ in:

$$\sigma_t^2 = \alpha_0 + \alpha_1^+ \varepsilon_{t-1}^2 + \delta_1 (\varepsilon_{t-1}^-)^2$$
$$+ \beta_1 \sigma_{t-1}^2 \qquad (16.32)$$

This specification is due to Glosten, Jagannathan and Runkle (1993), hereafter GJR. In the GJR model, α_1^+ is the coefficient on the positive (squared) shocks, and $\alpha_1^+ + \delta_1 = \alpha_1^-$ is the coefficient on the negative (squared) shocks.

The unconditional variance, $_u\sigma^2$, depends on the sign of the shocks. For positive and negative shocks the unconditional variances are:

$$_u\sigma_+^2 = \frac{\alpha_0}{(1 - \alpha_1^+ - \beta_1)} \quad \text{for positive shocks} \qquad (16.33a)$$

$$_u\sigma_-^2 = \frac{\alpha_0}{(1 - \alpha_1^- - \beta_1)} \quad \text{for negative shocks} \qquad (16.33b)$$

and $_u\sigma_-^2 > {}_u\sigma_+^2$ for $\delta_1 > 0$; that is the unconditional variance is larger for negative shocks.

The news impact curve for the GJR model is centred at ε_{t-1}, but is slope asymmetric about zero; that is, there are different slopes on positive and negative sides of $\varepsilon_{t-1} = 0$. On the positive side this is $2\alpha_1^+ \varepsilon_{t-1}$ and on the negative side this is $2(\alpha_1^+ + \delta_1)\varepsilon_{t-1}$; hence for $\delta_1 > 0$ the slope is steeper (in absolute value) on the negative side and so bad news has a bigger effect than good news. An example of the news impact curve for the GJR model is shown in Figure 16.6.

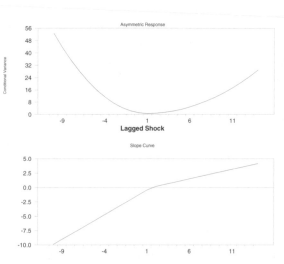

Figure 16.6   News impact curve for GJR model

A related asymmetric model that uses the conditional standard error rather than the conditional variance is due to Zakoian (1994), which he terms threshold GARCH – or TGARCH.

$$\sigma_t = \alpha_0 + \sum_{i=1}^{q} \alpha_i^+ \varepsilon_{t-1}^+ + \sum_{i=1}^{q} \alpha_i^- \varepsilon_{t-i}^-$$

$$+ \sum_{j=1}^{p} \beta_j \sigma_{t-j} \qquad (16.34)$$

Where ε_{t-1}^+ and ε_{t-1}^- are as defined before. Zakoian (*op. cit.*) suggests two advantages of modelling the standard error. First, Davidian and Carroll (1987) found that in the case of nonnormal distributions, absolute residuals give more efficient variance estimates than squared residuals; second, no positivity constraints are necessary as σ_t^2 will be positive whether σ_t is negative or positive.

16.7.4   Tests for asymmetry

Engle and Ng (*op. cit.*) suggest some test statistics which are useful in deciding whether asymmetry is present. Also the basic ARCH test described in section **16.4** is easily extended to test for slope asymmetry about zero. The Engle and Ng tests are designed to detect:

1. sign bias;
2. negative size bias;
3. positive size bias.

These tests can either be conducted on the raw data, that is without imposing a particular volatility model, or on the (scaled) residuals from a particular volatility model.

We first describe the general principles of the tests applied to the raw data. In step one estimate the model for the mean, that is $y_t = x_t\beta + \varepsilon_t$, and obtain the residuals $\hat{\varepsilon}_t$, where estimation is by OLS. In the case that returns, y_t, are unpredictable from the information set Ω_{t-1}, this is just a regression on a constant, otherwise it will be necessary to include variables predicting the

return in the regression; often a low order AR process is sufficient to 'filter' the raw returns data. Next define the following variables:

1. A dummy variable that indicates whether an estimated shock is negative, that is $S_t^- = 1$ if $\hat{\varepsilon}_t < 0$ and $S_t^- = 0$ if $\hat{\varepsilon}_t \geq 0$.
2. $\hat{\varepsilon}_{t-1}^- = \hat{\varepsilon}_{t-1}$ for $\hat{\varepsilon}_{t-1} < 0$
   $\equiv 0$ for $\hat{\varepsilon}_{t-1} \geq 0$
   These are the negative residuals, note that $\hat{\varepsilon}_t^- = S_t^- \hat{\varepsilon}_t$.
3. $\hat{\varepsilon}_{t-1}^+ = \hat{\varepsilon}_{t-1}$ for $\hat{\varepsilon}_{t-1} > 0$
   $\equiv 0$ for $\hat{\varepsilon}_{t-1} \leq 0$
   These are the positive residuals, note that $\hat{\varepsilon}_t^+ = (1 - S_t^-)\hat{\varepsilon}_t$.

In step two estimate the regression:

$$\hat{\varepsilon}_t^2 = a_0 + a_1 S_{t-1}^- + b_1 \hat{\varepsilon}_{t-1}^-$$

$$+ b_2 \hat{\varepsilon}_{t-1}^+ + \eta_t \qquad (16.35)$$

with the following interpretation. If the squared residuals are unaffected by the sign of the (lagged) residual then $a_1 = 0$, otherwise $a_1 \neq 0$ and sign matters. This is the sign bias test. If $b_1 \neq 0$ then the squared residuals are dependent on the size of the negative residual and, similarly, if $b_2 \neq 0$ then the squared residuals are dependent on the size of the positive residual. These tests could be carried out individually as 't' type tests, which are asymptotically normal distributed, or jointly as a $\chi^2(3)$ test calculated as T times R^2 from the regression (16.35), or as an (approximate) F test with 3 and $T - 4$ degrees of freedom. The test could be extended to consider the residuals at a longer lag length by defining S_{t-j}^-, $\hat{\varepsilon}_{t-j}^-$ and $\hat{\varepsilon}_{t-j}^+$ for $j \geq 1$. This might be particularly important for high frequency data, for example hourly, daily or weekly data. The test is referred to below as the EN test.

Carrying out these tests on the raw data is useful to indicate whether an asymmetric ARCH type model is needed. They could also be applied once a particular ARCH model has been estimated to test the adequacy of that model to departures from symmetry, and in this kind of application they are a useful model diagnostic test. The steps are similar to the case described above with two exceptions. First, the residuals (estimated shocks) and the indicator variables, $\hat{\varepsilon}_{t-1}^-$, $\hat{\varepsilon}_{t-1}^+$ and S_{t-1}^-, now relate to the ML estimator of the chosen ARCH specification. Second, the dependent variable in the auxiliary regression is the squared standardised (or scaled) residual $\hat{v}_t^2 = \hat{\varepsilon}_t^2/\hat{\sigma}_t^2$. (With raw data the null hypothesis includes the specification that $\sigma_t^2 = \sigma^2$, that is the conditional variance is constant, and the regression is unaltered if the dependent variable is multiplied by a constant, σ^{-1}; but in the ARCH case σ_t^2 is not constant and so this must be taken into account.)

The general test for the presence of an ARCH effect – see section **16.5** – can be modified to test for the possibility of asymmetric ARCH by distinguishing positive and negative residuals in the auxiliary regression. As before the first step is to estimate the mean (regression) by OLS to obtain the residuals $\hat{\varepsilon}_t$. The next step is to estimate the auxiliary regression:

$$\hat{\varepsilon}_t^2 = \varphi_0 + \rho_1^+(\hat{\varepsilon}_{t-1}^+)^2 + \cdots + \rho_q^+(\hat{\varepsilon}_{t-q}^+)^2$$
$$+ \rho_1^-(\hat{\varepsilon}_{t-1}^-)^2 + \cdots + \rho_q^-(\hat{\varepsilon}_{t-q}^-)^2 + \eta_t$$

(16.36)

The test statistic for the null hypothesis $\rho_i^+ = \rho_i^- = 0$ for $i = 1, \ldots, q$ is calculated as T times R^2 and asymptotically distributed as $\chi^2(2q)$ under the null of no symmetric *or* asymmetric ARCH effect. This will be referred to below as the MARCH (for modified ARCH) test. As before, the ARCH test is sometimes used in its F form here with $2q$ and $T - 2q - 1$ degrees of freedom.

An approach, which may be more informative, is to specify the regression to emphasise the difference from symmetry aspect of the alternative hypothesis, as in the GJR ARCH model. That is

$$\hat{\varepsilon}_t^2 = \varphi_0 + \rho_1^+\hat{\varepsilon}_{t-1}^2 + \cdots + \rho_q^+\hat{\varepsilon}_{t-q}^2$$
$$+ \kappa_1(\hat{\varepsilon}_{t-1}^-)^2 + \cdots + \kappa_q(\hat{\varepsilon}_{t-q}^-)^2 + \eta_t$$

(16.37)

The coefficients κ_i, $i = 1, \ldots, q$, are equal to 0 under the null of no asymmetric ARCH effects. The F test of this null against the alternative of asymmetric ARCH is approximately distributed as $F(q, T - 2q - 1)$ under the null. The alternative is that there are asymmetric ARCH effects (even if $\rho_i^+ = 0$ for $i = 1, \ldots, q$). If the null is not rejected then drop the $(\hat{\varepsilon}_{t-i}^-)^2$ terms and move to the standard test to see if there are any (symmetric) ARCH effects.

16.8   Examples

The first set of two examples, concerning the US inflation rate and the UK savings ratio, illustrate modelling the ARCH/GARCH process. The second set uses the resulting measure of volatility in the regression function and is, therefore, an example of ARCH-M modelling. The final example illustrates the importance of allowing for asymmetry in modelling returns on stock prices as represented by Standard and Poor's 500 index for the United States.

16.8.1   The US inflation rate

Bollerslev (1986) uses the model of inflation suggested in Engle and Kraft (1983) to illustrate the application of a GARCH process. The dependent variable is π_t defined as $100[\ln(P_t/P_{t-1})]$ where P_t is the implicit deflator for GNP and the sample period was 1948q2 to 1983q4 = 143 observations. An AR(4) model for π_t estimated by OLS resulted in (with 't'statistics in parentheses):

$$\pi_t = 0.240 + 0.552\pi_{t-1} + 0.177\pi_{t-2}$$
$$(3.00)\quad (6.650)\qquad (1.999)$$
$$+ 0.232\pi_{t-3} - 0.209\pi_{t-4} + \hat{\varepsilon}_t$$
$$(2.578)\qquad (-2.613)\qquad\qquad (16.38)$$
$$\hat{\sigma}_t^2 = \hat{\sigma}^2 = 0.282$$
$$(8.294)$$

Thus 0.282 is the assumed constant conditional variance. To gain an initial idea of whether an ARCH/GARCH model is necessary the autocorrelations in the squared OLS residuals, $\hat{\varepsilon}_t^2$, revealed significant values at lags 1, 3, 7, 9 and 10. The ARCH test was significant for $q = 1$, $q = 4$ and $q = 8$. These were pointers to an ARCH process with a long memory. That is high infla-tion leads to a high variance in inflation for several periods. The significant autocorrelations at long lags strongly suggest that an economical parameterisation of the conditional heteroscedasticity was as a GARCH rather than an ARCH process. Because of the long memory and the need to economise on the parameterisation, Engle and Kraft (*op. cit.*) fitted an ARCH(8) but with the coefficients restricted to decline linearly. Specifically their regression model with restricted ARCH(8) process estimated by ML was (with heteroscedastic consistent 't' statistics in {.} parentheses and asymptotic 't' statistics in (.) parentheses):

$$\pi_t = 0.138 + 0.423\pi_{t-1} + 0.222\pi_{t-2}$$
$$\{2.338\} \{5.222\} \qquad \{2.056\}$$
$$+ 0.377\pi_{t-3} - 0.175\pi_{t-4} + \hat{\varepsilon}_t$$
$$\{4.833\} \quad \{-1.683\} \qquad (16.39)$$

$$\hat{\sigma}_t^2 = 0.058 + 0.802 \sum_{i=1}^{8} \frac{(9-i)}{36} \hat{\varepsilon}_{t-i}^2$$

$$(1.757) \ (3.026) \qquad\qquad (16.40)$$

The LM test for including $\hat{\sigma}_{t-1}^2$ in the heteroscedasticity function was 4.57, which, compared to the 5% critical value of $\chi^2(1) = 3.84$, is significant. Hence, re-estimating using ML and assuming a GARCH(1, 1) seemed sensible and resulted in:

$$\pi_t = 0.141 + 0.433\pi_{t-1} + 0.229\pi_{t-2}$$
$$\{2.350\} \quad \{5.345\} \qquad \{2.082\}$$
$$+ 0.349\pi_{t-3} - 0.162\pi_{t-4} + \hat{\varepsilon}_t$$
$$\{4.532\} \quad \{-1.557\} \qquad (16.41)$$

$$\hat{\sigma}_t^2 = 0.007 + 0.135\hat{\varepsilon}_{t-1}^2 + 0.829\hat{\sigma}_{t-1}^2$$
$$(0.167) \ (1.928) \qquad (12.191) \qquad (16.42)$$

The LM statistic for the next higher order GARCH, that is GARCH(1, 2) or GARCH(2, 1), was 3.80 which is just not significant at the 5% level.

Some other aspects of the comparative results are worth mentioning. First, we can also derive the unconditional variance using the estimated ARCH/GARCH parameters. With no ARCH effects the estimate is 0.282; with the restricted ARCH(8) model it is 0.293 and with GARCH(1, 1) it is 0.194. The latter model offers tighter confidence intervals for the long-run forecast of inflation. Although attention is focused on the heteroscedasticity specification, there are some changes of note in the estimates of the coefficients in the AR(4) model; for example, the coefficient on π_{t-1} is variously 0.552, 0.423 and 0.433 depending on the specification of the conditional variance. Recall, however, that both OLS and ML yield consistent estimators. The difference is primarily in how a total effect is distributed over the lags. To see this we derive the implicit long run, equivalently the f step ahead forecast of inflation as $f \to \infty$. In the same order the estimates are: 0.967, 0.902, 0.934 (all % p.q.), and there is, thus, little difference in the long-run forecast of inflation.

16.8.2   The UK savings ratio

This example concerns the savings ratio, SR_t, for the United Kingdom, which is plotted in Figure 16.7A for the (overall) sample period 1955q1 to 1990q2. An AR(4) model for SR_t resulted in (with heteroscedasticity consistent 't' statistics in {.} parentheses):

$$SR_t = 0.009 + 0.427SR_{t-1} + 0.220SR_{t-2}$$
$$\{2.250\} \{4.313\} \qquad \{1.880\}$$
$$+ 0.100SR_{t-3} + 0.152SR_{t-4} + \hat{\varepsilon}_t$$
$$\{1.075\} \qquad \{1.788\}$$
$$(16.43)$$

1956q1 to 1990q2;
$\hat{\sigma}_t = \hat{\sigma} = 0.014$; dw $= 1.943$;
SC(4) $= 4.273[0.370]$; FF(1) $= 0.497[0.481]$;
JB(2) $= 1.868[0.393]$; HS(1) $= 2.459[0.117]$

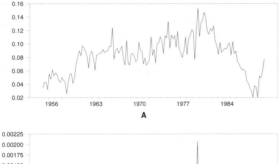

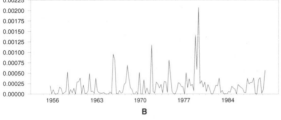

Figure 16.7 *The UK savings ratio. A – 1955q1 to 1990q2. B – Squared OLS residuals*

All the diagnostics are satisfactory. In particular there are no indications of either unaccounted for serial correlation, with SC(4) = 4.273 and an msl of 37%, or heteroscedasticity, with HS(1) = 2.459 and an msl of 11.7%. The squared residuals are graphed in Figure 16.7B. The clustering of $\hat{\varepsilon}_t^2$ is suggestive of an ARCH process; note, especially, the cluster of large $\hat{\varepsilon}_t^2$ at the end of the 1970s, and the cluster of small $\hat{\varepsilon}_t^2$ around 1984/1985.

To test for the presence of an ARCH effect, initially the fourth order auxiliary regression was estimated:

$$\hat{\varepsilon}_t^2 = 0.0001 + 0.154\hat{\varepsilon}_{t-1}^2 + 0.183\hat{\varepsilon}_{t-2}^2$$
$$(4.025) \quad (1.741) \quad\quad (2.043)$$

$$- 0.088\hat{\varepsilon}_{t-3}^2 + 0.008\hat{\varepsilon}_{t-4}^2 + \hat{\omega}_t$$
$$(-0.983) \quad\quad (0.093) \quad\quad\quad (16.44)$$

1957q1 to 1990q2;
$TR^2 = 134(0.0634) = 8.496[0.0748]$;
$F(4, 129) = 2.185[0.074]$;
't' statistics in parentheses.

The test statistic for ARCH(4) is $TR^2 = 8.496$ with msl = 7.48%; or in the *F* version $F(4, 129) = 2.187$ with msl = 7.43%. Note that the third and fourth lagged values are not significant and the

coefficient on the former is negative. Excluding these resulted in:

$$\hat{\varepsilon}_t^2 = 0.0001 + 0.138\hat{\varepsilon}_{t-1}^2 + 0.172\hat{\varepsilon}_{t-2}^2$$
$$(4.253) \quad (1.595) \quad\quad (1.992)$$

$$(16.45)$$

1957q1 to 1990q2;
$TR^2 = 134(0.0563) = 7.544[0.023]$;
$F(2, 131) = 3.915[0.022]$;
't' statistics in parentheses.

The LM test statistic for ARCH(2) has an msl of 2.3%, which, therefore, supports the view that there is an ARCH effect present in the conditional variance.

The results of ML estimation of the AR(4) equation for SR_t combined with different specifications of the ARCH/GARCH process are reported in Table 16.1. An ARCH(2) was specified first; however, despite the evidence from the LM test the estimated coefficient on $\hat{\varepsilon}_{t-2}^2$ was not significant, with an asymptotic 't' ratio of 0.016/ 0.197 = 0.080. An ARCH(1) process is reported next; the estimated coefficient on $\hat{\varepsilon}_{t-1}^2$ is 0.238 with an asymptotic 't' ratio of 1.897 and a one-sided msl of 3%. (The coefficient on SR_{t-3} is now insignificant, but omitting it did not alter the results.) For the ARCH(1) model, the estimated unconditional variance is

$$_u\hat{\sigma}^2 = 0.000147/(1 - 0.238) = 0.000193$$

compared to

$$_u\hat{\sigma}^2 = (0.01415)^2 = 0.00020$$

for OLS estimation. Even though there is some variation between OLS and ML estimates of the individual coefficients of the AR(4) model, the estimated long-run savings ratio is virtually identical at 8.76% and 8.74%, respectively.

Some alternative ARCH models are also reported in Table 16.1. A GARCH(1, 1) was estimated; however, the coefficient on $\hat{\sigma}_{t-1}^2$ was small and insignificant, with an asymptotic 't' ratio of 0.308, suggesting no GARCH as opposed to an ARCH effect. An EGARCH model was

Table 16.1   *ARCH/GARCH models for the UK savings ratio*

ARCH(2)				
constant	SR_{t-1}	SR_{t-2}	SR_{t-3}	SR_{t-4}
0.009	0.518	0.211	−0.164	0.182
(2.250)	(4.211)	(2.425)	(−1.325)	(2.092)
constant	$\hat{\varepsilon}_{t-1}^2$	$\hat{\varepsilon}_{t-2}^2$		
0.0001	0.229	0.016		
(11.480)	(1.163)	(0.080)		
ARCH(1)				
constant	SR_{t-1}	SR_{t-2}	SR_{t-3}	SR_{t-4}
0.009	0.520	0.213	−0.021	0.182
(2.053)	(5.781)	(2.509)	(−0.227)	(2.109)
constant	$\hat{\varepsilon}_{t-1}^2$	$\hat{\varepsilon}_{t-2}^2$		
0.0001	0.238	−		
(14.349)	(1.897)	−		
GARCH(1, 1)				
constant	SR_{t-1}	SR_{t-2}	SR_{t-3}	SR_{t-4}
0.009	0.513	0.214	−0.015	0.181
(2.050)	(5.349)	(2.479)	(−0.150)	(2.055)
constant	$\hat{\varepsilon}_{t-1}^2$	$\hat{\varepsilon}_{t-2}^2$	$\hat{\sigma}_{t-1}^2$	
0.0001	0.223	−	0.072	
(6.847)	(1.597)	−	(0.308)	
EGARCH(0, 1)				
constant	SR_{t-1}	SR_{t-2}	SR_{t-3}	SR_{t-4}
0.008	0.477	0.214	0.021	0.184
(3.950)	(4.318)	(2.548)	(0.191)	(2.017)
constant	$\dfrac{\hat{\varepsilon}_{t-1}}{\hat{\sigma}_{t-1}}$	$\left\|\dfrac{\hat{\varepsilon}_{t-1}}{\hat{\sigma}_{t-1}}\right\| - \mu$		
−8.589	0.143	0.297		
(6.847)	(1.196)	(1.471)		
ABSGARCH(1)				
constant	SR_{t-1}	SR_{t-2}	SR_{t-3}	SR_{t-4}
0.008	0.473	0.208	0.033	0.215
(1.772)	(5.089)	(2.402)	(0.354)	(2.400)
constant	$\|\hat{\varepsilon}_{t-1}\|$			
0.011	0.224			
(8.162)	(1.912)			

Notes: Estimation period, 1956q1 to 1990q2; ML asymptotic 't' statistics in parentheses.

estimated although, as there was no evidence of a GARCH effect, an EGARCH(0, 1) is reported. The estimated coefficient on the asymmetry term $\hat{\varepsilon}_{t-1}/\hat{\sigma}_{t-1}$ is 0.143 with an asymptotic 't' statistic of 1.196, which is not significant at conventional levels, so there appears no advantage of the EGARCH specification in this case. Finally, since there was a suggestion in the EGARCH(0, 1) model that the absolute value term was contributing something, the ABSGARCH(1) model was estimated. The coefficient on $|\hat{\varepsilon}_{t-1}|$ is 0.224 with an asymptotic 't' statistic of 1.912, and so is comparable to the ARCH(1) model.

Finally, the estimated conditional variances for the ARCH(1) and ABSGARCH(1) models are plotted Figures 16.8A and 16.8B, respectively. For the ARCH(1) model, apart from scale, the pattern is (as expected) close to that for the squared residuals in Figure 16.7B. The (conditional) heteroscedasticity is clearly evident.

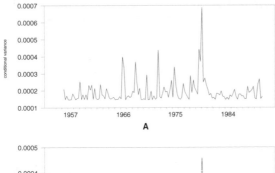

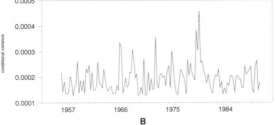

Figure 16.8 *The UK savings ratio. A – ARCH(1) conditional variance. B – ABSGARCH(1) conditional variance*

In the ABSGARCH case the conditional heteroscedasticity is 'flattened' slightly relative to the ARCH case but, nevertheless, still apparent.

16.8.3 ARCH-M applied to excess returns

ELR's application of the ARCH-M model to the excess holding period yield on a long bond relative to a short bond is instructive of the economics and econometrics of ARCH-M modelling. Consider an economy with two assets, the first yields a certain return of r_t, the second yields an uncertain total (comprising coupon and capital gain/loss) of q_t with mean return θ and variance ν, both initially assumed constant. The prices of the assets are normalised on the first which, therefore, has a price of 1 and the second has a price p_t (which we take to be expressed in 'dollars'). The excess return per dollar held in shares of the second (risky) asset is:

$$\text{excess return per dollar: } y_t = \frac{q_t}{p_t} - r_t \tag{16.46}$$

with mean

$$E\{y_t\} = \mu_t = \frac{\theta}{p_t} - r_t$$

and variance

$$\text{Var}(y_t) = \frac{1}{p_t^2} \nu$$

(p_t is assumed exogenous).

The cost to the investor of $y_t > 0$ is $\text{Var}(y_t) > 0$; that is while it might be possible to earn a positive excess return by investing in the uncertain asset relative to the sure asset, there is a probability that the investor takes a loss, that is $y_t < 0$. (A more precise notation as suggested in Chapter 3, would distinguish between the random variable excess returns, say y_t, and a particular outcome, say Y_t with, if y_t is normally distributed, $Y_t \in [-\infty, +\infty]$.)

The model in Tobin's (1958) classic article, briefly outlined in Chapter 10, fits into this framework. In Tobin's model there are two assets, cash and a capital uncertain asset, and the trade-off is between (expected) return and risk: a higher risk is compensated for by an increase in the expected return. If returns, which are a random variable, are normally distributed only the first two moments, that is the mean and the variance, matter for the trade-off. Assuming the (general) price level is constant, cash has a certain zero rate of return. Other assessments of the relation between return and risk include Fama and Schwert (1977), French, Schwert and Stambaugh (1987) and Engle, Ng and Rothschild (1990).

ELR formalise the intuitive notion that the mean excess return will be positively related to the risk as measured by the variance. This leads to the model

$$y_t = \mu_t + \varepsilon_t \tag{16.47}$$

with $\text{Var}(\varepsilon_t \mid \Omega) = \sigma_t^2$ where Ω represents all available information. There are two points to note about this specification. First, the mean excess return, μ_t, is not assumed constant; second, the conditional variance, σ_t^2, of ε_t is not assumed constant. The value added in ELR's model is to specify the conditional variance as an ARCH process; this is likely to account for the stylised empirical observation that large like signed excess returns tend to cluster together, as suggested by Mandelbrot (1963). Also, based on their extension of the Tobin type model of asset holding, the mean return, and hence the excess return, is specified as a positive function of the conditional standard deviation σ_t. That is the riskier the asset the larger the mean return. Together these result in the model:

$$y_t = \mu_t + \varepsilon_t \tag{16.48a}$$
$$\mu_t = \beta + \delta\sigma_t \tag{16.48b}$$
$$\sigma_t^2 \sim \text{ARCH}(q) \tag{16.48c}$$

β is a constant which might reflect a number of factors. μ_t may be a nonlinear function of σ_t, in which case a constant should be included in a linear approximation to this function; if investors work in preferred habitats – see Chapter 11 – then there may be a constant difference between yields on long and short bonds which is not arbitraged away. The specification of σ_t^2 is an empirical matter and might, for example, include other variables which represent risk, or a declining lag specification on ε_{t-i}^2. The presence of $\delta\sigma_t$ can be seen as capturing a time varying risk premium (or the volatility of excess returns).

ELR use yield data, for 1960q1 to 1984q3, on 6-month and 3-month US T-Bills, the former being the 'long' rate, denoted R_t and the latter the 'short' rate, denoted r_t, both rates expressed as % per quarter. To define the excess return y_t, as in Chapter 11, consider two strategies: first, invest A\$ long, to receive $A\$(1 + R_t)(1 + R_t) = A\$(1 + R_t)^2$ after two quarters; alternatively, invest A\$ short and rollover after one quarter to receive $A\$(1 + r_t)(1 + r_{t+1})$. There is no excess return if $(1 + R_t)^2 = (1 + r_t)(1 + r_{t+1})$. Divide both sides of this expression by $(1 + r_{t+1})$, and

then, to obtain a rate, subtract 1 from each side; this is the 'excess' rate of return y_t. That is

$$y_t \equiv \left[\frac{(1 + R_t)^2}{(1 + r_{t+1})} - 1\right] - ((1 + r_t) - 1)$$
$$\equiv \left[\frac{(1 + R_t)^2}{(1 + r_{t+1})} - (1 + r_t)\right] \tag{16.49}$$

The regression of y_t on a constant gave:

$$y_t = 0.142 + \hat{\varepsilon}_t \tag{16.50}$$
$$(4.04)$$
$$\hat{\sigma}_t = \hat{\sigma} = 0.351$$

OLS 't' statistic in parentheses.
ARCH test: $TR^2 = 10.1[0.000]$

This regression tells us that the (sample) mean excess return is 0.142% p.q. $= 0.568\%$ p.a. No other variables are included in this regression but it would be wise in applications of this model to check that there is no serial correlation in $\hat{\varepsilon}_t$ and, in particular, that y_t is not predictable from lagged y_t. The LM test for the absence of the ARCH effect was $TR^2 = 10.1$, which is distributed as $\chi^2(1)$ if the null is true, and is clearly significant (msl $= 0$).

An initial, linearly restricted, ARCH(4) model gave:

$$y_t = 0.048 + \hat{\varepsilon}_t \tag{16.51a}$$
$$(3.77)$$

$$\hat{\sigma}_t^2 = 0.004 + 1.90 \sum_{s=1}^{4} w_s \hat{\varepsilon}_{t-s} \tag{16.51b}$$
$$(0.95) \quad (7.30)$$

ML 't' statistics in parentheses; and $w_1 = 0.4$, $w_2 = 0.3$, $w_3 = 0.2$, $w_4 = 0.1$

Of particular note was the highly significant (asymptotic 't' $= 7.3$) coefficient of $1.90 > 1$ implying persistent shocks and a nonstationary variance. Including an ARCH effect (but not yet including it in the mean function) results in the mean excess return falling to 0.048% at a quarterly rate – about 0.2% at an annual rate.

After some experimentation the preferred ARCH-M model, that is now including a time varying risk premium in the mean function, was:

$$y_t = 0.355 + 0.135 \ln(\hat{\sigma}_t) + \hat{\varepsilon}_t \qquad (16.52a)$$
$$(4.38) \quad (3.36)$$

$$\hat{\sigma}_t^2 = 0.005 + 1.480 \sum_{s=1}^{4} w_s \hat{\varepsilon}_{t-s} \qquad (16.52b)$$
$$\phantom{\hat{\sigma}_t^2 = }(2.22) \quad (5.56)$$

ML 't' statistics in parentheses.

All coefficients are significant. The ARCH effect continues to be strong. The time varying risk premium is significant with estimated coefficient of the right sign, that is increased risk is associated with an increased excess return, and an asymptotic 't' statistic of 3.36. If all the shocks are zero, $\hat{\sigma}_t^2 = 0.005$ and, hence, the estimated excess return is

$$y_t = 0.355 + 0.135 \ln(\sqrt{0.005})$$
$$= -0.003\% \text{ p.q.}$$

which is plausibly close to zero.

16.8.4 Testing for asymmetry in the returns for Standard and Poor's 500 index for the United States

The tests for asymmetry of section **16.7.4** are illustrated with weekly data for Standard and Poor's 500 index for the United States over the period 1 January 1980 to 22 June 1998, a total of 963 observations. Denoting the level of the index as y_t. returns are then calculated as $R_t = 100[\ln(y_t/y_{t-1})]$. As ε_t has the interpretation of news, and should be unpredictable from information at $t - 1$, we first establish whether there is any autoregressive structure in the returns series that could be used to predict current returns. A 'general' model with five lags was estimated and then an F test was used to see if any of the lags were redundant. (That is first test whether lag 5 can be removed, then whether

lags 4 and 5 can be removed and so on.) The test sequence suggested lags 1 and 2 should remain, the $F(4, 954)$ statistic being 1.968 with an msl of just under 10%. Normally a sequence like this would use individual significance levels below 10% to avoid the cumulated type 1 error becoming too large; however, in this case the first and second lags were individually significant in the general regression with marginal significance levels of 0.4% and 2.1%, respectively. Removing the redundant lags resulted in a regression free from serial correlation in the residuals with $SC(5) = 4.474$, which has an msl of 48.3%. The estimated regression was:

$$R_t = 0.280 - 0.088R_{t-1} - 0.069R_{t-2} + \hat{\varepsilon}_t$$
$$(3.671)(-2.756) \quad (-2.142)$$
$$(16.53)$$

$dw = 2.002$, $SC(5) = 4.474[0.483]$
't' statistics in parentheses.

Estimated news is the residual $\hat{\varepsilon}_t$, which has a skewness coefficient of -2.688 indicating a skew to the left and a kurtosis coefficient of 39.301 indicating a leptokurtic distribution, which is too peaked and with long tails compared to the normal distribution (where the skewness and kurtosis coefficients are 0 and 3, respectively).

The first test is the standard one for ARCH effects – see section **16.5**. An initial regression with lags 1 to 5 of $\hat{\varepsilon}_{t-i}^2$ gave an ARCH test statistic of 6.728 distributed as $\chi^2(5)$, with msl of 24.1%, which is not significant. However, some of the lags were redundant and the regression could be reduced to the first two lags with no loss of fit. The test statistic is now significant with $ARCH(2) = 6.417$ and $msl = 4\%$. The resulting regression was:

$$\hat{\varepsilon}_t^2 = 4.910 + 0.027\hat{\varepsilon}_{t-1}^2 + 0.076\hat{\varepsilon}_{t-2}^2 + \hat{v}_t$$
$$\phantom{\hat{\varepsilon}_t^2 = }(4.240) \quad (0.845) \qquad (2.367)$$
$$\phantom{\hat{\varepsilon}_t^2 = xxxxxxxxxxxxxxxxxxxxxxxxxx}(16.54)$$

$ARCH(2) = 6.417[0.040]$
't' statistics in parentheses.

This regression suggests that it will be important to include the second lag of $\hat{\varepsilon}_t^2$ in subsequent tests for asymmetry, and that the ARCH specification should either directly include the second lag or, as in a GARCH specification, include a lag of the conditional variance so that higher order lags are implicitly included.

The simple extension of the ARCH test, which distinguishing the signs of the residuals, can be estimated in two alternative formulations. These gave, with (16.55) the parallel of (16.37) and (16.56) the parallel of (16.36):

$$\hat{\varepsilon}_t^2 = 5.146 - 0.037\hat{\varepsilon}_{t-1}^2 + 0.029\hat{\varepsilon}_{t-2}^2$$
$$(4.126)(-0.242) \qquad (0.189)$$
$$+ 0.674(\hat{\varepsilon}_{t-1}^-)^2 + 0.048(\hat{\varepsilon}_{t-2}^-)^2 + \hat{\eta}_t$$
$$(0.424) \qquad (0.304)$$
$$(16.55)$$

$$\hat{\varepsilon}_t^2 = 5.146 - 0.037(\hat{\varepsilon}_{t-1}^+)^2 + 0.029(\hat{\varepsilon}_{t-2}^+)^2$$
$$(4.126)(-0.242) \qquad (0.189)$$
$$+ 0.029(\hat{\varepsilon}_{t-1}^-)^2 + 0.078(\hat{\varepsilon}_{t-2}^-)^2 + \hat{\eta}_t$$
$$(0.902) \qquad (2.382)$$
$$(16.56)$$

MARCH(4) = 6.687[0.153]
$F(2, 956) = 0.135[0.873]$

$$\hat{\varepsilon}_t^2 = 5.156 + 0.029(\hat{\varepsilon}_{t-2}^+)^2 + 0.078(\hat{\varepsilon}_{t-2}^-)^2 + \hat{\eta}_t$$
$$(4.331) \quad (0.186) \qquad (2.409)$$
$$(16.57)$$

MARCH(2) = 5.803[0.055]
$F(1, 958) = 0.098[0.754]$
't' statistics in parentheses.

The first two regressions 'nest' the standard ARCH test regression. In the first version the coefficient on a typical lagged $\hat{\varepsilon}_t^-$ is κ_i, which is the difference between the coefficient on the squared residual and the squared negative residual. The test statistic for the null hypothesis that these are jointly 0, and hence there is no difference according to sign, is $F(2, 956) = 0.135$, which is not significant. Naturally the same test statistic results from the second regression on testing whether the coefficients on the positive and negative squared residuals are

equal. However, what the second regression indicates is that $\hat{\varepsilon}_{t-2}^-$ may be a key term in the regression. Dropping the first lags gives an almost unchanged fit and regression coefficients, so emphasising the role of $\hat{\varepsilon}_{t-2}^-$, see (16.57). Note that the coefficient on $\hat{\varepsilon}_{t-2}^-$ is considerably larger than the coefficient on $\hat{\varepsilon}_{t-2}^+$, so bad news does seem to have a bigger impact. Formally, though, the test that the coefficients are equal is not rejected with an msl of 75.4%. So at this stage there are ARCH effects, suggested by the significance of the standard ARCH test and the use of 5.5% for the MARCH(2) test statistic, but not yet evidence of asymmetry.

The Engle and Ng (*op. cit.*) tests for sign and size bias, allowing for a second lag, resulted in the following regression (these are the tests on the 'raw data').

$$\hat{\varepsilon}_t^2 = 4.523 - 1.020S_{t-1}^- - 4.109S_{t-2}^-$$
$$(1.416)(-0.323) \qquad (-1.300)$$
$$- 2.539\hat{\varepsilon}_{t-1}^- - 1.761\hat{\varepsilon}_{t-2}^- - 0.026\hat{\varepsilon}_{t-1}^+$$
$$(-3.118) \quad (-2.160) \quad (-0.023)$$
$$+ 0.071\hat{\varepsilon}_{t-2}^+ + \hat{\zeta}_t \qquad (16.58)$$
$$(0.063)$$

EN(6) = 17.873[0.006]
't' statistics in parentheses.

The test statistic for asymmetric effects is highly significant with EN(6) = 17.873, which has an msl of 0.6%. Individual tests suggest that the negative size bias for the first and second lags is what is important; the test statistic, distributed as $\chi^2(2)$ under the null of (just) no negative size bias, has a sample value of 15.214 with an msl of 0.

Overall, these tests suggest that modelling predictable volatility in the return should take account of the potential asymmetry. However, first, to establish a baseline, a standard GARCH(1, 1) was estimated resulting in:

Standard GARCH(1,1):
$$\hat{\sigma}_t^2 = 0.333 + 0.220\hat{\varepsilon}_{t-1}^2 + 0.746\hat{\sigma}_{t-1}^2 \quad (16.59)$$
$$(5.326) \quad (5.832) \qquad (14.422)$$

The estimated coefficients are plausible, but the test results suggest that an asymmetric GARCH is likely to be needed. Estimating an asymmetric GARCH resulted in:

$$\hat{\sigma}_t^2 = 1.339 + 0.027(\hat{\varepsilon}_{t-1}^+)^2 + 0.636(\hat{\varepsilon}_{t-1}^-)^2$$
$$(5.326)\ (0.815) \qquad\quad (6.028)$$
$$+ 0.464\hat{\sigma}_{t-1}^2 \qquad\qquad\qquad (16.60)$$
$$(6.937)$$

The estimated coefficients suggest a strong asymmetric effect with negative shocks, that is bad news, having a much greater impact than positive shocks. Imposing the constraint that the coefficients are equal gives the standard GARCH(1, 1) model, but results in a test statistic, which is distributed as $\chi^2(1)$ under the null of equality, of 32.822 with an msl of 0. Hence, symmetry is rejected. To check that there are no further asymmetric effects the test statistics for sign and size bias were calculated. The joint test was calculated from the following regression:

$$\hat{v}_t^2 = 1.169 - 0.173S_{t-1}^- - 0.145S_{t-2}^-$$
$$(5.550)(-0.817) \qquad (-0.690)$$
$$- 0.078\hat{\varepsilon}_{t-1}^- - 0.013\hat{\varepsilon}_{t-2}^- - 0.086\hat{\varepsilon}_{t-1}^+$$
$$(-0.566) \quad (-0.092) \quad (-0.542)$$
$$- 0.045\hat{\varepsilon}_{t-2}^+ + \hat{\zeta}_t \qquad\qquad (16.61)$$
$$(-0.284)$$

EN(6) = 1.294[0.972]
't' statistics in parentheses.
$v_t^2 = \hat{\varepsilon}_t^2/\hat{\sigma}_t^2$

The joint test statistic for asymmetry is 1.294 with an msl of 97% and none of the individual tests are significant.

The asymmetric effect means that estimates of the long-run variance depend on the sign of the originating shock. An interesting point about the coefficients is that while for a positive shock they indicate that the process is covariance stationary, this is not the case for a negative shock. The covariance stationary condition is that the sum of the coefficients on $\hat{\varepsilon}_{t-1}^2$ and $\hat{\sigma}_{t-1}^2$ should be between 0 and 1. For positive shocks this sum is $0.027 + 0.464 = 0.491 < 1$ and, hence, covar-

iance stationary, giving an estimate of the unconditional variance for positive shocks.

$$_u\hat{\sigma}_+^2 = \frac{\hat{\alpha}_0}{(1 - \hat{\alpha}_1^+ - \hat{\beta}_1)}$$

$$= \frac{1.339}{(1 - 0.027 - 0.464)} = 2.633 \quad (16.62)$$

The sample variance is 5.52 and so the difference between these two suggests that much of the sample variance is accounted for by negative shocks.

For negative shocks the sum of the coefficients is $0.636 + 0.464 = 1.1 > 1$ indicating an IGARCH process that is not covariance stationary. A review question considers whether these estimates satisfy Nelson's condition for strict stationarity. Further, the sum can be restricted to the covariance stationary region without loss in a statistical sense. For example, restricting the sum $\hat{\alpha}_1^- + \hat{\beta}_1$ to 0.99 and 0.95, respectively, gives a test statistic, distributed as $\chi^2(1)$ under the null, of 1.347 with msl of 24.6% and 3.004 with msl of 8.3%. If the sum $\hat{\alpha}_1^- + \hat{\beta}_1$ is restricted to 0.95, then the evidence of asymmetry remains with $\hat{\alpha}_1^- = 0.528$ ('t' = 7.571) and $\hat{\alpha}_1^+ = 0.031$ ('t' = 0.898).

An interesting proposal is that the IGARCH process for negative shocks might be a result of the bad news of the October 1987 crash, perhaps better characterised as a special 'bang' that should be treated as an outlier, rather than forcing the parameters of the model to be unduly influenced. This is particularly relevant for a process which squares the shocks, thus placing even greater weight on particular outlying observations. The estimated shock for the crash was -32.5, which was 6.25 times the estimated conditional standard error for the same period, and by itself led to a 3.5 increase in the (unconditional) sample variance for negative shocks. Figure 16.9 provides a graphic illustration of this point. The estimated conditional variance from equation (16.60) is plotted in the top panel and the variance of the negative and positive

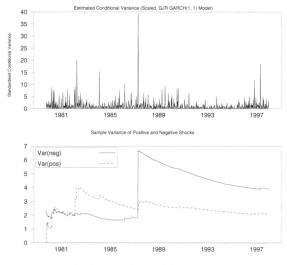

Figure 16.9 *Volatility for S&P 500*

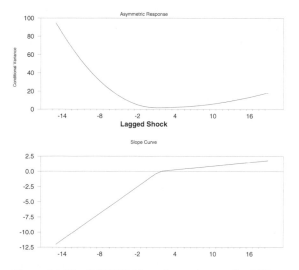

Figure 16.10 *S&P 500: News impact curve for GJR model*

shocks in the lower panel. Not only is the effect of the 1987 crash evident, but also the very different variances associated with the positive and negative shocks.

The asymmetric GARCH model was re-estimated for the before and after crash periods, with the following results.

Sample period: 4 February 1980 to 12 October 1987

$$\hat{\sigma}_t^2 = 1.988 + 0.003(\hat{\varepsilon}_{t-1}^+)^2 + 0.361(\hat{\varepsilon}_{t-1}^-)^2$$
$$\quad (3.758) \ (0.091) \qquad (5.398)$$

$$\quad + 0.047\hat{\sigma}_{t-1}^2 \qquad\qquad (16.63)$$
$$\quad (5.335)$$

$EN(6) = 4.256[0.642]; {}_u\hat{\sigma}_+^2 = 3.807; {}_u\hat{\sigma}_-^2 = 12.066$

Sample period: 30 November 1987 to 22 June 1998

$$\hat{\sigma}_t^2 = 1.751 + 0.051(\hat{\varepsilon}_{t-1}^+)^2 + 0.252(\hat{\varepsilon}_{t-1}^-)^2$$
$$\quad (3.628) \ (0.832) \qquad (2.431)$$

$$\quad + 0.364\hat{\sigma}_{t-1}^2 \qquad\qquad (16.64)$$
$$\quad (2.577)$$

$EN(6) = 6.267[0.394]; {}_u\hat{\sigma}_+^2 = 2.995; {}_u\hat{\sigma}_-^2 = 4.569$

The equations for both periods pass the EN tests for symmetry (that is no further asymmetric effects can be detected). In both equations it is the negative shocks that are driving the conditional variance, although their effects are not quite as strong as in the equation for the whole period. Also of note is the reduction in estimated persistence, as measured by $\hat{\alpha}_1^- + \hat{\beta}_1$, relative to the estimate for the complete period. There is no longer a suggestion that there is an IGARCH effect.

To illustrate, the news impact and slope curves are graphed in Figure 16.10 for the after-crash period. The news impact curve is still centred at 0, but its slope is $2(0.252)\varepsilon_{t-1}$ on the negative side but only $2(0.051)\varepsilon_{t-1}$ on the positive side.

16.9   Concluding remarks

One of the most interesting questions not addressed so far is what are the sources of the ARCH effect? The ARCH specification puts this question to one side. One aspect of the answer must concern the serial correlation of the process; interpreting shocks as news, means that the 'news arrival process' is serially correlated. One possibility, particularly relevant to financial markets, is that information, which was unforeseen and not incorporated into asset prices, comes to the market in 'lumps' rather than as a smooth process. At the risk of some simplification news comes in two forms. In one, information comes regularly and predictably but contains surprises. For example, officially published information on, for example, consumers' expenditure, inflation and company accounts only becomes available at certain times of the month or quarter, but contains departures from what was expected, which may affect asset prices. In the other form there is less predictability about the arrival of information, and the news is either in incorrect expectations about timing or in the information itself. Examples include natural disasters, changes of government and government policy.

With internationally based companies and internationally linked stock exchanges and financial markets, news from different parts of the world potentially impacts upon asset prices in episodes at discrete intervals. Thus markets may be tranquil and then volatile, volatile and then tranquil. These effects may be heightened by internal market dynamics as traders iterate to a common view and the news and volatility spills from one market to another before tranquillity is regained. With many markets trading at the same time volatility is transmitted internationally. The clustering of news and volatility spillovers are considered by Engle, Ito and Lin, EIL (1990), Hamao, Masulis and Ng (1990) and Lin, Engle and Ito (1994); and a model of market dynamics is provided by Kyle (1985). The EIL article prompted a number of studies using different frequencies of data and different trading areas. For example, Aggarwal and Park (1994) using daily data on US and Japanese equity prices, Booth, Martikainen and Tse (1997) on Scandinavian stock markets, Karolyi (1995) on US and Canadian stock markets and Brooks and Henry (1999) on US, Japanese and Australian stock markets.

Where to go next? A more technical treatment and survey of ARCH modelling including some estimation problems is Bera and Higgins (1995), which adds to the earlier Bollerslev, Chou and Kroner review of ARCH type specifications in financial econometrics that listed over 200 references. The most important area not covered in this chapter is multivariate ARCH specifications. These involve no new concepts, but rather a natural extension of ARCH principles to several series. For example, it is likely that asset prices in different geographical areas are linked; even though they are not precisely the same assets, news 'travels' and has ripple effects across several markets with spillover consequences. A leading example is the inter-market links between the leading stock exchanges, New York, London and Tokyo. Conceptually 'news' in New York affects returns in London and Tokyo, and news in London affects returns in New York and Tokyo – and so on. A way of modelling this process is to think of a multivariate ARCH process building upon a VAR model of N sets of returns, rather than a univariate model. We would then need to distinguish the ARCH inter-market links, defining news ε_{it} for $i = 1, \ldots, N$ markets and N linked conditional variances, σ_{it}^2. This gives rise to linked responses and multi-dimensional news impact curves with news from one market having an impact on the other markets. Analogously even within a single market different financial assets could be linked through their conditional variances and covariances. For an application to nominal exchange rates see Bollerslev (1990) and to Treasury Bills of different maturities see Engle, Ng and Rothschild (1990).

Review

1. The central theme of this chapter is that volatility matters, whether it is in determining, for example, asset prices, exchange rates or wage determination.

2. One way of measuring volatility is through the ARCH (autoregressive conditional heteroscedasticity) process due to Engle (1982).

3. The key distinction is between the unconditional variance and the conditional variance. The former can be constant while the latter is time varying.

4. For example, in the AR(1) model

$$y_t = \phi_0 + \phi_1 y_{t-1} + \varepsilon_t$$

the unconditional variance is a constant, $\sigma^2/(1 - \phi_1^2)$ where $E\{\varepsilon_t^2\} \equiv \sigma^2$, while the conditional variance

$$\text{Var}(y_t \mid y_{t-1}) \equiv \sigma_t^2$$

may vary over time.

5. Time varying conditional heteroscedasticity was suggested by Engle (1982). In the simplest case $\sigma_t^2 = \alpha_0 + \alpha_1 y_{t-1}^2$, so the conditional variance depends upon past values of squared y_{t-1}. This is an ARCH(1) process applied to the dependent variable.

6. Suppose y_t is inflation then an ARCH(1) process says high inflation last period leads to a large variance in inflation this period.

7. An ARCH(q) process is

$$\sigma_t^2 = \alpha_0 + \alpha_1 y_{t-1}^2 + \cdots + \alpha_q y_{t-q}^2$$

8. An important development is to extend the determination of the mean of y_t to a regression model, so that the ARCH process applies to the disturbance term. Now $y_t = x_t \beta + \varepsilon_t$ where

$$\varepsilon_t \equiv y_t - E\{y_t \mid X_t = x_t\} = y_t - x_t\beta$$

The ARCH(q) specification applied to the regression disturbance is: $\varepsilon_t = u_t\sigma_t$ and $\sigma_t^2 = \alpha_0 + \alpha_1\varepsilon_{t-1}^2 + \cdots + \alpha_q\varepsilon_{t-q}^2$.

9. A simple extension of the ARCH process is to GARCH processes. For example, the GARCH(1, 1) applied to the shocks is $\sigma_t^2 = \alpha_0 + \alpha_1\varepsilon_{t-1}^2 + \beta_1\sigma_{t-1}^2$.

10. The GARCH model can be interpreted as an infinite distributed lag on past ε_t^2. The general GARCH(p, q) is

$$\sigma_t^2 = \alpha_0 + \sum_{i=1}^{q} \alpha_i \varepsilon_{t-i}^2 + \sum_{j=1}^{p} \beta_j \sigma_{t-j}^2$$

11. As σ_t^2 is a variance it must be nonnegative (and will usually be positive); this imposes conditions on the ARCH/GARCH.

12. (i) In the ARCH(q) process for the unconditional variance to be finite and nonnegative we must have $\alpha_0 \geq 0$, $\alpha_i \geq 0$ and $0 \leq \sum_{i=1}^{q} \alpha_i < 1$.

    (ii) In the GARCH(p, q) process a necessary and sufficient condition for stationarity is $\sum_{i=1}^{q} \alpha_i + \sum_{j=1}^{p} \beta_j < 1$, this result is due to Bollerslev (1986, theorem 1).

13. In the widely applied GARCH(1, 1) model, $\sigma_t^2 = \alpha_0 + \alpha_1\varepsilon_{t-1}^2 + \beta_1\sigma_{t-1}^2$ estimation sometimes results in $\hat{\alpha}_1 + \hat{\beta}_1 \approx 1$, or even $\hat{\alpha}_1 + \hat{\beta}_1 > 1$. Engle and Bollerslev (1986) show that if $\alpha_1 + \beta_1 \geq 1$, the conditional variance is persistent to shocks.

14. By analogy to standard unit root processes, when $\alpha_1 + \beta_1 = 1$ the GARCH(p, q) model is said to be integrated, and is referred to as IGARCH(p,q), with drift α_0 if > 0. This looks like a random walk but Nelson (1990) points out that the analogy with a random walk is not precise.

15. In an ARCH(q) process with no lagged dependent variables in the regressors in the mean function, the OLS estimator of β is BLUE.

16. But OLS does not have minimum variance if we relax the class of estimators to include nonlinear rather than just linear estimators. In particular the maximum likelihood estimator is nonlinear and asymptotically efficient.

17. Testing for an ARCH(q) process is usually done with the LM principle which just requires estimation under the null hypothesis initially only requiring OLS estimation.

18. Estimate an auxiliary regression with squared OLS residuals $\hat{\varepsilon}_t^2$ regressed on a constant and $\hat{\varepsilon}_{t-1}^2, \ldots, \hat{\varepsilon}_{t-q}^2$. Then T times R^2 from this regression is asymptotically distributed as $\chi^2(q)$ when the null hypothesis is true. Rejection of the null hypothesis in favour of an ARCH(q) with q 'large', rule of thumb $q \geq 3$, is suggestive of a GARCH process.

19. In the absolute ARCH/GARCH model, as the name suggests, the absolute values of the innovations $|\varepsilon_t|$ are used. The GARCH(p, q) specification can then be applied either to the conditional variance, that is

$$\sigma_t^2 = \alpha_0 + \sum_{i=1}^{q} \alpha_i |\varepsilon_{t-i}| + \sum_{j=1}^{p} \beta_j \sigma_{t-j}^2$$

or alternatively to the conditional standard error

$$\sigma_t = \alpha_0 + \sum_{i=1}^{q} \alpha_i |\varepsilon_{t-i}| + \sum_{j=1}^{p} \beta_j \sigma_{t-j}$$

20. Nelson's EGARCH formulation has the advantage that it allows negative and positive shocks (innovations) to have different effects. The EGARCH(p, q) model is:

$$\ln(\sigma_t^2) = \alpha_0 + \sum_{i=1}^{q} \alpha_i \left[\frac{\varepsilon_t}{\sigma_t}\right]_{-i}$$

$$+ \sum_{i=1}^{q} \alpha_i^* \left[\left|\frac{\varepsilon_t}{\sigma_t}\right|_{-i} - \mu\right]$$

$$+ \sum_{j=1}^{p} \beta_j \ln(\sigma_{t-j}^2)$$

where $\mu = E\left\{\left|\frac{\varepsilon_t}{\sigma_t}\right|\right\} = \left[\frac{2}{\pi}\right]^{0.5}$ if $\varepsilon_t \sim N(0, 1)$.

21. Including the conditional variance or standard error in mean function, as in $y_t = x_t \beta + \delta \sigma_t + \varepsilon_t$, results in an ARCH-M model or a GARCH-M model. ARCH-M/GARCH-M

models have found widespread application where a time varying measure of risk is required.

22. The news impact curve summarises the effect of a shock, interpreted either as bad news (a negative shock) or good news (a positive shock), on the time varying conditional variance.

23. One problem with symmetric models of volatility, such as ARCH and GARCH, is that a one unit shock, $\varepsilon_t = +1$, or bad news, $\varepsilon_t = -1$, has the same impact on the conditional variance. However, the market may react differently to good and bad news.

24. The news impact curve is the relation between volatility σ_t^2 and news ε_{t-1}, with information dated at $t - 2$ or earlier held constant, and lagged conditional variances evaluated at the level of the unconditional variance.

25. The news impact curve is symmetric for ARCH and GARCH but asymmetric for EGARCH.

26. Another approach to asymmetry is to distinguish the sign of the shock as in the GJR (Glosten, Jagannathan and Runkle 1989) model.

27. Engle and Ng (1993) have suggested test statistics for sign bias, negative size bias and positive size bias. These tests can either be conducted on the raw data or on the (scaled) residuals from a particular volatility model.

28. Bollerslev (1986) uses the model of inflation suggested in Engle and Kraft (1983) to illustrate the application of a GARCH process. The dependent variable was US inflation.

29. Engle and Kraft (*op. cit.*) fitted an ARCH(8); however, Bollerslev found the more economically parameterised GARCH(1, 1) to fit well.

30. A second example concerned the UK savings ratio. An AR(4) model fitted the data well with satisfactory diagnostics for the absence of residual serial correlation and (conventional) heteroscedasticity. However, the LM test statistic for ARCH(2) has an msl of 2.3%,

suggesting a significant ARCH effect that was confirmed on estimating a number of alternative ARCH type specifications.

31. A third example, due to Engle, Lilien and Robins (1987), was of an ARCH-M model applied to the excess holding period yield on a long bond relative to a short bond. The LM test for the absence of the ARCH effect was $TR^2 = 10.1$, which is significant.

32. The log of the conditional standard error was included in the regression determining the mean excess return,

$$y_t = 0.355 + 0.135 \ln(\hat{\sigma}_t) + \hat{\varepsilon}_t$$

with a significant coefficient.

33. The final application was to weekly data for Standard and Poor's 500 index for the United States, with an emphasis on whether there was an asymmetric effect of 'news'.

34. The standard one for ARCH(2) effects was significant as was the test that distinguished the signs of the shocks (news). The Engle and Ng tests for asymmetry suggested an important negative sign bias.

35. Estimating a GJR asymmetric GARCH for the whole data period suggested a very significant asymmetric effect, with most of the work being done by bad news (that is negative shocks).

36. The sum of the coefficients on $(\hat{\varepsilon}_{t-1}^-)^2$ and $\hat{\sigma}_{t-1}^2$ was $0.636 + 0.464 = 1.1$, which indicates a process that is not covariance stationary. Splitting the overall period into before and after the October 1987 stock market crash resulted in a covariance stationary process for both periods and asymmetric with negative shocks more important than positive shocks.

Review questions

1. Given the AR(2) model

$$y_t = \phi_0 + \phi_1 y_{t-1} + \varepsilon_t$$

(i) Derive the unconditional variance. How does this differ from the conditional variance?

(ii) Derive the uncertainty of the prediction of y_{t+1}.

2. (i) In the ARCH(1) set-up of section **16.3.1** show that $\text{Cov}(\varepsilon_t, \varepsilon_s) = 0$ for $t \neq s$. (References: Bollerslev (1986, theorem 1) and Enders (1995, Chapter 3).)

(ii) If OLS is BLUE for β in the conditional expectation function,

$$(y_t \mid X_t = x_t) \sim N(x_t\beta, \sigma_t^2)$$

with σ_t^2 an ARCH(q) process, why is estimation by maximum likelihood preferable?

3. (i) Given the GARCH(1, 1) model

$$\sigma_t^2 = \alpha_0 + \alpha_0\varepsilon_{t-1}^2 + \beta_1\sigma_{t-1}^2$$

show that:

$$E\{\sigma_{t+f}^2 \mid \sigma_t^2\} = (\alpha_1 + \beta_1)^f \sigma_t^2$$

$$+ \alpha_0\left(\sum_{k=0}^{f-1}(\alpha_1 + \beta_1)^k\right)$$

(ii) Interpret this expression in terms of the persistence of shocks and their effect on the conditional variance. (Reference: Engle and Bollerslev (1986).)

4. Consider the following specification of a GARCH(1, 1) model.

$$\varepsilon_t = u_t\sigma_t; \quad E\{u_t\} = 0$$
$$\text{Var}(u_t) = E\{u_t^2\} = 1$$
$$\sigma_{t+1}^2 = \alpha_0 + \alpha_1\varepsilon_t^2 + \beta_1\sigma_t^2$$

Nelson (1990) shows that a sufficient condition for strict stationarity is:

$$E\{\ln(\alpha_1 u_t^2 + \beta_1)\} < 0$$

(i) Show that this condition is satisfied for $(\alpha_1 + \beta_1) = 1$ with $E\{u_t^2\} = 1$. (Use the following result, known as Jensen's inequality, $E\{\ln(w)\} < \ln(E\{w\})$.)

(ii) What other values of α_1 and β_1 such that $\alpha_1 + \beta_1 > 1$ satisfy Nelson's inequality?

(iii) Explain the difference between Engle and Bollerslev's (1986) conclusion that a GARCH(1, 1) model with $\alpha_1 + \beta_1 = 1$ is nonstationary and Nelson's (1990) result that it is strictly stationary.

(iv) Consider the example of section **16.8.4** which uses the S&P 500. The estimated coefficients in a GARCH(1, 1) model for the whole period are $\hat{\alpha}_1 + \hat{\beta}_1 = 0.636 + 0.464$. Do these estimates satisfy Nelson's condition for strict stationarity? (Nelson's Figure 8.1 is helpful for a quick assessment of whether the strict stationarity conditions are satisfied.)

5. (i) The Engle and Ng (1993) test for asymmetry involves defining a dummy variable that indicates whether the shock is negative, that is $S_t^- = 1$ if $\hat{\varepsilon}_t < 0$ and $S_t^- = 0$ if $\hat{\varepsilon}_t \geq 0$, and estimating the regression

$$\hat{\varepsilon}_t^2 = a_0 + a_1 S_{t-1}^- + b_1 \hat{\varepsilon}_{t-1}^-$$
$$+ b_2 \hat{\varepsilon}_{t-1}^+ + e_t \qquad (16.35)$$

(ii) What is the interpretation of the coefficients, a_0, a_1, b_1 and b_2?

(iii) Show that the following alternatives to the Engle and Ng specification give the same results.

(a) Define $S_t^+ = 1$ if $\hat{\varepsilon}_t > 0$ and 0 otherwise, and use S_{t-1}^+ instead of S_{t-1}^-.

(b) In the regression (16.35) drop the constant and use both S_{t-1}^+ and S_{t-1}^-.

6. Consider the VGARCH model – see Engle and Ng (*op. cit.*) – given by

$$\sigma_t^2 = \alpha_0 + \alpha_1 \left[\frac{\varepsilon_{t-1}}{\sigma_{t-1}} + \gamma \right]^2$$

$$+ \beta_1 \sigma_{t-1}^2 \quad \text{VGARCH}$$

(i) In what sense is this asymmetric?

(ii) What does the news impact curve look like for this model?

7. (i) Derive the news impact and slope curves for the EGARCH model.

(ii) Describe the asymmetry present in the EGARCH model.

8. (i) Data on stock returns often shows that the unconditional distribution has fatter tails than the normal distribution. Show that a GARCH(1, 1) model is able to generate this characteristic even though the assumption is made that the conditional distribution is normal. (References: Bollerslev (1986), Engle and González-Rivera (1991).)

(ii) Bollerslev (1987) found that the conditional distribution of monthly returns to S&P 500 was not normal. What could be done in such a case?

9. Check whether Nelson and Cao's necessary and sufficient conditions for non-negativity of the conditional variance are satisfied for the Engle, Ito and Lin model reported in section **16.3.4**.

Appendix

A16.1 The likelihood function for the ARCH model

First recall from Chapter 4 that an alternative to OLS is the method of maximum likelihood, ML. In the simple bivariate regression model with a constant conditional variance the log likelihood function, assuming a normal distribution for the conditional distribution of $(Y_t \mid X_t = x_t)$, is:

$$LL(\beta_1, \beta_2, \sigma_{Y|x}^2; y_t \mid x_t)$$

$$= \sum_{t=1}^{T} f(y_t \mid x_t; \beta_1, \beta_2, \sigma_{Y|x}^2)$$

$$= -\frac{T}{2} \ln 2\pi - \frac{T}{2} \ln \sigma^2$$

$$- \frac{1}{2\sigma^2} \sum_{t=1}^{T} (y_t - \beta_1 - \beta_2 x_t)^2 \qquad (A16.1)$$

For simplicity of notation we have defined $\sigma^2 \equiv \sigma^2_{Y|x}$. The critical difference for the ARCH model is that σ^2 is no longer constant and requires a time subscript, that is σ^2_t.

With the ARCH(q) specification the log likelihood function is:

$$\text{LL(ARCH)} = -\frac{T}{2}\ln 2\pi - \frac{T}{2}\ln \sigma^2_t$$

$$-\frac{1}{2\sigma^2_t}\sum_{t=1}^{T}(y_t - \beta_1 - \beta_2 x_t)^2$$

$$= -\frac{T}{2}\ln 2\pi - \frac{T}{2}\ln \sigma^2_t$$

$$-\frac{1}{2\sigma^2_t}\sum_{t=1}^{T}\varepsilon^2_t \qquad \text{(A16.2)}$$

$$\sigma^2_t = \alpha_0 + \alpha_1 \varepsilon^2_{t-1} + \cdots + \alpha_q \varepsilon^2_{t-q} \quad \text{where}$$
$$\varepsilon_t = y_t - \beta_1 - \beta_2 x_t$$

As in the standard case, the ML estimator is found by differentiating LL with respect to the unknown parameters, here β_1, β_2 and the ARCH parameters α_0, $\alpha_1, \ldots, \alpha_q$, and solving the first order conditions. Details of the maximisation of LL(ARCH) are given in Engle (1982). Within this set-up generalisations are straightforward. For example, the regression model can be extended to include more regressors some, or all, of which may be lagged dependent variables, and the ARCH specification could be changed to one of the alternatives. The 'in mean' variations are also easily accommodated by defining $\varepsilon_t = y_t - \beta_1 - \beta_2 x_t - \delta\alpha_t$, where $\delta\sigma_t$ captures the 'in mean' effect, and $\sigma_t = \sqrt{\sigma^2_t}$ is defined by a suitable ARCH process or variation.

A16.2 Nonnormality

ARCH models are usually estimated by maximum likelihood assuming normality for ε_t, the (conditional) innovations. Often with financial data this assumption is invalid; for example, with excess return models there is typically a greater chance of large and small shocks than the normal distribution would indicate. One possibility, programmed as a menu choice in MICROFIT, is to choose the t distribution, which has fatter tails than the normal distribution. A prior step is to initially assume normality and then examine the resulting residuals for departures from this assumption. In order to do this first define the standardised residuals $\hat{v}_t = \hat{\varepsilon}_t/\hat{\sigma}_t$, which will have a zero mean and unit variance. Standard diagnostics are to examine the skewness and excess kurtosis (relative to the normal distribution where the kurtosis coefficient is 3) of $\hat{v}_t$ – see Chapter 5, section **5.7.2**. These diagnostics are provided in most econometric packages (for example, Doan (1996, section 14-238) for RATS). The coefficient of kurtosis is 3 for the normal distribution and $3 + 6/(\lambda - 4)$ for the t distribution where λ is the degrees of freedom parameter. The relevant range of λ for fat tailed distributions starts with $\lambda = 5$ for which kurtosis $= 9$; kurtosis declines for $\lambda > 5$ and by about $\lambda = 13$ the distributions are not clearly different from the normal. If the ε_t are not normal, assuming normality in the log likelihood function involves an approximation and the estimator is referred to as Quasi-Maximum Likelihood; and an adjustment is available to obtain robust standard errors and a covariance matrix in order to construct robust 't' and cther statistics – see Bollerslev and Wooldridge (1992) and Engle and González-Rivera (1991).

A16.3 Properties of the maximum likelihood estimators in GARCH models

Weiss (1986) and Lumsdaine (1991, 1995) considered the theoretical properties of the ML estimator of the ARCH(q) model. They find that the ML estimators of the ARCH parameters are consistent and asymptotically normally distributed (assuming a finite fourth moment for ε_t). Lumsdaine (1991) showed that even if the conditional distribution of ε_t is not normal, and without the requirement of a finite fourth moment, the (quasi) maximum likelihood estimators of GARCH(1, 1) and IGARCH(1, 1) are consistent and asymptotically normally distributed. These are theoretical results and relate to asymptotic properties.

A related question, as we have seen in the context of estimators of cointegrating regressions, is do the asymptotic results provide a good guide to finite sample performance? Lumsdaine (1995) addresses some aspects of this question for the GARCH(1, 1) and IGARCH(1, 1) models, with a sample size of $T = 500$ and 500 replications. Larger sample sizes which are typical with daily and hourly data should conform to the asymptotic results. The DGP has a simple mean (regression) function where observations on y_t are regressed on a constant to obtain the residuals, which are modelled by a GARCH process. Lumsdaine (*op. cit.*) presents 'coverage' probabilities for her simulation results; that is the proportion of times the true value of the DGP parameter, for example β_1, falls within the confidence interval calculated as the simulation estimate $\pm \kappa$(e.s.e.), where $\kappa = 1.96$ for the 95% confidence interval and 1.645 for the 90% confidence interval and e.s.e. is the estimated standard error of the parameter. These proportions should be close to 95% and 90%, respectively, if the aysmptotic theory is a good guide. In practice they vary with the design of the simulation, which includes stationary GARCH, $\alpha_1 + \beta_1 < 1$ and IGARCH(1,1), $\alpha_1 + \beta_1 = 1$, with a variation in which there is not a finite fourth moment. For the 95% confidence intervals the proportions range between 83.6% and 93.0% for α_1 and 87.6% and 93.8% for β_1. There is no clear distinction between the different GARCH variations; certainly IGARCH is not at a disadvantage compared to GARCH. Generally the coverage probabilities understate the actual levels; that is the true values are too often outside the $(1 - \alpha)$% confidence intervals (that is the coverage probabilities are below 95% or 90% as the case may be). This suggests that the parameter κ is too small if $(\alpha/2)$% critical values from the normal distribution are used. In

standard 't' tests this implies an overrejection of the null hypothesis (that is the percentage of rejections when the null is true is greater than the size (significance) of the test). This is also what Lumsdaine (*op. cit.*, Table 2) finds for Wald, Lagrange-Multiplier and likelihood ratio tests of the IGARCH null hypothesis that $\alpha_1 + \beta_1 = 1$.

Lumsdaine (*op. cit.*) also obtained results for the 't' statistics on the four coefficients which, while similar for the varying GARCH specifications, differed depending on which coefficient was being considered. Denote these 't' statistics as t_c, t_{gc}, t_α and t_β for the constant in the mean function, the constant in the GARCH function, and $\hat{\alpha}_1$ and $\hat{\beta}_1$, respectively; then:

- t_c is approximately normal;
- t_{gc} is slightly skewed to the left (too much on the negative side);
- t_α is skewed to the left and not normal;
- t_β is skewed to the right and not normal; the skew is severe for the IGARCH models.

Thus, although the results for the estimation of the parameters seem acceptable, there is some concern about the distribution of the 't' statistics for $\hat{\alpha}_1$ and $\hat{\beta}_1$. It would be useful to know whether a small sample adjustment or correction is available which would give rather better finite sample properties.

A16.4 Practical ARCH/GARCH

Of course students do not literally have to write a program and solve the first order conditions in order to obtain ARCH estimates. Commercially available econometric software includes ARCH type options. One of the simplest to use is MICROFIT which contains a 'menu' of ready-made options covering the most frequently used variations. The savings ratio example of section **16.8.2** was estimated using the MICROFIT menu which treats ARCH(q) as a special case of GARCH(p, q) with $p = 0$; hence the user has to specify $p = 0$ in the GARCH menu to obtain

ARCH. In addition the user has to specify starting values for the unknown parameters. This is done quite simply for the regression parameters by first estimating the regression by OLS and using the estimates as starting values for ML estimation. A starting value for α_0 is obtained on noting that $\sigma_t^2 = \alpha_0$ if there is no ARCH type effect and, therefore, the conditional variance is constant. Hence, a reasonable starting value is the OLS estimate of the regression variance, $\hat{\sigma}_t^2 = \sum \hat{\varepsilon}_t^2/(T - k)$. Some experimentation may be needed in setting the starting values for the ARCH/GARCH parameters; generally, starting with small positive numbers will give good results. MICROFIT will remind you if the starting values do not satisfy the conditions for covariance stationarity; for example, $0 \leq \sum_{i=1}^{q} \alpha_i < 1$ for ARCH(q) or

$$\sum_{i=1}^{q} \alpha_i + \sum_{j=1}^{p} \beta_j < 1$$

for GARCH(p, q) models. Even with relatively good starting values the maximisation routine may not find an optimum quickly and you will be asked to increase the number of iterations by 20 at a time. MICROFIT and RATS output for the savings ratio, with ARCH(1) and ABSGARCH(1) as examples, follows this appendix.

An alternative to ready-made options is to write your own specification within a program. RATS deals with ARCH/GARCH estimation in this way. In order to understand this approach a basic appreciation of the likelihood function as given by (A16.2) is helpful. A typical RATS routine has the following steps:

1. Estimate the regression equation by OLS to provide starting values for ML estimation.
2. Define ε_t (resarch).
3. Define the ARCH function (archvar).
3. Define a typical element of the LL function (archlogl).
4. Specify the starting values.
5. Choose the estimation method.

The estimation routine 'maximise' is then chosen along with the method of solution, of which three are available, Simplex, BFGS and BHHH. Simplex does not provide standard errors, rather its use, since it is robust to poor starting values, is to provide starting values for one of the other two methods which can be quite slow in converging if the starting values for the ARCH parameters are poor. Initial starting values for the regression parameters are, as in MICROFIT, provided by a prior OLS regression. The terms in parentheses are the names used in the RATS output following this appendix.

Some examples of ARCH estimation using MICROFIT and RATS from section **16.8.2** and see Table 16.1.

1. MICROFIT estimation of an ARCH(1) model for the U.K Savings Ratio. Note that ARCH(1) is obtained as a special case of GARCH(p, q) with p = 0 and q = 1.

<pre>
                  GARCH(0,1) assuming a Normal distribution
                       converged after 20 iterations
****
Dependent variable is SR
138 observations used for estimation from 1956Q1 to 1990Q2
****
Regressor   Coefficient   Standard Error   T-Ratio[Prob]
INPT   .0088701   .0043206   2.0530[.042]
SR(-1)   .52049   .090030   5.7813[.000]
SR(-2)   .21334   .085022   2.5093[.013]
SR(-3)   -.021406   .094006   -.22771[.820]
SR(-4)   .18169   .086145   2.1092[.037]
****
R-Squared   .72132   R-Bar-Squared   .71294
S.E. of Regression   .014284   F-statistic F(4, 133)   86.0632[.000]
Mean of Dependent Variable   .083832   S.D. of Dependent Variable   .026660
Residual Sum of Squares   .027135   Equation Log-likelihood   393.3284
Akaike Info. Criterion   388.3284 Schwarz Bayesian Criterion   381.0103
DW-statistic   2.1180
****
Parameters of GARCH explaining H-SQ, the conditional variance of the error
****
                         Coefficient   Asymptotic T-Ratio
         GARCH constant .1470E-3   14.3438[.000]
         E-SQ(-1)   .23799   1.8970[.060]
****
</pre>

Note: H-SQ is the conditional variance denoted in the text by σ_t^2.

1. MICROFIT estimation of an ABSARCH(1) model for the U.K Savings Ratio.

<pre>
             Absolute value GARCH(0,1) assuming a Normal distribution
                       converged after 21 iterations
****
Dependent variable is SR
138 observations used for estimation from 1956Q1 to 1990Q2
****
Regressor   Coefficient   Standard Error   T-Ratio[Prob]
□
INPT   .0083191   .0046950   1.7719[.079]
□
SR(-1)   .47299   .092952   5.0886[.000]
SR(-2)   .20843   .086762   2.4023[.018]
SR(-3)   .0034489   .097474   .035383[.972]
SR(-4)   .21470   .089423   2.4009[.018]
****
R-Squared   .72324   R-Bar-Squared   .71492
S.E. of Regression   .014234   F-statistic F(4, 133)   86.8903[.000]
Mean of Dependent Variable   .083832   S.D. of Dependent Variable   .026660
</pre>

Residual Sum of Squares	.026948	Equation Log-likelihood	392.7722
Akaike Info. Criterion	387.7722	Schwarz Bayesian Criterion	380.4541
DW-statistic	2.0268		

****
Parameters of GARCH explaining H, the conditional S.E. of the error term
****

	Coefficient	Asymptotic T-Ratio
GARCH constant	.011289	8.1620[.000]
ABS(E(-1))	.22401	1.9118[.058]

****
Note: H is the conditional standard error denoted in the text by σ_t.

2. RATS estimation of an ARCH(1) model for the U.K Savings Ratio.

The data is first located. The model is then estimated and here all 3 methods (simplex, BFGS and BHHH) are used for illustration. There are some minor differences in the estimated coefficients and in the estimated standard errors. Provided the number of iterations taken exceeds the number of free parameters BFGS is preferred. The output for the OLS regression is suppressed in this output.

```
cal 1955 1 4
all 1990:2
smpl 1955:1 1990:2
open data uksr.dat
data(format = free, org = obs) / sr

***********************ARCH(1)
smpl 1956:1 1990:2
nonlin b0 b1 b2 b3 b4 a0 a1
frml resarch = sr - b0 - b1*sr{1} - b2*sr{2} - b3*sr{3} - b4*sr{4}
frml archvar = a0+a1*resarch(T-1)**2
frml archlogl = (V = archvar(T)), -0.5*(log(V) + resarch(T)**2/V)
linreg sr
#constant sr{1 to 4}
compute b0 = %beta(1), b1 = %beta(2), b2 = %beta(3), b3 = %beta(4), b4 = %beta(5)
compute a0 = 0.0001, a1 = 0.1
nlpar(subiterations = 500)
maximise(iterations = 200, method = simplex, recursive) archlogl
```

Estimation by Simplex
Quarterly Data From 1956:01 To 1990:02

Usable Observations	137	Degrees of Freedom	130
Total Observations	138	Skipped/Missing	1
Function Value		520.14194369	

	Variable	Coeff
		**************************************
1.	B0	0.008869726
2.	B1	0.520543279
3.	B2	0.213334464
4.	B3	-0.021425050
5.	B4	0.181673397
6.	A0	0.000147046
7.	A1	0.237665053

```
nonlin b0 b1 b2 b3 b4 a0 a1
frml resarch = sr - b0 - b1*sr{1} - b2*sr{2} - b3*sr{3} - b4*sr{4}
frml archvar = a0 + a1*resarch(T - 1)**2
frml archlogl = (V = archvar(T)), -0.5*(log(V) + resarch(T)**2/V)
linreg sr
#constant sr{1 to 4}
compute b0 = %beta(1), b1 = %beta(2),b2 = %beta(3), b3 = %beta(4),b4 = %beta(5)
compute a0 = 0.0001, a1 = 0.238
nlpar(subiterations = 500,criterion = coeffs)
maximise(iterations = 500, method = bfgs, recursive) archlogl
```

Estimation by BFGS
Iterations Taken 30
Quarterly Data From 1956:01 To 1990:02

Usable Observations	137	Degrees of Freedom	130	
Total Observations	138	Skipped/Missing	1	
Function Value		520.14194718		

	Variable	Coeff	Std Error	T-Stat	Signif
1.	B0	0.008870044	0.004052359	2.18886	0.02860706
2.	B1	0.520536817	0.059991939	8.67678	0.00000000
3.	B2	0.213287399	0.045796510	4.65728	0.00000320
4.	B3	-0.021374330	0.073728620	-0.28991	0.77188855
5.	B4	0.181672084	0.077218518	2.35270	0.01863761
6.	A0	0.000147017	0.000025051	5.86871	0.00000000
7.	A1	0.237968458	0.131908901	1.80404	0.07122560

```
nonlin b0 b1 b2 b3 b4 a0 a1
frml resarch = sr - b0 - b1*sr{1} - b2*sr{2} - b3*sr{3} - b4*sr{4}
frml archvar = a0 + a1*resarch(T - 1)**2
frml archlogl = (V = archvar(T)), -0.5*(log(V) + resarch(T)**2/V)
linreg sr
#constant sr{1 to 4}
compute b0 = %beta(1), b1 = %beta(2),b2 = %beta(3), b3 = %beta(4),b4 = %beta(5)
compute a0 = 0.0001, a1 = 0.238
nlpar(subiterations = 500,criterion = coeffs)
maximise(iterations = 500, method = bhhh, recursive) archlogl
```

Estimation by BHHH
Iterations Taken 14
Quarterly Data From 1956:01 To 1990:02

Usable Observations	137	Degrees of Freedom	130	
Total Observations	138	Skipped/Missing	1	
Function Value		520.14194749		

	Variable	Coeff	Std Error	T-Stat	Signif
1	B0	0.008870305	0.004271675	2.07654	0.03784400
2.	B1	0.520492418	0.085880382	6.06067	0.00000000
3	B2	0.213341524	0.094756643	2.25147	0.02435593
4.	B3	-0.021409175	0.099696418	-0.21474	0.82996717
5.	B4	0.181693822	0.089150308	2.03806	0.04154377
6.	A0	0.000147015	0.000024489	6.00322	0.00000000
7.	A1	0.237985395	0.157651235	1.50957	0.13115346

Notes:
the overall sample period is 1955q1 to 1990q2. Estimation of the sr equation specifies 4 lags hence 4 observations are 'lost' through lagging; one further observation is then lost because the ARCH(1) specification requires one lag of the squared residuals.
MICROFIT and BHHH in RATS give the same results apart from some minor differences in the estimated standard errors.

Appendix – Statistical tables

A1   The normal distribution
A2   The 't' distribution
A3   The χ^2 distribution
A4a&b The F distribution
A5a&b Critical values of the Durbin–Watson test

Acknowledgements: Tables A1 to A4 are based on *Biometrika Tables for Statisticians*, Cambridge University Press, Cambridge, edited by E.S. Pearson and H.O. Hartley (1970), reproduced by permission of the Biometrika trustees; Table A5 is based on J. Durbin and G.S. Watson (1951), Testing for Serial Correlation in Least Squares Regression, II, *Biometrika*, Vol. 38, pp. 159–178, reproduced by permission of the Biometrika Trustees.

Table A1   *Area under the standard normal distribution*

A table entry is the area between 0 and $+z$. For example, for $z = 1.96$ the area is 0.475 or 47.5%. Doubling this entry to 0.95 gives the area between -1.96 and $+1.96$. The critical values for a two-sided test at the 5% significance level are, therefore, ± 1.96. The critical value for a 5% (positive) one-sided test is $+1.645$, which corresponds to a table entry of halfway between 0.4495 and 0.4505.

z	0.00	0.01	0.02	0.03	0.04	0.05	0.06	0.07	0.08	0.09
0.0	0.0000	0.0040	0.0080	0.0120	0.0160	0.0199	0.0239	0.0279	0.0319	0.0359
0.1	0.0398	0.0438	0.0478	0.0517	0.0557	0.0596	0.0636	0.0675	0.0714	0.0753
0.2	0.0793	0.0832	0.0871	0.0910	0.0948	0.0987	0.1026	0.1064	0.1103	0.1141
0.3	0.1179	0.1217	0.1255	0.1293	0.1331	0.1368	0.1406	0.1443	0.1480	0.1517
0.4	0.1554	0.1591	0.1628	0.1664	0.1700	0.1736	0.1772	0.1808	0.1844	0.1879
0.5	0.1915	0.1950	0.1985	0.2019	0.2054	0.2088	0.2123	0.2157	0.2190	0.2224
0.6	0.2257	0.2291	0.2324	0.2357	0.2389	0.2422	0.2454	0.2486	0.2517	0.2549
0.7	0.2580	0.2611	0.2642	0.2673	0.2704	0.2734	0.2764	0.2794	0.2823	0.2852
0.8	0.2881	0.2910	0.2939	0.2967	0.2995	0.3023	0.3051	0.3078	0.3106	0.3133
0.9	0.3159	0.3186	0.3212	0.3238	0.3264	0.3289	0.3315	0.3340	0.3365	0.3389
1.0	0.3413	0.3438	0.3461	0.3485	0.3508	0.3531	0.3554	0.3577	0.3599	0.3621
1.1	0.3643	0.3665	0.3686	0.3708	0.3729	0.3749	0.3770	0.3790	0.3810	0.3830
1.2	0.3849	0.3869	0.3888	0.3907	0.3925	0.3944	0.3962	0.3980	0.3997	0.4015
1.3	0.4032	0.4049	0.4066	0.4082	0.4099	0.4115	0.4131	0.4147	0.4162	0.4177
1.4	0.4192	0.4207	0.4222	0.4236	0.4251	0.4265	0.4279	0.4292	0.4306	0.4319
1.5	0.4332	0.4345	0.4357	0.4370	0.4382	0.4394	0.4406	0.4418	0.4429	0.4441
1.6	0.4452	0.4463	0.4474	0.4484	0.4495	0.4505	0.4515	0.4525	0.4535	0.4545
1.7	0.4554	0.4564	0.4573	0.4582	0.4591	0.4599	0.4608	0.4616	0.4625	0.4633
1.8	0.4641	0.4649	0.4656	0.4664	0.4671	0.4678	0.4686	0.4693	0.4699	0.4706
1.9	0.4713	0.4719	0.4726	0.4732	0.4738	0.4744	0.4750	0.4756	0.4761	0.4767
2.0	0.4772	0.4778	0.4783	0.4788	0.4793	0.4798	0.4803	0.4804	0.4812	0.4817
2.1	0.4821	0.4826	0.4830	0.4834	0.4838	0.4842	0.4846	0.4850	0.4854	0.4857
2.2	0.4861	0.4864	0.4868	0.4871	0.4875	0.4878	0.4881	0.4884	0.4887	0.4890
2.3	0.4893	0.4896	0.4898	0.4901	0.4904	0.4906	0.4909	0.4911	0.4913	0.4916
2.4	0.4918	0.4920	0.4922	0.4925	0.4927	0.4929	0.4931	0.4932	0.4934	0.4936
2.5	0.4938	0.4940	0.4941	0.4943	0.4945	0.4946	0.4948	0.4949	0.4951	0.4952
2.6	0.4953	0.4955	0.4956	0.4957	0.4959	0.4960	0.4961	0.4962	0.4963	0.4964
2.7	0.4965	0.4966	0.4967	0.4968	0.4969	0.4970	0.4971	0.4972	0.4973	0.4974
2.8	0.4974	0.4975	0.4976	0.4977	0.4977	0.4978	0.4979	0.4979	0.4980	0.4981
2.9	0.4981	0.4982	0.4982	0.4983	0.4984	0.4984	0.4985	0.4985	0.4986	0.4986
3.0	0.4987	0.4987	0.4987	0.4988	0.4988	0.4989	0.4989	0.4989	0.4990	0.4990

Table A2 *Right tail critical values for the 't' distribution*
df is the degrees of freedom of the test. The column heading is the significance level of the test. For example, with df = 10, the critical values for a two-sided test at a 5% significance level are ±2.228. For small values of df these are noticeably larger, in absolute value, than the corresponding values for the normal distribution.

df	10% 5%	5% 2.5%	1% 0.5%	⇐ ⇐	2-sided test α% 1-sided test α%
1	6.314	12.706	63.657		
2	2.920	4.303	9.925		
3	2.353	3.182	5.841		
4	2.132	2.776	4.604		
5	2.015	2.571	4.032		
6	1.943	2.447	3.707		
7	1.895	2.365	3.499		
8	1.860	2.306	3.355		
9	1.833	2.262	3.250		
10	1.812	2.228	3.169		
11	1.796	2.201	3.106		
12	1.782	2.179	3.055		
13	1.771	2.160	3.012		
14	1.761	2.145	2.977		
15	1.753	2.131	2.947		
16	1.746	2.120	2.921		
17	1.740	2.110	2.898		
18	1.734	2.101	2.878		
19	1.729	2.093	2.861		
20	1.725	2.086	2.845		
21	1.721	2.080	2.831		
22	1.717	2.074	2.819		
23	1.714	2.069	2.807		
24	1.711	2.064	2.797		
25	1.708	2.060	2.787		
26	1.706	2.056	2.779		
27	1.703	2.052	2.771		
28	1.701	2.048	2.763		
29	1.699	2.045	2.756		
30	1.697	2.042	2.750		
40	1.684	2.021	2.704		
60	1.671	2.000	2.660		
120	1.658	1.980	2.617		
∞	1.645	1.960	2.576		

Table A3 *Right critical values for the χ^2 distribution*

df is the degrees of freedom of the test. A table entry is the value which cuts off α% of the distribution to the right. For example, for $\alpha = 0.05$ and df $= 2$, 5% of the area of the distribution is to the right of 5.99146. This is also known as the $(1 - \alpha)$% quantile, which is the area to the left of the table entry. Thus, 95% of the area is to the left of 5.99146. A significant value of a test statistic, distributed as $\chi^2(g)$ under the null hypothesis, at the α% significance level is one in excess of the table entry.

df	$\alpha = 0.995$	0.975	0.950	0.500	0.100	0.050	0.025	0.010	0.005
1	392704.10^{-10}	982069.10^{-9}	393214.10^{-8}	0.454936	2.70554	3.84146	5.02389	6.64390	7.87944
2	0.0100251	0.0506356	0.102587	1.38629	4.60517	5.99146	7.37776	9.21034	10.5966
3	0.0717218	0.215795	0.351846	2.36597	6.25139	7.81473	9.34840	11.3449	12.8382
4	0.206989	0.484419	0.710723	3.35669	7.77944	9.48773	11.1433	13.2767	14.8603
5	0.411742	0.831212	1.145476	4.35146	9.23635	11.0705	12.8325	15.0863	16.7496
6	0.675727	1.23734	1.63538	5.34812	10.6446	12.5916	14.4494	16.8119	18.5476
7	0.989256	1.68987	2.16735	6.34581	12.0170	14.0671	16.0128	18.4753	20.2777
8	1.34441	2.17973	2.73264	7.34412	13.3616	15.5073	17.5345	20.0902	21.9550
9	1.73493	2.70039	3.32511	8.34283	14.6837	16.9190	19.0228	21.6660	23.5894
10	2.15586	3.24697	3.94030	9.34182	15.9871	18.3070	20.4832	23.2093	25.1882
11	2.60322	3.81575	4.57481	10.3410	17.2750	19.6751	21.9200	24.7250	26.7568
12	3.07382	4.40379	5.22603	11.3403	18.5494	21.0261	23.3367	26.2170	28.2995
13	3.56503	5.00875	5.89186	12.3398	19.8119	22.3620	24.7356	27.6883	29.8195
14	4.07467	5.62873	6.57063	13.3393	21.0642	23.6848	26.1189	29.1413	31.3194
15	4.60092	6.26214	7.26094	14.3389	22.3072	24.9958	27.4884	30.5779	32.8013
16	5.14221	6.90766	7.96165	15.3385	23.5418	26.2962	28.8454	31.9999	34.2672
17	5.69722	7.56419	8.67176	16.3382	24.7690	27.5871	30.1910	33.4087	35.7185
18	6.26480	8.23075	9.39046	17.3379	25.9894	28.8693	31.5264	34.8053	37.1565
19	6.84397	8.90652	10.1170	18.3377	27.2036	30.1435	32.8523	36.1908	38.5823

Table A4a Right tail critical values of the F distribution (5%)

There are two degrees of freedom for the F test. The numerator degrees of freedom v_1 and the denominator degrees of freedom v_2. A table entry is the value which cuts off $\alpha\%$ of the distribution to the right, where $\alpha\% = 5\%$ for the first set of table entries and $\alpha\% = 1\%$ for the second set of table entries. For example, for $\alpha\% = 5\%$, $v_1 = 2$ and $v_2 = 10$, the upper 5% critical value is 4.10. A value in excess of this for a test statistic distributed as $F(2, 10)$ under the null is significant at the 5% level.

Upper 5% critical values

$v_2 \backslash v_1$	1	2	3	4	5	6	7	8	9	10	12	15	20	24	30	40	60	120	∞
1	161.4	199.5	215.7	224.6	230.2	234.0	236.8	238.9	240.5	241.9	243.9	245.9	248.0	249.1	250.1	251.1	252.2	253.3	254.3
2	18.51	19.00	19.16	19.25	19.30	19.33	19.35	19.37	19.38	19.40	19.41	19.43	19.45	19.45	19.46	19.47	19.48	19.49	19.50
3	10.13	9.55	9.28	9.12	9.01	8.94	8.89	8.85	8.81	8.79	8.74	8.70	8.66	8.64	8.62	8.59	8.57	8.55	8.53
4	7.71	6.94	6.59	6.39	6.26	6.16	6.09	6.04	6.00	5.96	5.91	5.86	5.80	5.77	5.75	5.72	5.69	5.66	5.63
5	6.61	5.79	5.41	5.19	5.05	4.95	4.88	4.82	4.77	4.74	4.68	4.62	4.56	4.53	4.50	4.46	4.43	4.40	4.36
6	5.99	5.14	4.76	4.53	4.39	4.28	4.21	4.15	4.10	4.06	4.00	3.94	3.87	3.84	3.81	3.77	3.74	3.70	3.67
7	5.59	4.74	4.35	4.12	3.97	3.87	3.79	3.73	3.68	3.64	3.57	3.51	3.44	3.41	3.38	3.34	3.30	3.27	3.23
8	5.32	4.46	4.07	3.84	3.69	3.58	3.50	3.44	3.39	3.35	3.28	3.22	3.15	3.12	3.08	3.04	3.01	2.97	2.93
9	5.12	4.26	3.86	3.63	3.48	3.37	3.29	3.23	3.18	3.14	3.07	3.01	2.94	2.90	2.86	2.83	2.79	2.75	2.71
10	4.96	4.10	3.71	3.48	3.33	3.22	3.14	3.07	3.02	2.98	2.91	2.85	2.77	2.74	2.70	2.66	2.62	2.58	2.54
11	4.84	3.98	3.59	3.36	3.20	3.09	3.01	2.95	2.90	2.85	2.79	2.72	2.65	2.61	2.57	2.53	2.49	2.45	2.40
12	4.75	3.89	3.49	3.26	3.11	3.00	2.91	2.85	2.80	2.75	2.69	2.62	2.54	2.51	2.47	2.43	2.38	2.34	2.30
13	4.67	3.81	3.41	3.18	3.03	2.92	2.83	2.77	2.71	2.67	2.60	2.53	2.46	2.42	2.38	2.34	2.30	2.25	2.21
14	4.60	3.74	3.34	3.11	2.96	2.85	2.76	2.70	2.65	2.60	2.53	2.46	2.39	2.35	2.31	2.27	2.22	2.18	2.13
15	4.54	3.68	3.29	3.06	2.90	2.79	2.71	2.64	2.59	2.54	2.48	2.40	2.33	2.29	2.25	2.20	2.16	2.11	2.07
16	4.49	3.63	3.24	3.01	2.85	2.74	2.66	2.59	2.54	2.49	2.42	2.35	2.28	2.24	2.19	2.15	2.11	2.06	2.01
17	4.45	3.59	3.20	2.96	2.81	2.70	2.61	2.55	2.49	2.45	2.38	2.31	2.23	2.19	2.15	2.10	2.06	2.01	1.96
18	4.41	3.55	3.16	2.93	2.77	2.66	2.58	2.51	2.46	2.41	2.34	2.27	2.19	2.15	2.11	2.06	2.02	1.97	1.92
19	4.38	3.52	3.13	2.90	2.74	2.63	2.54	2.48	2.42	2.38	2.31	2.23	2.16	2.11	2.07	2.03	1.98	1.93	1.88
20	4.35	3.49	3.10	2.87	2.71	2.60	2.51	2.45	2.39	2.35	2.28	2.20	2.12	2.08	2.04	1.99	1.95	1.90	1.84
21	4.32	3.47	3.07	2.84	2.68	2.57	2.49	2.42	2.37	2.32	2.25	2.18	2.10	2.05	2.01	1.96	1.92	1.87	1.81
22	4.30	3.44	3.05	2.82	2.66	2.55	2.46	2.40	2.34	2.30	2.23	2.15	2.07	2.03	1.98	1.94	1.89	1.84	1.78
23	4.28	3.42	3.03	2.80	2.64	2.53	2.44	2.37	2.32	2.27	2.20	2.13	2.05	2.01	1.96	1.91	1.86	1.81	1.76
24	4.26	3.40	3.01	2.78	2.62	2.51	2.42	2.36	2.30	2.25	2.18	2.11	2.03	1.98	1.94	1.89	1.84	1.79	1.73
25	4.24	3.39	2.99	2.76	2.60	2.49	2.40	2.34	2.28	2.24	2.16	2.09	2.01	1.96	1.92	1.87	1.82	1.77	1.71
26	4.23	3.37	2.98	2.74	2.59	2.47	2.39	2.32	2.27	2.22	2.15	2.07	1.99	1.95	1.90	1.85	1.80	1.75	1.69
27	4.21	3.35	2.96	2.73	2.57	2.46	2.37	2.31	2.25	2.20	2.13	2.06	1.97	1.93	1.88	1.84	1.79	1.73	1.67
28	4.20	3.34	2.95	2.71	2.56	2.45	2.36	2.29	2.24	2.19	2.12	2.04	1.96	1.91	1.87	1.82	1.77	1.71	1.65
29	4.18	3.33	2.93	2.70	2.55	2.43	2.35	2.28	2.22	2.18	2.10	2.03	1.94	1.90	1.85	1.81	1.75	1.70	1.64
30	4.17	3.32	2.92	2.69	2.53	2.42	2.33	2.27	2.21	2.16	2.09	2.01	1.93	1.89	1.84	1.79	1.74	1.68	1.62
40	4.08	3.23	2.84	2.61	2.45	2.34	2.25	2.18	2.12	2.08	2.00	1.92	1.84	1.79	1.74	1.69	1.64	1.58	1.51
60	4.00	3.15	2.76	2.53	2.37	2.25	2.17	2.10	2.04	1.99	1.92	1.84	1.75	1.70	1.65	1.59	1.53	1.47	1.39
120	3.92	3.07	2.68	2.45	2.29	2.17	2.09	2.02	1.96	1.91	1.83	1.75	1.66	1.61	1.55	1.50	1.43	1.35	1.25
∞	3.84	3.00	2.60	2.37	2.21	2.10	2.01	1.94	1.88	1.83	1.75	1.67	1.57	1.52	1.46	1.39	1.32	1.22	1.00

Table A4b *Right tail critical values of the F distribution (1%)*

Upper 1% critical values

v_2 \ v_1	1	2	3	4	5	6	7	8	9	10	12	15	20	24	30	40	60	120	∞
1	4052	4999.5	5403	5625	5764	5859	5928	5981	6022	6056	6106	6157	6209	6235	6261	6287	6313	6339	6366
2	98.50	99.00	99.17	99.25	99.30	99.33	99.36	99.37	99.39	99.40	99.42	99.43	99.45	99.46	99.47	99.47	99.48	99.49	99.50
3	34.12	30.82	29.46	28.71	28.24	27.91	27.67	27.49	27.35	27.23	27.05	26.87	26.69	26.60	26.50	26.41	26.32	26.22	26.13
4	21.20	18.00	16.69	15.98	15.52	15.21	14.98	14.80	14.66	14.55	14.37	14.20	14.02	13.93	13.84	13.75	13.65	13.56	13.46
5	16.26	13.27	12.06	11.39	10.97	10.67	10.46	10.29	10.16	10.05	9.89	9.72	9.55	9.47	9.38	9.29	9.20	9.11	9.02
6	13.75	10.92	9.78	9.15	8.75	8.47	8.26	8.10	7.98	7.87	7.72	7.56	7.40	7.31	7.23	7.14	7.06	6.97	6.88
7	12.25	9.55	8.45	7.85	7.46	7.19	6.99	6.84	6.72	6.62	6.47	6.31	6.16	6.07	5.99	5.91	5.82	5.74	5.65
8	11.26	8.65	7.59	7.01	6.63	6.37	6.18	6.03	5.91	5.81	5.67	5.52	5.36	5.28	5.20	5.12	5.03	4.95	4.86
9	10.56	8.02	6.99	6.42	6.06	5.80	5.61	5.47	5.35	5.26	5.11	4.96	4.81	4.73	4.65	4.57	4.48	4.40	4.31
10	10.04	7.56	6.55	5.99	5.64	5.39	5.20	5.06	4.94	4.85	4.71	4.56	4.41	4.33	4.25	4.17	4.08	4.00	3.91
11	9.65	7.21	6.22	5.67	5.32	5.07	4.89	4.74	4.63	4.54	4.40	4.25	4.10	4.02	3.94	3.86	3.78	3.69	3.60
12	9.33	6.93	5.95	5.41	5.06	4.82	4.64	4.50	4.39	4.30	4.16	4.01	3.86	3.78	3.70	3.62	3.54	3.45	3.36
13	9.07	6.70	5.74	5.21	4.86	4.62	4.44	4.30	4.19	4.10	3.96	3.82	3.66	3.59	3.51	3.43	3.34	3.25	3.17
14	8.86	6.51	5.56	5.04	4.69	4.46	4.28	4.14	4.03	3.94	3.80	3.66	3.51	3.43	3.35	3.27	3.18	3.09	3.00
15	8.68	6.36	5.42	4.89	4.56	4.32	4.14	4.00	3.89	3.80	3.67	3.52	3.37	3.29	3.21	3.13	3.05	2.96	2.87
16	8.53	6.23	5.29	4.77	4.44	4.20	4.03	3.89	3.78	3.69	3.55	3.41	3.26	3.18	3.10	3.02	2.93	2.84	2.75
17	8.40	6.11	5.18	4.67	4.34	4.10	3.93	3.79	3.68	3.59	3.46	3.31	3.16	3.08	3.00	2.92	2.83	2.75	2.65
18	8.29	6.01	5.09	4.58	4.25	4.01	3.84	3.71	3.60	3.51	3.37	3.23	3.08	3.00	2.92	2.84	2.75	2.66	2.57
19	8.18	5.93	5.01	4.50	4.17	3.94	3.77	3.63	3.52	3.43	3.30	3.15	3.00	2.92	2.84	2.76	2.67	2.58	2.49
20	8.10	5.85	4.94	4.43	4.10	3.87	3.70	3.56	3.46	3.37	3.23	3.09	2.94	2.86	2.78	2.69	2.61	2.52	2.42
21	8.02	5.78	4.87	4.37	4.04	3.81	3.64	3.51	3.40	3.31	3.17	3.03	2.88	2.80	2.72	2.64	2.55	2.46	2.36
22	7.95	5.72	4.82	4.31	3.99	3.76	3.59	3.45	3.35	3.26	3.12	2.98	2.83	2.75	2.67	2.58	2.50	2.40	2.31
23	7.88	5.66	4.76	4.26	3.94	3.71	3.54	3.41	3.30	3.21	3.07	2.93	2.78	2.70	2.62	2.54	2.45	2.35	2.26
24	7.82	5.61	4.72	4.22	3.90	3.67	3.50	3.36	3.26	3.17	3.03	2.89	2.74	2.66	2.58	2.49	2.40	2.31	2.21
25	7.77	5.57	4.68	4.18	3.85	3.63	3.46	3.32	3.22	3.13	2.99	2.85	2.70	2.62	2.54	2.45	2.36	2.27	2.17
26	7.72	5.53	4.64	4.14	3.82	3.59	3.42	3.29	3.18	3.09	2.96	2.81	2.66	2.58	2.50	2.42	2.33	2.23	2.13
27	7.68	5.49	4.60	4.11	3.78	3.56	3.39	3.26	3.15	3.06	2.93	2.78	2.63	2.55	2.47	2.38	2.29	2.20	2.10
28	7.64	5.45	4.57	4.07	3.75	3.53	3.36	3.23	3.12	3.03	2.90	2.75	2.60	2.52	2.44	2.35	2.26	2.17	2.06
29	7.60	5.42	4.54	4.04	3.73	3.50	3.33	3.20	3.09	3.00	2.87	2.73	2.57	2.49	2.41	2.33	2.23	2.14	2.03
30	7.56	5.39	4.51	4.02	3.70	3.47	3.30	3.17	3.07	2.98	2.84	2.70	2.55	2.47	2.39	2.30	2.21	2.11	2.01
40	7.31	5.18	4.31	3.83	3.51	3.29	3.12	2.99	2.89	2.80	2.66	2.52	2.37	2.29	2.20	2.11	2.02	1.92	1.80
60	7.08	4.98	4.13	3.65	3.34	3.12	2.95	2.82	2.72	2.63	2.50	2.35	2.20	2.12	2.03	1.94	1.84	1.73	1.60
120	6.85	4.79	3.95	3.48	3.17	2.96	2.79	2.66	2.56	2.47	2.34	2.19	2.03	1.95	1.86	1.76	1.66	1.53	1.38
∞	6.63	4.61	3.78	3.32	3.02	2.80	2.64	2.51	2.41	2.32	2.18	2.04	1.88	1.79	1.70	1.59	1.47	1.32	1.00

Table A5a *Lower and upper bounds of the Durbin–Watson statistic (5%)*
K is the number of regressors not including a constant; however, a constant is assumed to be present in the estimated regression. T is the number of observations. The null hypothesis is $\rho = 0$ in $\varepsilon_t = \rho\varepsilon_{t-1} + u_t$, and the alternative hypothesis is $\rho > 0$. For negative ρ, subtract the table entries from $+4$. At the 5% significance level, if $K = 3$ and $T = 30$, then d_L is 1.21 and d_U is 1.65. A sample value below 1.21 suggests rejection of the null hypothesis; a sample value in excess of 1.65 suggests nonrejection of the null hypothesis. A sample value between 1.21 and 1.65 is in the 'inconclusive' region.

5% lower and upper bounds

$K =$	1		2		3		4		5	
T	d_L	d_U	d_L	d_U	d_L	d_U	d_L	d_U	d_L	d_U
15	1.08	1.36	0.95	1.54	0.82	1.75	0.69	1.97	0.56	2.21
16	1.10	1.37	0.98	1.54	0.86	1.73	0.74	1.93	0.62	2.15
17	1.13	1.38	1.02	1.54	0.90	1.71	0.78	1.90	0.67	2.10
18	1.16	1.39	1.05	1.53	0.93	1.69	0.82	1.87	0.71	2.06
19	1.18	1.40	1.08	1.53	0.97	1.68	0.86	1.85	0.75	2.02
20	1.20	1.41	1.10	1.54	1.00	1.68	0.90	1.83	0.79	1.99
21	1.22	1.42	1.13	1.54	1.03	1.67	0.93	1.81	0.83	1.96
22	1.24	1.43	1.15	1.54	1.05	1.66	0.96	1.80	0.86	1.94
23	1.26	1.44	1.17	1.54	1.08	1.66	0.99	1.79	0.90	1.92
24	1.27	1.45	1.19	1.55	1.10	1.66	1.01	1.78	0.93	1.90
25	1.29	1.45	1.21	1.55	1.12	1.66	1.04	1.77	0.95	1.89
26	1.30	1.46	1.22	1.55	1.14	1.65	1.06	1.76	0.98	1.88
27	1.32	1.47	1.24	1.56	1.16	1.65	1.08	1.76	1.01	1.86
28	1.33	1.48	1.26	1.56	1.18	1.65	1.10	1.75	1.03	1.85
29	1.34	1.48	1.27	1.56	1.20	1.65	1.12	1.74	1.05	1.84
30	1.35	1.49	1.28	1.57	1.21	1.65	1.14	1.74	1.07	1.83
31	1.36	1.50	1.30	1.57	1.23	1.65	1.16	1.74	1.09	1.83
32	1.37	1.50	1.31	1.57	1.24	1.65	1.18	1.73	1.11	1.82
33	1.38	1.51	1.32	1.58	1.26	1.65	1.19	1.73	1.13	1.81
34	1.39	1.51	1.33	1.58	1.27	1.65	1.21	1.73	1.15	1.81
35	1.40	1.52	1.34	1.58	1.28	1.65	1.22	1.73	1.16	1.80
36	1.41	1.52	1.35	1.59	1.29	1.65	1.24	1.73	1.18	1.80
37	1.42	1.53	1.36	1.59	1.31	1.66	1.25	1.72	1.19	1.80
38	1.43	1.54	1.37	1.59	1.32	1.66	1.26	1.72	1.21	1.79
39	1.43	1.54	1.38	1.60	1.33	1.66	1.27	1.72	1.22	1.79
40	1.44	1.54	1.39	1.60	1.34	1.66	1.29	1.72	1.23	1.79
45	1.48	1.57	1.43	1.62	1.38	1.67	1.34	1.72	1.29	1.78
50	1.50	1.59	1.46	1.63	1.42	1.67	1.38	1.72	1.34	1.77
55	1.53	1.60	1.49	1.64	1.45	1.68	1.41	1.72	1.38	1.77
60	1.55	1.62	1.51	1.65	1.48	1.69	1.44	1.73	1.41	1.77
65	1.57	1.63	1.54	1.66	1.50	1.70	1.47	1.73	1.44	1.77
70	1.58	1.64	1.55	1.67	1.52	1.70	1.49	1.74	1.46	1.77
75	1.60	1.65	1.57	1.68	1.54	1.71	1.51	1.74	1.49	1.77
80	1.61	1.66	1.59	1.69	1.56	1.72	1.53	1.74	1.51	1.77
85	1.62	1.67	1.60	1.70	1.57	1.72	1.55	1.75	1.52	1.77
90	1.63	1.68	1.61	1.70	1.59	1.73	1.57	1.75	1.54	1.78
95	1.64	1.69	1.62	1.71	1.60	1.73	1.58	1.75	1.56	1.78
100	1.65	1.69	1.63	1.72	1.61	1.74	1.59	1.76	1.57	1.78

Table A5b *Lower and upper bounds of the Durbin–Watson statistic (1%)*

K is the number of regressors not including a constant; however, a constant is assumed to be present in the estimated regression. T is the number of observations. The null hypothesis is $\rho = 0$ in $\varepsilon_t = \rho \varepsilon_{t-1} + u_t$, and the alternative hypothesis is $\rho > 0$. For negative ρ, subtract the table entries from $+4$. At the 1% significance level, if $K = 3$ and $T = 30$, then d_L is 1.01 and d_U is 1.42. A sample value below 1.01 suggests rejection of the null hypothesis; a sample value in excess of 1.42 suggests nonrejection of the null hypothesis. A sample value between 1.01 and 1.42 is in the 'inconclusive' region.

1% lower and upper bounds

$K =$	1		2		3		4		5	
T	d_L	d_U	d_L	d_U	d_L	d_U	d_L	d_U	d_L	d_U
15	0.81	1.07	0.70	1.25	0.59	1.46	0.49	1.70	0.39	1.96
16	0.84	1.09	0.74	1.25	0.63	1.44	0.53	1.66	0.44	1.90
17	0.87	1.10	0.77	1.25	0.67	1.43	0.57	1.63	0.48	1.85
18	0.90	1.12	0.80	1.26	0.71	1.42	0.61	1.60	0.52	1.80
19	0.93	1.13	0.83	1.26	0.74	1.41	0.65	1.58	0.56	1.77
20	0.95	1.15	0.86	1.27	0.77	1.41	0.68	1.57	0.60	1.74
21	0.97	1.16	0.89	1.27	0.80	1.41	0.72	1.55	0.63	1.71
22	1.00	1.17	0.91	1.28	0.83	1.40	0.75	1.54	0.66	1.69
23	1.02	1.19	0.94	1.29	0.86	1.40	0.77	1.53	0.70	1.67
24	1.04	1.20	0.96	1.30	0.88	1.41	0.80	1.53	0.72	1.66
25	1.05	1.21	0.98	1.30	0.90	1.41	0.83	1.52	0.75	1.65
26	1.07	1.22	1.00	1.31	0.93	1.41	0.85	1.52	0.78	1.64
27	1.09	1.23	1.02	1.32	0.95	1.41	0.88	1.51	0.81	1.63
28	1.10	1.24	1.04	1.32	0.97	1.41	0.90	1.51	0.83	1.62
29	1.12	1.25	1.05	1.33	0.99	1.42	0.92	1.51	0.85	1.61
30	1.13	1.26	1.07	1.34	1.01	1.42	0.94	1.51	0.88	1.61
31	1.15	1.27	1.08	1.34	1.02	1.42	0.96	1.51	0.90	1.60
32	1.16	1.28	1.10	1.35	1.04	1.43	0.98	1.51	0.92	1.60
33	1.17	1.29	1.11	1.36	1.05	1.43	1.00	1.51	0.94	1.59
34	1.18	1.30	1.13	1.36	1.07	1.43	1.01	1.51	0.95	1.59
35	1.19	1.31	1.14	1.37	1.08	1.44	1.03	1.51	0.97	1.59
36	1.21	1.32	1.15	1.38	1.10	1.44	1.04	1.51	0.99	1.59
37	1.22	1.32	1.16	1.38	1.11	1.45	1.06	1.51	1.00	1.59
38	1.23	1.33	1.18	1.39	1.12	1.45	1.07	1.52	1.02	1.58
39	1.24	1.34	1.19	1.39	1.14	1.45	1.09	1.52	1.03	1.58
40	1.25	1.34	1.20	1.40	1.15	1.46	1.10	1.52	1.05	1.58
45	1.29	1.38	1.24	1.42	1.20	1.48	1.16	1.53	1.11	1.58
50	1.32	1.40	1.28	1.45	1.24	1.49	1.20	1.54	1.16	1.59
55	1.36	1.43	1.32	1.47	1.28	1.51	1.25	1.55	1.21	1.59
60	1.38	1.45	1.35	1.48	1.32	1.52	1.28	1.56	1.25	1.60
65	1.41	1.47	1.38	1.50	1.35	1.53	1.31	1.57	1.28	1.61
70	1.43	1.49	1.40	1.52	1.37	1.55	1.34	1.58	1.31	1.61
75	1.45	1.50	1.42	1.53	1.39	1.56	1.37	1.59	1.34	1.62
80	1.47	1.52	1.44	1.54	1.42	1.57	1.39	1.60	1.36	1.62
85	1.48	1.53	1.46	1.55	1.43	1.58	1.41	1.60	1.39	1.63
90	1.50	1.54	1.47	1.56	1.45	1.59	1.43	1.61	1.41	1.64
95	1.51	1.55	1.49	1.57	1.47	1.60	1.45	1.62	1.42	1.64
100	1.52	1.56	1.50	1.58	1.48	1.60	1.46	1.63	1.44	1.65

References

Abel, A., Dornbusch, R., Huizinga, J. and Marcus, A. (1979), Money Demand During Hyperinflation, *Journal of Monetary Economics*, Vol. 5, pp. 97–104.

Abidir, K.M. (1993), On the Asymptotic Power of Unit Root Tests, *Econometric Theory*, Vol. 9, pp. 189–221.

Abuaf, N. and Jorion, J. (1990), Purchasing Power Parity in the Long Run, *Journal of Finance*, Vol. 45, pp. 157–174.

Adler, M. and Lehman, B. (1983), Deviations from Purchasing Power Parity in the Long Run, *Journal of Finance*, Vol. 38, pp. 147–187.

Aggarwal, R. and Park, Y. (1994), The Relationship Between Daily US and Japanese Equity Prices: Evidence from Spot Versus Futures Prices, *Journal of Banking and Finance*, Vol. 18, pp. 757–773.

Ahn, S.K. and Reinsel, G.C. (1988), Nested Reduced-rank Autoregressive Models for Multiple Time Series, *Biometrika*, Vol. 80, pp. 855–868.

Ahn, S.K. and Reinsel, G.C. (1990), Estimation for Partially Nonstationary Multivariate Autoregressive Models, *Journal of the American Statistical Asociation*, Vol. 85, pp. 813–823.

Akaike, H. (1974), A New Look at Statistical Model Identification, *IEEE Transactions on Automatic Control*, Vol. 19, pp. 716–723.

Amemiya, T. (1985), *Advanced Econometrics*, Blackwell, Oxford.

Anderson, L.C. and Carlson, K.M. (1972), An Econometric Analysis of the Relation of Monetary Variables to the Behaviour of Prices and Unemployment, in O. Eckstein (ed.), *The Econometrics of Price Determination*, Board of the Governors of the Federal Reserve System, Washington.

Andrews, D.W.K. (1991), Heteroskedasticity and Autocorrelation Consistent Covariance Matrix Estimation, *Econometrica*, Vol. 59, pp. 817–858.

Andrews, D.W.K. (1993), Exactly Median-unbiased Estimation Of First Order, Autoregressive/Unit Root Models, *Econometrica*, Vol. 61, pp. 139–165.

Ashworth, J. and Evans, L. (1996), Functional Form of the Demand for Real Balances in the Cagan Model of Hyperinflation, *University of Durham Working Paper*, No. 167.

Baba, Y., Hendry, D.F. and Starr, R.M. (1992), The Demand for M1 in the USA, 1960–1988, *The Review of Economic Studies*, Vol. 59, pp. 25–61.

Balassa, B. (1964), The Purchasing Power Parity Doctrine: A Reappraisal, *Journal of Political Economy*, Vol. 72, pp. 584–596.

Ballie, R.T. and Bollerslev, T. (1989), The Message in Daily Exchange Rates: A Conditional Variance Tale, *Journal of Economic and Business Statistics*, Vol. 7, pp. 297–305.

Banerjee, A., Hendry, D.F. and Smith, G.W. (1986), Exploring Equilibrium Relationships in Economics Through Static Models: Some Monte Carlo Evidence, *Oxford Bulletin of Economics and Statistics*, Vol. 48, pp. 253–277.

Banerjee, A., Dolado, J.J., Galbraith, J.W. and Hendry, D.F. (1993), *Co-integration, Error-Correction and the Econometric Analysis of Non-stationary Data*, Oxford University Press, Oxford.

Barro, R.J. (1976), Integral Constraints and Aggregation in an Inventory Model of Money Demand, *Journal of Finance*, Vol. 31, pp. 77–86.

Baumol, W.J. (1952), The Transactions Demand for Cash – An Inventory Theoretic Appoach, *Quarterly Journal of Economics*, Vol. 66, pp. 545–556.

Bera, A.K. and Higgins, M.L. (1995), On ARCH Models: Properties, Estimation and Testing, Chapter 8 in L. Oxley, D.A.R. George, C.J. Roberts and S. Sayer. (eds) (1995), *Surveys in Econometrics*, Basil Blackwell, Oxford, pp. 215–272.

Berndt, E.R. (1991), *The Practice of Econometrics: Classic and Contemporary*, Addison-Wesley, Massachusetts.

Beveridge, S. and Oickle, C. (1993), Estimating Fractionally Integrated Time Series Models, *Economics Letters*, Vol. 43, pp. 137–142.

Bewley, R.A. (1979), The Direct Estimation of the Equilibrium Response in a Linear Model, *Economics Letters*, Vol. 3, pp. 357–361.

Bickel, P.J. (1978), Using Residuals Robustly 1: Tests for Heteroscedasticity, Nonlinearity, *The Annals of Statistics*, Vol. 6, pp. 266–291.

Bilson, J.F.O. (1978), Rational Expectations and the Exchange Rate, in H.F. Johnson and J.A. Frenkel (eds), *The Economics of Exchange Rates*, Addison-Wesley, Massachusetts.

Black, F. (1976), Studies of Stock Price Volatility Changes, *Proceedings of the 1976 Meetings Of The American Statistical Association, Business and Economic Statistics Section*, pp. 177–181.

Blough, S.R. (1992), The Relationship Between Power and Level for Generic Unit Root Tests in Finite Samples, *Journal of Applied Econometrics*, Vol. 7, pp. 295–308.

Bollerslev, T. (1986), Generalised Autoregressive Conditional Heteroskedasticity, *The Journal of Econometrics*, Vol. 31, pp. 307–327, reprinted as Chapter 3 in R.F. Engle (1995a), *ARCH Selected Readings*, Oxford University Press, Oxford, pp. 42–61.

Bollerslev, T. (1987), A Conditionally Heteroskedastic Time-Series Model for Security Prices and Rates of Return Data, *Review of Economics and Statistics*, Vol. 69, pp. 542–547.

Bollerslev, T. (1990), Modelling the Coherence in Short-Run Nominal Exchange Rates: A Multivariate Generalised ARCH Approach, *Review of Economics and Statistics*, Vol. 72, pp. 498–505, reprinted as Chapter 14 in R.F. Engle (1995a), *ARCH Selected Readings*, Oxford University Press, Oxford, pp. 300–313.

Bollerslev, T. and Wooldridge, J.M. (1992), Quasi-Maximum Likelihood Estimation and Inference in Dynamic Models with Time Varying Variances, *Econometric Reviews*, Vol. 11, pp. 143–172.

Bollerslev, T., Chou, R.Y. and Kroner, K.F. (1992), ARCH Modelling in Finance, a Review of the Theory and Empirical Evidence, *Journal of Econometrics*, Vol. 52, pp. 5–59.

Bomberger, W.A. (1993), Income, Wealth and Household Demand for Deposits, *American Economic Review*, Vol. 83, pp. 1034–1044.

Booth, G.G., Martikainen, T. and Tse, Y. (1997), Price and Volatility Spillovers in Scandinavian Stock Markets, *Journal of Banking and Finance*, Vol. 21, pp. 811–823.

Boswijk, H.P. (1994), Testing for an Unstable Root in Conditional and Structural Error Correction Models, *Journal of Econometrics*, Vol. 63, pp. 37–60.

Boswijk, H.P. (1996), Testing Identifiability of Cointegrating Vectors, *Journal of Business and Economic Statistics*, Vol. 14, pp. 153–160.

Box, G.E.P. and Jenkins, G.M. (1970), *Time Series Analysis, Forecasting and Control*, Holden-Day, San Francisco.

Box, G.E.P. and Pearce, D.A. (1970), Distribution of Residual Autocorrelations in Autoregressive Integrated Moving Average Time Series Models, *Journal of the American Statistical Association*, Vol. 65, pp. 1509–1526.

Braun, P.A., Nelson, D. and Sunier, A. (1995), Good News, Bad News, Volatility, and Betas, *Journal of Finance*, Vol. 50, pp. 1575–1603.

Breitung, J. and Gouriéroux, C. (1997), Rank Tests for Unit Roots, *Journal of Econometrics*, Vol. 81, pp. 7–27.

Breusch, T.S. (1978), Testing for Autocorrelation in Dynamic Linear Models, *Australian Economic Papers*, Vol. 17, pp. 334–355.

Breusch, T.S. and Pagan, A.R. (1979), A Simple Test for Heteroscedasticity and Random Coefficient Variation, *Econometrica*, Vol. 47, pp. 1287–1294.

Brooks, C. and Henry, O.T. (1999), Linear and Non-Linear Transmission of Equity Return Volatility: Evidence from the US, Japan and Australia, Mimeo, Univerisity of Reading.

Bureau of Economic Analysis (1992), *Business Statistics, 1963–91*, US Department of Commerce, Washington.

Bureau of Economic Analysis (1993a), *Fixed Reproducible Tangible Wealth in the United States, 1925–89*, US Department of Commerce, Washington.

Bureau of Economic Analysis (1993b), *National Income and Product Accounts of the United States* (NIPA), Vol. 2, US Department of Commerce, Washington.

Cagan, P. (1956), The Monetary Dynamics of Hyperinflation, in *Studies in the Quantity Theory of Money*, edited by M. Friedman, University of Chicago Press, Chicago, pp. 25–120.

Campbell, J.Y. (1996), A Defense of Traditional Hypotheses About the Term Structure of Interest Rates, *Journal of Finance*, Vol. XLI, pp. 183–193.

Campbell, J.Y. and Mankiw, N.G. (1987), Are Output Fluctuations Transitory?, *Quarterly Journal of Economics*, Vol. 102, pp. 857–880.

Campbell, J.Y. and Perron, P. (1991), Pitfalls and Opportunities: What Macroeconomists Should Know About Unit Roots, *NBER Macroeconomics Annual*, NBER, Cambridge, pp. 139–201.

Campbell, J.Y. and Shiller, R.J. (1984), A Simple Account of the Behaviour of Long-term Interest Rates, *American Economic Review*, Vol. 74, pp. 44–48.

Campbell, J.Y. and Shiller, R.J. (1987), Cointegration and Tests of Present Value Models, *Journal of Political Economy*, Vol. 95, pp. 1062–1088.

Campbell, J.Y. and Shiller, R.J. (1991) Yield Spreads and Interest Rate Movements: A Bird's Eye View, *The Review of Economic Studies*, Vol. 58, pp. 495–514.

Campbell, T.S. and Kracaw, W.A. (1993), *Financial Risk Management*, HarperCollins, New York.

Carlin, W. and Soskice, D.W. (1990), *Macroeconomics and the Wage Bargain: A Modern Approach to Employment, Inflation and the Exchange Rate*, Oxford University Press, Oxford.

Chang, W.W., Hamberg, D. and Hirata, J. (1983), Liquidity Preference as Behaviour Towards Risk is a Demand for Short-term Securities Not Money, *American Economic Review*, Vol. 73, pp. 420–427.

Charemza, W.W. and Deadman, D.F. (1992), *New Directions in Econometric Practice*, Edward Elgar, Aldershot.

Chen, B. (1995), Long-Run Purchasing Power Parity: Evidence from Some European Monetary System Countries, *Applied Economics*, Vol. 27, pp. 377–383.

Cheung, Y-W. (1993), Long Memory in Foreign-exchange Rates, *Journal of Business and Economic Statistics*, Vol. 11, pp. 93–101.

Cheung, Y-W. and Lai, K.S. (1993a), A Fractional Cointegration Analysis of Purchasing Power Parity, *Journal of Business and Economic Statistics*, Vol. 11, pp. 103–112.

Cheung, Y-W. and Lai, K.S. (1993b), Finite-Sample Sizes of Johansen's Likelihood Ratio Tests for Cointegration, *Oxford Bulletin of Economics and Statistics*, Vol. 55, pp. 313–328.

Cheung, Y-W. and Lai, K.S. (1994), Mean Reversion in Real Exchange Rates, *Economics Letters*, Vol. 46, pp. 251–256.

Cheung, Y-W. and Lai, K.S. (1995), Lag Order and Critical Values of the Augmented Dickey–Fuller Test, *Journal of Business and Economic Statistics*, Vol. 13, pp. 277–280.

Choi, I. (1993), Asymptotic Normality of the Least Squares Estimates for Higher Order Autoregressive Integrated Processes with Some Applications, *Econometric Theory*, Vol. 9, pp. 263–282.

Chow, G.C. (1960), Tests of Equality Between Sets of Coefficients in Two Linear Regressions, *Econometrica*, Vol. 28, pp. 591–605.

Christiano, L. (1987), Cagan's Model of Hyperinflation Under Rational Expectations, *International Economic Review*, Vol. 28, pp. 33–49.

Christiano, L.J. and Eichenbaum, M. (1990), Unit Roots in Real GNP: Do We Know and Do We Care?, *Carnegie-Rochester Conference Series on Public Policy*, Vol. 32. pp. 7–62.

Christie, A.A. (1982), The Stochastic Behaviour of Common Stock Variances: Value, Leverage, and Interest Rate Effects, *Journal of Financial Economics*, Vol. 10, pp. 407–432.

Clements, M. and Mizon, G.E. (1991), Empirical Analysis of Macroeconomic Time Series: VAR and Structural Models, *European Economic Review*, Vol. 35, pp. 887–917.

Cochrane, J.H. (1988), How Big is the Random Walk in GNP?, *Journal of Political Economy*, Vol. 96, pp. 893–920.

Cochrane, J.H. (1991), A Critique of the Application of Unit Root Tests, *Journal of Economic Dynamics and Control*, Vol. 15, pp. 275–284.

Cooper, J.C.B. (1994), Purchasing Power Parity: A Cointegration Analysis of the Australian, New Zealand and Singaporean Currencies, *Applied Economics, Letters*, Vol. 1, pp. 167–171.

Cox, D.R. and Hinkley, D.V. (1974), *Theoretical Statistics*, Chapman and Hall, London.

Cuthbertson, K.C. (1996a), *Quantitative Financial Economics*, John Wiley, New York.

Cuthbertson, K.C. (1996b), The Expectations Hypothesis of the Term Structure: The UK Interbank Market, *The Economic Journal*, Vol. 106, pp. 578–592.

Cuthbertson, K.C., Hayes, S. and Nitzsche, D. (1996), The Behaviour of Certificate of Deposit Rates in the UK, *Oxford Economic Papers*, Vol. 48, pp. 397–414.

Cuthbertson, K., Hall, S.G. and Taylor, M.P. (1992), *Applied Econometric Techniques*, Phillip Allan, New York.

Davidian, M. and Carroll, R.J. (1987), Variance Function Estimation, *Journal of the American Statistical Association*, Vol. 82, pp. 1079–1081.

Davidson, J. (1994), Identifying Cointegrating Regressions by the Rank Condition, *Oxford Bulletin of Economics and Statistics*, Vol. 56, pp. 105–110.

Davidson, J. (1995), *Stochastic Limit Theory*, Oxford University Press, Oxford.

Davidson, J., Hendry. D.F., Srba, F. and Yeo, S. (1978), Econometric Modelling of the Aggregate Time Series Relationship Between Consumers' Expenditure and Income in the United Kingdom, *The Economic Journal*, Vol. 88, pp. 661–692.

De Gregorio, J., Giovannini, A. and Krueger, T.H. (1994), The Behaviour of Nontradable Goods Prices in Europe: Evidence and Interpretation, *Review of International Economics,* Vol. 2, pp. 284–305.

De Gregorio, J., Giovannini, A. and Wolf, H.C. (1994), International Evidence on Tradables and Nontradables Inflation, *European Economic Review*, Vol. 38, pp. 1225–1244.

Deaton, A.S. (1977), Involuntary Saving Through Unanticipated Inflation, *American Economic Review*, Vol. 67, pp. 899–910.

Deb, P. and Sefton, M. (1996), The Distribution of a Lagrange Multiplier Test of Normality, *Economics Letters*, Vol. 51, pp. 123–130.

Demetriades, P.O. and Hussein, K.A. (1996), Does Financial Development Cause Economic Growth? Time Series Evidence from 16 Countries, *Journal of Development Economics*, Vol. 51, pp. 387–411.

Demetriades, P.O. and Luintel, K.B. (1997), The Direct Costs of Financial Repression: Evidence from India, *The Review of Economics and Statistics*, Vol. 52, pp. 311–319.

Desai, M. (1984), Wages, Prices and Unemployment a Quarter Century After the Phillips Curve, Chapter 9 in D.F. Hendry and K.F. Wallis (eds), *Econometrics and Quantitative Economics*, Blackwell, Oxford, pp. 253–274.

Dhrymes, P.J. (1970), *Econometrics*, Statistical Foundations and Applications, Harper International, New York.

Dhrymes, P.J. (1981), *Distributed Lags, Problems of Estimation and Formulation* (2nd edn), North-Holland, Amsterdam.

Dickey, D.A. (1975), Hypothesis Testing for Nonstationary Time Series, unpublished manuscript, Iowa State University, Iowa.

Dickey, D.A. and Fuller, W.A. (1979), Distribution of the Estimators for Autoregressive Time Series With a

Unit Root, *Journal of the American Statistical Association*, Vol. 74, pp. 427–431.

Dickey, D.A. and Fuller, W.A. (1981), Likelihood Ratio Statistics for Autoregressive Time Series With a Unit Root, *Econometrica*, Vol. 49, pp. 1057–1022.

Dickey, D.A. and Pantula, S.G. (1987), Determining the Order of Differencing in Autoregressive Processes, *Journal of Business and Economic Statistics*, Vol. 5, pp. 455–461.

Dickey, D.A. and Rossana, R.J. (1994), Cointegrated Time Series: A Guide to Estimation ad Hypothesis Testing, *Oxford Bulletin of Economics and Statistics*, Vol. 56, pp. 325–353.

Dickey, D.A., Bell, W.R. and Miller, R.B. (1986), Unit Roots in Time Series Models: Tests and Implications, *The American Statistician*, Vol. 40, pp. 12–26.

Dickey, D.A., Hasza, D.F. and Fuller, W.A. (1984), Testing for Unit Roots in Seasonal Time Series, *Journal of the American Statistical Association*, Vol. 79, pp. 355–367.

Diebold, F.X., Husted, S. and Rush, M. (1991), Real Exchange Rates Under the Gold Standard, *Journal of Political Economy*, Vol. 99, pp. 1252–1271.

Diebold, F.X., Husted, S. and Rush, M. (1993), The Monetary Approach to the Exchange Rate: Rational Expectations, Long-run Equilibrium and Forecasting, *I.M.F. Staff Papers*, Vol. 40, pp. 89–107.

Doan, A.T. (1996), *RATS User's Manual*, Estima, Evanston, US.

Doan, A.T., Litterman, R. and Sims, C.A. (1984), Forecasting and Conditional Projection Using Realistic Prior Distributions, *Econometric Reviews*, Vol. 3, pp. 1–100.

Dodds, J.C. and Ford, J.L. (1974), *Expectations, Uncertainty and the Term Structure of Interest Rates*, Martin Robertson, London.

Dolado, J.J., Jenkinson, T. and Sosvilla-Rivero, S. (1990), Cointegration and Unit Roots, *Journal of Economic Surveys*, Vol. 4, pp. 249–273.

Doornik, J.A. and Hendry, D.F. (1994), *PcGive 8.0: An Interactive Econometric Modelling System*, International Thomson Publishing, London.

Doornik, J.A. and Hendry, D.F. (1996), *PcGive Professional 9.0 for Windows*, International Thompson Publishing, London.

Dornbusch, R. and Fischer, S. (1981), *Macroeconomics*, McGraw-Hill, New York.

Durbin, J. and Watson, G.S. (1950), Testing for Serial Correlation in Least Squares Regression – I, *Biometrika*, Vol. 37, pp. 409–428.

Durbin, J. and Watson, G.S. (1951), Testing for Serial Correlation in Least Squares Regression – I, *Biometrika*, Vol. 38, pp. 159–178.

Durbin, J. and Watson, G.S. (1971), Testing for Serial Correlation in Least Squares Regression – III, *Biometrika*, Vol. 58, pp. 1–42.

Durlauf, S.N. and Phillips, P.C.B. (1988), Trends Versus Random Walks in Time Series Analysis, *Econometrica*, Vol. 56, pp. 1333–1354.

Elyasiani, E. and Nasseh, A. (1994), The Appropriate Scale Variable in the US Money Demand: An Application of Nonnested Tests of Consumption Versus Income Measures, *Journal of Business and Economic Statistics*, Vol. 12, pp. 47–55.

Enders, W. (1988), ARIMA and Cointegration Tests of PPP Under Fixed and Flexible Exchange Rate Regimes, *The Review of Economics and Statistics*, Vol. 70, pp. 504–511.

Enders, W. (1995), *Applied Econometric Time Series*, John Wiley, New York.

Engel, C. (1993), Real Exchange Rates and Relative Prices? An Empirical Investigation, *Journal of Monetary Economics*, Vol. 32, pp. 35–50.

Engle, R.F. (1982), Autoregressive Conditional Heteroskedasticity with Estimates of the Variance of United Kingdom Inflation, *Econometrica*, Vol. 50, pp. 987–1006, reprinted as Chapter 1 in R.F. Engle, (1995a), *ARCH Selected Readings*, Oxford University Press, Oxford, pp. 1–24.

Engle, R.F. (1995a), *ARCH Selected Readings*, Oxford University Press, Oxford.

Engle, R.F. (1995b), Introduction to R.F. Engle (1995a), *ARCH Selected Readings*, Oxford University Press, Oxford.

Engle, R.F. and Bollerslev, T. (1986), Modelling the Persistence of Conditional Variance, *Econometric Reviews*, Vol. 5, pp. 1–50.

Engle, R.F. and Chowdury, M. (1992), Implied ARCH Models from Option Prices, *Journal of Econometrics*, Vol. 52, pp. 289–311, reprinted as Chapter 17 in R.F. Engle (1995a), *ARCH Selected Readings*, Oxford University Press, Oxford, pp. 353–374.

Engle, R.F. and González-Rivera, G. (1991), Semiparametric ARCH Models, *Journal of Business and Economics Statistics*, Vol. 9, pp. 345–359, reprinted as Chapter 6 in R.F. Engle (1995a), *ARCH Selected Readings*, Oxford University Press, Oxford, pp. 115–144.

Engle, R.F. and Granger, C.W.J. (1987), Co-integration and Error Correction: Representation, Estimation and Testing, *Econometrica*, Vol. 55, pp. 251–276.

Engle, R.F. and Granger, C.W.J. (eds) (1991) *Long-Run Economic Relationships. Readings in Cointegration*, Oxford University Press, Oxford.

Engle, R.F. and Kraft, D. (1983), Multiperiod Forecast Error Variances of Inflation Estimated from ARCH Models, in A. Zellner (ed.), *Applied Time Series Analysis of Economic Data*, Washington, DC.

Engle, R.F. and Ng, V.K. (1993), Measuring and Testing the Impact of News on Volatility, *Journal of Finance*, Vol. 48, pp. 1749–1778, reprinted as Chapter 7 in R.F. Engle (1995a), *ARCH Selected Readings*, Oxford University Press, Oxford, pp. 145–175.

Engle, R.F. and Yoo, B.S. (1987) Forecasting and Testing in Cointegrated Systems, *Journal Of Econometrics*, Vol. 35, pp. 143–159.

Engle, R.F. and Yoo, B.S. (1991), Cointegrated Time Series: An Overview With New Results, Chapter 12 in R.F. Engle and C.W.J. Granger (eds) (1991), *Long-Run Economic Relationships. Readings in Cointegration*, Oxford University Press, Oxford, pp. 237–266.

Engle, R.F., Ito, T. and Lin, W. (1990), Meteor Showers or Heatwaves? Heteroskedastic Intra-daily Volatility in the Foreign Exchange Market, *Econometrica*, Vol. 58, pp. 525–542, reprinted as Chapter 18 in R.F. Engle (1995a), *ARCH Selected Readings*, Oxford University Press, Oxford, pp. 375–394.

Engle, R.F., Lilien, D.M. and Robins, R.P. (1987), Estimating Time-Varying Risk Premia in the Term Structure: The ARCH-M Model, *Econometrica*, Vol. 55, pp. 391–407, reprinted as Chapter 2 in R.F. Engle (1995a), *ARCH Selected Readings*, Oxford University Press, Oxford, pp. 24–41.

Engle, R.F., Ng, V.K. and Rothschild, M. (1990), Asset Pricing With a FACTOR-ARCH Covariance Structure: Empirical Estimates for Treasury Bills, *Journal of Econometrics*, Vol. 45, pp. 213–237, reprinted as Chapter 13 in R.F. Engle (1995a), *ARCH Selected Readings*, Oxford University Press, Oxford, pp. 277–299.

Engle, R.F., Granger, C.W.J., Hylleberg, S. and Lee, H.S. (1993), Seasonal Cointegration. The Japanese Consumption Function, *Journal of Econometrics*, Vol. 55, pp. 275–298.

Engsted, T. (1993), Cointegration and Cagan's Model of Hyperinflation Under Rational Expectations, *Journal of Money, Credit and Banking*, Vol. 25, pp. 350–360.

Ericsson, N.R. (1995), Conditional and Structural Error Correction Models, *Journal of Econometrics*, Vol. 69, pp. 159–171.

Ericsson, N.R., Hendry, D.F. and Prestwich, K.M. (1998), The Demand for Broad Money in the United Kingdom, 1878–1993, *Scandanavian Journal of Economics*, Vol. 100, pp. 289–324.

Ermini, L. (1989), Some New Evidence on the Timing of Consumption Decisions, *The Review of Economics and Statistics*, Vol. 70, pp. 643–650.

Evans, C.L. (1994), The Post-War U.S. Phillips Curve. A Comment, *Carnegie-Rochester Conference Series on Public Policy*, Vol. 41, pp. 221–230.

Evans, G.B.A. and Savin, N.E. (1981), Testing for Unit Roots: 1, *Econometrica*, Vol. 49, pp. 753–779.

Evans, G.B.A. and Savin, N.E. (1984), Testing for Unit Roots: 2, *Econometrica*, Vol. 52, pp. 1241–1269.

Evans, M.D.D. and Lewis, K.K. (1994), Do Stationary Risk Premia Explain it All?, *Journal of Monetary Economics*, Vol. 33, pp. 285–318.

Fama, E.F. and Schwert, G.W. (1977), Asset Returns and Inflation, *Journal of Financial Economics*, Vol. 5, pp. 115–146.

Faust, J. (1996), Near Observational Equivalence and Theoretical Size Problems With Unit Root Tests, *Econometric Theory*, Vol. 12, pp. 724–731.

Feige, E. and Parkin, M. (1971), The Optimal Quantity of Money, Bonds, Commodity Inventories and Capital, *American Economic Review*, Vol. 61, pp. 335–349.

Feller, W. (1968), *An Introduction to Probability Theory and its Applications*, Vol. 1 (3rd edn), John Wiley, New York.

Fellner, W. (1946), *Monetary Policies and Full Employment*, University of California Press, Berkeley, CA.

Fisher, I. (1926), A Statistical Relation Between Unemployment and Price Changes, *International Labour Review*, Vol. 13, pp. 785–792, reprinted in the *Journal of Political Economy* (1973), Vol. 81, pp. 496–502.

Flemming, J.S. (1976), *Inflation*, Oxford, Oxford University Press.

Franses, P.H. and Haldrup, N. (1994), The Effect of Additive Outliers on Tests for Unit Roots and Cointegration, *Journal of Business and Economic Statistics*, Vol. 12, pp. 471–478.

French, K., Schwert, G.W. and Stambaugh, R. (1987), Expected Stock Returns and Volatility, *Journal of Financial Economics*, Vol. 19, pp. 3–29, reprinted as Chapter 4 in R.F. Engle (1995a), *ARCH Selected Readings*, Oxford University Press, Oxford, pp. 61–86.

Frenkel, J.A. (1981), The Collapse of Purchasing Power Parities During the 1970s, *European Economic Review*, Vol. 16, pp. 145–165.

Friedman, M. (ed.) (1956), *Studies in the Quantity Theory of Money*, Chicago University Press, Chicago.

Friedman, M. (1968), The Role of Monetary Policy, *American Economic Review*, Vol. 58, pp. 1–17.

Friedman, M. (1975), Unemployment Versus Inflation, an Evaluation of the Phillips Curve, *Institute of Economic Affairs*, London, pp. 11–48.

Friedman, M. (1977), Nobel Lecture: Inflation and Unemployment, *Journal of Political Economy*, Vol. 85, pp. 451–472.

Fuller, W.A. (1976), *Introduction to Statistical Time Series*, John Wiley, New York.

Gagnon, J.E. and Knetter, M.M. (1991), Markup Adjustment and Exchange Rate Fluctuations: Evidence from Panel Data on Automobiles and Total Manufacturing, Federal Reserve Board of Governors, International Finance Discussion Paper No. 389.

Geweke, J.F. (1986), Comment on Modelling the Persistence of Conditional Variance, *Econometric Reviews*, Vol. 5, pp. 57–62.

Geweke, J.F. and Porter-Hudak, S. (1982), The Estimation and Application of Long Memory Time Series Models, *Journal of Time Series Analysis*, Vol. 4, pp. 221–238.

Ghysels, E. (1990), Unit Root Tests and the Statistical Pitfalls of Seasonal Adjustment: The Case of US Post

War Real GNP, *Journal of Business and Economic Statistics*, Vol. 8, pp. 145–152.

Ghysels, E. and Perron, P. (1993), The Effect of Seasonal Adjustment Filters on Tests for a Unit Root, *Journal of Econometrics*, Vol. 55, pp. 57–98.

Gil-Alana, L.A. and Robinson, P.M. (1997), Testing of Unit Root and Other Nonstationary Hypotheses in Macroeconomic Time Series, *Journal Of Econometrics*, Vol. 80, pp. 241–268.

Gilbert, C.G. (1976), The Original Phillips Curve Estimates, *Economica*, Vol. 43, pp. 51–57.

Gilboy, E.W. (1938/39a), The Propensity to Consume, *The Quarterly Journal of Economics,* Vol. LIII, pp. 120–140.

Gilboy, E.W. (1938/39b), The Propensity to Consume: Reply, *The Quarterly Journal of Economics*, Vol. LIII, p. 633.

Gilboy, E.W. (1940), Income–Expenditure Relations, *The Review of Economic Statistics*, Vol. 22, pp. 115–121.

Giovannini, A. (1988), Exchange Rates and Traded Goods Prices, *Journal of International Economy*, Vol. 24, pp. 45–68.

Glen, J.D. (1992), Real Exchange Rates in the Short, Medium and Long Run, *Journal of International Economy*, Vol. 33, pp. 147–166.

Glosten, L.R., Jagannathan, R. and Runkle, D.E. (1993), On the Relation Between the Expected Value and the Volatility of the Nominal Excess Return on Stocks, *Journal of Finance*, Vol. 48, pp. 1779–1801.

Godfrey, L.G. (1978a) Testing for Multiplicative Heteroscedasticity, *Journal of Econometrics*, Vol. 8, pp. 227–236.

Godfrey, L.G. (1978b) Testing Against General Autoregressive and Moving Average Error Models When the Regressors include Lagged Dependent Variables, *Econometrica*, Vol. 46, pp. 1293–1302.

Godfrey, L.G. (1978c), Testing for Higher Order Serial Correlation in Regression Equations Where the Regressors Include Lagged Dependent Variables, *Econometrica*, Vol. 46, pp. 1303–1310.

Godfrey, L.G. (1988), *Misspecification Tests in Econometrics*, Cambridge University Press, Cambridge.

Godfrey, L.G. (1999), Instrument Relevance in Multivariate Linear Models, *Review of Economics and Statistics*, Vol. 79, pp. 348–352.

Goldberger, A.S. (1991), *A Course in Econometrics*, Harvard University Press, Massachusetts.

Goldfeld, S.M. (1976), The Case of the Missing Money, *Brookings Papers on Economic Activity*, pp. 683–730.

Goldfeld, S.M. and Quandt, R. (1965), Some Tests for Homoscedasticity, *Journal of the American Statistical Association*, Vol. 60, pp. 539–547.

Goodfriend, M.S. (1982), An Alternative Method of Estimating the Cagan Demand Function in Hyper-inflation Under Rational Expectations, *Journal of Monetary Economics*, Vol. 9, pp. 43–57.

Graham, F.D. (1930), *Exchange, Prices and Production in Hyper-inflation Germany, 1920–23*, Princeton University Press, Princeton.

Granger, C.W.J. (1969), Investigating Causal Relationships by Econometric Models and Cross-spectral Methods, *Econometrica*, Vol. 37, pp. 424–438.

Granger, C.W.J. (1991), Developments in the Study of Cointegrated Economic Variables, Chapter 4 in R.F. Engle and C.W.J. Granger (eds) (1991), *Long-run Economic Relationships*, Oxford University Press, Oxford, pp. 65–80.

Granger, C.W.J. (1997), On Modelling the Long Run in Applied Economics, *The Economic Journal*, Vol. 107, pp. 169–177.

Granger, C.W.J. and Hallman, J. (1991), Nonlinear Transformations of Integrated Time Series, *Journal of Time Series Analysis*, Vol. 12, pp. 207–224.

Granger, C.W.J. and Newbold, P. (1974), Spurious Regressions in Econometrics, *Journal of Econometrics*, Vol. 2, pp. 111–120.

Granger, C.W.J. and Weiss, A.A. (1983), Time Series Analysis of Error-correction Models, in S. Karlin, T. Amemiya and L. Goodman (eds), *Studies in Econometrics, Time Series and Multivariate Statistics*, Academic Press, Academic Press.

Granger, C.W.J., Inoue, T. and Morin, N. (1997), Nonlinear Stochastic Trends, *Journal of Econometrics*, Vol. 81, pp. 65–92.

Greene, W.H. (1997), *Econometric Analysis* (3rd edn), Prentice-Hall, New York (now in 4th edn, 2000).

Gujarati, D.N. (1995), *Basic Econometrics* (3rd edn), McGraw Hill, New York.

Hakkio, C. (1984), A Re-examination of Purchasing Power Parity, *Journal of International Economy*, Vol. 17, pp. 265–277.

Haldrup, N. (1991), A Note on the Dickey–Fuller Regression With a Maintained Trend, University of Aarhus, Institute of Economics Working Paper.

Haldrup, N. (1994), Semiparametric Tests for Double Unit Roots, *Journal of Business and Economic Statistics*, Vol. 12, pp. 109–122.

Haldrup, N. and Hylleberg, S. (1991), Integration, Near Integration and Determininstic Trends, University of Aarhus, Institute of Economics Working Paper, pp. 1–43.

Hall, A.D., Anderson, H.M. and Granger, C.W.J. (1992), A Cointegration Analysis off Treasury Bill Yields, *The Review of Economics and Statistics*, Vol. 74, pp. 116–126.

Hall, A.R. (1994), Testing for a Unit Root in Time Series With Pretest Data-based Model Selection, *Journal of Business and Economic Statistics*, Vol. 12, pp. 461–470.

Hall, B.H. and Cummins, C. (1996), *TSP*, TSP International, Palo Alto, California.

Hallwood, C.P. and MacDonald, R. (1994), *International Money and Finance* (2nd edn), Blackwell: Oxford.

Hamao, Y., Masulis, R.W. and Ng, V.K. (1990), Correlations in Price Changes and Volatility Across International Stock Markets, *Review of Financial Studies*, Vol. 3, pp. 281–308.

Hamilton, J.D. (1994), *Time Series Analysis*, Princeton University Press, Princeton.

Hannan, E.J. and Quinn, B.G. (1979), The Determination of the Order of an Autoregression, *Journal of the Royal Statistical Society B*, Vol. 40, pp. 190–195.

Hansen, B.E. (1992), Efficient Estimation and Testing of Cointegrating Vectors in the Presence of Deterministic Trends, *Journal of Econometrics*, Vol. 53, pp. 87–121.

Hansen, B.E. and Phillips, P.C.B. (1990), Estimation and Inference in Models of Cointegration, in T.B. Fomby and G.F. Rhodes, Jr (eds), *Advances in Econometrics*, Vol. 8, JAI Press, Connecticut, pp. 225–248.

Hansen, H. and Juselius, K. (1995), *CATS in RATS*, Estima, Evanston, US.

Hansen, L.P. and Hodrick, R.J. (1980), Forward Exchange Rates as Optimal Predictions of Future Spot Rates: An Econometric Analysis, *Journal of Political Economy*, Vol. 88, pp. 829–853.

Hansen, P. and Johansen, S.J. (1998), *Workbook on Cointegration*, Oxford University Press, Oxford.

Hardouvelis, G.A. (1994), The Term Structure Spread and Future Changes in Long and Short Rates in the G7 Countries, is there a Puzzle?, *Journal of Monetary Economics*, Vol. 33, pp. 255–283.

Harris, R. (1995), *Using Cointegration Analysis in Econometric Modelling*, Prentice-Hall, Hemel Hempstead, UK.

Harrison, P.J. and Stevens, C.F. (1976), Bayesian Forecasting, *Journal of the Royal Statistical Society B*, Vol. 38, pp. 205–247.

Harvey, A.C. (1981), *The Econometric Analysis of Time Series*, Phillip Allen, Hemel Hempstead (now in 2nd edn, 1990).

Harvey, A.C. (1989), *Forecasting Structural Time Series Models and the Kalman Filter*, Cambridge University Press, Cambridge.

Harvey, A.C. (1997), Trends, Cycles and Autoregressions, *The Economic Journal,* Vol. 107, pp. 192–101.

Harvey, A.C., Ruiz, E. and Shepherd, N. (1994), Multivariate Stochastic Variance Models, *Review of Economic Studies*, Vol. 61, pp. 247–264, reprinted as Chapter 12 in R.F. Engle (1995a), *ARCH Selected Readings*, Oxford University Press, Oxford, pp. 256–276.

Hasza, D.P. and Fuller, W.A. (1979), Estimation for Autoregressive Processes With Unit Roots, *The Annals of Statistics*, Vol. 7, pp. 1106–1120.

Hatanaka, M. (1996), *Time-series-based Econometrics: Unit Roots and Cointegration*, Oxford University Press, Oxford.

Hendry, D.F. (1976), The Structure of Simultaneous Equations Estimators, *Journal of Econometrics*, Vol. 4, pp. 51–88.

Hendry, D.F. (1988), The Encompassing Implications of Feedback Versus Feedforward Mechanisms in Econometrics, *Oxford Economic Papers*, Vol. 40, pp. 132–149.

Hendry, D.F. (1995), *Dynamic Econometrics*, Oxford University Press, Oxford.

Hendry, D.F. and Mizon, G.E. (1990), Procrustean Econometrics: Or the Stretching and Squeezing of Data, in C.W.J. Granger (ed.) (1990), *Modelling Economic Time Series*, Oxford University Press, Oxford.

Hendry, D.F. and Mizon, G.E. (1993), Evaluating Dynamic Econometric Models by Encompassing the VAR, in P.C.B. Phillips (ed.), *Models, Methods, and Applications of Econometrics: Essays in Honour of A.R. Bergstrom*, Blackwell, Oxford.

Hendry, D.F. and Morgan, M.S. (1995), *The Foundations of Econometric Analysis*, Cambridge University Press, Cambridge.

Hendry, D.F. and Richard, J-F. (1982), On the Formulation of Empirical Models in Dynamic Econometrics, *Journal of Econometrics*, Vol. 20, pp. 3–33.

Hendry, D.F. and Richard, J-F. (1983), The Econometric Analysis of Time Series (with discussion), *International Statistical Review*, Vol. 51, pp. 111–163.

Hendry, D.F. and Richard, J-F. (1989), Recent Developments in the Theory of Encompassing, in B. Cornet and H. Tulkens (eds), *Contributions in Operations Research and Econometrics. The XXth Anniversary of Core*, MIT Press, Cambridge, Massachusetts, pp. 393–440.

Hendry, D.F. and Von Ungern-Sternberg, T. (1981), Liquidity and Inflation Effects on Consumers' Behaviour, Chapter 9 in A.S. Deaton (ed.), *Essays in the Theory and Measurement of Consumers' Behaviour*, Cambridge University Press, Cambridge, pp. 237–260.

Hodrick, R.J. (1978), An Empirical Analysis of the Monetary Approach to the Determination of the Exchange Rate, H. Johnson and J.A. Frenkel (eds), *The Economics of Exchange Rates*, Addison-Wesley, Massachusetts.

Hoffman, D.L. and Rasche, R.H. (1991), Long-run Income and Interest Elasticities of Money Demand in the United States, *The Review of Economics and Statistics*, Vol. 73, pp. 665–674.

Hong, Y. and Sheradeh, R.D. (1999), A New Test for ARCH Effects and its Finite Sample Performance, *Journal of Business and Economics Statistics*, Vol. 17, pp. 91–108.

Hosking, J.R.M. (1981), Fractional Differencing, *Biometrika*, Vol. 68, pp. 165–176.

Hseih, D.A. (1983), A Heteroscedasticity-consistent Covariance Matrix Estimator for Time Series Regressions, *Journal of Econometrics*, Vol. 22, pp. 281–290.

Hseih, D.A. (1993), Implications of Nonlinear Dynamics for Financial Risk Management, *Journal of Financial and Quantitative Analysis*, Vol. 28, pp. 41–64.

Hylleberg, S. (ed.) (1992), *Modelling Seasonality*, Oxford University Press, Oxford.

Hylleberg, S. and Mizon, G.E. (1989a), A Note on the Distribution of the Least Squares Estimator of a Random Walk With Drift, *Economics Letters*, Vol. 29, pp. 225–230.

Hylleberg, S. and Mizon, G.E. (1989b), Cointegration and Error Correction Mechanisms, *The Economic Journal*, Vol. 99, pp. 113–125.

Hylleberg, S., Engle, R.F., Granger, C.W.J. and Yoo, B.S. (1990), Seasonal Integration and Cointegration, *Journal of Econometrics*, Vol. 44, pp. 215–238.

Inder, B. (1993), Estimating Long-run Relationships in Economics, *Journal of Econometrics*, Vol. 57, pp. 53–68.

Isard, P. (1977), How Far Can We Push the Law of One Price?, *American Economic Review*, Vol. 65, pp. 942–948.

Jaeger, A. and Kunst, R.M. (1990), Seaonal Adjustment and Measuring Persistence in Output, *Journal of Applied Econometrics*, Vol. 5, pp. 47–58.

Jarque, C.M. and Bera, A.K. (1980), Efficient Tests for Normality, Homoscedasticity and Serial Independence fo Regression Residuals, *Economics Letters*, Vol. 6, pp. 255–259.

Jarque, C.M. and Bera, A.K. (1987), A Test for Normality of Observations and Regression Residuals, *International Statistical Review*, Vol. 55, pp. 163–172.

Johansen, S. (1988), Statistical Analysis of Cointegration Vectors, *Journal of Economic Dynamics and Control*, Vol. 12, pp. 231–254.

Johansen, S. (1992a), Determination of Cointegration Rank in the Presence of a Linear Trend, *Oxford Bulletin of Economics and Statistics*, Vol. 54, pp. 383–397.

Johansen, S. (1992b), Testing Weak Exogeneity and the Order of Cointegration in UK Money Demand Data, *Journal of Policy Modelling*, Vol. 14, pp. 313–334.

Johansen, S. (1992c) Cointegration in Partial Systems and the Efficiency of Single Equation Analysis, *Journal of Econometrics*, Vol. 52, pp. 389–402.

Johansen, S. (1992d), An I(2) Cointegration Analysis of the Purchasing Power Parity Between Australia and USA, in C. Hargreaves (ed.), *Macroeconomic Modelling of the Long Run*, Edward Elgar, London, pp. 229–248.

Johansen, S. (1992e), A Representation of Vector Autoregressive Processes Integrated of Order 2, *Econometric Theory*, Vol. 8, pp. 188–202.

Johansen, S.J. (1995a), *Likelihood-based Inference in Cointegrated Vector Autoregressive Models*, Oxford University Press, Oxford.

Johansen, S. (1995b), Identifying Restrictions of Linear Equations With Applications to Simultaneous Equations and Cointegration, *Journal of Econometrics*, Vol. 69, pp. 111–132.

Johansen, S. and Juselius, K. (1990), Maximum Likelihood Estimation and Inference on Cointegration With Applications to the Demand for Money, *Oxford Bulletin of Economics and Statistics*, Vol. 52, pp. 169–210.

Johansen, S. and Juselius, K. (1992), Testing Structural Hypotheses in a Multivariate Cointegration Analysis of the PPP and the UIP for the UK, *Journal of Econometrics*, Vol. 53, pp. 211–244.

Johansen, S. and Juselius, K. (1994) Identification of the Long-run and the Short-run Structure: An Application to the IS/LM Model, *Journal of Econometrics*, Vol. 63, pp. 7–36.

Johnson, P.A. (1994), On the Number of Common Unit Roots in the Term Structure of Interest Rates, *Applied Economics*, Vol. 26, pp. 815–820.

Judge, G.G. and Bock, M.E. (1978), *The Statistical Implications of Pre-test and Stein Rule Estimators in Econometrics*, North-Holland, New York.

Judge, G.G., Griffiths, W.E., Hill, R.C., Lütkepohl, H. and Lee, T-C. (1982), *Introduction to the Theory and Practice of Econometrics*, John Wiley, New York.

Judge, G.G., Griffiths, W.E., Hill, R.C., Lütkepohl, H. and Lee, T-C. (1985), *The Theory and Practice of Econometrics* (2nd edn), John Wiley, New York.

Juselius, K. (1994), On the Duality Between Long-Run Relations and Common Trends in the I(1) Versus I(2) Model. An Application to Aggregate Money Holdings, *Econometric Reviews*, Vol. 13, pp. 157–178.

Juselius, K. (1995), Do Purchasing Power Parity and Uncovered Interest Parity Hold in the Long Run? An Example of Likelihood Inference in a Multivariate Time Series Model, *Journal of Econometrics*, Vol. 69, pp. 211–240.

Karni, E. (1973), The Transactions Demand for Cash: Incorporation of the Value of Time into the Inventory Approach, *Journal of Political Economy*, Vol. 81, pp. 1216–1225.

Karolyi, G.A. (1995), A Multivariate GARCH Model of International Transmissions of Stock Retrun and Volatility: The Case of the United States and Canada, *Journal of Business and Economic Statistics*, Vol. 13, pp. 11–25.

Kasa, K. (1992), Adjustment Costs and Pricing to Market Theory and Evidence, *Journal of International Economy*, Vol. 32, pp. 1–30.

Kearney, C. and MacDonald, R. (1990), Rational Expectations, Bubbles and Monetary Models of the Exchange Rate: The Australian/U.S. Dollar Rate

During the Recent Float, *Australian Economic Papers*, Vol. 44, pp. 1–20.

Kendall, M. and Stuart, A. (1977). *The Advanced Theory of Statistics* (4th edn), Charles Griffin, London.

Kennedy, P. (1997), *A Guide To Econometrics* (4th edn), Oxford: Blackwell.

Keynes, J.M. (1936), *The General Theory of Employment, Interest and Money*, Macmillan, London.

Keynes, J.M. (1939), Professor Tinbergen's Method, *The Economic Journal*, Vol. 49, pp. 626–639.

King, R.G. and Watson, M.W. (1994a), The Post-War U.S. Phillips Curve: A Revisionist Econometric History, *Carnegie-Rochester Conference Series on Public Policy*, Vol. 41, pp. 157–219.

King, R.G. and Watson, M.W. (1994b), Rejoinder to Evans and McCallum, *Carnegie-Rochester Conference Series on Public Policy*, Vol. 41, pp. 243–250.

King, R.G., Stock, J.H. and Watson, M.W. (1995) Temporal Instability of the Unemployment–Inflation Relationship, *Economic Perspectives*, Federal Reserve Bank of Chicago, pp. 2–12.

Kirchgässner, G. (1991), Comment on M. Clements and G.E. Mizon, Empirical Analysis of Macroeconomic Time Series: VAR and Structural Models, *European Economic Review*, Vol. 35, pp. 918–922.

Kiviet, J.F. and Phillips, G.D.A. (1992), Exact Similar Tests for Unit Roots and Cointegration, *Oxford Bulletin of Economics and Statistics*, Vol. 54, pp. 349–368.

Kliebergen, F. and van Dijk, H.K. (1994), Direct Cointegration Testing in Error Correction Models, *Journal of Econometrics*, Vol. 63, pp. 61–103.

Knetter, M.M. (1989), Price Discrimination by U.S. and German Exporters, *American Economic Review*, Vol. 79, pp. 198–210.

Knetter, M.M. (1993), International Comparisons of Pricing-to-Market Behaviour, *American Economic Review*, Vol. 83, pp. 473–486.

Koenker, R. (1981), A Note on Studentizing a Test for Heteroscedasticity, *Journal of Econometrics*, Vol. 17, pp. 107–112.

Koreisha, S.G. and Pukkila, T. (1995), A Comparison Between Different Order-determination Criteria for Identification of ARIMA Models, *Journal of Business and Economic Statistics*, Vol. 13, pp. 127–131.

Kremers, J.J.M., Ericsson, N.R. and Dolado, J.J. (1992), The Power of Cointegration Tests, *Oxford Bulletin of Economics and Statistics*, Vol. 54, pp. 325–348.

Kwiatkowski, D., Phillips, P.C.B., Schmidt, P. and Shin, Y. (1992), Testing the Null Hypothesis of Stationarity Against the Alternative of a Unit Root, *Journal of Econometrics*, Vol. 54, pp. 159–178.

Kyle, A.S. (1985), Continuous Auctions and Insider Trading, *Econometrica*, Vol. 53, pp. 1315–1335.

Layard, R. and Nickell, S.J. (1985), The Causes of British Unemployment, *National Institute Economic Review*, Vol. 111, pp. 62–85.

Layard, R. and Nickell, S.J. (1986), Unemployment in Britain, *Economica*, Vol. 53, pp. S121–S169.

Leontief, W. (1947), Postulates: Keynes' General Theory and the Classicists, Chapter XIX in S. Harris (ed.), *The New Economics*, Knopf, New York.

Leybourne, S.J. and McCabe, B.P.M. (1994), A Consistent Test for a Unit Root, *Journal of Business and Economic Statistics*, Vol. 12, pp. 157–166.

Leybourne, S.J., McCabe, B.P.M. and Tremayne, A.R. (1996), Can Economic Time Series be Differenced to Stationarity?, *Journal of Business and Economic Statistics*, Vol. 14, pp. 435–446.

Lin, W.L., Engle, R.F. and Ito, T. (1994), Do Bears and Bulls Move Across Borders? International Transmission of Stock Returns and Volatility as the World Turns, *Review of Financial Studies*, Vol. 7, pp. 507–538.

Lipsey, R.G. (1960), The Relation Between Unemployment and the Rate of Change of Money Wage Rates in the United Kingdom, 1862–1957: A Further Analysis, *Economica*, Vol. 27, pp. 456–487.

Ljung, G. and Box, G.E.P. (1979), On a Measure of Lack of Fit in Time Series Models, *Biometrika*, Vol. 66, pp. 255–270.

Lothian, J.R. and Taylor, M.P. (1996), Real Exchange Rate Behaviour: The Recent Float from the Perspective of the Past Two Centuries, *Journal of Political Economy*, Vol. 104, pp. 488–510.

Lucas, R.E. (1972), Econometric Testing of the Natural Rate Hypothesis, in O. Eckstein (ed.), *The Econometrics of Price Determination*, Board of the Governors of the Federal Reserve System, Washington DC.

Lucas, R.E. (1973), Some International Evidence on Output–Inflation Tradeoffs, *American Economic Review*, Vol. 63, pp. 326–334.

Lucas, R.E. (1988), Money Demand in the United States, *Carnegie-Rochester Conference Series on Public Policy*, Vol. 29, pp. 137–168.

Lumsdaine, R.L. (1991), Asymptotic Properties of the Quasi-Maximum Likelihood Estimator in GARCH (1, 1) and IGARCH(1, 1) Models, unpublished manuscript, Princeton University, Department of Economics.

Lumsdaine, R. (1995), Finite-sample Properties of the Maximum Likelihood Estimator in GARCH(1, 1) and IGARCH(1, 1) Models: A Monte Carlo Investigation, *Journal of Business and Economic Statistics*, Vol. 13, pp. 1–10.

Lütkepohl, H. (1991), *Introduction to Time Series Analysis*, Springer-Verlag, Berlin.

MacDonald, R. (1993), Long-run Purchasing Power Parity: Is it for Real?, *The Review of Economics and Statistics*, Vol. 75, pp. 690–695.

MacDonald, R. (1996), Panel Unit Root Tests and Real Exchange Rates, *Economics Letters*, Vol. 75, pp. 7–11.

MacDonald, R. and Marsh, I.W. (1996), On Casselian PPP, Cointegration and Exchange Rate Forecasting, University of Strathclyde Discussion Paper No. 5.

MacDonald, R. and Marsh, I.W. (1997), On Fundamentals and Exchange Rates: A Casselian Perspective, *Review of Economics and Statistics*, Vol. 52, pp. 655–664.

MacDonald, R. and Speight, A.E. (1988), The Term Structure of Interest Rates in the UK, *Bulletin of Economic Research*, Vol. 40, pp. 287–299.

MacDonald, R. and Taylor, M.P. (1991), The Monetary Model of the Exchange Rate: Long Run Relationships and Coefficient Restrictions, *Economics Letters*, Vol. 37, pp. 179–185.

MacDonald, R. and Taylor, M.P. (1993), The Monetary Approach to the Exchange Rate: Rational Expectations, Long-run Equilibrium and Forecasting, *IMF Staff Papers*, 40, pp. 89–107.

MacDonald, R. and Taylor, M.P. (1994), The Monetary Model of the Exchange Rate: Long-run Relationships, Short-run Dynamics and How to Beat a Random Walk, *Journal of International Money and Finance*, Vol. 13, pp. 276–290.

MacKinnon, J. (1991), Critical Values for Cointegration Tests, in R.F. Engle and C.W.J. Granger (eds) (1991), *Long-run Economic Relationships*, Oxford University Press, Oxford, pp. 267–276.

MacKinnon, J. and White, H. (1985), Some Heteroscedasticity Consistent Covariance Matrix Estimators With Improved Finite Sample Properties, *Journal of Econometrics*, Vol. 19, pp. 305–325.

Mandelbrot, B. (1963), The Variation of Certain Speculative Prices, *Journal of Business*, Vol. 36, pp. 394–419.

Mankiw, N.G. and Miron, J.A. (1986), The Changing Behaviour of the Term Structure of Interest Rates, *Quarterly Journal of Economics*, Vol. 101, pp. 211–228.

Marriott, F.H.C. and Pope, J.A. (1954), Bias in the Estimation of Autocorrelations, *Biometrika*, Vol. 41, pp. 390–402.

McCallum, B.T. (1973), Friedman's Missing Equation: Another Approach, *The Manchester School*, Vol. 41, pp. 311–328.

McCallum, B.T. (1974), Wage Rate Changes and the Excess Demand for Labour: An Alternative Formulation, *Economica*, Vol. 41, pp. 269–277.

McCallum, B.T. (1975), Rational Expectations and the Natural Rate Hypothesis: Some Evidence for the United Kingdom, *The Manchester School*, Vol. 43, pp. 56–67.

McCallum, B.T. (1976), Rational Expectations and the Natural Rate Hypothesis: Some Consistent Estimates, *Econometrica*, Vol. 44, pp. 43–52.

McCulloch, J.H. (1990), The Term Structure of Interest Rates, appendix to Chapter 13 in B. Friedman and F. Hahn (eds), *The Handbook of Monetary Economics*, North-Holland, Amsterdam, pp. 672–715.

Meese, R.A. (1986), Testing for Bubbles in Exchange Markets: A Case of Sparkling Rates, *Journal of Political Economy*, Vol. 94, pp. 345–373.

Meese, E. (1990), Currency Fluctuations in the Post-Bretton Woods Era, *Journal of Economic Perspectives*, Vol. 4, pp. 117–134.

Mehra, Y.P. (1993), The Stability of the M2 Demand Function: Evidence from an Error Correction Model, *Journal of Money, Credit and Banking*, Vol. 25, pp. 455–460.

Michael, P., Nobay, A.R. and Peel, D.A. (1994), German Hyperinflation and the Demand for Money Revisited, *International Economic Review*, Vol. 35, pp. 1–22.

Mills, T.C. (1991), The Term Structure of UK Interest Rates: Test of the Expectations Hypothesis, *Applied Economics*, Vol. 23, pp. 599–606.

Mills, T.C. (1993), *The Econometric Modelling of Financial Time Series*, Cambridge University Press, Cambridge.

Mills, T.C. (1999), *The Econometric Modelling of Financial Time Series*, 2nd edn, Cambridge University Press, Cambridge.

Miron, J.A. (1991), Comment (on Campbell and Perron (1991)), *NBER Macroeconomics Annual*, NBER, Cambridge, pp. 211–218.

Modigliani, F. and Sutch, R. (1966), Innovations in Interest Rate Policy, *American Economic Review*, Vol. 56, pp. 178–197.

Montalvo, J.G. (1995), Comparing Cointegrating Regression Estimators: Some Additional Monte Carlo Results, *Economics Letters*, Vol. 49, pp. 229–234.

Muth, J. (1961), Rational Expectations and the Theory of Price Movements, *Econometrica*, Vol. 29, pp. 315–333.

Nelson, C.R. and Kang, H. (1981), Spurious Periodicity in Inappropriately Detrended Time Series, *Econometrica*, Vol. 49, pp. 741–751.

Nelson, C.R. and Plosser, C.I. (1982), Trends and Random Walks in Macroeconomic Time Series, *Journal of Monetary Economics*, Vol. 10, pp. 139–162.

Nelson, D.B. (1990). Stationarity and Persistence in the GARCH(1, 1) Model, *Econometric Theory*, Vol. 6, pp. 318–334, reprinted as Chapter 8 in R.F. Engle (1995a), *ARCH Selected Readings*, Oxford University Press, Oxford, pp. 176–192.

Nelson, D.B. (1991), Conditional Heteroskedasticity in Asset Returns: A New Approach, *Econometrica*, Vol. 59, pp. 347–370, reprinted as Chapter 5 in R.F. Engle (1995a), *ARCH Selected Readings*, Oxford University Press, Oxford, pp. 87–113.

Nelson, D.B. and Cao, C.Q. (1992), Inequality Constraint in the Univariate GARCH(1, 1) Model, *Journal of Business and Economic Statistics*, Vol. 10, pp. 229–235.

Newey, W. and West, K. (1987), A Simple Positive Semi-definite Heteroskedasticity and Autocorrelation Consistent Covariance Matrix, *Econometrica*, Vol. 55, pp. 703–708.

Noh, J., Engle, R.F. and Kane, A. (1994), Forecasting Volatility and Options Prices of the S&P 500 Index, *Journal of Derivatives*, pp. 17–30, reprinted as Chapter 8 in R.F. Engle (1995a), *ARCH Selected Readings*, Oxford University Press, Oxford, pp. 176–192.

Olekalns, N. (1994), Testing for Unit Roots in Seasonally Adjusted Data, *Economics Letters*, Vol. 45, pp. 273–279.

Orcutt, G.H. and Winokur, H.S. (1969), First Order Autoregression: Inference, Estimation and Prediction, *Econometrica*, Vol. 37, pp. 1–14.

Osborn, D.R., Chui, A.P.L., Smith, J.P, and Birchenall, C.R. (1988), Seasonality and the Order of Integration for Consumption, *Oxford Bulletin of Economics and Statistics*, Vol. 50, pp. 361–377.

Osterwald-Lenum, M. (1992), A Note on Quantiles of the Asymptotic Distribution of the Maximum Likelihood Cointegration Rank Test Statistic, *Oxford Bulletin of Economics and Statistics*, Vol. 54, pp. 461–472.

Ouliaris, S., Park, J.Y. and Phillips, P.C.B. (1988), Testing for a Unit Root in the Presence of a Maintained Trend, in B. Raj (ed.), *Advances in Econometrics and Modeling*, Kluwer Academic Publishers, Needham, MA.

Oxley, L., George, D.A.R., Roberts, C.J. and Sayer, S. (eds) (1995), *Surveys in Econometrics*, Basil Blackwell, Oxford.

Pantula, S.G. (1989), Testing for Unit Roots in Time Series Data, *Econometric Theory*, Vol. 5, pp. 256–271.

Pantula, S.G. (1991), Asymptotic Distributions of Unit-Root Tests When the Process is Nearly Stationary, *Journal of Business and Economics Statistics*, Vol. 9, pp. 63–71.

Pantula, S.G., Gonzalez-Farias, G. and Fuller, W.A. (1994), A Comparison of Unit Root Test Criteria, *Journal of Business and Economic Statistics*, Vol. 12, pp. 449–459.

Park, H.J. and Fuller, W.A. (1993), Alternative Estimators for the Parameters of an Autoregressive Process, unpublished manuscript, Iowa State University.

Park, J.Y. (1992), Canonical Cointegrating Regressions, *Econometrica*, Vol. 60, pp. 119–143.

Park, J.Y. and Phillips, P.C.B. (1988), Statistical Inference in Regressions With Integrated Processes: Part I, *Econometric Theory*, Vol. 4, pp. 468–497.

Patterson, K.D. and Pesaran, B. (1992), The Intertemporal Elasticity of Substitution in Consumption in the United States and the United Kingdom, *The Review Of Economics and Statistics*, Vol. 74, pp. 573–584.

Patterson, K.D. and Sowell, F. (1995), Consumption: Innovation Persistence and the Excess Smoothness Debate, *Applied Economics*, Vol. 28, pp. 1245–1255.

Pearson, E.S. and Hartley, H.O. (1970), *Biometrika Tables for Statisticians*, Cambridge University Press, Cambridge.

Peguin-Feissolle, A. (1999), A Comparison of the Power of Some Tests for Conditional Heteroscedasticity, *Economics Letters*, Vol. 63, pp. 5–17.

Perron, P.P. (1988), Trends and Random Walks in Macroeconomic Time Series: Further Evidence from a New Approach, *Journal of Economic Dynamics and Control*, Vol. 12, pp. 297–332.

Perron, P.P. (1989), The Great Crash, the Oil Price Shock and the Unit Root Hypothesis, *Econometrica*, Vol. 57, pp. 1361–1401.

Perron, P.P. (1997), Further Evidence on Breaking Trend Functions in Macroeconomic Variables, *Journal of Econometrics*, Vol. 80, pp. 355–385.

Pesaran, M.H. (1997), The Role of Economic Theory in Modelling the Long Run, *The Economic Journal*, Vol. 107, pp. 178–191.

Pesaran, M.H. and Pesaran, B. (1997), *MICROFIT 4.0, Interactive Econometric Analysis*, Oxford University Press, Oxford.

Phelps, E.S. (1967), Phillips Curves, Expectations of Inflation and Optimal Unemployment Over Time, *Economica*, Vol. 34, pp. 254–287.

Phelps, E.S. (1970), Money, Wage Dynamics and Labour Market Equilibrium, in E.S. Phelps, *Microeconomic Foundations of Employment and Inflation Theory*, Norton, New York.

Phelps-Brown, E.H. and Hopkins, S.V. (1950), The Course of Wage-Rates in Five Countries, 1860–1939, *Oxford Economic Papers*, Vol. 2, pp. 226–295.

Phillips, A.W. (1957), Stabilisation and the Time Form of Lagged Response, *Economic Journal*, Vol. 67, pp. 265–277.

Phillips, A.W. (1958), The Relation Between Unemployment and the Rate of Change of Money Wage Rates in the United Kingdom 1861–1957, *Economica*, Vol. 25, pp. 283–99.

Phillips, P.C.B. (1986), Understanding Spurious Regressions in Econometrics, *Journal of Econometrics*, Vol. 33, pp. 311–340.

Phillips, P.C.B. (1987), Time Series Regression With a Unit Root, *Econometrica*, Vol. 55, pp. 277–302.

Phillips, P.C.B. (1988), Reflections on Econometric Methodology, *The Economic Record* (Symposium on Econometric Methodology), Vol. 64, pp. 311–340.

Phillips, P.C.B. (1991), Optimal Inference in Cointegrated Systems, *Econometrica*, Vol. 59, pp. 283–306.

Phillips, P.C.B. and Hansen, B.E. (1990), Statistical Inference in Instrumental Variables Regression With I(1) Processes, *The Review of Economic Studies*, Vol. 57, pp. 99–125.

Phillips, P.C.B. and Ouliaris, S. (1988), Asymptotic Properties of Residual Based Tests for Cointegration, *Econometrica*, Vol. 58, pp. 165–193.

Phillips, P.C.B. and Perron, P. (1988), Testing for a Unit Root in Time Series Regression, *Biometrika*, Vol. 75, pp. 335–436.

Phylaktis, K. and Taylor, M.P. (1993), Money Demand, the Cagan Model and the Inflation Tax: Some Latin American Evidence, *The Review of Economics and Statistics*, Vol. 75, pp. 32–37.

Priestley, M.B. (1981), *Spectral Analysis and Time Series*, Academic Press, London.

Putnam, B.H. and Woodbury, J.R. (1980), Exchange Rate Stability and Monetary Policy, *Review of Business and Economic Research*, Vol. 15, pp. 1–10.

Ramsay, J.B. (1969), Tests for Specification Errors in Classical Linear Least Squares Regression Analysis, *Journal of the Royal Statistical Society B*, Vol. 31, pp. 350–371.

Ramsay, J.B. (1970), Models, Specification Error and Inference: A Discussion of Some Problems in Econometric Methodology, *Bulletin of the Oxford Institute of Economics and Statistics*, Vol. 32, pp. 301–318.

Rao, C.R. (1973), *Linear Statistical Inference and its Applications*, John Wiley, New York.

Reimers, H-E. (1992), Comparisons of Tests for Multivariate Cointegration, *Statistical Papers*, Vol. 33, pp. 335–359.

Reinsel, G.C. and Ahn, S.K. (1992), Vector Autoregressive Models With Unit Roots and Reduced Rank Structure: Estimation. Likelihood Ratio Test and Forecasting, *Journal of Time Series Analysis*, Vol. 13. pp. 353–375.

Richardson, J.D. (1978), Some Empirical Evidence on Commodity Arbitrage and the Law of One Price, *Journal of International Economy*, Vol. 8, pp. 341–351.

Rogers, J.H. and Jenkins, M.A. (1995), Haircuts or Hysteresis? Sources of Movements in Real Exchange Rates, *Journal of International Economy*, Vol. 38, pp. 339–360.

Rogoff, K. (1992), Traded Goods Consumption Smoothing and the Random Walk Behaviour of the Real Exchange Rate, *Bank of Japan Monetary and Economic Studies*, Vol. 10, pp. 1–29.

Rogoff, K. (1996), The Purchasing Power Parity Puzzle, *Journal of Economic Literature*, Vol. 34, pp. 647–668.

Rossana, R.J. and Seater, J.S. (1992), Aggregation, Unit Roots, and the Time Series Structure of Manufacturing Real Wages, *International Economic Review*, Vol. 33, pp. 159–179.

Said, S.E. and Dickey, D.A. (1984), Testing for Unit Roots in Autoregressive-moving Average Models of Unknown Order, *Biometrika*, Vol. 71, pp. 599–607.

Said, S.E. and Dickey, D.A. (1985), Hypothesis Testing in ARIMA ($p, 1, q$) Models, *Journal of the American Statistical Association*, Vol. 80, pp. 369–374.

Samavati, H., Dilts, D.A. and Deitsch, C.R. (1994), The Phillips Curve: Evidence for a 'Lady or Tiger Dilemma', *The Quarterly Review of Economics and Finance*, Vol. 33, pp. 333–345.

Samuelson, P. (1966), *Economics*, McGraw Hill, New York.

Samuelson, P.A. and Solow, R.M. (1960), Analytical Aspects of Anti-inflation Policy, *American Economic Review*, Papers and Proceedings, Vol. 50, pp. 177–194.

Santomero, A.M. and Seater, J.J. (1978), The Inflation–Unemployment Trade-off: A Critque of the Literature, *Journal of Economic Literature*, Vol. 16, pp. 499–544.

Sargan, J.D. (1964), Wages and Prices in the United Kingdom: A Study in Econometric Methodology, in P.E. Hart, G. Mills and J.K. Whitaker (eds), *Econometric Analysis for National Economic Planning*, Butterworth, London.

Sargent, T.J. (1971), A Note on the Accelerationist Controversy, *Journal of Money, Credit and Banking*, Vol. 3, pp. 50–60.

Sargent, T.J. (1973), Rational Expectations, the Real Rate of interest, and the Natural Rate of Unemployment, *Brookings Papers on Economic Activity*, Vol. 2, pp. 429–472.

Sargent, T.J. (1976), A Classical Macroeconometric Model for the United States, *Journal of Political Economy*, Vol. 84, pp. 207–237.

Sarno, L. and Taylor, M.P. (1998), Real Exchange Rate Under the Recent Float: Unequivocal Evidence of Mean Reversion, *Economics Letters*, Vol. 60, pp. 131–137.

Schwarz, G. (1978), Estimating the Dimension of a Model, *The Annals of Statistics*, Vol. 5, pp. 461–464.

Schwert, G.W. (1987), Effects of Model Specification Tests for Unit Roots in Macroeconomic Data, *Journal of Monetary Economics*, Vol. 20, pp. 73–103.

Schwert, G.W. (1989), Tests for Unit Roots: A Monte Carlo Investigation, *Journal of Business and Economic Statistics*, Vol. 7, pp. 147–160.

Seber, G.A.F. (1977), *Linear Regression Analysis*, John Wiley, New York.

Shaman, P. and Stine, R.A. (1988), The Bias of Autoregressive Coefficient Estimators, *Journal of the American Statistical Association*, Vol. 83, pp. 842–848.

Shea, G.S. (1992), Benchmarking the Expectations Hypothesis of the Term Structure: An Analysis of Cointegrating Vectors, *Journal of Business and Economic Statistics*, Vol. 10, pp. 347–365.

Shea, J. (1997), Instrument Relevance in Multivariate Linear Models: A Simple Message, *Review of Economics and Statistics*, Vol. 79, pp. 348–352.

Shiller, R.J. (1979) The Volatility of Long-term Interest Rates and Expectations Models of the Term Structure, *Journal of Political Economy*, Vol. 87, pp. 1190–1219.

Shiller, R.J. (1981), Do Stock Prices Move Too Much to be Justified by Subsequent Changes in Dividends?, *American Economic Review*, Vol. 71, pp. 421–436.

Shiller, R.J. (1989), *Market Volatility*, MIT Press, Cambridge, Massachusetts.

Shiller, R.J. (1990), The Term Structure of Interest Rates, Chapter 13 in B. Friedman and F. Hahn (eds), *The Handbook of Monetary Economics*, North-Holland, Amsterdam.

Shiller, R.J., Campbell, J.Y. and Schoenholtz, K.J. (1983), Forward Rates and Future Policy: Interpreting the Term Structure of Interest Rates, *Brooking Papers on Economic Activity*, Vol. 1, pp. 173–217.

Simpson, T.D. (1980), The Redefined Monetary Aggregates, *Federal Reserve Bulletin*, pp. 97–114.

Sims, C.A. (1988), Bayesian Skepticism on Unit Root Econometrics, *Journal of Economic Dynamics and Control*, Vol. 12, pp. 463–474.

Sims, C.A. (1991), Comment on M. Clements and G.E. Mizon, Empirical Analysis of Macroeconomic Time Series: VAR and Structural Models, *European Economic Review*, Vol. 35, pp. 922–932.

Sims, C.A., Stock, J.H. and Watson, M.W. (1990), Inference in Linear Time Series With Some Unit Roots, *Econometrica*, Vol. 58, pp. 113–144.

Snell, A. (1996), A Test of Purchasing Power Parity Based on the Largest Principal Component of Real Exchange Rates of the Main OECD Economies, *Economics Letters*, Vol. 51, pp. 225–231.

Sowell, F. (1992a), Maximum Likelihood Estimation of Stationary Univariate Fractionally Integrated Time Series Models, *Journal of Econometrics*, Vol. 53, pp. 165–188.

Sowell, F. (1992b), Modeling Long-run Behaviour With the Fractional ARIMA Model, *Journal of Monetary Economics*, Vol. 29, pp. 277–302.

Spanos, A. (1986), *Statistical Foundations of Econometric Modelling*, Cambridge University Press, Cambridge.

Stine, R.A. and Shaman, P. (1989), A Fixed Point Characterisation for Bias of Autoregressive Estimators, *The Annals of Statistics*, Vol. 17, pp. 1275–1284.

Stock, J.H. (1987), Asymptotic Properties of Least Squares Estimators of Co-integrating Vectors, *Econometrica*, Vol. 55, pp. 1035–1056.

Stock, J.H. (1991), Confidence Intervals for the Largest Autoregressive Root in U.S. Macroeconomic Time Series, *Journal of Monetary Economics,* Vol. 28, pp. 435–459.

Stock, J.H. and Watson, M.W. (1988), Testing for Common Trends, *Journal of the American Statistical Association*, Vol. 83, pp. 1097–2007.

Stock, J.H. and Watson, M.W. (1993), A Simple Estimator of Cointegrating Vectors in Higher Order Integrated Systems, *Econometrica*, Vol. 61, pp. 783–820.

'Student' (Gossett, N.S.) (1908), The Probable Error of a Mean, *Biometrika*, Vol. 6, pp. 1–25.

Susmel, R. and Engle, R.F. (1992), Hourly Volatility Spillovers Between International Equity Markets, Department of Economics, University of California at San Diego. Discussion Paper 92-08.

Sydsaeter, K. and Hammond, P.J. (1995), *Mathematics for Economic Analysis*, Prentice-Hall, New Jersey.

Taylor, M.P. (1988), An Empirical Examination of Long-run Purchasing Power Parity Using Cointegration Techniques, *Applied Economics*, Vol. 20, pp. 1369–1381.

Taylor, M.P. (1992), Modelling the Yield Curve, *The Economic Journal*, Vol. 102, pp. 524–537.

Taylor, M.P. (1995a), Modelling the Demand for U.K. Broad Money, 1871–1913, *Review of Economics and Statistics*, Vol. 77, pp. 112–117.

Taylor, M.P. (1995b), The Economics of Exchange Rates, *Journal of Economic Literature*, Vol. 33, pp. 13–47.

Thomas, R.L. (1997), *Modern Econometrics*, Addison-Wesley, New York.

Tinbergen, J. (1939a), *A Method and Its Application to Investment Activity. Statistical Testing of Business Cycle Theories.* Vol. I, League of Nations, Geneva.

Tinbergen, J. (1939b), *Business Cycles in the United States of America 1919–1932. Statistical Testing of Business Cycle Theories.* Vol. II, League of Nations, Geneva.

Tinbergen, J. (1940), On a Method of Statistical Research: A Reply, *Economic Journal*, Vol. 50, pp. 141–154.

Tobin, J. (1956), The Interest-Elasticity of Transactions Demand for Cash, *Review of Economic and Statistics*, Vol. 38, pp. 241–247.

Tobin, J. (1958), Liquidity Preference as Behaviour Towards Risk, *The Review of Economic Studies*, Vol. 25, pp. 65–86.

Urbain, J.P. (1995), Partial Versus Full System Modelling of Cointegrated Systems. An Empirical Illustration, *Journal of Econometrics*, Vol. 69, pp. 177–210.

Velu, R.P. and Reinsel, G.C. (1987), Reduced Rank Regression With Autoregressive Errors, *Journal of Econometrics*, Vol. 35, pp. 317–335.

Watson, M.W. (1994), Vector Autoregression and Cointegration, in *The Handbook of Econometrics*, Vol. IV, North-Holland, Amsterdam, pp. 2844–2915.

Whalen, E.L. (1966), A Rationalisation of the Precautionary Demand for Cash, *Quarterly Journal of Economics*, Vol. 80, pp. 314–324.

Weiss, A.A. (1986), Asymptotic Theory for ARCH Models: Estimation and Testing, *Econometric Theory*, Vol. 2, pp. 107–130.

West, K.D. (1988), Asymptotic Normality When Regressors Have a Unit Root, *Econometrica*, Vol. 56, pp. 1397–1418.

White, H. (1980), A Heteroskedasticity-consistent Covariance Estimator and a Direct Test for Heteroskedasticity, *Econometrica*, Vol. 48, pp. 817–838.

Yule, G.U. (1926), Why Do We Sometimes Get Nonsense Correlations Between Time Series? A Study in Sampling and the Nature of Time Series, *Journal of the Royal Statistical Society*, Vol. 89, pp. 1–64.

Zakoian, J-M. (1994), Threshold Heteroskedastic Models, *Journal of Economic Dynamics and Control*, Vol. 18, pp. 931–955.

Zellner, A. (1962), An Efficient Method of Estimating Seemingly Unrelated Regressions and Tests for Aggregation Bias, *Journal of the American Statistical Association*, Vol. 57, pp. 500–509.

Zivot, E. and Andrews, D.W.K. (1992), Further Evidence on the Great Crash, the Oil Price Shock and the Unit Root Hypothesis, *Journal of Business and Economic Statistics*, Vol. 10, pp. 251–270.

Author index

Subject index